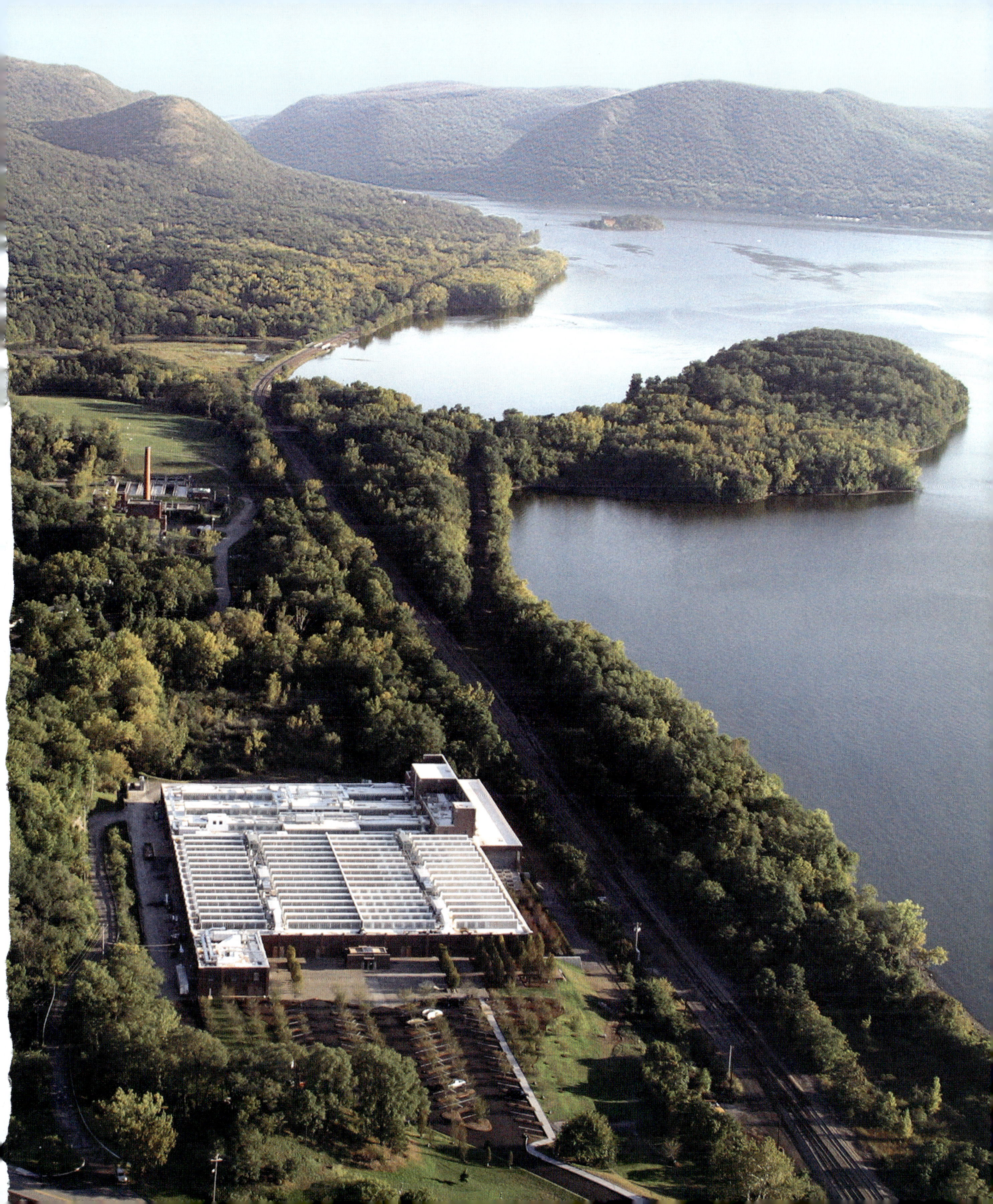

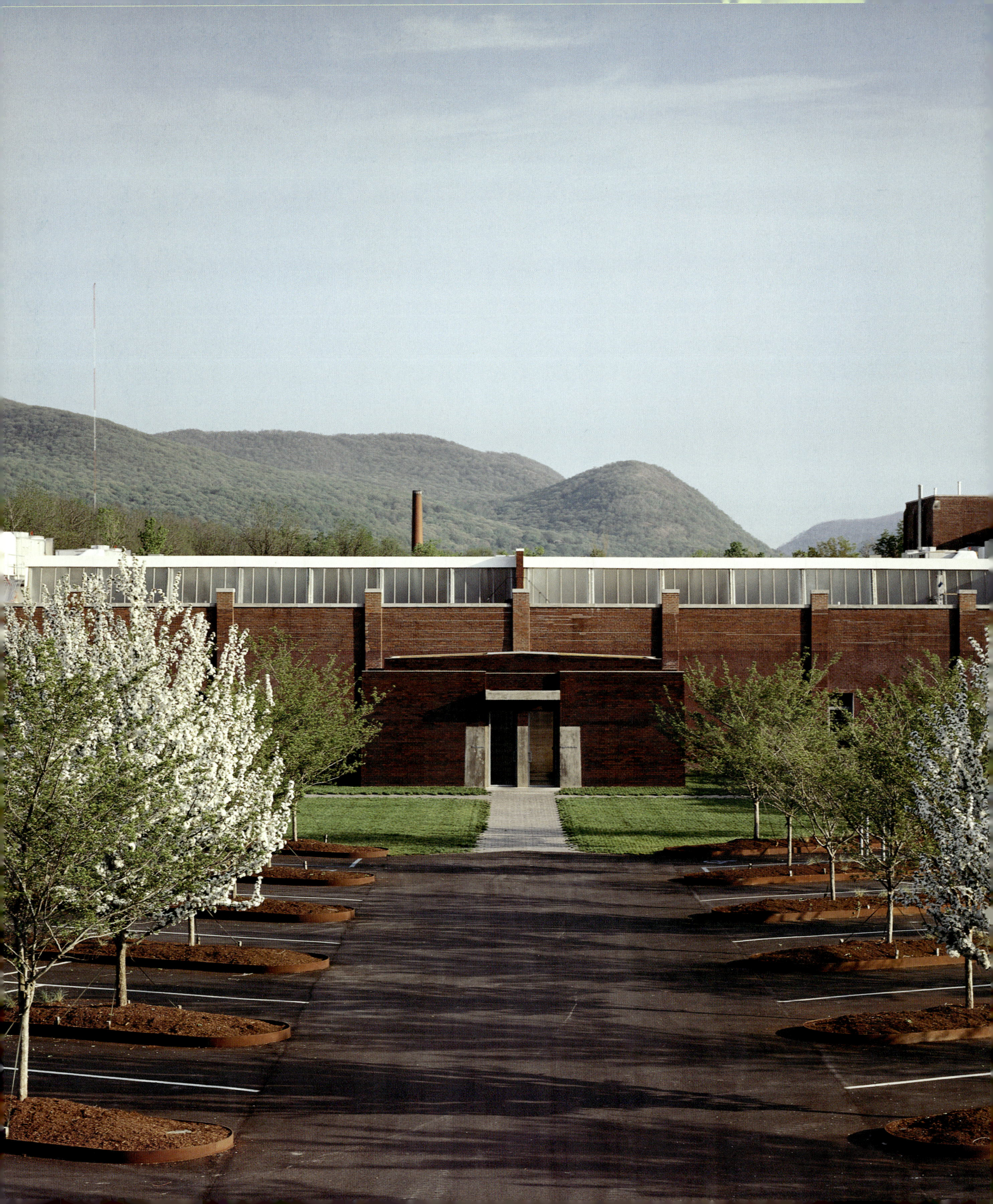

Dia:Beacon

Lynne Cooke and Michael Govan

Dia Art Foundation

Dia:Beacon

Dia:Beacon Riggio Galleries is named in honor of Louise and Leonard Riggio for their extraordinary generosity, which has made possible the realization of this museum dedicated to Dia Art Foundation's collection.

Significant capital funds were also contributed by Lannan Foundation, Ann Tenenbaum and Thomas H. Lee, and The Brown Foundation as well as Frances and John Bowes, Jay Chiat, Frances R. Dittmer, Angela and William L. Haines, and International Paper. Generous subsidies from public agencies were made available by the Office of Governor George E. Pataki through Empire State Development, the Dutchess County Industrial Development Agency, the City of Beacon, the New York State Office of Parks, Recreation, and Historic Preservation, and the New York State Council on the Arts. Capital support was also received from Constance R. Caplan, Carla Emil and Richard Silverstein, The Horace W. Goldsmith Foundation, Linda and Harry Macklowe, Lea H. Simonds, Louisa Stude Sarofim, and Barbara and Charles B. Wright.

This book commemorates the opening of Dia Art Foundation's museum Dia:Beacon Riggio Galleries on May 18, 2003.

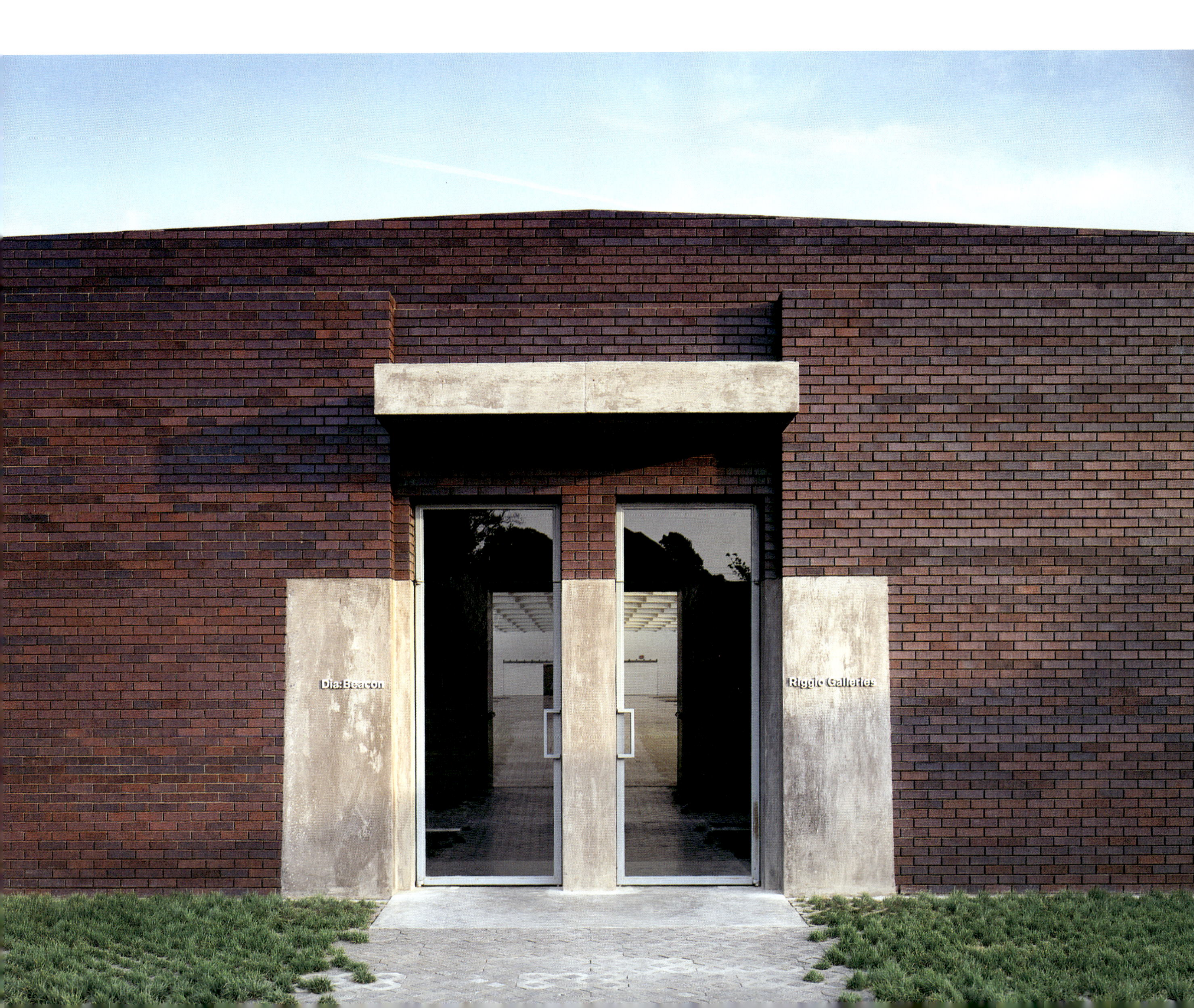

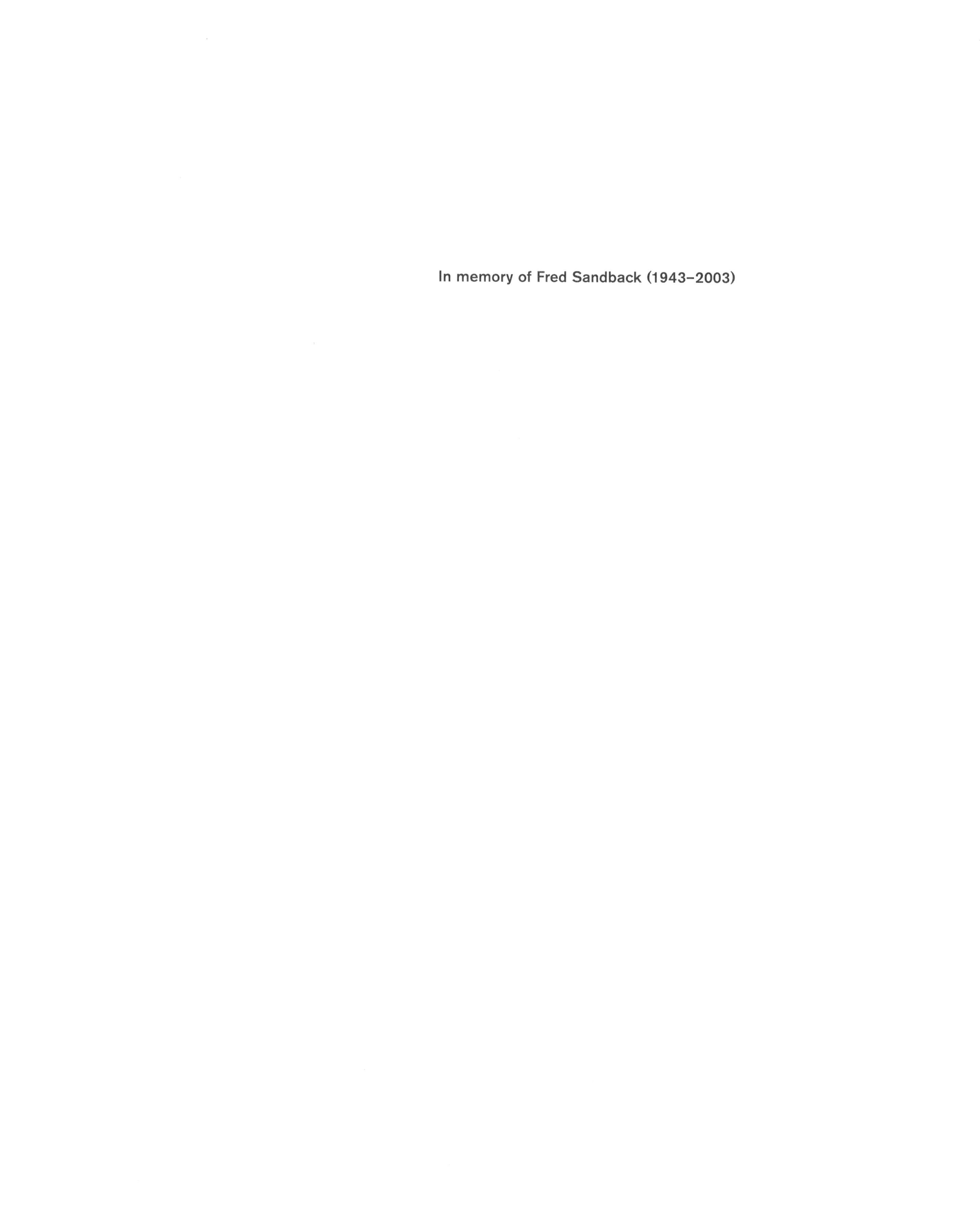

In memory of Fred Sandback (1943–2003)

Contents

Chairman's Statement

More than one hundred miles north of Las Vegas, Nevada, in a location as removed from contemporary civilization as Las Vegas attempts to be its center, Michael Heizer makes his art. There, in the rugged and pristine landscape that defines the great American West, Heizer works tirelessly, and will soon complete his own *City*, a project to which he has devoted every bit of his considerable energy and vision for the past thirty years. So, too, has James Turrell spent almost his entire adult lifetime working just north of Flagstaff, Arizona, at the edge of the Painted Desert, on his epic project known as the Roden Crater. Although these projects are similar in size, scale, and location, they are in fact as different from one another as the earth and the sky. Attempts at grouping them alongside Robert Smithson's *Spiral Jetty* and Walter De Maria's *The Lightning Field* as Land art are neither useful nor especially illuminating.

While Heizer and Turrell, together with the other artists in Dia's collection, are contemporaries, their monumental achievements can only be diminished by ascribing to them a collective vision. Clearly, their work is conceptual, yet they are not Conceptualists any more than Donald Judd, Dan Flavin, and others were Minimalists, or Andy Warhol was simply a Pop artist. More than in most other periods in art history, the work of the generation of artists who came to prominence in the 1960s and 1970s must be viewed individually, not collectively. Indeed, even the categorization implied by the phrase "art of the 1960s and 1970s" was long rejected by Judd, who preferred to define the period as "this time and place."

Dia:Beacon was built for these artists in the same way that Dia Art Foundation was formed to serve the works it commissioned and collected. The model for these galleries can be seen in many previous Dia collaborations, most particularly in Judd's own place, the Chinati Foundation in Marfa, Texas. Then and now, Dia remains rooted in a single ideal: to the greatest extent possible each artist should conceive the architecture, environment, and context in which his or her works are viewed.

My first visit to Dia in 1997 was to view the Richard Serra exhibition, "Torqued Ellipses": this began what has become a lifetime commitment to support this important foundation. It should be noted, however, that my early interest in Dia had nothing to do with its institutional objectives or even its standing in the world of art. The truth be told, I had little interest in museums, long holding the belief that too often they serve only themselves. My interest was in the artist Richard Serra and his work; more importantly, his work within the framework of the installation. Without knowing it, I had arrived at the essence of Dia.

In the years that followed, I have come to discover that defining Dia itself is as elusive as categorizing any of the artists in its collection. Questions such as what is Dia? where is Dia? even, why is Dia? remain open for me. During the course of finding a home for our permanent collection, which included the discovery of the magnificent site in Beacon, the board of trustees came to realize that the works of these artists—not the work of the institution—was our mission. Dia's contribution involves the sum total of the works we have sponsored and supported; our goal is to maintain the unique form of patronage for which we are known. True to the vision and largesse of founders Heiner Friedrich and Philippa de Menil, we seek not to become a center of the art world, but a place where a centering can occur.

The location of Dia:Beacon is more important for its distance from New York City than for its proximity to it. Situated on the banks of the Hudson River, Dia:Beacon is set in bucolic surroundings, in deliberate contrast to the conventional notion that all things cultural must exist in urban centers. This, too, is a concept given to us by the artists in our collection, many of whom have drawn their inspiration from the beauty of the American landscape and the inventiveness of the American spirit. Like Judd, many believe art should also be viewed outside the frame of a large city. At Dia:Beacon the uninitiated and the expert are invited not only to participate in a dialogue with the art but to interact with it.

Elsewhere in this volume we recognize many of the dedicated individuals who made this project possible. I would like to add my heartfelt appreciation for their efforts, especially to Dia's board of trustees for their support and their vision. Special tribute must also be given to Patrick Lannan and Lannan Foundation for their incredible generosity and their steadfast mission to encourage the depth and diversity of contemporary culture.

Finally, thanks to Michael Govan, one of the most dedicated, insightful, and talented human beings I have ever known. Dia:Beacon is the result of his brilliance. Working with Michael, with renowned curator Lynne Cooke, and with the many artists who have created a legacy for the ages has been the privilege of a lifetime.

Leonard Riggio
Chairman
Dia Art Foundation

Foreword

In November of 1997 I had the opportunity to give Dia trustee Jay Chiat and his guest Leonard Riggio a tour of Dia's new installation of Richard Serra's Torqued Ellipses in a building renovated primarily to house these large-scale steel constructions. The project was uniquely Dia's. A year earlier, Serra had shown a plan for his new work to Dia's curator, Lynne Cooke, and to me, but he had not determined who, if anyone, would be able to exhibit them: the works required a large level floor on grade, able to hold more than 120 tons of steel sculpture. The challenges for both the artist and the institution were evident and inviting. With the help of the architect Richard Gluckman, we rehabilitated a former garage of 8,000 square feet directly across the street from Dia's primary exhibition facility on West Twenty-second Street in Manhattan. A few subtle but significant changes to the building, including a new concrete floor, a rolling door, the extension of two interior brick walls, and the careful wire-brush cleaning of a beautiful timber truss supporting a roof with eleven skylights were all intended to provide an accommodating but nondistracting environment for the Torqued Ellipses. After intense experiment and labor, Serra completed and installed his three massive space-bending sculptures. Dissatisfied with any of the supplemental lighting systems we considered, we suggested that natural light from the skylights would be sufficient and appropriate to illuminate the works and that in the winter months, when days were short, we would close the gallery early. In fact, the opening reception for the show ended by sunset.

Len Riggio's enthusiasm for Serra's art was matched only by his appreciation of the artist's installation of the works, which took the space within and between the three Torqued Ellipses into account as a whole environment. "They should remain in this space exactly as the artist placed them," he said. And so the conversation became a discussion of Dia's history of commissioning and preserving artist-designed installations. It had been more than a decade since Dia had acquired new works, but Serra's new project seemed ideally suited to Dia's mission. Len talked with his wife, Louise, and with the artist and then proposed to acquire the works—all three—for Dia. Remarkable in itself, the Riggios' acquisition of the Ellipses on Dia's behalf also marked the recommencement of Dia's efforts to acquire both single projects and in-depth holdings by major artists of the 1960s and 1970s.

Less than a year later, as the ongoing discussion of the need to present Dia's collection to the public gained new strength on the board of trustees, now led by Len Riggio as chairman, we found a 300,000-square-foot factory space on the banks of the Hudson River in Beacon, New York. This space, a former Nabisco box-printing facility dating to 1929, has now become a museum for some of the most compelling artworks created in the last four decades. What made the museum possible was the substantial contributions made by the Riggios toward its construction and endowment, and toward several acquisitions, all motivated by their love of the art they support and manifest in Len Riggio's daily engagement and personal partnership in imagining the possibilities for Dia. This book commemorates the opening of Dia Art Foundation's new museum, Dia:Beacon Riggio Galleries, in May of 2003.

Dia Art Foundation was founded in 1974 as a vehicle for facilitating the making of some of the most ambitious work by some of the most important artists of the 1960s and 1970s, and for collecting that work in depth. The name "Dia," taken from the Greek word meaning "through" or "between," suggests the foundation's role in enabling the realization and preservation of extraordinary artistic projects and providing ongoing public access to them. As it developed under the guidance and patronage of Dia's founders, Philippa de Menil and Heiner Friedrich, Dia pursued this mission by generating long-term exhibitions and site-specific projects for each of a handful of artists represented in its collection.

Among Dia's most significant early accomplishments were Joseph Beuys's *7000 Eichen* (*7,000 Oaks)* project in Kassel, Germany; Walter De Maria's *The Lightning Field*, near Quemado, New Mexico, and *The Broken Kilometer* and *The New York Earth Room* in Manhattan; the Dan Flavin Art Institute in Bridgehampton, New York; and Donald Judd's Chinati Foundation in Marfa, Texas, with its permanent installations by Judd, Flavin, and John Chamberlain. Other artists for whom projects were planned and collections assembled included Imi Knoebel, Blinky Palermo, Fred Sandback, James Turrell, Cy Twombly, Andy Warhol, Robert Whitman, and La Monte Young.

The energy behind Dia's unique enterprise, inspired by the artists themselves, was then, as it is now, the product of a unique brand of patronage and the work of a small dedicated group of individuals. Along with Friedrich and de Menil, Helen Winkler helped found Dia and dedicated many years of her life to supporting its initial group of artists and projects. James Schaeufele joined Dia in 1981, in part to help Flavin complete his permanent installation in Bridgehampton, and became a key figure in facilitating many of Dia Art Foundation's installations and building renovations since then, including his role over the past four years as project director in the construction of the Beacon facility.

Reorganized in 1984, as a public institution by a board of trustees led by Chairman Ashton Hawkins, and with a new director, Charles Wright, Dia opened in 1987 an exhibition facility on West Twenty-second Street, New York, to present both work from its collection and newly commissioned projects in a unique format: individual artist-designed installations filling an entire 8,000-square-foot gallery for a year or more. Wright, Dia's director from 1984 to 1994, engaged a younger generation of artists and audiences through his establishment of exhibitions and a multidisciplinary program that included dance, poetry, and a series of lectures and symposia in what was renamed Dia Center for the Arts. (With the opening of Dia:Beacon, the exhibition space in Chelsea is now referred to as Dia:Chelsea.) Wright also spearheaded Dia's cofounding of the Andy Warhol Museum, Pittsburgh, in the mid-1990s, in collaboration with the Carnegie Institute and the Andy Warhol Foundation; and the creation of the Cy Twombly Gallery, Houston, in collaboration with the Menil Collection, providing permanent homes for Dia's own groups of paintings by these two artists. At the same time, he also initiated efforts to support Michael Heizer's *City* project in Nevada and began the drive to create a facility that would provide public access to Dia's extraordinary collection. In 1995 he stepped into the role of chairman of the board of trustees, a post he held until 1998. In 1991 Wright hired curator Lynne Cooke, who has developed Dia's exhibitions, publications, and programs to the level of international prominence that they hold today. By selecting artists for exhibition and for the collection, by her own critical thinking and writing, and by her invitations to numerous critics and scholars to speak and write for Dia, Cooke has put the foundation at the center of the discourse on contemporary art.

One of the unique aspects of Dia's history has been its effort to initiate, maintain, and help complete a group of epic-scale artworks in the American Southwest. Among Dia's first grants in 1974 supported James Turrell's Roden Crater project in Arizona, a huge undertaking that is ongoing thanks largely to the involvement and support of Lannan Foundation. De Maria's *The Lightning Field*, completed in 1977, remains Dia's most recognized icon. Judd's Chinati Foundation, in large part built with Dia's backing between Robert Smithson's *Spiral Jetty* was acquired by gift from the artist's estate in 1999. And Heizer's nearly complete *City* project in Nevada is a major focus of Dia's current efforts, with support from Lannan Foundation and the Brown Foundation.

In a historic agreement forged in 2000, Lannan Foundation made a series of grants for construction and endowments that allowed Dia's continued support for its projects in the Western states. Dia's collaboration with Lannan Foundation, led by its president, J. Patrick Lannan, Jr., is ongoing. Most recently, that partnership has added works by Chamberlain, Hanne Darboven, Heizer, Robert Irwin, Judd, On Kawara, Agnes Martin, Bruce Nauman, Smithson, Whitman, and Lawrence Weiner to Dia:Beacon. These acquisitions—noted as gifts and long-term loans from Lannan Foundation in this publication—are intended to be permanently on view at Dia:Beacon, dramatically extending the breadth and depth of the collection. The Lannan family, and its foundation board, have worked closely with many of Dia's artists and their projects, inside and outside the museum. Patrick has unstintingly given Dia his thoughtful counsel and his inspiring personal encouragement to pursue artistic projects outside the mainstream.

The generation of artists on which Dia has focused its support and collecting activities eschewed the confines of traditional galleries and museums. Working outdoors, these artists might resort to the vast and remote landscapes of the American Southwest; even their indoor works often demand large unencumbered spaces and are best situated in the raw and straightforward architecture of former industrial buildings. In most cases their art is intertwined with its environment, whether landscape or architecture, and requires the artist's involvement in or instructions for its installation.

No traditional museum could contain the geographically widespread, often large-scale achievements of this group of artists; few institutions, public or private, are willing or even always able to allow artists themselves to design not only their work but the manner of its presentation; and fewer still can allow the artists' installations and projects, even in remote locations, to remain on view permanently, providing future generations with direct experience of the work. Thus Dia's mission and purpose are defined by its ambitious accommodation of the special demands of a generation of artists who have created some of history's most compelling and lasting art, and by its belief that the intense, in-depth, immersive experience of these artists' works is of artistic, personal, and educational value to our society.

In describing Dia's early mission, Helen Winkler wrote, "We had a sequence of importance: the art, the artist, the public, and lastly, us." The *us* was the board of trustees and the patrons. A defining characteristic of Dia as an institution has been its unique patronage—often monumental in both scale and generosity of spirit. So idealistic were the founders that they did not see fit to incorporate their names into that of their new institution, but instead chose a word that defined its role as a vehicle, a means—certainly not an end. Since Dia became a charitable organization, in 1984, its contributors and supporters have numbered in the hundreds, both on its board of trustees among those who have made substantial gifts to its programs. But Dia has been particularly distinguished by a few visionary patrons—perhaps attracted by Dia's visionary artists.

Philippa de Menil and Heiner Friedrich poured the larger part of their human energy and wealth into the realization of a series of artists' projects, some of which would not otherwise even have been imagined. Dia's present board chairman Leonard Riggio and his wife, Louise, as major patrons, have remade Dia with the same sense of idealism and commitment shown by its founders. And Lannan Foundation has quietly and consistently supported Dia's exhibitions and collections as well as the most ambitious and remote individual artist's projects.

Key contributions to the realization of Dia's current projects and to Dia:Beacon have been made by the Brown Foundation; Dia's vice chair, Ann Tenenbaum, and her husband, Thomas H. Lee; and the State of New York, led by the Honorable Governor George Pataki. The people of the City of Beacon and its mayor, Clara Lou Gould, have become our colleagues.

The picturesque Hudson Valley is not new to Dia. In the late 1970s Dan Flavin lived and worked primarily in Cold Spring and Garrison, just south of Beacon. There Flavin and Dia envisioned a permanent installation of Flavin's light works as well as his and Dia's collection of nineteenth-century Hudson River school landscape drawings, in homage to those first American artists who were drawn to the light and beauty of that grand river and its surrounding valley. In 1976, with Dia's sponsorship, Flavin designed and installed a light installation on two platforms of Grand Central Terminal—along the tracks that connected New York City to his home on the Hudson, as they will now connect the vibrant population of the city to Dia's new home in Beacon.

Many artists have participated in the making of Dia:Beacon through both their artwork and their collaboration. Bernd and Hilla Becher, Louise Bourgeois, John Chamberlain, Hanne Darboven, Walter De Maria, Michael Heizer, On Kawara, Imi Knoebel, Sol LeWitt, Agnes Martin, Bruce Nauman, Robert Ryman, Fred Sandback, Richard Serra, and Lawrence Weiner have all had a hand in shaping the museum's presentations. Robert Irwin is responsible for designing much of the magical transformation of a factory into a museum. During the opening of Dia's museum in Beacon, work by artists La Monte Young and Robert Whitman can be experienced in New York City. And the spirits of artists no longer present are also embedded in Dia:Beacon through their work—particularly those of Joseph Beuys, Andy Warhol, Dan Flavin, and Donald Judd, who were primary architects of the ideas with which we live.

More than thirty years ago, Heiner Friedrich, imagining Dia, wrote of his desire to "make a new type of museum available to the public" where "the arts are not new or old, they are alive." The opening of Dia:Beacon is perhaps the most significant single event in Dia's history, for it encompasses not only our mission in the present, not only the energy and many accomplishments of Dia's past, but also our inspiration for the future.

Michael Govan
Director
Dia Art Foundation

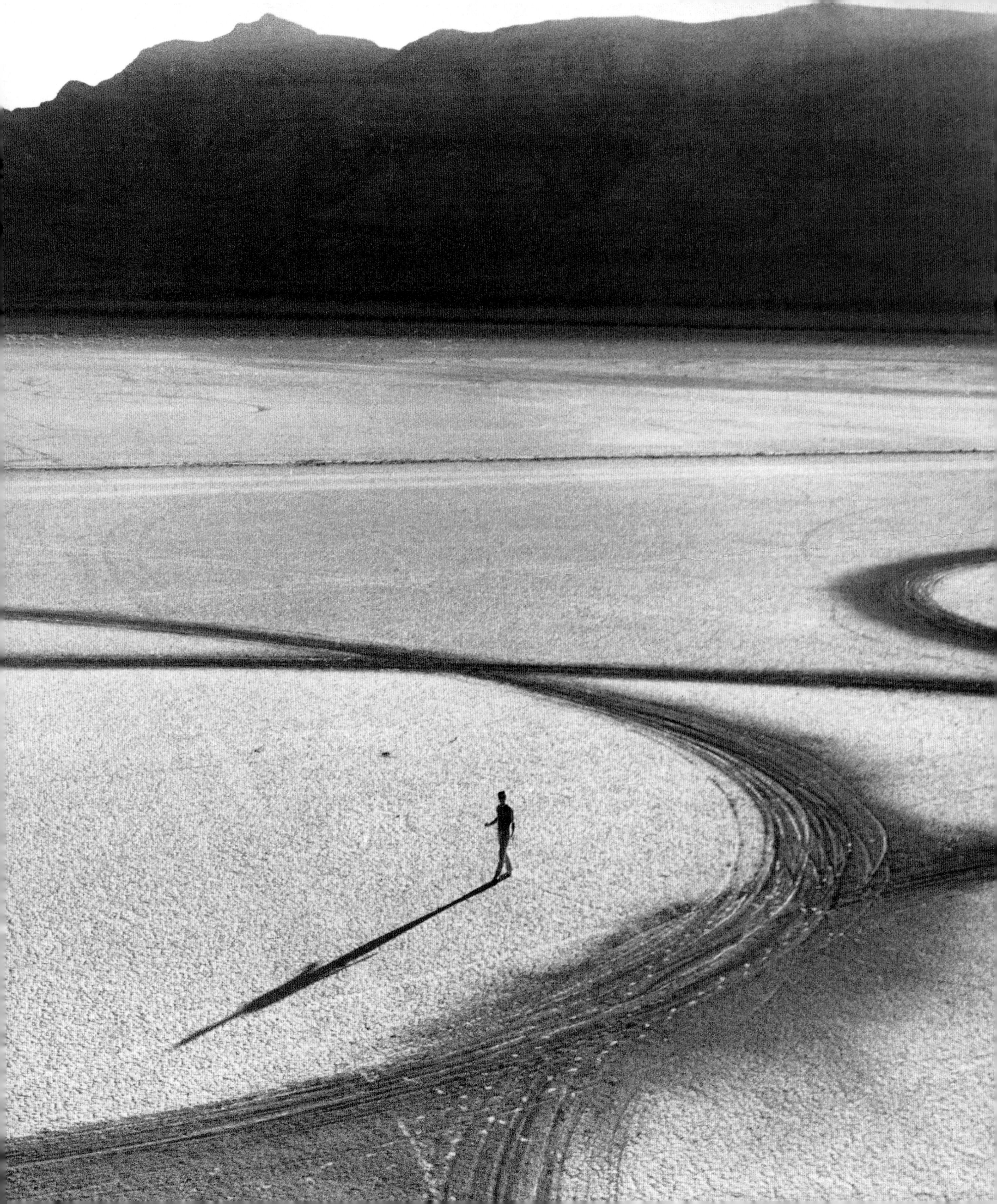

Introduction: Dia in Context MICHAEL GOVAN

First we change, and then we change our practices, and only later do we think to collectively change our institutions—to bring them in line with who we have become. —Robert Irwin

In the late 1940s Jackson Pollock was drawing lines of paint on canvases laid on his studio floor; by the mid-1960s Michael Heizer was using the wheels of his motorbike to inscribe lines on the vast canvas of a dry lake bed in the Mojave Desert. As Pollock took his canvas off the easel in his reinterpretation of the tradition of painting, Heizer and artists like him left the studio altogether, stretching the already elastic boundaries of modern art—in physical, temporal, and conceptual dimensions—to the point where traditional categories of painting and sculpture became nearly irrelevant.

The period of the 1960s and 1970s—the focus of Dia's collecting activities, and of the art on view at Dia's museum in Beacon—is widely considered one of the most radical and innovative in art history. Its breakthroughs echo those of the early twentieth century, including the birth of abstract painting and the advent of so-called modernism and its branches—Cubism, Constructivism, De Stijl, Dada, Surrealism, and other movements. In many ways the social and political unrest in Europe and America in the late 1960s, and the attendant convulsions in radical artistic production, may be compared with the similarly revolutionary outlook before World War I, the outlook that brought forth modernism—as if revolutionary times called forth revolutionary art.

How, then, can we describe the importance of the avant-garde art of the recent past represented at Dia's museum in Beacon? It must first be said that neither Dia's collection nor its presentation in Beacon is entirely representative of the historical period in question. Dia was founded by Heiner Friedrich and Philippa de Menil in 1974, not as a historical enterprise but as a vehicle for providing in-depth support to a handful of artists whom it sponsored to produce and present some of their most ambitious work. The result of the founders' monumental and energetic patronage in the late 1970s and early 1980s was a substantial collection of artwork and site-specific installations by a dozen artists. Then, however, their support subsided, leaving Dia financially unable to continue in its acquisitions and large-scale commissions. That abrupt break ended up forging a strong historical framework for the collection.

In 1987, Charles Wright, who was then the director of Dia Center for the Arts, initiated a series of ongoing exhibitions at Dia's Chelsea building to present work by artists in the collection, as well as to present work of similar scale and ambition by others. Memorable installations by a younger generation of artists, including Robert Gober, Jenny Holzer, and Ann Hamilton, were complemented by projects from Bernd and Hilla Becher, Hanne Darboven, Robert Irwin, On Kawara, Bruce Nauman, Gerhard Richter, Robert Ryman, Richard Serra, and Lawrence Weiner

Michael Heizer, *Circular Surface Planar Displacement Drawing*, 1970 (detail) Photo © Gianfranco Gorgoni

that allowed Dia to foster new connections with artists of the generation already represented in the collection and laid the groundwork for more recent acquisitions. Dia's collecting activities were reinitiated in 1998 thanks to the generosity of Louise and Leonard Riggio, who acquired Serra's Torqued Ellipses for Dia during their exhibition at the Chelsea galleries.

Dia once again began to collect, extending and augmenting the substantial founding collection of works by a relatively small number of artists who emerged in the 1960s and 1970s. But while Dia's collection now includes almost twice the original number of artists supported by the founders, recent acquisitions have focused, as in the past, on specific large-scale works and on in-depth holdings of works by a few artists with whom Dia has had long-term relationships. The collection, in sum, is distinguished by the artists themselves and by the degree of the institutions commitment to them, rather than by breadth or by thematic or didactic categories.

Despite the importance of the work exhibited in Beacon, it does not begin to represent the full range and historical relevance of Dia's collection. The founders' original vision was to present artists' work not only in depth but also in isolation, and in whatever location and circumstance were dictated by the artist and the needs of the work. That outlook corresponded with a strong impulse of the time to break free of the boundaries of the traditional gallery and museum.

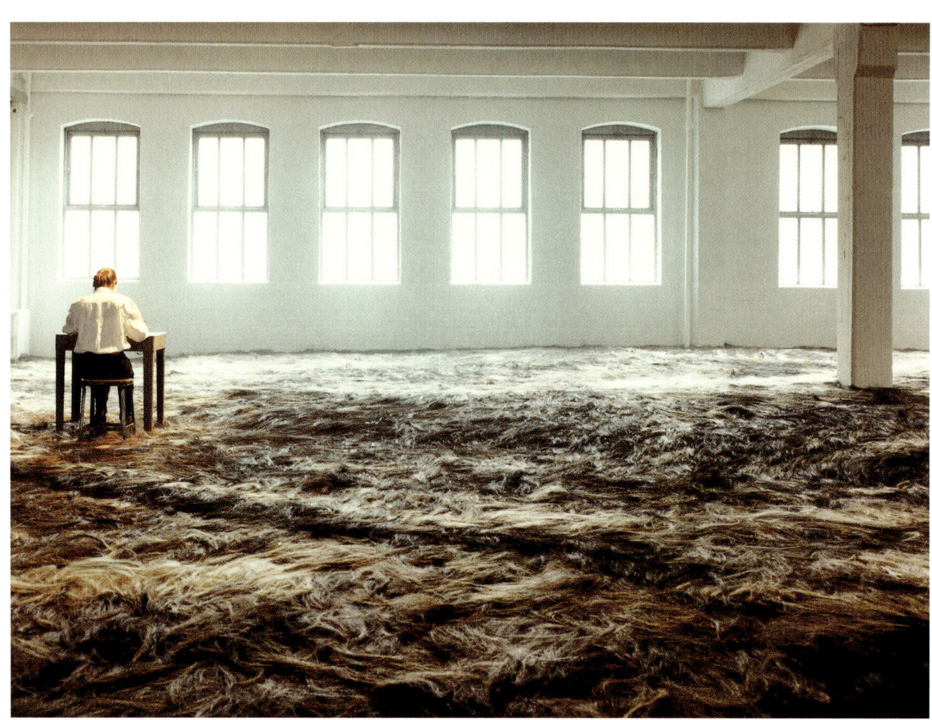

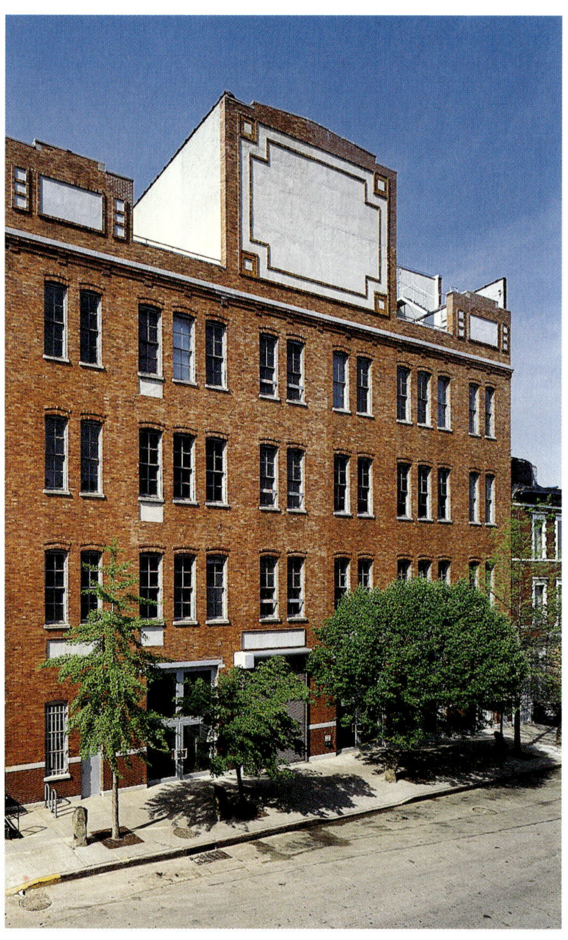

left Ann Hamilton, *tropos*, 1993, installation at Dia Center for the Arts, New York City
right Dia, 548 West 22nd Street, New York City, with Joseph Beuys's *7000 Eichen*, inaugurated in 1982, continued at Dia in 1988/1996

In the mid-1960s, Heizer and his colleague Walter De Maria struck out to the empty landscape of America's southwestern desert to create works of unprecedented grandeur. Robert Smithson and, later, Donald Judd and James Turrell, among others, were drawn to the same landscape for its scale and isolation. In the 1970s, Dia was instrumental in allowing many of these epic-scale projects to be realized.

It was not only in the Southwest that artists wished to present their work in a specific context. De Maria sited almost all of his works in unique environments and, with Dia's support, realized a number of permanent projects abroad (*The Vertical Earth Kilometer*, 1977, for example, in Kassel, Germany) and in New York City (*The New York Earth Room*, 1977, and *The Broken Kilometer*, 1979). Dia's "collection" extends across a vast geography including Dan Flavin's installations in Bridgehampton, New York; the more recent (during Wright's tenure) single-artist museums for Andy Warhol in Pittsburgh, Pennsylvania, and for Cy Twombly in Houston, Texas; and Smithson's *Spiral Jetty* (1970) in the Great Salt Lake, Utah. In addition, Dia's projects have encompassed ephemeral performance art that extended the definition of visual art in the 1960s and 1970s well beyond painting and sculpture, most notably Robert Whitman's groundbreaking performances and multimedia installations and many of La Monte Young's musical

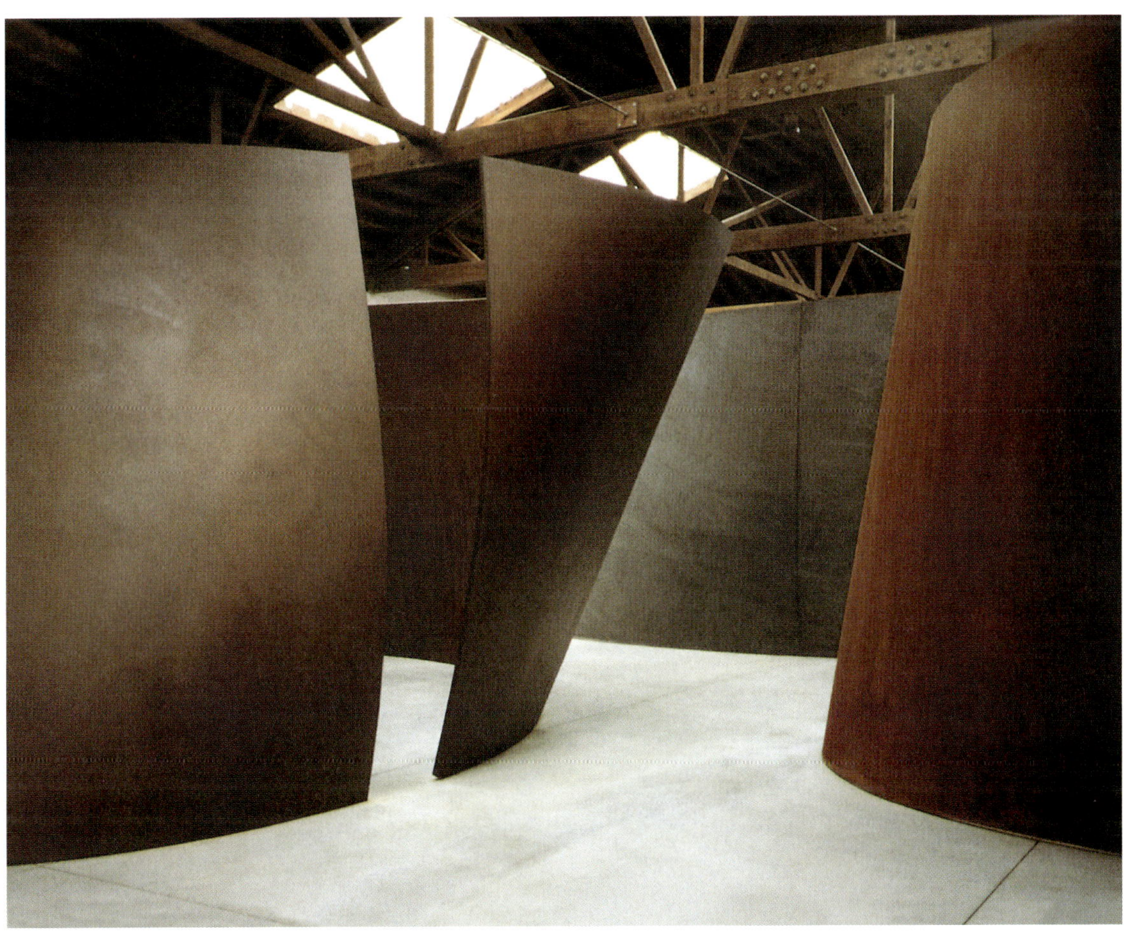

Richard Serra, "Torqued Ellipses," installation at Dia Center for the Arts, New York City, in 1997

and spatial events and installations, including the ongoing *Dream House*, (1995–present) in New York City.

Thus, Dia as an institution can be defined by no particular venue among its multiple manifestations across the United States, from Bridgehampton to the Great Salt Lake. Physically dispersed and at the same time sharply focused on individual artists, Dia emphatically resists broad categorizations. Even the museum in Beacon, comprising under one roof perhaps the most extensive and concentrated presentations anywhere of the work of the artists who emerged in the 1960s and 1970s, has been designed to isolate each artist's work in its own gallery and to provide a generous space between each viewing experience. It is also conceived as a targeted collection of these individual environments rather than a comprehensive presentation.

So the question remains, can anything be said broadly about the nature of the work on view at Dia:Beacon, or about the significance of the generation of artists concentrated in that collection? Selective rather than comprehensive, offering in-depth experiences rather than overviews, in addition to being stubbornly protective of individual artists' wishes and of the principle of

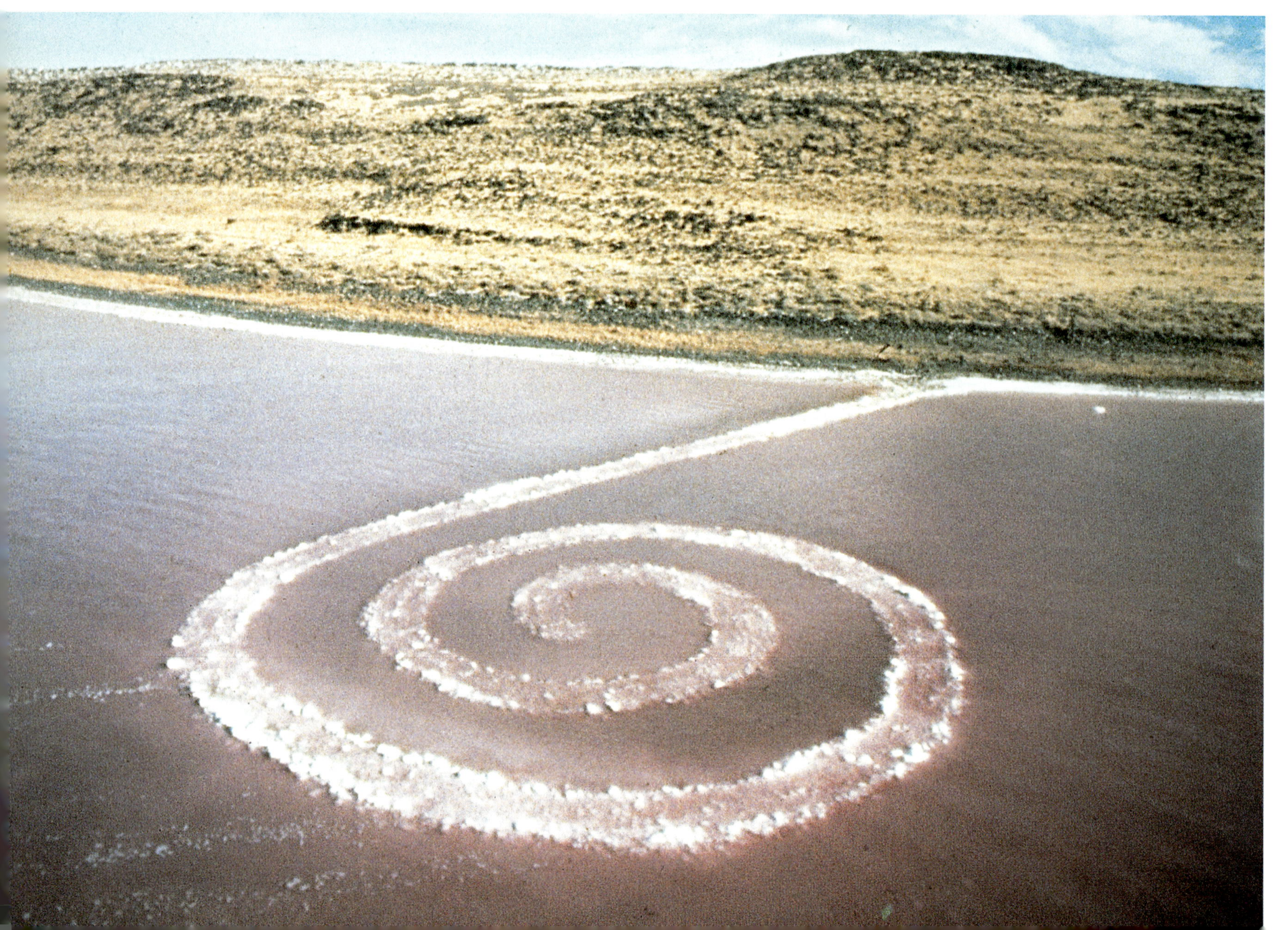

presenting those artists' works in isolation, Dia might seem a difficult example from which to draw conclusions about a historical era. Yet many of the artists Dia has supported and collected have in retrospect come to define the striking innovations of the time (loosely categorized as Pop, Minimal, Conceptual, Performance, and Earth art). And Dia, through its intense and direct involvement with those artists, since the 1970s has amassed a collection that has become an intimate portrait of that generation, a collection not essentially created as a museological synthesis of the history of the period but reflecting and in fact made of the specific ambitions of the artists and their works.

Perhaps the most definitive aspect of Dia:Beacon, and of the numerous manifestations of Dia's collection elsewhere, has to do not only with the artworks themselves, or even with the criteria by which the artists were selected, but rather with the idea of art in context. To the extent that the artists of the 1960s and 1970s were transgressing traditional boundaries and definitions of art—taking it outside the museum and gallery, expanding its scale, rethinking the material of its construction, and often dispensing with the object altogether (in favor of

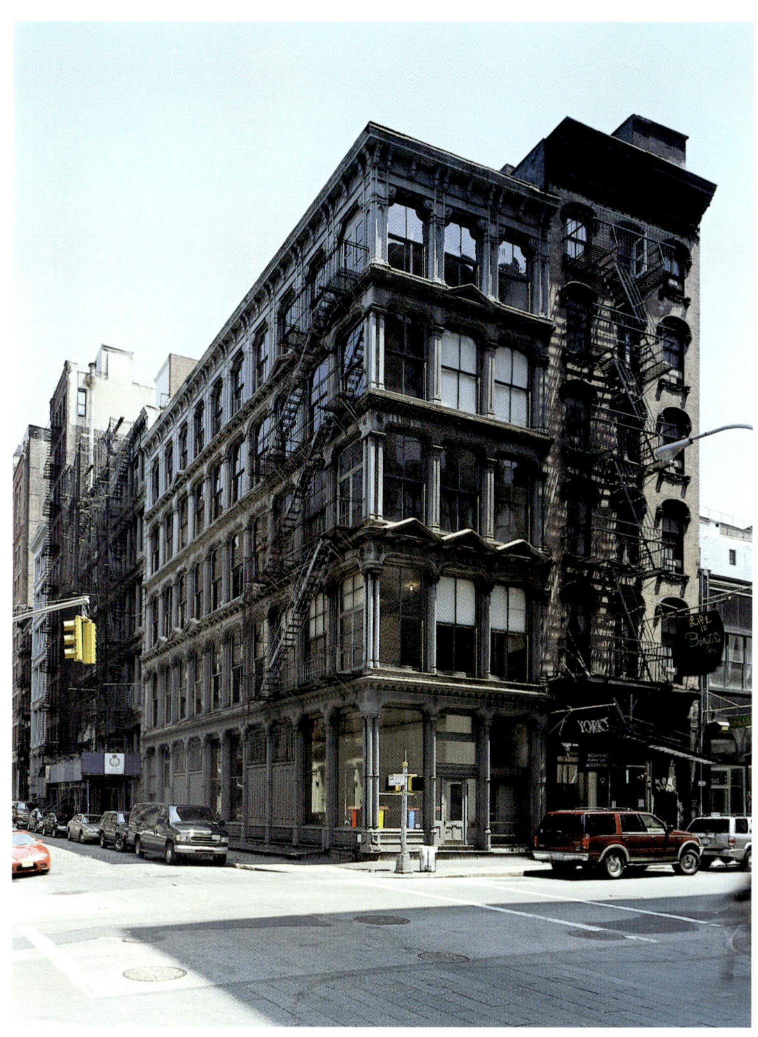

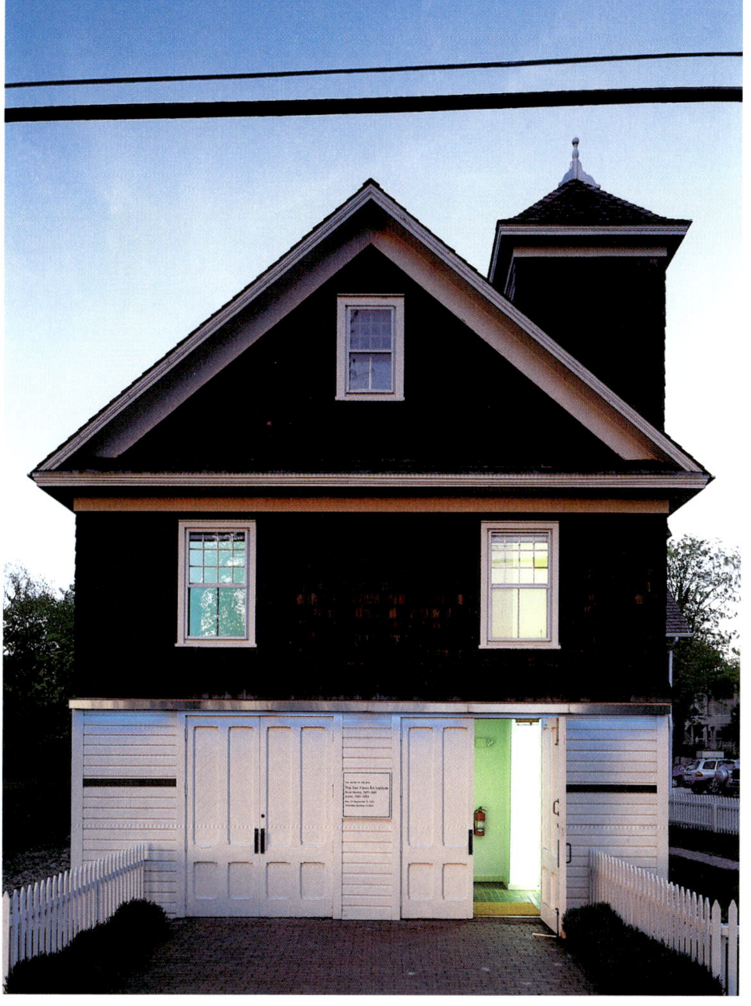

page 18 Robert Smithson, *Spiral Jetty*, 1970, Great Salt Lake, Utah
left Donald Judd's building, 101 Spring Street, New York City
right The Dan Flavin Art Institute, Bridgehampton, New York

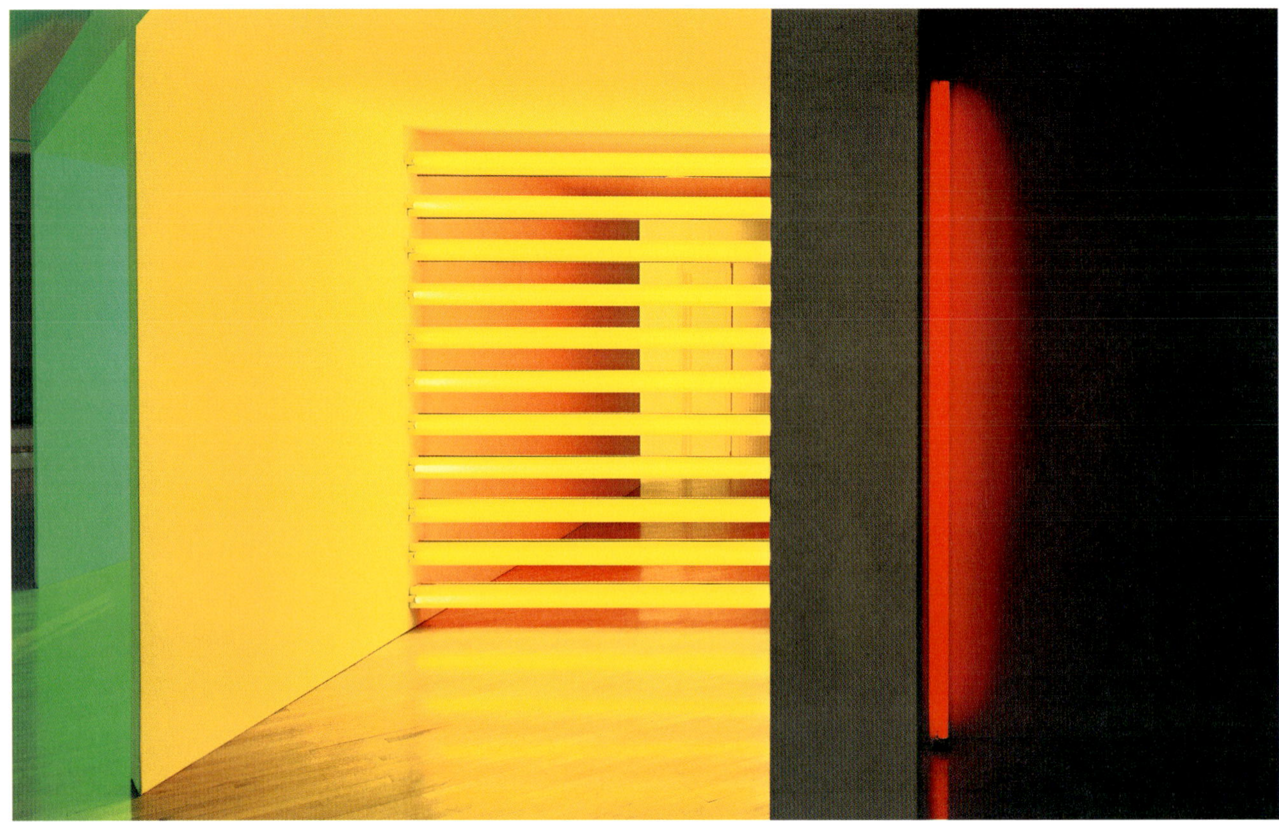

performance or pure ideas)—the work of the period was sometimes barely recognizable as art at all. This expansion of the definition of art necessitated a reconsideration of the field of its presentation. By a modernist, Duchampian dictate, of course, art could be anything named as such by the artist; but in practice that proposal is more complex. Marcel Duchamp's infamous readymades achieved their affect and meaning by being considered within an institutional or discursive framework of other artworks, and the same is true of even the most radical gestures of the 1960s and 1970s. More precisely, twentieth-century art became ever more sensitive to the context of its presentation, and artists took an ever increasing responsibility in defining the framework in which their work was presented. One of the fundamental differences between Pollock's drip paintings and Heizer's motorcycle drawings in the desert is that Heizer not only made a visual statement but also determined the circumstances in which it would be experienced and understood: a vast empty space that required an aerial perspective to be grasped entirely and that was isolated by hundreds of miles from anything resembling a traditional gallery. Flavin's "breakthrough" in the mid-1960s wasn't merely his selection of a ready-made, store-bought fluorescent light fixture as his primary medium but the fact that by making light constructions within the architectural frame of the gallery, he shifted the field of experience from an art object to an enveloping spatial experience.

The creation of the museum in Beacon has involved many artists in the present, and its conception was based on the principles and examples of some of Dia's founding artists, namely Flavin, Judd, and De Maria, who insisted on designing not only art but also the containers in which it

left and right Dan Flavin, "Nine Works (1971–1983)," installation at the Dan Flavin Art Institute, Bridgehampton, New York

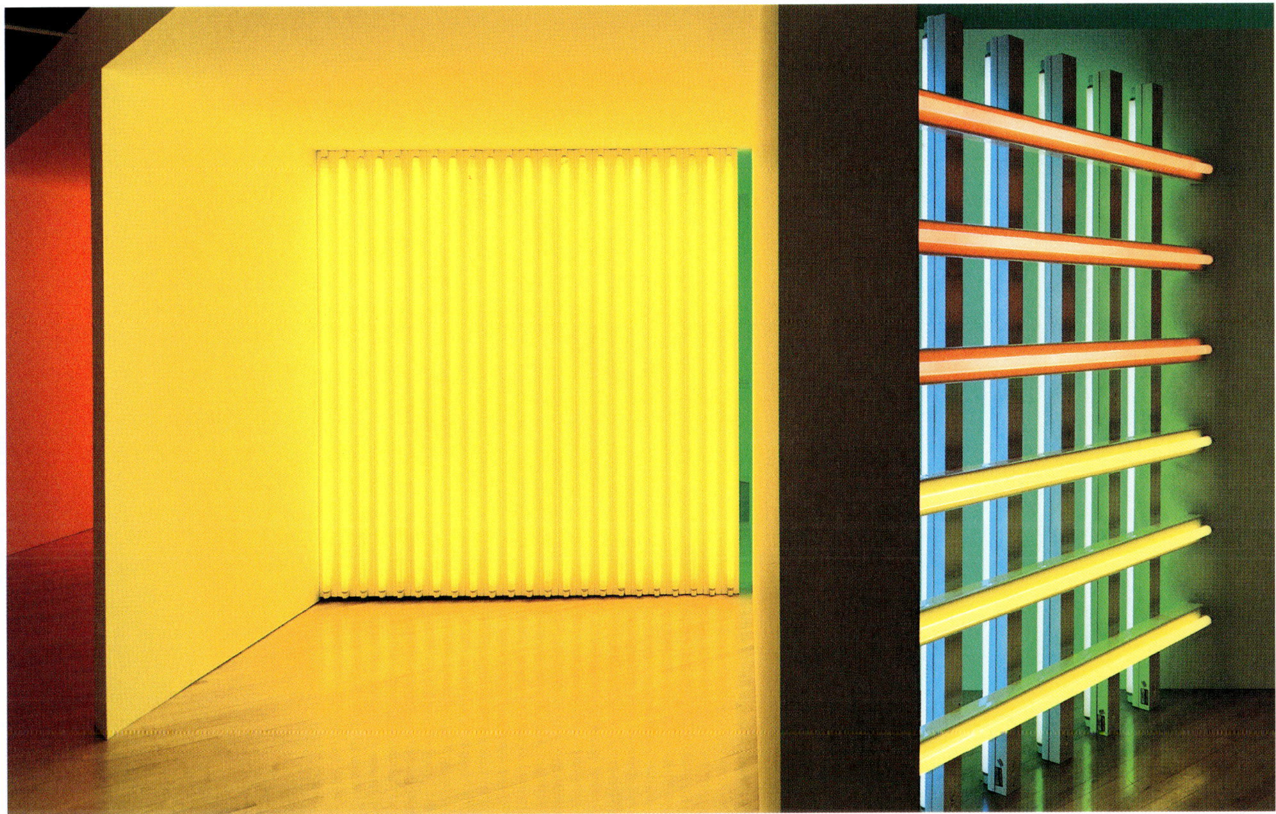

is experienced. The importance of this conjunction of art and environment is especially evident in Judd's writing and in his installations in New York City and in Marfa, in western Texas. Judd wrote that he often expended as much thought and energy on the placement of a work of art as on the work itself. Within that effort he found himself drawn to consider the selection and design of site, architecture, and even furniture in the presentation of his art. Finding existing museums deficient in the proper consideration of this intimate relationship between art and its environment, he set out to create his own contexts for his art, first in a nineteenth-century cast-iron building in SoHo, in downtown Manhattan, and later in abandoned buildings, including a former military base, in Marfa. His experiments in Texas, largely financed by Dia between 1974 and 1983, were designed to include presentations of work by two of his colleagues and fellow Dia artists, Flavin and John Chamberlain. Judd was especially insistent on the value of using existing buildings. "New land should not be built upon," he wrote. "And existing structures should be saved, 'important' and 'unimportant' alike."

When Flavin exhibited his art he was equally interested both in reusing existing buildings and in selecting or designing his own architectural environments, as evidenced in his permanent installation of nine works in a converted firehouse and former Baptist church in Bridgehampton, or in his unfinished project to install his work in Dick's Castle, an abandoned estate in Garrison, New York (ten miles south of Beacon), with commanding views of the Hudson River. In both cases the use of an existing structure provided a set of architectural limitations inspiring the spatial dialogue between light and architecture that lies at the core of Flavin's enterprise.

Flavin began working in pure fluorescent light in 1963 and realized his first entirely environmental installation, *greens crossing greens*, in Eindhoven, the Netherlands, in 1966. Taken for granted in today's art world, which is flooded with installations and environments of diverse objects and media, Flavin's all-encompassing gesture placed the viewer literally inside the glowing space of his art. This and his sole reliance on a common, commercially available medium, the fluorescent light fixture, helped overthrow traditional definitions of painting and sculpture. Unwilling to accept either term for his work, Flavin coined the term "proposals" for his light constructions and described his project as "electric light defining space." With Dia's collaboration, he accomplished numerous site-specific installations, of which several, in addition to the Dan Flavin Art Institute in Bridgehampton, exist today: a four-corner installation in the courtyard of the Kunstmuseum Basel, the two staircases of Dia's Chelsea exhibition facility, six barracks at Judd's Chinati Foundation in Marfa, and the Chiesa Rossa in Milan, Italy.

The relationship between art and architecture so evident among Flavin's and Judd's concerns can be compared to the relationship between art and its environment in De Maria's work

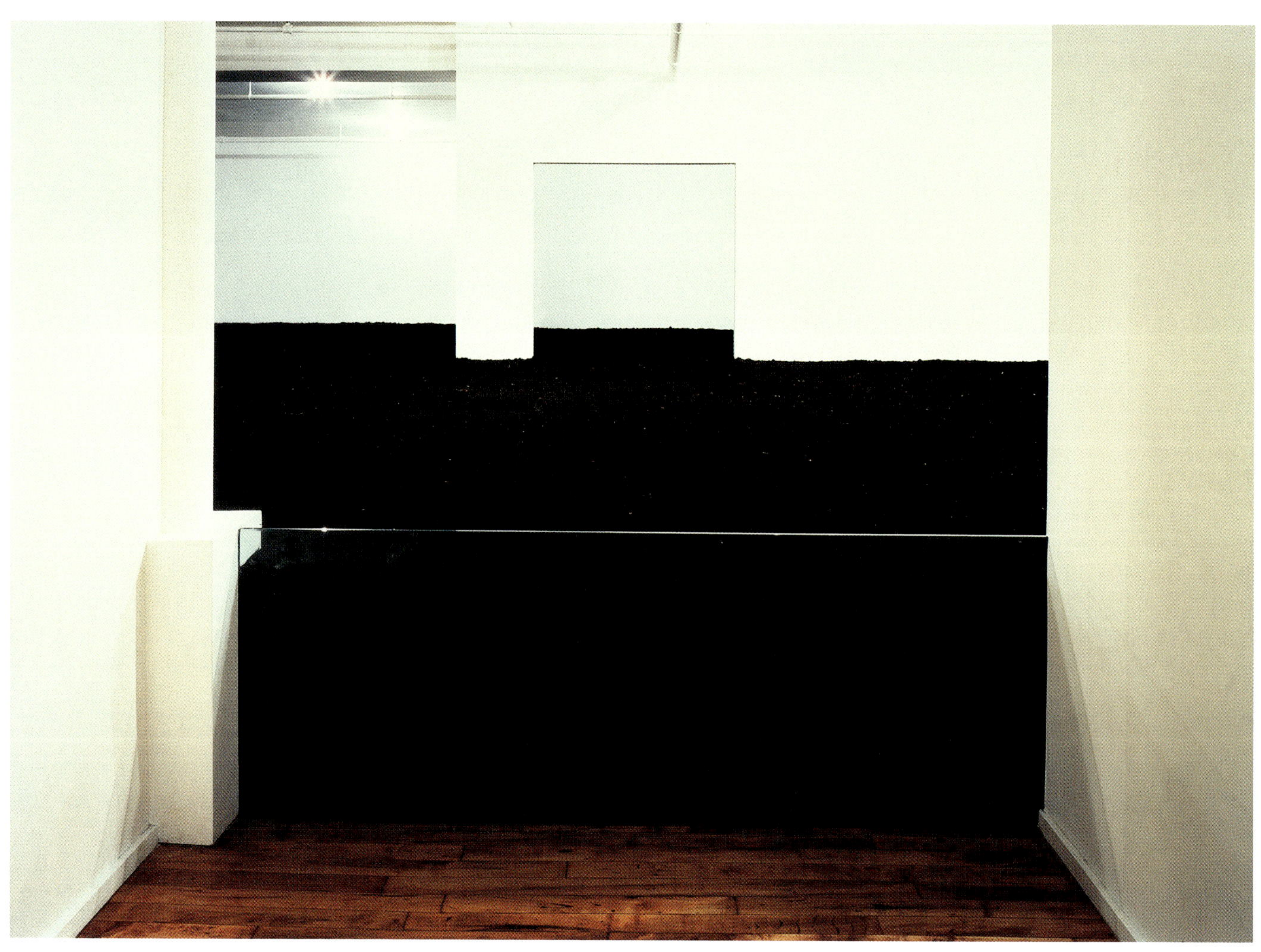

Walter De Maria, *The New York Earth Room*, 1977, 141 Wooster Street, New York City

(a major focus of Dia's support since the institution's beginnings). De Maria's *The New York Earth Room* and *The Broken Kilometer* in New York, and *The Lightning Field* (1977) in Quemado, New Mexico, all of them commissioned and maintained by Dia as part of its collection, stand as some of the most compelling large-scale sculptures of the period. Each appears within an immersive spatial frame designed or selected by the artist, and each involves a separation from the environment of everyday life. Viewing *The Lightning Field* requires a journey to the remote and empty landscape of the high desert of western New Mexico. To ensure a nearly solitary encounter with the work, and an experience of it over the course of a day and a night, no more than six people may visit it at one time; viewers, then, must make reservations in advance. Between May and October they meet at 2:30 pm in the afternoon of their visit in the small town of Quemado, itself a beautiful three-hour drive from Albuquerque, the nearest metropolis. They are driven on dirt roads still farther into isolation. Upon their arrival at the site, with the sun high, the sculpture—400 poles of polished stainless steel, two inches thick and some twenty feet tall, installed 220 feet apart in a grid measuring one mile by one kilometer—is nearly invisible in the vast, flat desert plateau

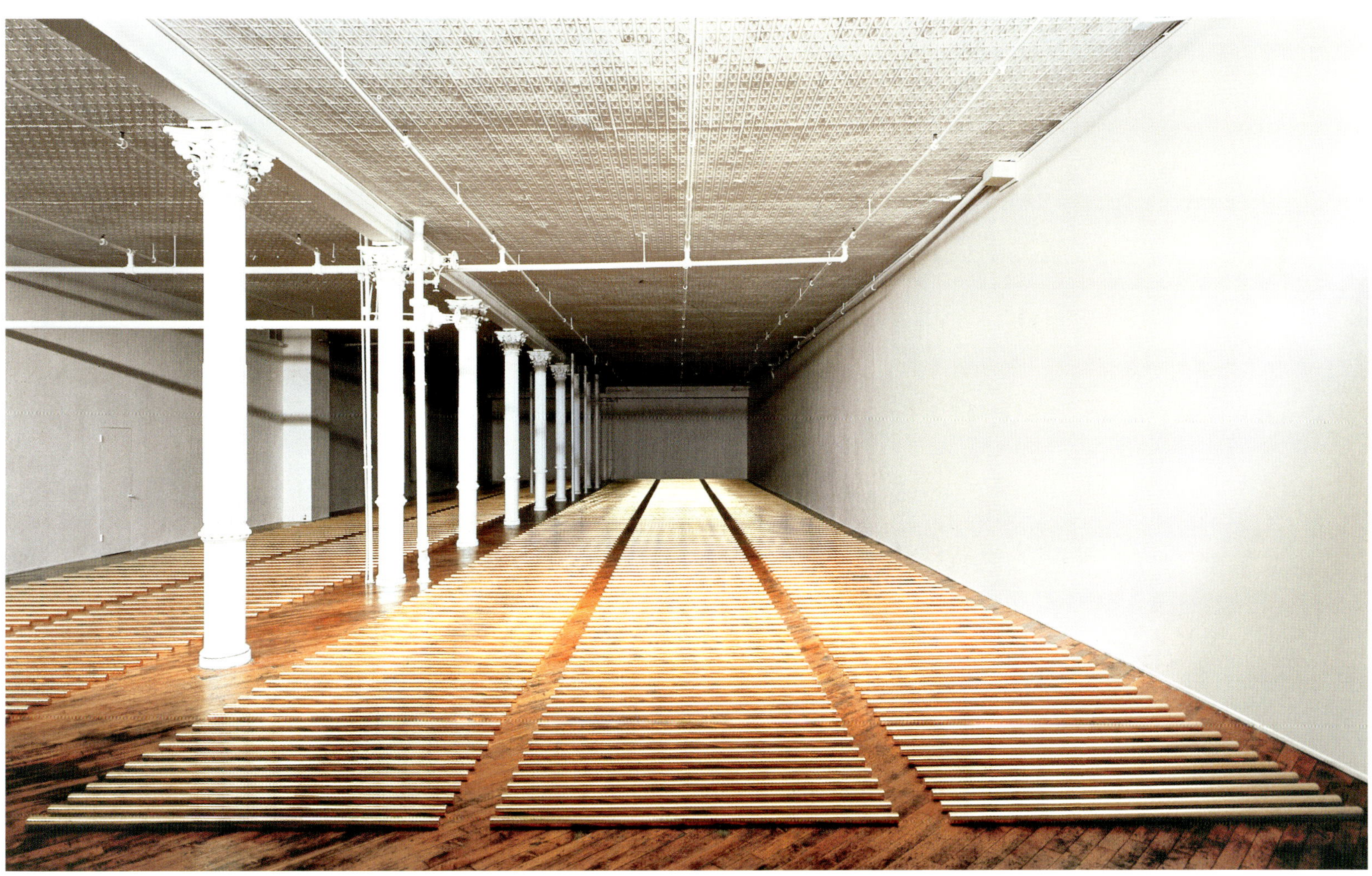

right Walter De Maria, *The Broken Kilometer*, 1979, 393 West Broadway, New York City

pages 24–25 Walter De Maria, *The Lightning Field*, 1977, Quemado, New Mexico

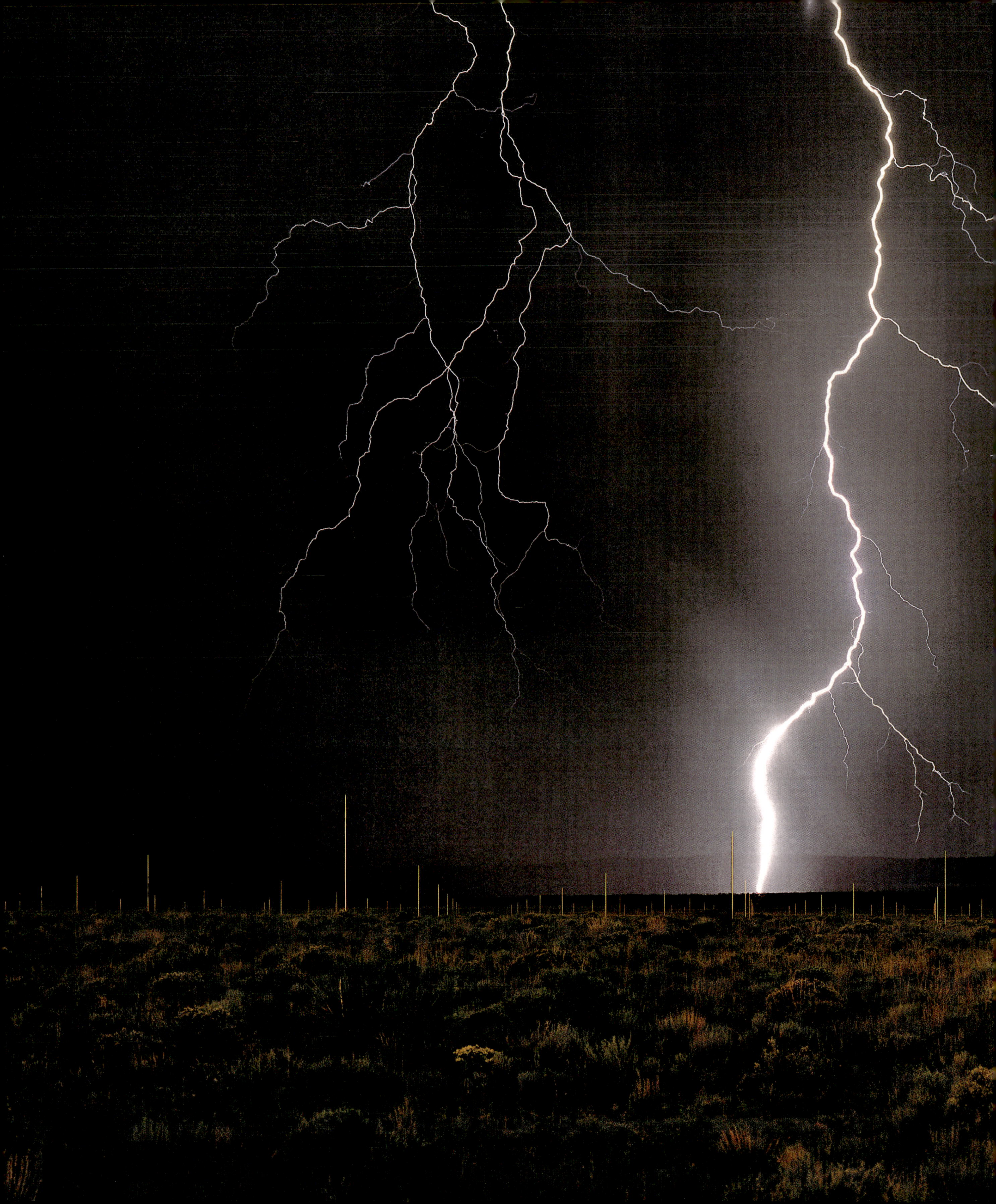

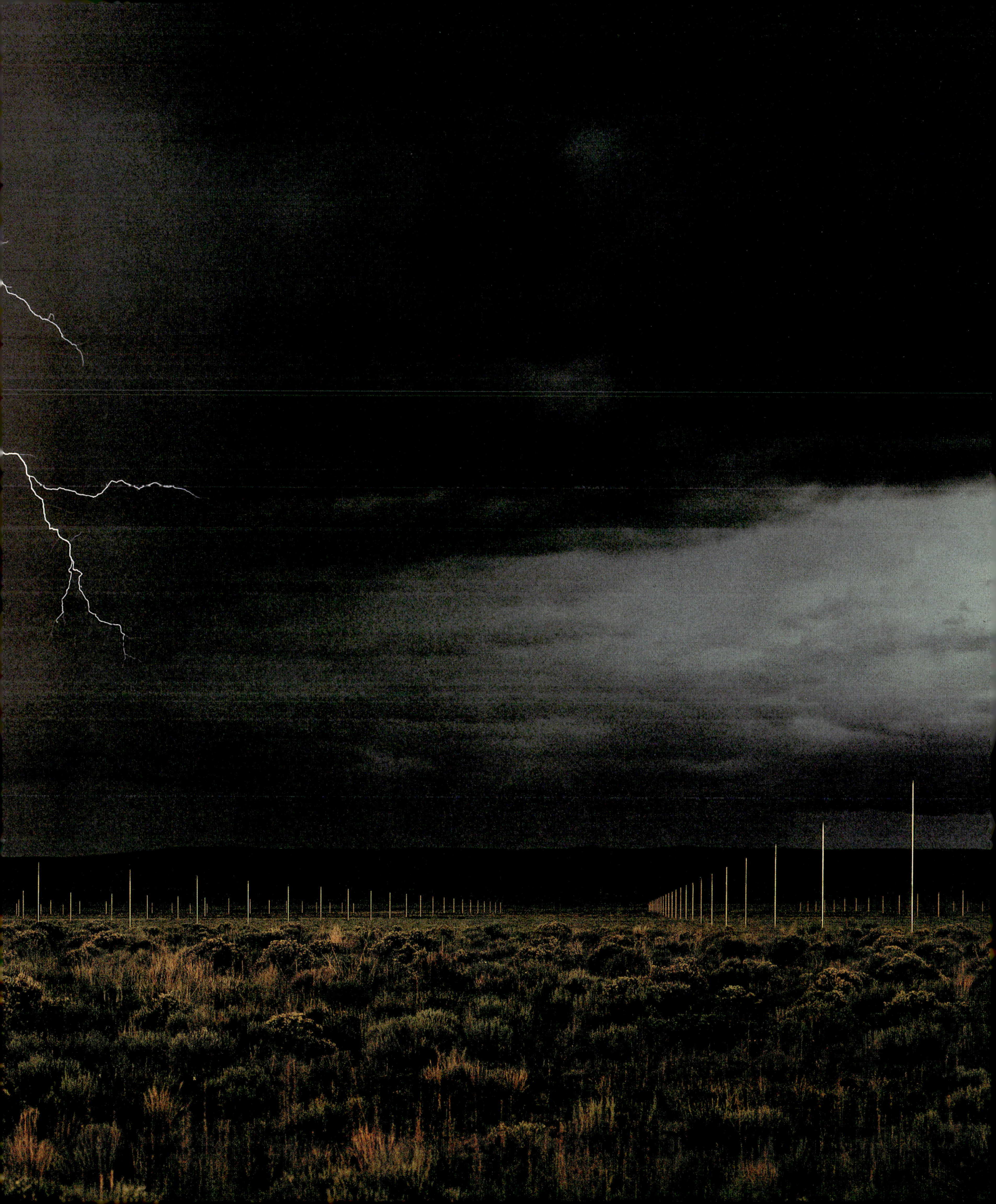

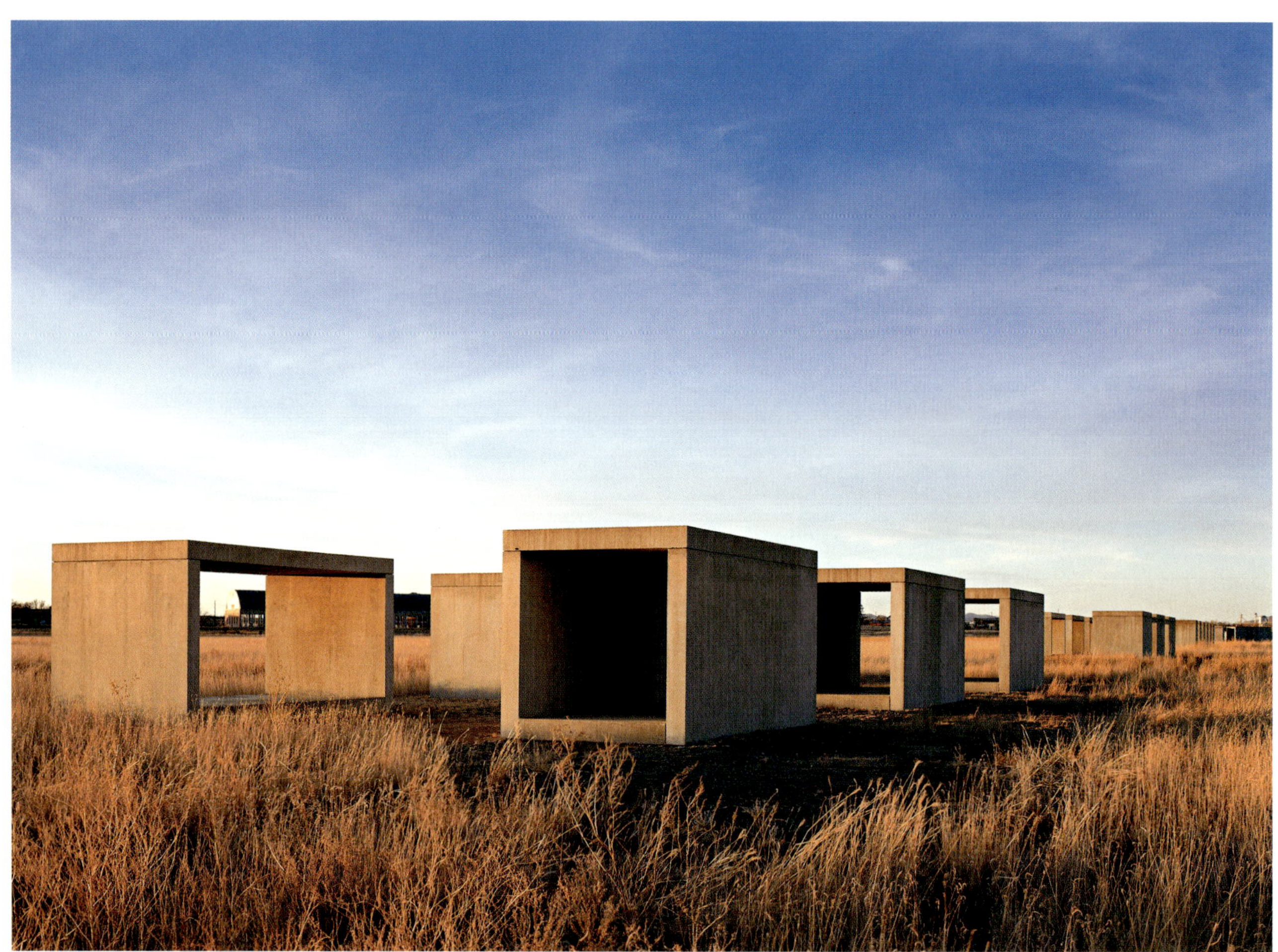

of low scrub surrounded by distant jagged peaks. The experience of the work relies on the experience of light. The visual presence of the poles emerges most sharply during the oblique morning and late-afternoon sun. And during the frequent summer thunderstorms of western New Mexico, the poles harness lightning from the sky, not only by beckoning it in their function as lightning rods (as seen in photographs, if not always on each visit) but by capturing its flash across the work's horizontal expanse. The isolation of the landscape, measured by the precise calibration of the poles, and the sharpened sensation of time marked by the changes of light, are integral elements of the experience of the work.

The relationship of *The Lightning Field* to the landscape is enhanced by the specificity of its situation and by its feeling of timelessness—its permanence. These senses of specific circumstance and of permanence are themes in many of Dia's projects. Both Judd and Flavin believed that their careful methods of installation could be applied with advantage to work besides their own; Judd's Marfa project and Flavin's art institute allowed for installations by other artists, setting precedents for Dia:Beacon. And like De Maria's *The Lightning Field* and other works, Judd's Marfa and Flavin's Bridgehampton installations were for the most part intended to be permanent. As Judd pronounced, "The art and architecture of the past that we know is that which remains. The best is that which remains where it was painted, placed, or built." In the establishment of Dia Art Foundation, Heiner Friedrich and Philippa de Menil set forth as part

Donald Judd, 15 untitled works in concrete, 1980–84, The Chinati Foundation, Marfa, Texas

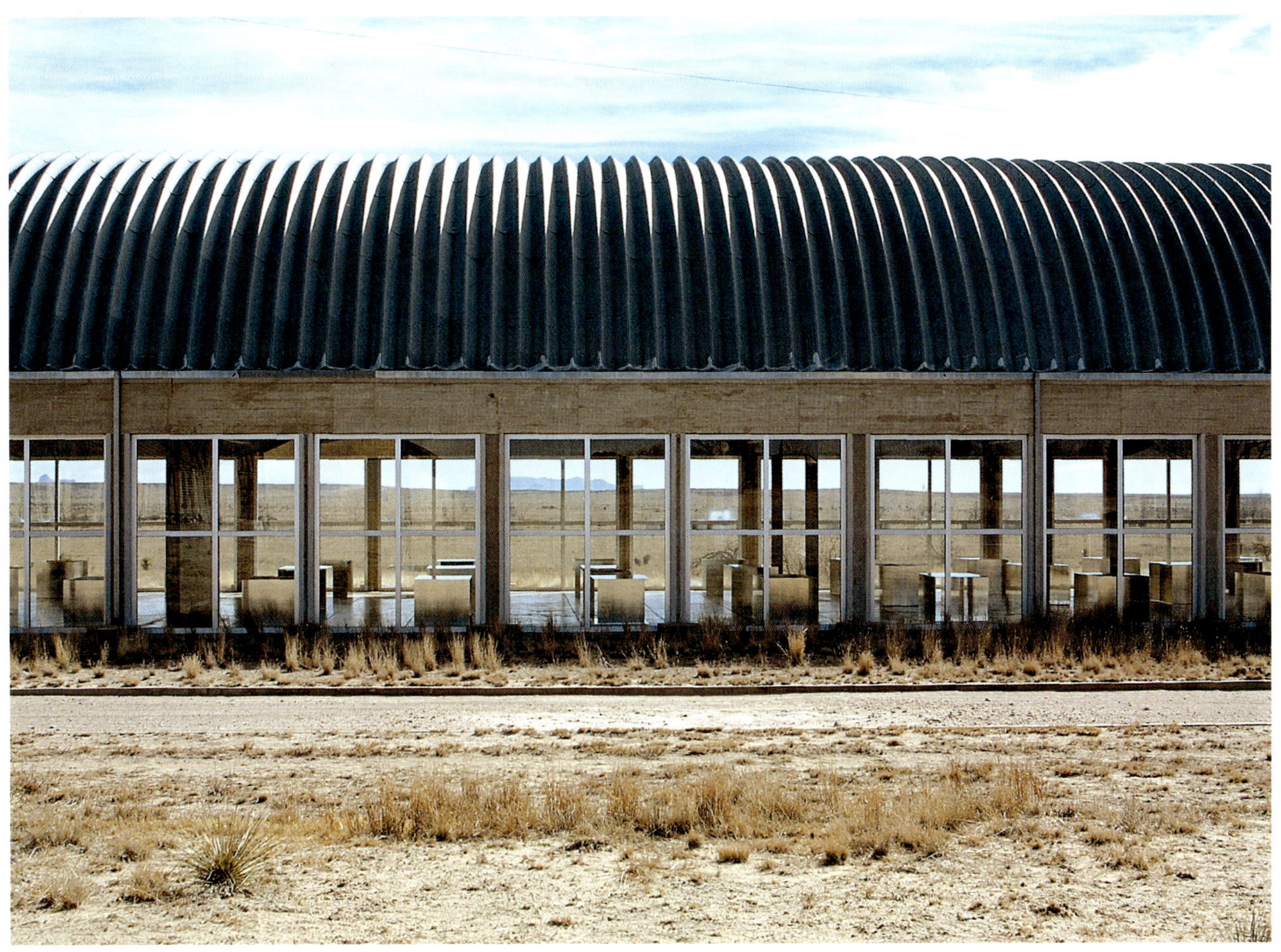

of their mission the idea not only of presenting single-artist installations but of making them permanent or at least long-term. The notion that Dia's projects should be single-artist, long-term, and engaged completely with their surroundings has been shared by patrons and artists alike who have worked with us, and has remained at the core of our mission to the present day. Even Dia's program of temporary exhibitions in Chelsea since the mid-1980s has accommodated single-artist exhibitions for a year or more.

Dia's museum in Beacon has been conceived as an extension of these fundamental tenets: the work of each artist is to be shown in relative isolation, most of the installations are intended to be long-term or permanent, and the spaces are either designed in consultation with the artist or are based on previous installations by the artist. Similarly, Dia:Beacon embodies Judd's and Flavin's interest in the reuse of existing buildings. The nineteenth-century cast-iron architecture of New York's SoHo neighborhood may have accommodated the many innovative avant-garde galleries of the 1970s, but it was Judd, on Spring Street in SoHo, and in Marfa, who raised aged, leftover nineteenth- and twentieth-century industrial and utilitarian structures to the status of ideal, permanent museum architecture for his and other contemporary art. He railed in numerous articles against the 1980s proliferation of architect-overdesigned new museums—completely inhospitable and insensitive to the art they were intended to exhibit—as well as against the never-ending torrent of special exhibitions. As Judd often repeated in different

Donald Judd, 100 untitled works in mill aluminum, 1982–86, The Chinati Foundation, Marfa, Texas

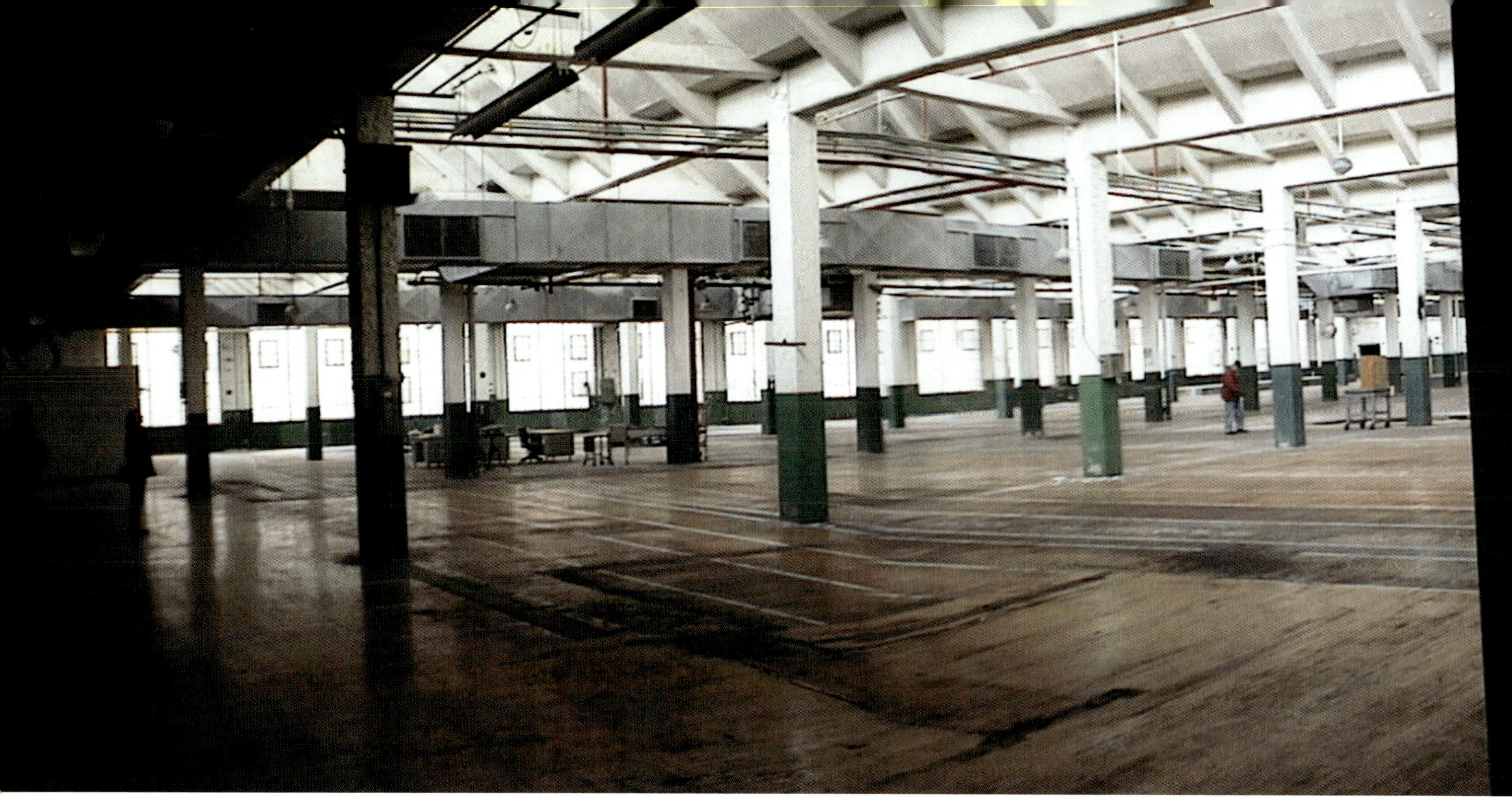

formulations, "The museum should be serious and competent and much is expected but it's a disappointment and a failure. . . . So much money spent on architecture in the name of art, much more than goes to art, is wrong, even if [the] architecture were good, but it's bad."

In Judd's philosophy, and Dia's, the use of existing utilitarian buildings has several advantages. As well as the moral and ecological rationales for renewing and reusing existing structures rather than building new, such reuse sets up a desirable ratio between expenditure on art and expenditure on architecture—giving art preference by all measures. Beyond that, an existing building provides a given set of conditions to inspire artists' installations, and those installations can in turn suggest further modifications to the structure, in a dialectical process of installation and renovation. A utilitarian existing building like the former Nabisco box-printing facility, dating to 1929, that has become Dia's museum in Beacon—and unlike so many architect-designed new museums, where the building itself is intended to have the qualities of a sculpture—does not impose its own overriding artistic signature onto the art. Equally important, the space can be subtly modified into collaboration with the artwork itself—as Judd beautifully demonstrated in Marfa, converting the artillery sheds of the former Fort D. A. Russell into translucent frames for 100 of his mill aluminum boxes. There he replaced roll-up doors with glass to let in light, and added standard galvanized-steel half-round Quonset roofs to better shed water and to grant the lowly warehouses some appropriate stature in the vast western Texas landscape. Rather than compromising his art to accommodate its setting, Judd changed the building to accommodate his art.

Ground floor of Dia:Beacon, 1999, before renovation

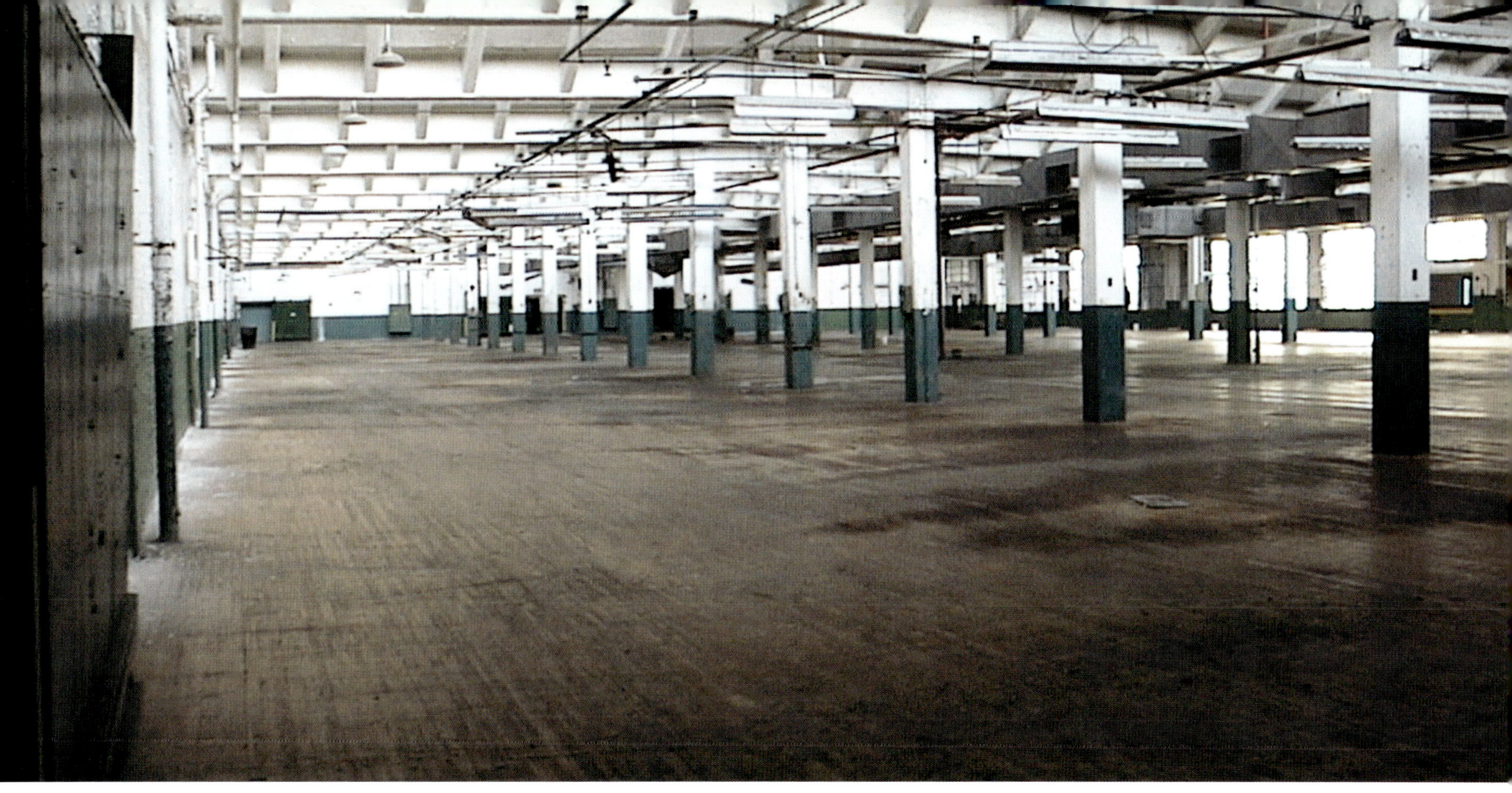

In the case of the Nabisco facility in Beacon, the functional design principles of good factory architecture—durable materials and generous space and light—are not only fitting heirs to the modernist codes of Constructivism and the Bauhaus, they produce the simple straightforward integrity sought by Judd and his peers. This made the building easy to identify as an ideal setting for Dia's permanent collection. Abundant, unvarying natural light from an extensive system of north-facing sawtooth skylights illuminates paintings and sculpture as brightly as it did the precision labor of printing colorful cracker boxes in 1929, without the aid of electric light. Concrete columns, generously placed to allow open spaces of 40 by 290 feet, accommodate some of Dia's largest works and, when provided with walls, create perfectly lit painting galleries. Maple floors look well as the base for floor-installed sculpture, warm the north light, and gently accept our steps, just as they softened the tread of factory workers before us. A total of 300,000 square feet has been shaped to house nearly all of the collection in generous, well-proportioned galleries, with room left over for ancillary public and staff space.

Judd and Flavin were always keenly interested not only in the aesthetic context of the spaces they chose for their work but in the historical one. In that sense it matters that the Beacon factory, sitting alongside the Hudson River, occupies a place of art-historical as well as political and industrial importance. The nearby stretch of the river in view of Storm King Mountain was the favorite of nineteenth-century painters such as John Frederick Kensett, Frederic Edwin Church, Thomas Cole, and Jasper Francis Cropsey. Later, in the 1970s, Flavin chose the Hudson Valley as his primary residence, and its natural beauty and rich artistic history inspired him to collect a series of nineteenth-century Hudson River school landscape drawings (many

Vera Lutter, *Nabisco Factory, Beacon, I: July 19–22, 1999*, 1999

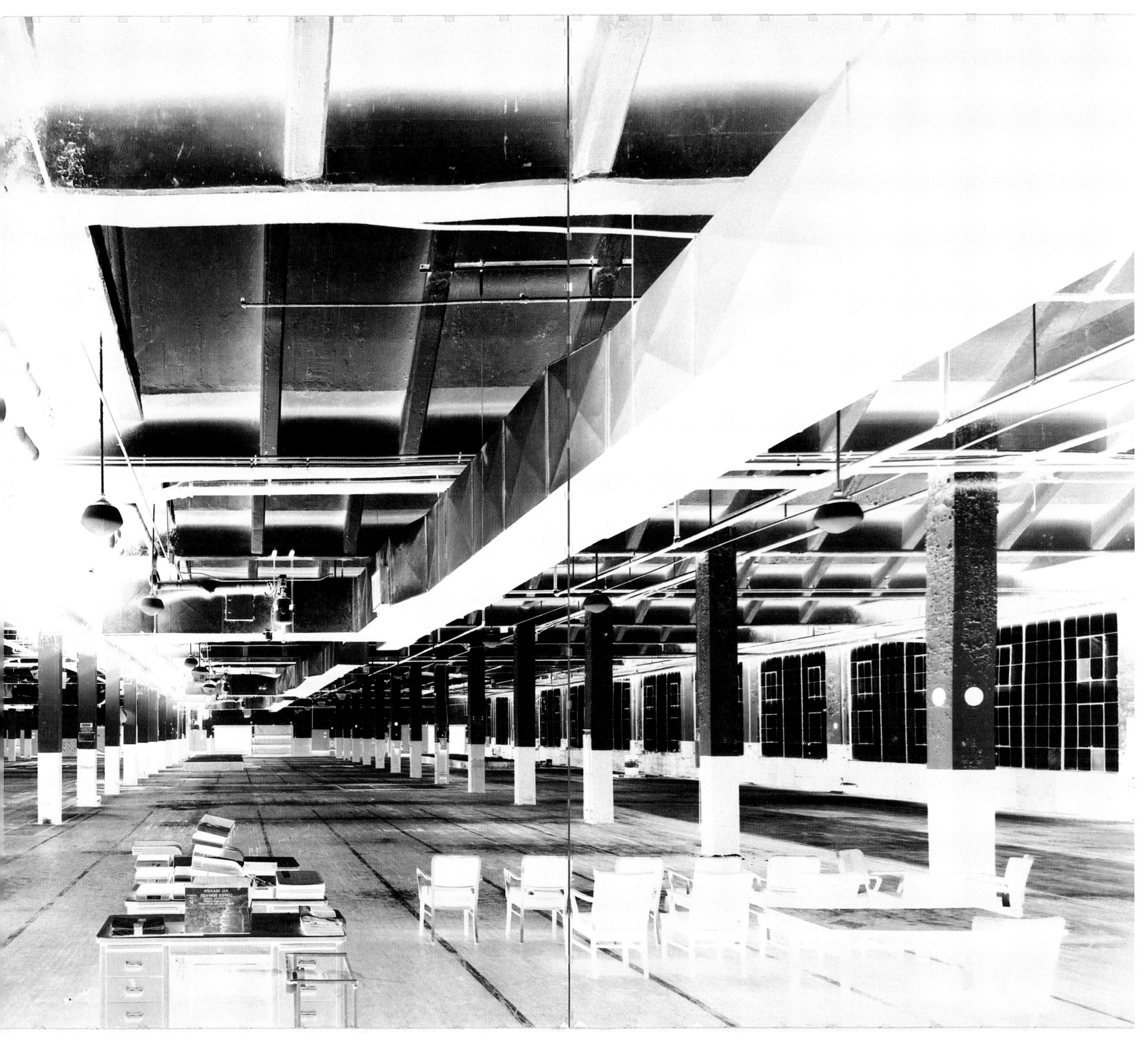

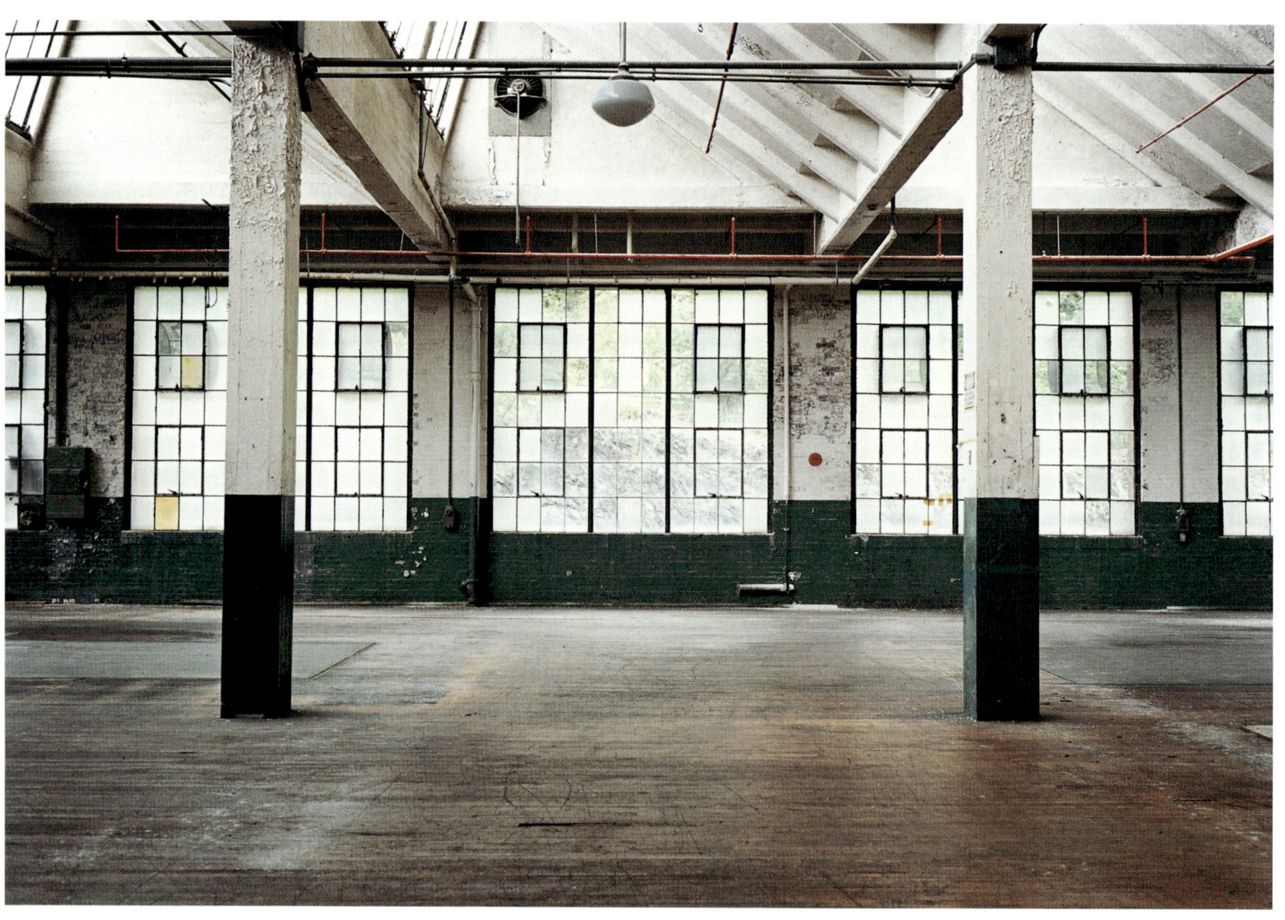

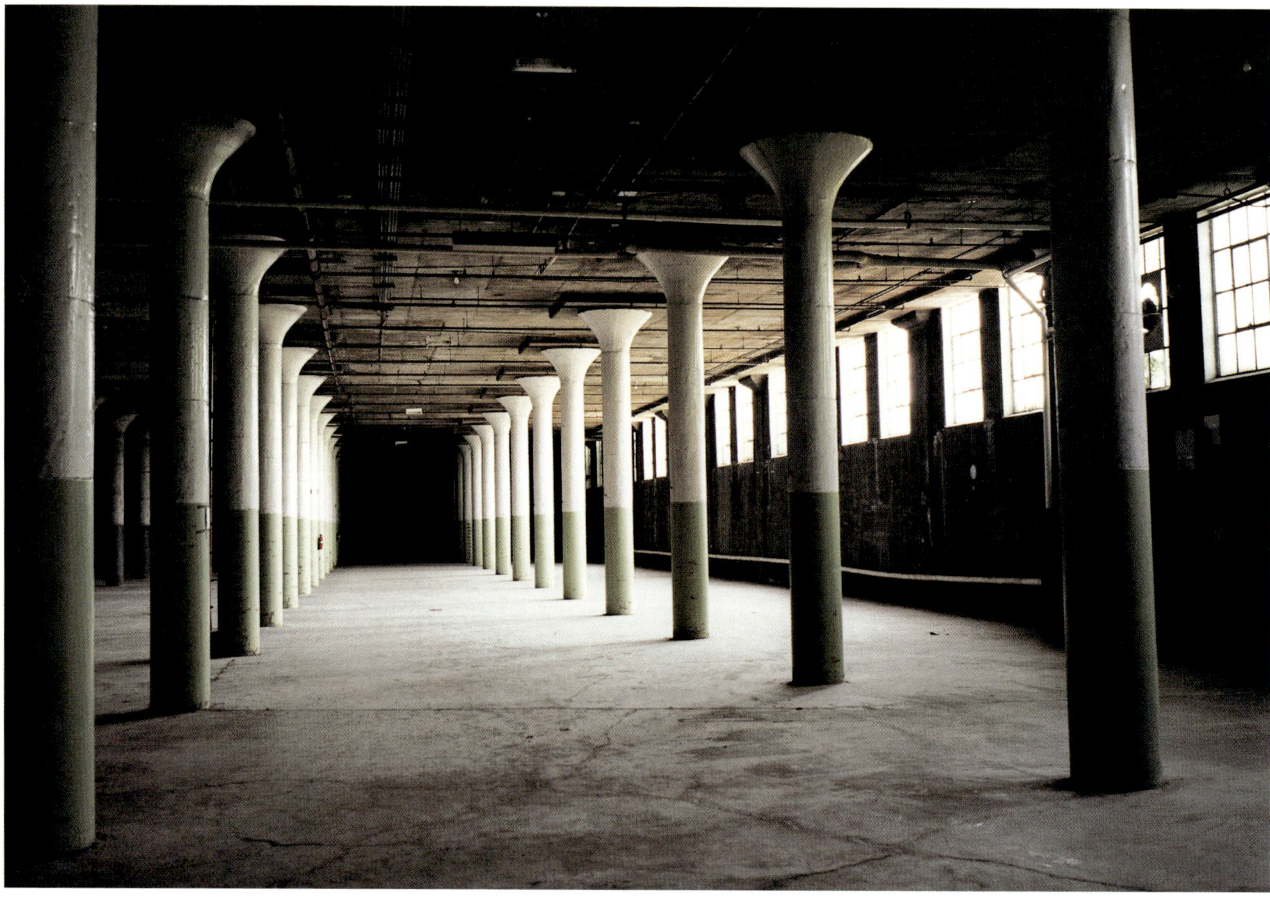

above Ground floor of Dia:Beacon, 1999, before renovation
below Basement of Dia:Beacon, 1999, before renovation

of which are now owned by Dia), which he proposed to exhibit around installations of his fluorescent-light works and his own landscape drawings in his never-realized project for Dick's Castle.

Beacon's manageable but measurable distance from the dense metropolis of New York City, rather than inconvenient, is very much in keeping with projects by De Maria, Flavin, and Judd, among others, which were set up as isolated destinations. For those who travel to Beacon, the pleasure of the drive, or of the scenic journey by train from Grand Central Terminal in Manhattan, only adds to the experience—an abbreviated version of the trek across the western landscapes to Marfa or Quemado.

The Beacon factory is well situated, then, and embodies the artists' standards for light and space in existing architecture. Its transformation into a museum for the twenty-first century, and one in the Dia tradition, called for the involvement of artists, not only in its internal gallery detail but in its organization. Artists represented in Dia's collection were accordingly consulted for their opinions on the project and its shape, and Robert Irwin, who had recently created a pair of installations for Dia Center for the Arts in New York City's Chelsea neighborhood (works that were subsequently purchased), was invited to collaborate with Dia in planning the interior and exterior renovations to the Beacon building that would allow it to accommodate art and public.

Irwin was uniquely suited to the task, not only through his preexisting relationships with Dia and with many of the artists represented in the collection, but also because his practice over the last three decades has involved the construction of environmental installations engaging issues of light and space, both interior and exterior, in both galleries and public spaces. In addition, he had

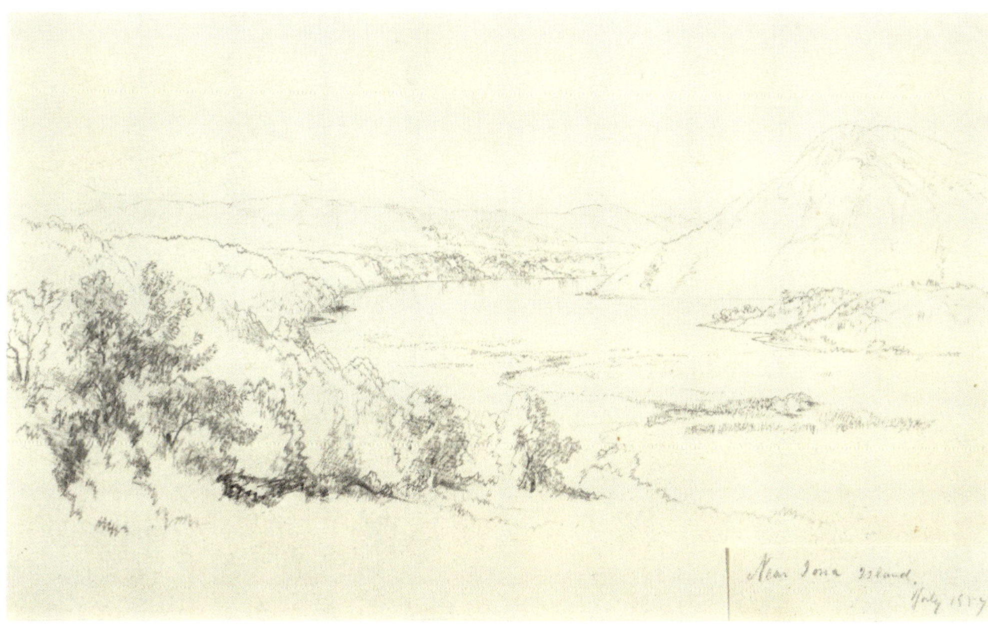

Aaron Draper Shattuck, *Near Iona Island*, 1857

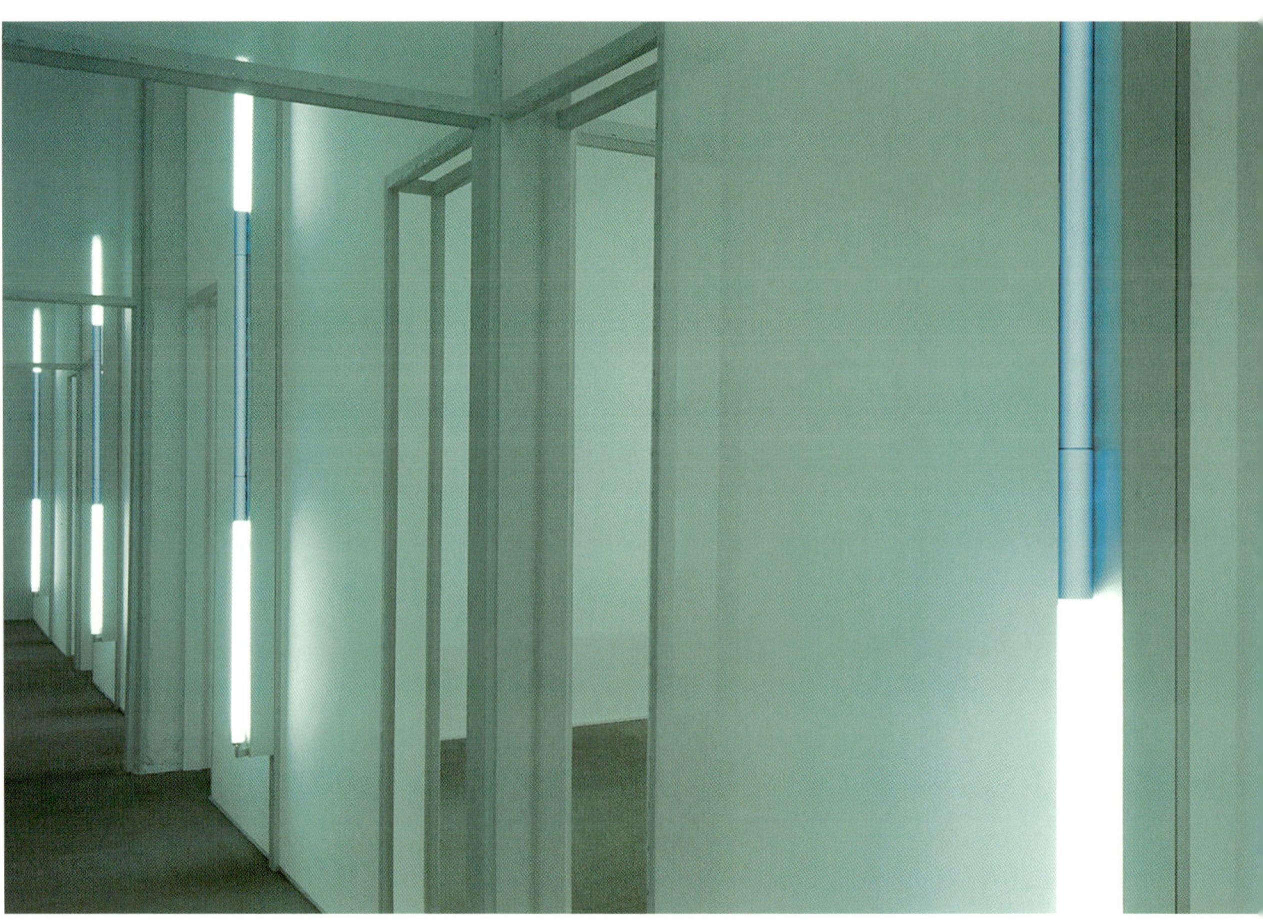

"museum design" experience as a member of the board of the Museum of Contemporary Art, Los Angeles, in the early 1980s, serving as a key advisor in planning the building program and commissioning architect Arata Isozaki to create a new museum. Most important, the innate architectural appeal of the Beacon factory lay in its extraordinary natural light, and Irwin had demonstrated his mastery and understanding of light throughout his career.

The invitation, which came in 1998, was interesting to Irwin because it dovetailed with his own efforts to extend his inquiry into the nature of the artist's practice. He had left the studio years earlier to explore site-specific problems in various given circumstances. Akin to Abstract Expressionist painting in the late 1950s, his art had yielded to ever more ethereal constructions—line paintings, dot paintings, and then convex painted "discs" distorting the atmosphere around a wall—that emphasized light over material, until, by the end of the 1960s, he had eschewed the object altogether to create room installations (like his 1998 Dia installation in Chelsea) constructed as devices for generating experiences rather than images. Since then, Irwin has often gone outside the gallery to work in public space, but he distinguishes his practice from "public art," that is, from art *placed* in public space. Instead, he affects public space directly by organizing both new and existing elements so as to heighten perception. As such, an Irwin work may not be noticed as "art" at all. In his writing and teaching, Irwin has called for a "conditional art" determined by circumstance and need rather than personal expression, and has further

Robert Irwin, *Part I: Prologue: x18*^{3}, 1998, installation at Dia Center for the Arts, New York City

limited his work to invitations he receives to engage specific conditional contexts. His most ambitious attempt to orchestrate a complex public space in experiential terms is an unrealized master plan, from 1986, for the renovation of the Miami airport. Most recently he devised a huge public garden in Los Angeles as the centerpiece of the new Getty Center designed by Richard Meier.

Armed with decades of thinking about such problems, in 1999 Irwin spent several months in Beacon studying the former Nabisco factory and its context, examining its fundamental physical attributes and spatial opportunities as well as the landscape around it. In the next phase of the design process he moved for a year to the Hudson Valley from his home in San Diego, in order, in his words, to "run my hands over the whole place," to "set up an intimacy with the place for myself and . . . create that same sense of intimacy for the future visitor to the museum." Following his method as an artist, Irwin began what he calls an "inquiry" rather than a design exercise. He considered all the experiential issues that would bear on the problem, from light to climate—none of which he could consider from a distance.

A few of the artists to be represented in Beacon had already identified preferred spaces for their works, and other placements were quickly narrowed down by practical considerations of such issues as light needs, dimension, weight, and wall size and arrangement. Irwin on several occasions brought Dia curator Lynne Cooke and me to Beacon for dialogues about both the physical materials of the building and the abstract qualities—time, space, light, symmetry, direction. He also forced us to be precise about the requirements of the artworks. Would the building be more powerful with a plan that agreed with its symmetries or with one that worked against them? What were the alternate qualities of eastern and western light? How did southerly and northerly paths through the building differ? As its shape was revealed by such questions, Irwin's inquiry felt more like a Socratic dialogue than a design initiative.

Irwin's problem solving was bounded by various constraints, primarily determined by the building itself and by the specific needs of the artworks as dictated by the artists and Dia. In addition, the building was to be nominated for the National Historic Register, and therefore neither its primary facades (to east and west) nor the fundamental character of its interior were to be altered. One of Irwin's tasks was to accommodate a number of necessary new emergency exits and a logical public circulation plan without destroying the historical or aesthetic integrity of the building's raw open space. He knew that the reuse of factory space as galleries would demand certain "qualitative" shifts, but in the face of the building's natural simplicity and beauty the working motto was "Don't screw it up."

Finally, in 2000, Irwin issued a series of proposals for organizing the experience of the museum to maximum effect. He also addressed the most pressing practical requirements outside the galleries, including intuitive circulation, fire egress, emergency lighting, parking, exterior access, and the need for rest space to allow breathing room between galleries. He noted that his proposals were subject to modification based on the needs of the artworks and that his "rules" (north-south and east-west axes, paths of circulation, light solutions) could and should be broken to accommodate specific installations but would still provide a subtle sense of overall structure.

Irwin imagined the potentially inhuman space of the parking lot as an experience in itself by proposing an orchard of flowering trees over the parked cars, complementing the building's mass and leaving open an intimate courtyard that would contain a modest new entry vestibule. The courtyard was proposed as a grid of permeable paving blocks of a material called Grasscrete—a pavement that grass would grow up through, except along two strong axial paths that would be filled in by stone. Surprising visitors with a courtyard of green grass emerging through concrete, the plaza would also allow access for cars and emergency vehicles. In serving as a solid visual plane, it would meanwhile strengthen the appearance of the factory's flat, low red-brick facade on this northern side—the least innately interesting wall of the existing structure (since it was originally intended to lie behind another structure that was never built), but, for the museum's purposes, necessarily the front entrance. The new entry vestibule, while involving an absolute minimum of construction in the building's native brick, would unequivocally direct people into the galleries and, in contrast to the overwhelming entrance of the typical museum, would mediate between exterior and interior rather than separate them.

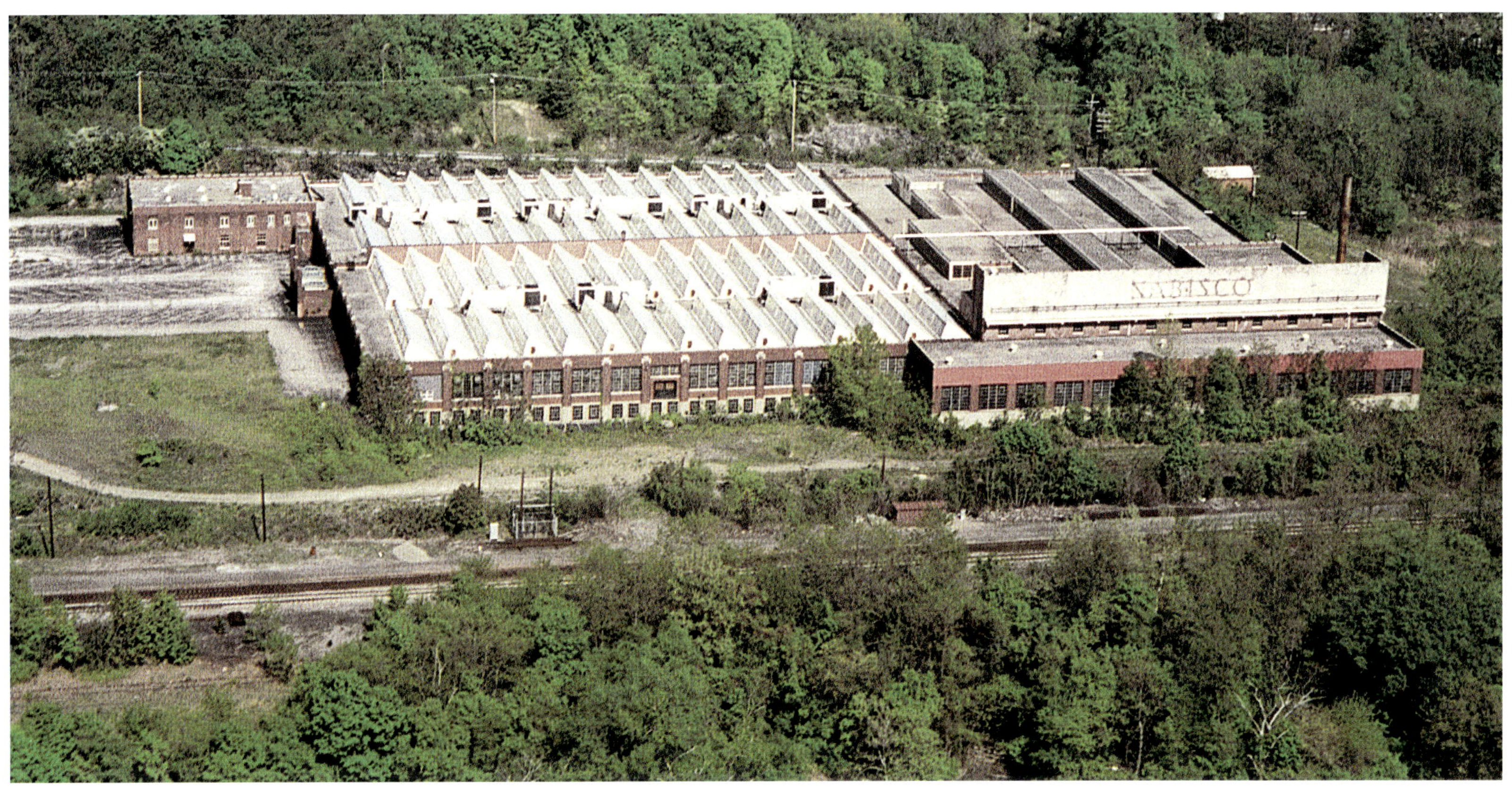

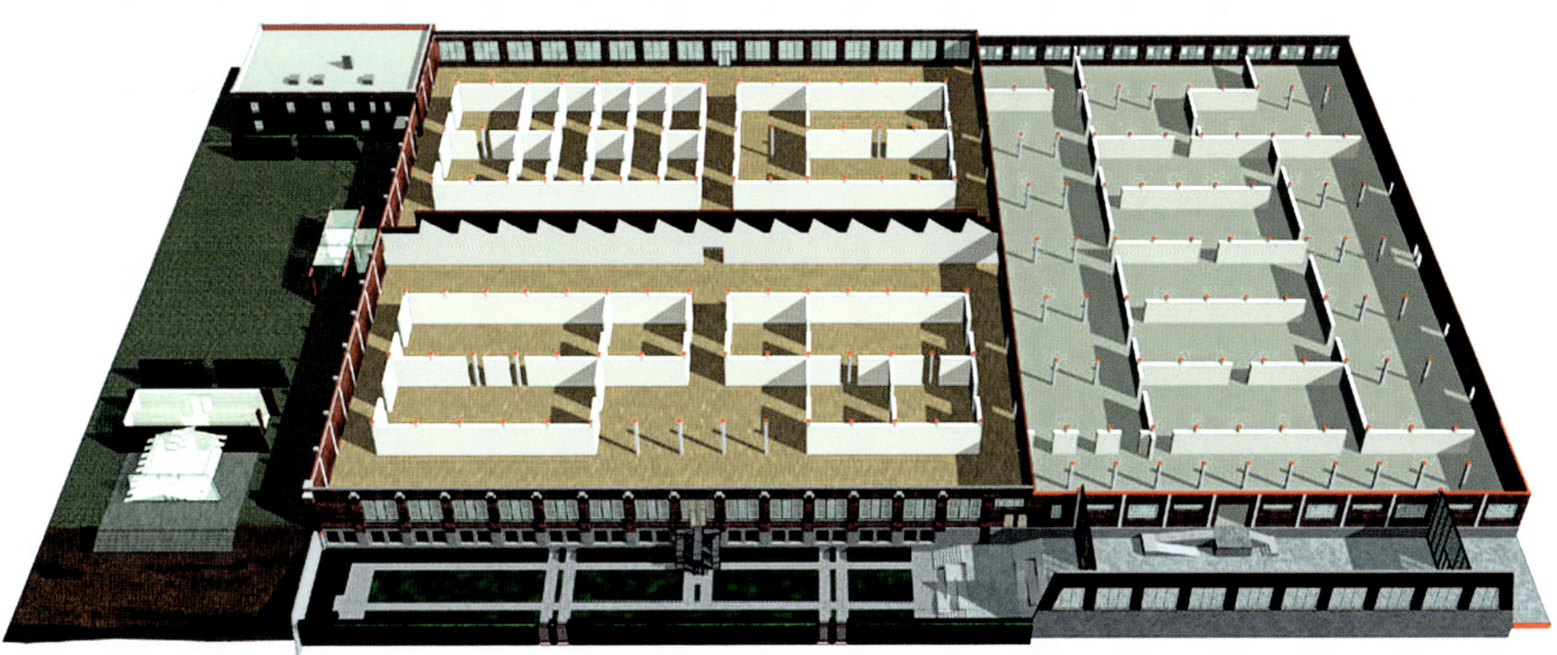

above Dia:Beacon, aerial view

below Robert Irwin, rendering of museum ground floor, 1999

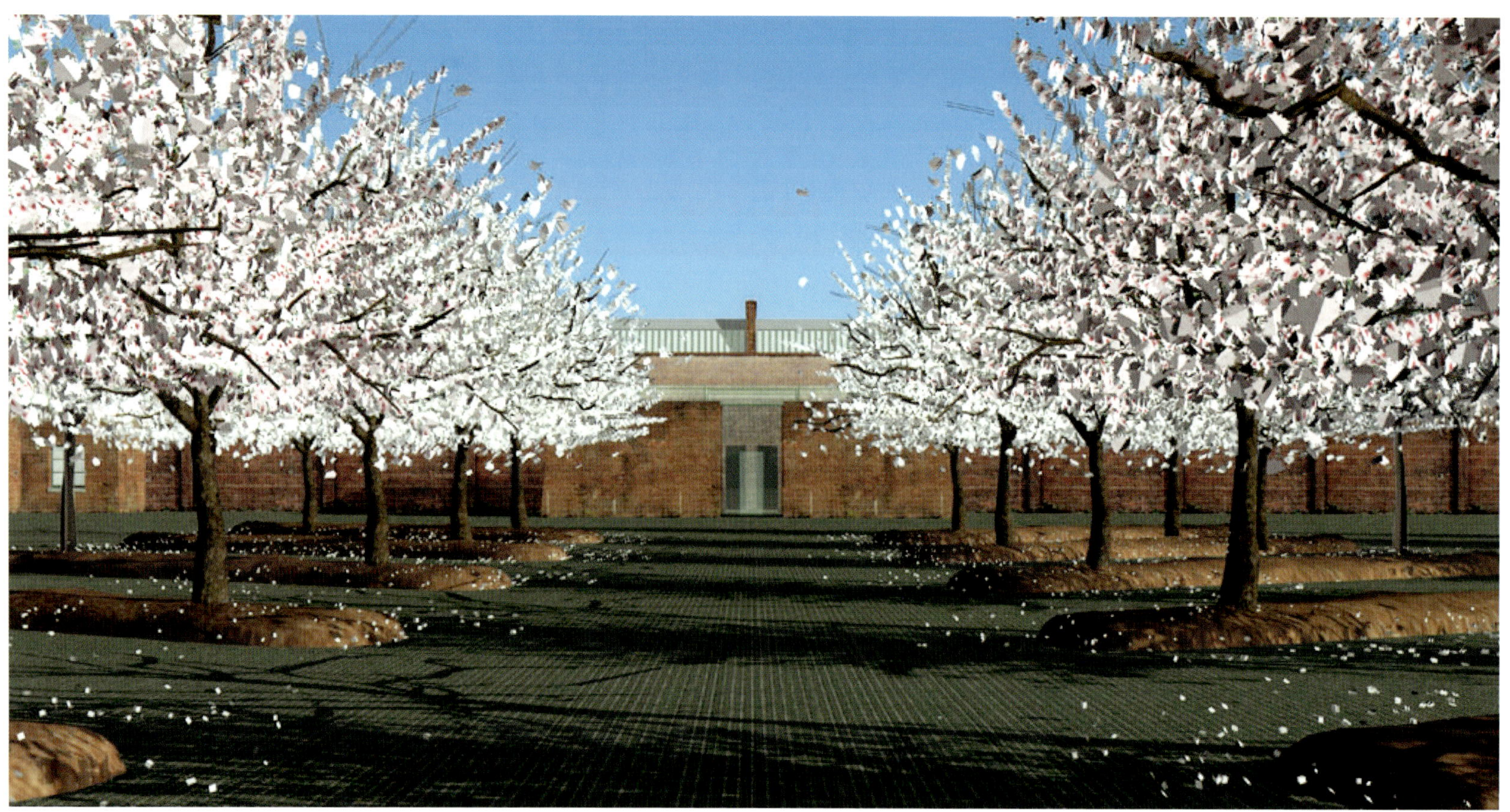

On the west side of the building, within the museum's security perimeter, Irwin proposed a formal garden. With its staircases connecting grade level to the building's three gallery floors, the garden would help solve circulation problems in addition to functioning as an outdoor gallery of plants and trees, providing respite from the cooler, more monochrome interior. Inside the building, Irwin suggested that the walls of the outer shell be stripped of paint and returned to their natural brick, emphasizing their material structure and visually defining the edges of the building from any of the long vistas through the interior. One of the mandated changes to the building, adding more than twenty emergency exits, became for Irwin an opportunity not only to bring additional light into the building along the relatively dark north and south walls but also to set up both rational directional axes through the space and primary and secondary symmetries along parallel facades, connecting the edges of the building with glimpses of light. Yet these powerful orienting symmetries were set up not to control the path of the visitors' experience but to provide tools and clues to keep them oriented, empowering them to make a series of free-flowing directional choices in defining their course through the galleries.

One nearly imperceptible modification called for sixteen panels of clear glass in four quadrants of each of the thirty-two major steel-frame exterior windows. The remaining forty-eight panes in each window were to be restored with the standard translucent factory wire-glass. This device was intended to solve an age-old problem of exterior windows in museums: large fields of frosted or other semiopaque glass, like factory glass, can create the same sense of closure as a wall; fields of clear glass, on the other hand, can overwhelm art with the color and chaos of the outdoors.

Robert Irwin, rendering of museum entrance, 1999

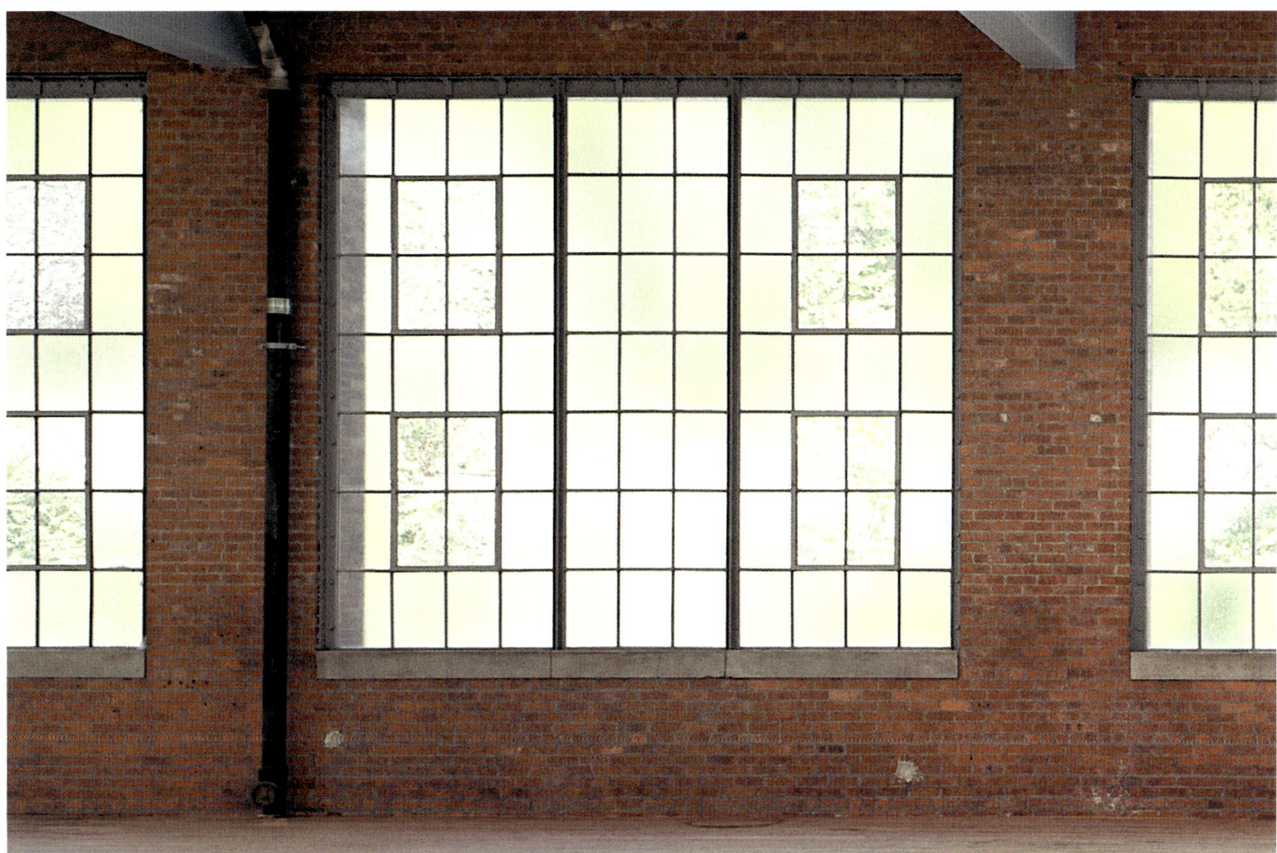

Irwin's hybrid windows, modified by nothing more than a variation in a few of their panes of glass, would create a permeable membrane of vision, protecting the clarity of the gallery space without closing off the exterior. An added bonus would be the flickering, filmlike experience of walking along a series of small framed glimpses of nature.

Open Office, a collaborative of New York architects, was chosen as the architectural firm for the project because its recent work had involved direct collaborations with artists in designing a series of proposed residences. Just as a Richard Gluckman had years earlier facilitated some of De Maria's and Flavin's installations as well as renovating Dia's Chelsea space, Open Office was assigned the task of hiring engineers and turning Irwin's, the artists', and Dia's ideas into architecture. James Schaeufele—the key figure who has directed Dia's building and art installation efforts since the early 1980s, including the construction of Flavin's Bridgehampton art institute—moved to Beacon to oversee the renovation. Together, Dia, Irwin, Open Office, and several artists collaborated in the final design.

The result was intended as a series of immersive experiences of individual artists' installations surrounded by Irwin's mediating exterior. The latter would welcome our visitors, the former would envelop them with art—from Warhol's 1978–79 *Shadows*, conceived as "one painting in . . . parts" and overflowing the more than 300 linear feet of a single gallery, to Agnes Martin's delicate series of eight paintings commissioned twenty years later for Dia:Beacon; from Serra's massive steel Torqued Ellipses, first exhibited at Dia's Chelsea galleries and now occupying the

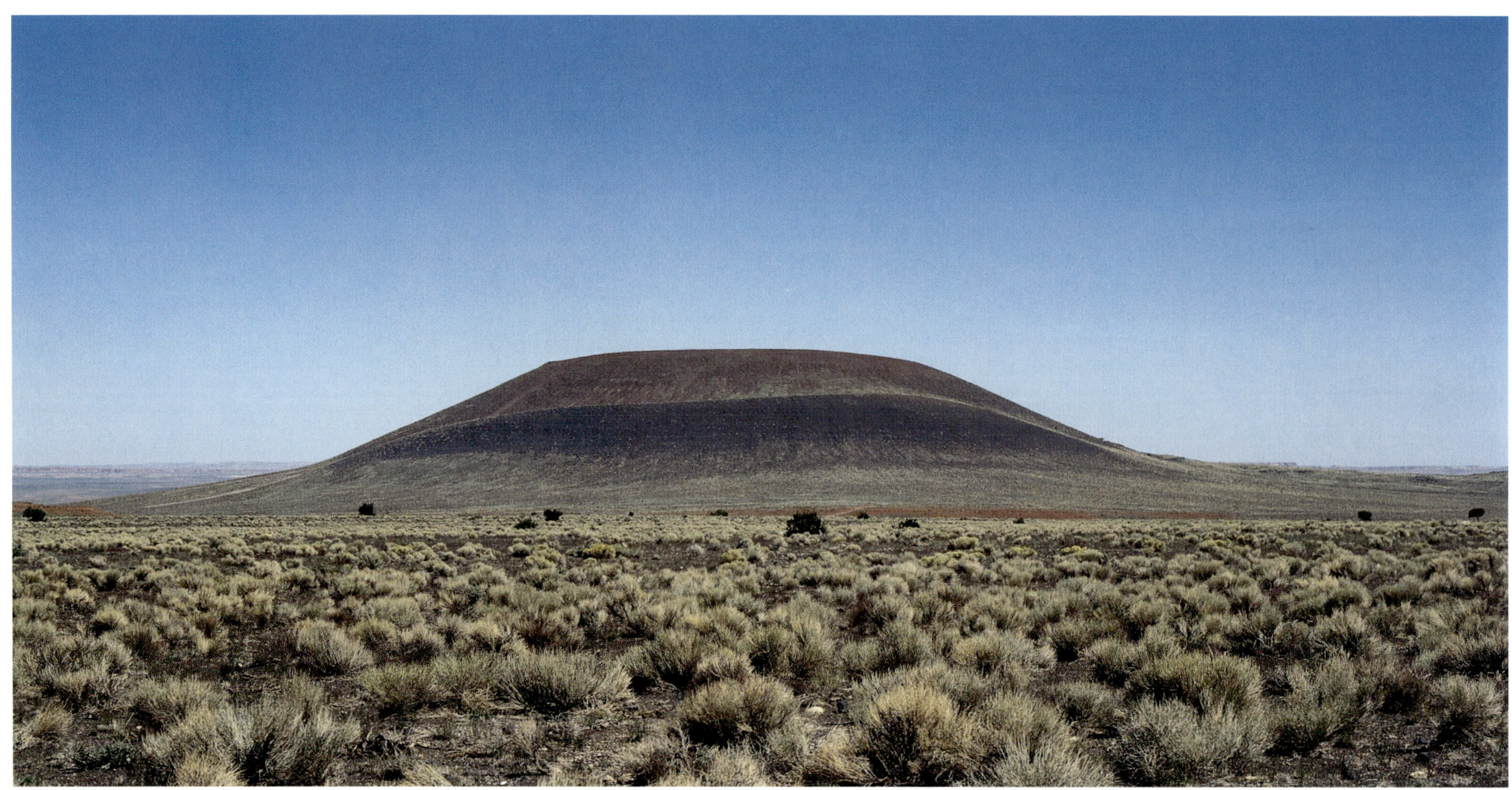

entirety of the Nabisco factory's former train depot, to Heizer's monumental "negative sculpture" *North, East, South, West*, conceived in 1967, now embedded permanently in a 150-by-40-foot concrete-floored gallery in the new museum.

These and many other artists' spaces at Dia:Beacon do suggest an abstract thematic related to the ideas of art in context and the construction of experience. Together they propose that most of the surprising formal innovations of the 1960s and 1970s—the prevalent use of ephemera, new media, and common nonart materials, the interest in performance, the relocation of art outside the gallery to public spaces or to remote, unpopulated landscapes—were aimed at tearing down the perceived wholeness, the commercial value, and the sanctity of the traditional objects of painting and of sculpture. The 1960s were a time when race and gender relations, government, and institutions—including museums and art schools—were searchingly revalued. But what came in their place? What alternatives were built by artists and activists?

One philosophical understanding that can be drawn out of the art of the 1960s and 1970s has to do with the importance of context. Sensitivity to and awareness of environment are easily discernible in Judd's frustration with most museums and in his ensuing quest to design his own—to determine the periphery as well as the focus of a visual experience. These concerns can be related to the social and political upheavals of the time. The movements for civil rights, feminism, sexual liberation, and the environment, the opposition to military and cultural imperialism, the tearing down of traditional institutions in general—all of these were as transgressive as the art that accompanied them. Yet each of these movements at its core involved

left and right James Turrell, Roden Crater, 1972–present, Painted Desert, Arizona

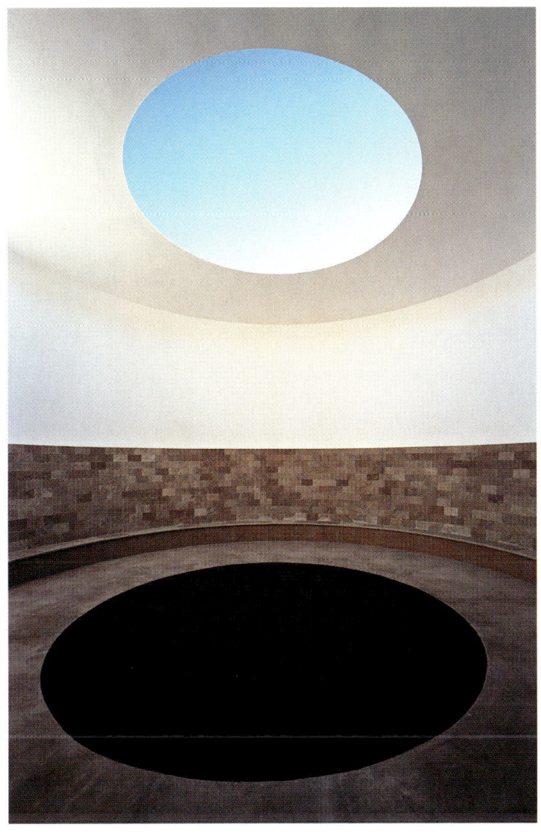
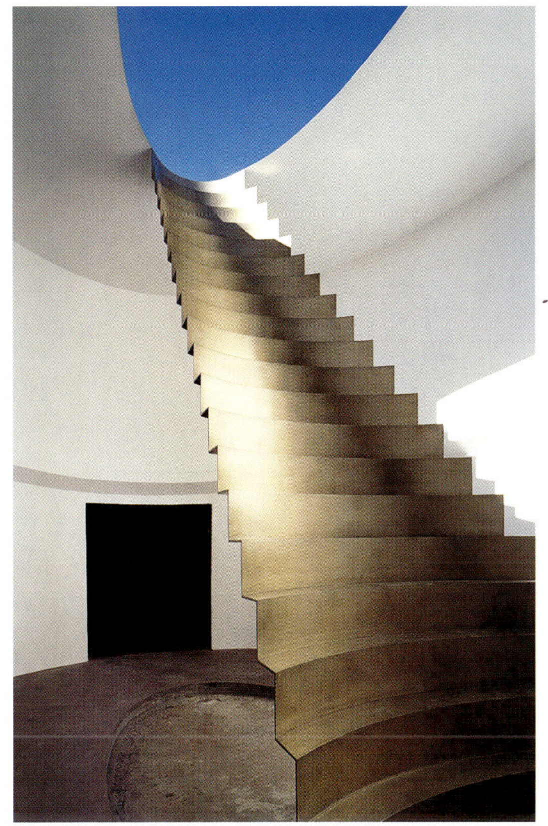

a heightened awareness of context. The basic principles of law, economy, and human rights had to be reconsidered in a larger field: a diverse world and a fragile environment. The visionaries of the time were those who enlarged our sense not only of what we experience but of the frame of reference in which we experience it. The civil rights and feminist movements, in particular, were aimed at destroying the false definitions and boundaries that had been historically and culturally constructed around people; the environmental movement, meanwhile, sought to make us understand that human existence could be neither contemplated nor even sustained without the survival of the world's natural resources. At the same time, the sixties generation witnessed increased emphases on the rights and the integrity of the individual.

The details of the relationship between the art of the 1960s and 1970s and the period's social and political revolutions lie outside the scope of this essay and perhaps suggest issues that need further historical and art-historical study. It is interesting to speculate, though, about the similar terms and conditions that might apply. In both cases, traditional institutional frames of reference were disregarded and new contexts built—first, around the integrity of the individual, and second, within a larger understanding about the fragile nature of our existence in relation to a larger environment.

These paradigmatic shifts in understanding can be distinguished from those of the early modern era, which were characterized by totalizing utopian visions (fueled, for example, by Marxist philosophy), by optimism about the redemptive social potential of technology and industry, and by a faith in the ability of art to play a fundamental role in the emerging transformations of of the twentieth-century world. The art of the Russian avant-garde—Kasimir Malevich's painting and theater projects, say, and Vladimir Tatlin's sculpture and architecture—is paradigmatic here. By the 1960s, though, the utopian project of modernism had been reassessed. Flavin's "monuments" for V. Tatlin (1964–90), a selection of which is on view at Dia:Beacon, are intended as an ironic but sympathetic commentary on the Russian Constructivist's proposed *Monument to the Third International*, of 1920, the apotheosis of the modernist ideal of integrating the arts and politics in the service of social change. The monument was never built, the postrevolutionary Russian authorities rejected modern art in favor of realist propaganda, and Tatlin died destitute and alone. Thus Flavin emphasized the "ironic humor" of his own temporary monuments, which "only survive as long as the light system is useful (2,100 hours)." He also dedicated his series of "monuments" to Tatlin's noble ambition but tragic life.

Interestingly, as the many large-scale projects in Dia's collection attest, the enormous ambition of modern art, and even the notion of the "monumental," were preserved, albeit reconsidered, by this new generation of artists. Heizer has continued to pursue his most ambitious art outside the confines of the museum, working since 1970 on an enormous sculptural construction of space, earth, and concrete in a remote and empty desert valley in southern Nevada. Entwining monumentally sized sculptural elements, shaped mounds, and carved-out "negative" spaces in complex visual and spatial relationships, Heizer's epic project, appropriately titled *City*, literally sets up an alternative world of experience. Its civic-scale abstract forms fuse ancient and supermodern associations in an all-encompassing, seemingly endless region of visceral sensation that must be traversed in time, like the landscape or the cityscape, rather than viewed in a single gestalt. Constructed in a language of pure abstraction without didactic purpose, the work, still under construction, will offer an utterly immersive field of experience of enormous depth and suggestive power, provoking the construction of meaning in the viewer rather than imposing meaning through the art.

One of Dia's earliest, most ambitious (and as yet unfinished) initiatives was to support Turrell's Roden Crater. In the Painted Desert of northern Arizona in the early 1970s, Turrell had found a natural volcanic crater that he proposed to transform into a variety of experiences of light,

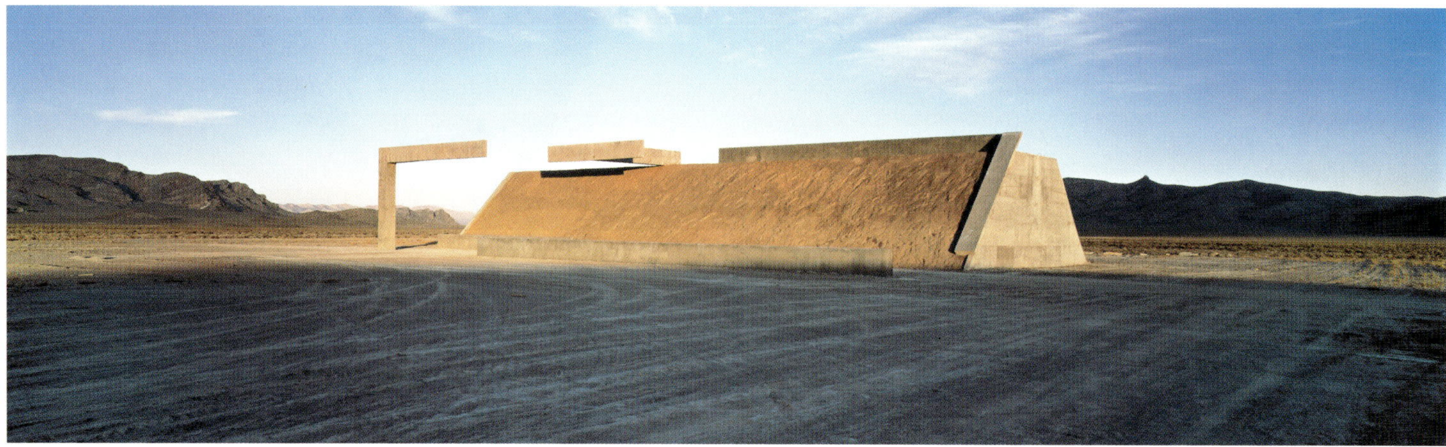

Michael Heizer, *Complex One/City*, 1972–74, Nevada

space, and celestial phenomena. He would generate these experiences by slightly reshaping the interior of the crater bowl and by creating a series of chambers and tunnels that would direct and hold light while simultaneously allowing navigation through the mountain. From the center of the bowl, once its rim had been evened out, the sky would appear as a huge physical dome, a phenomenon known as "celestial vaulting." From a slightly different viewpoint—from lower down, in a space at the center of the crater with a large circular opening in its ceiling—the sky would appear not as a dome but as a flat disk, and one of a much deeper blue: a ceiling of intense color close enough to touch. The conclusion to be drawn from these two visions of the sky—each radically different from our everyday sense of the ubiquitous, amorphous atmosphere —is that it is through the mechanism of our human perception, and the specific frame of reference within which we see, that, as Turrell says, "we make the shape and the color of the sky." The context in which we see the sky matters, and we form our image and understanding from that context. Turrell's art dramatizes the truth of the relativity of our perception as we negotiate our delicate relationship with our universe.

With its 240,000 square feet of galleries making it for the moment the largest museum of modern or contemporary art in the world, Dia:Beacon itself begs the question of monumentality. Yet its scale is dictated by the immersive environmental qualities of the art it contains, and is driven by a need to establish distinctive and dramatic contexts for each work—analogous to Heizer's drive to leap from the canvas to the desert. Discussing the museum's formal entrance through orchard and plaza—a processional, axial, symmetrical approach—and the surprisingly grand interior vistas through its vast galleries, Irwin describes the design as "ceremonial without being ceremonious." Its monumentality, like the scale of projects by De Maria, Heizer, Judd, and Turrell, is intended not to mark a national or historical event, or even to clear space in art history, but to put individual human perception in the context of a larger environment, examining and asking questions about that liaison and celebrating the rich and surprising subjectivity of our human relationship to the world.

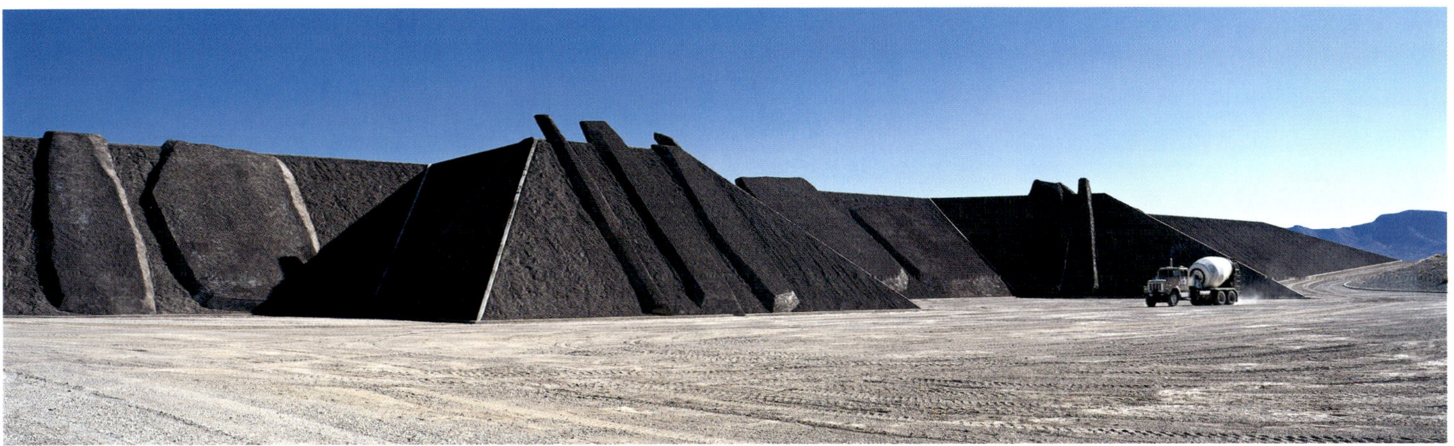

right Michael Heizer, *Complex Two/City*, 1980–99, Nevada

pages 44–45 Dia:Beacon, interior with partial view of Walter De Maria's *The Equal Area Series*, 1976–77

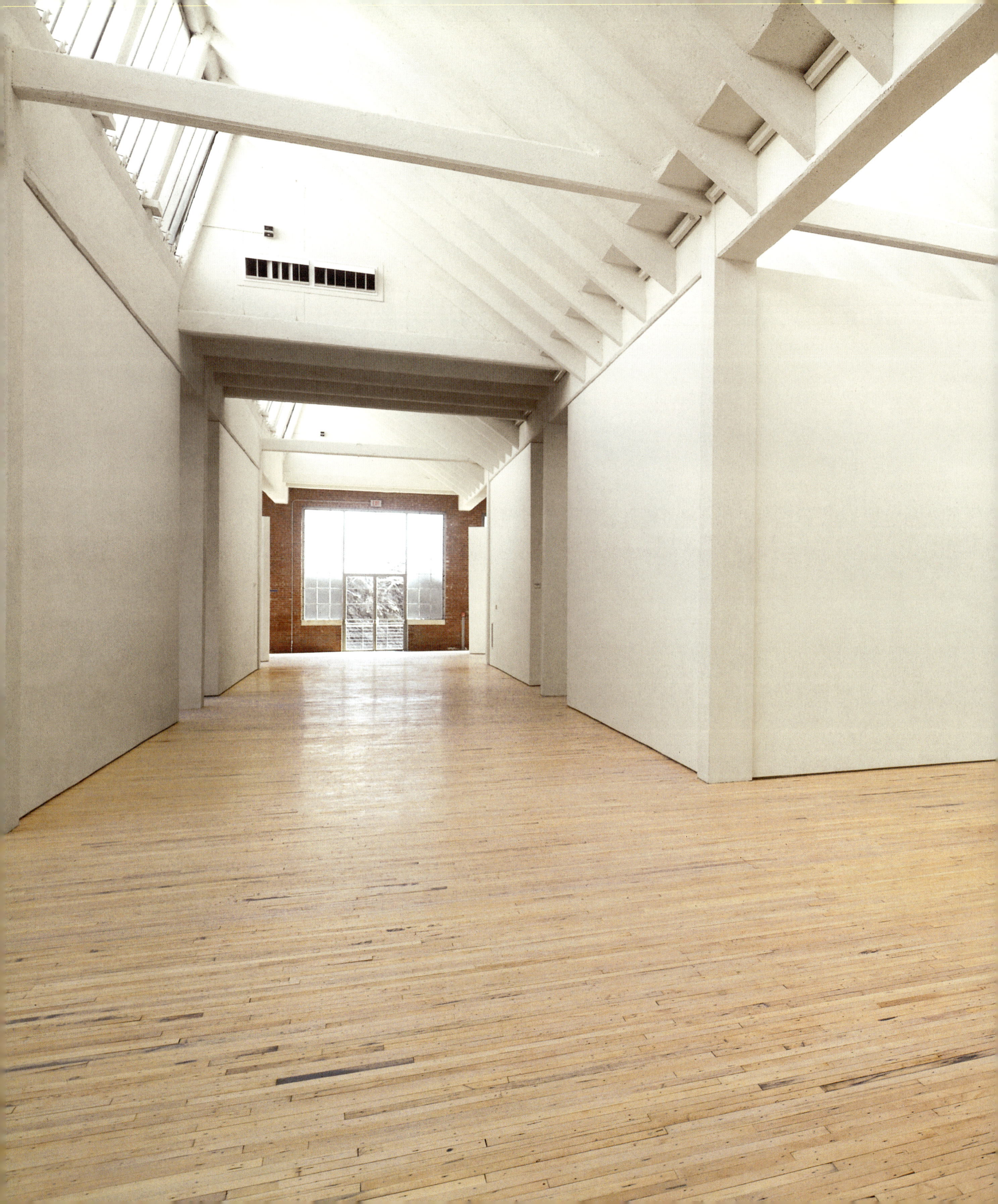

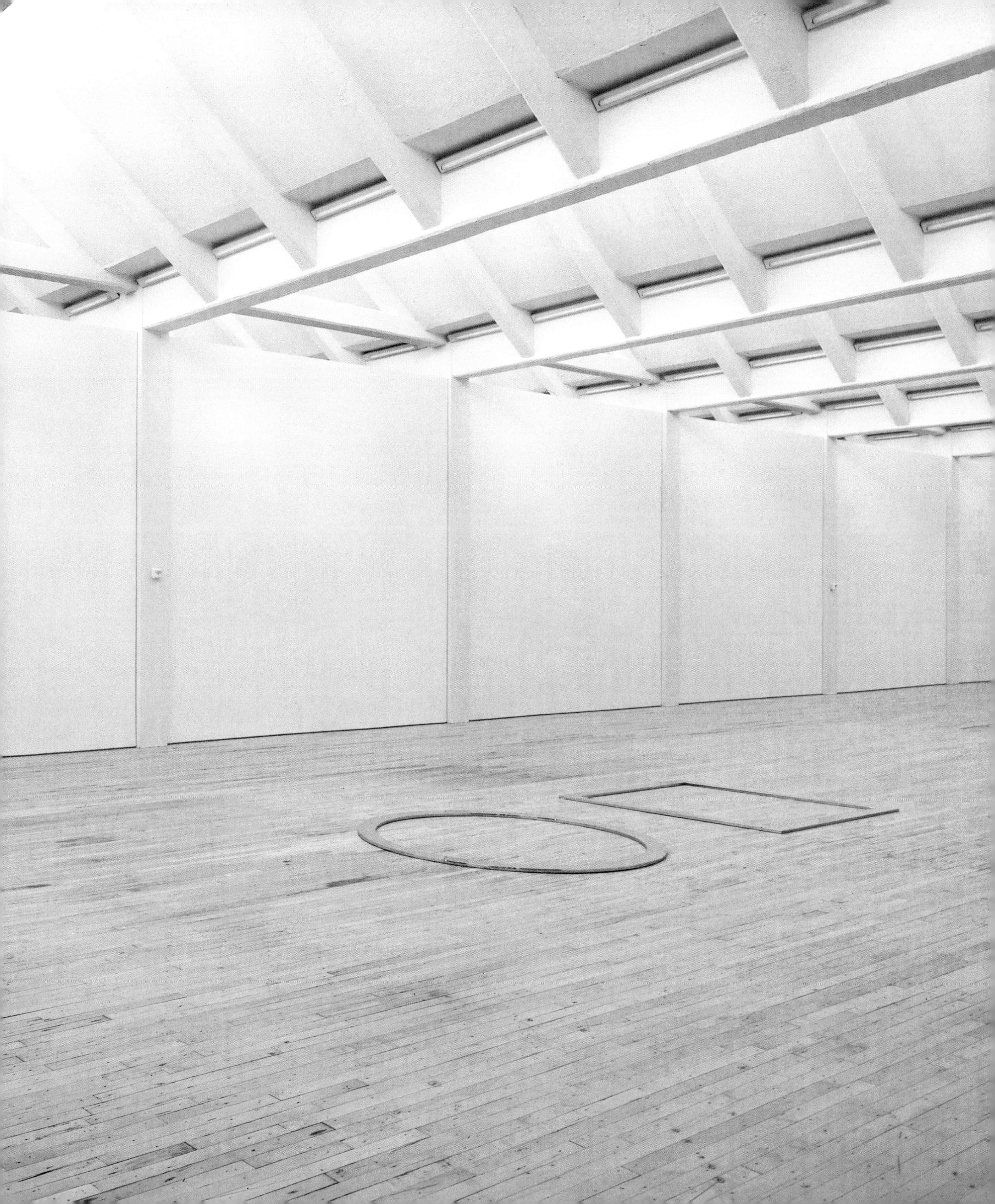

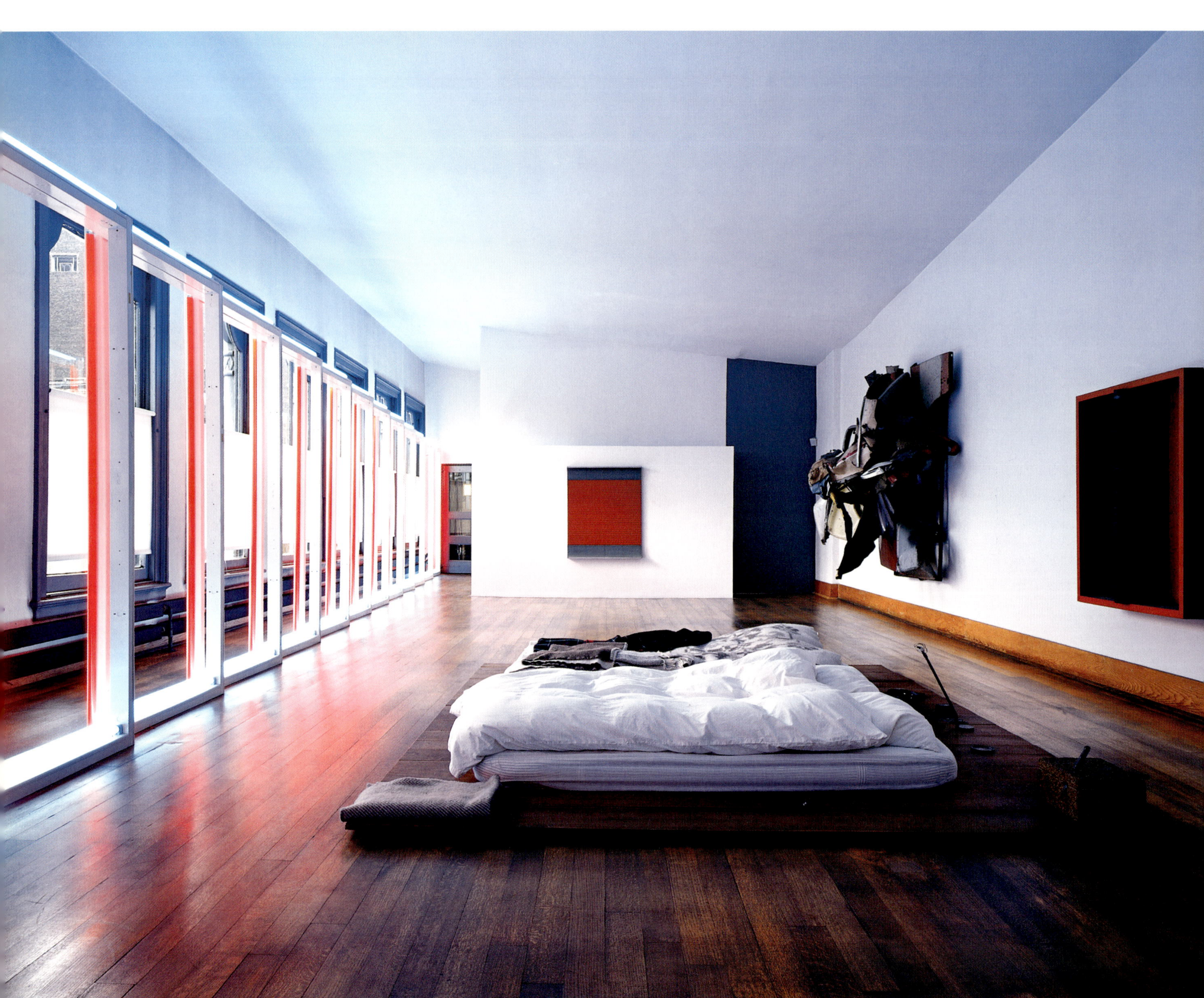

Never No More No Literature? LYNNE COOKE

"It's freshman English forever and never no more no literature," was Donald Judd's gloomy assessment of the growing tendency of museums of modern art to construct and present their collections on the model of the anthology.[1] "The installation and context for the art being done now is poor and unsuitable," Judd argued in 1982. "The correction," he asserted with characteristically terse acuity, "is a permanent installation of a good portion of the work of each of the best artists. . . . The main reason is to be able to live with the work and think about it, and also to see the work placed as it should be."[2] This model was one he himself had long tried to implement. Offering a radical counter to the prevailing anthologizing trend, his succinctly limned vision was to yield a deferred legacy several decades later in Beacon, a small blue-collar town upstream from New York City—coincidentally but not inappropriately the locus, more than a century earlier, of some of America's first significant artistic statements, the visionary works of the Hudson River school.[3]

In May 2003 in Beacon, Dia Art Foundation is opening a museum very much in tune with this blueprint, in order to showcase a major part of its collection of contemporary art, which features—not coincidentally and quite appropriately—several outstanding works by Judd. Dia's collection is singular in its formation, its compass, and, arguably, its contribution. Comprising works by a relatively small number of artists who reached maturity in the 1960s, it had its genesis in the mid-1970s. Although it has broadened its scope in recent years, it has not become a representative survey or cross-section of a historical era. Nor, despite its strong holdings in Minimal and Land art, does it offer an in-depth study of any movement or stylistic tendency. Art-historical categories meant little to its founders, Americans Philippa de Menil and Helen Winkler, and German gallerist Heiner Friedrich. As indifferent to the notion of the encyclopedic collection as to that of the anthology of a particular period, their vision was never encumbered by theoretical classifications.

Indeed, collecting was not their first impulse. Incorporated in 1974, Dia Art Foundation was established with the aim of commissioning and realizing exceptional projects and soon embraced proposals by James Turrell, Dan Flavin, Walter De Maria, Michael Heizer, Judd, Joseph Beuys, and La Monte Young and Marian Zazeela.[4] These projects were intended to be maintained in perpetuity by Dia or its beneficiaries. It was only several years later, when, in May 1976, Lone Star Foundation was incorporated as a companion organization to facilitate the formation of a collection, that acquiring in more conventional terms became a significant aspect of the founders' multifaceted involvement with contemporary art.

Bedroom of Donald Judd's home on 101 Spring Street, New York City, showing, clockwise from left: Dan Flavin's *untitled* (1970); Judd's untitled, 1963; John Chamberlain's *Mr. Press*, 1961; Judd's untitled, 1962; and Lucas Samaras's *Box 46*, 1966 Photo © Todd Eberle

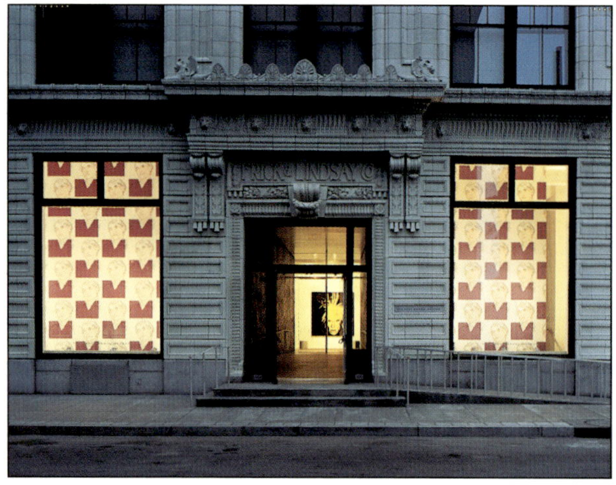

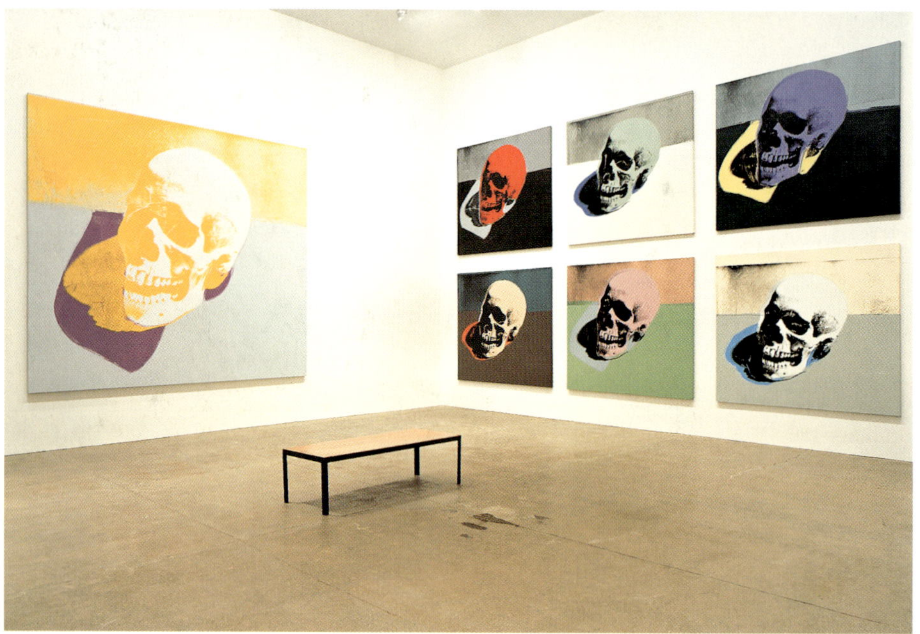

(Lone Star and Dia would eventually merge in 1980.) In this arena, too, their focus on individual artists, as distinct from movements or chronological periods, was unwavering and unqualified. In parallel with the large-scale, widely dispersed projects that Dia sponsored in the American Southwest and elsewhere, between 1976 and 1980 it amassed substantial groupings of autonomous works—that is, works devised specifically for gallery and museum venues.

This rapidly growing collection represented not only De Maria and Judd but a number of their peers whose practices were grounded in more conventional systems of production, distribution, and reception. Yet even in these cases Dia's founders exhibited a preference for monumentally and environmentally scaled work and for work conceived in extended series. Notable among such acquisitions are Blinky Palermo's magnum opus, *To the People of New York City* (1976–77), an environmental suite of paintings in fifteen parts; and Beuys's epic reprise of his multifarious "actions" and interventions, *Arena—dove sarei arrivato se fossi stato intelligente!* (*Arena—where would I have got if I had been intelligent!*), 1970–72, comprising 100 panels of photographs plus several sculptural components. A like impulse purportedly prompted Friedrich when, in 1978, he encountered Andy Warhol at work on the early stages of what were to become *Shadows* and commissioned the artist to create a suite of 100 works on the theme, which Dia would subsequently acquire. In other cases where such an approach was neither feasible nor prudent, notably those of John Chamberlain, Barnett Newman, and Cy Twombly, individual works were purchased, often in closely related groups or series.

The goal underlying this almost obsessive preoccupation with a few crucial figures was to realize multiple institutions, each dedicated to the long-term, in-depth public presentation of one artist's work. The small museum devoted to changing installations of Fred Sandback's sculpture, established in collaboration with the artist in Winchendon, Massachusetts, in 1981 (closed in

left The Andy Warhol Museum, Pittsburgh
right "Andy Warhol: Skull, 1976," exhibition at the Andy Warhol Museum, Pittsburgh, 1988

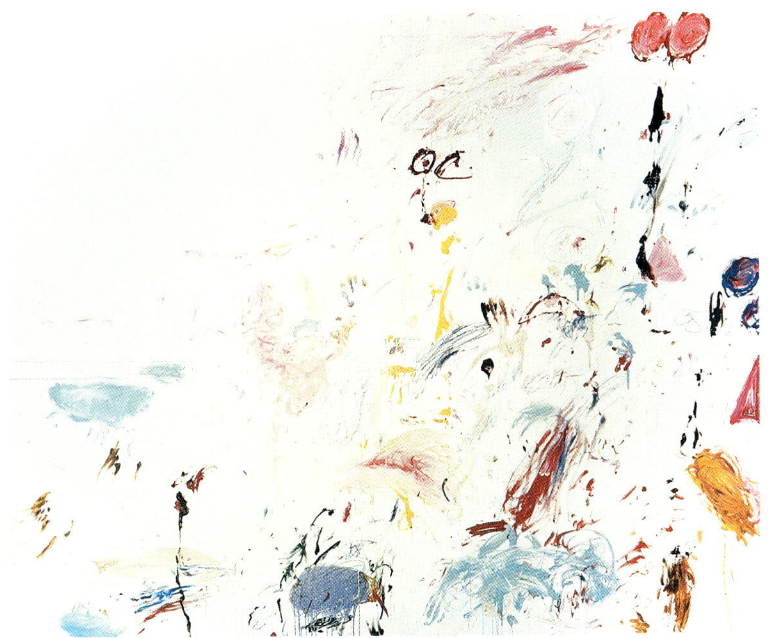

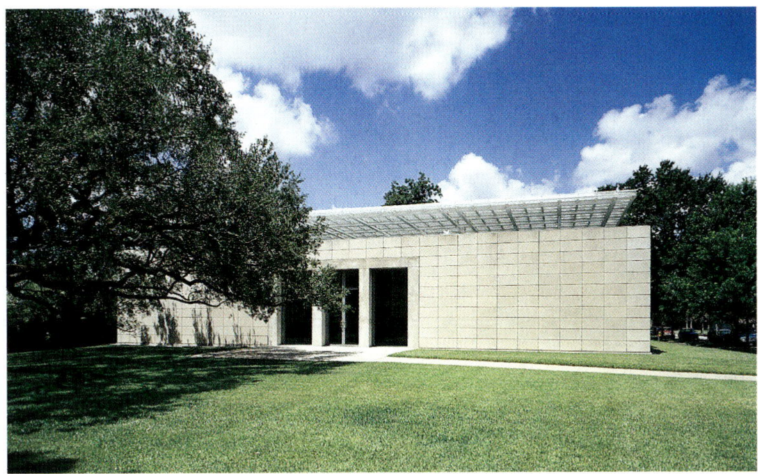

1996), and the Dan Flavin Art Institute in Bridgehampton, New York (1983–present)—a former fire station and later a church, converted under Flavin's direction into a permanent presentation of nine of his works in fluorescent light—are among the clearest manifestations of these ambitions. Variants on this model were devised for artists with somewhat different practices in that they related to the performing arts. Thus in 1979 a warehouse was purchased on West Nineteenth Street in Chelsea, New York City, to be converted into rehearsal spaces and studios for the documentation, production, and presentation of work by Robert Whitman. That same year, a building suitable for the creation of *Dream House*, archival facilities, and a performance space for Young and Zazeela was secured at 6 Harrison Street in lower Manhattan. (The facility was later transferred to 275 Church Street, nearby.) More than a decade later, when Dia was under a new directorship and governing board, the launching of the Andy Warhol Museum in Pittsburgh in 1993 and of the Cy Twombly Gallery in Houston in 1995 confirmed Dia's ongoing commitment to the original plan for the disposition of the collection.[5] Whenever possible, the principle of directly consulting with the artists on their projects had continued to be strictly maintained.

The pantheon of some dozen German and American artists who by the early 1980s occupied the center stage of Dia's activities was selected according to a predetermined plan.[6] A list drawn up at the incorporation of Lone Star Foundation contains the following names: Carl Andre, De Maria, Flavin, Judd, Imi Knoebel, Palermo, Sandback, and Twombly. Four months later an additional five were appended: Beuys, Chamberlain, Newman, Franz Erhard Walther, and Warhol.[7] The contents of the collection were closely shaped by associations that Friedrich had forged during the later 1960s through his gallery in Munich. In 1970, in Cologne, he had opened a second space that featured essentially the same roster of artists until it closed, in 1980. When, in 1973, he established a third gallery, this time

left Cy Twombly, *Bay of Naples*, 1961
right Cy Twombly Gallery, The Menil Collection, Houston, Texas

in New York City, De Maria, Palermo, Judd, Flavin, and Chamberlain were again given solo shows.[8]

Even in Munich, Friedrich had not been bound by conventional gallery presentations. Palermo's site-specific wall paintings occupied the gallery in the winter of 1968–69 and again in the spring of 1971; in 1969 Mel Bochner presented "Measurements," in situ works inscribed on the gallery walls. The first of De Maria's three incarnations of the Earth Room was presented in September 1968. Young's and Zazeela's *Dreamhouse—A Continuous Environment in Sound and Light with Singing from Time to Time* was on view for a week in July 1968. In May 1972, films by Marcel Broodthaers were shown. Prophetic of Friedrich's subsequent ventures in the United States was the large-scale (but temporary) environmental piece *Munich Depression*, which Heizer constructed under the auspices of the Friedrich gallery in an undeveloped urban site in May 1969: some thousand tons of earth were displaced in this monumental outdoor sculpture, creating a declivity fifteen feet deep and 100 feet in diameter.[9] Friedrich had also been instrumental in encouraging the German industrialist Karl Ströher to embark on a large-scale commitment to the work of Beuys, whom he himself strongly supported. This ultimately resulted in an unparalleled site-specific bequest of Beuys's work to the Hessisches Landesmuseum Darmstadt in 1969. In an ongoing collaboration with the donor, the collection was installed in the museum by the artist, in perpetuity, in a suite of dedicated galleries. This exceptional project, called "Beuys Block," closely prefigured Friedrich's plans for the artists he would support in the United States, Beuys included.[10]

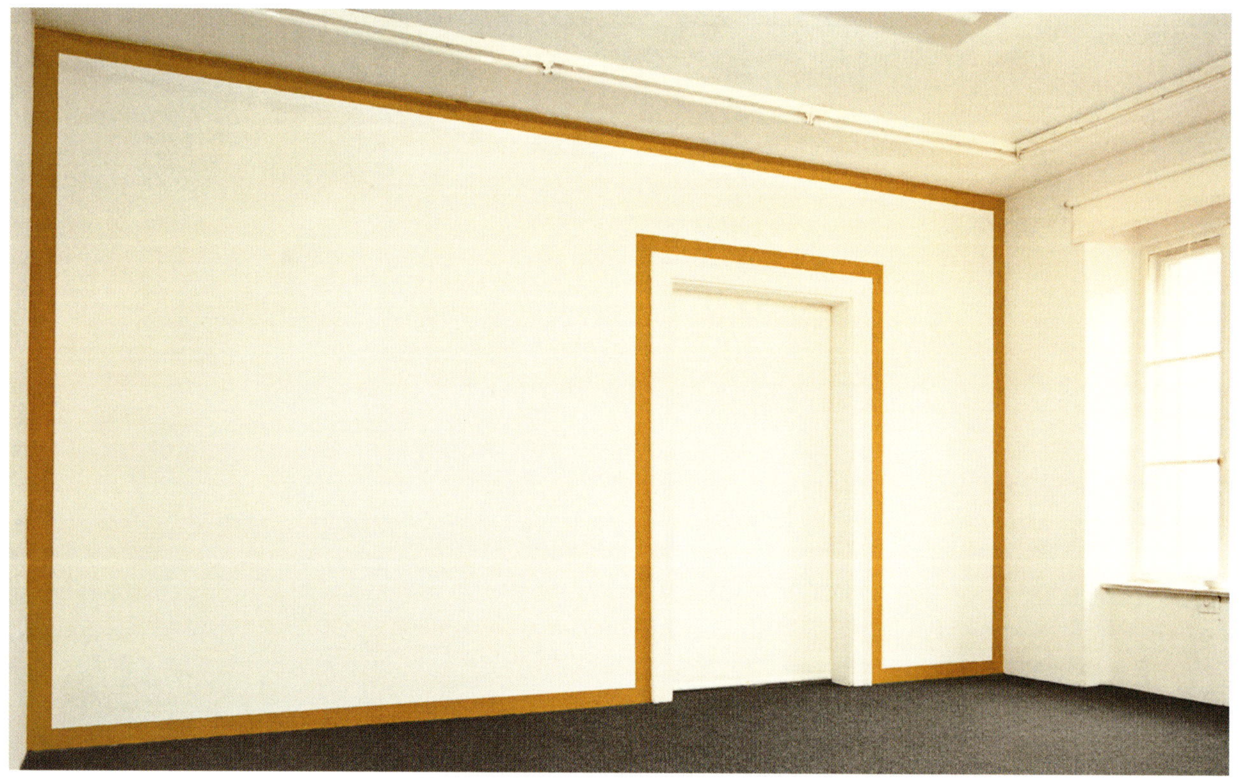

Blinky Palermo, *Wall Painting on Two Opposite Walls*, 1971, Galerie Heiner Friedrich, Munich

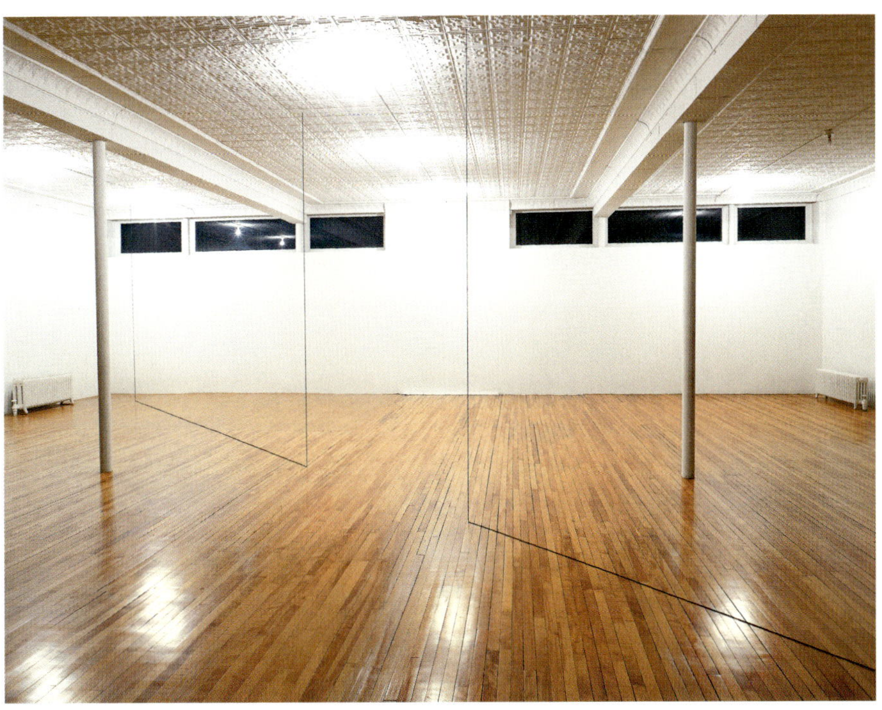

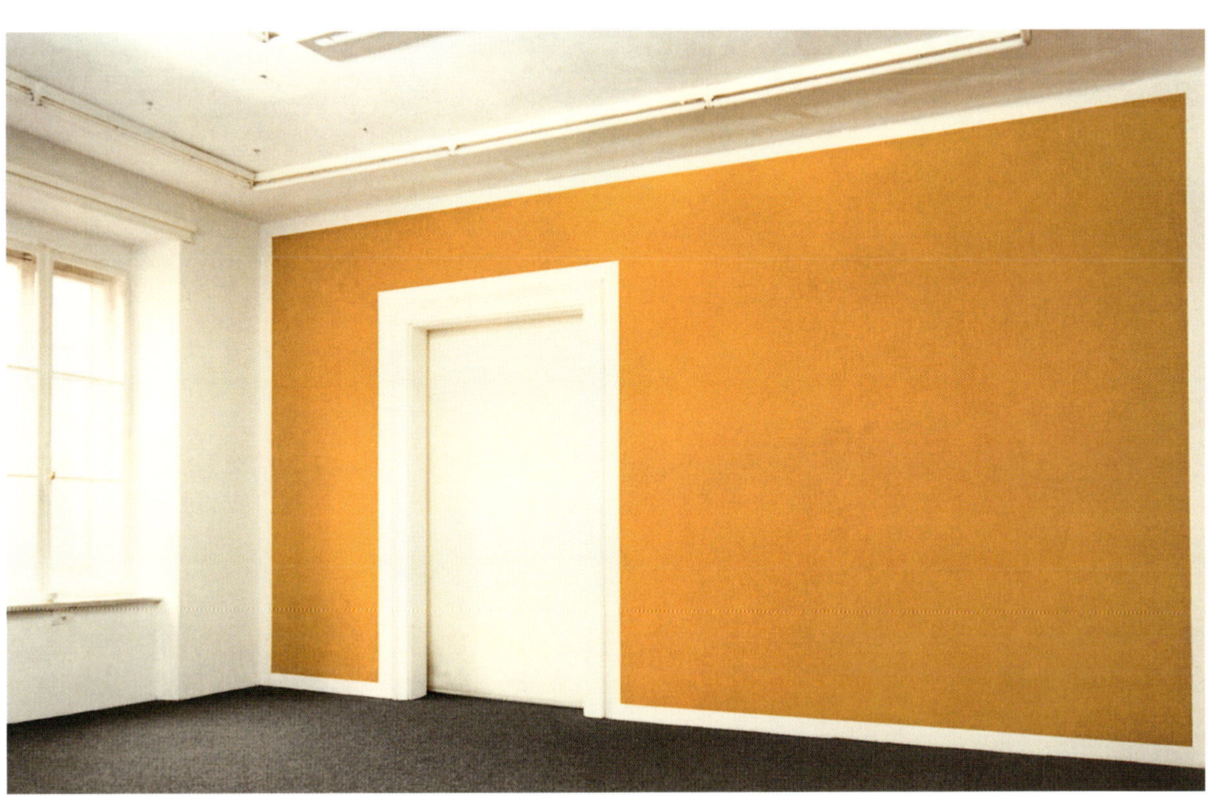

above Fred Sandback, *untitled*, 1976/1981, The Fred Sandback Museum, Winchendon, Massachusetts
below Blinky Palermo, *Wall Painting on Two Opposite Walls*, 1971, Galerie Heiner Friedrich, Munich

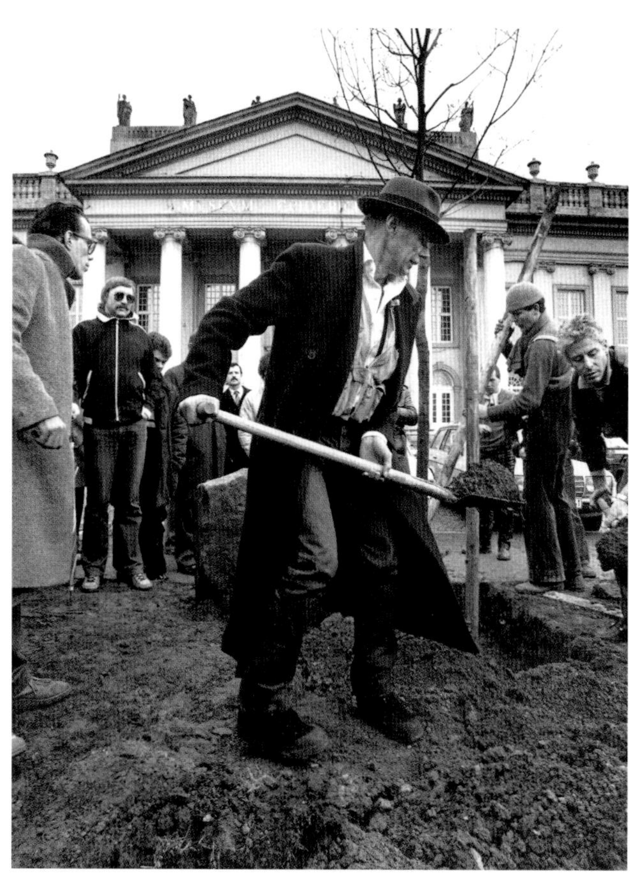

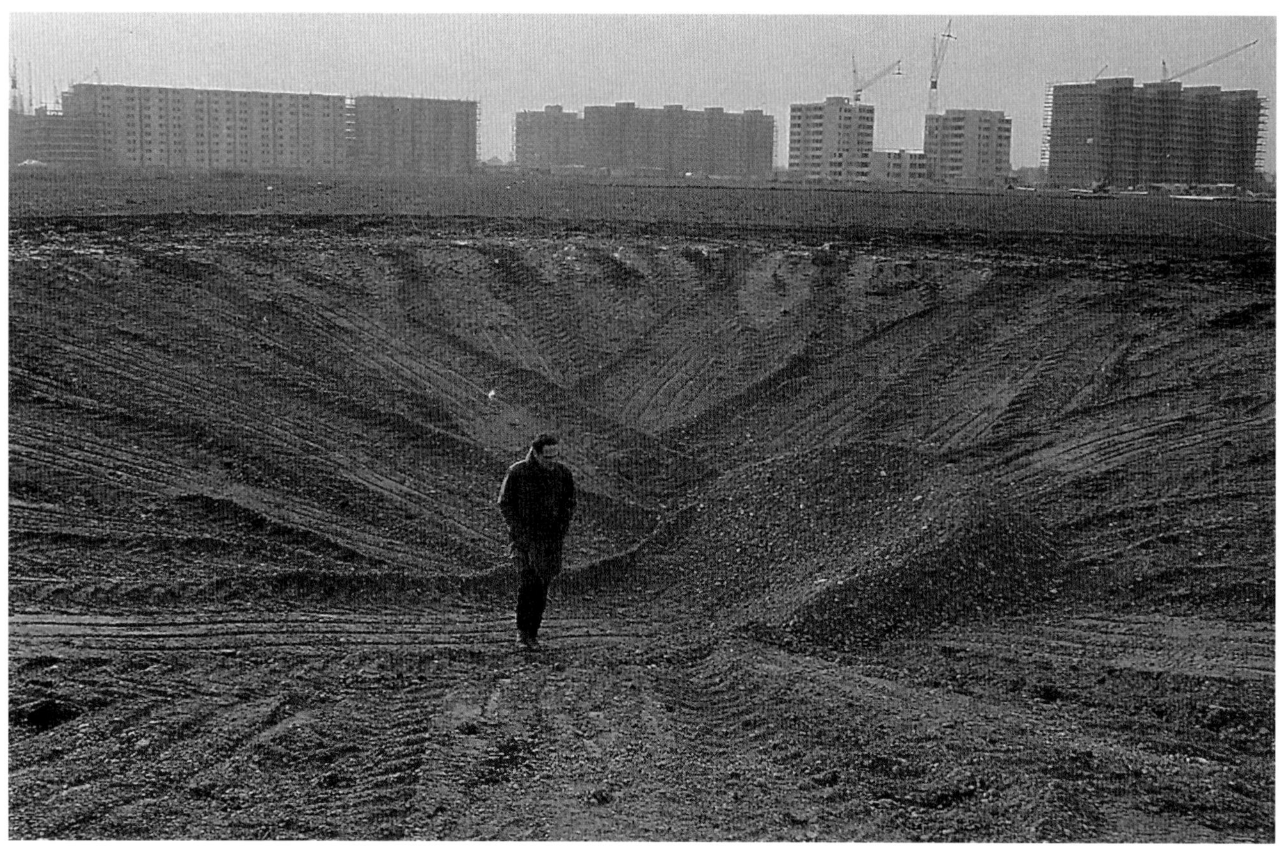

above Joseph Beuys planting the first tree of *7000 Eichen* in Kassel, Germany, for Documenta 7 in 1982
below Michael Heizer, *Munich Depression*, 1969

Friedrich's roster of artists—wide-ranging in Munich, then consolidated in Cologne—betrayed certain clear alignments, notably to Minimal art, its offshoots and affiliates; to the leading German painters of the day, Sigmar Polke, Gerhard Richter, and Georg Baselitz; and to a group loosely descended from Beuys, including Walther, Palermo, and Knoebel. Other associations may have been confirmed through the advice or partisan lobbying of certain artists: when Judd was an occasional art critic, for instance, he had repeatedly championed Chamberlain's sculpture, and Chamberlain became one of the select few whose art he personally collected from an early date. Amassed mostly in the later 1970s and early 1980s, Dia's holdings of Chamberlain's works are today unrivaled.[11] A formative friendship linked De Maria and Young, who as musicians as well as artists had played and worked together in San Francisco before moving to New York at the beginning of the 1960s. De Maria also manifests a point of confluence with Whitman, with whom he teamed up soon after arriving in New York to rent a space on Great Jones Street in Greenwich Village, where they planned to present exhibitions, film screenings, and other events. Several of Whitman's early performances, which included De Maria among the participants, had their debut in that short-lived venture. It was Whitman who met Friedrich first, in the mid-1960s, then introduced him to De Maria several years later. Whitman later exhibited drawings in what, by 1974, had become Friedrich's multiples gallery in Munich. De Maria in turn may have been Heizer's principal conduit to Friedrich, who, by late 1968, was providing funding for Heizer's first work requiring earth-moving equipment, *Five Conic Displacements*, excavated in Coyote Dry Lake in the Mojave Desert in January 1969. Heizer had previously invited De Maria to travel to the Mojave Desert with him, which resulted in De Maria's making his first in situ Land art work, *Mile Long Drawing*, in 1968. Anomalous as the sole representative of a previous generation in Dia's collection, Newman was the Abstract Expressionist artist most deeply revered by younger colleagues from widely differing vantages. His work was to have a decisive impact on many of the artists in this coterie, from Judd to Flavin, Palermo to Whitman.[12]

During the 1960s an ambitious model of collecting emerged that entailed the amassing of large numbers of works by a select group of vanguard artists. In addition to the Panza collection in Italy, the Marx and Ströher collections in Germany became renowned.[13] What distinguished the Dia–Lone Star approach was not its intense focus on the individual artist—verging on a crusade—but that focus' dual character. One strand of Dia's two-pronged program was devoted to the establishment of "customized" single-artist institutions, presenting concentrated groups of works in buildings that had been renovated or redesigned in consultation with the artist to suit the work's needs and its long-term maintenance. The second aspect involved the commissioning, again for long-term public presentation, of ambitious projects from the visual and performing arts, in whatever location or situation was deemed most appropriate. The result would be a multisite organization comprised of semi-independent satellites whose main links to the mother ship are administrative and financial.

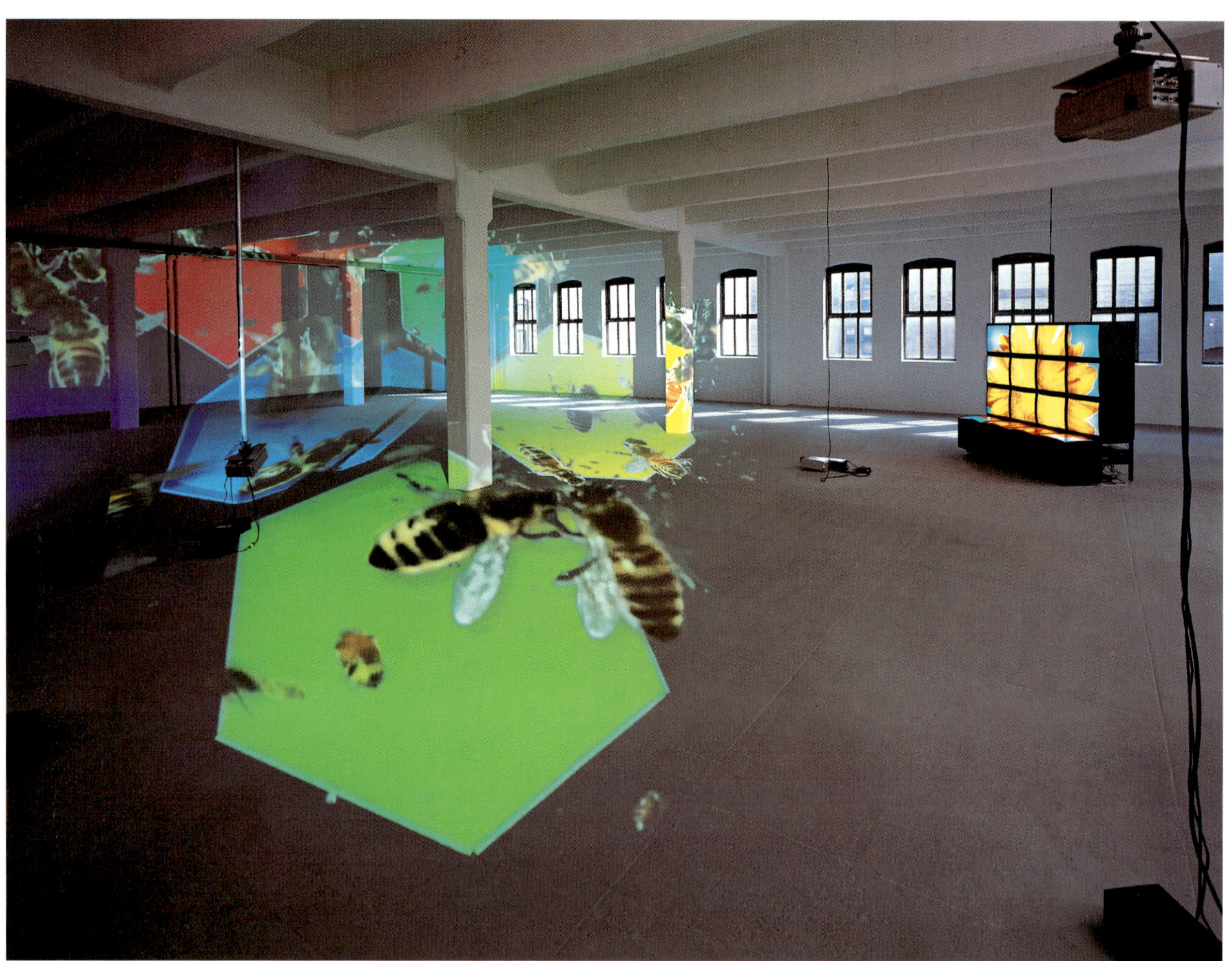

Fate, in the guise of the oil crisis of the late 1970s, caused a sharp decline in the foundation's resources, so that Dia was soon no longer able to continue its extensive program of commissioning and collecting.[14] After 1981, no further works were acquired for the collection for more than a decade. And excepting Beuys's project *7000 Eichen* (*7,000 Oaks*), realized at Documenta 7 in Kassel, Germany, in 1982, with support from Dia, no new commissions were undertaken in the early 1980s. Following its reconstitution as a public charitable institution from a private foundation under the leadership of Charles Wright in the mid-1980s, Dia embarked on a revised mission that nonetheless adhered to its founding principles while interpreting them anew. Rather than expanding its collection, it strove to put more of the works on public view. And while it continued to commission new work on an ambitious scale, the commissions were now tailored to a specific site, an exhibition facility located in a renovated warehouse in the semi-industrial Chelsea neighborhood of New York City. The focus continued to be placed on the individual artist, on the display of concentrated bodies of work in tailored spaces, and on a relatively long-term presentation of one year's duration for each exhibition. The program of what was renamed Dia Center for the Arts can be simply summarized as "one artist, one floor, one year." Opening in 1987 with a trio of shows, each dedicated to an artist in its collection—Beuys, Palermo, and Knoebel—this program has continued for more than fifteen years to weave

Diana Thater, *Knots & Surfaces*, 2001, installation at Dia Center for the Arts, New York City

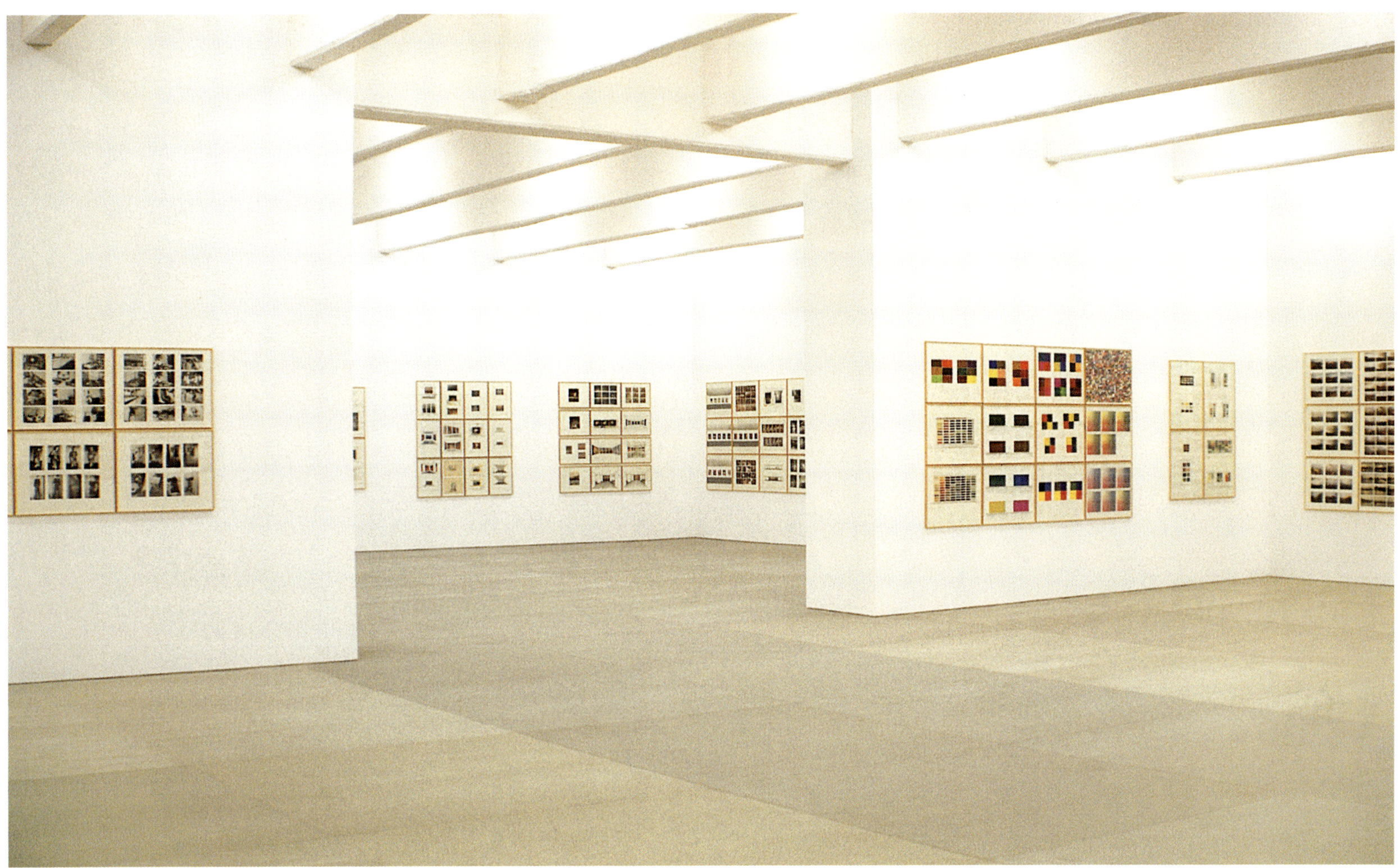

together three interrelated strands: shows based on works in the collection; shows comprising key works by other artists who are of that sixties generation but are not represented in the collection; and shows resulting from commissions for new work from artists of both the founding generation and the next.

The choice of a vernacular industrial building and its location was fully in the spirit of earlier ventures by Judd, first on Nineteenth Street in New York City, later downtown from there on Spring Street in SoHo, and later still in Marfa, Texas. In all of these places he converted warehouses and other utilitarian spaces for the presentation of his art and that of select peers.[15] At Dia in Chelsea, too, the renovation was basic and inexpensive, leaving the almost raw space as a set of given conditions, straightforward, unencumbered, and highly flexible. The fact that the location was at that time peripheral to the New York art scene meant that a considered decision to venture there was required of the public, forestalling a too-casual consumption; this, too, was fully in keeping with Judd's belief in purposive unhurried viewing. Between 1987 and 2003, collection shows were devised from works by Beuys, Chamberlain, Flavin, Judd, Sandback, Warhol, and Whitman. Among their peers, Jo Baer, Bernd and Hilla Becher, Alighiero e Boetti, Frédéric Bruly Bouabré, Hanne Darboven, Alfred Jensen, Panamarenko, Richter, Bridget Riley, Robert Ryman, Richard Serra, and Gilberto Zorio were invited to exhibit. Typically, the work Dia commissioned

Gerhard Richter, *Atlas*, 1964–present, installation at Dia Center for the Arts, New York City, 1995

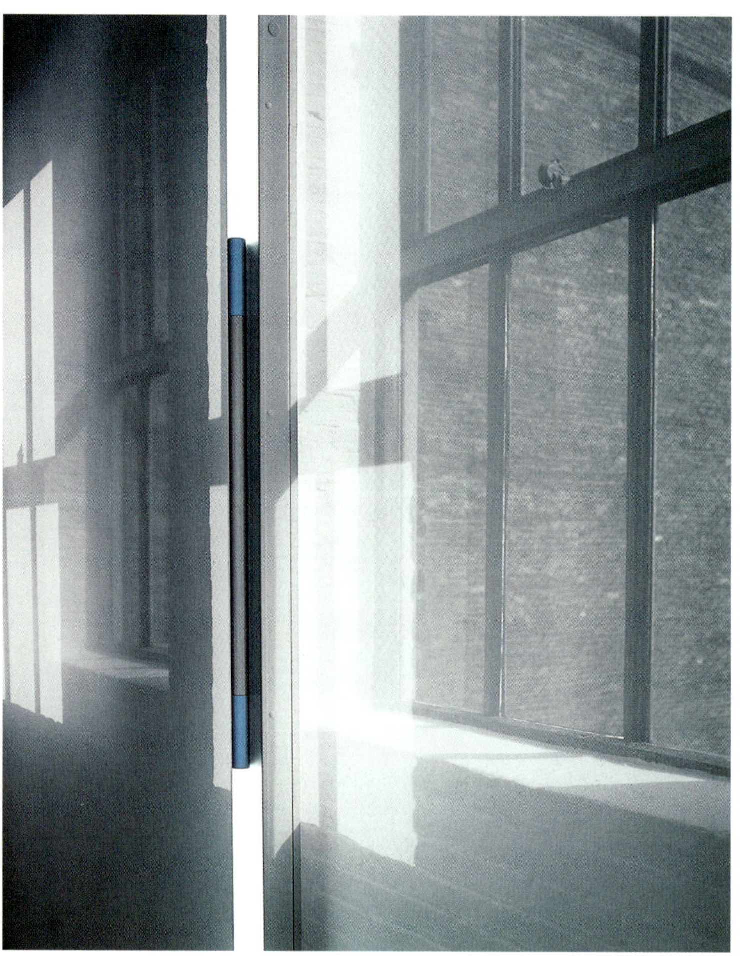

after 1987 again proved to be monumental and site-specific in character or, at the least, site-related and epic in scale. Among many memorable installations were those by Lawrence Weiner (1990), Robert Gober (1991), Ann Hamilton (1993), On Kawara (1993), Jessica Stockholder (1994), Juan Muñoz (1996), Robert Irwin (1998), and Diana Thater (2000). Long-term commissions have included Dan Graham's *Rooftop Urban Park Project* (1991) and Flavin's last public project, in the building's paired stairwells. In the early 1990s plans to make more of the collection public through the purchase and renovation of an additional warehouse in Chelsea, in which each floor would be devoted to one artist's work, were drawn up but then shelved. The single-artist museums devoted to Warhol and Twombly were realized, however, in conjunction with partnering institutions, in 1993 and 1995, respectively.

Commissioning supplanted acquisition until the later 1990s. The gift by Louise and Leonard Riggio in1997 of the three sculptures from Richard Serra's exhibition, "Torqued Ellipses," presented in Dia's new Chelsea annex at 545 West Twenty-second Street, dramatically changed this situation. The long-standing plan to put more of the collection on public view was revisited and revitalized. Forsaking Manhattan, where suitable and affordable real estate was increasingly rare, the search, spearheaded by Dia's director, Michael Govan, expanded beyond the city. Once again, priority was given to existing, generic industrial structures, which could be renovated to provide an appropriate frame, over proposals to construct a new building, an architectural

Robert Irwin, *Part I: Prologue: x18³*, 1998, installation at Dia Center for the Arts, New York City

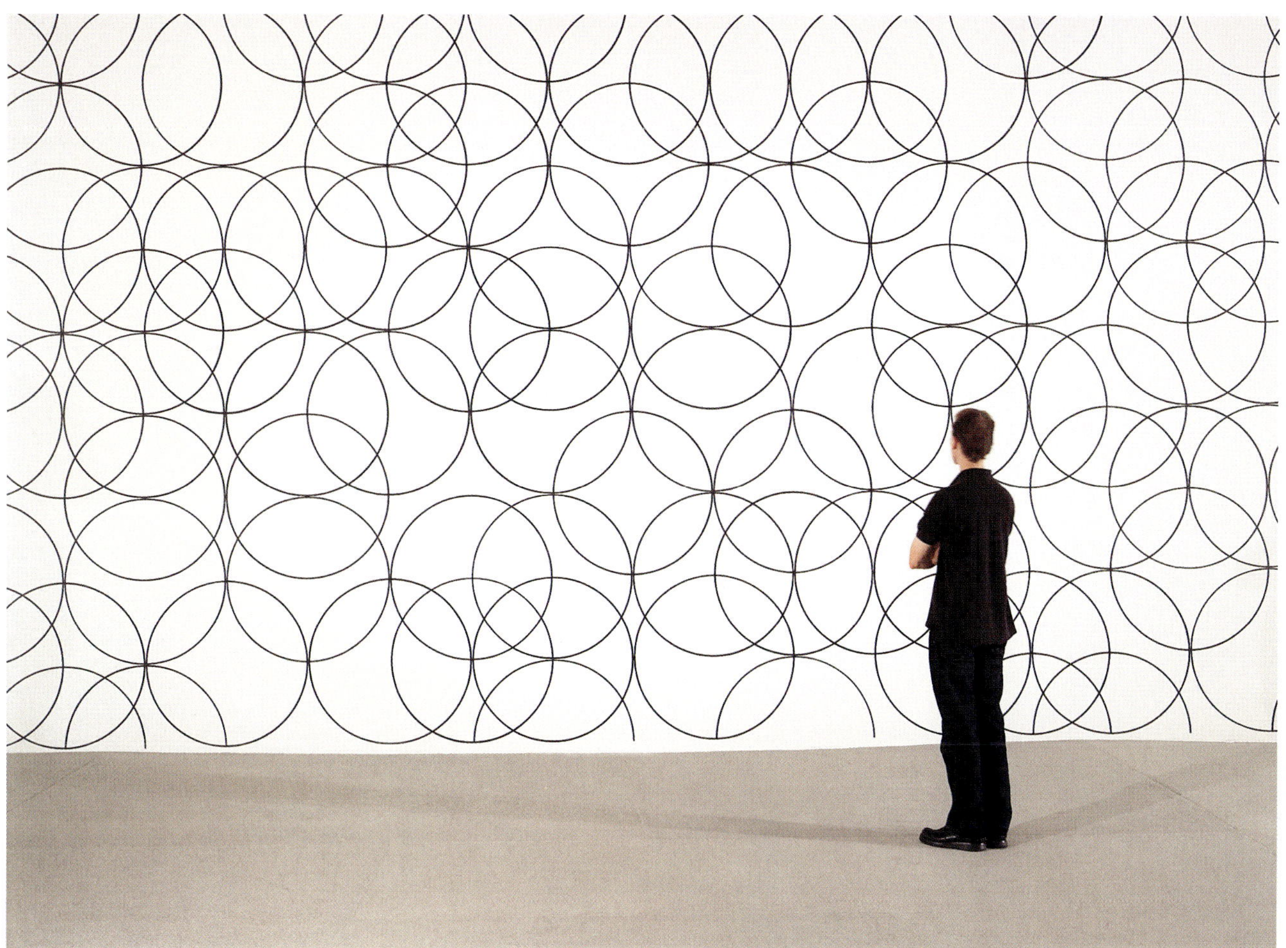

symbol. Contributing to this willingness to look farther afield was a growing belief in the value of purposive travel to a relatively isolated destination, a point of repose, where the visitor would encounter concentrated bodies of work in dedicated spaces designed for unhurried scrutiny. Here again, Judd's model and example in Marfa, Texas, were pertinent.[16]

In anticipation of realizing this project, which soon focused on the former Nabisco box-printing facility in Beacon, new works have recently been added to the collection.[17] In accordance with the acquisition policy formalized by Dia's Board of Trustees in 2001, key works or series of works by yet other artists from the generation that emerged in the 1960s have been added: these include historical pieces by Sol LeWitt, Agnes Martin, Bruce Nauman, Ryman, and Robert Smithson. *Kulturgeschichte 1880–1983* (*Cultural History 1880–1983*), 1980–83, an encompassing work by Darboven that was exhibited in 1997 at Dia in Chelsea, was also procured, as was a site-specific installation created by Irwin in 1999; *Composition with Circles 2* (2000), a vast wall drawing from Riley's show in 2000; and Nauman's multiprojection installation *Mapping the Studio I (Fat Chance John Cage),* 2001, all of which had had their debuts at Dia. Moreover, the representation of certain artists already in the collection has been strengthened by additional pieces. Thus, to complement Whitman's unparalleled suite of twenty-seven double-sided drawings known as the *Dante Drawings* (1974–75), which was acquired in 1976, major Whitman works in other media have been secured in the past two years: the pioneering

Bridget Riley, *Composition with Circles 2*, 2000, wall drawing at Dia Center for the Arts, New York City

laser installation *Solid Red Line* (1967), the canonical performance *Prune Flat* (1965), and the multimedia projection *Spyglass (Film Images 1960–1976)*, 1976/2003. Not least, Dia has acquired a substantial group of works by Judd, beginning with untitled (1976) and ending with an innovative untitled late work of 1991, six plywood wall boxes with red and blue Plexiglas.

Art-historical hindsight today plays a substantial role in determining the addition of artists to the original roster, in contrast to the more personal, passionate, and intuitive basis on which the founders made their decisions. New acquisitions are designed to be complementary; there is no pressure to be comprehensive. Irrespective of how coherent and cohesive the inclusions may prove in terms of current art-historical orthodoxies, they are not decided on by adhering narrowly to academic notions of artistic style or aesthetic tendency. Acquisition usually follows an extended period of discussion and collaboration, which may entail an exhibition of new works and/or the offer of works on loan, as, for example, in the case of the Bechers. At present few other additions are planned to this constellation of some twenty artists.

Responsibility for the furtherance of the collection has occasioned an examination of the discursive protocols in which it originated as much as of the formative conditions and circumstances. What is remarkable is the degree to which the theoretical debate that surrounded and shaped the gestation of these oeuvres was first formulated by the artists themselves. Polymaths, they on occasion also served as critics and curators. Three of the landmark shows that defined emerging trends in the 1960s were organized by artists. "Eleven Artists," an exhibition curated by Flavin at the Kaymar Gallery, New York, in March 1964 that included the work of Jo Baer, Flavin,

Max Neuhaus, 2002 study for *Times Square*, 1977/2002

Judd, LeWitt, Ryman, and Frank Stella, among others, is widely heralded as the public debut of Minimalism. In 1967 Robert Morris orchestrated "Nine in a Warehouse," which marked the transition to various forms of Post-Minimalism: it included Giovanni Anselmo, Eva Hesse, Nauman, Alan Saret, Serra, Keith Sonnier, and Zorio. "Earth Works," at Dwan Gallery, New York, in 1968, largely masterminded by Smithson, is credited with announcing what was to become known as Land art.

An exceptional artistic colloquy based in theoretical debate marked the mid-1960s in New York, where many of these artists were resident. To a degree rare in the history of modernism, theoretical debate both generated by artists and governing their practices played a seminal role in determining the principal aesthetic issues of the time. Its legacy continues to shape not only the discourse of current art practice but those of museology and criticism as well.[18] Manifesto-like statements, declarations of intent, jeremiads, speculative essays, as well as more familiar forms of critical reviewing often proved highly influential. A telling instance of the persuasiveness of such polemics may be seen in Judd's fervent advocacy of the work of Chamberlain. Still arguably the best texts written on that artist's work, they offer keys to understanding how it might have come to be included on de Menil's and Friedrich's momentous 1976 list.[19] A discerning if somewhat quirky critic, Smithson identified in the art of Judd certain features and proclivities to which few others have attended, a service he later performed for LeWitt as well.[20] His articles, like many of Judd's, illuminate his own practice. More recently, Serra, too, has proven a generous advocate for a number of artists, often of very different persuasions from his own, not least Louise Bourgeois.[21] Furthermore, it was on Serra's urging that Dia recently began a dialogue with Max Neuhaus that resulted in the commissioning of a public project for Beacon (as yet unrealized), together with the gift in 2002 of that artist's landmark *Times Square* (1977) project to Dia's collection. Such examples are not instances of mere camaraderie among fellow artists, of mutual advocacy extending across a generation (one that is often better known for its acrimonious rivalries and bitter feuds). Judd, Smithson, and Serra all devised rigorous theoretical premises that grounded their own practices and informed their appreciation of those of others. Stringent, demanding, and formidable critics, they rapidly moved beyond a concern with the artwork in and of itself to the question of its presentation and reception. Given that ambient space was integral to the art object as they and many of their peers conceived it, issues of presentation and reception soon proved inextricable from the work, not only for these artists but for many of their peers.

Judd's clarion call for "a permanent installation of a good proportion of the work of the best artists" consequently implied more, and was more urgent, than might at first be evident. Such a wish could seem a natural desire for any close-knit group of self-consciously vanguard artists, whether the Impressionists or the Cubists, although not the schismatic Abstract Expressionists. But what was at stake for Judd and his cohorts was not simply the desire for a stable public

Barnett Newman, *Anna's Light*, 1968

presentation but also the provision of certain conditions of display that were preconditions for the apprehension of this work, and that were hence integral to its meaning. Their art is experienced in real space and actual time; it is therefore inflected by and in turn impacts upon the spatial matrix it occupies. In contrast to more autonomous, hermetic works such as a conventional painting or a sculpture on a plinth, it exists in the same spatio-temporal framework as the viewer, and hence can easily be encroached upon by other work that is differently premised, and by architecture that becomes intrusive or preemptive. *Anna's Light* (1968), Newman's great painting formerly in Dia's collection, exemplifies this: its vast scale and brilliant light impact upon its immediate context, transforming the viewers' role into one of active spectatorship. Rather than scanning the painting to investigate its formal resolution or the properties of its medium, they are drawn to explore the perceptual consequences of its intervention in its ambient site.

Close-knit artistic cadres, tight-knit networks that shaped and in turn were shaped by their labile but potent theoretical discourse, provide the intellectual substratum for the conjunction of artists in Dia's collection. In place of a single unifying aesthetic credo, certain premises and presuppositions concerning the presentation and reception of their art are held in common (but are not exclusive to this constellation). What, in short, constitutes mutual ground is a concern with the relation of the work to its site. By "site" is meant the physical ambience, its scale, dimension, and spatial and architectural boundaries. These primarily formal qualities define a context that is considered a neutral container. Discrete, unobtrusive, and straightforward, it is a supporting frame rather than an equal partner in a dialogue. In this formulation the architecture is visible, the institution invisible. There is no politicized subversion of the gallery/museum nexus, although there are explorations of its relationship to sites located geographically outside its matrix (in the case of Smithson's 1970 film, *Spiral Jetty*) or to other modes of distribution (via such reproductive channels as the posters, artist's books, and films favored by Weiner). While these representational strategies evidence the self-reflexive criticality implicit in many of these artists' practices, no direct critique of the institution of art of the kind espoused by Daniel Buren, Michael Asher, or Hans Haacke emerges here. None of these artists is primarily preoccupied with probing the ideologies subtending art's venues and infrastructures, its conventions of display, and its commodification.

Nor is an investigation of the role of a socially constructed and gendered spectator, as emerged concurrently in the work of Graham, Vito Acconci, and fellows, to be found here—even though elsewhere such issues have engaged certain of these artists. As critic Hal Foster argues, by considering perception in phenomenological terms "as somehow before or outside history, language, sexuality, and power . . . [art of the kind found in this collection did] not regard the subject as a sexed body positioned in a symbolic order any more than it regards the gallery or the museum as an ideological apparatus."[22] Reception is defined as a phenomenologically grounded experience, a contingent, bodily based act of seeing in which the work of art is

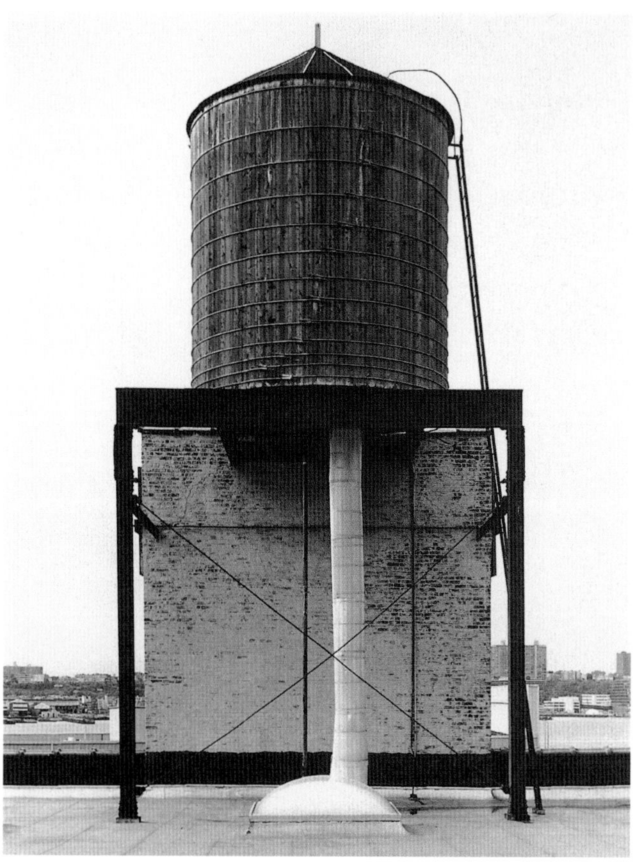

apprehended palpably—space is engaged viscerally as well as visually—and temporally, for multiple viewpoints, an aspectual diversity, involve the viewer in an interchange that unfolds in real time. Maurice Merleau-Ponty's dictum "Perception does not give me truths like geometry but presences" distills something at the core of the aesthetic of most of the artists in this pantheon, a tension between what Morris termed "the known constant and the experienced variable."[23] Not all of these artists—Weiner and LeWitt, for example—necessarily require that a work be fabricated, but when it is, its content may be only marginally affected by the site, and then primarily in formal terms; as witnessed in LeWitt's luminous, magisterial wall drawing of 1969, or the incisive conjuring of haptic form, structure, mass, and composition through textual and diagrammatic representations in Weiner's *5 Figures of Structure* (1987). Constructing his own quasi-architectural or topographic sites, Nauman entices the viewer into charged spaces whose impact, psychologically as well as phenomenologically, is difficult to resist. Unassumingly fabricated from inexpensive materials, these works are offered less as aesthetic artifacts to be savored in their own right than as vehicles in an investigation of what art might be. Knoebel's prophetic early work parses the question of installation somewhat differently, in that the artist improvises a solution in response to each individual site. Sometimes, as here, the work may be tightly compacted, as if held *in potentia* or in storage. On other occasions it treats the gallery as a volumetric support for the creation of an encompassing spatialized environment. With few exceptions, the works exhibited at Dia:Beacon are not examples of installation art, yet the question of their installation proves crucial in almost every individual case.[24]

Bernd and Hilla Becher, *Water Tower, 548 West 22nd Street, New York, U.S.A.*, 1989

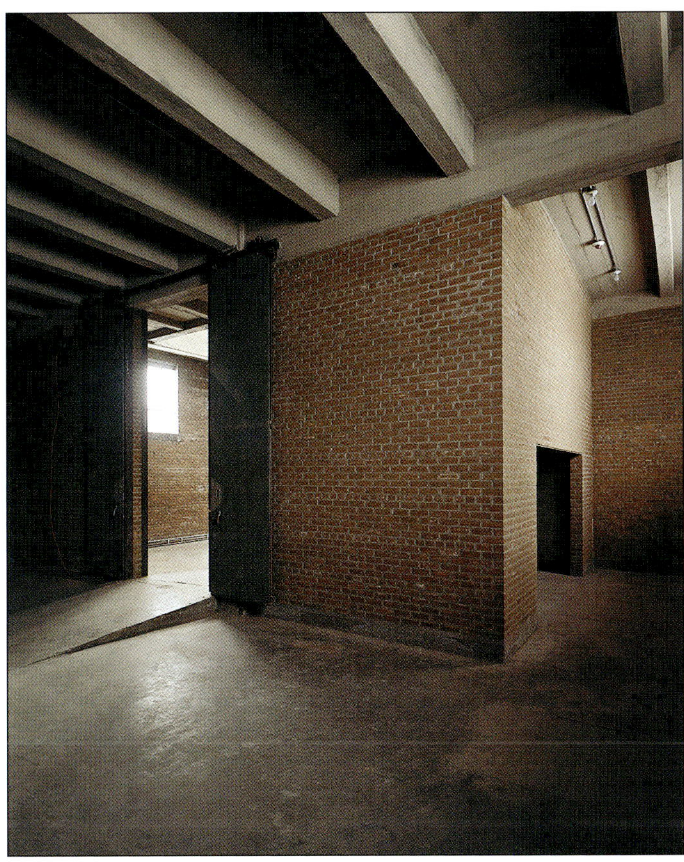

This is the fundament on which this presentation is assayed. Since architecture conceived as a frame for the work rather than as an art form in its own right is key to this conception, the renovation project has been carried out under the leadership of an artist—Irwin—in lieu of a renowned architect.[25] Decisions and procedures relating to installation have been similarly governed. Each artist's work occupies one or more galleries as required; works by several artists are never mixed together in one space. Where possible, each artist has chosen or designed his or her own space to conform to the requirements of the work to be displayed. The location of any particular body of work in the museum is conditioned by its needs rather than by any reference to art-historical chronologies or typologies. Consequently, paintings are sited in the two front buildings, where the north-facing skylights produce a limpid diffuse light. Sculpture is mostly located in the back building, where the east-west-oriented clerestory windows filter shifting light that casts shadows over the course of a day, and the heavier concrete floor provides a more substantial-seeming ground than do the maple floors in the pavilions containing paintings and wall drawings. Works that, for reasons of medium or materials, require low light levels, such as the Bechers' photographs and Beuys's *Arena . . .*, are hung in more somber and more intimately scaled spaces. Necessitating a clear, open area roughly square in configuration, Judd's series of plywood boxes has occasioned the one substantial architectural intervention in the project, the raising of the roof in the center of the third building.

Neither painting nor sculpture but engaging notions proper to both, Richter's *Six Gray Mirrors* (2003) serve as a pivot at the core of the whole facility, animating and inflecting

Attic of Dia:Beacon during renovation in 2003

the context and foregrounding issues of spectatorship. As they engage pictorial mythemes of painting as a window onto the world or a mirror held up to nature, they act architectonically, destabilizing the certainties that would ground place and space. By contrast, On Kawara eschews ocularcentric (re)visioning. Conflating an address of the spirit with an address of the mind and body, he counterpoints the ineluctable passage of time lost—inscribed by registering human history in a painting made on one particular day and recording that date on which it was executed—with a restorative shift, charging the atmosphere in this gallery by a process of ionization. The vivid painterly metallic surfaces in Chamberlain's sculptures brilliantly negotiate the light of the setting sun as it streams through the west facade. Conversely, Bourgeois's work suits well the penumbral mood of the attic. Left raw, this space has a pronounced expressive quality redolent of a previous era, rife for catalyzing encounters with traces and relics of a haunting past. At odds with the open, spacious luminosity that is a hallmark of the newly constructed galleries below, these claustral rooms solicit the kind of fateful but fortuitous immersion in disused or marginalized spaces so beloved of the Surrealists. Serra meanwhile selected the former train depot, legacy of a bygone industrial era, to accommodate his massive torqued steel sculptures. His choice finds a melancholic echo in the Bechers' photographic project of archiving what have often become obsolete forms of mechanical production.

No single route through the museum is supplied or imposed. The threshold signals that no pathway is privileged, no itinerary choreographed: from the small entrance vestibule, designed by Irwin, visitors must choose to enter by either the left or the right door. That these options are equivalent but different is intimated in the placement of De Maria's sculpture *The Equal Area Series* (1976–77) to straddle two buildings that are mirror images of each other. Poised on the threshold, momentarily arrested in front of the central column in Irwin's intimate low-lit annex, visitors initially glimpse De Maria's elegant work as if it were laid out in a single immense field. From this preliminary vantage point the wall that divides the two buildings cannot be seen. This apparent unity is temporary and elusive: it dissipates as soon as one door is chosen over the other. Thereafter the trajectory is unpredictable. The principal north-south and east-west axes are revealed at various stages in the navigation of the museum, their uninterrupted vistas offering means of orientation and respite. They order without predetermining visitors' movements. Neither coercively linear nor confusingly labyrinthine, the layout eschews any climactic resolution, literally as well as metaphorically and conceptually. In this as in other ways Dia:Beacon is designed to resist and preempt the kinds of spectacularization produced by bravura displays of architectural rhetoric. Ultimately circuitous, the journey ends where it began: the modest entrance also serves as the principal exit.

This disposition of the artworks is designed to escape not only strict chronological or typological ordering but all implications of hierarchical placement and of resolution into a synoptic overview or master narrative. This intention is reinforced by the fact that the museum is for

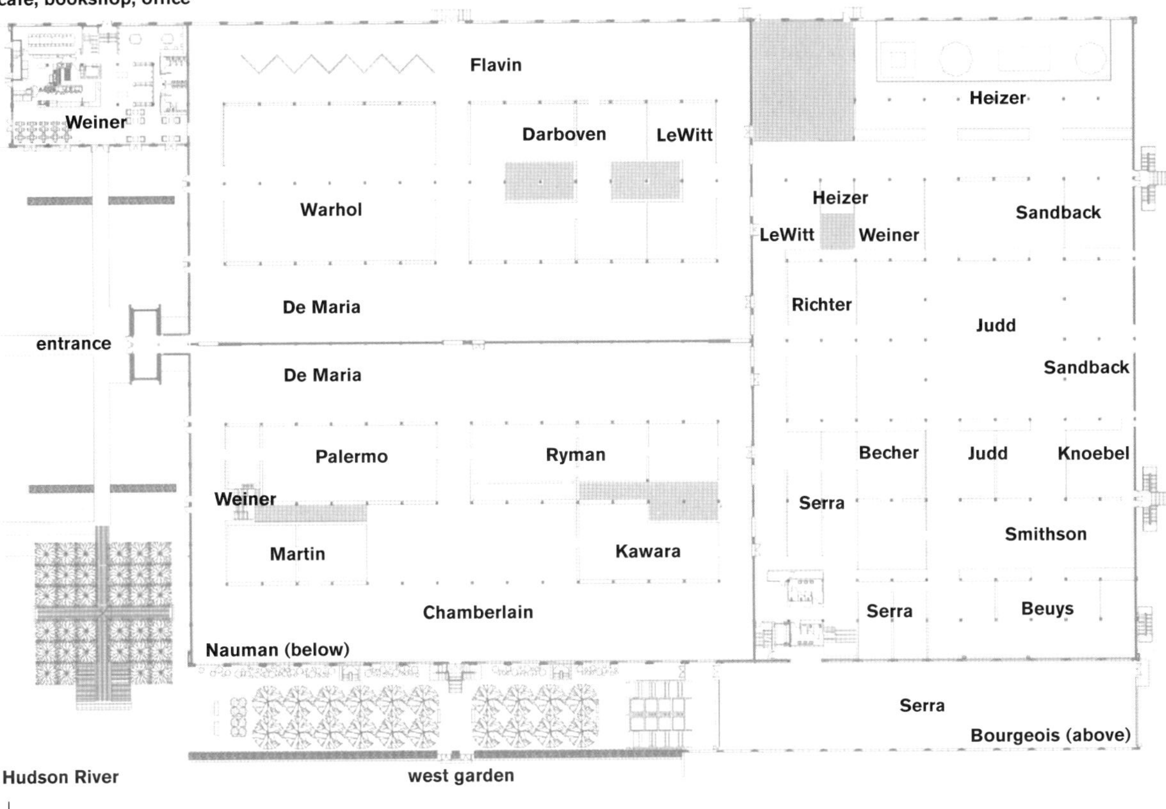

the most part laid out horizontally, a standardized regular grid largely determining its form and structure. The principal exception is found in the vertical linkage of the basement, densely forested with columns, to the sequestered attic. The renovation here is minimal; little has been done other than insert such required services as light, heat, air circulation, and fire and security systems. From this putative alignment of Nauman, Beuys, and Bourgeois, something unexpected emerges: reorienting and disorienting, it suggests other ways of apprehending based in the psychological, in memory and history, and in the performative. In the works of these three artists the space of subjective fantasy, reverie, and retrospection—of the imaginary, in short—is inseparable from that of the phenomenal. Distinct in tenor and reference, this congeries offers a salutary reminder of modalities not present elsewhere, whether deliberately excluded, repressed, or suppressed. Irrespective of how deftly if not seamlessly woven the tapestry of affinity, proximity, and similitude in Dia:Beacon may appear, its threads are always fragile, for they are woven of filigree—hypothesis, conjecture, and contention.

This museum presents only part of the totality of the collection.[26] And, as outlined above, the collection represents only half of the Dia Art Foundation's bifurcated heritage and mandate. If Dia:Beacon can succeed in presenting what T. S. Eliot termed "a perception, not only of the pastness of the past, but of its presence," it will do so because of the other element in the institution's program. For, as that arch modernist insisted in his influential essay "Tradition and

Dia:Beacon floor plan

the Individual Talent": "The existing monuments form an ideal order among themselves, which is modified by the introduction of the new (the really new) work of art among them."[27] Dia's museum in Chelsea thus remains an integral component. The site for commissions of exceptional projects, the second premise on which Dia was founded, it offers the opportunity for "the new (the really new)" to catalyze that which is known. Concurrent with the launch of Dia:Beacon, an installation of video projections and wall sculptures by the German artist Rosemarie Trockel, devised specifically for the second-floor gallery of the facility in New York City's Chelsea neighborhood, will be on extended view. Exhibitions in this building are bracketed by Graham's *Rooftop Urban Park Project* and Jorge Pardo's *Project* (2000), the latter encompassing the bookstore, lobby, and exhibition space on the first floor. Each the result of a commission, these two very different site-specific interventions represent another historical moment, one informed by significantly altered values and premises from those in which the artists of the 1960s matured. Both Graham's and Pardo's works incorporate utilitarian operations; both create a porous, fluid interrelationship among art, architecture, and design; both engage spectators in questions of spectatorship that dialectically question their relationship to the artwork, the institution, and its auxiliary functions.

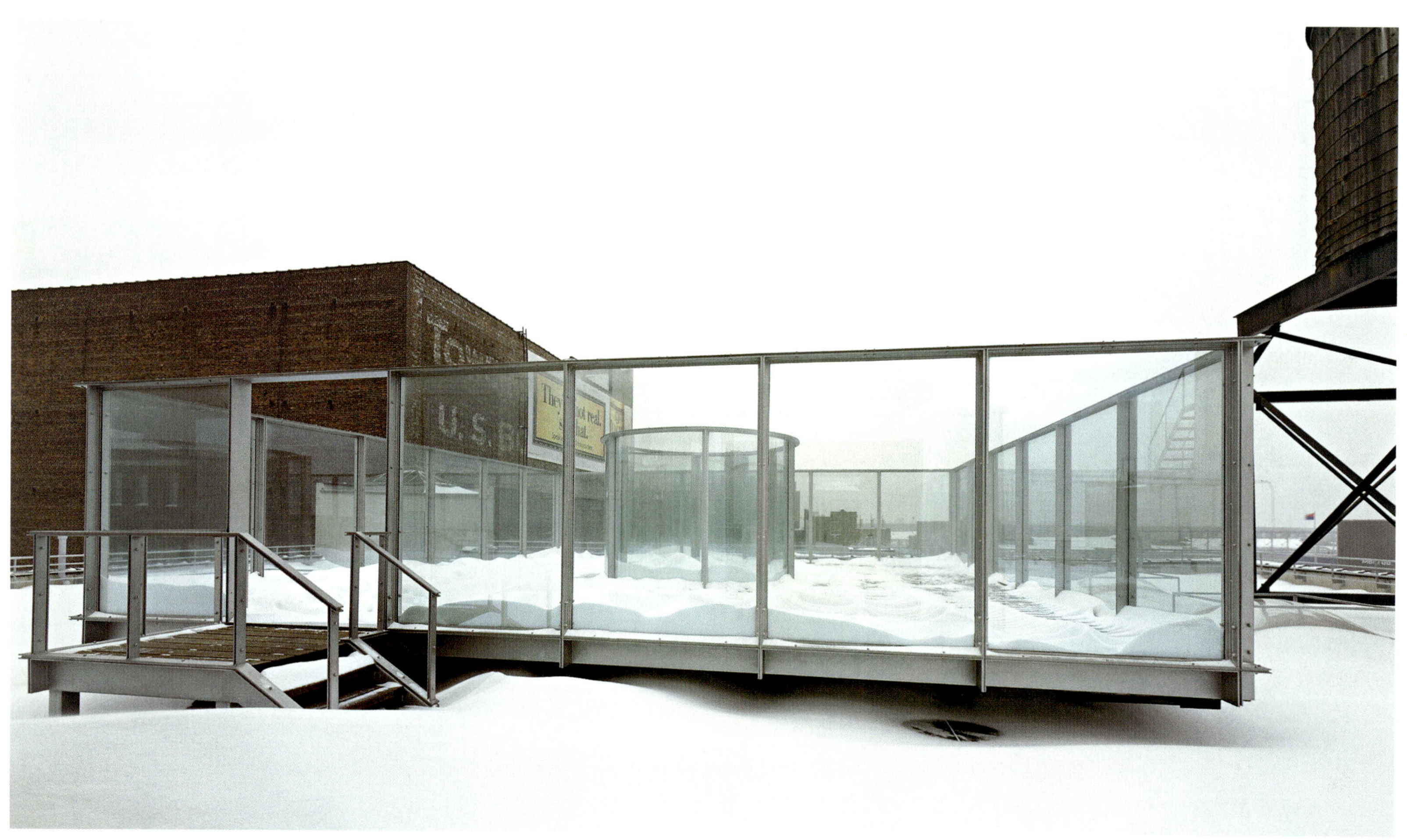

Dan Graham, *Rooftop Urban Park Project*, 1991, Dia Center for the Arts, New York City

Installation today is often considered an art form in its own right. Irrespective of whether this is justified, the practice of taking a "space" as a set of given conditions in relation to which the artist will generate a work has become an identifiable convention: a mode of working in situ. Among its origins are those occasions when the previous generation of artists, such as Judd or Serra, reacted to a particular venue, adapting or reworking or transforming works the better to accommodate the particularities of the new situation. In 1974, for example, Judd remade an untitled work, a series of plywood boxes, in order to install it in his Spring Street residence when it failed to sell in his show at the Castelli Gallery. The realignments required in the positioning of the pieces to fit the architecture, together with the elimination of two of the original seven elements, were sufficient for him finally to consider it a new work: that is, although the physical components themselves remained unchanged, their spatial relationships were for him so altered that it became a different piece. A like approach fueled the interventions of Kawara and Weiner years later as they reconceived existing works, or the relations between existing works, as the basis for new shows, unprecedented in their oeuvres, in Dia's Chelsea galleries. This, too, is the basis on which Trockel's current show is predicated. Such examples contribute to and exemplify the ways in which a space or place or site is today determined discursively,

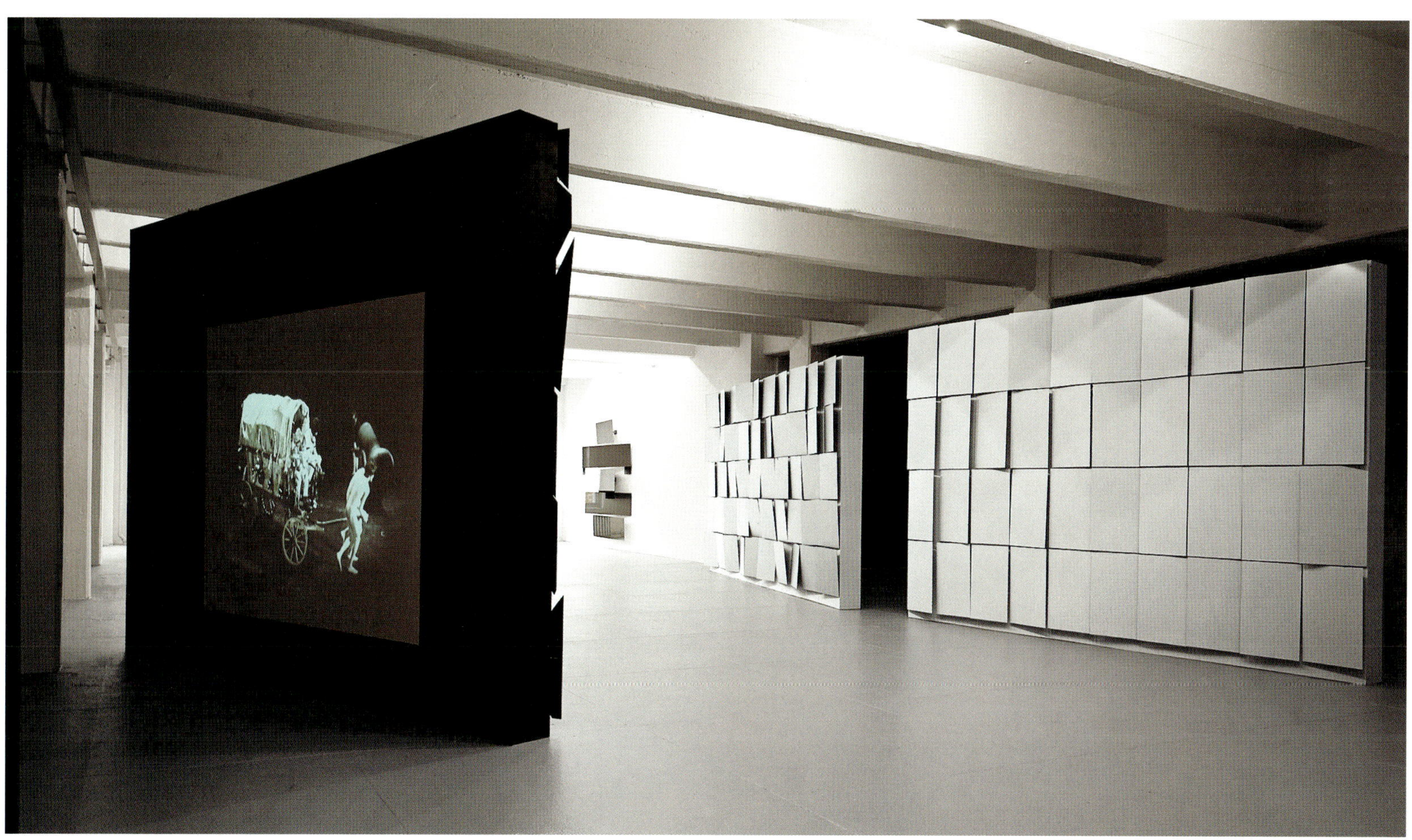

Rosemarie Trockel, "Spleen," installation at Dia Center for the Arts, New York City, 2002

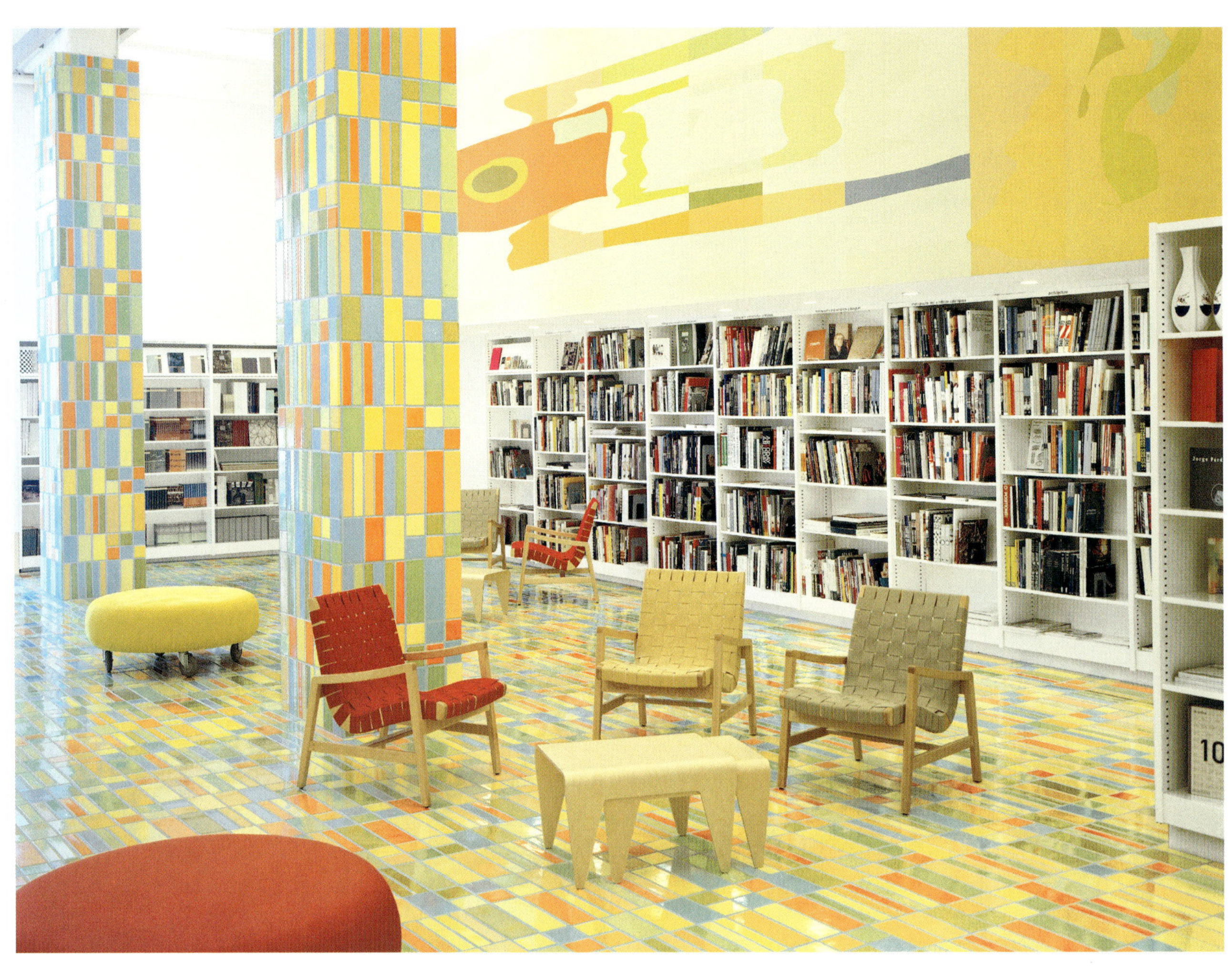

Jorge Pardo, *Project*, 2000, bookshop, Dia Center for the Arts, New York City

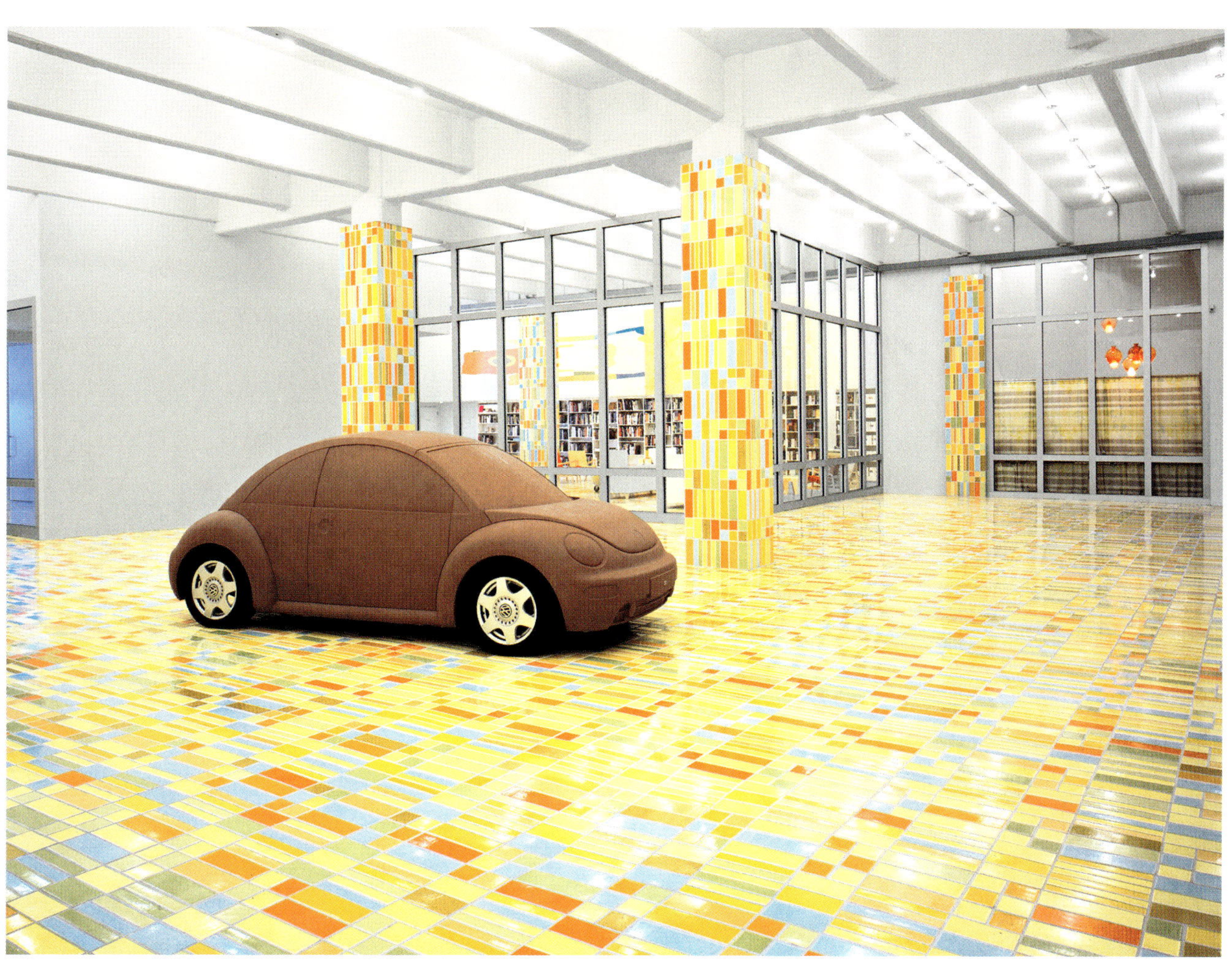

Jorge Pardo, *Project*, 2000, exhibition space with model of Volkswagen's New Beetle, Dia Center for the Arts, New York City

via relations based in history, gender, representation, and institutional politics.[28] This typological model of a space defined as a given set of conditions in a converted industrial building, as distinct from the traditional white-cube gallery of the modern art museum, has become the venue most favored by artists of a generation who has developed, questioned, and challenged the multifaceted vanguard legacy of the 1960s and 1970s.

Complementing this ongoing program based in site-related commissions, a series of more historically based exhibitions will be undertaken, mostly at Dia:Beacon. In tandem with the in situ projects, such presentations as "Playback," the retrospective of Whitman's work currently on view at Dia in Chelsea, will serve to probe and clarify the contribution and character of what is held in permanent trust. Shaped by a powerful formative vision that, tellingly, was most persuasively articulated by an artist—namely Judd—and consolidated by history and circumstance, Dia's collection is open to constant and critical revision. Its very singularity ensures that it lays claim to no ideological, absolute, or fixed historical account, and yet, given the highly important role that artists' visions and prescripts have played in forging its mandate and articulating the exigent model embraced by both the founders and their successors alike, it is far from being ahistorical, arbitrary, or serendipitous. It is perhaps best described as a response to the gauntlet thrown down by Judd in 1986: "Somewhere, just as the platinum-iridium meter guarantees the tape measure, a strict measure must exist for the art of this time and place."[29]

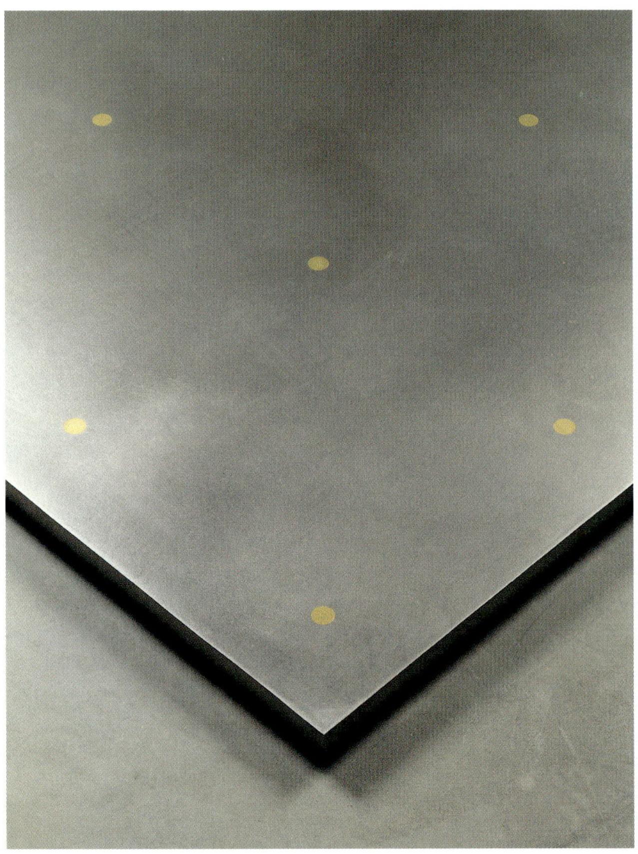

Walter De Maria, *Gold Meters*, 1976 (detail)

notes

1 Donald Judd, "On Installation," 1982, reprinted in *Donald Judd: Complete Writings 1975–1986* (Halifax: The Press of Nova Scotia College of Art and Design, in association with New York University Press, 1975), p. 21.

2 "After the work itself, my effort for some eighteen years, beginning in a loft on Nineteenth Street in New York, has been to permanently install as much work as possible, as well as to install some work by other artists. . . . The installations provide a considered, unhurried measure by which to judge hurried installations of my own and others in unfamiliar and often unsuitable places." Ibid., p. 19. Judd's list of the "best artists" was not so different from the core list that Dia's founders drew up in 1976 (ibid., p. 23): It comprised "Serra, Oldenburg, Flavin, Chamberlain, Bell, Andre, or myself."

3 Dan Flavin lived in this region in the 1970s, in Garrison, and worked on a project for Dick's Castle, a building just outside Cold Spring, adjacent to Beacon, funded by Dia in 1979. The extensive presentation of Flavin's work proposed for Dick's Castle was never realized. Under Dia's auspices, Flavin formed a substantial collection of drawings and watercolors by the Hudson River landscape painters.

4 Helen Winkler was critical to the implementation of many of these projects, from Walter De Maria's *The Lightning Field* (1977) to James Turrell's Roden Crater (1972) to Robert Whitman's performance retrospective in 1976. The third partner in the formation of both Dia Art Foundation and the companion Lone Star Foundation, she had many critical roles, not least bringing the two principals together, steering aesthetic policy, and administering Dia Art Foundation. Reflecting Dia's unusual openness to questions of location were two projects realized by Flavin: one was a site-specific installation in the courtyard of the Kunstmuseum Basel, which Dia gifted to that institution in 1975; the second was a joint institutional project (no longer extant) involving his work at Grand Central Terminal, New York, in 1976. The realization of temporary environmental projects and installations was widely pursued by the mid-1970s; the highlight of the landmark 1976 Venice Biennale, for example, was the series of large-scale installation works titled "Ambiente Art," which included such artists as Maria Nordman and Douglas Wheeler. In this context Dia's commissions were exceptional on account of their projected longevity. Dia's project with La Monte Young and Marian Zazeela involved annual series of concerts staged over an extended period of several months, reflecting the commitment to the performing as well as the visual arts as expressed in Dia Art Foundation's 1974 certificate of incorporation.

5 Dia donated all of its Warhol works to the Andy Warhol Museum with the exception of *Shadows* (1979), which it reserved on the grounds that the work's large-scale, environmental character was fully commensurate with other works in the collection. There are in fact 102 paintings in Dia's series, two having been added to the original commission of 100 at the time of purchase.

6 I am indebted for this information, as for much of the documentation of Dia's early history here, to Stephan Urbaschek, "Dia Art Foundation: Institution und Sammlung 1974–1985," Ph.D. Humboldt University, Berlin, 2002. This list of artists was preceded by a broader and more extensive one drawn up as part of a sketch or plan for a museum and its program by Friedrich and Winkler in 1972. The bare outlines of this institution reveal a far more conventional set of precepts than the program that Dia–Lone Star realized after 1976.

7 Very few works by Carl Andre or Franz Erhard Walther were in fact acquired. Two of the three paintings by Barnett Newman that Dia acquired were offered at auction at Sotheby's, New York, on November 11, 1985: *Anna's Light* (1968) and *Genesis—The Break* (1946). *Genesis—The Break* was bought in, and remains in Dia's collection, the sole work by Newman in its holdings. The third work, *The Moment I* (1962), was sold separately.

8 Friedrich opened the Munich gallery in 1963, in partnership with Franz Dahlem. It was at first devoted mostly to group shows of contemporary German, British, Italian, and American artists, but from 1965 (when Dahlem left to open his own space) until 1978 (when it came under the direction of Six Friedrich and Sabine Knust), solo exhibitions predominated. Notable exhibitions were those by Twombly (1964), Gerhard Richter (1964, 1966, 1967), Robert Rauschenberg (1965), Palermo (1966, 1967, 1968, 1971), Chamberlain (1967), Sigmar Polke (1967, 1970), Walther (1967, 1969, 1971–72, 1973), Andre (1968), De Maria (1968), Flavin (1968), Sol LeWitt (1968), Robert Ryman (1968, 1969), Sandback (1968), Warhol (1968), Hanne Darboven (1969), Michael Heizer (1969, 1970), La Monte Young and Marian Zazeela (1969, 1970, 1972 [this last a concert]), Knoebel (1971, 1972, 1973), Georg Baselitz (1972, 1975, 1976, 1977), and Judd (1972, 1973). See Urbaschek, Appendix, "Dia Art Foundation." Urbaschek cautions that there remains some ambiguity about whether the New York shows were made under the auspices of the Heiner Friedrich Gallery or Dia Art Foundation.

9 On Friedrich's activities in the context of the contemporary German art scene, see Wibke von Bonin, "Germany: The American Presence," *Arts Magazine* (March 1970), pp. 53–56.

10 See *Eva, Wenzel, and Jessyka Beuys, Joseph Beuys: Block Beuys* (Munich: Schirmer/Mosel, 1990).

11 See, for example, Judd, "Chamberlain: Another View," *Art International* 7 (January no. 10 1964), pp. 38–39. *Mr. Press* (1961), a wall sculpture by Chamberlain, hung in Judd's Spring Street residence from 1974 until his death, in 1994. In Marfa, he devoted a building purchased by Dia in the winter of 1978–79 to a presentation of works by Chamberlain, gifted by Dia.

12 Judd writes, "It's easy to imagine the magnificence of a museum in New York containing a couple of dozen paintings by [Jackson] Pollock or by Newman. It's too late to make such an installation for Pollock, almost for Newman." "On Installation," 1982, p. 22. In a long analysis of Abstract Expressionist art, one work Judd singles out for study is Newman's masterpiece *Anna's Light*, which was for a while a part of Dia's collection. "Abstract Expressionism," 1983, in *Donald Judd: Complete Writings 1975–1986*, p. 47.

13 See Germano Celant, *Das Bild einer Geschichte 1956/1976. Die Sammlung Panza di Biumo* (Milan: Electa, 1980), and Heiner Bastian, ed., *Joseph Beuys, Robert Rauschenberg, Cy Twombly, Andy Warhol: Sammlung Marx* (Munich: Prestel, 1983). On Ströher, see *Eva, Wenzel, and Jessyka Beuys, Joseph Beuys: Block Beuys*. In 1984, the Crex collection opened in a former textile factory in Schaffhausen, Switzerland. It features strong and concentrated groupings of works by many artists of the 1960s and 1970s found also in Dia's collection: Andre, Beuys, Flavin, Judd, Jannis Kounellis, LeWitt, Richard Long, Robert Mangold, Mario Merz, Bruce Nauman, Ryman, and Lawrence Weiner. Tellingly, the Marx, Ströher, and Panza collections, in different guises, have all entered major museums in recent years. The concentrations of works by specific individuals that they or the Dia or Crex collection offer have become, in accord with Judd's vision, the highly desired model. By contrast, earlier in the twentieth century the need of museums was to showcase modern art on a changing basis, prioritizing a changing exhibition program in order to educate a wide public. See, for example, two essays by Alfred H. Barr, Jr., proposing a model for New York's Museum of Modern Art, "A New Art Museum" and "A New Museum," in *Defining Modern Art. Selected Writings of Alfred H. Barr, Jr.*, eds. Irving Sandler and Amy Newman (New York: Harry N. Abrams, 1986), pp. 69–76. With the end of the "grand narratives" of the modernist era, even the pedagogical value of anthologizing collections, one of the foremost arguments in their support, has lost ground.

14 In addition, Dia was forced to auction a number of works in the collection, including key paintings by Newman, and to default on certain financial commitments. Among these, funding was curtailed to Turrell's Roden Crater project, which was subsequently administered by the newly established and soon-independent Skystone Foundation, and to Judd's Chinati Foundation, which was wrested from Dia and reestablished under the artist's control. After Whitman's performance space failed to make itself self-supporting, it was sold to The Kitchen in 1985. By mutual consent of the artist and the institution, Sandback's Winchendon museum was finally closed in 1996.

15 The seeds of this approach may be found not only in Judd's theories but in his example. When he purchased a cast-iron building at the corner of Spring and Mercer Streets in SoHo in 1974, he was finally able to realize long-cherished ideas concerning the segregation yet not complete separation of artistic from everyday activities, together with the reinstallation or reconfiguration of individual works of his own and others with respect to the space, scale, and dimensions of the site.

16 On Judd's Marfa project, see Judd, "Marfa, Texas," in *Donald Judd: Complete Writings 1975–1986*, pp. 96–102, and "Statement for the Chinati Foundation/La Fundación Chinati," in ibid., pp. 110–14.

17 Since 2000, Lannan Foundation has gifted works to Dia's collection and provided long-term loans for permanent exhibition as well as crucial funds for a number of large-scale projects. It has also provided ongoing support for Dia's

affiliated projects in the American Southwest, including Turrell's Roden Crater in Arizona and Heizer's *City* in Nevada.

18 The key texts initially defining Minimalism were Judd's "Specific Objects," 1965, first published in *Arts Yearbook* 8, 1965, and reprinted in *Donald Judd: Complete Writings 1959–1975*, pp. 181–89; Robert Morris's series "Notes on Sculpture," Parts I–III, published in *Artforum* in February 1966, October 1966, and Summer 1967; and Michael Fried's "Art and Objecthood," published in *Artforum* 5, no.10 (Summer 1967), pp. 12–23. Tellingly, all three were published in art magazines, *Artforum* becoming by the late 1960s the preeminent vehicle for vanguard debate. "The art world's players were very nearly obsessed with theoretical self-definition and self-justification. Aesthetic and philosophical positions were taken and held passionately. . . . *Artforum* was *the* paramount institution and its writers the voices that others responded to—in *this* arena at *this* time, as the Museum of Modern Art and Alfred Barr had been in the two previous decades," contends art historian Amy Newman in her chronicle of that highly influential journal: Newman, *Challenging Art: Artforum 1962–1974* (New York: Soho Press, 2000), pp. 3, 11. Among its key issues was one devoted to American sculpture, published in the summer of 1967, which contained both Fried's "Art and Objecthood" and part III of Morris's "Notes on Sculpture" series, as well as Robert Smithson's "Towards the Development of an Air Terminal Site" and LeWitt's landmark "Paragraphs on Conceptual Art."

19 See in particular, Judd, "In the Galleries: John Chamberlain," *Arts Magazine* 36, no. 6 (March 1962), reprinted in *Donald Judd: Complete Writings 1959–1975*, p. 46; "Chamberlain: Another View;" "John Chamberlain," 7 *Sculptors* Philadelphia: Institute of Contemporary Art, 1965), reprinted in *Complete Writings 1959–1975*, p. 190; and "Chamberlain Building," in *Donald Judd: Architektur* (Münster: Westfälischer Kunstverein, 1989), pp. 78–79. In 1989 Judd brought together all his writing on Chamberlain along with notes on Pollock and other remarks to constitute the essay for a catalogue accompanying a show of Chamberlain's new work; see Judd, "John Chamberlain," in *John Chamberlain: New Sculpture* (New York: Pace Gallery, 1989), pp. i–xi.

20 See *The Collected Writings of Robert Smithson*, ed. Jack Flam, 1979 (reprint ed. Berkeley: University of California Press, 1996), pp. 4–6, passim.

21 See Richard Serra, *Writings Interviews* (London and Chicago: The University of Chicago Press, 1994). A less wide-ranging and prolific writer than either Judd or Smithson, both of whom were essayists as well as critics, Serra has written occasional pieces on individual artists, often in response to direct requests. See his "Rage," in *Louise Bourgeois: The Locus of Memory. Works 1982–1993* (New York: The Brooklyn Museum in association with Harry N. Abrams, 1994), p. 80. The quantity as well as the quality of the writings of the sixties generation is notable. Only Newman and Ad Reinhardt among their immediate forebears were similarly prolific.

22 Hal Foster, "The Crux of Minimalism," 1986, reprinted in Foster, *The Return of the Real* (Cambridge, Mass.: The MIT Press, 1996), p. 43. The boundaries dividing these types of work are more permeable than this formulation suggests; works such as Serra's *Tilted Arc* (1981) notably elide many of these distinctions.

23 Maurice Merleau-Ponty, quoted in Jan Butterfield, *The Art of Light and Space* (New York: Abbeville Press, 1993), p. 8. Morris's much quoted phrase is cited, for example, in Foster, "The Crux of Minimalism," p. 47.

24 Judd says much that is pertinent here in his essay "On Installation," pp. 23–24: "A good installation is too much work and too expensive and if the artist does it, too personal, to then destroy. Paintings, sculptures and other three-dimensional work cannot withstand the constant installation and removal and shipping. . . . One building [that contains my art in Marfa] . . . has two large rooms and the other has one. Each of the two took two years of thinking and moving pieces around. The one room took about a year. One of the two rooms was the basis for the installations in the exhibition of my work at The National Gallery of Canada in 1975. . . . None of my work that's installed is lent nor is that by other artists." Although site-specific work was rare in Judd's practice, he was keenly alert to the opportunity that a museum on the model he proposed would offer for new works to be added, created specifically by the artist for the venue. "Permanent installations are also important for the development of larger and more complex work," he contended (p. 24). Not limited to the amassing of existing works, this model is meant to offer opportunities for ambitious projects on a large scale. At Dia:Beacon, this impulse has been variously manifested: in Heizer's *North, East, South, West* (1967/2002); in a series of paintings, *Innocent Love* (1999), created by Agnes Martin in anticipation of their acquisition for Dia:Beacon; and in a commissioned suite of gray-glass panels from Richter. A further variation on this model was proposed by Sandback for Winchendon and will be continued in Dia:Beacon. The artist has reinstalled different groups of his works selected from the collection and will periodically make new works for exhibition, thereby treating the museum in part as a laboratory.

25 For a fuller discussion of Irwin's role in this project, see Michael Govan's introduction, "Dia in Context," pp. 14–43, and "Robert Irwin," pp 156–165.

26 Not all of the works could be accommodated, including two monumental versions of De Maria's *I Ching* (1981). Bridget Riley's landmark *Composition with Circles 2* (2000) will be on loan to the retrospective of her work at Tate Britain in summer 2003. Not all of the artists in the collection are featured in this opening presentation: those not here will be included in future presentations. While the installation of works in many of the galleries is long-term, several will cycle, primarily for reasons of conservation.

27 T. S. Eliot, "Tradition and the Individual Talent," 1920, in *Selected Essays* (New York: Harcourt, Brace and World, Inc., 1964) pp. 4–5.

28 See Miwon Kwon, *One Place after Another: Site Specific Art and Locational Identity* (Cambridge, Mass.: The MIT Press, 2002), for a fuller discussion of this shifting focus. In contrast to environmentally scaled work, installation art can be defined as work that offers a heightened immersive experience, requiring an activated spectatorship armed with a critical consciousness. It is usually decentered, in that there is no ideal or privileged position from which to survey the work but a multiplicity of contingent points of view. Large-scale serial work, such as Judd's untitled plywood boxes of 1975, implies aspectual diversity as part of a phenomenologically grounded apprehension, that is, one that involves a heightened immediacy in the spectator's perceptual faculties. By contrast, installation art tends to a more visceral, sensory, and kinesthetic experience, as found in Ann Hamilton's *tropos* (1993), or via the sort of counterpointing of the illusory and actual found in Diana Thater's *Knots & Surfaces* (2001). Engaging the site conceptually as well as physically, such work typically treats it as a locus set apart for an encounter that, at best, is always and constantly circumscribed by a self-reflexive critical awareness, creating a dialectical interplay between psychically and physically grounded experiences. Here, too, it contrasts with environmentally scaled pieces, like Judd's, based in an interplay between the conceptual and the perceptual. Thus installation art as it came to be defined in the 1980s has few precedents in Dia's collection. Irwin creates site-specific works, such as the one he presented at Dia in Chelsea 1998–99. Beuys adopted this mode infrequently, for example in *Aus Berlin: Neues vom Kojoten* (*From Berlin: News from the Coyote*), 1979, to which he accorded a fixed presentation secured by a detailed template drawing that precisely positions each component in the mise-en-scène. More typically, though, Beuys readjusted existing works to fit the occasion. Thus, he installed *Arena. . .* in several permutations and configurations depending on the space available and the conceptual as well as material circumstances. For a fuller discussion see *Joseph Beuys, Arena—where would I have got if I had been intelligent!* (New York: Dia Center for the Arts, 1994).

29 Judd, "Statement for the Chinati Foundation/La Fundación Chinati," p. 111.

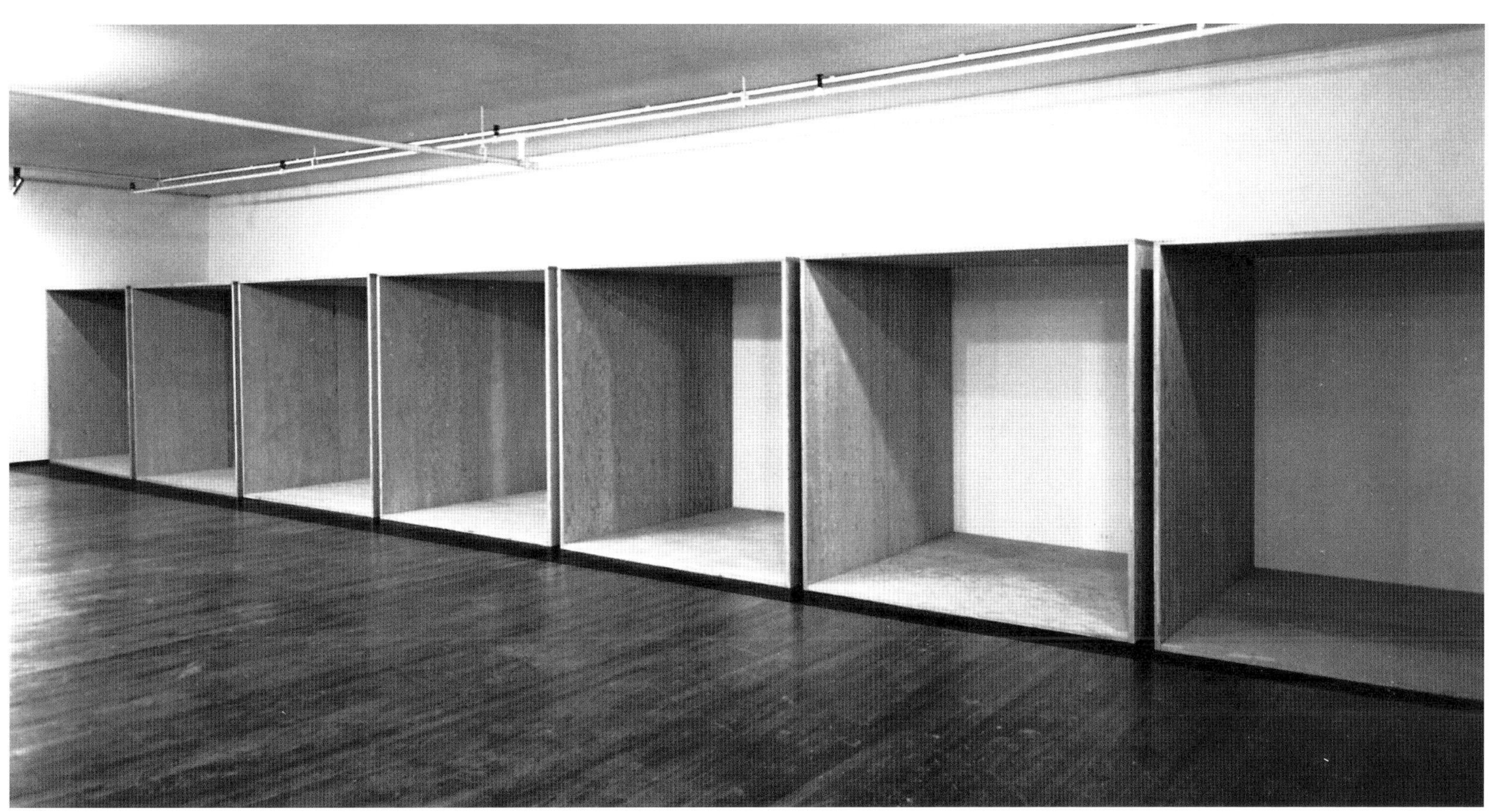

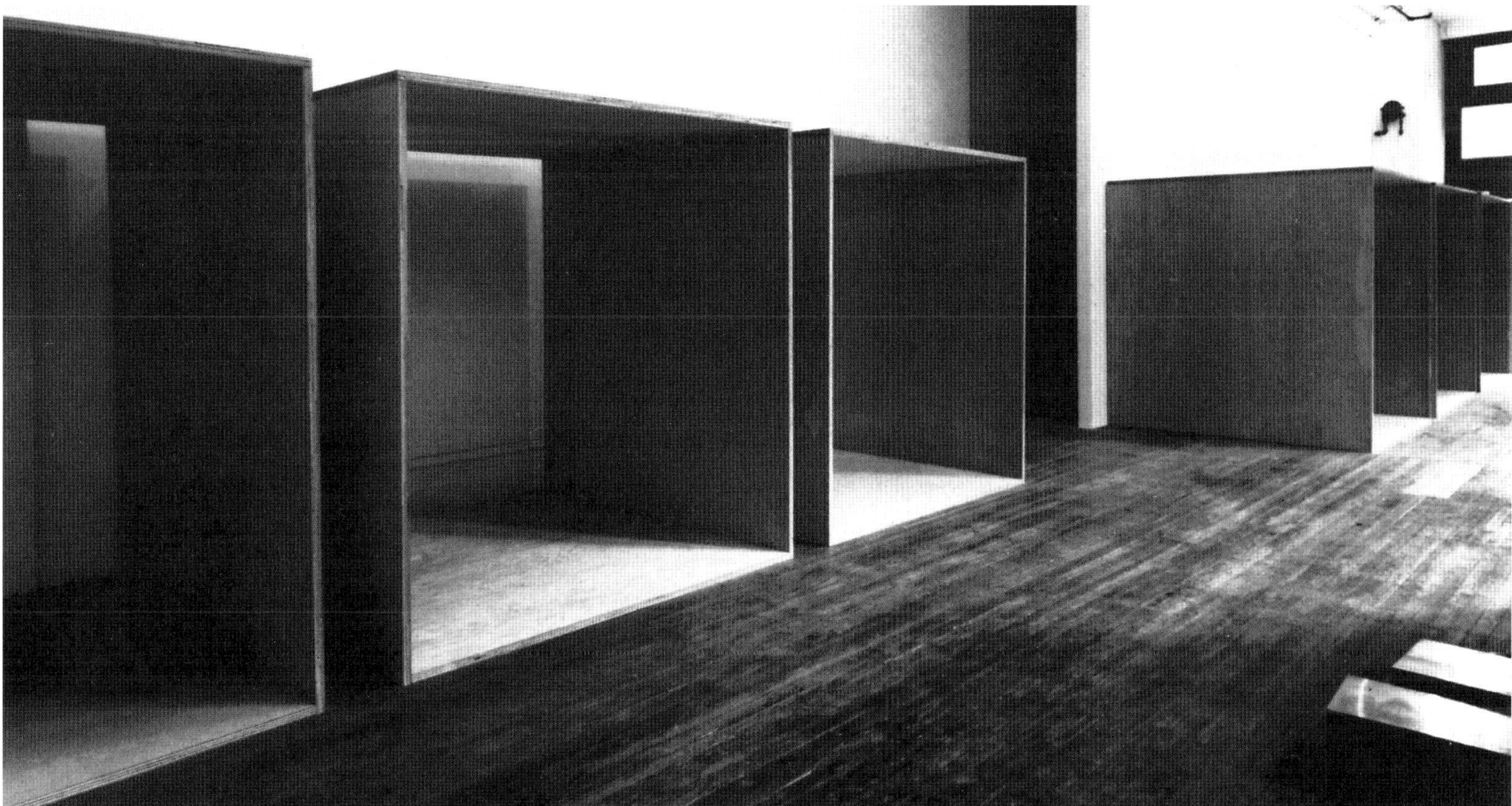

above Donald Judd, untitled, at Leo Castelli Gallery, New York City, 1973
below Donald Judd, untitled, at 101 Spring Street, New York City, 1974

Artists

Bernd and Hilla Becher

Joseph Beuys

Louise Bourgeois

John Chamberlain

Hanne Darboven

Walter De Maria

Dan Flavin

Michael Heizer

Robert Irwin

Donald Judd

On Kawara

Imi Knoebel

Sol LeWitt

Agnes Martin

Bruce Nauman

Blinky Palermo

Gerhard Richter

Robert Ryman

Fred Sandback

Richard Serra

Robert Smithson

Andy Warhol

Lawrence Weiner

Robert Whitman

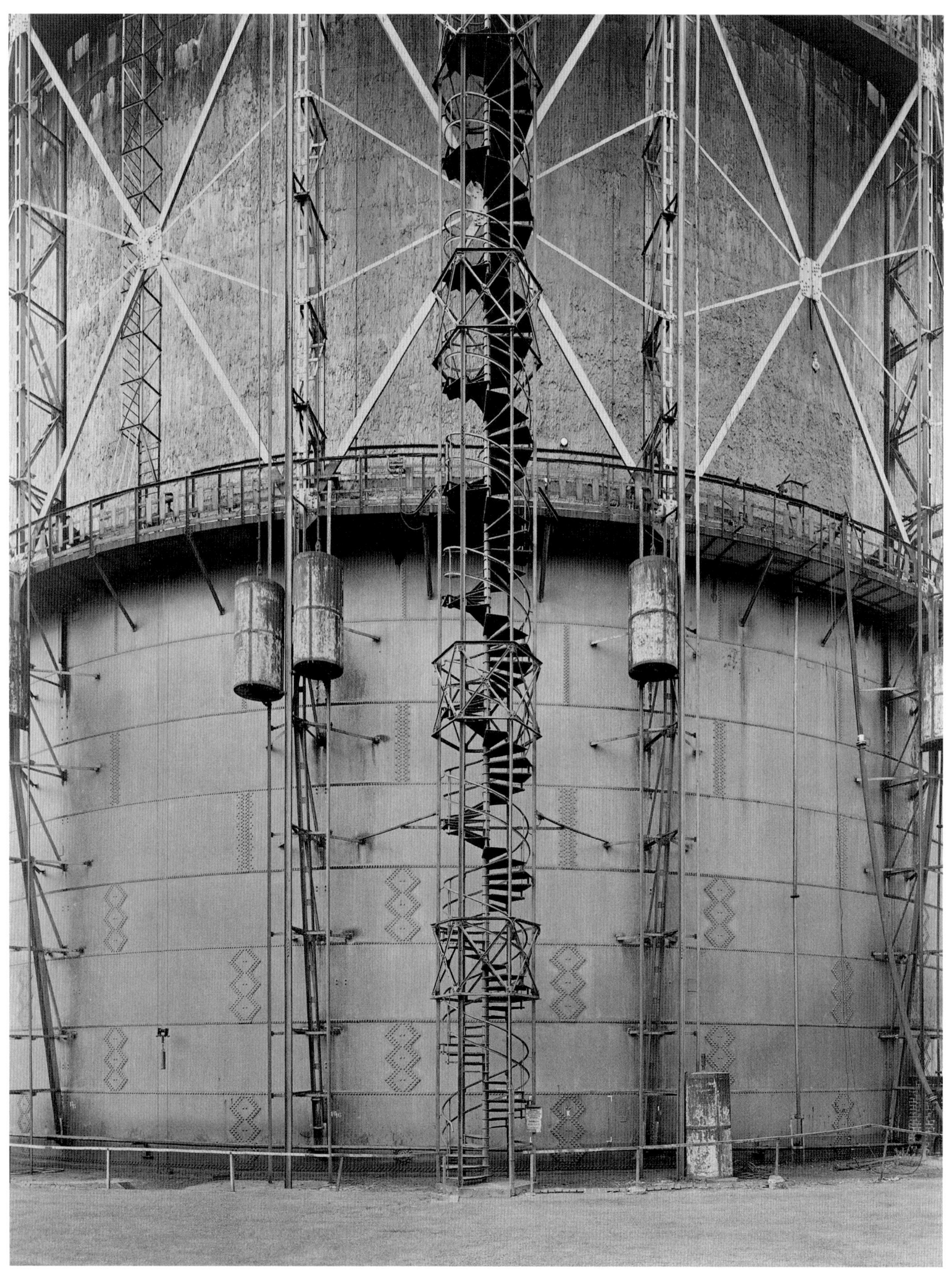

Bernd and Hilla Becher

Bernd Becher was born in Siegen, Germany, in 1931. Hilla Becher was born Hilla Wobeser in 1934, in Potsdam, Germany. They met at the Kunstakademie Düsseldorf, where they both studied painting in the late 1950s, and began to collaborate in 1959. Their first gallery exhibition took place in 1963 at the Galerie Ruth Nohl in Siegen. Since then, their work has been shown in Documentas 5 (1972), 6 (1977), 7 (1982), and 11 (2002), and at the São Paulo Bienal, in 1977. The Stedelijk Van Abbemuseum, Eindhoven, organized a retrospective of the artists' work in 1981. Their exhibition at Dia in 1989–91 included photographs of grain elevators, hot-blast stoves, mineheads, and other industrial structures. After winning the 1991 Leone d'Oro award at the Venice Biennale, the Bechers reworked their Venice installation for a retrospective exhibition at the Kunstverein Cologne. Highly influential teachers at the Kunstakademie Düsseldorf, they were awarded the Erasmus Prize of 2002, which honors achievements in society and culture.

Partial View of Gas Tank, Coal Mine "Anna," Alsdorf/Aachen, Germany, 1992

Vernacular industrialized architecture has been the sole subject of Bernd and Hilla Becher's work for some forty years. Their vast photographic inventory now ranges geographically from western Europe through North America and taxonomically across an enormous array of heterogeneous building types, many verging on obsolescence—mine shafts, lime kilns, silos, cooling towers, blast furnaces, tipples, gasometers—all classified by reference to function. The initial impetus that led the young Bernd Becher to begin photographing such subjects in the late 1950s was purely practical: he wanted to use his recordings as raw material for the paintings he was then making in a Neue Sachlichkeit style. In those same years Hilla Becher, née Wobeser, apprenticed and briefly worked in a professional advertising studio, where she developed a passion for photographing technical and mechanistic subjects. Once husband and wife started working together, in 1957, they assumed identical roles: tasks are not separately assigned to one or the other; both are involved in scouting sites, negotiating with the owners and other authorities, setting up the cameras, and printing. The art they have produced does not fall within conventional categories of documentary photography, though it has many affiliations with that long-standing tradition. The disciplined ethic with which this dedicated German couple defined, then refined, their project of recording for posterity the increasingly neglected relics of the industrial era, with its domestic offshoots, has yielded not just an aesthetic but a vision.

From their earliest publication, titled tellingly *Anonyme Skulpturen: Eine Typologie technischer Bauten* (*Anonymous Sculpture: A Typology of Technical Buildings*), 1970, the Bechers' work has circulated within the realm of contemporary art practice and discourse. Certain features of their art, the hallmark of which is, in Charles Wright's felicitous phrase, "a controlled beauty," make this positioning particularly apt—though the Bechers themselves do not regard the issue as of great import.[1] Typically, their works present each industrial motif in what soon evolved into a rigorous, disciplined signature manner whose focus is an exploration of the relation between the subject's function and the resulting photographic representation. Isolated, centered, and frontally framed, each motif is shot in as objective a manner as possible. The combination of large-format cameras and finely grained black-and-white film ensures a remarkable tonal range in each print. By working only under slightly overcast skies and early in the morning during the seasons of spring and fall, the Bechers are ensured of an even, diffuse light with minimal shadows, a lambent ambience that enhances their intensive focus on the motif, which is revealed in crystalline detail, grounded in a formal factual clarity. All anecdotal incident, such as intrusive foliage, stray animals, and humans, is sedulously avoided: nothing disturbs the systematic ascetic neutrality. Tellingly, the vantage point tends to be subtly elevated. "Looking at an object from a point half way up it [causes] it to appear before you in its full reach and free of distortion," they explain.[2] The raised camera position also causes the horizon to appear to recede, the surroundings to become more panoramic, and the object to stand forth prominently so that, while clearly related to its environment, it simultaneously appears somewhat removed, apart, an effect enhanced by the expansive neutral skies. The results evidence a brilliant understanding of scale relations—of how a vast structure can be made to fit a small-sized pictorial format—without rhetoric or expressive distortion.

By the mid-1960s the Bechers had also settled on a preferred presentational mode: the grid. Groupings of prints, each print measuring sixteen by twelve inches or smaller, either framed discretely or encased within a single large frame, facilitate direct, immediate comparison between motifs, which are arrayed without hierarchy, according to type, function, and/or material. Juxtaposition permits industrial structures that at first might appear prevailingly similar, even uniform, to register as significantly different one from another. Given that most viewers know little about the economic, engineering, and functional requirements that determine the generic forms and characters of these structures, comparison of the several components in any of these multipartite works operates primarily at a formal level—that is, in an aesthetic dimension. Differences and similarities among related motifs consequently appear as variations on an ideal form, given that the structures are family members from the same species. Specific subjects are interpreted as anonymous plastic forms—as anonymous sculpture.

In 1989–91, for an exhibition at Dia in New York, the Bechers introduced a second format into their oeuvre: single images that are larger in size—twenty-four by twenty inches—and presented individually rather than as gridded tableaux. Several galleries within this extensive exhibition were devoted to a specific subject, a strategy that allowed new typologies to cohere. This presentational strategy was heralded in part by a series of finely printed publications that they had begun to produce, beginning with *Framework Houses*, in 1977. This was soon followed by, among others, *Water Towers* (1988), *Blast Furnaces* (1990), and *Pennsylvania Coal Mine Tipples* (1991), the latter timed to mark the Dia show. Devoted to one kind of

Lime Kilns, Dieversburg, Holland, 1968

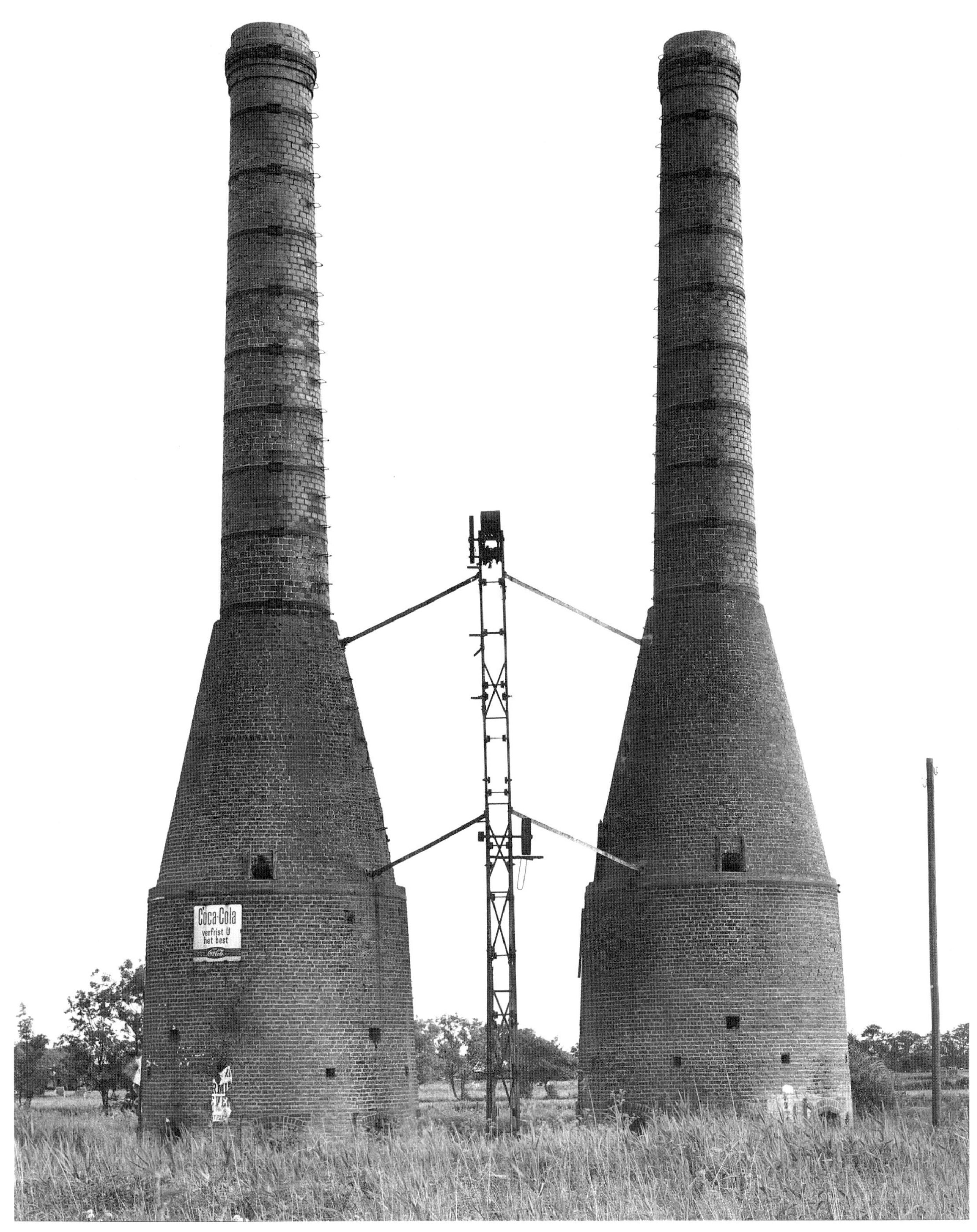
Coca-Cola
verfrist U
het best
Coca-Cola

industrialized plant, this ongoing series of books constitutes a type-by-type corpus documenting a rapidly dying industrial age. The brief texts that the artists wrote to accompany the first books in the series provided information on the genesis of the various typologies, offering a historical positioning that corresponded to the inclusion, in the captions, of the date on which each building was constructed together with the year in which the photograph was taken. In more recent publications this approach has been superseded by accounts that concentrate on how the plants function, an approach paralleled by the elimination of the plants' dates from the captions. Taken together, these decisions further abstract the subjects from their sociohistorical ambience in favor of a concentration on the typological relation of the individual instance to the generic, of the single member to the species or class.

For Dia:Beacon the Bechers ring further changes on their presentational modalities by capitalizing on the fact that the gallery they selected for their work is divided into two equal parts. All the photographs in one half of the space are partial views, which are relatively unusual in their oeuvre. Some of these are sequenced by type into small subsets. For example, three of the Winding Towers are installed on one wall; the Blast Furnaces hang on another. A diptych–a format they rarely employ–occupies one of the two short walls that bisect the gallery. Most of these images, which have seldom been exhibited, were recorded in the late 1980s and early 1990s, reflecting a subtle shift of focus in their work. The one "vintage" image, from 1968, is formally no different, testimony both to the roots of this reorientation in certain early forays and to the remarkable consistency and cohesion of their methodology and aesthetic.

The other half of the gallery is devoted to Aggregates, that is, to details of large-scale machinery, pipes, conduits, and metallic containers that belong to a diverse range of plants. A suite of eight lime kilns, vessels of one of the oldest and most commonplace processes long proceeding the onset of the industrial age, and hence frequently found in their archive, are counterpointed by images of plants that involve what are, for them, unusually contemporary procedures and processes–notably, Styrofoam and petrochemical production.

Tracing the history of a rapidly declining industrial era many of whose older technical processes and functions are now defunct, and of individual buildings decaying or threatened with destruction, is an important impulse in the Bechers' practice. Well aware of the fine-art and commercial portrayal of industry by previous specialists and by trade photographers alike, they have gradually assembled a second archive to probe and survey the recording of this thematic from other perspectives. Primarily heuristic in function, the counterarchive both expands and focuses their knowledge of their subject matter. In contrast to those predecessors whose work constitutes a traditional industrial archaeology, a particular level of self-conscious awareness and reflexivity defines and distinguishes their enterprise.

While foregrounding the urgency of their archival mission, the Bechers also stress their concern for canonical documentary procedures, such as ensuring the legibility of the image: "The photographs should always show all the details and the textures of the materials," they insist,[3] adding that they let "the forms speak for themselves and become readable," that they refuse "to hide or exaggerate or depict anything in an

Partial View of Water Cooler, Coal Mine "Anna," Alsdorf/Aachen, Germany, 1992

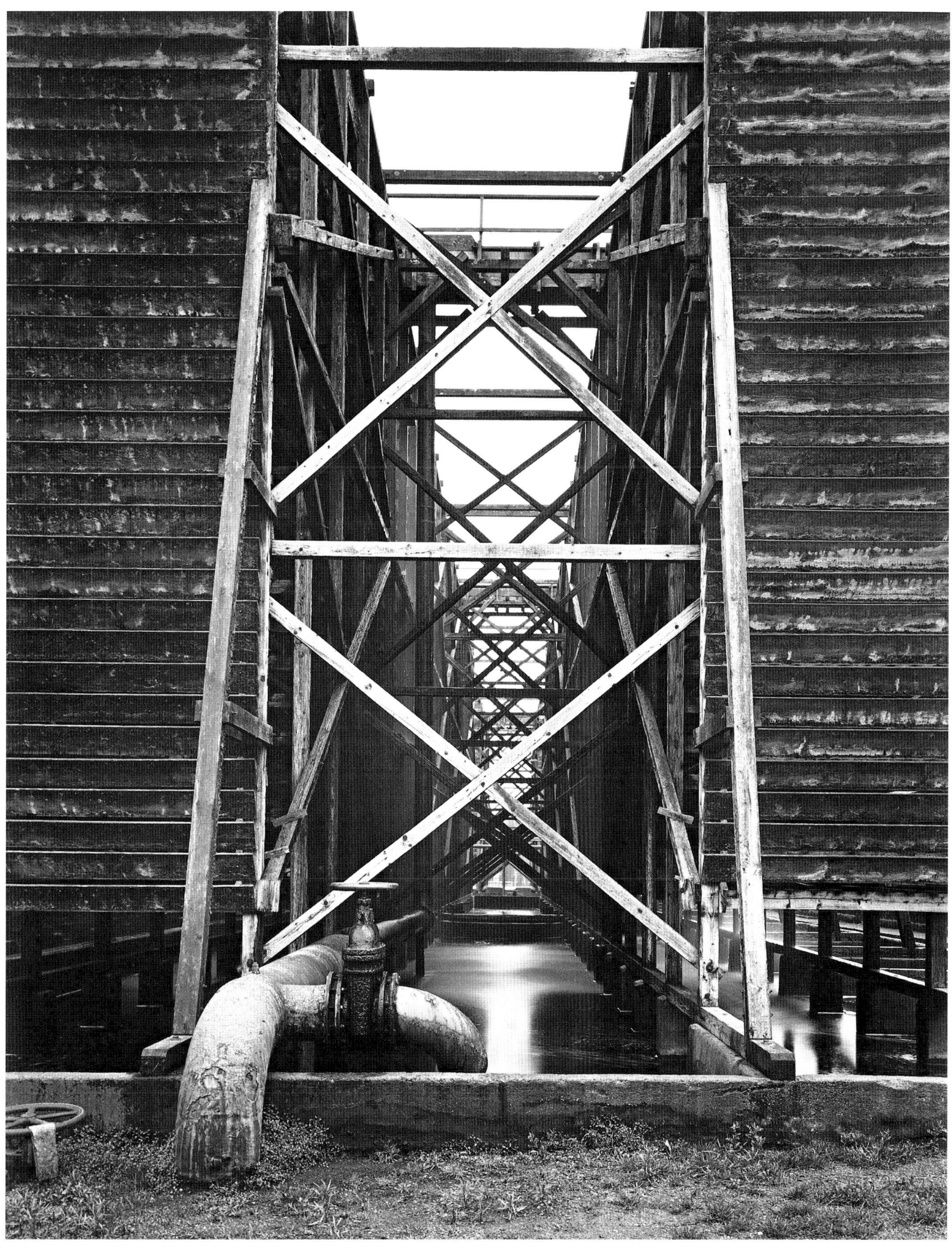

untrue fashion."[4] Viewed in this light, their work may be placed in a lineage stemming from such early modernist luminaries as Eugène Atget and August Sander, rather than in relation to artisanal modes of the kind that subtend industrial archaeology. Sander sought to classify into a pictorial catalogue, in a "style devoid of style," the professional and social types that made up modern Germany. The resonant formal uniformity of his lifelong project *Menschen des 20. Jahrhunderts* (*Man in the Twentieth Century*) exceeds the strictly documentary, becoming a cornerstone in the history of twentieth-century modernism. The Bechers are today the foremost exponents of that revered legacy.

They are nonetheless fully attuned to the contemporaneous practices of many fellow artists who, in the 1960s, began to use the camera as a convenient tool for recording and documenting. Notable among these artists were Robert Smithson, whom they assisted when he arrived in the Ruhr district in 1968 to explore the demise of the industrial era from a very different perspective, and Hanne Darboven, whose project engaging collective cultural memory, *Kulturgeschichte 1880–1983* (*Cultural History 1880–1983*), 1980–83, shares certain impulses, methodologies, and techniques with the Bechers. Other parallels may be drawn with such artists as Sol LeWitt, Donald Judd, Carl Andre, and Ed Ruscha (with his deadpan early book projects), who based their compositional and structural modalities on seriality and permutation. In addition, Judd and many of his peers shared the Bechers' appreciation for and knowledge of anonymous industrial structures, vernacular building types, and early modern as well as contemporary engineering.[5] These affinities and confluences generated the discursive context for the initial reception of their work, one that subsumed archaeological, sociological, and strictly photography-based critiques into a late modernist agenda centered in formal, structural, and serial procedures. Highly influential as teachers, the Bechers have in turn shaped another generation of artists both orthodox and aberrant, notable among them Thomas Struth, Candida Höfer, and Thomas Ruff, their former students from the Kunstakademie Düsseldorf.

L.C.

notes

1 Charles Wright, "Foreword," in Bernd and Hilla Becher, *Pennsylvania Coal Mine Tipples* (New York: Dia Center for the Arts, 1991), n.p. "The question if this is a work of [fine] art or not is not very interesting for us," Hilla Becher has stated on a number of occasions. See, for example, Carl Andre, "A Note on Bernhard and Hilla Becher," *Artforum* 11, no. 5 (December 1972), p. 59.

2 Bernd and Hilla Becher, quoted in "Interview mit Bernd und Hilla Becher," in *Bernd und Hilla Becher* (Munich: WB Verlag, 1989), p. 14.

3 Bernd and Hilla Becher, quoted in Angela Grauerholz and Anne Ramsden, "Photographing Industrial Architecture: An Interview with Bernd and Hilla Becher," *Parachute* 22 (Spring 1981), p. 15.

4 Ibid., p. 18.

5 Donald Judd's review of the 1964 exhibition "Twentieth Century Engineering" at the Museum of Modern Art, New York, is telling here. See Judd, "Month in Review," *Arts Magazine* 39, no. 1 (October 1964), reprinted in *Donald Judd: Complete Writings 1959–1975* (Halifax: The Press of Nova Scotia College of Art and Design, and New York: New York University Press, 1975), pp. 136–39.

right *Plant for Styrofoam Production, Wesseling near Cologne, Germany,* 1997

pages 84–85 *Mines of Giraumont, Lorraine, France,* 1985

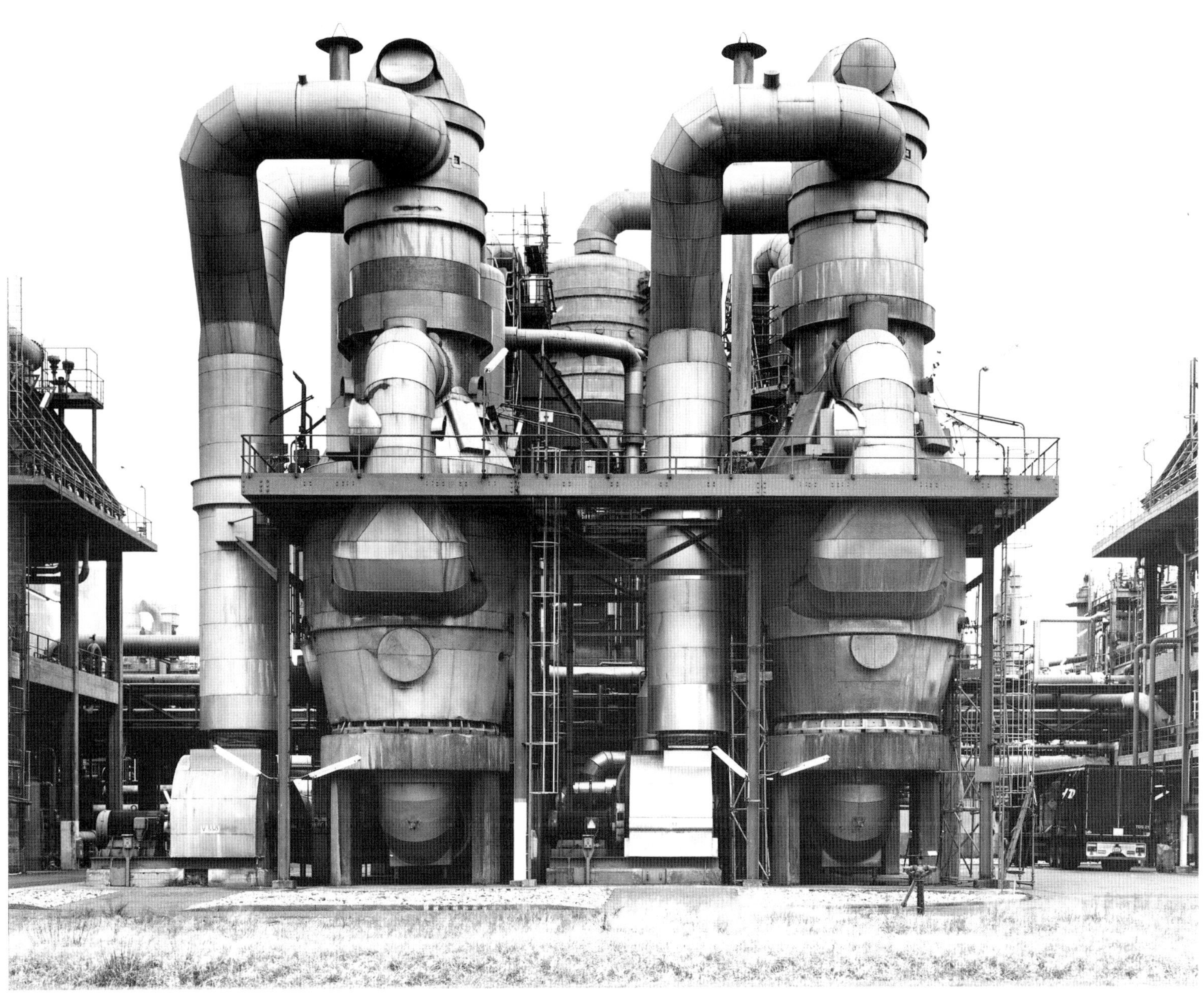

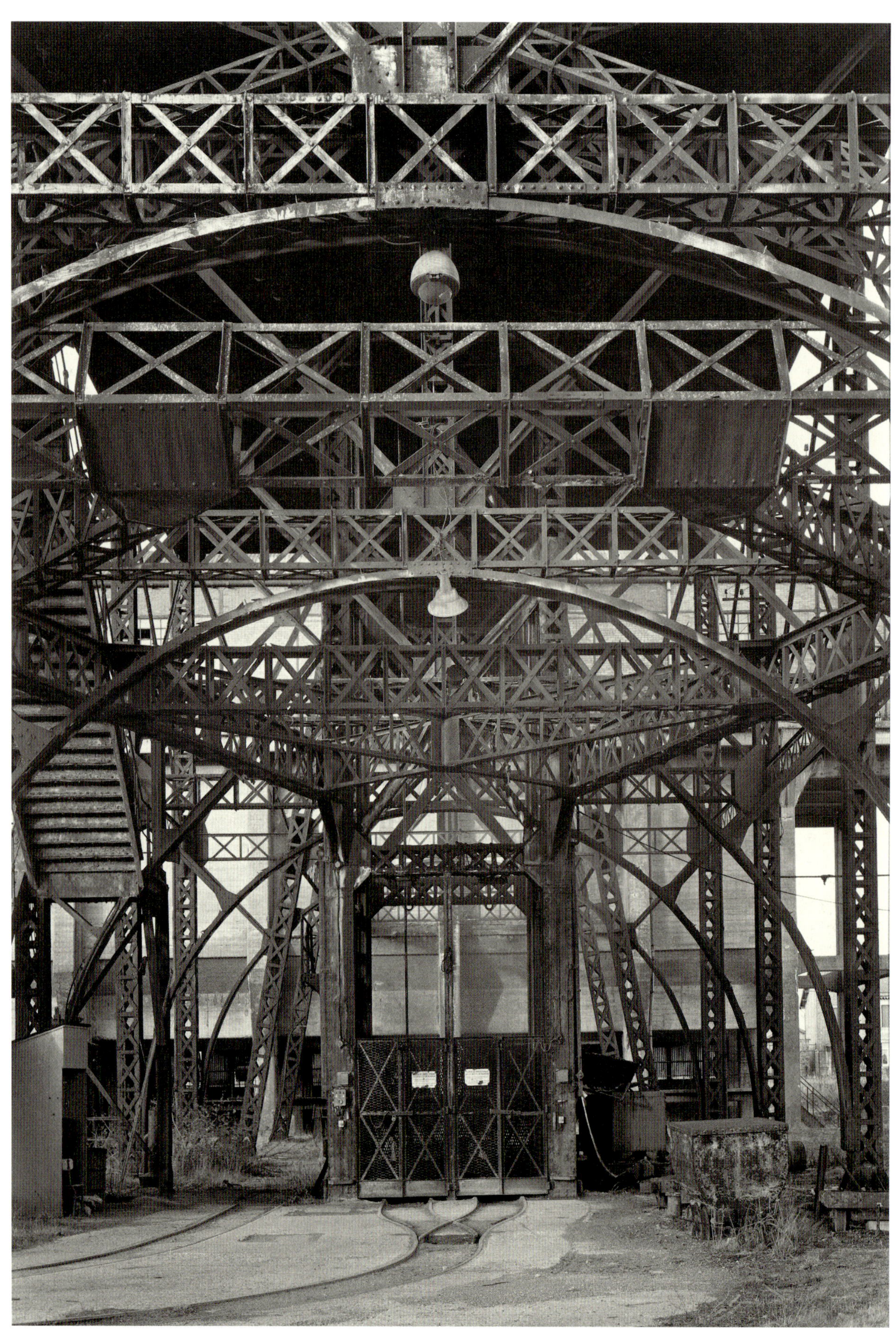

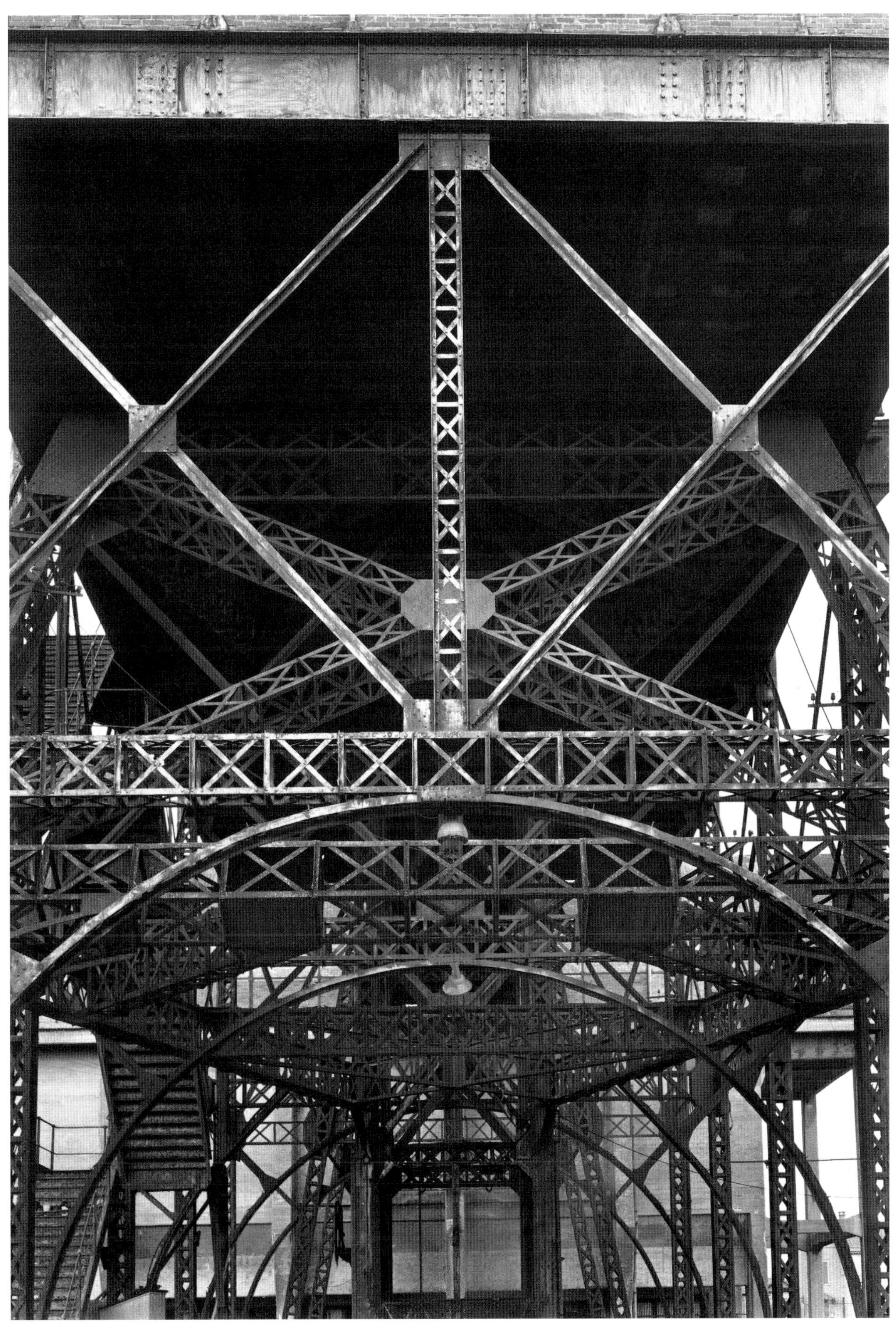

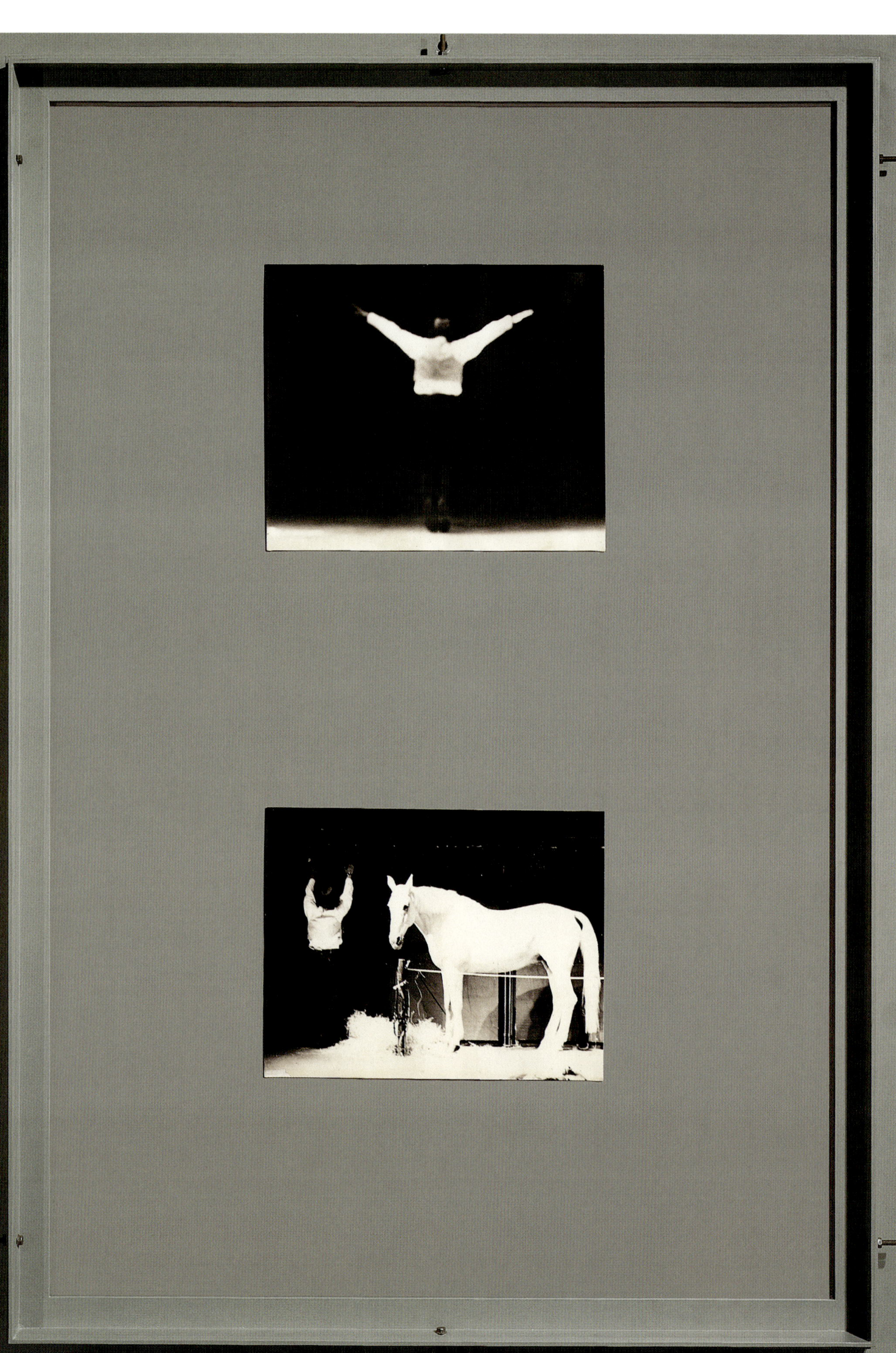

Joseph Beuys

Joseph Beuys was born in 1921 in Krefeld, Germany. He trained at the Kunstakademie Düsseldorf from 1947 to 1951, then taught there as a professor of sculpture from 1961 until his controversial dismissal, in 1972. Beuys's first one-person exhibition of his sculpture and drawings was in 1953, at the house of the collectors Franz Joseph and Hans van der Grinten. In the early 1960s he became involved with the Fluxus group, taking part in concerts and performances and devising his own "actions," which for a time became his principal aesthetic mode. In 1970 the Beuys Block—a large collection of Beuys's work formed under his own aegis from the Sammlung Karl Ströher—was installed in the Hessisches Landesmuseum Darmstadt; it remains his most important public collection. Dia held exhibitions of Beuys's work in 1987, 1992, and 1998, and has planted trees and basalt columns in New York City as part of his *7000 Eichen*, a project he began in 1982 for Documenta 7 in Kassel, Germany, with initial funding from Dia Art Foundation. Beuys died in Düsseldorf in 1986.

Arena—dove sarei arrivato se fossi stato intelligente!, 1970–72, frame no. 66

In 1982, Dia facilitated the realization of Joseph Beuys's proposal for Documenta 7, *7000 Eichen* (*7,000 Oaks*), a project that called for the planting of seven thousand trees, each paired with a columnar basalt marker, throughout the city of Kassel, Germany. Dia's association with Beuys, an artist known for his theory and practice of a "social sculpture" that was largely based in political involvement, environmental concerns, and performance, illustrates its willingness to help artists develop projects that are ephemeral and conceptual in nature.

The encyclopedic work, *Arena—dove sarei arrivato se fossi stato intelligente!* (*Arena—where I would have got if I had been intelligent!*) discloses the ambitious motivations of this highly influential German artist in 100 panels containing several hundred photographs taken over the span of his career up to 1972.[1] Traces of ephemeral activities, the photographs include multiple shots of some of Beuys's most important actions and concerts woven across a number of panels. A single found photograph, of the Roman amphitheater at Verona, speaks to his overriding conception of the work as dealing with the "arena" of life.

In assembling *Arena* . . . Beuys treated the prints in ways that draw attention to their status as reproductions. Many negatives were bleached, solarized, or otherwise manipulated; the roughness of their printing, reminiscent of an Arte Povera aesthetic, was enhanced by casually torn edges and perforations. In addition, most of the prints' surfaces were worked over, often with a layer of wax; in other cases, fat and *Braunkreuz* (an oil-based medium that was part of Beuys's signature vocabulary) were applied. Alongside the panels containing photographs, Beuys incorporated three panels made from colored glass—two in royal blue, one in golden yellow. For him, Caroline Tisdall contends, these monochrome panels were redolent of "blue sky for the cold clarity of the north . . . [and] the warm yellow of sulphur and southern sun."[2] An oilcan and two piles of blocks of wax and fat interspersed with sheets of copper and iron serve as freestanding sculptural and material components.

Like many of Beuys's works, *Arena . . .* was developed and modified over several years. An early, untitled version was shown in Edinburgh in 1970, when Beuys performed the action *Celtic (Kinloch Rannoch) Scottish Symphony*. In the two years before its next exhibition—at Lucio Amelio's Modern Art Agency, Naples, in 1972, under the title *Arena—dove sarei arrivato se fossi stato intelligente!* Beuys completely reworked it, adding specially designed frames of heavy aluminum, as well as the sculptural stacks and oilcan. As finally realized, *Arena . . .* constitutes not so much an autobiographical statement as an allegorical portrait of Beuys's artistic persona. Favoring evocation over documentation, it functions as an artistic summa, drawing together images of Beuys's "actions" and collaborative performances, his sculptural objects and drawings.

The ideal configuration that Beuys imagined for *Arena . . .* was within a circular space containing all of the panels (as he outlined in a related, undated drawing that was the sketch for the announcement card). He nevertheless adjusted the presentation of the work according to the specifics of the site, variously condensing or expanding the layout as space permitted. In its fifth and last installation, in his extensive retrospective at the Solomon R. Guggenheim Museum, New York, in 1979, he displayed the work in a singularly succinct fashion. All 100 panels were grouped into three piles that were propped against a low wall. At the front of each pile was one of the colored glass panels, which took on the role of filters, only partially revealing the layers of images beneath. The oilcan and the stacks of wax, fat, and metal were positioned nearby. This presentation, the most condensed one possible, massed the elements into a block, or *Fond*—the collective term Beuys coined for batteries that send, store, and receive energy, recurrent presences in his work. By adapting the Fond form to *Arena . . .* he turned the piece into a work *in potentia*: dormant in this guise, it awaited other occasions for its unfolding, its enactment.

The dense, compact structure of the Fond was used constantly in installations, actions, and objects throughout Beuys's oeuvre. He cherished its self-contained structure for its implicit promise of transformation. An archaic English word for "fundament" or "basis," Fond indicates a source or repository—simple, massive, and elemental—from which other, more complex works might grow and vital energy might be dispersed.

In *Brasilienfond* (*Brazilian Fond*), *Fond III/3*, and *Fond IV/4*, all made in 1979, Beuys again left the configuration of the individual parts open, to be determined by the requirements of each new exhibition site and situation. Made of piles of felt and stacks of metal, these Fonds employ his distinctive material vocabulary. For Beuys, materials carried a symbolic resonance within his overall conception of social sculpture: like the fat in the stacks of *Arena . . .* , felt symbolized protective insulation, while metals implied transmission. And he favored copper for its conductive properties, iron for its rootedness to the earth. Drawing on the anthroposophical writings of Rudolf Steiner and on

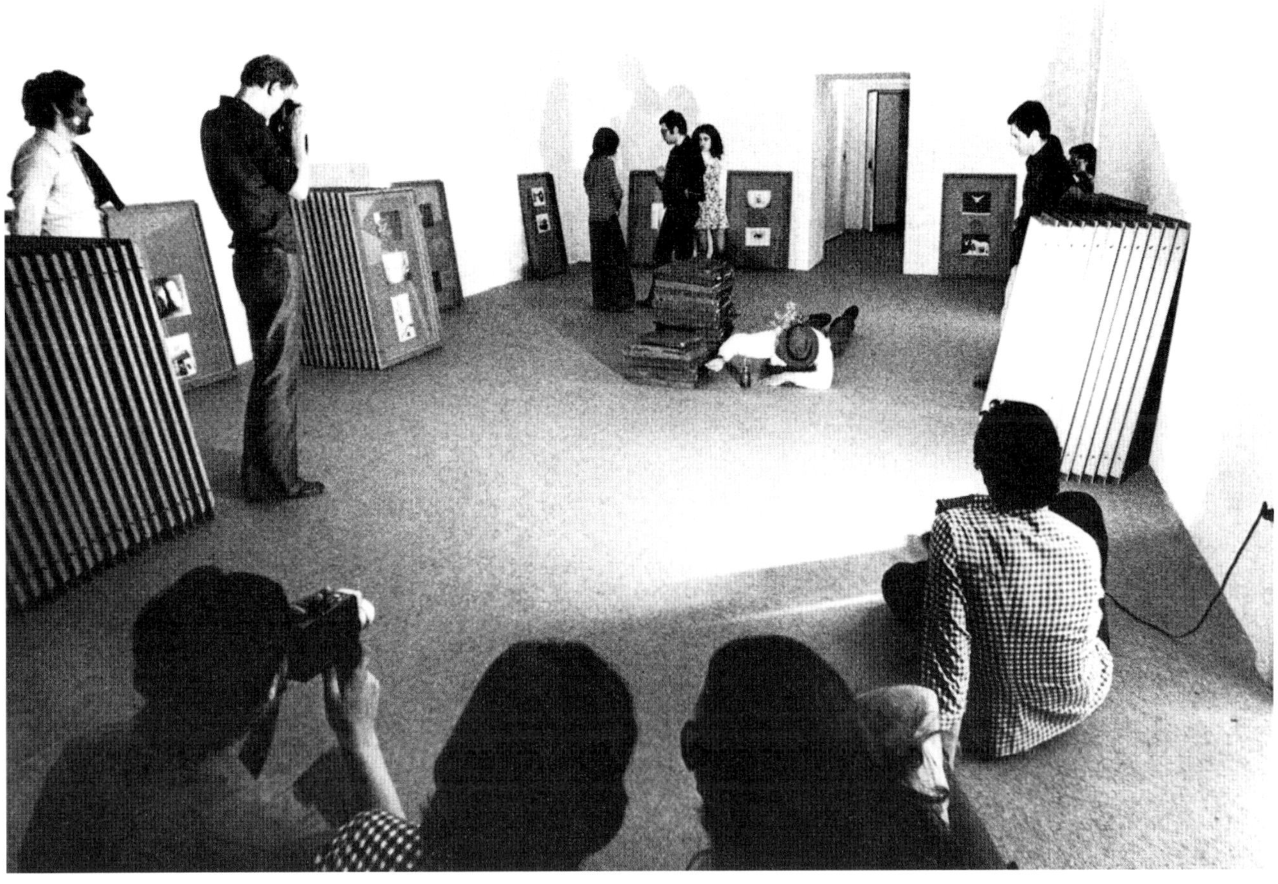

Vitex agnus castus, 1972, performance at the Modern Art Agency, Naples

the Fluxus postulate that the interchange of energies is the principal form of communication through art, Beuys developed an idealistic vision in which the role of the artist is akin to that of a shaman and art is a means to a social utopia.

Aus Berlin: Neues vom Kojoten (*From Berlin: News from the Coyote*), 1979, is composed of rubble and plaster lathe from the former René Block Gallery in Berlin, plus elements from Beuys's first project in the United States, the action *I like America and America likes Me*, which took place in the New York branch of Block's gallery in the spring of 1974. For that performance Beuys traveled from Germany to Manhattan wrapped in felt, then spent a week in a room with a coyote, engaging it in a number of ritualistic encounters. Revered as a deity by Native Americans for its wiliness and its supposed ability to transform itself at will, this wild animal served for Beuys as a fitting New World counterpart to the hare and the stag, which, as subjects of Celtic mythology and European folklore, were key motifs in his pantheon—resonant vehicles through which to extend the range of the viewer's experience and understanding beyond the narrowly anthropomorphic.

The theatricality of *I like America . . .* also informs *Aus Berlin*. Conceived like a stage set, its almost barren "landscape" is lit by a projector and a series of miner's lamps elevated on sticks. A felt hat—a talismanic insignia of Beuys's—is juxtaposed with various other staples of the artist's visual language. A walking stick, a musician's triangle, and certain articles of apparel are accoutrements relating to the figure of the magus. Meticulously recorded, the original installation has been re-created here in a space whose dimensions replicate those of Ronald Feldman's gallery in New York, where it was first realized.

Considered collectively, this group of works can be seen as embodying the potent yet cryptic and open-ended nature of Beuys's thinking. Neither inert nor empty, material remnants, like relics, limn the course of the artist's life and work.

L.C.

notes

1 According to unpublished records in Dia's archive, Beuys may once have planned to continue to update *Arena*... by adding further photographs in new panels. In fact he never did. Nonetheless, the proposal reaffirms the open character that this work retained for him.

2 Caroline Tisdall, *Joseph Beuys* (New York: Solomon R. Guggenheim Museum, 1979), p. 225.

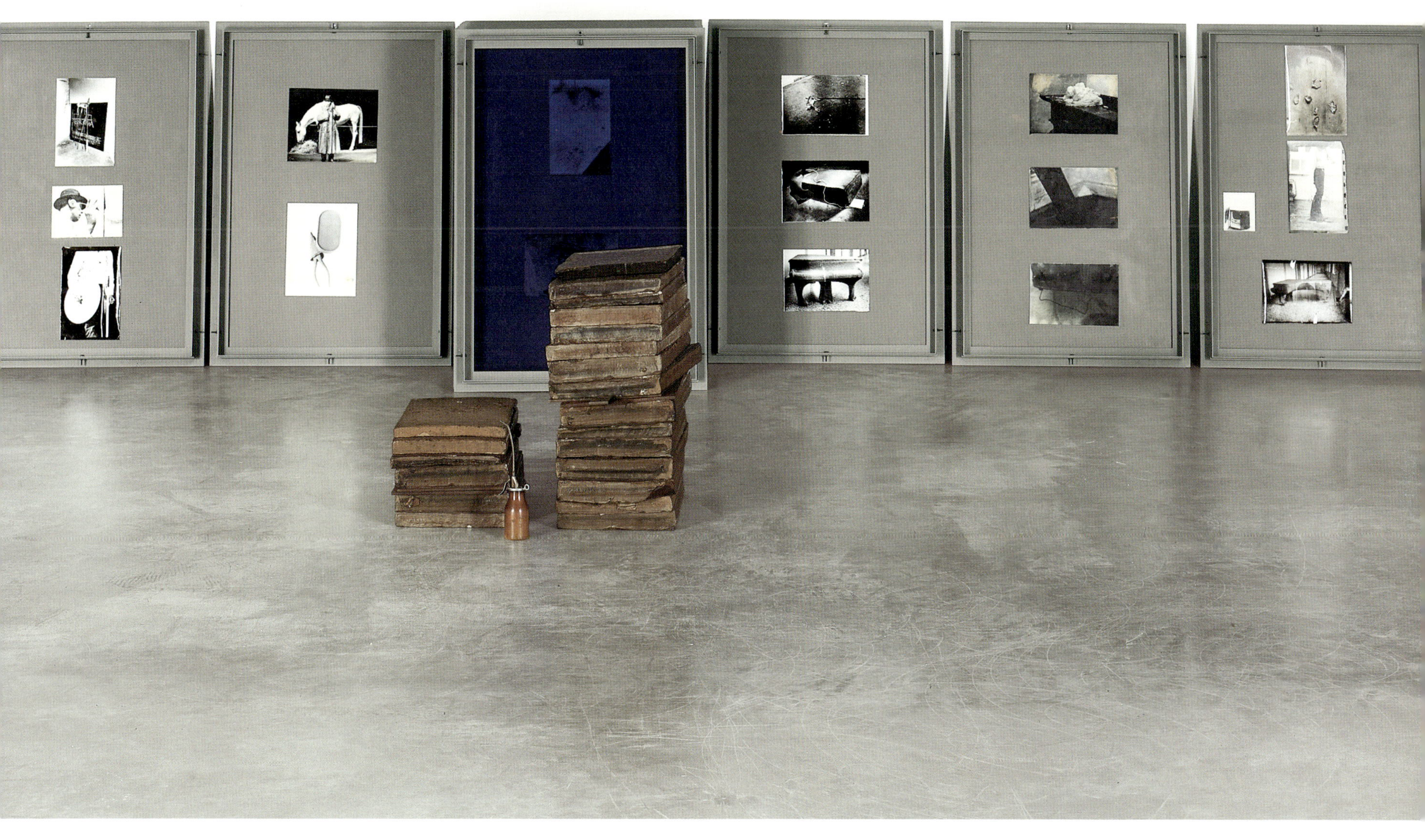

Arena—dove sarei arrivato se fossi stato intelligente!, 1970–72

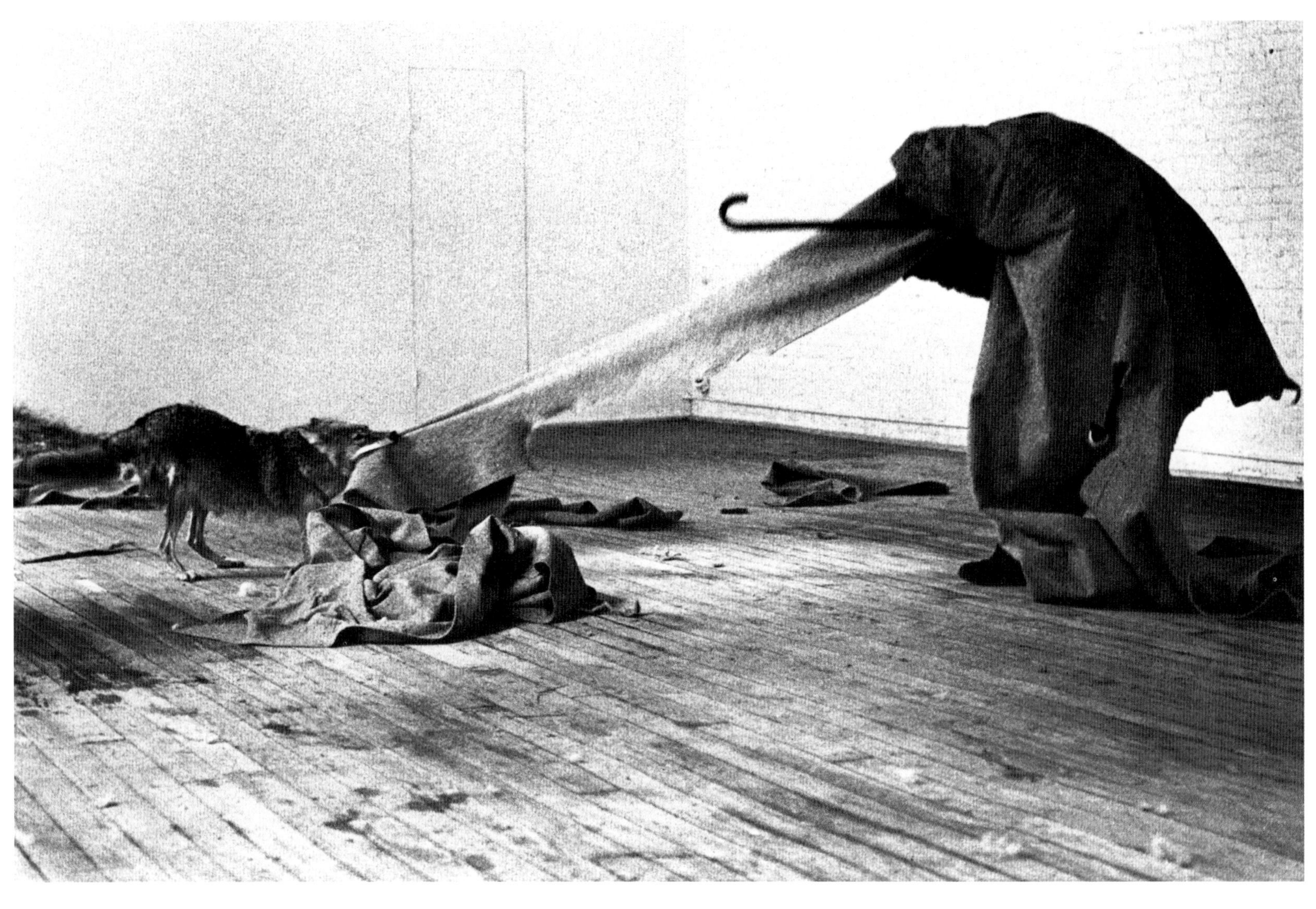

I like America and America likes Me, 1974, performance at René Block Gallery, New York

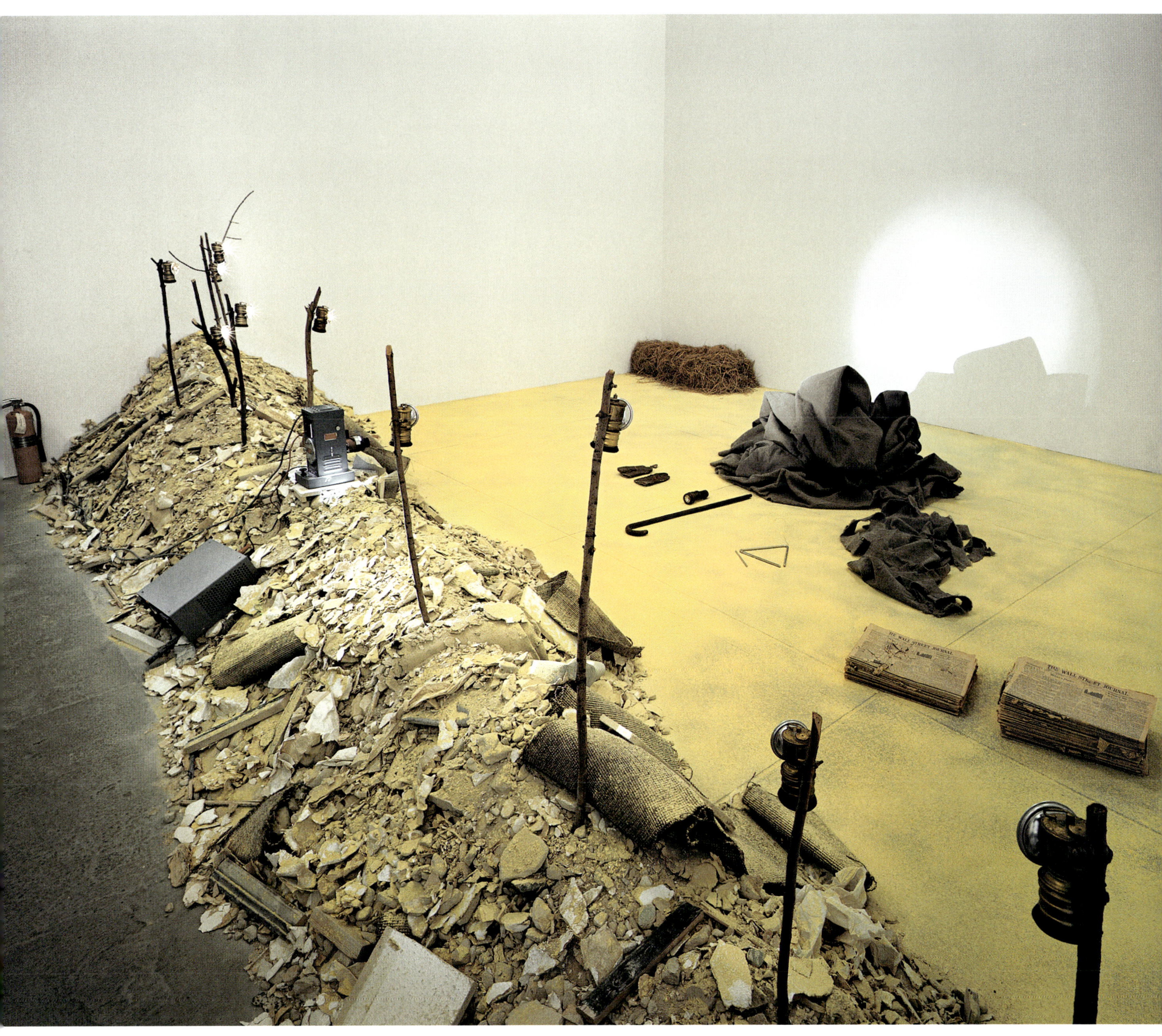

Aus Berlin: Neues vom Kojoten, 1979

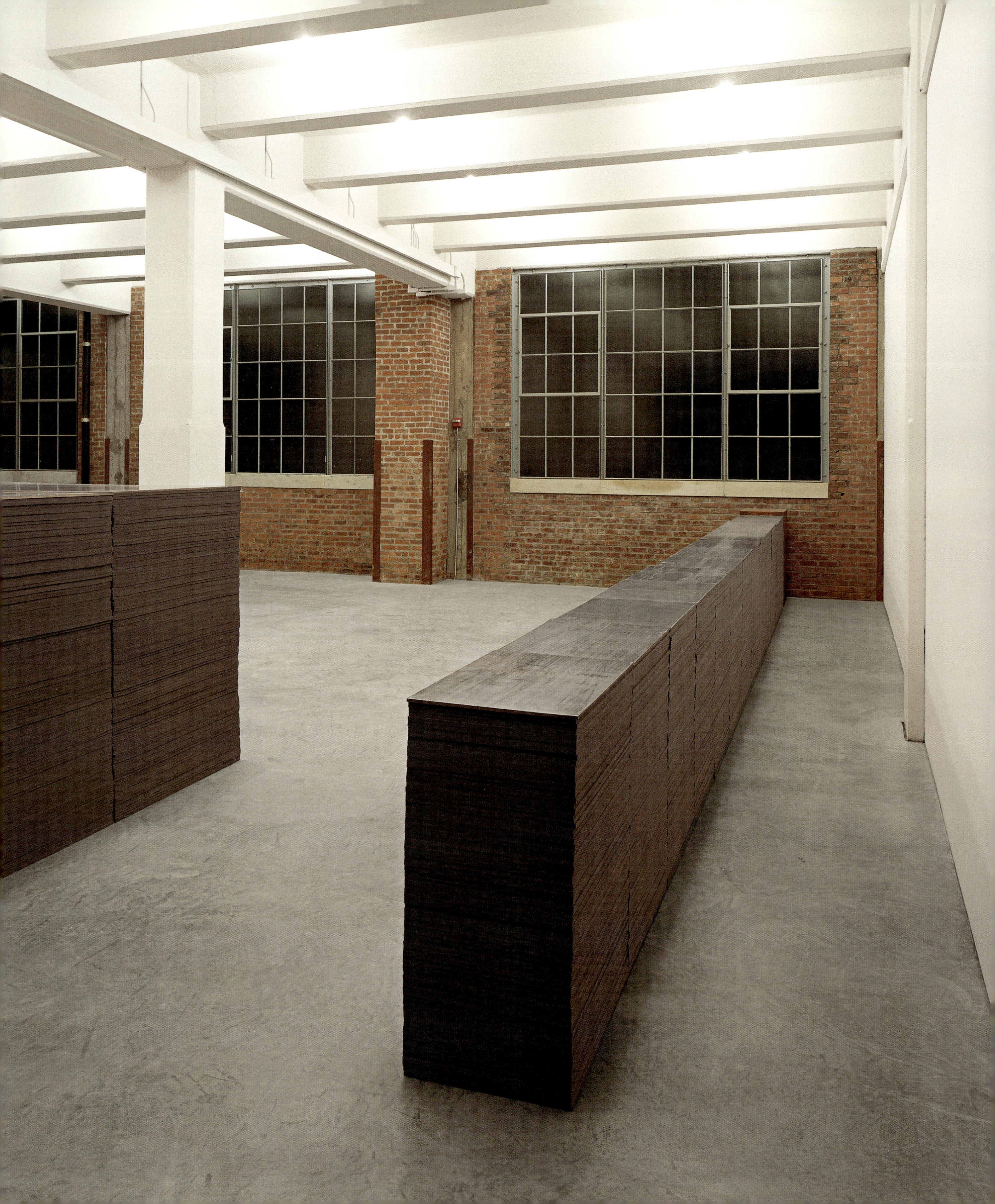

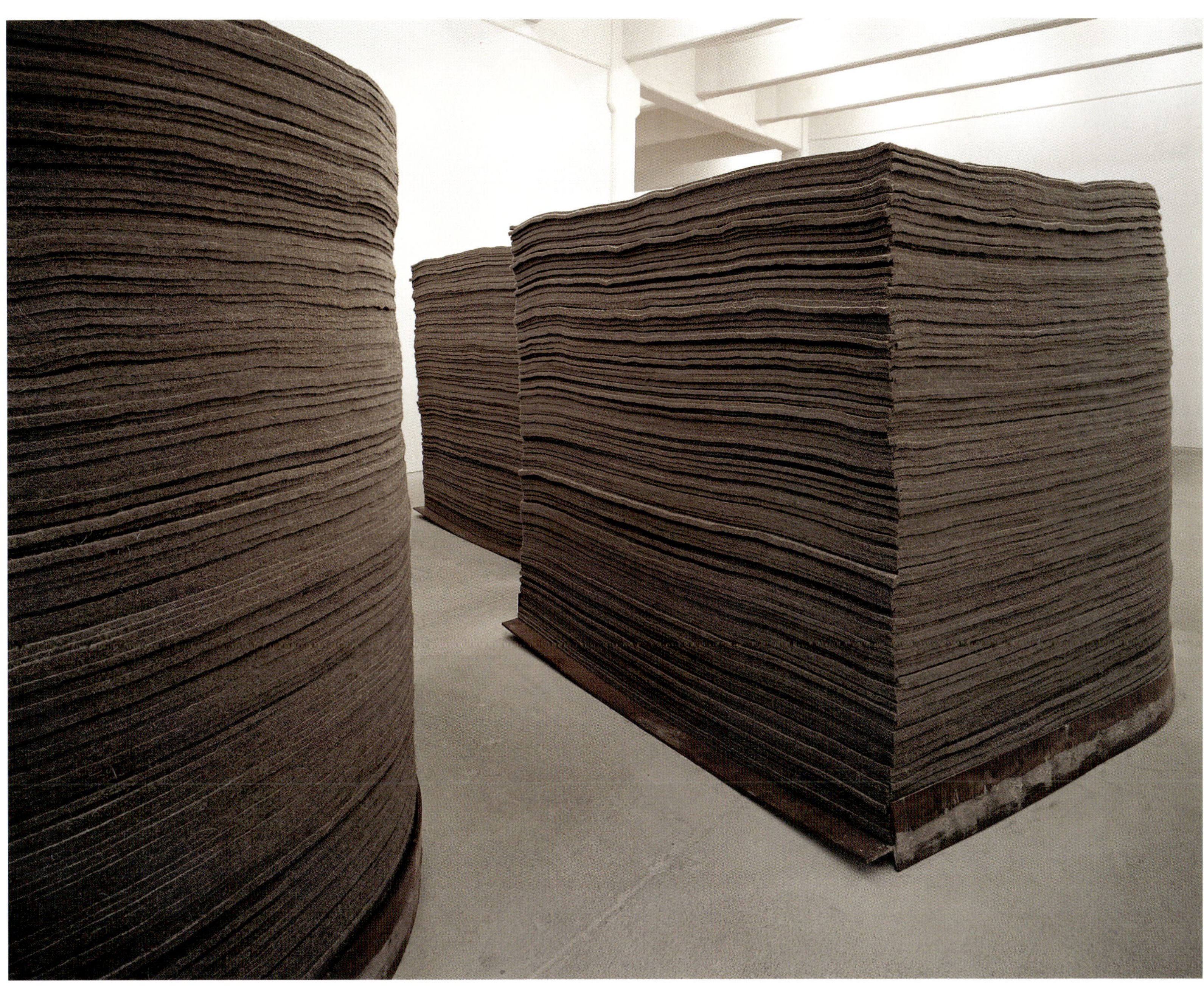

left Installation view of *Fond III/3*, 1979, and *Fond IV/4*, 1979
right *Brasilienfond*, 1979

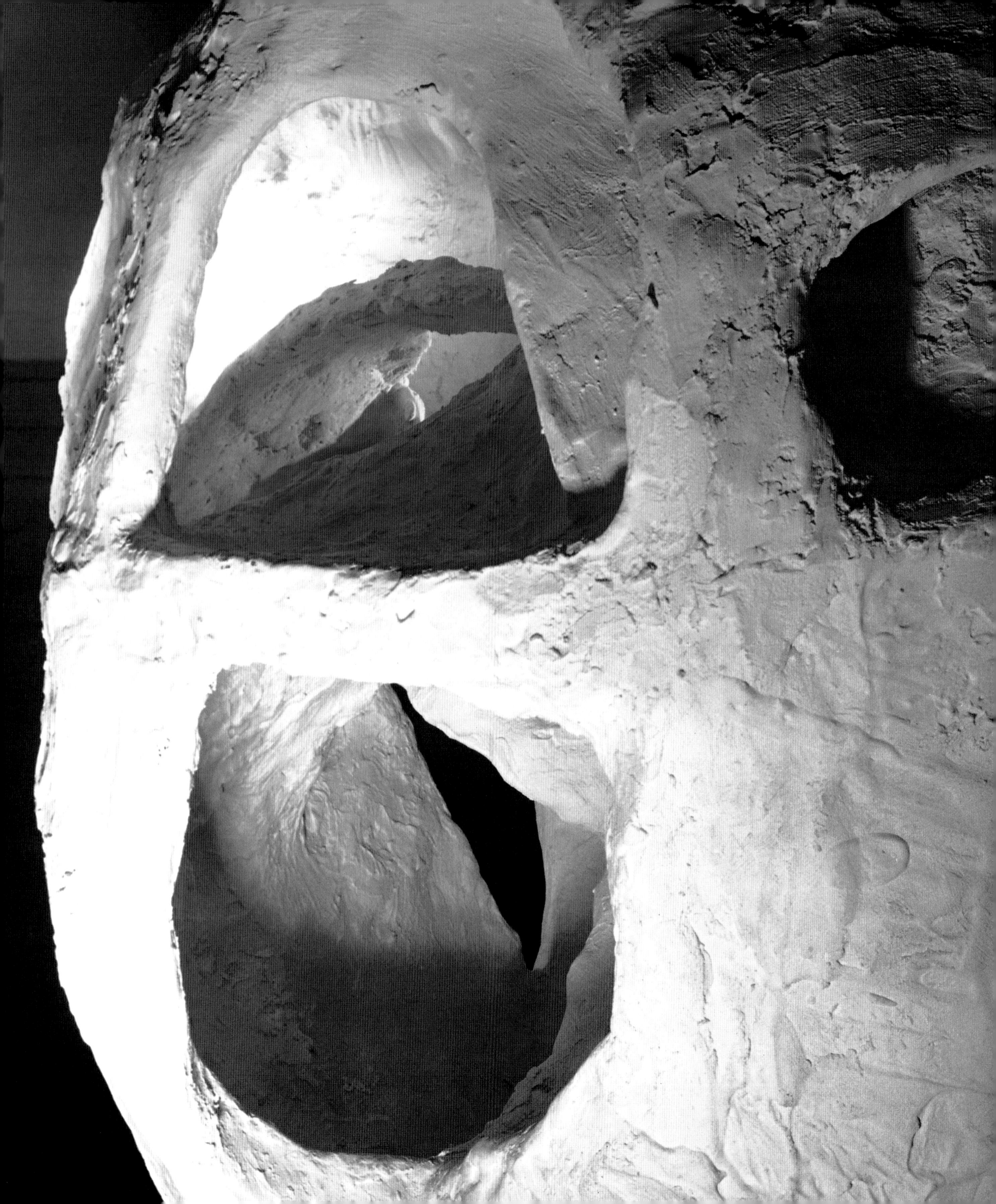

Louise Bourgeois

Louise Bourgeois was born in 1911 in Paris. She entered the Sorbonne to study mathematics in 1932 but turned to art the next year, enrolling at several art schools, including the Ecole des Beaux-Arts in Paris, in addition to apprenticing in artists' studios in Montparnasse and Montmartre. She emigrated to New York, in 1938, and continued her studies at the Art Students League. Her first one-person exhibition was held at the Bertha Schaefer Gallery, New York, in 1945, and her sculpture was first shown in 1949 at the Peridot Gallery, New York. In 1982 the Museum of Modern Art, New York, organized a retrospective, which traveled to various American venues. Her work has since been shown internationally, including in Documenta 9 (1992) and the São Paulo Bienal of 1996. Bourgeois's first European retrospective was organized in 1989, traveling from the Frankfurter Kunstverein to the Städtische Galerie im Lenbachhaus, Munich, and the Fundació Antoni Tàpies, Barcelona, among other venues. Bourgeois represented the United States at the Venice Biennale in 1993.

Fée Couturière, 1963 (detail) Photo © Peter Moore

In his seminal study *The Poetics of Space*, Gaston Bachelard contended that "our house . . . is our first universe, a real cosmos in every sense of the word."[1] A fundamental thematic in Louise Bourgeois's practice, which now spans more than six decades, this notion has been continually and compulsively probed by an address to tectonic space that fuses the body with architecture. "Space does not exist, it is just a metaphor for the structure of our existence," Bourgeois claims.[2] The barely refurbished, dimly lit rooms in which her work is installed at Dia:Beacon in effect constitute the museum's attic. In the marginalized and outmoded spaces that typify an attic, the past is evoked literally and metaphorically, physically and psychically. The relation of past to present, a central dialectic in Bourgeois's art, here becomes highly charged. If the present is returned to the past, the result is an immersion in a bygone world: a regression, in short. Conversely, if the past returns to the present, the effect is of a resurgence of the repressed, an uncanny revenant (since the past, having been repressed, cannot return benignly). Suspended between regression and a return of the repressed, seeking a means to negotiate these competing contradictory lures, the spectator enveloped in Bourgeois's matrix discovers in reflexive reenchantment a mode of critical resistance.

Ranging from smaller sculptures made in the 1960s to the landmark installation *The Destruction of the Father* (1974) to one of the most complex of Bourgeois's recent series of monumental Spiders, many of the works assembled here variously engage with forms of tectonic space. The critical discourse surrounding her art is almost entirely grounded in biographical and psychosexual narratives, which are considered the most viable vehicles for constructing a cohesive structure that can encompass the work's formal diversity. Yet other tropes, namely that of a spatialized body in the guise of a housed body—or *femme maison*, to borrow her phrase—may provide more apt and illuminating tools. The fusion of the body with architecture that marks her first mature works, the series known as Femme Maison (1946–47), evolves in the 1960s into the Soft Landscapes and related Lairs. Albeit obliquely, these works manifest her longstanding fascination with mathematics, which burgeoned while she was briefly a student at the Sorbonne, Paris, in 1932. Eventually she would concentrate less on Euclidean geometry, that is, on constants whose hallmark is a consistency of scale and structure, than on the science of topology. Here, there are neither rigid bodies nor consistency in measurement or form, for all shapes are subject to constant deformation through processes of twisting and stretching, or endless inversions of inside and outside. Such forms consequently become relational rather than abstract in their configurations.[3]

Many of Bourgeois's works from the 1960s that engage plastic space as a metaphoric hybrid, a body/house, shift between a quasi-geometric architectonics and a fluid topological articulation. In the various Lairs, for example, labyrinthine inchoate extrusions and convoluted incremental aggregations seem to improvise their own centers of gravity: poised between the poles of deliberated structure and organic amorphousness, they construct both their inner and outer limits. Not surprisingly, Bourgeois places little meaning in the materials and processes she uses to construct these sculptural realms: a belief in *architecture parlante*, that is, in architecture deployed as a symbolic language, underpins her approach to spatialized form. Whether shelter or prison—lair, haven, sanctuary, retreat, fortress, habitat, cage, or cavern—spatialized form signifies principally in psychic terms.

In the late 1950s, as Bourgeois turned from carving to modeling and from tectonic to biomorphic idioms, her vocabulary came to be dominated by womblike and cocoonlike sanctums that blend the organic and the anthropomorphic, part and whole, microscopic and monumental, in radically new conflations of sexuality and habitat. The sexualized spaces of these modestly scaled sculptures often seem either grounded in experiences that precede gender distinctions or, alternatively, constructed as composite entities composed of multiple genders. Melding the contraries of confinement and refuge, these sites no longer pertain exclusively to anthropomorphic realms but reference domains utilized by many forms of sentient being. Engagement in this world is mediated tactilely as well as visually, that is, through erogenous polymorphous play. Subsuming the visual into the visceral and corporeal, such environments are best experienced proprioceptively, through the fingers as well as the eyes. Engendered by processes of fusing, splitting, multiplying, magnifying, and proliferating, these plastic spaces and forms often collapse distinctions between inside and outside, body and environment. They consequently invite interpretations culled from fantasies of a body riven by drives and undifferentiated by gender, that is, in relation to regressive infantile experiences.

Profiting from her fascination with topology to morph rather than fracture spatial interconnections, Bourgeois undermines many of the basic dichotomies fundamental to normative architecture: public/private, male/female, nature/culture. By virtue of their complex, seamless, continuously flowing or burgeoning surfaces, which appear to bend, warp, torque, and twist space, these tectonic forms become harbingers of a new architectural language, environments of liquid spatiality predicated on a labile structural skin. Contrarily, they also evoke some of the most primal of organic shelters, namely, carapaces and other shell-like protuberances.

A small group of works that allude to flayed and eviscerated bodies or body parts, including *Fillette (Sweeter Version)* (1968/1999), *Torso (Self-Portrait)*, (1963–64), and *Rabbit* (1970), offer a disturbing counterpoint to the 1960s groups of architectonic and topological works. A two-foot-long phallus, roughly made from latex, that Bourgeois describes as a doll—*her* doll—*Fillette* is riddled with transgressive, subversive humor. As so often in her oeuvre, a body part is isolated, enlarged, doubled, divided, multiplied or flayed so that, as Mignon Nixon argues, "it resists, absorption, possession, [and] sublimation as a complete or intact whole."[4] For Bourgeois, cathexis, the projection of her desire onto an object, is coupled, Nixon claims, "with self-representation, or more precisely, with a projection of the self onto the object which becomes its substitute."[5] As seen in the Janus series, strategies of cathexis and substitution for the self, or, better, for some lost part of it, are manifest as a constant reworking of certain motifs and forms, in the translation of certain works from one material to another, and in their reinvocation later in other contexts and guises. Ghoulish trophies and fetishes, these phallic symbols are recuperated for female subjects through a delirious upstaging of stereotypical images of potency.[6] Exuberantly fantastical incarnations of an uninhibited desire for dominance and seduction, their dense, compact, swollen forms are the antipodes of the feminized spaces of the lairs and the tumulous landscapes.

The visceral morphologies and confining spaces that characterize these parallel bodies of work are combined in *The Destruction of the Father*, the underlying motivations for which are radically different from those that catalyzed her previous sculpture. Bourgeois has supplied a vivid, pathological familial narrative involving dismemberment and cannibalism as the genesis of this eerily macabre installation, which is imbued with a Gothick violence unprecedented in her oeuvre.[7] In a secret chamber, a claustrophobic alcove opening within the very fabric of the museum, a bulbous terrain is glimpsed, created from grotesque globular latex forms that swell up from the plateaulike ground plane or erupt sinisterly from the cavernous ceiling. Strewn among these "female" forms are remains of animal parts suggesting eviscerated relics casually discarded in some bizarre ritual. The whole is garishly illumined by an oppressive red light, which enhances the aura of violence and mayhem permeating the tableau, at once a sacrificial altar and a weirdly primeval landscape.

In general, less lurid autobiographical tales serve as the points of departure for many of Bourgeois's more complex environmental works from the later 1980s—the series of haunting Cells, made from assemblages of mostly familiar everyday objects. Once again, the role accorded the spectator is that of a voyeuristic witness to a cloistered world, but one that is now made from found material rather then fashioned from formless inchoate matter. In these tightly bordered enclaves, objects are contextualized not according to their respective historical heritages, as in authentic dioramas, but in fictive, often fantastical environments governed by the oneiric dictates of the artist's imagination. Embodying a range of emotional states relating to pain, loss, frustration, hysteria, and longing, or to obsessions and compulsions too nuanced or inflected to be easily labeled with words, they may occasionally be entered, inviting interaction. Irrespective of whether the transition is literal or only figurative, crossing the threshold is a portentous step, for edges, limits, and boundaries are crucial to the maintenance and integrity of any entity, both physical and psychological.

Spider (1997) fuses the preoccupations underpinning many of Bourgeois's Cells with the most potent motif to dominate her work in the mid-1990s, the spider. With its tall thick legs supporting a cagelike enclosure, this architectonic sculpture is at once a potent metaphor for the protective mother and a representation of a nightmarish predator, which threatens to trap the viewer not in its proverbial web but in a metal cage. Arachne the weaver, in mythic times, transformed herself into a spider. Bourgeois, who as a child assisted her parents in their family business of repairing tapestries, has in recent years returned to sewing as her preferred medium. Fragments of venerable textiles drape the mesh walls; other pieces of fabric clothe the worn armchair. Outside, the enormous legs of the insect wrap as they shield the cage, in what proves an eloquent reworking and interweaving of the multiple modalities through which Bourgeois has transformed the spatialized body into a species of *femme maison*. As elsewhere in this veteran's art, this is a singular place, one where reenchantment must negotiate a precarious route between regression and an unseemly return of the repressed.

L.C.

notes

1 Gaston Bachelard, *The Poetics of Space*, trans. Maria Jolas (Boston: Beacon Press, 1969), p. 4.

2 Louise Bourgeois, quoted in Lynne Cooke, "Farewell to the Doll House," *Louise Bourgeois: Memory and Architecture* (Madrid: Museo Nacional Centro de Arte Reina Sofia, 1999), p. 63.

3 See Jerry Gorovoy, "Louise Bourgeois and the Nature of Abstraction," in *Louise Bourgeois* (New York: Bellport Press, 1986), n.p.

4 Mignon Nixon, "Louise Bourgeois's *Fillette*," *Parkett*, no. 27 (1991), p. 49.

5 Ibid. See also Rosalind E. Krauss, "Portrait of the Artist as Fillette," in *Louise Bourgeois* (Frankfurt: Frankfurter Kunstverein, in association with Stemmle, Schaffhausen, Switzerland, 1989).

6 If Bourgeois's formative intellectual milieu was shaped by such nineteenth-century luminaries as Norwegian playwright Henrik Ibsen, French neurologist Jean-Martin Charcot, and the French Symbolists, among others, and inflected later by aspects of Surrealism, the nascent feminism of the late 1960s freed her to mine psychic trauma and suppressed memory more overtly and directly.

7 This account has frequently been published. See, for example, Beatriz Colomina, "The Architecture of Trauma," in *Louise Bourgeois: Memory and Architecture*, p. 32.

right *The Destruction of the Father*, 1974
page 102 *Fée Courturière*, 1963 Photo © Peter Moore
page 103 *The Quartered One*, 1964–65 Photo © Peter Moore
pages 104–105 *Spider*, 1997

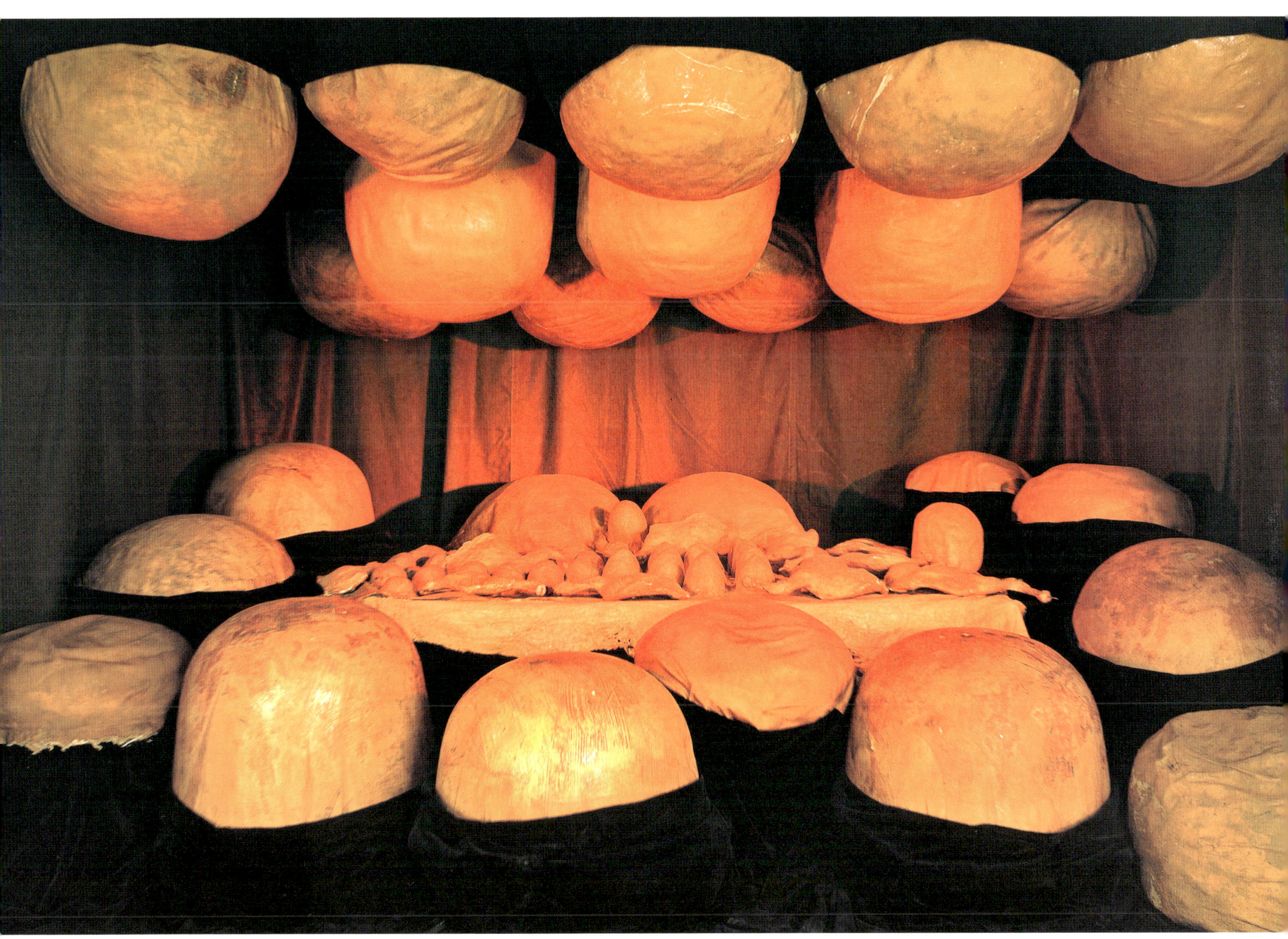

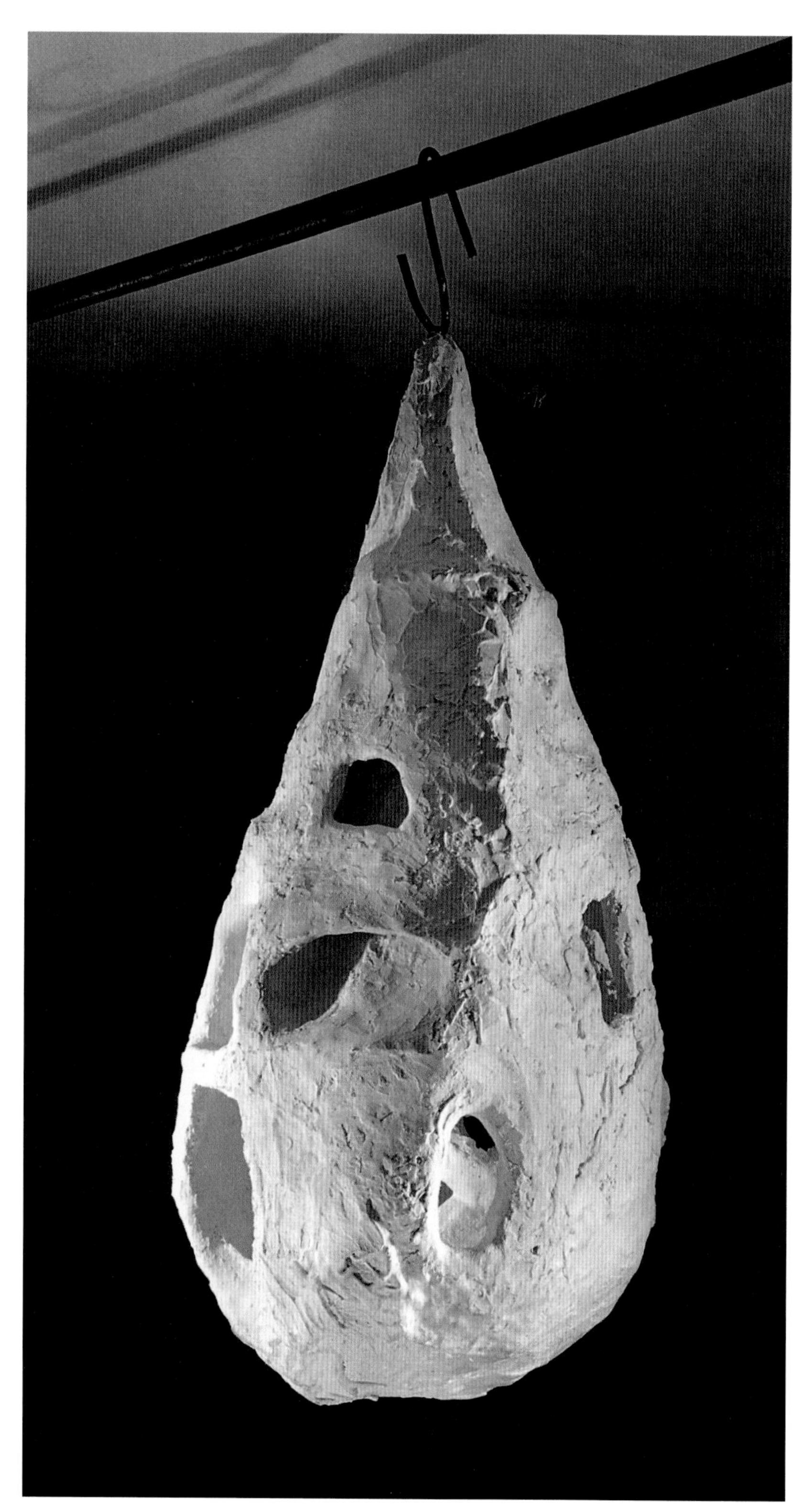

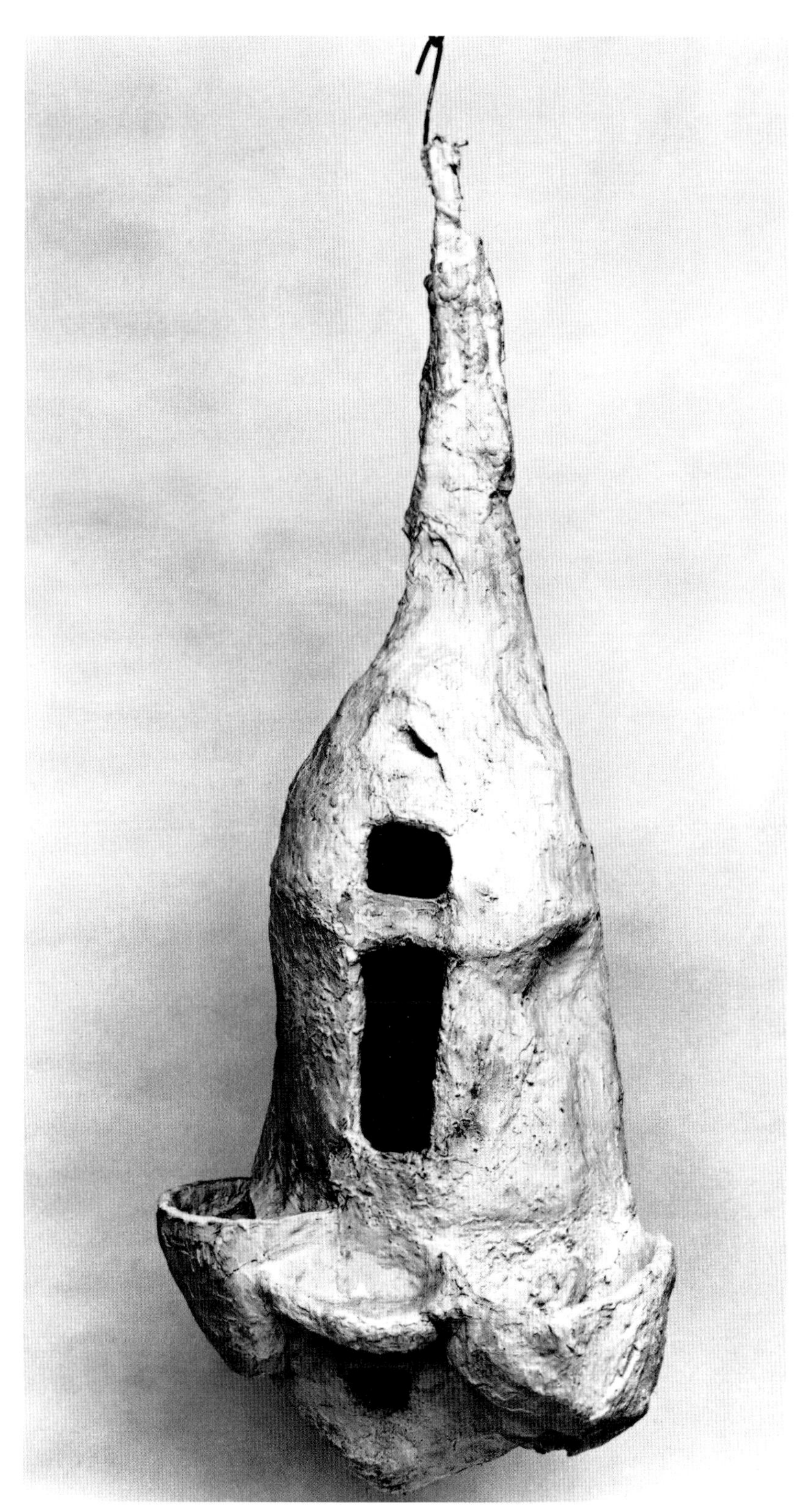

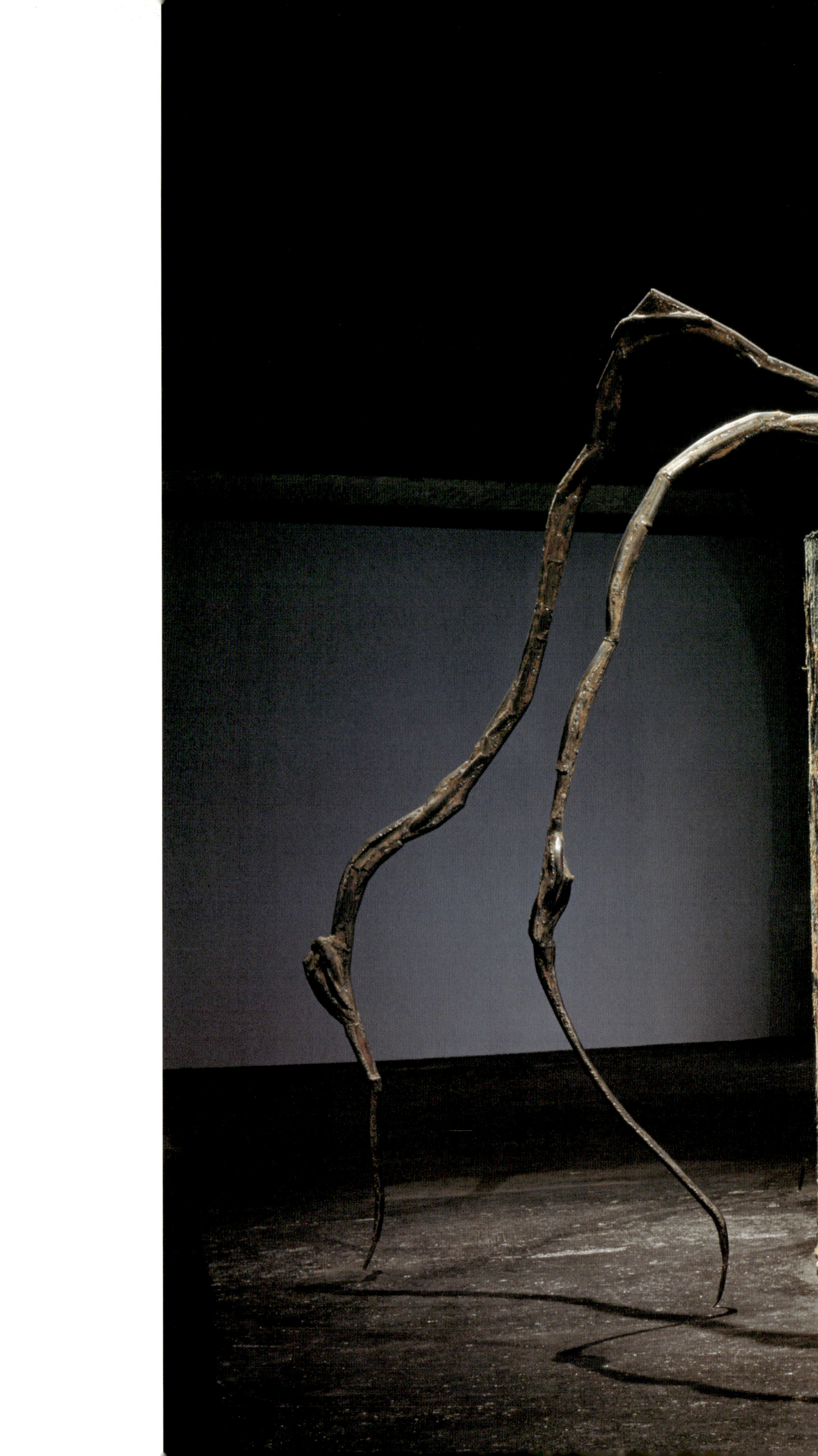

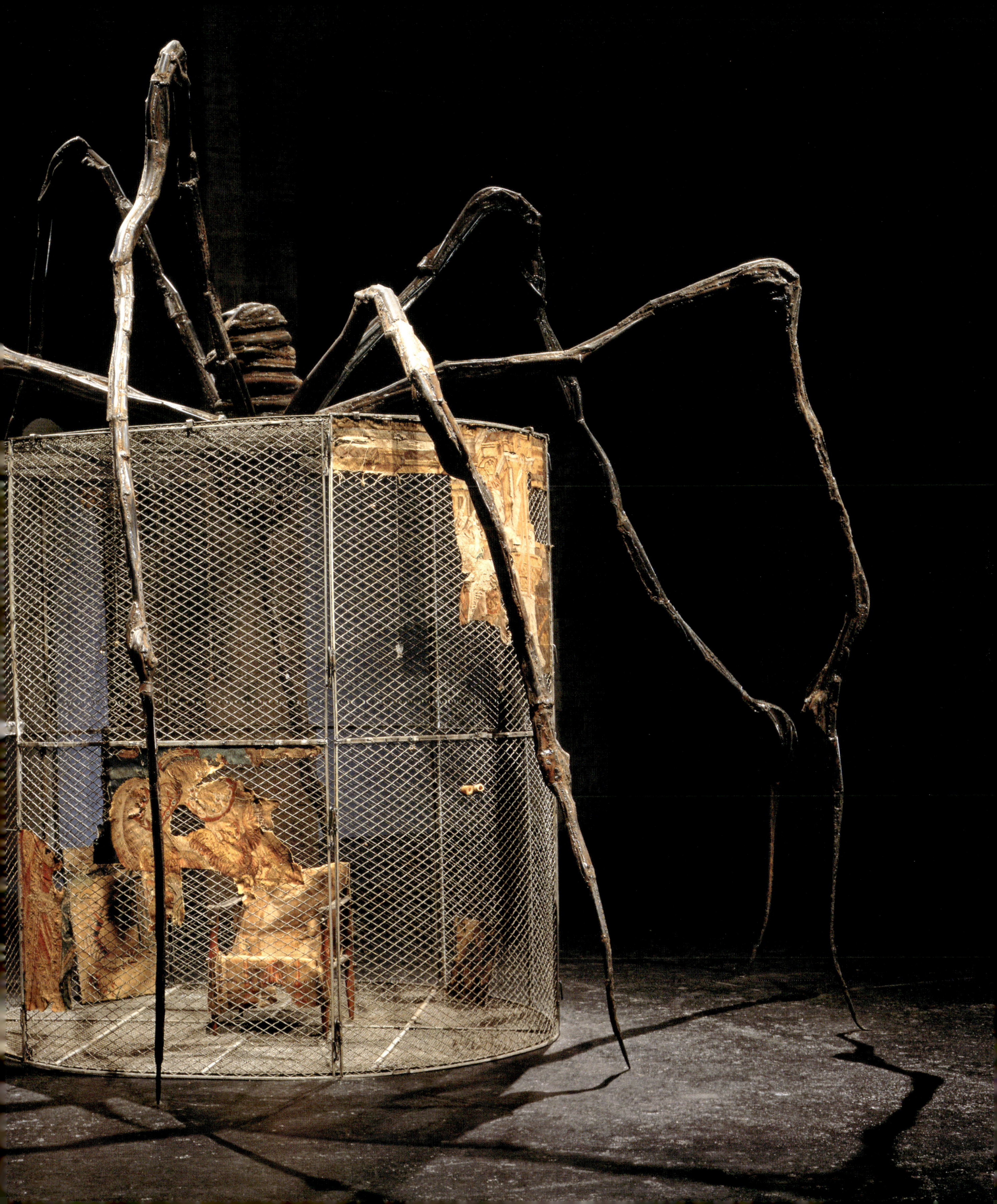

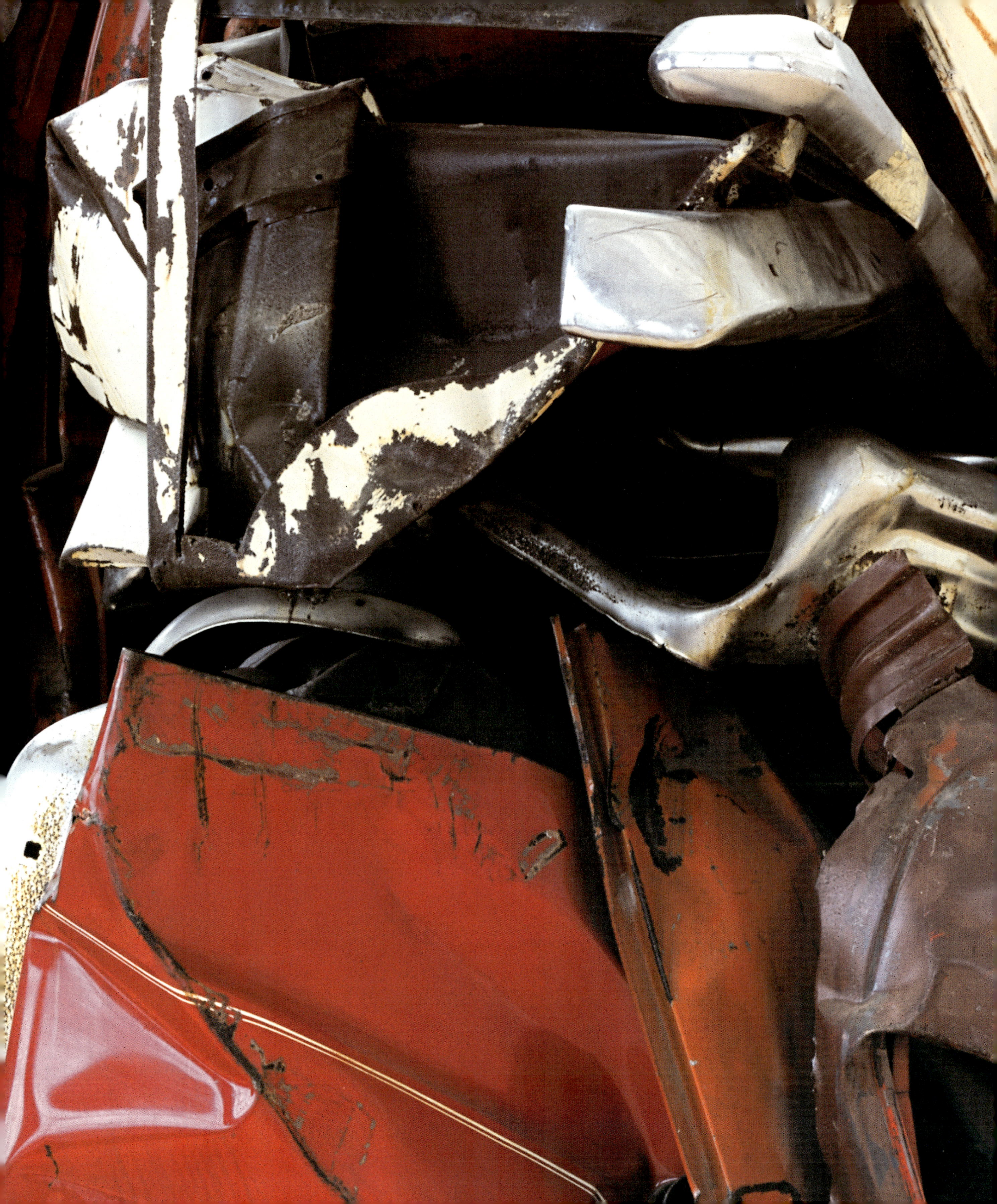

John Chamberlain

Born in 1927 in Rochester, Indiana, John Chamberlain grew up in Chicago. After serving in the United States Navy from 1943 to 1946, he attended the Art Institute of Chicago (1951–52) and Black Mountain College (1955–56). Chamberlain moved to New York in 1956 and the following year made *Shortstop*, his first sculpture incorporating automobile parts. His work was included in the "Art of Assemblage" exhibition at the Museum of Modern Art, New York, in 1961, and he began showing at Leo Castelli's New York gallery in 1962. Chamberlain had his first retrospective in 1971, at the Solomon R. Guggenheim Museum, New York, and the Museum of Contemporary Art, Los Angeles, held a second retrospective in 1986. He currently lives and works on Shelter Island, New York.

Luftschloss, 1979 (detail)

There has never been a consensus on how to classify and evaluate the art of John Chamberlain. In the early 1960s, when his art matured, it seemed to many to be the quintessential, if belated, Abstract Expressionist sculptural statement; its vigorously gestural, visceral abstract idiom was seen as falling within a direct line of descent from the art of Willem de Kooning and Franz Kline.[1] To others who focused less on its form than on its material—crushed automobile parts in sweet, hard colors, redolent of Detroit cars of the 1950s—it was more appropriately aligned with the contemporary work of many Pop artists.

By the end of the 1960s, Chamberlain had replaced his signature materials initially with galvanized steel, then with urethane foam and mineral-coated Plexiglas, and finally with aluminum foil, all in the guise of pristine raw material that was variously wadded, compacted, and compressed according to its individual structural properties. Alignments with Process art were then discerned. Affinities with the art of Donald Judd, Chamberlain's longtime supporter and most discerning critic, were also detected, as at other moments in this heteroclite's career. In the mid-1970s, further eluding easy classification and forestalling prediction, he reverted to using automotive parts after a seven-year-long sabbatical.

Chamberlain has since continued to deploy this distinctive material in increasingly inventive ways. While encouraging assistants to improvise freely on his established set of elements by further cutting, crushing, torquing, and crimping them, he has also elaborated their enameled surfaces by spraying, stenciling, dribbling, graffitiing, and airbrushing additional coats of brilliant hues—hot, jazzy, tropical, and even raucously patterned. Ever ready to capitalize on accidental and chance occurrences, Chamberlain has occasionally resorted to a more restricted palette of, say, luscious black, cream, and chrome, as found in *Dooms Day Flotilla* of 1982. Such temporary restraints only enhance the sumptuous efflorescence of his usual ebullient rainbow spectrum.

Chamberlain's range of given forms has likewise expanded over the years. As an indigent young artist he was drawn to scrap metal primarily because it was free and plentiful. Consequently, he embraced a miscellany of secondhand metals, found in such diverse objects as kitchen cabinets, buckets, and steel benches, as well as the more ubiquitous crushed car parts.[2] He later ordered boxes constructed to his specifications in galvanized steel or Plexiglas and appropriated metal barrels fresh from the fabricator. When he returned to automotive material in the mid-1970s, he streamlined his repertoire by concentrating selectively on particular car parts—fenders and bumpers at one moment, truck chassis at another. The recent works' parts—which have been transfigured into narrow, crenellated, ribbonlike forms—have less decipherable industrial origins: devoid of rust or other evidence of aging, they bear few traces of their past lives. Such formal shifts and feints in Chamberlain's vocabulary over a period of some four decades reveal the restlessness of this obsessive, agile artist, whose oeuvre extends beyond sculpture and related modes to film, printmaking, painting, relief, language, environmental sculpture, and even more exploratory vehicles, not least of which are the remarkable "barges" and smaller foam couches.

In the early 1960s, Chamberlain created sculpture that introduced volume and color into this three-dimensional art form in wholly new ways. As Judd astutely and presciently noted, Chamberlain's welters of voluminous forms swell and furl, bend and fold, in and around a hollow spatial core, limning, demarcating, and ordering it contingently rather than absolutely, provisionally rather than fixedly. Without displacing this negative inner space with solid form, they create a plastic art that remains resolutely porous and airy.[3] Individual components fit together through an assemblage technique that requires the parts to interlock literally and organically to create the form. For Chamberlain only resorts to spot welding after a work is resolved, and then merely to ensure that it remain stable and secure once it has left the studio. Grounded in an intuitive method of collaging, his intractable, large-scale painterly shapes—abstract and neutral in form as well as reference—can be thought of as three-dimensional equivalents to the gestural vocabularies wielded by de Kooning and Kline, and as freely, rapidly, and spontaneously deployed in ways that, like theirs, preclude any after-the-fact tinkering, any retrospective adjusting of composition, color, or balance. As formative to Chamberlain's burgeoning aesthetic as the example of these Action painters was his encounter at Black Mountain College in 1955–56 with the poets Charles Olsen, Robert Creeley, and Robert Duncan, who were teaching there that semester. This interaction further confirmed his understanding of the ways in which everyday elements—be they words or bits of colored metal—could be mobilized in novel conjunctions to make unexpected kinds of sense: fresh, immediate, direct, and thus divested (particularly in the case of poetry) of narrative and commentary, as well as (in the case of sculpture) of image, referent, and subject.[4]

In 1980 Chamberlain relocated from New York to Sarasota, Florida, in quest of an affordable studio

Luftschloss, 1979

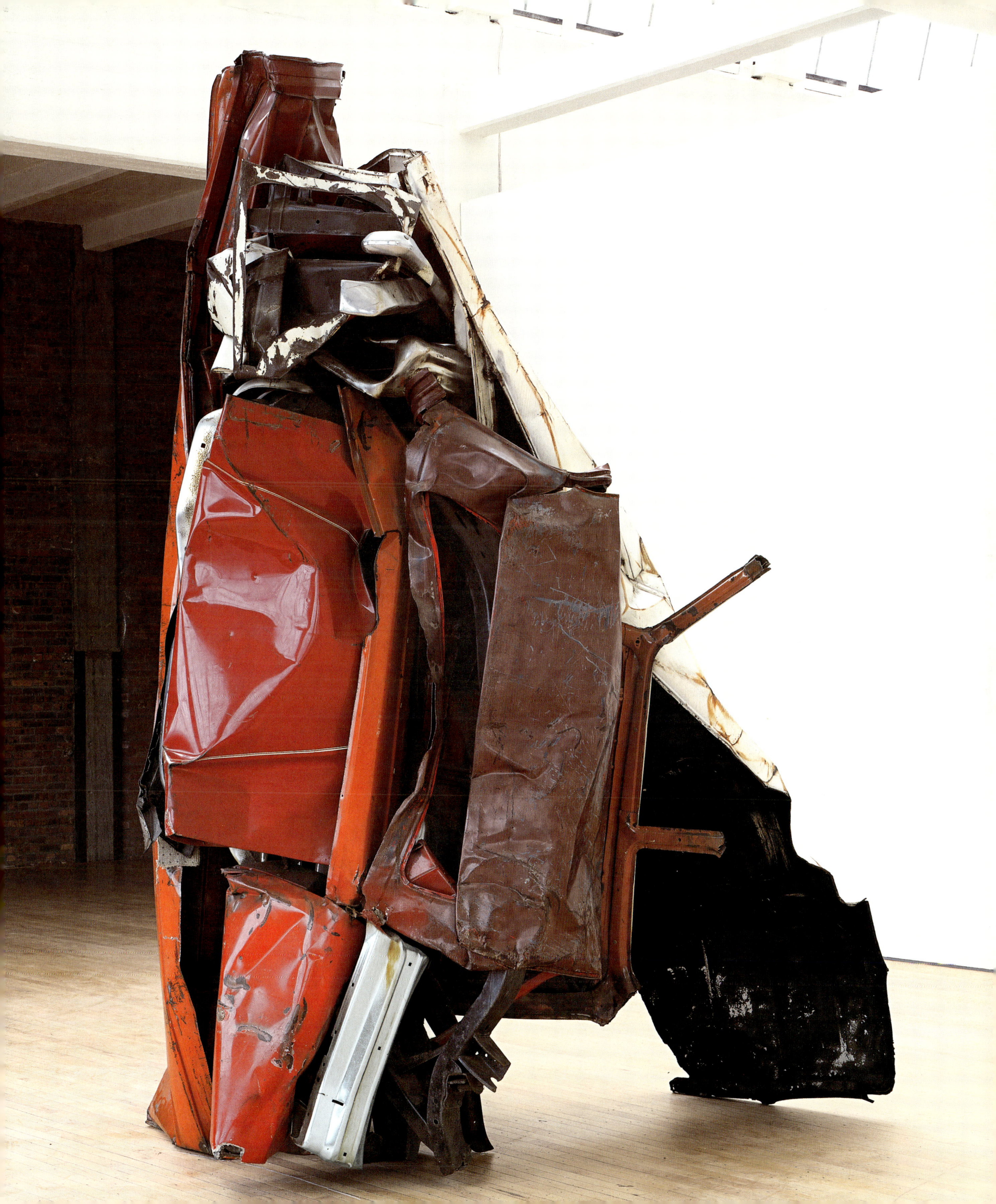

with high ceilings and abundant space. As evidenced in the extravagant densities of *The Line Up (Dedicated to the Sarasota Police Department)* (1982), his work soon became more monumental, whether it was confined to the wall or freestanding–or somewhere in between. Paradoxically, the first body of work he produced in Sarasota was a series of low-slung, meandering works made from small planar elements threaded into, draped over, and perched on horizontal linear armatures forged from dismembered truck chassis. Each of these works, the Gondolas (1981–82), is dedicated to a poet whose work he had first encountered at Black Mountain College. Responding to latent aspects of his familiar material, Chamberlain for the first time created compositions that build incrementally from one element to another along the etiolated scaffolding, the ground-hugging spine. Structure, composition, color, line, plane, shape, and surface are all to a certain degree discrete, verging at points on fragmentation. The works therefore require a more attenuated, more leisurely mode of apprehension in space and time than had his more densely impacted congeries, which only slowly and after repeated scrutiny reveal inner order and resolution beyond the seemingly happenstance and inchoate, the nonchalant and promiscuous.

Many of the subsequent works Chamberlain made in Florida revert to more volumetric, compact configurations, often aligned on a vertical axis. As seen in the so-called Giraffe series (circa 1982–83), for example, linear patterns cavort over multicolored surfaces–the results of sandblasting the metal, removing the paint, and exposing the raw surface beneath. The process counterpoints scarred, pitted, and peeling industrial hues with discordantly confectionary tones.

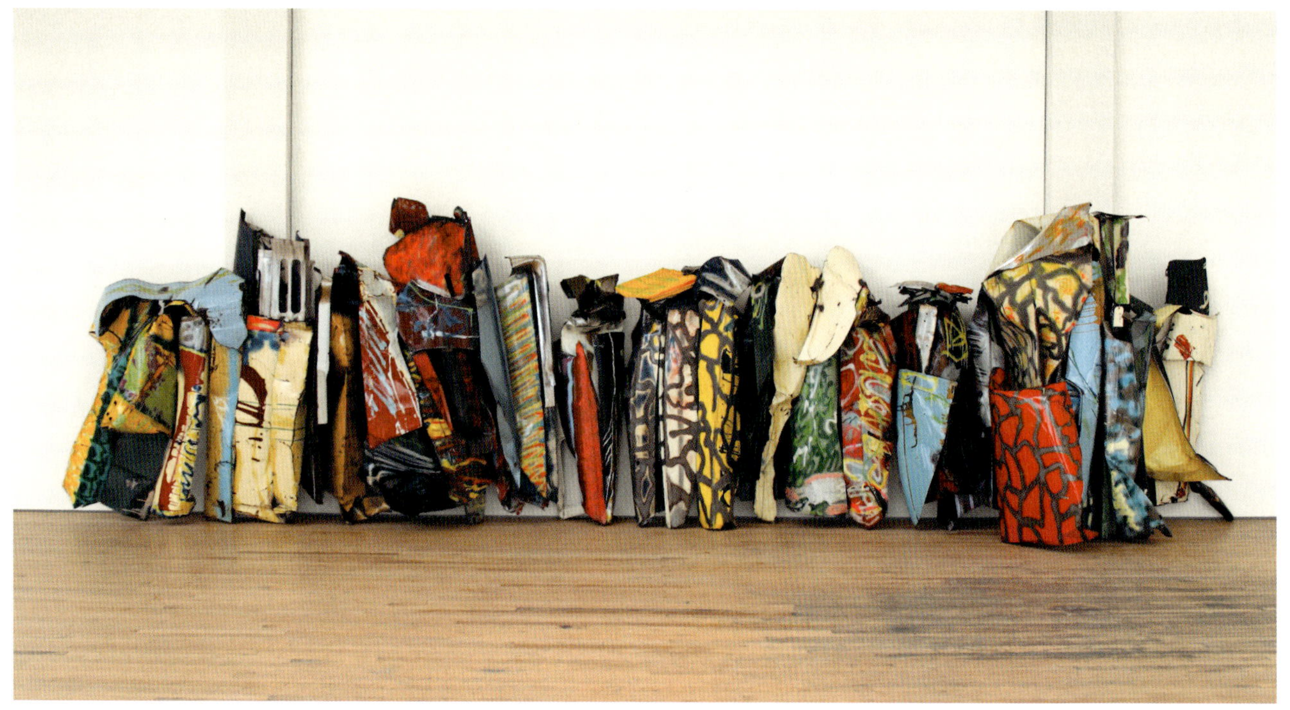

The Line Up (Dedicated to the Sarasota Police Department), 1982

In the late 1980s, Chamberlain again reinvigorated his signature mode, this time by confining himself to more regular geometric forms in which the works' lithe, ribbonlike components are evenly articulated to create an allover field that is more or less symmetrically weighted; the forms also introduce an atypical degree of referentiality. *The Privet* (1997), the key work in an exhibition he playfully titled "Chamberlain's Fauve Landscape" (1998), is among his largest sculptures to date. Intertwining fronds of metal tendrils corkscrew into a dense, candy-colored skein, a tracery that is as pictorial as it is plastic as once more he revisited the interface of painting and sculpture, ever at the crux of his practice. Appropriate to the belatedness of his engagement with a morphology once closely associated with Minimalism is his sly sidestepping of questions of gravity and *gravitas* in favor of grace, wit, and élan. Necessarily less improvisational and intuitive than his previous work, *The Privet* manifests the artist's abiding drive to wrest a new terrain from a deliberately restricted style, a terrain located on the edges of the known and expected.

L.C.

notes

1 See, for example, William C. Agee, "The Year of John Chamberlain," *The New Criterion* 6, no. 3 (November 1987), pp. 49–53, and Michael Auping, "John Chamberlain," in *Art of Our Time: The Saatchi Collection* (New York: Rizzoli, 1985), pp. 12-16. John Chamberlain himself states that he felt intuitively connected to the Abstract Expressionists; he especially admired Willem de Kooning's dexterous compositional complexities and Franz Kline's muscular speed and power.

2 "In the early sculptures I used anything made of steel that had color on it. There were metal benches, metal signs, sand pails, lunch boxes, stuff like that. . . . Body shops would cut parts away and I would choose *what* I wanted from whatever was in their scrap pile. . . . I wasn't interested in the car parts *per se*. I was interested in either the color or the shape or the amount. I didn't want engine parts, I didn't want wheels, upholstery, glass, oil, tires, rubber, lining . . . none of that. Just the sheet metal. It already had a coat of paint on it, and some of it was formed. . . . *I believe that common materials are the best materials*." Chamberlain has reiterated this credo many times. Chamberlain, in Julie Sylvester, "Auto/Bio: Conversations with John Chamberlain," in *John Chamberlain: A Catalogue Raisonné of the Sculpture 1954–1985* (New York: Hudson Hills Press, in association with the Museum of Contemporary Art, Los Angeles, 1986), pp. 15, 17.

3 Donald Judd remains the most astute of Chamberlain's many critics. His laconic, phlegmatic tone and spare, Hemingwayesque style frame his incisive assertions, such as the following: "Initially and recurrently the metal is neutral, pretty much something as anything is something." Judd, quoted in *John Chamberlain: New Sculpture* (New York: Pace Gallery, 1989), pp. III; reprinted in *Art International* 7, no. 10 (1964), p. 39.

4 For a fuller account, see Sylvester, "Auto/Bio." Chamberlain's titles, of which *Taoist Toast* (1994) is representative, isolate, then juxtapose individual words; these often derive from the experiments in wordplay he made at Black Mountain College.

pages 112–113 *Dooms Day Flotilla*, 1982
pages 114–115 *The Privet*, 1997

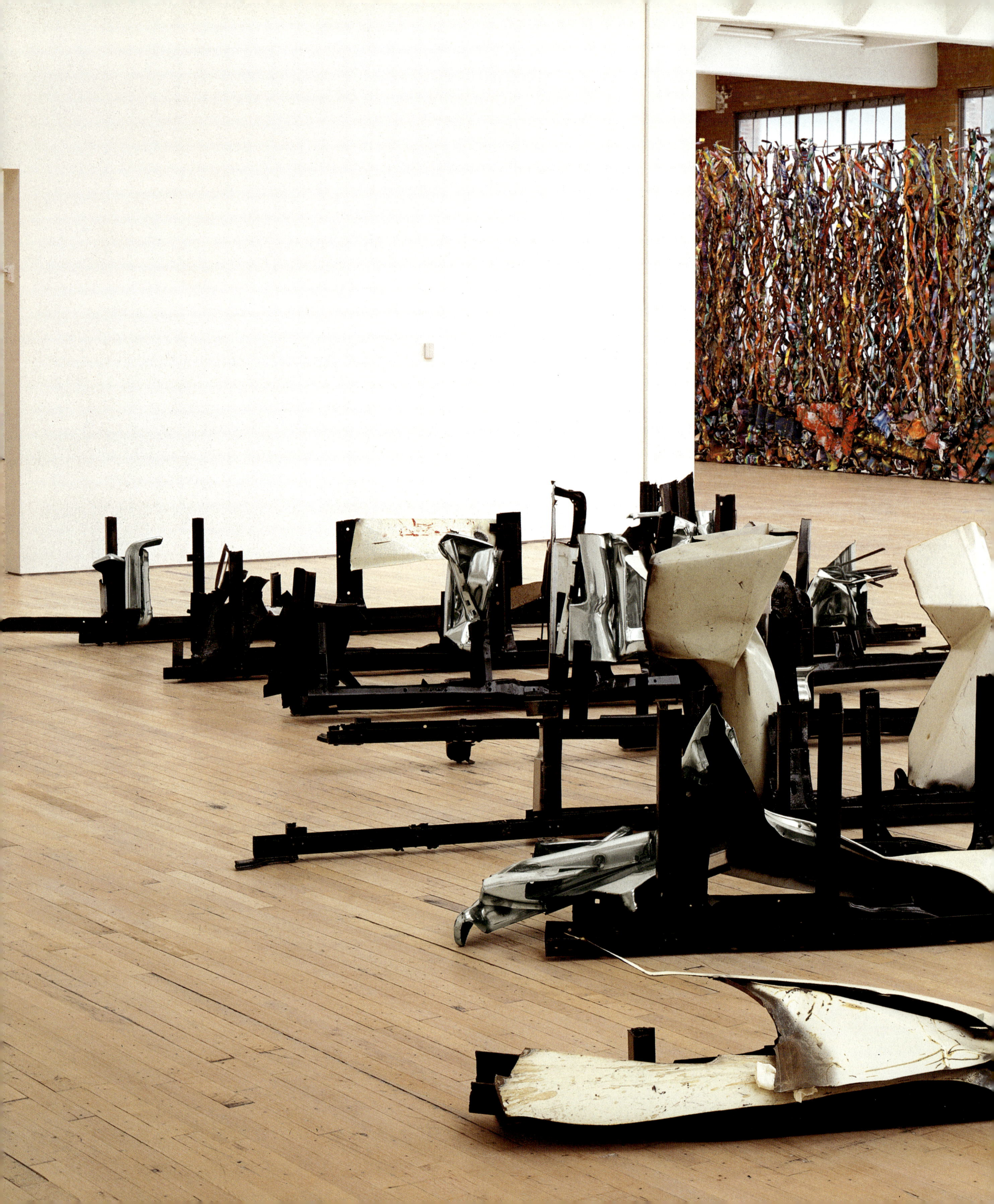

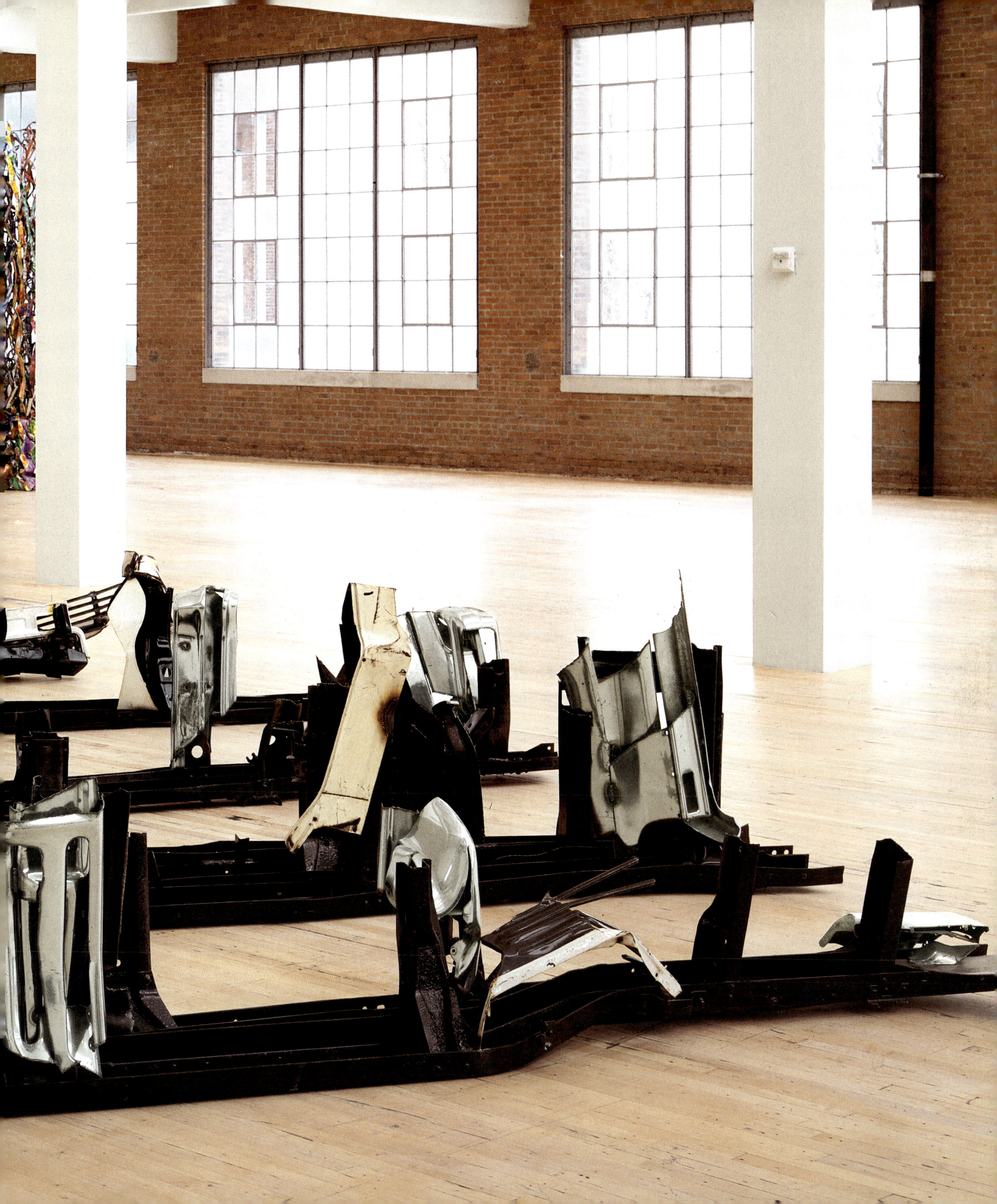

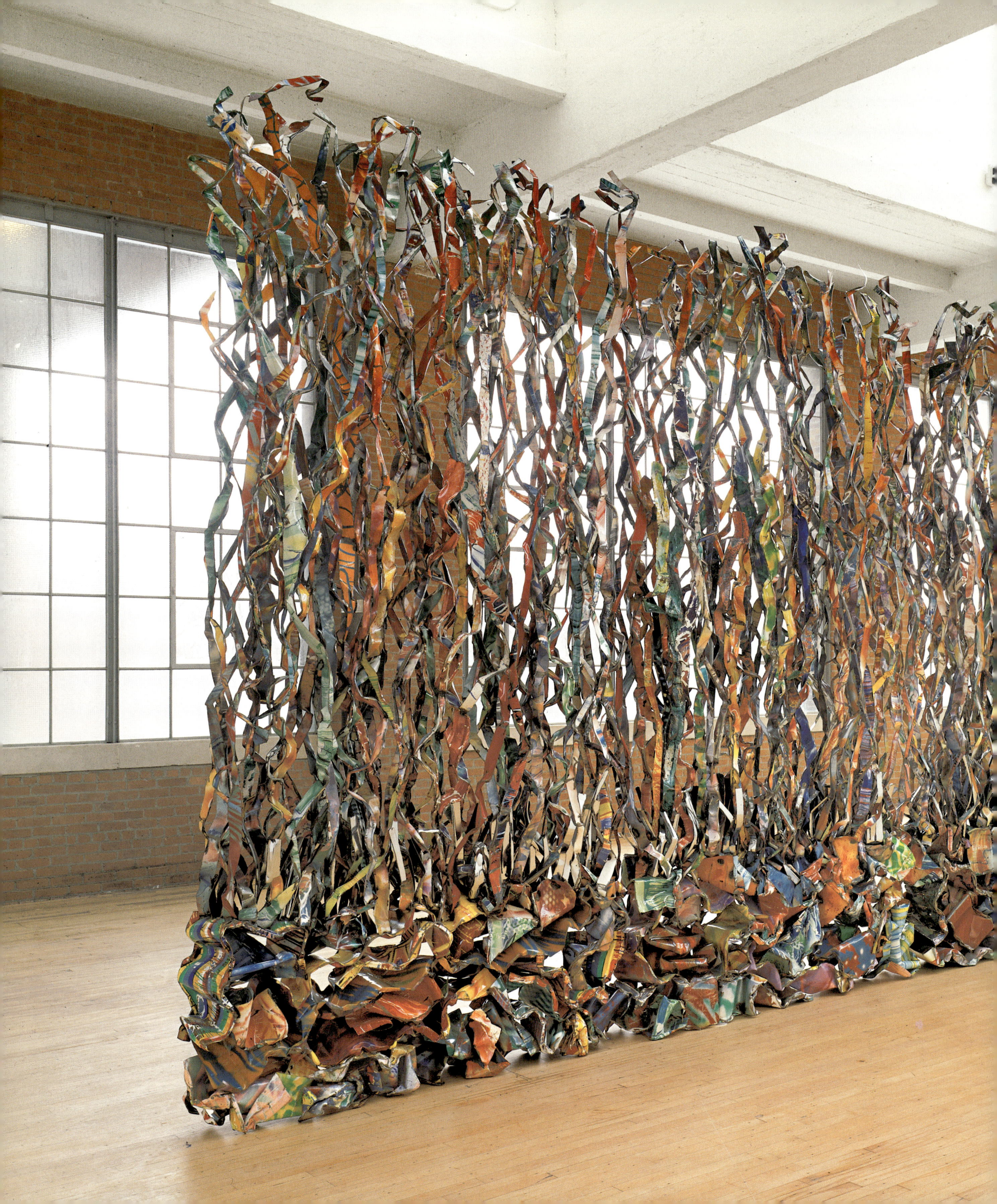

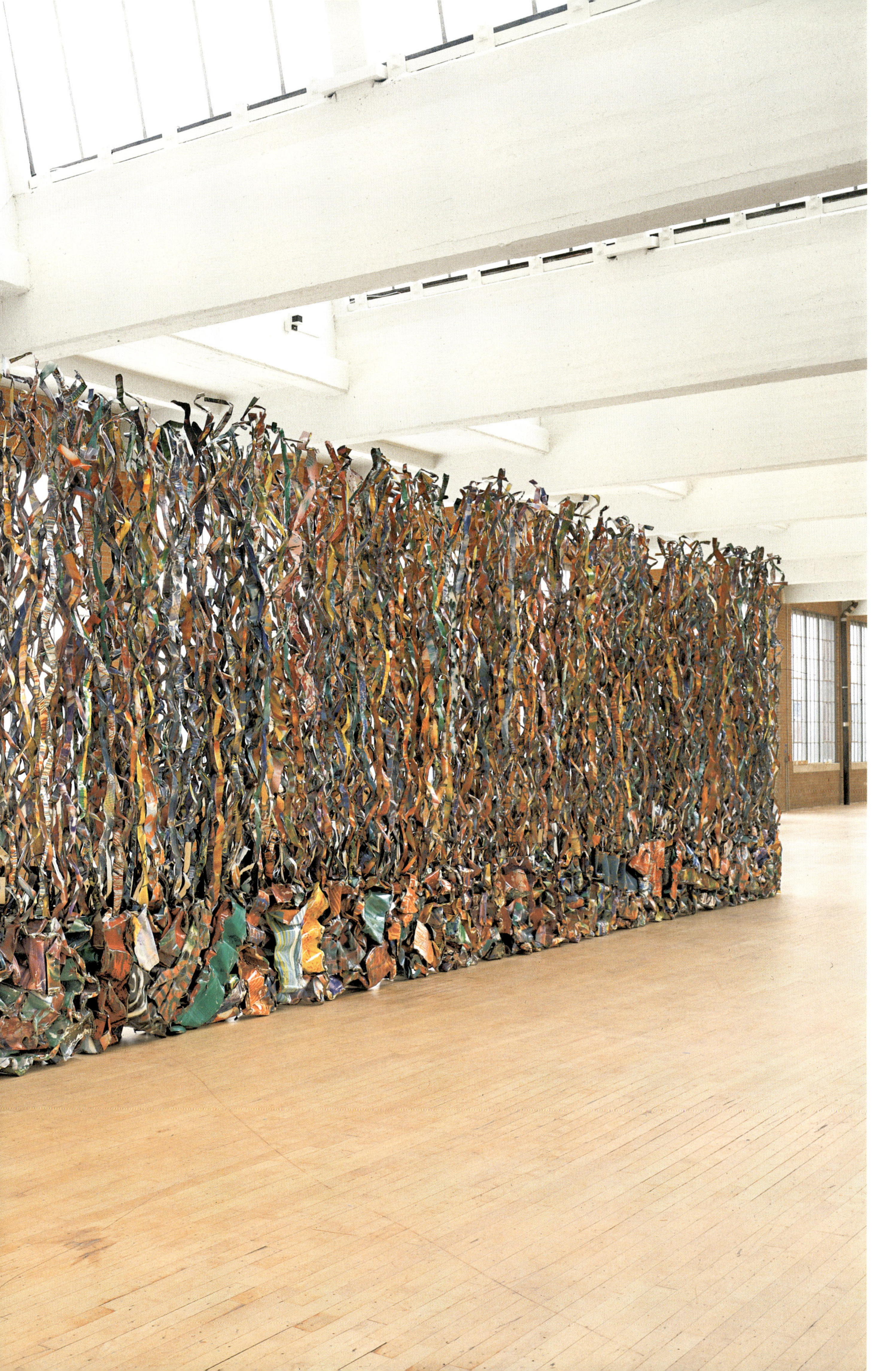

2

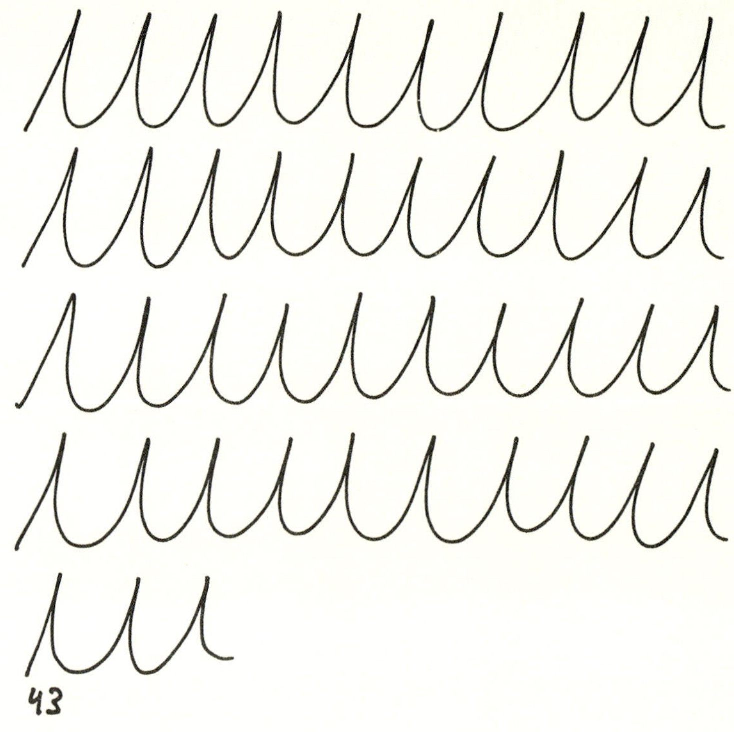

2.) Index: 01, 10, – 2X

3 K – 44 K / 42 No

1 + 1 + 0 + 1 – 3 ——— 42 No ——— 31 + 12 + 0 + 1 – 44

1 + 1 + 1 + 0 – 3 ——— 42 No ——— 31 + 12 + 1 + 0 – 44

3 K ———————————→ 44 K

Hanne Darboven

Hanne Darboven was born in Munich in 1941. Following a brief episode as a pianist, she studied painting at the Staatliche Hochschule für Bildende Künste, Hamburg. Between 1966 and 1969 she lived intermittently in New York City, then returned to her family home in Hamburg, where she continues to live and work. Her first one-person show was at the Galerie Konrad Fischer, Düsseldorf, in 1967. Darboven has participated in many international exhibitions, including Documentas 5 (1972), 6 (1977), 7 (1982), and 11 (2002), in Kassel; the 1973 São Paulo Bienal; and the 1982 Venice Biennale. She has also had numerous one-person shows in Europe and North America, including major presentations at the Ydessa Hendeles Foundation, Toronto, in 1991, the Staatsgalerie Stuttgart, in 1997, and the Museum für Moderne Kunst, Frankfurt, in 1999. Dia exhibited *Kulturgeschichte 1880–1983* in 1996–97.

left *Kulturgeschichte 1880–1983*, 1980–83 (detail)
pages 119–120; 122–125 *Kulturgeschichte 1880–1983*, 1980–83

Time today is no longer a principle of intelligibility . . . let alone a principle of identity. . . . So it is with an image of excess—excess of time—that we can start defining the situation of supermodernity.

—Marc Augé

From the moment in the mid-1960s when Hanne Darboven moved to New York City, after a highly academic training at the Staatliche Hochschule für Bildende Künste in Hamburg, her work has been informed by Conceptual art practices. Based by the late 1960s on various forms of numerical writing, her systematic work securely occupied the realm of abstraction and universality.

> *I only use numbers because it is a way of writing without describing. . . . It has nothing to do with mathematics. Nothing! I choose numbers because they are so constant, confined, and artistic. Numbers are probably the only real discovery of mankind. A number of something (two chairs, or whatever) is something else. It's not pure number and has other meanings.*[1]

Over time, time has become the focus of Darboven's art. For her, Annelie Pohlen argues, time constitutes the primary and essential structure of human life—it is "a basically intangible measure for the totality of the indices determining being; it is the content of consciousness; it exists beyond human comprehension."[2] The calendar, which subsequently formed the foundation of Darboven's art practice, again offered a universal orientation, embodying a given, prefabricated, ready-made temporal system. Calibrated in her work in many ways over almost three decades, it has provided the basis of an arbitrary artistic system that has the appearance of objectivity. Conjoining a rigorous numerical process with free-associative roots, and tight rational thought with intellectual freedom,

Darboven's capricious sense of time has resulted in diverse monumental works that may span a month, a year, even a century, all recorded day by day.

In the early 1970s Darboven introduced a kind of writing into her work that took the form of an even cursive script. Although executed by hand, this script was standardized and regulated, systematic and abstract. Its resistance to decoding conformed to a basic tenet of the artist's, epitomized in a quotation she borrowed from the Dutch politician Wiert Pauwel Berghuis: "A working method is not a system of thought. We do not believe that even the most ingenious of systems could completely illuminate life in its totality."[3] In 1973 she began to incorporate texts–transcribed directly because, she has claimed, they could not be bettered–from various writers, initially Heinrich Heine and Jean-Paul Sartre. These texts spoke both to her recognition of the failure of the grand narratives of Enlightenment thought to provide convincing, encompassing interpretations and, equally, to her fundamentally romantic existentialist position. Then, in 1978, she introduced visual documentation alongside her numbers and looping texts, primarily in the form of found and rephotographed images, which allowed her to address specific historical issues for the first time. Shortly thereafter, she invented a system of musical notation, based on her system of numbering dates, which she has used since 1979 to compose scores for organ, double bass, string quartet, and chamber orchestra. Darboven sees her music as she does her "mathematical writing," a highly abstract language functioning in an entirely self-referential manner; it thus serves as an abstract correlative to the concrete, visual nature of her artwork.

Comprising 1,590 sheets, each measuring 27½ x 19¾ inches, and nineteen sculptural objects, *Kulturgeschichte 1880–1983* (*Cultural History 1880–1983*), 1980–83, is one of Darboven's grandest, most epic works to date. Weaving together cultural, social, and historical references with autobiographical documents, it synthesizes collective memory with personal history, the social with the private. Braided among the vast numbers of postcards, caches of film- and rock-star pinups, documentary references to the First and Second World Wars, geometric diagrams for textile weaving, a heterogeneous sampling of New York doorways and portals, illustrated covers from major newsmagazines, the contents of an exhibition catalogue on postwar European and American art, and a kitsch literary calendar are extracts from certain of Darboven's earlier works, exhibition catalogues from solo shows, and other mementos of previous exhibitions. The result resembles an encyclopedia rather than an archive; it feels exhaustive but logically cannot be. Like an encyclopedia, the work catalogues and displays information without subordinating it to a dominant narrative form. Panels are sequenced and grouped, and then the groups are juxtaposed; although they are physically contiguous, they are seldom cognitively connected. In contrast to many of Darboven's previous large-scale works, no overriding calendrical system structures this work. Such is the magnitude of its scale that it invites, not a reading, but a visual experience. An image of information, it might best be unraveled by meandering through the site, wandering from panel to object, object to panel, part to part, aided by neither a strict nor an exclusive methodology. Installed in a tight-knit formation around the walls of a large space, it takes on a spectacular panoramic quality.

If accumulativeness is the effect created by too few objects and fragmentation the effect of too many, then between these extremes lies a point, precariously

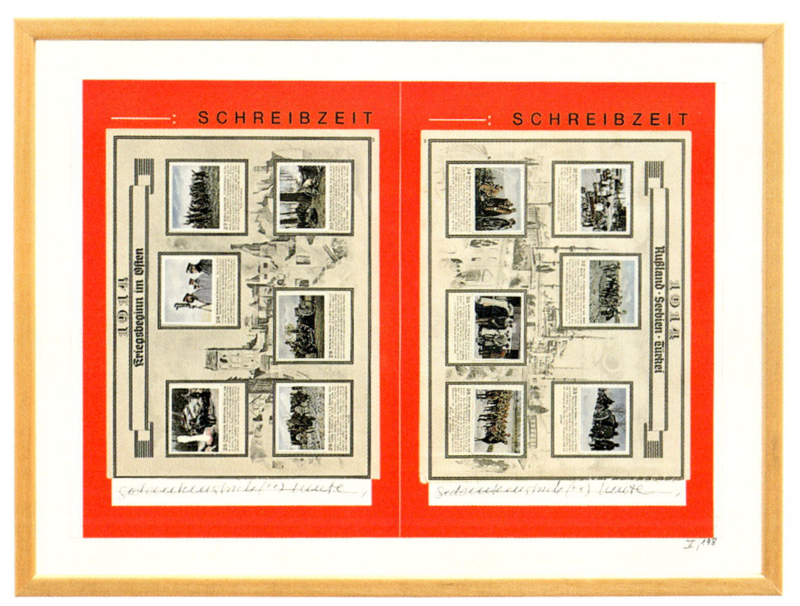
SCHREIBZEIT
SCHREIBZEIT
1914
Kriegsbeginn im Osten
1914
Rußland · Serbien · Türkei

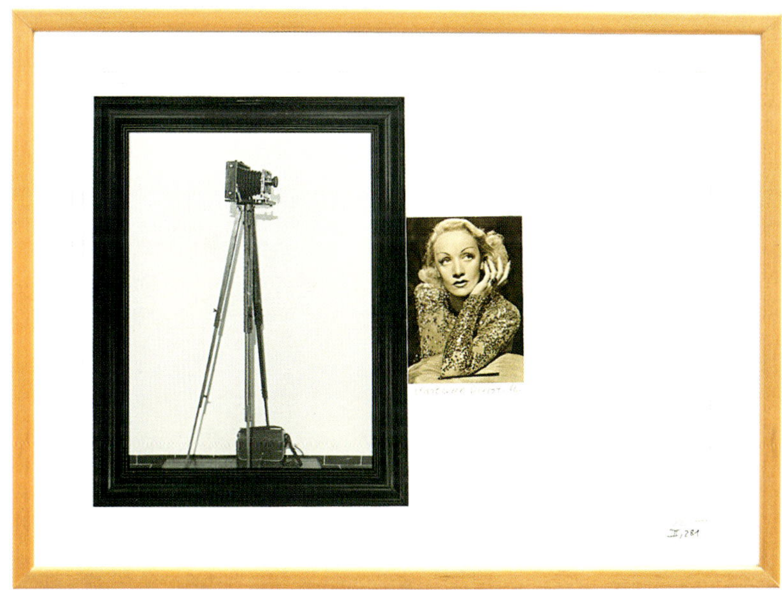

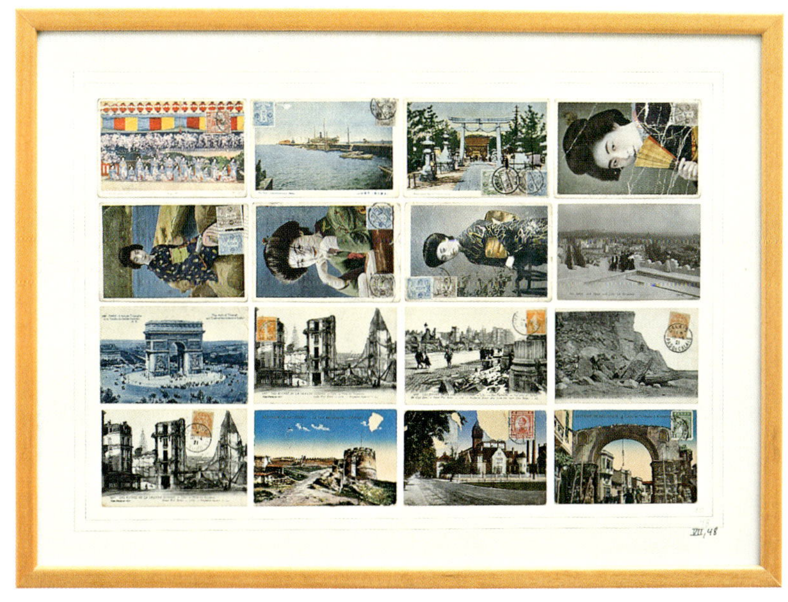

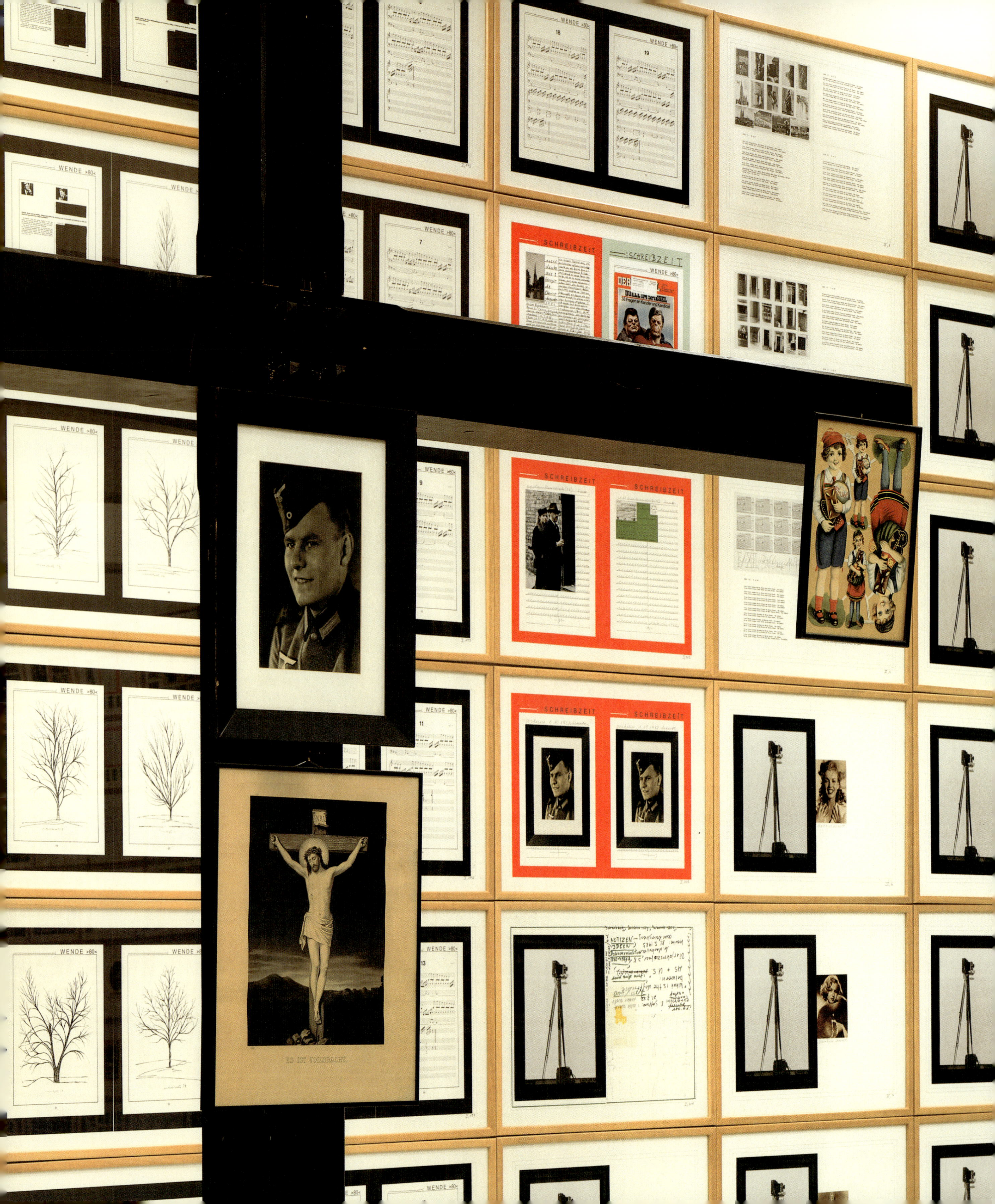
WENDE >80<
SCHREIBZEIT
DUELL IM SPIEGEL
NOTIZEN
ES IST VOLLBRACHT.

held in *Kulturgeschichte 1880–1983*, where quantity instills its own visual structure. At a microlevel, Darboven's use of the grid provides a taut formal structure that appears endless and infinitely repeatable; larger sections cohere by color and morphology rather than by subject matter per se. Repetition within any one section, or the rephrasing of a part later within the whole, creates a subtle rhythmic pattern of sameness and difference, such that the work ultimately escapes the twin poles of intolerable monotony and loss of aesthetic identity.

Perhaps more than any other work in Darboven's extensive oeuvre, an oeuvre that contains works of rich philosophical and political import, *Kulturgeschichte 1880–1983* incorporates both a sense of spectacle and a charged emotional register. Supermodernity, as French anthropologist Marc Augé defines it, "makes the old (history) into a specific spectacle, as it does with all exoticism and all local particularity. History and exoticism play the same role in it as the 'quotations' in a written text."[4]

Kulturgeschichte 1880–1983 produces a kind of libidinal exuberance, an effect nonetheless shot through with pathos. Whereas in most of her work Darboven arrests the flow of time by recording it, here, divesting herself of a constraining temporal structure, she seems to surrender to its excess. Attempts to try to synthesize this vast array, to decode it or otherwise render it coherent, are futile. A patchwork of modes, its atomized epistemological structure calls into question the artist's former, Sartrean-derived position, which held that in the final analysis the universal is the truth of the specific. Nonetheless, within this grand, apparently unbridled display Darboven inserts the possibility, albeit qualified, of individual demurral.

"At the end of the twelfth chapter of the Günter Grass book *Das Treffen in Telgte* (*The Encounter* [sic] *in Telgte*) is a passage that reflects exactly what I think," Darboven once stated.[5] That passage reads,

> *Heinrich Schütz, who had attended the debate as though absent, answered the question: For the sake of the written words, which poets alone had the power to write in accordance with the dictates of art. And also to wrest from helplessness—he knew it well—a faint "and yet."*[6]

L.C.

notes

1 Hanne Darboven, quoted in Lucy Lippard, "Hanne Darboven: Deep in Numbers," *Artforum* 12, no. 2 (October 1973), pp. 35–36. (Translation modified.)

2 Annelie Pohlen, "Hanne Darboven's Time: The Content of Consciousness," *Artforum* 21, no. 8 (April 1983), p. 52.

3 Wiert Pauwel Berghuis, quoted in Kathryn Hixson, "Chicago in Review," *Arts* 64, no. 7 (March 1990), p. 123.

4 Marc Augé, *Non-places: Introduction to an Anthropology of Supermodernity* (New York: Verso, 1995), p. 110.

5 Darboven, quoted in Amine Haase, "An Interview with Hanne Darboven," trans. Michael Schultz, reprinted in *Hanne Darboven: Primitive Time/Clock Time* (Philadelphia: Goldie Paley Gallery, Moore College of Art and Design, 1990), p. 14.

6 Günter Grass, *Das Treffen in Telgte*, published in English as *The Meeting at Telgte*, trans. Ralph Manheim (New York: Harcourt, Brace, Jovanovich, 1990), pp. 68–69.

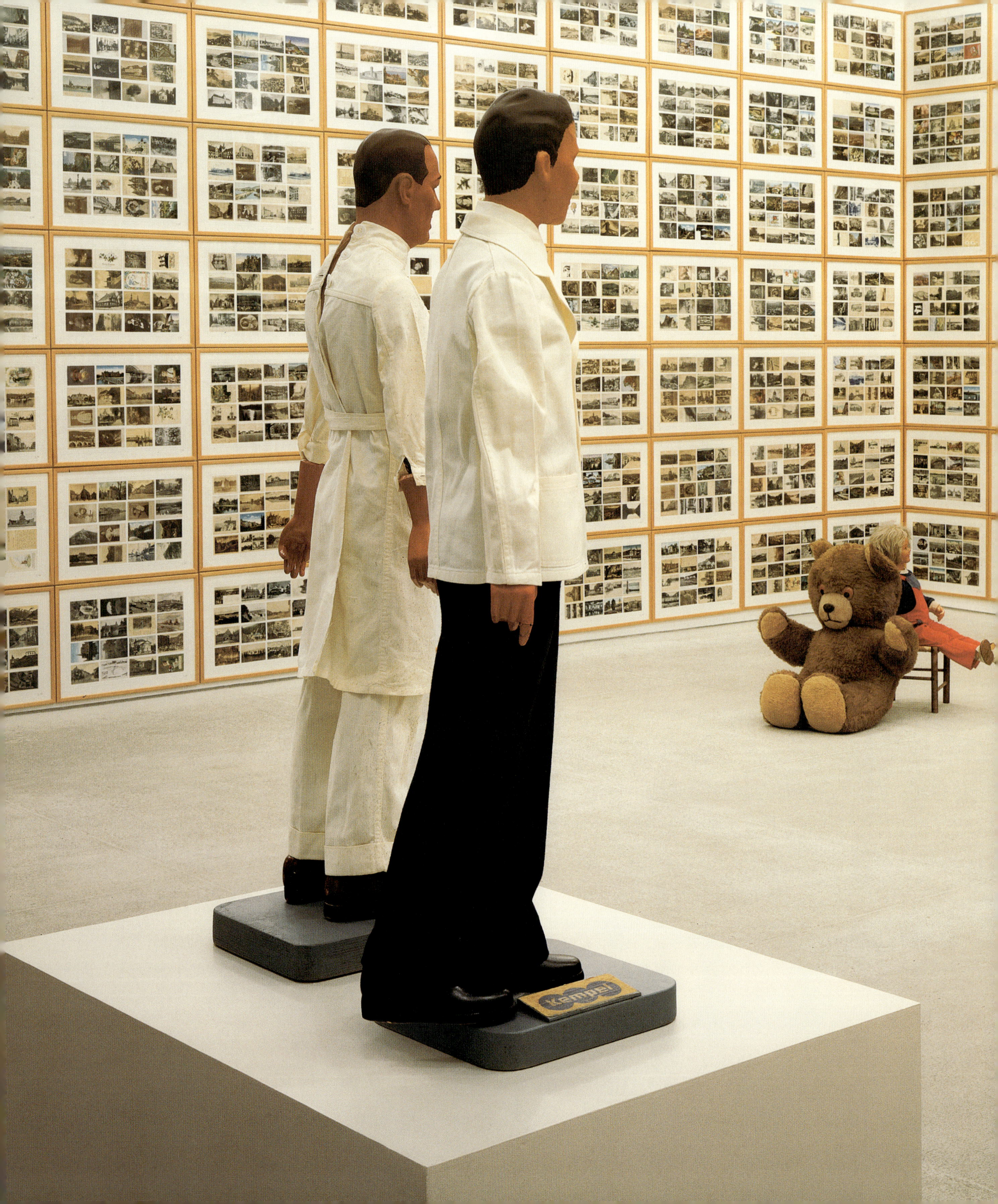
Kempel

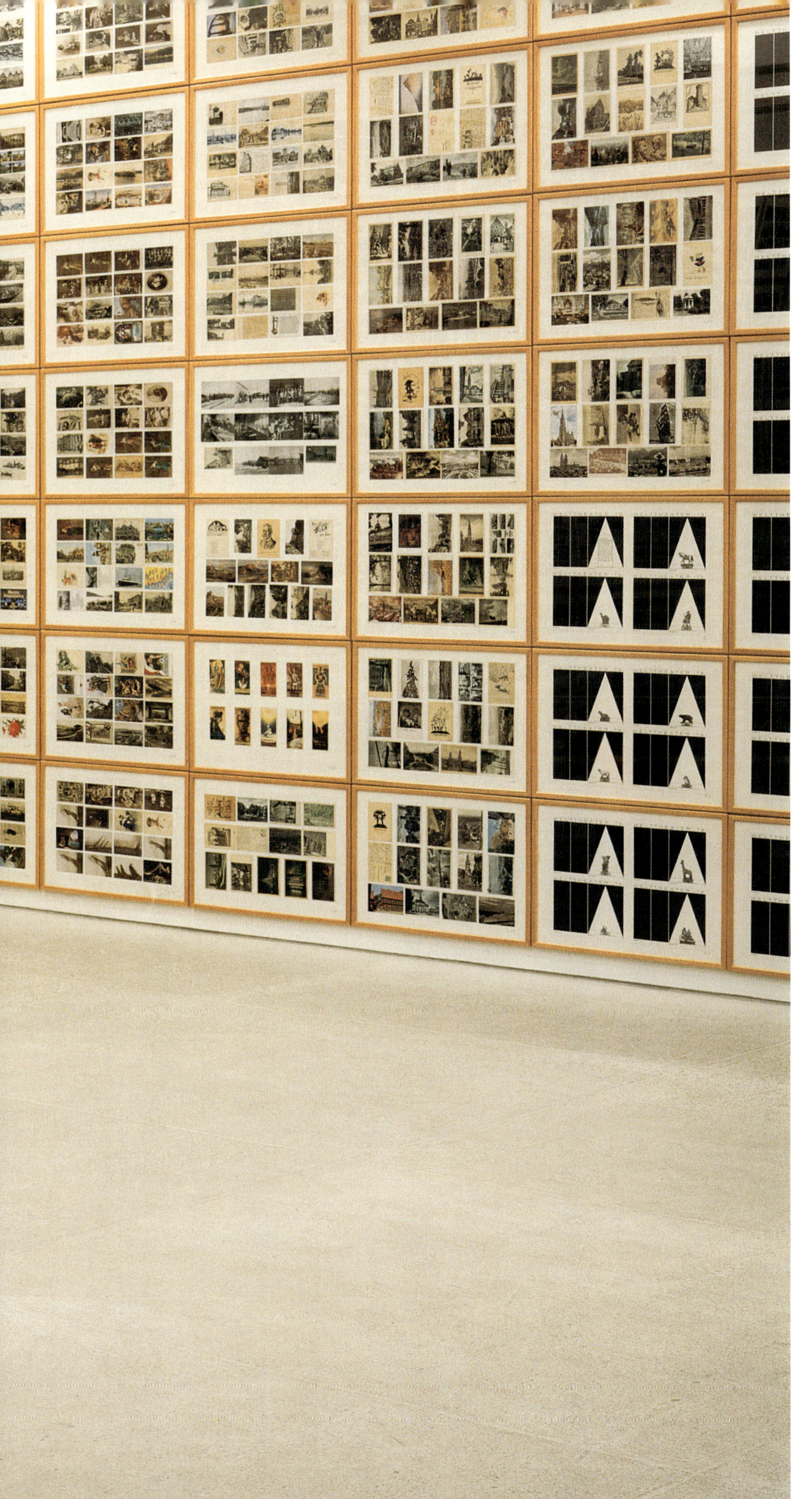

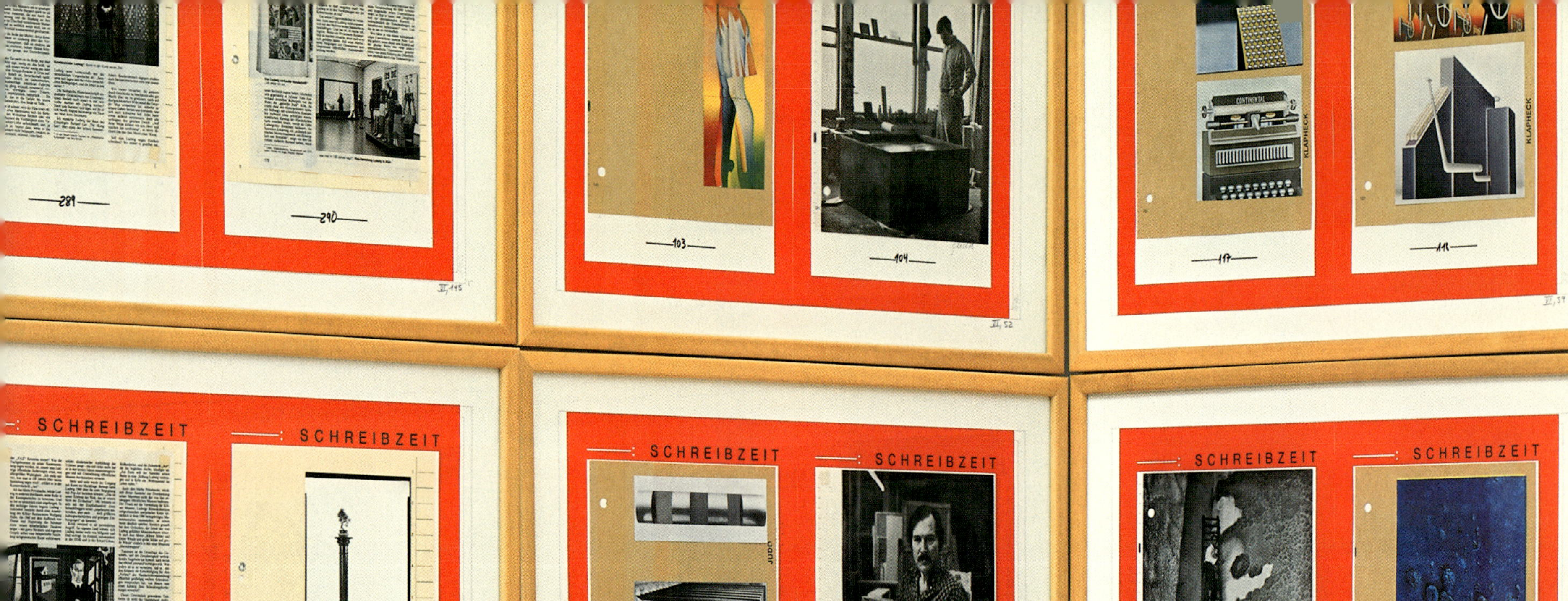
KLAPHECK
KLAPHECK

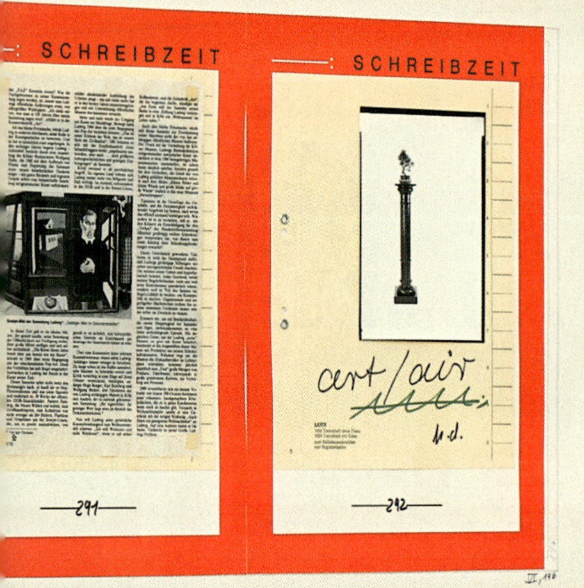
SCHREIBZEIT
SCHREIBZEIT

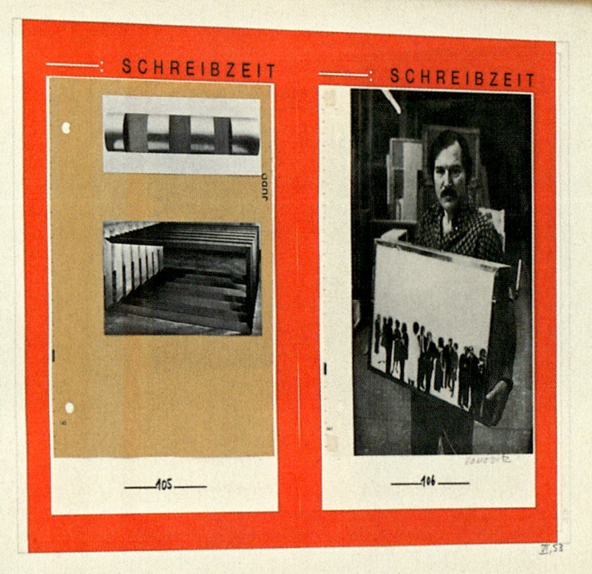
SCHREIBZEIT
SCHREIBZEIT
JUDD

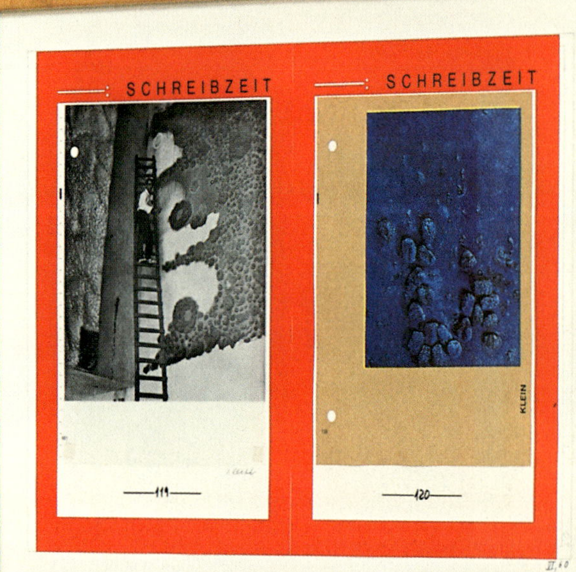
SCHREIBZEIT
SCHREIBZEIT
KLEIN

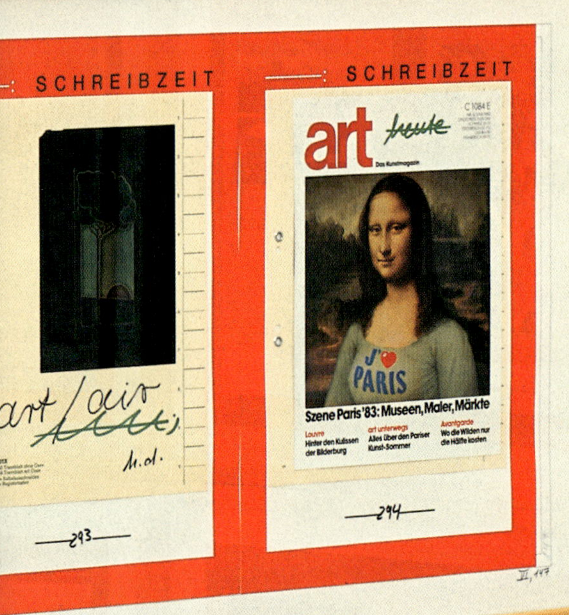
SCHREIBZEIT
SCHREIBZEIT
art
Das Kunstmagazin
PARIS
Szene Paris '83: Museen, Maler, Märkte

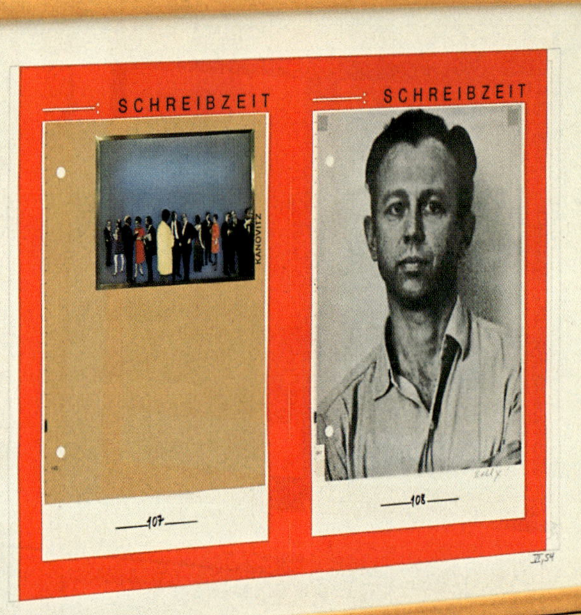
SCHREIBZEIT
SCHREIBZEIT
KANOVITZ

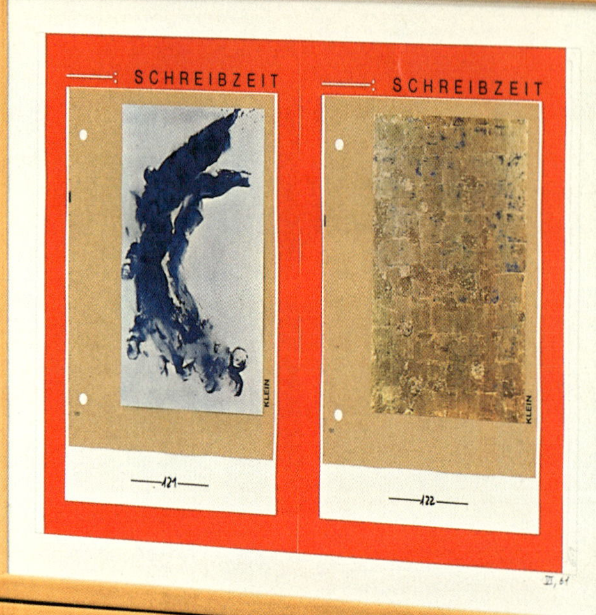
SCHREIBZEIT
SCHREIBZEIT
KLEIN
KLEIN

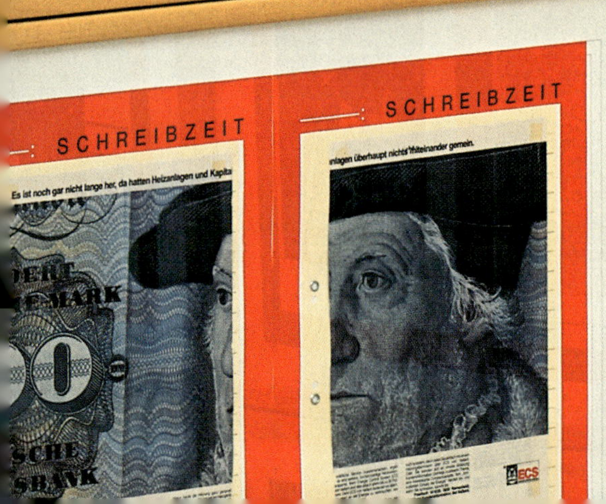
SCHREIBZEIT
SCHREIBZEIT

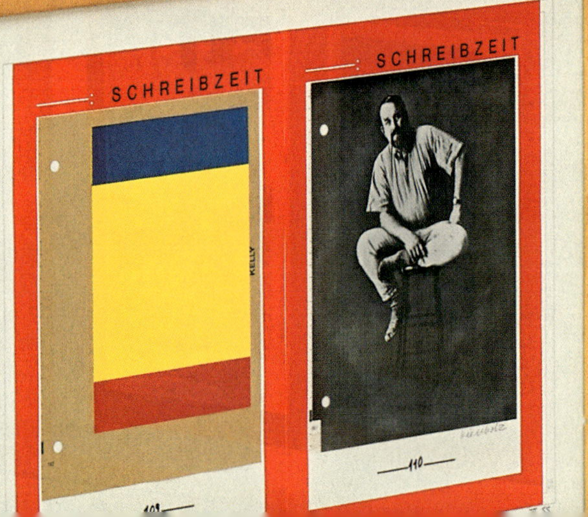
SCHREIBZEIT
SCHREIBZEIT
KELLY

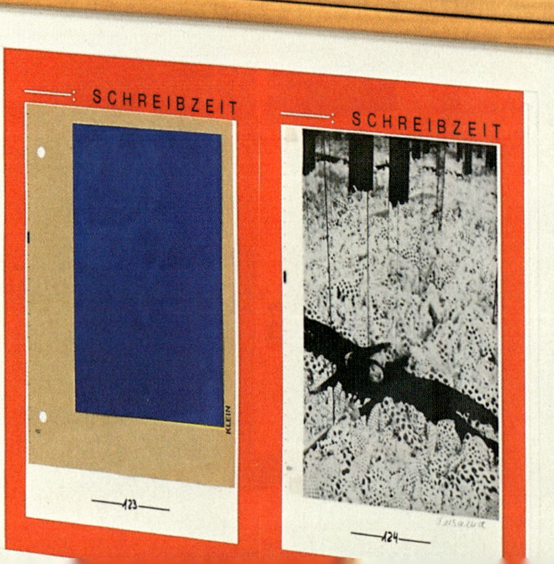
SCHREIBZEIT
SCHREIBZEIT
KLEIN

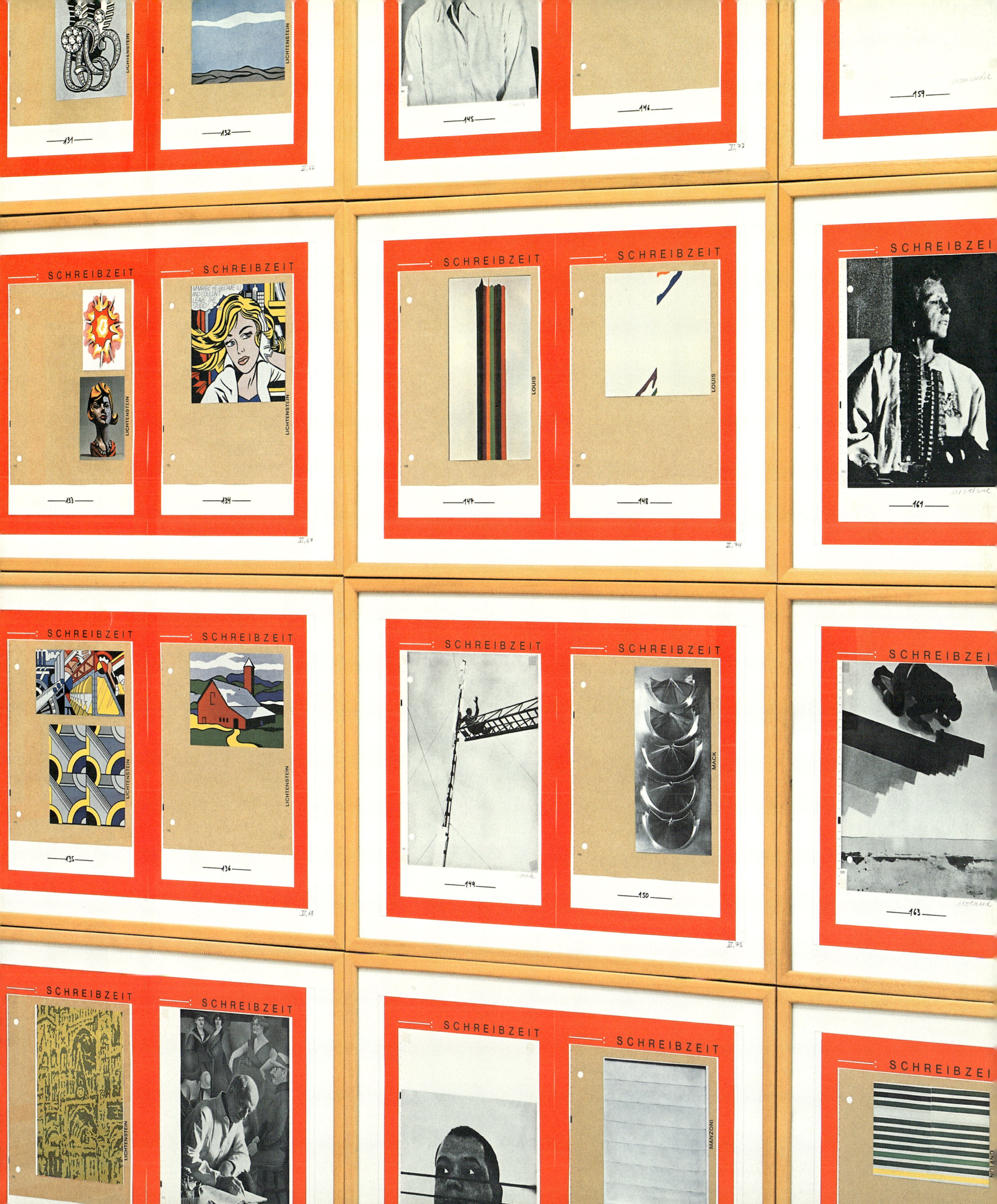

LICHTENSTEIN
131
132
145
146
159
SCHREIBZEIT
133
134
LOUIS
147
148
161
M-MAYBE HE BECAME ILL AND COULDN'T LEAVE THE STUDIO!
135
136
MACK
149
150
163
MANZONI

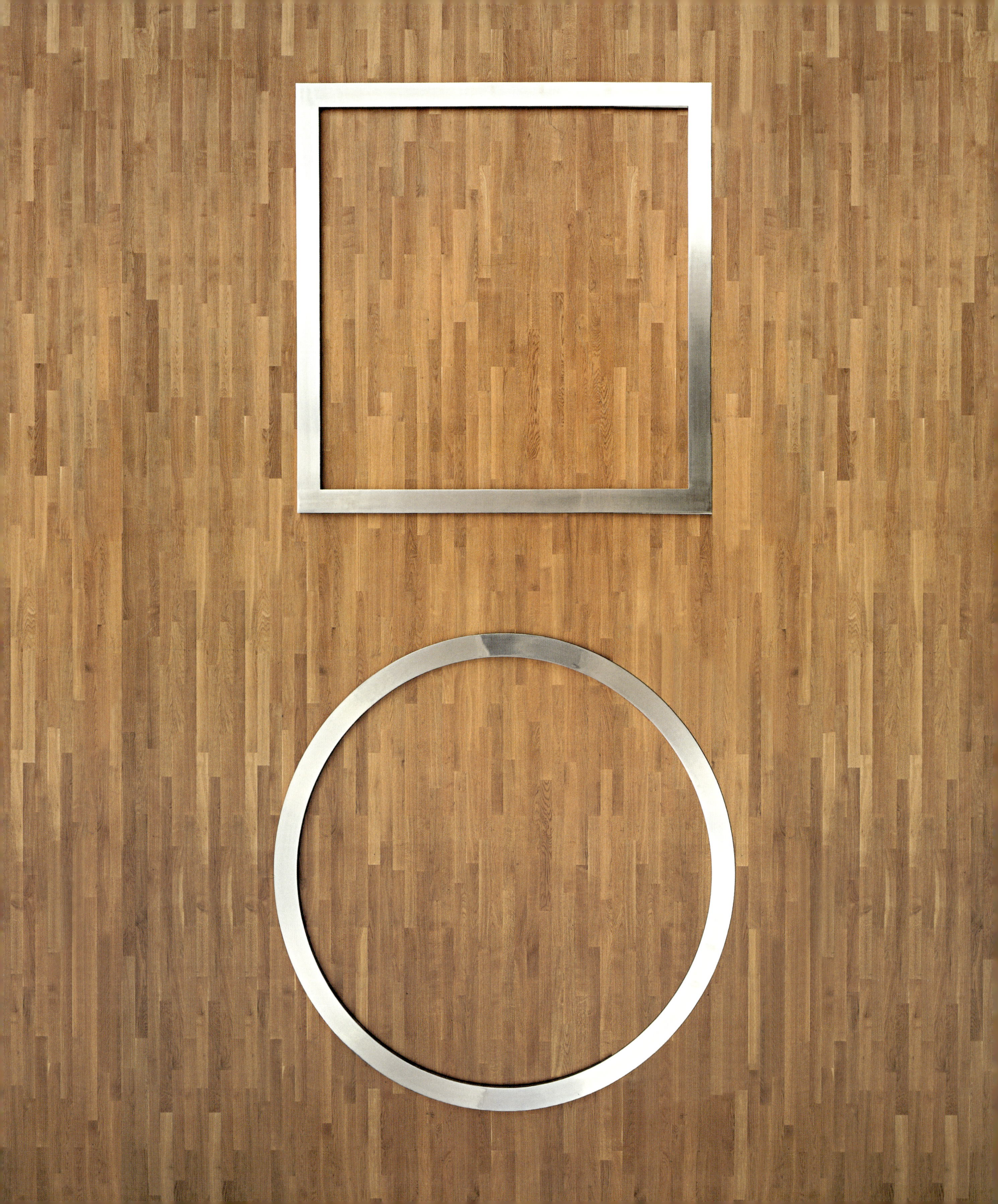

Walter De Maria

Walter De Maria was born in 1935 in Albany, California, and studied history and art at the University of California, Berkeley. In 1960 he moved to New York City, where he continues to live and work. With Robert Whitman, De Maria cofounded a gallery at 9 Great Jones Street, Manhattan, in 1963, and held a show of his sculptures there that year. His work was included in the "Primary Structures" exhibition at the Jewish Museum, New York, in 1966. De Maria has had numerous international shows, at venues including the Kunsthaus Zürich (1999), the Museum für Moderne Kunst, Frankfurt (1991), the Staatsgalerie Stuttgart (1987), and the Museum Boymans-van Beuningen, Rotterdam (1984).

The Equal Area Series, 1976–77 (detail)

The Equal Area Series (1976–90) is one of several large-scale works by Walter De Maria in Dia's collection. Beginning in the mid-1970s, Dia commissioned and now maintains for visitors some of De Maria's most significant permanent site-specific installations, including *The Lightning Field* (1977), on a remote desert plateau near Quemado, New Mexico, and *The Broken Kilometer* (1979) and *The New York Earth Room* (1977), both in downtown Manhattan, New York.

De Maria's early work of the 1960s included music, performance, and writing as well as sculptural and conceptual works. The principal pieces of the latter kind, such as *4' x 8' Box* (1961), also in Dia's collection, and the proposal for *Mile-Long Parallel Walls in the Desert* (1964), foreshadowed much of the Minimal, Conceptual, Installation, and Land art movements, which would radically change aesthetic practice through the next two decades.

The Equal Area Series comprises twenty-five pairs of circles and squares that are formed by highly polished solid stainless-steel plate, 5 inches wide by 7/8 of an inch thick. The works are installed flat on the floor. Each pair differs slightly in size from each of the others and is considered an individual sculpture. As the title of the work implies, each circle in a pair defines an area of the same size as its corresponding square. The smallest pair in the series, for example, is made up of a square 6 feet wide and a circle with a diameter of 6 feet 8 inches; the area inscribed by each is nearly exactly the same–3,844 and 3,848 square inches respectively. The next largest square is one inch wider, at 6 feet 1 inches; the circle that corresponds to it, in order to maintain the same area, has a diameter of 6 feet 9 1/8 inches, or 1 1/8 inches larger than the circle in the smaller pair. The squares increase incrementally in size by the same measure—one inch—for each subsequent pair in the series. The largest square is 8 feet wide and the largest circle is almost 9 feet in diameter (see chart).

The first thirteen pairs, their squares running from six feet to seven feet wide inclusively, were made from 1976 to 1977 and first exhibited at a temporary rented storefront on Waverly Place, New York City, October 1977 to January 1978. The second, larger twelve pairs were fabricated in two phases—pairs fourteen through nineteen were made in 1983 and pairs twenty through twenty-five in 1990. At Dia:Beacon the artist has placed the first twelve pairs of the series in a continuous line through the museum's two symmetrical central galleries. The polished geometric perfection of the circles and squares, and the subtly increasing size of each pair in the installation, focus the eye equally on the individual pairs and on the breathtaking scale of the overall arrangement. The pairs increase in

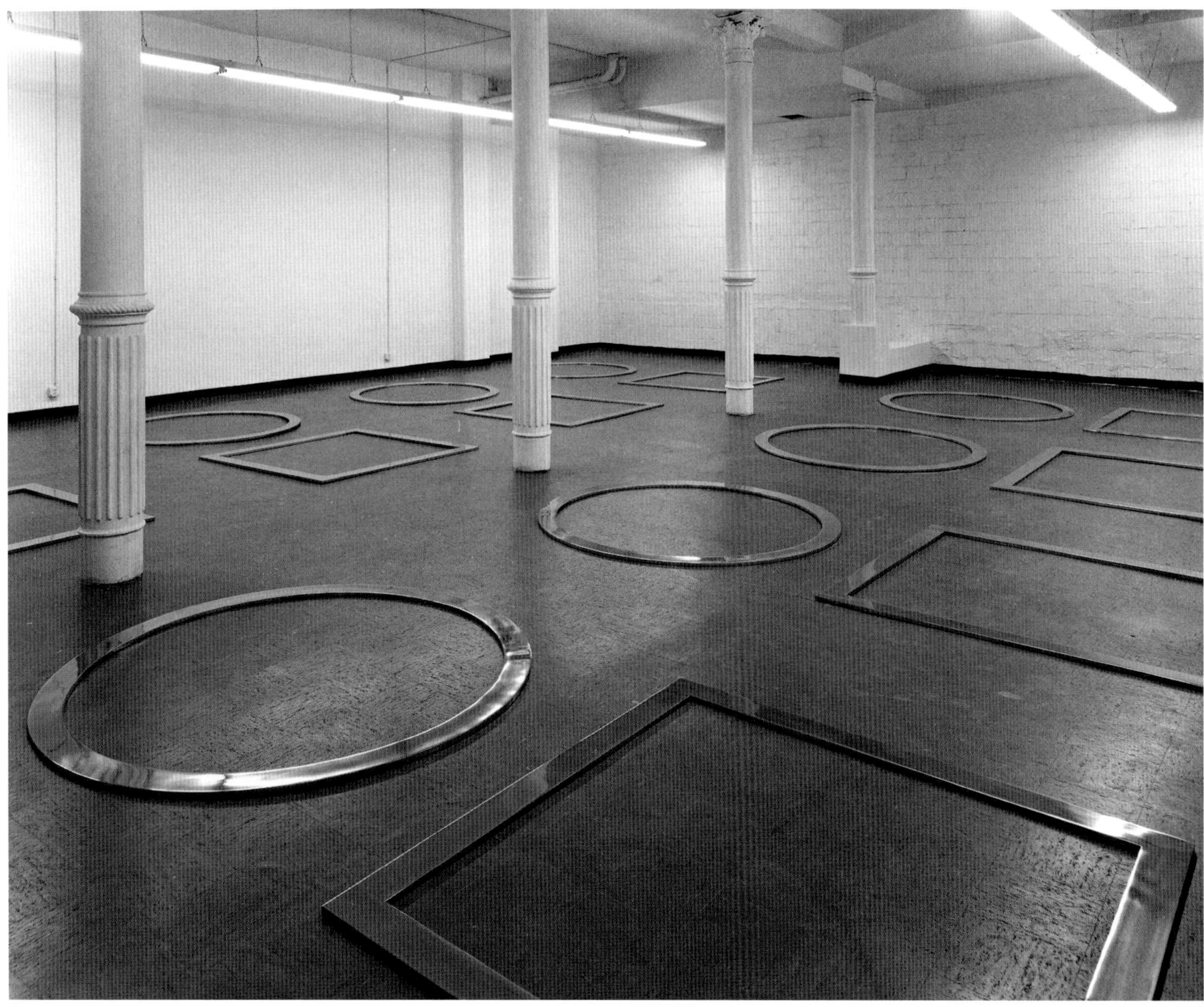

The Equal Area Series, 1976–77, installation at Waverly Place, New York

THE EQUAL AREA SERIES
DIMENSIONS

Pairs 1 thru 15 use the fixed system of increasing 1 inch per square and 1 1/8 inch per circle.

Pairs 16 thru 25 continue to use the fixed system of increasing 1 inch per square but change to a flexible system for increasing the circle. The circle increases by 1 inch plus a variable number to within a 64th of an inch. In this way the equal area relationship between the circles and the squares will always be within 1 square inch.

	Pair No.	Square Width	Circle Diameter	Square Area	Circle Area
	1	6'	6' 8"	3,844 sq. in.	3,848 sq. in.
	2	6' 1"	6' 9-1/8"	3,969 sq. in.	3,973 sq. in.
	3	6' 2"	6' 10-1/4"	4,096 sq. in.	4,100 sq. in.
	4	6' 3"	6' 11-3/8"	4,225 sq. in.	4,229 sq. in.
	5	6' 4"	7' 1/2"	4,356 sq. in.	4,359 sq. in.
	6	6' 5"	7' 1-5/8"	4,489 sq. in.	4,492 sq. in.
1976-77	7	6' 6"	7' 2-3/4"	4,624 sq. in.	4,626 sq. in.
	8	6' 7"	7' 3-7/8"	4,761 sq. in.	4,763 sq. in.
	9	6' 8"	7' 5"	4,900 sq. in.	4,902 sq. in.
	10	6' 9"	7' 6-1/8"	5,041 sq. in.	5,042 sq. in.
	11	6' 10"	7' 7-1/4"	5,184 sq. in.	5,185 sq. in.
	12	6' 11"	7' 8-3/8"	5,329 sq. in.	5,329 sq. in.
	13	6' 12"	7' 9-1/2"	5,476 sq. in.	5,476 sq. in.
	14	7' 1"	7' 10-5/8"	5,625 sq. in.	5,625 sq. in.
	15	7' 2"	7' 11-3/4"	5,776 sq. in.	5,775 sq. in.
1983	16	7' 3"	8' 59/64"	5,929 sq. in.	5,930 sq. in.
	17	7' 4"	8' 2-1/64"	6,084 sq. in.	6,084 sq. in.
	18	7' 5"	8' 3-9/64"	6,241 sq. in.	6,241 sq. in.
	19	7' 6"	8' 4-17/64"	6,400 sq. in.	6,399 sq. in.
	20	7' 7"	8' 5-13/32"	6,561 sq. in.	6,562 sq. in.
	21	7' 8"	8' 6-17/32"	6,724 sq. in.	6,725 sq. in.
1990	22	7' 9"	8' 7-21/32"	6,889 sq. in.	6,889 sq. in.
	23	7' 10"	8' 8-25/32"	7,056 sq. in.	7,056 sq. in.
	24	7' 11"	8' 9-29/32"	7,225 sq. in.	7,224 sq. in.
	25	8'	8' 11-3/64"	7,396 sq. in.	7,397 sq. in.

scale *against* the force of diminishing perspective in one gallery and, turning the corner, increase *with* perspective in the other, leaving the smallest pair and the largest pair installed on either side of the threshold of the gallery and providing a subtle but perceptibly different feeling in each of two mirror-image rooms. The polished steel geometric outlines incorporate the building's dramatic architecture into their presence, nearly dematerializing in certain light. From some angles they can appear dark, and from others they channel the light of the skylights onto their bright surfaces on the floor.

The precise mathematics of *The Equal Area Series* are unavailable to even the most observant eye, but measure and number are essential to most of De Maria's sculptures. *The Lightning Field*, for example, is made up of 400 poles (also of stainless steel) in a grid measuring one mile by one kilometer. *The Broken Kilometer*, true to its name, comprises 500 solid round bars each two meters long, so that together they total one kilometer in length. In its companion piece, *The Vertical Earth Kilometer* (1976), also commissioned by Dia, a brass pole one kilometer long has been driven into the ground in Kassel, Germany, so that only its top, two inches in diameter, is visible on the earth's surface.

Counting and arithmetic progressions also feature prominently in much of De Maria's other works, such as *A Computer Which Will Solve Every Problem in the World/3–12 Polygon* (1984). It comprises seventy-five stainless-steel polygonal bars, each of them one meter long, arranged in rows on the floor. Each row differs from the others in the number of sides on its bars, a number that in turn corresponds to the number of bars in the row: the first row contains three three-sided bars, the second contains four four-sided bars, and so on through twelve rows. Also, although the bars vary in the number of their sides, they are all of equal area and weight. *A Computer . . .*, like *The Equal Area Series*, suggests an infinitely expandable progression. That same progression was further extended in another work, *13, 14, & 15 Meter Rows* in 1985.

The particular numerology and geometry in each of De Maria's sculptures offer a starting point for expanding consideration of the artwork beyond its immediate visual gestalt, but by no measure exhausts the work's layered meanings and its visceral effect. Within the powerful sense of dramatic scale and seemingly absolute geometric perfection commanded by De Maria's installations, there are many dynamic relationships, for example, the play between the universal underlying cosmic continuum of natural abstract mathematics and our arbitrary culturally defined units of measurement.

In *The Equal Area Series*, within the continuous expansion and progression of measure, De Maria poses the opposition of the circle and the square—the perfect curve versus the perfect rectangle—perhaps the most essential of geometric contrasts. The pairing of the circle and the square suggests a binary opposition—like male and female, 0 and 1, black and white, or yin and yang—that underlies the essence of our world—procreation, counting and computing, light and visibility, and so on. This totalizing binary conjunction is integral to other of De Maria's works in Dia's collection, including the two versions, one white and one black, of the *360° I-Ching* (1981), that are intended to be exhibited together in an arrangement of sixty-four elements in a square grid surrounded by sixty-four elements in a circle.

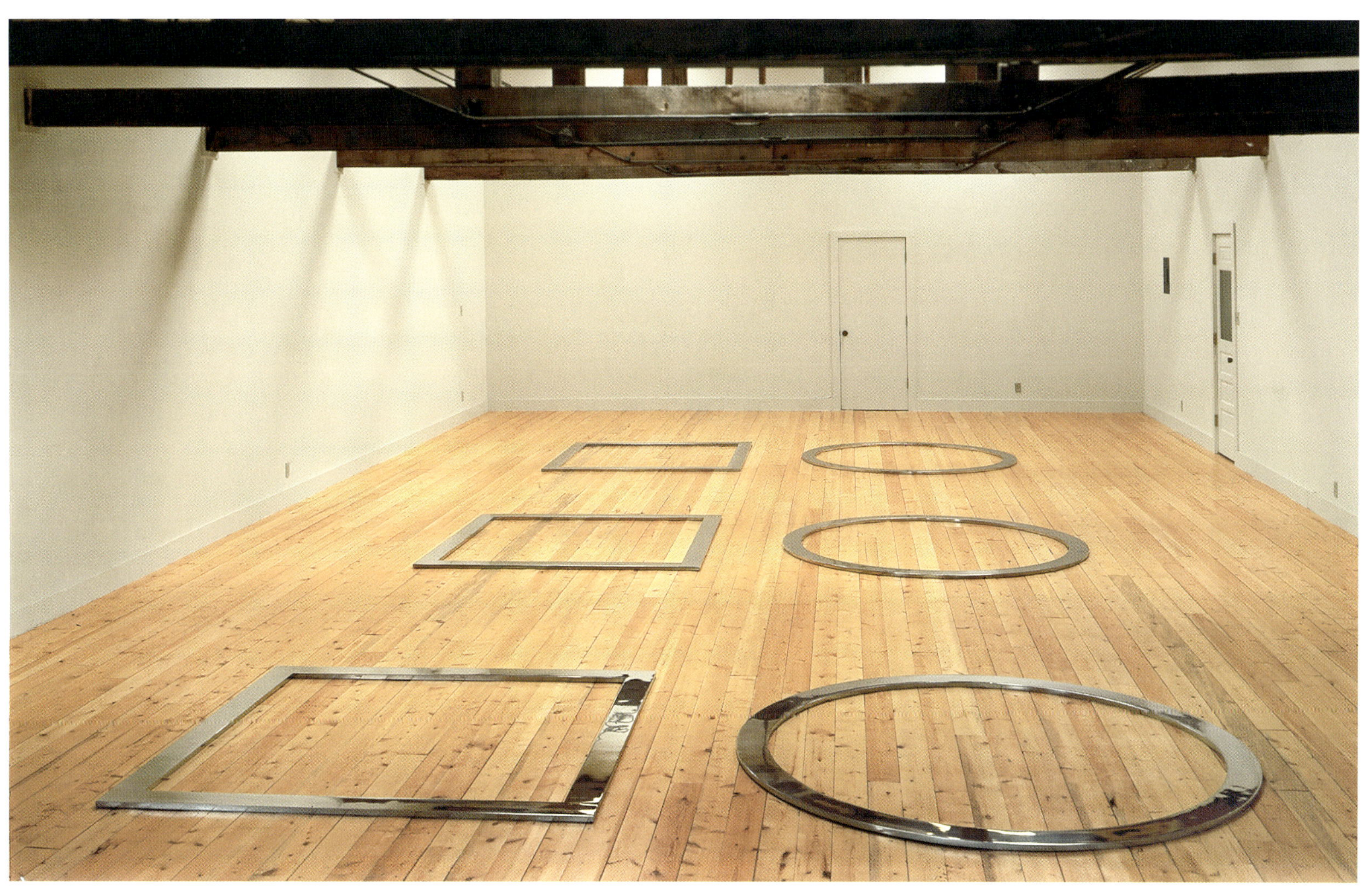

The Equal Area Series, 1976–77, installation in Quemado, New Mexico

Many qualities of De Maria's work–their large scale, the serial, gridlike arrangement of simple but precisely shaped individual elements, the use of pure materials–are shared by the work of some of his contemporaries, particularly Dan Flavin and Donald Judd as represented in Dia's museum in Beacon. De Maria, Flavin, Judd, and their peers have been labeled Minimalists because of their use of simple, geometric, serially repeating forms and unveneered materials, but they are anything but minimal in their complex intentions, the spectacular nature of their work's phenomenal effect, and the far-reaching conceptual implications that may be gleaned from close observation and sustained thought.

Perhaps most clearly in *The Lightning Field*, precise design and measure serve, among other things, to channel the sublime cosmic scale and explosive power of the natural environment into the artwork. As defined in large part by eighteenth-century artists and writers concerned with reconciling our human-dimensioned existence with overwhelming qualities in the natural world and the greater universe, the sublime is a function less of scale, grandeur, or even beauty, all of which might be measured or comprehended, than of the transcendent implications of the incomprehensible. The sublime is sensed, but not grasped, through emotions of awe or terror in the face of nature. The philosopher Immanuel Kant described the "supersensible" quality of things beyond the grasp of the senses and the imagination as a kind of infinity, which he called "the mathematically sublime." As such, the subtly expanding dimensions of each pair in *The Equal Area Series* might suggest larger phenomena, perhaps even the notion of the infinitely expanding celestial universe. But that metaphoric description would have to be counterpoised against absolute, specific facts of the artwork, facts that correspond with our own centered, if fleeting, experience of viewing it: the absolute eternity of the universe versus the absolute human now.

In sum, the notion of the sublime suggests a continuum between the experience given to us by our senses, the thoughtfulness given to us by our minds, and some other zone inaccessible to us. The immediate visual sensation of De Maria's sculpture withholds another reality of calculated mathematical measure that must be understood in the mind and that, in turn, may refer to some unknown universal order. As is implied by the title of a recent work of De Maria's, *Seen/Unseen Known/Unknown*, an installation in Naoshima Contemporary Art Museum, Japan, the visible is only one aspect or layer of the aesthetic experience, and hence of our existence.

M.G.

pages 133, 134, 135 *The Equal Area Series*, 1976–77

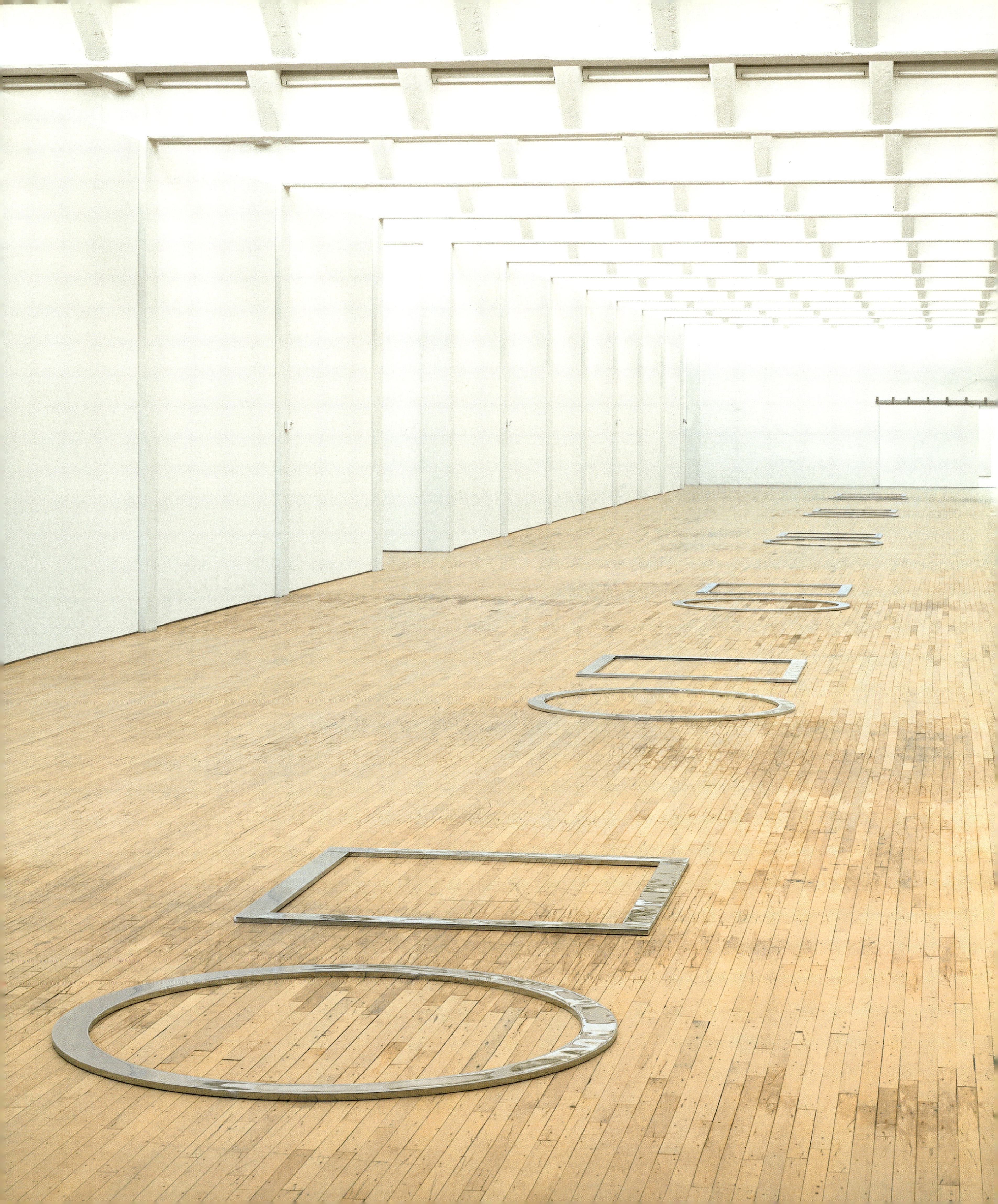

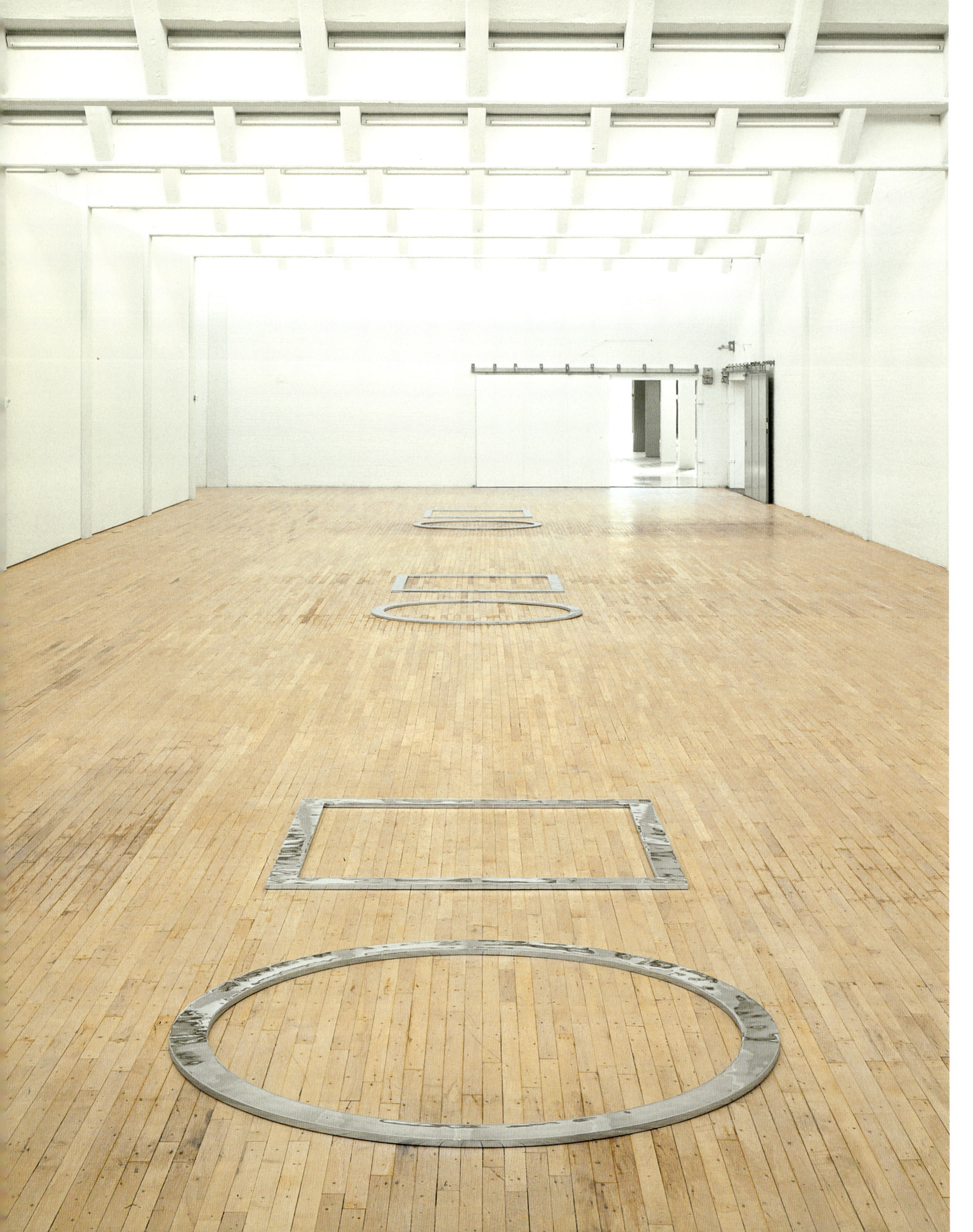

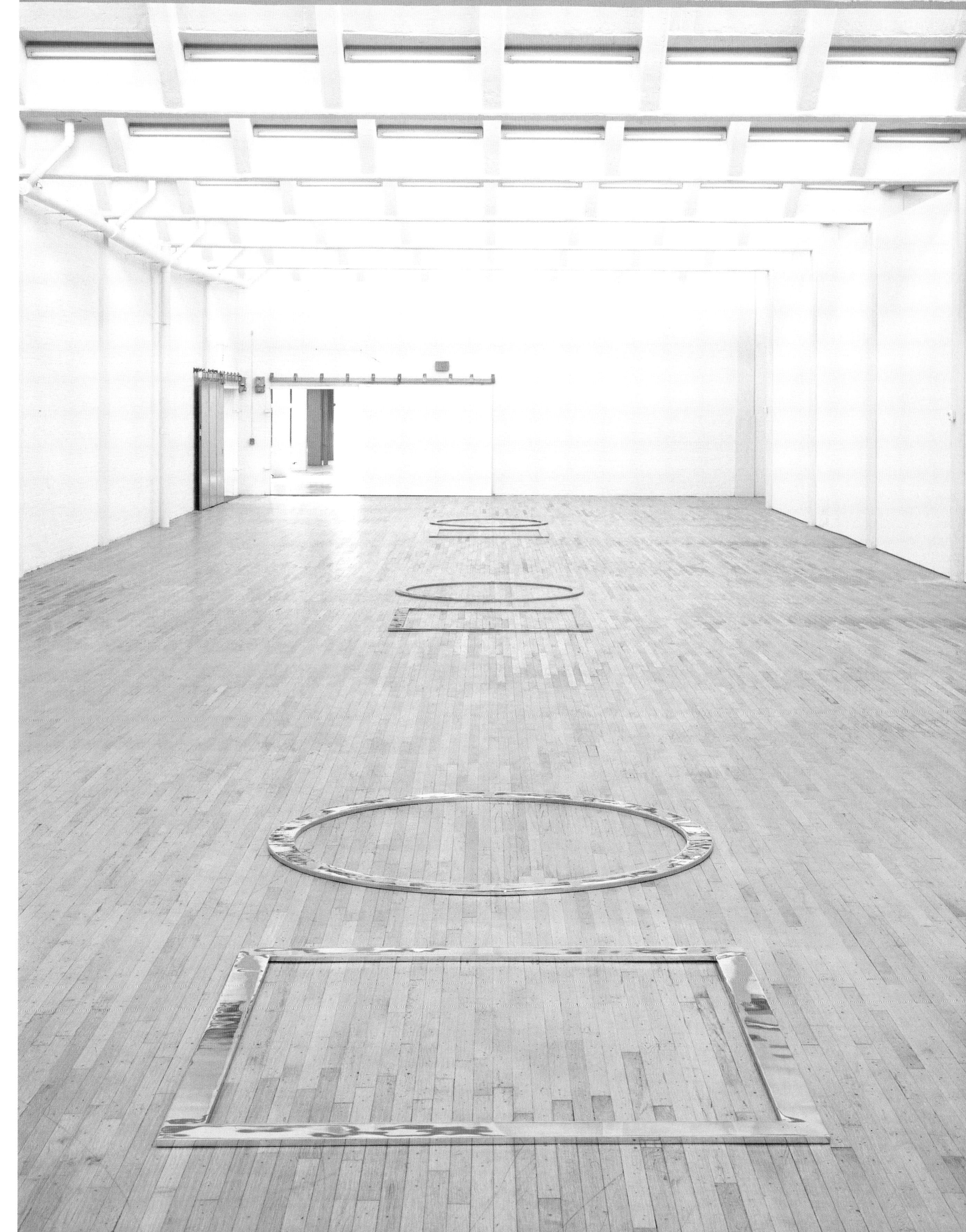

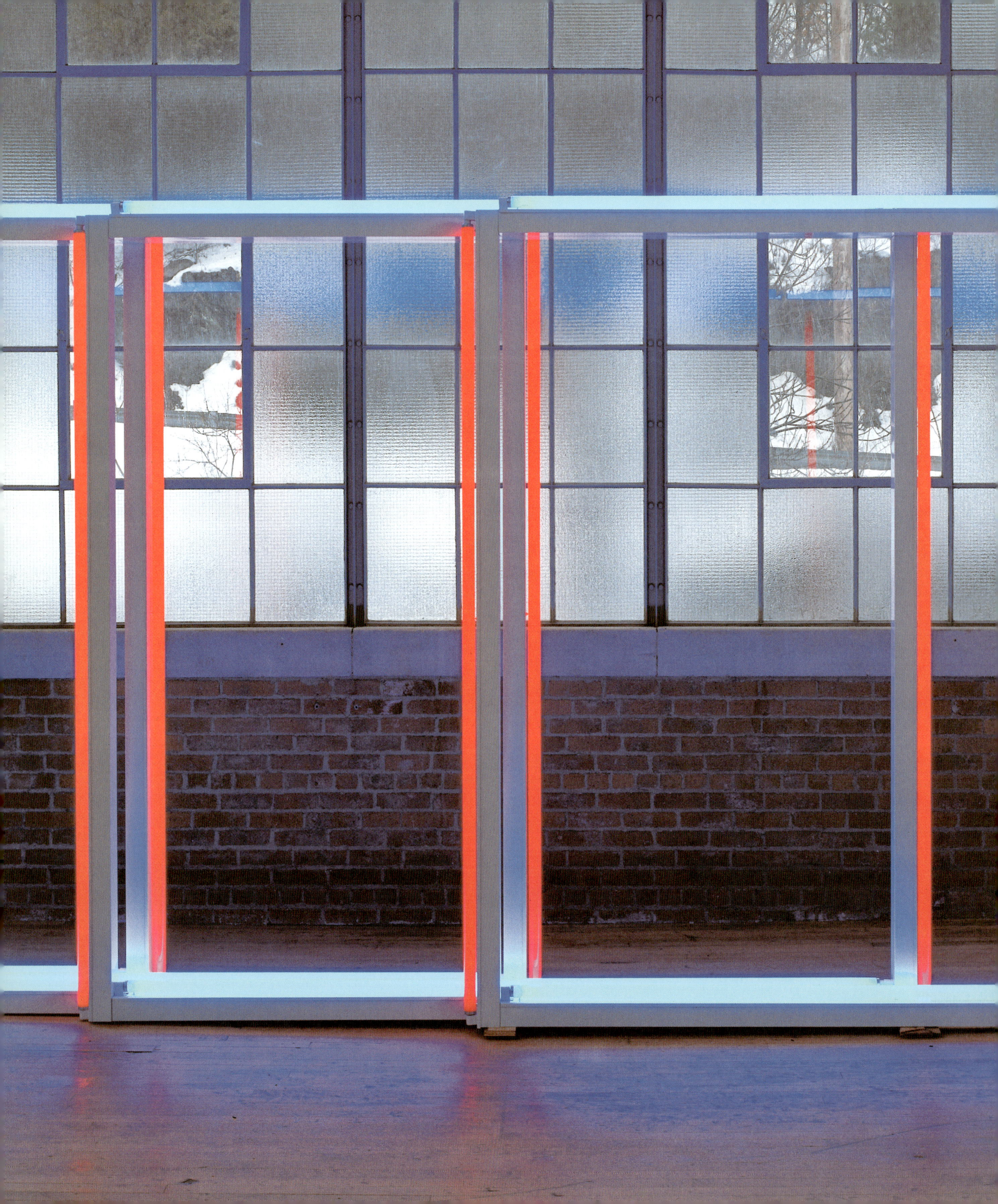

Dan Flavin

Dan Flavin was born in 1933 in New York City, where he later studied art history at the New School for Social Research (1956) and Columbia University (1957–59). His first solo show was at the Judson Gallery, New York, in 1961. Flavin made his first work with electric light that same year, and he began using commercial fluorescent bulbs in 1963. Major exhibitions of Flavin's work include those at the Museum of Contemporary Art, Chicago (1967), the National Gallery of Canada, Ottawa (1969), and the Staatliche Kunsthalle, Baden-Baden (1989). In 1983, Dia opened the Dan Flavin Art Institute in Bridgehampton, New York, a permanent exhibition designed by the artist in a converted firehouse and open to the public each summer. In 1992 Flavin created a monumental installation for the reopening of the Solomon R. Guggenheim Museum, New York. He died in 1996, leaving designs for a light installation for Milan's Chiesa Rossa that was realized posthumously with Dia's support. Flavin's last completed work, *untitled* (1996) occupies the stairwell at Dia's exhibition space in Chelsea.

untitled, 1970 (detail)

Outside painting and sculpture, few artists are more identified with a particular medium than Dan Flavin. After 1963, and except for his drawings and prints, Flavin's work was composed almost entirely of light, in the form of commercially available fluorescent tubes in ten colors (blue, green, pink, red, yellow, ultraviolet, and four whites) and five shapes (one circular and four straight fixtures of different lengths).

It was in 1962 that Flavin introduced his first experiments with electric light art: square monochrome paintings with attached fixtures and bulbs, which he deemed "icons." He used the term ironically in relation to its traditional religious context, explaining,

> *My icons differ from a Byzantine Christ held in majesty; they are dumb–anonymous and inglorious. They are as mute and indistinguished [sic] as the run of our architecture. My icons do not raise up the blessed savior in elaborate cathedrals. They are constructed concentrations celebrating barren rooms. They bring a limited light.*[1]

By 1963 Flavin had come to eschew any medium of painting or collage in favor of simple, unadorned, commercially produced fluorescent light fixtures and tubes. And by 1965 he had effectively summed up the major components of his art:

> *In time, I came to these conclusions about what I had found in fluorescent light, and about what might be done with it plastically: Now the entire interior spatial container and its parts–wall, floor, and ceiling–could support this strip of light but would not restrict its act of light except to enfold it. . . . Realizing this, I knew that the actual space of a room could be broken down and played with by planting illusions of real light (electric light) at crucial junctures in the room's composition. For example, if you press an eight-foot fluorescent lamp*

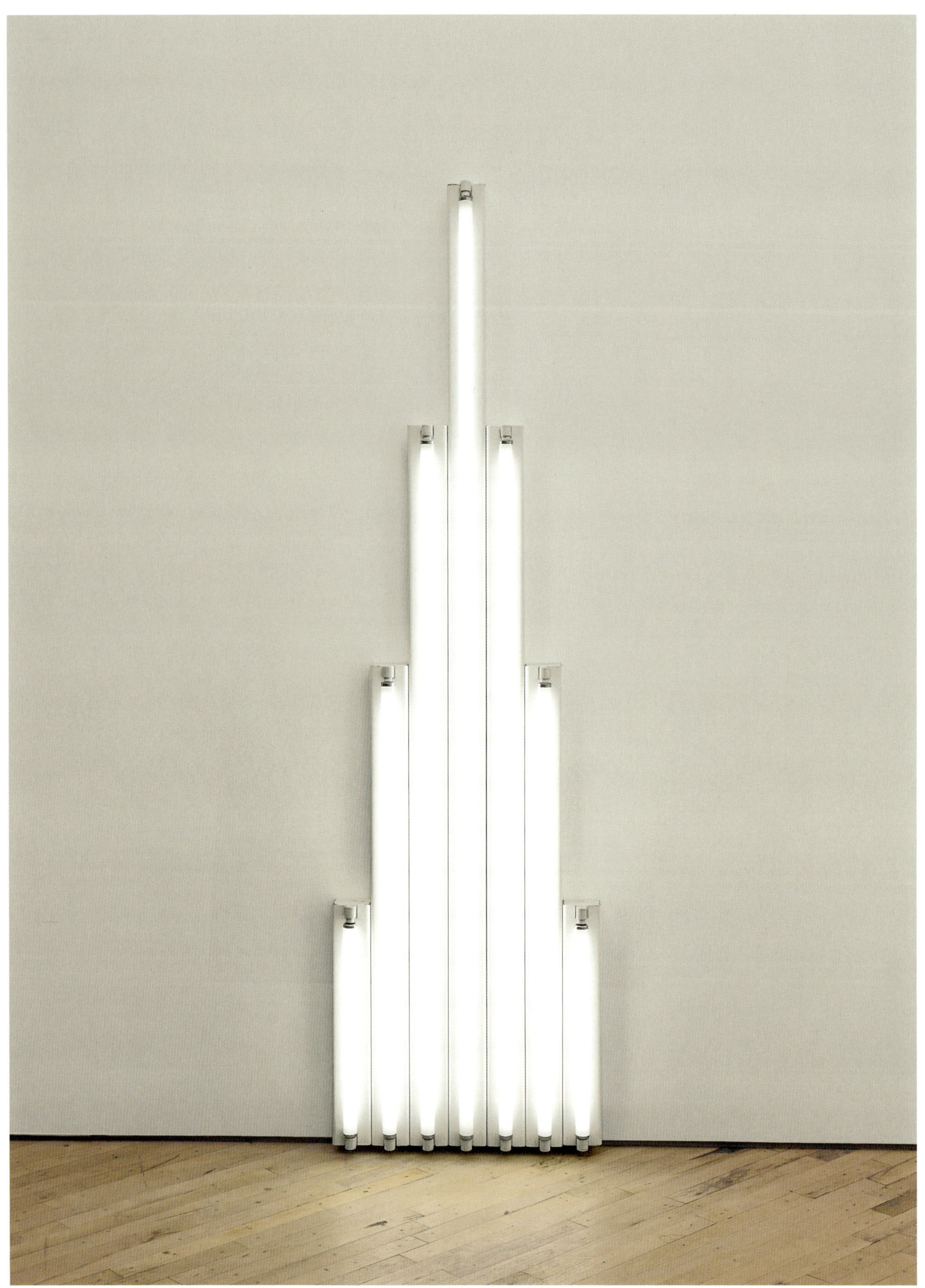

> *into the vertical climb of a corner, you can destroy that corner by glare and doubled shadow. A piece of wall can be visually disintegrated from the whole into a separate triangle by plunging a diagonal of light from edge to edge on the wall; that is, side to floor, for instance. . . . What has art been for me? In the past, I have known it (basically) as a sequence of implicit decisions to combine traditions of painting and sculpture in architecture with acts of electric light defining space.*[2]

Despite his dedication of each untitled work to a person or a personal reflection, and his own deep awareness of the historical symbolism of light in art,[3] Flavin always refused to attach any symbolic or referential significance to his works:

> *It is what it is, and it ain't nothin' else. . . . Everything is clearly, openly, plainly delivered. There is no overwhelming spirituality you are supposed to come into contact with. I like my use of light to be openly situational in the sense that there is no invitation to meditate, to contemplate. It's in a sense a "get-in-get-out" situation. And it is very easy to understand. One might not think of light as a matter of fact, but I do. And it is, as I said, as plain and open and direct an art as you will ever find.*[4]

Flavin's simplified formal vocabulary can be related to the work of contemporaries such as Carl Andre, Walter De Maria, and Donald Judd, all of whom have been called Minimalist artists for their reduction of formal devices, their emphasis on serial and rational rather than gestural forms, and their promotion of phenomenological rather than symbolic or narrative strategies. These artists had gained much of their inspiration from the fundamental structures of certain modernist predecessors, such as Constantin Brancusi. Flavin's admiration for Brancusi's *Endless Column* (1918) was made manifest when he dedicated his first work in fluorescent light, *the diagonal of personal ecstasy (the diagonal of May 25, 1963)*, to the Romanian artist. "Both structures had a uniform elementary visual nature, but they were intended to excel their obvious visible limitations of length and their apparent lack of complication," he wrote.[5] The systematic repetition of form seen in *Endless Column* persisted in Flavin's work, albeit usually oriented horizontally, as in *untitled* (1970), a large-scale barrier in red and blue light (the first version of which was made for Judd's loft on Spring Street, New York). Flavin had invented the "barrier" in 1966 as a freestanding series of fixtures that physically block a passageway or a segment of a space with light.

Flavin also proclaimed respect for the work of other modernist abstract artists, most notably perhaps the innovators of the Russian avant-garde, particularly Vladimir Tatlin, to whom he dedicated his most sustained series of works, "monuments" for V. Tatlin (1964–90). The far-from-incidental relationship of these works to Tatlin's illuminates both formal inventions in Flavin's work and its context within the history of art.

Tatlin's first major public work was the sculptural installation of collaged industrial materials that he displayed in a 1915 exhibition with Kasimir Malevich's painting *Black Square*. Both works were installed in corners of the gallery, thereby claiming the unused margins of their exhibition space, while also overtly referring to the religious icons that traditionally hung in the corner of a room in many Russian homes. Tatlin's and Malevich's occupations of the corners with their new abstract "icons" were an attempt to create a radical, unique, and dynamic artistic vocabulary that expressed the human aspirations of the impending industrial and social revolution of the twentieth century.

"monument" 1 for V. Tatlin, 1964

Flavin's career-long preoccupation with the corner of the gallery implicitly echoes the Russians' gesture of engaging spaces traditionally not utilized for painting and sculpture; nevertheless, his corner works refute the simultaneous religious symbolism and utopian social ambition that are epitomized by Tatlin's sculpture.

Tatlin's greatest work was *Monument to the Third International* (1920), the planned but unrealized spiral tower for which Flavin's "monuments" are named. Yet Flavin noted, "I always use 'monuments' in quotes to emphasize the ironic humor of temporary monuments. These 'monuments' only survive as long as the light system is useful (2,100 hours)."[6] Flavin presented his appropriation of commercial light fixtures—quintessential products of our industrialized society—not as a timeless celebration of a revolutionary culture, as Tatlin's work was intended to be, but as ontological fact, tangible and temporal. He used his humorous historical reference to Tatlin precisely to separate his work from the kind of symbolic significance to which Tatlin aspired. At the same time, though, he clearly revered Tatlin as a tragic human individual, and his "frustrated, insistent attitude to attempt to combine artistry and engineering."[7]

Having employed generic mass-produced light fixtures in order to deny his light art any transcendental significance, and having also denied those same light fixtures their simple utilitarian function by calling them art, the irony of Flavin's gestures and use of terms like "icon" is obvious. Less obvious is the almost limitless plastic potential the artist devised and demonstrated in his systematic application of the limited vocabulary of commercially available light fixtures and light bulbs.

M.G.

notes

1 Dan Flavin, in *Dan Flavin: three installations in fluorescent light* (Cologne: Wallraf-Richartz-Museum and Kunsthalle Köln, 1973), p. 83. This comment is taken from a "record" book entry dated August 9, 1962.

2 Flavin, "' . . . in daylight or cool white': an autobiographical sketch," *Artforum* 4, no. 4 (December 1965), p. 24. Flavin later revised and republished this text in several exhibition catalogues.

3 Flavin attended a Roman Catholic seminary; although he rejected that path, he began his art education with religious art. He was also a knowledgeable collector of art past and present.

4 Flavin, quoted in Michael Gibson, "The Strange Case of the Fluorescent Tube," *Art International* 1 (Autumn 1987), p. 105.

5 Flavin, "' . . . in daylight or cool white': an autobiographical sketch," p. 24.

6 Flavin, quoted in Suzanne Muchnic, "Flavin Exhibit: His Artistry Comes to Light," *Los Angeles Times*, April 23, 1984. sec. 6, p. 2.

7 Ibid. Muchnic is quoting from a wall text Flavin wrote for "'monuments' to V. Tatlin from Dan Flavin," an exhibition at the Temporary Contemporary space of the Museum of Contemporary Art, Los Angeles, in 1984.

right *"monument" for V. Tatlin*, 1968, and *"monument" for V. Tatlin*, 1969
pages 142–143 *"monument" for V. Tatlin XI*, 1964, *"monument" for V. Tatlin*, 1966, *"monument" for V. Tatlin*, 1966–69, and *untitled*, 1970
pages 144–145 *untitled*, 1970

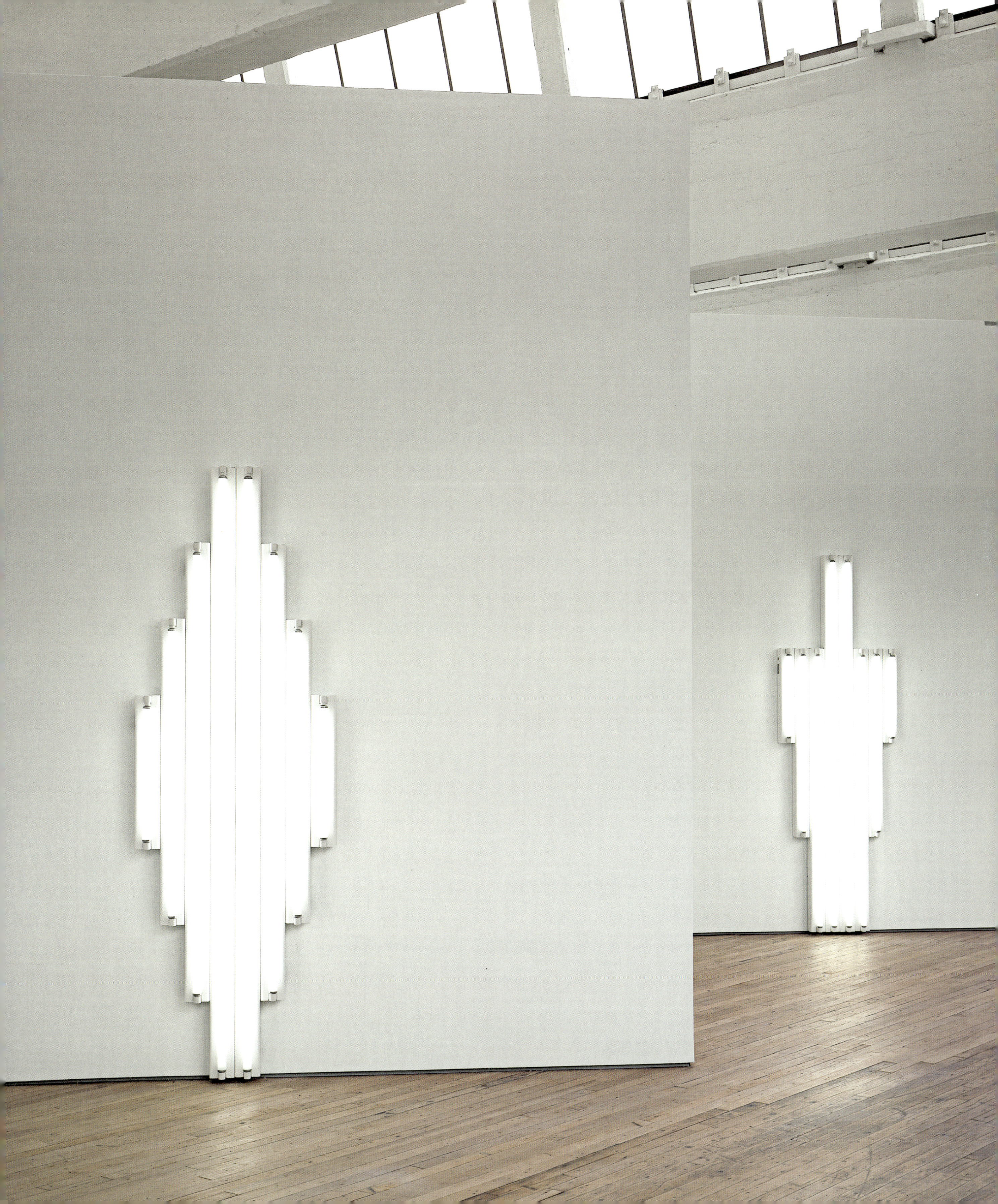

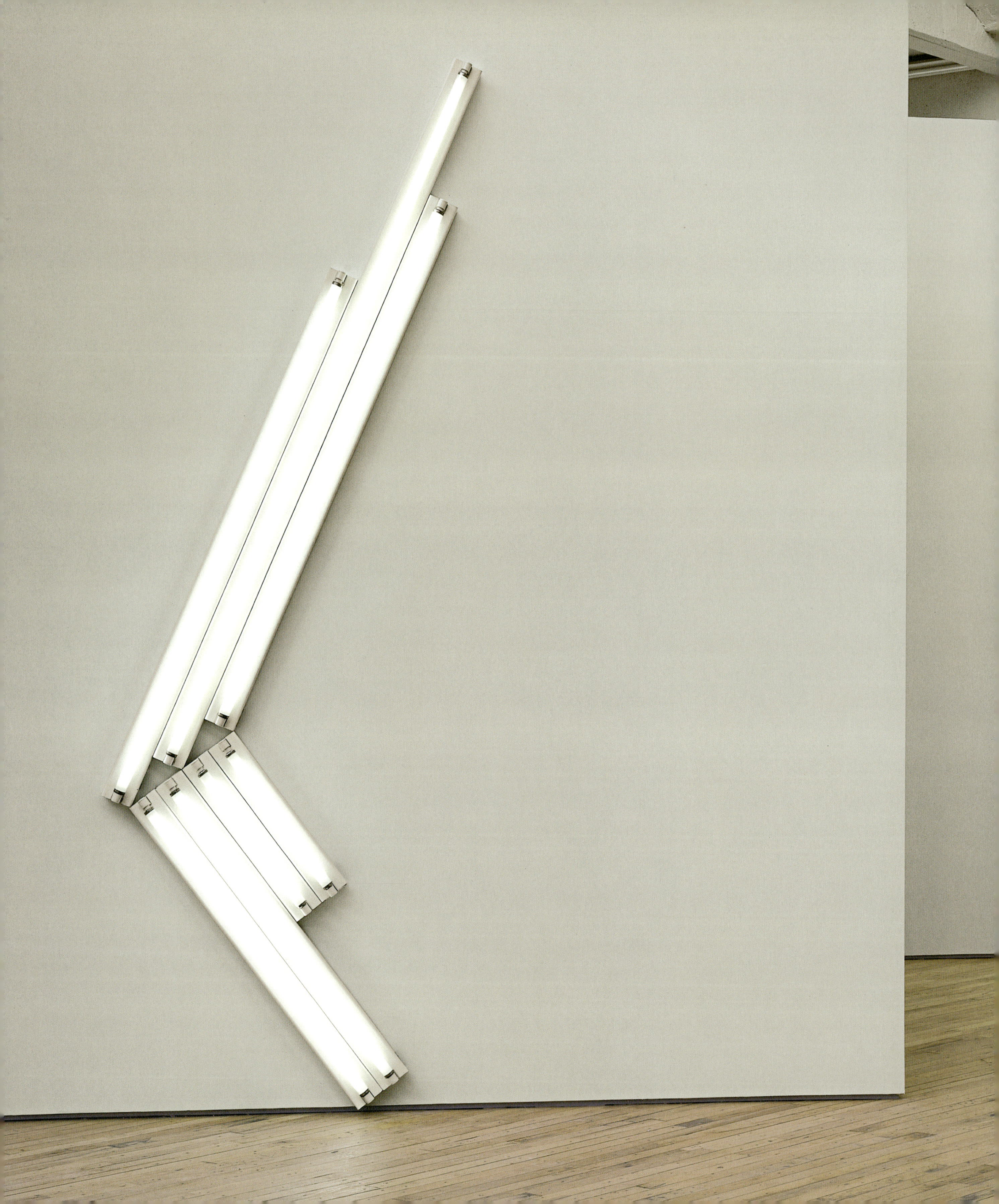

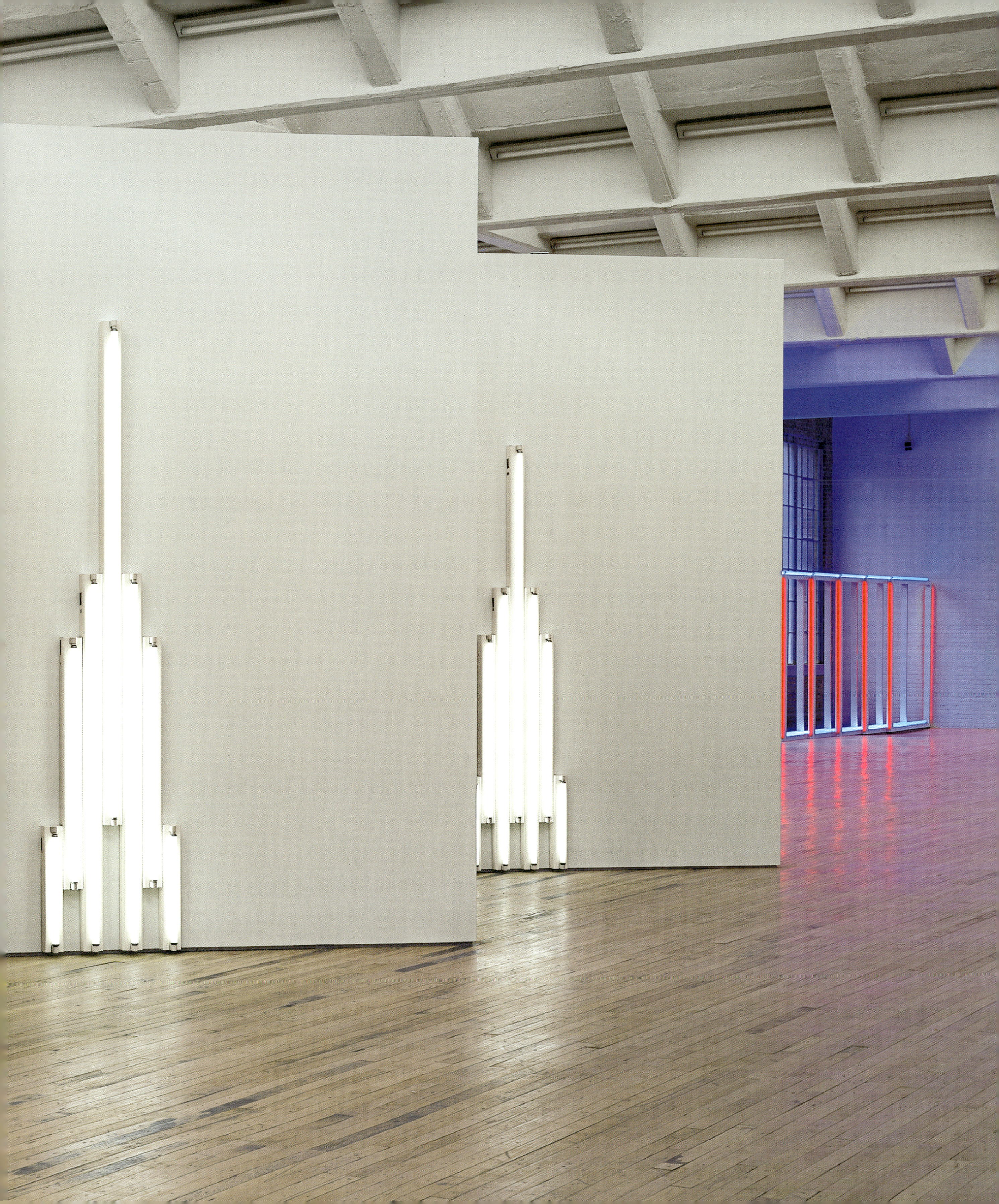

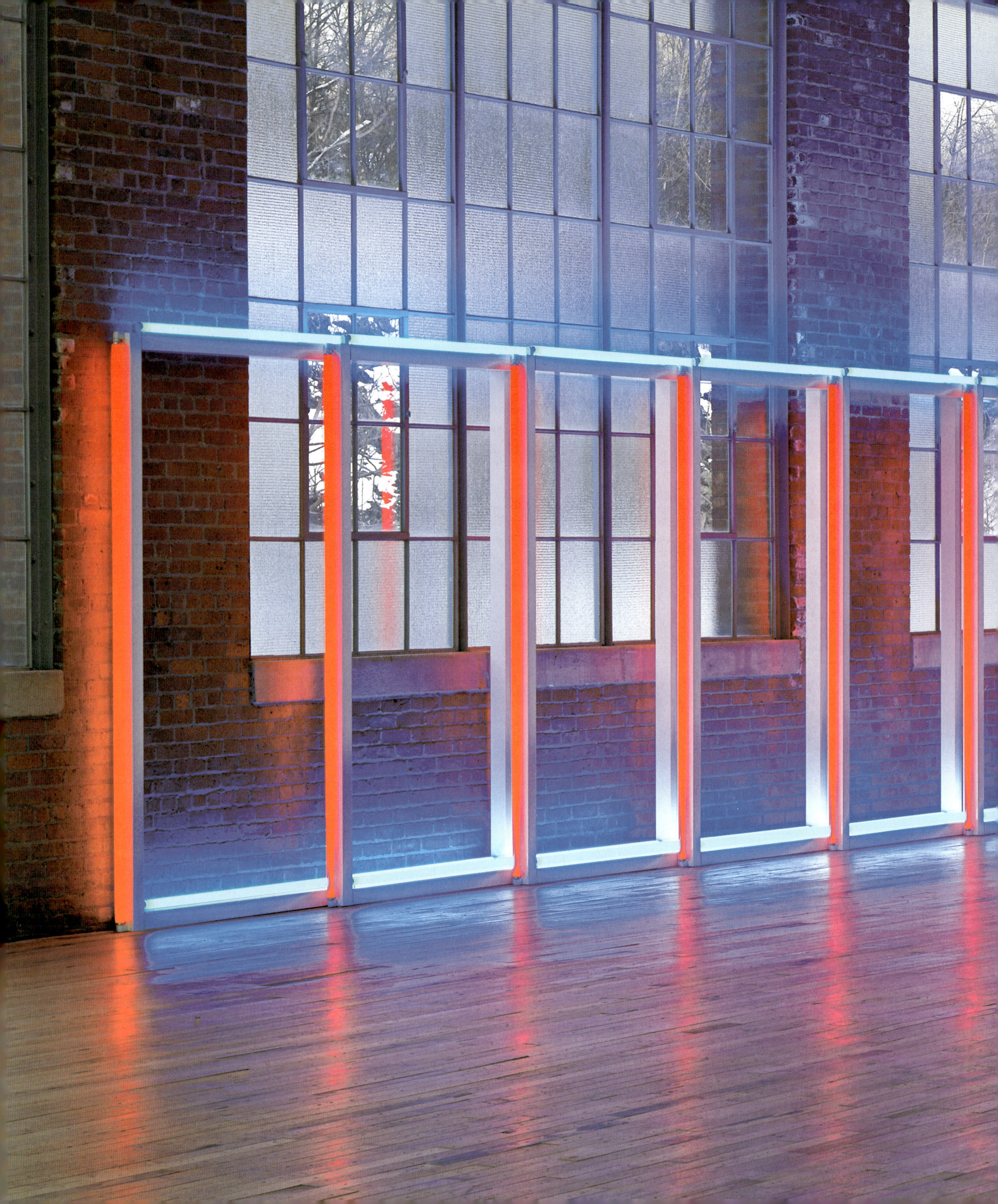

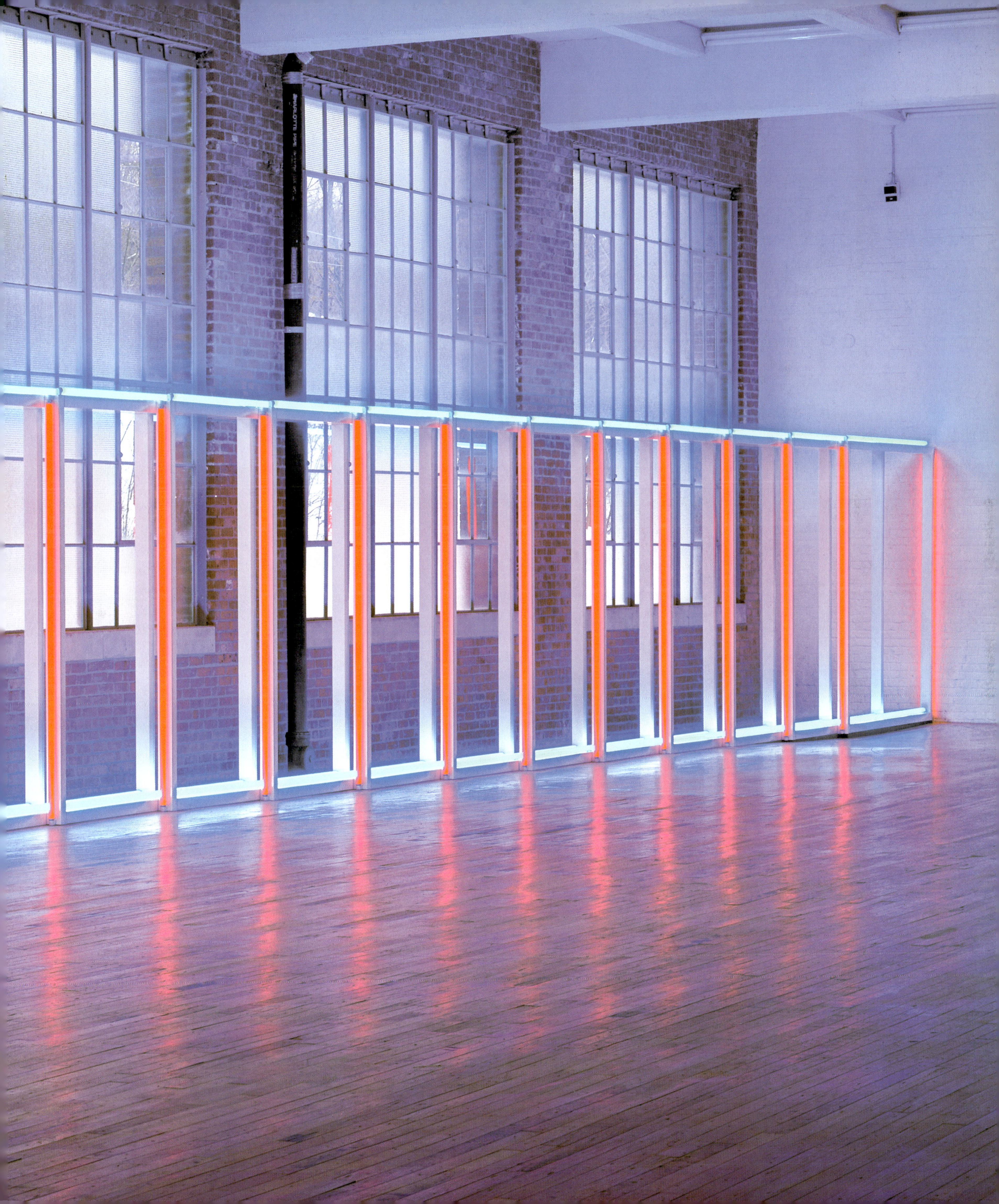

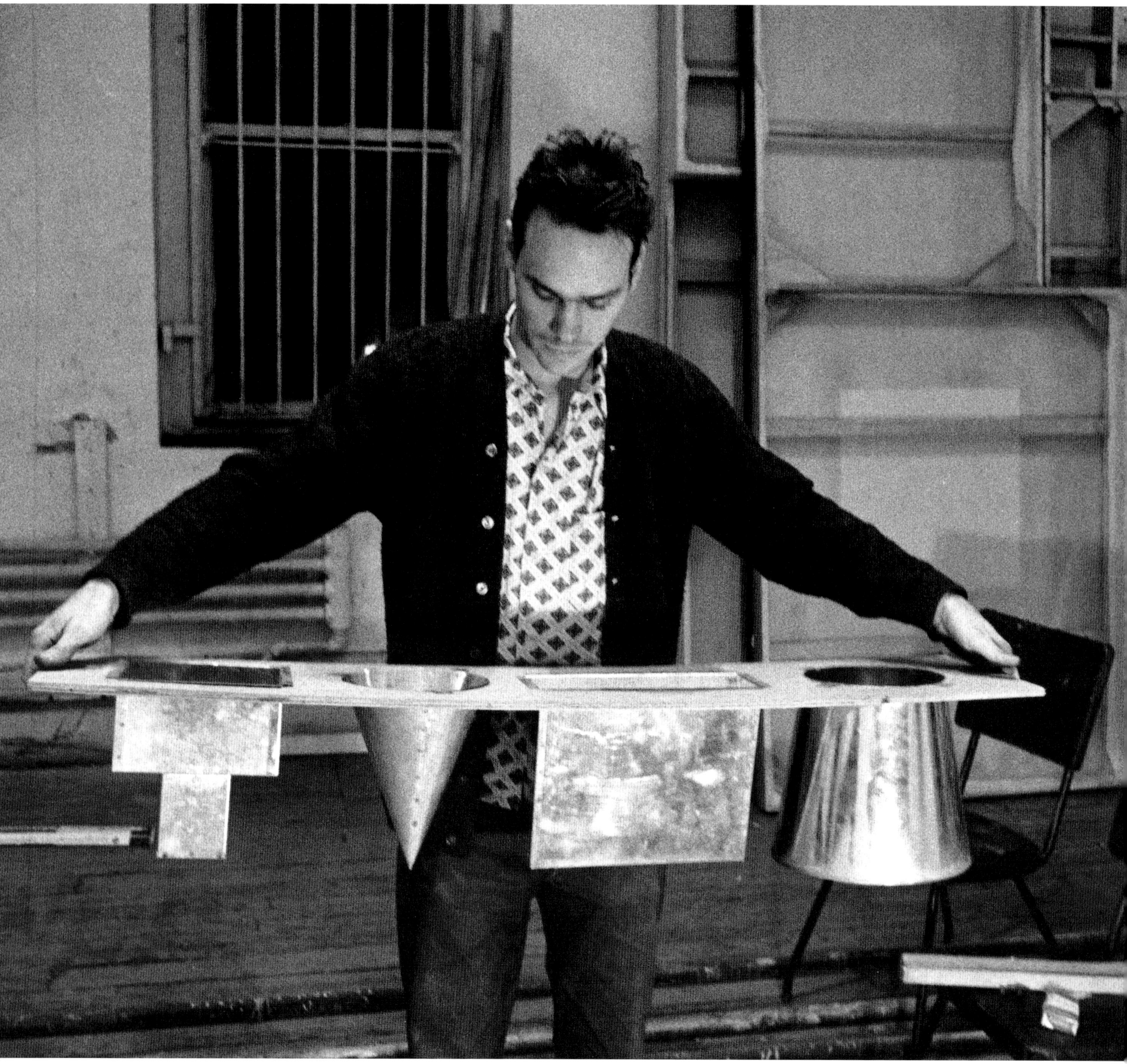

Michael Heizer

Michael Heizer was born in Berkeley, California, in 1944, the son of the anthropologist Robert Heizer. After briefly attending the San Francisco Art Institute in 1963–64, he moved to New York in 1966. In 1967 Heizer began creating large Earthworks, primarily in California and Nevada. For his first one-person show, at the Galerie Heiner Friedrich, Munich, in 1969, he removed 1,000 tons of earth in a conical shape to create *Munich Depression*. He followed this with *Double Negative*, a displacement of over 240,000 tons of earth to make two vast incisions opposite one another on the edge of Virgin River mesa, Nevada. Heizer's next one-person show was at the Dwan Gallery, New York, in 1970, and that same year he exhibited in the International Pavilion at the Venice Biennale. Major exhibitions of his work have been staged at institutions such as the Museum Folkwang, Essen (1979), and the Museum of Contemporary Art, Los Angeles (1984). Heizer lives in Nevada, where he continues to work on *City*, a sculptural complex begun in 1970 currently supported by Dia and Lannan Foundation.

Michael Heizer in 1967 with model for *North, East, South, West*, 1967

In the mid-1960s, during the same period that Michael Heizer was making large-scale, shaped, "negative" paintings in his New York City studio, he began a series of trips to his home states of Nevada and California to experiment on the expansive raw canvas of the American desert landscape, where he created "negative" sculpture. The genre that he and his colleague Walter De Maria invented there–later dubbed "Earth art" or "Land art"–changed the course of modern art history. Working largely outside the confines of the gallery and the museum, Heizer went on to redefine sculpture in terms of scale, mass, gesture, and process, creating a virtual lexicon of three-dimensional form.

Heizer's *Double Negative* (1969) comprises two giant rectangular cuts (and the space in between them) in the irregular cliff edges of a tall desert mesa near Overton, Nevada. This monumental piece is iconic of the period and of works made in and of the landscape, as are Robert Smithson's later *Spiral Jetty* (1970), in Utah, and De Maria's *The Lightning Field* (1977), in New Mexico. Facing each other in the cliffs on either side of a wide cleft in the mesa, the cuts define rectilinear spaces from which bulldozers have removed the sandstone strata and rock. These spaces, which would roughly absorb the Empire State Building lying on its side, might as aptly be compared to the large-scale feats of modern engineering, or to the monumental earthen architecture of ancient times, as to sculpture. Thus, Heizer's work constitutes a challenge to sculpture's long history.

Although the "sculptural volume" of *Double Negative* was created by a massive movement of earth, performed with the help of heavy machinery, it isn't physical at all. Instead it is made literally of nothing, of negative space: the volume that traditionally defines a sculpture is described in these works by a void, by absence rather than presence. The first such "negative" form in Heizer's work was *North, East, South, West*, which the artist produced in wood and sheet metal in 1967, putting two of the four elements, *North* and *South*, in the ground in the Sierra Nevada in California. The work has now been constructed in its entirety as a permanent feature of Dia's museum in Beacon, in the size and material (weathering steel) that Heizer originally specified for it. These four diverse sculptural elements—two stacked cubic forms, one larger and one smaller (*North*); a cone (*South*); a triangular trough (*West*); and an inverted truncated cone (*East*)—together measure more than 125 feet in length, and sink from the floor of the gallery to a depth of 20 feet. When the work was first developed, such dimensions had no precedent in the art of recent times.

Heizer prefers the term *size* to *scale* in descriptions of his work, in part to emphasize the factual and visual implications of the actual distance traversed by the eye or on foot in viewing it. The sheer physical dimensions of *North, East, South, West*, and its physical integration into, or displacement of, the fabric of the Dia building, force an entirely different viewing experience from that of traditional sculpture in the round, an experience that is a function less of movement to allow multiple viewpoints than of the extended journey in time and space required to comprehend it. And the fact that the sculpture literally displaces the floor on which the visitor walks creates a sense of potential physical danger that further challenges the viewing experience.

The architectural scale and construction of Heizer's work, particularly *Double Negative* and *City*, begun in 1970 and still under construction in Nevada, often call forth comparisons to the megalithic monuments of ancient cultures. The son of an anthropologist, Heizer acknowledges numerous ancient sources for some of his forms but sees the comparison as more apt in the realm of effect than of specific reference:

> *It is interesting to build a sculpture that attempts to create an atmosphere of awe. Small works are said to do this but it is not my experience. Immense, architecturally sized sculpture creates both the object and the atmosphere. Awe is a state of mind equivalent to religious experience, I think if people feel commitment they feel something has been transcended. . . . I think that large sculptures produced in the '60s and '70s by a number of artists were reminiscent of the time when societies were committed to the construction of massive, significant works of art.*[1]

The simplified, monumental geometric forms of *North, East, South, West* also share affinities with futuristic Constructivist sculpture and modernist architecture. In sum, the piece suggests the underlying Euclidean lexicon of basic three-dimensional forms—box, cone, and wedge—essential for all sculpture, ancient and modern. Going more deeply still, the forms suggest the molecular crystalline morphology from which all physical shapes in matter are derived.[2]

The emphasis on elemental vocabularies of form and gesture is key to Heizer's work. His most massive single (positive) sculptural shape, *45°, 90°, 180°/Geometric Extraction*, is a focal point of his ongoing *City* project; he also created a slightly smaller version (made of industrial corrugated cardboard) of it for an exhibition at the Museum of Contemporary Art, Los Angeles, in 1984. The work comprises eighteen diverse geometric forms, but its title refers to its feature

North, East, South, West, 1967, Sierra Nevada (*South* on left; *North* on right)

elements, three rectangular blocks respectively placed at a forty-five-degree angle, vertically, and horizontally. Set on a rectangular plaza, the forms are separate volumes cut from a single triangular monolith that was itself a by-product of a drilling plan that Heizer originally developed for the removal of masses of stone block from a cliff for a vertical sculpture. As in *Dragged Mass* (1971), which is the result of earth displaced by literally dragging a massive thirty-ton block of stone over the ground, Heizer's "forms" are sometimes less designs than the results of a practical physical process.

Another outdoor work, *Adjacent, Against, Upon* (1976), comprises three poured-concrete geometric shapes, each so paired with a comparably huge natural rock as to enumerate the possible relationships between a movable object and a fixed one: as the title describes, one rock is adjacent to, one is against, and one stands upon its concrete counterpart.[3] The title *45°, 90°, 180°* describes another essential axiom of three-dimensional potential: any object can stand, lean, or lie in relationship to a horizontal and a vertical plane. Similarly, the title *North, East, South, West*—defining the cardinal points of the compass as well as describing in total the 360° plane of the floor or ground—suggests a primary set of conditions that rest at the core of more complex variations.

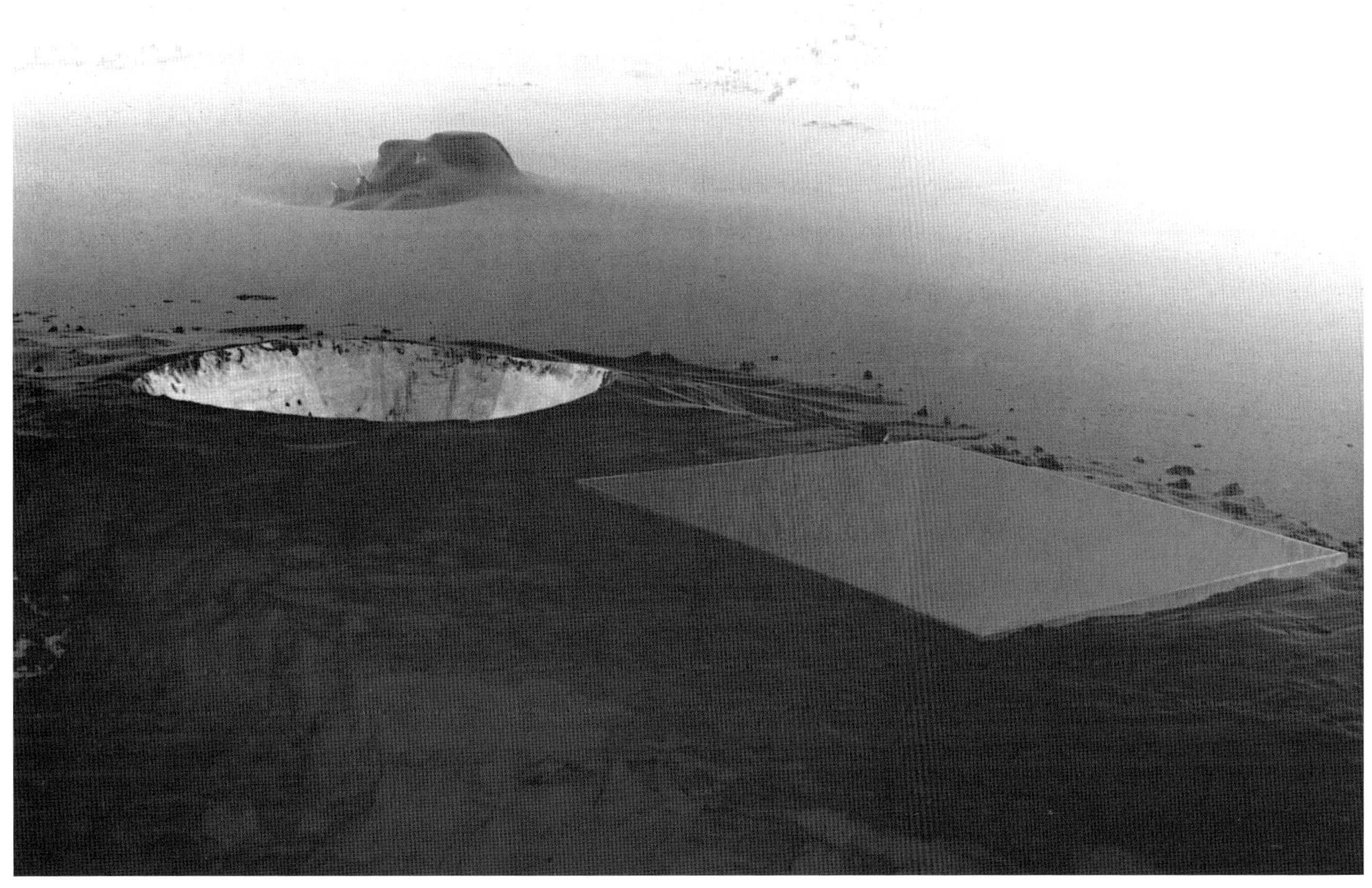

Described like this by the artist himself in his titles, Heizer's work can seem less art than a collection of data or a list of fundamental laws of sculpture. Yet, to the contrary, these matter-of-fact titles only partially account for the experiential effects of each sculpture, because the translation of any abstract principle into actual form in time and space involves countless formal decisions. Even the most minimal artistic intentions, then, are infused with the unique perspective and biases of the artist and of the culture within which the work is made. The "minimal" shapes in Heizer's sculpture abound with references to the objects and architectures of ancient cultures, to the language of sculpture, and even to the underlying crystalline morphology defining all shapes. But what lies at the core of Heizer's art is his extreme reduction of such myriad specific sources.

Ancient sculpture may have specific commemorative or religious meaning to convey, but for Heizer it generates its sense of awe through its intense "commitment" to making an "architecturally sized" work that becomes "both the object and the atmosphere." Those issues of commitment and scale can equally be embodied in the contemporary artist's intense and self-reflexive process of abstraction—even negation—with the same overall results.

M.G.

notes

1 Michael Heizer, in an interview with Julia Brown, in Brown, ed., *Michael Heizer: Sculpture in Reverse* (Los Angeles: Museum of Contemporary Art, 1984), p. 33.

2 On crystalline morphology, Heizer references James D. Dana, *Manual of Mineralogy and Petrography* (New York: John Wiley & Sons, 1889).

3 The two materials, concrete and natural rock, are also contrasted by their different crystalline morphology.

right Drawing for *North, East, South, West,* 1999
pages 152, 154–155 *North, East, South, West,* 1967/2002
page 153 Detail showing *North,* 1967

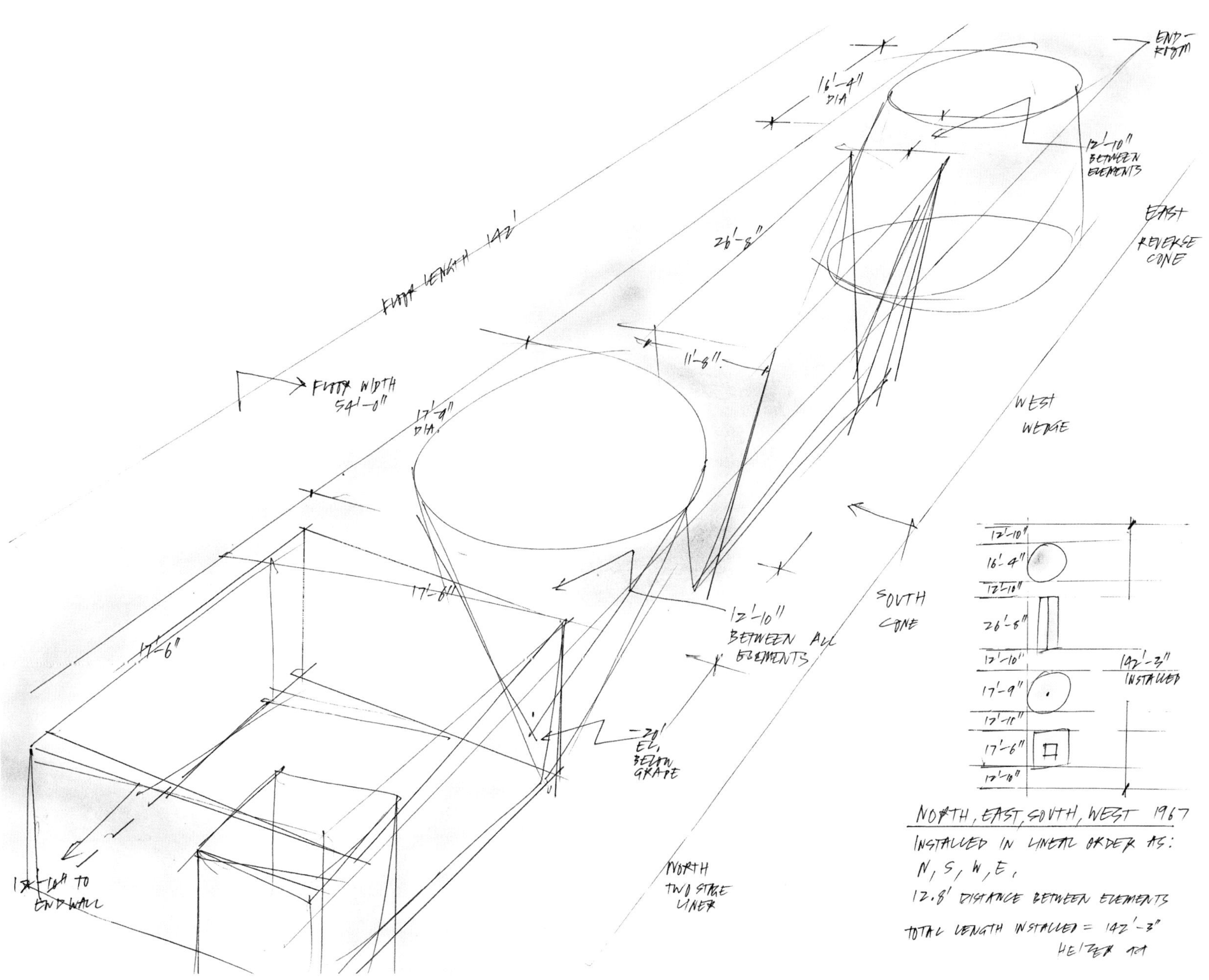

16'-4"
DIA
12'-10"
BETWEEN
ELEMENTS
EAST
REVERSE
CONE
26'-8"
FLOOR LENGTH 142'
FLOOR WIDTH
54'-0"
17'-9"
DIA.
11'-8"
WEST
WEDGE
17'-6"
12'-10"
BETWEEN ALL
ELEMENTS
SOUTH
CONE
20'
EL.
BELOW
GRADE
TO
ENDWALL
NORTH
TWO STAGE
LINER
12'-10"
16'-4"
12'-10"
26'-8"
12'-10"
142'-3"
INSTALLED
17'-9"
12'-10"
17'-6"
12'-10"
NORTH, EAST, SOUTH, WEST 1967
INSTALLED IN LINEAL ORDER AS:
N, S, W, E,
12.8' DISTANCE BETWEEN ELEMENTS
TOTAL LENGTH INSTALLED = 142'-3"

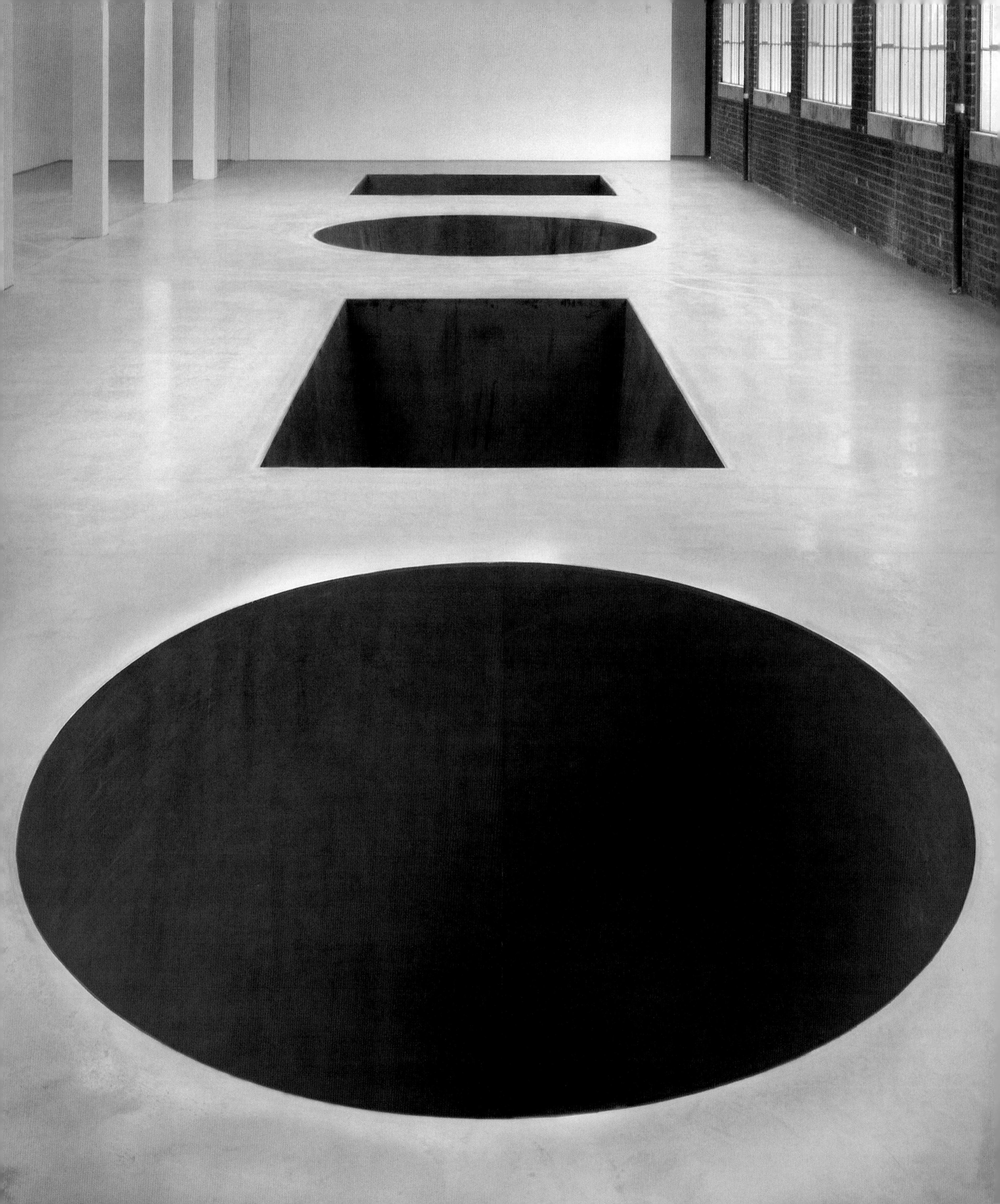

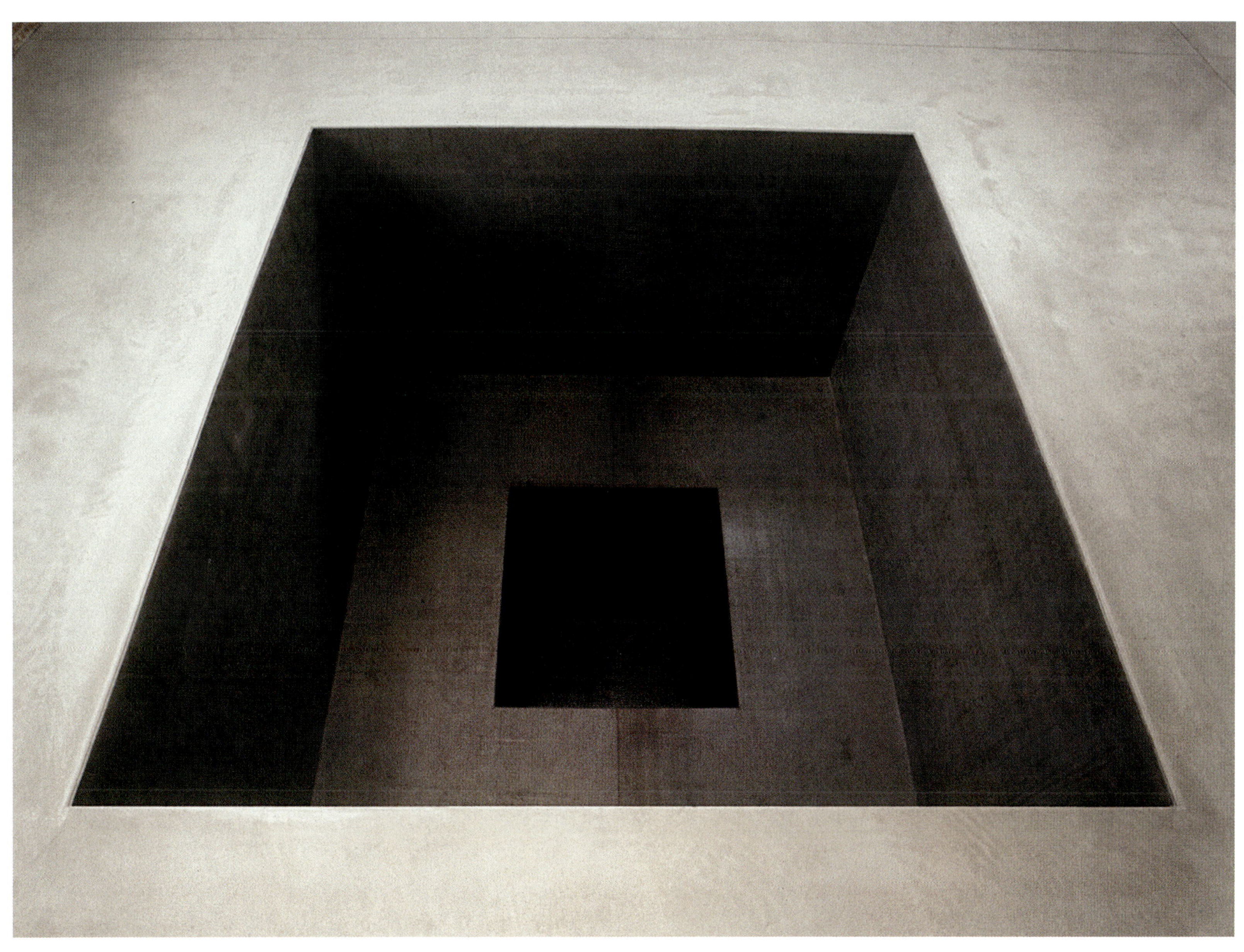

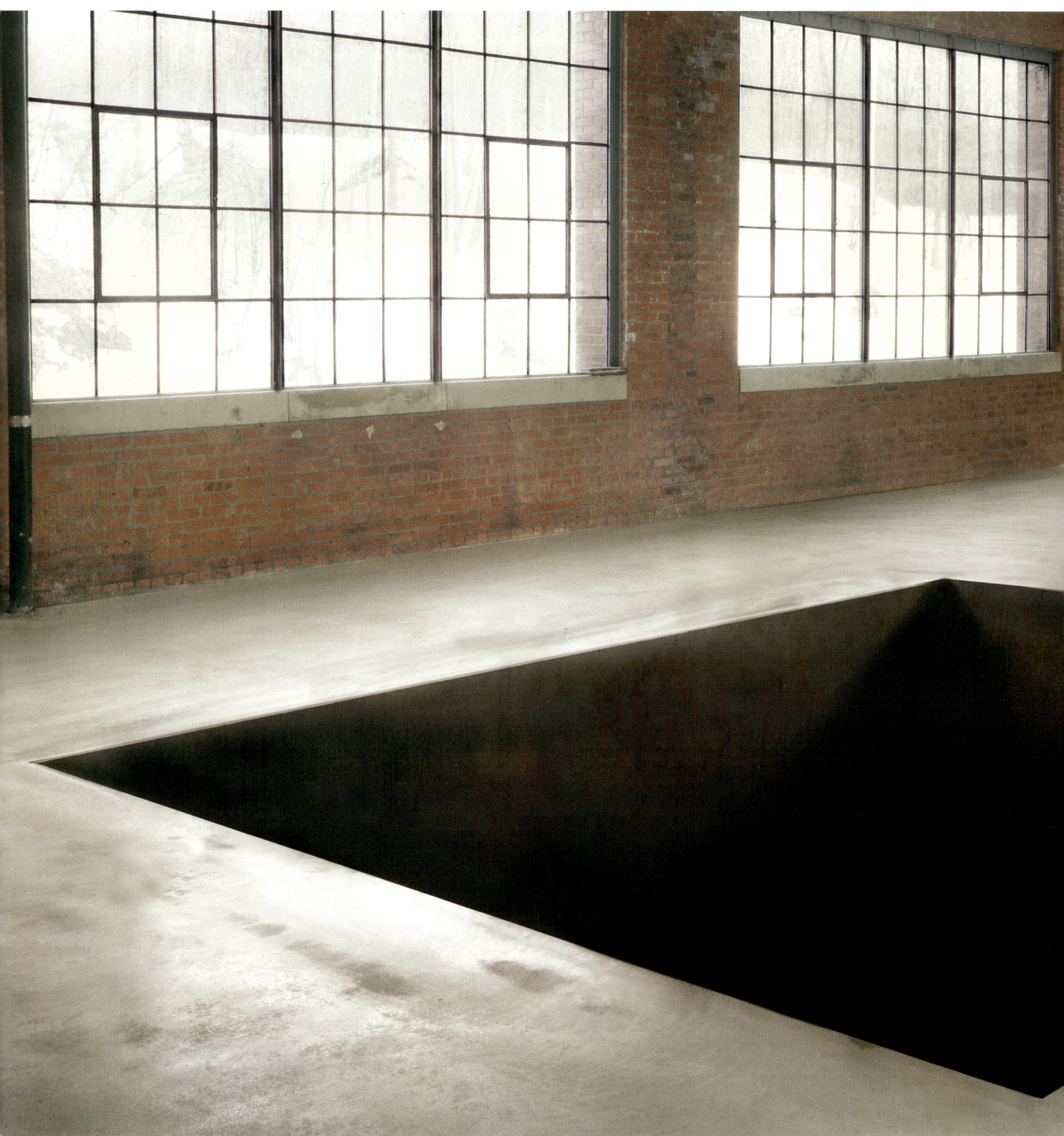

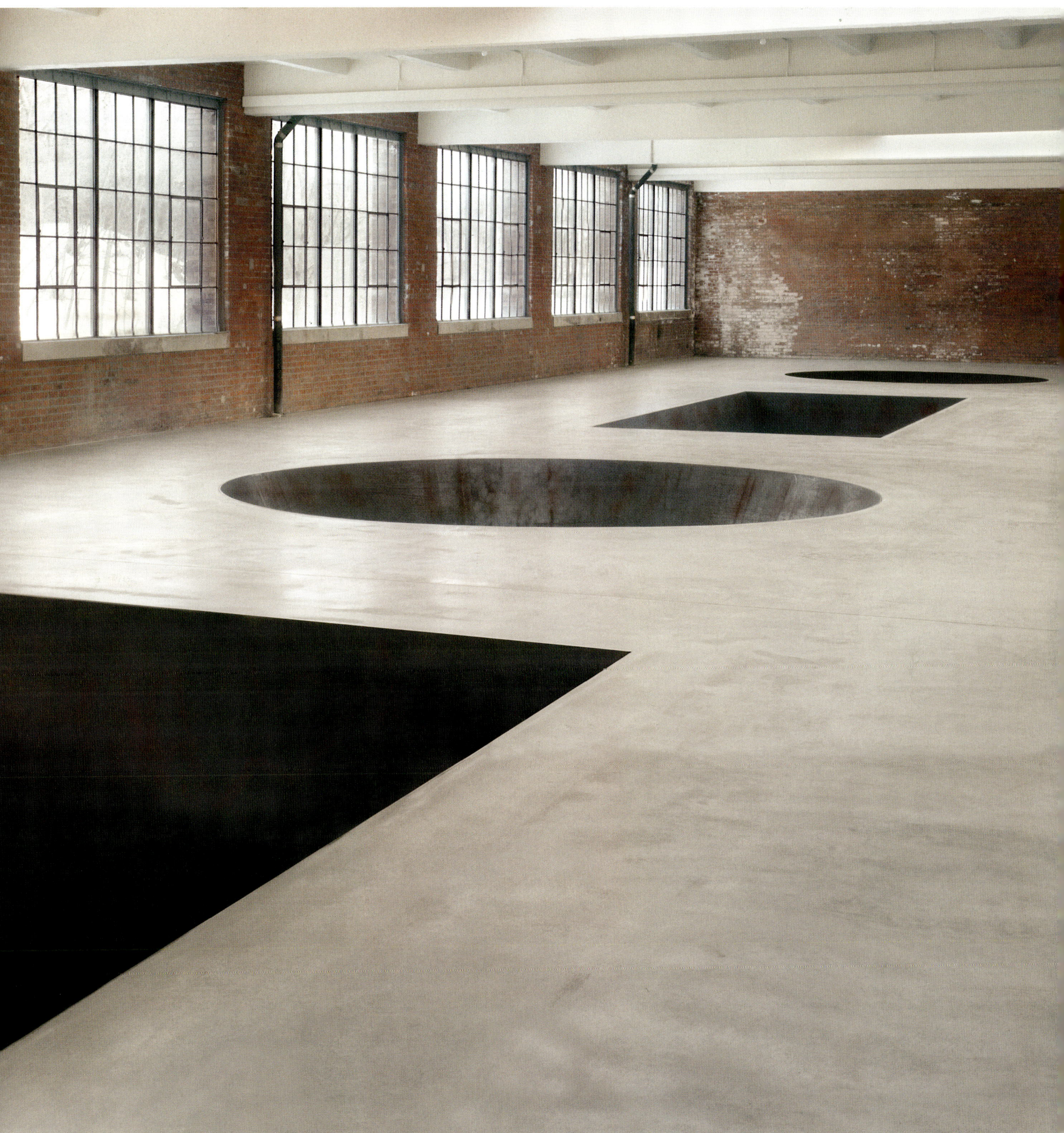

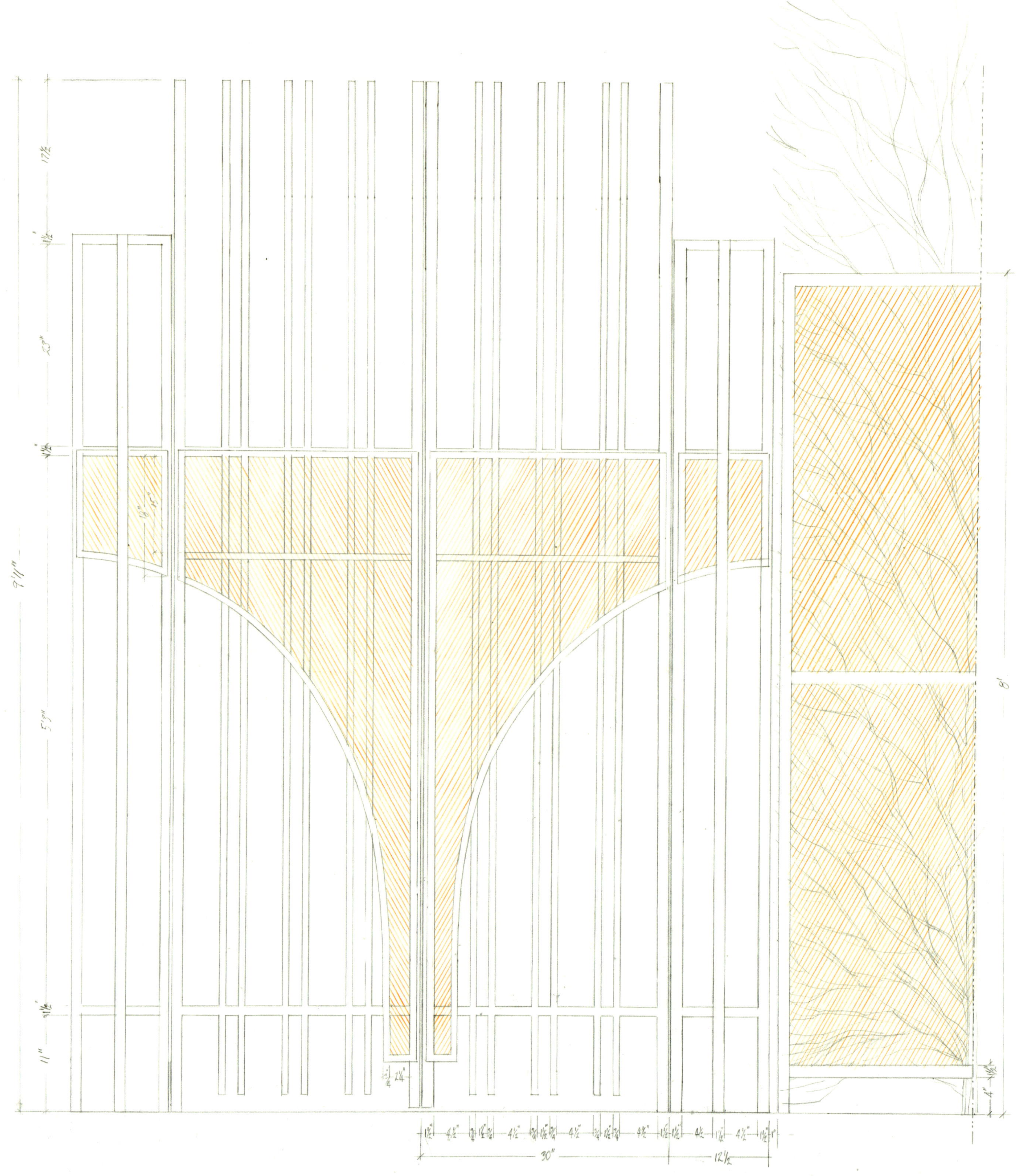

17½
23"
9'4"
53"
11"
8'
30"
12½

Robert Irwin

Robert Irwin was born in Long Beach, California, in 1928, and studied in Los Angeles at the Otis Art Institute (1948–50), the Jepson Art Institute (1951), and the Chinouard School of Art (1952–54). Since his first solo exhibition, at the Landau Gallery, Los Angeles, in 1957, he has exhibited widely in galleries and museums in North America and abroad. Irwin received a MacArthur Fellowship in 1984. In 1993, the Museum of Contemporary Art, Los Angeles, initiated a major retrospective of his work, which subsequently traveled to Paris, Madrid, and Cologne. Among his numerous public projects, the most recent is the monumental garden he designed for the Getty Center in Los Angeles, which opened in 1997. Dia held a two-part exhibition of Irwin's work in 1998–99, showing two site-specific installations, *Prologue: x18*[3] and *Excursus: Homage to the Square*[3]. Irwin currently lives and works in San Diego.

Rendering of iron gate for Dia:Beacon, 2001–2002

Robert Irwin's work at Dia:Beacon may elude the casual visitor. It consists of a master plan for the museum and its outdoor spaces, as well as design work on numerous aspects of the project, most notably the extensive landscape environment, where Irwin was involved in every aspect of the plantings, paving and fencing, and windows and doors.

Most important, Irwin helped Dia consider the design of the Beacon project in experiential and environmental terms as a totality—from the visitor's entrance, by car or by foot, down a driveway marked at its top by a gate and a new copper beech tree, through an orchard that serves as a parking lot, into a plaza that signals one's arrival at the museum, into either a café and bookshop or the newly constructed entrance to the galleries, and from there down any of a number of possible paths through the museum's interior and into the artists' spaces, each specifically designed by the artist in question and/or by Dia to accommodate the work on view. Irwin's work in Beacon lay across the borders of a number of different roles—landscape designer, architect, aesthetic philosopher—in a manner completely consistent with his practice as an artist, in which, among other things, he has questioned exactly where the boundaries lie around the role of the artist today.

At the beginning of the twentieth century, artists such as Kasimir Malevich and Piet Mondrian proposed that the basis of painting could change, from representational relationships with an external world to a play of formal relationships within a work itself—Mondrian's *culture of determined relations*, as Irwin often calls it. As if in search of the reduced essence of painting, Mondrian's career moved dramatically from landscape painting, through a Cubist-inspired dissolution of pictorial space, to the rarefied and entirely abstract paintings for which he is best known. Irwin's early development moves along a similarly reductive trajectory, from Abstract Expressionist painting in the late 1950s, to more rigorously optical hand-painted line and dot paintings, to metal and plastic circular discs and prismatic columns that nearly dissolve visually at the same time that they channel and shape the light and space around them. Finally, in the early 1970s, Irwin eschewed the discrete object entirely in favor of totally environmental works that involved modifying and augmenting indoor and outdoor spaces themselves. He sees this development as foreshadowed by Mondrian, who predicted "the end of art as a thing separated from our surrounding environment." But that would not mean the end of art, Mondrian continued: "By the unification of architecture, sculpture and painting, a new plastic reality will be created. Painting and sculpture will not manifest themselves as separate objects . . . but being purely constructive will aid the creation of a surrounding not merely utilitarian or rational but also pure and complete in its beauty."[1]

For *Soft Wall*, a 1974 installation at Pace Gallery in New York City, Irwin simply cleaned and painted a rectangular gallery and hung a thin, translucent white theater scrim eighteen inches in front of one of the long walls, creating the effect of an empty room in which one wall seemed permanently out of focus. Because of its quality as a substance that defines space by slowing or heightening vision rather than creating an impenetrable barrier, scrim is a prevalent material in many of Irwin's projects, in various manifestations as fabric, translucent film, fencing, or even the branches, raw and dense in winter, of the European hornbeam trees that frame the Dia:Beacon entrance plaza.

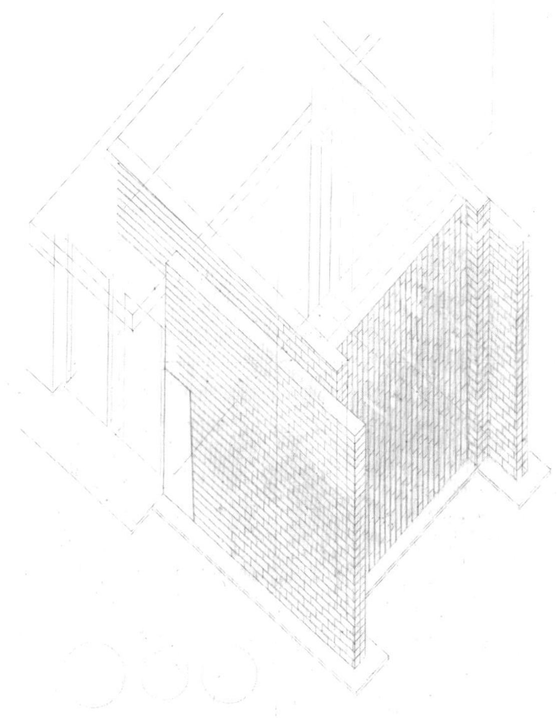

In 1975–76, at the Museum of Contemporary Art, Chicago, Irwin similarly cleared out a gallery but this time placed one long strip of black tape on the floor to create, in conjunction with the reveal below three bounding walls, a continuous dark line forming a square around an existing standard square structural column. By this simple gesture the column became eerily isolated and newly discovered as a prominent object in an austere room. Commissioned to make an installation at the Museum of Contemporary Art, San Diego, in a gallery overlooking the Pacific Ocean, Irwin removed a square of glass from each of two corner windows and one central large window. The deletions from the gray-tinted glass created a strange and entirely new relationship between the museum and its spectacular outdoor context: Framed by a suddenly

Rendering of entrance building for Dia:Beacon, 2000

blurry and dense-seeming barrier of glass, the cutouts put the outdoors into sharp focus while also objectifying it, like small cubes of nature. Similarly, the decision to replace just a few panes of Dia:Beacon's long east and west rows of opaque factory-glass windows with clear glass completely changes the relationship between the galleries and the exterior. And the decision to create two windows in the south boundary of the building, directly opposite the double doors at the museum's new north entrance, has the effect from outside the front doors of momentarily collapsing the 490-foot view through the entire building into two punctures of light.

In the early 1980s, Irwin was invited to participate as a collaborating artist in designs for the rejuvenation and improvement of the Miami International Airport. The daunting task of creating some overall structure for the chaotic and unruly environment of an airport was an ideal challenge for Irwin, whose ambition it is to show that an artist can use his or her trained sense of vision to reshape any experience simply through a creative reorganization of elements such as directional paths and seating. An artist, for example, can create an overriding order, while also taking visual and experiential complexities as opportunities for discoveries in perception. The politics of the airport's huge construction project eventually defeated Irwin's proposals—but not before he had worked intensely to develop a master plan that included a process for identifying and then working with other artists on the project, as well as his own proposal to plant a large new grove of cypress trees in place of an old parking garage. He had also gotten a worthwhile taste of the possibilities of working on a complex, large-scale public project. More recently, Irwin completed a more discrete project for the Getty Center in Los Angeles, a large-scale public garden. Both of those projects were important precedents for his work at Dia's museum in Beacon.

The primary medium of Irwin's art is neither steel nor glass, neither trees nor pavement, but our perception, our curiosity, and our desire to make sense of the world around us. By subtly manipulating our environment in unexpected ways, his gestures provoke us to see differently, to question our assumptions, and to pay an attention to phenomena that in turn cause us to redraw our mental picture of the world. The role of the artist, in Irwin's terms, is to learn to see not only a physical, *quantitative* reality but the *qualitative* aspects of a situation, and to empower the viewer to gain access to that vision as well—to engage in a process of discovery. The real subject of Irwin's art is not the object, then, but the viewer:

> *As artists, the one true inquiry of art as a pure subject is an inquiry of our potential to know the world around us and our actively being in it, with a particular emphasis on the aesthetic. This world is not just somehow given to us whole.* We perceive, we shape the world, *and as artists we discover and give value to our human potential to "see" the infinite richness (beauty?) in everything, creating an extended aesthetic reality.*[2]

Through a self-directed study of philosophy, psychology, and art history, Irwin has come to understand art not within its traditional social, cultural, and commercial practice of object making but as a process of "pure inquiry," as he says, and "pure subject." Art for him need not result in a discrete object or even a discrete experience. The work of the artist might then be defined as a process of investigation subject to a particular set of circumstances (a place, an invitation to work, a problem to solve) that may or may not result in a thing called artwork.

"If you asked me the sum total—what is your ambition?" Irwin told his friend and biographer Lawrence Weschler. "Basically it's just to make you a little more aware than you were the day before of how beautiful the world is. It's not saying that I know what the world should look like. It's not that I'm rebuilding the world. Basically what artists do is to teach you how to exercise your own potential—they always have, that's the one thread that goes all the way through."[3] By Irwin's measure, a work of art succeeds when it challenges our perceptions to such a degree as to cause us to reconsider our environment and invest it, and ourselves, with greater potential. In the case of his work at Dia:Beacon, it was only after he had sensed and assessed the degree to which he had carried out his responsibilities to solve practical problems, as well as the total aesthetic effect of his myriad of individual and dispersed gestures, details, and proposals—some of which are described in his drawings in the following pages—that he was satisfied that his efforts operated within those terms and could be considered a work in his oeuvre and in Dia's collection.

M.G.

notes

1 Piet Mondrian, quoted in Robert Irwin, *Being and Circumstance: Notes Toward a Conditional Art* (Larkspur Landing, Calif.: Lapis Press, in conjunction with the Pace Gallery and the San Francisco Museum of Modern Art, 1985), p. 23.

2 Irwin, "The Hidden Structures of Art," in *Robert Irwin*, ed. Russell Ferguson (Los Angeles: The Museum of Contemporary Art, and Rizzoli, New York, 1993), p. 35.

3 Irwin, quoted in Lawrence Weschler, "Playing It as It Lays & Keeping It in Play: A Visit with Robert Irwin," in ibid., p. 173.

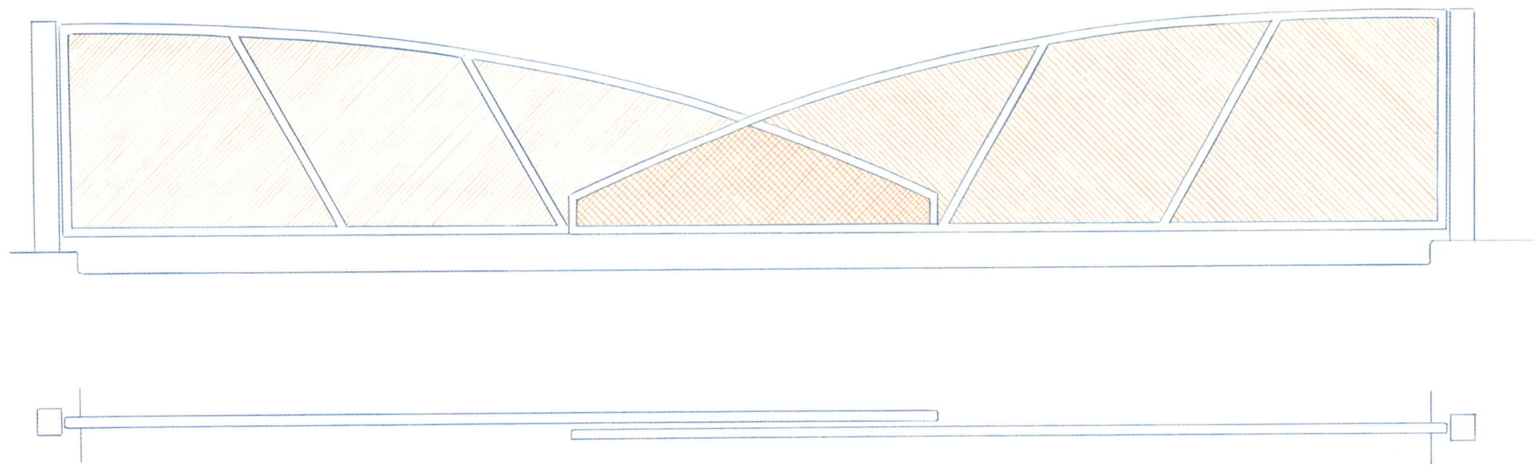

left Rendering of iron gate for Dia:Beacon, 2001
right Rendering of forecourt for Dia:Beacon, 2001

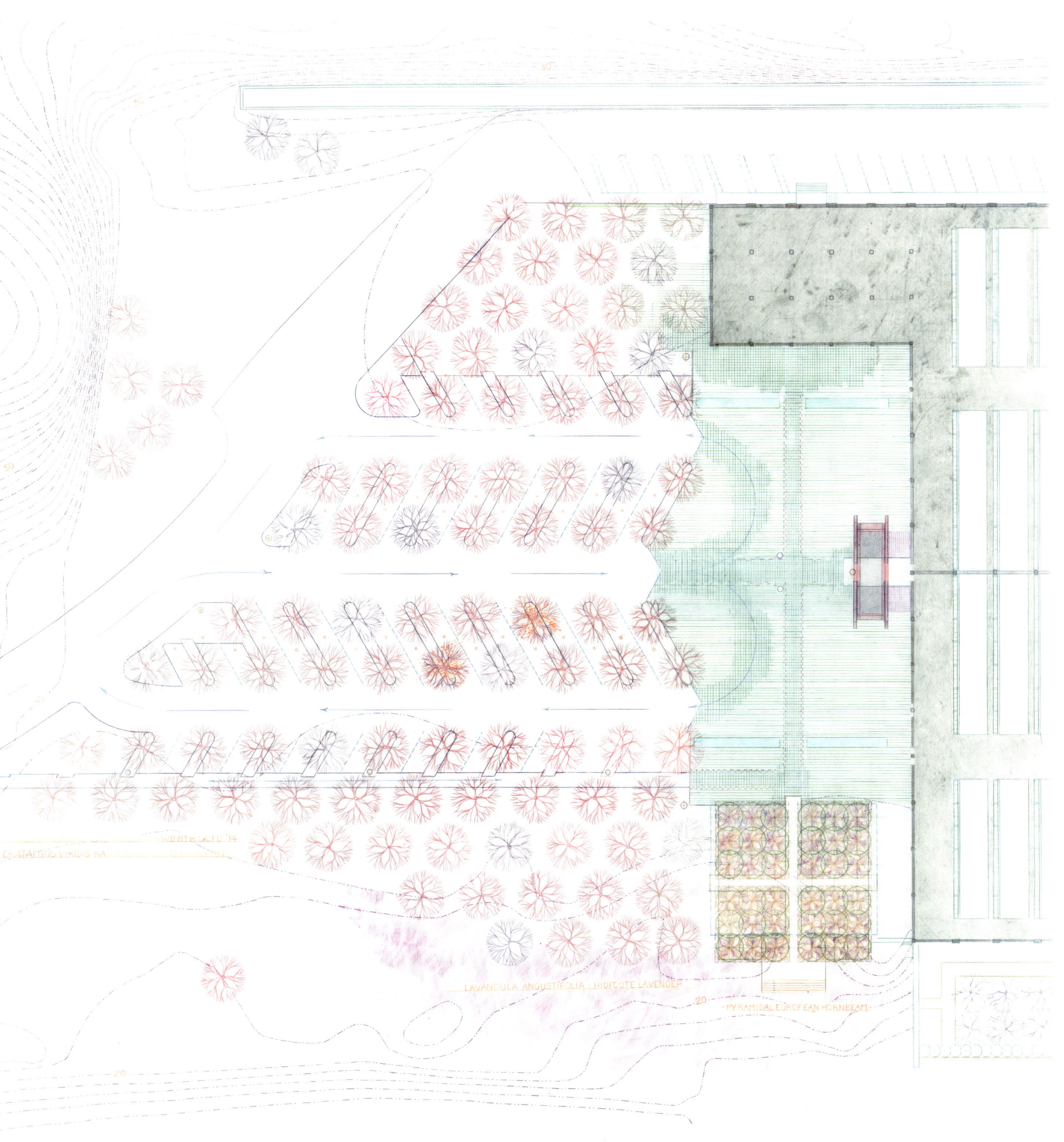

30
50
60
CRATAEGUS VIRIDIS
LAVANDULA ANGUSTIFOLIA - HIDCOTE LAVENDER
20
PYRAMIDAL EUROPEAN HORNBEAM

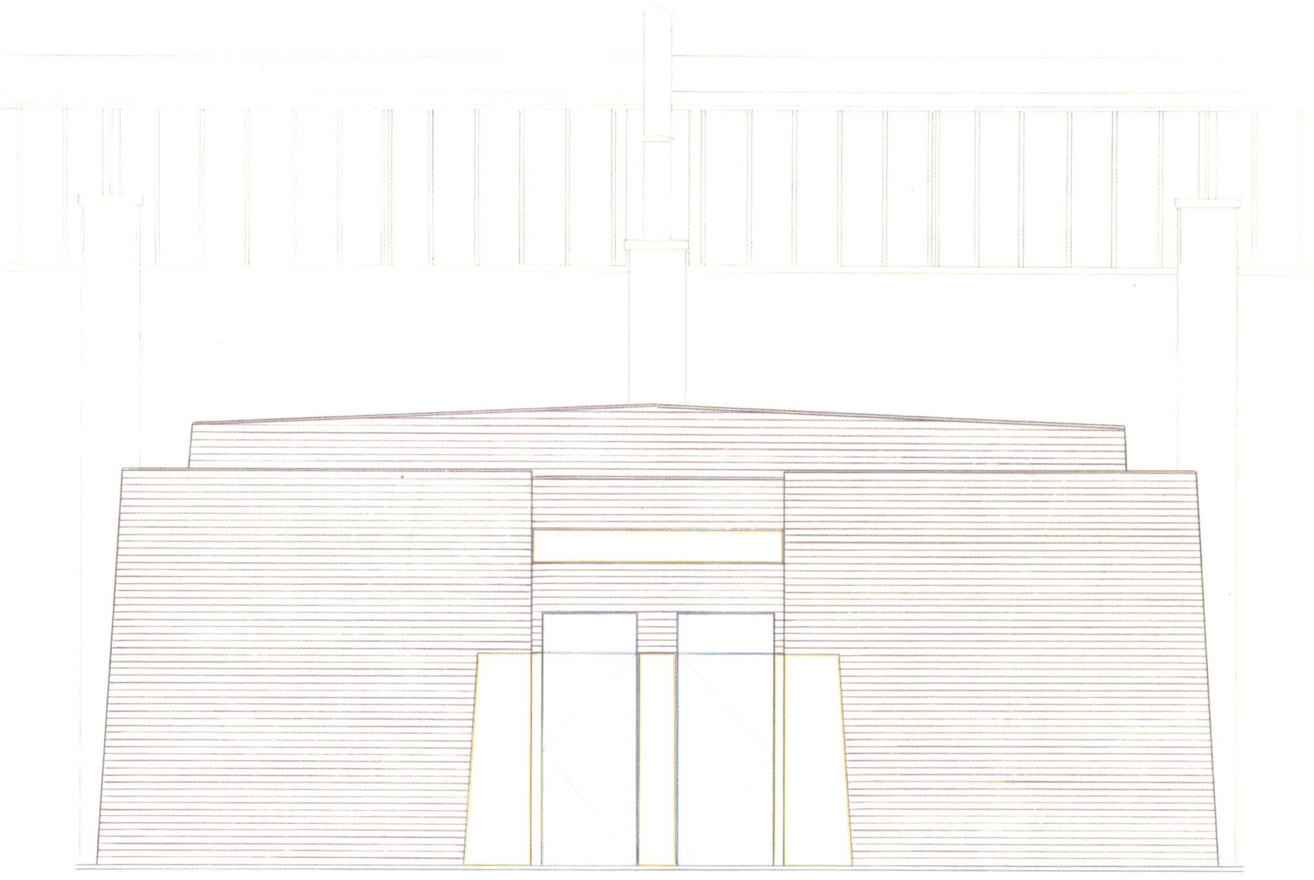

Rendering of entrance building for Dia:Beacon, 2000

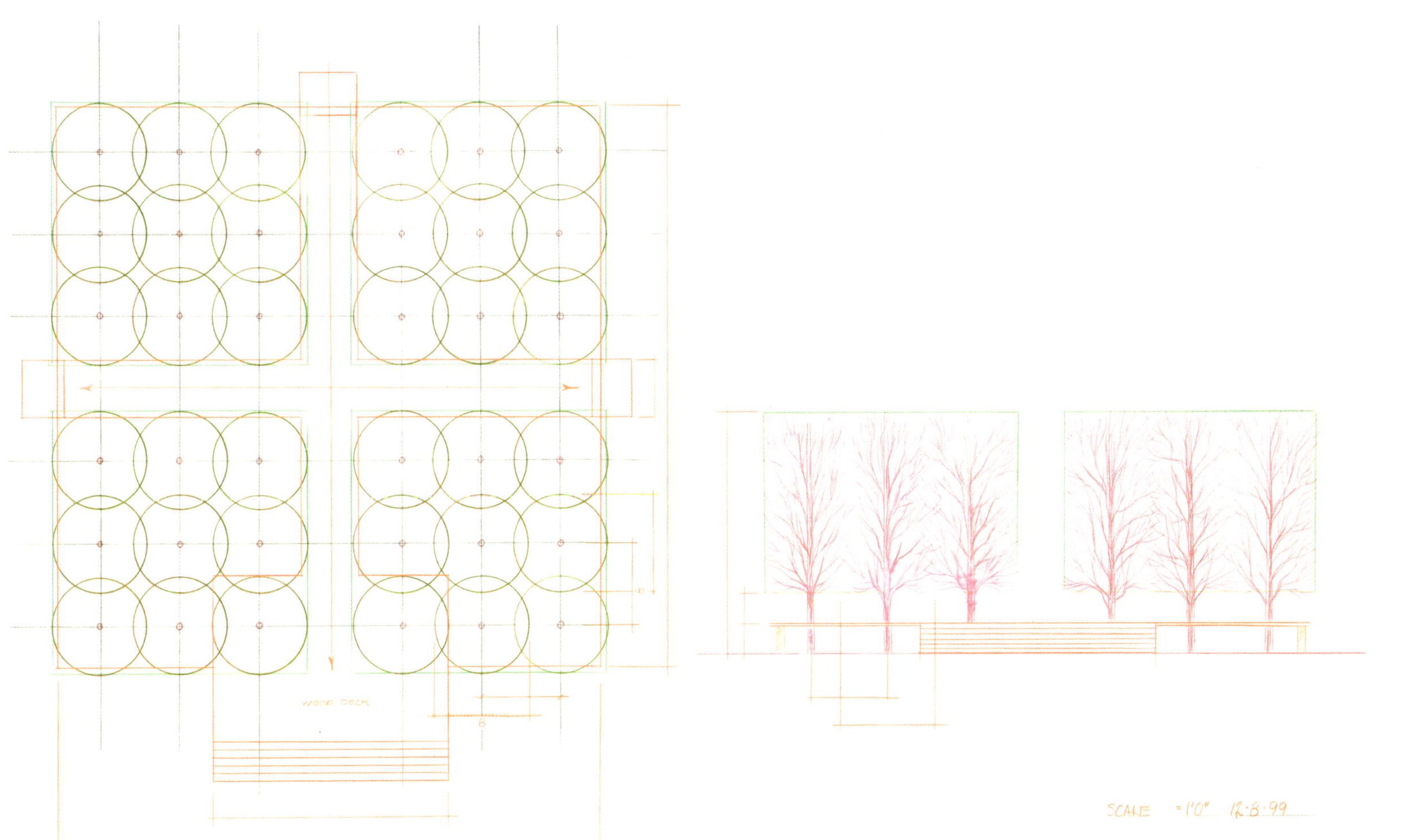

Rendering of platform with European hornbeam trees for Dia:Beacon, 1999

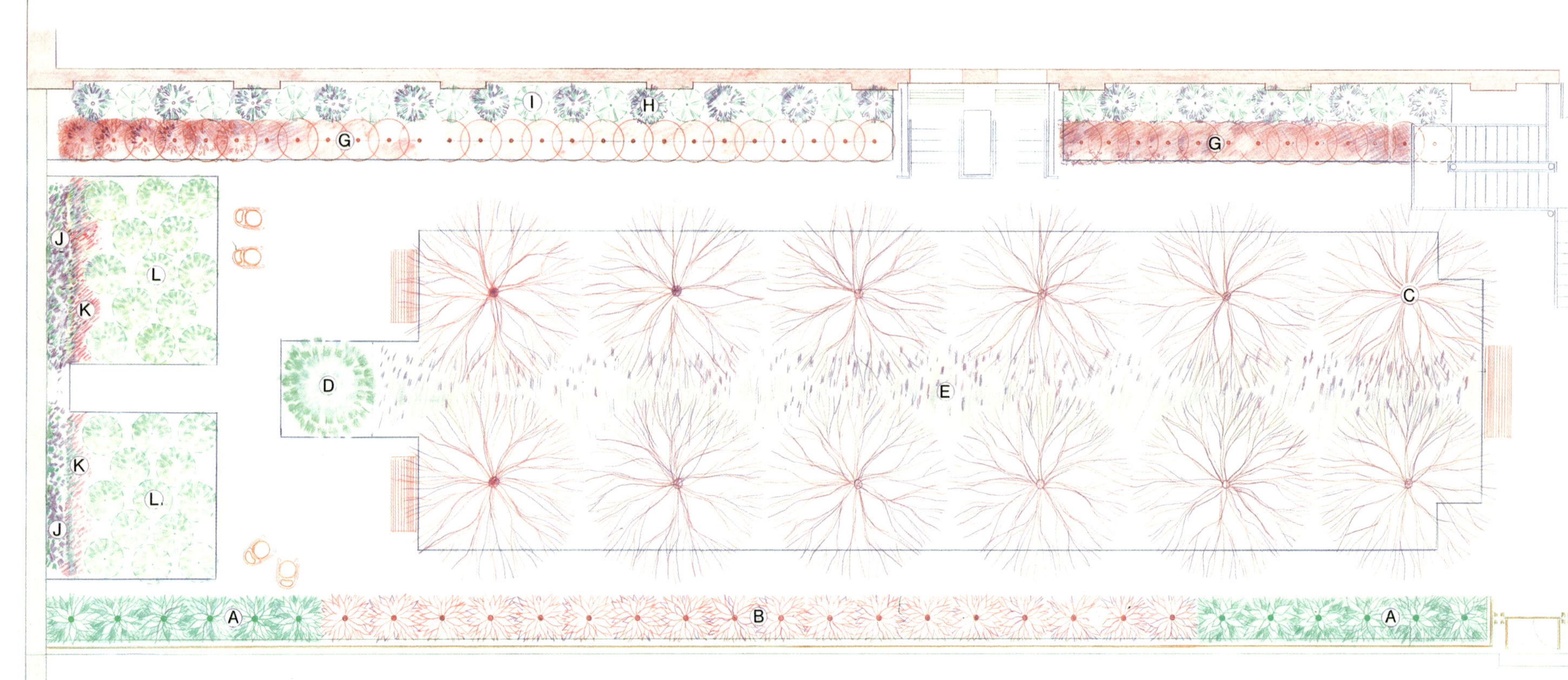

Rendering of West Garden for Dia:Beacon, 2001

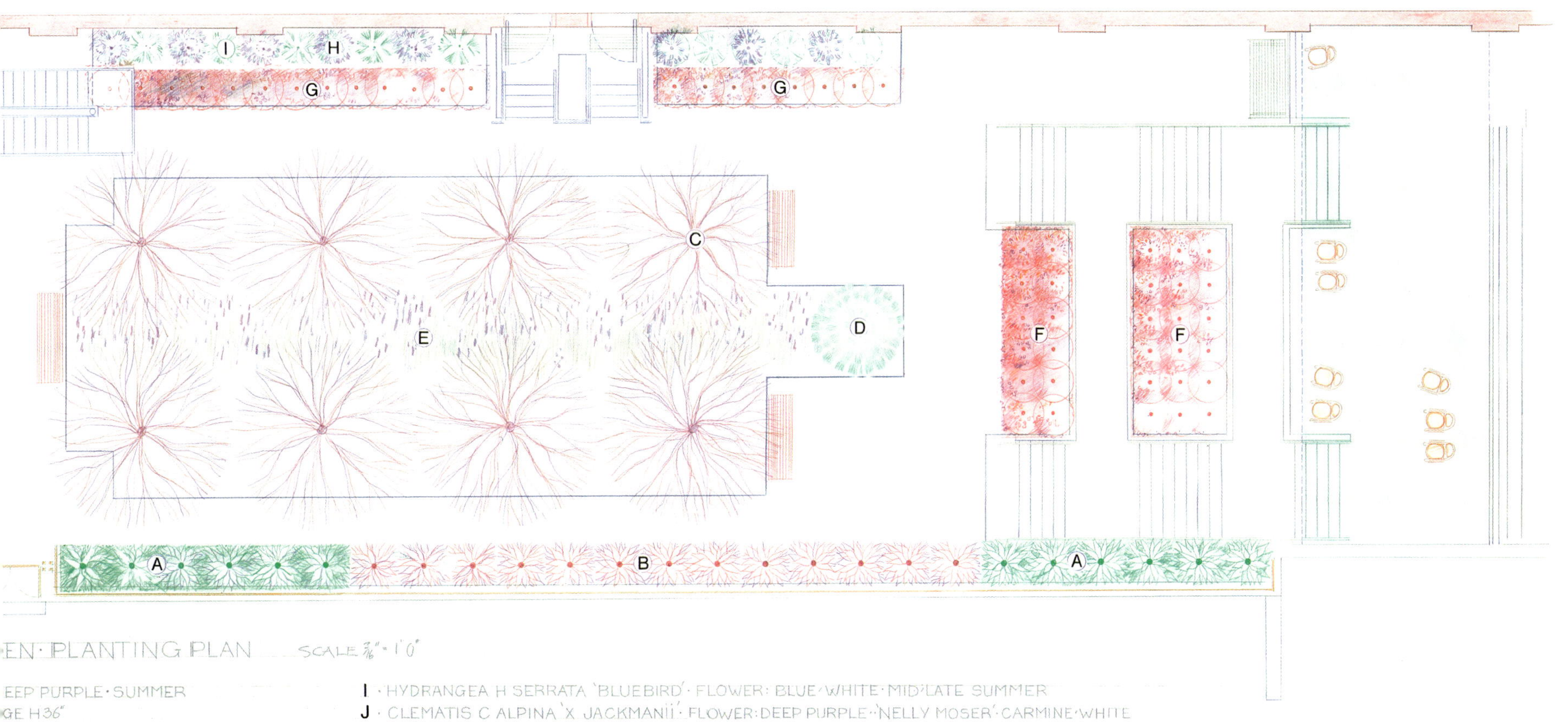
I
H
G
G
C
E
D
F
F
A
B
A
EN · PLANTING PLAN
SCALE 3/16" = 1'0"
EEP PURPLE · SUMMER
GE H36"
ER · WHITE · RED FLECK · EARLY SPRING
I · HYDRANGEA H SERRATA 'BLUEBIRD' · FLOWER: BLUE/WHITE · MID/LATE SUMMER
J · CLEMATIS C ALPINA 'X JACKMANII' · FLOWER: DEEP PURPLE · 'NELLY MOSER' · CARMINE/WHITE
K · CLLUNA VULGARIS · 'DARKNESS' · FLOWER: DEEP CARMINE · SUMMER/AUTUMN
L · ROSA 'ICEBERG' FLORIBUNDA · FLOWER: WHITE · SPRING/FALL

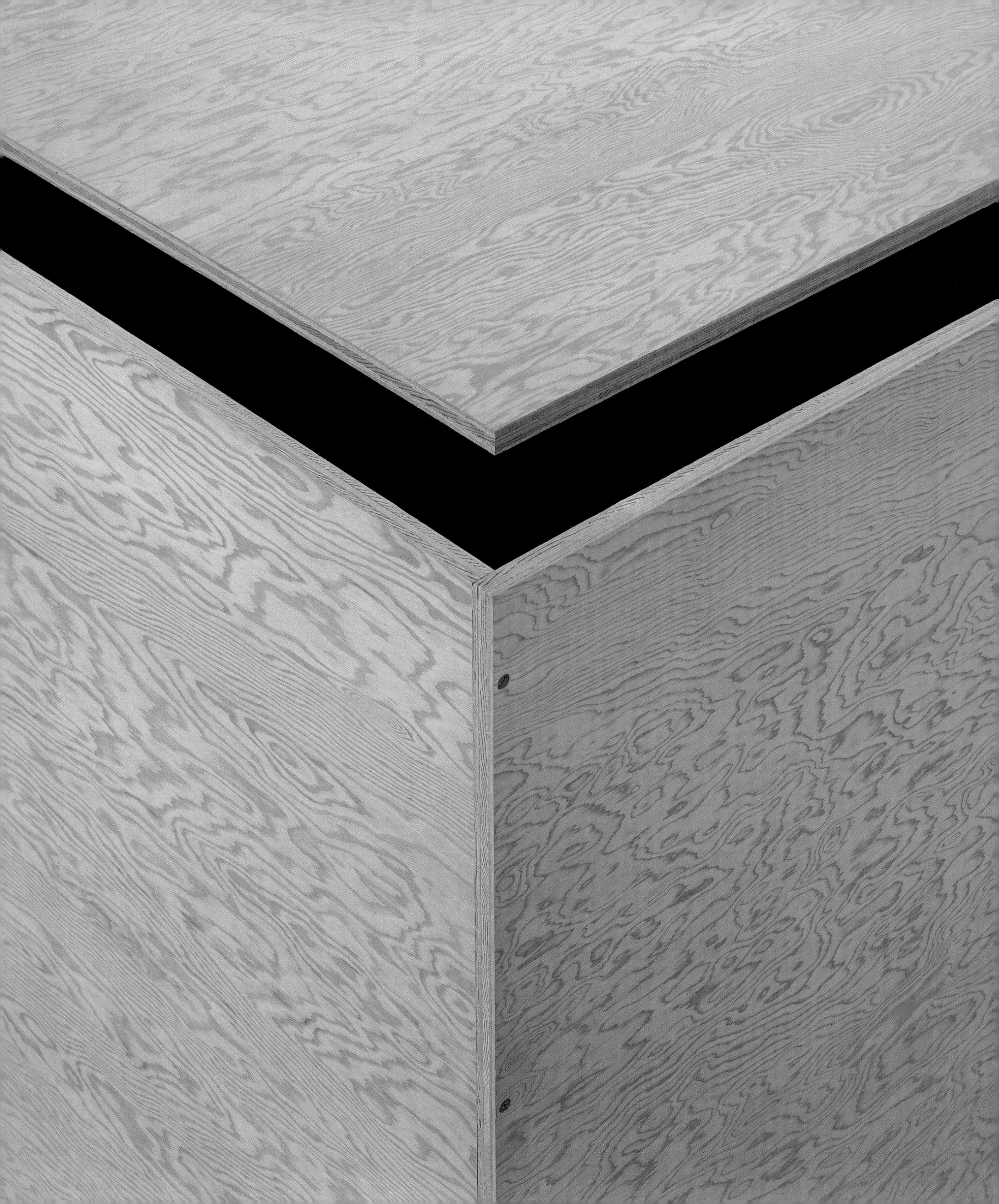

Donald Judd

Donald Judd was born in Excelsior Springs, Missouri, in 1928. He attended Columbia University, New York, studying philosophy from 1949 to 1953 and art history with Meyer Schapiro from 1957 to 1962. At the same time that he launched an impressive career as an art critic and polemicist, he began to produce his earliest paintings. He had forged his mature aesthetic by 1965. After a retrospective at the Whitney Museum of American Art, New York, in 1968, Judd's most important solo museum exhibition was held at the National Gallery of Canada, Ottawa, in 1975, and he exhibited widely throughout the world. In 1986 a permanent installation of his work opened at the Chinati Foundation in Marfa, Texas. Donald Judd died in 1994.

Untitled, 1976 (detail)

In a remarkably fertile though brief period in the early 1960s, Donald Judd not only forged his aesthetic but also determined the iconography, materials, and forms that were to ground his practice for the remainder of his career. Celebrated as a preeminent Minimalist, despite his antipathy to the term, Judd refined, honed, and parlayed his rigorous visual vocabulary through an enormous range of industrial materials, most of which had never been extensively employed in art production: anodized aluminum, stainless steel, brass, copper, Plexiglas, plywood, and galvanized iron (often enameled or anodized) were among those he preferred. His simple geometric forms, whose mode of fabrication is directly exposed and immediately legible, are presented as single works, or combined serially into greater wholes, or composed according to conventional mathematical progressions. Typically, these lucid forms are declaratively simple and obdurately factual, and their surfaces sensuous, even sumptuous, so that, as Judd stated, "the image, all of the parts, and the whole shape are coextensive."[1] Commensurate with his stringent conceptualizing, his works were fabricated with an elegant regard for niceties of finish and detail by a range of technical specialists.

In relentlessly probing issues of similarity and difference, likeness and identity, Judd required that each of his works be closely and attentively scrutinized. The recognition of the specificity of each element informs the viewer's appreciation of the relation of the individual to the collective, of the singular entity to the larger series, and of repetition to order. Such recognition has implications that are as much social and ethical in character as they are aesthetic. "Aspectual diversity"—the sequence of distinct vantage points required to navigate each work, and to negotiate its multiple faces, in an engagement that necessarily takes place in real time and actual space—plays a fundamental role in the apprehension of his work.

Change rather than evolution characterizes the shifts in Judd's practice during the 1960s. In the early 1970s his art increased in scale and complexity, as he closely engaged with issues of site and presentation and accorded greater emphasis to the problem of created space (as opposed to space treated as simply an empty surround).[2] Comprising fifteen plywood boxes fabricated from the finest Douglas fir, an untitled work of 1976 manifests this development. From the first glance the viewer recognizes that, while the dimensions of every box are identical, each is different, each is unique. Certain boxes immediately capture attention, notably one whose top seems to be suspended over a four-inch spatial gap; by contrast, others—most obviously the most bare container—appear austerely uninflected. Yet others—among them one with a compound slope, whose lid tilts from an upper corner to the opposite corner at the bottom of the box— are almost unreadable. Just as no rigid system has been exhaustively explored to determine all the different configurations possible with this elementary module, so no identifiable system accounts for their overall sequence—that is, for the juxtaposition of any one box with its often quite distinctively different neighbors.[3] Nevertheless, a sense of order can be apprehended, one that eschews both a hierarchical placement and the suppression of the individual to the whole. As art historian Dieter Koepplin aptly stated, Judd favored "free individuation" over structural subordination, the likely outcome of uniformity.[4] Each box consequently retains its autonomy and identity. A multipartite entity, the work is constructed collectively, by consensus, as it were, neither given nor preordained.[5]

Composed of twelve stainless-steel boxes with deep blue Plexiglas panels forming the back plane of each interior, untitled (1975) contrasts tellingly with the plywood piece discussed above, in that here all the units are identical. Once again, though, appearances change radically as the viewer explores each element in the sequence. For example, the color of the inner spaces fluctuates according to the play of light, the back plane at times darkening almost to black—like the negative of a mirror—at other moments swelling with a sumptuous blue that diffuses the crystalline interior into a softly glowing ambience. A hue relatively new to Judd's palette in 1975, ultramarine inevitably compromised the effects of "transparent factuality" (formerly considered axiomatic), since it permits shadow to modulate light, eroding angles and edges and rendering space indefinite.[6]

Even as Judd tempered his desire for the uninflected clarity that had been a hallmark of his early endeavors, his approach was not fundamentally altered: rather, he now more fully acknowledged the contingencies inherent in the act of looking.[7] His conviction that his works be lit by natural, even light, in preference to artificial illumination, also remained firm. In these opulent metal boxes, the interior spaces appear to expand or to contract, so that at moments they become perceptually at variance with the same spaces as they are defined externally by planes and edges whose precise configurations from most vantages read as strictly controlled. Given their high polish, reflections render the components unstable, diffusing their svelte surfaces and divesting them, albeit intermittently, not only of mass and weight but even of shape and surface. Relatively small in size, these compact wall boxes approximate in proportion to a double cube, yet they

Untitled (slant piece), 1976

are subtly tempered in ways that further enhance the sense of stable harmonious balance—that is, of visual resolution. Since their interiors appear slightly shallower than their exterior depths, even a lateral viewpoint affirms the finely calibrated horizontality of the work as a whole.

Conceptual presuppositions constantly founder before the particularity—the specificity—of each of Judd's finely honed works, given that every encounter is always phenomenologically determined, as untitled (slant piece) (1976), the third work in Dia's collection from this midpoint in Judd's oeuvre, vividly attests. First exhibited at the Paula Cooper Gallery in New York's SoHo in 1976, this singular sculpture was devised for that location; the length of the back wall of the room, as well as the given dimensions of a sheet of plywood, governed its dimensions. Scale and placement were consequently a function of this particular site and were attuned to such aspects as the distance of the gallery entrance from the piece.[8] The given width of the material determined the degree of the angle of the sloping plane. Only when the work is approached closely does the role of the secant plane that modulates the void into two equal spaces, one visible and the other concealed, become fully apparent.

Unequivocally abstract, this work, like the two others discussed above, reveals itself in ways that both structurally and formally parallel certain familiar experiences generated in the natural as well as the built environment. A resolutely materialist art grounded in abstraction, Judd's work eschews metaphor and association. It nonetheless garners meaning and affect from its engagement with space, time, and existence, with what French philosopher Henri Bergson termed

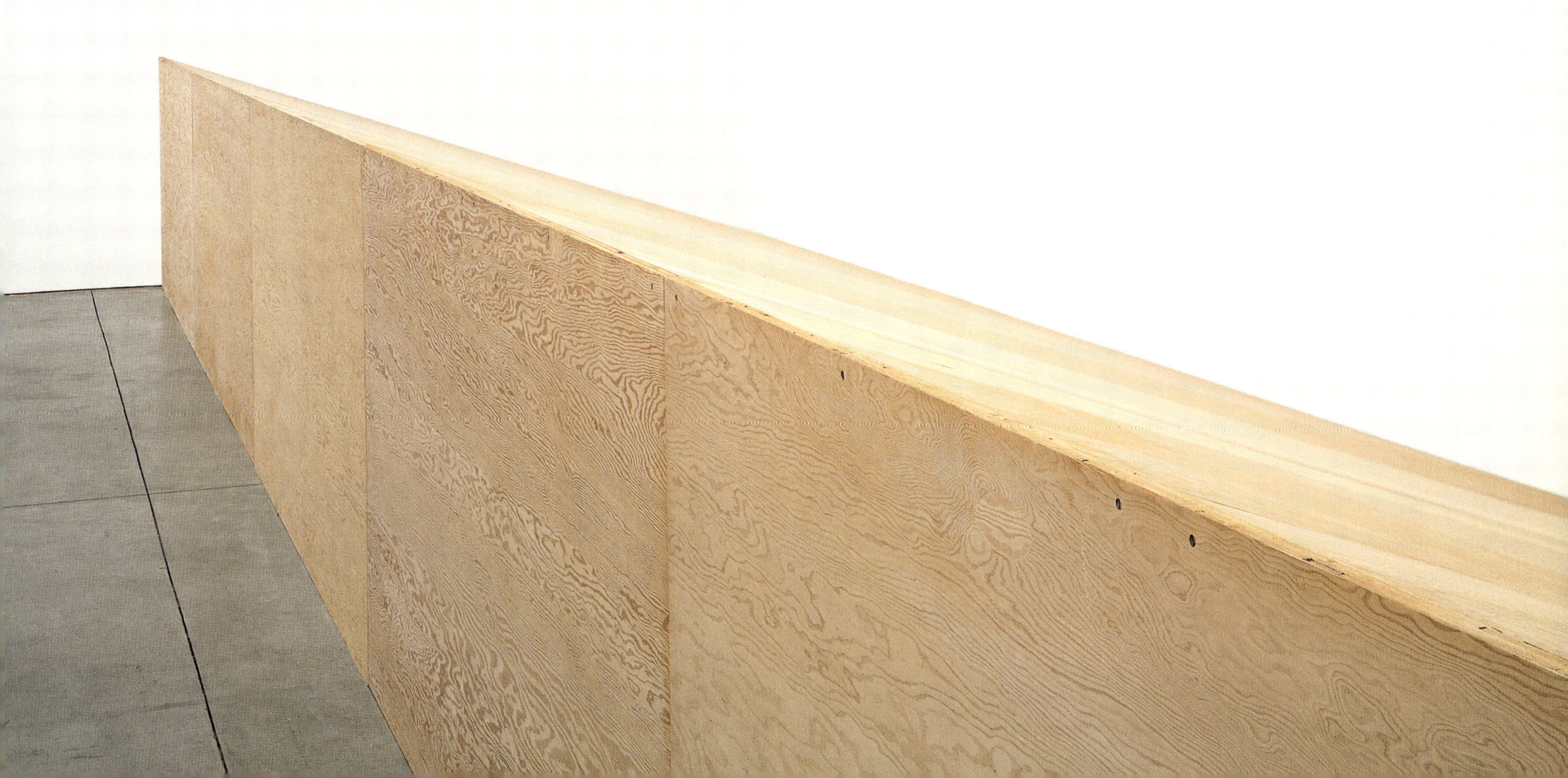

la durée.[9] An elective affinity links his work with that of Bridget Riley, Agnes Martin, Robert Irwin, and Robert Ryman, among others, who have also explored an abstract art based in phenomenological and perceptual experience, rather than in transcendental or idealist visions of the kind that informed much of the radical nonfiguration of the 1910s and 1920s. In this regard, the definition of Judd's sculpture as a hermetically formalist Minimalism seems too confining a rubric.

L.C.

notes

1 Donald Judd, "Specific Objects," in *Donald Judd: Complete Writings 1959–1975* (Halifax: The Press of the Nova Scotia College of Art and Design, in association with New York University Press, 1975), pp. 181–89. See also Judd, "Local History," in ibid., pp. 148–55.

2 Yve-Alain Bois has acutely explored the way that space in Judd's later work is purposely made, that is, formed like a solid. Treated equally, he contends, space and solid symbiotically define each other. Bois, "The Inflection," in *Donald Judd: Sculpture 1991* (New York: Pace Gallery, 1991), n.p.

3 The box entered Judd's repertoire as his principal form in 1963. From the early 1970s, the motif of an open box with multiple modalities increasingly preoccupied him, as he constantly explored different materials, proportions, scales, and compositions. From 1971, works constructed from plywood were fabricated by master craftsman Peter Ballantine. A number of related works—plywood boxes with the same overall dimensions but configured differently—were executed at this time. Sixteen boxes were made for an exhibition at Heiner Friedrich's gallery, New York, in 1977; see *Donald Judd: Fifteen Works* (New York: Heiner Friedrich Gallery, 1977); Thomas B. Hess, "Boxing Day," *New York*, 11 April, 1977, pp. 70–72; and Kenneth Baker, "Donald Judd: Past Theory," *Artforum* 15, no. 10 (Summer 1977), pp. 46–47. Judd decided to exhibit only fifteen, however, and these were then kept together as one work, untitled (1976), now in Dia's collection. An identical second set was sold as separate works.

4 Dieter Koepplin, *Donald Judd: Zeichnungen/Drawings 1956–1976* (Halifax: The Press of the Nova Scotia College of Art and Design, in association with New York University Press, and Basel: Kunstmuseum Basel, 1976), p. 9.

5 Order was an issue that much preoccupied the artist. Refusing the a priori, which he linked to rationalistic procedures, he instead sought a logical method, which he defined as "a local order, just an arrangement, barely order at all," and on another occasion as "one thing after another," a modus operandi that for him ensured autonomy and immediate accessibility for the components of any multipartite work. For a fuller discussion see Lynne Cooke, "Donald Judd: Reordering Order," in *Donald Judd* (London: Waddington Galleries, 1989), pp. 5–10. Order is often proposed in opposition to composition, which Judd relates to part-to-part assembling—a practice he abhorred, for he sought a holistic form, a totality. For a fuller discussion see "Don Judd: An Interview with John Coplans," in *Don Judd* (Pasadena: Pasadena Art Museum, 1971), pp. 19–44.

6 Among the first works in Judd's oeuvre made from stainless steel, these boxes were fabricated by Bernstein Brothers in Queens, who had previously made many of Judd's works in other metals. As with Judd's other wall-mounted works, these sculptures are affixed to the supporting surface by techniques customarily used with lightweight industrial objects, such as cabinets and appliances. For Judd, these techniques had to be practical and conventional; for him, cantilevering should not require engineering solutions. For a fuller discussion see "Don Judd: An Interview with John Coplans" pp. 19–44.

7 Rosalind E. Krauss brilliantly acknowledged the role of illusion in this and related works in "The Material Uncanny," in *Donald Judd: Early Fabricated Work* (New York: Pace Wildenstein, 1998), pp. 7–13.

8 It is possible to expand this work to fit a similarly sized but not identical location, for it is not site specific but site related. In principle, Judd would reinstall these and other more environmental works on an appropriate occasion. The dimensions of the standard plywood sheet he used are four feet by eight feet.

9 Judd's clearest account of this comes in a text written in 1983, in a discussion of the work of Jackson Pollock and Barnett Newman, his most important forebears: "Pollock and Newman have no immediate emotion of the kind [found in the art of Clyfford Still and Mark Rothko]. The thought and emotion of their work is of the more complex kind, unidentifiable by name, underlying, durable, and concerned with space, time, and existence. It's what Bergson called 'la durée.'" Judd refers again to this notion, a governing precept of his own aesthetic, when he concludes, "I think the extension of extremes in a work of art is classical, again for lack of a better word. The greater the polarity of the elements in a work, the greater the work's comprehension of space, time, and existence." Judd, "John Chamberlain," in *John Chamberlain: New Sculpture* (New York: Pace Gallery, 1989), pp. ix–x.

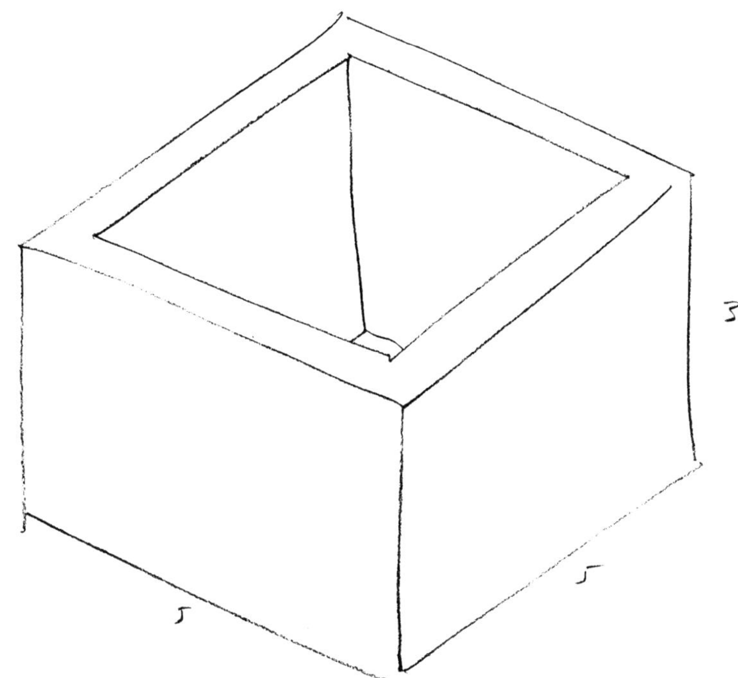

left Drawing for untitled, 1976

right and pages 172–173 Untitled, 1976

page 174 Untitled, 1975

page 175 Untitled, 1991

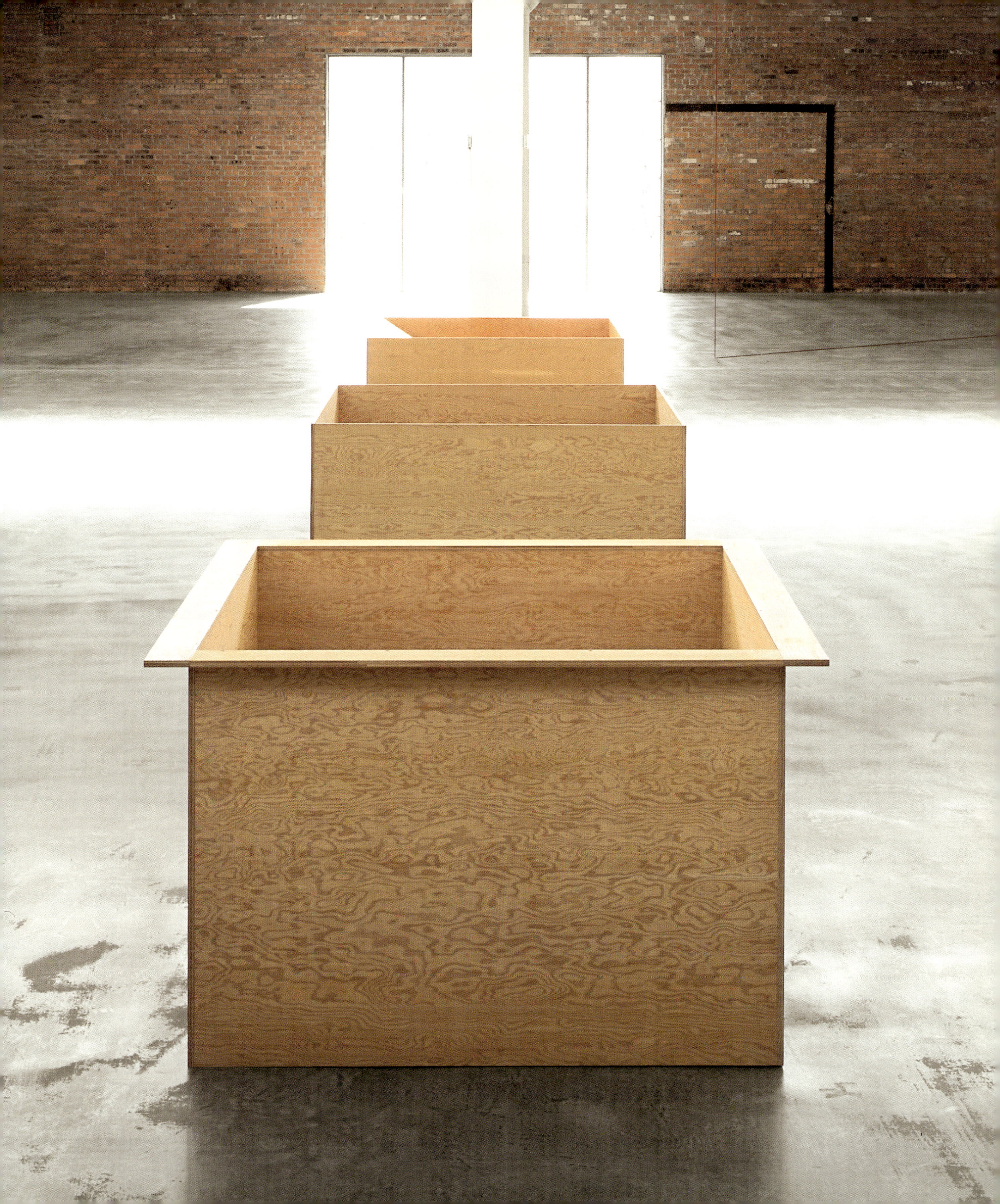

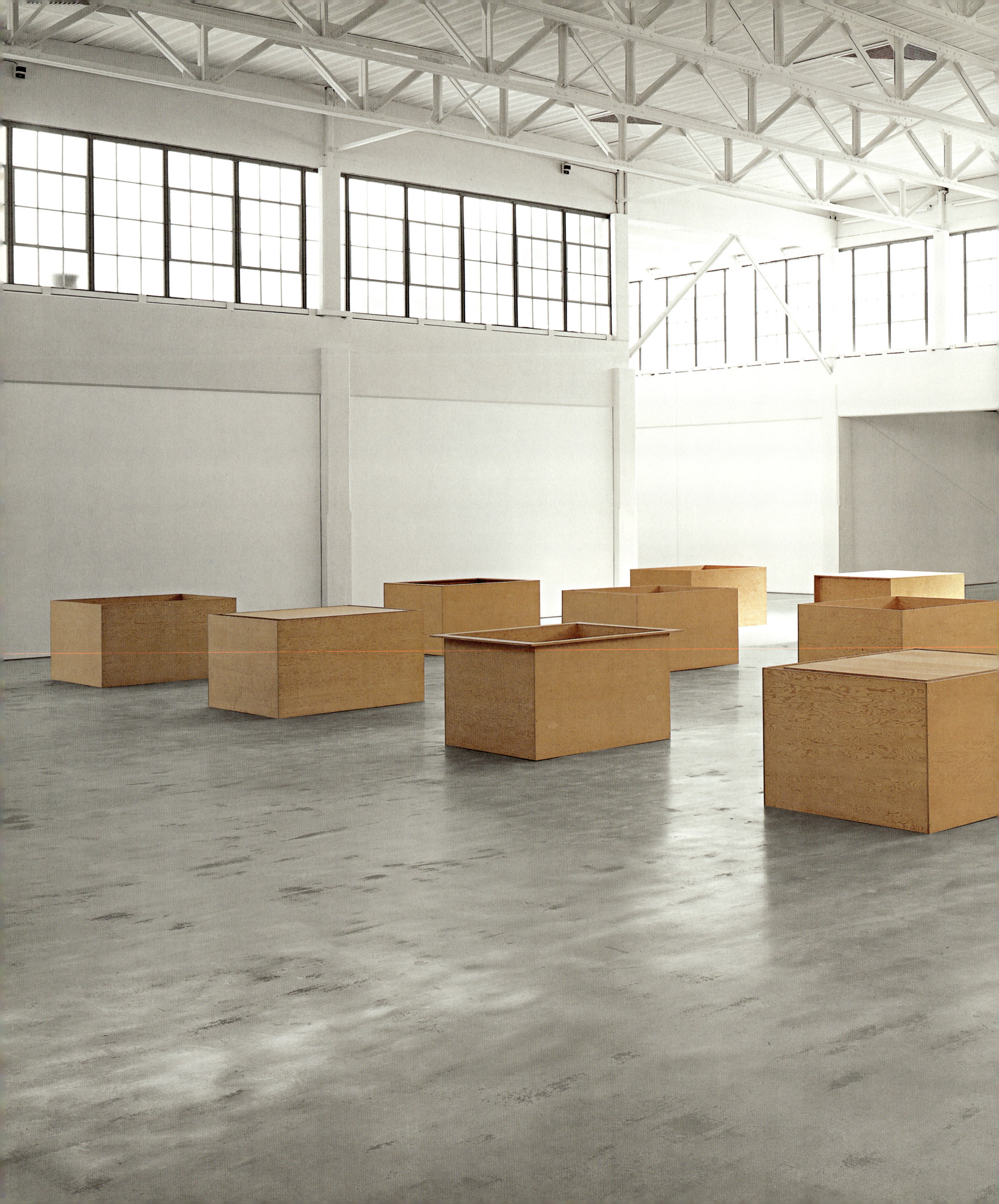

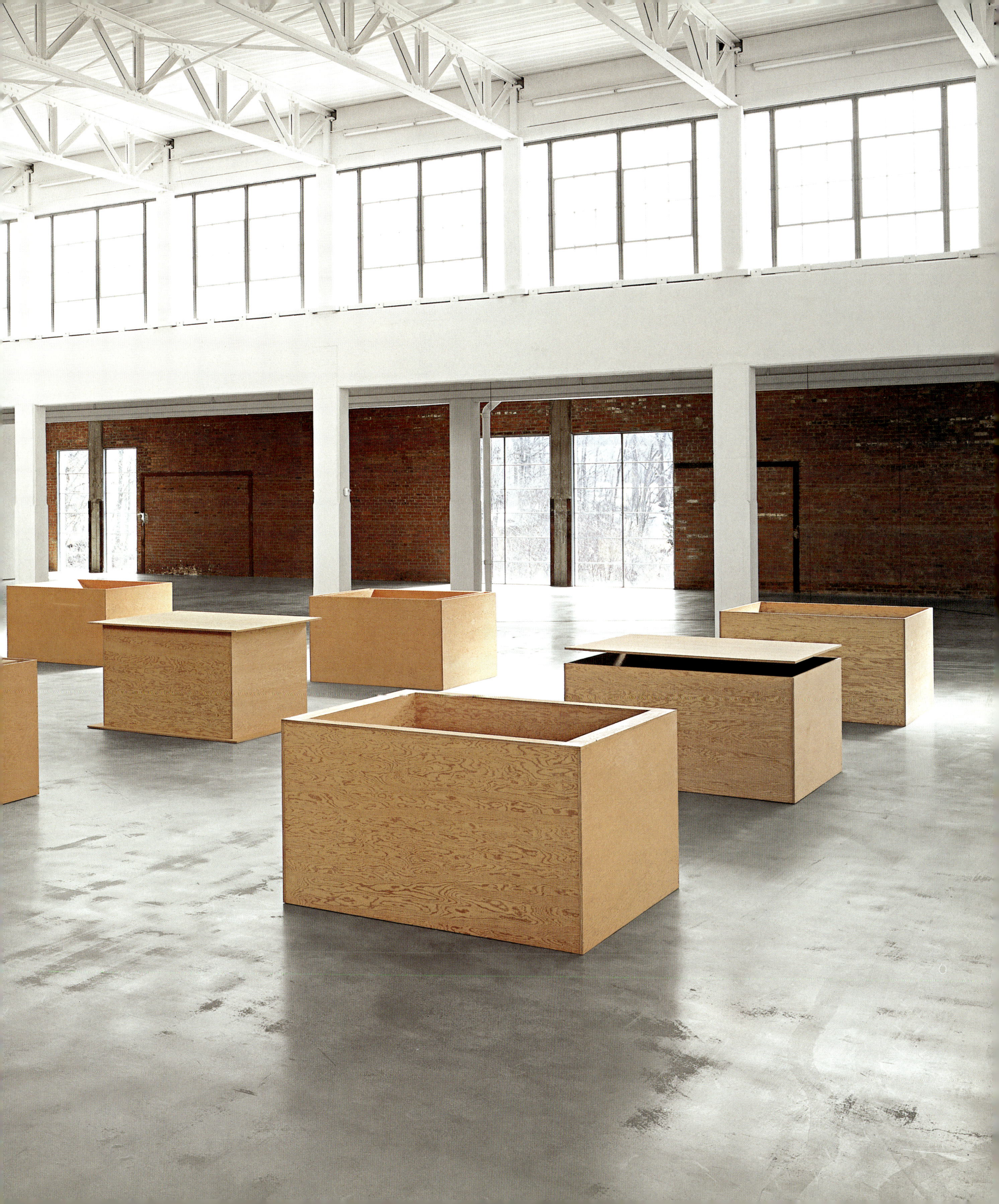

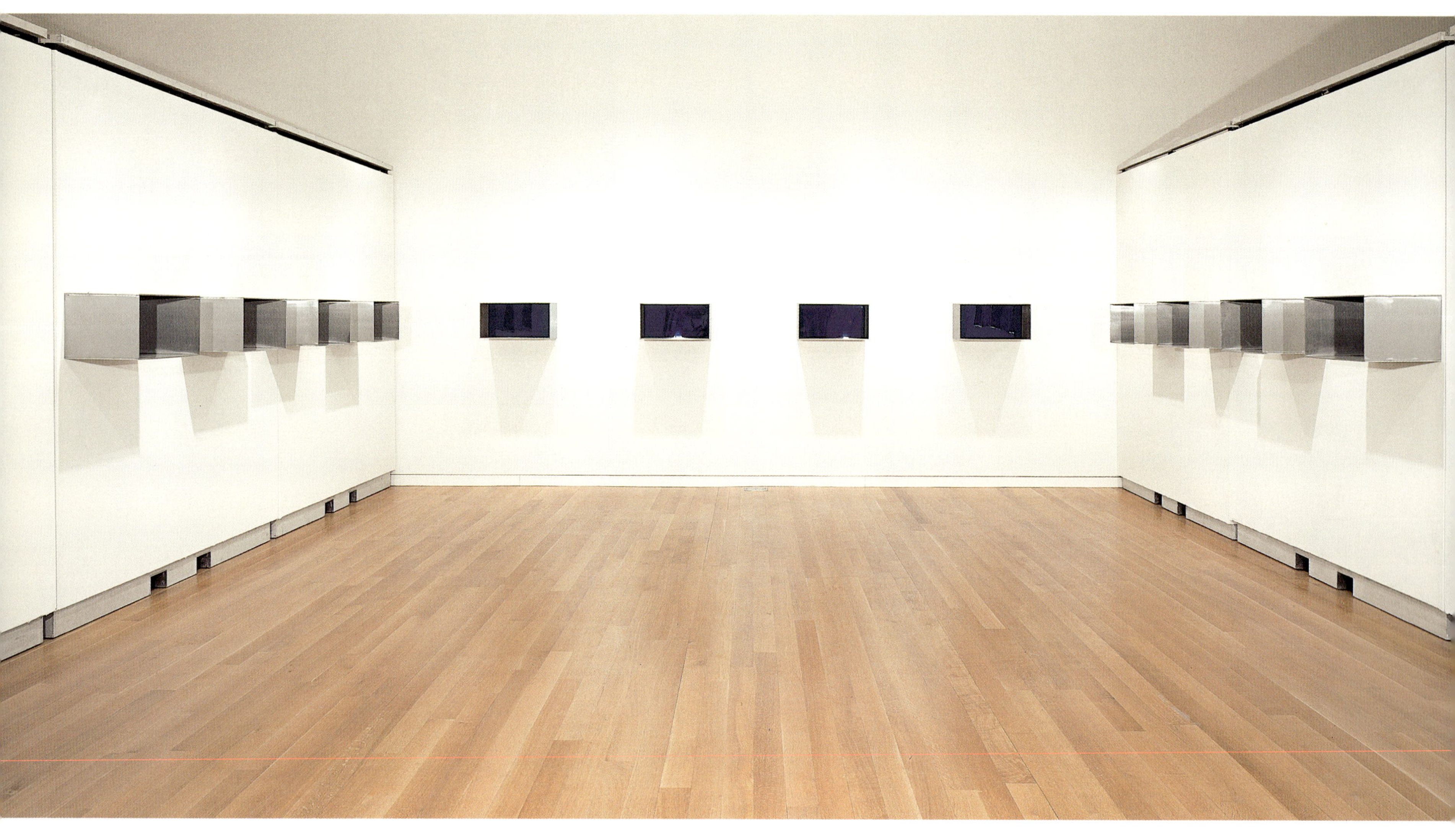

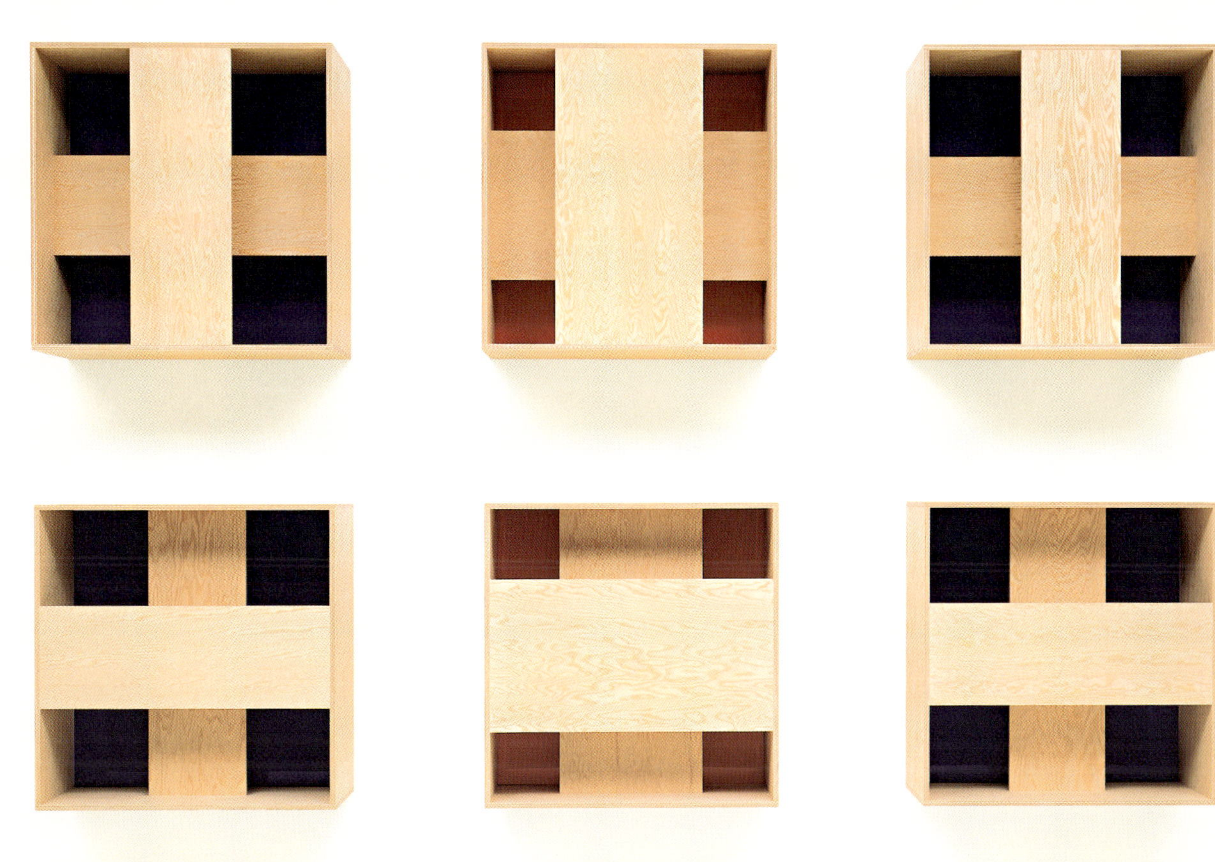

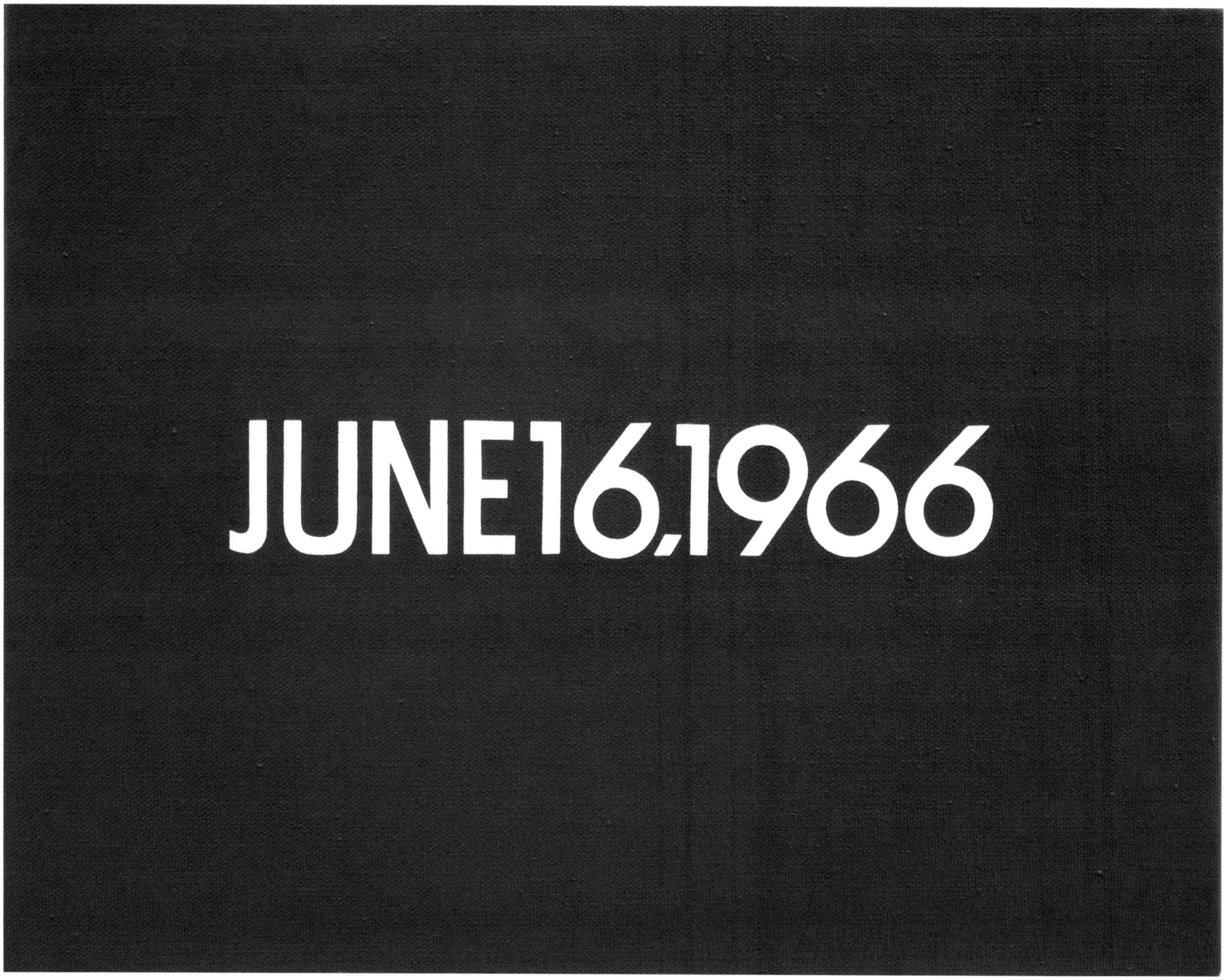

JUNE 16, 1966

On Kawara

On Kawara, 25,712 days (May 18, 2003). Kawara's first exhibitions include the first Nippon Exhibition, at the Tokyo Metropolitan Art Museum, in 1953, and at the Takemiya and Hibiya galleries the following year. He began traveling throughout the world in 1959, then settled in 1965 in New York City, where he has been an intermittent resident ever since. His work was exhibited at New York's Dwan Gallery in 1967, and his one-person exhibition "One Million Years" was shown in Düsseldorf, Paris, and Milan in 1971. Kawara's work was included in Documentas 5 (1972), 7 (1982), and 11 (2002), in Kassel, and in the Tokyo Biennale (1970), the Kyoto Biennale (1976), and the Venice Biennale (1976). He won the Carnegie Prize in 1991 and the Kunstpreis Aachen the following year. In 1993, Dia held the yearlong exhibition "One Thousand Days, One Million Years," for which Kawara installed paintings from the *Today Series* that had been executed in New York City. The exhibition also included his book work *One Million Years (Past)*, and a sound work, *One Million Years (Future)*.

JUNE 16, 1966, "Two tankers and two tugboats crashed in a fiery disaster in Lower New York Bay.", 1966, from *Today Series*, 1966–present

Time, as registered in its familiar increments of days, years, centuries, and eons, has preoccupied On Kawara since the mid-1960s, when he began his magnum opus, the *Today Series*. Each of the Date Paintings that constitute this ongoing work is a monochrome field on which is inscribed the date of the day on which the individual painting is executed, in the language and according to the calendrical conventions of the country in which Kawara is present when he begins it.[1] If he does not complete it by midnight he destroys it. Some days he makes more than one; very occasionally, a third is added to that second before the midnight deadline strikes. Most days he makes none.

Certain sets of limitations govern this series, as they do Kawara's other bodies of work. Every painting in the *Today Series* conforms to one of eight predetermined sizes, all horizontal in orientation, ranging from eight by ten inches to sixty-one by eighty-nine inches. And for every painting the artist mixes the color afresh, so that the chroma of each is unique. Colors and tonalities in the brown-gray and blue-black areas of the spectrum have become prevalent in recent years; earlier, cerulean blues and clear reds were more frequently employed. Four or five coats of acrylic are evenly applied to the surface of the canvas, on the sides as well as the frontal plane, and each layer is sanded down before the next is added, creating a dense matte surface. The whole is self-evidently an object, a three-dimensional entity. Letters, numbers, and punctuation marks are then meticulously built up across the center of the monochrome field. Eschewing stencils in favor of hand-drawn characters, Kawara skillfully renders the script, initially an elongated version of Gill Sans, later a quintessentially modernist Futura. Whatever slight variations and adjustments in the letters may be discerned over the years, they are

THE NEW YORK TIMES, THURSDAY, NOVEMBER 20, 1969

recision in Landing Proves Feasibility of Most Ambitious of Future Apollo Proj

hief Surprise Is Dust That Rocket Stirred Up

By WALTER SULLIVAN

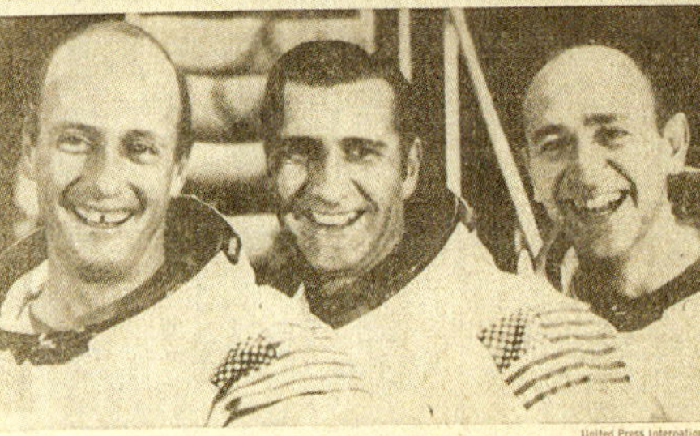

The Apollo 12 crewmen are, from left, Comdr. Charles Conrad Jr., mission leader; Comdr. Richard F. Gordon Jr., command module pilot; Comdr. Alan L. Bean, lunar lander pilot.

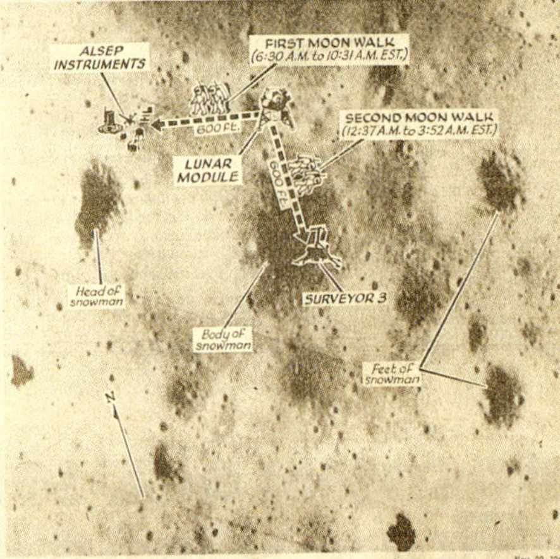

The Apollo 12 lunar ferry made precise landing 600 feet from Surveyor 3, as indicated on map photo above. Four craters known as the Snowman aided Commanders Conrad and Bean in finding target. On first of two moon walks, they distributed parts of Apollo Lunar Surface Experiments Package (ALSEP). Second walk plan included visiting Surveyor.

Walking—and Talking—on the M

Pinpoint Landing Goal Fulfilled by Apollo 12

Ample Oxygen and Energy Are Left After Moon Walk

NOV.20,1969

no more significant than the often minute differences in hue. Nor is the choice of color more expressive or connotative than the measurements that determine the size of an individual work.

Each painting is stored in its own handmade cardboard box, alongside a clipping from a newspaper published in the same city and on the same day that the artist made the painting. History as recorded in daily events, whether global, national, or local, is bound together with the residues of individual activity and memorialized under the rubric of the date. In addition to the title, determined by the day on which the work was executed, a subtitle may be appended. These vary widely from diaristic notes to impersonal records, as the following examples from January 1966 attest: "I thought about memory and sense," "Janine came to my studio," "I am painting this painting," "USA began to bomb North Vietnam again." In counterpoint to the dialectic between order and chance–that is, between the regularity and standardization imposed by calendrical and linguistic conventions and the arbitrarily determined strictures governing size and color–there is a modicum of subjectivity: in the subtle traces of manual execution, clear evidence is offered of the act of making.[2] A constant traveler, Kawara has now created Date Paintings in more than 112 cities worldwide, in a project that will end only with his death.

Other, related works in his oeuvre confirm the existentialism at the heart of his metaphysics.[3] For example, in 1970 he began intermittently to send telegrams to friends and professional colleagues that always contain the same message: I am still alive.[4] Once a medium of urgent news, the telegram has become almost obsolete as a means of communication. Normally it announces timely or memorable events, such as unexpected deaths, but Kawara's messages invert these customary practices: given that everyone is assumed to be alive until the contrary is announced, Kawara's reassurance that he is still living seems gratuitous–absurd. Moreover, even though it was true at the moment it was sent, it may not be so by the time it is received. Imbued in equal measure with humor and pathos, these terse missives nonetheless offer testimony to a fundamental state: consciousness, a precondition to all other forms of being. Although destined initially for the attention of a single recipient, they were immediately understood to be a form of Conceptual art and hence soon exhibited or published in catalogues and monographs on the artist.

Kawara has long shown the *Today Series* both as single paintings and as groups, and with or without their boxes. Recently, however, more far-reaching premises have occasioned different types of presentation. In 1993, he planned an exhibition unprecedented in his career for Dia. Titled "One Thousand Days One Million Years," it opened on January 1, 1993, and closed on December 31 of the same year. Complexly structured, it involved three components. The largest was a selection of a thousand works from the *Today Series*, all executed in New York City, where this Japanese-born artist has partially resided since 1965. Heralded by the originary canvas, dated January 4, 1966, different groups of the paintings were installed in the gallery at the beginning of each month over the course of the year, so that the visitor who wished to experience fully the exhibition was required to return time and again in order to view the unfolding of the thousand days from its inception onward. Concurrently, and for the duration of the show, in a small room adjacent to the principal exhibition space,

NOV. 20, 1969, "Ascent stage and command ship dock. Comdrs. Charles Conrad Jr. and Alan L. Bean crawl through tunnel to rejoin Comdr. Richard F. Gordon Jr.", 1969, from *Today Series*, 1966–present

One Million Years (Past) was exhibited in its original form, as a ten-volume book in which the dates of the one million years preceding are typed in Arabic numerals in neat rows of nine columns, a decade per line, with every century slightly separated from the preceding, as in a paragraph, and five hundred years to each page. A dedication, "For all those who have lived and died," introduces the work. Its companion, *One Million Years (Future)*, which opens with the inscription "For the last one," was first executed some ten years after the completion of *One Million Years (Past)*, also in the guise of an edition of leather-covered binders. But at Dia, for the first time, it was presented as a recording, in which a male and a female voice counting continuously, year upon year, into the future were audible in the museum spaces.

Over a succession of visits, visitors to "One Thousand Days One Million Years" not only experienced the lapse of real time, that is, lived time, but were faced with a future that, as mapped in Kawara's sound piece, had passed according to a quite differently calibrated temporality. As they surveyed the seemingly random dates on the paintings aligned sequentially around the gallery, some canvases might, fortuitously, have seemed significant; those marked with the birthday of a friend, a family anniversary, the beginning of a war. History and memory were invoked but ultimately yielded little that proved telling. The reiteration of countless dates served as the vehicle of ontological meditation rather than epistemological inquiry: time came to be experienced as a lived abstraction. Through this telling juxtaposition of three different works, Kawara subtly restated an abiding preoccupation in his practice: the conviction that temporality and duration, while objectively determined—that is, determined according to standardized systems and concepts—are nonetheless always and finally subjectively experienced in and through the present moment.

In two recent projects Kawara deployed the *Today Series* in a more redemptive spirit, though once again via channels that challenge linguistically based forms of communication. In "Pure Consciousness," a traveling exhibition initiated in 1998, seven paintings from consecutive days are installed in kindergartens so that, as part of the classroom decor along with teaching aids and the pupils' artwork, they are available to students and teachers in their daily activities. For young children taking elementary lessons in reading, writing, and mathematics, in drawing, in history and various forms of literature and storytelling, these works may prove pertinent as models—they may offer alternatives to prevailing paradigms.[5]

For Dia:Beacon, Kawara proposed that a gallery be constructed to house thirty-six paintings from the *Today Series*, registering each year from its beginning in 1966 until the millennium. Executed in the same small format and in similar dark tonalities, they were made in various cities around the world, from Tokyo to Stockholm, from New York to the town of North East Margaree, Nova Scotia. Their starting point, a day in the mid-1960s, is contemporary with some of the earliest works in Dia's collection, and their span corresponds to the period currently covered by the collection. Yet their relation to that time is at once central and peripheral. Given the conditions under which they were produced, they are as locked into that historical moment as any other artworks on view here. But, in contrast to almost all of the work in Dia's collection, their address of a bodily based mode of experiencing is no longer primarily ocular-centric.[6] For the installation contains a second, key component:

right "Pure Consciousness," 1998–present, installation of Date Paintings from 1997, from the *Today Series* (1966–present), at the Center for the Protection of Children, Institute of Social Formation, Abidjan, 2000

pages 182–185 36 Date Paintings of 35 years from the *Today Series*, 1966–present

the air in the room has been ionized, purifying the atmosphere. This redemptive gesture may affect viewers in ways that they consciously register, but knowledge of the agent's presence does not necessarily assist in facilitating that process, for any recuperative effect is experienced by the spirit, or consciousness, via the sensate body rather than the mind. Although there can be no certainty that the intervention of the ionizers will be felt (and no means of calibrating or quantifying it), spending time in the space is a minimal requirement. The subtitle to the Date Painting for July 26, 1972, a quote from the Russian astrophysicist Nikolai Kozyrev, is as pertinent to this project as to most others Kawara has undertaken in recent years: "Time is thin around the cause and dense around the effect."

L.C.

notes

1 For Japanese, Korean, and other languages that do not use Roman letters, Kawara uses Esperanto to write the date.

2 On December 28, 1972, Kawara wrote, in Swedish (because he was then in Stockholm), the last of these subtitles: "I don't know." Since then the only subtitle has been the weekday on which that Date Painting was executed. This last testimony can be seen as yet another instance of Kawara's increasingly radical intellectual skepticism.

3 Jean-Paul Sartre's novel *La Nausée*, 1938 (*Nausea*), had a formative influence on the young Kawara. Since the 1970s, however, he has become more engaged with the ideas of the Russian-Armenian mystic George Ivanovitch Gurdjieff, for whom linguistic communication was inadequate in the search for a "primordial condition," a state of consciousness or "aspect of the mind higher than ordinary thought."

4 These telegrams followed three he sent for the "18 Paris IV.70" exhibition: "I am not going to commit suicide—don't worry" (December 5, 1969); "I am not going to commit suicide—worry" (December 8, 1969); and "I am going to sleep—forget it" (December 11, 1969).

5 In 1962 Kawara visited the cave paintings of Altamira, which made a profound impression on him. Rather than considering them prehistoric, he saw them as "beyond history" and "beyond language": for him, they make a direct appeal outside time. Moreover, given that they were executed in artificial light, they bear witness to an extension of diurnal time unprecedented in human history.

6 In the mid-1960s Kawara made a number of works involving braille or self-invented visual codes. See Jonathan Watkins, "Where 'I Don't Know' Is the Right Answer," in *On Kawara* (New York: Phaidon, 2002), p. 82.

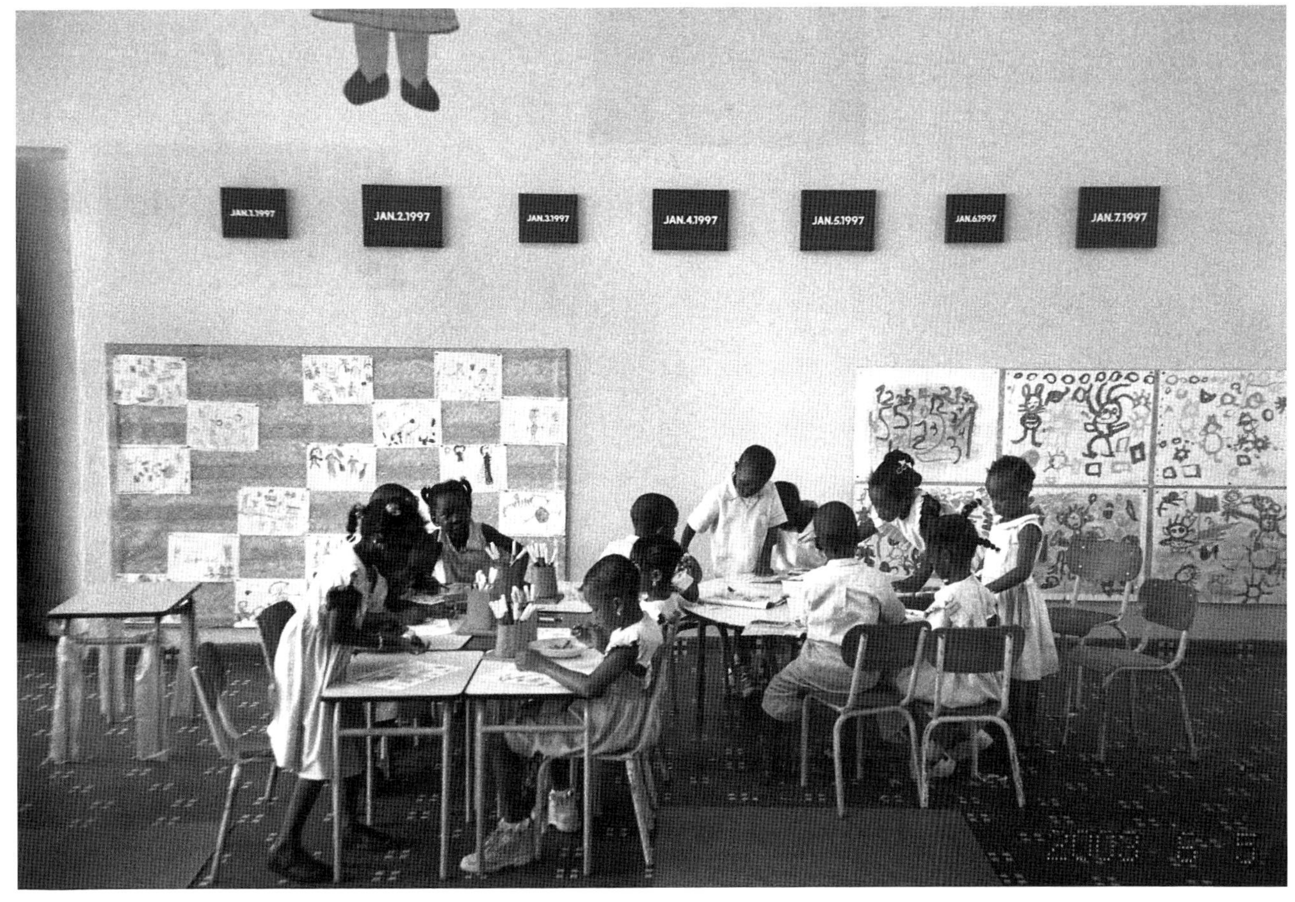

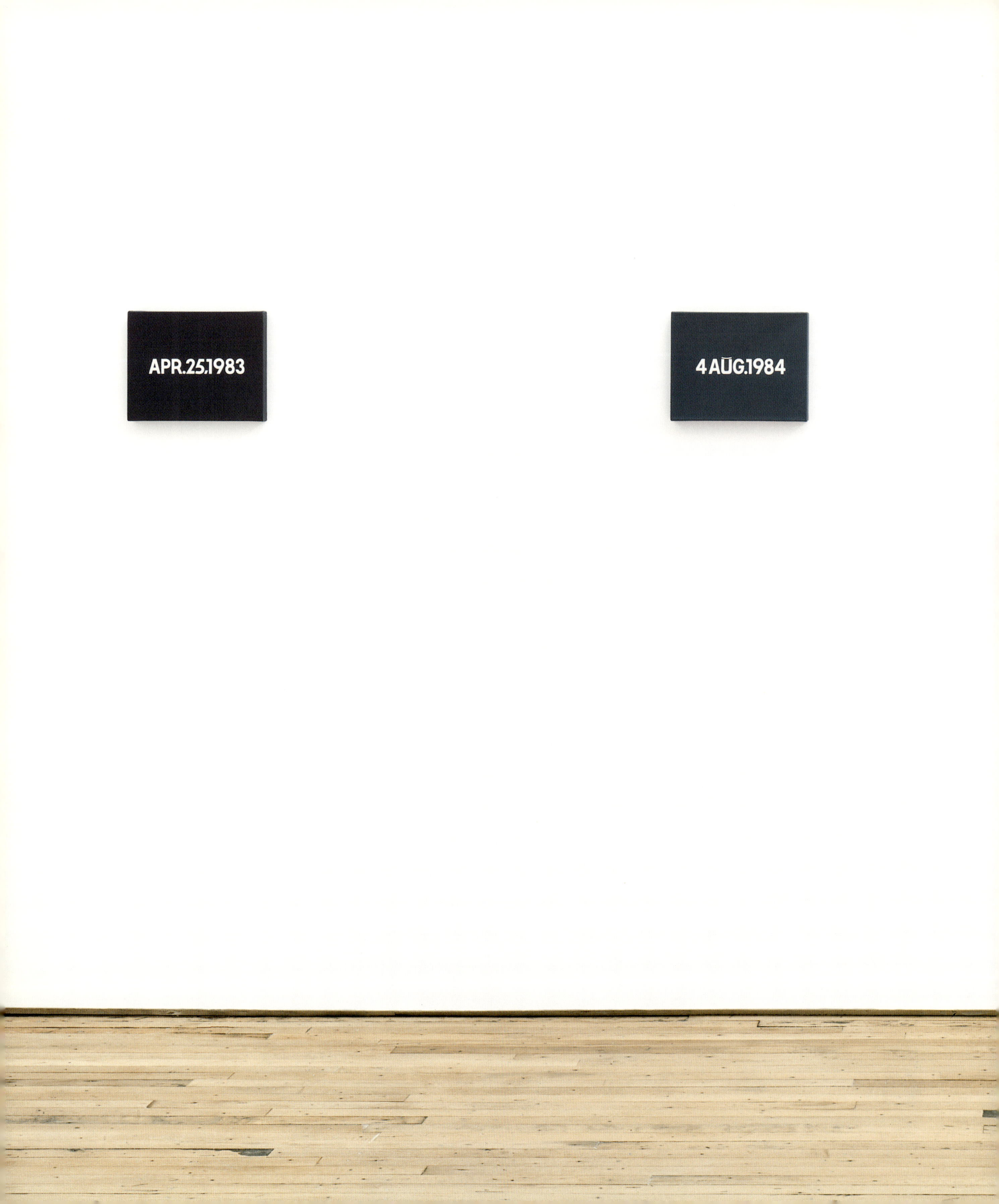

APR.25,1983

4 AUG.1984

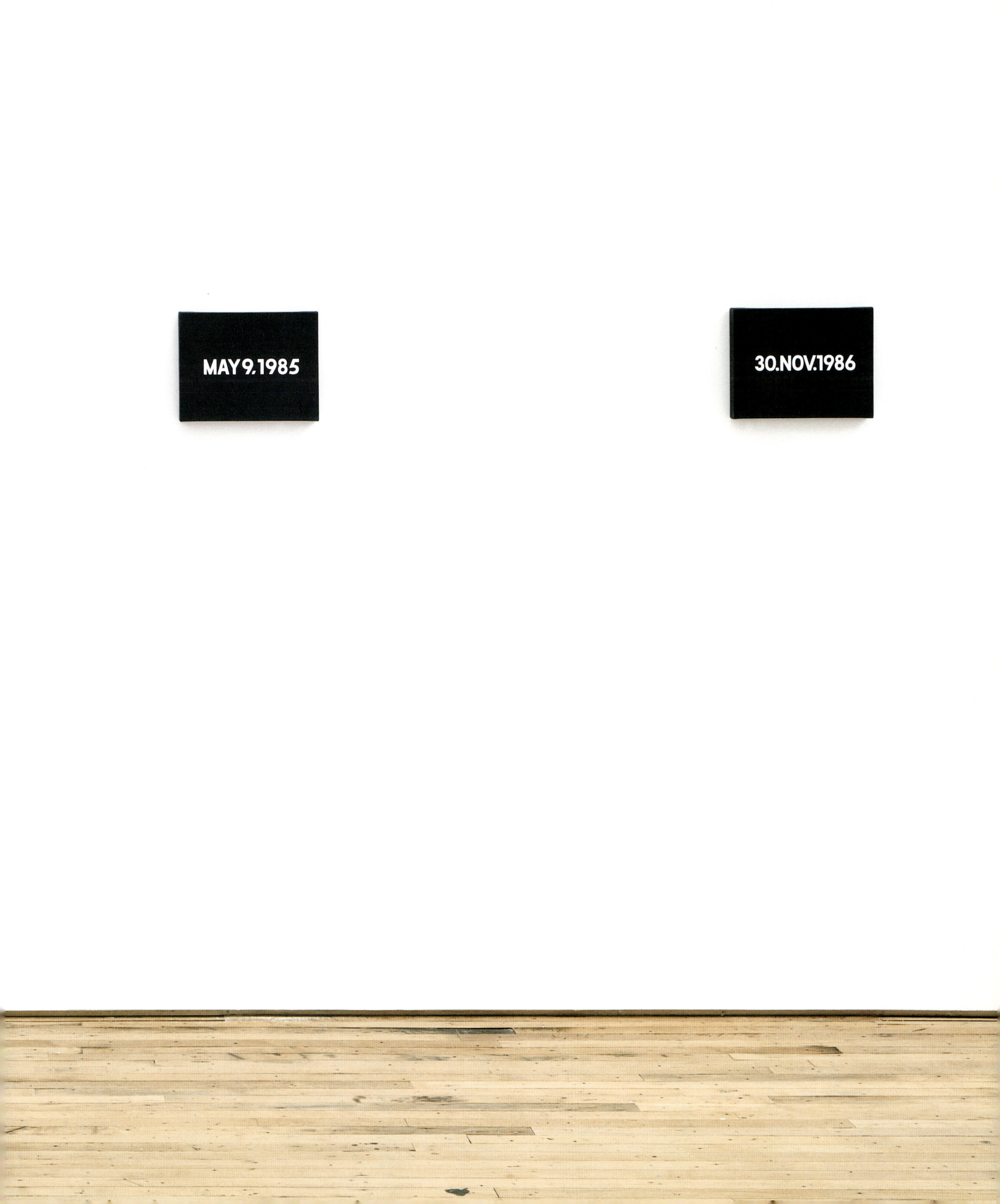

MAY 9, 1985

30.NOV.1986

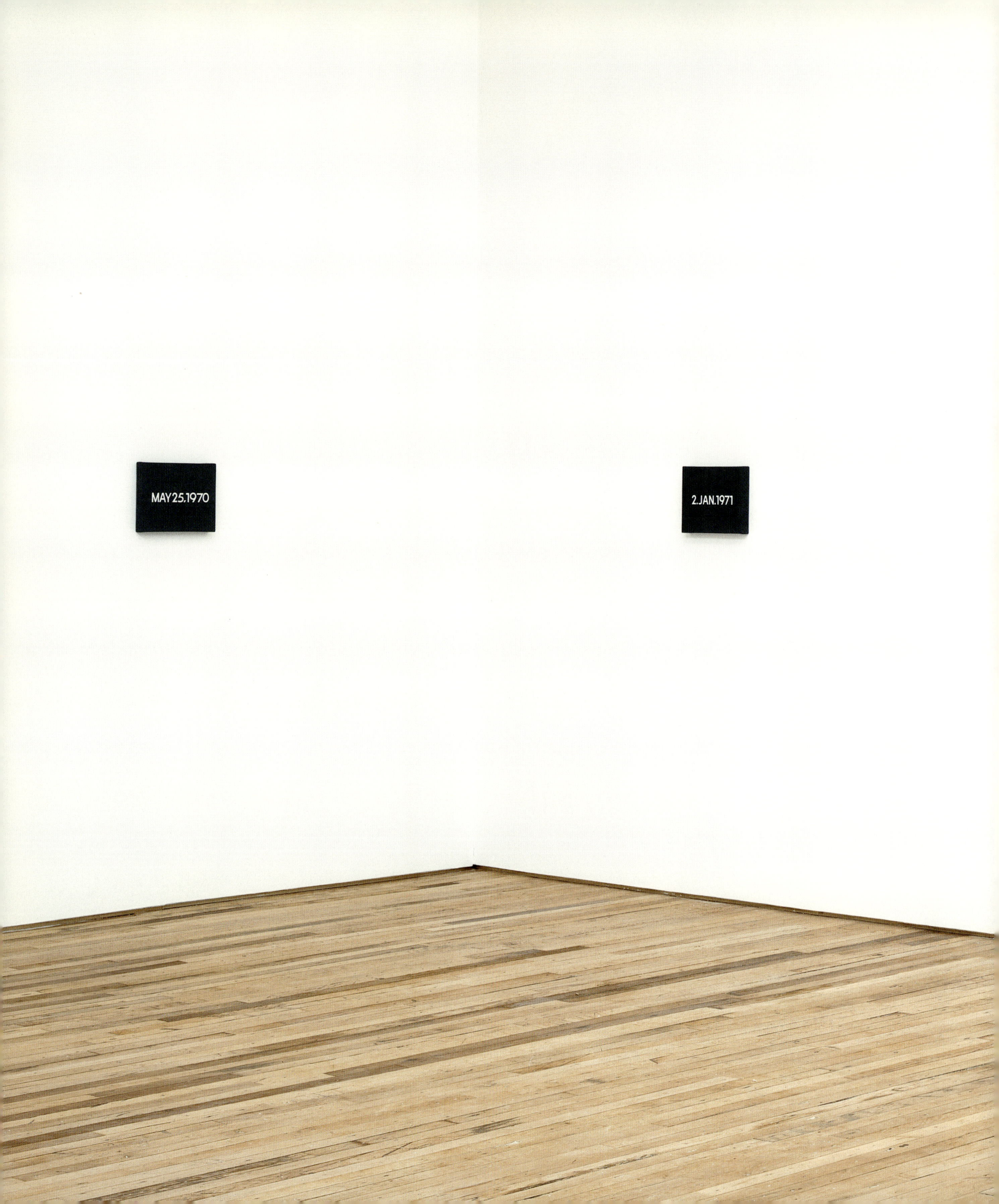

MAY 25.1970
2.JAN.1971

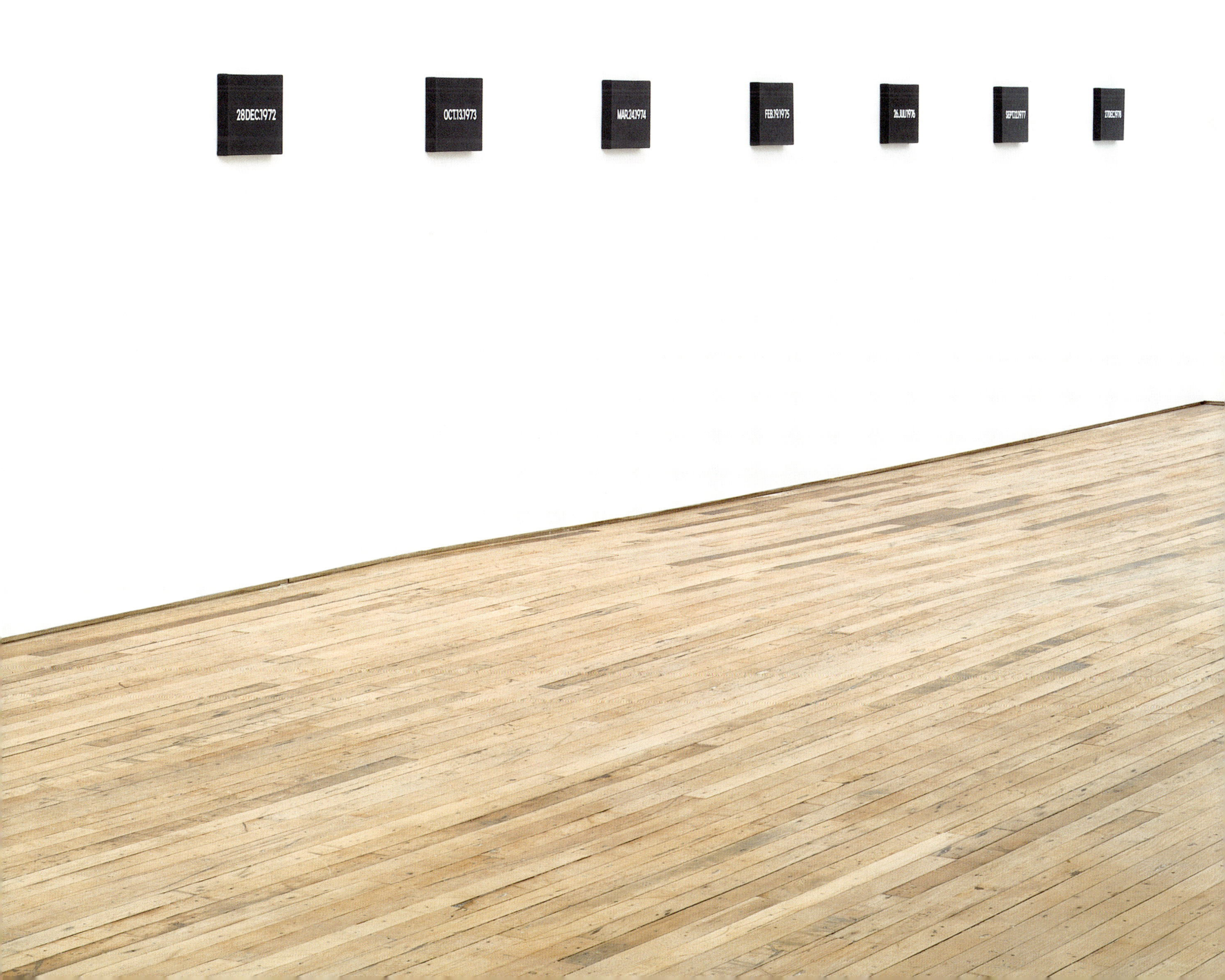
28DEC.1972
OCT.13,1973
MAR.24,1974
FEB.19,1975
26.JULI.1976

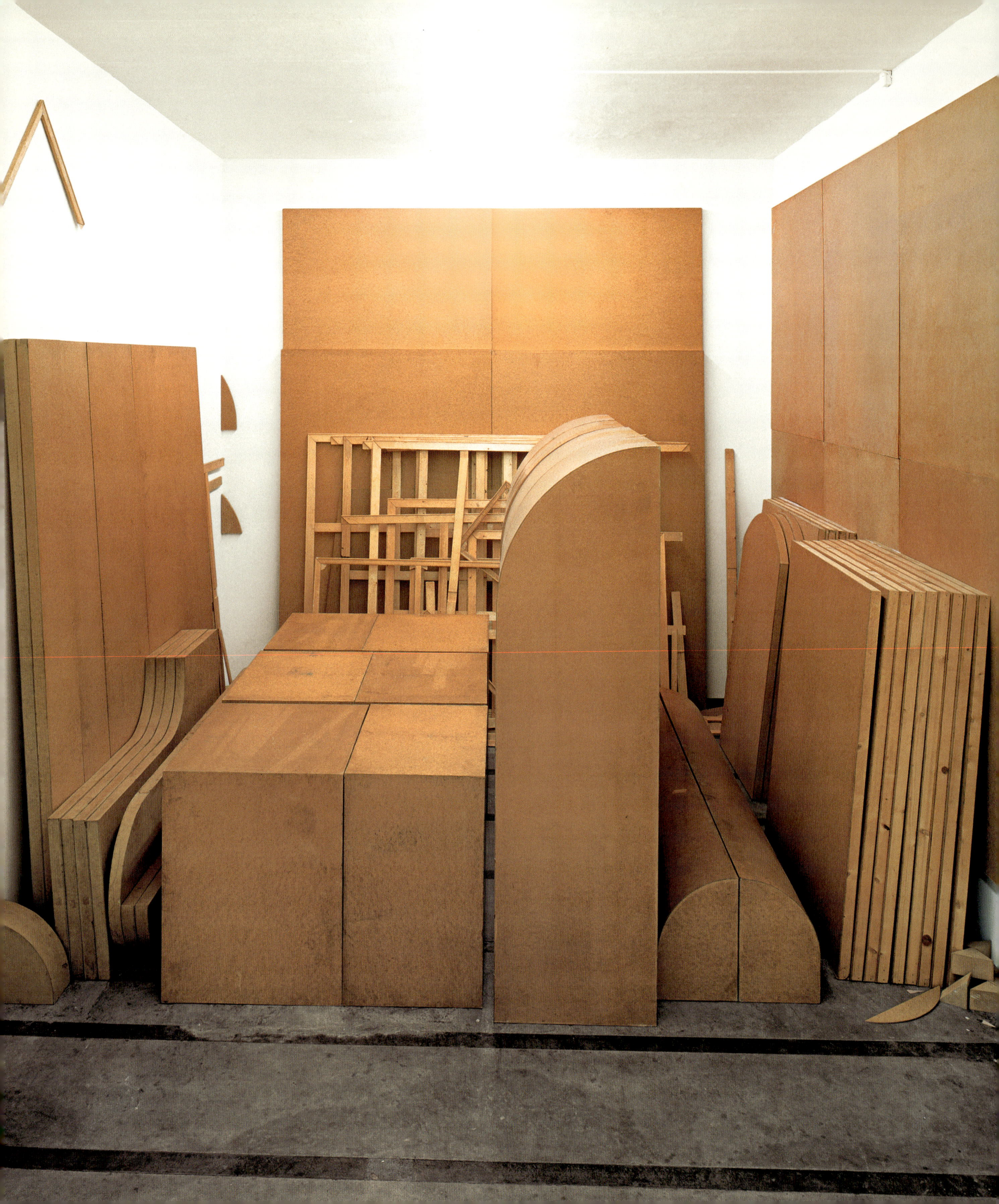

Imi Knoebel

Imi Knoebel was born in Dessau, Germany, in 1940. He was a student of Joseph Beuys at the Kunstakademie Düsseldorf from 1964 to 1971. His first exhibition, "IMI + IMI," with Imi Giese, a fellow student of Beuys's, was held in Copenhagen, in 1968. Knoebel has since exhibited his works in Documentas 5 (1972), 6 (1977), 7 (1982), and 8 (1987), and at Sonsbeek '71. In 1987 Knoebel oversaw an installation of his own work, as well as those of Beuys and Blinky Palermo for the inaugural exhibitions at Dia's galleries on West Twenty-second Street in New York City. A retrospective of his work traveled, in 1996–97, throughout Europe, including such venues as Haus der Kunst, Munich; Stedelijk Museum, Amsterdam; and Institut Valencià d'Art Modern, Centre Julio González, Valencia. He lives and works in Düsseldorf.

Raum 19, 1968, installation at Galerie Heiner Friedrich, Cologne, 1977

Raum 19 (*Room 19*), 1968 is a key work in Imi Knoebel's oeuvre, prescient of his mature aesthetic and practice. Created while he was still a *Meister-student* under Joseph Beuys, it took its title from the place of its execution, the number of his studio in the Kunstakademie Düsseldorf.[1] All seventy-seven parts—stretchers, planar elements, stereometric and rectangular volumes—are fabricated from wood and fiber-board, which has been used "raw," in an untreated state; the pristine condition of these simple geometric components gives the impression that they await future deployment. A commonplace building material then rarely used for the making of artworks, Masonite soon became one of Knoebel's preferred materials on account of its quotidian serviceability and ready availability. This humble ordinariness, together with the straightforward carpentry techniques it presupposes, signals his belief that the artist's practice is as banal and pragmatic as that of a farm laborer, an urban worker, or an architect. Notwithstanding his abiding reverence for Kasimir Malevich and Beuys, he claims that an artist's role today has little to do with that of a visionary creator inspired by mystical beliefs.

Also prophetic of much of Knoebel's later work is the way these ineluctably nonobjective forms elide the realm of painting with those of sculpture and architecture. But not only does *Raum 19* dispense with illusion in favor of corporeal presence, it also restricts metaphoric and referential content. From the stretchers and stretcher parts to the picture frames, from the variously scaled planar surfaces, in the guise of both individual "canvases" and sections of mural-sized compositions, to the bland, simple sculptural volumes, it arrays the constituents and components of a painterly practice reduced to its rudimentary essentials: form, material, surface, space, support. Given its embrace of both the plastic and the tectonic, *Raum 19* may also serve as an ideal model for a creative revisioning of the world, but Knoebel's works never create a metastructure of reality: "[They] take part in this world as *things*," Christoph Schenker argues. Moreover, in seeking to function as "instruments of the pure experience of 'image,' excluded from the realm of language," they remain, he contends, "at the very limits of communicability."[2]

The polymorphous elements of *Raum 19* can be variously assembled depending on the context, that is, depending on the gallery space and the artist's impulses. Since no fixed set of relationships binds the components, the work can expand to an environmental scale or may be densely compacted so that it appears as if in storage, as was the case when Knoebel exhibited it at Dia's exhibition facility in New York City, in 1987, alongside a range of other works. Given that the ensemble is permutable, and that its particular configuration, dimensions, and internal relations are dependent on the artist's decisions in situ, form becomes an event–sometimes chaotic, sometimes ordered; sometimes impenetrable, sometimes lucid; sometimes austere, sometimes abundant; sometimes confined, sometimes boundless. Though unique, every event remains contingent. Since any single installation is only ever one among innumerable possible compositions in this open system, emphasis shifts to notions of presentation per se, to staging as an abstract condition.

Knoebel's precocious preoccupation with questions of installation betrays a considerable debt to Beuys. Not only were the older artist's performances–his "actions"–undertaken in relation to the specifics of a situation, but his larger sculptural works, such as *Arena–dove sarei arrivato se fossi stato intelligente! (Arena–where would I have got if I had been intelligent!)*, 1970–72, were also adapted to the context in which they were to be shown. *Arena . . .* could be tightly compacted into three densely layered stacks, as in his retrospective at the Solomon R. Guggenheim Museum, New York, in 1979, or hung in a panoramic sweep so that every panel was visible, testimony to the breadth and character of his performance work–its very subject–over some fifteen years. When compressed, *Arena . . .* became for Beuys a battery, a repository of potential energy, and hence a prime instrument in the social revolution he hoped his art would ultimately effect.

Knoebel in large part eschewed Beuys's ideology, with the important proviso that he adhered to his mentor's guiding belief in the regenerative function of creativity. Thus, although from the outset of his career he variously explored the notion of a state of storage, a condition in which the work of art is not revealed but held at the ready, works such as *Raum 19*, in contrast to Beuys's Fonds, or batteries, carry no metaphysical meaning beyond a recuperative reflection on strategies of disposition as vehicles for constructing an aesthetic totality–as opposed to the sociopolitical totality that Beuys sought to engage. For Knoebel this focus on a creative revisioning of the spatiomaterial world required a stubbornly pragmatic investigation of the formal properties, syntax, and protocols that determined its identity. Several years later he explored this problematic further in a companion piece, *Genter Raum* (*Ghent Room*), 1980. Comprising more than 450 elements, its hallmark is not the greatly enhanced scale but the addition of color, which, manifest in all its fullness and unpredictability, assumes the form of monochrome panels in brilliant enameled and reflective acidic hues. In installation, once again a subjective response to a set of given conditions, *Genter Raum* is based on color as event. While it, too, may be presented as if in a stored state, *in potentia*, its expansive tectonic and territorial capacity on occasion enables it (as in 1991 when exhibited at the Kunstmuseum Winterthur) to incorporate within its frame certain historical works from the permanent collection of the museum in which it has been placed on temporary view.[3]

Shortly after devising *Raum 19*, Knoebel began a series of drawings that were kept in boxed portfolios housed in specially designed cabinets. When put on public view, the six cabinets that constitute *Untitled* (1973–75) can be opened under supervision to make a selection of their contents available to viewers. Realizing that this vast project was potentially limitless, the artist curtailed it at the point when he had filled more than 900 portfolios with a quarter of a million pencil drawings, each a typewriter-format sheet of paper limned with thin vertical rules varying in number and spacing. This combination of a monumental scale (and concomitant ambition) with a willingness to maintain the work in what might be deemed a truncated state bears a close relation to works by several of Knoebel's contemporaries, notably Hanne Darboven, for whom the book as "stored time" serves as an important structural modality, and Franz Erhard Walther, who typically presents his "demonstration materials" in a "stored state."[4]

Purging his frugal ascetic materials of vestigial metaphoric or allusory meanings, Knoebel sought to focus on the originary forms and bases of painting, and on its relation to sculpture and to architecture, by means of installations conceived as an aesthetic totality. His work consequently assumes an abstract, generic condition: it seeks to become a universal statement. At odds with contemporary formalist theories propounded by Clement Greenberg and his followers in the United States in the 1960s, Knoebel was profoundly shaped by a formative encounter with Malevich's book *The Non-Objective World* (1926), and by his landmark painting *Black Square* (1915), which became a touchstone for the young German painter.[5] Seeking "the zero of form," Malevich created an art that is as far from the reductive as it is from the doctrinaire.[6] Although Knoebel's work is by contrast unequivocally secular, he derived from the Russian mystic a notion of art that is essentially utopian, that is, of an art that in assuming a tabula rasa as its point of departure resists language and the discursive. Friedrich Schiller's philosophical poem "The Veiled Image at Sais," which Knoebel reprinted in 1991 as the preface to one of his catalogues, provides further

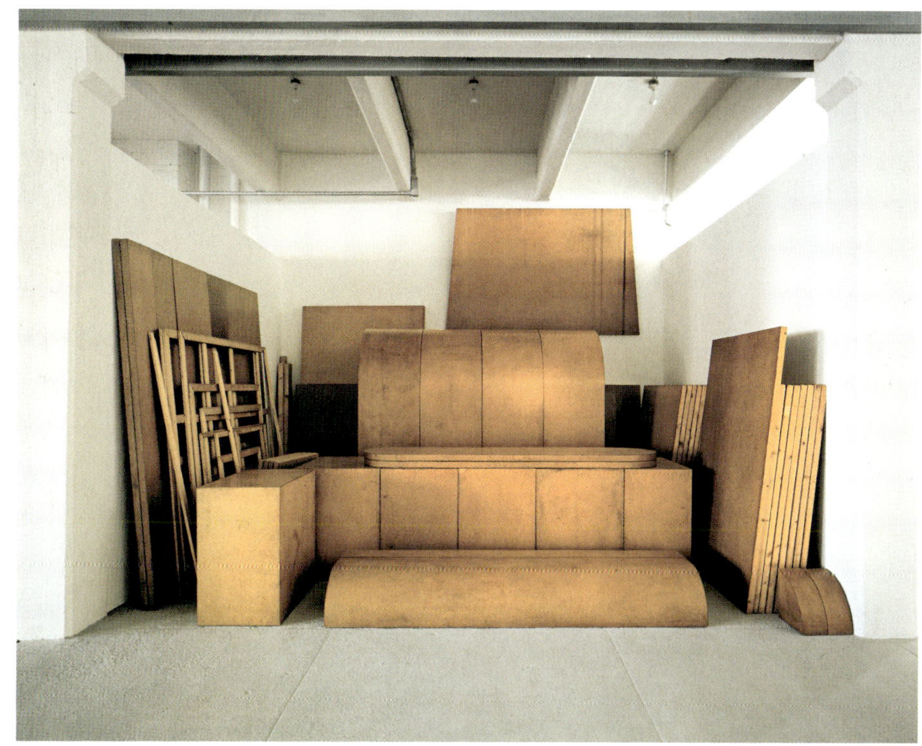

Raum 19, 1968, installation at Dia Art Foundation, New York City, 1987

elucidation of this aesthetic.[7] Schiller posits an ideal Truth that in its purest form is unattainable, or, better, that is revealed only to those who at mortal risk lift its veil. At issue, however, is less the protagonist's efforts to transgress the prohibition on lifting the veil than the aspiration toward Absolute Truth, incarnate as a hieratic shrouded image. According to Schiller, what is not disclosed, what remains pure possibility—what is, in short, utopic—takes emblematic visual form. That this iconic image resists verbal communication and comprehension is manifest in the poem's refusal to elaborate on it, indeed to do more than demonstrate its fatal effect on those who seek complete disclosure, who relentlessly privilege the finality of the definitively fixed and absolute.

Inspired by his lodestar Malevich, shaped by his mentor Beuys, Knoebel inserted a structured profusion at the very heart of *Raum 19*, his protean, pioneering statement. Suspended between amorphous and crystalline principles, this insistently reticent work has been reassembled anew at Dia:Beacon. In some future incarnation elsewhere in the building it may become an enveloping spatialized entity that will treat the gallery as a volumetric support; for the moment, it responds to its assigned location in the museum as warehousing, as a conventional storage site. The irony of this ploy is not lost on the artist.

L.C.

notes

1 From 1965 Imi Knoebel shared this studio with Imi Giese. For a short time Jörg Immendorf and Blinky Palermo also used it. The two Imis only gave up the studio when Beuys's own atelier, next door at number 20, became impossibly overcrowded owing to the master's controversial policy of accepting every student who applied to join his class. This open policy became the pretext for Beuys's eventual dismissal from the Kunstakademie in 1972, the year after Knoebel graduated. See Johannes Stüttgen's interview with Knoebel, "'Der Ganze Riemen': Imi & Imi 1964–1969," 1982, reprinted in *Imi Knoebel* (New York: Dia Art Foundation, 1987), pp. 26–32. *Raum 19* is sometimes known by an alternative title, *Hartfaser Raum* (*Fiberboard Room*), derived from its materials.

2 Christoph Schenker, "Imi Knoebel: The Limits of Communicability," *Flash Art*, 24, no. 161 (November/December 1991), p. 107.

3 See ibid., pp. 103–07.

4 See Rudolph Bumiller, "Working with Success—Working with Unsuccess," *Parkett*, no. 32 (1992), pp. 38–43.

5 Marianne Brouwer's text "For Imi and Carmen" well captures the significance of *Black Square* for Knoebel: "It is a painting against metaphysics. . . . In its substance, matter and mass, the black square that isn't a [perfect] square, absorbs like a black hole all language, all 'worldviews.' . . . It absorbs and renders silent but it does not kill. I mean it does not kill speech or existence by denying a representational world. For by its counterpart: radiation, the white, nothingness, it suddenly opens to us, like an explosion of the eye, the existence of another logic, in which everything, paradoxically, lives and lives therein. . . . Because the painting is so precise, and because it isn't the rendering of the thought of the square (not a geometrical abstraction), it is a reality, [it is] a world seen . . . not a mathematical, idealist, immaterial painting of perfection." In *Imi Knoebel* (Otterlo: Rijksmuseum Kröller-Müller, 1985), n.p.

6 See Kasimir Malevich, "From Cubism and Futurism to Suprematism: The New Painterly Realism," 1916, reprinted in John E. Bowlt, ed., *Russian Art of the Avant Garde: Theory and Criticism, 1902–1934* (New York: Viking, 1976), p. 128.

7 Friedrich Schiller, "The Veiled Image at Sais," 1795, in *Imi Knoebel: Acht Portraits* (Berlin, Galerie Fahnemann, 1991), n.p. Knoebel has only permitted a single interview with him to be published; see note 1.

Untitled, 1973–75, installation at Dia Art Foundation, New York City, 1987

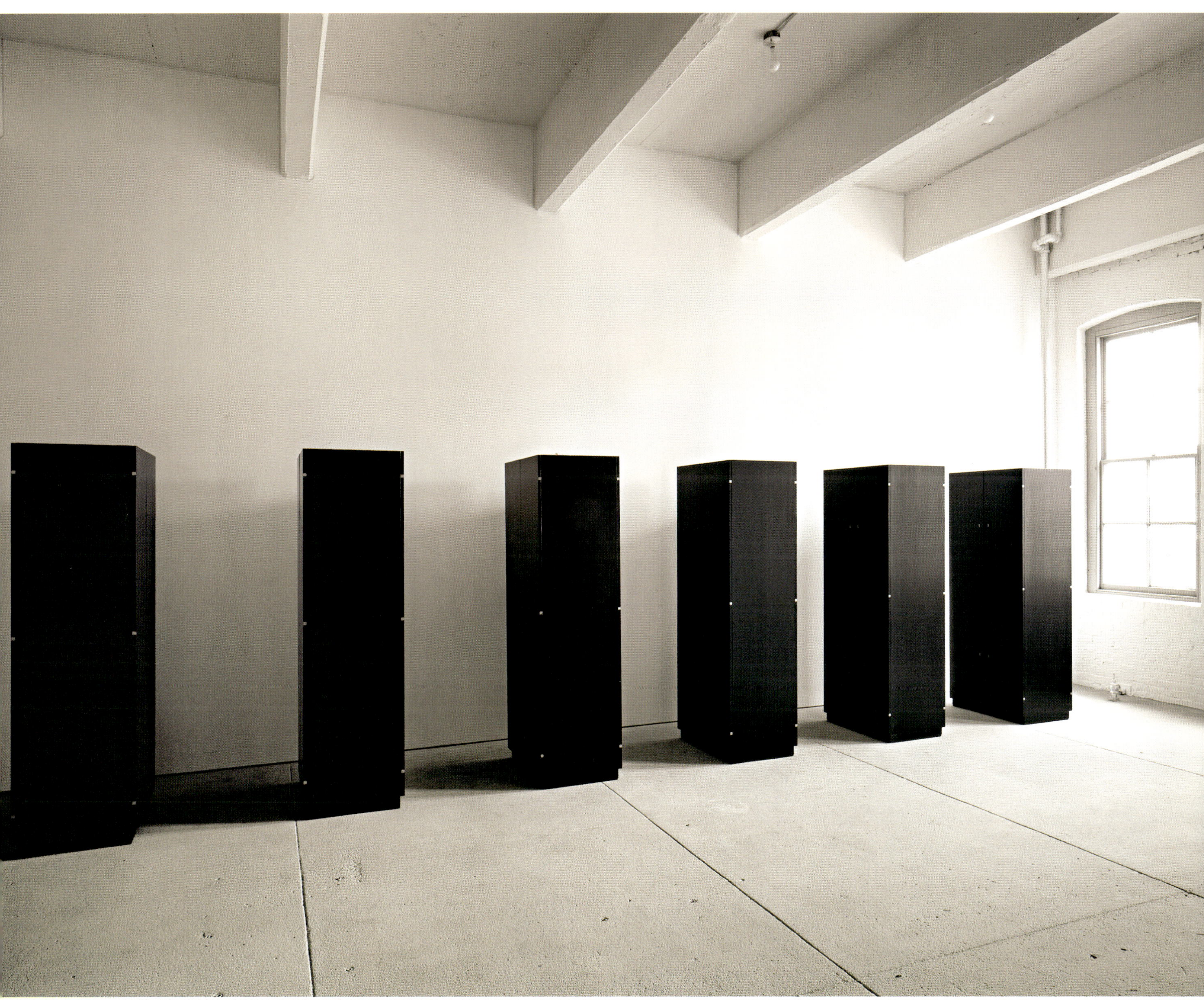

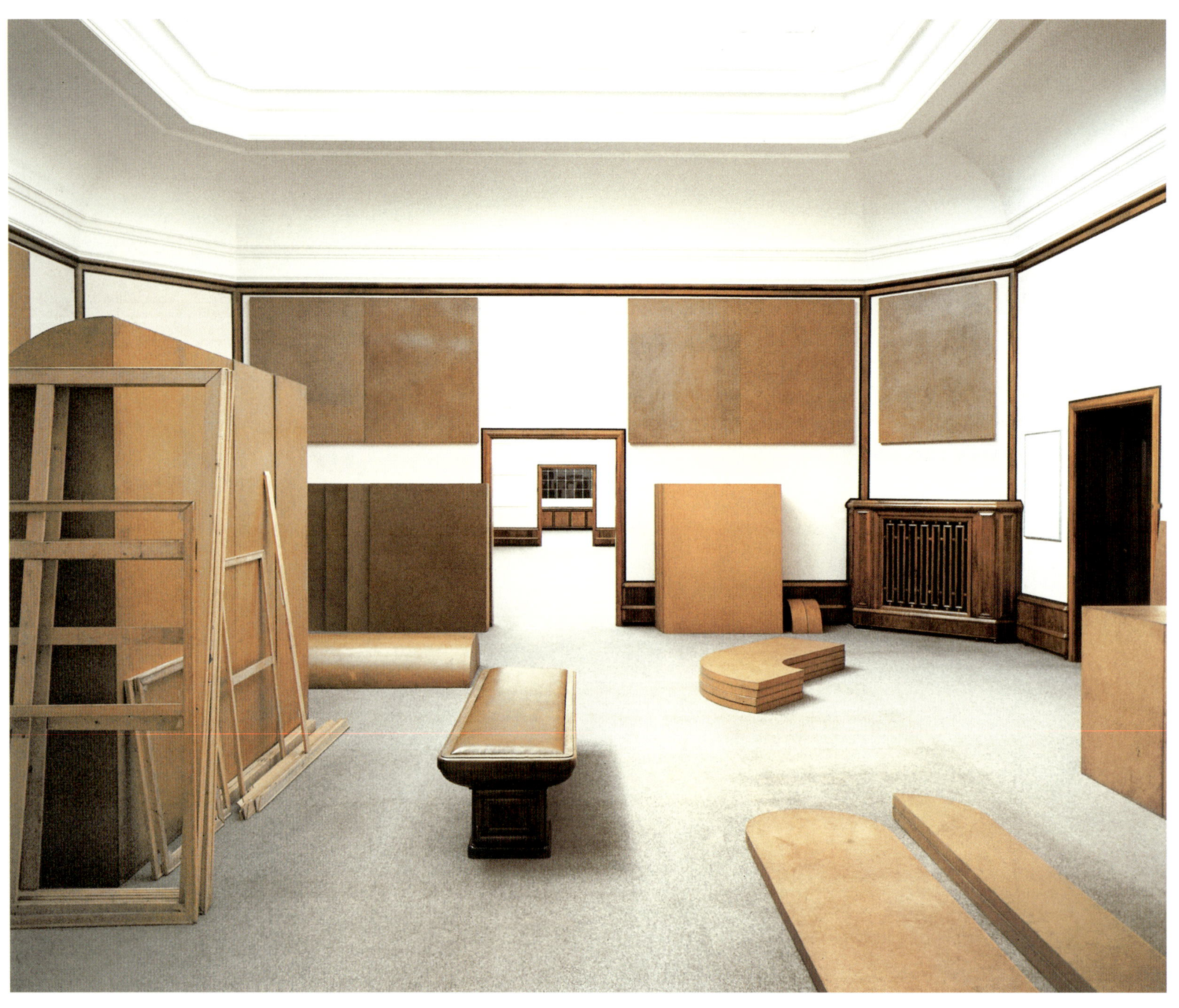

left and right *Raum 19*, 1968, installation at Kunstmuseum Winterthur, 1983

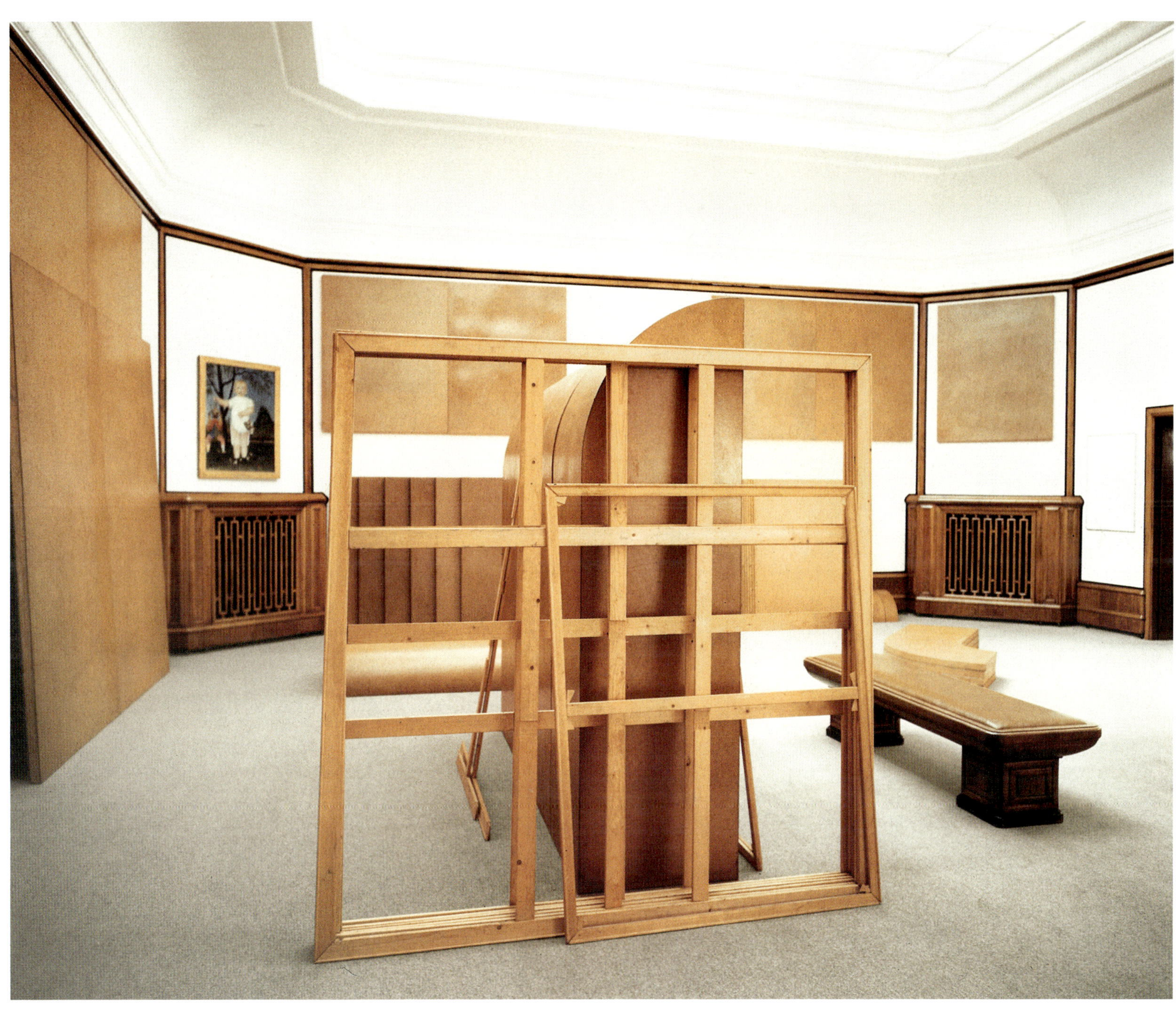

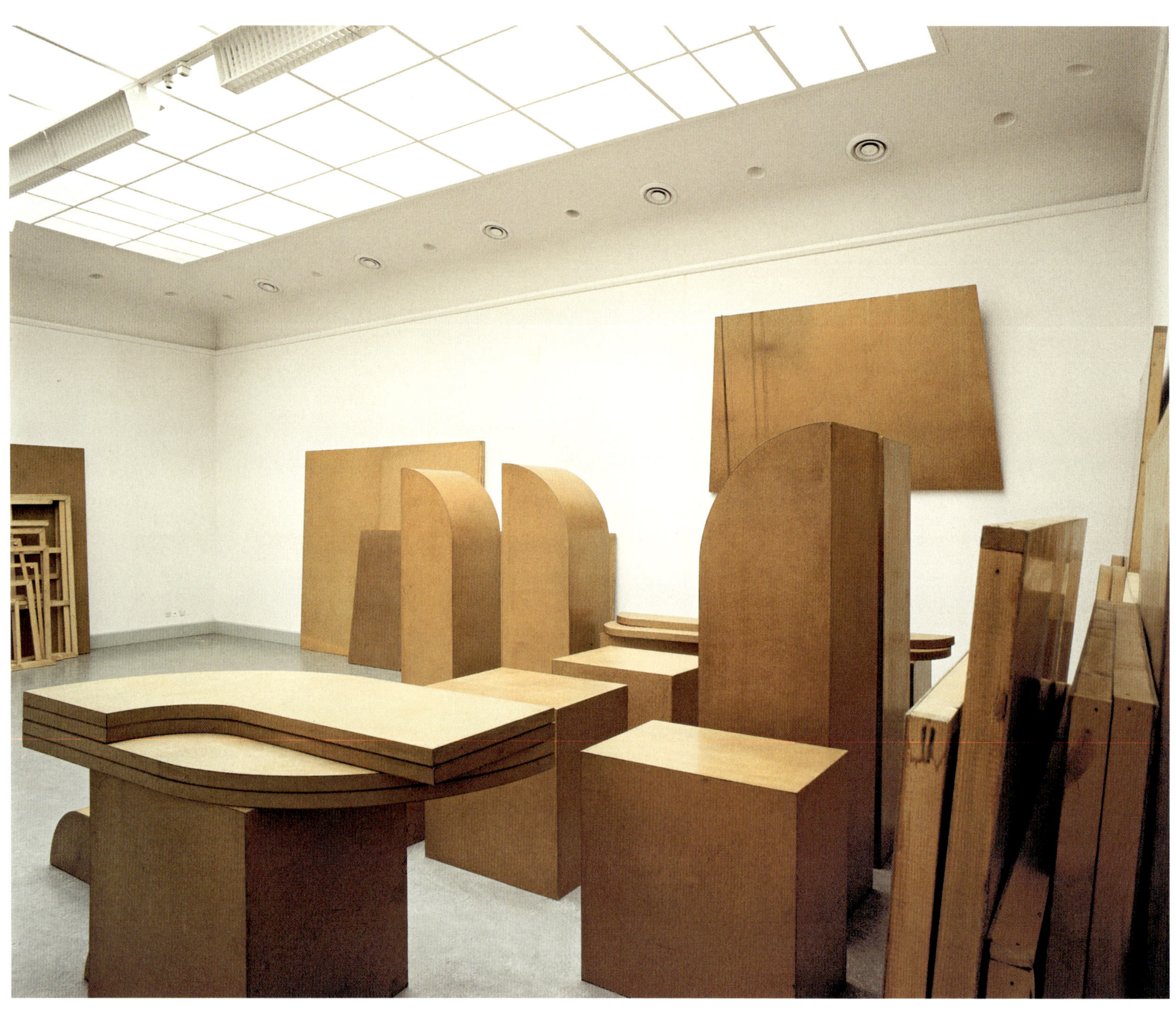

left and right *Raum 19*, 1968, installation at Van Abbemuseum, Eindhoven, 1982

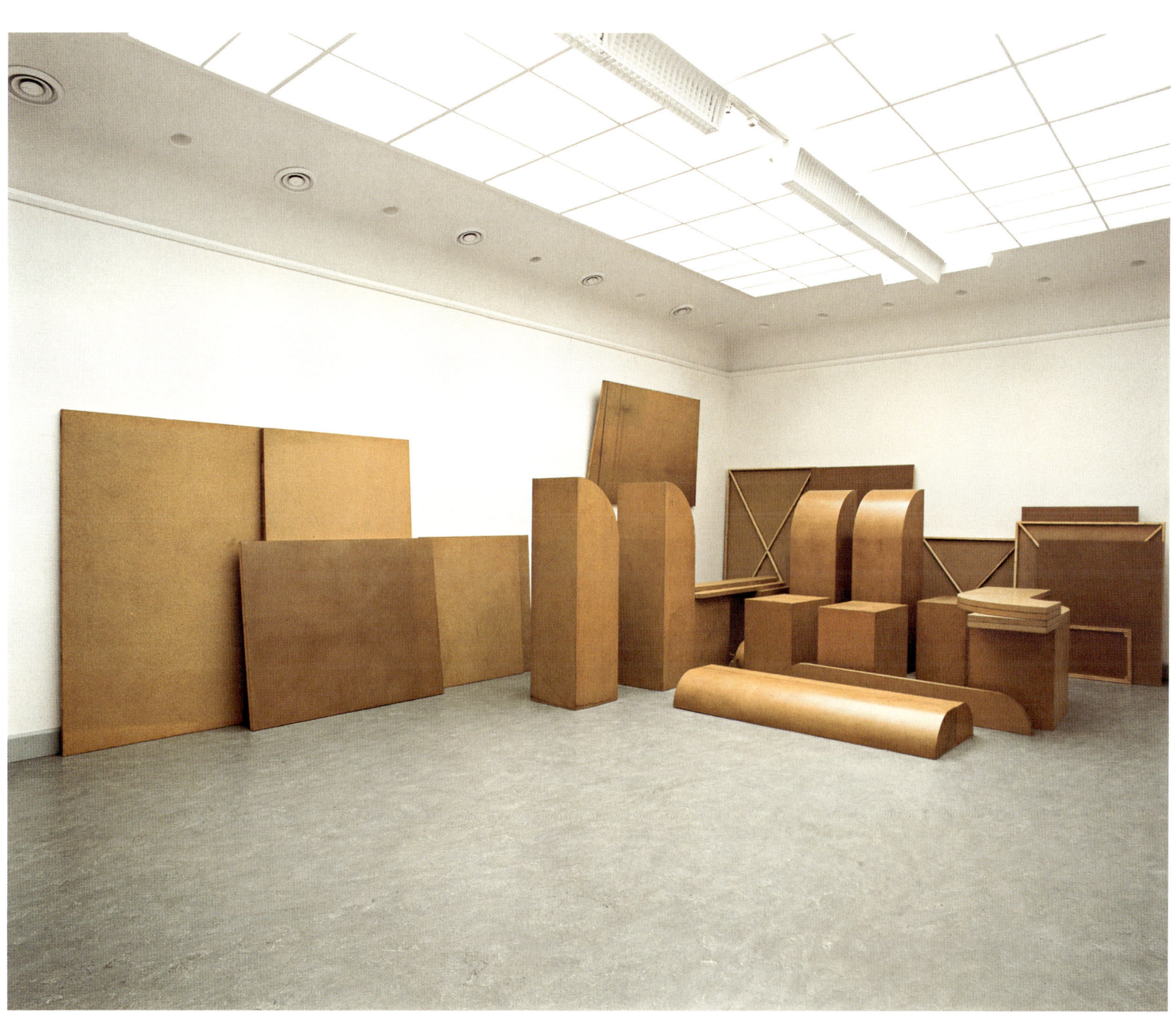

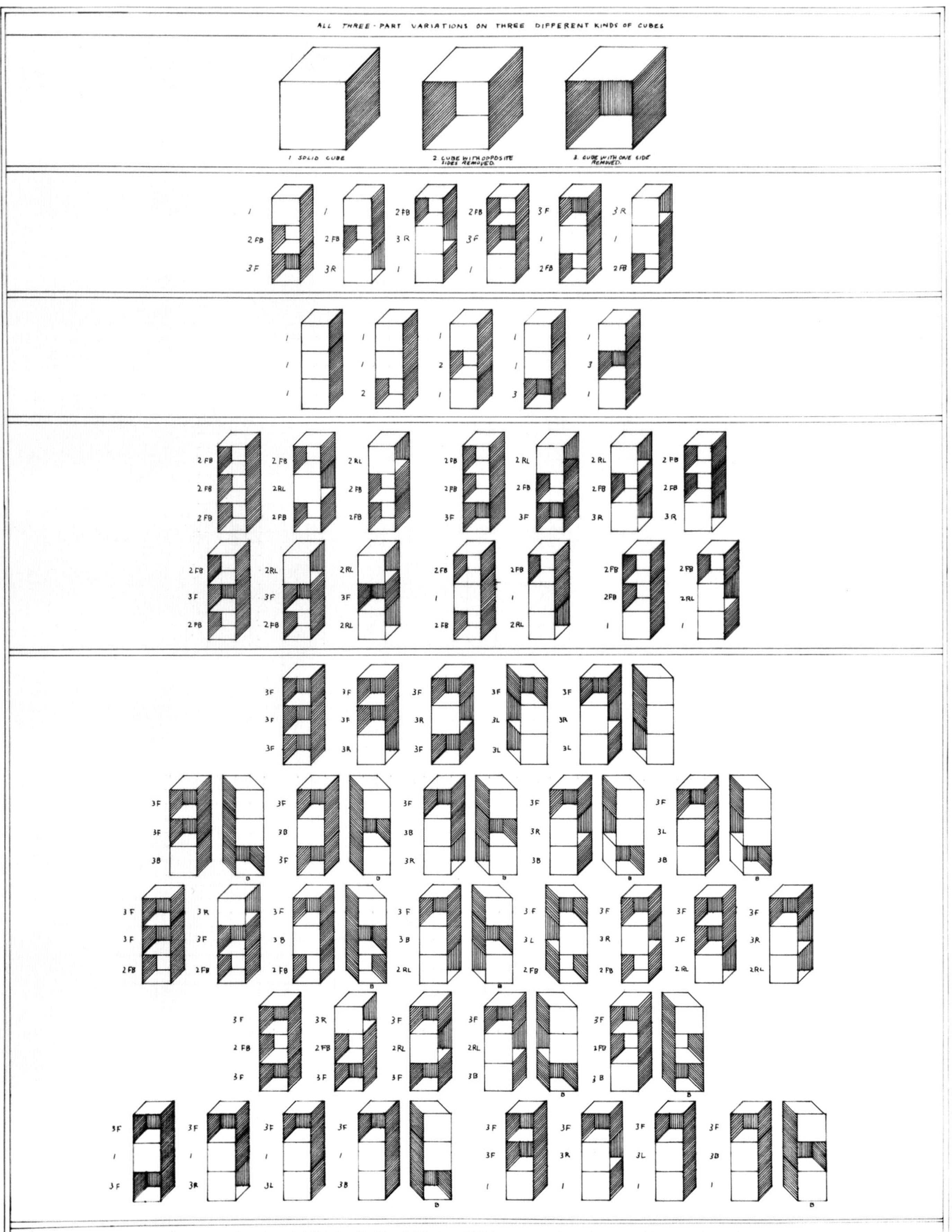
ALL THREE-PART VARIATIONS ON THREE DIFFERENT KINDS OF CUBES
1 SOLID CUBE
2. CUBE WITH OPPOSITE SIDES REMOVED.
3. CUBE WITH ONE SIDE REMOVED.
F, B, R & L : FRONT, BACK, RIGHT & LEFT AND REFER TO OPEN SIDES OF THE CUBES. BACK VIEWS ARE SHOWN WHEN NECESSARY. SOL LEWITT

Sol LeWitt

Sol LeWitt was born in Hartford, Connecticut, in 1928, and attended Syracuse University. After serving in the Korean War as a graphic artist, he moved, in 1953, to New York, where he worked as a draftsman for the architect I. M. Pei. LeWitt had his first solo exhibition at the Daniels Gallery, New York, in 1965, and the following year Dwan Gallery, New York, mounted the first in a series of solo exhibitions. He participated, during the late 1960s and early 1970s, in several significant group exhibitions of Minimalist and Conceptual art, including "Primary Structures," at the Jewish Museum, New York, in 1966, and "When Attitude Becomes Form," at the Kunsthalle Bern, Switzerland, in 1969. His renowned text "Paragraphs on Conceptual Art" was published in 1967. LeWitt's work was included in Documentas 6 (1977) and 7 (1982) in Kassel, as well as the 1987 Skulptur Projekte in Münster and the 1989 Istanbul Biennial. Major retrospectives of his works were organized by the Museum of Modern Art, New York, in 1978, and the San Francisco Museum of Modern Art, in 2000.

All Three-Part Variations on Three Different Kinds of Cubes, 1969

"Serial components are multipartite pieces with regulated changes," Sol LeWitt argued in 1966. "The differences between the parts are the subject of the composition."[1] Such works, which have constituted the mainstay of his practice since the mid-1960s, "are to be read by the viewer in a linear or narrative manner . . . even though," he conceded, "in its final form many of these sets would be operating simultaneously, making comprehension difficult."[2] LeWitt first articulated his long-standing commitment to seriality as a mode of composition and a thematic as his practice was evolving from its roots in Minimalism to a pioneering Conceptualism. In response to seminal works by peers such as Donald Judd and, more particularly, Dan Flavin, LeWitt, too, pared his vocabulary to simple geometric forms. Focusing on the cube and square, he fabricated neutral three-dimensional structures, in a pristine white, which he then parsed in permutational progressions or finite preset series. For example, *1 2 3* (1967–2003) manifests all possible variations on three different kinds of cubes. Eliminating the play of the arbitrary, the expressive, and the subjective, eschewing all trace of his hand and taste, LeWitt accorded priority to underlying ideas over their physical counterparts: "In conceptual art the idea or concept is the most important aspect of the work," he stated in his landmark 1967 credo, "Paragraphs on Conceptual Art."[3]

At first highly rational and logical, LeWitt's foundational precepts veered in unforeseen ways once they entered a two-dimensional arena. Inspired by Flavin's *the nominal three (to William of Ockham)* (1963), he increasingly explored the inherent potential of wall-based works to engage with their surrounds, that is, not only with the space but with the contours of the site in which they are realized. But whereas Flavin focused on the ways in which light shaped and inflected the work's environment, LeWitt began to limn his graphite lines directly onto the architecture, which he thereby made physically integral to the work. By dispensing with the conventional support—whether paper or, as in the case of Agnes Martin, canvas—he fused his grids of closely drawn, evenly toned pencil lines with the planar field in which the work had its being. In his earlier graphite works, among which *Drawing Series—Composite, Part I–IV, #1–24, A+B* (1969) is a key example, the dimensions of the individual drawing were fixed and hence independent of the scale and size of any venue. Gradually, however, LeWitt began to adjust the overall frame of the works as they were given material existence to the proportions and measurements of the site, so that they now engaged the whole wall. Yet each work exists initially as an idea, in the guise of textual instructions accompanied by a diagrammatic representation: it need not assume concrete form as a monumental physical entity. Its existence, then, is always contingent: not only its dimensions but its duration is provisional.[4]

Drawing Series. . . exemplifies LeWitt's singular yet highly influential practice on manifold counts. Formulated from an initial idea outlined in a diagrammatic sketch accompanied by a set of instructions, it has been installed here by a team of trained assistants supplemented by volunteers, who rigorously followed the artist's directives, including his determination of its placement in relation to the particular configuration of Dia's galleries.[5] In the work of Judd and other Minimalists, the specifics of the modular system underpinning any individual work are not necessarily overtly legible, although they may be intuited. In LeWitt's art, by contrast, the conceptual program that determines the composition is always self-evident. Irrespective of the resulting degree of complexity, the point of departure—the preset schema—is literally stated, in the title, the accompanying diagrammatic instructions, or both. The straightforward formulation of the preset idea of *Drawing Series. . .* has here been exhaustively realized: all 192 permutations of the black pencil version are present.[6]

The work's basic unit, a square measuring one meter per side and divided into quarters, which are each quartered again for a total of sixteen modules, is grouped to make a larger square of four equal units, then stacked into four rows centered on each of the four walls of the gallery. A recurrent form in LeWitt's early drawings, the square, like the cube, from which most of his early sculptures were composed, is for him among the "least emotive" of any possible forms.[7] "A more complex form would be too interesting in itself and obstruct the meaning of the whole. There is no need to invent new forms," he contends. "The square and cube are efficient and symmetrical."[8] This elementary syntax constitutes "the best form to use as a base unit for any more elaborate function, the grammatical device from which the work may proceed."[9] The four directions assumed by the lines in *Drawing Series. . .* represent the basic directions in which lines may be drawn: vertical, horizontal, diagonal from top left to bottom right, and diagonal from top right to bottom left. In accordance with the artist's preset plan, these lines have been overlaid in every possible combination so that the resulting sequence methodically exhausts every variation that may be derived from the given logic and within the formal limits established by the location. Light-toned and applied evenly with a near-uniform thickness and spacing, the lines create grids of varying tonality that nonetheless preserve the integrity of the surface plane even as they appear at one with it.

The measured logic and reasoning evidenced here betray neither a dogmatic commitment to mathematical calibration nor a belief in the transcendence of thought, of mind.[10] On the contrary, obsession pushed to the limit of paradox and absurdity is as fundamental to LeWitt's practice as any axiomatic intellectualizing–witness a key statement in his 1967 credo "Paragraphs on Conceptual Art": "Irrational thoughts should be followed absolutely and logically."[11] It was precisely this fascination with the contradictory that Robert Smithson so presciently identified when he acclaimed LeWitt's concepts as "prisons devoid of reason."[12] In their monumental physical guise his works reveal a compelling, luminous beauty that speaks as much to the senses as to the intellect. For even though the preset programs can be readily grasped, what is unexpected is their exhilarating presence. Experienced as a kind of aesthetic excess, this is the sensory equivalent of their conceptual address to "the purposelessness of purpose."[13]

L.C.

notes

1 Sol LeWitt, "Serial Project No. 1," *Aspen*, section 17, nos. 5–6, 1966, n.p., reprinted in Gary Garrels, ed., *Sol LeWitt: A Retrospective* (San Francisco: San Francisco Museum of Modern Art, in association with Yale University Press, New Haven, Conn., 2000), p. 373.

2 Ibid.

3 LeWitt, "Paragraphs on Conceptual Art," *Artforum* 5, no. 10 (June 1967), pp. 79–83, reprinted in Garrels, ed., *Sol LeWitt: A Retrospective*, p. 369.

4 Number 10 in LeWitt's "Sentences on Conceptual Art," 1969, asserts, "Ideas alone can be works of art: they are in a chain of development that may eventually find some form. All ideas need not be made physical." *Art-Language*, no. 1 (May 1969), pp. 11–13, reprinted in Garrels, ed., *Sol LeWitt: A Retrospective*, p. 372.

5 Certain minimal requirements are basic to the execution of LeWitt's wall drawings. A degree of skill and concentration, which practice may enhance, is required. Thus, although he does not privilege aesthetic training per se, LeWitt has come to realize that not everyone who tries can meet his standards. His decision to employ readily available everyday materials has similarly been determined: the hard–6H–graphite lead used here was the tool for the earliest wall drawings.

6 Another drawing with the same title is executed in colored pencils–red, blue, yellow, and graphite 6H leads. This companion work is not owned by Dia and will not be presented concurrently in Dia:Beacon. Completed in1969, this work does appear in full in an untitled book published by Sperone/Fischer, and printed by Petrino-Torino, in 1974 in an edition of 1,500.

7 LeWitt, "The Cube," quoted in Afdachiara Zevi, ed., *Sol LeWitt: Critical Texts* (Rome: Libri de AEIOU, 1995), p. 72.

8 LeWitt, "Serial Project No. 1," p. 373.

9 LeWitt, "The Cube," p. 72.

10 In a discussion of complex patterning, Ernst Gombrich contrasts the ability of "God and higher intelligences" to apprehend "the whole of Truth in the immediacy of direct intuition" with that of ordinary mortals who see all existing correlations in succession. "The limit of our capacity is not a liability but a gain," he contends. "For such higher Intelligences who take in the whole of the pattern at once it could not possibly have the same interest and beauty it has for us." Ernst H. Gombrich, *The Sense of Order: A Study in the Psychology of Decorative Art* (Ithaca, N.Y.: Cornell University Press, 1979), p. 148. For LeWitt, seriality, like pattern as defined by Gombrich, requires apprehension "in a linear or narrative manner"; its heuristic potential lies in these contrasting modes of apprehension.

11 LeWitt, "Paragraphs on Conceptual Art," in Garrels, ed., *Sol LeWitt: A Retrospective*, p. 371.

12 Robert Smithson, "A Museum of Language in the Vicinity of Art," *Art International*, no. 1 (May 1969), p. 11.

13 This term comes from what remains one of the key texts on LeWitt's art, Rosalind E. Krauss, "LeWitt in Progress," *October*, no. 6 (Fall 1978), pp. 46–60.

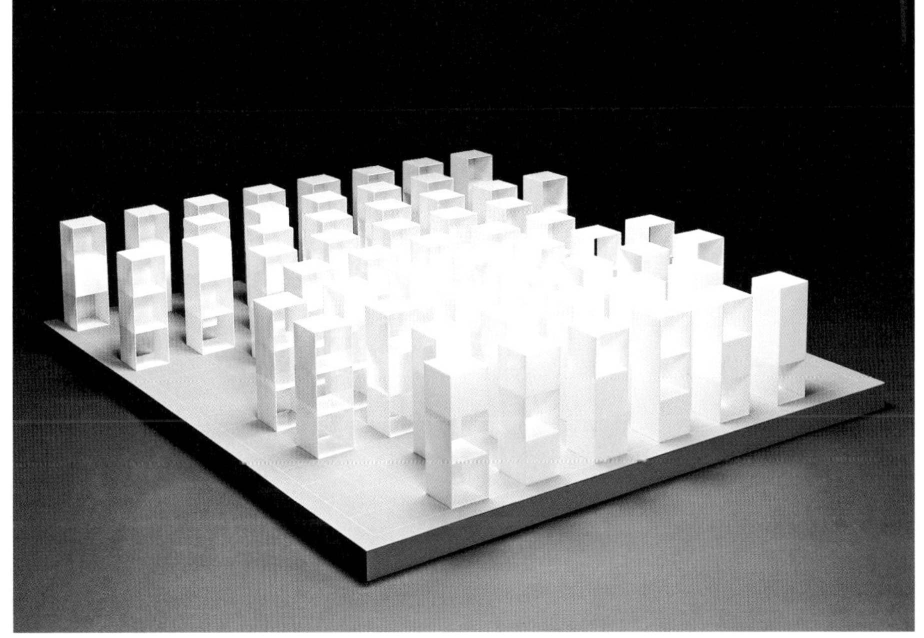

right Maquette for *1 2 3*, 1967–2003

pages 200–205 *Drawing Series—Composite, Part I–IV, #1–24, A+B*, 1969

I

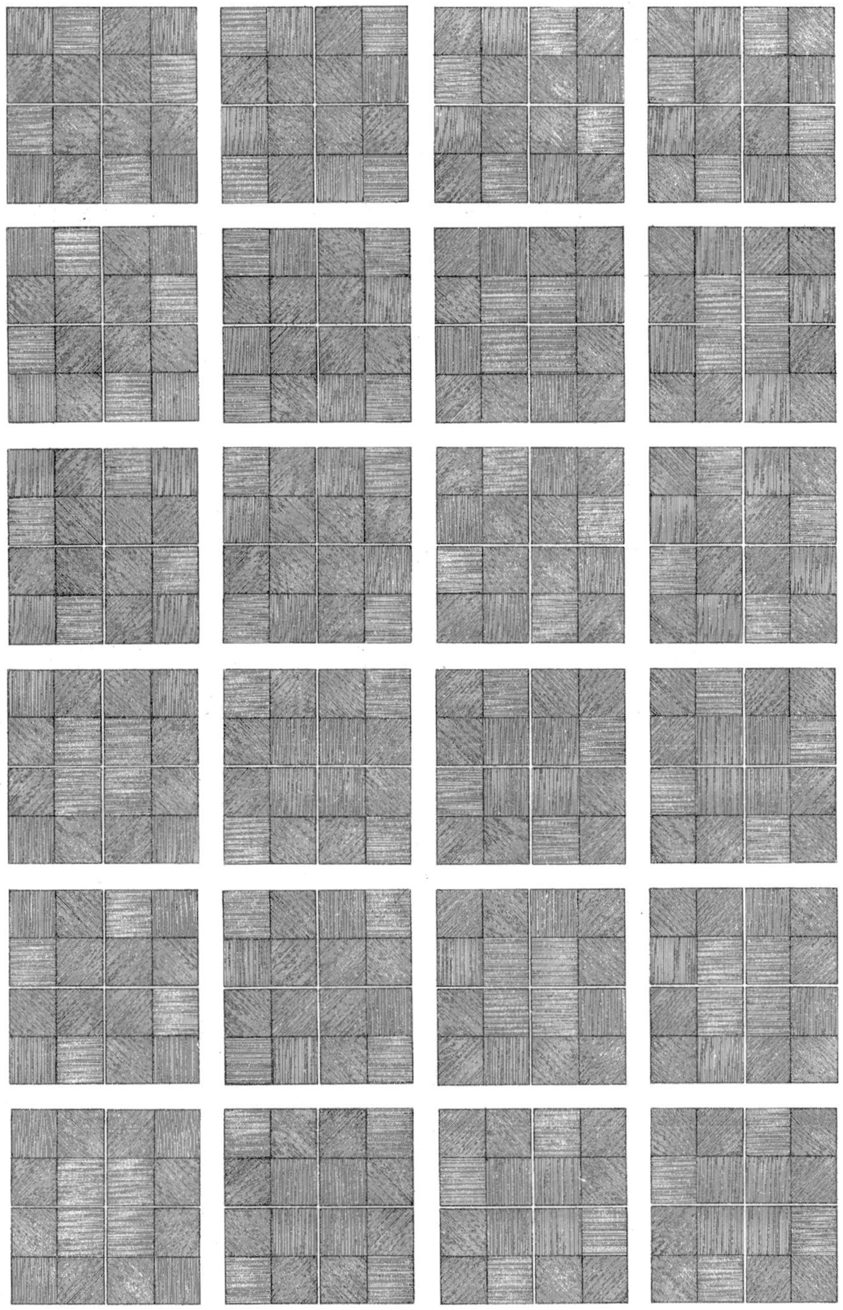

II

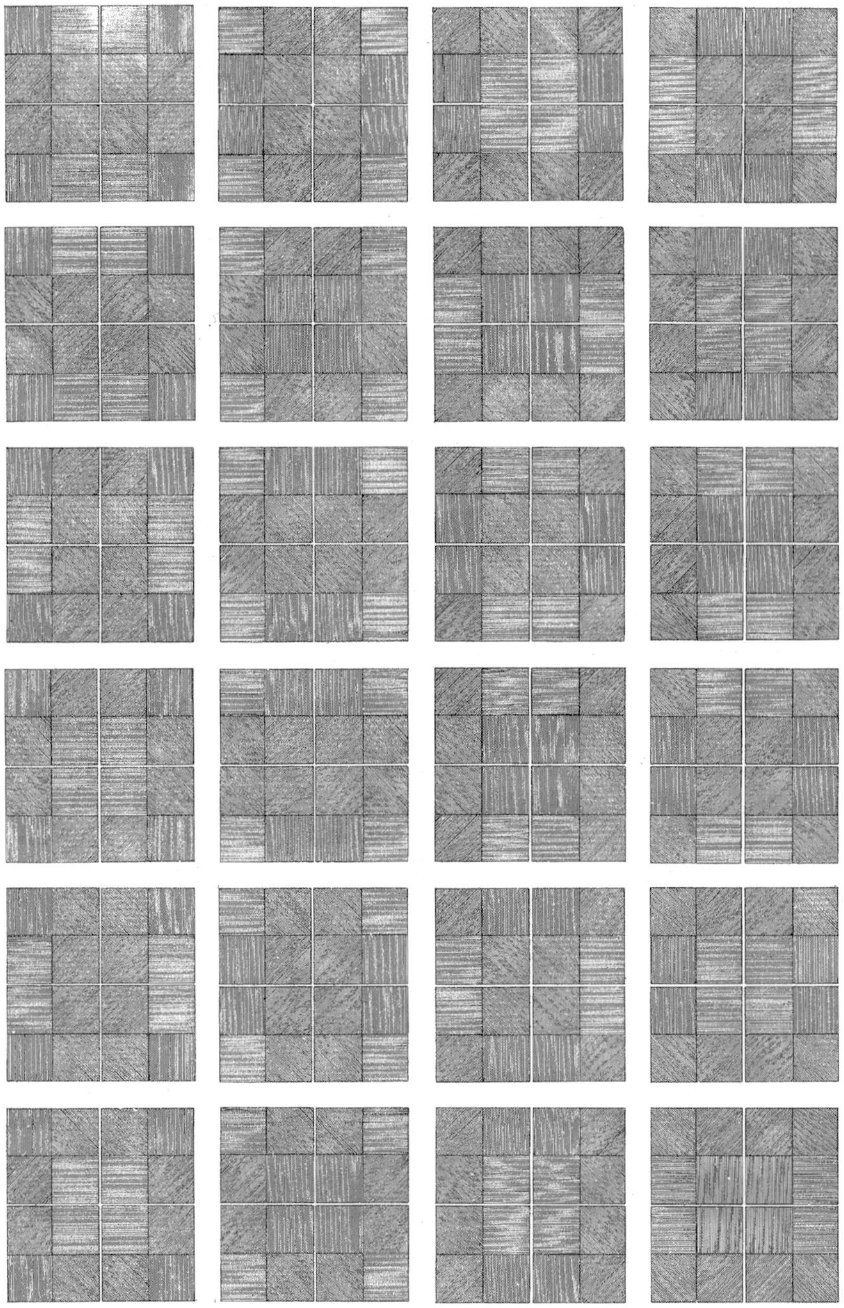

III IIII

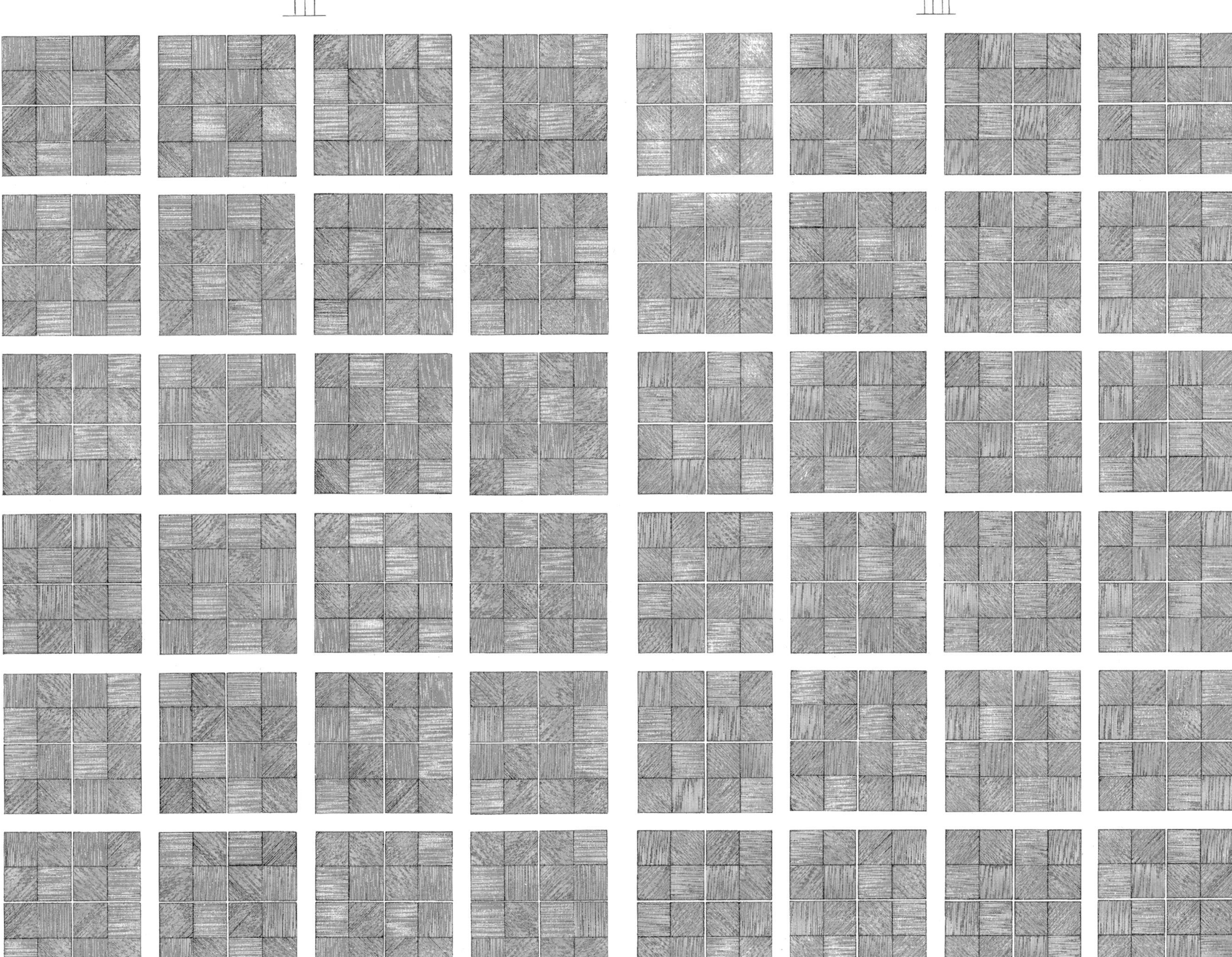

I

II

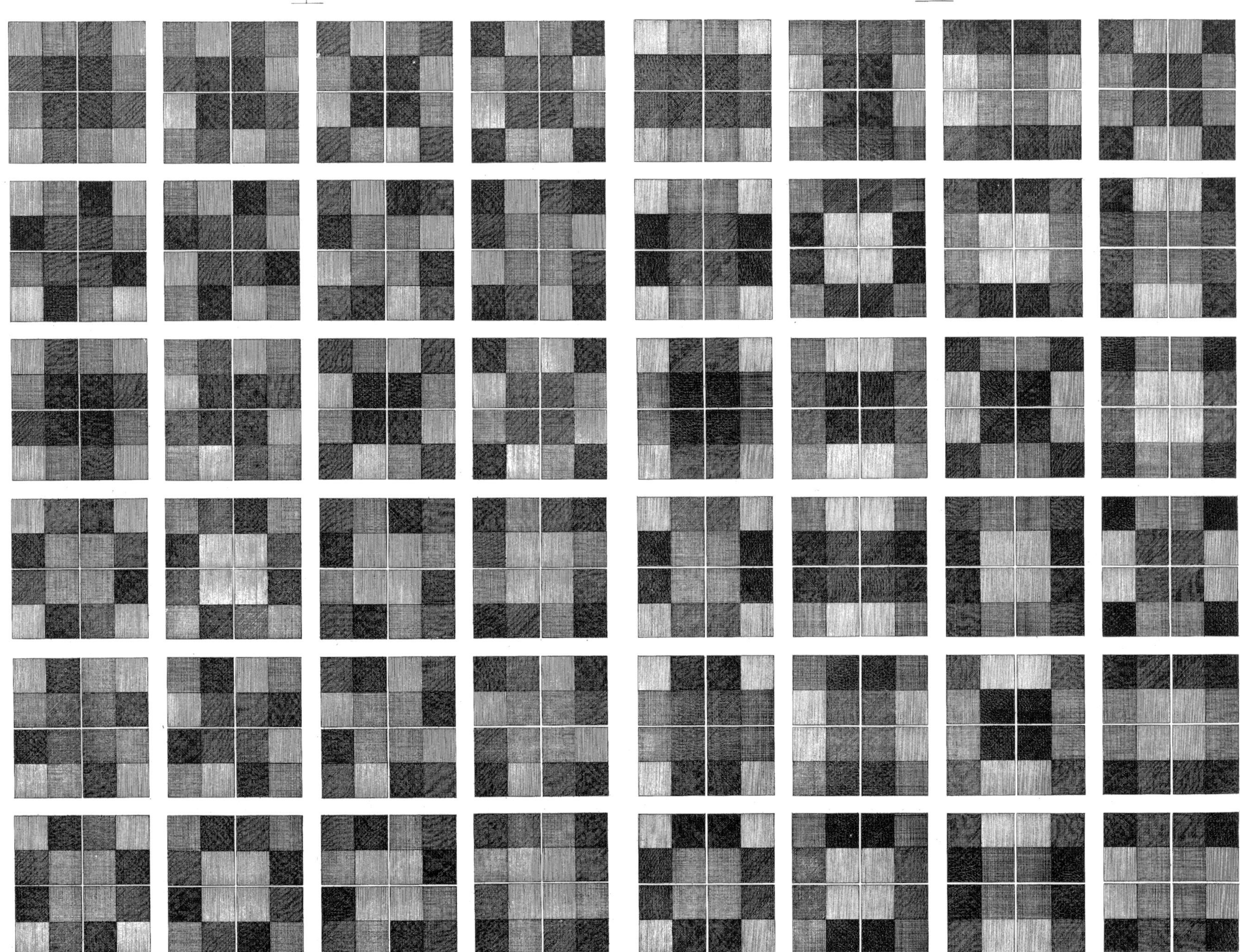

III

IIII

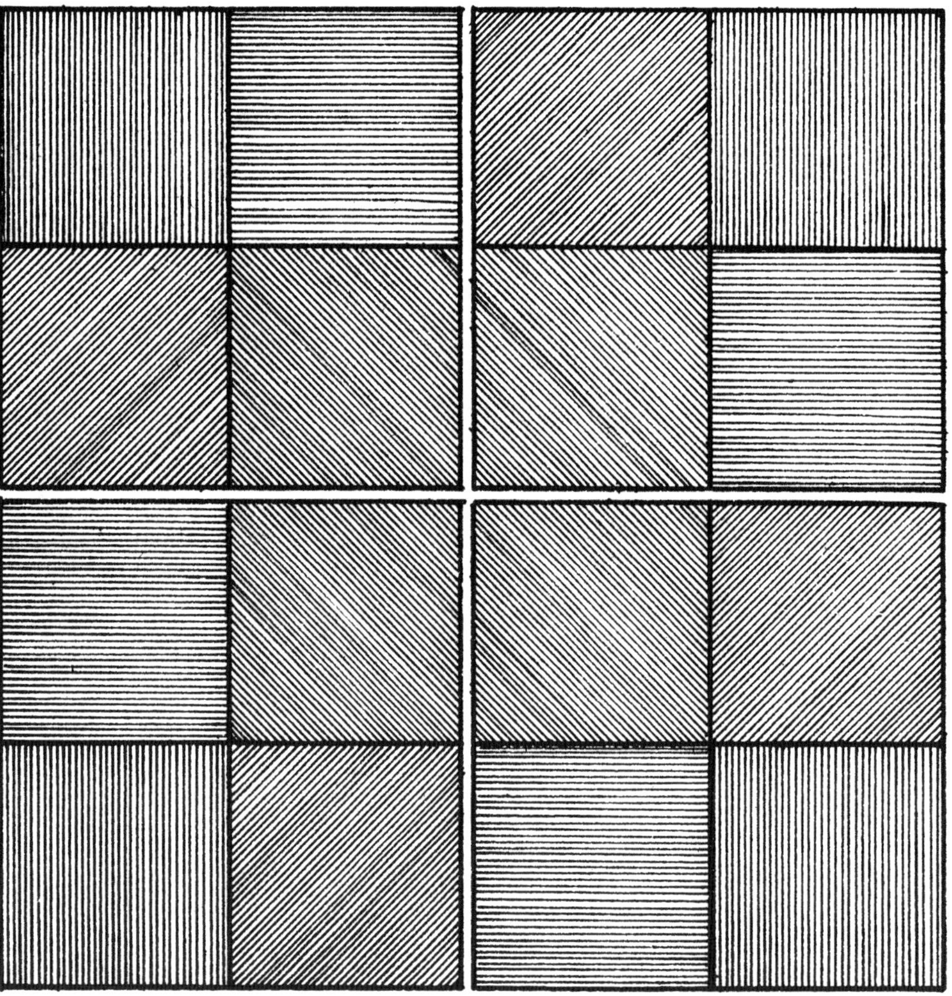

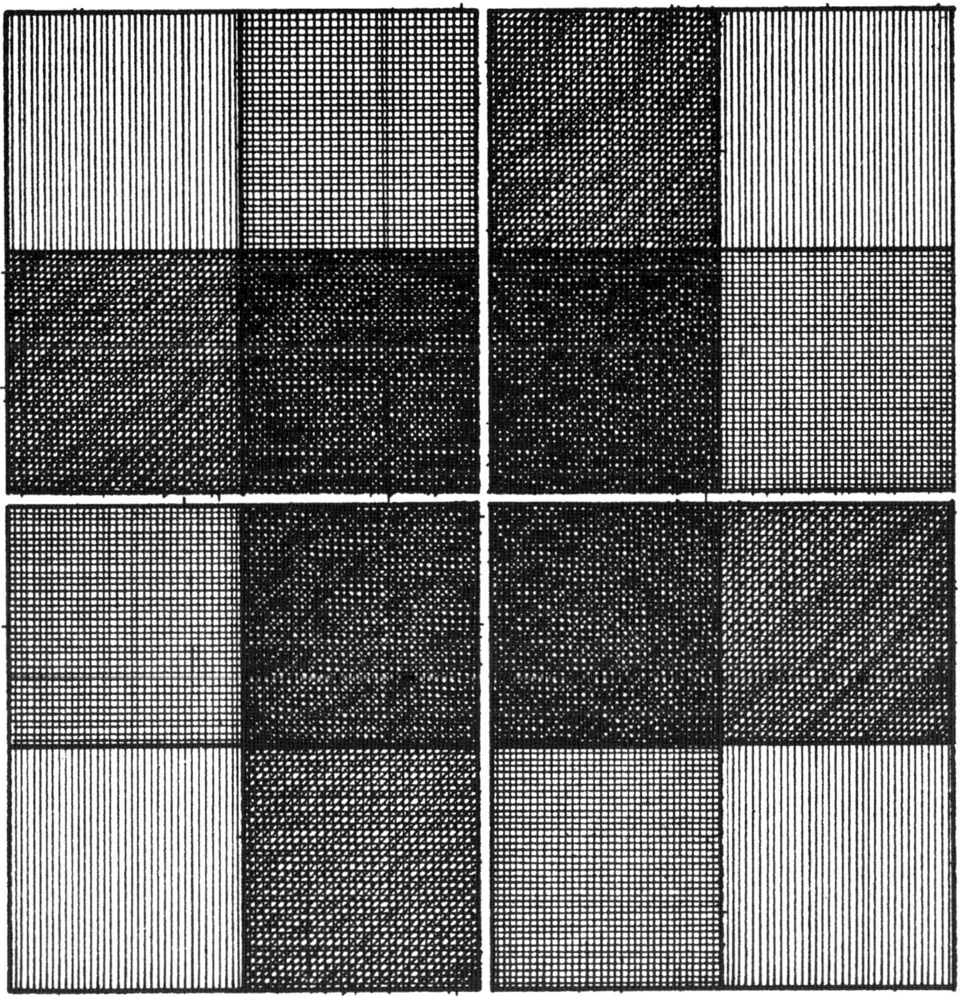

Agnes Martin

Agnes Martin was born in Macklin, a town in Saskatchewan, Canada, in 1912. She grew up in Vancouver, then moved to Bellingham, Washington, in 1932. Martin studied art and art education at Columbia University, New York (1942), and the University of New Mexico, Albuquerque (1946). Alternately living in New Mexico and on Coenties Slip in downtown Manhattan, where her neighbors included the artists Robert Indiana, Ellsworth Kelly, James Rosenquist, Leonore Tawney, and Ann Wilson, Martin had her first one-person exhibition at the Betty Parsons Gallery, New York, in 1958. Surveys of her work have been presented at venues including the Institute of Contemporary Art at the University of Pennsylvania, Philadelphia (1973), the Stedelijk Museum, Amsterdam (1991), the Whitney Museum of American Art, New York (1992), and the Menil Collection, Houston (2002). Martin continues to live and work in Taos, New Mexico.

The Peach, 1964 (detail)

Born in 1912, and having long outlived all her contemporaries of the Abstract Expressionist generation, Agnes Martin has created a four-decade-long body of work that could equally be described as ahead of its time and as timeless. In the mid-1960s, Martin was applauded as a herald of the cool geometric Minimalism that was emerging in the aftermath of Abstract Expressionism, but she herself declined that claim, for she saw the Minimalist approach as impersonal and dispassionate. Her own abstractions use a combination of ideal geometry and the lightest touch of the artist's hand to achieve a pitch of emotion and feeling.

Martin grew up in the Pacific Northwest, then in the 1940s, as a student, was drawn to the arid, open landscape of New Mexico. The vast Southwestern desert, which cannot be justly represented in painting, was a defining experience for her; as she later described it, "I used to paint mountains here in New Mexico and I thought/my mountains looked like ant hills/I saw the plains driving out of New Mexico and I thought/the plain had it/just the plane."[1] At the urging of her dealer, Betty Parsons, Martin lived and worked in New York in the late 1950s and early 1960s, when Abstract Expressionism was at its zenith in the city and the Pop and Minimalist movements were soon to be born. In her Lower Manhattan studio at Coenties Slip—the downtown nexus of a group of young artists including Ellsworth Kelly and Robert Indiana, with Jasper Johns and Robert Rauschenberg also living nearby—Martin discontinued her soft biomorphic abstractions and began to develop sparse geometric constructions often based on grids.

A four-foot-square canvas from 1959, *The Spring*, introduces a geometric vocabulary within a square

The Peach, 1964

format: a series of three gray horizontal lines painted between upper and lower rectangles prefigures the artist's career-long focus on variations of horizontal lines and fields. Two untitled works from 1959 introduce the potential for the grid, and the subtle relationship between square and rectangle, as bases of Martin's developing language: in one, a small rectangle of thick, smooth white paint is articulated by a delicate grid inscribed with the sharp edge of a palette knife, in the other, also white, two rectangles float on a nearly raw six-foot-square canvas. The six-foot square soon became the support for nearly all of Martin's paintings until 1985, when the square was reduced to five by five feet.

The repetitive marks and lines of the continuous allover grid paintings that Martin began in the early 1960s earned her the reputation of being an inspiration for the Minimalists. Yet the grid that underlies the paintings, as the artist says, is never mechanical and never rigid: "My formats are square, but the grids never are absolutely square; they are rectangles, a little bit off the square, making a sort of contradiction, a dissonance, though I didn't set out to do it that way. When I cover the square surface with rectangles, it lightens the weight of the square, destroys its power."[2]

Through simple geometry, Martin found, she could pursue a classical perfection that she described as absent from nature, held only in the mind. Using rectangles, squares, and grids of points and lines, she virtually dispensed with traditional notions of composition in painting. Even the inventors and heroes of abstraction, from Dutch artist Piet Mondrian and the Russian Kasimir Malevich to her own Abstract Expressionist contemporaries, had clung to the powerful dynamics of painterly composition. Martin's delicate rectangular grids of pencil lines, on the other hand, lightly echoing the weave of her square canvases, as in *The Beach* (1963) or *The Peach* (1964), border

left *The Spring*, 1959
right *Untitled*, 1959

on the edge of being paintings at all. Merging the classical abstract ideal of Platonic geometry with an empty, egoless Taoist meditation, Martin dematerializes the canvas into a transparent, nonhierarchical field of vision, perhaps suggesting the experience (rather than the image) of the landscape of the Southwest desert.

In the 1966 exhibition "Systemic Painting," at the Solomon R. Guggenheim Museum, New York, Martin's grids were celebrated as quintessential examples of the new Minimalist art and were hung among works by artists including Sol LeWitt, Robert Ryman, and Donald Judd. Indeed, these grids could have formed the Minimalists' armature and seemed to prefigure the disappearance of traditional painting into nonhierarchical two- and three-dimensional rhythms of theme and variation. Meanwhile, however, Martin was coming to reject much of her own work, along with that of the Minimalists, as too material, and New York City as too distracting to be conducive to inspiration. In 1967 she moved permanently to the Southwest, and she also gave up painting for close to a decade. Alone, living on an empty mesa in Cuba, New Mexico, Martin built her own adobe house, where she pursued isolation as a means of seeking inspiration. "I suggest to artists," she wrote, "that you take every opportunity of being alone."[3] Not until the mid-1970s did she reemerge with new work on canvas, blending pencil lines with translucent washes of pale color.

Martin's recent paintings–epitomized by her 1999 *Innocent Love* series, made specifically for Dia–seem to emanate light rather than reflect it. Gently insistent horizontal lines suggest an infinite space beyond the serial grid of the eight five-foot-square canvases. The theme of innocent love may be related to the artist's descriptions of the "untroubled state of mind" (often referred to in her journals) that allows for "moments of inspiration," which "added together make what we call sensibility."[4] Young children, innocent and untroubled, have many more inspirations than adults, Martin writes. She has also said that it was in thinking about the innocence of trees that she first considered the grid. A pure, abstract, egoless, untroubled state of mind is conveyed through these nearly immaterial works and through Martin's infinite vision.

M. G.

notes

1 Agnes Martin, *Writings—Schriften* (Winterthur: Kunstmuseum Winterthur, in association with Cantz, Ostfildern-Ruit, 1991), pp. 36–37.

2 Ibid., p. 29.

3 Ibid., p. 117.

4 Ibid., p. 62.

Untitled, 1959

The Beach, 1963

left *Love* (from *Innocent Love* series), 1999

right *Contentment* (from *Innocent Love* series), 1999

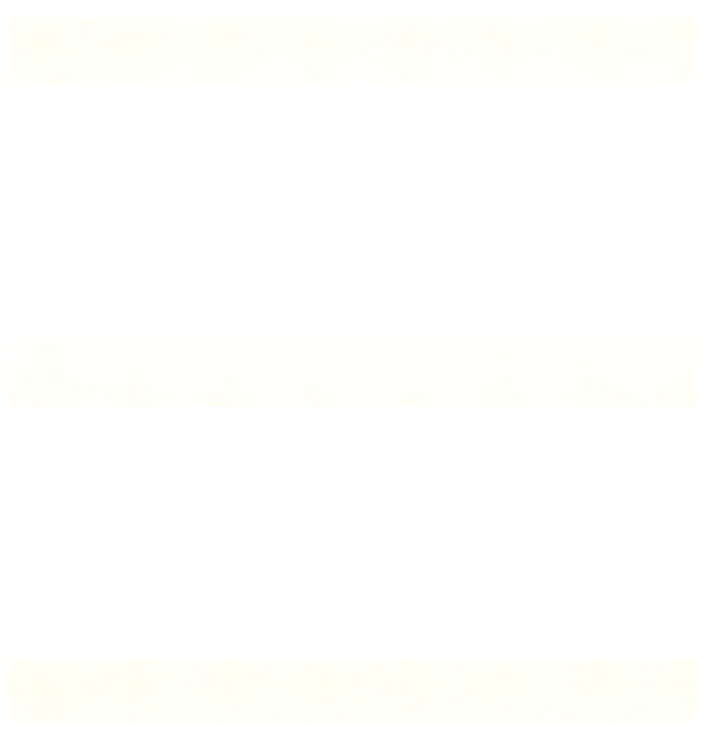

left *Innocent Living* (from *Innocent Love* series), 1999
right *Happiness* (from *Innocent Love* series), 1999

left *Innocent Happiness* (from *Innocent Love* series), 1999
right *Perfect Happiness* (from *Innocent Love* series), 1999

left *Innocent Love* (from *Innocent Love* series), 1999

right *Where Babies Come From* (from *Innocent Love* series), 1999

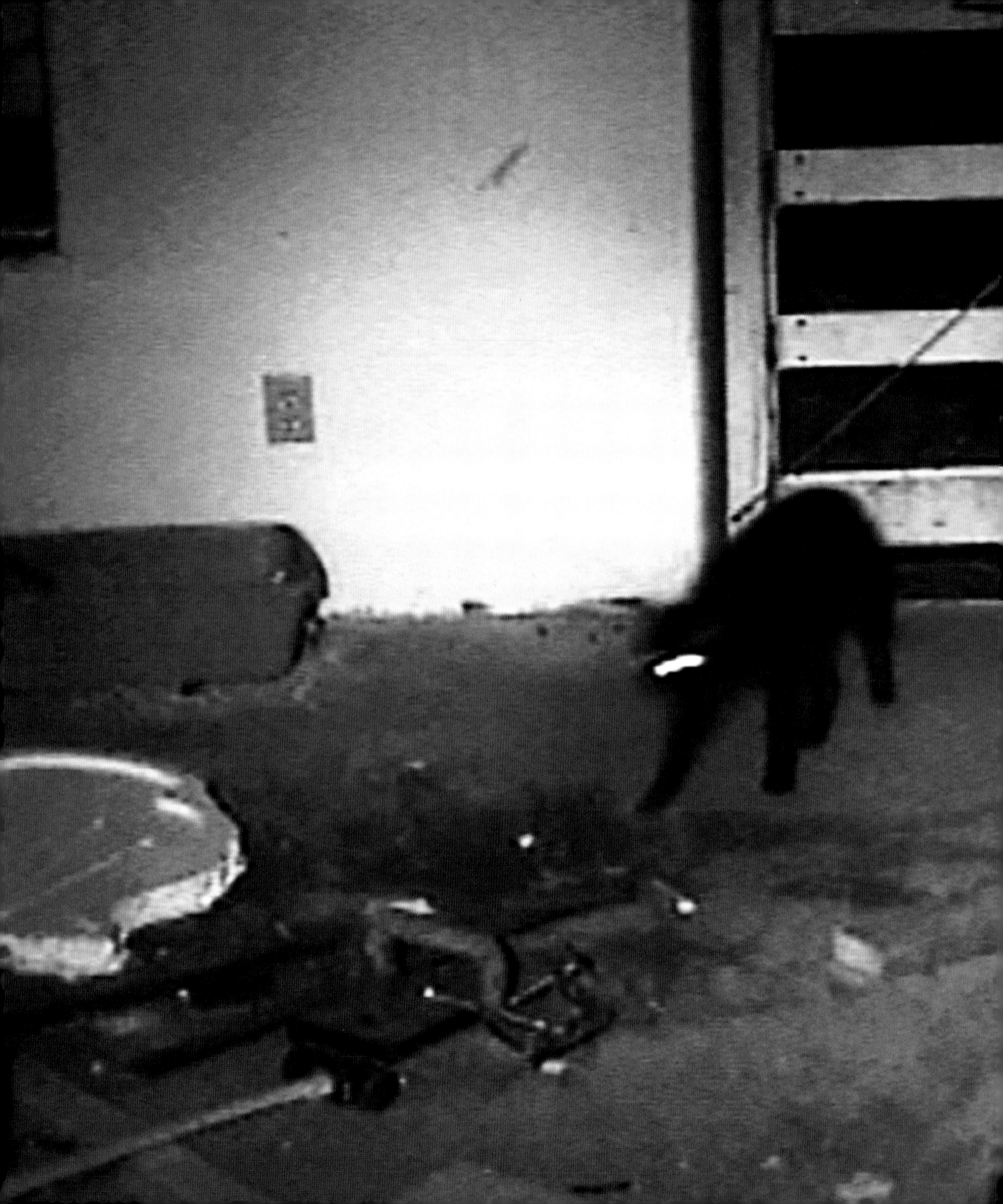

Bruce Nauman

Bruce Nauman was born in Fort Wayne, Indiana, in 1941. After studying at the University of Wisconsin from 1964 to 1965, he acquired an M.F.A. from the University of California, Davis, in 1966. His debut show was at the Nicholas Wilder Gallery, Los Angeles, in 1966, and since then he has exhibited widely in North America and Europe, including contributions to Documentas 4 (1968), 5 (1972), and 7 (1982), in Kassel, Germany, and to the Whitney Biennials of 1984, 1991, and 1997. Several major exhibitions of his work toured, principally in Europe, in the 1980s, and in 1994–95 the Walker Art Center, Minneapolis, and the Hirshhorn Museum and Sculpture Garden, Washington, D.C., organized a retrospective. He won the Golden Lion prize at the Venice Biennale in 1999. Nauman has lived on a ranch near Galisteo, New Mexico, since 1979, where, in addition to his studio practice, he breeds horses.

Video still from *Mapping the Studio I (Fat Chance John Cage)*, 2001

Art is a means of acquiring an investigative attitude.

—Bruce Nauman

Mice invaded Bruce Nauman's studio in the summer of 1999. In response, he bought an inexpensive video camera and an infrared lamp to track their nocturnal activity. In late August he began recording, having established seven camera positions that mapped junctions of wall and floor around the perimeter of his studio, a prefabricated building on his ranch near Galisteo, New Mexico. Continuing to shoot intermittently over the next three months, he amassed some forty-five hours of footage, which he then edited and compressed to five hours forty-five minutes.

The presentation of *Mapping the Studio I (Fat Chance John Cage)* (2001) figuratively overlays Nauman's studio on a structure made from semitransparent scrim, which makes it possible to read the images from outside as well as when enclosed in the interior. The arrangement of the projections mimics the original camera placement. Each projection is accompanied by its own stereo soundtrack, which consists mostly of ambient noises: trees rustling in a gale, a heavy rainstorm, the occasional barking of a dog, a train passing in the distance, a cat's plaintive meow. When shown at Dia in Chelsea, New York City, a log pinned to the gallery's entrance wall charted the key visual and aural events within each projection—a temporal corollary to the spatial map within. Standard office stools offer long-term viewers the opportunity to rest as they wait, anxiously expectant.

These recordings of the studio reveal evidence of daily activity, as well as accumulated residues from the past. Depending on the work carried out during the day, the paraphernalia shifts around or even disappears:

a ladder, for example, is removed midway through the cycle; a screen door shuts, presumably as the weather cools. A couple of chairs, stacks of videocassettes, and several monitors create a kind of oasis near the center of the room–the site for reviewing the previous night's footage. Occasionally a blurred figure can be glimpsed crossing the camera's sight line as the artist exits the room after inserting a new cassette into the camera. Odd moths and other insects interrupt the static mise-en-scène, their brief trajectories limning eerie staccato gestures. But the real stars are Toonsis the tailless cat, more bored than excited by the invasion of potential prey, and the effervescent mice that have appropriated the studio as their stage.

Mapping the Studio I reprises key themes and preoccupations that Nauman has mined and honed over a career spanning some thirty years. *Fishing for Asian Carp* (1966), one of his first ventures with film, lasts just under three minutes, the length of time it took for the protagonist (William Allen) to capture his quarry.[1] Like several other films Nauman shot about this time, *Fishing for Asian Carp* reflects the strong impression made on him as a student by an industrial training film depicting an elevator in operation, its doors mechanically and repetitively opening and closing.

It was in the late 1960s, when he was a recent graduate, that Nauman began his exploration of the practice of artmaking and of the role of the artist. Performances that put his own body under duress were matched by those that demanded as much of paid performers or of spectators: compare the physically exhausting *Slow Angle Walk (Beckett Walk)* (1968) with *Untitled (Performance Project for Leverkusen)* (1969) or *Body Pressure* (1974), exacting mental exercises in which an actor and viewers respectively are required through intense concentration to try to suffuse themselves into the architecture of the room. Sometimes these works were orchestrated for the camera in the studio, to become single-monitor video pieces; sometimes they were choreographed for a gallery or museum situation.

With *Performance Corridor* (1969) Nauman transformed a prop that had initially been built for one such piece into an autonomous work. Moored to the wall of the gallery, the long, narrow, plywood structure teases the visitor to venture into its claustrophobic recesses. This seminal sculpture soon spawned numerous related progeny, some of which incorporate surveillance cameras and closed-circuit video systems that function as a kind of electronic mirror. Both these virtual mirrors and the real mirrors Nauman used elsewhere allowed spectators to see places that they did not imagine they would be able to see. Typical of these works is the way a frustrating denial of physical access to what can be seen engenders a strange sense of removal or dislocation. Yet other corridor pieces, notably *Left or Standing, Standing or Left Standing* (1971), saturate the space with a garish luminosity, tiring and taxing the viewer's perception before producing disturbing purplish afterimages. The laconic text placed on monitors at each entrance to the structure reprises as it skews the disjunctive architectonic experience: paradoxically it is more concrete in defining the sources of the unsettling fear than its eerie physical counterpart. "Perhaps the space was insufficient," Nauman conceded. "In a way it's a poem that stands by itself, next to the space, without describing it. The writing is about language; it includes a kind of anxiety that the space seemed to generate."[2]

From assailing viewers' stamina and resilience in directly confrontational situations, Nauman gradually adopted less overtly controlling means to challenge their psychic and physical equilibrium.[3] In *Cones Cojones* (1973–75) he used masking tape to redraw the topography of the gallery. The concentric arcs limned on the floor are meant to represent cross sections of giant cones that begin at the center of the earth and project into the universe, immersing the viewer at their disorienting core. A disjunctive text of fragmentary typewritten phrases pasted on two large sheets of paper accompanies the graphic floor piece. Syllogisms riddled with wordplays, snippets of stream-of-consciousness ramblings, and quasi-scientific statements are randomly juxtaposed "like a bunch of fortune cookies lying on a dinner table."[4] Slipping seamlessly from "Let's talk about control" to "We are talking about control," an anonymous interlocutor finally commands, "Placate my art." If, in the past, Nauman posited the artist as a seer or visionary–the revealer of "mystic truths"–more recently he has offered a far more sinister paradigm, authoritarian, manipulative, implacable. Occasionally, as evidenced in *South America Circle* (1981), his abiding preoccupation with issues of power as they pertain to the realm of the aesthetic–to the relation between artist, artwork, and beholder–expands to take on wider political reference.

Typically low-key and low-budget in their form and their fabrication, these deceptively heterogeneous sculptures imply that the struggle to conceive a work of art is more likely to involve hours of tedious repetitive activity, or bleak periods of seemingly fruitless inactivity, than macho manipulations of recalcitrant material, virtuoso displays of craftsmanship, or transcendent insights. But, irrespective of whether externally imposed or, more frequently these days, self-determined, Nauman's discipline of limited means produces works that are disarmingly nonchalant, unassumingly rough-edged, even blackly humorous as they relentlessly pillory received notions of inspiration and creativity, of the role and image of the artist, and of artistic practice. At once impassioned and deeply impersonal, his practice approaches more closely the activities of a protagonist in a Samuel Beckett play than it does the standard Hollywood movie treatment of a great artist driven by unwavering instinct, be it Picasso or Pollock.

L.C.

notes

1 For a detailed study of this and all works in Bruce Nauman's oeuvre, see the catalogue raisonné: *Bruce Nauman*, ed. Joan Simon (Minneapolis: Walker Art Center, in association with Distributed Art Publishers, New York 1994).

2 Nauman, quoted in Coosje van Bruggen, *Bruce Nauman* (New York: Rizzoli, 1988), p. 193.

3 "I mistrust audience participation," Nauman stated in 1970. "That's why I try to make these works as limiting as possible." "Bruce Nauman Interviewed by Willoughby Sharp," *Arts Magazine* 44, no. 5 (March 1970), p. 23. The spectator or the hired performer therefore does "something similar to what I would do." "Bruce Nauman Interviewed by Willoughby Sharp," *Avalanche*, no. 2 (Winter 1971), p. 27.

4 Nauman, quoted in van Bruggen, p. 195.

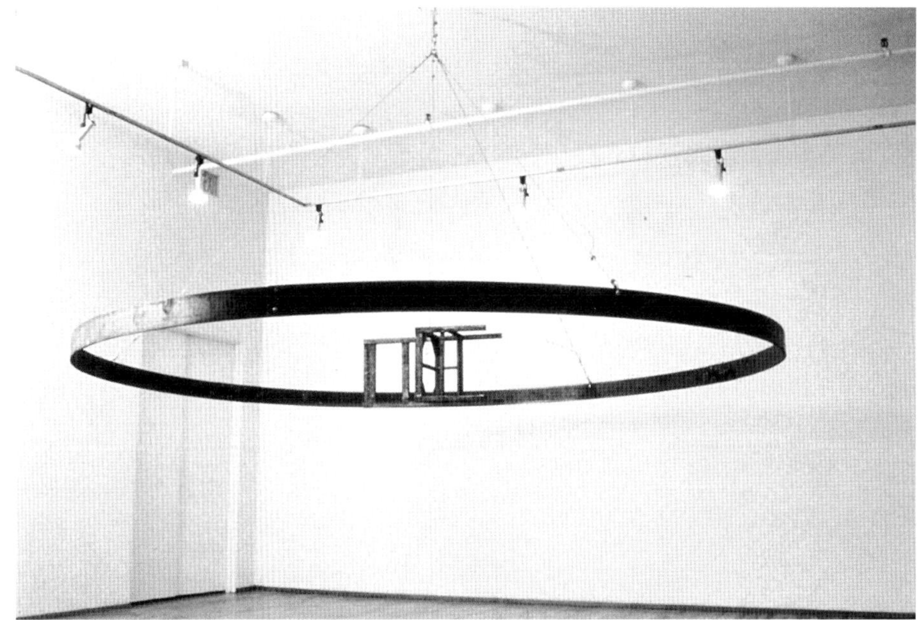

South America Circle, 1981

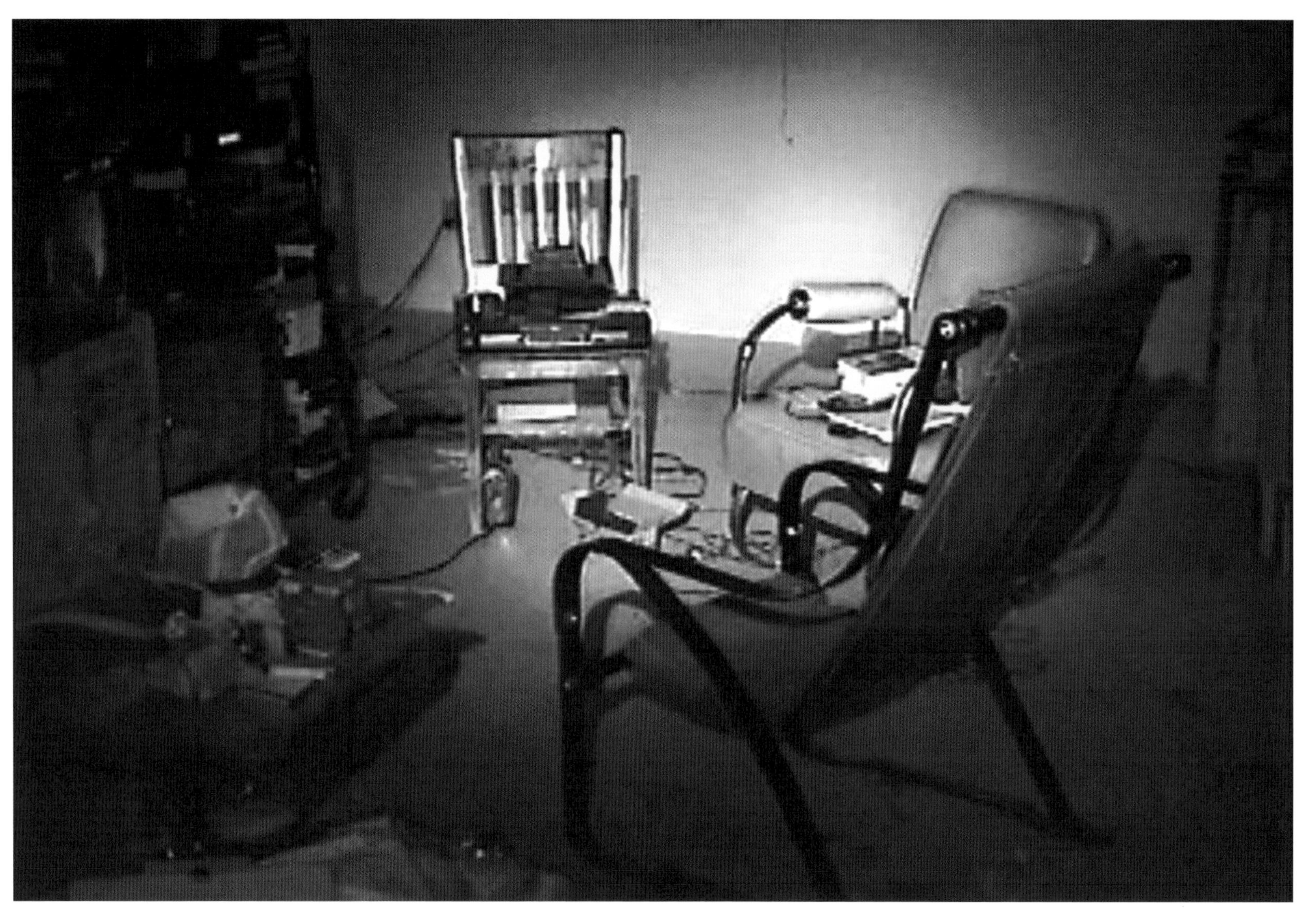

left and right Video still from *Mapping the Studio I (Fat Chance John Cage)*, 2001

pages 222–223 *Mapping the Studio I (Fat Chance John Cage)*, 2001

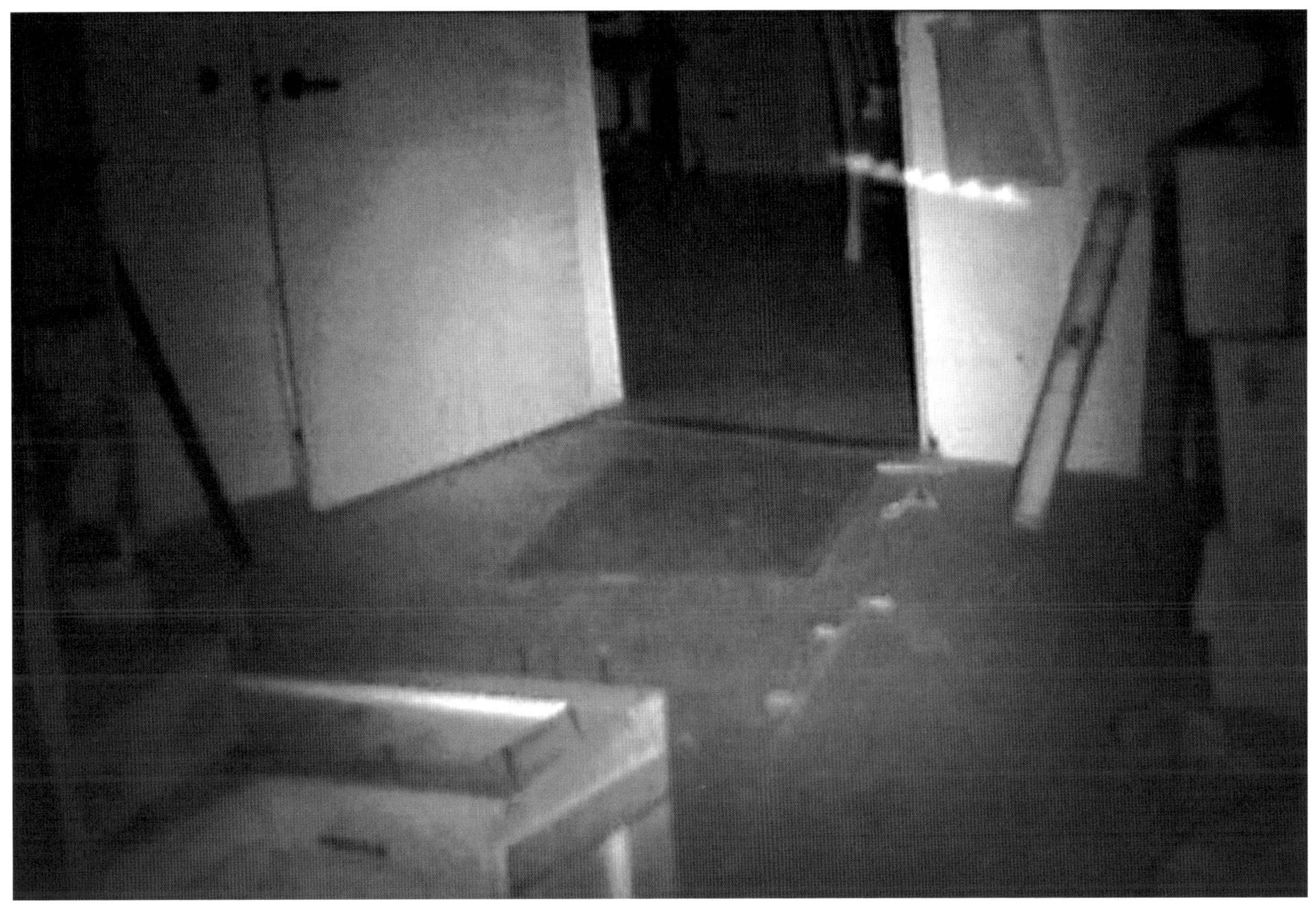

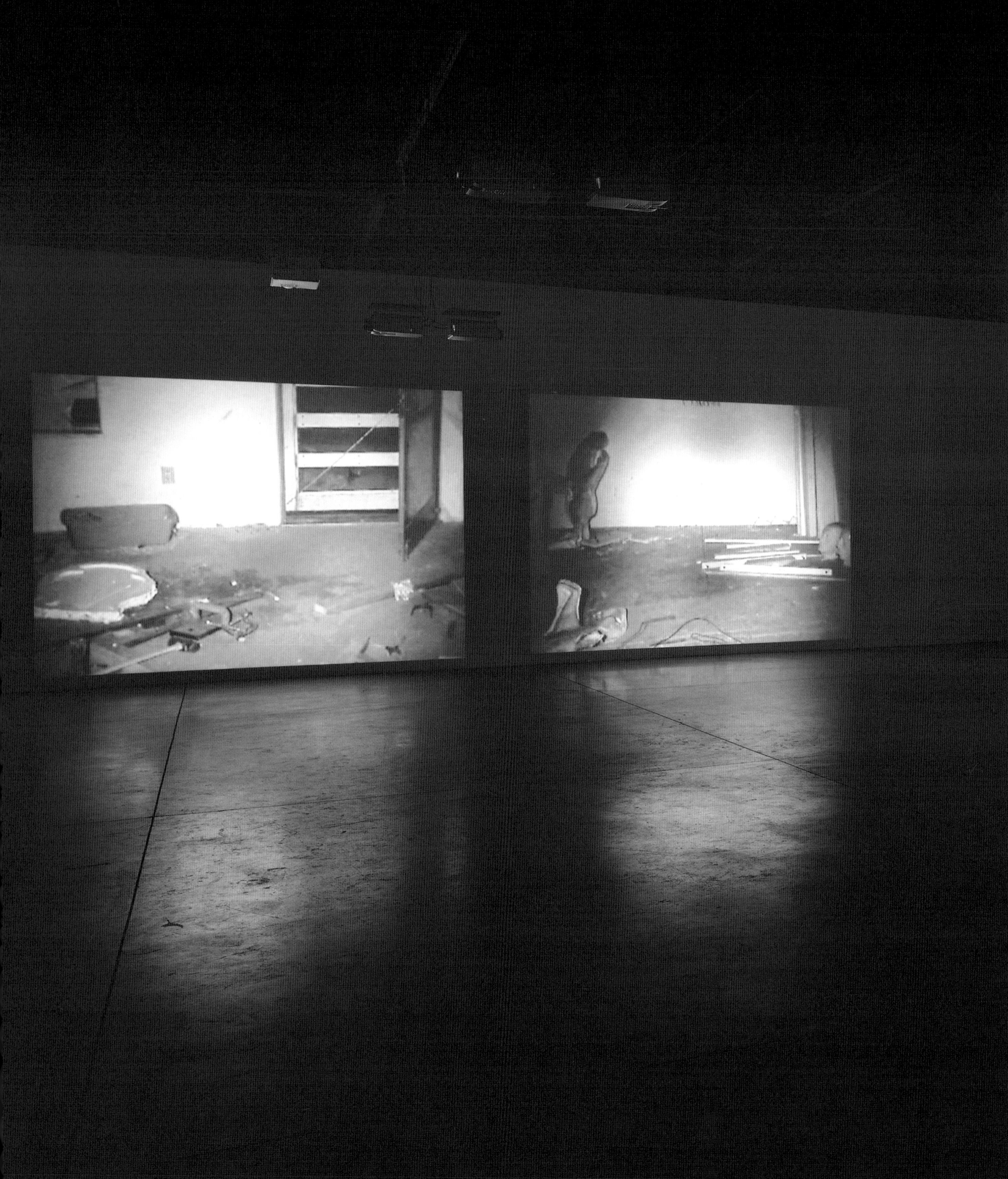

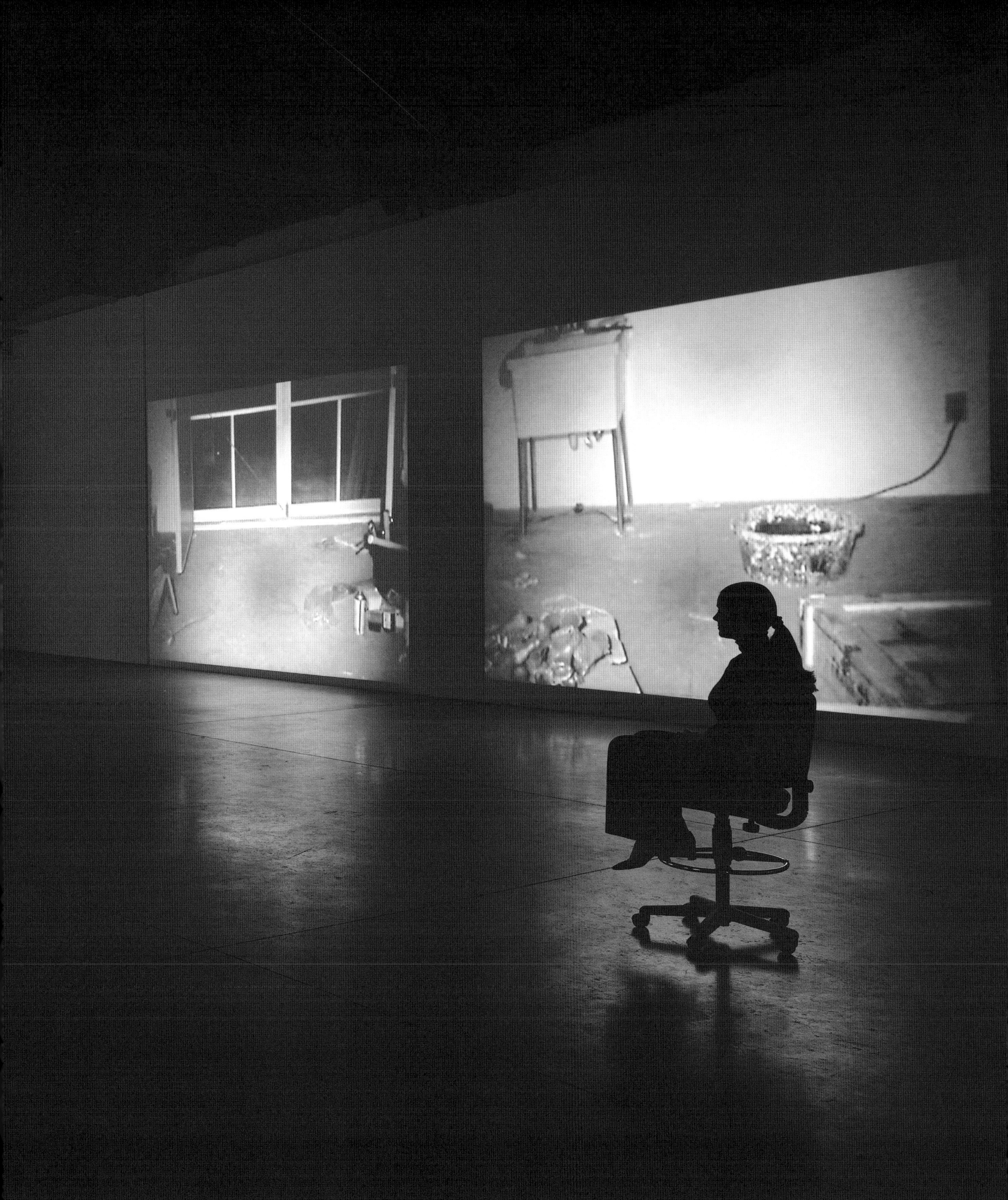

Left or Standing

His precision and accuracy suggesting clean cuts, leaving a vacancy, a slight physical depression as though I had been in a vaguely uncomfortable place for a not long but undeterminable period; not waiting.

Standing or Left Standing

His preciseness and acuity left small cuts on the tips of my fingers or across the backs of my hands without any need to sit or otherwise withdraw.

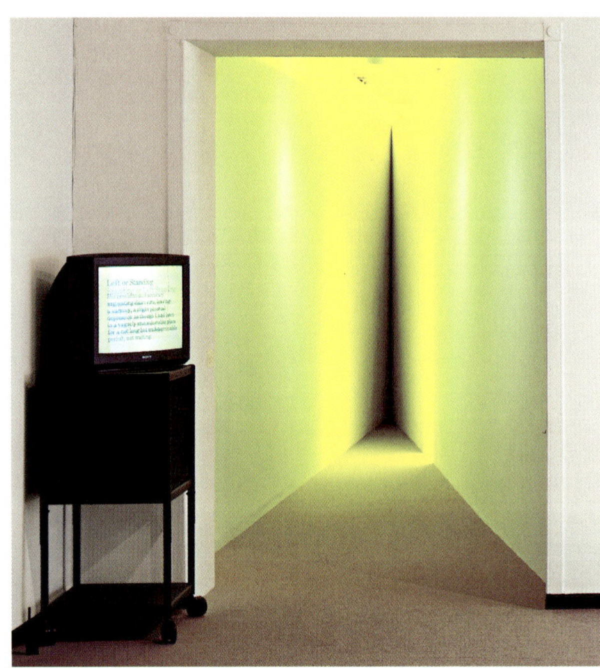

left and right *Left or Standing, Standing or Left Standing*, 1971

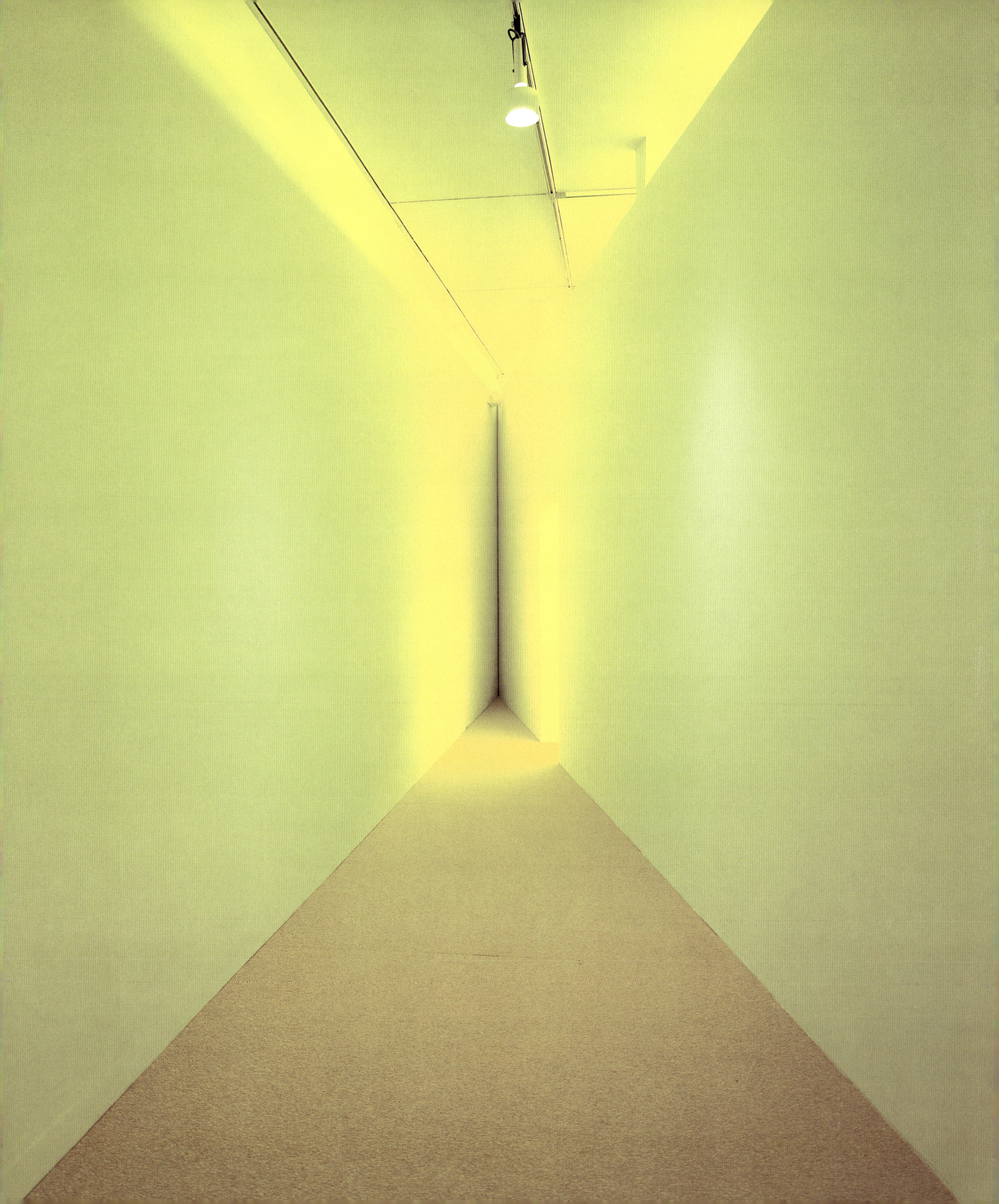

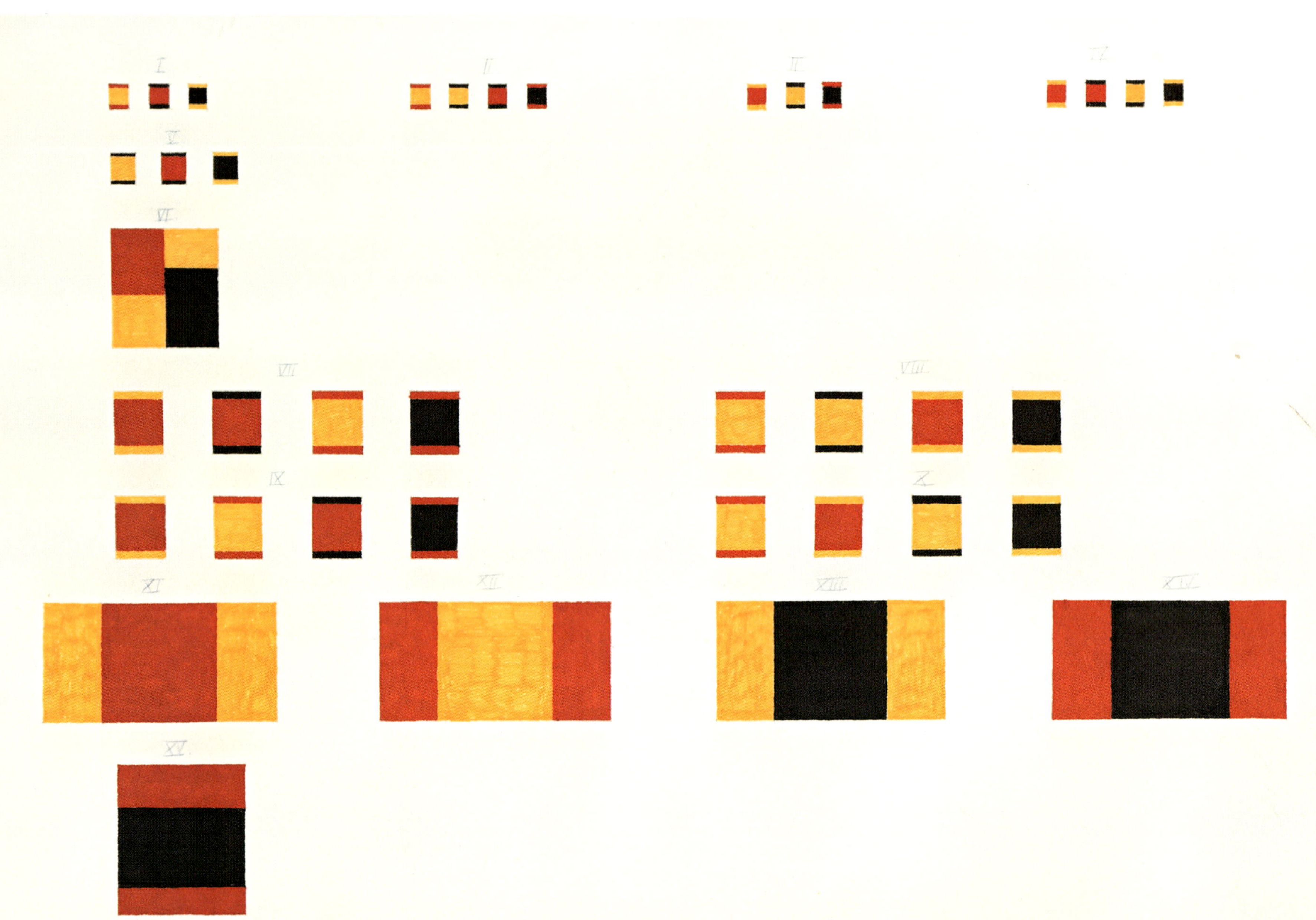
to the people of N.Y.C.
acrylic on aluminum
Palermo 76

Blinky Palermo

Blinky Palermo was born Peter Schwarze in Leipzig in 1943. He and his twin brother, Michael, grew up as adopted children under the name Heisterkamp. In 1962 he entered the Kunstakademie Düsseldorf, where he studied with Joseph Beuys and, in 1964, adopted the name "Blinky Palermo," which he appropriated from an American boxing promoter and mafioso. In 1968 Palermo showed his Wall Drawings at the Galerie Heiner Friedrich, Munich. After visiting New York with Gerhard Richter in 1970, he established a studio there in 1973. Palermo died in 1977, while traveling in the Maldives. His last work, *To the People of New York City* (1976), was shown at the Heiner Friedrich Gallery, New York, in 1977, and at Dia in 1987. Before his death, Palermo participated in more than seventy exhibitions and represented Germany at the São Paulo Bienal in 1975. He has had posthumous retrospectives at the Kunstmuseum Winterthur (1984) and the Kunstmuseum Bonn (1993).

Sketch for *To the People of New York City*, 1976

To the People of New York City (1976), by the German artist Blinky Palermo, is a fifteen-part work comprising thirty-nine individual paintings. Palermo completed it in January 1977, not long before his untimely death. Although he had relocated to New York in the last few years of his life, he realized the work in his studio in Düsseldorf. The cycle was shown from May to June 1977 at the Heiner Friedrich Gallery, New York, and again ten years later at Dia.

Belonging to a group of works called the *Metallbilder* (Metal Paintings), initiated in 1974, *To the People of New York City* may be seen as a coda to a career defined by several distinct aesthetic approaches. Works classified as Objects date from 1964 through 1974; the *Stoffbilder* (Fabric Paintings) first appear in the latter half of 1966; and Palermo began his Wall Drawings and Paintings at the end of 1968. He continued to create *Stoffbilder* until 1972 and Wall Drawings and Paintings until 1973. In 1976 he exhibited a work that was more installation than painting at the Venice Biennale. In each case Palermo variously redefined conventional ideas of painting as a planar rectangular surface conveying an image.

The thirty-nine single elements of *To the People of New York City* require a sizeable amount of wall. While the spaces between each of the fifteen sets of paintings are variable, the distances between the panels of each grouping must be equal to their respective width. All thirty-nine paintings are painted in cadmium red, cadmium yellow, and black. Notably, Palermo applied his acrylic paint to thin aluminum panels rather than to canvas, disqualifying reference to the weave of a fabric support without diminishing the effect of color-bearing paint. He applied the paint by hand but did so evenly, eliminating any sense of gestural activity and allowing the brush to leave only slight striations or irregularities subtly apparent.[1] While thus refraining from signaling an authorial presence, he nonetheless retained the actual and notional quality of an artist's handling of paint.

Nine of the work's fifteen separate parts comprise either three or four panels each. The size of the panels varies but remains consistent within each group. These small-scale panels display a horizontal format with, at top and bottom, narrow strips of color that band a central rectangle. The areas of red, yellow, and black in Part XV are not symmetrically proportioned, as they are in the other parts. Parts XI–XIV are larger, measuring 3¼ x 6½ feet, and have a horizontal format, while Part VI is uniquely sectioned into four disparately scaled rectangles—one red, one black, and two yellow.

Palermo's decision to use the same three hues throughout the work as a whole gave him the foundation for a set of combinations with which to set forth a controlled permutational color scheme. The scheme, however, evinces no regularized, inflexible system. Even while it takes full advantage of the visual power of repetition, it spares itself of an unyielding, mathematically determined seriality.

Free from representational obligation within a single rectangular unit, the colors of red, yellow, and black carry the eye from panel to panel and around the room without enforcing a sequence. Although Palermo refuses to impose a definite system of color arrangement, viewers may tend to want to look for one, a desire that encourages them not to dwell on any one panel. Instead they participate in the experience of observing unenclosed, resonating hues that—despite a deliberate allusion to the colors of the German flag—"float and breathe in the space of the gallery,"[2] having escaped referential responsibility and subjugation to the strictures of formal delineation. The compositional relationships among the colors foster a sense of the color as disembodied from the unframed aluminum panels, which are almost imperceptible, projecting only minimally from the wall by hidden fasteners. These chromatic relationships are marked by their inherent potential for an open-ended interplay between individual panels and sets of panels.

The *Metallbilder*, concluding with *To the People of New York City*, were a new departure for Palermo toward the end of his short career. Like the Objects, the *Stoffbilder*, and the Wall Drawings and Paintings, they succeeded in broadening the parameters of painting, even while remaining unconditionally flat and rectangular. The Objects, on the other hand, had been conspicuous for their break from the customary planarity and rectilinearity of painting.

In the Objects, form is freed from dependence on a separately delimited background. *Kissen mit Schwarzer Form* (*Cushion with Black Shape*), 1967, for example, resembles an upright cushion, as its title suggests. Made of foam rubber covered with cloth and attached to the wall, it is painted a red-rust color on its rounded outer edges and bright orange on its rectangular face. A curvilinear black shape cuts eccentrically through the center. Stuffed like a pillow but richly imbued with brushwork, *Kissen mit Schwarzer Form* is a three-dimensional object whose presence is painterly and tactile. The emphatic black shape on its surface, moreover, assumes an autonomy that it would not possess on the surface of a flat picture plane. Thus superimposed on a protruding object, the shape's own flatness "stands out."

Palermo constructed his Objects so as to enhance the autonomy of painted shape. In the case of *Schmetterling II* (*Butterfly II*), 1969, a long, thin, irregular, vertical shape almost touches a decidedly irregular polygon placed high on the wall to its left. *Tagtraum II* (*Daydream II*), 1966, also a two-part work, is constructed out of a wood T shape and a nonspecific rounded shape covered with beige and purple silk, and thickly painted in uneven areas of white, violet, black, and orange. Instead of containing the form on a two-dimensional rectangular surface, Palermo outlined the entire painting-object so that it would function indiscriminately as both a form and a support.

While he was working on the Objects, Palermo embarked on the *Stoffbilder*, which he fabricated, literally, from bolts of colored cloth that he purchased from department stores. Unlike the Objects but like the *Metallbilder*, the *Stoffbilder* not only have pristine surfaces but are rectangular and two-dimensional rather than irregularly shaped. Tautly attached to a stretcher, the fabrics create smooth rectangular planes of color, one above the other. With the exception of early or experimental pieces in satin, silk, or white fabrics such as muslin or linen, the *Stoffbilder* are made of matte cotton yardage with surface textures and weaves that do not distract from the direct perception of the abutted areas of two or three separate areas of color, which are neatly, almost imperceptibly stitched together. The standard available width of fabric determined the maximum possible dimensions of the colored rectangles, which Palermo matched and scaled intuitively.

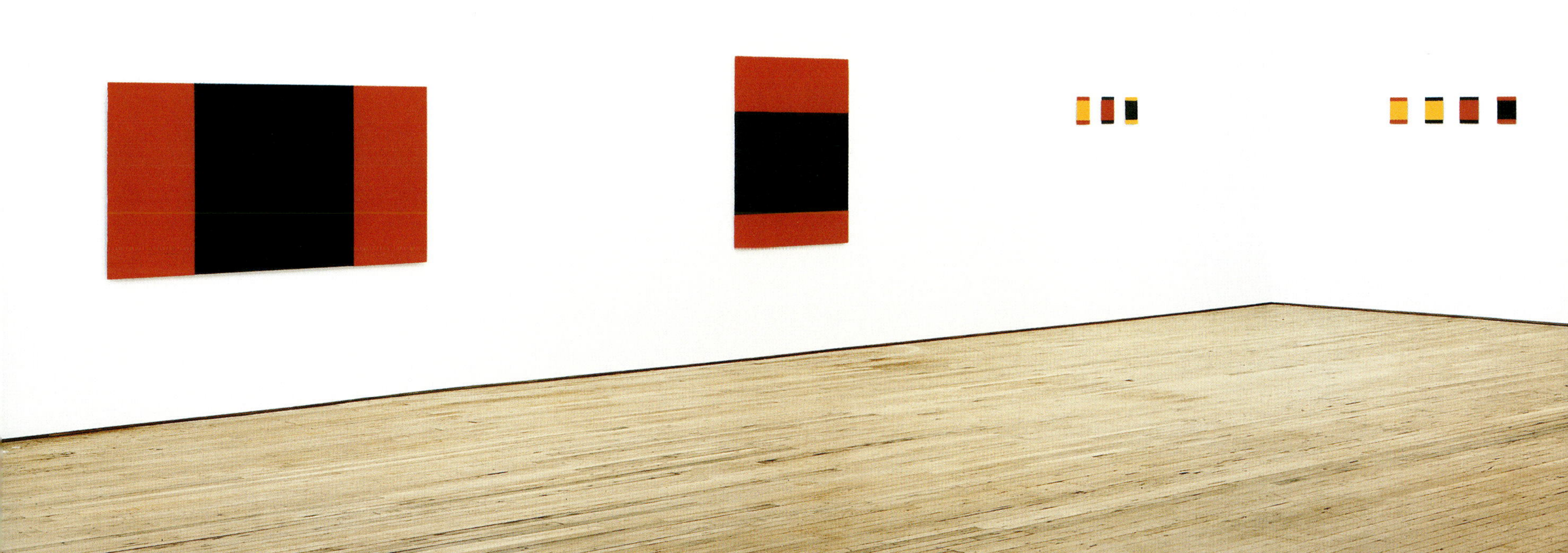

The broad bands of cotton in the *Stoffbilder* are perceived as unobstructed fields of solid color. Commercially available fabric stands in for oil or acrylic on canvas; expanses of dyed cotton substitute for a painted ground. Color and form, surface and support, fuse into a single, united presentation. Released from identification with any external referent, color is not subordinate to rectilinearity but instead announces its field as an independent reality unimpeded by any need to suggest illusionistic space.

Palermo's Wall Drawings and Paintings mark a radical yet logical extension of the ideas underlying the Objects and the *Stoffbilder*. Dispensing with the canvas, an intermediary support, they ally instead with a more all-embracing support, the architecture of the exhibition space. Between 1968 and 1973 Palermo realized more than twenty of these projects and recorded them in sketches and photographic documentation. (They themselves, however, having been affiliated with their place of installation, are no longer extant.) For a solo exhibition in 1971 at Galerie Heiner Friedrich in Munich, for example, Palermo painted one of the gallery's four walls in ocher and one in white. Then he outlined these walls with a border a hand's width wide, encompassing the door frames. The wall painted ocher was outlined in white; the wall painted white was outlined in ocher. In precocious manner, Palermo extended painting to embrace its usually unattended architectural support—a support that here served also to determine the work's formal properties.

In *To the People of New York City*, form follows the dictates of rectilinearity rather than those of the surrounding architecture. Functioning through multiplicitous juxtapositions of red, yellow, and black rectangular areas, released from representational duties and from participation in hierarchies of composition, color receives a chromatic life of its own as the very subject and image of the work.

A. R.

notes

1 See Gary Garrels, "Technical Notes and Schematic Outline," in *Blinky Palermo* (New York: Dia Art Foundation, 1987), for a close descriptive analysis of the work overall, including the nature of the paint handling, and for accompanying schematic diagrams pertaining to each panel's size and color scheme.

2 Richard Lorber, "Blinky Palermo, Heiner Friedrich Gallery," *Artforum* 16, no. 1 (September 1977), p. 77.

right *To the People of New York City*, 1976, Part XII
page 232 *To the People of New York City*, 1976, Part VIII
page 233 *To the People of New York City*, 1976, Part IX
pages 234–235 *To the People of New York City*, 1976

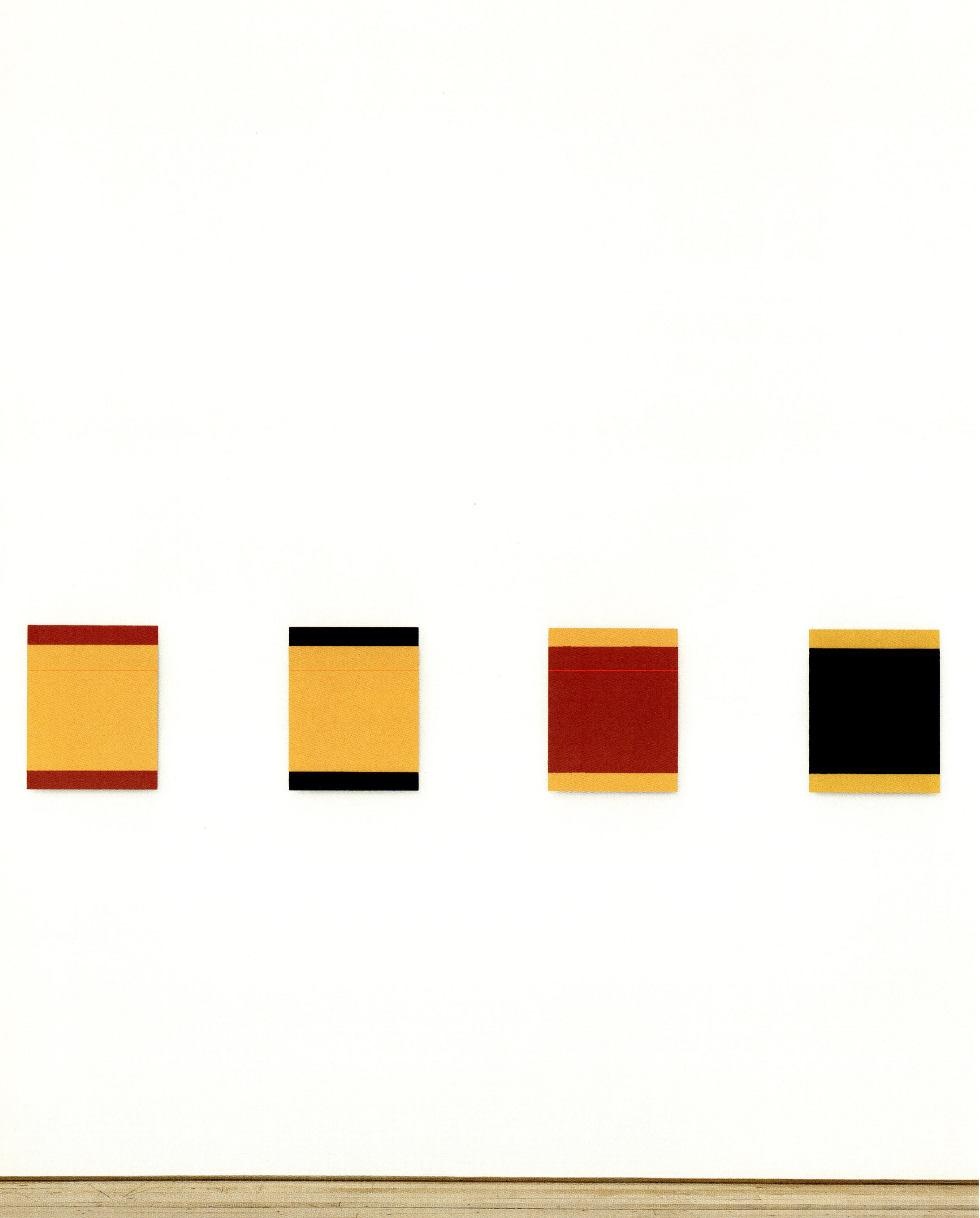

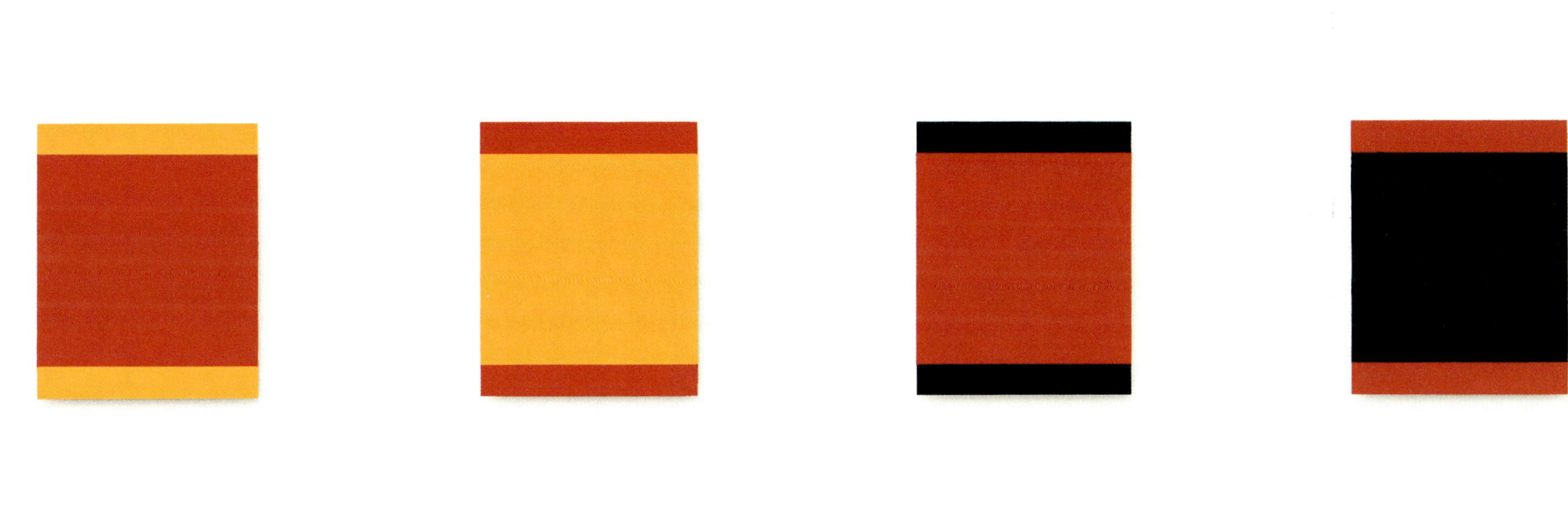

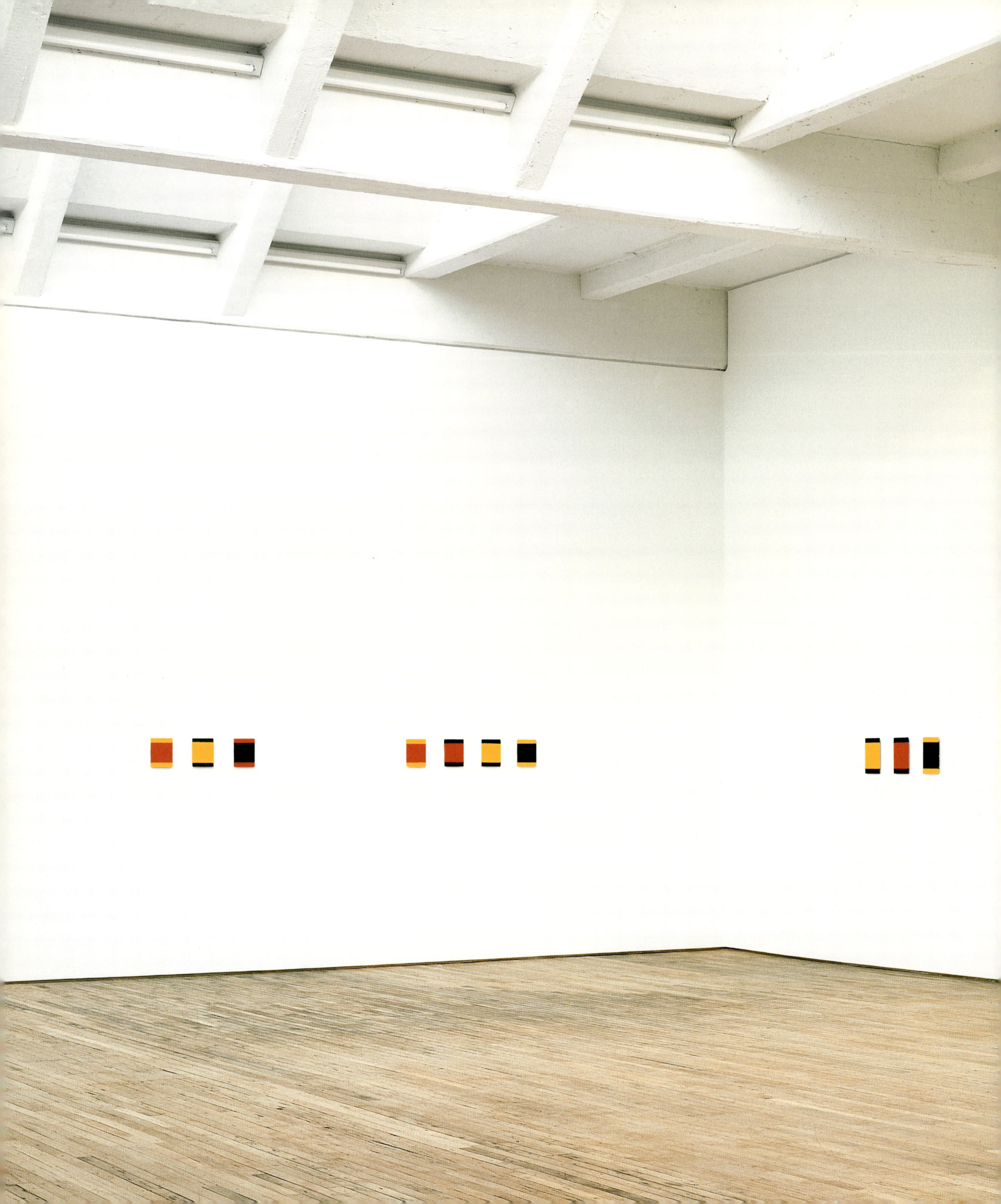

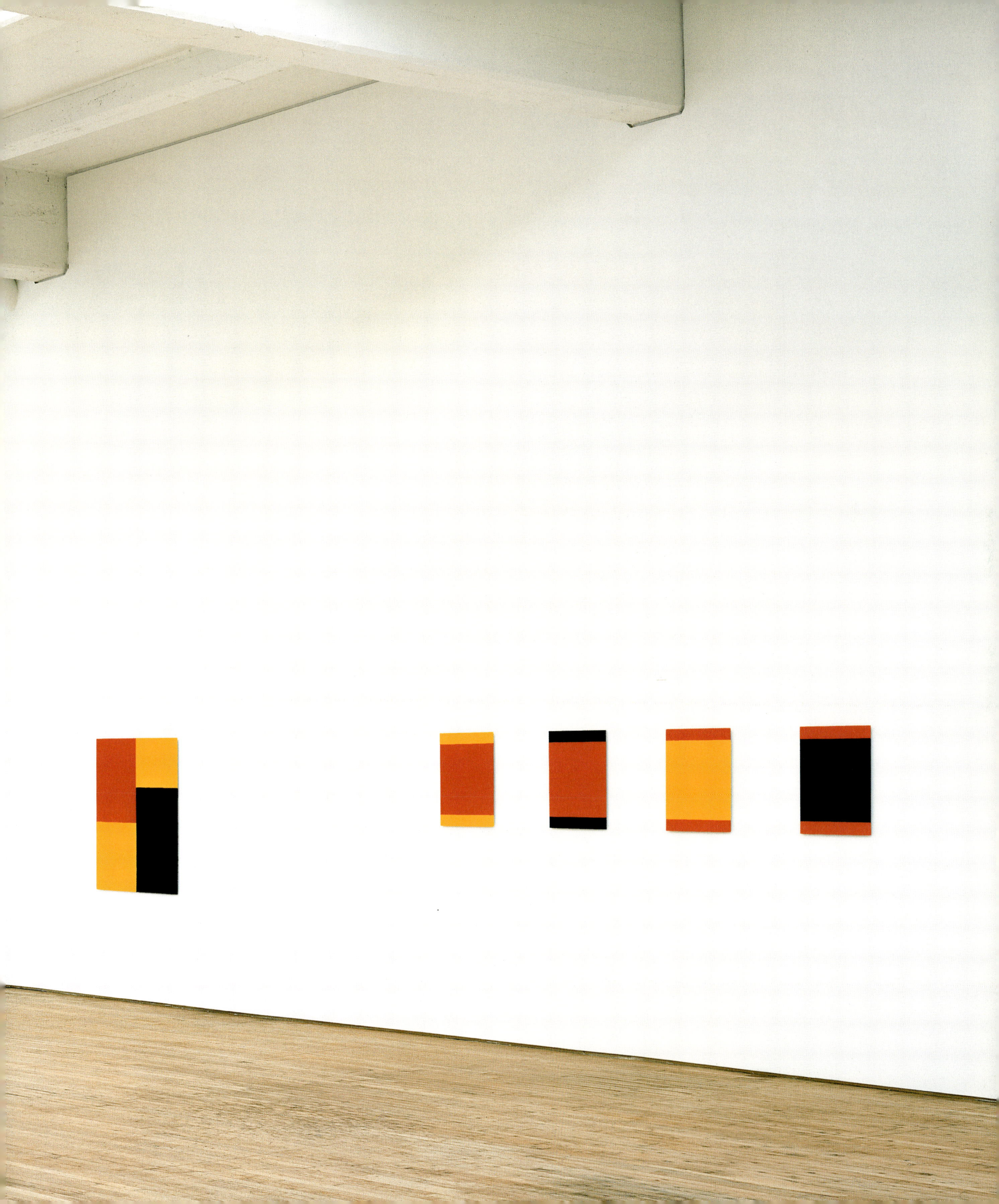

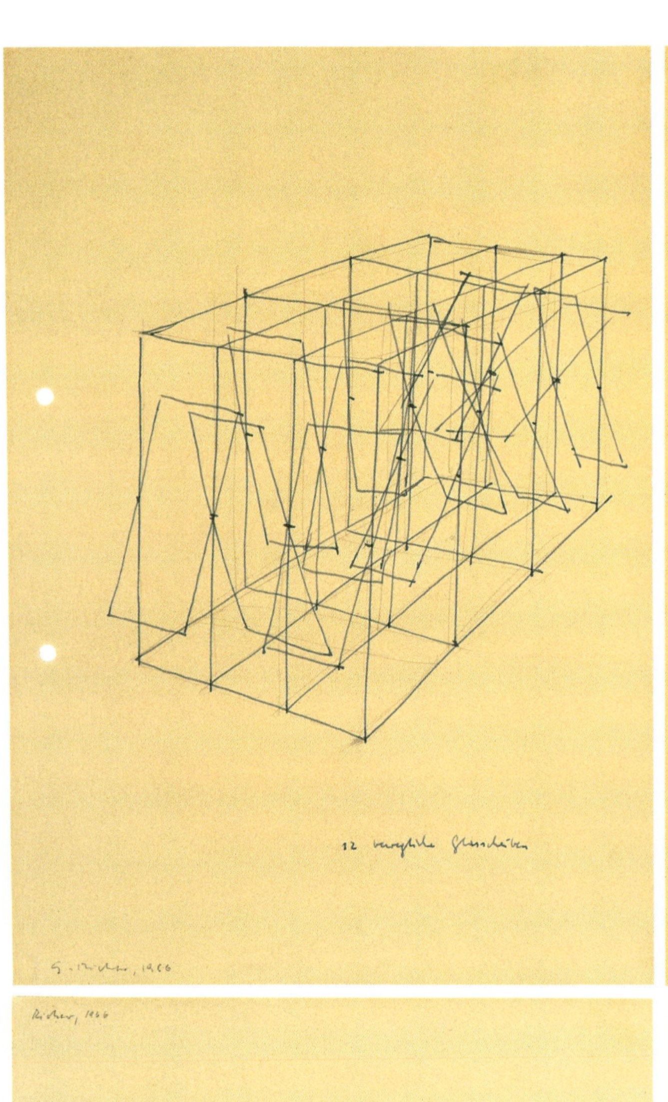

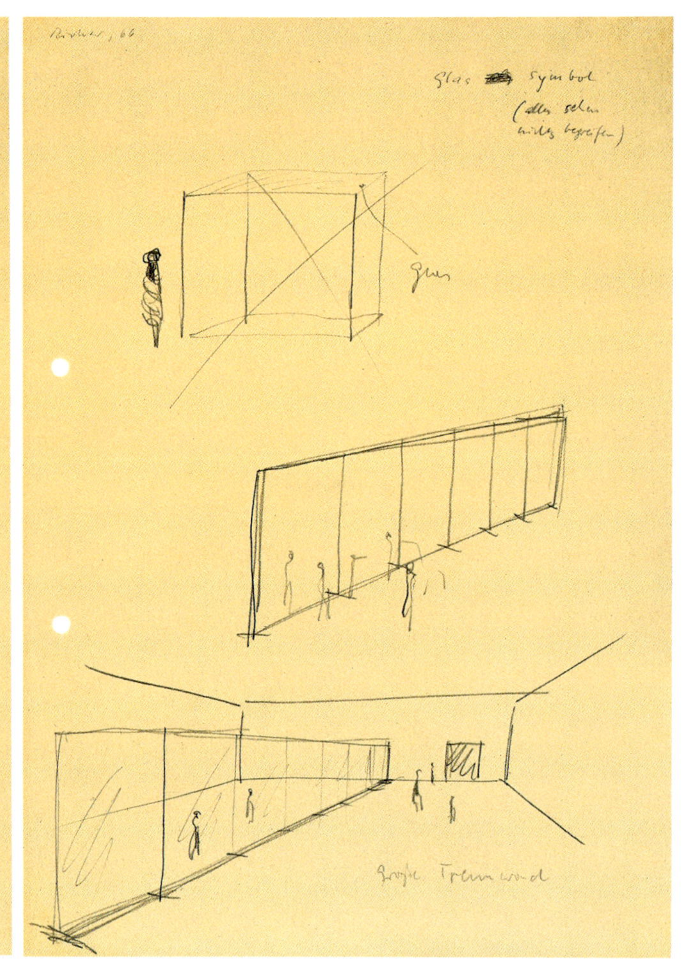
Glas Symbol
Glas
Große Trennwand

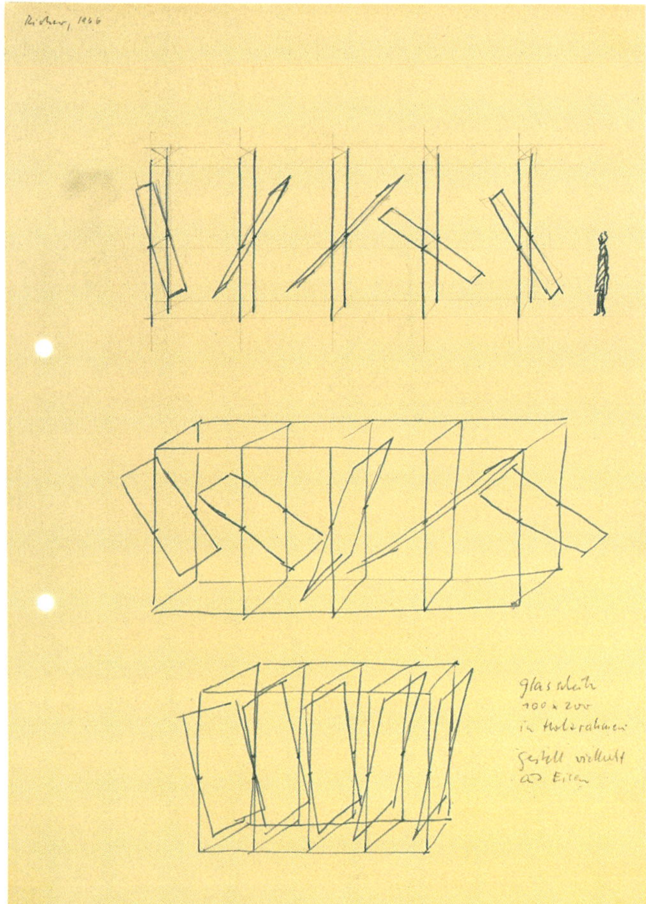

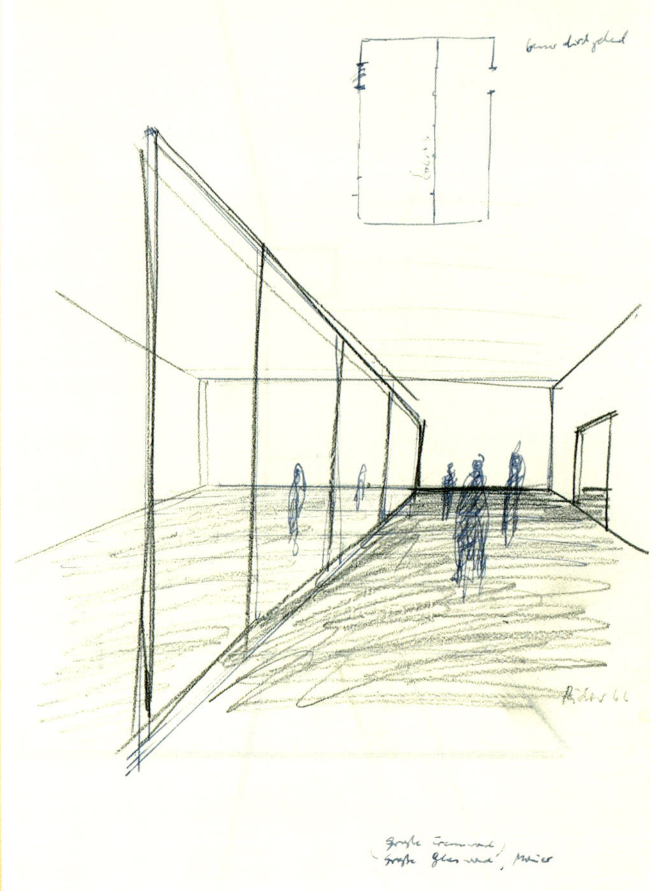

Gerhard Richter

Gerhard Richter was born in Dresden in 1932. He studied at the art academy in Dresden between 1951 and 1956 and at the Kunstakademie Düsseldorf from 1961 to 1963, becoming a professor there in 1971. Since his first solo show at Galerie René Block in Berlin in 1964, Richter has exhibited in many international venues, including Documentas 5 (1972), 7 (1982), 8 (1987), 9 (1992), and 10 (1997). In 1998, the Art Gallery of Ontario and the Museum of Contemporary Art, Chicago, co-organized Richter's first North American retrospective. During its 1995–96 season, Dia exhibited *Atlas*, Richter's ongoing encyclopedic work composed of photographs, reproductions, and illustrations; during Dia's 2002–03 season, Richter presented, with Jorge Pardo, "Refraction," an exhibition in *Project*, Pardo's redesign of Dia's bookshop, lobby, and first-floor exhibition gallery in Chelsea. In 2002, the Museum of Modern Art, New York, presented a major retrospective of Richter's paintings, which traveled throughout the United States.

Study for *4 Panes of Glass*, 1966
Study for *Glass Wall*, 1966
Study for *4 Panes of Glass*, 1966
Study for *Glass Wall*, 1966

Gerhard Richter exhibited his first signature works in a furniture store in Düsseldorf in 1963. A relatively recent immigrant to the West from the East German city of Dresden, where he had been born, raised, then trained as a painter, Richter demonstrated in this group of works, in a style he called "Capitalist Realism," a preoccupation with both the context in which painting was received and how that framing operated—physically, socially, historically, and conceptually. Photographs gleaned from newspapers and other popular sources, and snapshots from family albums, provided the point of departure for these early works, which explored ways in which photography, as the dominant visual language of the modern era, challenges and impacts upon the production and the reception of painting. Through questioning the role of painting, Richter also addressed an ocular-centrism now inextricably enmeshed with the spectacle, an issue that has become increasingly foregrounded in his art in recent years.

In the later 1960s, when many of his colleagues abandoned painting for other art forms ranging from performance to installation-based and still more experimental modes, Richter focused self-critically on his practice. Under pressure to justify, if not restore, painting's vanguard position as a viable expressive language, he embarked on an exigent scrutiny of its history and ontology. The results included a number of strategies devised to explore its origins in mimesis. The key mythemes grounding Western painting derive from the notion of a painting as either a window offering a view on to a world beyond or a mirror reflecting whatever is held before it. These two tropes, the window and the mirror, which metaphorically figure painting's relation to visuality, now became his subjects. A group of some twelve pencil studies from

1965–67 for glass constructions are all based in his ongoing critique of painting as a form of illusionistic picturing.[1] However, only one of these, the landmark *4 Glasscheiben* (*4 Glass Panes*), 1967, was executed at this time. Poised between architecture and painting, this seminal work invokes mythemes of glass, including the German Romantics' reverence for it as a mystical substance, the German Expressionists' fascination with it as the inculcation of a visionary new world, and salient modernist preoccupations with it, such as the embrace of transparency by Walter Gropius and his peers as integral to a utopian functionalist architecture.

Concurrently, in a series of paintings titled *Fenster* (*Window*), begun in 1967, Richter directly addressed abstraction, modernism's primary pictorial language. Wittily and subtly reformulating the axiom that any representation is necessarily an abstraction, he simultaneously postulated the converse: abstraction is inherently referential. All languages of representation, the mimetic as well as the nonfigurative, are constructs whose formulations depend on the establishment of governing pictorial codes and conventions.

More forthrightly, the monochrome, the paradigm of modernist abstraction, became the focus of Richter's attention in the Gray Paintings series, initiated in 1975. While invoking influential precedents by Kasimir Malevich, Aleksandr Rodchenko, and other pioneering early twentieth-century abstractionists, Richter's dour works ambiguously mourn what are irretrievably lost registers of pictorial experience: mimetic representation, individuated subjective expressiveness, psychic inscription, virtuoso craftsmanship, sensual gratification, etc. Subtle but telling differences among these reductive, manifestly impersonal works serve eloquently as "a memory of the past of painting," rendering the ongoing series mute testimony to "the elegiac conditions of painting."[2] In one of the bleakest of his many commentaries accompanying his work, the artist himself described this series as "the welcome and only possible correlative for indifference, apathy, refusal to make a statement, formlessness."[3]

Literally and metaphorically, Richter's works increasingly incorporated the walls on which they were hung and the spaces in which they confronted each other.[4] For example, in 1981, for a two-person show with Georg Baselitz in Düsseldorf, he produced the first of the monumental transparent mirrors that appear intermittently thereafter in his oeuvre.[5] Purged of all evidence of the maker's presence, they absorb as their content the ambient world before them in all its transitory serendipity. Subsuming spectators into that fluctuating matrix, depriving them of any clear, fixed, stable relationship to space and place, his mirrors seductively undermine the viewers' authorial independence and autonomy by dissembling traditional hieratic perspectival systems of perception. *Sieben stehende Scheiben* (*Seven Standing Panes*), 2002, the first in a recent series of three-dimensional glass works stemming from those seminal sketches of 1965–67, confounds what is seen with what is represented. Filtering, refracting, and inflecting its environment, it affectlessly incorporates its surroundings, venturing yet another compelling if double-edged variant on the problematics of the in situ or environmental artwork.

The strongly synesthetic basis of Richter's practice, evident early in his career in a virtuoso interplay of disparate traditions and techniques, has turned increasingly in recent years to a fusion of the normally discrete registers of architecture, painting, decor, and sculpture, as witnessed in the ensemble of paintings and colored mirrors he presented in a special pavilion designed in collaboration with architect Paul Robbrecht at Documenta 9 in Kassel, Germany, in 1992. Interweaving abstract paintings, a floral still life, and two colored mirrors, this installation foregrounded protocols of exhibition and display. In this unprecedented spatialized ensemble Richter realized what, only several years before, he had described as a "dream of mine—that the pictures will become an environment or become architecture—that would be even more effective."[6]

"I do perceive an unchangeable basic attitude, a constant concern that runs through all my works," the artist averred in 1991.[7] Now spanning some forty years, Richter's oeuvre confirms his continued engagement with fundamental pictorial problems in the broadest sense, for from his first exhibition in the Düsseldorf department store he has been highly attentive to issues of presentation and reception.[8] At the same time, his unwavering commitment to the media and materials conventionally associated with the practice of painting—oil pigment, acrylic, watercolor—allows him to probe the viability of this art form by situating his work in dialogue with its most hallowed traditions.

Richter's proposal for Dia:Beacon is an installation comprising a suite of six large reflecting glass surfaces, a fusion of the monochrome gray paintings that he has executed for almost thirty years and the earlier glass and mirror works originating in those prophetic sketches of 1965–67. He describes his hybrid colored mirrors as a "Neither/Nor," noting, "which is what I like about it."[9] At his request the space where his work is installed has been redesigned so that the building's articulated structure of column and beam has been masked, transforming it into a more conventional white-cube gallery lit by a clerestory. The gray enameled panels of glass cantilevered from the walls on steel supports will be tilted at various angles.[10] Their crepuscular depths not only reflect approaching visitors but respond to shifting weather conditions, as light is refracted through the high windows, conflating the registers of architecture, sculpture, painting, and photography into a synthetic environmental whole.

The culmination of a pursuit that began with *4 Glasscheiben*, the Dia:Beacon project *Six Gray Mirrors*, 2003, is more a sequel to than a reprise of

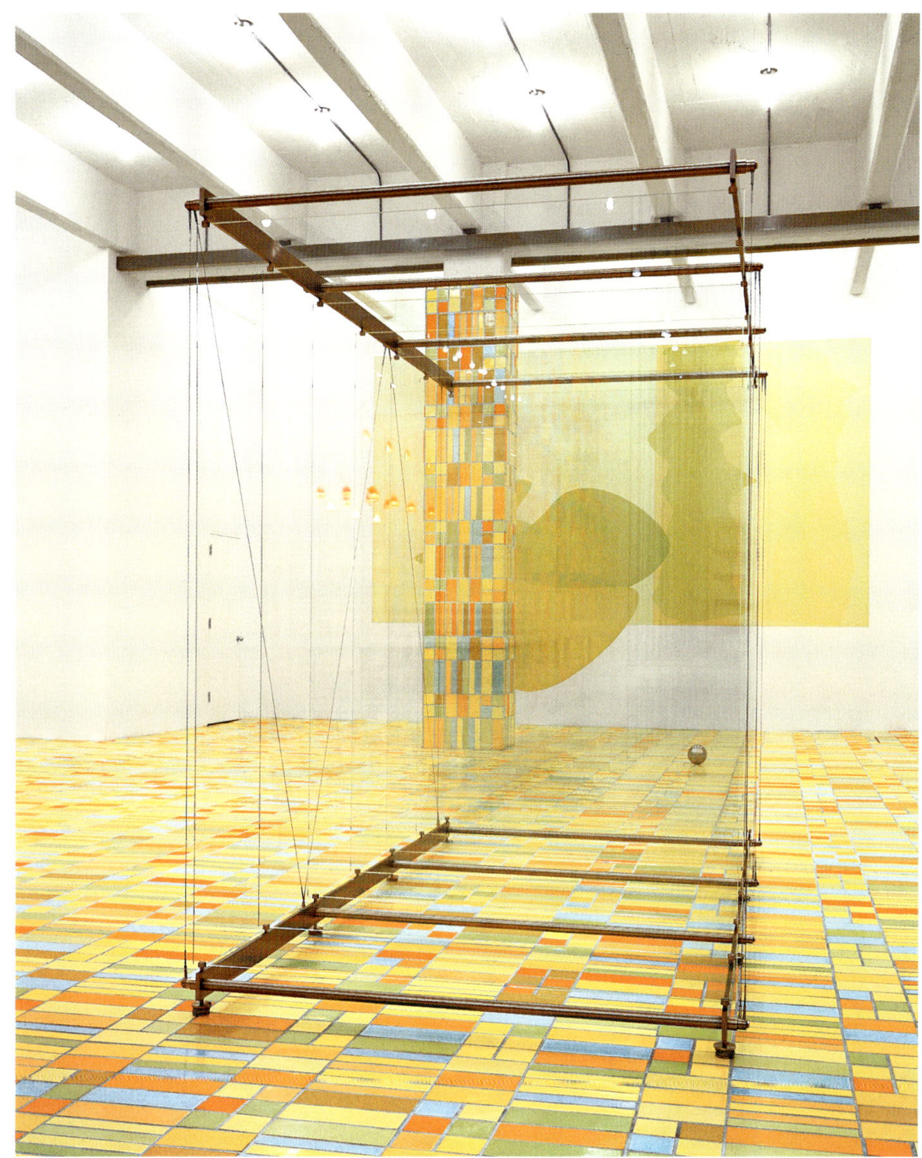

Seven Standing Panes, 2002, installation view, "Gerhard Richter and Jorge Pardo: Refraction," Dia Center for the Arts, 2002

Acht Grau (*Eight Gray*), 2002; commissioned for the Deutsche Guggenheim, Berlin, in 2002 that grand, austere installation was as profoundly destabilizing in its relation to site and place as it was solemnly elegiac.[11] "Glas Symbol (alles sehen nichts begreifen)" (Glass symbol [to see everything to understand nothing]), Richter wrote in 1966 on the edge of one of the sketches limning *4 Glasscheiben*. This brief note succinctly formulates his abiding doubt that perception will vouchsafe understanding, and, by extension, that light, with glass as its preeminent transmitter, can still serve as the embodiment of transcendental experience—in short, that the Enlightenment project has any viability today. Drained of memory, repulsing history, these penumbral surfaces obscure as they reflect. At once somber veils and surfaces of pure unblemished radiance, they offer no reconciliation between the contraries of opacity and reflection, painterly paradigms for the monochrome and the window. Refuting the Enlightenment's belief in the power of illumination, and, with it, the promise of seeing as a transcendental experience, Richter proffers a stance that is, however, less unrelievedly pessimistic than that which underpinned his Gray Paintings in the mid-1970s. A qualified skepticism informs his Neither/Nor.[12]

L.C.

notes

1 René Magritte was very much on Gerhard Richter's mind at this moment, as a singular untitled painting from 1967, made on a found framed mirror, attests. It is not published in the catalogue raisonné.

2 These apt phrases were coined by Benjamin H. D. Buchloh, Richter's foremost critic and historian. The first is quoted in Martin Hentschel, "On Shifting Terrain: Looking at Richter's Abstract Paintings," in *Gerhard Richter 1998* (London: Anthony D'Offay Gallery, 1998), p. 11; the second comes from Buchloh, "The Allegories of Painting," in *Gerhard Richter: Documenta IX, 1992 • Marian Goodman Gallery, 1993* (New York: Marian Goodman Gallery, 1993), p. 14.

3 The statement, made in 1982 to Heribert Heere, is quoted in Hentschel, "On Shifting Terrain," p. 13.

4 Several sketches in *Atlas*, the encyclopedic work that Richter began in 1964, depict vast galleries containing his monumental paintings. These are obviously fantastical projections, but *Atlas* also contains technical drawings and designs for built and buildable structures, including furniture and architecture.

5 See Jürgen Harten, ed., *Georg Baselitz—Gerhard Richter* (Düsseldorf: Städtische Kunsthalle, 1981).

6 Richter, quoted in an interview by Dorothea Dietrich, *The Print Collector's Newsletter* 16, no. 4 (September–October 1985), p. 130.

7 Richter, quoted in "Interview with Jonas Storsve," 1991, reprinted in *Gerhard Richter: The Daily Practice of Painting. Writings and Interviews 1962–1993*, ed. Hans-Ulrich Obrist (Cambridge, Mass.: The MIT Press, in association with Anthony D'Offay Gallery, London 1995), p. 229.

8 This may owe something to Richter's formative years in East Germany, where he painted a number of murals under a socialist aesthetic. More pertinent, perhaps, are such modernist predecessors as El Lissitzky's *Abstract Cabinet* (1926–28), for Dresden and Hannover.

9 Richter, in "Interview with Jonas Storsve," p. 226.

10 The colored mirrors are glass paintings made by a technique in which pure pigment is fused in a heating process to the back of a glass sheet. Variations in tone and hue are found among the various groups of Gray Mirrors as well as among the brighter hues.

11 See Buchloh's excellent study, to which this text is much indebted, "Gerhard Richter's *Eight Gray*: Between *Vorschein and Glanz*," in *Gerhard Richter: Eight Gray 2002* (Berlin: Deutsche Guggenheim Berlin, 2002), pp. 13–28.

12 Buchloh offers a more critical interpretation than that found here: "we encounter a definition of visuality that seems to suggest that it is far from liberating and transcendental, that it is in fact deeply inscribed in or causally connected to other formations, the regulations of institutional interests and control or the processes of systematic fetishization." Ibid., p. 28.

right *Eight Gray*, 2001, studio view, Cologne

page 242 *Mirror, Gray*, 1991

page 243 *Gray Mirror*, 1991, installation view, The Saint Louis Art Museum

pages 244–245 *Six Gray Mirrors*, rendering for installation at Dia:Beacon, 2003

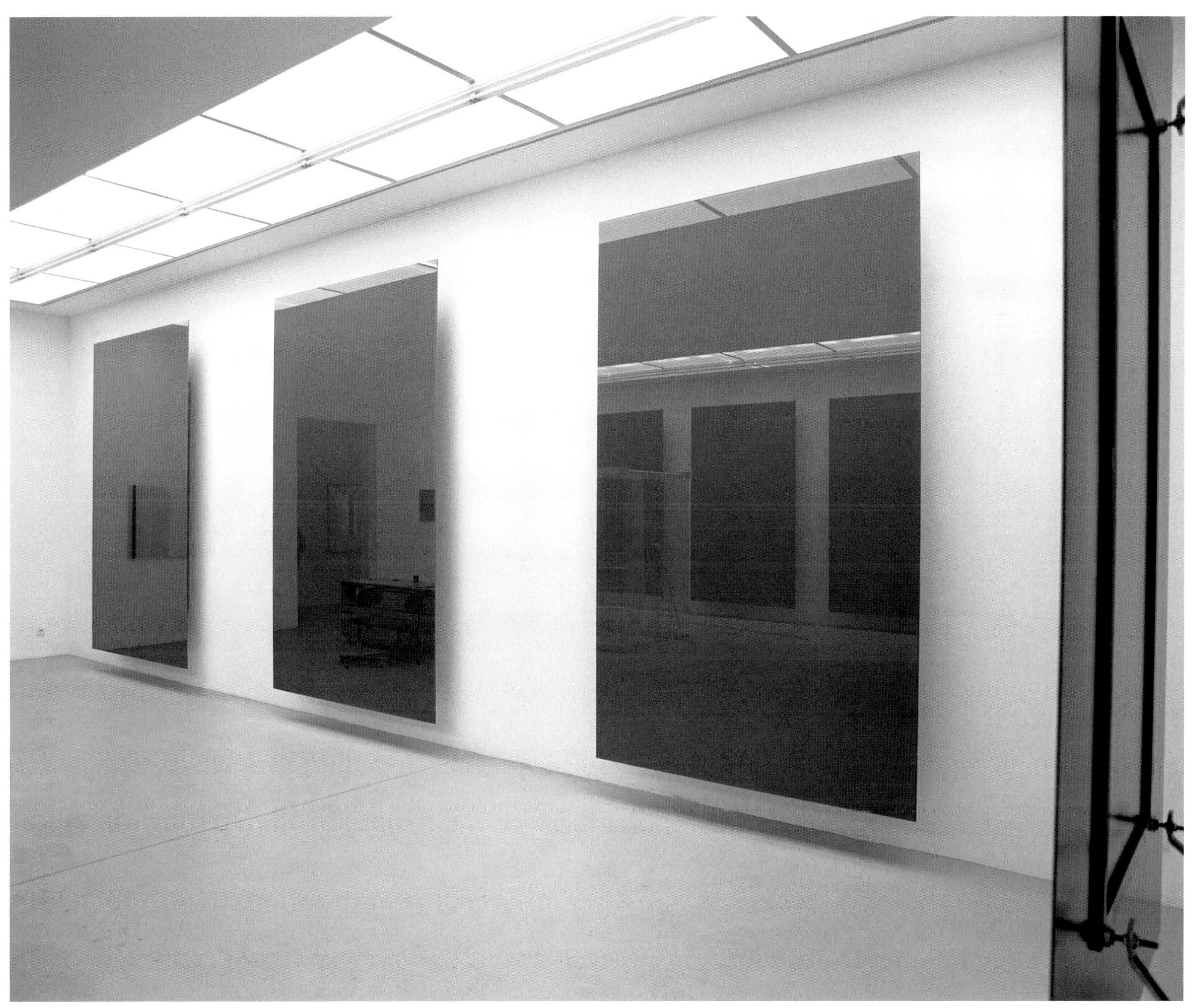

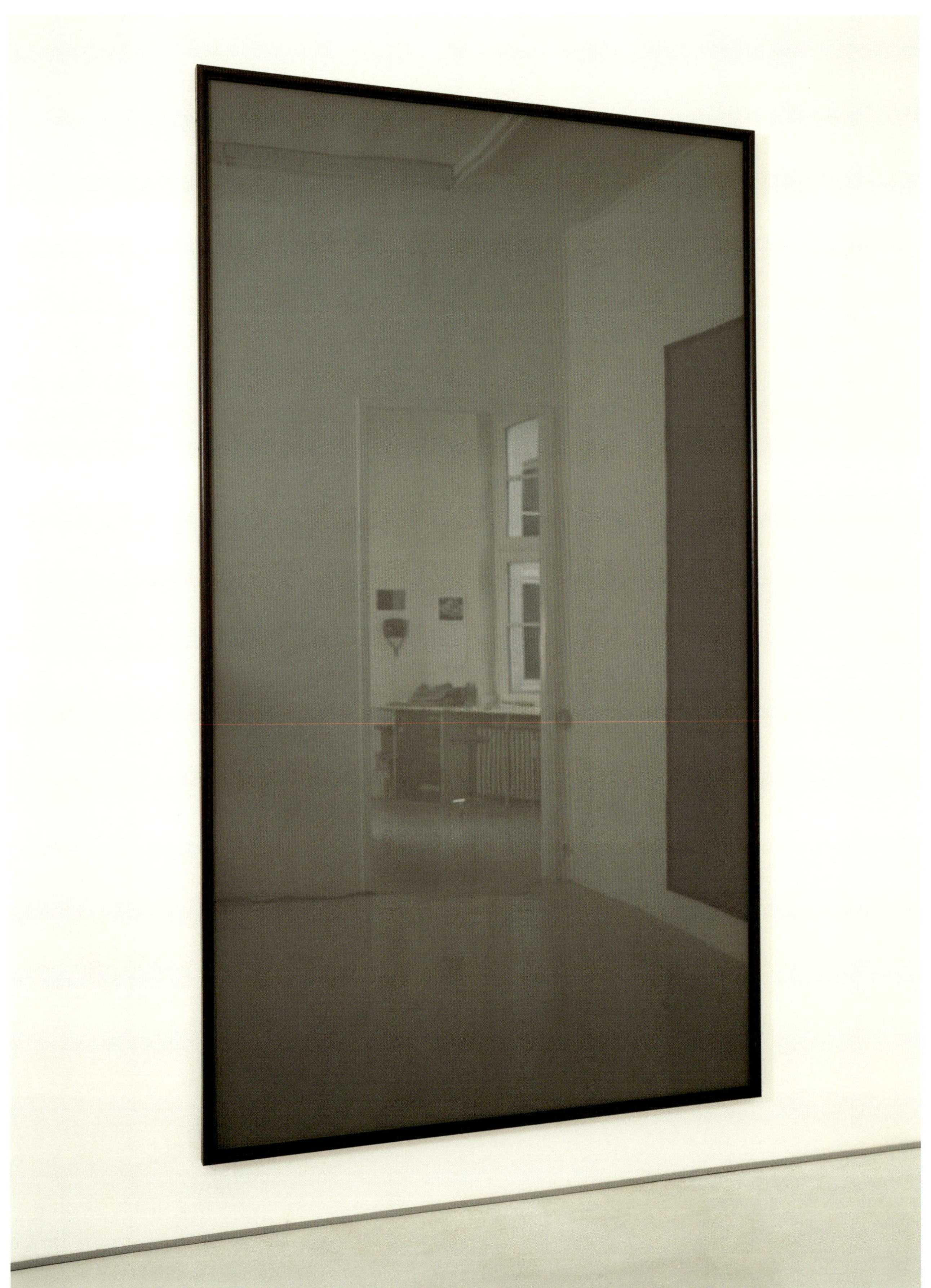

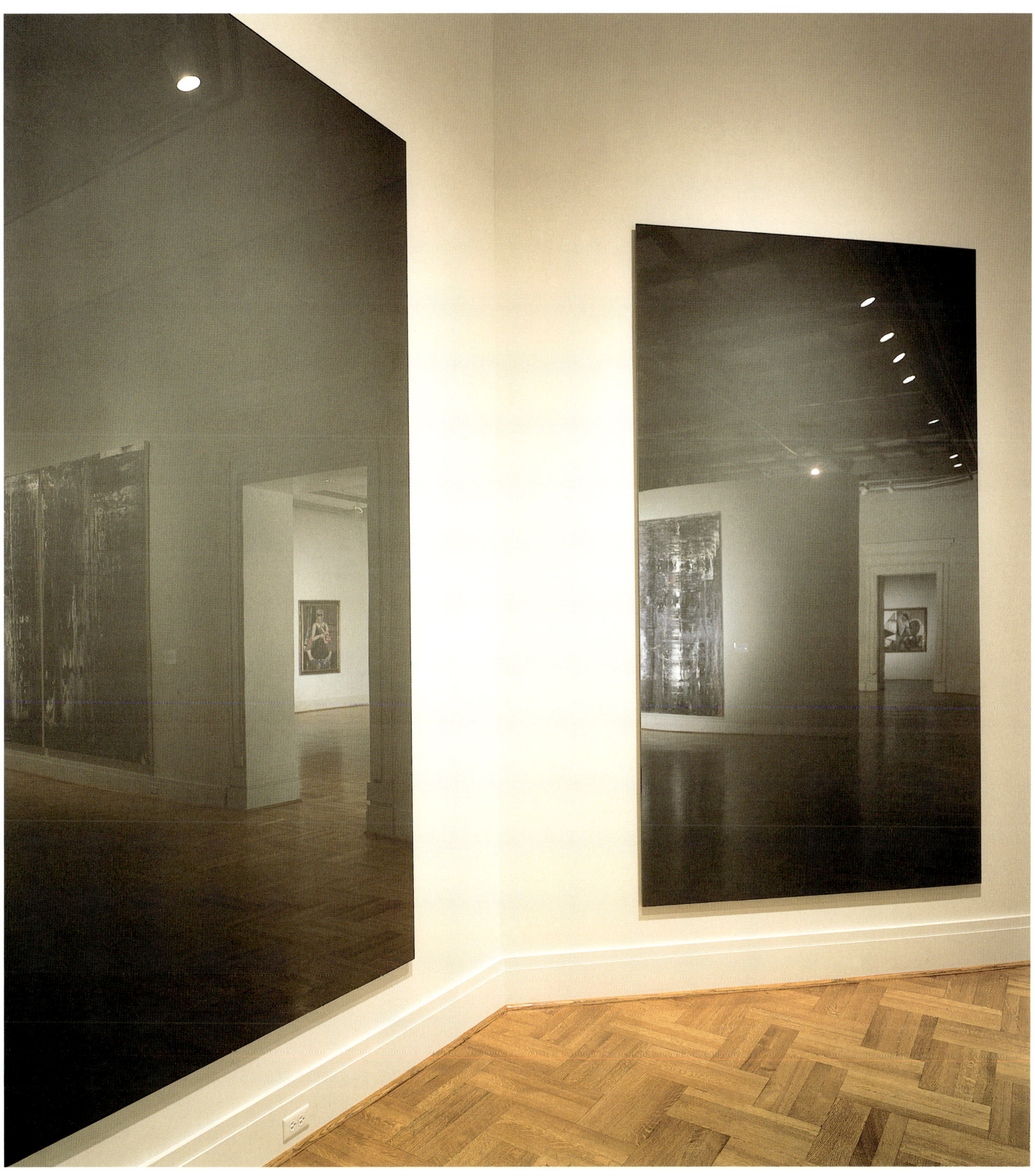

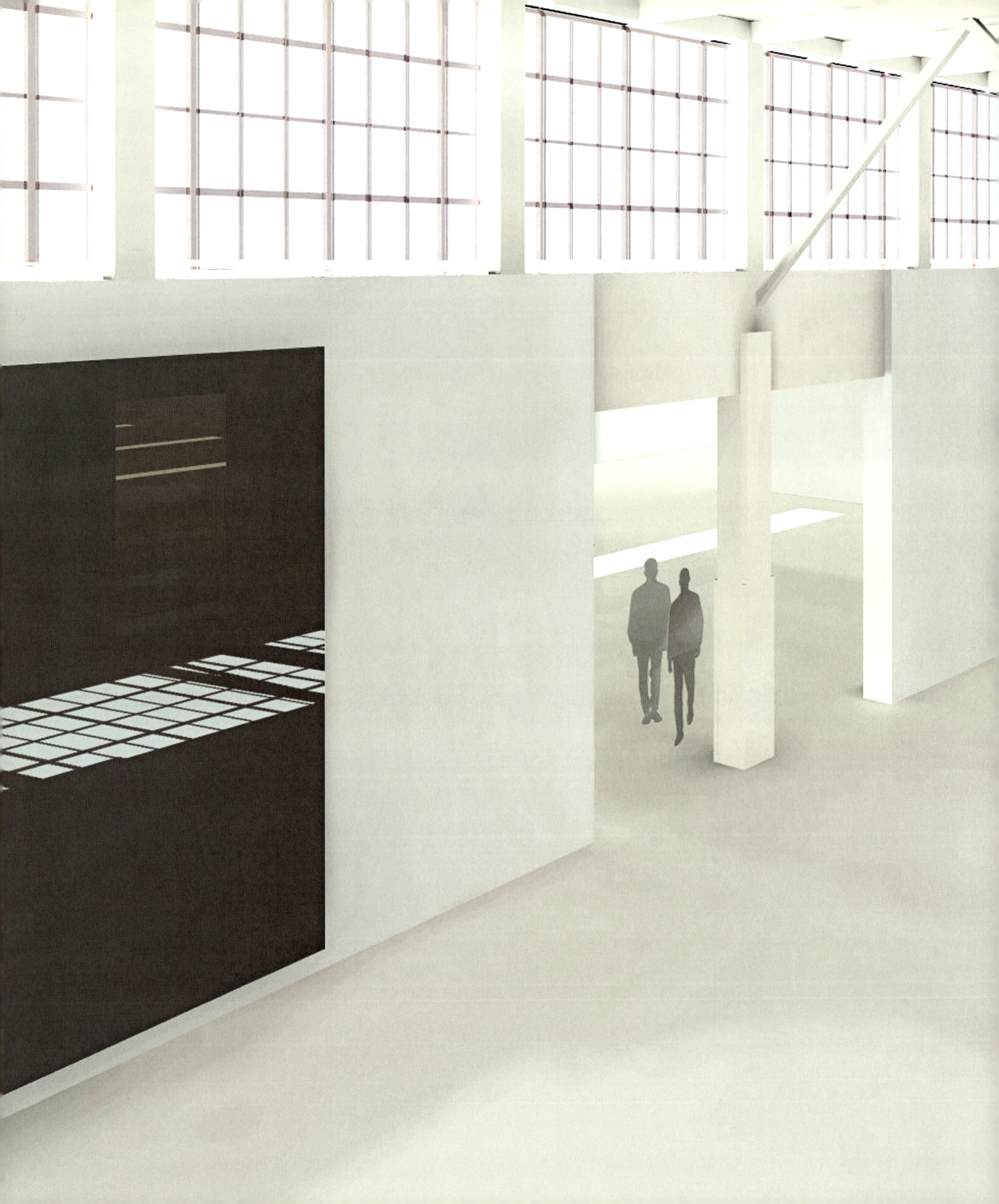

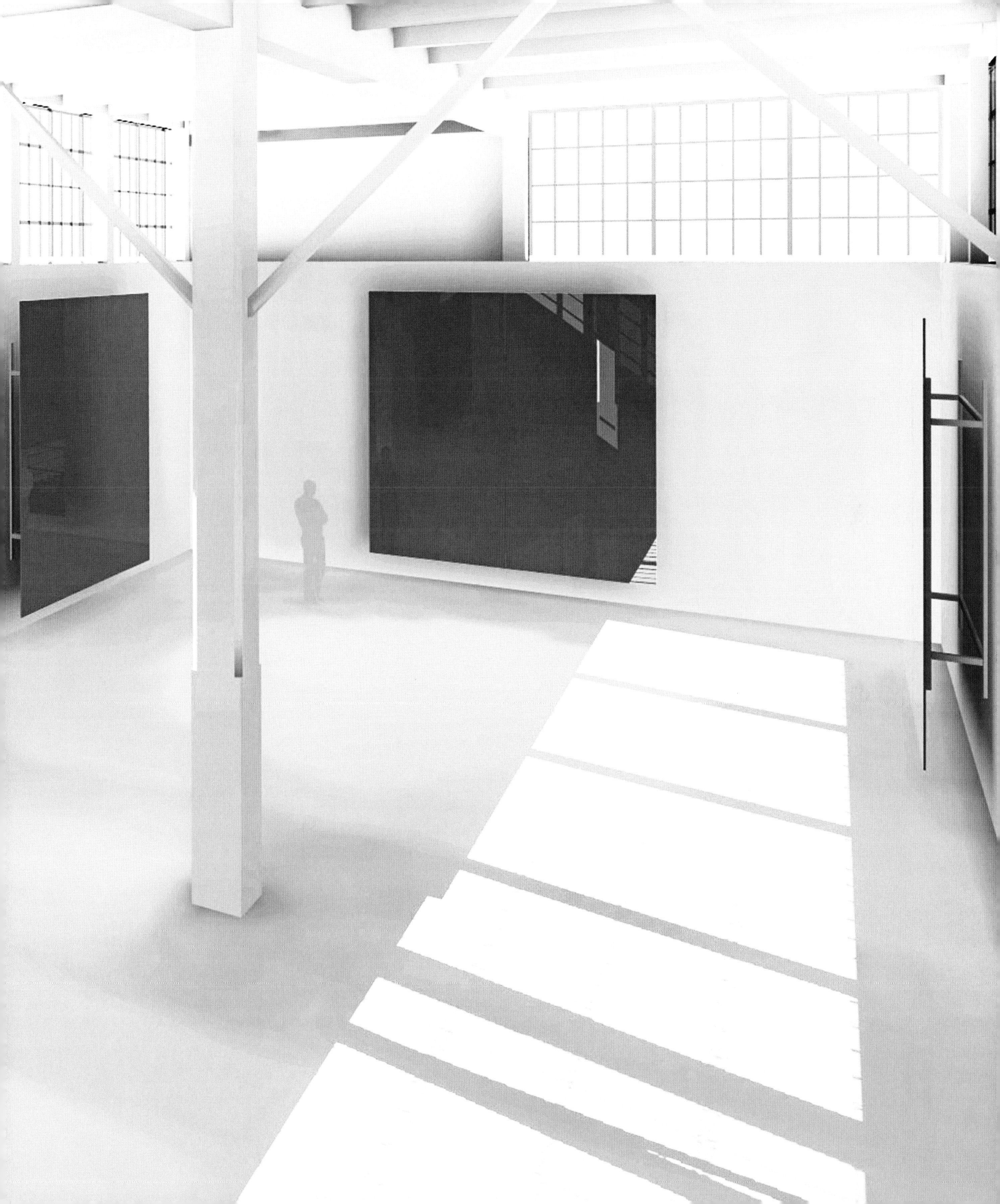

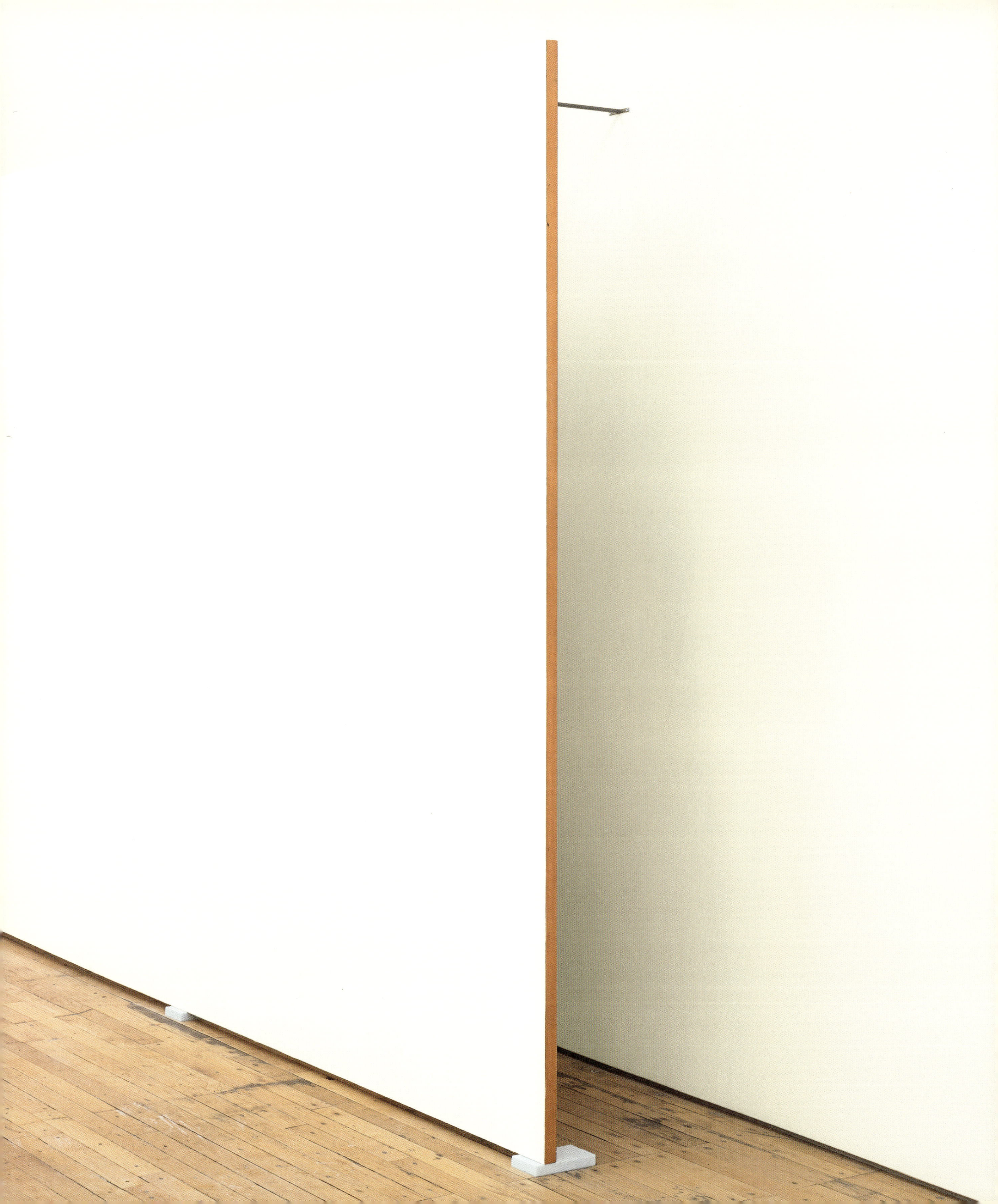

Robert Ryman

Born in Nashville, Tennessee, in 1930, Robert Ryman attended Tennessee Polytechnic Institute and the George Peabody College for Teachers (1948–49). After serving in the United States Army Reserve Corps from 1950 to 1952, he moved to New York City, intending to pursue a career in jazz by studying with the pianist Lenny Tristano. In 1953, however, Ryman began working as a guard at the Museum of Modern Art, and that same year he was inspired to make his first painting. His first one-person exhibition was held at the Paul Bianchini Gallery, New York, in 1967, and his first show in Europe came the following year at the Galerie Heiner Friedrich, Munich. Ryman's works were represented in Documentas 5 (1972), 6 (1977), and 7 (1982), in Kassel, in the Venice Biennale of 1976, and in the Whitney Biennial of 1987. His first retrospective was organized by the Stedelijk Museum, Amsterdam, in 1974; Dia mounted a show of his works in 1988, and he had a retrospective at the Museum of Modern Art, New York, in 1993.

Varese Wall, 1975 (detail)

Robert Ryman's lifelong inquiry into the notion of painting as a medium and a verb—that is, into paint as a viscous material that articulates its support—began as early as the mid-1950s. His principal concern over the decades has been with the presentation of a painted surface in relation to its underlying support. This ongoing investigation has yielded ever-new visual possibilities, however nuanced these may be.

In Ryman's oeuvre the work's "image" results from the nature of the surface that arises when paint is applied to a canvas or any other material support in a particular manner. "What the painting is, is exactly what [people] see," he remarked in a relatively early interview.[1] With greater emphasis on the "see" than on the "is" of his statement, Ryman later elaborated on his basic thesis:

> *We have been trained to see painting as "pictures," with storytelling connotations, abstract or literal, in a space usually limited and enclosed by a frame which isolates the image. It has been shown that there are possibilities other than this manner of "seeing" painting. An image could be said to be "real" if it is not an optical reproduction, if it does not symbolize or describe so as to call up a mental picture. This "real" or "absolute" image is only confined by our limited perception.*[2]

Ryman's aesthetic practice is further illuminated by his observation in the late 1960s that "there is never a question of what to paint, but only how to paint. The how of painting has always been the image—the end product."[3] For his part he has "wanted to make a painting getting the paint across"—meaning getting paint literally across the surface and, more idiomatically, getting it across as an idea.[4]

Occupied from the outset with ways of letting paint engage with its surface, Ryman has continuously sought to activate the painted surface, often subtly, while simultaneously approaching the support as if it were the proscenium of a stage. Unlike *Untitled* (*Orange Painting*) (1955–59), which he considers his first mature painting, his works typically use white paint, because of its neutrality as a color, and more often than not they are square in format. The exclusion of other hues, and the equalizing of all sides of the support, minimize distraction from the paint as an area warranting the full attention of the viewer.

Untitled (1959) is indicative of his overriding interest in imbuing paint with the power to act on its own behalf. Multidirectional, interwoven, overlapping brushwork and residual globules of paint signify the performance of paint itself, rather than suggesting some quality beyond its own physicality and its behavior in response to the brush. Moreover, the artist's painted signature, the vertically upended "R Ryman," intervenes in the overall activity of the paint. According to Ryman, the signature, "an accepted element of all painting," functions saliently here as a line meant to avert symbolism, and to prevent the painting from being mistaken as "trying to say something."[5] Simultaneously a painted sign and an authorial one, the orange-toned signature is engulfed in the all-encompassing field of paint. Close in color to the orange-yellow tint of the work's raw cotton canvas, the signature-as-line-as-physical-paint mediates between the entirety of the painted field and the partially revealed cloth support beneath it.

The paints Ryman has used since the 1950s have varied immensely in viscosity and finish, whether glossy, semiglossy, matte, or dull.[6] These many paint qualities, along with the multifarious methods with which Ryman handles them, interact with one another in concert with the material of the painting's support and in view of the painting's scale.

Both *Vector* (1975/1997) and *Varese Wall* (1975) are large in scale, and both are painted on wood panels. The evenhanded approach to paint application in these works brings up a question: what differentiates the paint of the painting from the paint of the white wall behind it? The two works pose this question somewhat differently by virtue of their respective supports. *Vector* comprises eleven wood units of the same size, hung equidistant from one another; *Varese Wall*, on the other hand, appears as one extended surface, propped up from the floor on five small bluish blocks of foam. Measuring eight feet high and twenty-four feet long, the work is braced to stand just over a foot and a half from the wall.[7]

The wall plays an active role in the experience and meaning of Ryman's works, whatever their size and no matter what the interaction between paint and support. "If you were to see any of my paintings off of the wall, they would not make any sense at all . . . unlike the usual painting where the image is confined within the space of the paint plane," the artist has pointed out.[8] In *Vector*, the empty spaces between the painted panels echo the forms of the panels themselves. Ryman initially painted this work in vinyl acetate, a pigmented commercial glue, at the Kunsthalle Basel for his exhibition there in the summer of 1975. A couple of years later the eleven panels were separated into two artworks, one of five panels (*Vector I*) and one of six (*Vector II*), but they were reunited in 1979. In 1997, Ryman painted over the original, vertically brushed vinyl acetate with oil paint, leaving a new, horizontally brushed surface as impassive as the earlier one. In effect, the paint quality of *Vector* nearly matches that of the wall, from which, however, the panels may be distinguished in that their thin left sides are made of a clear pine wood and their right sides are of redwood. As the light plays on the work's painted surfaces, the panels seem to float ever so slightly away from the wall. In this way the work demonstrates how painted surface, wall, light quality, and overall spatial confines converge to form an image that simultaneously incorporates and contradicts the formerly blank space of a wall.

Varese Wall, like *Vector*, also exhibits the fine line between a painting and its background wall. Here, in fact, the painting–its title a reference to the walls leading to the villa of Count Panza di Buomo in Varese, Italy–is also a wall of sorts. This painting-cum-wall creates a dialectic with the wall of its given exhibition space, a wall that presumably is painted but is not in any sense a painting. With his introduction of metal fasteners that visibly hold his paintings to their walls, in 1976, Ryman overtly acknowledged the symbiosis between a painting and its supporting wall. *Varese Wall* furthermore remains ever freshly painted, as does any "real" exhibition wall, since the artist gives it another coat of vinyl acetate whenever it is installed anew.

Vector and *Varese Wall* anticipate later works of Ryman's in that they verge on obliterating the distinction between the thematic aspect of painting and a painting as a physical object, but never quite do–in fact, this is a distinction they insist upon. These works fully express the idea that the relationship of paint to support, though born of material practicality, is ultimately grounded in the ideational capacity of painting to be about its own activity. Ryman's paintings detail different possibilities for the application of paint. For him, painting remains an ongoing reflection on itself, and in his work it becomes ever more mindful of its differentiation from, yet necessary, attachment to a wall.

A. R.

notes

1 Robert Ryman, quoted in Phyllis Tuchman, "An Interview with Robert Ryman," *Artforum* 9, no. 9 (May 1971), p. 53.

2 Ryman, in *Wall Painting* (Chicago: Museum of Contemporary Art, 1979), p. 16.

3 Ryman, in *Art in Process*, vol. 4 (New York: Finch College Museum of Art/Contemporary Wing, 1969–70), n.p.

4 Ryman, in Tuchman, "An Interview with Robert Ryman," p. 49.

5 Ryman, in Robert Storr, *Robert Ryman* (New York: The Museum of Modern Art, in association with the Tate Gallery, London, 1993), p. 70.

6 For a full explication of Ryman's working methods and materials, see Robert Storr, "Simple Gifts," in ibid., pp. 9–45.

7 I thank Amy Baker Sandback for unpublished information on these paintings from her forthcoming catalogue raisonné of Ryman's work.

8 Ryman, in Gary Garrels, "Interview with Robert Ryman," in *Robert Ryman* (New York: Dia Art Foundation, 1988), p. 13.

pages 250–251 *Varese Wall*, 1975

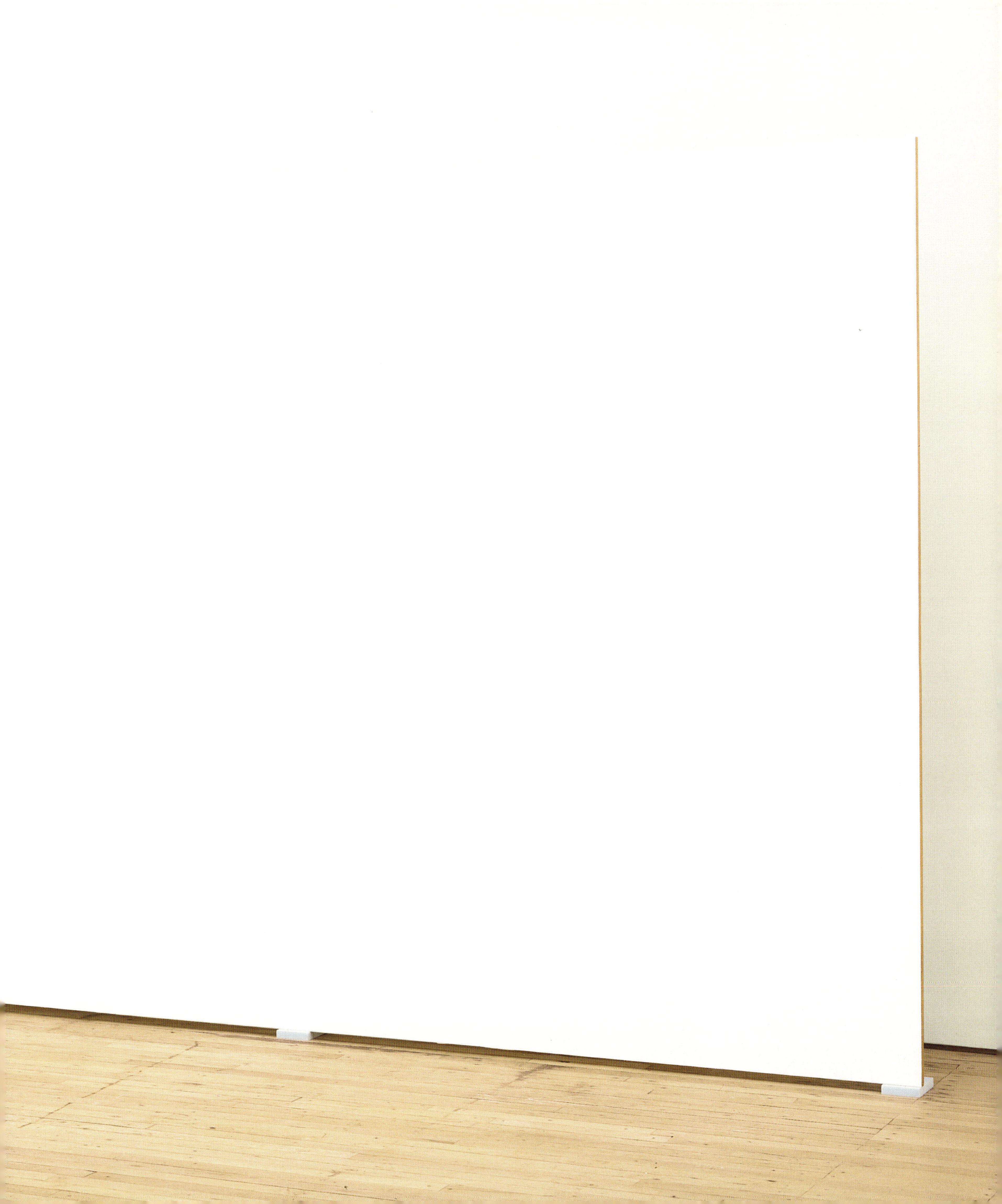

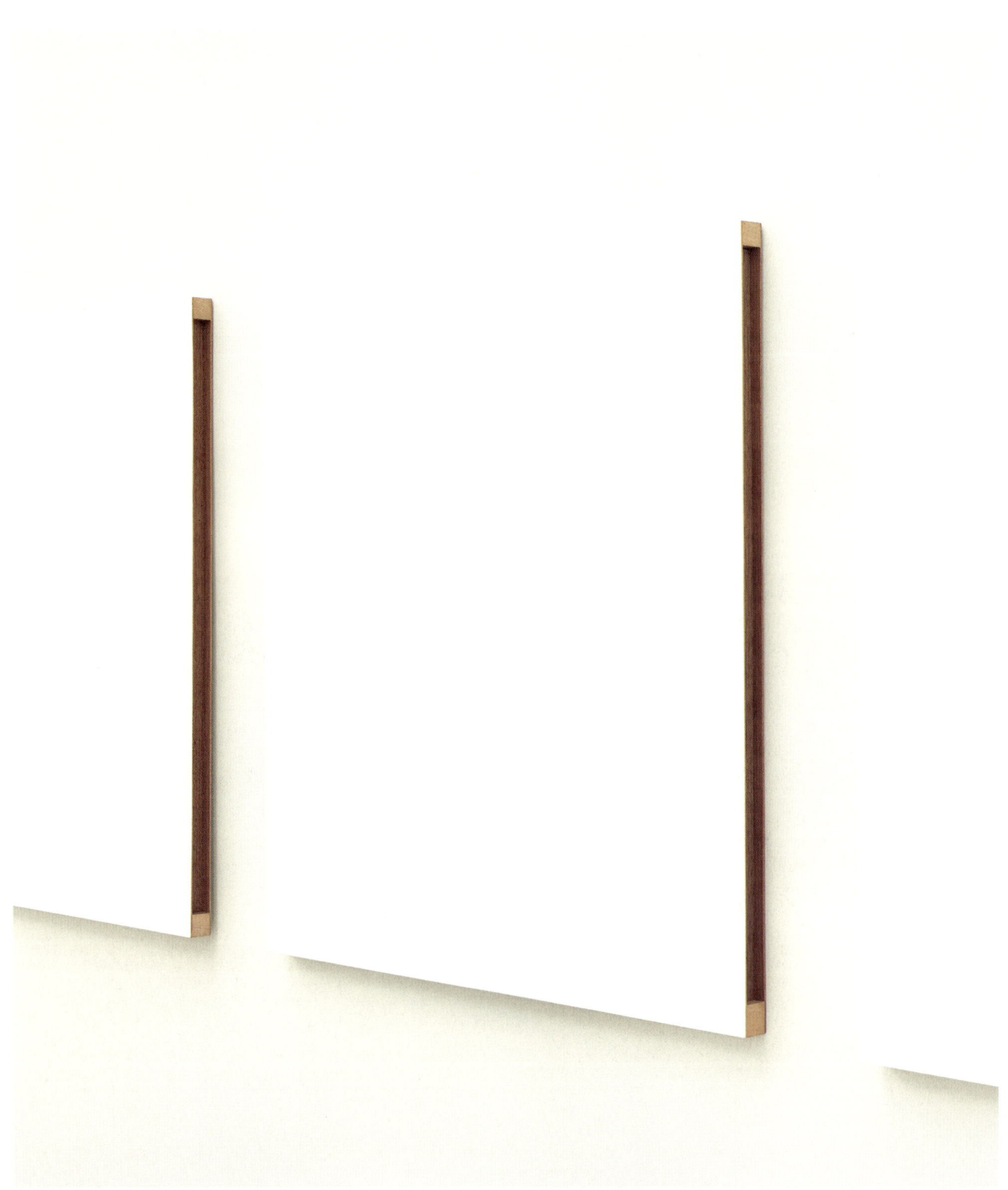

left and right *Vector*, 1975/1997 (detail)
pages 254–255 *Vector*, 1975/1997

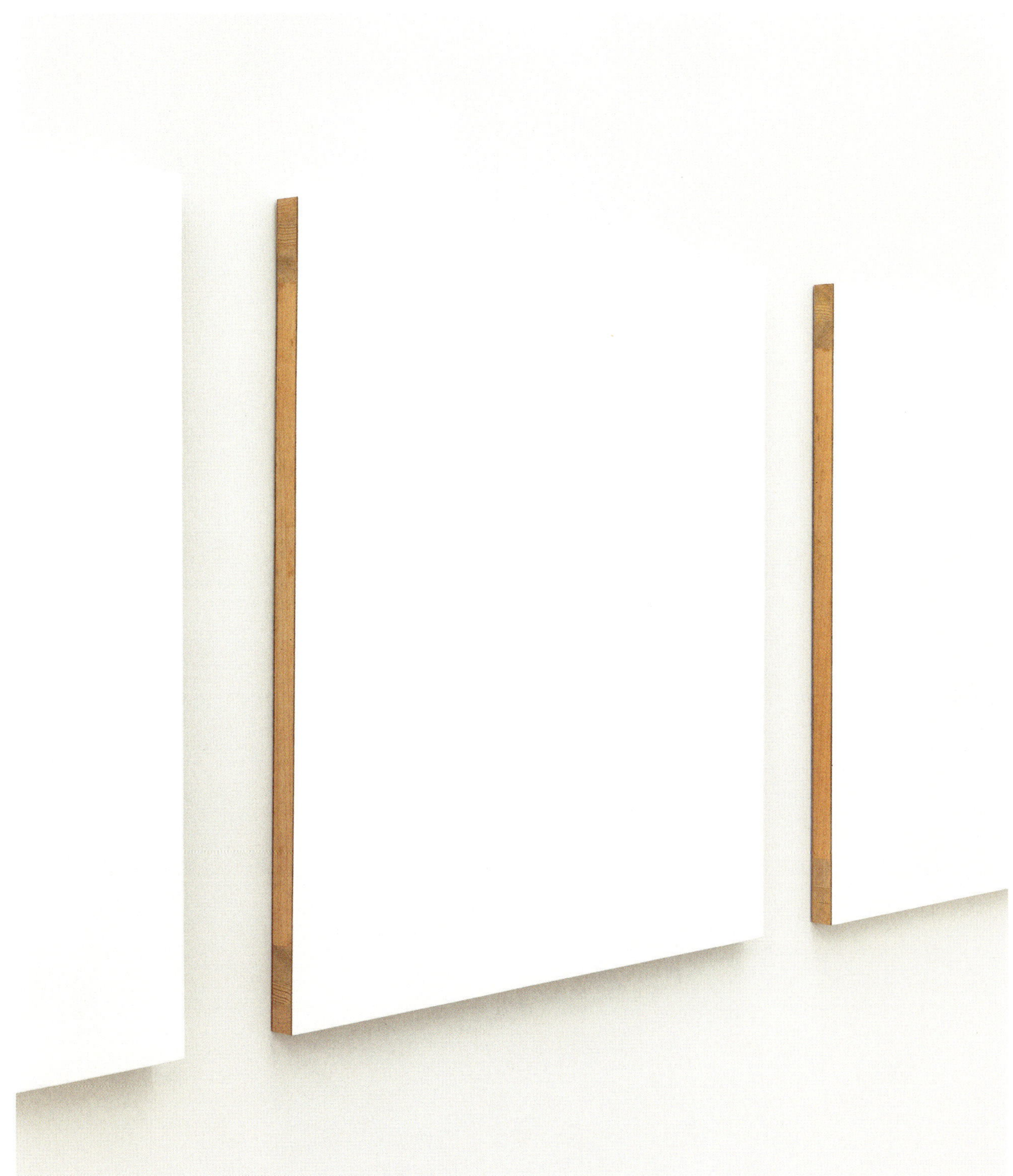

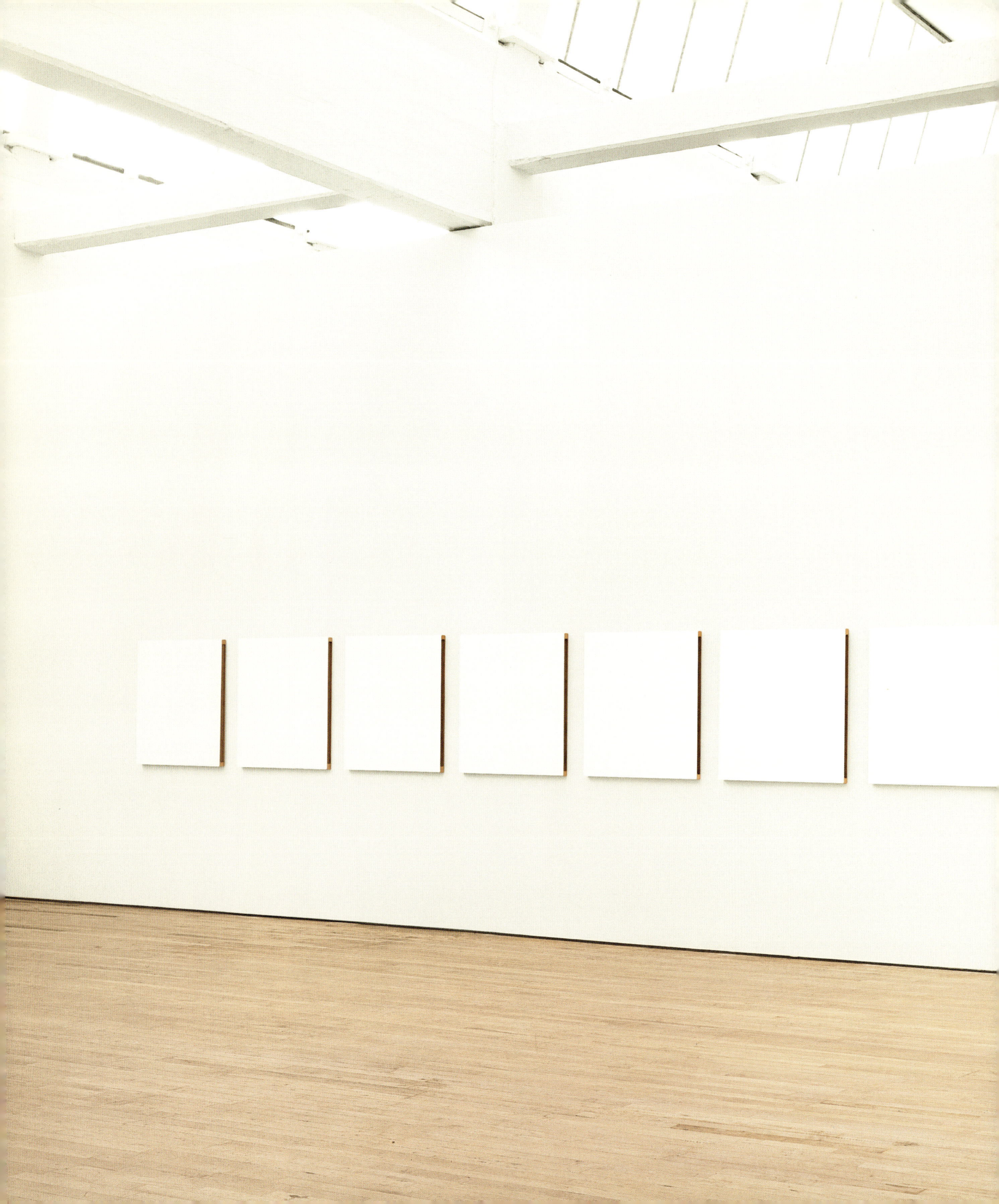

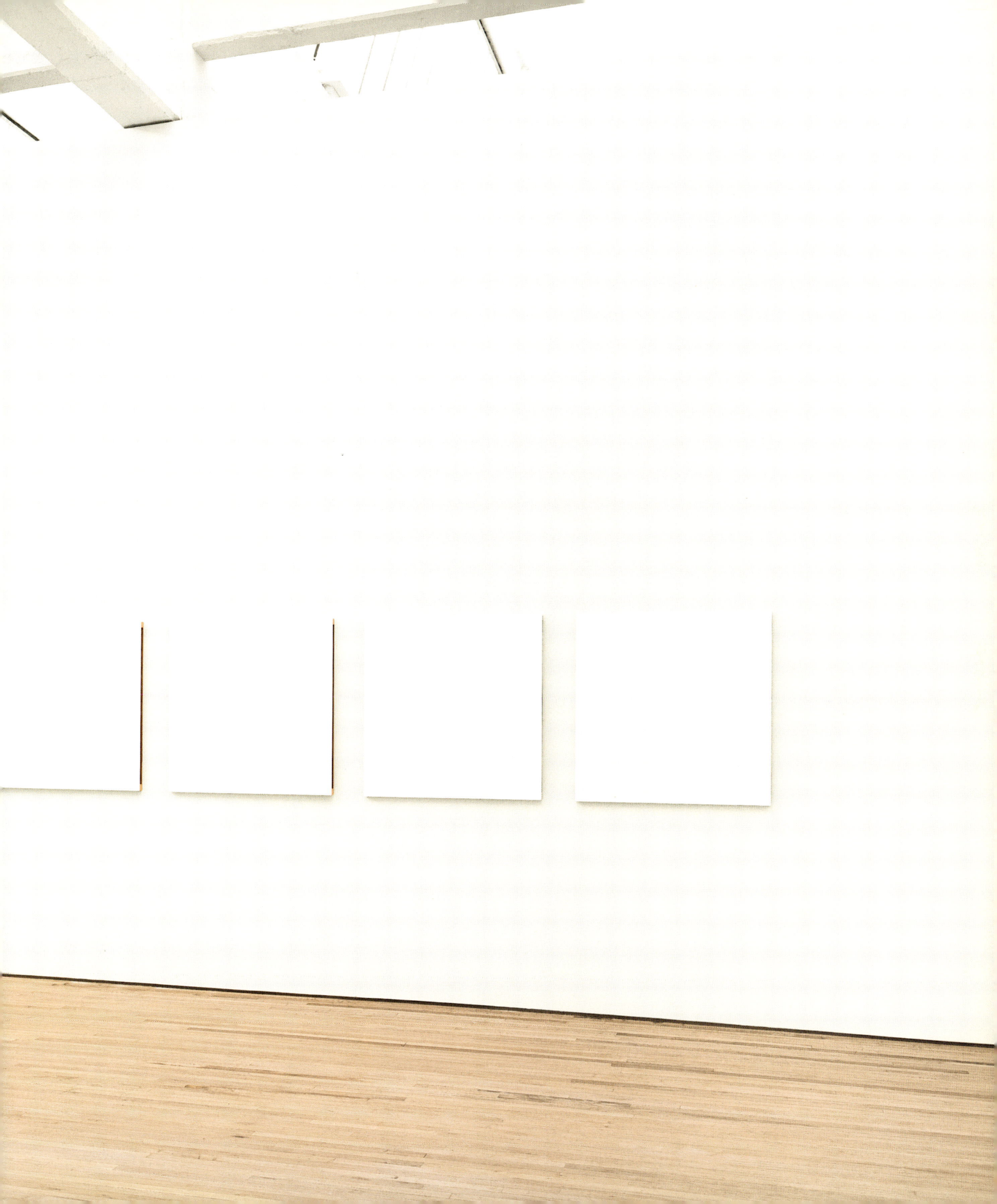

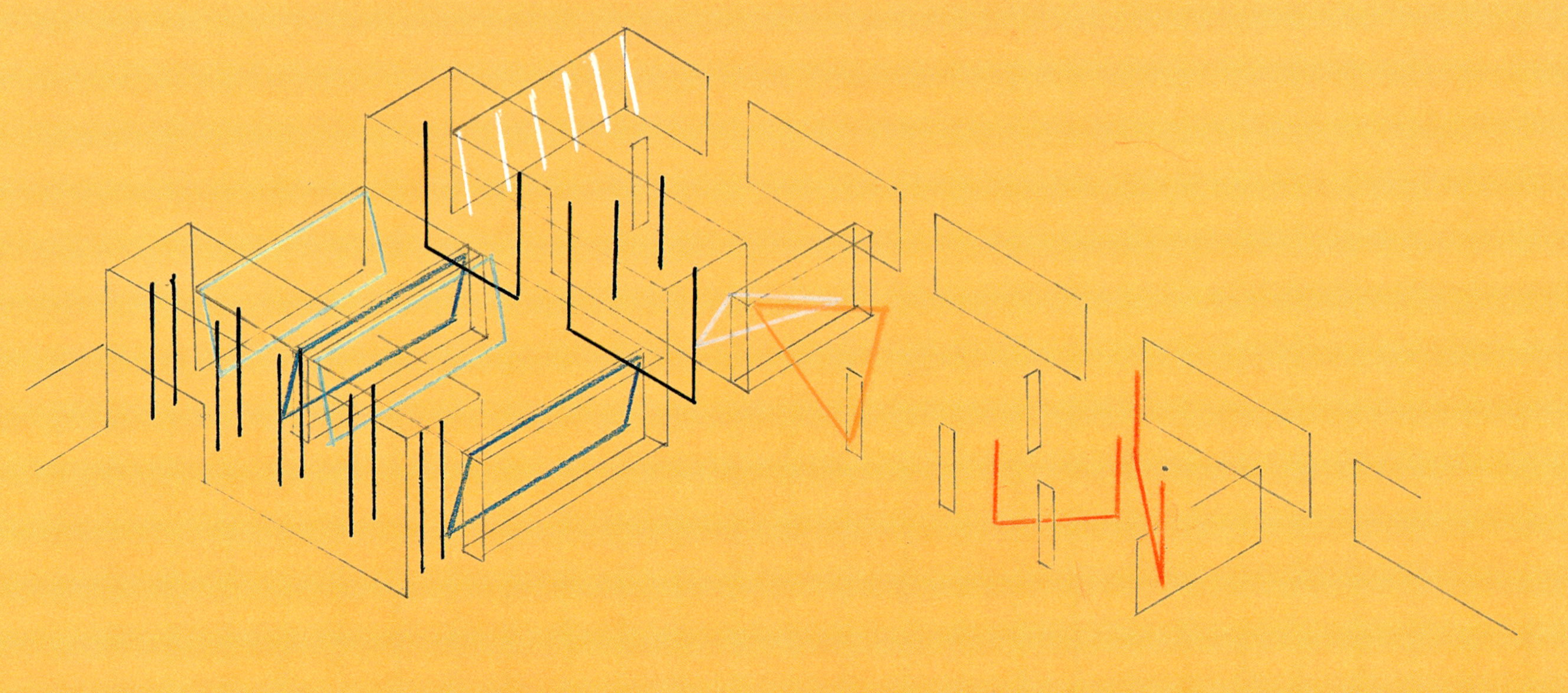

Fred Sandback

Fred Sandback was born in Bronxville, New York, in 1943. After receiving a B.A. in philosophy at Yale, he studied sculpture, with Donald Judd and Robert Morris, at the Yale University School of Art and Architecture. Sandback's first one-person exhibitions were at the Galerie Konrad Fischer, Düsseldorf, and the Galerie Heiner Friedrich, Munich, both in 1968. Since then he exhibited widely both in the United States and abroad. His work was included in the Whitney Museum of American Art's Annual exhibition of 1968, the Biennale of Sydney, 1976, and the Biennial Exhibition of American Artists at the Art Institute of Chicago in 1979. In 1981 the Dia Art Foundation initiated and maintained a museum of his work, the Fred Sandback Museum in Winchendon, Massachusetts, which was open until 1996. Dia itself presented exhibitions of his works in 1988 and in 1996–97. Sandback died in 2003.

Isometric drawing, 2003

"The first sculpture I made with a piece of string and a little wire was the outline of a rectangular solid . . . lying on the floor. It was a casual act, but it seemed to open up a lot of possibilities for me," Fred Sandback wrote in 1986, looking back over twenty years of activity to a seminal sculpture he had executed in 1966.[1] The key implications of that determining impulse remain at the heart of his practice today. In wanting to create sculpture that did not have an inside, he found through this seemingly "casual act" the means to "assert a certain place or volume in its full materiality without occupying and obscuring it."[2]

For more than three decades, Sandback has pursued these governing insights with remarkable consistency and inventiveness, creating a body of work that is informed by a signature style and yet, as a result of the close interdependence of each piece with the architectural site in which it is realized, ever different in its manifestations. Arguably still the best commentator on his own work, he has elucidated his abiding wish "to be in some sort of constituting material relationship with my environment" in limpid forthright terms: "My feeling persists," he avowed, in that same article from 1986, "that all my sculpture is part of a continuing attitude and relationship to things. . . . The sculptures address themselves to the particular space and time that they're in, but it may be that the more complete situation I'm after is only constructed in time slowly, with the individual sculptures as its constituent parts."[3]

For his presentation at Dia:Beacon, Sandback has seamlessly integrated older pieces with newer ones to orient and ground the viewer in a particular place, a specific situation. A rigorous selection from his deliberately circumscribed lexicon, each sculpture is newly parsed for the site: "I don't feel that once a piece is made, then it's done with," he explained. "I continue to work with older schemata and formats, and often begin to get what I want out of them only after many reworkings. Though the same substructure may be used many times, it appears each time in a new light. It is the measure of the relative success of a piece, not necessarily that a new structure emerges, but that a familiar one attains, in its present manifestation, a particular vibrancy or actuality."[4]

The character of any particular work is relative to its site, its proportions and form subtly calibrated in response to the architectonics of the area it inhabits. Thus not only the specific measurements and proportions but also the tone or hue of the yarn may be adapted or altered as the artist intuitively adjusts a work to both its neighbors and its new location. In these sculptures, space is both defined and imbued with an incorporeal palpability, so that often the spectator concentrates less on the edges, on the yarn demarcating the forms, than on the planar or volumetric components contained within. Whether transparent geometries, as in *Untitled* (1977)–a two-part vertical construction–and *Untitled* (1996)–two triangles–or simple linear trajectories, as in *Untitled* (1996)–a six-part vertical construction–Sandback's sculptures unequivocally occupy the same physical site as the viewer. Inhabiting what the artist has dubbed "pedestrian space"–the ordinary matter-of-fact space coextensive with that of the spectator and of the site–they reveal themselves over time, from different vantages, and according to different perspectives.[5] While any apprehension of his works involves a process of kinesthetic viewing, a phenomenological experiencing of each piece in situ, Sandback has been careful to distinguish his sculpture from so-called Installation art, from the creation of a holistic place, set apart, in and of itself, sui generis. His work is never environmental, if that implies transforming the context. On the contrary, as he states, "It incorporates specific parts of the environment, but it's always coexistent with that environment, as opposed to overwhelming or destroying that environment in favor of a different one."[6]

In a low gallery that opens off an installation of Donald Judd's plywood boxes aligned in strictly serried rows, two works have been introduced that are initially glimpsed from afar, as brightly colored vectors skimming through the air. When confronted directly they radically reorient the spectator's relation to the dominant axial configuration of the architecture, dramatically skewing one's circuit away from the strongly accented horizontal and vertical sight lines that elsewhere prevail. The vivid terracotta contours of the two-part vertical construction limn two planes positioned at right angles to each other, creating dynamic diagonal vectors on the west side of the gallery. To the east, a vibrant ocher triangle tilting out from the wall ventures beyond its half of the space to invade the transitional passage linking this gallery to the adjacent one. As the viewer passes into this room, a second triangle, angled almost parallel to the back side of the dividing wall, is revealed. Although canted more modestly off the vertical, and more subdued in hue, it deftly counters and stabilizes the bold thrust of its more monumental partner. By actively incorporating the wall as a pivot that balances in delicate equilibrium a pair of contending components (rather than treating it simply, and conventionally, as a passive element whose function is to separate the two spaces), the artist in characteristically adroit fashion engages the viewer actively in the immediate context–in the world at hand.

Like the other works on view here, these two sculptures are made from acrylic yarn, a material that for Sandback carries no significant connotations. He prefers it over other materials because its soft, slightly fuzzy contours conjure a less crisp, less rigid line than that produced by metal, and its matte surface absorbs rather than reflects light. When required, a more strongly accentuated edge can easily be made by doubling or trebling the strings. Taken together these qualities permit the yarn works to coexist more subtly and diversely with their ambience than did their predecessors made from wire or metal rods.

Emerging during the heyday of Minimalism, Sandback's art has distinguished and differentiated itself from that of his immediate forebears by its eschewal of the reductively literal and of the material as its primary modes of being.[7] In his exploration of physical relationships via the incorporeal rather than through concrete matter—via the interplay of vacancy and volume—he recognizes that the illusory and the factual are inextricably intertwined. "Fact and illusion are equivalents," he asserts; "Trying to weed one out in favor of the other is dealing with an incomplete situation."[8] Nevertheless, he stresses that "in no way is my work illusionistic. Illusionistic art refers you away from its factual existence towards something else. My work is full of illusions, but they don't refer to anything."[9]

L. C.

notes

1 Fred Sandback, "Remarks on My Sculpture 1966–1986," in *Fred Sandback Sculpture 1966–1986* (Mannheim: Kunsthalle, 1986), p. 12.

2 Ibid.

3 Ibid., pp. 12–13.

4 Ibid., p. 13.

5 Sandback and a friend coined the term *pedestrian space* to define space that was "literal, flatfooted, and everyday. The idea was to have the work right there along with everything else in the world, not up on a spatial pedestal. The term also involved the idea of utility—that a sculpture was there to be actively engaged, and it had utopian glimmerings of art and life happily cohabitating." Ibid.

6 Sandback, quoted in *74 Front Street: The Fred Sandback Museum, Winchendon, Massachusetts* (New York: Dia Art Foundation, 1982), p. 4.

7 In 1967, as a student at the Yale School of Art and Architecture, Sandback took courses from both Robert Morris and Donald Judd.

8 Sandback, quoted in *74 Front Street*, p. 4.

9 Ibid.

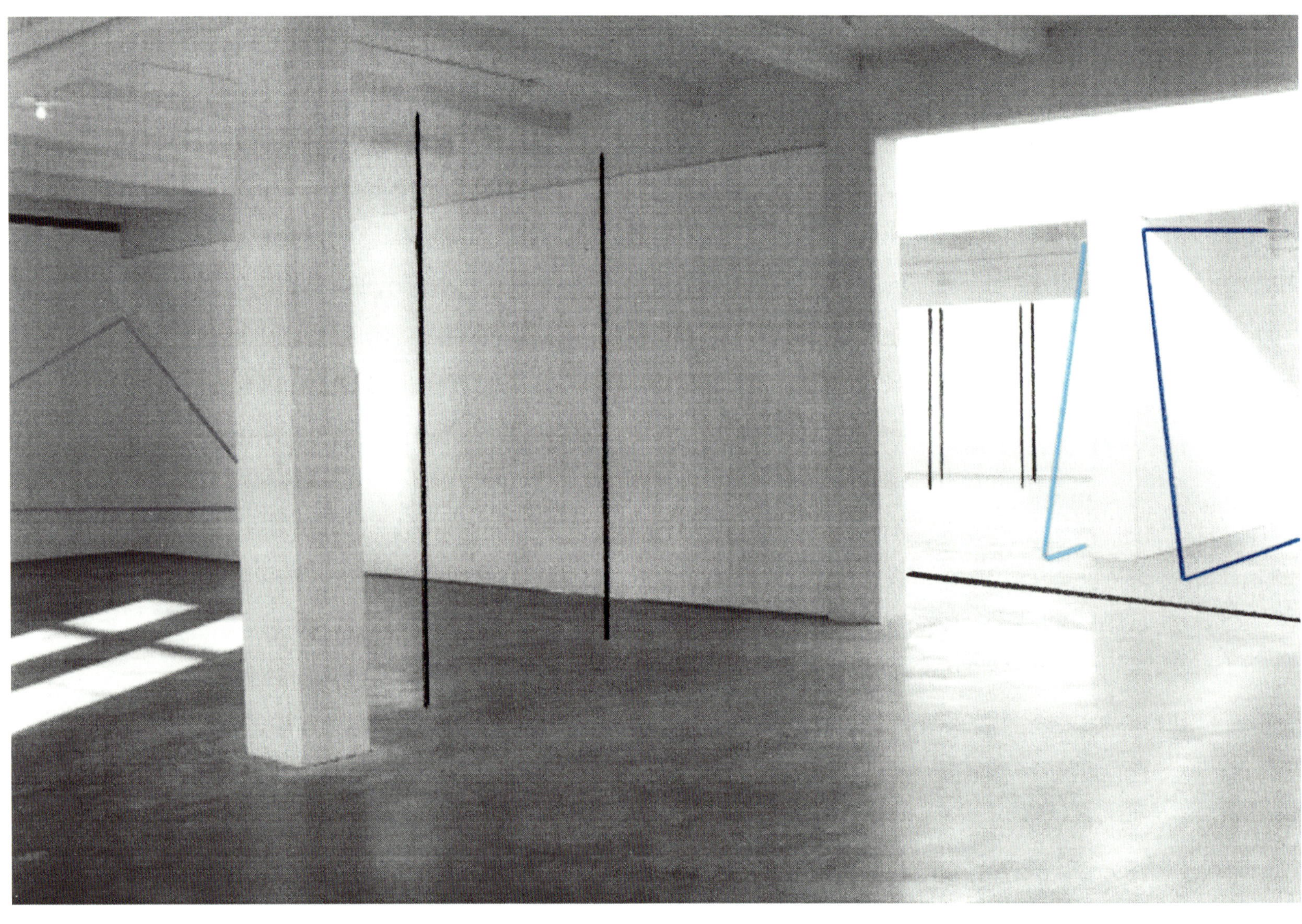

left and right installation drawing for Dia:Beacon, 2003

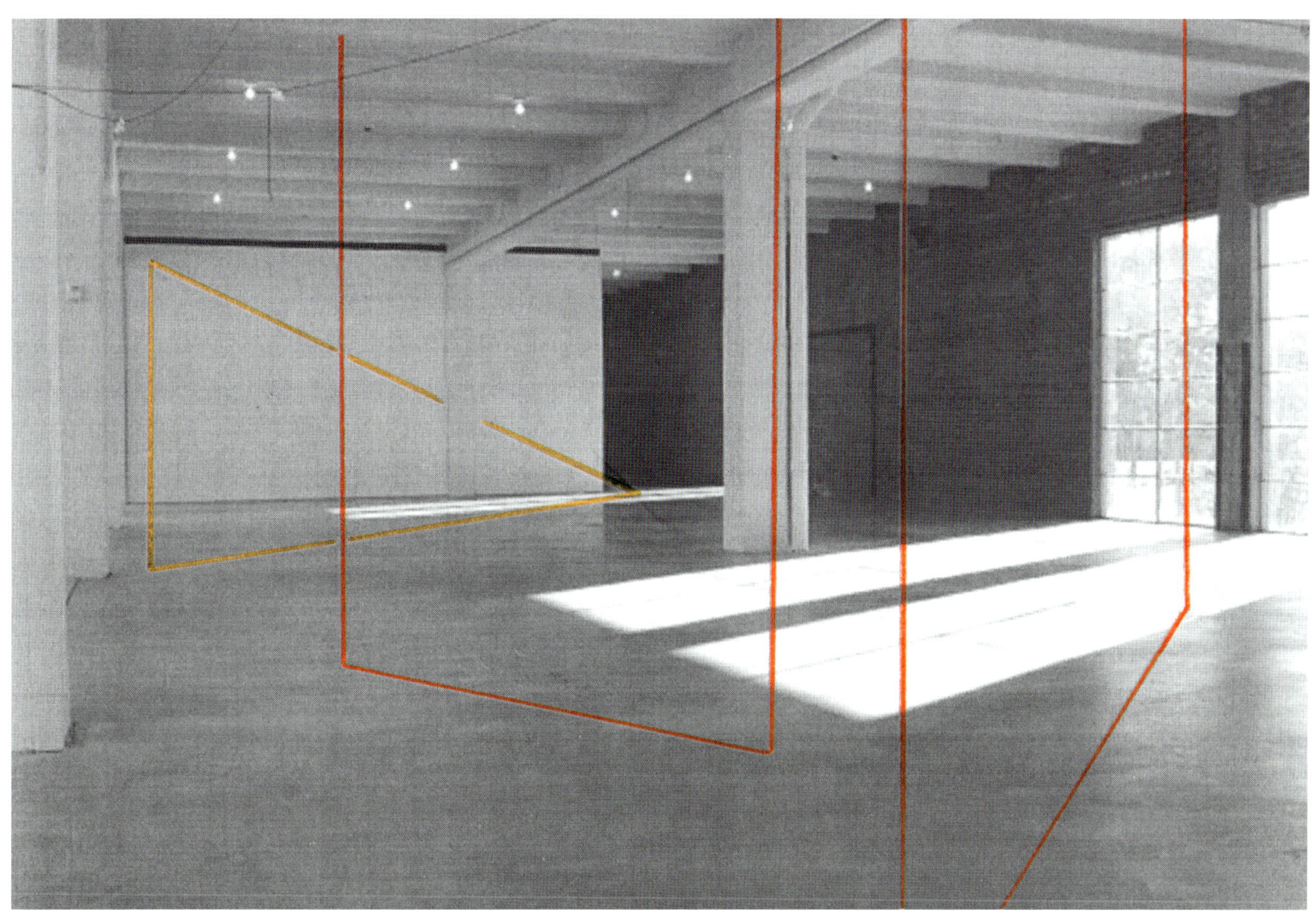

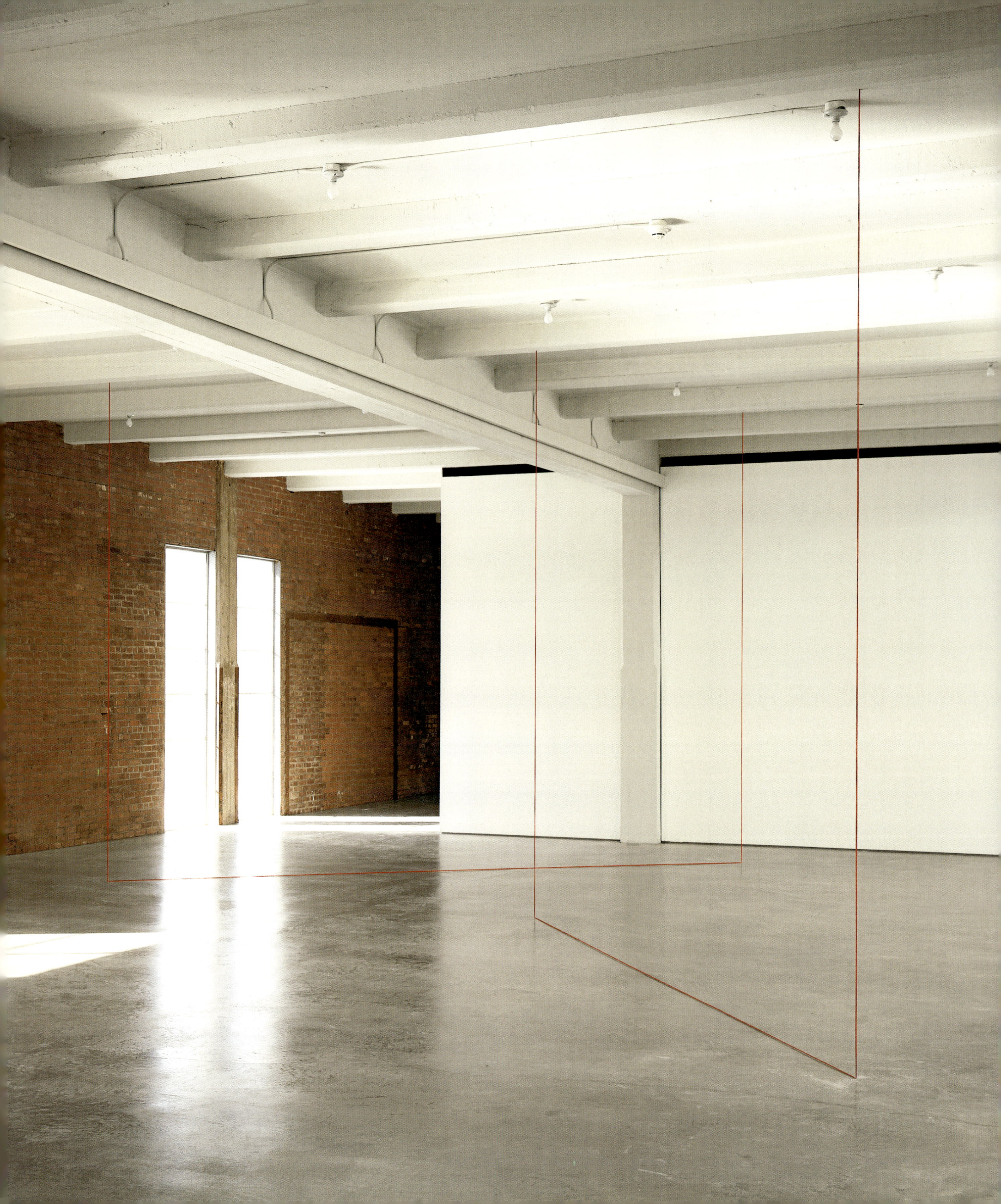

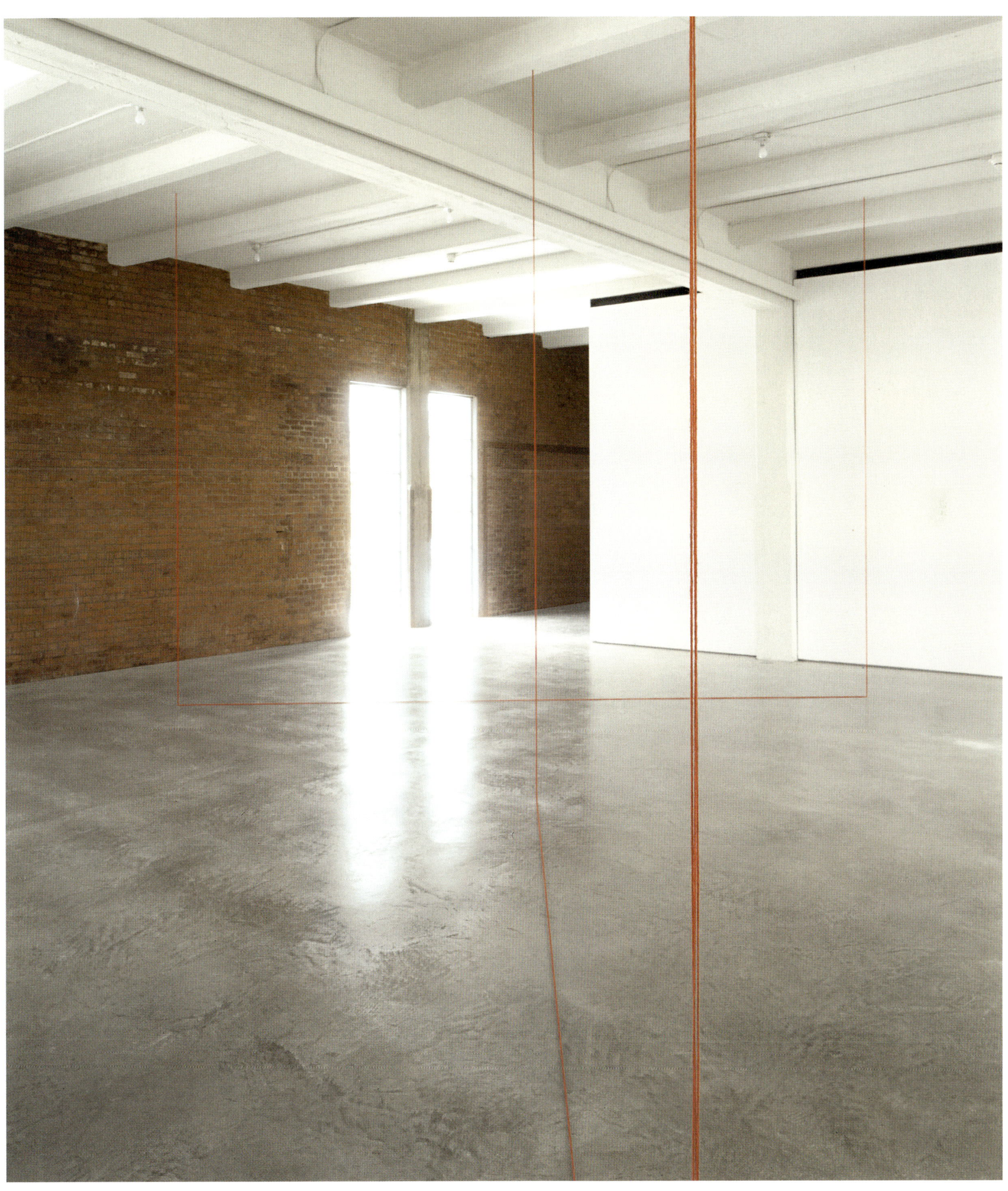

left and right *Untitled* (from *Ten Vertical Constructions*), 1977
pages 264–265 *Untitled* (from *Ten Vertical Constructions*), 1996

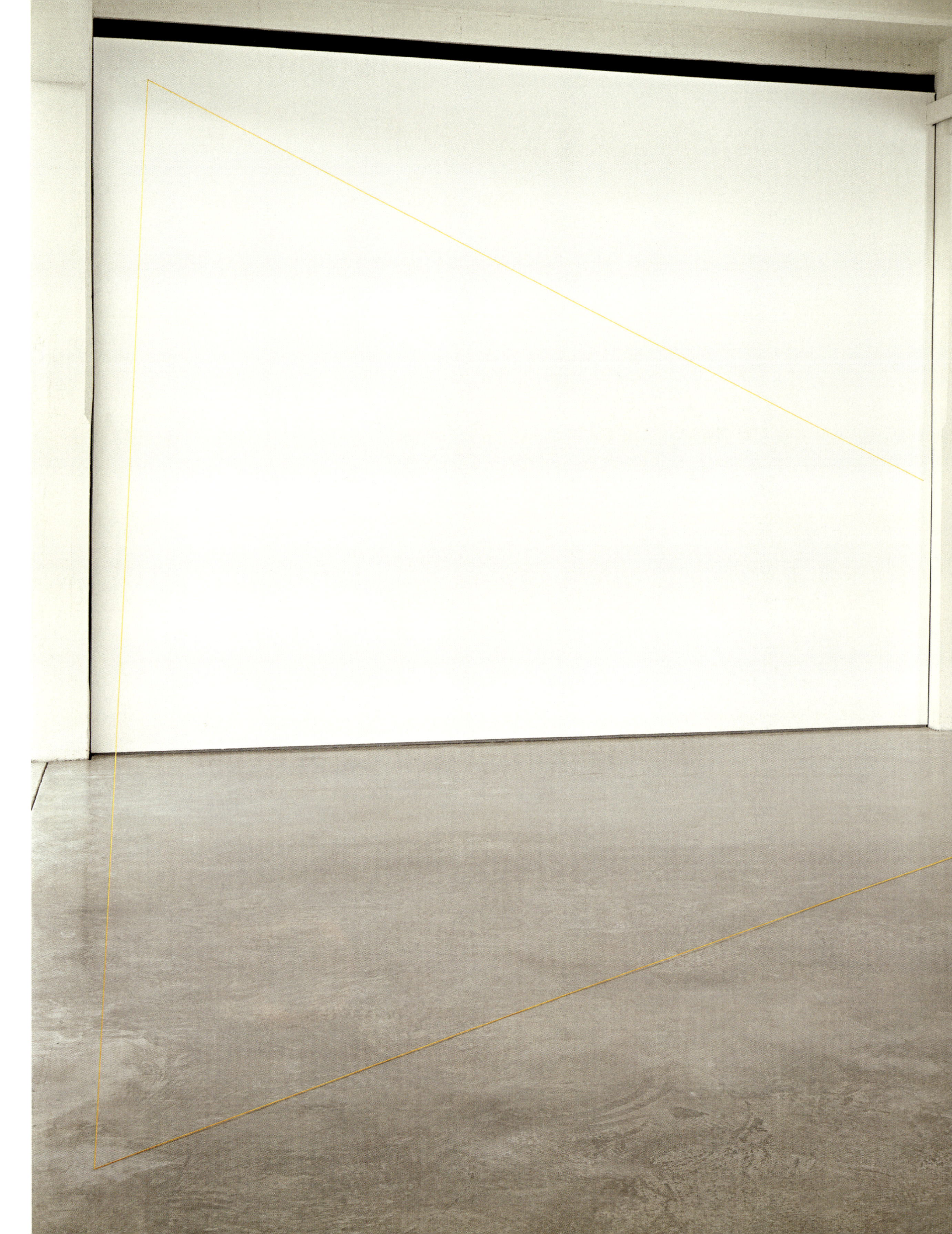

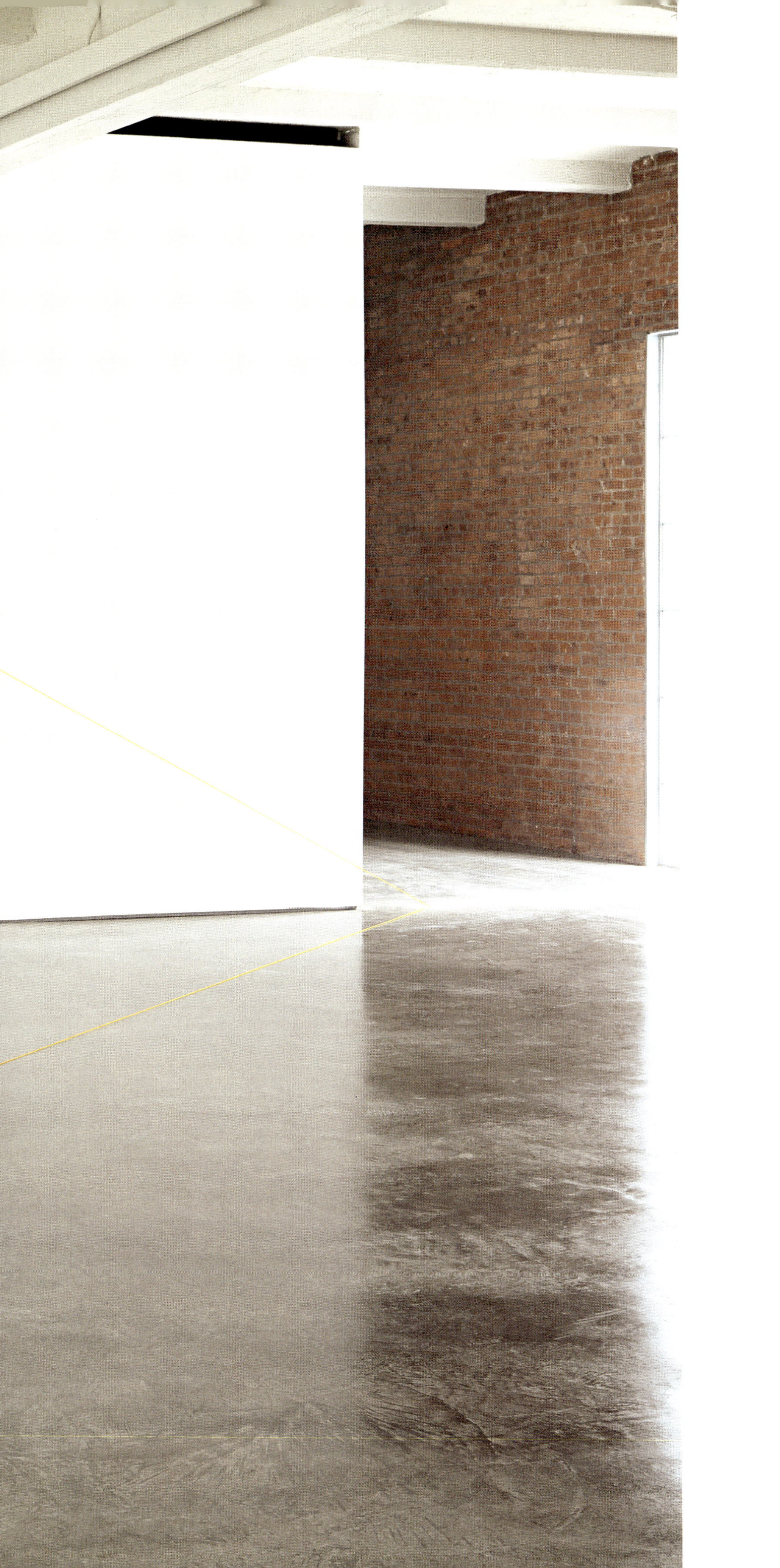

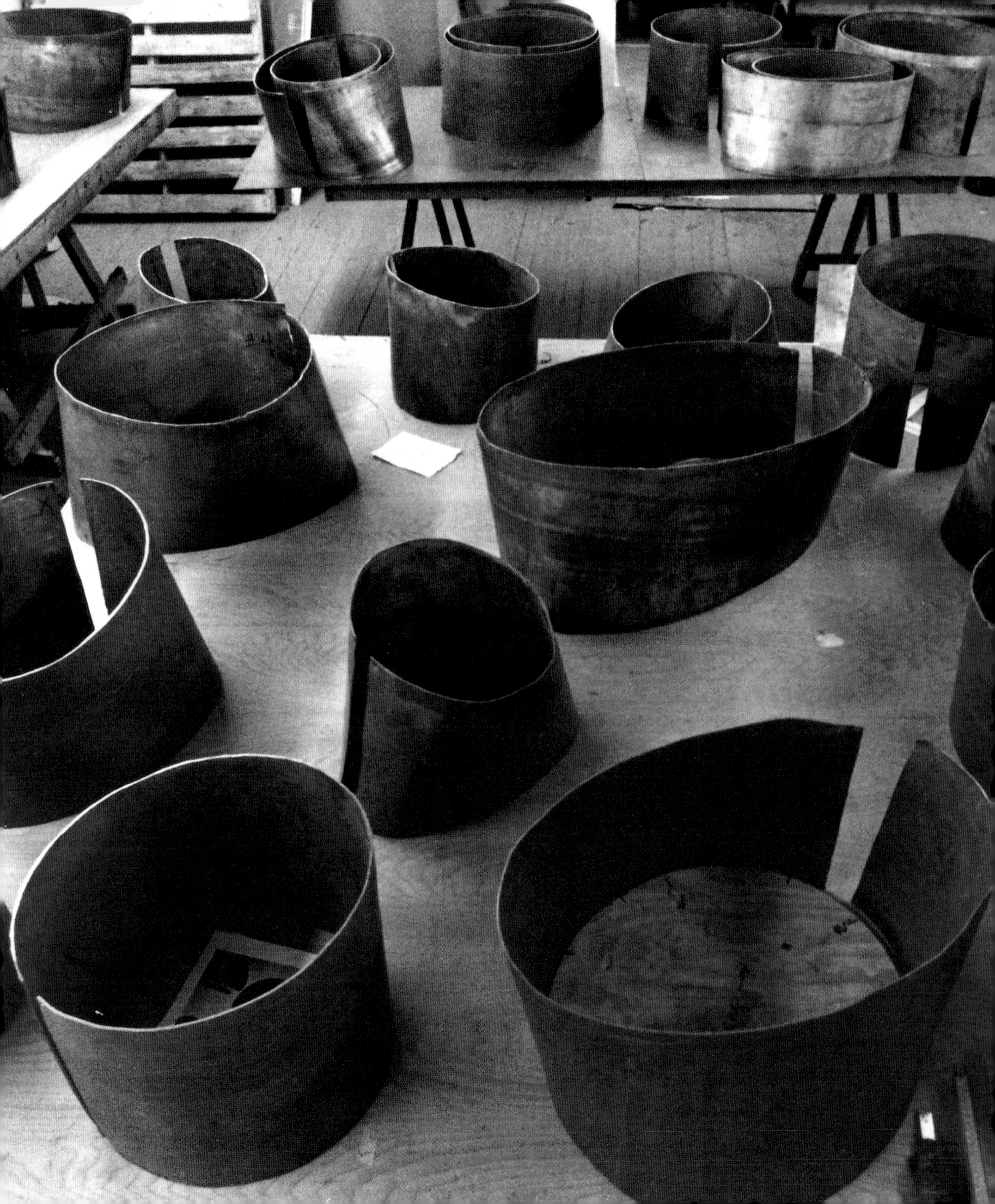

Richard Serra

Richard Serra was born in San Francisco in 1939. He graduated from the University of California, Santa Barbara, in 1961, with a degree in English, then studied art at Yale University until 1964, taking classes with Josef Albers and others. After receiving his M.F.A., Serra spent two years traveling in Europe before settling in 1966 in New York City, where he continues to live and work. The following year he began to show his work in museums and galleries in New York, and since then he has exhibited extensively throughout the world, including representation in Documentas 5 (1972), 6 (1977), 7 (1982), and 8 (1987), in Kassel, the Venice Biennales of 1984 and 2001, and the Whitney Museum of American Art's Annual and Biennial exhibitions of 1968, 1970, 1973, 1977, 1979, 1981, and 1995. Retrospectives of Serra's work have been organized by the Museum of Modern Art, New York (1986), and the Museum of Contemporary Art, Los Angeles (1998). He has also created numerous site-specific sculptures in public and private venues in both North America and Europe. In 1997, Dia exhibited for the first time Serra's landmark Torqued Ellipses.

Models for Torqued Ellipses, 1994–98

What interests me is the opportunity for all of us to become something different from what we are, by constructing spaces that contribute something to the experience of who we are.

–Richard Serra

Concerns quintessentially sculptural have engaged Richard Serra for more than thirty years, although as a young artist in New York in the late 1960s he was strongly affected by the work of a number of contemporary dancers, above all Yvonne Rainer. Such work prompted him to consider "ways of relating movement to material and space," he has explained, in that it allowed him "to think about sculpture in an open and extended field in a way that is precluded when dealing with sculpture as an autonomous object. . . . I found very important the idea of the body passing through space, and the body's movement not being predicated totally on image or sight or optical awareness, but on physical awareness in relation to space, place, time, movement."[1] A visit to a number of Zen gardens in Kyoto while on a trip to Japan in 1970 reinforced Serra's growing preoccupation with work that was defined through the processes of its reception. There he discovered that "your vision is peripatetic and not reduced to framing an image. It includes and is dependent upon memory and anticipation. . . . The relationship of time, space, walking, and looking–particularly in arcs and circles–constitutes the only way you can see certain Japanese gardens."[2]

Redefining this requirement of extended temporality and nomadic vision, Serra's recent series of Torqued Ellipses elaborates concerns with orientation and movement into tightly contained sculptures that radically challenge modernist notions of sculptural space. For in these works space shifts and moves in wholly unpredictable and unprecedented ways: so destabilizing yet so beguiling is this sensation of movement that the spectator quickly gets caught up in an exploration of extended duration.

Rolled-steel plates, each two inches thick and weighing twenty tons, stand abutted. This forthright, direct presentation, characteristic of Serra's aesthetic, gives little hint of the fundamental newness and potency of the experience offered in these monumental works—and also fails to betray the prolonged and difficult process of their realization. By Serra's account, the initial idea for this body of work was breathtakingly simple: take an elliptical volume of space and torque it. After an inspirational visit to Francesco Borromini's San Carlo alle Quattro Fontane church in Rome in the early 1990s, he began to try to devise such a space. Experimenting with two small wood ellipses held parallel but angled to each other by a dowel, he created a "wheel" from which he cut and rolled a template in lead. By varying the angles at which the ellipses were set to each other, or by modifying the overall proportions, or by introducing a second component within the first, he gradually assembled some thirty models for large-scale sculptures. With the aid of a computer program, he then calculated the positions and angles at which sheets of steel would need to be bent in order to realize such works at full scale.

The problem next confronting Serra was to find a steel mill capable of this exacting task, a difficulty

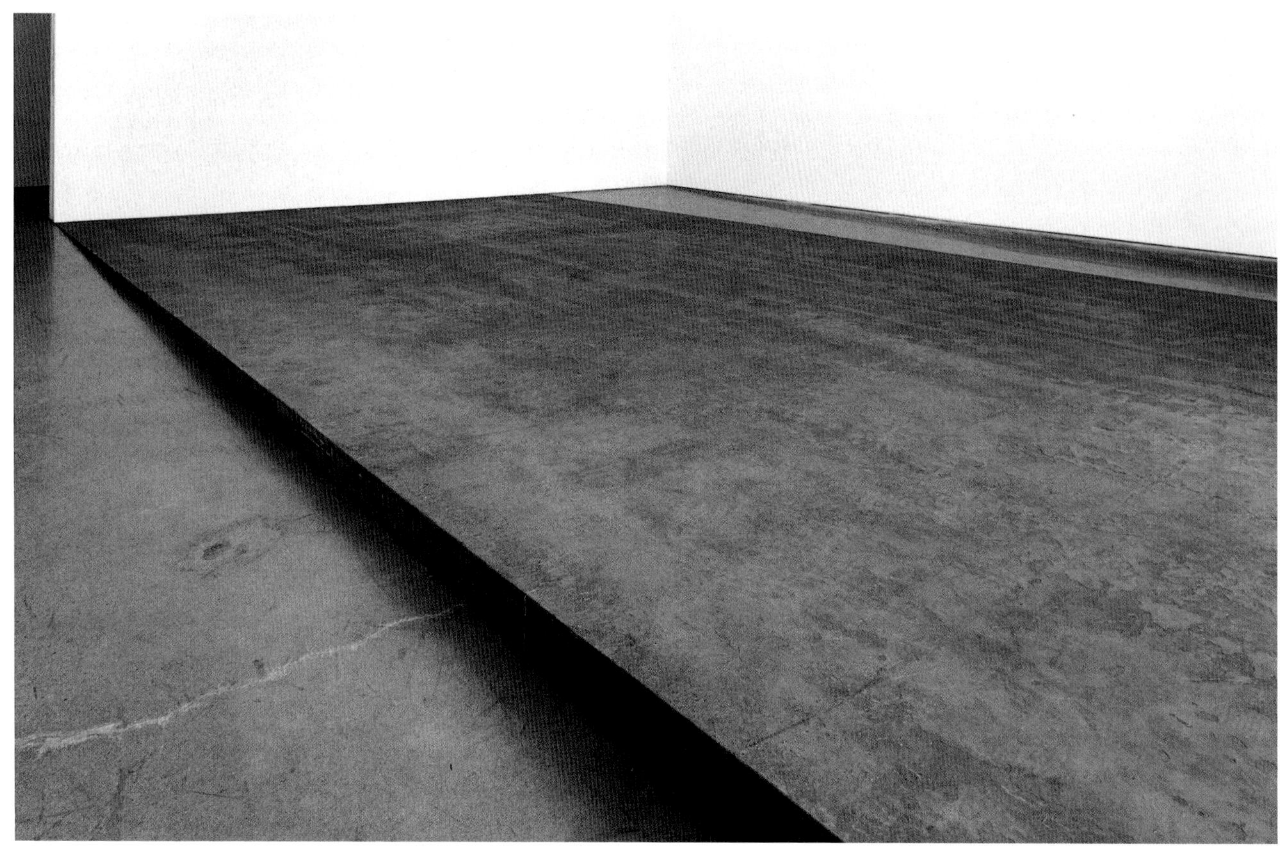

left *Elevational Wedge*, 2001
right *Union of the Torus and the Sphere*, 2001

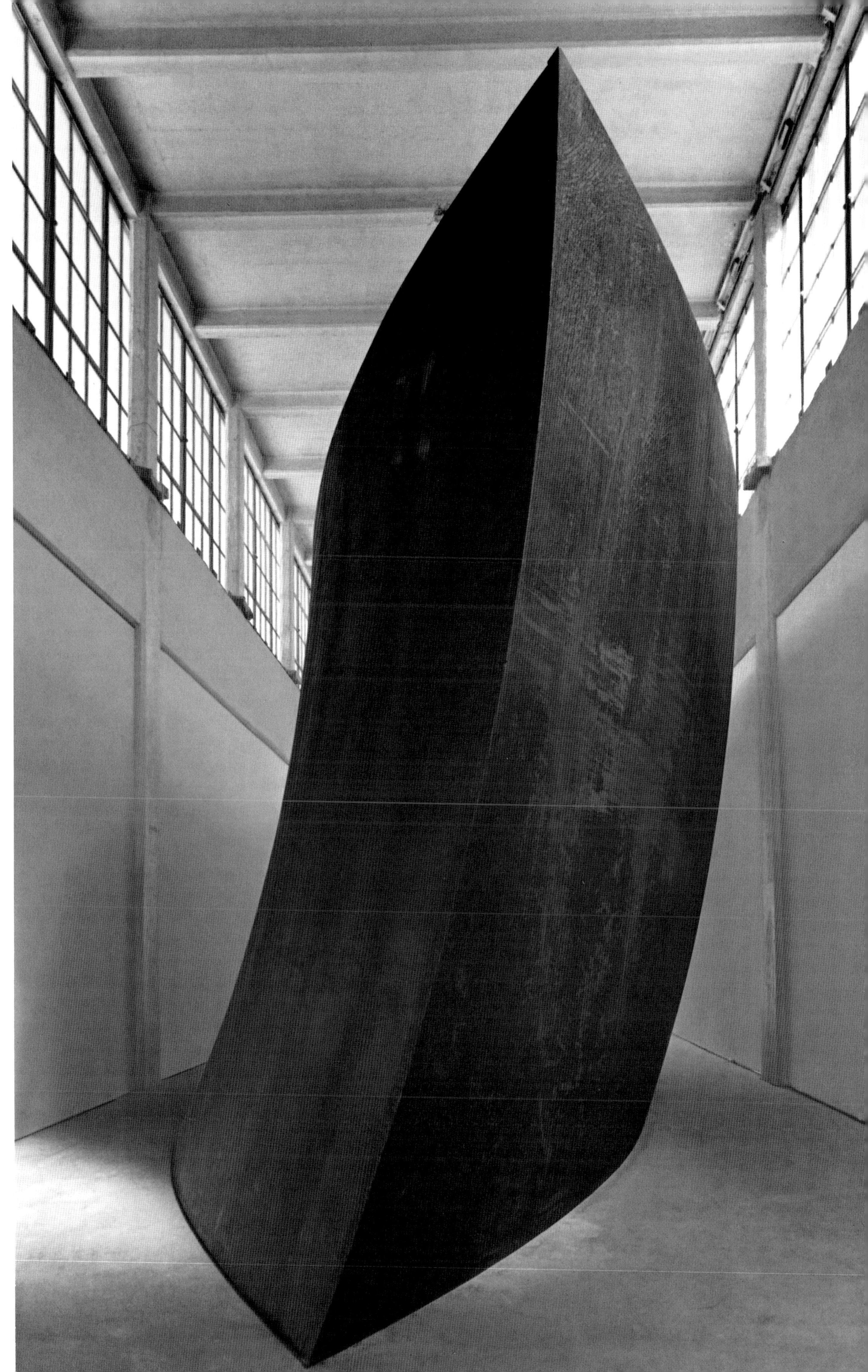

compounded by the fact that the job required a special type of roller and by his need to work with the maximum-size plate available, that is, with sixteen-foot sheets. After considerable research, it became apparent that there were perhaps only two rollers in existence that could carry out the project. Beth Ship, a shipyard and rolling mill outside Baltimore, agreed to undertake the work without fully comprehending the complexities entailed. Several trials were required before the first sculpture was completed, in late 1996.

The results are informed by his signature clarity, stringency, and rigor. In tracking the exteriors of the sculptures (in the particular configuration installed in the former train depot at Beacon), one is always in close proximity to the steel skins, and this sets up a dramatic tension between one's bodily awareness and one's vision. Inside, the converse of what is occurring at one's feet seems to be happening over one's head; the works consequently generate bodily based movements and responses that are neither necessarily nor exclusively initiated by looking or seeing. Though it is arguably even more difficult to follow visually the motion of the curving walls leading to the interior of these works than to track the exterior modulations, only there do the footprint of the sculpture and the shape of its upper profile become evident. Each is a perfect ellipse, and each has the same radius; these ellipses never align, however, instead angling one to the other. Therein lie both the structural and the compositional sources of such unprecedented spatial experiences.

Union of the Torus and the Sphere (2001), one of the latest works to extend this vocabulary, presents a closed form, an exception in Serra's oeuvre: extravagantly tilting, obviously hollow, it encourages a kind of vertigo as the viewer edges around the deliberately constricted space, a site selected by the artist for its snug fit and for the dramatic immediacy of the encounter. In contrast, *Elevational Wedge* (2001) evolves directly from earlier bodies of work, as it subtly alters the proportions of the room in which it is located, testing perceptual and conceptual apprehension of the relation between the assumed horizontal plane and the ground, and tempering routine assumptions regarding the built environment and the spectator's relationship to it.

L.C.

notes

1 Richard Serra, in an interview with Lynne Cooke and Michael Govan, in *Richard Serra: Torqued Ellipses* (New York: Dia Center for the Arts, 1997), pp. 27–28.

2 Ibid, pp. 28–29.

pages 271, 272 Installation view Dia:Beacon
page 273 *Double Torqued Ellipse*, 1997
pages 274, 275 *2000*, 2000

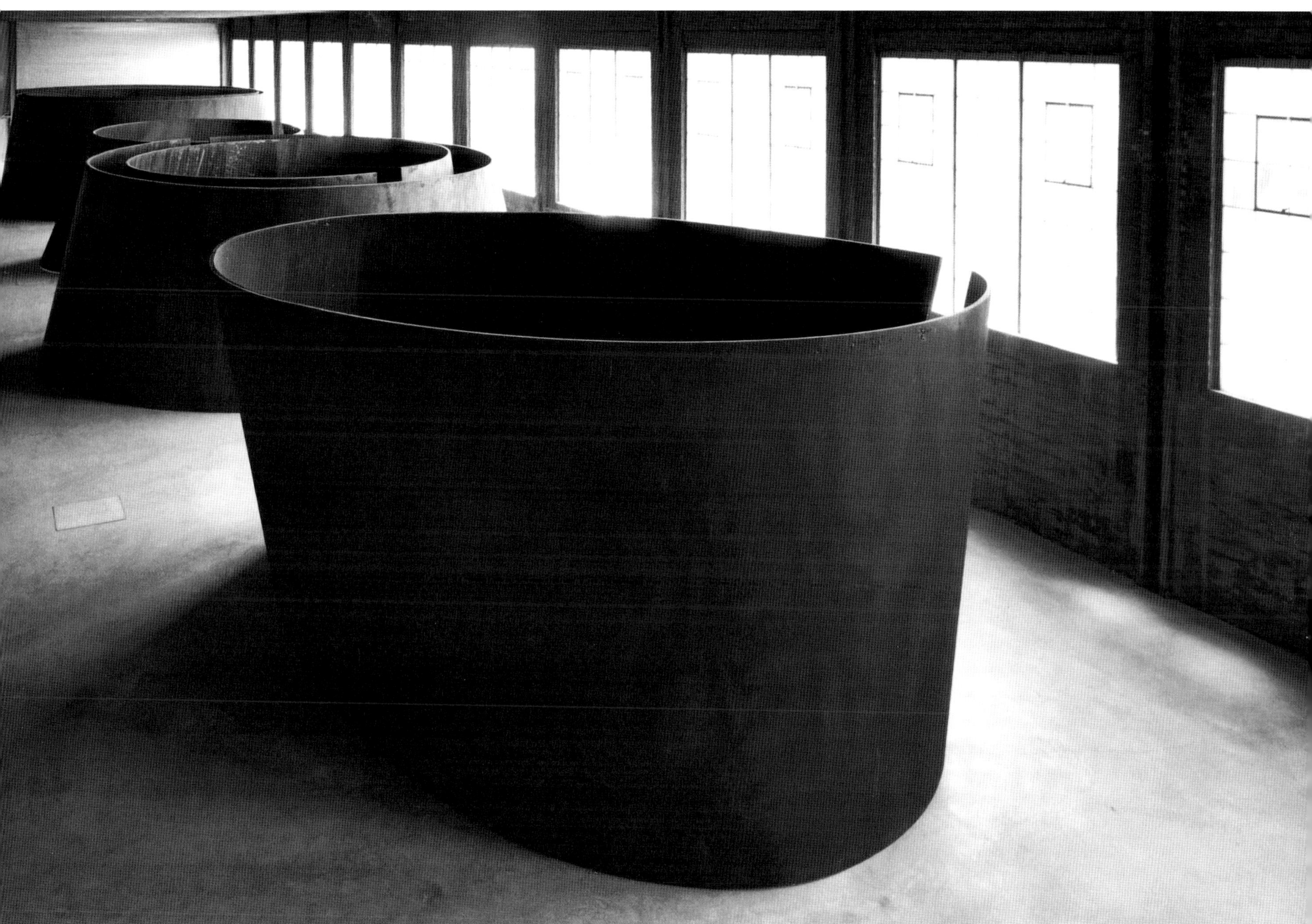

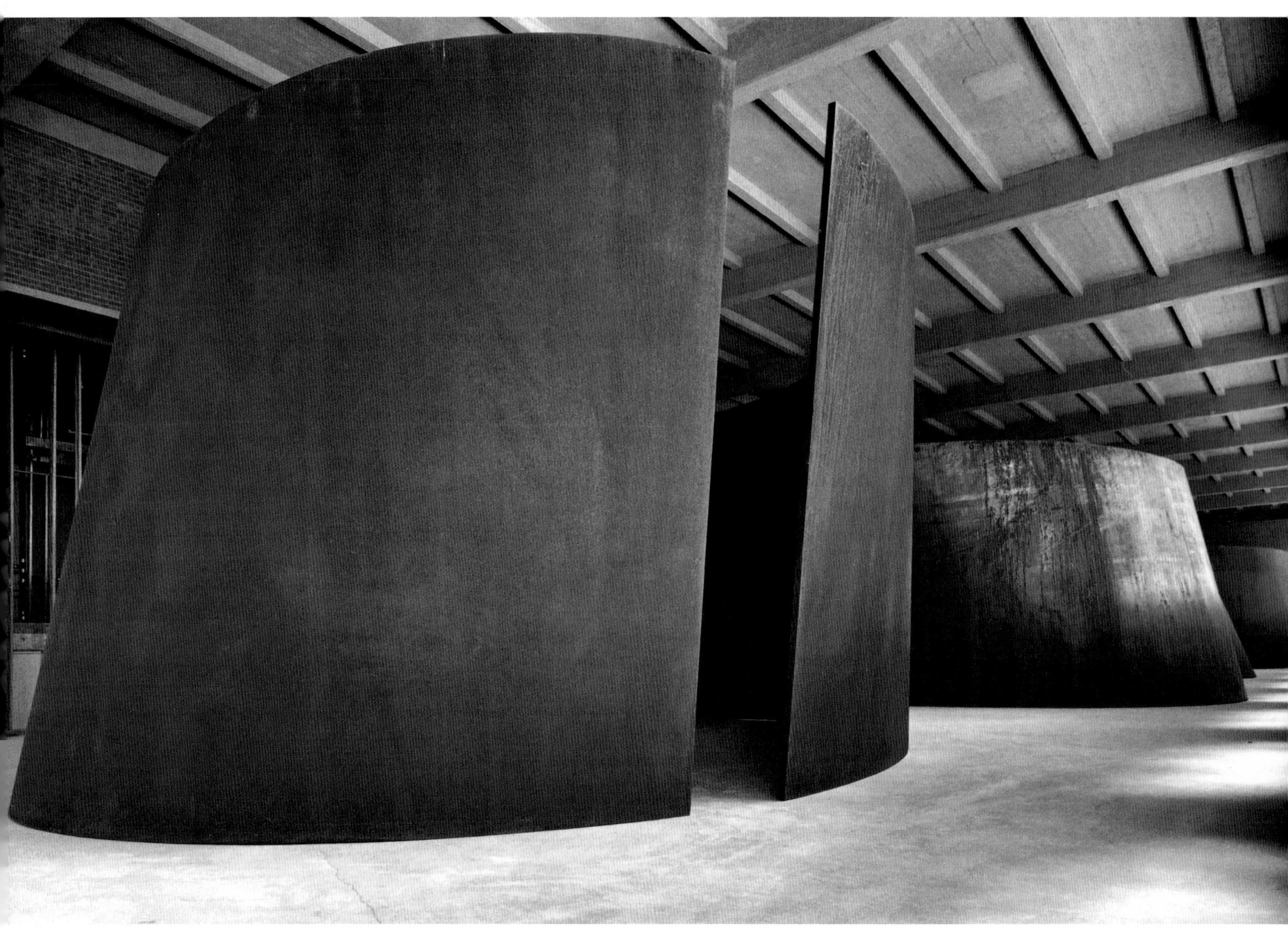

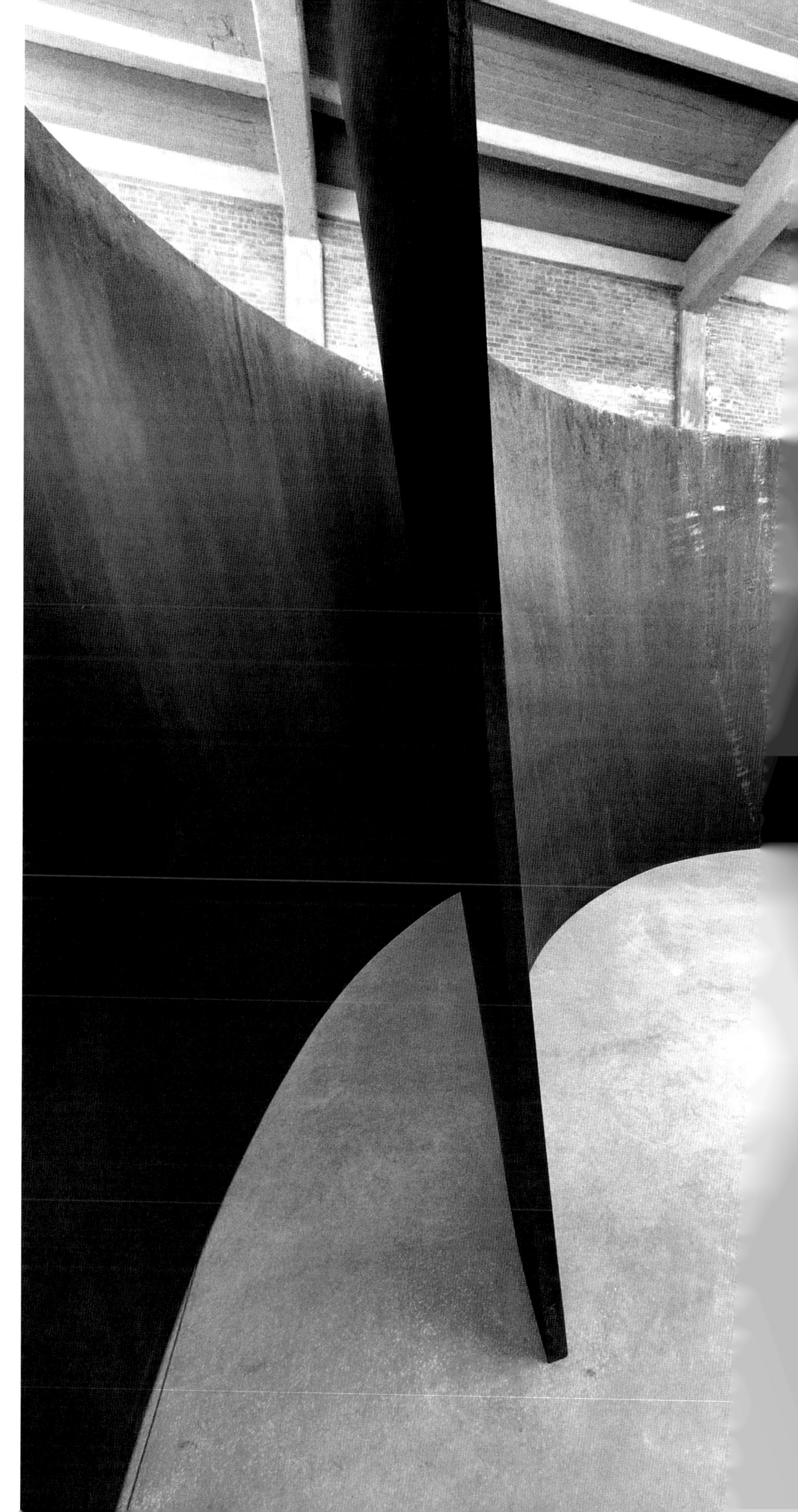

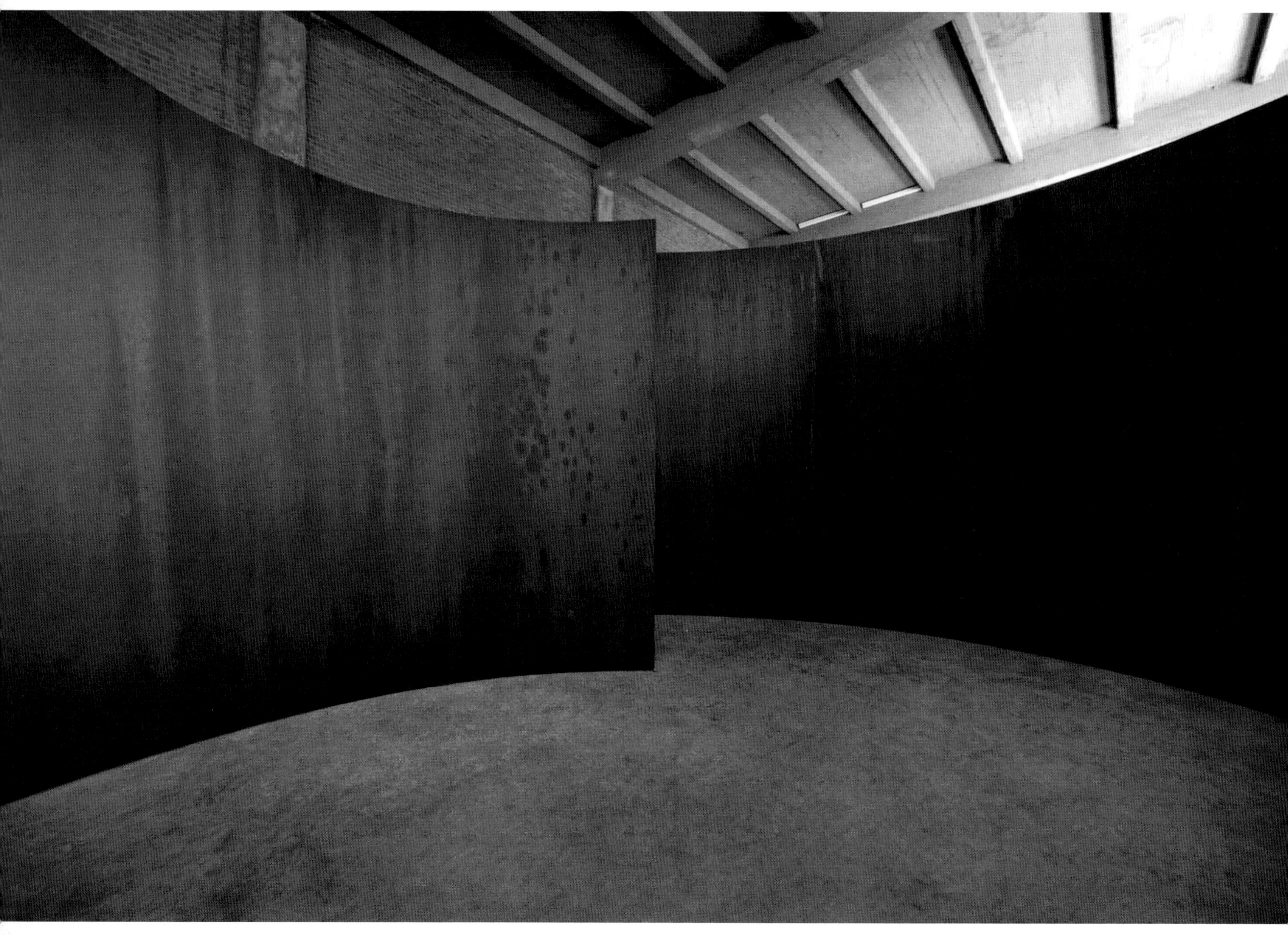

ROBERT SMITHSON GREAT SALT LAKE UTAH

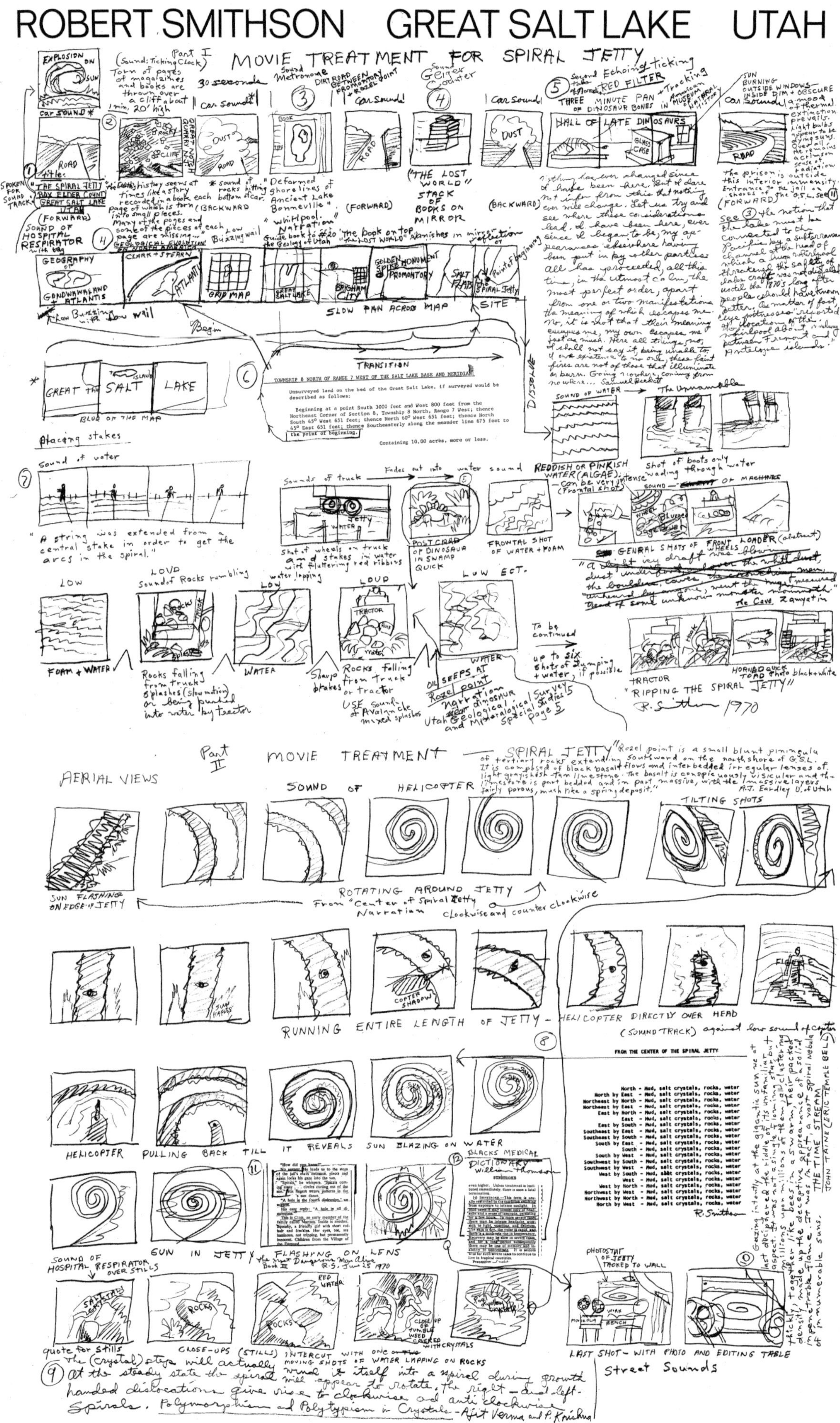

DWAN 29 WEST 57 STREET NEW YORK OPENING OCTOBER 31 TO NOVEMBER 25
A 16 MM, 35 MINUTE, COLOR AND SOUND FILM ON THE SPIRAL JETTY WILL BE SHOWN DAILY AT 2:00 IN THE GALLERY FOR DURATION OF EXHIBITION

Robert Smithson

Robert Smithson was born in Rutherford, New Jersey, in 1938. In 1953, as a high-school student, he won a scholarship to New York's Art Students League, where he studied in the evenings for the next two years, also taking classes at the Brooklyn Museum School in 1956. Smithson's first solo exhibition was in 1959, at the Artist's Gallery, New York. He began to produce what he considered his first mature works of writing and sculpture in 1964. Smithson used black basalt rocks and earth from the site surrounding the Great Salt Lake in Utah, to create the monumental Earthwork *Spiral Jetty* (1970), a coil 1,500 feet long and fifteen feet wide that stretches out counterclockwise into the translucent red water of the lake. Smithson died in a plane crash in Amarillo, Texas, in 1973, while working on *Amarillo Ramp*. Major retrospectives of his work have been organized by the Herbert F. Johnson Museum of Art, Ithaca, New York (1980), the Institut Valencià d'Art Modern, Centre Julio González, Valencia (1993), and the National Museum of Contemporary Art, Oslo (1999). In 1999, Dia acquired his *Spiral Jetty* as a gift of his estate.

Poster for Dwan Gallery exhibition, 1970

Robert Smithson is surely best known for *Spiral Jetty* (1970), an Earthwork on nature's grandest scale at Rozel Point on Utah's Great Salt Lake. Made with a bulldozer, the sculpture comprises the materials of its location: mud, salt crystals, rocks, water. Smithson died in a plane crash in 1973 while he was working on another large Earthwork, *Amarillo Ramp*. As works like these show, he focused in his forward-looking and influential career on a reconsideration of the nature of sculpture—or, rather, of sculpture in relation to "nature," as nature is constituted in our time. Three of the four sculptures shown at Dia:Beacon—*Gravel Mirrors with Cracks and Dust* (1968), *Closed Mirror Square (Cayuga Salt Mine Project)* (1969), and *Leaning Mirror* (1969)—are intended for indoor display unlike Earthworks such as *Spiral Jetty*. Nevertheless, they set up contrapuntal relationships between the institutional indoors and the great outdoors by importing natural and industrial materials previously foreign to art into the exhibition space.

These and the fourth sculpture here, *Map of Broken Glass (Atlantis)* (1969), relate directly to the works of 1968 titled Nonsites, which evolved out of earlier works of Smithson's based on crystalline and geological structures. The Nonsites employ cartographic and occasionally photographic documentation in conjunction with language: maps serve to identify the origin of a work's materials, and a typed text offers commentary. The materials, which Smithson obtained from outlying quarries or industrial sites, far from the art-supply store, include slag, lava, sand, cinders, different varieties of rock, and the like. These materials may be presented either singly or serially and are contained in geometrically shaped bins of painted metal. Wall documentation—the cartographic and linguistic representations—connects the rubble imported into the exhibition space with the place from which it was taken. As Smithson wrote in the accompanying text panel for *Nonsite (Palisades–Edgewater, N.J.)* (1968), "Instead of putting a work of art on some land, some land is put into the work of art." Through the alliance between the unshaped material piled in the bins, the three-dimensional geometric forms of the bins themselves, and the documentary information provided in the two-dimensional form of typed or printed language and maps, the Nonsites extend the notion of sculpture beyond the traditional one of the discrete consolidated object.

Like the Nonsites, the Site/Nonsite pieces presented at Dia:Beacon are constructed of materials collected from the natural debris of the earth or the detritus of industrial fabrication. Sand, gravel, rock salt, shards of glass, and other such materials are heaped together to form sculptures unshaped by handcrafting and thus divested of content pertaining either to the persona or skill of their maker or to any traditional narrative or emotive subject matter. These works differ from the Nonsites, however, in dispensing with linguistic and cartographic elements and, with the exception of *Map of Broken Glass (Atlantis)*, in including mirrors. This latter inclusion is crucial to the self-reflexive character of the sculptures, which broke away from concepts of sculptural self-containment through their address of notions of site. Through their reflective elements, these works visually and thematically embody both their surroundings and their viewers within their own materiality.

Each of the Dia works accomplishes this task in a slightly different manner. In *Gravel Mirrors with Cracks and Dust*, twelve abutting, three-foot-high mirrors sit on the floor and run eighteen feet along the wall. Their shining upright surfaces reflect the piles of stone laid in front of them; at the same time, they expand the work to twice its size and create the illusion that it stretches out on the other side of the gallery wall. Furthermore, as Robert Hobbs has noted, the gravel was dropped so that it cracked the glass in several places, imbuing the work with an incident of accident.[1] Asymmetrical yet symmetrically duplicated by the mirrors' reflectiveness, these fissures, and the dust accruing from the process, deliberately mar the pristine surface of the glass while bringing chance operations into play as part of the work as a whole.

Closed Mirror Square (Cayuga Salt Mine Project) resulted from Smithson's participation in the exhibition "Earth Art," at the Andrew Dickson White Museum of Art, Cornell University, Ithaca, New York, in 1969. Here, in the gallery and not far away in the Cayuga Salt Mine (now owned by Cargill, Inc.), Smithson realized what is considered his most ambitious Site/Nonsite.[2] Located on the floor in a sizeable room, *Closed Mirror Square* . . . , which was reconstructed for later display after the artist's death, combines the strictures of geometric form with the free-form aspect of the granular, lapidary, sharp, or crystalline substances that subtend Smithson's reflective container: a square-shaped mound of rock salts from the Cayuga Salt Mine supports an opened mirrored cube. As Smithson observed, "There's no order outside the order of the material."[3] In other words, Smithson's sculpture overtly demonstrates how material and form mutually interact upon each other, under the guidance—but not the manual workmanship—of the artist.

Leaning Mirror further emphasizes the important role played by the mirror in Smithson's redefinition of sculpture. A double-sided mirror is wedged on a slant into a pile of sand. As the mirror reflects the work's setting in a museum or gallery space, it also relieves sculpture of its static nature by capturing the movements of visitors and opening up the work for multifaceted viewing.

The several tons of shattered glass forming *Map of Broken Glass (Atlantis)* are layered both literally and figuratively. As the title suggests, the work is to be seen not simply as a large pile of flat, sharp, transparent fragments but also as a map of a legendary lost continent–almost certainly, however, a fictional one. Smithson's map of Atlantis proffers the idea that the concrete materiality of sculpture depends on the ability of the mind to "see" metaphorically in order to comprehend multifaceted meanings within the language of art.

Overall, these four works of Smithson's bear witness to his interest in revising the formal, material, and contextual properties of traditional sculpture. Explicitly divesting the art object of its supposedly autonomous standing in both physical and cultural space, and breaking new ground in the dialogue between work and site, Smithson made sculptures that must take their place among the radical innovations in the art of the late 1960s.

A. R.

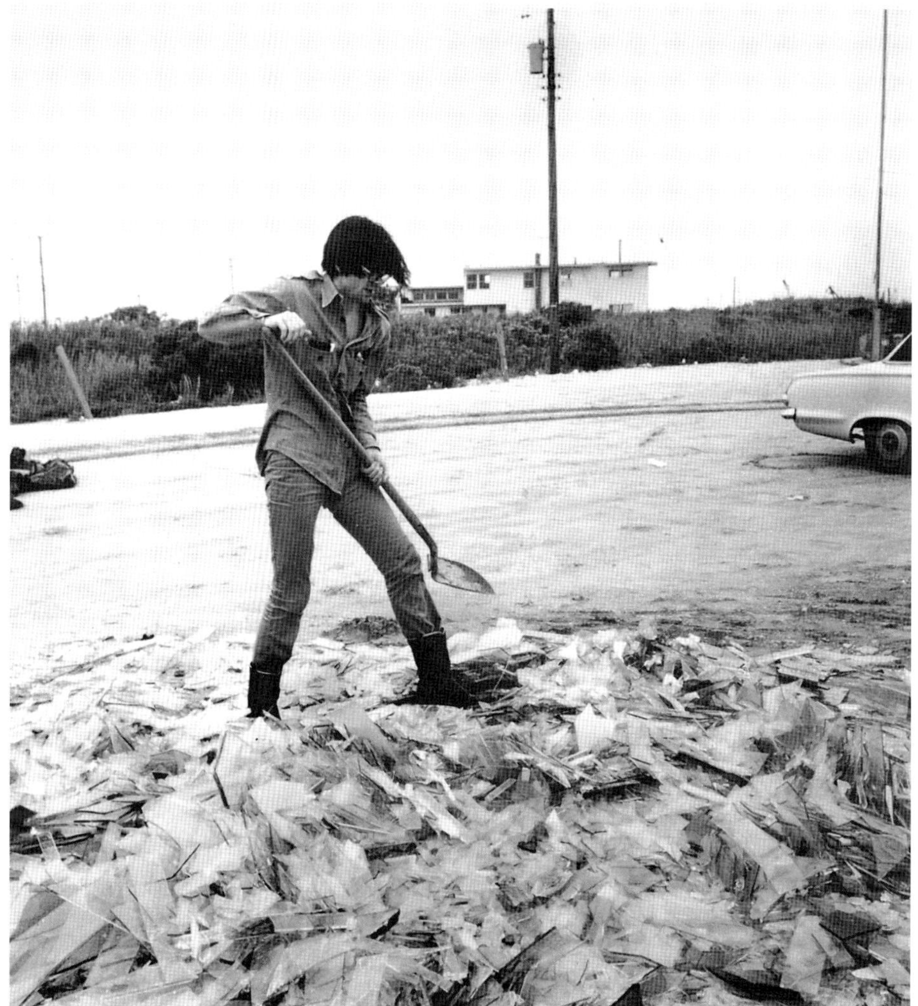

notes

1 See Robert Hobbs, *Robert Smithson: Sculpture* (Ithaca: Cornell University Press, 1981), p. 120.

2 See ibid., pp. 132–38.

3 Robert Smithson, in ibid., p. 136.

Robert Smithson constructing *Map of Broken Glass (Atlantis)*, 1969

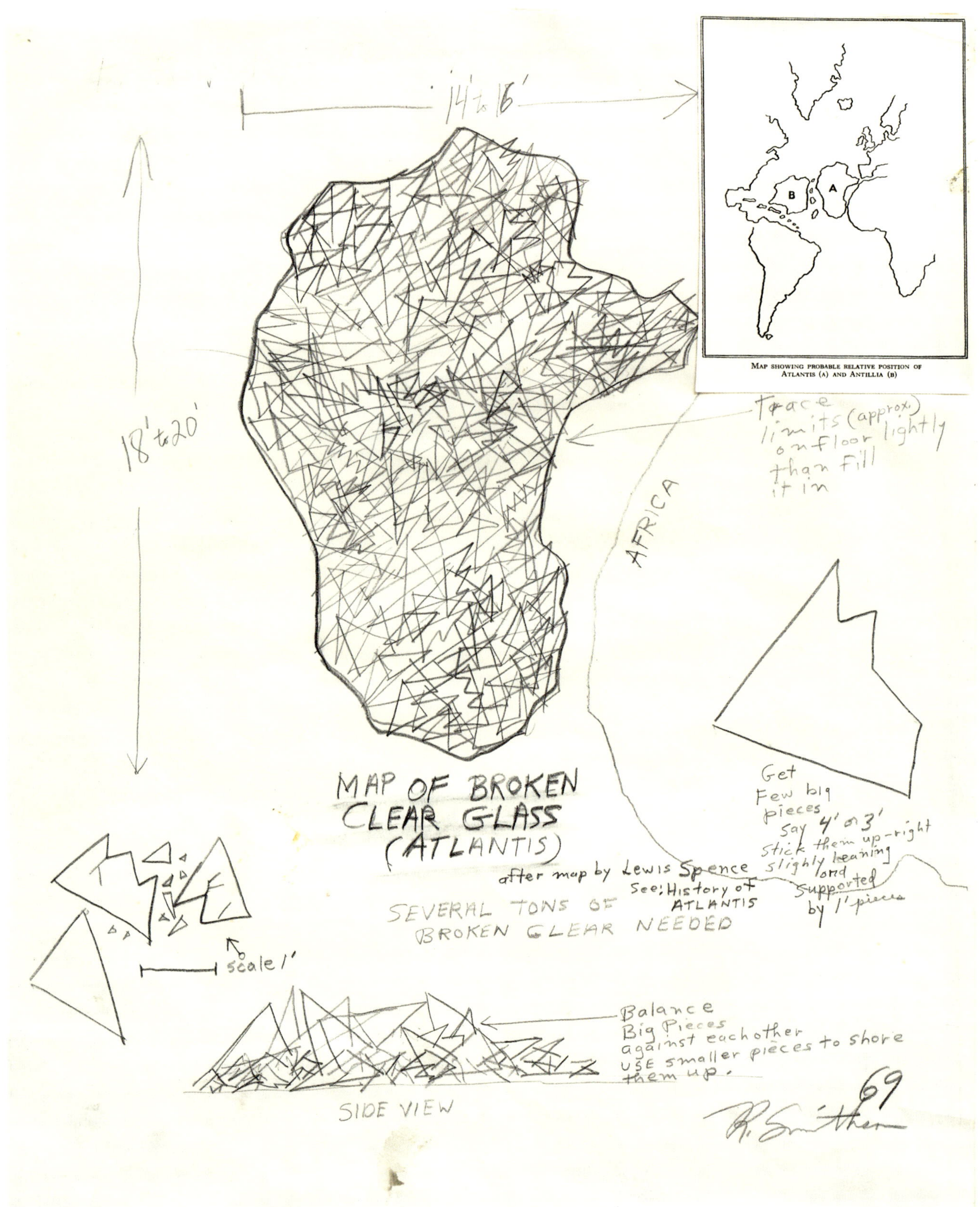

Map of Broken Clear Glass (Atlantis, After Map by Lewis Spence), 1969

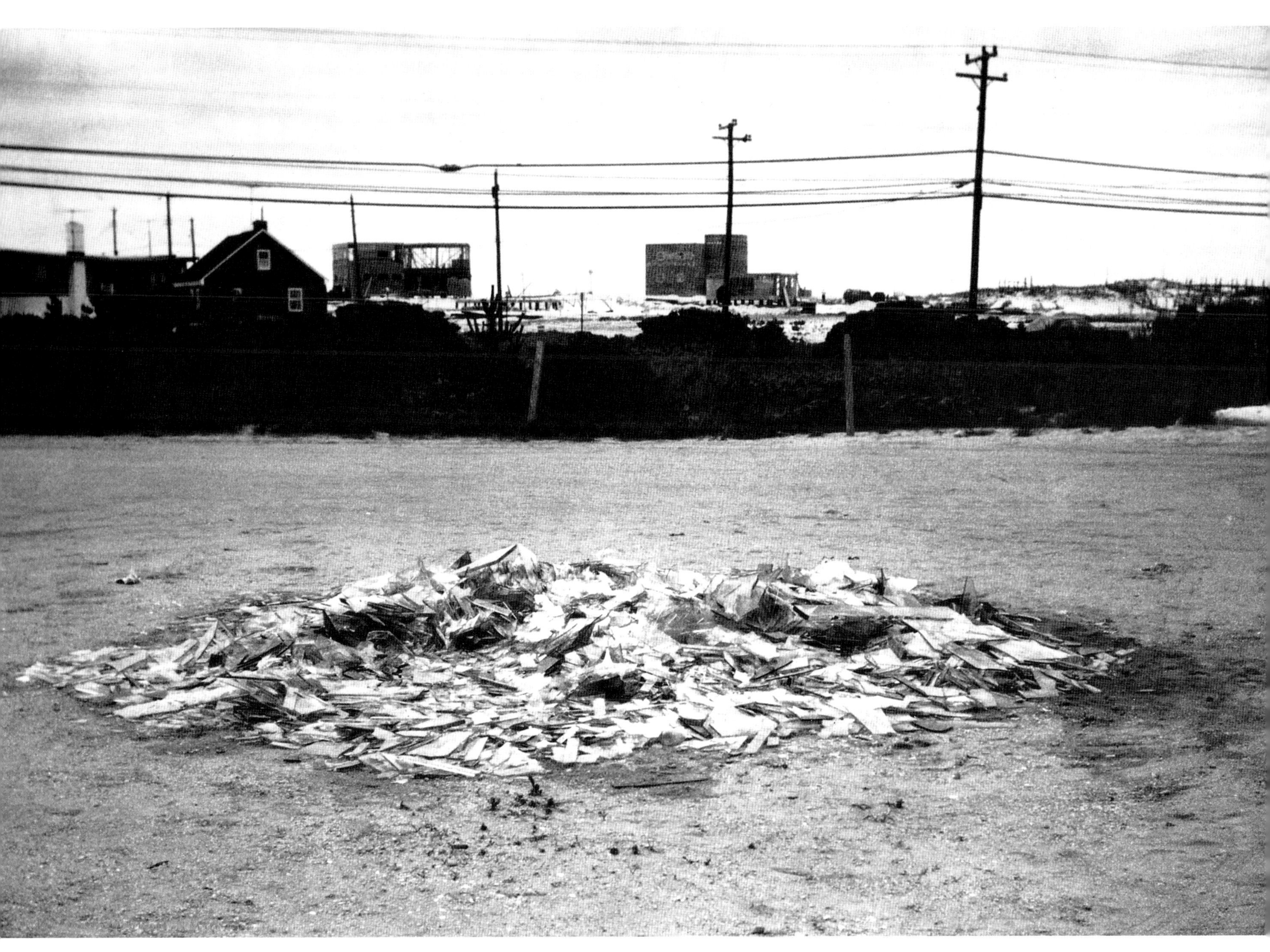

Map of Broken Glass (Atlantis), 1969

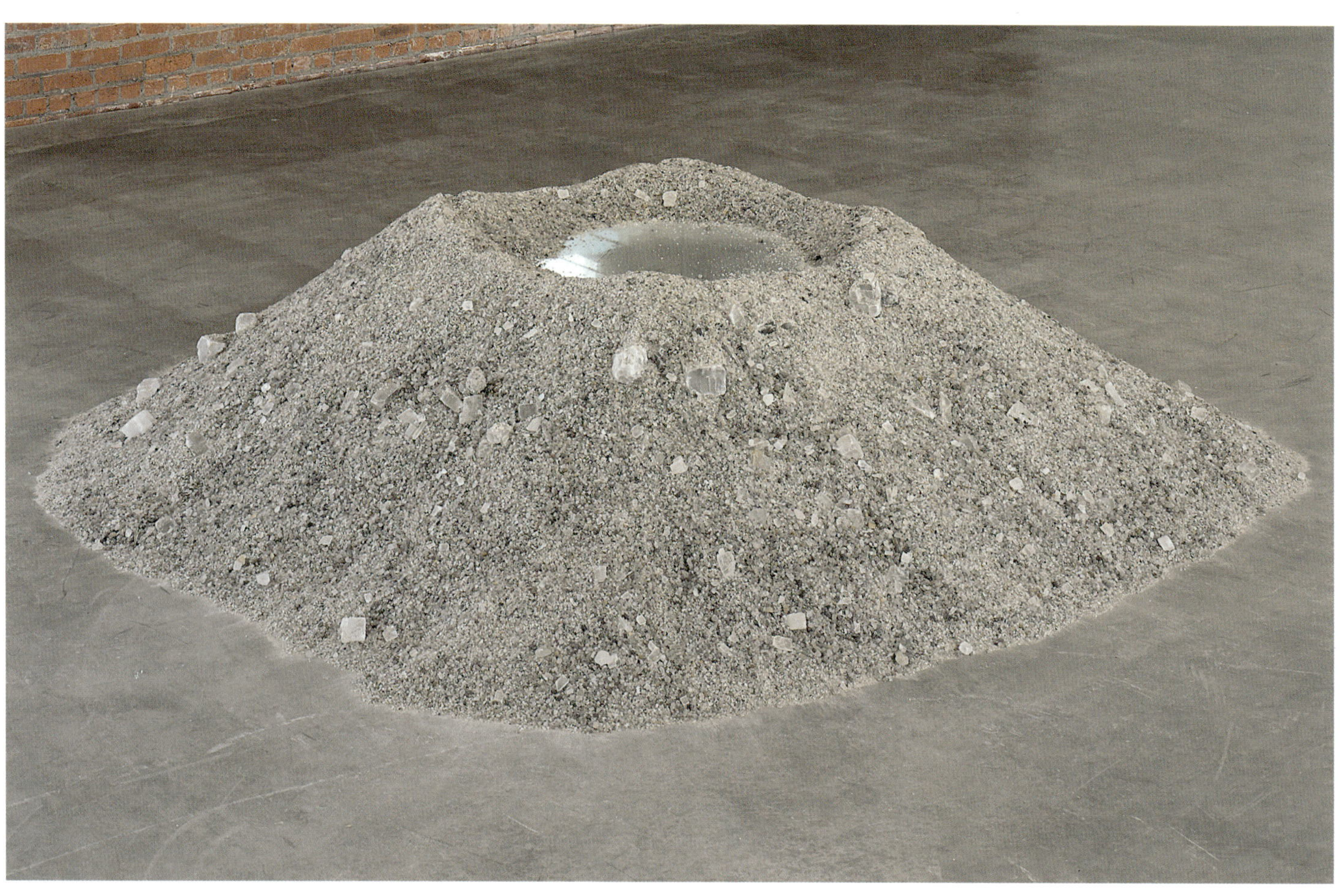

Closed Mirror Square (Cayuga Salt Mine Project), 1969

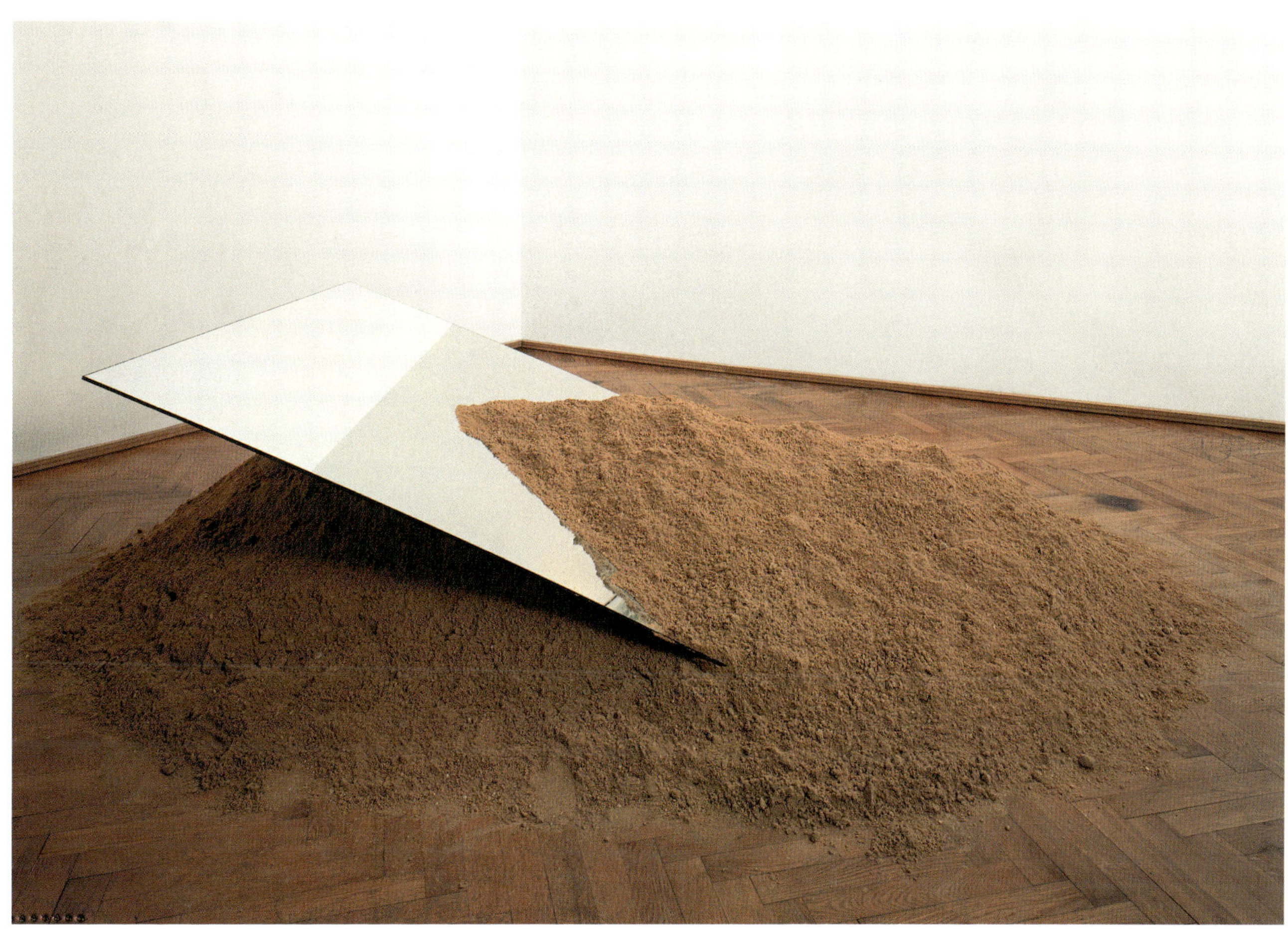

above *Leaning Mirror*, 1969

pages 284–285 *Gravel Mirrors with Cracks and Dust*, 1968

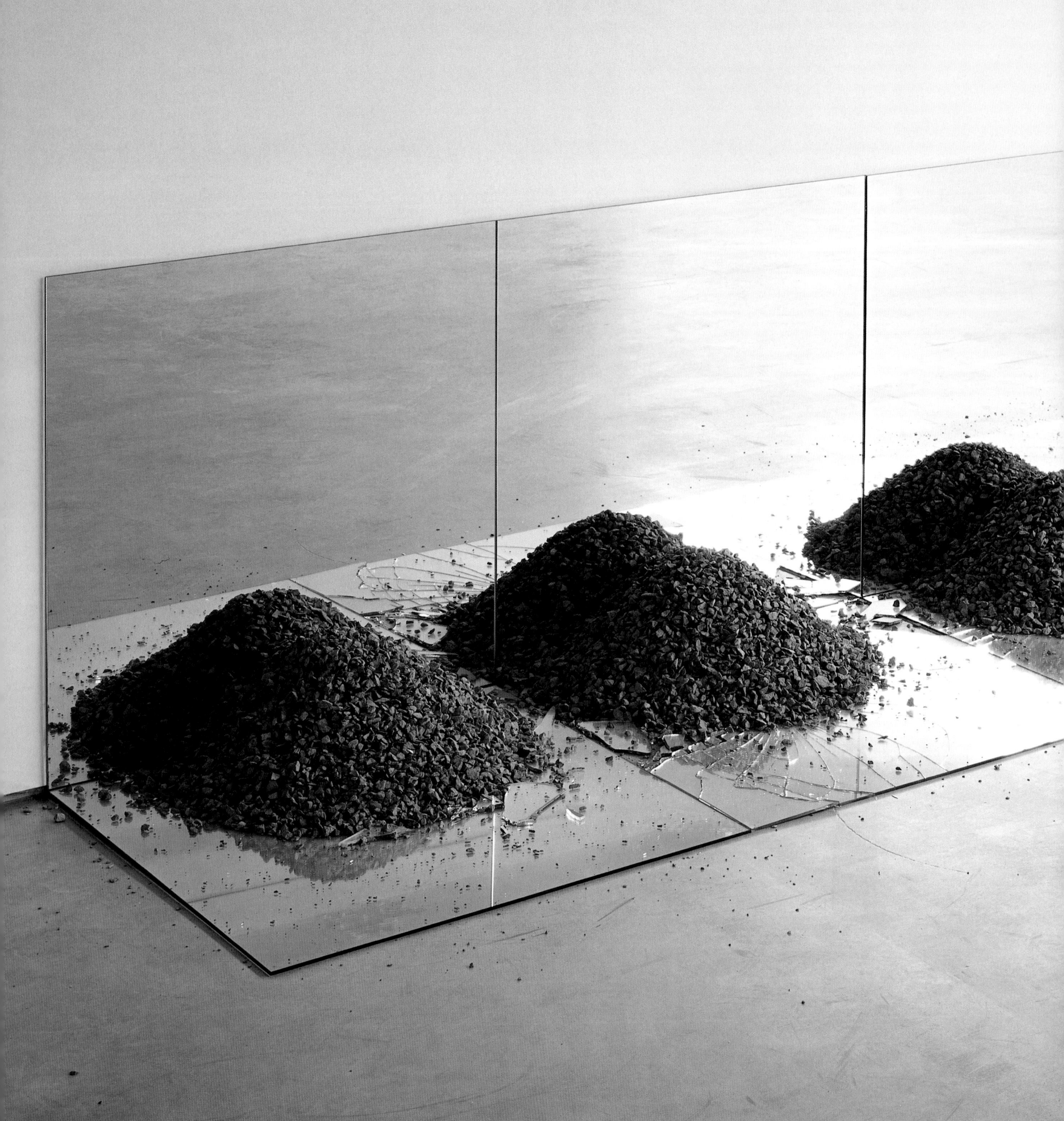

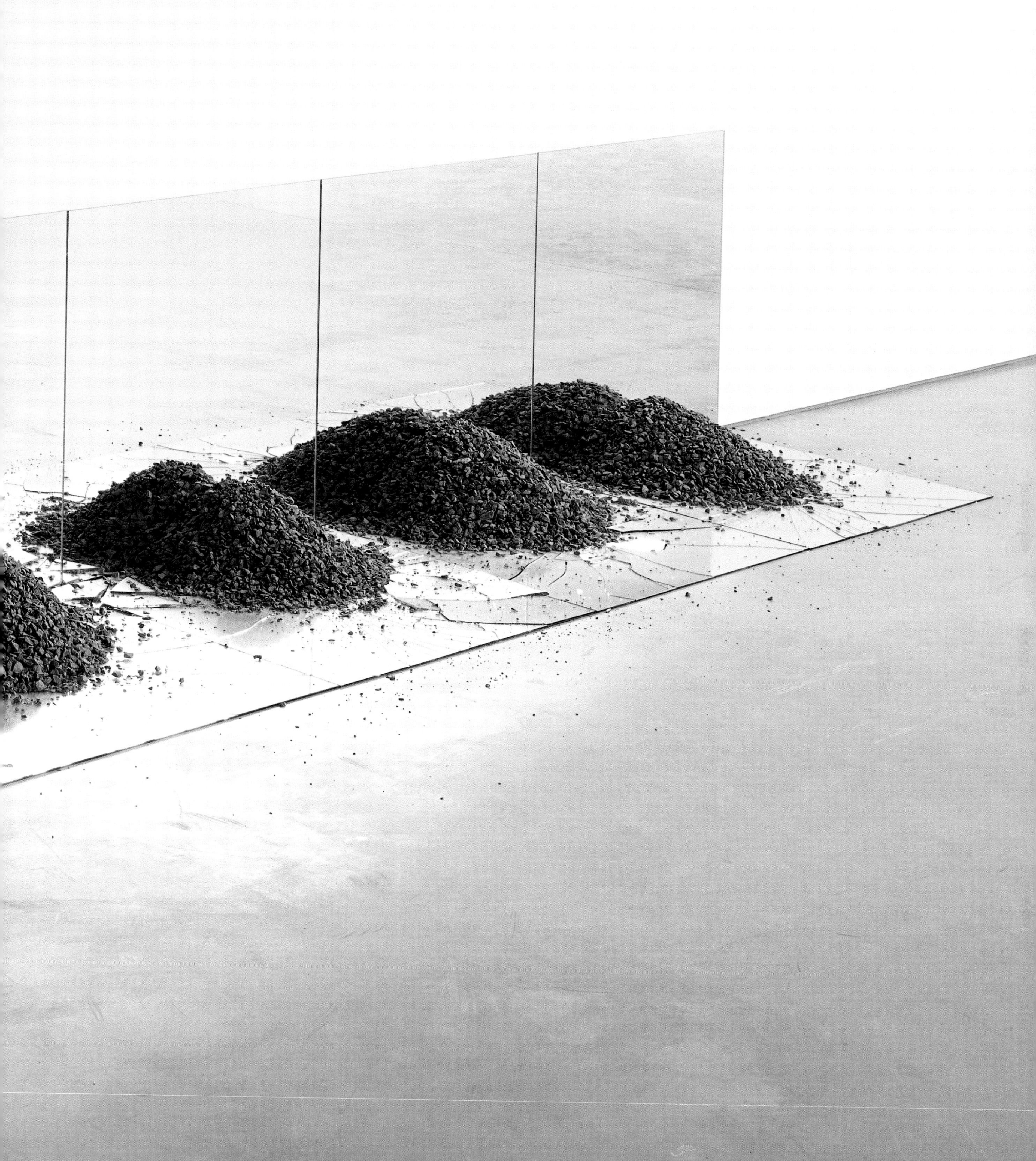

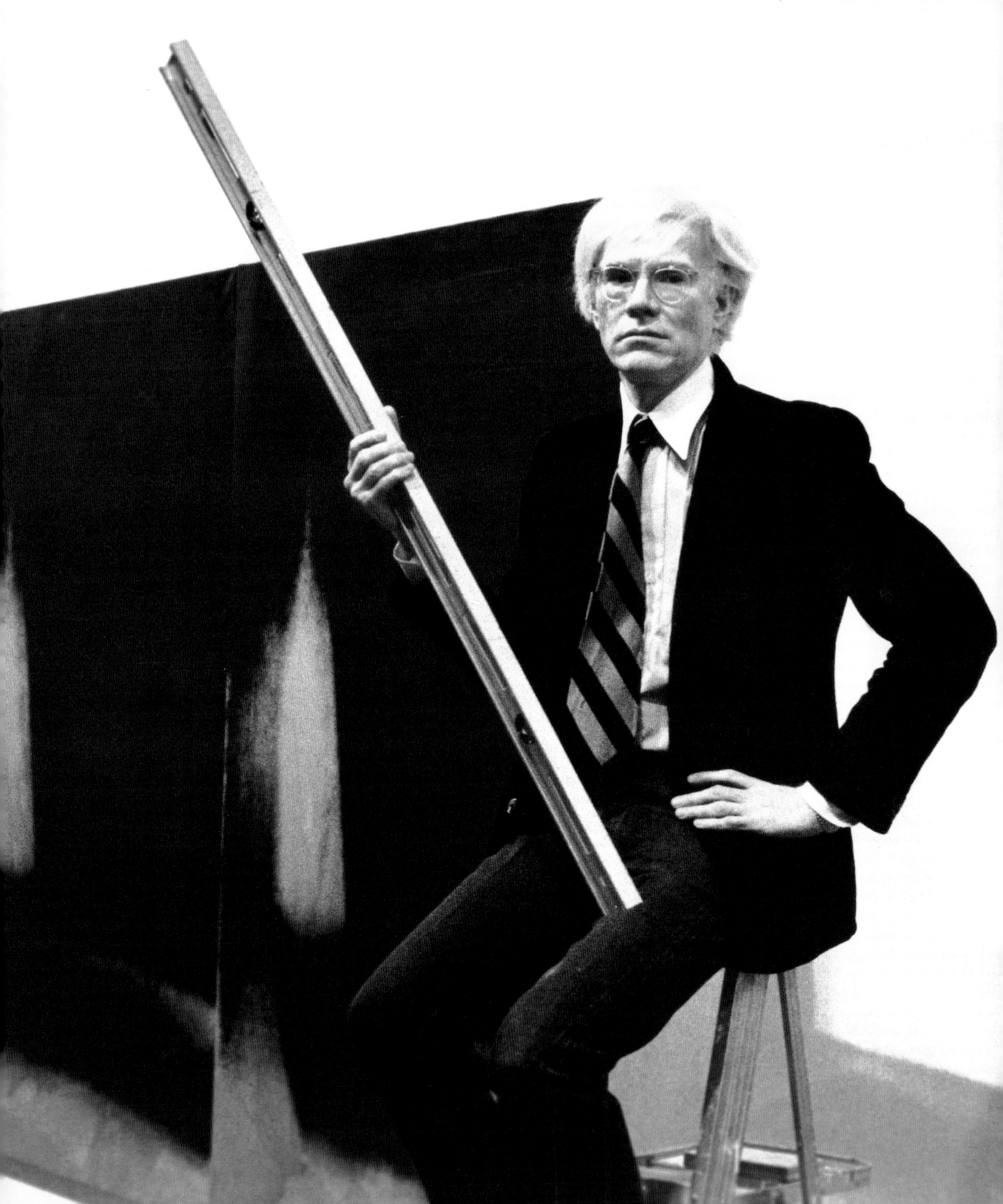

Andy Warhol

Andy Warhol was born in 1928 in Pittsburgh to immigrant parents from Czechoslovakia. He studied pictorial design at the city's Carnegie Institute of Technology, then moved to New York City upon graduation. Relinquishing a successful and acclaimed career as a commercial illustrator in New York in the 1950s, he began exhibiting paintings with silkscreened Pop imagery in 1962. In 1963 he began to produce films and other projects, including *Interview* magazine, which was begun in 1969. Retrospectives of his work have been organized by the Pasadena Art Museum (1970), the Museum of Modern Art, New York (1989), and the Neue Nationalgalerie, Berlin (2002). *Shadows* (1979) was first exhibited at Heiner Friedrich's gallery at 393 West Broadway, New York City, in January 1979, and most recently at Dia in 1998–99. Dia's other exhibitions of Warhol's work include "Andy Warhol: Disaster Paintings, 1963" (1986), "Andy Warhol: Hand-Painted Images, 1960–62" (1987), and "Andy Warhol: Skulls" (1987–88). Warhol died in 1987. In 1994, Dia collaborated with the Carnegie Institute and the Andy Warhol Foundation for the Visual Arts to open the Andy Warhol Museum in Pittsburgh.

Andy Warhol in the 1979 installation of *Shadows*, 1978–79, at Heiner Friedrich's gallery, 393 West Broadway, New York City

In the mid-1970s, shadows increasingly began to haunt Andy Warhol. In the Still Life drawing series of 1975 and the Hammer and Sickle series of 1977 (also titled Still Life), they assume an idiosyncratic, almost independent existence as compositional elements; in the Skulls of 1976, they become more expressive and fanciful in character. Finally, in 1978–79, in a brief but concentrated foray, Warhol confronted shadows as a subject in their own right. The result was an exceptional series of paintings, notably one vast environmental work in 102 parts, together with sundry others in different formats and with different motifs.

The precise sources for these enigmatic images remain contested. Notwithstanding the artist's own lapidary description of their genesis in "a photo of a shadow in my studio," alternate and conflicting accounts of their origins have been offered, among which the most persuasive is that given by Warhol's studio assistant at the time, Ronnie Cutrone, who remembers Warhol asking him to take photographs of shadows generated by maquettes devised expressly to create abstract forms.[1]

Of the seven or eight different compositions in the series, Warhol used two extensively, the remainder very seldom. Only the preferred pair are employed in Dia's environmental work *Shadows*. With two silver exceptions, the tall, narrow form dubbed "the peak" always appears as a black positive on a colored ground. These grounds, which range in hue from a Day-Glo acid green to a majestic purple, from a lurid turquoise to a sober brown, are mostly treated as a flat matte surface. Occasionally, however, they are broadly handled so that bravura brushwork irregularly fills the canvas, creating a lively field onto which the motif is then silkscreened. The second form, known as "the cap," is shorter and more organic in form, and always appears, paradoxically, as a negative in a black milieu: an "absent" shadow. Also monochromatic, these panels partake of the same palette as their counterparts.

Purchased as a single entity by Lone Star Foundation (now the Dia Art Foundation), this cycle of paintings was first exhibited in January 1979, at 393 West Broadway in New York City.[2] Its current presentation in Dia:Beacon mimics that debut, for it, too, incorporates as many canvases, hung edge to edge and close to the floor, as will fit the space, but it sequences the works by acquisition number–an equally random order. Warhol left decisions regarding the initial order of the paintings to Cutrone and his assistants. In adhering to no system, they conformed to Warhol's own practice when he chose the colors for the grounds, or selected prints from contact sheets to be made into screens. Yet his method was far from completely arbitrary: restricting the vocabulary of the group to two compositional formats, confining the total number of hues to seventeen, and limiting each canvas to a single color, Warhol filtered a controlled and circumscribed serendipity through the proclivities of taste to create an environmental ensemble that pertains as much to decor as it does to high art. In fact, in typically disarming fashion, Warhol referred to *Shadows* not as art but as "disco decor."[3] Soon after the exhibition, he employed it as a backdrop in a fashion shoot for the April 1979 edition of his magazine *Interview*.

The work's multiple roles and ambiguous status derive from the innovative and often provocative approach to installation that Warhol developed over the course of his career. For his first European retrospective, which opened at the Moderna Museet, Stockholm, early in 1968, he covered the building's Neoclassical facade with his Cow wallpaper. At the Whitney Museum of American Art, New York, in 1971, for the final appearance of a second and more comprehensive retrospective that had toured the United States the previous year, he hung paintings directly over the Cow wallpaper, which now covered the gallery interiors. When he presented his Mao series at the Musée Galliera, Paris, in 1974, he devised a landmark installation that superimposed paintings and prints of the Chinese leader over wallpaper that also depicted him, producing "a colorful, decorative salon."[4] Finally, just before his death, Warhol proposed installing his small camouflage paintings directly on their larger counterparts, which differed only in the scale of the motif and the color combinations.

If Warhol's own exhibition history contains precedents for the installation of *Shadows*, other models for the notion of a single monumental work in many parts were also readily at hand, not least in Blinky Palermo's *To the People of New York City* (1976). This composite abstract painting, arranged in fifteen parts, had been shown the previous January in the same space as Warhol's 1979 installation, and again subsequent to its acquisition by the Lone Star Foundation. Related formal strategies likewise appear in Minimal art, and specifically in the oeuvres of Donald Judd and Carl Andre, both of whom installed large-scale works composed of serially repeated units contiguously along the gallery wall(s) near the junction with the floor.

Ultimately, however, the examples that occasioned Warhol's preoccupation with abstraction were not those of his peers but those of the Abstract Expressionists. Even today this Pop painter's practice is routinely regarded as the nemesis of that movement, and indeed, when embarking on this hallowed terrain,

Warhol adopted a far from direct or reverential approach. Read as a homage to Jackson Pollock, his Oxidation series (1978) was as sardonic as it was celebratory; if allusion to Franz Kline may be discerned in *Shadows*, so may associations with "apocalyptic wallpaper,"[5] a term frequently applied to Action Painting by its detractors.

In its iconography and consequently in its metaphysics, the series is conceptually more akin to work by Marcel Duchamp, longtime exemplar for Warhol, than to that of any American artist. Duchamp's cryptic *Tu m'* (1918) rehearses many of the subjects raised in Warhol's series in its complex and subtle play with issues of representation and with discourses of reality and illusion, presence and absence.[6] In taking up this subject Warhol must also have been aware of experiments made by Man Ray, such as *Interrogation of Shadows* from 1919 and the series of Rayographs from 1921, several of which exist mysteriously in both positive and negative guise.

The shadow, which holds a seminal role in the originary accounts of both painting and photography as art forms, assumes in Warhol's depictions a paradigmatic identity: devoid of identifiable source, detached from its maker or creator, it exists in and of itself, a purposefully made image of "nothing." As Julian Schnabel asserted in the preface to the catalogue marking the first comprehensive exhibition of these works, in 1989, "There is almost nothing on them. Yet they seem to be pictures of something." In a telling afterthought, he added that they are "as full of imagery as any of Andy's other paintings."[7]

L.C.

notes

1 Ronnie Cutrone, telephone conversation with the author, November 26, 1998. Mark Francis cites a slightly different account by Cutrone, suggesting that the images were produced by children's small building blocks. See Francis, "No There There or Horror Vacui: Andy Warhol's Installations," *Andy Warhol: Paintings 1960–1986* (Lucerne: Kunstmuseum, 1995), p. 72. Other proposals include the shadow cast by an erect penis or by the Empire State Building.

2 The initial commission from Lone Star was for a cycle of 100 paintings. Warhol decided to make an additional eight paintings in this vein for his own purposes. In the end, Lone Star's acquisition comprised 102 paintings.

3 Warhol, "Painter Hangs His Own Paintings," *New York*, February 5, 1979. Reprinted in *Warhol Shadows* (Houston: Menil Collection, 1987), n.p.

4 Francis, "No There There," p. 70.

5 The term was originally coined by Harold Rosenberg to describe Action Painting, which he thought lacked "the dialectical tension of a genuine act, associated with risk and will." See Rosenberg, "The American Action Painters," *Art News* 51, no. 8 (December 1952), p. 22.

6 Commissioned by the collector Katherine S. Dreier, *Tu m'*, which measures 27½ by 123¼ inches, is the largest painting in Marcel Duchamp's oeuvre. The artist himself confessed that he "never liked it because it is too decorative." Quoted in Arturo Schwarz, *The Complete Works of Marcel Duchamp* (New York: Delano Greenridge Editions, 1996), 2:658.

7 Julian Schnabel, preface to *Andy Warhol: Shadow Paintings* (New York: Gagosian Gallery, 1989), p. 4.

pages 290–91, 292–93, 294–95 *Shadows*, 1978–79

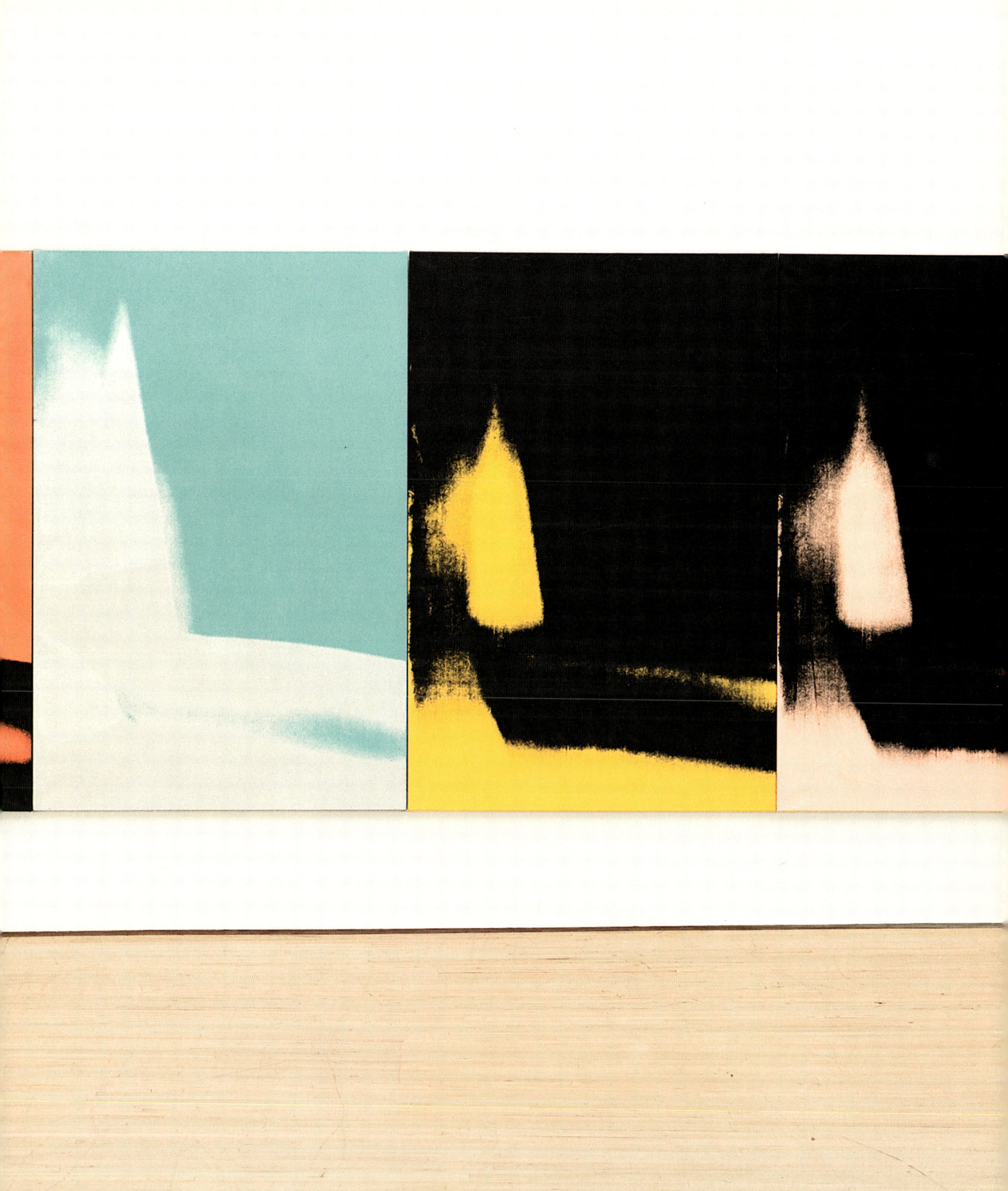

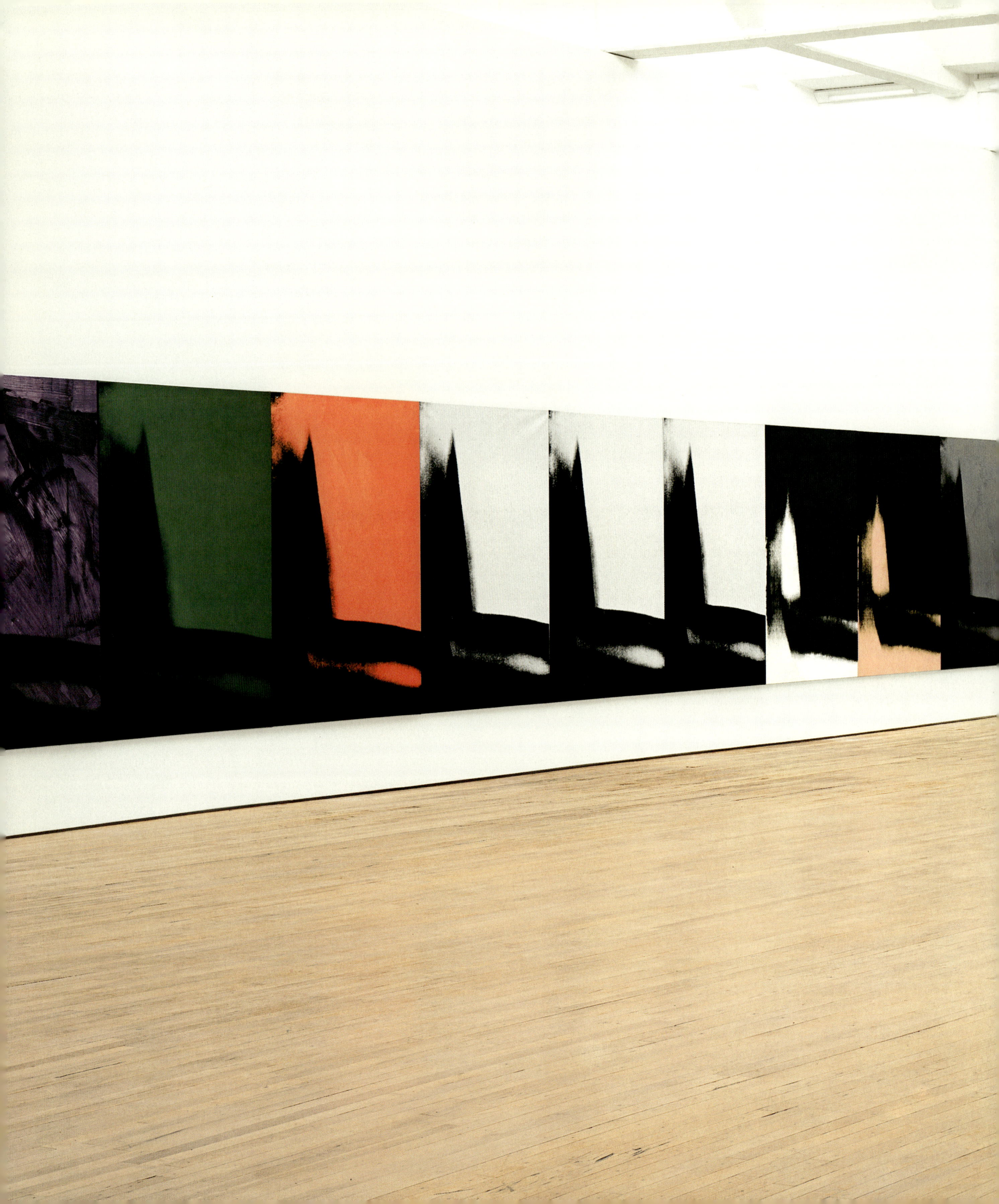

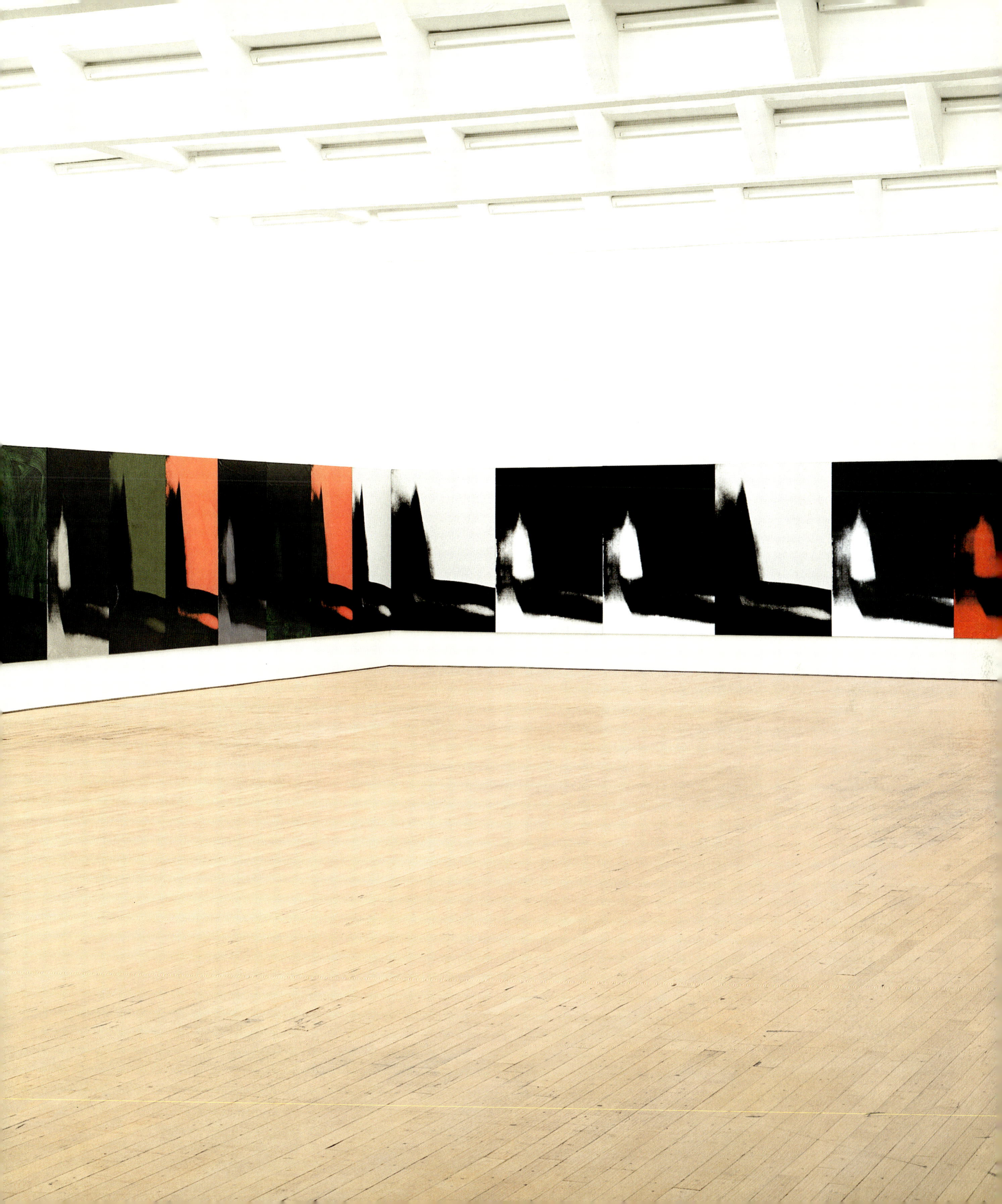

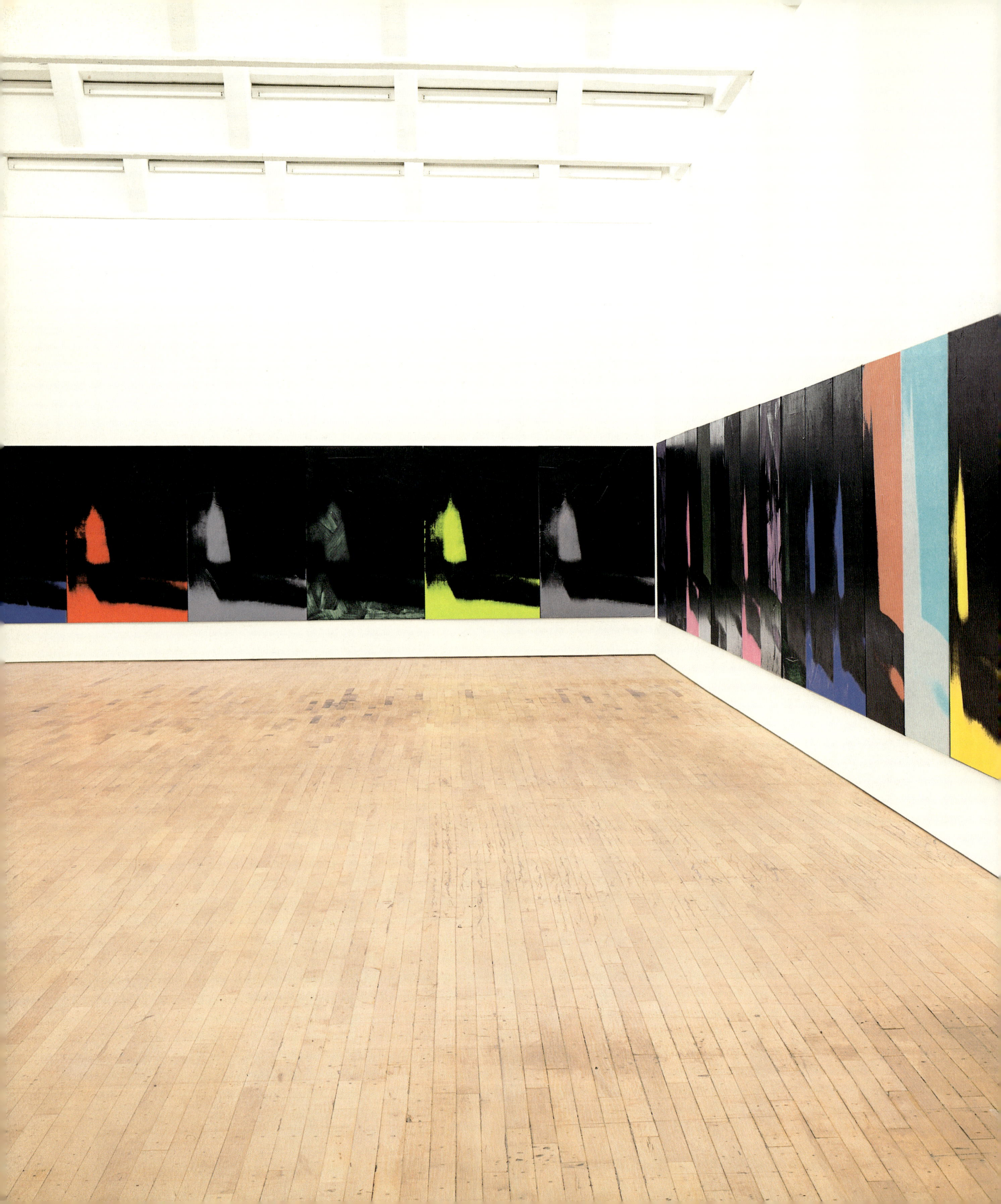

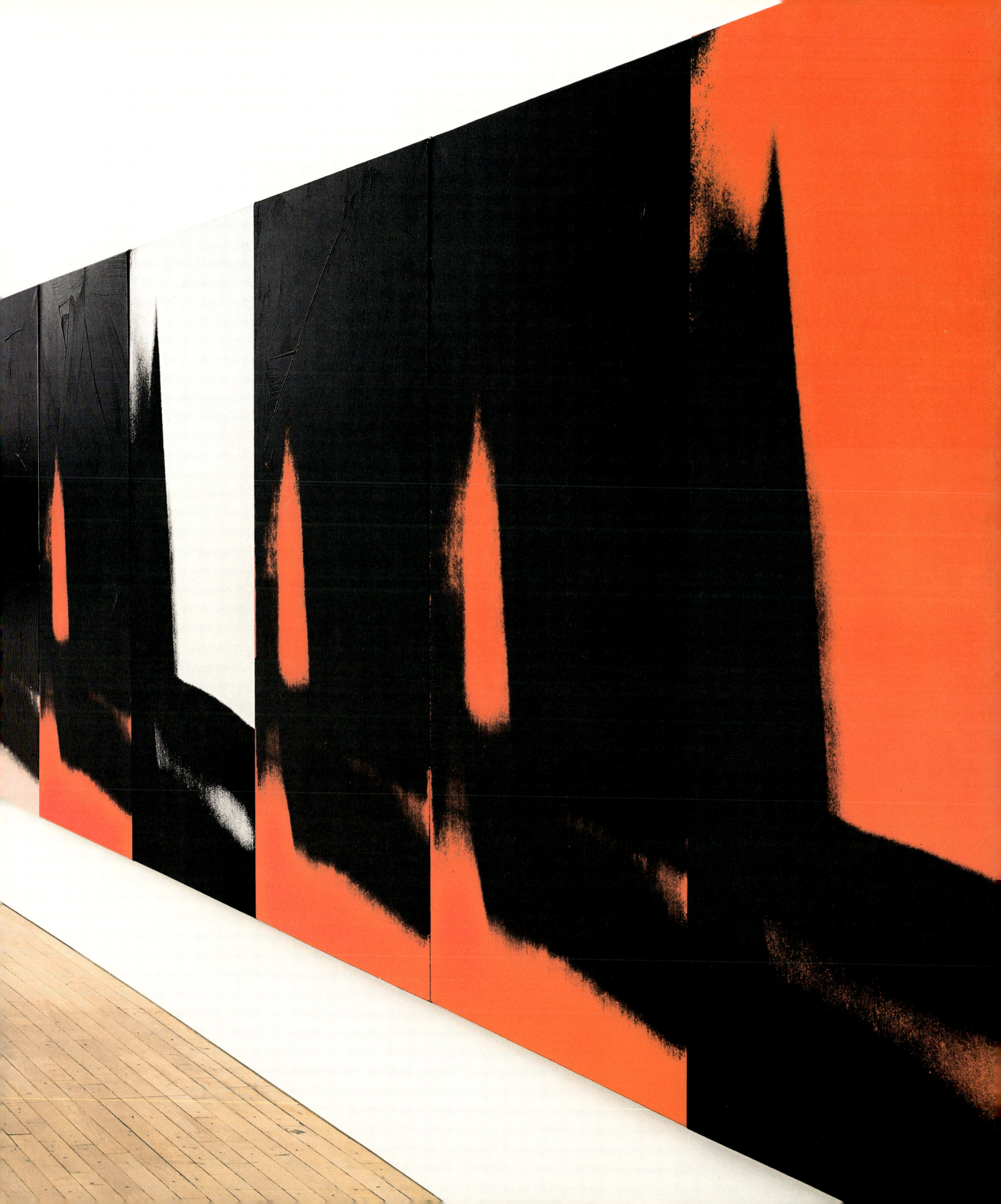

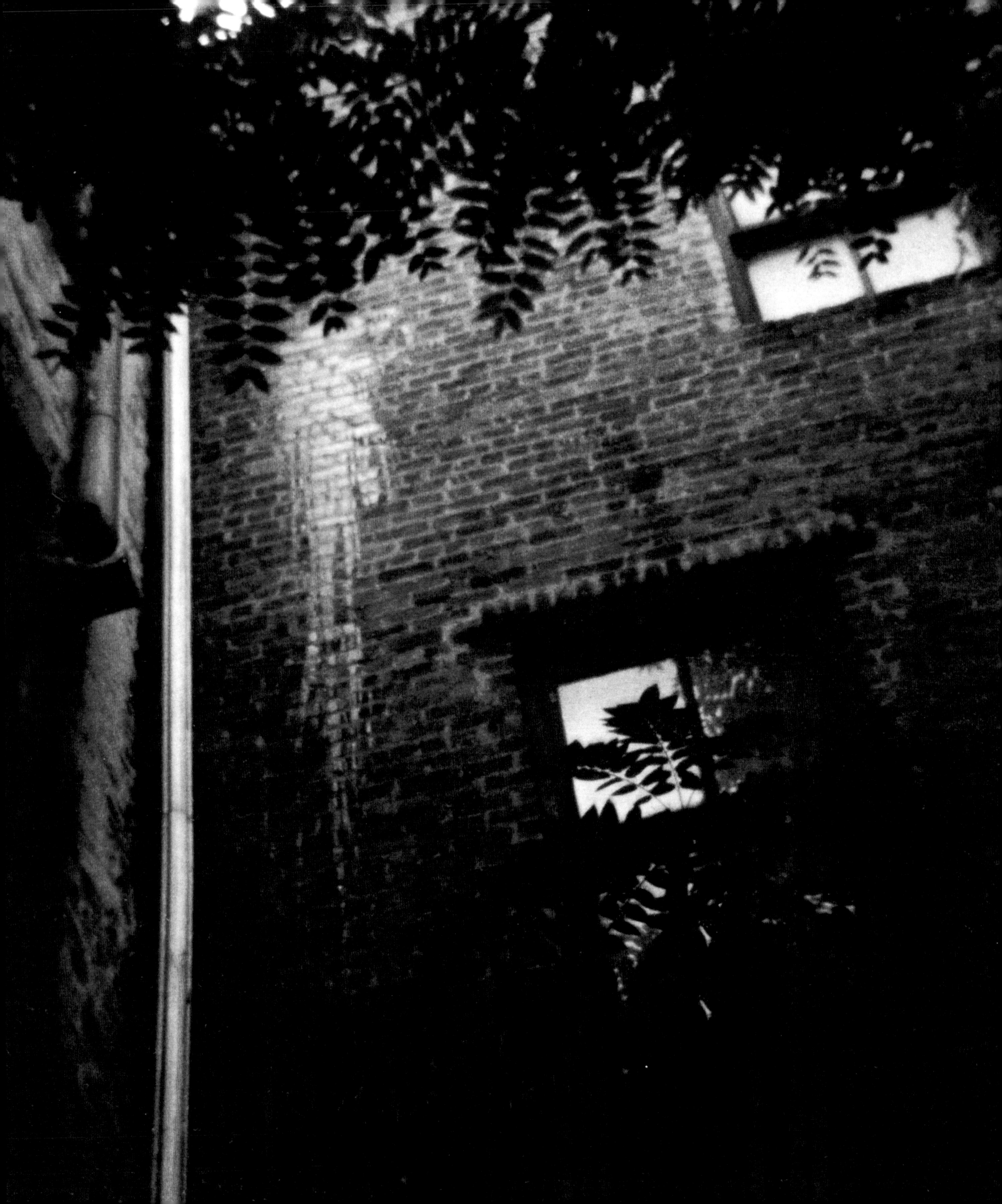

Lawrence Weiner

Lawrence Weiner was born in the Bronx, New York, in 1942. After graduating from high school, he traveled across the country to California, where, in 1960, he used dynamite to create his Cratering Pieces in Mill Valley. His first one-person show was held at the Seth Siegelaub Gallery, New York, in 1964. In 1968 he presented *Statements*, a book of works composed solely of language, in another show at Siegelaub's gallery, and since then he has continued to explore the capacities and presentation of language as a sculptural medium. The museums in which Weiner has had solo exhibitions have included the Kunstmuseum Wolfsburg (2000), the Walker Art Center, Minneapolis (1994), and the Hirshhorn Museum and Sculpture Garden, Smithsonian Institution, Washington, D.C. (1990). In 1991 Dia presented his work *Displacement* and published an accompanying book of the same title. Weiner currently lives in New York City and Amsterdam.

ONE QUART EXTERIOR GREEN INDUSTRIAL ENAMEL THROWN ON A BRICK WALL, 1968

Since 1967 Lawrence Weiner's work has been formulated by recourse to language rather than the more conventional idioms of painting or sculpture. In language, Weiner found a medium and tool for representing material relationships in the external world in as objective a manner as possible, one that could eliminate all references to authorial subjectivity—all traces of the artist's hand, his skill, or his taste. "ART IS NOT A METAPHOR UPON THE RELATIONSHIP OF HUMAN BEINGS TO OBJECTS & OBJECTS TO OBJECTS IN RELATION TO HUMAN BEINGS BUT A REPRESENTATION OF AN EMPIRICAL EXISTING FACT," he argues. "IT DOES NOT TELL THE POTENTIAL & CAPABILITIES OF AN OBJECT (MATERIAL) BUT PRESENTS A REALITY CONCERNING THAT RELATIONSHIP."[1] This often-quoted contention is spelled out in characteristically succinct spare terms: it posits the allusive and hypothetical as the negative of that which *is*, an objectively observable or verifiable concrete reality.

By focusing on generalities rather than specifics, Weiner has been able to constitute these material relationships and conditions as abstractions. And by utilizing, wherever possible, semantic and grammatical symbols such as capitalization, brackets, parentheses, ampersands, and the plus and equal signs, or, more recently, arrows and related graphic devices, he has articulated his work in unequivocally direct terms. Clear, concise, lapidary, and affectless, such sculpture in the guise of statements is designed, in the artist's words, to offer "a universal common possibility of availability."[2] Eschewing the literary or poetic, this former philosophy student concentrates on empirically observable properties, materials, states, conditions, processes, behaviors, and functions of matter.

An individual work need never actually be realized, Weiner contends, since "each being equal and consistent with the intent of the artist, the decision as to condition rests with the receiver upon the occasion of receivership."[3] Shifting the onus onto the audience, delegating the responsibility of instantiation to the owner or custodian, this fundamental tenet of his practice was appended to a Declaration of Intent set forth in 1969:

1. THE ARTIST MAY CONSTRUCT THE WORK
2. THE WORK MAY BE FABRICATED
3. THE WORK NEED NOT BE BUILT

Because Weiner's works are conceived as nonspecific, as endlessly adaptive representations of states or processes grounded in but not bounded by material reality, they can be viewed in countless possible situations and manifestations. Although material relations at the level of generalities and abstractions embody the content–the thematics–of his art, presentation and context impact upon and cannot be divorced from the content of any individual work whenever and wherever it is realized. Since presentation and context are always determined only when, and if, a particular work is installed, the choice of medium–whether, for example, the letters are stenciled, painted, or mounted in relief, and in what typeface, size, proportions, placement, and color–varies with the site; similarly, the context–whether a poster, artist's book, gallery wall, mural, or other public arena–necessarily inflects not only the work's form but its very meaning. In David Batchelor's felicitous phrase, "The site doesn't so much receive the work as the work receives a voice from the site."[4]

Seldom site specific, Weiner's works can be tellingly site related, that is, strategically conceived or adapted to the venue and circumstances. In *Displacement*, for example, an environmental-scale project at Dia in Chelsea in 1991, he painted an abbreviated version of the Statement of Intent in a hopscotch grid on the floor. Immediately to the left of the entrance he placed a small work, BITS & PIECES PUT TOGETHER TO PRESENT A SEMBLANCE OF A WHOLE (1991). On the opposite side of the gallery, on the longest available wall, he installed CADMIUM & MUD & TITANIUM & LEAD & FERROUS OXIDE & SO ON . . . (1991); an aggregation of an indeterminate, heterogeneous array of materials, this work exemplifies the postulates set forth in the piece on the threshold.

In *Displacement* Weiner stipulated the identity of a set of material components but not their quantity or proportion. Elsewhere he has focused on other sculptural aspects: spatial and structural relationships, composition, and mass. When *5 Figures of Structure* was first realized, at the Arts Club of Chicago in 1987, it took the form of words in Franklin Gothic Condensed typeface outlined in charcoal on the textured gallery walls.[5] At the Marian Goodman Gallery, New York, in 1999, the dense sanserif script appeared as solid black letters compacted into weighty blocks stacked one above another on a single wall, the relevant diagrams adjacent. At Dia:Beacon, the weighty massiveness of this quintessentially sculptural work is embodied in an interplay between optical quiddity and physical proximity, between the semantic solidity and the silhouetted graphic paradigms. Visual and textual "figures" are cadenced to mime the conditions they embody, in what proves almost a tautological imbrication of text, inscription, context, and site.

"I really believe the subject matter of my art is–art," Weiner asserted in 1969.[6] In the thirty-odd years since he made that claim his work has ranged widely, from early pieces strongly connected to painting to others evoking the sculptural, which has ultimately become his primary focus. In its constituents, techniques, and formal concerns, ONE QUART EXTERIOR GREEN INDUSTRIAL ENAMEL THROWN ON A BRICK WALL (1968) alludes self-evidently to the art of painting and especially to that of Jackson Pollock, a revered icon when this work was conceived. Yet in boldly eschewing that art's defining or established conventions, notably the rectangular pictorial field and intentional mark making, it eloquently invokes more contemporary, process-based genres.[7]

Exemplary of Weiner's earliest works, ONE QUART EXTERIOR GREEN INDUSTRIAL ENAMEL . . . was initially conceived in the form of a statement; when not printed in books or catalogues, such works existed as typed sheets of paper that could simply be mounted on the walls of the gallery for exhibition. With some few others, it was also fabricated by the artist, who, in hurling paint against the facade of his home, effectively extended Pollock's gesture into the real world. Only after 1972, when Weiner began to work directly in situ in art venues as well as less orthodox frameworks, did it assume multiple guises. Among its many memorable incarnations are a rapidly daubed graffito on a grimy residential streetscape and a modestly scaled bilingual Japanese-English presentation that, in conforming to each language's respective conventions, appeared both vertically and horizontally on the same wall. Given their inherent variety and versatility, Weiner's works may well commandeer physically dispersed sites–as found in Beacon, where they are set among the galleries devoted to sculpture, in a stairwell, and in the café-bookstore. Reflecting his desire that his works not be confined to "aesthetically contracted spaces," that they exist in the culture at large, the Declaration of Intent is suspended high over the admissions desk. As it offers vivid testimony to his belief that irrespective of placement "art always institutionalizes itself," it also reminds visitors that the work of art is completed in the act of "receivership," or reception.[8] Above all, in this context it becomes less a gentle admonition than a promise.

L.C.

notes

1 Lawrence Weiner, "Notes from Art (4 pages)," in Clive Phillpot, ed., "Words and Word Works," *Art Journal* 42, no. 2 (Summer 1982), p. 122.

2 Weiner, quoted in Benjamin H. D. Buchloh in "Conversation with Lawrence Weiner," in *Lawrence Weiner* (London: Phaidon, 1998), p. 19. Only rarely does Weiner engage in double entendres, or figures of speech, by the choice of imbricated literal and metaphoric idioms, as in AROUND THE BEND (1970) and OVER THE HILL (1970). A more telling exception to the tenor of his written statements occurs when the text is spoken or, especially, sung, as in several of his recent CDs, including MONSTERS FROM THE DEEP (1997), with Ned Sublette. In such works the neutral, objective monotone of the abstract statement in its written guise becomes imbued with affect: in short, since the voice is inherently expressive, it could be said to offer another location. See Batchelor, "MANY COLORED OBJECTS PLACED SIDE BY SIDE TO FORM A ROW OF MANY COLORED OBJECTS," in *Lawrence Weiner*, pp. 74–83.

3 This statement has been used in many presentations since its first publication in *ARTnews* in the fall of 1968 and its republication in the catalogue for the group show "January 5–31 1969," at the Seth Siegelaub Gallery, New York, in 1969. See Buchloh, ed., *Lawrence Weiner: Posters November 1965–April 1986* (Halifax: The Press of Nova Scotia College of Art and Design, in association with Art Metropole, Toronto, 1986), p. 173.

4 Batchelor, "MANY COLORED OBJECTS PLACED SIDE BY SIDE," p. 83. This is obviously more true when the work is positioned outside the white cube of the traditional museum or gallery, but even there the presence of works by other artists potentially impacts upon the viewer's reading of the piece. Even when permanently sited in a specific context, Weiner's works may always be reinstalled, not least because the artist retains the right to an exhibition copy.

5 See Anne Rorimer, "Sculpture: Figures of Structure. The Work of Lawrence Weiner," in *Lawrence Weiner: 5 Figures of Structure* (Chicago: The Arts Club of Chicago, 1987), n.p.

6 Weiner, quoted in "Art without Space: A Symposium Moderated by Seth Siegelaub with Lawrence Weiner, Robert Barry, Douglas Huebler, and Joseph Kosuth, 1969," reprinted in *Lawrence Weiner*, p. 96.

7 One of Weiner's formative artistic experiences was a visit he made as a child to the Museum of Modern Art, New York, where he saw a painting by Jackson Pollock. See Weiner, "The Possibility of Language Functioning as a Representation of Non Metaphorical Reality, e.g. Art," 1997, reprinted in *Lawrence Weiner*, pp. 137, 140. Films and photographs of Pollock at work in his barn, pouring paint onto his canvas on the floor or onto a sheet of glass, were widely circulated, and much lampooned, in the popular press during Weiner's adolescence. Buchloh contextualized ONE QUART EXTERIOR GREEN INDUSTRIAL ENAMEL . . . in relation to more contemporary practices when he asked Weiner, "Do these strategies and materials not add up to an internal criticism of the false heroization of even the last layer of industrial materials that was still dominating the aesthetics of minimal and postminimal sculpture?" "Exactly," was Weiner's reply. "Benjamin Buchloh in Conversation with Lawrence Weiner," pp. 16–17.

8 Weiner, quoted in Robert C. Morgan, "A Conversation with Lawrence Weiner," *Reallife*, nos. 11–12 (Winter 1983), p. 36.

pages 300–303 *5 Figures of Structure*, 1987
page 304 *5 Figures of Structure*, 1987, installation at Marian Goodman Gallery, 1999
page 305 ONE QUART EXTERIOR GREEN INDUSTRIAL ENAMEL THROWN ON A BRICK WALL, 1968

ONE SLAB + ANOTHER SLAB RESTED AGAINST
EACH OTHER ON TOP OF A HORIZONTAL
SLAB SET INTO THE GROUND

ONE SLAB PUT TOP TO BUTT OF ANOTHER SLAB
SET ABOVE ANOTHER SLAB SET TOP TO BUTT
WITH THE GROUND

ONE SLAB + ANOTHER SLAB SET
ATOP A SLAB RESTING ON THE GROUND

TWO SLABS PLACED AGAINST EACH OTHER
TO FORM A FORM WITH ANOTHER SLAB LYING
ON THE GROUND

ONE SLAB SET ABOVE THE GROUND EXPOSED
BETWEEN ONE SLAB SET IN LINE WITH
ANOTHER SLAB

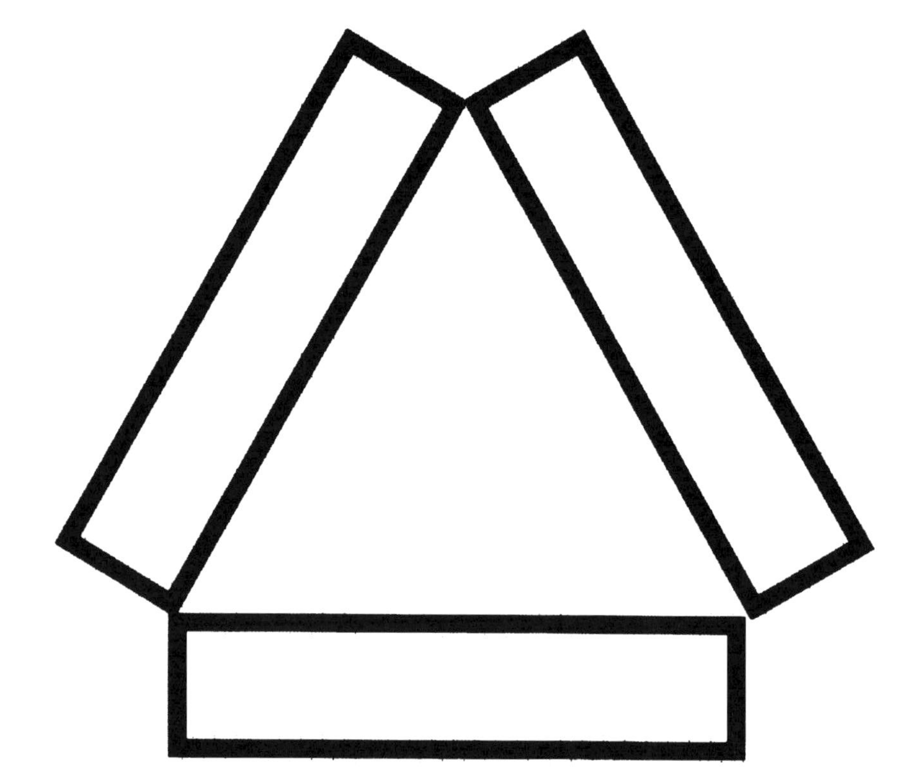

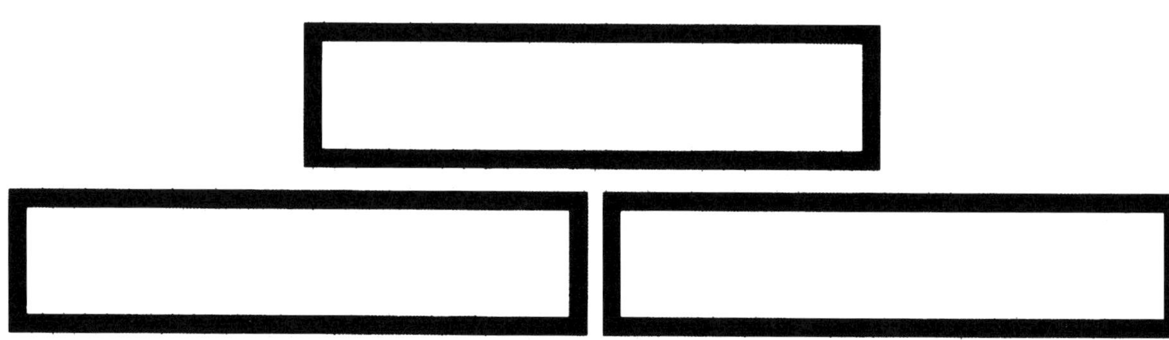

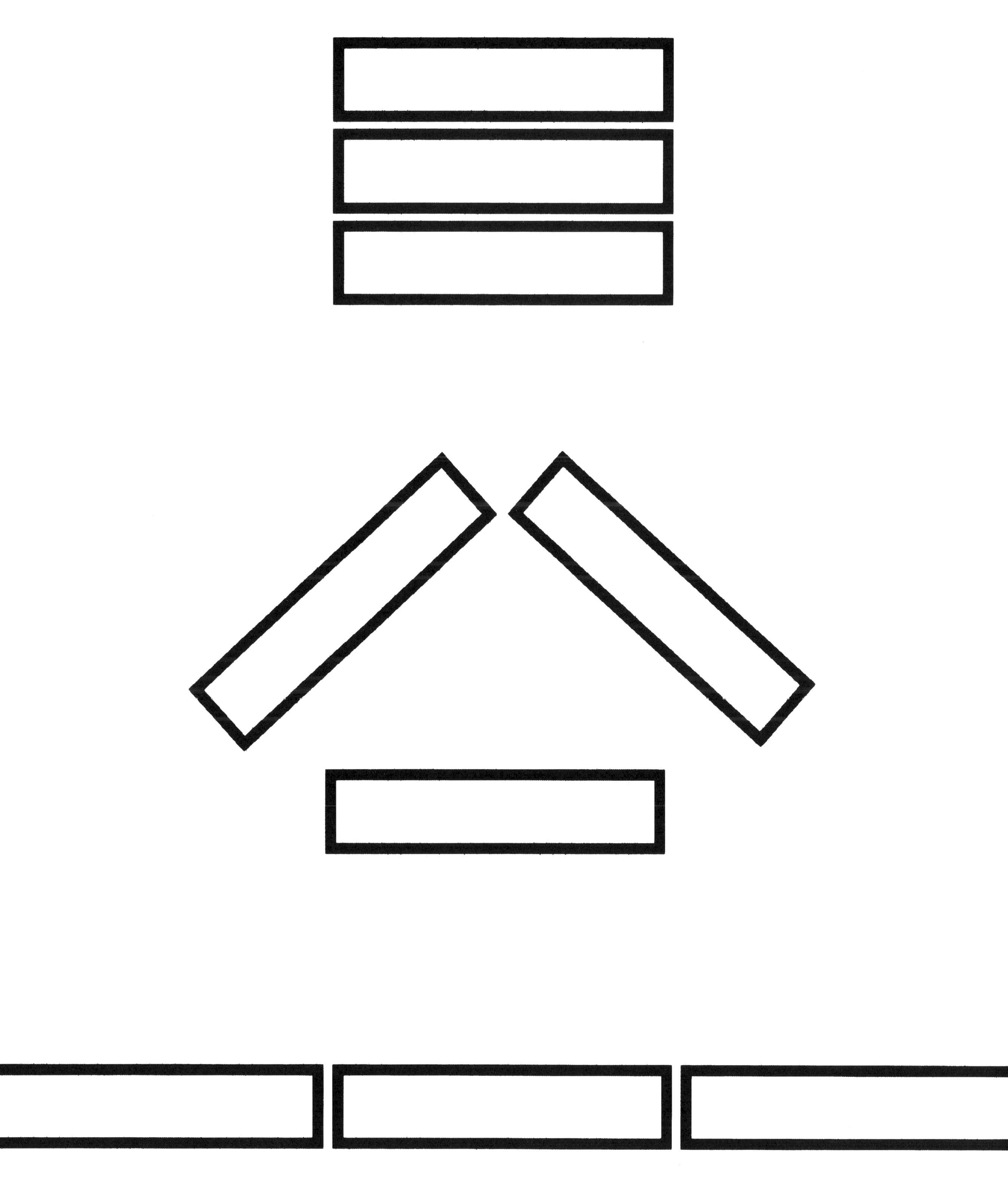

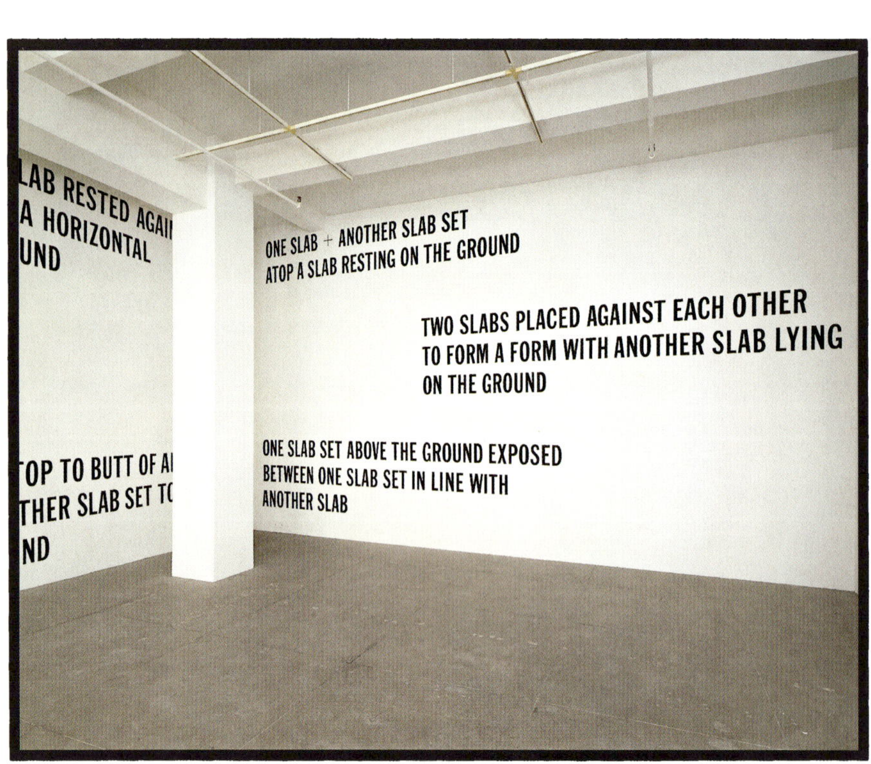
ONE SLAB + ANOTHER SLAB SET
ATOP A SLAB RESTING ON THE GROUND
TWO SLABS PLACED AGAINST EACH OTHER
TO FORM A FORM WITH ANOTHER SLAB LYING
ON THE GROUND
ONE SLAB SET ABOVE THE GROUND EXPOSED
BETWEEN ONE SLAB SET IN LINE WITH
ANOTHER SLAB

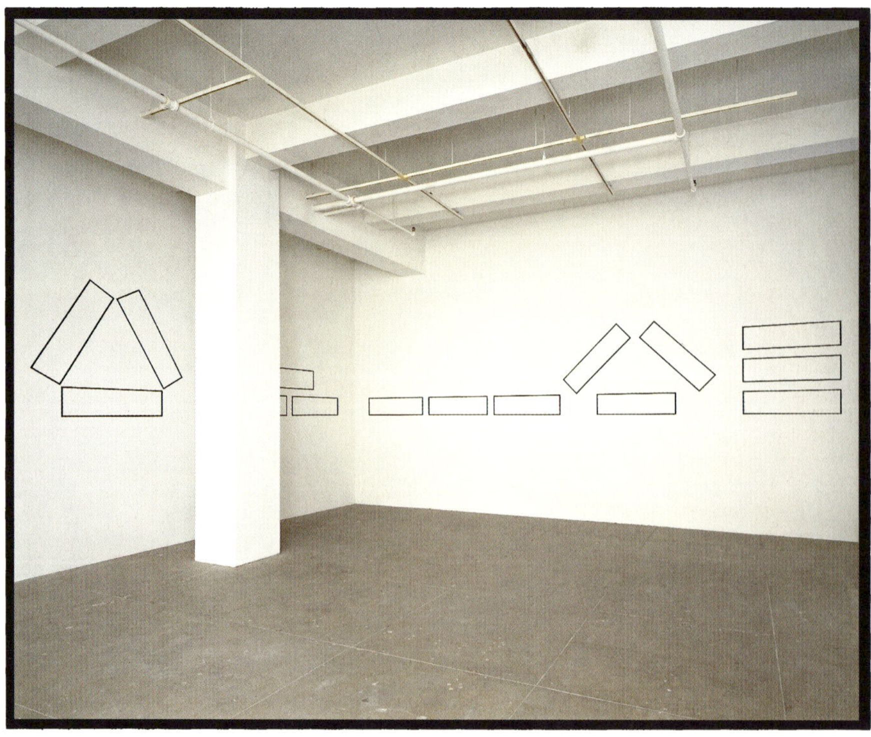

ONE QUART EXTERIOR GREEN INDUSTRIAL ENAMEL THROWN ON A BRICK WALL

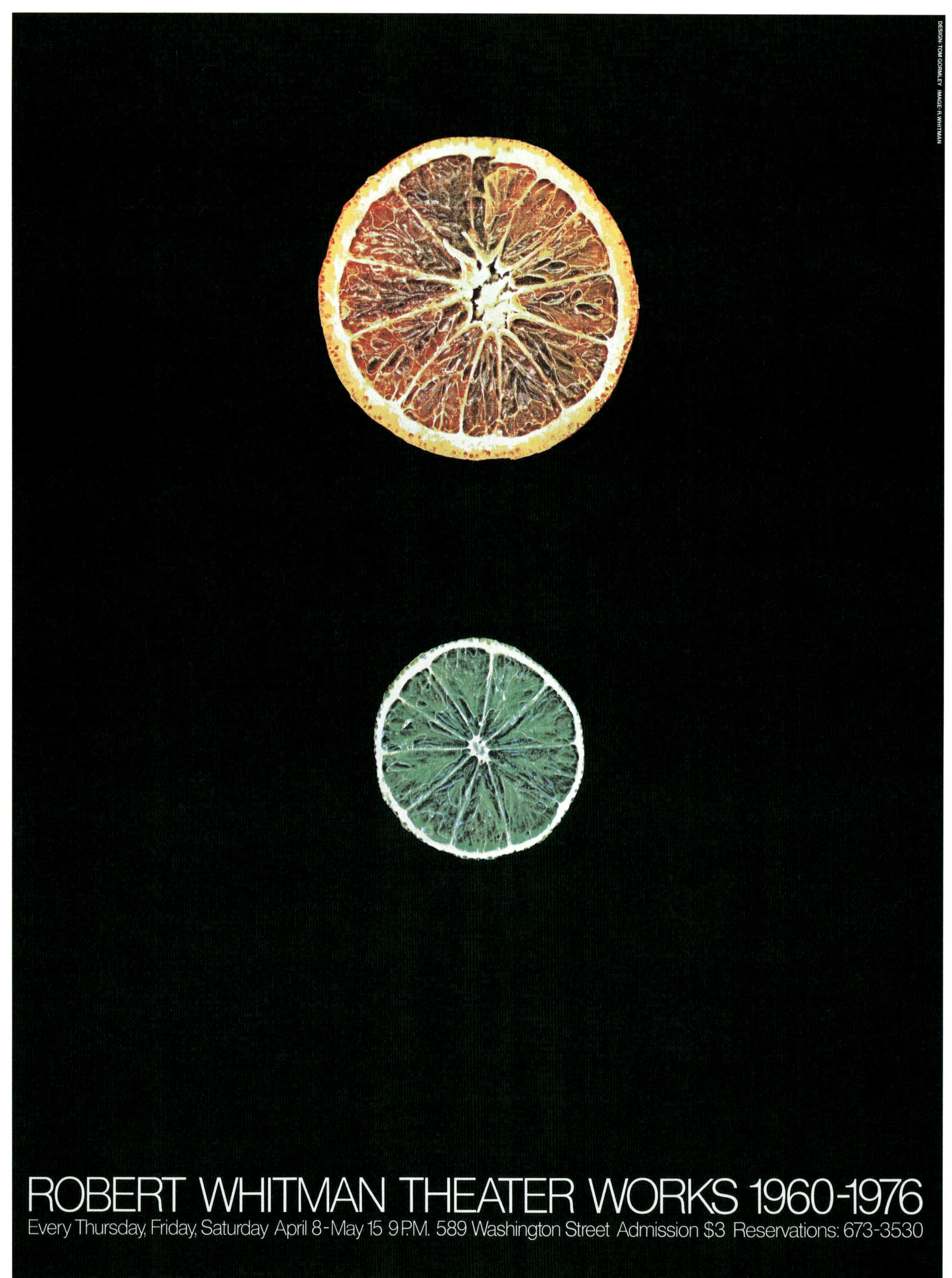
DESIGN: TOM GORMLEY IMAGE: R. WHITMAN
ROBERT WHITMAN THEATER WORKS 1960-1976
Every Thursday, Friday, Saturday April 8-May 15 9 P.M. 589 Washington Street Admission $3 Reservations: 673-3530

Robert Whitman

Robert Whitman was born in New York City in 1935. He studied literature at Rutgers University from 1953 to 1957 and art history at Columbia University in 1958. He began in the late 1950s to present performances and to exhibit his multimedia work in some of New York's more influential experimental galleries, including the Hansa, Reuben, and Martha Jackson galleries. With the scientists Fred Waldhauer and Billy Klüver and artist Robert Rauschenberg, Whitman founded, in 1966, Experiments in Art and Technology (E.A.T.), a loose-knit association that organized collaborations between artists and scientists. His one-person exhibitions include such venues as the Jewish Museum, New York (1968), the Museum of Contemporary Art, Chicago (1968), and the Museum of Modern Art, New York (1973). Dia organized a retrospective of Whitman's theater works in 1976. Several theater projects have also toured to various European venues, including the Moderna Museet, Stockholm (1987 and 1989) and the Centre Pompidou, Paris (2001 and 2002).

Poster for "Robert Whitman: Theater Works 1960–1976," 1976

Robert Whitman's pioneering performances of the early 1960s "alchemically transmuted the most quotidian objects and images into improbably fantastic events [imbued with] a magical, mythic aura."[1] Among the earliest in a coterie of heterogeneous artists who adopted the nascent idiom of performance on the cusp of the decade, Whitman soon devised a distinctive signature mode: in contrast to the assertively banal literalism fundamental to Allan Kaprow's Happenings and the louche ambience of street and gutter that was integral to those of Claes Oldenburg, his were distinguished by a poetics grounded in fugitive phantasms. A statement from the mid-1960s succinctly outlines his credo:

> *I intend my works to be stories of physical experience and realistic, naturalistic descriptions of the physical world. . . . At a certain point, fantasy is an object in the physical world. It is like a street or rain. It is a product of physical events. . . . The fantasy exists as an object, as a central physical entity, and as part of the story that you tell about other objects.*[2]

To distill the illusory as well as the actual into an oneiric physical reality, Whitman employed a variety of projected forms, ranging from cast shadows to slides to film, that mimicked, echoed, or presaged their material counterparts, themselves devised, typically, from makeshift props and improvised antics.

Critical to this hallucinatory vision was the inspiration he gleaned both from originary, atavistic, or visionary forms of theater—forms closer to ritual than to reportage—and from silent film.[3] Georges Méliès and Buster Keaton occupy the highest tier in his (otherwise anonymous) pantheon of the elect.[4] Lured by cinema's capacity to create a realm of wonder, a waking dream, with structural laws of its own, Whitman, like his predecessors, reveled in the editorial possibilities it offered for overlaying, suturing, and interweaving discrete fragments of the unexceptional with the uncanny.

Whitman's approach to performance was unique in this period in that he "scored" his works to permit subsequent presentation: few were strictly site specific. In place of the frenetic, almost violently aggressive spirit of such early works as *American Moon* (1960), *Prune Flat* (1965), his signature piece from the 1960s, is imbued with a lyrical reverie. A "realistic" dream in which the focus has veered from action to image, from the dramatic to the filmic, it probes a cinematic ontology through a cadence of events, actions, and images shorn of all narrative and text.

The momentum propelling this multimedia performance vanguard was undercut once mainstream organizations appropriated its innovations, stifling it in the process. Although Whitman remains committed to creating "theater works" (his preferred term for his performance pieces), in the mid-1960s he began to gravitate toward collaborations of other types. Turning to engineers, scientists, and related specialists, he explored more arcane optical effects and representations than those he had first broached in *Prune Flat*, still his most renowned theater piece. Among the most elegantly succinct of these is *Solid Red Line* (1967), in which a piercing light traces a horizontal plane across the ambience of the gallery, then rewinds, erasing itself. Soon, however, his persistent attraction to the transient and mutable effloresced into more diverse and encompassing installations.

The new alliances forged between artists interested in electronic technologies and scientists attracted by the possibility of working collaboratively in interdisciplinary exchanges fueled Experiments in Art and Technology (E.A.T.), founded in September 1966 by Whitman, Robert Rauschenberg, and scientists Fred Waldhauer and Billy Klüver. Its legendary *9 Evenings: Theater and Engineering*, held at the Sixty-ninth Regiment Armory, New York, in the fall of 1966, privileged innovative processes over resolved staging. The climax of the group's experimentation, however, was the spectacular pavilion commissioned by Pepsi-Cola for Expo '70 in Osaka in 1970, for which Whitman devised a vast mirrored dome—a site of uncanny apparitions, an evanescent realm of pure visuality.[5]

In 1976 a related but less technically ambitious work, *Untitled (Film Images, 1960–1976)*, had its debut on the occasion of a retrospective of Whitman's seminal performances, "Theater Works 1960–1976," commissioned by Dia. Its definitive form, retitled *Spyglass (Film Images, 1960–1976)* (realized in 2003), is configured as an octagon whose sides are made from four mirrors interspersed with four screens of the same dimensions on which film images are continuously projected. Multiplied endlessly in a *mise-en-abîme* of reflections of reflections, spectators lose themselves amid the myriad beautiful but lusciously perverse images: traffic slowly gliding backward across the street; a capsicum burning incandescently without disintegrating; glowing lights unearthed from the soil; matches flaring miraculously in water. The effect is one of a time outside time, "a kind of dream with meaning around the corners."[6]

Whitman's 1976 retrospective of theater works ended with *Light Touch*, a new commission. In reviving the spare vocabulary of simple props and costumes particular to *Prune Flat*, it too drew inspiration from its venue (a truck depot in this instance, an actual cinema in the case of its predecessor), which it made integral to the staging and the thematic of the piece. Characteristically, it is at once disarmingly simple yet psychically deep-rooted. Projected images of familiar commonplace objects—a brick, a cup, a burning paper bag—are "unloaded" from the back of the real vehicle pulling into a loading dock and carried through the space to be stacked neatly nearby, as, shortly after, are their physical counterparts. Once again, Whitman's abiding precept was to collaborate with the space, neither hiding it nor being governed by it as in site-specific work: "I either find some place to perform a piece [which requires] specific architecture, or I make a particular space consistent with the image of the work," he declared.[7]

For Whitman, issues relating to vision, whether figurations of visuality or modalities of perception, are not historically delimited but are constantly available for reexamination. "Optics is age-old, the Greeks knew about optics," he said in 1979, reflecting on his governing concerns.[8] In consequence, "hardware" has only ever been for him a means to an end: whether a work employs advanced technological equipment or makeshift secondhand materials, whether it involves transient actions or is confined to paper and graphite, is never significant in itself.[9] What counts, he contends, are the underlying abstract relationships that specify and individuate an experience—color, form, rhythm, the deep structure of time and space, condensed and distilled into what he has defined as the implicit "image" of any work.

L.C.

notes

1 Sally Banes, "Dream Time in a Warehouse," *The Village Voice*, November 23, 1982, p. 105.

2 Robert Whitman, "A Statement," in Michael Kirby, *Happenings: An Illustrated Anthology* (New York: E. P. Dutton, 1965), pp. 134, 135.

3 Parallels have been made between Whitman's practices and Antonin Artaud's theories on theater. Although Whitman did not read it until much later, Artaud's *La théâter et son double* (*The Theater and Its Double*), 1938—first published in the United States by Grove Press in 1958—was widely acclaimed by others close to him.

4 See Mimi Crossley, "Artistic Image-Maker Robert Whitman Bringing Visual Theater to Houston," *The Houston Post*, November 26, 1977, p. 126.

5 See *Pavilion: Experiments in Art and Technology*, eds. Billy Klüver, Julie Martin, and Barbara Rose (New York: Dutton, 1972).

6 This suggestive phrase was coined by Harriet Janis and Rudi Blesh with respect to *American Moon* (1960), Whitman's first important performance, which they found "mysterious out of all proportion." See Janis and Blesh, *Collage: Personalities, Concepts, Techniques* (Philadelphia: Chilten, 1967), p. 276.

7 Whitman, typescript, n.d., Dia Art Foundation archive. For the 1976 retrospective, *American Moon, Prune Flat*, and the four additional works on the program were adapted to the temporary site, a Lower Manhattan warehouse, in anticipation of their future relocation to a dedicated performance venue purchased and converted by Dia at 512 West Nineteenth Street in Manhattan, today the home of The Kitchen: Center for Video, Music, Dance, Performance, Film, and Literature.

8 Whitman, quoted in Barbara Rose, "Interview with Robert Whitman," in *Robert Whitman: Palisade* (Yonkers: The Hudson River Museum, 1979), n.p.

9 Whitman had first conceived a project based on Dante's *Divine Comedy* while a student at Rutgers in the mid-1950s. Focusing on its part *Paradise*, the *Dante Drawings*, 1974–75, were finally realized concurrently with his performance retrospective. Featuring an iconography of elementary, even rudimentary, motifs that relates as much to the romantic Sublime as to the visions of outsider artists, this unprecedented suite of twenty-seven double-sided sheets reprises Whitman's abiding fascination with the speculative, the mysterious, and the wondrous. The fantastical dreamworld of sublimated desire—sometimes atavistic, sometimes futuristic—that gave his early work its indelible magic is transformed here into a mystical meditation on Dante's account of what he experienced in a state of "Pure Vision," a state that in being beyond time and space almost defies recollection and communicability.

pages 310–311 *Dante Drawings*, 1974–75

pages 312–315 *Prune Flat*, 1965, performance at Dia's 1976 Retrospective

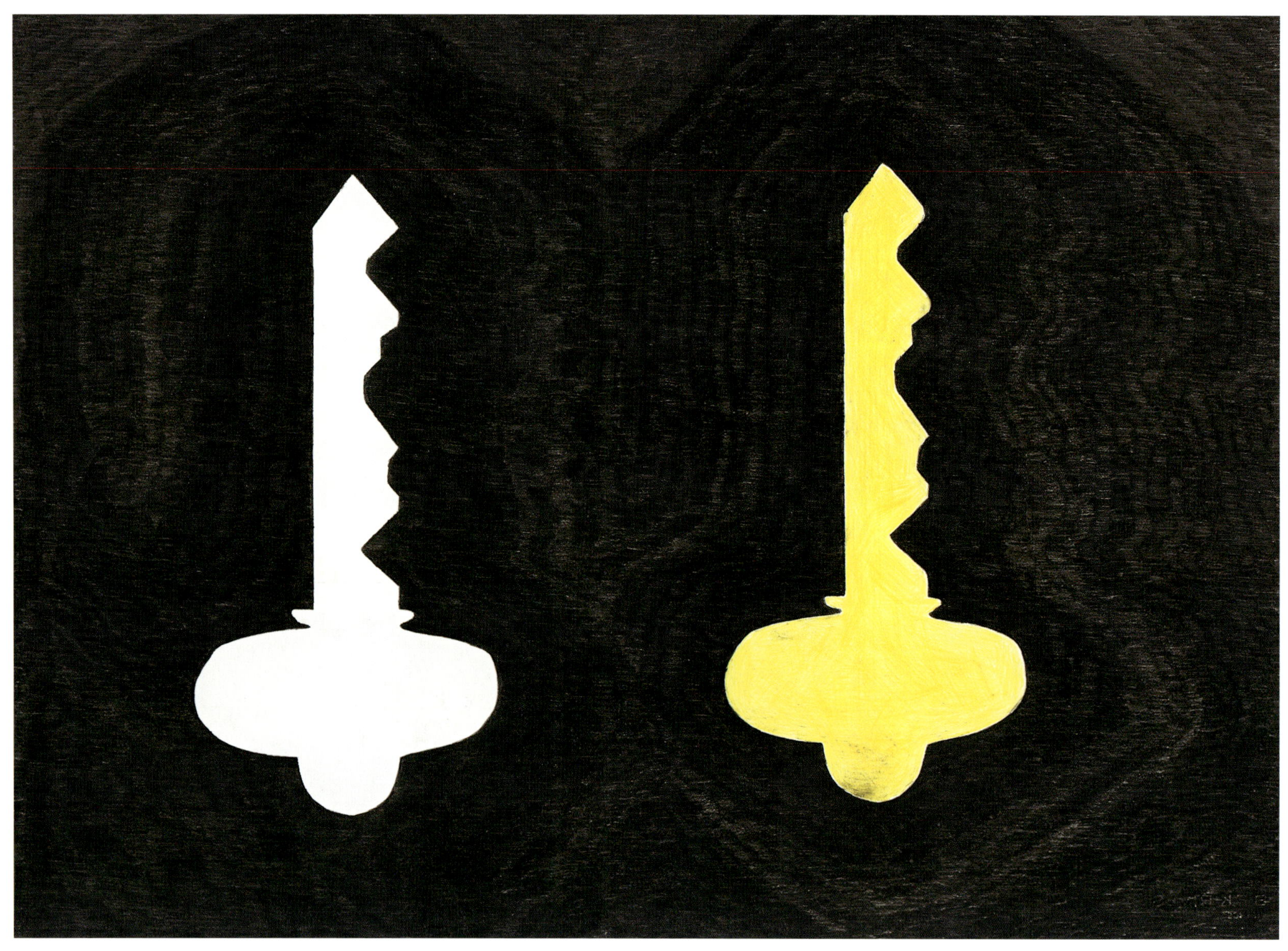

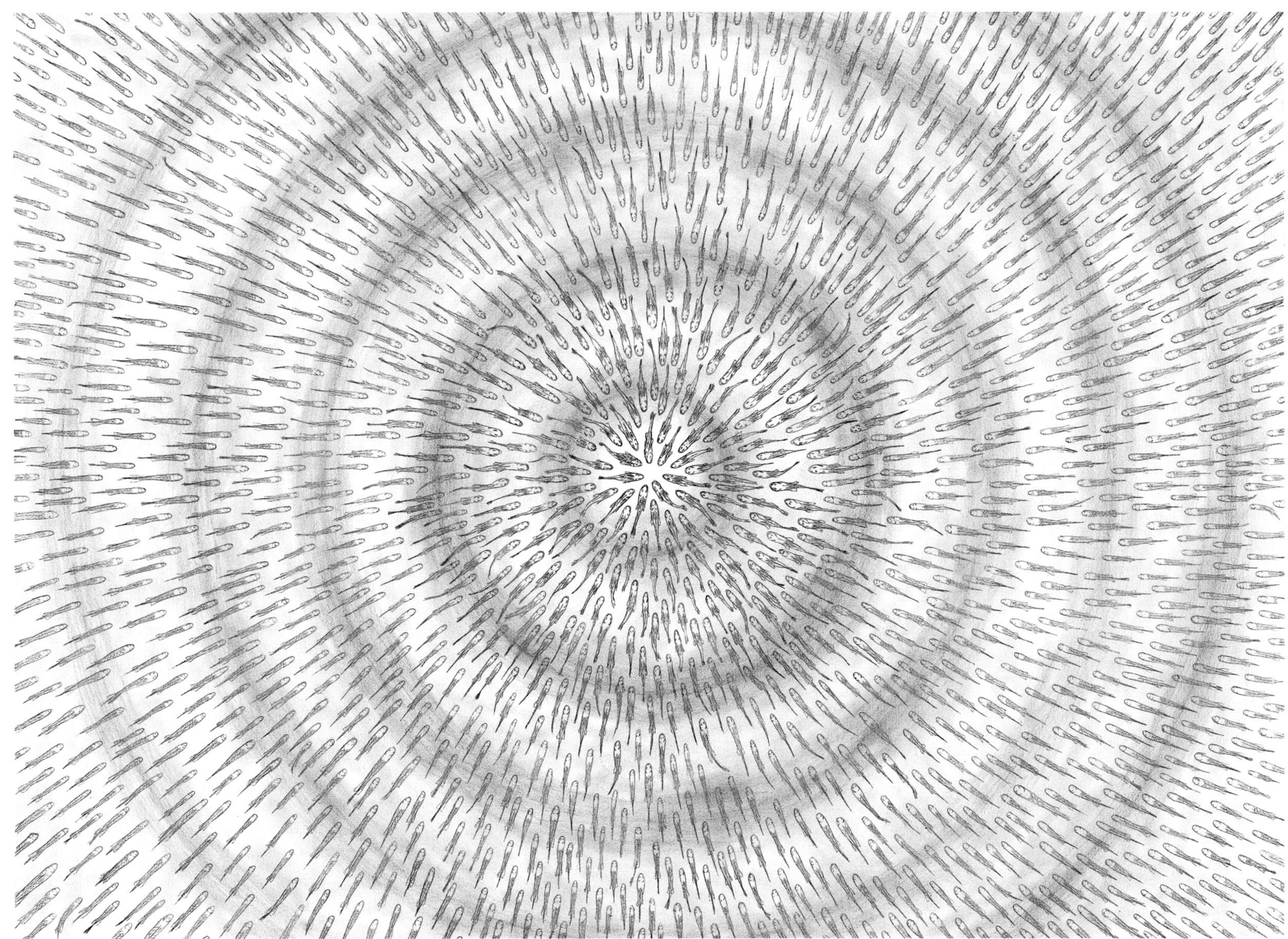

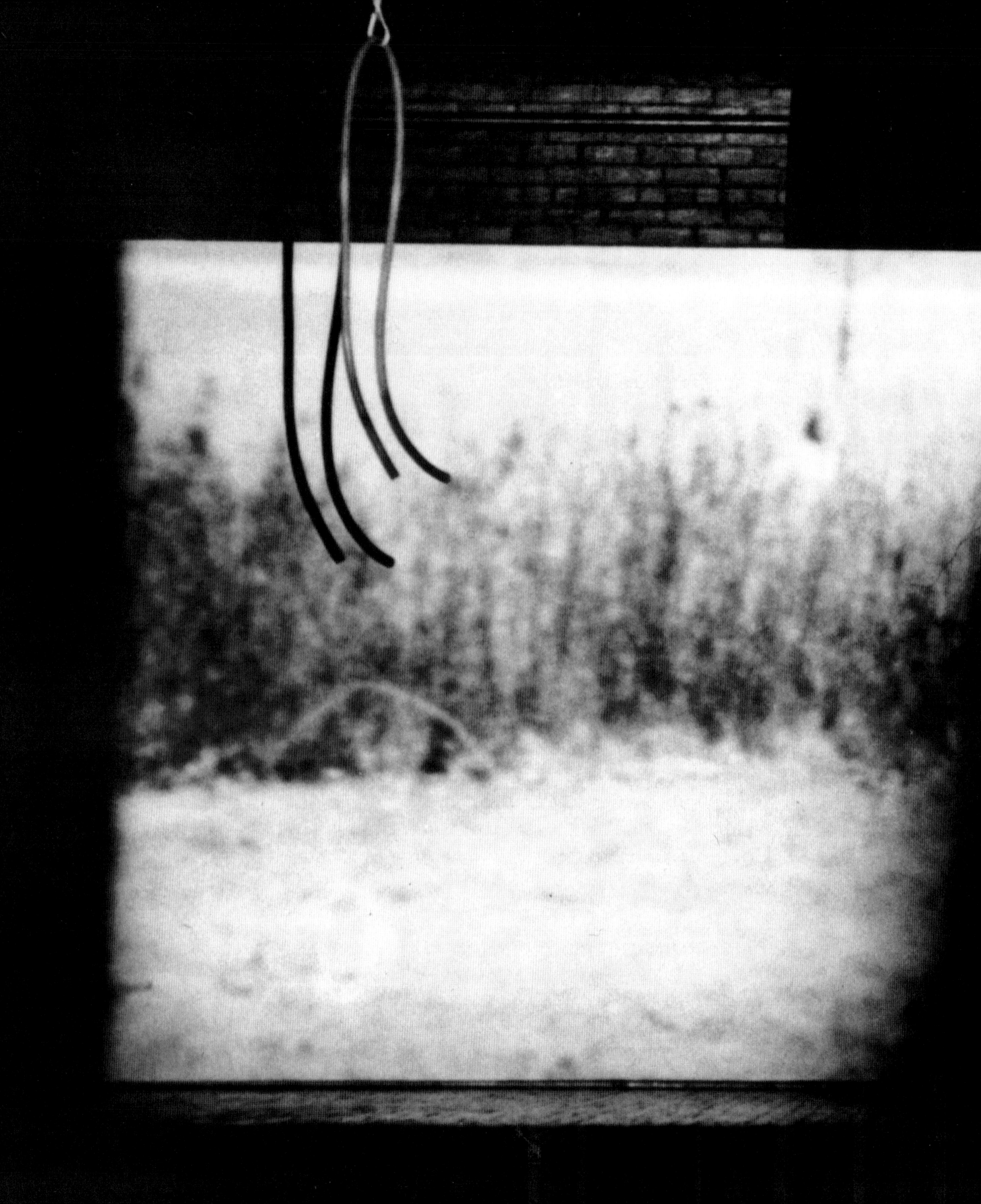

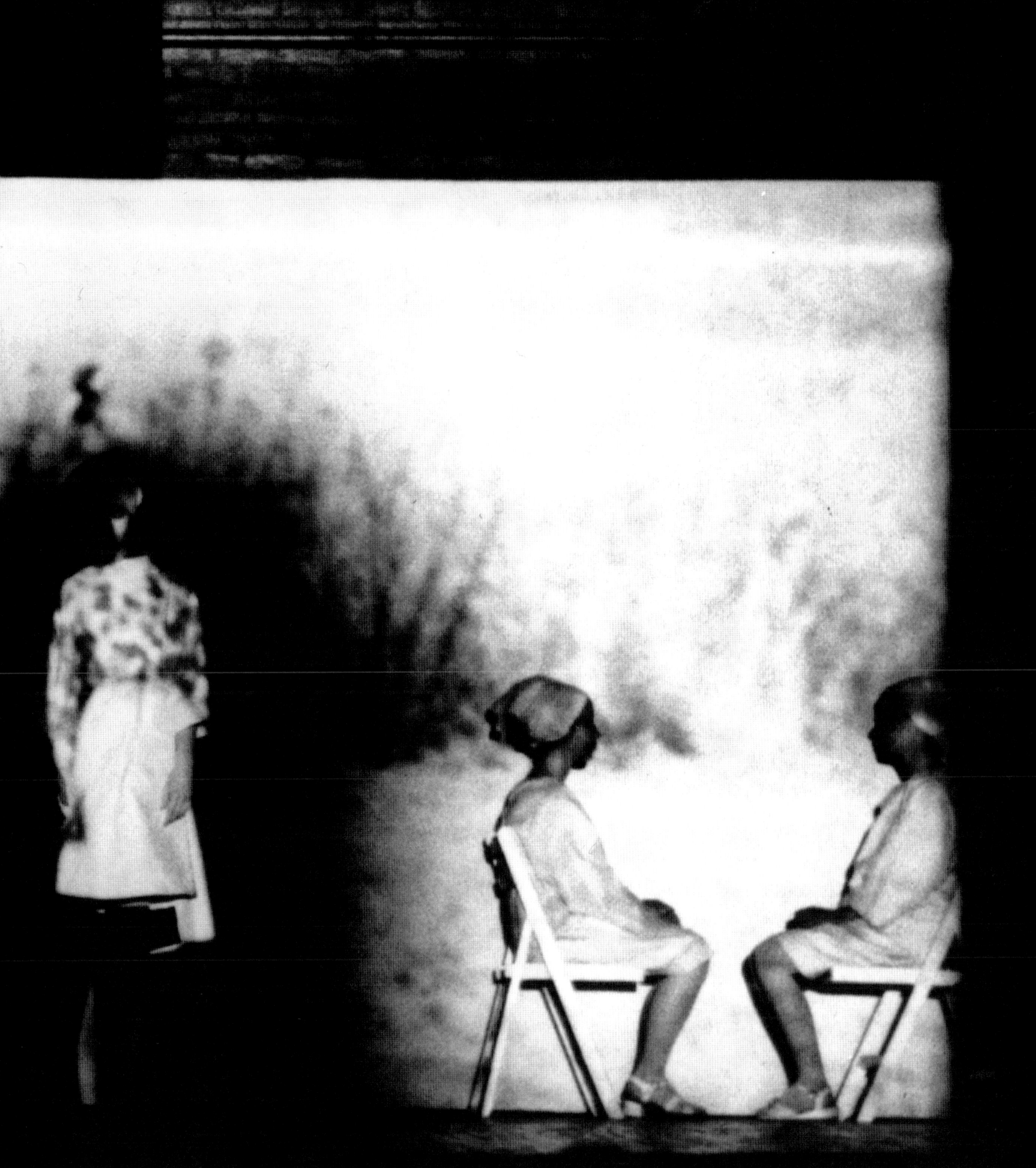

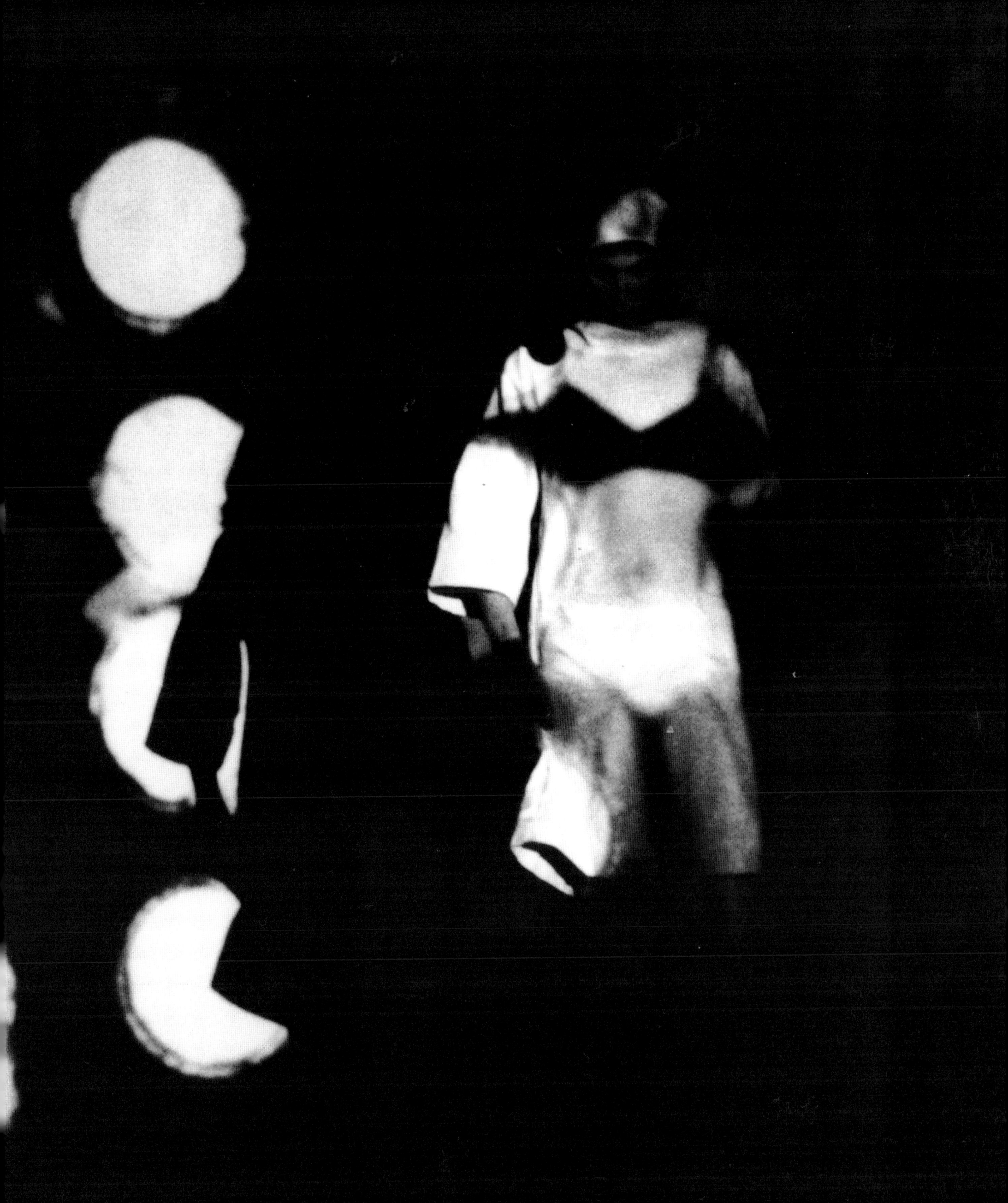

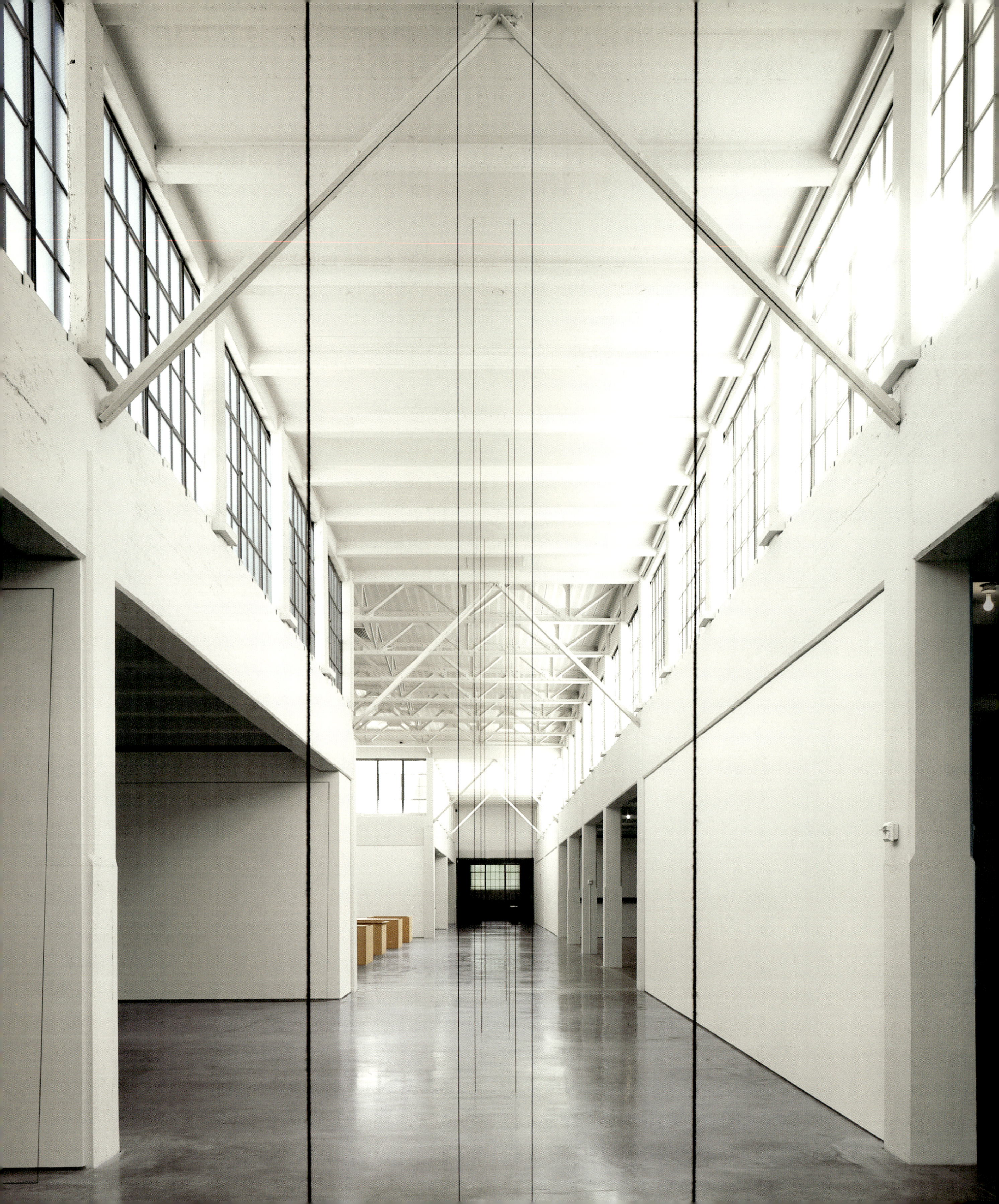

Selected Bibliographies

BERND AND HILLA BECHER

Bernd und Hilla Becher: Anonyme Skulptur. Eine Typologie technischer Bauten. Düsseldorf: Art-Press Verlag, 1970.

Bernd and Hilla Becher. London: Arts Council of Great Britain, 1974. Text by Lynda Morris.

Bernd & Hilla Becher: Pennsylvania Coal Mine Tipples. New York: Dia Center for the Arts, 1992. Introduction by Bernd and Hilla Becher.

Lange, Susanne. *Bernd und Hilla Becher: Häuser und Hallen*. Frankfurt am Main: Museum für Moderne Kunst, 1992.

Bernd and Hilla Becher: Basic Forms. New York: teNeues Publishing Company, 1999. Text by Thierry de Duve.

Bernd und Hilla Becher: Festschrift. Erasmuspreis 2002. Ed. Susanne Lange. Munich: Schirmer/Mosel, 2002. Texts by Jean-Christophe Ammann, Els Barents, Klaus Bußmann, Rudi Fuchs, Candida Höfer, Klaus Honnef, Douglas Huebler, Volker Kahmen, Susanne Lange, Karl Ruhrberg, Lothar Schirmer, Illeana Sonnabend, and Armin Zweite.

JOSEPH BEUYS

Joseph Beuys. New York: Solomon R. Guggenheim Museum, 1979. Texts by Joseph Beuys and Caroline Tisdall.

Joseph Beuys: Life and Works. Ed. Götz Adriani, Winfried Konnetz, and Karin Thomas. Trans. Patricia Lech. Woodbury, N.Y.: Barron's, 1979.

Joseph Beuys: Skulpturen und Objekte. Ed. Heiner Bastian. Berlin: Martin Gropius Bau, in association with Schirmer/Mosel, Munich, 1988. Texts by Götz Adriani, Heiner Bastian, Franz Joseph van der Grinten, Franz-Xaver Kaufmann, Helmut Martin, Karin v. Maur, Thomas McEvilley, Theodora Vischer, and Armin Zweite.

Joseph Beuys: Arena—where would I have got if I had been intelligent! Ed. Lynne Cooke and Karen Kelly. New York: Dia Center for the Arts, in association with Distributed Arts Publishers/D.A.P., New York, 1994. Texts by Lynne Cooke, Pamela Kort, and Christopher Phillips.

Joseph Beuys: Drawings After the Codices Madrid of Leonardo da Vinci. Ed. Lynne Cooke and Karen Kelly. New York: Dia Center for the Arts, in association with Richter Verlag, Düsseldorf, 1998. Texts by Lynne Cooke, Martin Kemp, Cornelia Lauf, and Ann Temkin.

Joseph Beuys: Mapping the Legacy. Ed. Gene Ray. Sarasota, Fla.: The John and Mable Ringling Museum of Art, in association with Distributed Arts Publishers/D.A.P., New York, 2001. Texts by Lukas Beckmann, Benjamin H. D. Buchloh, Mel Chin, Pamela Kort, Kim Levin, Peter Nisbet, Gene Ray, Max Reithmann, and Joan Rothfuss, and an interview by Georg Jappe.

LOUISE BOURGEOIS

Louise Bourgeois. Ed. Deborah Wye. New York: The Museum of Modern Art, 1982. Text by Deborah Wye.

Louise Bourgeois: The Locus of Memory. Works 1982–1993. Ed. Joanna Ekman. Brooklyn: The Brooklyn Museum, 1994. Texts by Charlotta Kotik, Terrie Sultan, and Christian Leigh.

Louise Bourgeois: Sculptures, environnements, dessins 1938–1995. Paris: Musée d'art moderne de la ville de Paris, 1995. Texts by Lynne Cooke, Alain Cueff, Béatrice Parent, and Robert Storr. (Published in German by Deichtorhallen, Hamburg, in 1996.)

Louise Bourgeois: Blue Days and Pink Days. Ed. Jerry Gorovoy and Pandora Tabatabai Asbaghi. Milan: Fondazione Prada, 1997. Text by Paulo Herkenhoff.

Louise Bourgeois: Destruction of the Father, Reconstruction of the Father. Writings and Interviews 1923–1997. Ed. Marie-Laure Bernadac and Hans-Ulrich Obrist. London: Violette Editions, 1998. Texts by Marie-Laure Bernadac and Hans-Ulrich Obrist.

Louise Bourgeois: Memory and Architecture. Madrid: Museo Nacional Centro de Arte Reina Sofía, 1999. Texts by Mieke Bal and Jennifer Bloomer, Beatriz Colomina, Lynne Cooke, Jerry Gorovoy and Danielle Tilkin, Joseph Helfenstein, and Christiane Terrisse.

JOHN CHAMBERLAIN

John Chamberlain: A Retrospective Exhibition. Ed. Diane Waldman. New York: Solomon R. Guggenheim Museum, 1971. Interviews by Elizabeth C. Baker, Donald Judd, and Diane Waldman.

John Chamberlain: Reliefs, 1960–1982. Sarasota, Fla.: The John and Mable Ringling Museum of Art, 1983. Text and interview by Michael Auping.

John Chamberlain: A Catalogue Raisonné of the Sculpture, 1954–1985. Ed. Julie Sylvester. New York: Hudson Hills Press, in association with The Museum of Contemporary Art, Los Angeles, 1986. Text by Klaus Kertess.

John Chamberlain: Gondolas and Dooms Day Flotilla. New York: Dia Center for the Arts, 1991. Interviews by Julie Sylvester and Lawrence Weiner.

John Chamberlain. Baden-Baden: Staatliche Kunsthalle, in association with Cantz, Ostfildern, 1991. Texts by Angelika Beckmann, John Chamberlain, Donald Judd, and Jochen Poetter.
DeKooning, Chamberlain: Influence and Transformation. New York: PaceWildenstein, 2001. Text by Bernice Rose.

HANNE DARBOVEN

Lippard, Lucy R. "Hanne Darboven: Deep in Numbers." *Artforum* 12, no. 2 (October 1973), pp. 35–39.

Pohlen, Annelie. "Hanne Darboven's Time: The Content of Consciousness." *Artforum* 21, no. 8 (April 1983), pp. 52–53.

Fred Sandback, *Untitled* (from *Ten Vertical Constructions*), 1977/2003

Bordaz, Jean-Pierre. "Hanne Darboven, or the Dimension of Time and Culture." *Parkett* 10 (September 1986), pp. 104–11.

Hanne Darboven: Primitive Time/Clock Time. Philadelphia: Goldie Paley Gallery, Moore College of Art and Design, 1990. Texts by Coosje van Bruggen, Klaus Honnef, and Elsa Longhauser, and an interview by Amine Haase.

Hanne Darboven: Kulturgeschichte 1880–1983. Cologne: Walther König, in association with Edition Cantz, Ostfildern, 2002.

Newman, Michael. "Remembering and Repeating: Hanne Darboven's Work." In *Robert Lehman Lectures on Contemporary Art*, vol. 2. Ed. Lynne Cooke and Karen Kelly. New York: Dia Center for the Arts, 2003.

WALTER DE MARIA

Hess, Thomas B. "Walter De Maria, or the Emperor's New Cat Box." *New York*, 31 October 1977, pp. 102–03.

Smith, Roberta. "De Maria: Elements." *Art in America* 66, no. 3 (May–June 1978), pp. 103–05.

De Maria, Walter. "The Lightning Field." *Artforum* 18, no. 8 (April 1980), pp. 52–59.

Walter De Maria: Two Very Large Presentations. Stockholm: Moderna Museet, 1989. Texts by J. C. Cooper, Olle Granath, Pontus Hultén, Cecilia Lindqvist, Lars Nittve, Mario Perniola, and Ingrid Rein.

Wakefield, Neville. "Walter De Maria: Measure and Substance." *Flash Art* 28, no. 182 (May–June 1995), pp. 91–94.

Walter De Maria: 1999 Milano 2000. Milan: Fondazione Prada, 1999. Text by Germano Celant.

DAN FLAVIN

Dan Flavin: fluorescent light etc. Ottawa: National Gallery of Canada for the Queen's Printer, 1969. Texts by Mel Bochner, Dan Flavin, Donald Judd, and Brydon Smith.

"monuments" for V. Tatlin from Dan Flavin, 1964–1982. Chicago: Donald Young Gallery in association with The Museum of Contemporary Art, Los Angeles, and Leo Castelli Gallery, New York, 1989. Text by Dan Flavin.

Dan Flavin. Buenos Aires: Fundación Proa, 1998. Texts by Dan Flavin, Michael Govan, and Julio Sánchez.

Cattedrali d'Arte: Dan Flavin per Santa Maria in Chiesa Rossa. Ed. Germano Celant. Milan: Fondazione Prada, 1998. Texts by Carlo Bertelli, Christine Buci-Glucksmann, Germano Celant, Hubert Damish, Renato Diez, Michael Govan, Vittorio Gregotti, Fulvio Irace, Pierluigi Lia, Mario Perniola, Pier Paolo Rinaldi, and Gianni Vattimo.

Dan Flavin: The Architecture of Light. Ed. J. Fiona Ragheb. New York: Solomon R. Guggenheim Foundation, 1999. Texts by Tiffany Bell, Frances Colpitt, Jonathan Crary, Dan Flavin, Michael Govan, Joseph Kosuth, Michael Newman, J. Fiona Ragheb, and Brydon E. Smith.

Dan Flavin. London: Serpentine Gallery, 2001. Text by Michael Govan.

MICHAEL HEIZER

Michael Heizer. Essen: Museum Folkwang, in association with the Rijksmuseum Kröller-Müller, Otterlo, 1979. Texts by Zdenek Felix, Michael Heizer, and Ellen Joosten.

Michael Heizer: Sculpture in Reverse. Ed. Julia Brown. Los Angeles: Museum of Contemporary Art, 1984. Texts by Rainer Crone, Paula Deitz, Barbara Heizer, and Sam Wagstaff, and an interview by Julia Brown.

Michael Heizer: Dragged Mass Geometric. New York: Whitney Museum of American Art, 1985. Interview by David Whitney.

McGill, Douglas C. *Michael Heizer: Effigy Tumuli.* New York: Abrams, 1990.

Michael Heizer: Double Negative—Sculpture in the Land. New York: Rizzoli, in association with The Museum of Contemporary Art, Los Angeles, and the Nevada Institute for Contemporary Art at the University of Nevada, Las Vegas, 1991. Text by Mark C. Taylor.

Michael Heizer. Milan: Fondazione Prada, 1996. Text by Germano Celant.

ROBERT IRWIN

Robert Irwin. New York: The Jewish Museum, 1968. Text by John Coplans.

Robert Irwin. Chicago: Museum of Contemporary Art, 1975. Text by Ira Licht.

Robert Irwin. New York: Whitney Museum of American Art, 1977. Text by Robert Irwin.

Irwin, Robert. *Being and Circumstance: Notes toward a Conditional Art.* Ed. Lawrence Weschler. Larkspur Landing, Calif.: Lapis Press, in conjunction with the Pace Gallery and the San Francisco Museum of Modern Art, 1985.

Robert Irwin. Ed. Russell Ferguson. Los Angeles: The Museum of Contemporary Art, in association with Rizzoli, New York, 1993. Texts by Arthur C. Danto, Jeremy Gilbert-Rolfe, Robert Irwin, Klaus Kertess, John Hallmark Neff, Lawrence Weschler, and Sally Yard.

Robert Irwin: Getty Garden. Los Angeles: The J. Paul Getty Museum, 2002. Text and interview by Lawrence Weschler.

DONALD JUDD

Donald Judd. Ottawa: National Programme of the National Gallery of Canada, 1975. Catalogue raisonné by Brydon Smith. Texts by Dan Flavin and Roberta Smith.

Donald Judd: Complete Writings, 1959–1975. Ed. Kasper Koenig. Halifax: The Press of Nova Scotia College of Art and Design, in association with New York University Press, New York, 1975.

Donald Judd: Complete Writings, 1975–1986. Eindhoven: Van Abbemuseum, 1987.

Judd, Donald. *Architektur*. Ed. Marianne Stockebrand. Trans. Brigitte Kalthoff. Münster: Westfälischer Kunstverein, 1989.

Donald Judd: Sculpture 1991. Trans. Gregory Sims. New York: Pace Gallery, 1991. Text by Yve-Alain Bois.

Donald Judd: Early Fabricated Work. New York: PaceWildenstein, 1998. Texts by Rosalind E. Krauss and Robert Smithson.

ON KAWARA

On Kawara: Date Paintings in 89 Cities. Rotterdam: Museum Boymans Van Beuningen, 1991. Texts by Teresa O'Connor, Anne Rorimer, and Karel Schampers.

Kawara, On. *I Went, I Met, I Read. Journal: 1969*. 4 vols. Cologne: Walther König, 1992.

On Kawara: Whole and Parts, 1964–1995. Ed. Xavier Douroux and Franck Gautherot. Villeurbanne: Institut d'art contemporain, in association with Les presses du réel, Paris, 1996. Texts by On Kawara et al.

Wall, Jeff. "Monochrome and Photojournalism in On Kawara's Today Paintings." In *Robert Lehman Lectures on Contemporary Art*, vol. 1. Ed. Lynne Cooke and Karen Kelly. New York: Dia Center for the Arts, 1996, pp. 135–156.

Kawara, On. *One Million Years (Future)*. New York: Dia Center for the Arts, 1999. Audio CD.

On Kawara. London: Phaidon, 2002. Texts by René Denizot, Stuart Hameroff and Roger Penrose, Jonathan Watkins, et al.

IMI KNOEBEL

Wechsler, Max. "Imi Knoebel: Kunstmuseum, Winterthur." *Artforum* 22, no. 2 (October 1983), p. 86.

Imi Knoebel. New York: Dia Art Foundation, 1987. Texts by Franz Dahlem, Kubinski/Dubost, Katharina Schmidt, and Johannes Stüttgen.

Schenker, Christoph. "Imi Knoebel: The Limits of Communicability." *Flash Art*, no. 161 (November–December 1991), pp. 103–07.

Imi Knoebel: Oeuvres de 1968 à 1996. Grenoble: Musée de Grenoble, 1996. Texts by Rudi Fuchs, Serge Lemoine, Johannes Stüttgen, and Max Wechsler.

Imi Knoebel: Genter Raum. Düsseldorf: Kulturstiftung der Länder, with the Kunstsammlung Nordrhein-Westfalen, 2001. Text by Anette Kruszynski.

SOL LEWITT

Krauss, Rosalind E. "LeWitt in Progress." *October*, no. 6 (Fall 1978), pp. 46–60.

Sol LeWitt. Ed. Alicia Legg. New York: The Museum of Modern Art, New York, 1978. Essays by Lucy R. Lippard, Bernice Rose, and Robert Rosenblum.

Sol LeWitt: Wall Drawings 1984–1992. Bern: Kunsthalle, 1992. Text by Ulrich Loock.

Sol LeWitt. Structures 1962–93. Oxford: The Museum of Modern Art, 1993. Texts by David Batchelor, David Elliott, Chrissie Iles, and Rosalind E. Krauss.

Sol LeWitt: Critical Texts. Ed. Adachiara Zevi. Rome: Libri de AEIOU, 1995.

Sol LeWitt: A Retrospective. Ed. Gary Garrels. San Francisco: San Francisco Museum of Modern Art, in association with Yale University Press, New Haven, 2000. Texts by Martin Friedman, Andrea Miller-Keller, Brenda Richardson, Anne Rorimer, John S. Weber, and Adam D. Weinberg.

AGNES MARTIN

Agnes Martin. Philadelphia: Institute of Contemporary Art, University of Pennsylvania, 1973. Texts by Lawrence Alloway, Agnes Martin, and Ann Wilson.

Agnes Martin: Paintings and Drawings, 1957–1975. London: Arts Council of Great Britain, 1977. Texts by Dore Ashton and Agnes Martin.

Agnes Martin: Writings—Schriften. Ed. Dieter Schwarz. Winterthur: Kunstmuseum Winterthur, in association with Edition Cantz, Ostfildern-Ruit, 1991.

Agnes Martin. New York: Whitney Museum of American Art, New York, 1992. Texts by Anna C. Chave, Barbara Haskell, Rosalind E. Krauss, and Agnes Martin.

Simon, Joan. "Perfection Is in the Mind: An Interview with Agnes Martin." *Art in America* 84, no. 5 (May 1996), pp. 82–89, 124.

Agnes Martin: Paintings and Writings. New York: PaceWildenstein, 2000. Texts by Arne Glimcher and Agnes Martin.

BRUCE NAUMAN

Bruce Nauman: Work from 1965 to 1972. Los Angeles: Los Angeles County Museum of Art, in association with Praeger, New York, 1972. Texts by Jane Livingston and Marcia Tucker.

Bruce Nauman: Neons. Baltimore: The Baltimore Museum of Art, 1982. Text by Brenda Richardson.

van Bruggen, Coosje. *Bruce Nauman*. New York: Rizzoli, 1988.

Bruce Nauman. Ed. Joan Simon. Minneapolis: Walker Art Center, in association with Distributed Art Publishers/D.A.P., New York, 1994. Catalogue raisonné and texts by Neal Benezra, Kathy Halbreich, Paul Schimmel, and Robert Storr.

Bruce Nauman: Interviews, 1967–1988. Ed. Christine Hoffmann. Dresden: Verlag der Kunst, 1996.

Gary Hill, Bruce Nauman: International New Media Art. Canberra: National Gallery of Australia, 2002. Texts by Lynne Cooke, George Quasha, and Jörg Zutter.

BLINKY PALERMO

Rorimer, Anne. "Blinky Palermo: Objects, 'Stoffbilder,' Wall Paintings." *Artforum* 12, no. 3 (November 1978), pp. 28–35.

Blinky Palermo. New York: Dia Art Foundation, 1987. Text by Gary Garrels.

Blinky Palermo. New York: Sperone Westwater, 1987. Text by Anne Rorimer.

Blinky Palermo. Leipzig: Galerie für Zeitgenössische Kunst and Museum der Bildenden Künste, in association with Edition Cantz, Ostfildern, 1993. Texts by Bernhard Bürgi, Johannes Cladders, Erich Franz, Laszlo Glozer, Susanne Küper, Thomas Alfred Lange, Bernhart Schwenk, Dierk Stemmler, Max Wechsler, and Klaus Werner.

Palermo: Werkverzeichnis, 2 vols. Ed. Thordis Moeller. Bonn: Kunstmuseum, in association with Oktagon Verlag, Stuttgart, 1995. Texts by Thordis Moeller, Klaus Schrenk, and Christoph Schreier.

Palermo: To the People of New York City. Basel: Öffentliche Kunstsammlung Basel, Museum für Gegenwartskunst, 1995. Texts by Frank O'Hara and Katharina Schmidt.

GERHARD RICHTER

von Drathen, Doris. "Gerhard Richter: Les pouvoirs de l'abstraction." *Les Cahiers du Musée National d'Art Moderne* (Paris) 40 (Summer 1992), pp. 67–85.

Gerhard Richter: Catalogue Raisonné of Paintings and Sculptures 1962–1993, 3 vols. Ed. Benjamin H. D. Buchloh and Kasper König. Bonn: Bundeskunsthalle, and Musée d'art moderne de la ville de Paris, 1993.

Wood, Paul. "Truth and Beauty: The Ruined Abstraction of Gerhard Richter." In *Art Has No History*. Ed. John Roberts. London: Verso, 1994, pp. 180–99.

Gerhard Richter: The Daily Practice of Painting. Writings and Interviews 1962–1993. Ed. Hans-Ulrich Obrist. Cambridge, Mass.: The MIT Press, in association with Anthony d'Offay Gallery, London, 1995.

Fer, Briony. "Postscript: Vision and Blindness." In *On Abstract Art*. New Haven, Conn.: Yale University Press, 1997, pp. 153–69.

Buchloh, Benjamin H. D. "Gerhard Richter's *Eight Gray*: Between *Vorschein and Glanz*." In *Gerhard Richter: Eight Gray 2002*. Berlin: Deutsche Guggenheim, 2002, pp. 13–28.

ROBERT RYMAN

Robert Ryman. London: Whitechapel Art Gallery, 1977. Texts by Robert Ryman and Naomi Spector.

Robert Ryman. Paris: Centre Georges Pompidou, 1981. Texts by Yve-Alain Bois and Christel Sauer.

Robert Ryman. New York: Dia Art Foundation, 1988. Interview by Gary Garrels.

Robert Ryman: New Paintings. New York: Pace Gallery, 1990. Text by Yve-Alain Bois.

Robert Ryman. Paris: Espace d'art contemporain, in association with Hallen für neue Kunst, Schaffhausen, 1991. Texts by Urs Raussmüller, Robert Ryman, Christel Sauer, and Robert Storr.

Robert Ryman. New York: The Museum of Modern Art, in association with Tate Gallery, London, 1993. Text by Robert Storr.

FRED SANDBACK

74 Front Street: The Fred Sandback Museum, Winchendon, Massachusetts. New York: Dia Art Foundation, 1982. Text by Fred Sandback.

Fred Sandback: Diagonal Constructions/Broken Lines. Skulpturen und Zeichnungen. Hannover: Kestner-Gesellschaft, 1987. Texts by Carsten Ahrens, Carl Haenlein, and Fred Sandback.

Fred Sandback: Sculpture. New Haven, Conn.: Yale University Art Gallery, in association with Contemporary Arts Museum, Houston, 1991. Texts by Suzanne Delehanty, Richard S. Field, Sasha M. Newman, and Phyllis Tuchman.

Fred Sandback. Bregenz: Kunstverein, 1997. Interview by Joan Simon.

Fred Sandback Escultura. Mexico City: Museo Rufino Tamayo, 2002. Text by Lynne Cooke and an interview by Joan Simon.

Taylor, Mark C. "Apprehension." In *Robert Lehman Lectures on Contemporary Art*, vol. 2. Ed. Lynne Cooke and Karen Kelly. New York: Dia Center for the Arts, 2003.

RICHARD SERRA

Richard Serra: Sculpture. Ed. Laura Rosenstock. New York: The Museum of Modern Art, 1986. Texts by Douglas Crimp and Rosalind E. Krauss.

Richard Serra: Writings, Interviews. Chicago: The University of Chicago Press, 1994. Texts by Richard Serra. Interviews by Friedrich Teja Bach, Liza Bear, Patricia Bickers, Lizzie Borden, Lynne Cooke, Douglas Crimp, Peter Eisenmann, Mark Francis, Bernard Lamarche-Vadel, Annette Michelson, Robert C. Morgan, Alfred Pacquement, Brenda Richardson, Mark Rosenthal, Nicholas Serota, David Sylvester, and Clara Weyergraf.

Richard Serra: Torqued Ellipses. New York: Dia Center for the Arts, 1997. Text by Mark C. Taylor, and an interview by Lynne Cooke and Michael Govan.

Richard Serra: Sculpture, 1985–1998. Los Angeles: Museum of Contemporary Art, 1998. Text by Hal Foster, and an interview by David Sylvester.

Richard Serra. Ed. Hal Foster and Gordon Hughes. Cambridge, Mass.: The MIT Press, 2000. Texts by Yve-Alain Bois, Benjamin H. D. Buchloh, Douglas Crimp, Hal Foster, Rosalind E. Krauss, and Annette Michelson.

Richard Serra: Torqued Spirals, Toruses and Spheres. New York: Gagosian Gallery, 2001. Text by Hal Foster.

ROBERT SMITHSON

Robert Smithson: Sculpture. Ed. Robert Hobbs. Ithaca: Cornell University Press, 1981. Texts by Lawrence Alloway, John Coplans, Robert Hobbs, and Lucy R. Lippard.

Robert Smithson: Photo Works. Los Angeles: Los Angeles County Museum of Art, in association with University of New Mexico Press, Albuquerque, 1993. Text by Robert A. Sobieszek.

Robert Smithson: Operations on Nature. Toronto: Art Gallery of Ontario, 1994. Texts by Iain Baxter, Robert Fones, Rodney Graham, and Matthew Teitelbaum.

Smithson, Robert. *The Collected Writings*. Ed. Jack Flam. Berkeley: University of California Press, 1996. Text by Robert Smithson, and interviews with Liza Bear, Paul Cummings, Bruce Kurtz, Thomas W. Leavitt, William C. Lipke, Patsy Norvell, Gregoire Müller, Gianni Pettena, Eva Schmidt, Anthony Robbin, Moira Roth, Alison Sky, Paul Toner, and Dennis Wheeler.

Robert Smithson Retrospective: Works 1955–1973. Oslo: National Museum of Contemporary Art, in association with Moderna Museet, Stockholm, and Arken Museum of Modern Art, Ishøj, 1999. Texts by Per Boym, Stian Grøgaard, Tim Martin, Anette Østerby, and Vibeke Petersen.

Reynolds, Ann. *Robert Smithson: Learning from New Jersey and Elsewhere*. Cambridge, Mass.: The MIT Press, 2002.

ANDY WARHOL

Warhol Shadows. Houston: The Menil Collection, 1987.

Andy Warhol: A Retrospective. Ed. Kynaston McShine. New York: The Museum of Modern Art, 1989. Texts by Benjamin H. D. Buchloh, Marco Livingstone, and Robert Rosenblum.

The Work of Andy Warhol. Ed. Garrels, Gary. Discussions in Contemporary Culture, no. 3. New York: Dia Art Foundation, in association with Bay Press, Seattle, 1989. Texts by Benjamin H. D. Buchloh, Rainer Crone, Trevor Fairbrother, Nan Rosenthal, Charles F. Stuckey, and Simon Watney.

Andy Warhol: Abstrakt. Basel: Kunsthalle and Österreichisches Museum für angewandte Kunst, Vienna, in association with Prestel, Munich, 1993. Texts by Callie Angell and Thomas Kellein.

Krauss, Rosalind E. "Warhol's Abstract Spectacle." In *Abstraction, Gesture, Ecriture: Paintings from the Daros Collection*. New York: Scalo, 1999, pp. 123–33.

Hickey, Dave. "The Importance of Remembering Andy." In *Robert Lehman Lectures on Contemporary Art*, vol. 2. Ed. Lynne Cooke and Karen Kelly. New York: Dia Center for the Arts, 2003.

LAWRENCE WEINER

Lawrence Weiner: Posters November 1965–April 1986. Ed. Benjamin H. D. Buchloh. Halifax: Press of Nova Scotia College of Art and Design, in association with Art Metropole, Toronto, 1986. Text by Benjamin H. D. Buchloh.

Lawrence Weiner: Works from the Beginning of the Sixties towards the End of the Eighties. Ed. Marja Bloem. Amsterdam: Stedelijk Museum, 1988. Texts by Wim Beeren, Marja Bloem, Rudi H. Fuchs, Edward Leffingwell, and Anne Rorimer.

Lawrence Weiner: Books 1968–1989. Catalogue Raisonné. Ed. Dieter Schwarz. Cologne: Walther König, in association with Le Nouveau Musée, Villeurbanne, 1989. Text by Dieter Schwarz.

Show (&) Tell: The Films & Videos of Lawrence Weiner. A Catalogue Raisonné. Ed. Bartomeu Mari. Ghent: Imschoot, 1992. Texts by Rudi H. Fuchs, Bartomeu Mari, Dieter Schwarz, Alice Weiner, and Lawrence Weiner.

Rorimer, Anne. "Lawrence Weiner: *Displacement*." In *Robert Lehman Lectures on Contemporary Art*, vol. 1. Ed. Lynne Cooke and Karen Kelly. New York: Dia Center for the Arts, 1996, pp. 19–41.

Lawrence Weiner. London: Phaidon, 1998. Texts by Alexander Alberro, David Batchelor, Benjamin H. D. Buchloh, Lawrence Weiner, W. B. Yeats, and Alice Zimmerman, and an interview by Benjamin H. D. Buchloh.

ROBERT WHITMAN

Whitman, Robert. "A Statement." In Michael Kirby, *Happenings: An Illustrated Anthology*. New York: E. P. Dutton, 1965, pp. 134–83.

Robert Whitman: 4 Cinema Pieces. Chicago: Museum of Contemporary Art, 1968. Text by Jan Van der Mark and an EvaTone Soundsheet by Robert Whitman.

Rose, Barbara. "Considering Robert Whitman." In *Projected Images: Peter Campus, Rockne Krebs, Paul Sharits, Michael Snow, Ted Victoria, Robert Whitman*. Minneapolis: Walker Art Center, 1974, pp. 38–45.

Palisade: Robert Whitman. Yonkers, N.Y.: Hudson River Museum, 1979. Interview by Barbara Rose.

Off Limits: Rutgers University and the Avant-Garde, 1957–1963. Ed. Joan Marter. New Brunswick, N.J.: Rutgers University Press, in association with Newark Museum, Newark, N.J., 1999. Interview with Joseph Jacobs.

Robert Whitman: Playback. New York: Dia Art Foundation, 2003. Texts by George Baker, Lynne Cooke, David Joselit, Ben Portis, and Robert Whitman.

Dia:Beacon
Works on view, May 2003

Page numbers indicate works illustrated

BERND AND HILLA BECHER

Collection of the artists

p. 79
Lime Kilns, Dieversburg, Holland, 1968
Black-and-white photograph
24 1/2 x 20 inches (62 x 51 cm)

Partial View of Winding Tower, Coal Mine "Amalie," Bochum-Werne, Germany, 1968
Black-and-white photograph
24 1/2 x 20 inches (62 x 51 cm)

Partial View of Winding Tower, Coal Mine "Friedrich Heinrich," Kamp-Lintfort, Germany, 1982
Black-and-white photograph
24 1/2 x 20 inches (62 x 51 cm)

pp. 84, 85
Mines of Giraumont, Lorraine, France, 1985
Two black-and-white photographs
24 1/2 x 20 inches (62 x 51 cm) each

Air Filter for Steel Plant, Neuves-Maisons, France, 1986
Black-and-white photograph
24 1/2 x 20 inches (62 x 51 cm)

Gas Cooler in Cokery Plant, Coal Mine "Emscher-Lippe," Ruhr District, Germany, 1986
Black-and-white photograph
24 1/2 x 20 inches ((62 x 51 cm)

Gas Cooler in Cokery Plant, Coal Mine "Heinrich-Robert," Hamm, Ruhr District, Germany, 1987
Black-and-white photograph
24 1/2 x 20 inches (62 x 51 cm)

Partial View of Winding Tower, Coal Mine "Minister Stein," Dortmund, Germany, 1987
Black-and-white photograph
24 1/2 x 20 inches (62 x 51 cm)

Partial View of Winding Tower, Coal Mine "Minister Stein," Dortmund, Germany, 1987
Black-and-white photograph
24 1/2 x 20 inches (62 x 51 cm)

Partial View of Preparation Plant, Coal Mine, Waterschei, Belgium, 1988
Black-and-white photograph
24 1/2 x 20 inches (62 x 51 cm)

Partial View of Winding Tower, Coal Mine, Winterslag, Belgium, 1988
Black-and-white photograph
24 1/2 x 20 inches (62 x 51 cm)

Gas Cooler in Cokery Plant, Coal Mine "Scholven," Gelsenkirchen, Ruhr District, Germany, 1991
Black-and-white photograph
24 1/2 x 20 inches (62 x 51 cm)

Partial View of Blast Furnace, Duisburg-Bruckhausen, Germany, 1991
Black-and-white photograph
24 1/2 x 20 inches (62 x 51 cm)

Partial View of Blast Furnace, Unterwellenborn, Thüringen, Germany, 1991
Black-and-white photograph
24 1/2 x 20 inches (62 x 51 cm)

Partial View of Blast Furnace, Unterwellenborn, Thüringen, Germany, 1991
Black-and-white photograph
24 1/2 x 20 inches (62 x 51 cm)

Partial View of Winding Tower, Coal Mine "Minister Stein," Dortmund, Germany, 1991
Black-and-white photograph
24 1/2 x 20 inches (62 x 51 cm)

Detail of Petrochemical Plant, Wesseling near Cologne, Germany, 1992
Black-and-white photograph
24 1/2 x 20 inches (62 x 51 cm)

Gas Cooler in Cokery Plant, Coal Mine "Anna," Alsdorf/Aachen, Germany, 1992
Black-and-white photograph
24 1/2 x 20 inches (62 x 51 cm)

Lime Kilns, near Diez/Lahn, Germany, 1992
Black-and-white photograph
24 1/2 x 20 inches (62 x 51 cm)

Partial View of Blast Furnace, Rombas, Lorraine, France, 1992
Black-and-white photograph
24 1/2 x 20 inches (62 x 51 cm)

Partial View of Blast Furnace, Uckange, Lorraine, France, 1992
Black-and-white photograph
24 1/2 x 20 inches (62 x 51 cm)

p. 76
Partial View of Gas Tank, Coal Mine "Anna," Alsdorf/Aachen, Germany, 1992
Black-and-white photograph
24 1/2 x 20 inches (62 x 51 cm)

Partial View of Lime Plant, Dugny/Verdun, France, 1992
Black-and-white photograph
24 1/2 x 20 inches (62 x 51 cm)

Partial View of Lime Plant, Dugny/Verdun, France, 1992
Black-and-white photograph
24 1/2 x 20 inches (62 x 51 cm)

p. 81
Partial View of Water Cooler, Coal Mine "Anna," Alsdorf/Aachen, Germany, 1992
Black-and-white photograph
24 1/2 x 20 inches (62 x 51 cm)

Lime Kilns, Jemelle, Belgium, 1996
Black-and-white photograph
24 1/2 x 20 inches (62 x 51 cm)

Lime Kilns, Jemelle, Belgium, 1996
Black-and-white photograph
24 1/2 x 20 inches (62 x 51 cm)

Lime Kilns, Marche-les-Dames, Belgium, 1996
Black-and-white photograph
24 1/2 x 20 inches (62 x 51 cm)

Lime Kilns, Kaltestal, Harz Mountains, Germany, 1997
Black-and-white photograph
24 1/2 x 20 inches (62 x 51 cm)

Lime Kilns, Kaltestal, Harz Mountains, Germany, 1997
Black-and-white photograph
$24^1/_2$ x 20 inches (62 x 51 cm)

Lime Kilns, Rübeland, Harz Mountains, Germany, 1997
Black-and-white photograph
$24^1/_2$ x 20 inches (62 x 51 cm)

p. 83
Plant for Styrofoam Production, Wesseling near Cologne, Germany, 1997
Black-and-white photograph
20 x $24^1/_2$ inches (51 x 62 cm)

JOSEPH BEUYS

pp. 86, 91
Arena—dove sarei arrivato se fossi stato intelligente! (*Arena—where would I have got if I had been intelligent!*), 1970–72
Aluminum and glass panels in metal frames with 264 photographs, wax, paint, acid, and other substances; stacks of fat and waxed blocks, copper and iron plates; oilcan
100 panels, $44^3/_4$ x $32^1/_4$ inches (114 x 82 cm) each, framed; two stacks, $9^7/_8$ x 12 x $19^1/_4$ inches (25 x 30 x 49 cm) and $25^7/_8$ x 13 x $22^1/_2$ inches (66 x 33 x 57 cm)
Dia Art Foundation

p. 93
Aus Berlin: Neues vom Kojoten (*From Berlin: News from the Coyote*), 1979
Felt blanket, gloves, toenail clippings, animal and human hair balls, cigar box, fire extinguishers, walking stick, flashlight, musician's triangle and striker, hay, bundles of the *Wall Street Journal*, felt hat, plaster rubble, and lathe, 10 acetylene lanterns on sticks, arc light, and sulfur
16 feet 6 inches x 20 feet (502 x 610 cm)
Dia Art Foundation

p. 95
Brasilienfond (*Brazilian Fond*), 1979
Stacks comprising approximately 155 U-shaped felt sheets on U-shaped copper base; one iron horseshoe
Four stacks, 70 x 99 x $79^1/_2$ inches (178 x 250 x 200 cm) each; dimensions variable overall
Dia Art Foundation

p. 94
Fond III/3, 1979
Stacks comprising 111 felt sheets and one copper sheet each
Nine stacks, $57^3/_4$ x 79 x $39^1/_2$ inches (146 x 200 x 100 cm) each
Dia Art Foundation

p. 94
Fond IV/4, 1979
Stacks comprising felt, iron, and copper sheets
12 felt and iron stacks, $38^3/_4$ x $27^3/_4$ x 19 inches (98.4 x 70.5 x 48.3 cm) each; one copper and iron stack, $40^1/_2$ x 28 x 19 inches (103 x 71 x 48.3 cm)
Dia Art Foundation

LOUISE BOURGEOIS

Collection of the artist

Clutching, 1962
Plaster
12 x 13 x 12 inches (30.5 x 33 x 30.5 cm)

Labyrinthine Tower, 1962
Edition 2/6
Bronze
18 x 12 x $10^1/_2$ inches (45.7 x 30.5 x 26.7 cm)

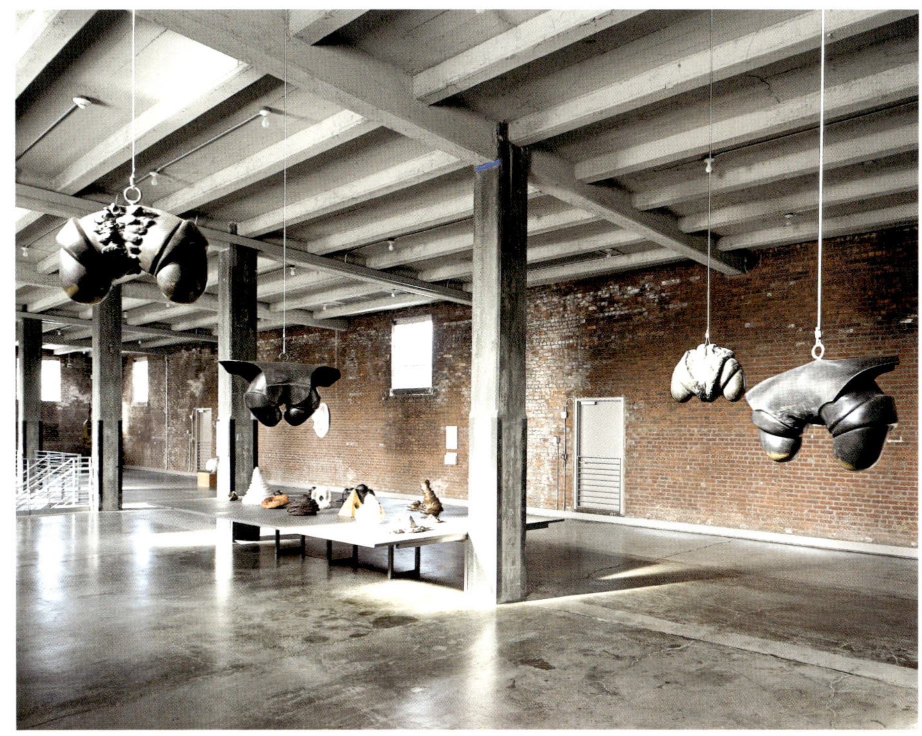

Lair, 1962
Edition 2/6
Bronze
16 x 15 x 15 inches (40.6 x 38 x 38 cm)

Lair, 1962
Plaster and wire
22 x 22 x 22 inches (56 x 56 x 56 cm); 29 inches (73.6 cm) diameter with wire coil

Lair, 1962–63
Plaster
$18^1/_2$ x $29^1/_8$ x $21^3/_8$ inches (47 x 74 x 54.3 cm)

pp. 96, 102
Fée couturière, 1963
Plaster
$39^1/_2$ x $22^1/_2$ x $22^1/_2$ inches (100 x 57 x 57 cm)

Lair, 1963
Latex
$9^1/_2$ x $16^3/_4$ x $14^3/_8$ inches (24 x 42.5 x 36.5 cm)

Portrait, 1963
Latex
$10^1/_2$ x 7 x 3 inches (26.7 x 17.8 x 7.6 cm)

Rondeau for L, 1963
Plaster
11 x 11 x $10^1/_2$ inches (28 x 28 x 26.7 cm)

Soft Landscape, 1963
Latex and plaster
7 x 8 x 8 inches (17.8 x 20.3 x 30.3 cm)

Amoeba, 1963–65
Plaster
$37^1/_2$ x $28^1/_2$ x $13^1/_4$ inches (95.3 x 72.4 x 33.7 cm)

p. 103
The Quartered One, 1964–65
Plaster
$62^1/_4$ x 24 x 20 inches (158 x 61 x 50.8 cm)

Louise Bourgeois, installation view

Resin Eight, 1965
Resin over hemp
2 x 7 x 2 1/2 inches (5 x 17.8 x 6.4 cm)

Le Regard, 1966
Latex and cloth
5 x 15 1/2 x 14 1/2 inches (12.7 x 39.4 x 36.8 cm)

End of Softness, 1967
Edition 3/6
Bronze with gold patina
7 x 20 3/8 x 15 1/4 inches (17.8 x 51.8 x 38.7 cm)

Germinal, 1967
Edition 2/6
Bronze
5 5/8 x 7 3/8 x 6 1/4 inches (14.3 x 18.7 x 16 cm)

Sleep II, 1967
Marble
23 3/8 x 30 1/4 x 23 3/4 inches (59.4 x 76.8 x 60.3 cm)

Soft Landscape, 1967
Aluminum
6 3/4 x 19 3/4 x 17 1/4 inches (17 x 50 x 43.8 cm)

Soft Landscape I, 1967
Plastic
4 x 12 x 11 inches (10.2 x 30.5 x 28 cm)

Soft Landscape II, 1967
Plastic
6 7/8 x 14 5/8 x 9 5/8 inches (17.5 x 37 x 24.4 cm)

Unconscious Landscape, 1967–68
Edition 1/6
Bronze
12 x 22 x 24 inches (30.5 x 56 x 61 cm)

Hanging Janus with Jacket, 1968
Edition 1/6
Bronze
10 5/8 x 20 5/8 x 6 3/8 inches (27 x 52.4 x 16.2 cm)

Janus, 1968
Edition 1/6
Bronze
10 x 13 x 7 inches (25.4 x 33 x 17.8 cm)

Janus fleuri, 1968
Edition 1/6
Bronze
10 1/8 x 12 1/2 x 8 3/8 inches (25.7 x 31.8 x 21.3 cm)

Janus in Leather Jacket, 1968
Edition 2/6
Bronze
12 x 22 x 6 1/2 inches (30.5 x 56 x 16.5 cm)

Noir veine, 1968
Marble
23 x 24 x 27 inches (58.4 x 61 x 68.6 cm)

The Fingers, 1968
Bronze
Diptych, 3 x 12 1/2 x 8 inches (7.6 x 31.8 x 20.3 cm) overall

Avenza, 1968–69
Edition 1/6
Latex
21 x 30 x 46 inches (53.3 x 76.2 x 117 cm)

Fillette (Sweeter Version), 1968/1999
Edition 3/3
Latex over plaster
23 1/2 x 10 1/2 x 7 3/4 inches (59.7 x 26.7 x 19.7 cm)

Le Trani Episode, 1971
Plaster and latex
16 1/2 x 23 1/8 x 23 1/4 inches (42 x 58.7 x 59 cm)

p. 101
The Destruction of the Father, 1974
Plaster, latex, wood, fabric, and two 85-watt flood lamps, each with red diffusion gel
93 5/8 inches x 11 feet 10 inches x 97 7/8 inches (238 x 361 x 249 cm)

pp. 104–05
Spider, 1997
Steel, tapestry, perfume bottle, chair, bones, lockets with photographs, and other objects
14 feet 7 inches x 19 feet 10 inches x 17 feet (445 x 665 x 518 cm)

JOHN CHAMBERLAIN

Royal Ventor, 1967
Galvanized steel and aluminum
61 3/8 x 57 1/8 x 46 3/8 (156 x 145 x 117 cm)
Dia Art Foundation

Norma Jean Risen (formerly *Norma Jean Rising*), 1967/1984
Galvanized steel and paint
66 x 38 x 38 inches (167.6 x 96.5 x 96.5 cm)
Dia Art Foundation

Lucy and Ricky, 1973
Aluminum foil, polyester resin, and paint
46 5/8 x 57 1/2 x 44 inches (118.4 x 146 x 112 cm)
Dia Art Foundation

Daddy-O-Springs, 1975
Painted and chromium-plated steel
70 x 67 x 26 inches (178 x 170 x 66 cm)
Dia Art Foundation

Toasted Hitlers (From E.J.), 1977
Painted and chromium-plated steel
85 3/4 x 51 1/4 x 43 3/4 inches (218 x 130 x 111 cm)
Dia Art Foundation

. . . and his hair was perfect, 1978
Painted and chromium-plated steel
78 x 50 x 22 inches (198 x 127 x 56 cm)
Dia Art Foundation

Chickmeat, 1979
Painted and chromium-plated steel
77 x 8 feet 10 inches x 24 inches (196 x 269 x 61 cm)
Dia Art Foundation

The Hot Lady from Bristol, 1979
Painted and chromium-plated steel
83 x 51 x 50 inches (211 x 129.5 x 127 cm)
Dia Art Foundation

pp. 106, 109
Luftschloss, 1979
Painted and chromium-plated steel
148 x 9 feet 8 inches x 96 1/2 inches (386 x 261.6 x 211 cm)
Dia Art Foundation

Coup d'Soup, 1980
Painted steel
8 feet 4 1/4 inches x 51 x 26 inches (259 x 129.5 x 66 cm)
Dia Art Foundation

Grandma's Hat, 1981
Painted and chromium-plated steel
69 1/2 x 41 1/2 x 45 inches (176.5 x 105.4 x 114 cm)
Dia Art Foundation

pp. 112–13
Dooms Day Flotilla, 1982
Painted and chromium-plated steel
Seven units varying from 27 inches x 13 feet 5 1/2 inches x 6 inches (70 x 410 x 15.2 cm) to 41 inches x 17 feet x 26 inches (105.5 x 518 x 66 cm); dimensions variable overall
Dia Art Foundation

King King Minor, 1982
Painted steel
98 1/2 x 63 1/2 x 56 inches (250 x 161 x 142 cm)
Dia Art Foundation

p. 110
The Line Up (Dedicated to the Sarasota Police Department), 1982
Painted and chromium-plated steel
81 inches x 16 feet 6 inches x 49 inches (208 x 504 x 126 cm)
Dia Art Foundation

Daddy in the Dark, 1988
Painted and chromium-plated steel
9 feet 4 1/4 inches x 65 inches x 51 1/2 inches (285 x 165 x 132 cm)
Dia Art Foundation; Promised gift of Louise and Leonard Riggio

pp. 114–15
The Privet, 1997
Painted mild steel and chromium-plated steel
12 feet 6 inches x 61 feet 6 inches x 30 inches (381 cm x 18.7 m x 76.2 cm) overall
Lannan Foundation; Long-term loan

Potawatami Falls, 2002
Painted and chromium-plated and stainless steel
9 feet 8 1/4 inches x 48 inches x 53 1/4 inches (295 x 122 x 135 cm)
Collection of the artist

HANNE DARBOVEN

pp. 116, 119, 120, 122–23, 124–25
Kulturgeschichte 1880–1983 (*Cultural History 1880–1983*), 1980–83
Postcards, magazine clippings, photographs, and mementos mounted on paper sheets; sculptural objects
1,590 sheets, 20 7/8 x 28 11/16 inches (53 x 73 cm) each, framed; 19 sculptural objects, varying in size from 11 x 8 x 3 inches (28 x 20 x 7.6 cm) to 12 feet 6 inches x 8 feet 4 inches x 6 inches (381 x 254 x 15.2 cm)
Lannan Foundation; Long-term loan

WALTER DE MARIA

pp. 126, 128, 131, 133, 134, 135
The Equal Area Series, 1976–77
Stainless steel
12 from a series of 25 pairs, each comprising one circle and one square; circle from 80 inches (203 cm), increasing 1 1/8 inches (2.9 cm) diameter in each pair; square from 72 inches (183 cm), increasing 1 inch (2.54 cm) in each pair; 7/8 inch (2.2 cm) in thickness each
Dia Art Foundation

DAN FLAVIN

"monument" for V. Tatlin, 1964
Edition 4/5
Seven cool white fluorescent lights
Height 96 inches (244 cm)
Dia Art Foundation

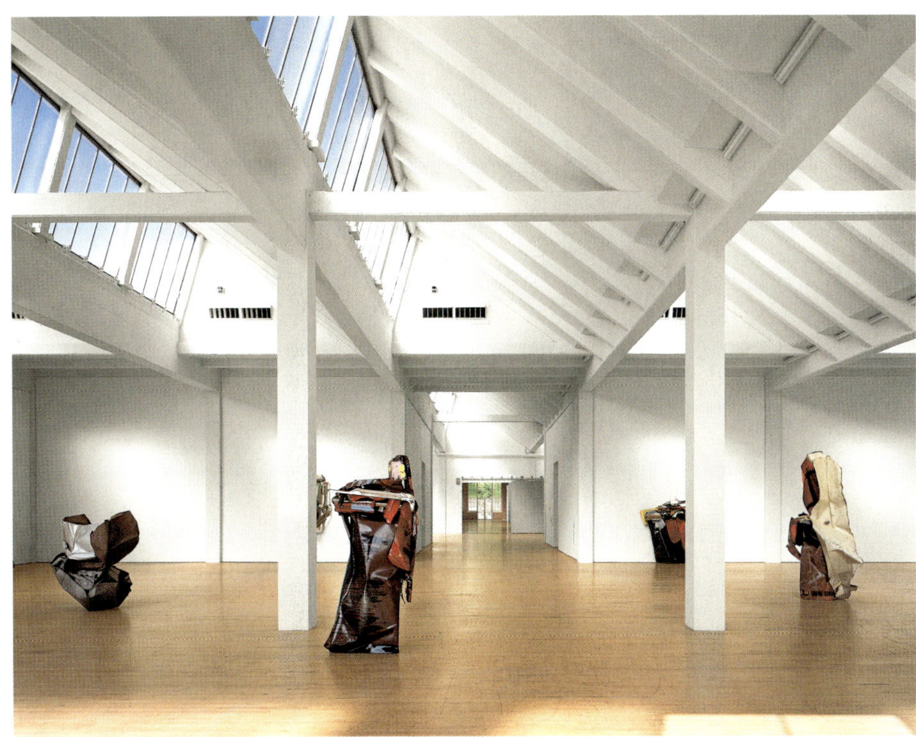

John Chamberlain, installation view

"monument" for V. Tatlin, 1964
Edition 4/5
Seven cool white fluorescent lights
Height 10 feet (305 cm)
Dia Art Foundation

"monument" for V. Tatlin 6 VI, 1964
Edition of 5
Seven cool white fluorescent lights
Width 14 feet (427 cm)
Dia Art Foundation

"monument" for V. Tatlin XI, 1964
Edition of 5
Seven cool white fluorescent lights
Height 11 feet (335 cm)
Dia Art Foundation

p. 138
"monument" 1 for V. Tatlin, 1964
Edition 3/5
Seven cool white fluorescent lights
Height 96 inches (244 cm)
Dia Art Foundation

"monument" 7 for V. Tatlin, 1964
Edition 4/5
Seven cool white fluorescent lights
Height 10 feet (305 cm)
Dia Art Foundation

pp. 142–43
"monument" XI for V. Tatlin, 1964
Edition 4/5
Seven cool white fluorescent lights
Height 96 inches (244 cm)
Dia Art Foundation

"monument" 12 for V. Tatlin, 1964
Edition 4/5
Seven cool white fluorescent lights
Height 96 inches (244 cm)
Dia Art Foundation

pp. 142–43
"monument" for V. Tatlin, 1966
Edition 4/5
Seven cool white fluorescent lights
Height 10 feet (305 cm)
Dia Art Foundation

"monument" for V. Tatlin, 1966
Edition 4/5
Seven cool white fluorescent lights
Height 12 feet (366 cm)
Dia Art Foundation

pp. 142–43
"monument" for V. Tatlin, 1966–69
Edition 4/5
Seven cool white fluorescent lights
Height 9 feet (274 cm)
Dia Art Foundation

p. 141
"monument" for V. Tatlin, 1968
Edition 4/5
Eight cool white fluorescent lights
Height 96 inches (244 cm)
Dia Art Foundation

"monument" for V. Tatlin 45, 1968
Edition of 5
Eight cool white fluorescent lights
Width 14 feet (427 cm)
Dia Art Foundation

p. 141
"monument" for V. Tatlin, 1969
Edition 4/5
Eight cool white fluorescent lights
Height 96 inches (244 cm)
Dia Art Foundation

"monument" for V. Tatlin, 1969
Edition 4/5
Eight cool white fluorescent lights
Height 96 inches (244 cm)
Dia Art Foundation

"*monument" for V. Tatlin*, 1969
Edition 4/5
Seven cool white fluorescent lights
Height 96 inches (244 cm)
Dia Art Foundation

"monument" for V. Tatlin, 1969
Edition 4/5
Seven cool white fluorescent lights
Height 10 feet (305 cm)
Dia Art Foundation

"monument" for V. Tatlin, 1970
Edition 4/5
Eight cool white fluorescent lights
Height 96 inches (244 cm)
Dia Art Foundation

"monument" for V. Tatlin, 1981
Out of edition, exhibition copy
Five fluorescent lights: three daylight, one yellow, and one red
Height 96 inches (244 cm)
Dan Flavin Estate

"monument" for V. Tatlin, 1981
Edition of 5
Five fluorescent lights: four daylight and one red
Height 96 inches (244 cm)
Dia Art Foundation

pp. 136, 142–43, 144–45
untitled, 1970
Blue and red fluorescent lights
97 1/2 inches x variable length x 3 3/4 inches (248 x variable length x 9.5 cm); 97 1/2 inches x 72 feet x 3 3/4 inches (248 x 219 x 9.5 cm), at Dia:Beacon
Dia Art Foundation

MICHAEL HEIZER

pp. 152, 153, 154–55
North, East, South, West, 1967/2002
Weathering steel
North (square), 17 feet 6 inches x 17 feet 6 inches x 20 feet (533 x 533 x 610 cm); *East* (truncated cone), 15 feet 4 inches increasing to 21 feet 11 inches (diameter) x 20 feet (467 increasing to 668 cm x 610 cm); *South* (cone), 17 feet 6 inches in diameter tapering to 16 inches x 20 feet (533 tapering to 406 cm x 610 cm); *West* (wedge), 11 feet 2 inches x 26 feet 8 inches x 20 feet (340 x 813 x 610 cm); 142 feet x 39 feet 2 inches x 20 feet below floor level (43.3 m x 11.9 m x 610 cm) overall
Dia Art Foundation; Gift of Lannan Foundation

Negative Megalith #5, 1998
Diorite granite and steel
15 feet 8 inches x 78 inches x 26 inches (477.5 x 198 x 66 cm)
The Menil Collection, Houston, gift of Mr. and Mrs. James A. Elkins, Jr., in memory of Dominique de Menil; Extended loan

ROBERT IRWIN

Beacon Project, 1999–2003
Irwin's work comprises a master plan that includes the forecourt, a grove of flowering trees, the museum vestibule, and the west garden, among other components.

DONALD JUDD

Untitled, 1970
Anodized aluminum
8 1/4 inches x 13 feet 5 inches x 8 inches (21 x 409 x 20.3 cm)
Judd Foundation

Untitled, 1970
Anodized aluminum
8 1/4 inches x 21 feet 2 inches x 8 inches (21 x 645 x 20.3 cm)
Judd Foundation

p. 174
Untitled, 1975
Stainless steel and Plexiglas
12 units, 12 x 24 x 14 inches (30.5 x 61 x 35.5 cm) each
Lannan Foundation; Long-term loan

pp. 166, 171, 172–73
Untitled, 1976
Douglas fir plywood
15 boxes, 36 x 60 x 60 inches (76 x 152 x 152 cm) each
Dia Art Foundation; Gift of The Brown Foundation

p. 169
Untitled (slant piece), 1976
Douglas fir plywood
48 inches x length variable x 10 feet 9 inches (122 cm x length variable x 328 cm); 48 inches x 33 feet 10 inches x 10 feet 9 inches (122 cm x 10.3 m x 328 cm), at Dia:Beacon
Dia Art Foundation; Gift of Louise and Leonard Riggio

Untitled, 1980
Anodized aluminum and galvanized iron
8 1/4 inches x 13 feet 5 inches x 8 inches (21 x 409 x 20.3 cm)
The Chinati Foundation

Untitled, 1980
Anodized aluminum and brass
8 1/4 inches x 21 feet 2 inches x 8 inches (21 x 645 x 20.3 cm)
The Chinati Foundation

p. 175
Untitled, 1991
Douglas fir plywood and Plexiglas
Six units, 39 3/8 x 19 5/8 inches (100 x 100 x 50 cm) each
Dia Art Foundation; Gift of Louise and Leonard Riggio

ON KAWARA

pp. 176, 178, 182–83, 184–85
36 Date Paintings (1966–2000), from the *Today Series* (1966–present)
Acrylic on canvas in handmade cardboard box
10 x 13 inches (25.4 x 33 cm), except *18 MAI 2000*, 10 x 13 1/2 inches (25.4 x 34.3 cm)
Dia Art Foundation
Lannan Foundation; Long-term loan
Collection of the artist

JUNE 16, 1966, "Two Tankers and two tugboats crashed in a fiery disaster in Lower New York Bay." 1966

FEB. 14, 1967, "Da Vinci's manuscripts which were produced between 1491 and 1505." 1967

5 ABR. 68, "La violencia y el odio racial envuelven a los Estados Unidos." 1968

NOV. 20, 1969, "Ascent stage and command ship dock. Comdrs. Charles Conrad Jr. and Alan L. Bean crawl through tunnel to rejoin Comdr. Richard F. Gordon Jr." 1969

MAY 25, 1970, "The withdrawal of all United States ground troops from Cambodia is to be completed ahead of the June 30 deadline under present plans of the Nixon Administration, senior Government officials said today in Washington." 1970

2 JAN. 1971, "2 JAN. 1971." 1971
28 DEC. 1972, "Jag vet inte." 1972
OCT. 13, 1973, "Saturday." 1973
MAR. 24, 1974, "Sunday." 1974
FEB. 19, 1975, "Wednesday." 1975
26. JULI 1976, "Montag." 1976
SEPT. 12, 1977, "Monday." 1977
27 DEC. 1978, "Merkredo." 1978
MAY 22, 1979, "Tuesday." 1979
OCT. 11, 1980, "Saturday." 1980
AUG. 3, 1981, "Monday." 1981
JAN. 21, 1982, "Thursday." 1982
APR. 25, 1983, "Monday." 1983
4 AUG. 1984, "Sabato." 1984
MAY 9, 1985, "Thursday." 1985
30. NOV. 1986, "Sonntag." 1986
JAN. 28, 1987, "Wednesday." 1987
15 JUL. 1988, "Vendredo." 1988
NOV. 3, 1989, "Friday." 1989
NOV. 3, 1989, "Friday." 1989
26 OTT. 1990, "Venerdi." 1990
6 MRT. 1991, "Woensdag." 1991
AUG. 29, 1992, "Saturday." 1992
JAN. 1, 1993, "Friday." 1993
JUNE 7, 1994, "Tuesday." 1994
27 MARS 1995, "Lundi." 1995
SEPT. 8, 1996, "Sunday." 1996
FEB. 11, 1997, "Tuesday." 1997
19 DEC. 1998, "Sabato." 1998
APR. 30, 1999, "Friday." 1999
18 MAI 2000, "Jeudi." 2000

100 Years Calendar (24,698 Days), August 6, 2000
Ink and silkscreen on paper
27 1/2 x 51 5/8 inches (70 x 129.5 cm)
Collection of the artist

IMI KNOEBEL

pp. 186, 189, 192, 193, 194, 195
Raum 19 (*Room 19*), 1968
Fiberboard and wood
77 units, varying from 1 5/8 x 3 1/2 x 24 inches (4 x 9 x 61 cm) to 63 3/8 x 101 5/8 x 2 inches (161 x 258 x 5 cm) each; dimensions variable overall
40 feet x 26 feet (12.2 m x 792.5 cm), at Dia:Beacon
Dia Art Foundation

SOL LEWITT

1 2 3: All Three-Part Variations on Three Different Kinds of Cubes, 1967/2003
Enamel on steel
48 x 16 x 16 inches (122 x 40.6 x 40.6 cm) each
Collection of the artist

p. 196
All Three-Part Variations on Three Different Kinds of Cubes, 1969
Ink and graphite on paper
29 x 23 inches (73.7 x 58.4 cm)
Collection of the artist

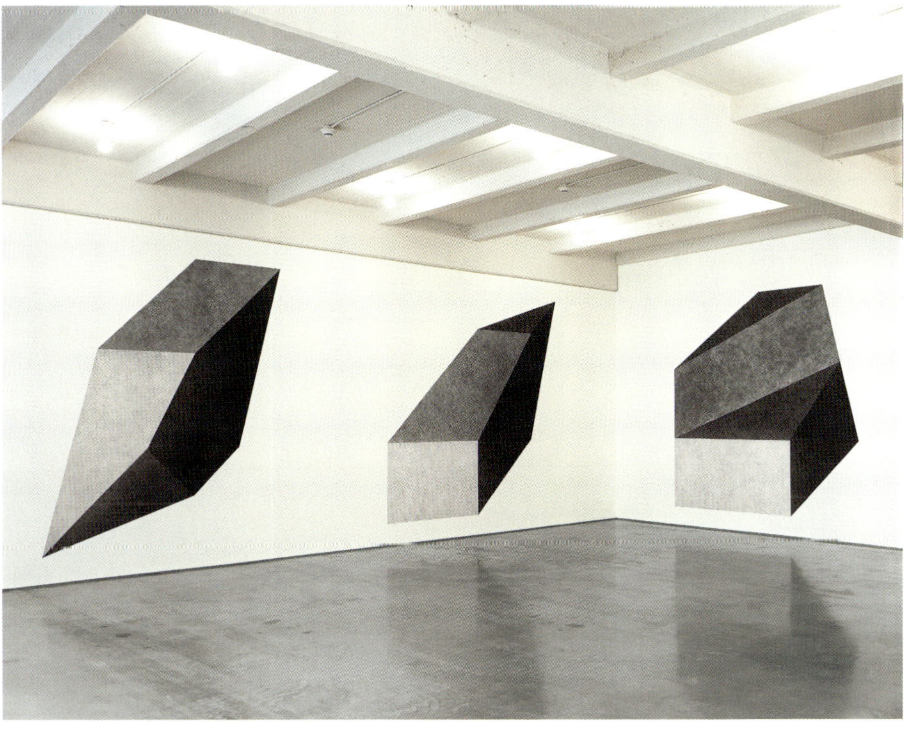

Sol LeWitt, left to right, *Wall Drawing #411b: Isometric figure with progressively darker gradations of gray ink wash on each plane,* 1984, *Wall Drawing #411d: Isometric figure with progressively darker gradations of gray ink wash on each plane,* 1984, and *Wall Drawing #411e: Isometric figure with progressively darker gradations of gray ink wash on each plane,* 2003

Wall Drawing #1085: Drawing Series—Composite, Part I–IV, #1–24, B, 1969
6H graphite on wall
96 drawings, 40 1/4 x 40 1/4 inches (103 x 103 cm) each
Drawn by Takeshi Arita, Sachiko Cho, Stephen Gunn, John Hogan, Eric Hongisto, Emily Ripley, Anthony Sansotta, and Hans Viets, April–May 2003
Dia Art Foundation; Gift of Melva Bucksbaum and Raymond Learsy and The Martin Bucksbaum Family Foundation

Wall Drawing #411b: Isometric figure with progressively darker gradations of gray ink wash on each plane, 1984
Ink wash on wall
Dimensions variable; within 10-foot (25.4 cm) square, at Dia:Beacon
Drawn by Hidemi Nomura and Jo Watanabe, May 2003
Dia Art Foundation; Gift of the artist

Wall Drawing #411d: Isometric figure with progressively darker gradations of gray ink wash on each plane, 1984
Ink wash on wall
Dimensions variable; within 10-foot (25.4 cm) square, at Dia:Beacon
Drawn by Hidemi Nomura and Jo Watanabe, May 2003
Dia Art Foundation; Gift of the artist

Wall Drawing #411e: Isometric figure with progressively darker gradations of gray ink wash on each plane, 2003
Ink wash on wall
Dimensions variable; within 10-foot (25.4 cm) square, at Dia:Beacon
Drawn by Hidemi Nomura and Jo Watanabe, May 2003
Dia Art Foundation; Gift of the artist

AGNES MARTIN

p. 211
The Beach, 1963
Acrylic and graphite on canvas
75 1/2 x 74 3/4 inches (192 x 190 cm)
Lannan Foundation; Long-term loan

pp. 206, 208
The Peach, 1964
Oil and graphite on canvas
72 x 72 inches (183 x 183 cm)
Dia Art Foundation; Promised gift of Louise and Leonard Riggio

Untitled #5, 1977
Ink, graphite, and gesso on canvas
72 x 72 inches (183 x 183 cm)
Anonymous loan

Untitled X, 1982
Acrylic and graphite on canvas
72 x 72 inches (183 x 183 cm)
Anonymous loan

Untitled #12, 1984
Acrylic, gesso, and graphite on canvas
72 x 72 inches (183 x 183 cm)
Anonymous loan

pp. 212–15
Innocent Love series, 1999
Acrylic and graphite on canvas
60 x 60 inches (152.4 x 152.4 cm) each
Lannan Foundation; Long-term loan

Love
Contentment
Innocent Living
Happiness
Innocent Happiness
Perfect Happiness
Innocent Love
Where Babies Come From

Untitled #16, 2002
Acrylic and graphite on canvas
60 x 60 inches (152.4 x 152.4 cm)
Dia Art Foundation; Gift of the artist

Untitled #20, 2002
Acrylic and graphite on canvas
60 x 60 inches (152.4 x 152.4 cm)
Dia Art Foundation; Gift of the artist

BRUCE NAUMAN

Corridor Installation (Nick Wilder Installation), 1970
Three video cameras, scanner and mount, four video monitors, videotape player, and 1/2-inch videotape (black-and-white, silent, 2 hours), wallboard
10 x 40 x 20 feet (305 cm x 12.2 m x 610 cm)
Flick Collection

pp. 224, 225
Left or Standing, Standing or Left Standing, 1971
Two monitors, two video laser disk players, two video laser disks (color), fluorescent lights, text on video, wallboard
12 x 48 x 40 feet (366 cm x 14.6 m x 12.2 m) overall
Lannan Foundation; Long-term loan

Cones Cojones, 1973–76
Masking tape and text on paper
Largest tape circle, dimensions variable, approximately 68 feet (20.7 m) diameter; two sheets of paper with tape, 39 15/16 x 25 15/16 inches (101.4 x 66 cm) each
Collection of the artist

Body Pressure, 1974
Text on paper
25 3/16 x 16 1/2 inches (64 x 42 cm)
Flick Collection

p. 219
South America Circle, 1981
Steel, cast iron, wire
168 inches (427 cm) diameter, suspended 60 inches (152.4 cm) above floor
Lannan Foundation; Long-term loan

Indoor Outdoor Seating Arrangement, 1999
Steel and wood bleachers
4 units, 96 inches x 15 feet 6 inches x 21 feet (243 x 472 x 640 cm) each; one unit, 10 feet x 11 feet 6 inches x 21 feet (304 x 350 x 640 cm)
Flick Collection

pp. 216, 220, 221, 222–23
Mapping the Studio I (Fat Chance John Cage), 2001
DVD projections (black-and-white, sound, 5 hours 45 minutes), office chairs
Seven projections and seven chairs, 13 x 62 x 56 feet (396 cm x 18.9 m x 17.1 m) overall
Lannan Foundation; Long-term loan

BLINKY PALERMO

Times of the Day I, 1974–75
Acrylic on aluminum
4 panels, 22 3/8 x 20 1/2 inches (56.8 x 52 cm) each
Dia Art Foundation

Times of the Day II, 1975
Acrylic on aluminum
4 panels, 22 3/8 x 20 1/2 inches (56.8 x 52 cm) each
Dia Art Foundation

pp. 229, 231, 232, 233, 234–35
To the People of New York City, 1976
Acrylic on aluminum panels
15 parts, including 40 panels ranging from 8 1/4 x 6 5/16 inches (21 x 16 cm) to 39 3/8 x 78 3/4 inches (100 x 200 cm)
Dia Art Foundation

GERHARD RICHTER

Six Gray Mirrors, 2003
Tempered and enameled glass with stainless-steel mount
Six parts, 13 feet 1 1/2 inches x 13 feet 1 1/2 inches x 19 11/16 inches (400 x 400 x 50 cm) each
Dia Art Foundation

ROBERT RYMAN

The Paradoxical Absolute, 1958
Casein and graphite on printed paper
7 1/4 x 7 3/8 inches (18.4 x 18.7 cm)
Dia Art Foundation; Promised gift

Untitled, 1959
Gouache and casein on printed paper
11 x 11 inches (28 x 28 cm)
Dia Art Foundation; Promised gift

Untitled, 1960
Oil on linen canvas
36 x 36 inches (91.4 x 91.4 cm)
Dia Art Foundation; Promised gift

Untitled, 1962
Oil and primer on unstretched linen canvas
19 x 19 inches (48.3 x 48.3 cm)
Dia Art Foundation; Promised gift

Stretched Drawing, c. 1963
Charcoal on cotton canvas
7 x 7 inches (17.8 x 17.8 cm)
Dia Art Foundation; Promised gift

Stretched Drawing, c. 1963
Charcoal on cotton canvas
8 1/4 x 8 1/4 inches (21 x 21 cm)
Dia Art Foundation; Promised gift

Stretched Drawing, 1963
Charcoal on cotton canvas
14 1/2 x 14 3/8 inches (36.8 x 36.5 cm)
Dia Art Foundation; Promised gift

Untitled, 1965
Enamel on linen canvas
62 1/2 x 12 1/2 inches (159 x 159 cm)
Dia Art Foundation; Promised gift

Untitled, c. 1965–66
Oil on linen canvas
11 1/4 x 11 1/4 inches (28.6 x 28.6 cm)
Dia Art Foundation; Promised gift

Untitled, Delta, c. 1965–66
Oil on cotton canvas
8 feet 9 1/4 inches x 8 feet 9 1/4 inches (267 x 267 cm)
Dia Art Foundation; Promised gift

Medway, 1968
Acrylic on paper, masking tape
79 1/2 x 77 1/2 inches (202 x 197 cm) overall
Dia Art Foundation; Promised gift

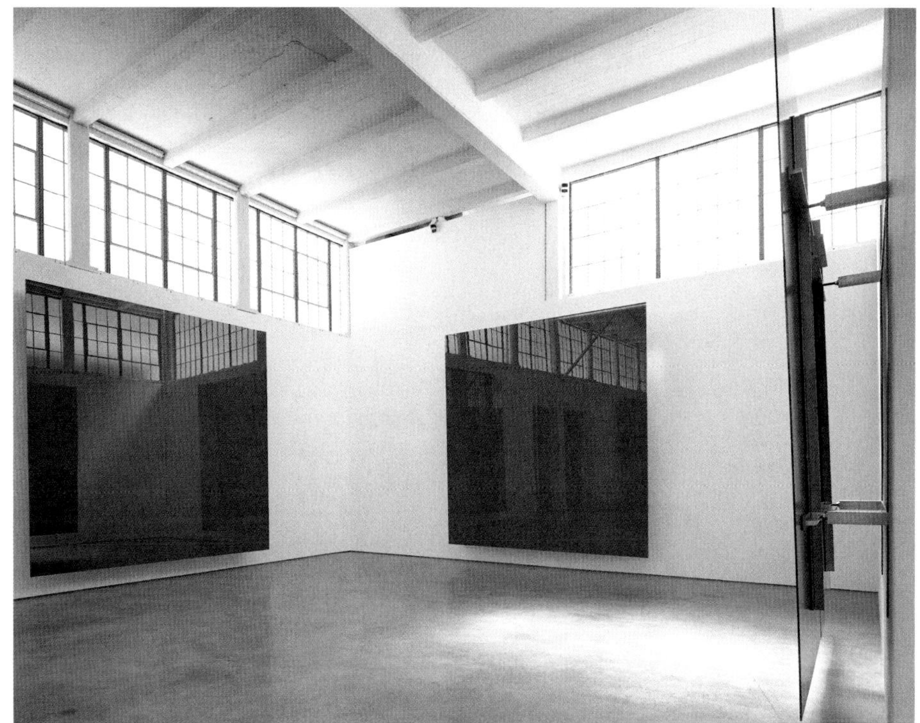

Stations, 1969
Enamelac on corrugated cardboard panels
Four panels, 60 x 60 inches (152.4 x 152.4 cm) each
Dia Art Foundation; Promised gift

pp. 246, 250–51
Varese Wall, 1975
Vinyl acetate emulsion on wood panels, metal bars, and foam blocks
96 x 24 feet x 20 inches (2.4 m x 7.3 m x 50.8 cm) overall
Dia Art Foundation; Promised gift

pp. 252, 253, 254–55
Vector, 1975/1997
Oil over vinyl acetate emulsion on wood panels with clear pine and mahogany inserts
11 panels, 37 3/8 x 37 3/8 inches (95 x 95 cm) each; 7 inches (17.8 cm) between panels; 37 3/8 inches x 40 feet 1 3/8 inches (95 cm x 13 m) overall
Dia Art Foundation; Promised gift of Judy and Michael Ovitz

Tower I, 1976
Oil on Acrylivin, Plexiglas panel, and sanded Plexiglas fasteners with pentagonal steel bolts
17 1/8 x 14 inches (43.5 x 35.6 cm)
Dia Art Foundation; Promised gift

Tower II, 1976
Acrylic on Acrylivin and sanded Plexiglas fasteners with pentagonal cadmium-plated steel bolts
15 5/8 x 14 inches (40.7 x 35.6 cm)
Dia Art Foundation; Promised gift

Phoenix, 1979
Polyurethane on steel panels, fasteners with bolts
Panel 1, 13 3/8 x 13 3/8 inches (34 x 34 cm); panel 2, 13 3/8 x 13 3/8 inches (34 x 34 cm); panel 3, 15 1/2 x 15 1/2 inches (39.4 x 39.4 cm); panel 4, 14 1/8 x 13 1/2 inches (36 x 34 cm); panel 5, 14 1/8 x 13 1/2 inches (36 x 34 cm); panel 6, 17 1/2 x 14 1/2 inches (44.5 x 36.8 cm); panel 7, 18 1/2 x 15 inches (47 x 38 cm); panel 8, 18 1/2 x 15 inches (47 x 38 cm)
Panel sequence variable; 1, 8, 7, 3, 2, 5, 6, and 4, at Dia:Beacon
Dia Art Foundation; Promised gift

Gerhard Richter, *Six Gray Mirrors*, 2003

Factor, 1983
Oil over acrylic (recto) and acrylic with varnish (verso), on fiberglass with epoxy edge and metal rods with oval attachments
92 3/4 x 45 x 14 3/4 inches (236 x 114 x 37.5 cm)
Dia Art Foundation; Promised gift

Pair Navigation, 1984
Oil on fiberglass with redwood edge, metal frame, four rod fasteners, and metal dowels
9 x 47 1/2 x 47 1/2 inches (23 x 121 x 121 cm)
Dia Art Foundation; Promised gift

Measure, 1987
Acrylic on Gatorboard and steel bolts
27 x 27 inches (68.6 x 68.6 cm)
Dia Art Foundation; Promised gift

Transfer, 1987
Acrylic on Gatorboard and four steel bolts
30 3/4 x 31 1/2 inches (78 x 79 cm)
Dia Art Foundation; Promised gift

Consort, 1988
Acrylic on fiberglass and four cadmium-plated bolts
123 x 123 inches (313 x 313 cm)
Dia Art Foundation; Promised gift

Cord, 1994
Oil and Enamelac on acrylic and fiberglass panel, nails
24 x 24 inches (61 x 61 cm)
Dia Art Foundation; Promised gift

Place IV, 1998
Encaustic and graphite on sized paper mounted on stretched linen canvas over aluminum panel
24 x 24 inches (61 x 61 cm)
Dia Art Foundation; Promised gift

Third Prototype 2003, 2003
Acrylic and varnish on vinyl panels
14 panels, 24 x 24 inches (61 x 61 cm) each; 26 1/2 x 36 feet 4 inches with varnish
(67.3 cm x 11 m) overall
Dia Art Foundation; Promised gift

FRED SANDBACK

Untitled (from *133 Variations for Heiner Friedrich*), 1969
Acrylic yarn (double strand, blue and green)
Construction of four parallel leaning planes, dimensions variable; 11 feet 3 inches x 35 feet 6 inches x 54 feet 6 inches (342 cm x 10.82 m x 16.61 m) overall, at Dia:Beacon
Estate of the artist

pp. 262, 263
Untitled (from *Ten Vertical Constructions*), 1977
Acrylic yarn (three strands, red variation)
Two-part vertical construction, dimensions variable; approximately 13 feet 11 inches x 27 feet 6 inches x 24 feet (424 x 878 x 731 cm) overall, at Dia:Beacon
Dia Art Foundation

Untitled (from *Ten Vertical Constructions*), 1977
Acrylic yarn (single black strand)
Two-part vertical construction of two unequal planar figures, dimensions variable; approximately 23 feet 9 inches x 1/8 inch x 53 feet 4 inches (724 cm x 0.12 cm x 16.26 m) overall, at Dia:Beacon
Dia Art Foundation

Untitled (from *Ten Vertical Constructions*), 1977/2003
Acrylic yarn (single black strand)
Eight- or ten-part vertical construction, dimensions variable; approximately 23 feet 9 inches x 14 inches x 53 feet 4 inches (7.24 x 0.36 x 16.25 m) overall, at Dia:Beacon
Dia Art Foundation

Untitled, 1979
Acrylic yarn (single black strand)
Two-part vertical construction, dimensions variable; approximately 39 inches x 1/8 inch x 9 feet (4 m x 0.12 cm x 22.9 m) overall, at Dia:Beacon
Estate of the artist

Untitled, 1996
Acrylic yarn (single white strand)
Six-part construction (leaning verticals), dimensions variable; approximately 12 feet 2 inches x 2 feet 2 inches x 31 feet 9 inches (3.7 m x 66 cm x 9.7 m) overall, at Dia:Beacon
Dia Art Foundation

pp. 264–65
Untitled, 1996
Acrylic yarn (single strand, ochre and beige)
Two-part construction (two triangles), dimensions variable; 12 feet 2 inches x 28 feet x 34 feet 4 inches (3.08 x 2.03 x 2.25 m) overall, at Dia:Beacon
Estate of the artist

RICHARD SERRA

Scatter Piece, 1967
Rubber latex, metal rods, rubber-covered wire
Dimensions variable overall, approximately 20 inches x 25 feet x 25 feet (50.8 x 762 x 762 cm), at Dia:Beacon
Judd Foundation

p. 271
Torqued Ellipse I, 1996
Weatherproof steel
13 feet 1 inch x 29 feet 11 inches x 20 feet 7 inches (398 x 912 x 627 cm)
Dia Art Foundation; Gift of Louise and Leonard Riggio

p. 271
Torqued Ellipse II, 1996
Weatherproof steel
12 feet x 29 feet x 20 feet 5 inches (366 x 884 x 622 cm)
Dia Art Foundation; Gift of Louise and Leonard Riggio

pp. 271, 273
Double Torqued Ellipse, 1997
Weatherproof steel
Outer ellipse, 13 feet 1 inch x 33 feet 6 inches x 27 feet 1 inch (398 cm x 10.2 m x 10.8 m); inner ellipse, 13 feet 1 inch x 25 feet 11 inches x 20 feet 11 inches (398 x 790 x 638 cm)
Dia Art Foundation; Gift of Louise and Leonard Riggio

p. 271
2000, 2000
Weatherproof steel
Outer spiral, 13 feet 7 inches x 42 feet 6 inches x 35 feet 5 inches (414 cm x 13 m x 10.8 m); inner spiral, 13 feet 7 inches x 31 feet 6 inches x 25 feet 7 inches (414 x 960 x 780 cm)
Dia Art Foundation

p. 268
Elevational Wedge, 2001
Hot rolled steel
5 inches tapering to 1/8 inch x 10 feet 10 inches x 21 feet 7 1/8 inches (12.7 tapering to 0.32 cm x 3.3 x 658 cm)
Dia Art Foundation; Gift of Louise and Leonard Riggio

p. 269
Union of the Torus and the Sphere, 2001
Weatherproof steel
11 feet 10 inches x 37 feet 9 inches x 10 feet 5 inches (360 cm x 11.5 m x 317.5 cm) overall
Dia Art Foundation

Consequence, 2003
Paint stick on linen
Two parts, 6 feet 11 3/4 inches x 55 feet (213 cm x 16.7 m) each
Collection of the artist

ROBERT SMITHSON

pp. 284–85
Gravel Mirrors with Cracks and Dust, 1968
Mirrors and gravel
12 mirrors, 36 x 36 inches (91.4 x 91.4 cm) each; 36 inches x 18 feet x 36 inches
(91.4 x 549 x 91.4 cm) overall
Lannan Foundation; Long-term loan

p. 282
Closed Mirror Square (Cayuga Salt Mine Project), 1969
Rock salt, mirror, and glass
One glass and one mirror element, 36 x 36 inches (91.4 x 91.4 cm) each; four mirror elements, 12 x 36 inches (30.5 x 91.4 cm) each; 25 x 96 x 96 inches (63.5 x 244 x 244 cm) overall, at Dia:Beacon
Lannan Foundation; Long-term loan

p. 283
Leaning Mirror, 1969
Mirrors (back to back), sand
2 mirrors, 72 x 72 inches (183 x 183 cm) each; approximately 33 x 88 x 108 inches (83.8 x 224 x 274 cm) overall, at Dia:Beacon
Lannan Foundation; Long-term loan

pp. 279, 281
Map of Broken Glass (Atlantis), 1969
Glass
28 inches x 20 feet x 16 feet (71 x 610 x 488 cm)
Lannan Foundation; Long-term loan

ANDY WARHOL

pp. 290–91, 292–93, 294–95
Shadows, 1978–79
Installation of 72 of 102 paintings
Acrylic, variously silkscreened and painted on canvas
76 x 52 inches (193 x 132 cm) each
Dia Art Foundation

LAWRENCE WEINER

pp. 300, 301, 302, 303, 304, 305
5 Figures of Structure, 1987
Matte enamel-painted (black) lettering (Franklin Gothic Extra Condensed) on wall
Height of letters approximately 12 inches (30.5 cm); dimensions variable overall
Lannan Foundation; Long-term loan

p. 297
ONE QUART EXTERIOR GREEN INDUSTRIAL ENAMEL THROWN ON A BRICK WALL, 1968
Glossy enamel-painted (Pantone Green 348) lettering (Franklin Gothic Extra Condensed) on wall
Height of letters 4 1/2 inches (11.4 cm); dimensions variable overall
Collection of Alice Zimmerman-Weiner; Long-term loan

Statement of Intent, 1969
Paint and lettering (FF Offline) on wall
Height of large letters 12 inches (30.5 cm), small letters 6 inches (15.3 cm); dimensions variable overall
Public Freehold; Courtesy of the artist

ROBERT WHITMAN

pp. 312–13, 314–15
Prune Flat , 1965
Theater work, 50 minutes (September 2003 stagings)
Dia Art Foundation

Light Touch, 1976
Theater work (September 2003 stagings)
Collection of the artist

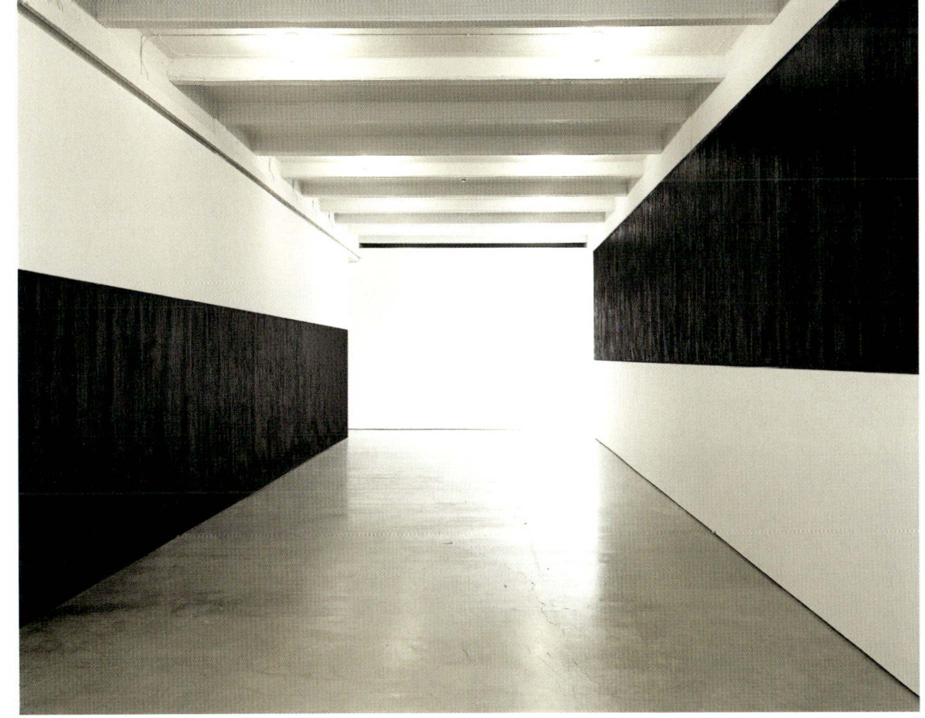

Richard Serra, *Consequence*, 2003

Additional works illustrated

JOSEPH BEUYS

p. 89
Vitex agnus castus, 1972
Performance at the Modern Art Agency, Naples

p. 92
I like America and America likes Me, 1974
Performance at René Block Gallery, New York

MICHAEL HEIZER

p. 146
Maquette for *North, East, South, West*, 1967
Stainless steel
$25^{3}/_{5}$ x $51^{1}/_{8}$ x $17^{3}/_{4}$ inches (65 x 130 x 45 cm)
Collection of the artist

p. 149
North, East, South, West, 1967 (now dismantled)
South: sheet metal, 48 inches diameter x 48 inches deep (121 cm diameter x 121 cm deep)
North: painted wood, 48 x 48 x 48 inches (121 x 121 x 121 cm)

p. 151
Drawing for *North, East, South, West*, 1999
Graphite and ink on paper
18 x 24 inches (45.7 x 61 cm)
Dia Art Foundation

ROBERT IRWIN

p. 156
Rendering of iron gate for Dia:Beacon, 2001–2
Graphite and colored pencil on vellum
24 x $17^{1}/_{2}$ inches (61 x 44.5 cm
Dia Art Foundation

p. 158
Rendering of entrance building for Dia:Beacon, 2000
Graphite on vellum
22 x 18 inches (56 x 47 cm)
Dia Art Foundation

p. 160
Rendering of iron gate for Dia:Beacon, 2001
Colored pencil on vellum
12 x 28 inches (30.5 x 71 cm)
Dia Art Foundation

p. 161
Rendering of forecourt for Dia:Beacon, 2001
Graphite and colored pencil on vellum
36 x 36 inches (91.5 x 91.5 cm)
Dia Art Foundation

p. 162
Rendering of entrance building for Dia:Beacon, 2000
Graphite and colored pencil on vellum
24 x $28^{1}/_{2}$ (61 x 72.5 cm)
Dia Art Foundation

p. 163
Rendering of platform with European hornbeam trees for Dia:Beacon, 1999
Graphite and colored pencil on vellum
$13^{3}/_{4}$ x 18 inches (35 x 46 cm)
Dia Art Foundation

pp. 164–65
Rendering of west garden for Dia:Beacon, 2001
Graphite and colored pencil on vellum
18 x 56 inches (46 x 142 cm)
Dia Art Foundation

DONALD JUDD

p. 170
Page from *Donald Judd: Fifteen Works* (New York: Lone Star Foundation, 1977).

IMI KNOEBEL

p. 191
Untitled, 1973–75
Drawings on paper in 912 boxes in painted wood cabinets
Six cabinets, 80 x $30^{1}/_{4}$ x 22 inches (203 x 76.8 x 55.9 cm) each;
250,000 drawings, $11^{11}/_{16}$ x $8^{1}/_{4}$ inches (29.7 x 21 cm) each
Dia Art Foundation

SOL LEWITT

p. 199
Maquette for *1 2 3: 56 Three-Part Variations on Three Different Kinds of Cubes*, 1967/2003
Masonite, wood, plastic, paint, pencil
56 parts, 9 x 3 x 3 inches (22.9 x 7.6 x 7.6 cm) each; base, 54 x 48 x 2 inches (137 x 213 x 5 cm)
Collection of the artist

pp. 200–05
From artist's book outlining Wall Drawing #1085: *Drawing Series—Composite, Part I–IV, #1–24, A + B*, 1969/2003 (Published by Sperone/Fischer, 1974)

AGNES MARTIN

p. 209
The Spring, 1959
Oil on canvas
48 x 48 inches (122 x 122 cm)
Dia Art Foundation; Anonymous gift

p. 209
Untitled, 1959
Oil on canvas
$69^{1}/_{2}$ x $69^{1}/_{2}$ inches (176.5 x 176.5 cm)
Dia Art Foundation; Anonymous gift

p. 210
Untitled, 1959
Oil and graphite on canvas
$47^{1}/_{2}$ x 24 inches (120.6 x 61 cm)
Dia Art Foundation; Anonymous gift

BLINKY PALERMO

p. 226
Sketch for *To the People of New York City*, 1976
Acrylic on paper, on cardboard
$9^{7}/_{16}$ x $12^{3}/_{4}$ inches (24 x 32.5 cm)
Private collection

GERHARD RICHTER

p. 236 (top left)
Study for *4 Glasscheiben* (*4 Panes of Glass*), 1966
Ink on paper
$11^{11}/_{16}$ x $8^{1}/_{4}$ inches (29.7 x 21 cm)
Herbert Collection, Ghent

p. 236 (bottom left)
Study for *4 Glasscheiben* (*4 Panes of Glass*), 1966
Ink and graphite on paper
$11^{11}/_{16}$ x $8^{1}/_{4}$ inches (29.7 x 21 cm)
Herbert Collection, Ghent

p. 236 (top right)
Study for *Glaswand* (*Glass Wall*), 1966
Graphite on paper
$11^{11}/_{16}$ x $8^{1}/_{4}$ inches (29.7 x 21 cm)
Herbert Collection, Ghent

p. 236 (bottom right)
Study for *Glaswand* (*Glass Wall*), 1966
Ink and graphite on paper
$11^{11}/_{16}$ x $8^{1}/_{4}$ inches (29.7 x 21 cm)
Herbert Collection, Ghent

p. 239
Sieben stehende Scheiben (*Seven Standing Panes*), 2002
Glass and steel
$92^{1}/_{2}$ x 63 x $125^{1}/_{4}$ inches (235 x 160 x 318 cm)
Courtesy the artist and Marian Goodman Gallery, New York

p. 241
8 Grau (*8 Gray*), 2001
Enameled glass and steel
8 panes, 10 feet 6 inches x $78^{3}/_{4}$ inches x 9 feet $3^{3}/_{16}$ inches
(320 x 200 x 30 cm) each
21st Century Museum of Contemporary Art, Kanazawa, Japan

p. 242
Spiegel, Grau (*Mirror, Gray*), 1991
Enameled glass
9 feet $2^{1}/_{4}$ inches x 65 inches (280 x 165 cm)
Musée des Beaux-Arts de Nantes

p. 243
Grauer Spiegel (*Gray Mirror*), 1991
Enameled glass
Four parts, 118 x $68^{7}/_{8}$ inches (300 x 175 cm) each
The Saint Louis Art Museum; Gift of the artist

p. 244–45
Proposal for *Six Gray Mirrors*, 2003
Computer rendering

FRED SANDBACK

p. 256
Isometric drawing, 2003
$8^{1}/_{2}$ x $10^{3}/_{4}$ inches (21.6 x 27.3 cm)
Pencil on paper
Estate of the artist

p. 260
Installation drawing
$8^{1}/_{2}$ x 11 inches (27.9 x 21.5 cm)
Colored pencil on photocopy
Estate of the artist

p. 261
Installation drawing
$8^{1}/_{2}$ x 11 inches (27.9 x 21.5 cm)
Colored pencil on photocopy
Estate of the artist

RICHARD SERRA

p. 266
48 models for Torqued Ellipses, 1994–98
Lead
Various sizes
Dia Art Foundation; Gift of the artist

ROBERT SMITHSON

p. 276
Poster for Dwan Gallery exhibition, 1970
38 x 22 inches (96.5 x 56 cm)
Courtesy James Cohan Gallery

p. 280
Map of Broken Clear Glass (Atlantis, After Map by Lewis Spence), 1969
Graphite and collage on paper
$16^{3}/_{4}$ x $13^{7}/_{8}$ inches (42.5 x 35.2 cm)
Dia Art Foundation

ROBERT WHITMAN

p. 306
Poster for "Robert Whitman: Theater Works 1960–76," 1976
24 x 31 inches (61 x 78.7 cm)
Dia Art Foundation

pp. 310, 311
Two drawings from *Dante Drawings*, 1974–75
Graphite, colored pencil, pastel, wax crayon, and aluminum foil on paper
27 double-sided sheets, $29^{1}/_{2}$ x $41^{1}/_{2}$ inches (74.9 x 105.4 cm) each
Dia Art Foundation

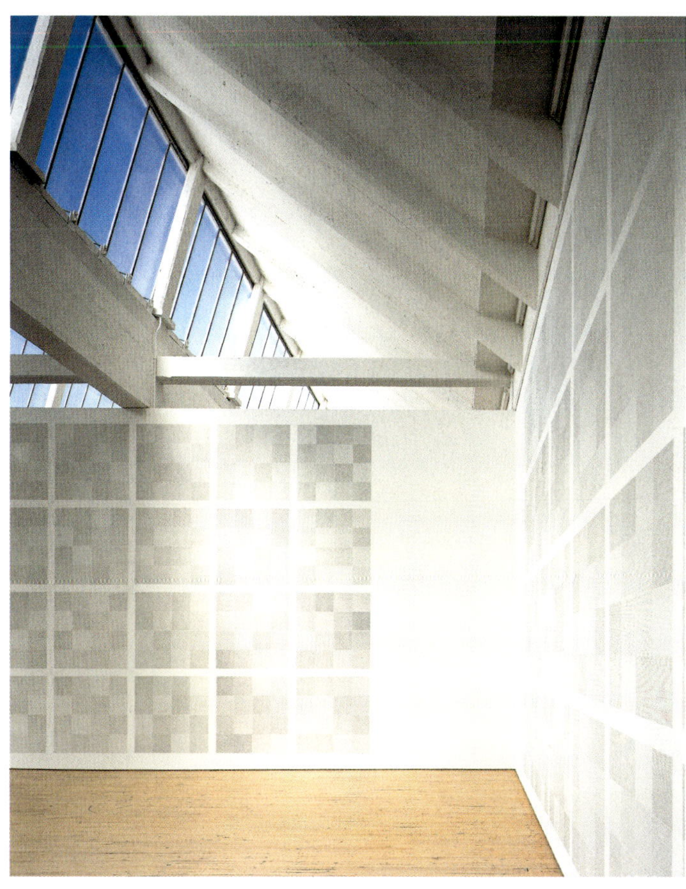

Sol LeWitt, *Wall Drawing #1085: Drawing Series—Composite, Part I–IV, #1–24, B*, 1969

Acknowledgments

Dia:Beacon is the result of the inspiration, creativity, and hard work of many individuals, paricularly important among them the artists it presents, most of whom have been working for over four decades. A special contribution was made by those who not only gave us their art but shaped the experience of it in these galleries as the museum was built, including Bernd and Hilla Becher, Louise Bourgeois, John Chamberlain, Hanne Darboven, Walter De Maria, Michael Heizer, Robert Irwin, On Kawara, Imi Knoebel, Sol LeWitt, Agnes Martin, Bruce Nauman, Gerhard Richter, Robert Ryman, Fred Sandback, Richard Serra, Lawrence Weiner, and Robert Whitman. The late Joseph Beuys, Dan Flavin, Donald Judd, Blinky Palermo, Robert Smithson, and Andy Warhol are equally present through both their work and their example.

Museums and artworks are left to us by artists and also by patrons. Dia's chairman, Leonard Riggio, and his wife, Louise, through their passionate advocacy of Dia and its artists and their daily involvement in the museum's work, are largely responsible for the creation of these galleries that will bear their name, and for the acquisition of many of the artworks contained therein. This book also describes the visionary achievements of Dia's founding figures, Heiner Friedrich, Philippa De Menil, and Helen Winkler. Dia's strong but silent partner in nearly all of its major endeavors over the last decade—exhibitions in New York City, the ambitious projects in the West, and the acquisition of many significant artworks for Beacon—is the Lannan Foundation, under the principled direction of its president, J. Patrick Lannan, Jr.

Other primary contributions to the capital construction and art acquisitions for Dia:Beacon were made by Ann Tenenbaum and Thomas H. Lee, who have been steadfast in their encouragement, and the Brown Foundation, Houston, represented in the heartfelt generosity of Dia trustee Nancy Brown Negley. The International Paper Corporation generously donated the former Nabisco box-printing facility in Beacon that we have now transformed into a museum. Dia trustees and their spouses Frances and John Bowes, Frances R. Dittmer, and Angela and William Haines have made sizable gifts of capital funds as well as of time and expertise. And trustee Jay Chiat, who, sadly, did not live to see the museum open, was one of its most outspoken and generous champions.

The Honorable George E. Pataki, Governor, made Dia's new museum a cultural priority for New York State and the Hudson Valley, and he and other regional officials, most visibly Beacon's own esteemed mayor, Clara Lou Gould, have supplied the project with both funds and encouragement. We deeply appreciate the warm welcome that the citizens of Beacon have given us into their community, and we are grateful for contributions from many New York sources including Empire State Development, the Dutchess County Industrial Development Agency, the City of Beacon, the New York State Office of Parks, Recreation, and Historic Preservation, and the New York State Council on the Arts.

The National Trust for Historic Preservation and its Community Partners division led by John Leith-Tetrault helped identify the 1929 factory in Beacon, designed by Louis Wirsching, Jr. as an architectural landmark worthy of being listed on the National Register of Historic Places. It helped classify the renovation project as eligible to receive federal Historic Tax Credits, a step encouraged by the New York State Parks Department and the U.S. Park Service and supported through the financial partnership of Banc of America Historic Tax Credit Fund.

Important contributions to the construction project were also made by Constance R. Caplan, Carla Emil and Richard Silverstein, the Horace W. Goldsmith Foundation, Linda and Harry Macklowe, Lea H. Simonds, Louisa Stude Sarofim, and Barbara and Charles B. Wright.

Dia is blessed with a supportive board of trustees and a remarkably dedicated and talented staff. A presence in both categories over the past two decades has been Charles Wright, Dia's former director, former chairman of the board, current board member and contributor, and constant advocate. Wright has been a force in Dia's history, revitalizing it in the mid-1980s with new programs in Chelsea, creating separate museums for its holdings of the art of Andy Warhol and Cy Twombly, and initiating its effort to build a permanent home in Beacon for the balance of its collection.

Dia's curator, Lynne Cooke, has organized its exhibition program in Chelsea for over a decade, building its reputation in the contemporary art community on an international scale. She has also been my collaborator throughout the development of the Beacon project, bringing her close relationships with many of the artists, as well as her critical insight, to bear on the shape of the museum.

Jim Schaeufele, Dia's guru of installation and construction since the early 1980s, relocated with his family to Beacon four years ago to direct the renovation of the factory into modern galleries. His dedication and long hours were matched only by those of his deputy, Steven Evans, who is now devoting himself to Dia:Beacon as its director of operations. Working with Jim and Steven, Jim Bauerlein, Curtis Harvey, and Gary Shakespeare committed themselves to the difficult task of directing efforts and solving problems in the field.

Dia's assistant director Stephen Dewhurst has spent an equally intense eight years of his career guiding the institution administratively through a financial restructuring, a capital campaign, several building projects, and the complex work of the financing and operations of the Beacon plan while simultaneously managing Dia's ongoing operations. And Amy Weisser has served for three years as assistant director for Beacon, nurturing the birth of the new museum and acting as a dedicated liaison and spokesperson for Dia in its new Hudson Valley community, through, among other things, the establishment of a new arts-education program in the Beacon schools. In the context of her responsibilities associated with Dia's development efforts and external relations, Laura Raicovich, secretary to the board, has skillfully managed the complex task of organizing Dia:Beacon's inaugural events.

The huge and precise effort of assembling and installing the artworks in Beacon has been deftly directed by John Bowsher, Dia's art administrator. Working with John, Jang Park and Eric Magnuson supervised the skilled crew of Joel Bacon, Dennis Bellone, Pedro Cruz-Castro, Cara Erskin, Heidie Giannotti, Ian Holman, Kimberly Lowe, James Nelson, Arwen O'Reilly, Gene Schmidt, Hans Viets, Sarah Wood, and Collin Zaug. Special thanks to Vickie Arndt, who coordinated the transit of the collection to Beacon.

This book results from the collaboration of many gifted and determined people. Mary DelMonico, an invaluable advisor on many aspects of the Beacon project, led this team. She and Karen Kelly established the conceptual structure and content of the book, while Barbara Schröder, with skill and consideration, managed its myriad components. Laura Fields transformed these diverse elements into an elegant and lucid design. The text is enhanced by

Anne Rorimer's contributions and by David Frankel's insightful editing. Stephan Urbaschek's research was a useful resource. And the striking images of works on view at Dia:Beacon are the efforts of photographers Richard Barnes, Florian Holzherr, Bill Jacobson, Nic Tenwiggenhorn, and Tom Vinetz with assistants Tim Lehmacher and Ralf Maier. Finally, Harri Christ and Klaus Prokop demonstrate their color-separating and printing expertise in these pages.

In sum, the creation of the new museum involved the intelligence and hard work of nearly every member of Dia's staff. Many devoted long hours specifically to the realization of the Beacon project, including Katherine Carl, Bettina Funcke, Patrick Heilman, Jennifer Mackiewicz, Michelle Marozik, Jennifer Minnen, Kirsten Nash, Justine Pizzo, Armelle Pradalier, Amy Sandback, Sarah Thompson, and Sara Tucker. Dia's interns, Nele Brauner, Amanda Cachia, Alexandra Hennig, Elizabeth Millquist, Christiane Schneider, and Tina Teufel also provided necessary support. Dia is also indebted to the staff working at the Beacon site, especially Kelly Adams, Rendell Archibald, Kathleen Fekete Bauerlein, Kurt Diebboll, Scott Fulmer, Rupert Goldsworthy, Jason Kendell, Charles Rodstrom, John Sprague, Marcel Walker, Mark Walker, and Rita Wise.

The design of the museum is the product of an unusual collaboration, between Dia, artist Robert Irwin, architectural firm Open Office—Alan Koch, Lyn Rice, Galia Solomonoff, and Linda Taalman with Jay Hindmarsh—and a team of skilled professionals, bolstered on occasion by generous time and assistance from several key members of the architectural firm of Skidmore, Owings, and Merrill, with the encouragement and enthusiasm of Roger Duffy as well as Frank Ruggiero, Calvin Smith, and Walt Smith. In addition, Katie Andresen and Georgie Stout from the graphic design group 2x4 worked with Dia to produce a comprehensive signage system and numerous handsome printed materials for Dia:Beacon.

Numerous technical and legal consultants assisted Dia throughout in critical phases of the project's design and implementation, including Jennifer Van Tuyl with Charles Bazydlo of Cuddy & Feder & Worby LLP; Donoghue, Thomas, Auslander, & Drohan; Irving Fisher; Ed Hayes; Highridge Farms; Matterhorn Nursery; Ove Arup & Partners; Elliot Rosenfeld; Ross Dalland P.E.; John Servino; Aryeh Siegel; Henry Gold of Strategic Environmental Solutions; and T.M. DePuy Engineering & Land Surveying. Throughout the process of securing federal historic tax credits for the restoration, we are indebted to preservation consultant Jeffrey Shrimpton, our counsel Thomas Glynn, and Al Shehadi at the National Trust. Dia is also deeply appreciative of the army of construction specialists, contractors, laborers, and crafts people who renovated our former industrial facility.

Dia is especially grateful for the creative and technical contributions to the bookshop and café from Barnes & Noble's amazing staff namely Modesto Alcala, Gina Casella, Melissa Church, Mindy Droutman, Theresa Fitzgerald, Suzanne Kundro, Lou Ann Leary, Richard Lederman, Kevin Luhrs, Dotty McNally, Lori Mitros, Dennis O'Neil, Sylvia Oleck, Carol Pankiw, Miriam Peters, John Petrocelli, Terese Profaci, Jane Shea, Melissa Stemple, Lee Stern, and Christopher Troia.

Many offices within New York State government assisted Dia's efforts, especially John Cahill, Kevin Carpenter, Dale Desnoyers, and Sue McCormick from the New York State Department of Environmental Conservation. In addition, many City of Beacon officials and employees, such as Joseph Braun, Tim Dexter, and Etha Grogan, helped Dia realize this complex project.

As new residents of Beacon and the Hudson Valley, Dia has made friends and partnerships with a variety of organizations working continuously to improve the quality of life and the environment here. Scenic Hudson and its staff have worked closely with Dia in developing the Beacon waterfront for public use, for example, collaborating with Dia and the City of Beacon, with the assistance of Minetta Brook and its director Diane Shamash, in commissioning artist George Trakas to create a master plan for the river's edge. Metro North is improving the accessibility of its railway station for both the town of Beacon and new development there such as Dia's. Numerous regional artists, art organizations, and businesses have welcomed Dia to their community.

Dia:Beacon's wide-reaching public relations plan was crafted and executed by Jeanne Collins with her staff of Libby Mark, Hillary Murray, Lucy O'Brien, and Lisa Russman. MF Productions's team, Melissa Feldman with Allison Brown, Bryan Langston, and Emily Powers, helped to plan and manage the sizable inaugural celebrations. There were also many volunteer advocates for Dia at the project's inception, among them Barry Garfinkel, John Harris, Kathleen Plunkett, Michael Rips, and Daniel Tomson.

Artists are at the core of our endeavor but are not alone in their work: they are supported not only by the museum but also by their families and by assistants, galleries, and collectors, who care for the many aspects of their art. Among those who have assisted Dia and the artists in Beacon (a few by loaning key works to supplement those from Dia, Lannan, and the artists) are Peter Ballantine, Mary Livingstone Beebe, Elizabeth Childress, William Dwyer, Konstanze Ell, Andrea Feldman, Elyse Goldberg, Jerry Gorovoy, Narendra Gosain, Stephen Gunn, Bethany Izard, Hiroko Kawahara, Carmen Knoebel, Susanne Küper, Norm Laich, Doris Lohmann, Steve Morse, Trina McKeever, Juliet Myers, Anthony Sansota, Susanna Singer, and Wendy Williams. In particular Friedrich Christian Flick was willing, from the project's inception, to make pieces available for loan from his outstanding collection of Bruce Nauman's work.

It would be impossible to list all of the many other individuals, foundations, companies, and government representatives who have advanced the cause of this project and help bring it to fruition. Dia sincerely appreciates each of their multifarious contributions to Dia:Beacon.

M.G.

Dia Art Foundation

FOUNDERS

Philippa de Menil and Heiner Friedrich
Lannan Foundation
Louise and Leonard Riggio

PATRONS

The Brown Foundation
Ann Tenenbaum and Thomas H. Lee

BENEFACTORS

The Bohen Foundation
Frances and John Bowes
Jay Chiat
Frances R. Dittmer
Mimi and Peter Haas
Angela and William Haines
International Paper
The Andrew W. Mellon Foundation

DIA CORPORATE SPONSORS

Altria Group, Inc.
Barnes & Noble
Bloomberg
Donna Karan
Timothy and Karin Greenfield-Sanders
International Paper
Kroger Electric Company
Skadden, Arps, Slate, Meagher & Flom LLP
SOM

DIA SUPPORTERS

Dutchess County Industrial Development Agency
Empire State Development Corporation
National Endowment for the Arts
New York City Department of Cultural Affairs
New York State Council on the Arts
New York State Office of Parks, Recreation, and Historic Preservation
The Andrew W. Mellon Foundation
The Andy Warhol Foundation for the Visual Arts
Art for Art's Sake, New York
The Arthur M. Blank Family Foundation
ArtPace, A Foundation for Contemporary Art
The Brown Foundation
The Carnegie Corporation of New York
The Elizabeth Firestone-Graham Foundation
The Getty Grant Program
The Greenwich Collection Ltd.
The Helena Rubinstein Foundation
The Henry Luce Foundation, Inc.
The Horace W. Goldsmith Foundation
J. M. Kaplan Fund
Jean and Louis Dreyfus Foundation
The Juliet Lea Hillman Simonds Foundation
Lannan Foundation
Lila Acheson Wallace Theater Fund at Community Funds, Inc.
The Liman Foundation
Peter Norton Family Foundation
Richard Florsheim Art Fund
Robert Lehman Foundation, Inc.
J. P. Morgan Chase & Co.
Lutz and Carr LLP

DIA ART COUNCIL

Harley Baldwin and Richard Edwards
Lee Balter
Douglas Baxter
Jo and Douglas Berlin
Carolyn Marks Blackwood
Harry Blain
Frances and John Bowes
Sandra J. Brant
Edye and Eli Broad
Melva Bucksbaum and Raymond Learsy
Constance R. Caplan
Eileen Cohen
Jan Cowles
Rosa and Carlos de la Cruz
Joan Davidson
Frances R. Dittmer
Alexandra Loeb Driscoll and Joe Driscoll
Cheryl Cohen Effron and Blair Effron
Ruth Lloyds and William Ehrlich
Carla Emil and Rich Silverstein
Charlene Engelhard
Valerie and John C. Evans
Meghan Ferrill
Roger and Yvonne Ferris
Edmée de Montmollin Firth and Nicholas Firth
Linda and Gregory Fischbach
Doris and Donald Fisher
Wendy and Jason Flom
Michael Formica and Robert Hiemstra
Fariha and Heiner Friedrich
Glenn R. Fuhrman
Barbara Gladstone
Milly and Arne Glimcher
Marian Goodman
Geraldine and Noam Gottesman
Ray A. Graham III
Nan and Steven Grand-Jean
Mimi and Peter Haas
Angela and William Haines
Ydessa Hendeles
Jane Hertzmark
Marieluise Hessel
Audrey M. Irmas
Elizabeth R. Kabler
J. Alan Kahn
Simone and Paulo Klabin
Michèle Gerber Klein and Jeffrey Klein
Pentti Kouri
Werner Kramarsky
Anne Lannan
Rachel and Jean-Pierre Lehman
Toby Lewis
Warren Lichtenstein
Linda and Harry Macklowe
Anne and John Marion
Richard Massey
Susan and Francois de Menil
Stavros Merjos
Ann Lawrance Morse
Peter Morton
Alberto Mugrabi
Nancy Brown Negley
Brooke and Daniel Neidich
Judith Neisser
Peter Norton
Susan and Roy O'Connor
Catherine Orentreich
Linda Pace
Giovanna and Giuseppe Panza di Biumo
Lisa and Richard Perry
Peggy and Bradford J. Race
Cindy and Howard Rachofsky
Louise and Leonard Riggio
Jeanne Greenberg Rohatyn and Nicolas Rohatyn
Deedie and Rusty Rose
Kathy and Keith Sachs
Mary and Jon Shirley
Lea H. Simonds
Ake Skeppner
Suzanne Slesin and Michael Steinberg
Melissa and Robert Soros
Ann M. and Chris Stack
Axel Stawski
Sue and Marco Stoffel
Ann Tenenbaum and Thomas H. Lee
Alice and Tom Tisch
Edwina von Gal
Susy and Jack Wadsworth
Artur Walther
Diana Bowes Weller and Felton Weller
Manuela and Ivan Wirth
Barbara and Charles B. Wright
Virginia and Bagley Wright
Don and Christina Zacharia
Nina and Michael Zilkha
Mary and Harold Zlot
Monica and Bryan Zuriff

As of April 1, 2003

DIA ART FOUNDATION STAFF

Michael Govan *Director*

Mariah Adin *Building Attendant, Beacon*

Rich Aldrich *Book Sales Assistant*

Rendell Archibald *Facility Assistant, Beacon*

Vickie Arndt *Exhibitions Manager*

Mary Berning *Visitor Services, Chelsea*

Chad Bowen *Building Attendant, Beacon*

John Bowsher *Administrator, Art Programs*

Nele Brauner *Curatorial Intern*

Lauren Canelli *Admissions Cashier, Chelsea*

Katherine Carl *Development*

Carolyn Kay Carson *Finance Manager*

Lynne Cooke *Curator*

Keisha Cruz *Café Assistant, Beacon*

Stephen Dewhurst *Assistant Director*

Patrice Dilworth *Gallery Attendant, The Broken Kilometer*

William Dilworth *Gallery Attendant, The New York Earth Room*

Ivan Diodonet *Buildings Assistant, Chelsea*

Steven Evans *Operations Deputy*

Lacey Fekishazy *Gallery Attendant, Beacon*

Laura Fields *Graphics*

Junior Forde *Facility Assistant, Beacon*

Bettina Funcke *Publications and Special Programs Associate*

Gale Griffiths *Receptionist, Beacon*

Wade Guyton *Cafe and Video Library Manager, Chelsea*

Christine Hanaway *Book Sales Assistant Manager*

Curtis Harvey *Building Manager, Beacon*

Patrick Heilman *Digital Media Specialist*

Corrie Hogg *Gallery Attendant, Chelsea*

Paul Hrusa *Gallery Attendant, Chelsea*

Brad Jackson *Manager of Visitor Services, Beacon*

Nina Jesberger *Book Sales Assistant Manager*

Palyzeh Kashi *Gallery Attendant, Chelsea*

Karen Kelly *Director of Publications and Special Programs*

Dion Kliner *Buildings Manager, Chelsea*

Tonya Kostenko *Café Manager, Beacon*

Nathan Lowman *Gallery Attendant, Chelsea*

Jason Lujan *Visitor Services, Chelsea*

Jennifer Mackiewicz *Director's and Operations Office, Beacon*

Victoria Manning *Gallery Attendant, Beacon*

Michelle Marozik *Book Sales Manager*

Kate McKeown *Gallery Attendant, Beacon*

Bryan Messenbourg *Gallery Attendant, The Dan Flavin Art Institute*

Jennifer Minnen *Development Associate*

Marika Miya *Café Assistant, Beacon*

Brighde Mullins *Director of Poetry Series*

Kirsten Nash *Operations and Events*

Adrienne Parks *Receptionist and Office Manager*

Jill Petrush *Book Sales Assistant*

Justine Pizzo *Development Assistant*

Armelle Pradalier *Curatorial Associate*

Laura Raicovich *Secretary to the Board*

Suzanne Read *Gallery Attendant, Beacon*

Victoria Robinson *Assistant Manager of Visitor Services, Beacon*

Charles Rodstrom *Building Attendant, Beacon*

Amy Sandback *Director of Collection Research*

James Schaeufele *Director of Operations*

Caroline Schneider *Admissions, Beacon*

Barbara Schröder *Publications Assistant*

Kathleen Shields *Administrator, The Lightning Field*

Tina Teufel *Curatorial Intern*

Sarah R. Thompson *Public Affairs Associate*

Melissa Toth *Gallery Attendant, Beacon*

Sara Schnittjer Tucker *Director of Digital Media*

Mark Walker *Construction Manager*

Karren Weathers *Caretaker, The Lightning Field*

Robert Weathers *Caretaker, The Lightning Field*

Dina Weiss *Education Associate*

Amy S. Weisser *Assistant Director for Beacon/Director of External Affairs*

Rita Wise *Facility Assistant, Beacon*

Aaron Young *Gallery Attendant, Beacon*

Fernando Zelaya *Finance Assistant*

As of May 18, 2003

PHOTOGRAPH AND REPRODUCTION CREDITS

Bill Jacobson: cover, pp. 57, 62, 176, 182–85, 206, 208–215, 229, 246, 250–55; Michael Govan: pp. 1, 27–29, 32, 37 (above); Richard Barnes: pp. 2, 5, 316, 323, 325, 327, 329, 331, 333, and 344; Gianfranco Gorgoni: p. 14; Thibault Jeansen: p. 16 (left); Florian Holzherr: pp. 16 (right), 19, 39–41; Ivory Serra, © 2003 Richard Serra / Artists Rights Society (ARS), New York: p. 17; Nancy Holt, © Estate of Robert Smithson/Licensed by VAGA, New York: p. 18; Florian Holzherr, © 2003 Estate of Dan Flavin / Artists Rights Society (ARS), New York: pp. 20–21, 136; John Cliett: pp. 22, 24–25, 131; Jon Abbott: p. 23; Florian Holzherr, © Donald Judd Foundation/Licensed by VAGA, New York: pp. 26; Stuart Tyson: pp. 30–31; Thibault Jeansen, © 2003 Robert Irwin / Artists Rights Society (ARS), New York: pp. 34–35, 56; Florian Holzherr, © James Turell: pp. 40–41; Tom Vinetz: pp. 42, 43, 152–55; Nic Tenwiggenhorn: pp. 44–45, 63, 66, 133–135, 186, 189, 191–195, 262–65; Todd Eberle, © Donald Judd Foundation/Licensed by VAGA, New York: p. 46; Paul Rocheleau, 1994, courtesy The Andy Warhol Museum, Pittsburgh, © 2003 Andy Warhol Foundation for the Visual Arts / Artists Rights Society (ARS), New York: p. 48; Hickey-Robertson, © Cy Twombly Gallery, courtesy of The Menil Collection, Houston: p. 49 (right); Erika Fischer, © 2003 Artists Rights Society (ARS), New York / VG Bild-Kunst, Bonn: pp. 50–51 (below); David Ludlow: p. 51 (above); Dieter Schwerdtle, © 2003 Artists Rights Society (ARS), New York / VG Bild-Kunst, Bonn: p. 52 (above); courtesy Michael Heizer: pp. 52 (below), 146, 149; Frederick Nilsen: p. 54; Cathy Carver: pp. 55, 68–69, 178, 310–11; Gamma One Conversions, pp. 58, 151, 156, 158, 160–65, 306; courtesy Kawamura memorial museum of art, © 2003 Barnett Newman Foundation / Artists Rights Society (ARS), New York: p. 60; David Allison: p. 67; Attilio Maranzano: p. 70; Rudolph Burckhardt, © Donald Judd Foundation/Licensed by VAGA, New York: p. 73 (above); Paul Katz, © Donald Judd Foundation/Licensed by VAGA, New York: p. 73 (below); Lawrence Beck: pp. 76, 79, 81, 83–85; Cathy Carver, © 2003 Artists Rights Society (ARS), New York / VG Bild-Kunst, Bonn: p. 86; courtesy Lucio Armelio, Naples, © 2003 Artists Rights Society (ARS), New York / VG Bild-Kunst, Bonn: p. 89; Bill Jacobson, © 2003 Artists Rights Society (ARS), New York / VG Bild-Kunst, Bonn: p. 91; Caroline Tisdall, © 2003 Artists Rights Society (ARS), New York / VG Bild-Kunst, Bonn: p. 92; Cathy Carver, © 2003 Artists Rights Society (ARS), New York / VG Bild-Kunst, Bonn: pp. 93, 95; Nic Tenwiggenhorn, © 2003 Artists Rights Society (ARS), New York / VG Bild-Kunst, Bonn: p. 94; Peter Moore, © Estate of Peter Moore/Licensed by VAGA, NYC: pp. 96, 102–103; Rafael S. Lobato, courtesy Cheim & Read, New York, © Louise Bourgeois/Licensed by VAGA, New York: p. 101; Frédéric Delpech, courtesy Cheim & Read, New York, © Louise Bourgeois/Licensed by VAGA, New York: pp. 104–05; Bill Jacobson, © 2003 John Chamberlain / Artists Rights Society (ARS), New York: pp. 106, 109; Michael Govan, © 2003 John Chamberlain / Artists Rights Society (ARS), New York: p. 110; Nic Tenwiggenhorn, © 2003 John Chamberlain / Artists Rights Society (ARS), New York: pp. 112–15; Cathy Carver, © Hanne Darboven, 1980-83: pp. 116, 119 (middle), 120, 122–23; Bill Jacobson, © Hanne Darboven, 1980-83: pp. 119 (above, below), 124–125; Tord Lund, © 1989 Moderna Museet, Stockholm: p. 126; Bevan Davies: p. 128; Bill Jacobson, © 2003 Estate of Dan Flavin / Artists Rights Society (ARS), New York: pp. 138, 141–45; Bill Jacobson, © Donald Judd Foundation/Licensed by VAGA, New York: pp. 166, 171–73, 175; Tom Powel, courtesy Paula Cooper Gallery, © Donald Judd Foundation/Licensed by VAGA, New York: p. 169; courtesy Lannan Foundation, © Donald Judd Foundation/Licensed by VAGA, New York: p. 174; Andre Magnin, courtesy Hiroko Kawahara: p. 181; Robert E. Mates and Paul Katz, © 2003 Sol LeWitt / Artists Rights Society (ARS), New York: p. 196; John Groo, courtesy the artist, © 2003 Sol LeWitt / Artists Rights Society (ARS), New York: p. 199; © Sol LeWitt, pp. 200–05; video capture: Patrick Heilman, © 2003 Bruce Nauman / Artists Rights Society (ARS), New York: pp. 216, 220, 221; courtesy Lannan Foundation, © 2003 Bruce Nauman / Artists Rights Society (ARS), New York: p. 219; Stuart Tyson, © 2003 Bruce Nauman / Artists Rights Society (ARS), New York: pp. 222–23; courtesy Sperone Westwater, © 2003 Bruce Nauman / Artists Rights Society (ARS), New York: pp. 224–25; courtesy Thordis Moeller, © 2003 Artists Rights Society (ARS), New York / VG Bild-Kunst, Bonn: p. 226; Bill Jacobson, © 2003 Artists Rights Society (ARS), New York / VG Bild-Kunst, Bonn: pp. 231–35; courtesy Gerhard Richter: p. 236, 241; David Allison: p. 239; Friedrich Rosenstiel, Cologne, courtesy Gerhard Richter: p. 242; Bob Kolbreuer, courtesy The Saint Louis Art Museum: p. 243; Dirk Reinartz, © 2003 Richard Serra / Artists Rights Society (ARS), New York: pp. 266, 268–69, 271–75; Cathy Carver, © Estate of Robert Smithson/Licensed by VAGA, New York: p. 276; Estate of Robert Smithson, courtesy James Cohan Gallery © Estate of Robert Smithson/Licensed by VAGA, New York: pp. 279, 281; Bill Jacobson, © Estate of Robert Smithson/Licensed by VAGA, New York: pp. 280, 282, 284–85; courtesy John Weber Gallery, New York © Estate of Robert Smithson/Licensed by VAGA, New York: p. 283; Arthur Tress, © 2003 Andy Warhol Foundation for the Visual Arts / Artists Rights Society (ARS), New York: p. 286; Bill Jacobson, © 2003 Andy Warhol Foundation for the Visual Arts / Artists Rights Society (ARS), New York: 290–95; courtesy of the artist, © 2003 Lawrence Weiner / Artists Rights Society (ARS), New York: p. 296; courtesy of the artist and Marian Goodman Gallery, New York, © 2003 Lawrence Weiner / Artists Rights Society (ARS), New York: p. 304; Babette Mangolte: pp. 312–15.

This book was published on the occasion of the opening of Dia Art Foundation's museum, Dia:Beacon.

Project Director: Mary DelMonico

Director of Publications: Karen Kelly

Publication and Curatorial Coordinator: Barbara Schröder

Designer: Laura Fields

Editor: David Frankel

Research: Bettina Funcke

Publication Assistant: Martin Fox

Proofreader: Richard Gallin

Color separations by C+S Repro, Germany

Printed and bound in Germany by Cantz

LIBRARY OF CONGRESS CATALOGING-IN-PUBLICATION DATA

Cooke, Lynne.
Dia: Beacon / Lynne Cooke and Michael Govan.
p. cm.
Includes bibliographical references.
ISBN 0-944521-47-9 (alk. paper)
1. Dia: Beacon (Art museum) 2. Art, Modern--20th century. 3.
Art--New York (State)--Beacon. I. Govan, Michael. II. Dia Art
Foundation. III. Title.
N6487.B43C66 2003
708.147'33--dc21
2003043915

ISBN 0-944521-47-9

535 West 22nd Street
New York, NY 10011
www.diaart.org

Third edition 2003

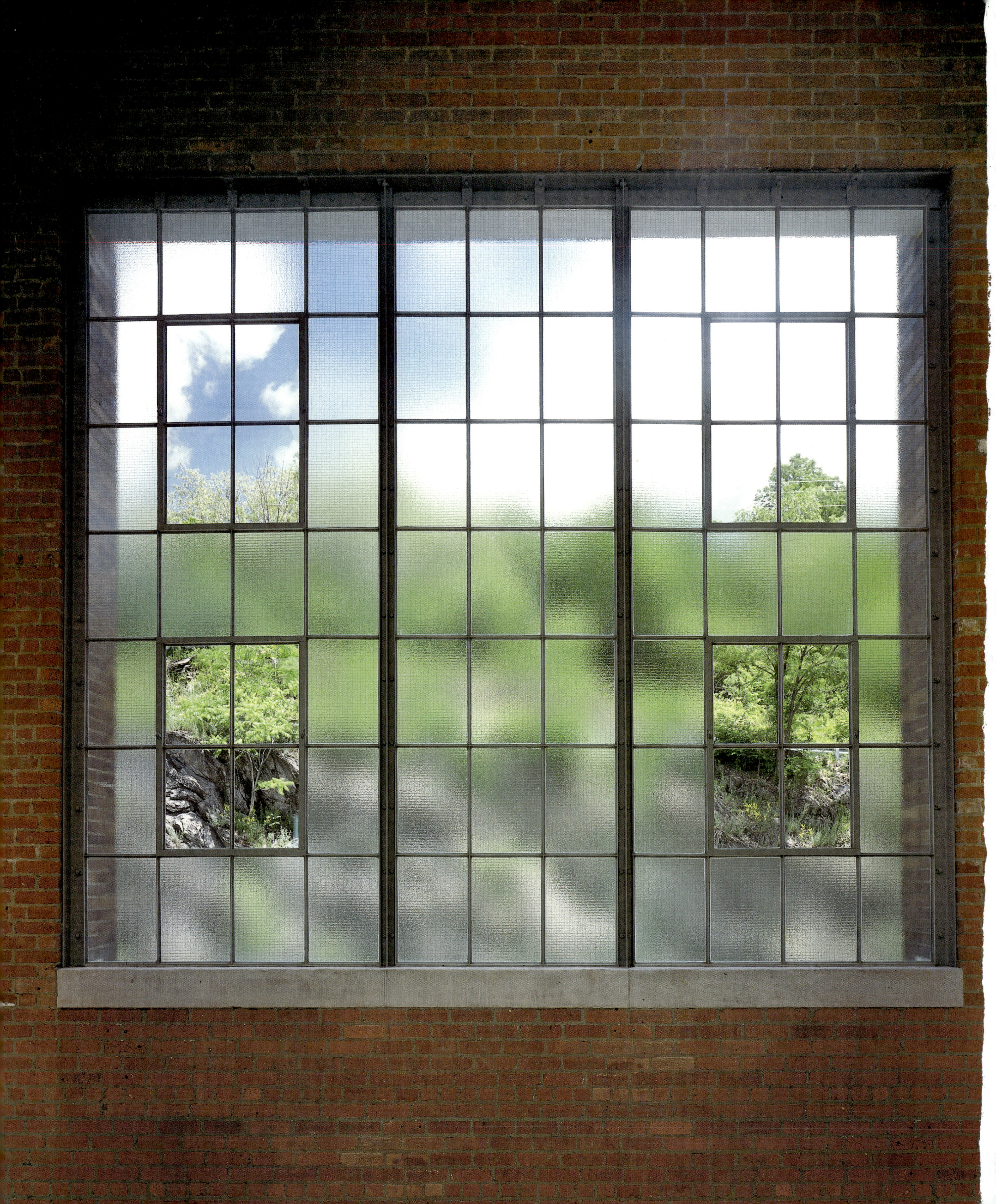

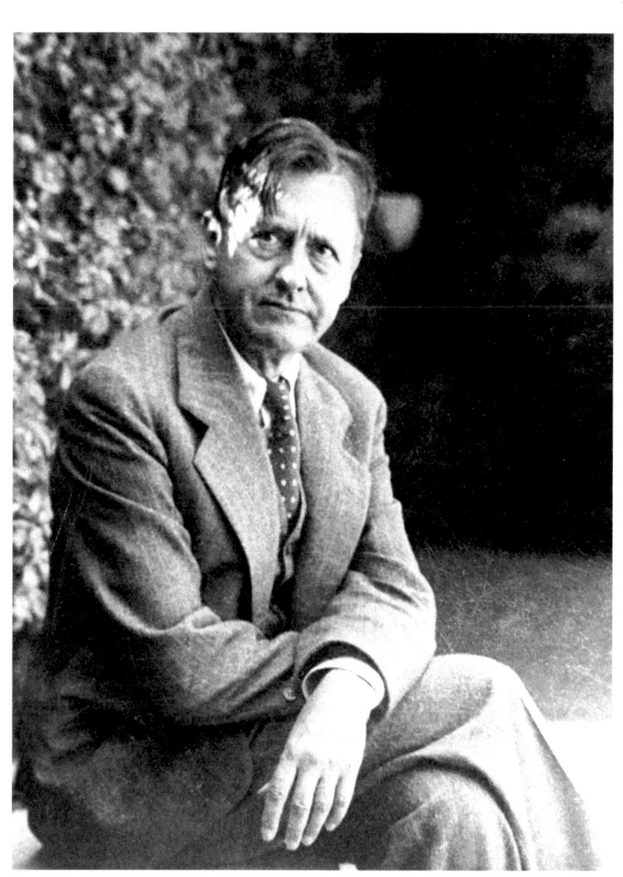

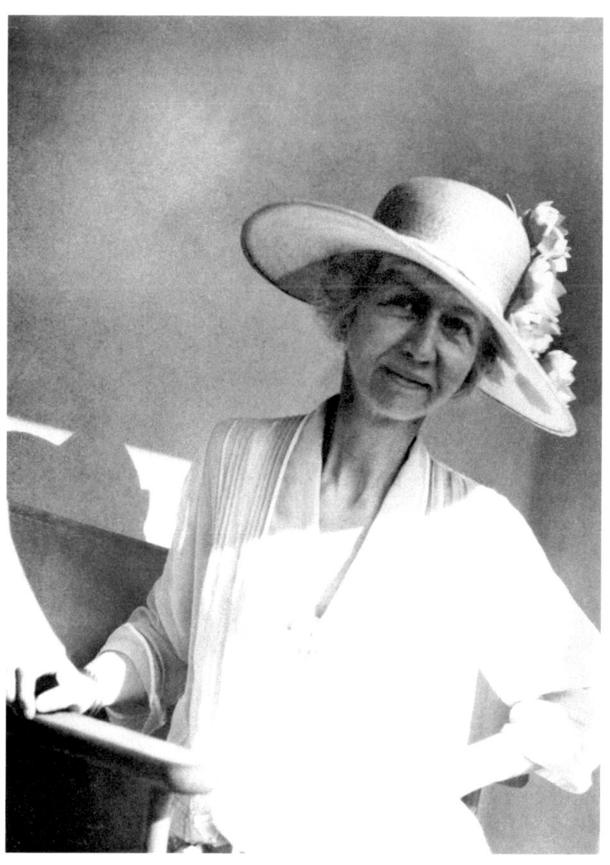

H O L L Y W O O D

ARENSBERG

Avant-Garde Collecting in Midcentury L.A.

MARK NELSON
WILLIAM H. SHERMAN
ELLEN HOOBLER

GETTY RESEARCH INSTITUTE LOS ANGELES

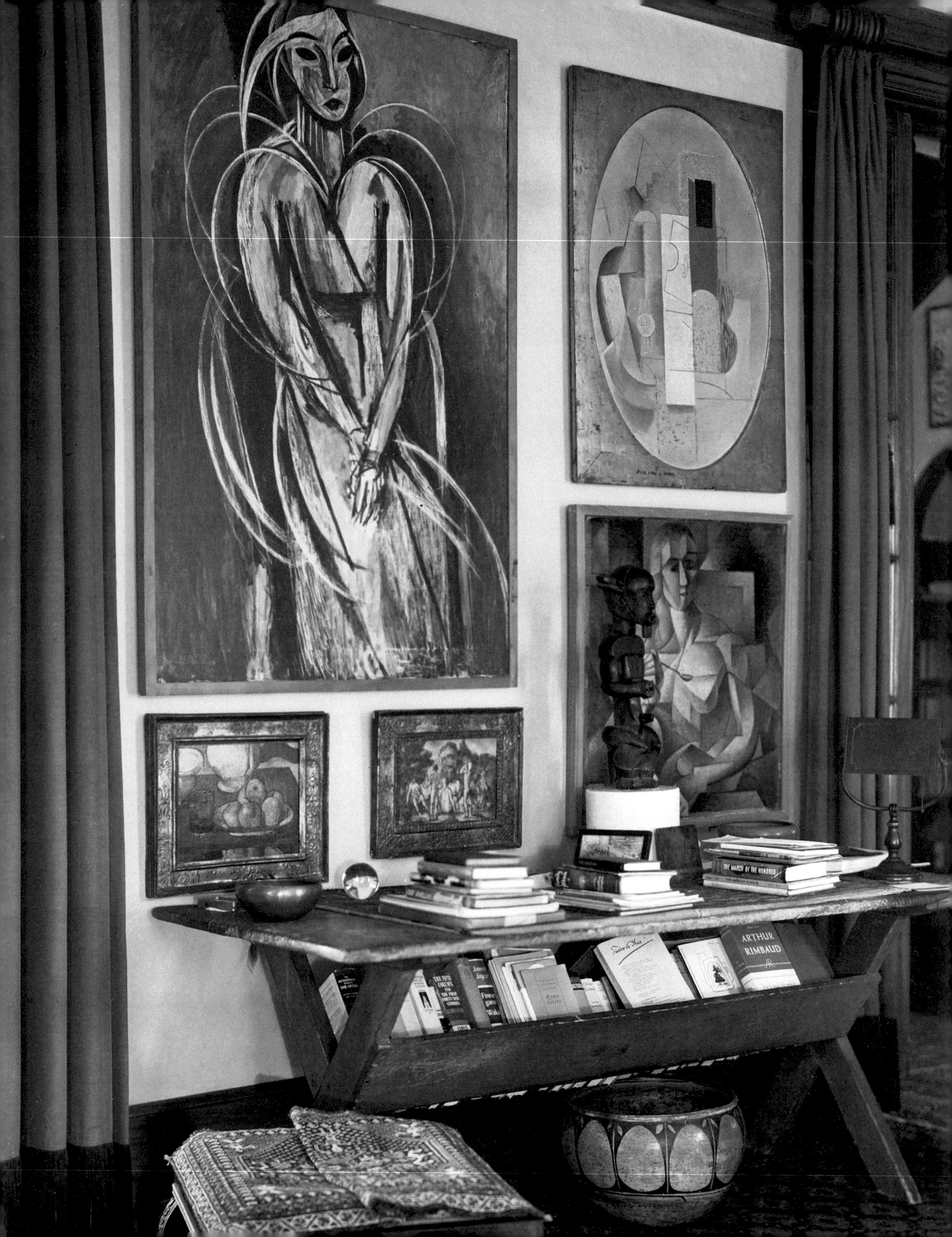
THE MARCH OF THE HUNDRED
THE AMERICAN SCHOLAR
THE OPERA
THE FIFTH COLUMN AND THE FIRST FORTY-NINE STORIES
Twice a Year
ARTHUR RIMBAUD

CONTENTS

7065 HILLSIDE AVENUE, the house at the center of this book, is located in the heart of charming 1920s and 1930s Hollywood. It was here that Louise and Walter Arensberg assembled the spectacular modern and pre-Columbian art collection and Francis Bacon materials that the couple are known for, and it was here that they connected to their neighbor, the gallerist Earl Stendahl, who would ultimately purchase 7065 Hillside. All told, the house was in the hands of these two families for almost one hundred years.

Over the course of Walter and Louise Arensberg's nearly thirty years at the house, the couple's lives would become intertwined with those of the Stendahl family next door, who were the proprietors of the Stendahl Galleries. Throughout the years, the Stendahl Galleries would occupy various sites around Los Angeles—including the Ambassador Hotel—before ultimately moving to 7065 Hillside Avenue after the deaths of the Arensbergs. Best known today for their sales of pre-Columbian art, the Stendahls also sold Brancusi sculptures and Modigliani paintings; when they could, they would secure old master paintings as well as their broad inventory of ancient Mexican offerings, an assemblage of materials that also characterized the works within the Arensberg home.

The neighbors had much to teach one another. Educated in the best settings (Harvard for Walter, a finishing school in Dresden for Louise), the Arensbergs were sophisticated in ways that their neighbors could only dream of. But Earl and Enid Stendahl, educated in the public schools of Menomie, Wisconsin, were canny and quick students of the world, and Earl Stendahl was an astute businessman. Happy to share what he had learned of the world, he did not, for example, hesitate to write an extensive letter to the newly minted curator of ancient Mexico and Central America at the American Museum of Natural History in 1947, schooling him up in the style and significance of Maya figurines of the eighth and ninth centuries, with some advice about the rampant forgeries in circulation. The Arensbergs and the Stendahls saw their fair share of such falsifications, both learning as the Stendahl Galleries made pre-Columbian art far more familiar to American consumers. That they became fast friends and trusted associates attests to their shared interests, especially in the power of visual material. It was no small matter that Earl Stendahl wanted these prominent collectors—yes, the Arensbergs, but also the Honorable Robert Woods Bliss in Washington, DC, who, with his wife Mildred, cofounded the Dumbarton Oaks collection—to underscore the insight and acumen of the dealer.

Intertwined in life, the archival records of the Arensbergs and Stendahls remain so today, in the references to one and the other in notes and works. The principal homes of Arensberg records are the Huntington Library and the Philadelphia Museum of Art. These records are often accessed together through the microfilm copies at the Smithsonian's Archives of American Art. Stendahl Galleries archival documentation of the business regarding largely, but not exclusively, California artists (7.5 linear feet) has been held by the Smithsonian's Archives of American Art since 1976, and this, too, is usually accessed through the microfilms of the Archives. But the families and their business interests come together at the Getty Research Institute (GRI), which acquired the rest of the Stendahl Galleries archives, with particular focus on the pre-Columbian, in 2017. It is in the archives' stock books that one sees sale after sale to the Arensbergs. Item 744, a typically undated stock book entry, a jade stone figure acquired from William Spratling in Mexico, was sold to the Arensbergs for $350; they make acquisitions on every page of the stock books of the 1940s, set amid acquisitions by rival Bliss, in DC, as well as individuals whose names jump off the page today, such as Vincent Price and Man Ray.

This story will continue, especially now that the GRI launched, in 2019, the Pre-Hispanic Art Provenance Initiative to document the origins, sales, and acquisitions of pre-Hispanic art across the United States and Europe. The Arensberg collections are prominent in these inventories, which will serve as a launchpad for new rounds of research, much of it starting at 7065 Hillside Avenue. The GRI is pleased to recognize that the story of California collections has room to grow, and *Hollywood Arensberg* is a key study that will stimulate investigations for years to come.

MARY MILLER
Director, Getty Research Institute

Has the house ever been photographed?
It should be documented from cellar to attic. For in these days of emphasis on installation, when for valid educational reasons we tend to isolate and canonize the work of art, it is sobering to think upon a successful exception to rule. The Arensberg pictures stand belligerently close together, but they do not fight. Their hanging breaks every museum precept of height, space and light, but you see them clearly, one by one, and remember them in detail for a long time afterward.

—JAMES THRALL SOBY[1]

"HAS THE HOUSE EVER BEEN PHOTOGRAPHED?" James Thrall Soby wondered in March 1945. If it never had been, this book would not exist.

The house in question was the Hollywood residence of Louise and Walter Arensberg at 7065 Hillside Avenue. In the first half of the twentieth century, the Arensbergs assembled one of the most important private collections of art in the United States, as well as the world's largest private library of works by and about Sir Francis Bacon. The collection took shape in the couple's Manhattan apartment (pages 10–11), where they gave Marcel Duchamp his first American home and presided over the salon that brought Dada to New York, and it expanded rapidly after their move to Los Angeles in 1921. By the time Louise and Walter Arensberg died—in 1953 and 1954, respectively—they had acquired some four thousand rare books and manuscripts and nearly one thousand works of art, including hundreds of Mesoamerican objects, world-class specimens of cubism, surrealism, and primitivism, and the bulk of Duchamp's oeuvre.

When Soby wrote the words that serve as our epigraph, he had just finished a stint as director of the Department of Painting and Sculpture at New York's Museum of Modern Art and was consolidating his own position as a leading collector of contemporary art. He was therefore ideally placed to recognize the Arensbergs' remarkable achievement not just in acquiring so many valuable objects but also in giving them a vitality that bordered on the supernatural: "The house is invested with magic," Soby observed, "as if it were a studio in which nearly all the finest modern artists had worked together, with what they created still holding the warmth and excitement of original discovery."

Soby knew that photographs would capture the exceptional quality of the works that filled nearly all available space in every room of the house (including the bathrooms). A lens aimed at the living room fireplace, for instance, would take in three Picassos, three Braques, three Rousseaus, three Klees, four iconic pieces by Brancusi, and four major Duchamp works, interspersed with original letters written by Sir Francis Bacon and his mother, a leaf from a 1462 Mainz Bible, a monolithic figure from Easter Island, a Peruvian mask, Persian rugs of various shapes and sizes, and at least a dozen pre-Columbian sculptures. A full photographic survey of the remaining rooms would register no fewer than nineteen works by Brancusi and more than forty Duchamps (including all three versions of his notorious painting *Nude Descending a Staircase*). But Soby was also struck by the interaction between the Arensbergs' art and the Arensbergs' home: the truly startling lesson, for him, was the fact that the dense and eccentric display, while breaking every curatorial rule, could bring the works clearly before the eyes and give them a lasting place in the mind. In calling for thorough documentation, Soby wanted the Arensbergs' house to have an enduring place in our cultural memory as well.

As it happens, the first few glimpses of the couple's home were published in *Vogue* magazine the same month that Soby's essay in *View* was being prepared for printing (fig. 1). Over the next six years, the house and its collections were photographed at least five more times, for a variety of purposes. The pictures that make up *Hollywood Arensberg*'s room-by-room, wall-by-wall, object-by-object tour of the home were taken between around 1939 and early 1951, as the Arensbergs' vast collection of art and books was approaching the form that would be handed down to posterity. Very few of these images were published, however, and

1. Epigraph and all included quotations in the preface are James Thrall Soby, "Marcel Duchamp in the Arensberg Collection," in "Marcel Duchamp Number," special issue, *View: The Modern Magazine* 5, no. 1 (1945): 10–12.

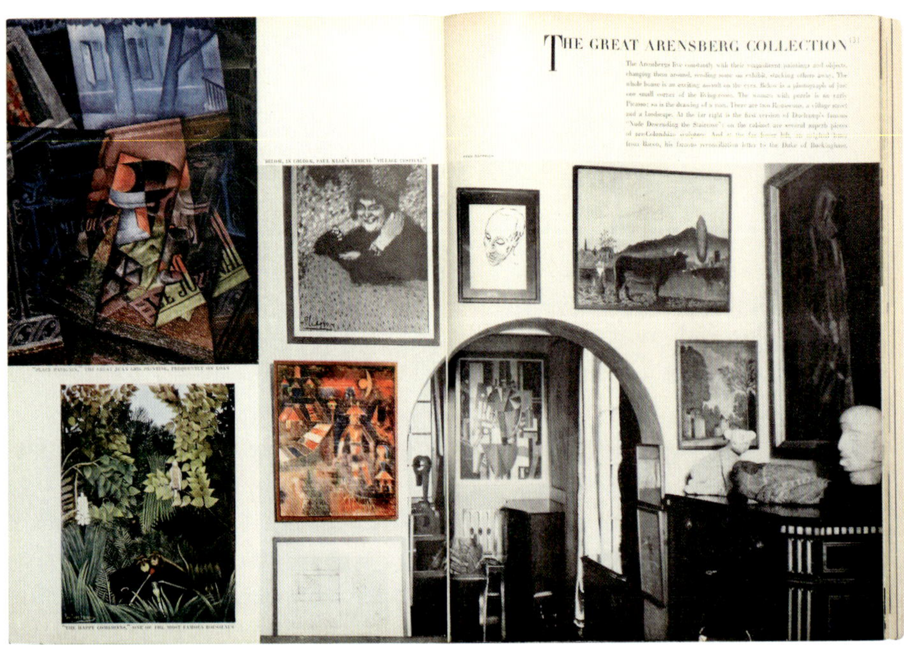
THE GREAT ARENSBERG COLLECTION

1. A SPREAD FROM THE ARTICLE "GREAT ART . . . IN FOUR CALIFORNIA HOUSES: THE GREAT ARENSBERG COLLECTION," IN THE 1 FEBRUARY 1945 ISSUE OF *VOGUE*

some have not been seen in decades. This volume marks the first time that they have been brought together in a single place, set in sequence, and put in context.

Because none of the photographers independently captured every wall in every room, images taken by all of them have been collected and arranged here to give the best possible representation of the house and its holdings. Many of these pictures have been sourced from beautiful archival prints and original negatives, but some of lesser quality have also been included because they offer the only record of a particular surface or view. While they vary in artistic and technical quality, collectively the photographs have the power to take us back in time and guide us through a domestic space where the "warmth and excitement of original discovery" experienced by Soby and so many others can still be felt.

To construct a logical path through the home, emphasis is placed on the spatial relationships between objects and rooms, rather than on the chronology of the photographs. In other words, space trumps time as an organizing tenet. Still, the temporal dimension is not altogether absent. This sequence shows the house in different states of order and disorder, illustrating how artworks were moved from one room to another, and how they might have been perceived differently as their display was changed. Organized in this manner, the photographs provide an overall snapshot of a collection in motion and convey how much pleasure the Arensbergs took in creating arrangements that were never fixed or static. The photographs also reveal a great deal about the couple's famously private personalities, sometimes for what they do not show as much as for what they do.

Readers of the book's plates section will enter the house, as visitors did, through the audacious foyer designed by Henry Palmer Sabin to hold two contrasting sculptures by Brancusi. They will proceed through a circuit beginning in the home's public spaces (living room, dining room, and sunroom) and moving toward its more private spaces (bedrooms and offices) before finishing outdoors with the sculptural displays on the patios.

These photographs testify to the elaborate arrangements that once brought paintings, sculptures, and drawings into close contact with leather-bound volumes, exotic carpets, historical furniture, and indigenous artifacts. This was a collection that cut across periods, cultures, and media, establishing a dialogue between art and books, the European and the American, the ancient and the avant-garde. The patterns that made such a vivid impression on so many guests, from famous artists to local students, are harder to see now that the collection is split between two public institutions—the Philadelphia Museum of Art and the Huntington Library in San Marino, California—and further divided among the departments within them.

Louise and Walter Arensberg saw their diverse holdings as part of a single enterprise, and they gathered them under the umbrella of the Francis Bacon Foundation, established in 1938 and run from an office on the second floor of their home. The Arensbergs had wanted to keep their collections together and hoped to find an arrangement that would allow them to remain in Los Angeles. Ultimately, though, the art and art-related archives went to the Philadelphia Museum of Art, while the Baconian books, Walter's working papers, and many of the couple's personal documents stayed behind in Southern California, finding their way, in 1996, to the Huntington. The organizational diagram on page 74 charts the complex path the Arensberg collection took as it made its transition from private home to public institutions, explaining what has ended up where and (when possible) why. It is meant to help readers follow the abbreviations used in identifying and discussing specific objects and locate up-to-date descriptions of them in finding aids and catalogs, and to serve, more generally, as a map for future scholarship on the Arensbergs' legacy.

Hollywood Arensberg asks—some seventy years after Soby's call—what can be learned by seeing these disparate materials as part of a single vision, framed by a unique domestic space at the heart of Hollywood's burgeoning artistic scene. Few of the people who visit Duchamp's modern masterpieces in Philadelphia today are aware that the man who collected them spent most of his time studying the writings of Sir Francis Bacon, and few of the readers who consult the Bacon books now housed at the Huntington have any idea that they once sat side by side with some of the twentieth century's most radical works of art. Reuniting these objects and communities has been a principal motivation for this project, but our hosts have not made this job easy. While the Arensbergs were surprisingly happy to open their doors to visitors, they greatly disliked publicity, refusing to be photographed among their collection and writing little about its history or rationale. Given Walter's willingness to publish on other subjects—his output included translations of Italian and French literature, experimental poetry, studies of Dante's cryptic symbolism, and increasingly elaborate books arguing for Bacon's authorship of the plays attributed to Shakespeare—his reticence about his work as a collector and curator is all the more conspicuous. His only detailed statement on the subject can be found in the transcript of a previously unpublished interview from about 1951 conducted by Kenneth Ross, cultural critic and director of the Los Angeles Municipal Arts Department, which we have reproduced in its entirety. That interview conveys the ease and enthusiasm with which Walter moved between early modern books and modernist paintings, and expresses the qualities of a mercurial mind that reveled in allegory, excelled at chess, and never tired of looking for hidden meanings. And it goes some way toward explaining why an almost comprehensive collection of Marcel Duchamp's work came to be owned by something called the Francis Bacon Foundation—and indeed why Duchamp himself served as one of its trustees.

Our introductory essay, "The King and Queen Surrounded: The Arensberg Collection in Context," supplies the background needed to follow this story. It explains the personal, aesthetic, and intellectual forces that prepared the Arensbergs for their approach to collecting and tracks the evolution of their collections as they moved from New York to Los Angeles. We present the Hollywood home not only as a studio (to borrow Soby's metaphor) but also as a cabinet of curiosities combining artifacts from the new world and the old, as a chessboard where pieces could be moved according to the rules of various games, and as a laboratory where experimental art could come into contact with other forms of knowing and making—the mythical and the magical, the covert and the subconscious. Such an approach makes the Arensbergs look less like wealthy hoarders of priceless objects and more like scholar-collectors for whom configurations of words and images in space could be vehicles for discovery and invention.

As the photographic record makes clear, these configurations took on an extra dimension as the Arensbergs became fixated on pre-Columbian art, eventually giving it an equal place alongside their modern art and Renaissance books. Previous accounts of the Arensbergs have not fully explored this radical development—despite its importance to the milieus of modernist art and California collecting—so we were delighted when Ellen Hoobler, the William B. Ziff, Jr., Associate Curator of Art of the Americas at the Walters Art Museum, expressed an interest in returning to her earlier work on the Arensbergs. In her essay, "Smoothing the Path for Rough Stones: The Changing Role of Pre-Columbian Art in the Arensberg Collection," Hoobler provides the first full account of how the couple's appreciation of the ancient art of the Americas shifted over the decades, setting them alongside peers and competitors in the field, including John Quinn and Robert Woods Bliss.

She details their first years as serious collectors in New York in the 1910s, where they were initially advised by the Mexican artist, critic, and dealer Marius de Zayas and the artist Walter Pach (organizer of the Armory Show, which had first stimulated their interest in modern art). Hoobler shows how, by the mid-1930s, the Arensbergs had become interested in pre-Columbian objects as "American Sources of Modern Art," as the Museum of Modern Art labeled them in a 1933 exhibition. Guided by the Mexican artist Roberto Montenegro and the Hollywood film producer Kenneth Macgowan, and facilitated by California's premier dealer (and the couple's next-door neighbor) Earl Stendahl, the Arensbergs bought hundreds of pre-Columbian works, including the monumental central Mexican sculptures that dominated their outdoor patios.

In Soby's eyes, the Arensbergs had "created something for which the word 'collection' seems too dispassionate a term, though theirs, certainly, is one of the greatest collections of contemporary art in the world." To the Arensbergs' credit, many of the objects they collected are still highly prized, and this book seeks to restore the extra charge they take on when considered in the context of their common history in such an electric space. The Arensberg home was a challenge and an inspiration to innumerable visitors for nearly thirty formative years in the first half of the twentieth century, and it continues to prompt new questions today. This book is an invitation to travel back to Hollywood's singularly modern past. Dial GLadstone 1628 to make an appointment—Louise and Walter will gladly receive you.

MARK NELSON | WILLIAM H. SHERMAN

HOLLYWOOD ARENSBERG builds upon pioneering studies of Louise and Walter Arensberg by Naomi Sawelson-Gorse and Francis M. Naumann. Sawelson-Gorse wrote both her master's thesis and doctoral dissertation on the couple and has gone on to publish several significant essays about them. She worked closely with the Arensbergs' trusted assistant, Elizabeth Wrigley, at the Francis Bacon Library in Claremont, California, and after Wrigley's death played a key role in transferring the Arensbergs' art-related papers to the Philadelphia Museum of Art. Both her published and unpublished work on the Arensbergs are essential reading for anyone seeking a broader understanding of the couple's impact on the development of modernism in the United States generally and Marcel Duchamp's rise to art-historical prominence specifically. Naumann's expertise on the couple's early years in New York and his voluminous body of work on Duchamp have provided significant context for our interest in the Arensbergs' later years in Los Angeles. Naomi and Francis have been extraordinarily supportive of our work and generous with their time and resources: their knowledge of Arensberg minutiae and their responses to the material we present in this book have contributed immensely to our project.

In a 1980 article for the *Philadelphia Museum of Art Bulletin* that anticipated the approach we have taken in this book, Naumann identified every object visible in Charles Sheeler's photographs, taken ca. 1919, of the Arensbergs' New York apartment (pages 10–11), highlighting how quickly the couple's collection had grown after their introduction to the European avant-garde only six years earlier. Naumann later took his project further by constructing a life-size replica of the apartment's main room for *Making Mischief: Dada Invades New York*, his 1996 exhibition at the Whitney Museum of American Art.

Our own reconstruction of the Hollywood house—including the floorplans and elevations drawn for this book by Siobhán Burke and Jonathan Giffin of Lyric Design and Planning—would not have been possible without the tremendous hospitality of Ronald and April Dammann, who opened their doors to us at 7065 Hillside Avenue. We are deeply grateful for their friendship and trust. Ron, grandson of the art dealer Earl Stendahl, continued to operate the Stendahl Galleries from the Arensbergs' former home, extending the business's run to an impressive 106 years of continued operation before he retired in 2016. April's enthusiasm for the gallery's history (documented in her own book, *Exhibitionist: Earl Stendahl, Art Dealer as Impresario*) was infectious. In addition to donating significant archival materials to the Getty Research Institute, Ron and April ensured that the Arensberg and Stendahl legacies would be better protected by securing landmark status for 7065 Hillside from the Cultural Heritage Commission of the Los Angeles Department of City Planning. There can be little doubt that this decision substantially reduced the potential pool of buyers, and even less doubt that, by consequence, the right one would be found.

As we write this, Jonathan Browning and Marco Heithaus, the new owners of 7065 Hillside, are lovingly restoring it, turning their eyes toward both its social history and its architectural eccentricities. Their discoveries have reshaped our understanding of the house and its history. Jonathan and Marco have kept the doors of 7065 Hillside open to us, and we in turn are happy to have assisted them in their goal of restoring the house to its original condition.

We were fortunate to talk to a number of people who visited the home when the Arensbergs lived there, including Andrew Baker, whose first wife, Carol Irene Bruns Baker, was one of Walter Arensberg's secretaries; and Elaine Lustig Cohen, whose first husband, Alvin Lustig, did graphic-design work for both the Arensbergs and Earl Stendahl. Their vivid memories did as much as any photograph to bring the house, its contents, and its owners back to life. It has also been a pleasure sharing this project with (and learning from) members of the Arensbergs' extended family, including Suzi Arensberg, the late Charles Arensberg and his son, Charles C. M. Arensberg, and Susan McMillan Arensberg. We are very grateful for their enthusiasm for our work.

Over the many years it took to complete this book, individuals from the two institutions most closely associated with the Arensberg legacy—the Philadelphia Museum of Art (PMA) and the Huntington Library, Art Museum, and Botanical Gardens in San Marino, California—provided essential access and encouragement as we explored the materials in their care.

At the PMA, in the Library and Archives, our deepest gratitude goes to Kristen Regina, Susan Anderson Laquer, Rose Chiango, Miriam Cady, and Margaret Huang. We also thank Conna Clark, Holly Frisbee, and Giema Tsakuginow.

Among the museum's staff, Timothy F. Rub deserves our thanks along with Michael R. Taylor. Taylor introduced us to Ashley McKeown, who, with the help of Sebastien LeClercq and Chris Havlish, moved hundreds of objects around on our behalf. Michael's successor, Matthew Affron, shared his expertise on Duchamp with us and has championed this book with key colleagues. John Vick read the first essay, "The King and Queen Surrounded," carefully and provided crucial insights. Hiromi Kinoshita and Jessica Kwasniak provided new information on the Arensbergs' Chinese objects. Other individuals at the museum assisted us with questions large and small: Brooks Rich and James Wehn both deserve thanks, as do Jennifer Otte Vanim and Emily Rice.

At the Huntington, we were first introduced to the Arensberg materials by Robert C. (Roy) Ritchie and Alan Jutzi. We also owe a debt of gratitude to Henry "Hank" Gibbons, who—along with Steve Hindle—enabled our studies in San Marino with grants from the Francis Bacon Foundation, the research institute founded by Louise and Walter Arensberg in 1938. Hank's support and interest helped us to feel—as well as to get—closer to the subjects of our study.

Our research at the Huntington was facilitated with great patience by Suzanne Oatey, who helped us to navigate the Arensbergs' unprocessed archive and later produced its essential finding aid. Among the many others in the library who advanced our work, we must single out David Zeidberg, Sandra Brooke, Laura Stalker, Mary L. Robertson, Vanessa Wilkie, Dan Lewis, Stephen Tabor, and Jenny Watts. We are grateful, finally, for the assistance of June Li, who contributed significantly to our knowledge of the Arensberg collection at the Huntington.

Our reconstruction of the Arensbergs' Hollywood house has found an ideal home at the Getty, and our book would not have made it into print without the efforts of many individuals. At the Getty Research Institute, we thank Mary Miller, Gail Feigenbaum, and Andrew Perchuk for their advocacy and enthusiasm. We also extend our gratitude to Sally McKay and Aimee Calfin for allowing us access to the Stendahl archives before they were fully processed. At Getty Research Institute Publications, we thank Michele Ciaccio for preparing us for peer and committee reviews; and Laura Santiago, who turned her keen eyes and sharp red pencil to our texts. At Getty Publications, Kara Kirk and Maureen Winter embraced this project wholeheartedly and shepherded it through to completion with aplomb; Megan Ro worked creatively and diligently to ensure we found an audience; Amita Molloy and Victoria Gallina assisted with production; and Allison McCann, Karen Ehrmann, Clare Davis, and Leslie Rollins ensured that our t's were crossed.

Massimo Tonolli, Alberto Adami, Nadia Bottacini, and all of our other friends at Trifolio SRL, Verona, deserve our profound gratitude not only for ensuring this book was printed and bound with care but also for believing it needed to be made in the first place and helping to make that happen.

This book would also not exist without the goodwill of those who care for the estates of the photographers whose pictures appear in *Hollywood Arensberg*. We are indebted, first, to Karl Bissinger's son, David Fechheimer, who died unexpectedly in April 2019, and to David's son Zachary Fechheimer, who graciously assisted us after his father's passing on behalf of himself, his brother, Samuel Fechheimer, and his mother, Diane Roxas. We also thank L. Rebecca Johnson Melvin, who manages the Bissinger Archive at the University of Delaware Library for the Fechheimer family, for her long engagement with the project.

We are grateful to Roland Jaeger, who manages the estate of Fritz (Fred) Block for the photographer's heirs, Gustav and Ingrid Levy-Hünebergart. As author of the monographs *Block and Hochfeld, die Architekten des Deutschlandhauses: Bauten und Projekte in Hamburg 1921–1938, Exil in Los Angeles* and *Photo-Eye Fritz Block: New Photography, Modern Color Slides*, Jaeger has ensured that Block's work as both an architect and a photographer will be remembered, and he has spent a significant amount of time examining Block's history on our behalf.

Likewise, we are honored to have had the assistance and trust of Kevin Wallace at the Beatrice Wood Center for the Arts & Happy Valley Cultural Center, Ojai, who looks after the estate of Beatrice Wood; and of the contemporary family of Floyd Harold Faxon, including Floyd's recently deceased grandson Craig Faxon and his wife, Mary Faxon, his great-grandchildren Sean Faxon and Kelly Ross, and his grandnephew Bob Faxon.

Though we could not find any record of Corporal F. W. Lumbord, we were able to make contact with the family of Don Schloat, one of the soldiers depicted in his photographs. Schloat became an animator for Disney and published a memoir about his wartime experiences, *Freedom! Bataan—POW—PVT*. Sadly, he died prior to being identified for our book. We thank Schloat's nephew, Andrew Schloat, for helping us understand more about his uncle.

We extend our thanks also to everyone at the Historic New Orleans Collection (THNOC), which protects and manages the archives of Clarence John Laughlin. We encourage future scholars of the Arensbergs to spend some time in the Laughlin archive reviewing the extensive materials we could not include in this volume. At THNOC, we thank Daniel Hammer, John H. Lawrence, Alfred Lemmon, and Rebecca Smith for their engagement with this project.

Thanks are due also to Karen E. Haas and Sue Bell at the Museum of Fine Arts, Boston, for their assistance with the photographs of the Arensbergs' New York apartment and Hollywood home taken by Charles Sheeler; and to Jocelyn Gibbs and Julia Larson of the Architecture and Design Collection in the Art, Design & Architecture Museum at UC Santa Barbara, for help with the images in the Henry Palmer Sabin archive. Additionally, we are appreciative of Catharine Karl Millikan, granddaughter of Milton R. Inman, for letting us use his photograph of Fred Dapprich; and Robert and Sheila Frampton, son and daughter-in-law, respectively, of Robert "R. C." Frampton, who took the images of Elizabeth Wrigley and the Francis Bacon Library.

We are grateful to the late Murray Ross, son of Kenneth Ross, who was excited to see his father's previously unpublished interview with Walter Arensberg in print. Its inclusion has allowed us to share one of the few statements about the collection in the collectors' own voices. We are saddened that Murray didn't live to see the finished book.

Many experts—among them Susan Delson, Isabelle Fleuriet, Frederique Joseph-Lowry, Alfred Pacquement, and Don Quaintance—reviewed this book and offered useful feedback. The late Robert Pincus-Witten always provided a wellspring of encouragement; he is deeply missed. The indefatigable Charles Stuckey spent a great deal of time engaging with this material, offering ideas and assistance: his suggestions, without fail, made our work better. Our good friend Anna Jardine helped us keep our text tight and clear prior to its submission to the Getty.

We also benefited from the timely invitation to participate in the 2014 seminar on Contemporary and Modern Art Perspectives in a Global Age (C-MAP) at the Museum of Modern Art (MoMA), New York, and we would like to thank Jay A. Levenson and Luis Pérez-Oramas for their invitation, along with C-MAP's counselors—Mieke Bal, Homi Bhabha, Thierry de Duve, and David Joselit—for their thoughtful responses. Among the staff at MoMA, we would like to thank Glenn D. Lowry, Leah Dickerman, Anne Umland, Ann Temkin, Cornelia H. Butler (now at the Hammer Museum), David Platzker, Doryun Chong (now at M+ Museum, Hong Kong), and David Frankel. Milan R. Hughston and Michelle Elligott deserve special thanks for their interest and assistance.

At other libraries and archives, we would like to acknowledge Paul Barron and Jeffrey Kozak of the Library and Archives at the George C. Marshall Foundation; Michael Bonnet at the University of Southern California, Dornsife College of Letters, Arts and Sciences; Simon Elliott at the Charles E. Young Research Library at the University of California, Los Angeles (UCLA); Michelle Harvey at MoMA Library Special Collections; Carrie Marsh and Adam Rosenkranz at the Honnold/Mudd Library, Claremont, California; Florence Palomo at Condé Nast Publications; Barbara Rominski, formerly of the San Francisco Museum of Modern Art; and Judy Harvey Sahak of the Ella Strong Denison Library at Scripps College, Claremont, California.

For assistance with other collections and historical background, we are grateful to Yaëlle Biro, Asher Miller, and Joanne Pillsbury at the Metropolitan Museum of Art, New York; Bill Deverell of the Huntington-USC Institute on California and the West; Rex Koontz at the University of Houston and the Museum of Fine Arts, Houston; Victoria Lyall at the Denver Art Museum; Leonardo López Luján of the Proyecto Templo Mayor at the Instituto Nacional de Antropología e Historia, Mexico; Teresa Montaner at the Fundació Joan Miró in Barcelona; Matthew H. Robb at the Fowler Museum, UCLA; Antonio Saborit García Peña at the Museo Nacional de Antropología, Mexico; Jo Anne Van Tilburg at the UCLA Rock Art Archive and Cotsen Institute of Archaeology, UCLA; and Karole Vail and Grazina Subelyte of the Peggy Guggenheim Collection, Venice.

For their help and friendship, we are grateful to Anthony Atlas, Joe Avery, Lisa Anderson-Zhu, Stefan Banz, Sarah Hudson Bayliss, Chris Beekman, Sue Bergh, Verónica Betancourt, Jeremy Braddock, Maureen Bray, Amelia Brown, Patricia Brundage, our friends at *Cabinet* magazine (Sina Najafi, Alexander Nagel, Graham Burnett, and Jeff Dolven), Nicole Cadoret, Matt Carr, Lisa Chaney, Anna Clarkson, Clemency Coggins, Billy Copley, Claire Copley, Victoria Dailey and Steve Turner, Charles Dibble, James Doyle, Mark Eastment, Angie Elliott, T. R. Ericsson, Diana Fane, Lori Anne Ferrell, Juliet Fleming, Carter Foster, Enrique Fuentes Castilla, Joanna Gohmann, Stacy Goodman, Blake Gopnik, Brett Gorvy, Sandy Gross, Agnes Gund, Maricruz Gutierrez-Villa, Tom Hackney, Deborah Harkness, Selva Hernández, Jonathan Hernández-Otañez, Anne Higonnet, John Hoopes, Loren Houchins, Laura Howell, Ellie Hughes, Beth Huseman, Jan Jancourt, Elinor Jansz, Garrick Jones, Julie Jones, Michael Joo, Joni Joseph, Jennifer Josten, Winnie Kho, Lock Kresler, Sandy Leichtman, Dominique Lévy, Daniel Mercurio López Casillas, Alejandro López González, Vicki Mahaffey, Laura Marcus, Simon Martin, Sonia Mattheus, Anthony and Annabel McCall, Jeff McMillan, Jay Miller, Peter Miller, Debbie Nagao, Joseph Newland, James Oles, María del Refugio Paisano Rodríguez, Jerry Passannante, Esther Pasztory, Susanne Mack Payott and Marc Payott, Sonia Arlette Pérez, Vicki Phillips, Rick Poynor, George Quasha, Alanna Radlo-Dzur, Kim Richter, Kelsey Roberts, Sandy Rodríguez, Leila Saadai, Michael Sand, Marc Sapir, Jasper Schad, Richard and Clara Serra, Ezra Shales, James Shapiro, Eve Snyder, Emilio Steinberger, Kevin Tervala, Clara Touboul, Michael Tower, Beth Turk, Andrew Turner, Mark Uhen, Emily Umberger, Javier Urcid, Rebeca Vega, Khristaan Villela, Michael White, Lehua Yim, Leon Yugrakh, and Lucas Zwirner.

We are grateful to each one of the McCall Associates—past and present—who have helped make this project a success. David Zaza's belief that a business should contribute something to our culture beyond the transactional is profoundly inspiring. He is truly *our* Silent Guard. Sarah Wolberg's rigorous reading and rereading of our texts, and especially her help managing our endnotes, ensured we would cross the finish line; simply said, we couldn't have done it without her. And we cannot thank Michelle Nix, Marijane Kubow, Logan Myers, Elin Miller, Doug Clouse, John Calmeyer, and Meg Becker (nor former McCall interns Chloe Lee, Andrew Nelson, Yeonjae Yuk, and Alexandra Zsigmond) enough for letting this project occupy our shared space for so long.

Finally, for their love, patience, and understanding, we thank Brigid, Ava, and Margot Nelson; Gerald Nelson; Paul and Eric Nelson and their families; Claire MacDonald; Tom and Ronna Sherman; Dorothy and Thomas Hoobler; and Mandar Banavadikar. This book is for Sandra Nelson.

MARK NELSON | WILLIAM H. SHERMAN | ELLEN HOOBLER

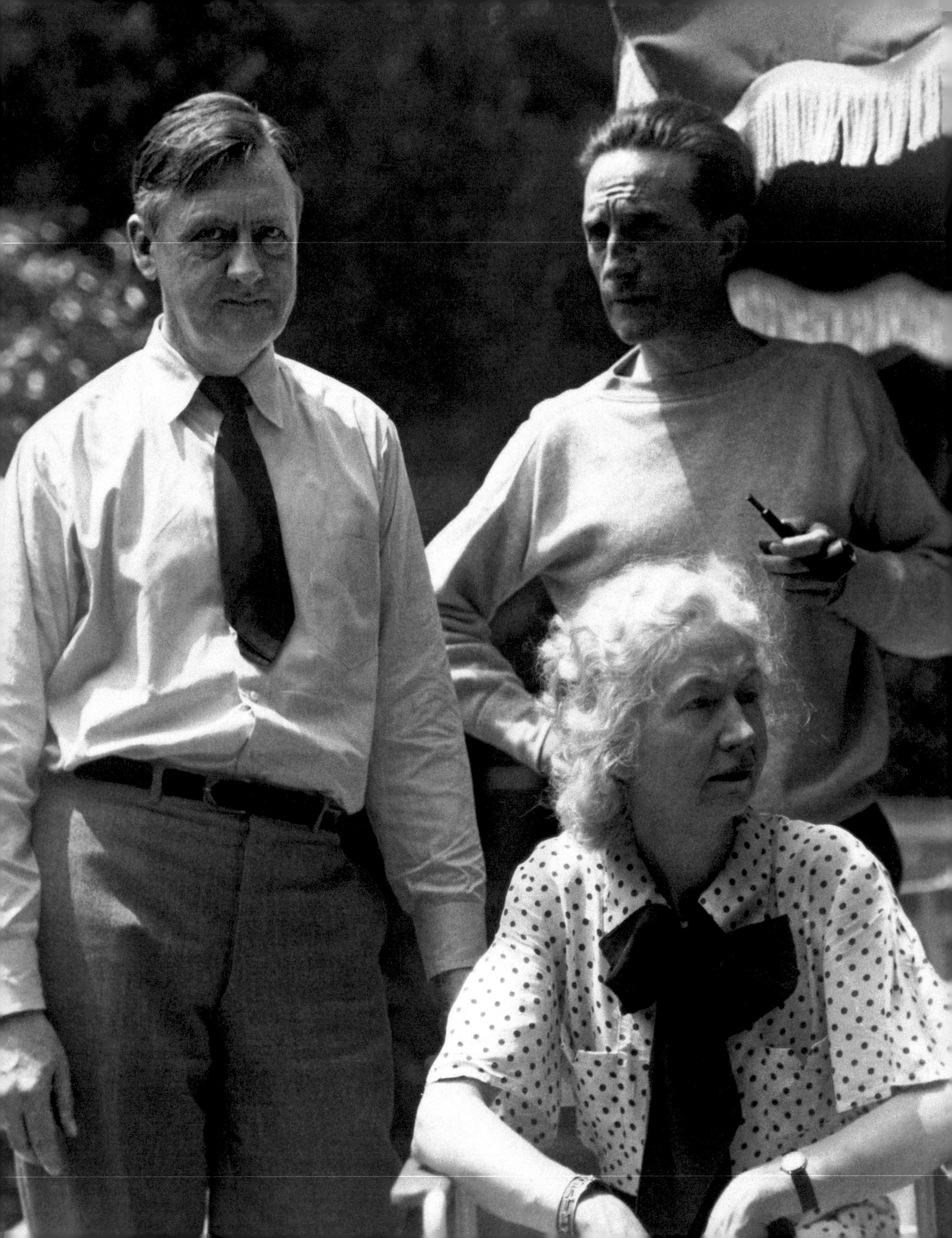

THE KING AND QUEEN SURROUNDED

The Arensberg Collection in Context

WILLIAM H. SHERMAN | MARK NELSON

BEATRICE WOOD. LOUISE ARENSBERG, WALTER ARENSBERG, AND MARCEL DUCHAMP IN THE GARDEN AT 7065 HILLSIDE AVENUE, LOS ANGELES, 17 AUGUST 1936. PHILADELPHIA MUSEUM OF ART, LIBRARY AND ARCHIVES, ALEXINA AND MARCEL DUCHAMP PAPERS (PMA-MDP), BOX 30, FOLDER 17. GIFT OF JACQUELINE, PAUL, AND PETER MATISSE IN MEMORY OF THEIR MOTHER, ALEXINA DUCHAMP. REPRODUCED COURTESY OF BEATRICE WOOD CENTER FOR THE ARTS / HAPPY VALLEY FOUNDATION

No two figures ever lived in art more indomitable than these two,
"The King and Queen Surrounded by Swift Nudes."
Light is immovable by comparison, marble is mobile,
and yet they are caught, trapped, encircled, bound.

—**HELEN FREEMAN CORLE**[1]

I

Opening Moves

IN 1949, at the end of a whistle-stop tour of America's finest art collections, the *New York Times* critic Aline Louchheim found herself in front of a "large, rather nondescript and very un-Hollywood house in Hollywood, Calif." (fig. 1). When the owners, Louise and Walter Arensberg, opened the door, Louchheim encountered one of the most extraordinary installations of art ever assembled in a private home. Having grown accustomed to "expensive Impressionists . . . in elaborate Louis XV frames," she was amazed by both the radical art on the walls and its idiosyncratic methods of display.

Louchheim described the scene to *Times* readers in vivid detail: "Paintings were jammed and crowded on every available space from floor to ceiling. They filled the porch, trembled on the backs of doors . . . [and] lined the bathrooms." The house held nearly forty artworks by Marcel Duchamp; paintings by Pablo Picasso, Georges Braque, Paul Klee, Henri Matisse, Joan Miró, and other modern masters hung edge to edge in every room. The dense array extended beyond the walls to the floors and other surfaces: interspersed with nearly twenty sculptures by Constantin Brancusi "there were a mass of other objects—ex-votos, bits of Americana, Indian sculpture . . . [and] African and Pre-Columbian carvings." Significant specimens of American and European furniture rested on a patchwork of Persian rugs—piled, in some places, two or three deep. "How astounding," she reported, "these gentle, gracious, past middle-aged people who are my hosts are as at home with this art, as unself-conscious and unpretentious about it as one's grandmother was about Victorian chromos and doodabs."[2]

Louchheim's astonishment was understandable. Los Angeles was surprisingly slow to embrace modernism in its many forms: new artistic initiatives often met with hostility, and the city did not establish a permanent museum dedicated to modern art until 1961, nearly a decade after the Arensbergs' deaths.[3]

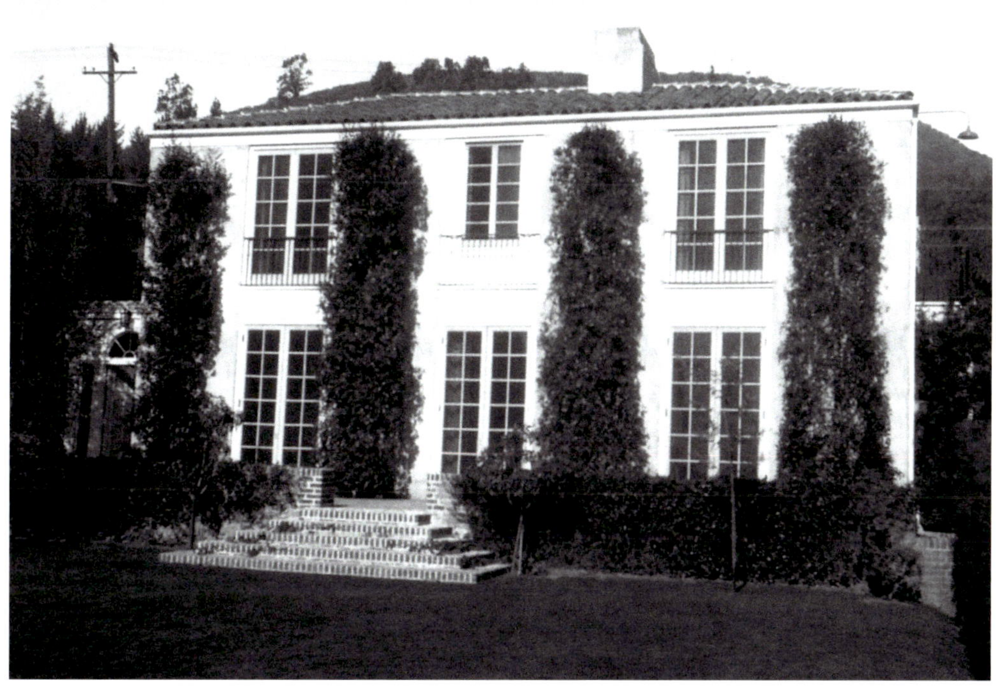

1. 7065 HILLSIDE AVENUE, LOS ANGELES, AFTER 1928 BUT BEFORE 1933. PHOTOGRAPHER UNKNOWN.
PHILADELPHIA MUSEUM OF ART, LIBRARY AND ARCHIVES, ARENSBERG ARCHIVES (PMA-WLA), BOX 54, FOLDER 8

Yet for more than twenty years, from the late 1920s to the early 1950s, Louise and Walter Arensberg generously opened their Hollywood home to a constant stream of visitors. Most of them were friends from their wide circle of artists, authors, and actors, but many were members of the general public hoping for a glimpse of the couple's legendary collection. One of their earliest and most persistent guests was Charis Wilson, an aspiring writer who later became the photographer Edward Weston's collaborator and wife. Wilson was introduced to the Arensbergs in 1929 while still a student at nearby Hollywood High, and in her memoir, *Through Another Lens*, she recalled her first visit to their house:

> Walter Arensberg himself took me on a brief tour. There, on the walls throughout the home, were famous paintings I had heard about but never seen.... I knew from the moment I entered that exotic living room—where Rousseau's apes peered out of their jungle at Matisse's *Woman in Blue*, and Picasso's *Guitar Player* fraternized with Miró's primary-colored, geometrical creatures—that I would return as often as possible.[4]

After taking a job only a few streets away, Wilson found it "a daily struggle to refrain from ringing the doorbell." Walter welcomed her often enough to extend her education with longer tours of the collection, during which he invited her comments on the placement of particular pictures and dazzled her with explanations of the complex symbolism he found in them. "My delight in his wordplay, puns, conundrums, and cryptic meanings behind cryptic meanings was so stimulating I felt buoyed up for days after a visit," she wrote.[5]

These puzzles grew out of Walter's intellectual preoccupations as a practicing poet and amateur scholar of Renaissance culture, and they point to another (much less known) part of the Arensbergs' collection. Throughout the house, there were thousands of books stacked on tables and crammed onto shelves, on topics ranging from mythology to cryptography and featuring the world's largest private library of works by the Renaissance-era scientist and statesman Sir Francis Bacon.[6] Long celebrated for inventing the scientific method, reforming the British legal system, developing the essay form in English, and producing one of history's most ingenious cipher systems, Bacon—rather than Shakespeare—was considered by many to be the preeminent writer of the English Renaissance. Indeed, many people were persuaded that Bacon was the true author of Shakespeare's plays—among them Walter, who spent many years searching for the evidence that would support this claim, poring over books in his office and explaining his theories to anyone who expressed an interest in the subject (fig. 2). Wilson found Walter's lessons intoxicating: "Under his influence I even began writing a novel in my late teens which turned out to be so densely packed with symbolism it was close to unfathomable."[7]

When Louchheim visited some two decades later, Walter's passion for symbols was undiminished:

> One is not surprised to learn that Mr. Arensberg's other great interest is literary—he is a passionate Baconian who has written extensively on the Shakespeare-Bacon controversy. The inclination toward Cubist and Surrealist art may well be explained by a basic literary taste, for in much of this art the problem is to make ideas visual rather than to start with images and let ideas and emotions evolve.[8]

Louchheim understood that many of the Arensbergs' artworks were fundamentally conceptual, even as their owners "chose almost infallibly those works which succeeded best in visual terms."[9] She concluded

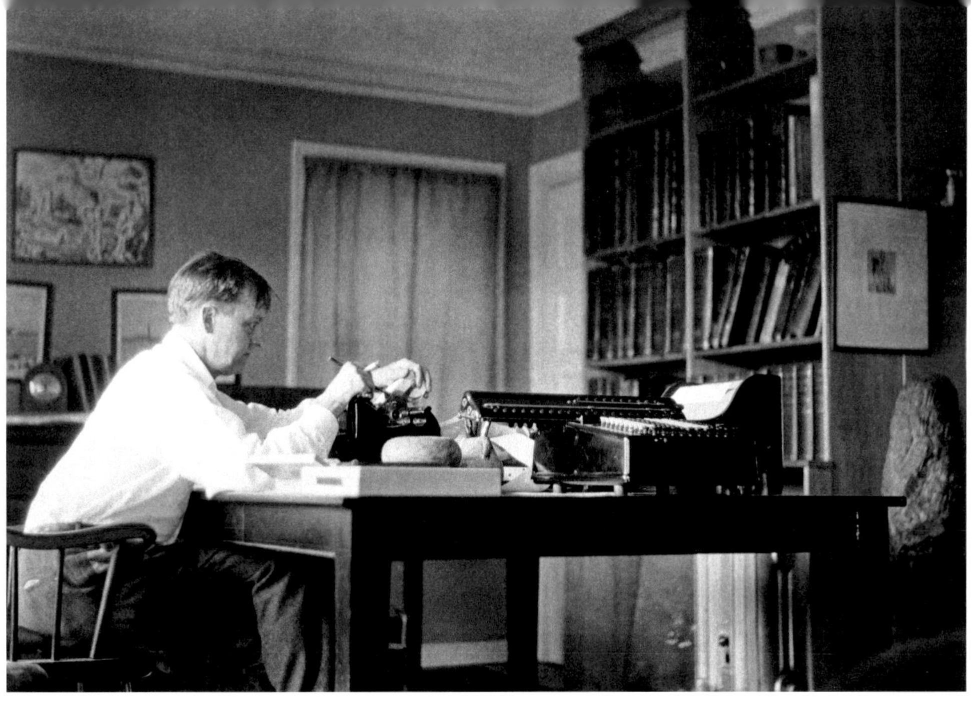

2. BEATRICE WOOD. WALTER ARENSBERG USING HIS ADDING MACHINE IN HIS HOME OFFICE AT ONE OF THE HOUSES HE AND LOUISE RENTED PRIOR TO PURCHASING 7065 HILLSIDE AVENUE IN 1927. THE HUNTINGTON LIBRARY, FRANCIS BACON LIBRARY ARCHIVE, WALTER AND LOUISE ARENSBERG PAPERS (HEH-FBLA), BOX 104, FOLDER 9. REPRODUCED COURTESY OF BEATRICE WOOD CENTER FOR THE ARTS / HAPPY VALLEY FOUNDATION

her article by celebrating an achievement some four decades in the making: "The singleness of purpose, the completeness of what it undertakes, the courage of conviction and the perspicacity of selection set the Arensberg Collection apart."[10]

Louchheim's article was titled "The Arensbergs Bought Cubists Then." It was prompted by the opening of the first public display of the couple's collection, at the Art Institute of Chicago in 1949, but the *then* in her title referred to the years immediately following 1913, when the International Exhibition of Modern Art brought some of Europe's most radical paintings and sculptures to New York—none more controversial than Marcel Duchamp's *Nude Descending a Staircase (No. 2)* (fig. 3).[11] Both the painting and the exhibition—the Armory Show, as it came to be known—took the American public by storm and hit the Arensbergs, as Walter's Harvard classmate William Ivins later recalled, "between wind and water." Another of Walter's college friends, the poet Wallace Stevens, concurred: "I don't suppose there is anyone to whom the Armory Show of 1913 meant more than it did to him," though "Mrs. Arensberg," Stevens was careful to note, "was as much interested as he was" (fig. 4).[12]

The exhibition affected the couple so profoundly that by early 1914 they had abandoned their settled life at the historic house known as Shady Hill in Cambridge, Massachusetts, for a bohemian existence in an apartment on Manhattan's Upper West Side.[13] Regretting their tentative purchases at the show itself—where they lost out to John Quinn, Arthur Jerome Eddy, and Frederic C. Torrey on the most adventurous pieces—they soon began (in the words of Milton Brown) "an assiduous search to assemble all those works [they] had missed the first time around."[14] Within a year, they had established themselves as preeminent patrons of the show's most infamous artist, Marcel Duchamp: they put him up in their own home when he moved to New York in the summer of 1915 and then arranged a studio for him in their building, paying his rent in exchange for ownership of *The Bride Stripped Bare by her Bachelors, Even*, also known as *The Large Glass* (see fig. 37), a work that Walter considered "perhaps the supreme monument of Marcel's genius."[15]

Over the next few years, the Arensbergs' apartment became the lively American salon for the European Dada movement, prompting their frequent visitor, the artist Francis Picabia, to dub Walter "the true Dada of New York."[16] In doing so, Picabia acknowledged not only the Arensbergs' role as patrons in chief to the city's avant-garde artists but also the active part they played in shaping the artistic and literary ventures associated with Dada itself, including exhibitions, galleries, and magazines. Among the seminal Dada

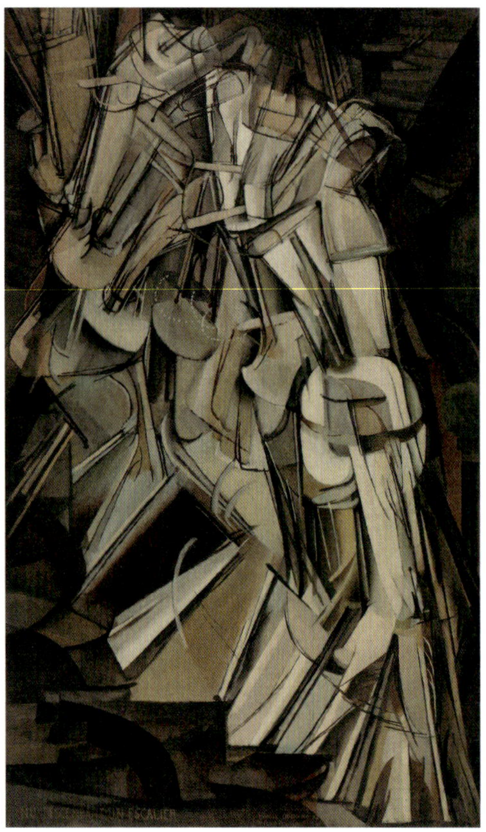

3. MARCEL DUCHAMP. *NUDE DESCENDING A STAIRCASE (NO. 2)*, 1912. OIL ON CANVAS, 147 × 89.2 CM. PHILADELPHIA MUSEUM OF ART, THE LOUISE AND WALTER ARENSBERG COLLECTION, 1950-134-59

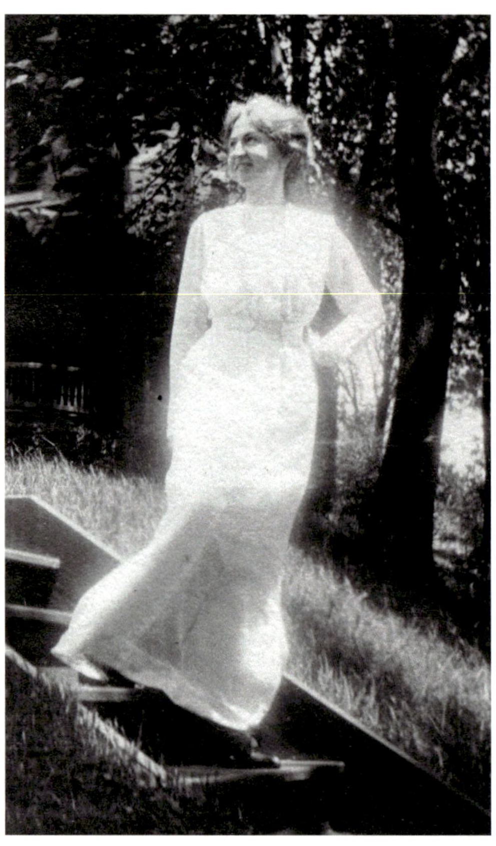

4. LOUISE STEVENS ARENSBERG DESCENDING A STAIRCASE, CA. 1917. PHOTOGRAPHER UNKNOWN. PHILADELPHIA MUSEUM OF ART, LIBRARY AND ARCHIVES, ARENSBERG ARCHIVES (PMA-WLA), BOX 50, FOLDER 13

publications that can be linked to the Arensbergs were *Blind Man* and *391*, in which Walter's name was given a prominent position in drawings by Picabia that charted the "movement" and "molecular construction" of Dada (figs. 5, 6). Walter and Duchamp also appeared alongside Picabia in a group manifesto published in *Dada* no. 6.[17]

Just as the Arensbergs' artistic tastes had been transformed by their encounter with the work in the Armory Show, Walter's efforts as an author and editor became decidedly experimental after the move to New York. His interest in writing had first taken root during his undergraduate years at Harvard, where he was editor of the *Harvard Monthly* and president of the university's literary society, and where he performed as Class Poet at his graduation ceremony in 1900.[18] Insofar as Walter had a *career* during the decades in Boston and New York—and the trust funds that he and Louise were able to draw on meant that work was never a necessity—it was as a writer.[19] By 1916, he had published two volumes of traditional verse (both issued by Houghton Mifflin) and funded the production of a radical new magazine called *Others*, edited by the poet and playwright Alfred Kreymborg. Five of Walter's most experimental poems opened the magazine's first anthology, in 1917, appearing alongside early work by Wallace Stevens, Marianne Moore, William Carlos Williams, and Mina Loy.[20] With titles such as "Ing" and "Arithmetical Progression of the Verb 'To Be,'" Walter's new poems set out to do for the word what Duchamp's *Nude* had done for the image.[21] As in the early work of Stevens and Williams, Walter broke apart received poetic forms, using multiple perspectives, shifting syntax, and enigmatic titles to unsettle the traditional relationships between things and representations. The *Others* anthologies carried the bold motto "The old expressions are with us always, and there are always others," and nowhere was Walter's break with the past more apparent than in the provocative portrait of his former Cambridge home, "For 'Shady Hill'":

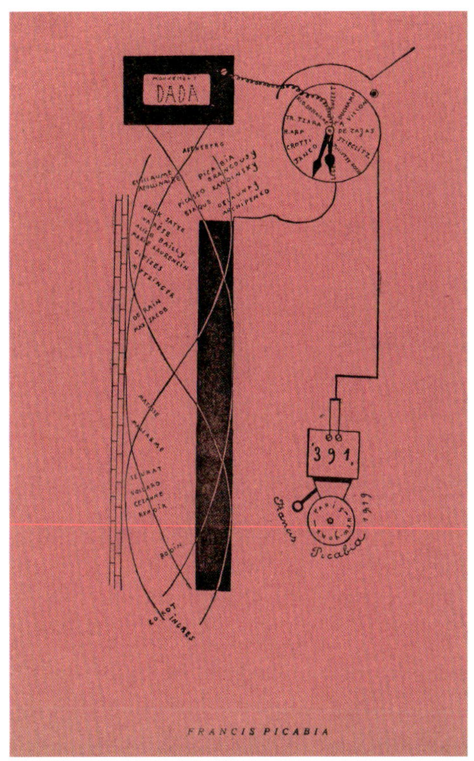

5. FRANCIS PICABIA. *DADA MOVEMENT*, 1919. DRAWING PRINTED IN "ANTHOLOGIE DADA," ED. TRISTAN TZARA, SPECIAL ISSUE, *DADA*, NO. 4/5 (15 MAY 1919). PICABIA'S DADA MACHINE DRAWING INCLUDES WALTER ARENSBERG'S NAME NEAR THE TOP. YALE UNIVERSITY, BEINECKE RARE BOOK & MANUSCRIPT LIBRARY, CALL NUMBER 1978 FOLIO S63 4-5

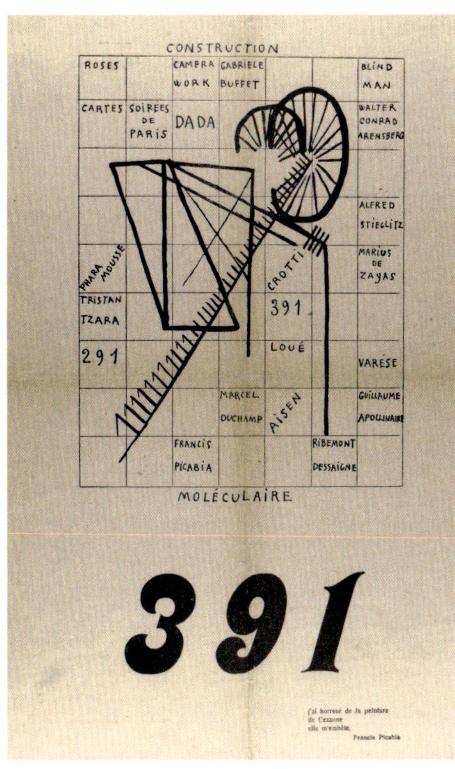

6. FRANCIS PICABIA. *MOLECULAR CONSTRUCTION*, 1919. FRONT COVER FOR *391*, NO. 8 (FEBRUARY 1919). PICABIA'S DADA MACHINE DRAWING INCLUDES WALTER ARENSBERG'S NAME IN THE TOP RIGHT CORNER, UNDER THE TITLE OF THE DADA JOURNAL *BLIND MAN*. NATIONAL GALLERY OF ART LIBRARY, WASHINGTON, DC. DAVID K. E. BRUCE FUND

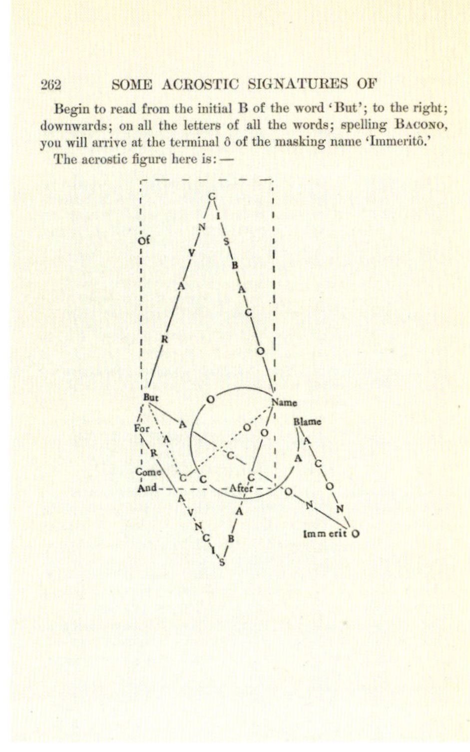
262 SOME ACROSTIC SIGNATURES OF

Begin to read from the initial B of the word 'But'; to the right; downwards; on all the letters of all the words; spelling Bacono, you will arrive at the terminal ô of the masking name 'Immeritô.'

The acrostic figure here is: —

7. AN EXAMPLE OF A ROUTE TRACING THE LETTERS OF BACON'S NAME IN ANOTHER "MASKING" TEXT, IN WALTER ARENSBERG'S COPY OF WILLIAM STONE BOOTH, *SOME ACROSTIC SIGNATURES OF FRANCIS BACON* (LONDON: A. CONSTABLE, 1909), 262. HUNTINGTON LIBRARY, RARE BOOKS COLLECTION (HEH-RBC), CALL NUMBER 613575

As at the end of an equation of two to green,
which have the butters of extra broken
on badges biting a needle to partners
if only the bridge is fluent
let it not nice.
INTERFERE IN ORDER TO MORrow was once
upon a timePIECE OF MY MInd you do not.[22]

Walter's experimental turn and his pronounced interest in verbal/visual play (fig. 7) are hardly surprising, given that these poems were produced between the word games and chess games he played with his friend and neighbor Duchamp. A photograph taken at the time, during an outing of the *Others* group to the writers' colony in Ridgefield, New Jersey, indicates how close the two men had grown: they stand arm in arm, with the artist casting a fond and mischievous look at the grinning poet (figs. 8a, b). They look as if they are sharing a secret, and considering the various strategies they devised during these years for teasing out multiple meanings—from Walter's obsession with Bacon's theories of allegory to Duchamp's explorations of extra dimensions and liminal states—they probably were. Their joint experiments are recorded in scribbled notes in the Arensbergs' archive and more publicly displayed in Duchamp's collaborative "readymades" of 1916, including *Comb* and *With Hidden Noise*.[23] The former was a comb used for grooming the Arensbergs' dog, onto which Duchamp meticulously painted a French phrase written by Walter, containing a hidden (though nonsensical) substitution cipher. The latter comprised a ball of twine—sandwiched between two brass plates, each bearing a cryptic inscription and held together by four long bolts—into

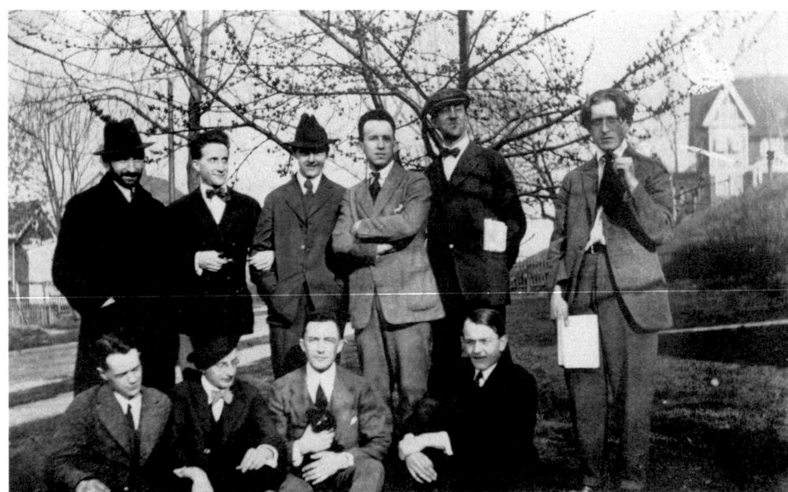
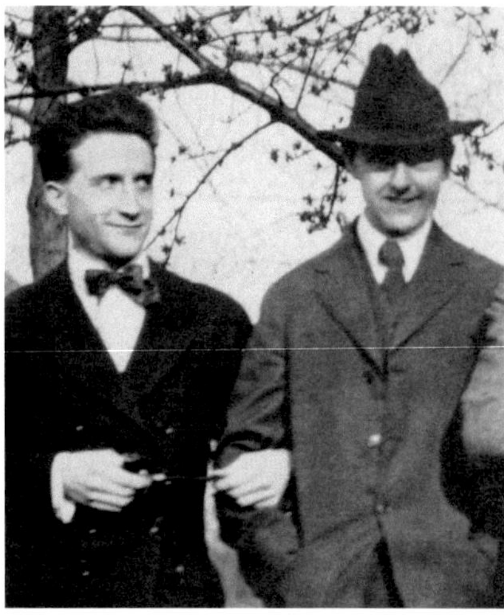

8A, B. THE *OTHERS* GROUP AT WILLIAM CARLOS WILLIAMS'S HOUSE IN RUTHERFORD, NEW JERSEY, APRIL 1916; DETAIL (B) SHOWS MARCEL DUCHAMP NEXT TO WALTER ARENSBERG. PHOTOGRAPHER UNKNOWN. UNIVERSITY AT BUFFALO, THE STATE UNIVERSITY OF NEW YORK, THE POETRY COLLECTION OF THE UNIVERSITY LIBRARIES, WILLIAM CARLOS WILLIAMS COLLECTION, 1902–1960, BOX 76, FOLDER G111, PCMS-0024

which Walter inserted a mysterious, noise-making object (see plate 57.23). Walter withheld the identity of the object even from Marcel, and the work served, as Duchamp later put it, as "a sort of secret" between them.[24]

Turning found objects into artworks was one of Duchamp's signature moves, but the cryptic texts inscribed on these two pieces derived from Walter's long-standing interest in cryptographic systems.[25] The origins of what would become a lifelong obsession can be traced once again to Walter's years at Harvard, where his literary studies were supplemented by lectures in philosophy, lessons in psychoanalysis, and endless games of chess. His first publication to draw fully on that training came in 1921, in a book-length decoding of *The Divine Comedy* called *The Cryptography of Dante*. In his conviction that there were hidden messages encrypted in Dante's works, Walter took encouragement from two men, both of whom he had met over the chessboard. The first was Elmer Ernest Southard, a neuropsychiatrist who headed the Boston Psychopathic Hospital. Walter credited Southard with helping him to move beyond simplistic readings of the sexual symbolism found in Freudian psychoanalysis, discovering in Dante's allegory a world of oblique and latent meanings. The second was a charismatic lumber merchant, librarian, and literary scholar named William Stone Booth (1864–1926), who introduced Walter to the then-popular theory that Bacon had written the works attributed to Shakespeare and to the pleasures of searching for secret structures embedded in Renaissance texts—hidden, as the would-be decoder would have it, in plain sight. Booth's *Some Acrostic Signatures of Francis Bacon* (1909) would have been particularly attractive to Walter. With many striking diagrams illustrating how new messages could be created by selecting significant letters from old texts (see fig. 7), *Some Acrostic Signatures* provided both the initial argument and the general method Walter took to unprecedented extremes in his later work on Dante and Bacon.

By the time the Arensbergs moved to New York, Walter had immersed himself in the history of technical cryptography—in which Bacon played a pioneering role, having produced the first published account of ciphers in English.[26] But he never left behind the looser codes that could be used to make one thing mean something else, or indeed nothing at all; and alongside the readymades produced with Duchamp there are countless signs in the archive of the pair's experiments with multilingual puns, free association, and other forms of wordplay.[27]

The private games played by Walter and Marcel found a more public outlet at the now legendary all-night salons hosted by the Arensbergs. During these years, Walter and Louise were the king and queen of an artistic court that brought together an ever-changing cast of painters, writers, and performers. As the art historian Naomi Sawelson-Gorse explains:

> There were want-to-be's, would-be's, and soon-to-be's. The Arensbergs' apartment was *the* place to be, whether one was a luminary like Isadora Duncan, a low-level diplomat on the way up the ladder like Henri Pierre Roché, a composer trying to make a mark like Edgard Varèse, a boxer-poet like Arthur Cravan, a rising stage actress like Fania Marinoff, or a struggling *ingénue* like Beatrice Wood. Of all [those] who frequented the salon, in general four distinct groups peopled it.... There were the old Cambridge chums (including Pitts Sanborn, Wallace Stevens, and Elmer Ernest Southard); the group of émigrés, mostly French, with the majority visual artists (such as Marcel Duchamp, Francis Picabia, Gabrielle Buffet-Picabia, Albert Gleizes, Marius de Zayas, the Baroness Elsa von Freytag-Loringhoven, Yvonne Chastel, and Jean Crotti); American artists, whether [by] birth or in past emigration (like Charles Sheeler, Walter Pach, Charles Demuth, Marsden Hartley, Man Ray, Morton Schamberg, Joseph Stella, Frances Simpson Stevens, Clara Tice, and John Covert, Walter's cousin); and the literary crowd, including those associated with salon-sponsored little magazines like *Rogue* and *Others* (for instance, Williams Carlos Williams, Mina Loy, Carl Van Vechten, Louise Norton, Robert Carlton Brown, Donald Evans, Robert Allerton Parker, Sophie Treadwell, Allen Norton, and Alfred Kreymborg).[28]

The Arensbergs were not the only hosts of artistic salons in these heady years, and in New York the one organized by Alfred Stieglitz at his gallery, 291, was better known to the public. As Robert M. Crunden has argued, however, the Arensbergs' was the most significant in terms of its long-range impact:

> In poetry, painting, and music it was crucial in numerous ways; and in that nebulous genre which should exist to include machine art and readymades, it was always preeminent. There, far more than in the Stieglitz salon which it often overlapped, vital issues of two-dimensional and four-dimensional art came up for discussion; and there, far beyond the dreams of anyone in 291, Europe and America not only met and intermingled, but cross-fertilized: sexually, obscenely, mechanically, comically, interdisciplinarily, linguistically, and even artistically.[29]

Unfortunately, this activity is notably absent from Charles Sheeler's iconic photographs of the Arensberg apartment, taken sometime after March 1919 (figs. 9a–d).[30] Though these images supply the primary visual record of the Arensberg collection during its formative years in New York, they were produced after the Arensberg salon had run its course and its "dynamo" (as Sawelson-Gorse described Duchamp) had departed for Buenos Aires.[31]

Even after the parties had ended, however, the New York apartment continued to elicit the liveliest of responses. In 1920, when the *Dial*'s art critic Henry McBride profiled the Arensbergs for his column, Modern Forms, he found the apartment still animated by the spirit of the salons and the playful ruses of Duchamp:

> "Do you want to see Marcel's latest work of art?" Walter Arensberg asked me, upon the occasion of my first visit to the studio and after we had had a long and easy conversation without a word of reference to Matisse, the Brancusi, and the other marvels, all of which I had seen perfectly without looking at them. From the grin upon his face, I knew Marcel's latest was something larky. When Arensberg lifted a glass bulb with a curious tail to it from the protecting cottons of a wooden box I saw that my premonitions had not played me false.

9A–D. CHARLES SHEELER.
FOUR VIEWS OF THE LIVING ROOM OF LOUISE AND WALTER ARENSBERG'S APARTMENT AT 33 WEST SIXTY-SEVENTH STREET, NEW YORK, AFTER MARCH 1919. MUSEUM OF FINE ARTS, BOSTON, THE LANE COLLECTION. PHOTOGRAPHS © 2020, MUSEUM OF FINE ARTS, BOSTON

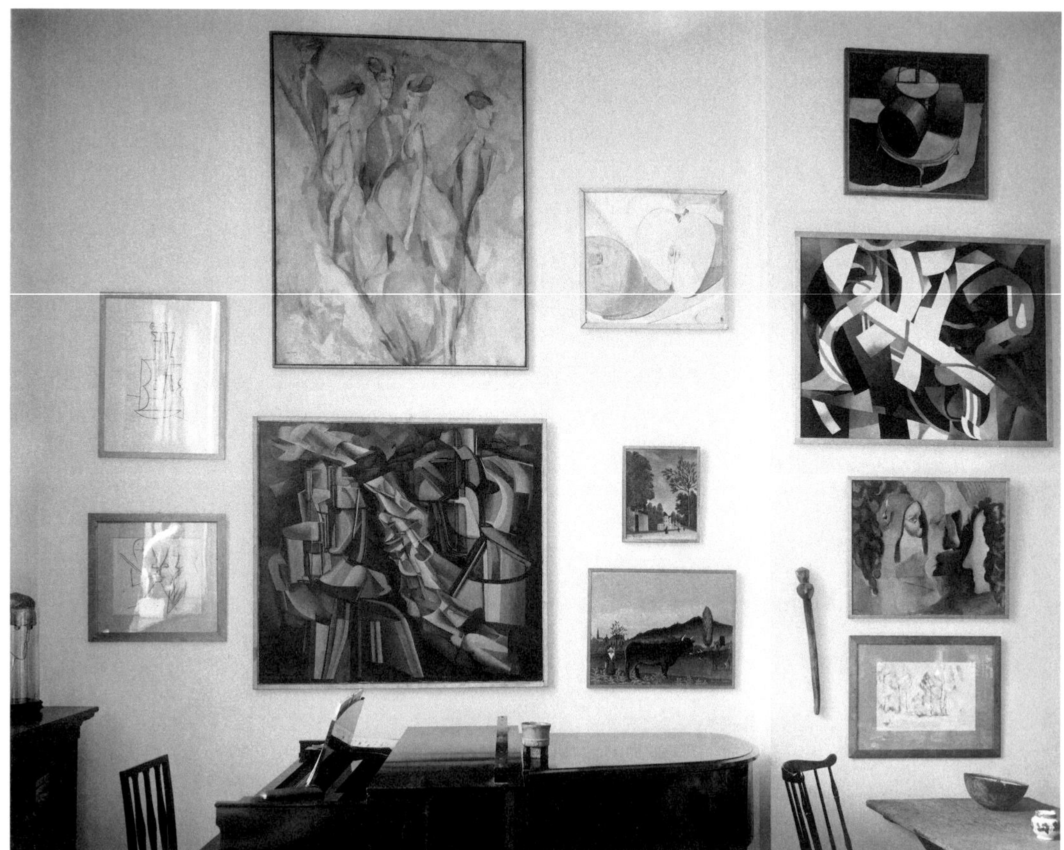

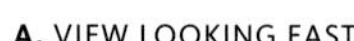

A. VIEW LOOKING EAST

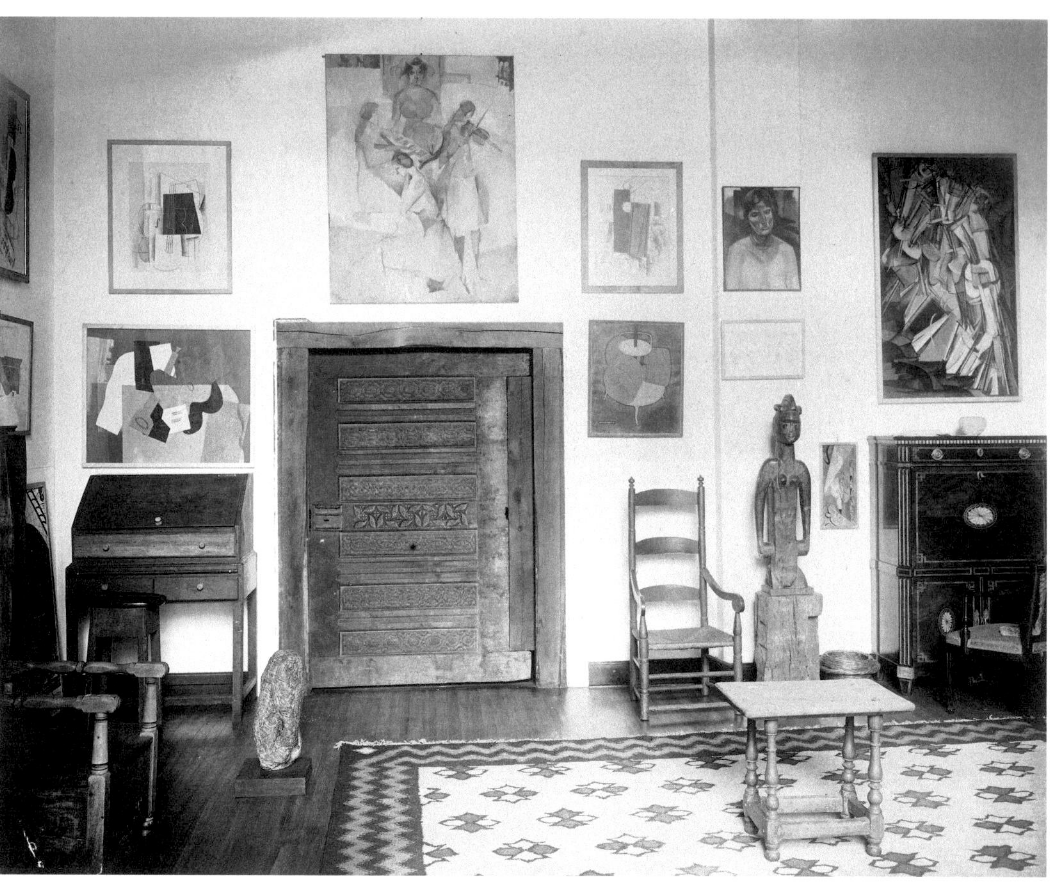

C. VIEW LOOKING SOUTH, SHOWING *NUDE DESCENDING A STAIRCASE (NO. 2)*

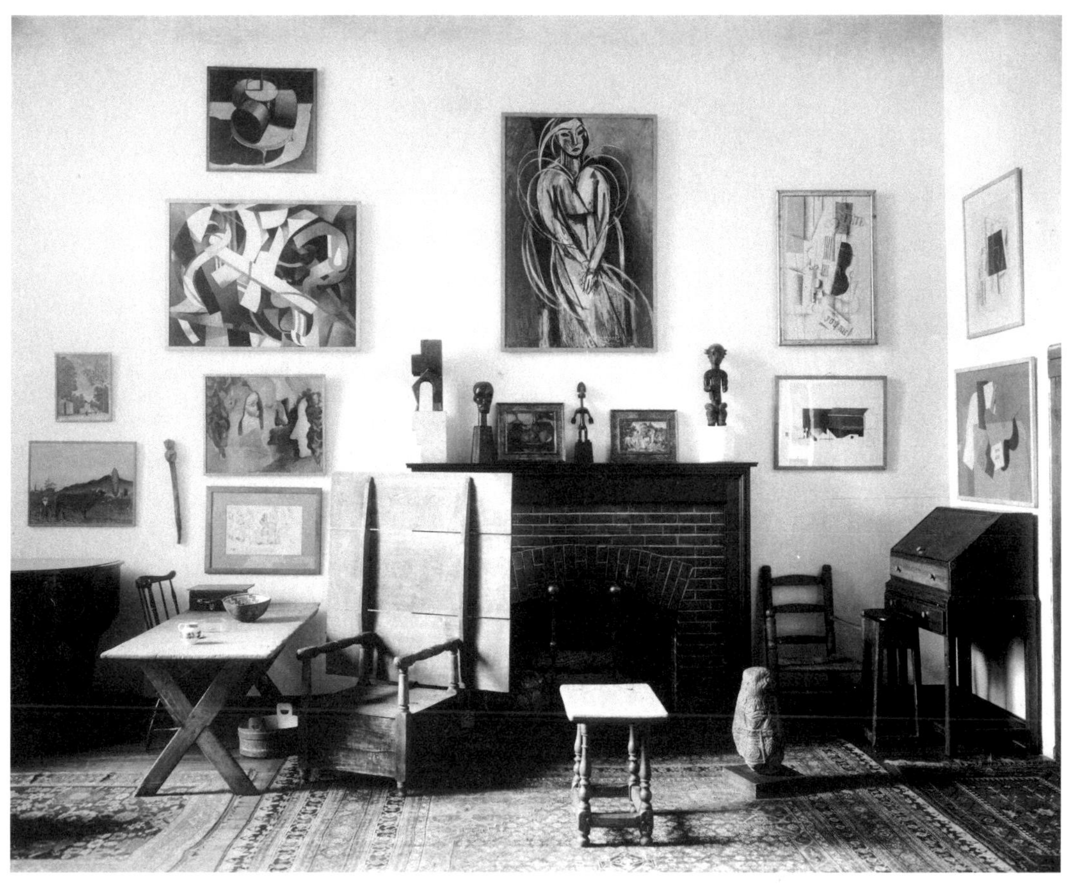

B. VIEW LOOKING EAST

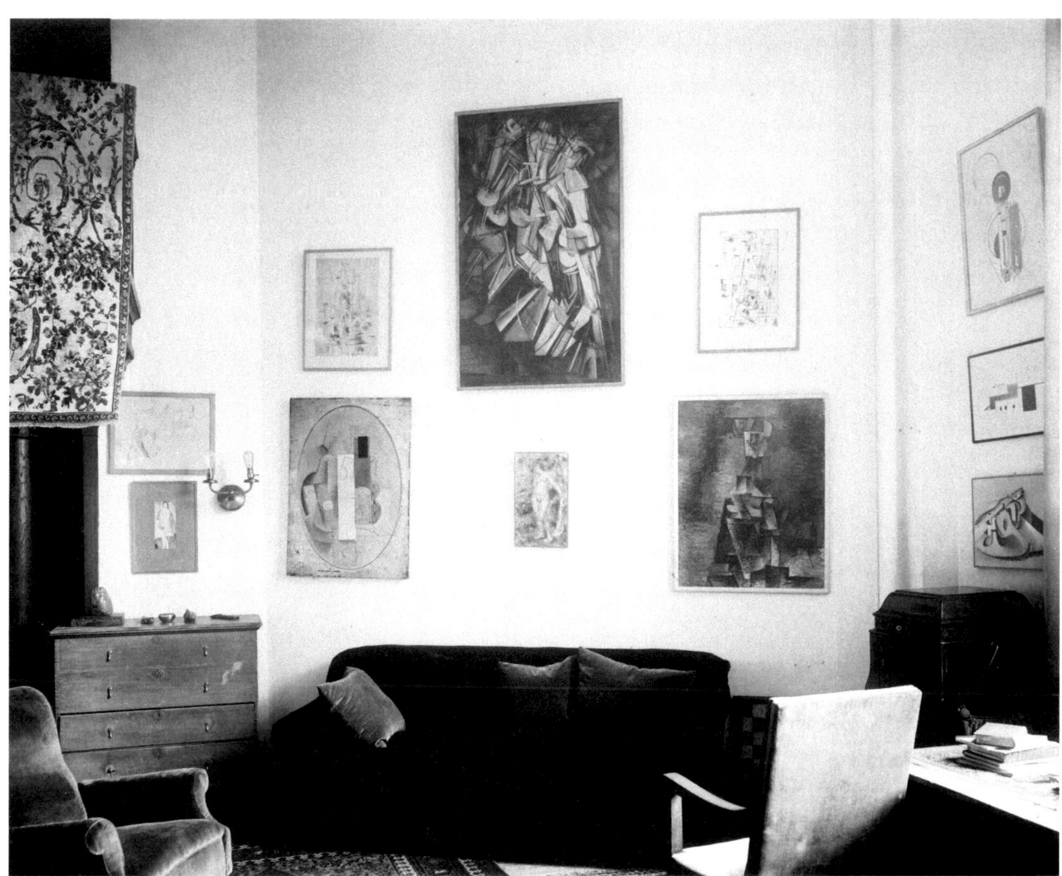

D. VIEW LOOKING NORTH, SHOWING *NUDE DESCENDING A STAIRCASE (NO. 3)*

10. MARCEL DUCHAMP. *50 CC OF PARIS AIR*, 1919. GLASS AMPOULE (BROKEN AND LATER RESTORED), 13.3 × 6.4 CM. PHILADELPHIA MUSEUM OF ART, THE LOUISE AND WALTER ARENSBERG COLLECTION, 1950-134-78

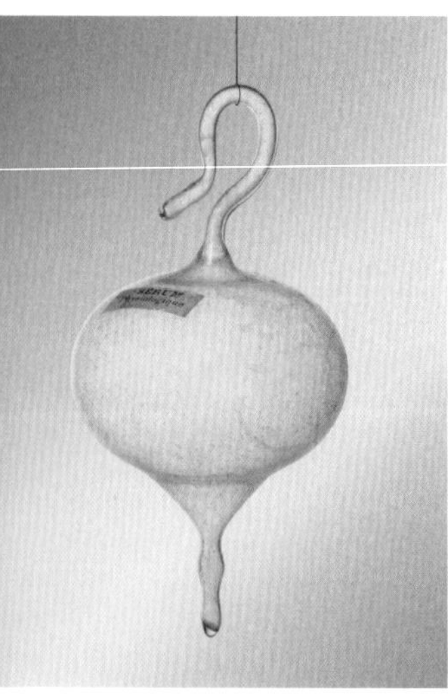

"It's air from Paris," said my host, "hermetically sealed at a particular street corner in that city." ... Like Arensberg, I laughed. As a work of art "Marcel's latest" seemed pleasant and droll.

McBride's attention moved from this small sealed vial (fig. 10) to "the big, and still uncompleted, chef-d'oeuvre in glass [*The Bride Stripped Bare by Her Bachelors, Even*, see fig. 37]...posed near the entrance." Given the size and novelty of *The Large Glass*, we may now find it surprising that *The Large Glass* struck McBride as having "the reticence of...a Rembrandt in the Metropolitan Museum of Art" compared to the other paintings and sculptures around the room:

> Things by Gris, Braque, and Metzinger in vivid colours... pull the eye of him who enters the door.... Furthermore, there is one of Picasso's "reasoned derangements" in paint, some particularly dynamic African fetish carvings, and plenty of the latest local outpourings in cubism. Some of the works individually verge towards violence, but they have been so carefully placed by the mad owners of the establishment that not only a perfect balance but a genuine if hitherto unheard of harmony has been attained.[32]

McBride's description of the Arensbergs as "mad" may have been intended as a celebration of their aesthetic audacity, but the couple he encountered were in fact heading for an emotional and financial breakdown.

For nearly a decade, they had indulged their every whim and were on the brink of insolvency. Walter philandered and drank to excess while Louise, bored, began an affair of her own with Roché.[33] Drifting away from her husband and feeling the physical strain of their lifestyle, she threatened divorce if he didn't try to save their marriage by taking a break out west. Exhausted and nearly bankrupt, Walter somehow had the wherewithal to submit a completed manuscript of *The Cryptography of Dante* to his publisher, Alfred A. Knopf, and the couple finally found the money and strength to make the journey to Los Angeles in the early spring of 1921.

Invigorated by California's easy climate and lifestyle, the Arensbergs began to rebuild the foundations of their marriage. For Louise, the effect of the change of setting was dramatic, as her health and confidence returned; and within a year Walter, too, was transformed. Now much more sober, he shifted his cryptographic campaign from Dante to Bacon: in 1922 he published *The Cryptography of Shakespeare*, his first work devoted to the thesis that Bacon wrote the texts attributed to the Bard. Walter's Harvard classmate Pitts Sanborn provided one of the book's few positive reviews, while holding back from endorsing its conclusions:

> To the rank outsider the whole matter...may seem the most hopeless sort of labyrinth, but if he enters the maze under the expert guidance of Mr. Arensberg, whether or not he comes out of it convinced that the thesis so elaborately supported by his pilot is correct, he will at least have the satisfaction of studying a fascinating hypothesis in the company of an extraordinary mind functioning most ingeniously.[34]

In spite of the Arensbergs' renewed health and industriousness, the next few years were filled with personal and professional upheaval. Walter struggled to accept his declining status within the intellectual establishment, and the couple's financial situation remained precarious. Thinking they had no other choice, Louise and Walter consigned all but their most beloved artworks to Charles Sheeler to sell through the

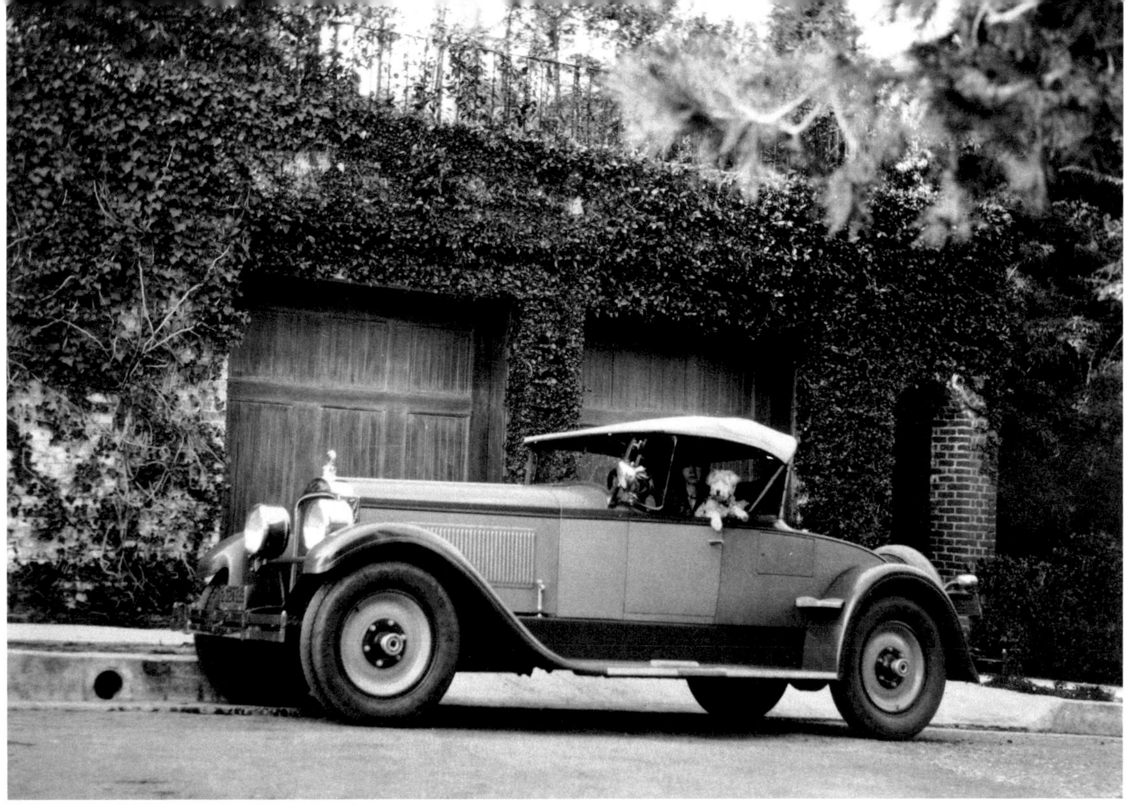

11. LOUISE STEVENS ARENSBERG WITH HER DOG, LOLLIE, IN FRONT OF THE WILLIAM LEE WOOLLETT–DESIGNED GARAGES AND FRONT ENTRANCE TO 7065 HILLSIDE AVENUE, LOS ANGELES, CA. 1930S. PHOTOGRAPHER UNKNOWN. PHILADELPHIA MUSEUM OF ART, LIBRARY AND ARCHIVES, ARENSBERG ARCHIVES (PMA-WLA), BOX 53, FOLDER 25

gallery of Marius de Zayas. Their prized pieces, however, found purchasers only in John Quinn, who bought very little, and in Katherine Dreier, to whom they sold *The Large Glass*. Though the Arensbergs were expecting a windfall, one was not forthcoming. They instead put their art in storage.

Perhaps believing they would someday live again on the East Coast, they made return visits frequently during their early years in California. And they jumped between several rental houses, including a brief and unhappy stint as the first residents in Residence A at Olive Hill, the cluster of buildings designed by Frank Lloyd Wright for the oil heiress and theater impresario Aline Barnsdall.[35] The Arensbergs decided in the summer of 1925 to live more permanently in California. They traveled again to New York that fall—where they saw Duchamp and met Brancusi—but beyond attending to the estates of their recently deceased relatives and enjoying the amusements of the city, they found little reason to stay. As Sawelson-Gorse observes, the Arensbergs' return to Hollywood by December 1926 confirmed for others what they already knew: "Their temporary destination [had become] their permanent one."[36]

In September 1927, the Arensbergs finally settled into 7065 Hillside Avenue, a large house nestled in the hills just north of Hollywood Boulevard. It had been built in 1920 for the lumber tycoon Lee B. Menefee, who had commissioned it from William Lee Woollett, best remembered today as the interior architect of one of the first "movie palaces" in the United States: Sid Grauman's Million Dollar Theater in downtown Los Angeles.[37] Designed by Woollett in an L-shaped plan, the Arensbergs' new home featured a front facade of rough-troweled stucco punctuated by symmetrical French doors and matching casement windows under a clay-tiled, slightly hipped roof.[38] Set back from the street behind a generous front yard, with gating and foliage along the sidewalk and a two-car garage also designed by Woollett (fig. 11), the house was almost completely hidden from view, and the privacy it afforded surely appealed to the couple. Though it was a conservative and relatively typical example of the Mediterranean Revival–style architecture then at the height of its popularity in Southern California, the home's spacious interior must have seemed to the Arensbergs a fine fit for their maturing relationship, its high walls the perfect blank slate on which to reimagine their art collection (figs. 12, 13).

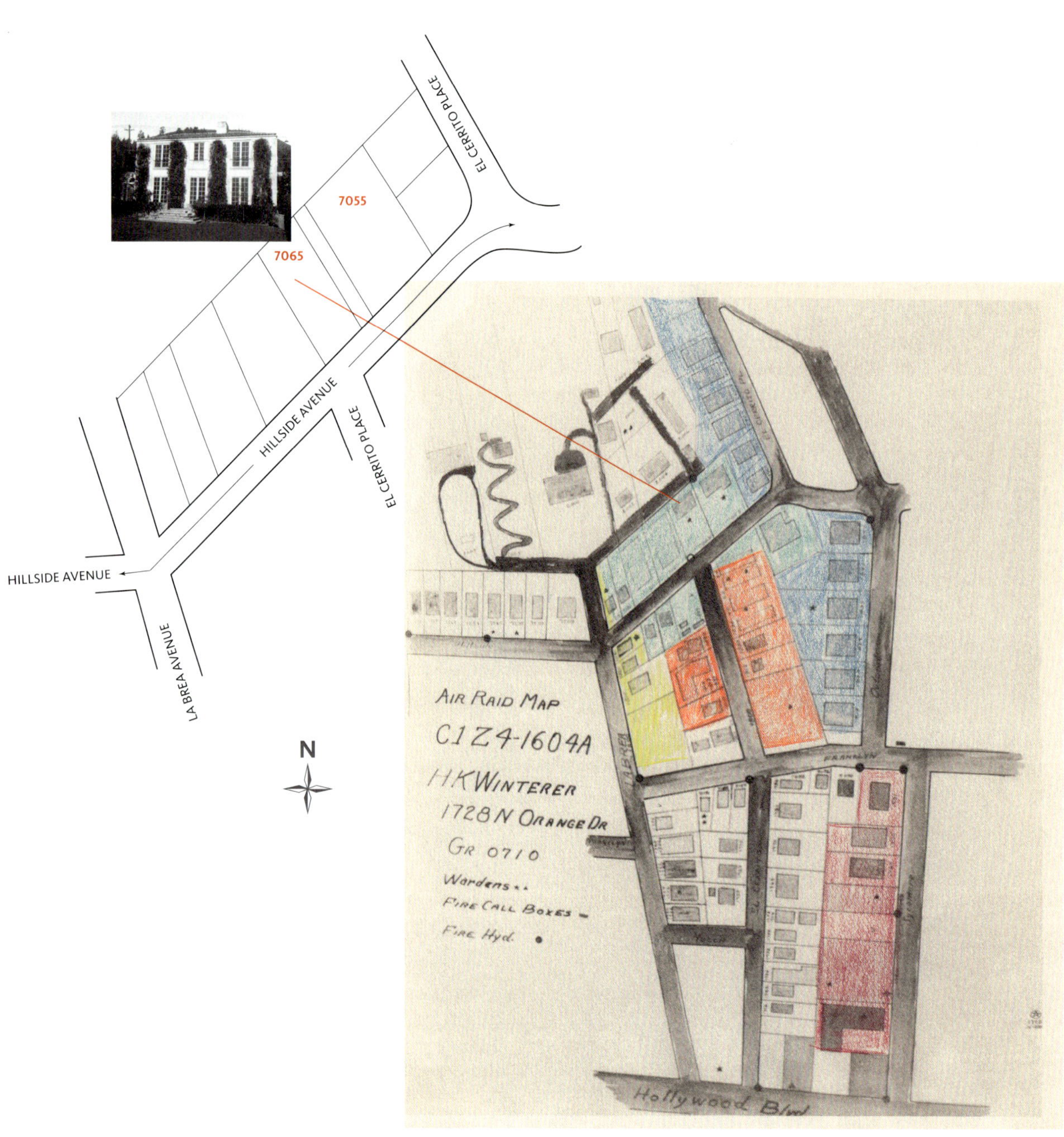

12. MAP OF THE ARENSBERGS' HOLLYWOOD NEIGHBORHOOD, SHOWING THE AREA THAT WALTER AND HIS NEIGHBOR EARL STENDAHL MONITORED AS AIR-RAID WARDENS DURING WORLD WAR II. THE HUNTINGTON LIBRARY, FRANCIS BACON LIBRARY ARCHIVE, WALTER AND LOUISE ARENSBERG PAPERS (HEH-FBLA), BOX 82, FOLDER 2

HAVING LIVED AT 7065 HILLSIDE AVENUE SINCE 1927, THE ARENSBERGS PURCHASED THE NEIGHBORING PROPERTY (7055 HILLSIDE) IN 1939, INITIALLY THINKING IT MIGHT ONE DAY HOUSE THEIR COLLECTION. ABANDONING THAT PLAN IN 1941, THEY INSTEAD GAVE IT TO STENDAHL TO SETTLE INVOICES ON PRE-COLUMBIAN ART OBJECTS THEY HAD PURCHASED FROM HIM. AFTER THE ARENSBERGS' DEATHS, STENDAHL PURCHASED 7065 HILLSIDE.

13. SITE PLAN OF 7065 HILLSIDE AVENUE, LOS ANGELES, NOTING THE ARCHITECTS OF RECORD AND THE ARCHITECTURAL MODIFICATIONS COMMISSIONED BY LOUISE AND WALTER ARENSBERG (OWNERS, 1927–54) AND BY ENID AND EARL STENDAHL (OWNERS, 1954–66)

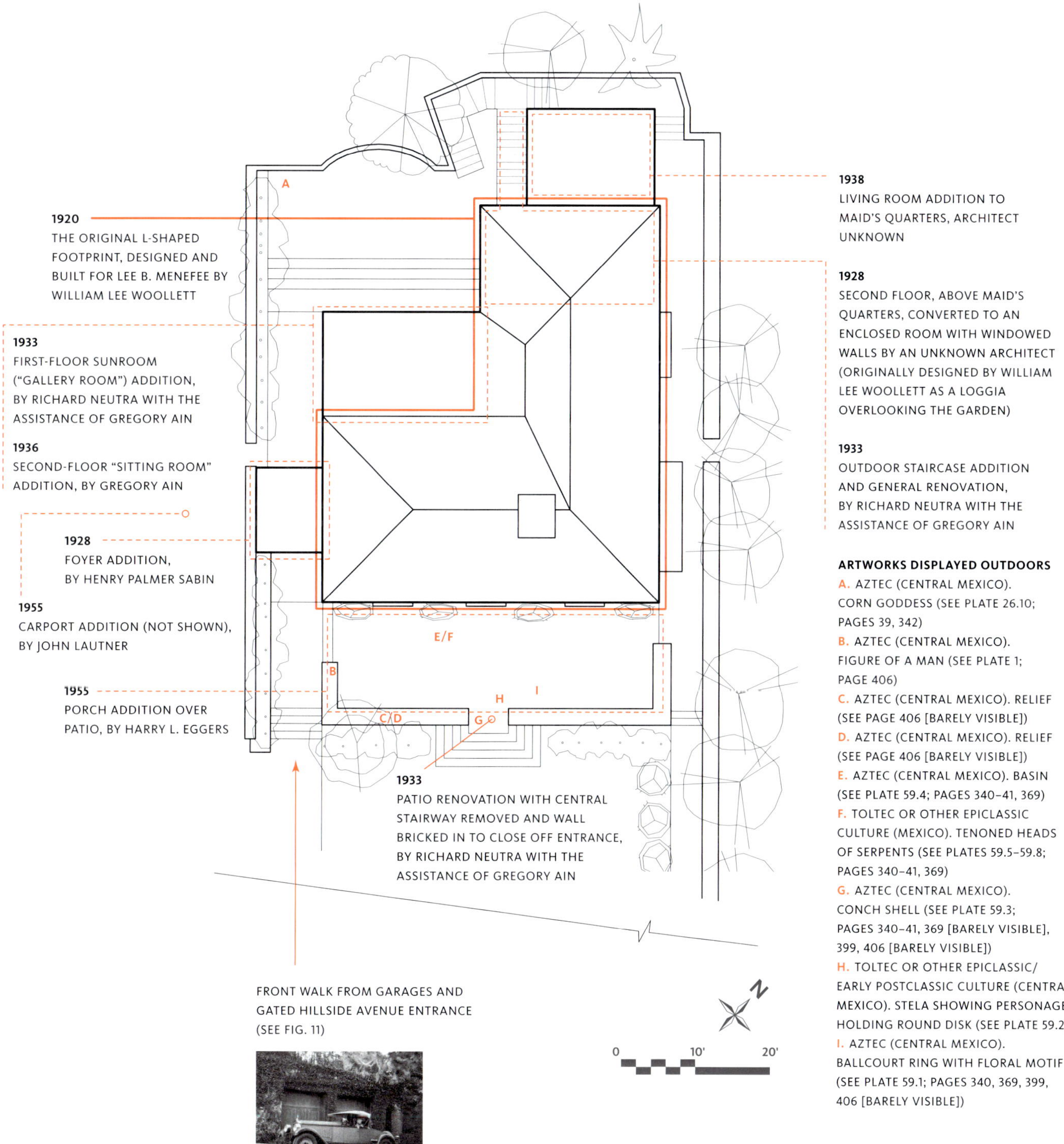

ARTWORKS DISPLAYED OUTDOORS

A. AZTEC (CENTRAL MEXICO). CORN GODDESS (SEE PLATE 26.10; PAGES 39, 342)
B. AZTEC (CENTRAL MEXICO). FIGURE OF A MAN (SEE PLATE 1; PAGE 406)
C. AZTEC (CENTRAL MEXICO). RELIEF (SEE PAGE 406 [BARELY VISIBLE])
D. AZTEC (CENTRAL MEXICO). RELIEF (SEE PAGE 406 [BARELY VISIBLE])
E. AZTEC (CENTRAL MEXICO). BASIN (SEE PLATE 59.4; PAGES 340–41, 369)
F. TOLTEC OR OTHER EPICLASSIC CULTURE (MEXICO). TENONED HEADS OF SERPENTS (SEE PLATES 59.5–59.8; PAGES 340–41, 369)
G. AZTEC (CENTRAL MEXICO). CONCH SHELL (SEE PLATE 59.3; PAGES 340–41, 369 [BARELY VISIBLE], 399, 406 [BARELY VISIBLE])
H. TOLTEC OR OTHER EPICLASSIC/ EARLY POSTCLASSIC CULTURE (CENTRAL MEXICO). STELA SHOWING PERSONAGE HOLDING ROUND DISK (SEE PLATE 59.2)
I. AZTEC (CENTRAL MEXICO). BALLCOURT RING WITH FLORAL MOTIF (SEE PLATE 59.1; PAGES 340, 369, 399, 406 [BARELY VISIBLE])

II

A "tour"

DUCHAMP HAD NOT SET EYES on his patrons for a decade when he made his first visit to California in August 1936 (fig. 14). By then the walls of the Arensbergs' Hollywood house were far from empty: they now held so much of Duchamp's work that as the artist embarked on the project *Box in a Valise* (*Boîte-en-valise*)[39]—a portable retrospective with miniature reproductions of his major works—he could reacquaint himself with many of the originals in the new house of his old friends.[40] In the intervening years, Duchamp had continued to act as an agent in the building of the Arensbergs' collection, corresponding regularly about purchases and loans, but he had not seen most of his works in full size and color since 1926, and he had never seen them all displayed together in a single space. To celebrate the occasion, the Arensbergs threw a series of soirees in honor of the artist who had, as the *Los Angeles Times* reported, "quit painting for chess."[41] Walter's protégée Charis Wilson was on hand at the largest of these parties to describe the couple's fitting tribute:

> Their house was swarming with a who's who of names from the art and literary worlds. Some people followed a "tour" that took them past every painting and sculpture, visiting bedrooms and bathrooms as well as the more usual sites—carefully guarding their wine glasses against spillage as they passed on the stairs.[42]

Wilson's quotation marks around "tour," and her recollection of passing by *every* artwork, suggest that this was no ordinary viewing of the collection—and not just because it was unusually thorough or took the guests to parts of the house that were normally off-limits. The route she described resembles a very particular kind of tour, one familiar to students of chess since ancient times. In chess parlance, a "tour" refers to a series of movements whereby a particular piece (usually the knight or king) visits all of the board's sixty-four squares in turn, touching each position only once. Mathematicians have worked for centuries on the permutations needed to cover the whole board without repetition;[43] and during the first half of the twentieth century, a number of artists in the Arensberg circle were fascinated by the patterns produced when these movements were mapped—with different pieces generating different shapes (thanks to the rules of the game). John Covert, for example, who actively participated in the Arensbergs' New York salon, made many elaborate diagrams illustrating variants on the Knight's Tour (fig. 15).[44] And the artist Man Ray, one of Duchamp's closest friends, engaged with the patterns produced by this age-old problem too: in the early 1940s (while living near the Arensbergs in Hollywood) he created a painting called *The Knight's Tour*, depicting a web of lines crisscrossing an eight-by-eight grid of black and white squares.[45]

The Knight's Tour was shown in 1944 at Julien Levy's landmark exhibition, *The Imagery of Chess*, for which Duchamp designed the invitation to the opening party. The party featured the blindfolded grand master George Koltanowski (later famous for his public performances of memorized Knight's Tours) playing games simultaneously with five of the art world's leading figures.[46] For Duchamp, playing games on the chessboard and in the art gallery went hand in hand.

Indeed, from the late 1930s, Duchamp served as curator of numerous exhibitions presenting the work of his fellow artists in playful and provocative scenographies. These included the 1938 Exposition International du Surréalisme in Paris, in which visitors carried flashlights through dark grottoes that were covered with coal sacks, and 1942's *First Papers of Surrealism* show, housed in New York's Whitelaw Reid Mansion, where Duchamp wove a dense web of twine between the temporary partitions holding the exhibition's paintings.

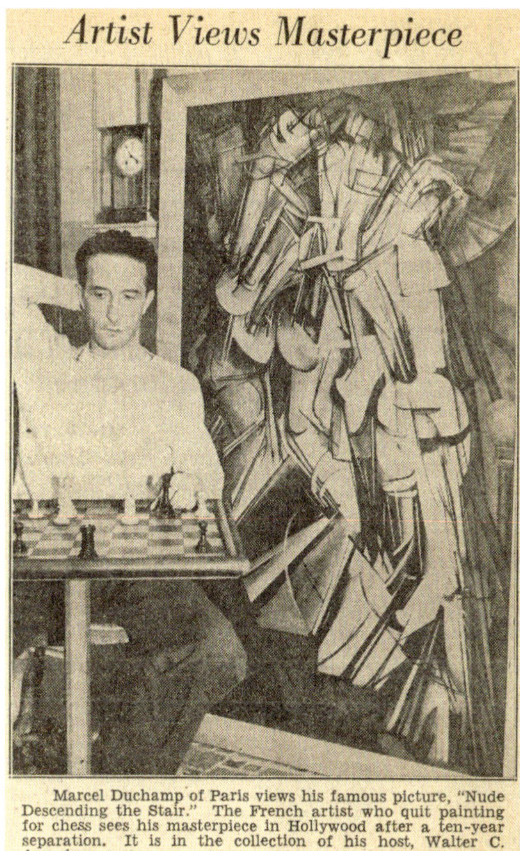

Artist Views Masterpiece

Marcel Duchamp of Paris views his famous picture, "Nude Descending the Stair." The French artist who quit painting for chess sees his masterpiece in Hollywood after a ten-year separation. It is in the collection of his host, Walter C. Arensberg.

Times photo

14. "PAINTER HITS ART THEORY: FRENCH ARTIST VISITS CITY," *LOS ANGELES TIMES*, 16 AUGUST 1936, SEC. 2, P. 2 (DETAIL). PHILADELPHIA MUSEUM OF ART, LIBRARY AND ARCHIVES, ARENSBERG ARCHIVES (PMA-WLA), BOX 41, FOLDER 14

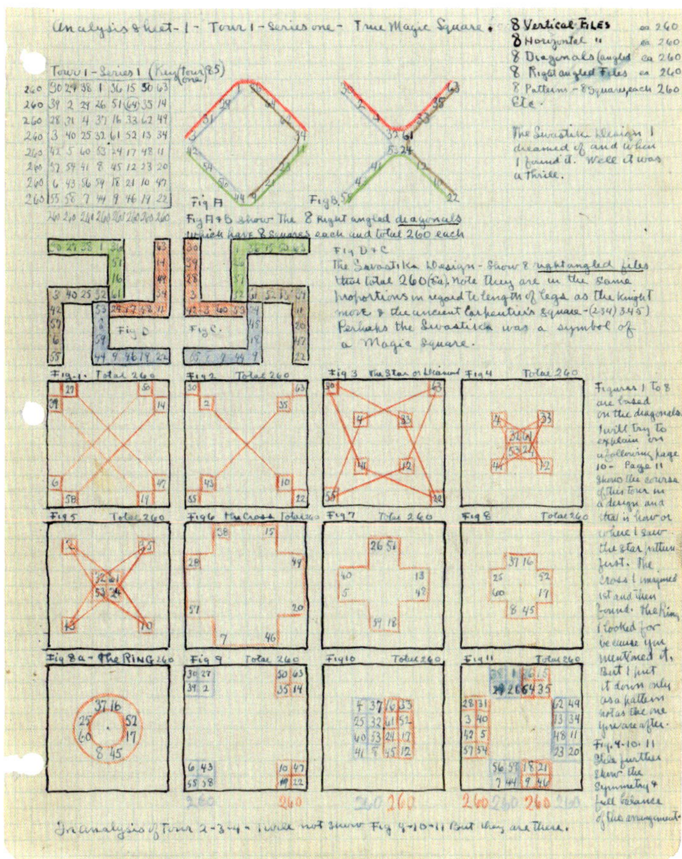

15. JOHN COVERT. DIAGRAMS OF KNIGHTS' TOURS, CA. 1915–25. PHILADELPHIA MUSEUM OF ART, LIBRARY AND ARCHIVES, JOHN RAPHAEL COVERT PAPERS (PMA-JRC), BOX 1, FOLDER 28

"The net result... forever gets between you and the assembled art and in doing so creates the most paradoxically clarifying barrier imaginable," according to *New York Times* critic Edward Alden Jewell.[47]

At the time of his 1936 visit with the Arensbergs, however, Duchamp was busy preparing a radical new display of his own work. It took the form, as he later put it to James Johnson Sweeney, of a box in which "reproductions of those paintings that I loved so much... would be mounted like in a small museum, a portable museum, so to speak."[48] Duchamp scholar Elena Filipovic describes the resulting *Box in a Valise* (figs. 16a, b) as "an unstable, unbounded structure with a collapsing frame, sliding panels, movable parts, and an endlessly reconfigured exhibition space," one that stands in stark opposition to both the monographic book and the "static, solid, and stable architecture... of the museum."[49] But books and museums were not the only models available to Duchamp in 1936: he encountered just such a space—a fluid and dynamic environment for art—in the Arensbergs' Hollywood house.

The alternatives presented by the "house-*cum*-museum" (to borrow the phrase used by Naomi Sawelson-Gorse to describe this phase of the Arensberg collection) blurred the boundaries between creating, collecting, and curating.[50] Jeremy Braddock has argued that this was a particular feature of the modernist moment to which the Arensbergs belonged, identifying "the two most prominent forms of modernist collecting [as] the privately assembled, but publicly exhibited, art collection and the interventionist literary anthology."[51] Braddock touches on Walter's work with Kreymborg on *Others* in his discussion of the latter phenomenon, but the example he provides of the former is the Merion, Pennsylvania, home and foundation of Dr. Albert C. Barnes.[52] Barnes displayed his equally diverse collection in similarly surprising ways, combining art and furniture from various periods and cultures in elaborate "wall ensembles" (as they have

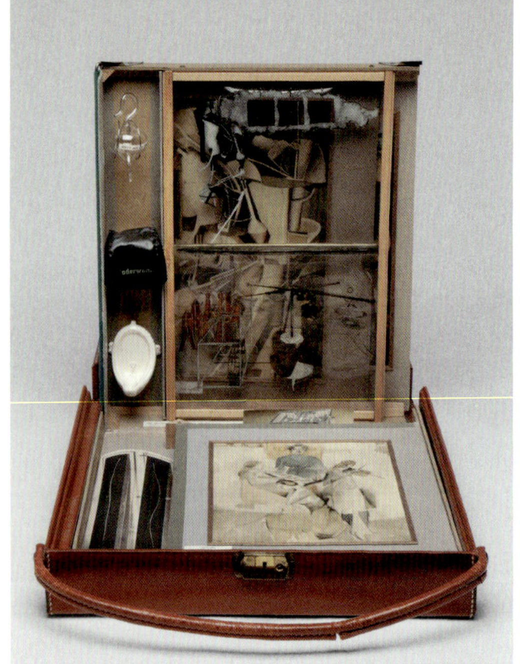

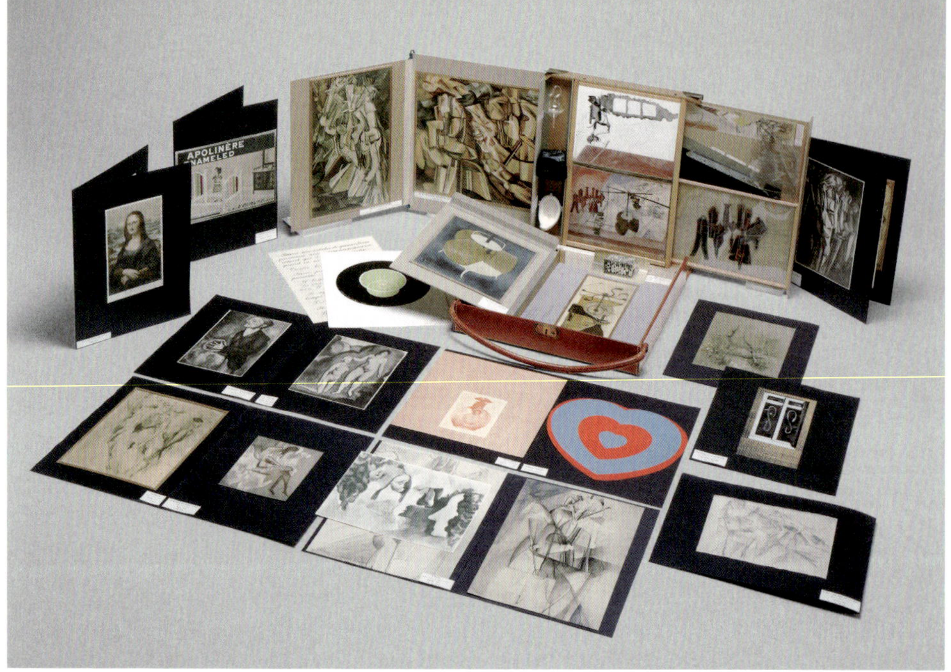

16A, B. MARCEL DUCHAMP. *FROM OR BY MARCEL DUCHAMP OR RROSE SÉLAVY (BOX IN A VALISE)*, 1935–41 (CONTENTS); 1938 (COLLOTYPE). LEATHER VALISE CONTAINING A BOX WITH SIXTY-NINE MINIATURE REPLICAS AND PRINTED REPRODUCTIONS AND ONE HAND-COLORED COLLOTYPE, *VIRGIN (NO. 2)*, 1938. EDITION: SERIES A (SPECIAL DELUXE EDITION), 0/XX FOR LOUISE AND WALTER ARENSBERG, 1943. VALISE (CLOSED): 40.6 × 37.5 × 10.8 CM. PHILADELPHIA MUSEUM OF ART, THE LOUISE AND WALTER ARENSBERG COLLECTION, 1950-134-934

come to be known) that embodied his aesthetic theories and served the educational program he initiated to improve public understanding of art. Unlike the Arensbergs, who never published an account of their approach as collectors, Barnes explained at great length how his art ought to be analyzed. In 1925, a few years after his foundation opened its doors to the public, he produced a 500-page treatise called *The Art in Painting*, outlining the formal qualities (light, line, color, space) through which an artist communicates his or her vision—following up, over the next fifteen years, with two expanded editions, along with detailed studies of Matisse, Pierre-Auguste Renoir, and Paul Cézanne.[53]

Barnes's pedagogical program was reflected in an evolving sequence of gallery rooms, organized primarily in terms of visual relationships rather than movements, techniques, or subjects (figs. 17a, b). In the words of the Barnes Foundation's former chief curator Judith Dolkart, "The ensembles, densely installed in multiple tiers of metalwork and paintings, astound, provoke, and overwhelm. With [them], Barnes challenged expectations of chronology, style, and geography, as well as traditions of exhibition and interpretation."[54] While there was a strong emphasis on formal symmetry in Barnes's arrangements, Braddock finds traces of other systems of association in play, ranging from visual puns (including "the placement of a fine pair of scissors next to a painting of Christ's circumcision" in Room IV and the pairings of skulls and mountains found in Rooms II and XIV) to cryptic conceits (such as the cluster of sexualized animals in Room XXIII).[55]

For the Arensbergs, as for Barnes, these were more than aesthetic decisions, and the patterns produced were more than simply visual. As Aline Louchheim had observed when she visited the Hollywood house in the late 1940s, Walter was a student of literature as well as a patron of painters and sculptors, a writer of poetry and criticism as well as a collector of art. And as Walter himself observed, in an interview with Kenneth Ross carried out around the time of Louchheim's visit and published for the first time in this volume, he and Louise were drawn to modern works where the artist

> intends to compel the spectators to engage in an active cooperation of interpretation. [Such work] is an attempt to make the spectator a co-creator, because the spectator who really penetrates this mystery of forms . . . is becoming active instead of passive. . . . This is very true of all the great Cubists, and is particularly true of Duchamp too.[56]

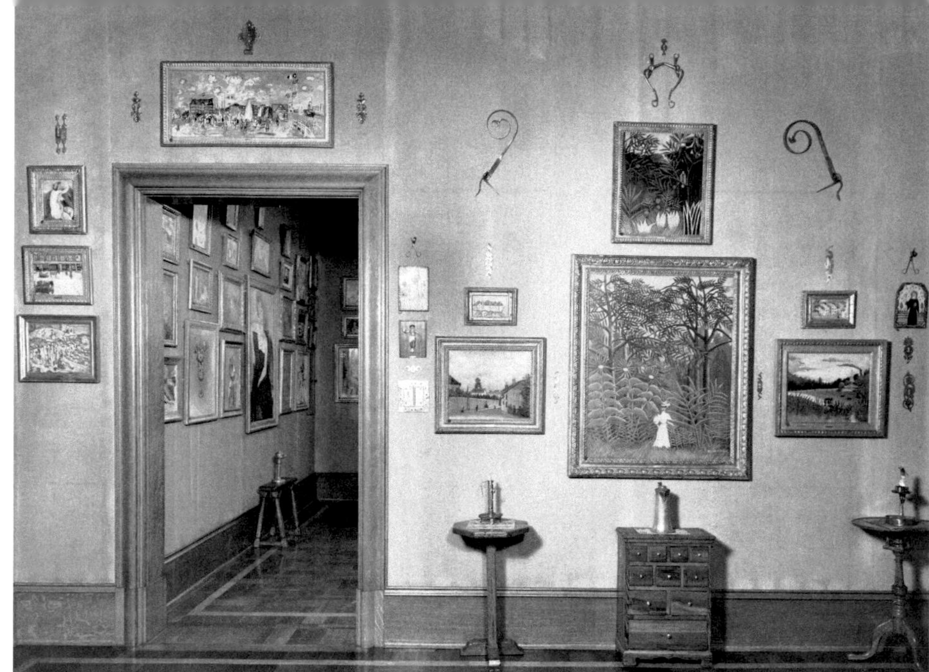

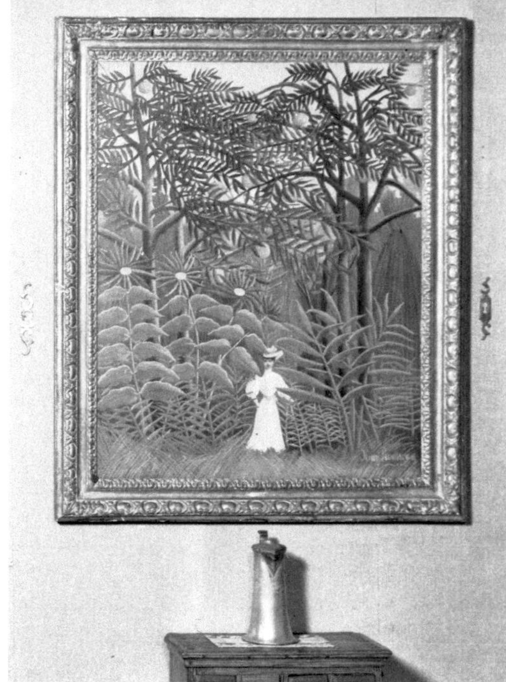

17A, B. ANGELO PINTO. GALLERY 11, VIEW OF THE NORTH WALL IN THE BARNES FOUNDATION CRET GALLERY, MERION, PENNSYLVANIA, CA. 1952. THE DETAIL AT RIGHT ILLUSTRATES HOW BARNES JUXTAPOSED OBJECTS IN HIS COLLECTION TO ACCENTUATE THEIR FORMAL AND VISUAL SIMILARITIES. HERE, FOR EXAMPLE, HE PAIRED HENRI ROUSSEAU'S 1905 PAINTING *WOMAN WALKING IN AN EXOTIC FOREST* WITH A FLAGON OF 1729 BY AN UNIDENTIFIED MAKER (CF. PLATE 23). BARNES FOUNDATION ARCHIVES, PHOTOGRAPH COLLECTION. IMAGE © 2018 THE BARNES FOUNDATION

This conception of spectator as cocreator is frequently credited to Duchamp, but it seems to have been part of the broader conversation around art in the years when modernism was becoming more readily accepted. In her "Analytical Reflection" on *The Large Glass*, Katherine Dreier claimed that "Marcel Duchamp was the first to paint the image per se, to be completed by an act of consciousness on the part of the spectator," but Barnes, in *The Art in Painting*, may in fact have been the first to articulate this theory in print.[57] Walter would have bristled at these associations—he was competitive with Dreier and despised Barnes—but he and Louise would likely have enjoyed the irony in their having created the conditions through which Marcel, during his 1936 visit, became the spectator of his own life's work.

At this time, Duchamp might well have welcomed the Arensbergs' participation (interpretive or otherwise) in his art. He had both short- and long-term designs for his own posterity, and significant reason therefore to ensure that his relationship with the owners of most of his pieces was healthy. But there were difficulties to overcome: the natural gulf created by years of geographic and cultural separation was widened because Louise and Walter believed that Duchamp was colluding with Roché to inflate prices on works the couple wanted to acquire.[58] Despite this tension, enough good feeling remained intact over the course of Duchamp's sixteen-day visit for the Arensbergs to facilitate his initial ambitions for the *Box in a Valise* project: they commissioned a local photographer, Sam Little, to take photographs of Duchamp's works for him, and they allowed the artist to wander through their house at will, recording the colors and other details of these pieces so he could reproduce them later at small scale with the help of various technicians.[59]

Returning to his home in Paris, Duchamp spent the next five years using elaborate and time-consuming production processes to create the individual components of the *Box* project. Crucially, during this time he also grew closer to a long-term acquaintance, the heiress Peggy Guggenheim, advising her on purchases and programming for Guggenheim Jeune, the London-based gallery she founded in 1937. And when Guggenheim decamped for Paris in early 1940 with the idea of buying "a picture per day" in order to start a museum of her own, Duchamp provided introductions to the most renowned galleries and artists' studios around the city.[60] In just a few months, Guggenheim acquired more than seventy major works of art with Duchamp's assistance (hers was now the third major collection he had helped to assemble) but by the summer of that same year the approaching Nazis declared all Jewish-owned property subject to

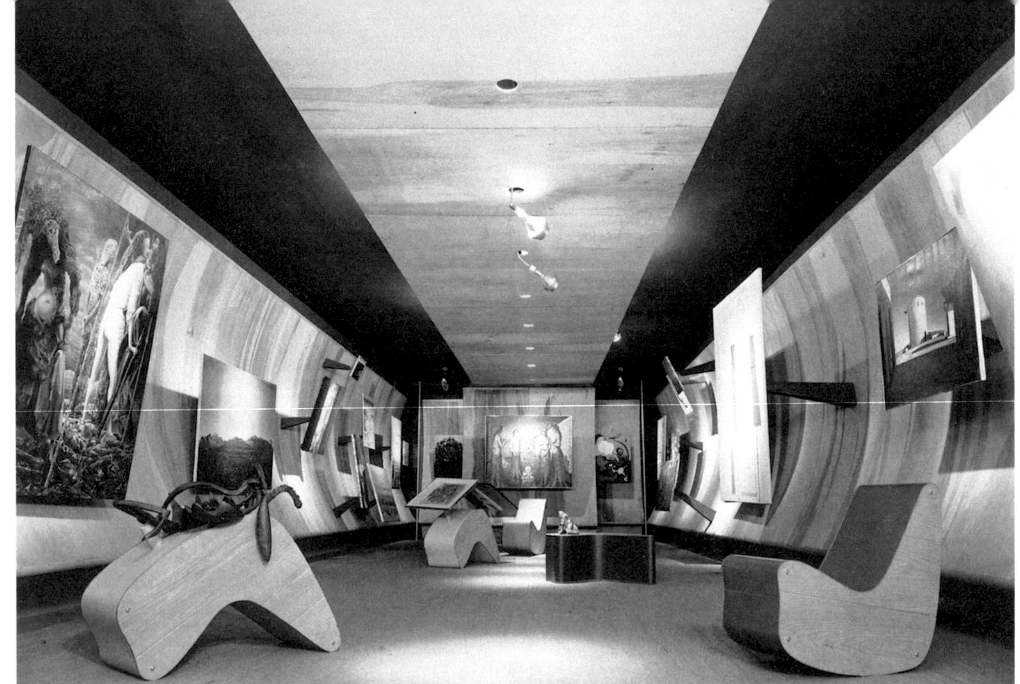

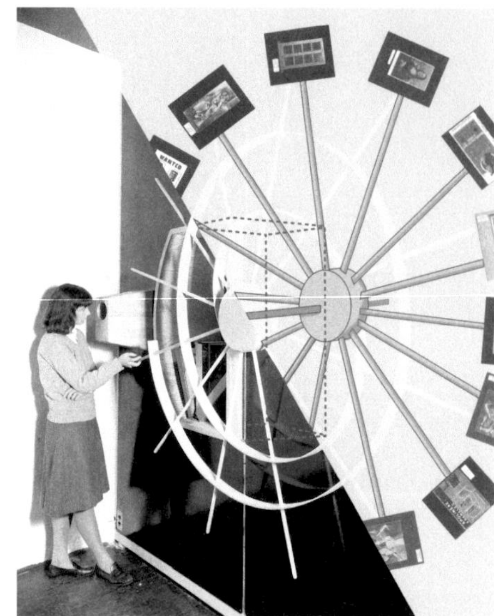

18. BERENICE ABBOTT. SOUTH-LOOKING INSTALLATION VIEW OF THE SURREALIST GALLERY IN PEGGY GUGGENHEIM'S NEW YORK GALLERY, ART OF THIS CENTURY, 1942.

19. DON QUAINTANCE. CUTAWAY SCHEMATIC REPRESENTATION OF THE VIEWING MECHANISM FOR DUCHAMP'S *BOX IN A VALISE*, SHOWING HOW THE INTERNAL WHEEL HOLDING THE ARTWORK'S LOOSE FOLDERS MAY HAVE FUNCTIONED. SEE ALSO FIG. 16B

confiscation, and her safety was no longer guaranteed. Pleading with the Louvre for the protection of her art, she was told that it was "not worth saving."[61] Guggenheim escaped from Paris on 12 June, just days before the German occupation of the city.

As wartime conditions worsened, Duchamp managed to assemble in the early months of 1941 a few completed examples of *Box in a Valise*, the first of which was purchased by Guggenheim. She had found temporary storage for her collection at the Musée de Grenoble and was secretly working from a room in the basement to catalog it. With assistance from a French shipping agent, she managed to arrange safe passage of her artworks to the United States and, remarkably, was also able to include in the shipment fifty crates of Duchamp's working materials for *Box in a Valise*. Guggenheim, and an extended entourage under her care, finally escaped to New York via Portugal in July 1941.[62]

As an American citizen with considerable resources, Guggenheim easily landed on her feet. She traveled west soon after her Stateside arrival, visiting the Arensbergs in California and taking "daily expeditions along the coast" in search of a property suitable for her "home-plus-museum."[63] She ultimately decided, to the great relief of a traveling companion, Jimmy Ernst, that "California was not ready to house her museum."[64]

The Arensbergs had only recently abandoned a similar plan: in 1939, they had purchased the house next door to their own (7055 Hillside; see fig. 12), hoping it might one day serve as a museum for their collection. Barely a month before Guggenheim's 1941 visit, however, they decided that the idea was untenable and gave the house to the art dealer Earl Stendahl to resolve unpaid invoices on pre-Columbian sculpture they had purchased from him. On the other side of the country, Dreier, too, had become urgently concerned for the well-being of her artworks—and especially for *The Large Glass*, which she felt should not be moved—unsuccessfully proposing to Yale University between 1939 and 1941 that they turn her house into a "Country Museum."[65] Thus, as Duchamp languished under continually worsening conditions, so, too, did his legacy, entwined as it was with those of his three patrons, each of them living with a part of Duchamp's life's work and each of them struggling with the realities of protecting it for posterity. It is unsurprising, therefore, that when Duchamp was finally extracted from Europe in June 1942 with the help of the Arensbergs, the Museum of Modern Art's director Alfred Barr, and Varian Fry of the Emergency Rescue Committee, one of his first orders of business was to complete his work on the first edition of *Box in a Valise*.[66]

Resettling in New York, Duchamp lived for a while in Guggenheim's Manhattan apartment, assembling his *Boxes* and acting as an adviser of sorts for Peggy and their mutual friend the architect Frederick Kiesler. Guggenheim and Kiesler were working together on Guggenheim's new gallery, Art of This Century, which they had begun planning a few months before Duchamp arrived. As the curator Susan Davidson has written, "Kiesler had acquired a reputation among vanguard circles as an innovator in display techniques and as a visionary architect.... Peggy gave [him] great freedom to create a 'new exhibition method.'"[67] The result of this collaboration, Davidson has noted, was

> an ideal showcase for Peggy's magnificent collection. The unusual surroundings in which it was displayed—curved gumwood walls for the Surrealist Gallery [fig. 18] and an undulating blue canvas curtain for the Abstract Gallery—only added to the praise for the collection's quality.... Three decades of artistic experimentation were on view, giving many Americans their first comprehensive view of the modern aesthetic.[68]

The art historian Don Quaintance has written that the gallery's opening, in October 1942, "provoked an intense response not unlike that caused by the 1913 Armory show 30 years earlier... [arousing] extraordinary curiosity, word-of-mouth buzz, and press attention."[69] *Box in a Valise* was one of the exhibited works; indeed, among the many novel methods of display utilized in this radical new exhibition space was a manually operated mechanism by which a visitor could view pieces of *Box* through a peephole that was probably equipped with a magnifying device (fig. 19).[70]

As Guggenheim's gallery and its Kiesler-designed "flexible hanging systems"[71] were animating the art world, Duchamp finally sent the Arensbergs a copy of *Box*, which included a hand-colored collotype of *Virgin (No. 2)* (see plate 33.12).[72] Probably expecting something more akin to a traditional book, it took some time for the couple to come to terms with the final form of Duchamp's "portable museum." On 6 May 1943, Walter wrote the following to Marcel:

> We should have acknowledged long ago the arrival of the wonderful box, but it has been difficult to know exactly what to say of such an epitome of a life work. You have invented a new kind of autobiography. It is a kind of autobiography in a performance of marionettes. You have become the puppeteer of your past.[73]

The art historian Ecke Bonk has described this "miniature, folding exhibition space"[74] as the embodiment of Duchamp's curatorial approach:

> The manifold overlaps and cross-references in his work as a whole are reflected in the spatial construction of the *Boîte*, as well as in the arrangement of the reproductions. His artistic statements and achievements, in all their heterogeneous and many-sided profusion, are presented here by Duchamp as a carefully ordered whole.[75]

And while Duchamp's approach to the presentation of his life's work derives from what Bonk calls "the synthesis of his paradoxical principles," it in fact bears a very close resemblance to the arrangement mindset of the Arensbergs, within whose home the project first took shape.

In turn, Duchamp's *Box in a Valise* may have inspired the Arensbergs to become much more interested in preserving and presenting their collection as a whole. It is perhaps no coincidence that the earliest pictures of the house collected and arranged in *Hollywood Arensberg*—those by Fritz (Fred) Block (part of a slide series he published in 1943) and Fred R. Dapprich (taken in late 1944 and published in part in *Vogue* the following year)—occur around the time the Arensbergs received their copy of *Box in a Valise*. When arranged alongside others in a carefully ordered whole, these photographs allow us to see the patterns and puzzles that Louchheim, Wilson, and Duchamp saw as they encountered the Arensbergs' wall ensembles.

Immediately upon walking through the front door, visitors to the Arensbergs' house in Hollywood were put in a position to consider what it might mean to place the work of one artist next to that of another or to consider how a sculpture by Brancusi might be interpreted differently when accompanied by an Aztec goal ring or a dinosaur print. Likewise, readers of this book are taken on a tour through a series of spaces in which (as our short descriptions in the following pages begin to suggest and as the testimonies of contemporary visitors confirm) we find traces of the intellectual and biographical associations that brought the collection to life for the couple who created it. As we move from room to room, we can watch the collectors playing a kind of chess with their art—and we can even become players in the game ourselves.

THE FOYER

In 1928, almost immediately after moving into 7065 Hillside, the Arensbergs commissioned Henry Palmer Sabin to redesign the main entryway, then a heavy paneled door set into the wall on the southwest side of the house. Sabin extended this entrance by building a symmetrical structure around it, an enclosed foyer with two additional exterior doors—one paneled, the other glass-paned for a view of the back garden—each framed by Palladian-style sunburst windows and sidelights (see plate 1).[76]

The little structure's pièce de résistance was to be found not in any structural or stylistic novelty but, rather, in the function of its northwest wall, which was designed to highlight two artworks by Constantin Brancusi: *Arch* and *Princess X* (fig. 20). Wood pilasters set against this brick wall were precisely measured to visually align with, and provide support for, the vertical posts of *Arch*, an artwork Brancusi had made from salvaged architectural remnants (see plate 2).[77] Sabin set clerestory windows atop this wall to frame *Arch*'s massive curved lintel, and he built a shallow niche with a barrel-vault arch within it so that natural light from the room's many windows showcased the gleaming brass of *Princess X*. Placed directly across from the original (and still functioning) door, the arrangement could be seen from the living room or closed off from view, as desired. Some time later, the Arensbergs installed a large stone sculpture of an Aztec corn goddess near the wall at the far end of the back garden, framed by the glass of the foyer's rear door (see fig. 27; page 342). Here, the skillful utilization of architectural sightlines provided one of the first hints that the couple saw their house as a configurable space for interactions between objects and viewers.

The artist Elaine Lustig Cohen, who visited the Arensbergs' home frequently as a young woman, recalled being "thunderstruck" when she first entered the foyer, saying, "Every time I passed through and saw [*Princess X* in the *Arch*] I would hold my breath. It left me breathless."[78] Indeed, the audacity of this design is notable because it marks one of the first times that an architectural feature was purpose-built into an American home specifically to hold modern art.

How much of this originality can be attributed to Sabin is unclear. The Massachusetts Institute of Technology–educated architect was no philistine, having lived and worked extensively in Europe and South America before opening his own office in Pasadena, California, in 1928.[79] However, the foyer was among the first commissions awarded to his burgeoning practice, and even he may not have fully realized how dynamic *Princess X* and *Arch*—"by owner, contracted to be set as directed," as he noted on his elevational drawings—would look once installed.[80] Given the room's classical lines and pleasing proportions, as well as the slightly uneasy formal relationship between the clerestory windows and *Arch*'s lintel, it seems

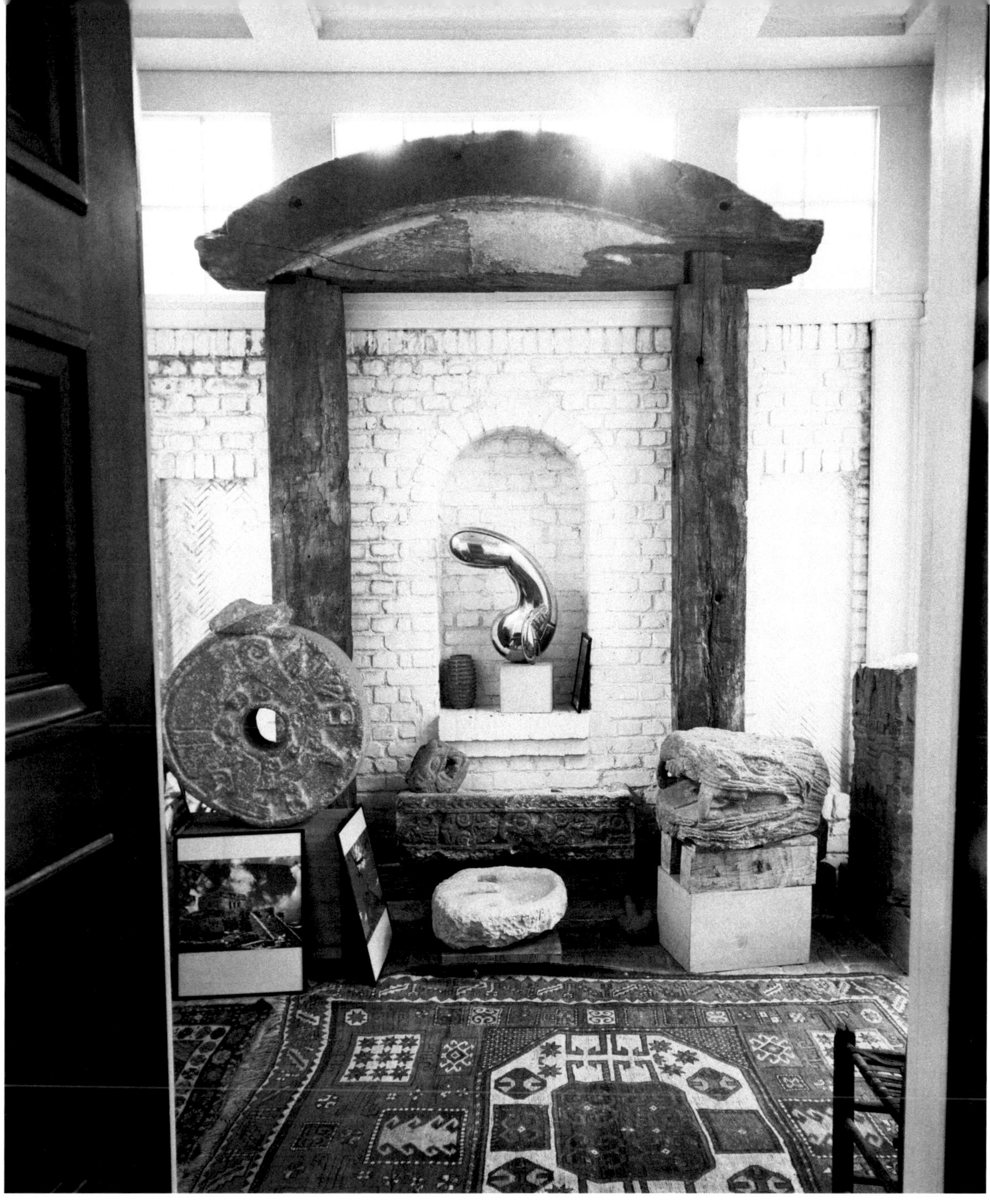

20. KARL BISSINGER. VIEW FROM THE ARENSBERGS' LIVING ROOM INTO THE FOYER DESIGNED BY HENRY PALMER SABIN, 7065 HILLSIDE AVENUE, LOS ANGELES, 16 MARCH 1950. THE STRUCTURE WAS CUSTOM-BUILT TO HOUSE THE TWO PICTURED WORKS BY CONSTANTIN BRANCUSI, *ARCH* AND *PRINCESS X*. UNIVERSITY OF DELAWARE LIBRARY, NEWARK, SPECIAL COLLECTIONS, KARL BISSINGER ARCHIVE (MSS0682). © THE ESTATE OF KARL BISSINGER. SEE ALSO PLATE 2; PAGE 350

reasonable to suggest that Sabin did not expect that the sculptures would remain in the foyer permanently. Yet, after the work had been completed, he may have been as astonished as his contemporaries that such simple material and ideational juxtapositions could create such an exhilarating effect. In this small space, classicism and modernity leaned into each other, and the echo of religious veneration in the inset niche was all the more jarring for the sexual suggestiveness of the sculpture set inside it (fig. 21).

Sawelson-Gorse has conjectured that the design in its totality was so sophisticated that Duchamp or Brancusi perhaps played a role in its conception.[81] (Brancusi had met the Arensbergs in New York in 1926[82] and had said on more than one occasion that he wanted to "build a temple."[83]) More importantly, she has argued that "the permanence of its installation as part of an ensemble" laid the foundation for a permanent collection that the Arensbergs grew, refined, and prepared for posterity over the last two decades of their lives.[84]

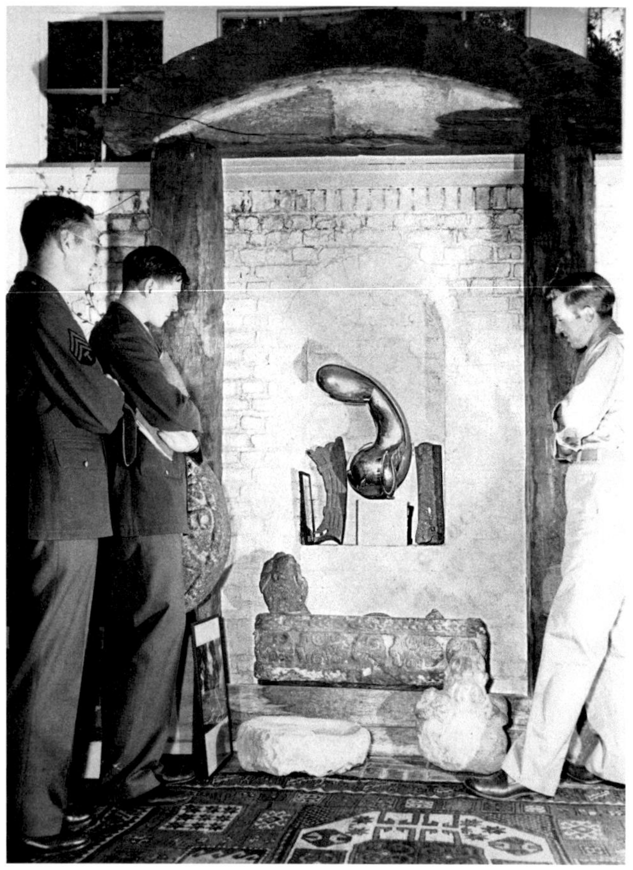

21. SOLDIERS FROM NEARBY BIRMINGHAM GENERAL HOSPITAL VISITING THE ARENSBERGS, CA. APRIL 1945. PHOTOGRAPH BY CORPORAL F. W. LUMBORD. PHILADELPHIA MUSEUM OF ART, LIBRARY AND ARCHIVES, ARENSBERG ARCHIVES (PMA-WLA), BOX 53, FOLDER 51

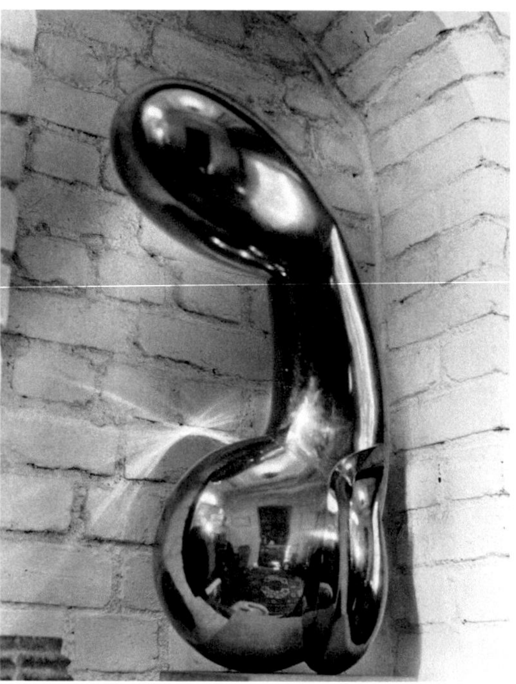

22. CLARENCE JOHN LAUGHLIN. *THE VORACIOUS PRINCESS*, 1 MAY 1950. THE CLARENCE JOHN LAUGHLIN ARCHIVE AT THE HISTORIC NEW ORLEANS COLLECTION. FOR THE COPY OF THIS PRINT THAT LAUGHLIN GAVE TO THE ARENSBERGS, SEE PHILADELPHIA MUSEUM OF ART, THE LOUISE AND WALTER ARENSBERG COLLECTION, 1950-134-979

Close study of *Princess X*'s reflective surface, as shown in a photograph by Clarence John Laughlin (fig. 22), reveals that the Arensbergs later hung two additional works by Brancusi, *Study for "The Newborn"* and *Study for "The Princess,"* on the opposite wall on each side of the door leading into the living room, completing an interior shrine to an artist whose work had entranced them.[85] The Arensbergs gave unusual access to Laughlin, who was best known for his "symbolic" photographs combining Southern buildings and landscapes with surrealist-inspired effects.[86] During a 1950 visit, Laughlin produced thirteen dramatically lit portraits of individual works in the Arensbergs' collection, experimental pictures that inspired him to undertake a long-running series of interpretations of sculptures in American homes and museums. Like many visitors to the couple's house, Laughlin was moved to put what he saw into words, providing poetic captions for his photographs. Of *Princess X* he wrote,

> *The Voracious Princess:*
> The golden metal is like a congealed object of dark liquid, with the lower portion enclosing the room beyond (even the rug), while the curve in the top of the sculpture is echoed in the curved brick arch. To one side of the lower portion the light re-appears as though it came to birth in the metal figure, and had been then re-born upon the wall.[87]

In the concentrated space of the foyer, the Arensbergs had effectively created an antechamber to a museum within a home. Showcasing one of their most dramatic pieces, it prepared visitors for the jarring arrangements they would encounter as they crossed the threshold into the house.

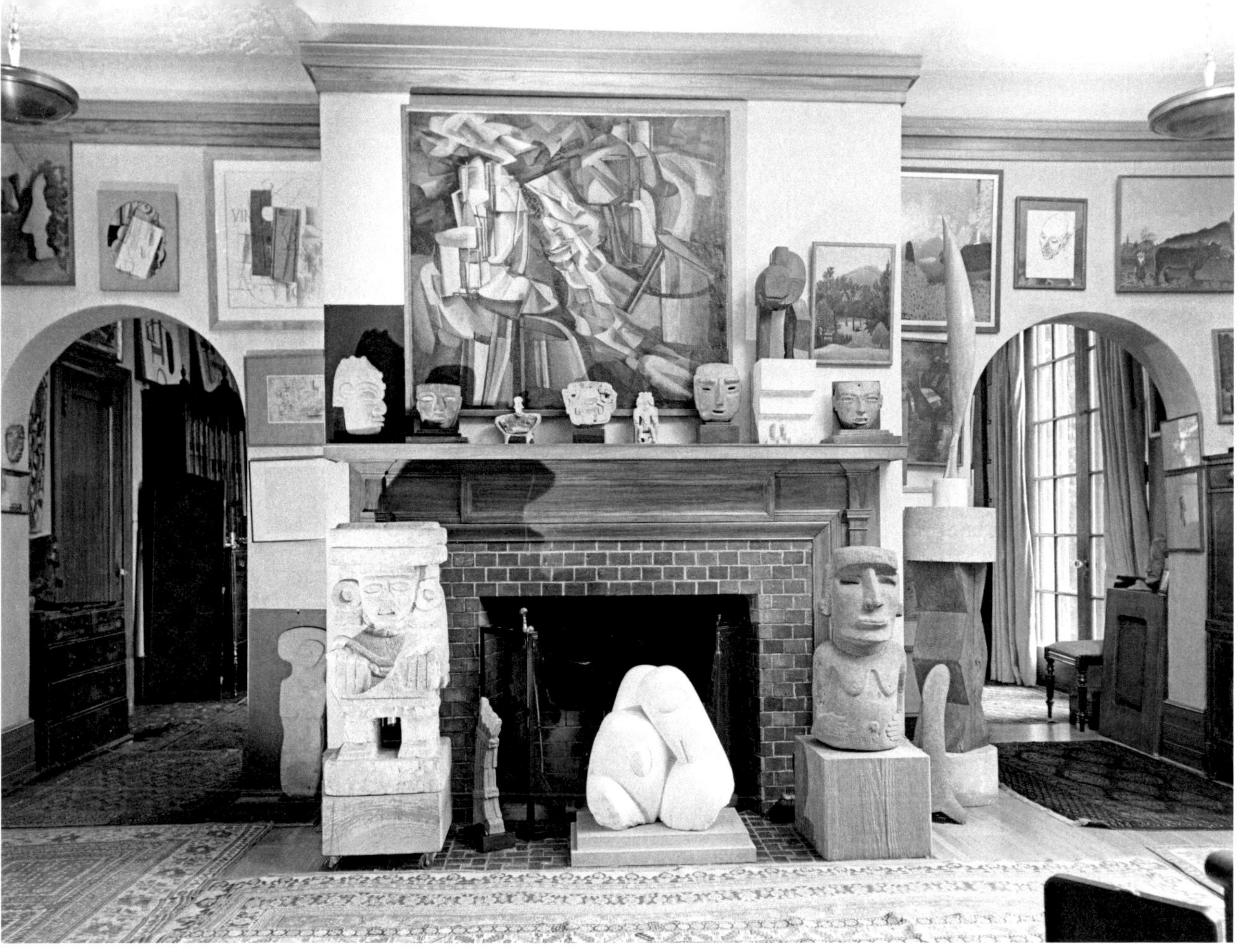

23. KARL BISSINGER. VIEW OF LOUISE AND WALTER ARENSBERG'S LIVING ROOM AT 7065 HILLSIDE AVENUE, LOS ANGELES, 16 MARCH 1950. PICTURED AMONG OTHER WORKS ARE MARCEL DUCHAMP'S *THE KING AND QUEEN SURROUNDED BY SWIFT NUDES*, CONSTANTIN BRANCUSI'S *PRODIGAL SON*, AND, IN FRONT OF IT, TWO MINIATURE MEZCALA FIGURES WITH "MR. ARENSBERG" AND "MRS. ARENSBERG" ETCHED INTO THEIR ACRYLIC BASES. IN FRONT OF THE FIREPLACE SITS BRANCUSI'S *THREE PENGUINS*, FLANKED BY A MESOAMERICAN GODDESS AND THE DEIFIED ANCESTOR OF AN EASTER ISLANDER. UNIVERSITY OF DELAWARE LIBRARY, NEWARK, SPECIAL COLLECTIONS, KARL BISSINGER ARCHIVE (MSS0682). SEE ALSO PLATES 3–5

THE LIVING ROOM

As a photograph of soldiers visiting from nearby Birmingham Hospital illustrates, the spacious living room was the social hub of the Arensbergs' home (see plate 3).[88] Here, the couple hosted a new series of salons for debating Walter's theories on the Shakespeare authorship controversy, and when they were alone or among confidants, Louise, "an exquisite *bel canto* soprano," sang and played the piano near the French doors looking out over the front patio.[89] As it had been during their early years in New York, the living room was the set piece of their collection.

Entering from the foyer, visitors would have been immediately drawn to Duchamp's *The King and Queen Surrounded by Swift Nudes* (figs. 23, 24; see fig. 53), a commanding painting some fifty inches across that dominated the intricate arrangement of art and artifacts set above and around the mantel. Duchamp painted this picture in May 1912: it was the culmination of a series of chess-related drawings representing the king and queen as well as the fluid movement of other pieces around them. Stepping closer, visitors may have noticed two pre-Columbian statuettes on the mantel below, with the words *Mr. Arensberg* and *Mrs. Arensberg* etched into their acrylic bases (fig. 25). Set in front of Brancusi's *Prodigal Son*,[90] the stone statuettes were about the size of chess pieces. Most likely gifts from the Arensbergs' neighbor (and LA's preeminent dealer of pre-Columbian art) Earl Stendahl (fig. 26), these objects offered a playful parallel between Duchamp's king and queen and the formidable couple who presided over the collection.

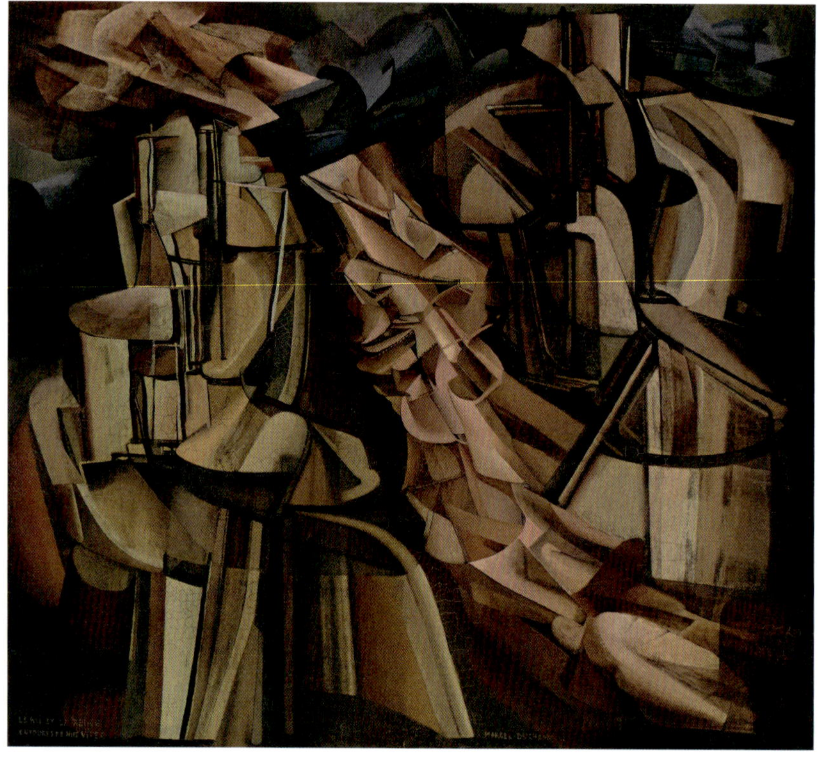

24. MARCEL DUCHAMP. *THE KING AND QUEEN SURROUNDED BY SWIFT NUDES*, 1912.
OIL ON CANVAS, 114.6 × 128.9 CM. PHILADELPHIA MUSEUM OF ART, THE LOUISE AND WALTER ARENSBERG COLLECTION, 1950-134-63A. SEE ALSO PLATES 3.12, 4.22, 5.24

The King and Queen Surrounded by Swift Nudes made a dramatic impression on another regular visitor to the house, the actress Helen Freeman Corle; in fact, she put it at the center of a sixty-page essay (from which the epigraph opening this essay is taken) attempting one of the first sustained assessments of Duchamp's artistic output:

> It has been my strange fortune to stand many times in the room commanded by this canvas and surrounded by the finest examples of Picasso, Léger, Braque, Matisse, to mention only a few. The latter are somehow diminished. Le Roi et La Reine (the King and the Queen) overshadow and swallow them all up.[91]

This painting occupied such an important place in Duchamp's development as an artist, and such a signal position in the Arensbergs' collection, that it is worth stepping back to survey it once more from the entrance foyer (fig. 27). From this vantage point, with Brancusi's princess behind them framed by her two arches, visitors would have faced Duchamp's king and queen framed by the two arched doorways leading to the dining room beyond, and by two stone sculptures on either side of the fireplace, one representing a Mesoamerican goddess and the other a deified ancestor of an Easter Islander (see plates 5.6, 5.9).[92] Directly below the mantel, they would have seen Brancusi's *Three Penguins*—inspired by the "Kings" and "Emperors" encountered during the first Antarctic expeditions (see plate 5.8).[93] Turning to the left, visitors would have again seen the corn goddess framed behind the glass of the foyer door.

Stepping across the threshold and looking back into the foyer from the center of the living room (fig. 28), they would have noticed Brancusi's princess flanked by another princess, Ariadne, in Giorgio de Chirico's *The Soothsayer's Recompense* (see plate 18.7); and a second king and queen, in Marcel Duchamp's *The King and Queen Traversed by Swift Nudes at High Speed* (see plate 18.18).

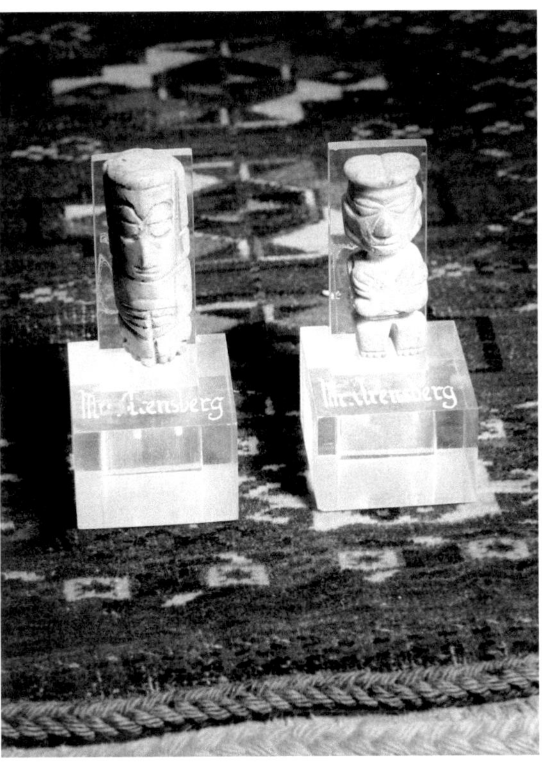

25. FRED R. DAPPRICH. TWO MINIATURE MEZCALA FIGURES. THESE OBJECTS, POSSIBLY GIFTS FROM EARL STENDAHL, SAT ON THE LIVING ROOM MANTEL NEXT TO MARCEL DUCHAMP'S *THE KING AND QUEEN SURROUNDED BY SWIFT NUDES*. PHILADELPHIA MUSEUM OF ART, LIBRARY AND ARCHIVES, ARENSBERG ARCHIVES (PMA-WLA), BOX 58, FOLDER 94. SEE ALSO PLATES 5.21, 5.22

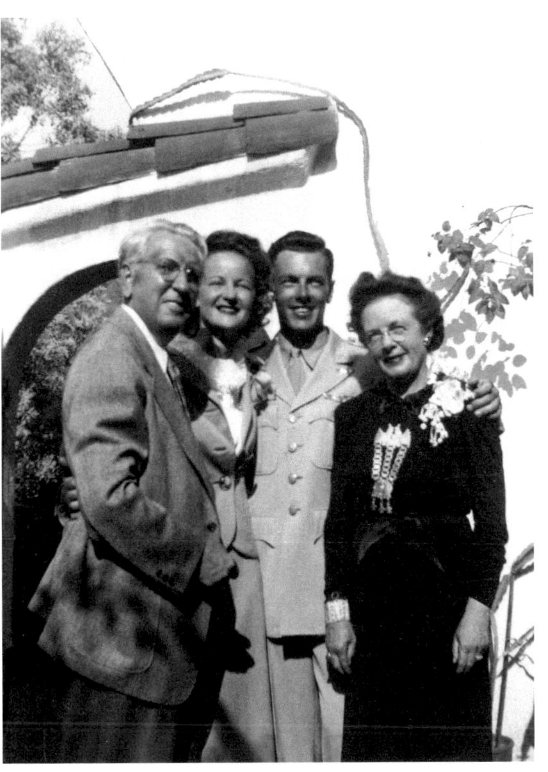

26. EARL AND ENID STENDAHL (FAR LEFT AND FAR RIGHT) WITH THEIR SON, ALFRED, AND HIS BRIDE, URSULA, ON THEIR WEDDING DAY, 31 JULY 1943. PHOTOGRAPHER UNKNOWN. THIS PHOTOGRAPH WAS TAKEN AT THE WHITLEY HEIGHTS HOME OF URSULA'S PARENTS, KARL "KEM" WEBER AND ERIKA WEBER. PHILADELPHIA MUSEUM OF ART, LIBRARY AND ARCHIVES, ARENSBERG ARCHIVES (PMA-WLA), BOX 53, FOLDER 39

The invisible lines connecting these works reinforce the couple's close relationship with Duchamp and their mediation of his ideas through the display of their art and artifacts. According to the art historian Francis M. Naumann,

> the male and female identities [in the work of Duchamp] represent established polarities of opposition, like the black and white pieces in a chess game.... [These] works...mark the beginning of Duchamp's first systematic efforts to develop an iconographic content unique to his own work, one that harbored meaning only within the narrowly established confines of an extremely personal, highly individualistic and self-reflexive narrative context.[94]

In positioning their pieces this way, the Arensbergs extended Duchamp's game outward, pitting gods and royals against each other on a chessboard of walls and floors.

Well before their move to Hollywood, Louise and Walter had been aware of how these ideas of opposition informed more than just Duchamp's art making; how dramatically, in fact, they had changed the trajectory of his life and career. "I am all set to become a chess maniac," Duchamp had told them in a letter of 1919 as he began to pursue the game professionally. "I find all around me transformed into knight or queen and the outside world holds no other interest for me than its transposition into winning and losing scenarios."[95]

Recasting Duchampian dynamics as a means of personal expression was just one of the ways in which the Arensbergs used the strategic placement of particular works to turn their living room—indeed, their whole house—into the "kind of microcosm or little model of the Universe" that Walter had found (as he explained in his interview with Ross) in the work of Dante and Bacon.[96] There the couple created a cosmos

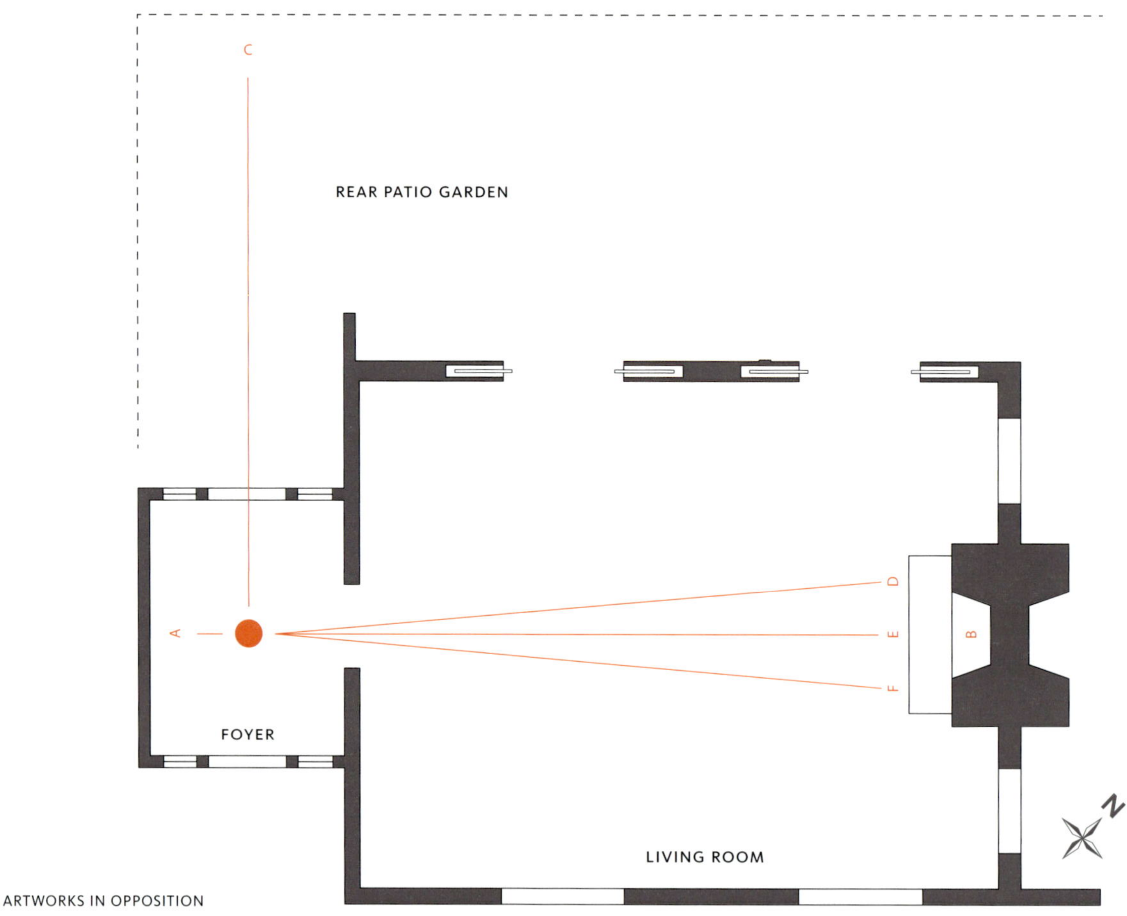

27. ARTWORKS IN OPPOSITION

A. CONSTANTIN BRANCUSI. *PRINCESS X* (SEE PLATE 2.2)
B. MARCEL DUCHAMP. *THE KING AND QUEEN SURROUNDED BY SWIFT NUDES* (SEE PLATE 5.24)
C. AZTEC (CENTRAL MEXICO). CORN GODDESS (SEE PLATE 26.10)
D. TEOTIHUACAN (CENTRAL MEXICO). GODDESS FIGURE (SEE PLATE 5.6)
E. CONSTANTIN BRANCUSI. *THREE PENGUINS* (SEE PLATE 5.8)
F. ARTIST/MAKER UNKNOWN (EASTER ISLAND). FIGURE OF A MAN (SEE PLATE 5.9)

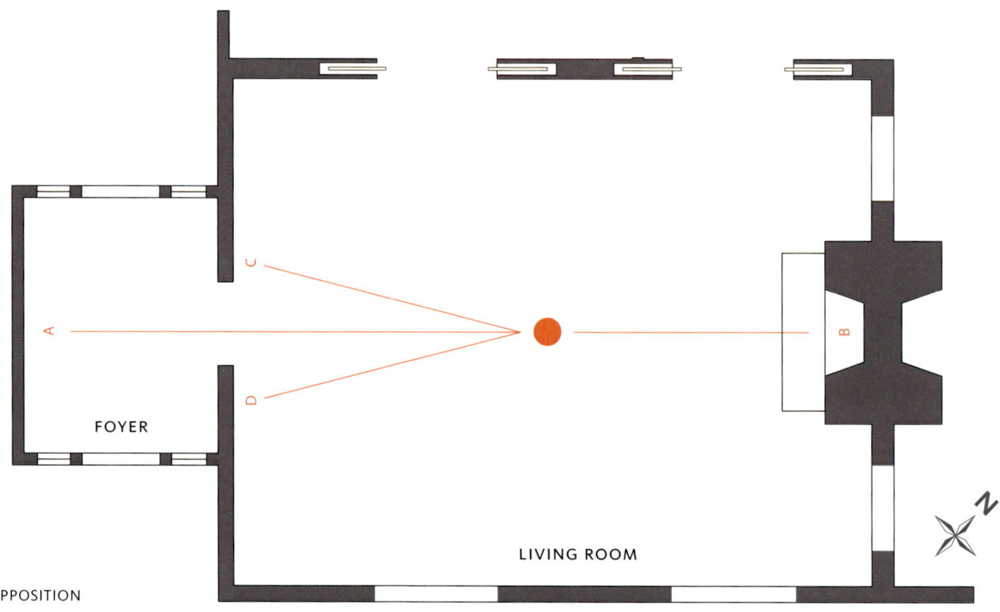

28. ARTWORKS IN OPPOSITION

A. CONSTANTIN BRANCUSI. *PRINCESS X* (SEE PLATE 2.2)
B. MARCEL DUCHAMP. *THE KING AND QUEEN SURROUNDED BY SWIFT NUDES* (SEE PLATE 5.24)
C. MARCEL DUCHAMP. *THE KING AND QUEEN TRAVERSED BY SWIFT NUDES AT HIGH SPEED* (SEE PLATE 18.18)
D. GIORGIO DE CHIRICO. *THE SOOTHSAYER'S RECOMPENSE* (SEE PLATE 18.7)

of their own invention, populating it with a changing cast of sculpted and painted characters, including a trio of zoomorphic sculptures by Brancusi—the *Three Penguins* in front of the fireplace, *Bird in Space (Yellow Bird)*, and *Fish*, which swam on a mirrored base (see plates 5.8, 5.12, and 6.23).

In one particularly playful arrangement (see plate 23), the Arensbergs placed three Mesoamerican sculptures in front of Henri Rousseau's *The Merry Jesters*, combining two- and three-dimensional works to trompe l'oeil effect. One of these sculptures, a figure of a pre-Columbian nude woman from Nayarit, also completed a triangle of nudes with Picasso's cubist *Female Nude* and Duchamp's *The King and Queen Traversed by Swift Nudes at High Speed*. Because the Arensbergs were certainly aware that Rousseau had influenced cubism generally—and Picasso specifically—this photograph (along with others printed here) suggests that the couple's pairings or groupings of artworks may have provided visitors with lessons in art history. It also illustrates the enjoyment they took in juxtaposing works based on similarities of various kinds. Notice, for example, how the two central monkeys in Rousseau's painting seem a twinned pair with the king and queen in Duchamp's work; how Picasso's *Female Nude* seems a distorted reflection of the Nayarit nude figure below it; and how the almost fractal shapes in both of those paintings seem to pick up where the wild foliage depicted in Rousseau's canvas leaves off.

For the Arensbergs—especially Walter, whose stock-in-trade had always been wordplay—the power of a pun was not to be underestimated.[97] On the reading desk positioned against the north wall, for example, they placed a lamp in front of Juan Gris's painting *Lamp* (see plate 19.18). Under Georges Braque's *Table* (see plate 32.13), they set a small table. And they conspicuously positioned Jean Metzinger's *Landscape with Roofs* above the doorway at the highest point on the wall, wedging it against the molding that ran along the ceiling (see plate 18.8).

It was *The Soothsayer's Recompense*, however, that activated some of the home's most elaborate visual punning. In his reading of Fred Dapprich's photograph of the living room (see plate 18), the artist Michael Minelli has noticed the "odd visual correspondence" between the slab on which the figure of Ariadne reclines and the couch that sat directly below it.[98] He has also connected the arch in the painting to the pre-existing archways—joining living room and dining room—that framed the entire scene. "Whether by fluke or by design," he observes, "this is where the boundaries between...the Arensbergs' room and de Chirico's painting begin to blur."[99] As we have already seen, this play on arches extended farther, back through the open door to Brancusi's *Arch* and the curved niche in the foyer designed by Sabin, strongly suggesting intention rather than chance and further dissolving boundaries between art and home.

The placement of *The Soothsayer's Recompense* also points to artful associations that dissolved the boundaries separating the walls of the home and the grid of the city. Visitors taking in the palm trees and clear sky of de Chirico's painting from the same vantage point as Dapprich might have felt that they were looking not just into a mythical Mediterranean landscape but also out to the actual beachfront of the Pacific Ocean a few miles away. And this is not the only case of a painting that can be read in relation to the orientation of the Arensbergs' house (fig. 29). If we follow Fernand Léger's *The City (Fragment, Third State)* out from its position on the southeast wall, we arrive in central Los Angeles. Likewise, the relationship between lake, hill, and houses in Roger de La Fresnaye's *Landscape*, on the dining room's northernmost wall, evokes the Hollywood Reservoir, located a little farther up the hill to the northeast. Given that the couple rarely traveled from their city once they had settled, it is easy to see how the home became the center point of their compass. Yet few houses brought so many times and places into a single compass: within a rather conventional shell, in a barely developed neighborhood, the Arensbergs assembled a panoramic survey of scenes from ancient empires and modern utopias, representations of the natural world and glimpses of the supernatural.

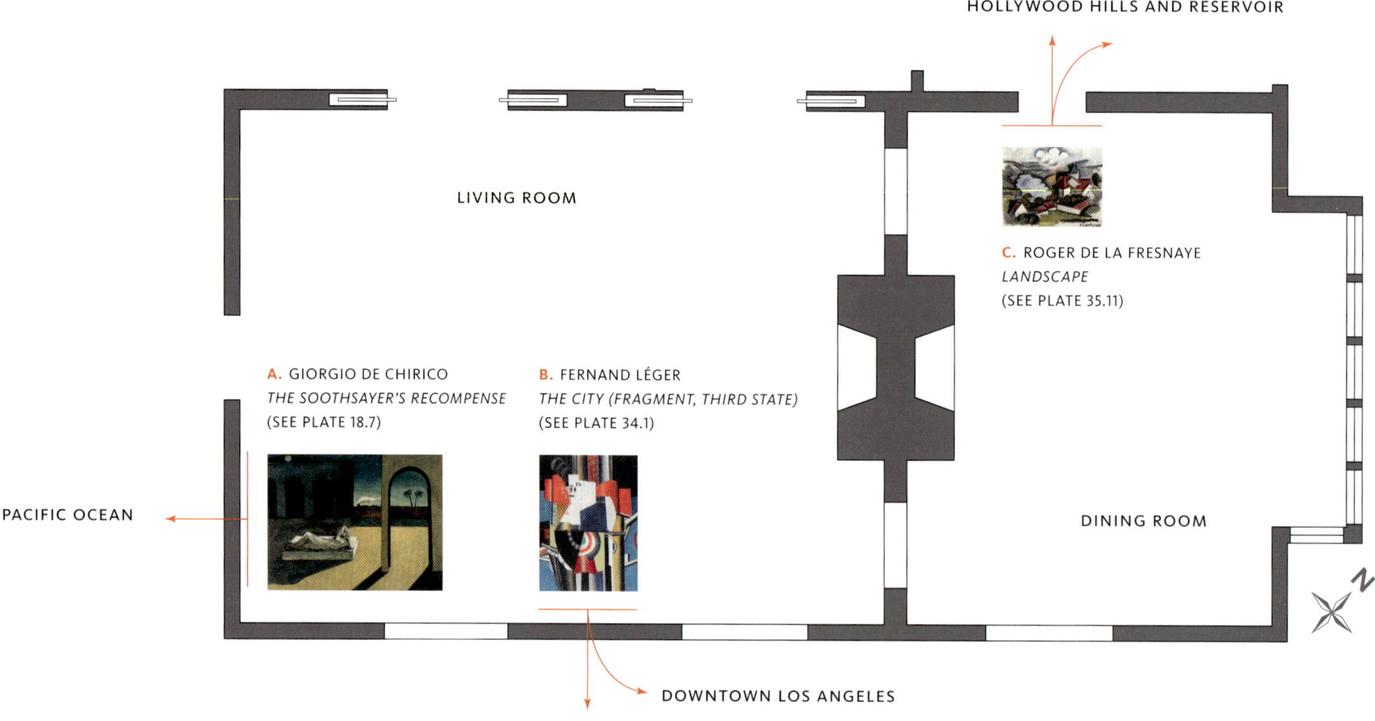

29. THE HOME AS COMPASS. LEFT TO RIGHT:
A. GIORGIO DE CHIRICO. *THE SOOTHSAYER'S RECOMPENSE*, 1913. OIL ON CANVAS, 135.6 × 180 CM. 1950-134-38
B. FERNAND LÉGER. *THE CITY (FRAGMENT, THIRD STATE)*, 1919. OIL ON CANVAS, 129.9 × 97.1 CM. 1950-134-124
C. ROGER DE LA FRESNAYE. *LANDSCAPE*, 1912. OIL ON CANVAS, 47.6 × 60.3 CM. 1950-134-90
ALL ARE PHILADELPHIA MUSEUM OF ART, THE LOUISE AND WALTER ARENSBERG COLLECTION. SEE ALSO PLATES 18, 34, 35

THE DINING ROOM

In the dining room, where the Arensbergs ate the simple meals prepared by their live-in housekeeper, examples of this "microcosmic" compression were communicated via human and animal forms from places as diverse as China, Costa Rica, Gabon, and Mexico (fig. 30). Carlos Mérida's *Deer Dance*, Paul Klee's *Animal Terror*, and André Masson's *Animal Caught in a Trap* extended the bestial themes to the walls, while Brancusi's abstract sculptural portrayal of the Chimera (fig. 31)—the mythological creature combining lion, goat, and snake—stood guard over the scene. Representations of humans in the dining room included a large canvas by Duchamp called *Portrait (Dulcinea)* (see plate 9.2), featuring a woman stripped of her clothing through a sequence of five blurred positions; Roger de La Fresnaye's contorted *Nude (The Italian Girl)* (see plate 10), which may have been intentionally placed in proximity to Duchamp's painting; Brancusi's *Torso of a Young Man [I]* (see plate 15.5), an abstract wood sculpture chopped at its neck and thighs; and many pre-Columbian figures portrayed as bent, disfigured, or dead.

Some of the Arensbergs' guests—among them the well-known food writer M. F. K. Fisher—found this heady presentation overwhelming. Thanking the Arensbergs for an evening spent in their company, Fisher wrote:

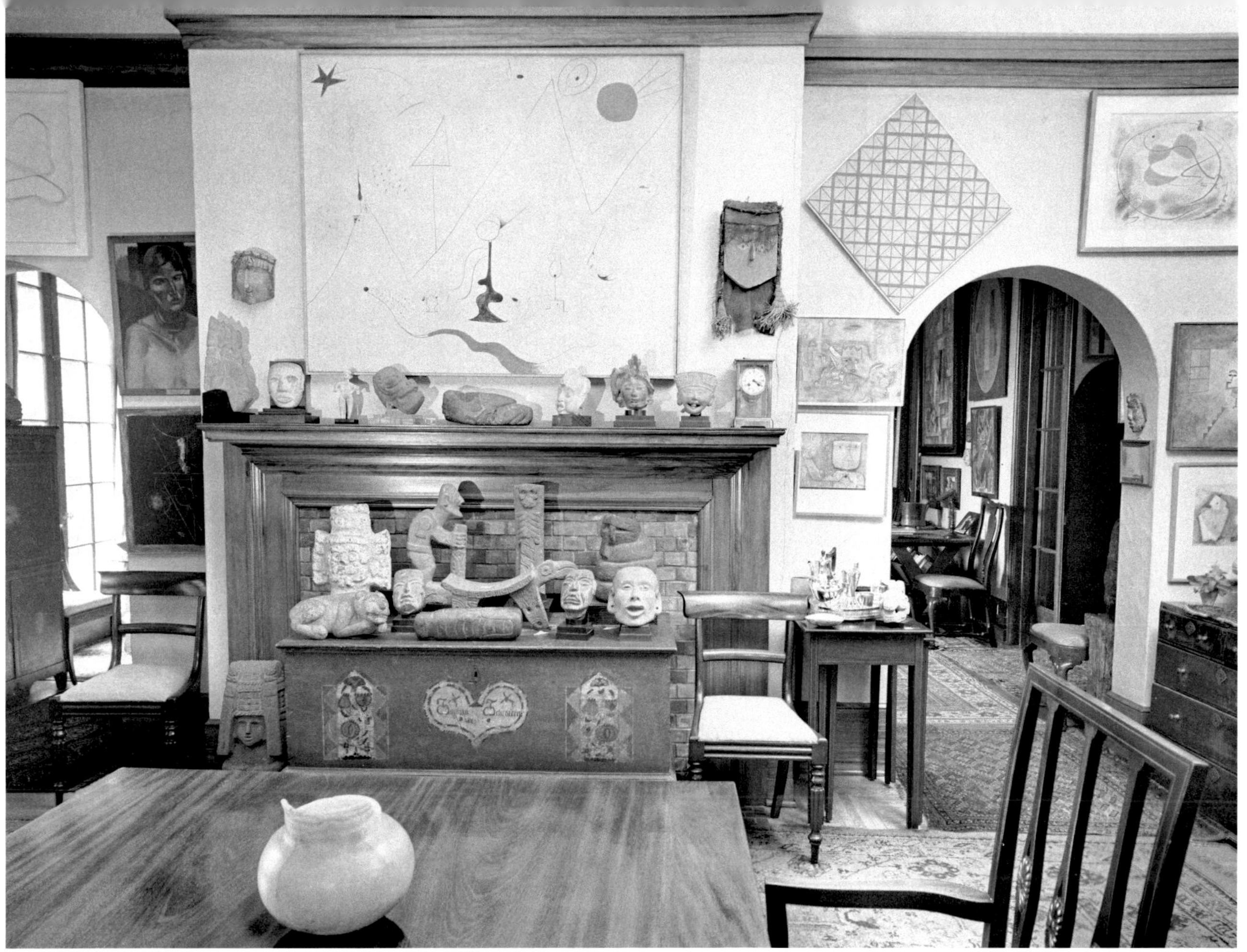

30. KARL BISSINGER. VIEW OF LOUISE AND WALTER ARENSBERG'S DINING ROOM, 7065 HILLSIDE AVENUE, LOS ANGELES, 16 MARCH 1950. PICTURED AMONG OTHER WORKS ARE CARLOS MÉRIDA'S *DEER DANCE*, PAUL KLEE'S *ANIMAL TERROR*, ANDRÉ MASSON'S *ANIMAL CAUGHT IN A TRAP*, PIET MONDRIAN'S *COMPOSITION IN BLACK AND GRAY* OR *COMPOSITION WITH GRID 4 (LOZENGE)*, AND JOAN MIRÓ'S *THE HERMITAGE*. UNIVERSITY OF DELAWARE LIBRARY, NEWARK, SPECIAL COLLECTIONS, KARL BISSINGER ARCHIVE (MSS0682). © THE ESTATE OF KARL BISSINGER. SEE ALSO PLATES 13–17

> It was one of the most exciting [nights] in my life for some time, and of course one of the most disturbing. Undoubtedly you are used to hearing of that reaction from people who see for the first time your fabulous collection. I found it almost unbearably fatiguing, since I have grown unaccustomed to the impact of creation. I hope I shall see it again, and be able to stand it longer.[100]

As in the living room, artworks and arrangements highlighting the Arensbergs' relentless sense of play contributed to the overall environment (see fig. 31). Juan Gris's early cubist painting *Open Window*, for example, was hung beside the outwardly opening bay windows that framed the trees marking the home's property line—its abstracted windows and trees making a clever, if obvious, pun with the surrounding environment. And František Kupka's *Disks of Newton (Study for "Fugue in Two Colors")*, a vibrant work hanging in the same alcove, was likely very important to Walter given his lifelong interest in Renaissance science: Kupka had been partially inspired, as the title suggests, by Sir Isaac Newton's discovery that the light of the sun is composed of seven principal colors spread across a spectrum.[101] Kupka was also among the first artists to achieve, by 1911, pure abstraction in painting, a development whose origins were actively debated by the Arensbergs and their associates.[102] When Germain Seligman, a New York dealer from whom the Arensbergs occasionally purchased artworks, offered Walter a chance to purchase a contemporaneous painting, Robert Delaunay's *Simultaneous Contrasts: Sun and Moon*, he asserted that it was "one of the most, if not the most,

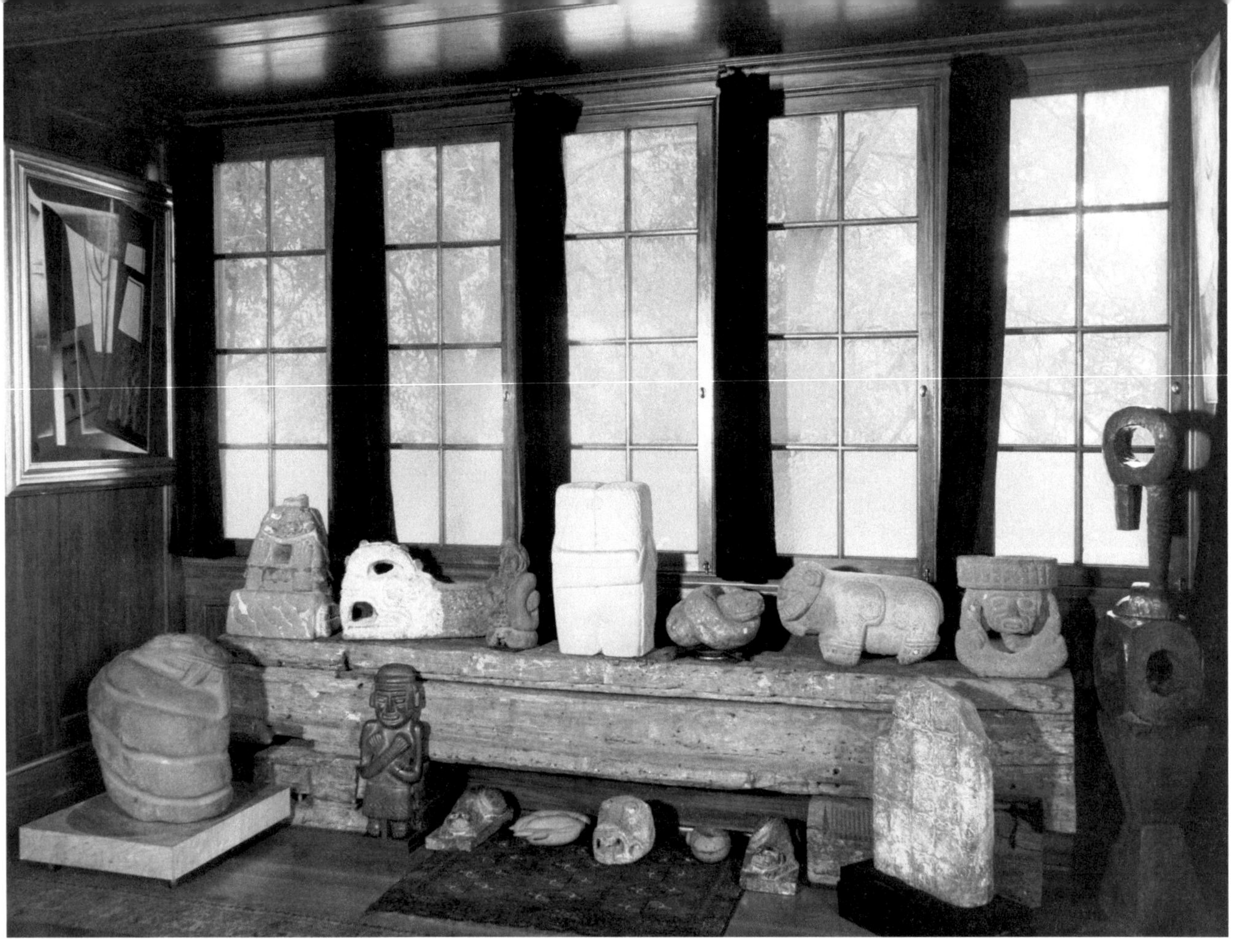

31. FRED R. DAPPRICH. VIEW OF LOUISE AND WALTER ARENSBERG'S DINING ROOM ALCOVE, 7065 HILLSIDE AVENUE, LOS ANGELES, CA. 1945–50. JUAN GRIS'S *OPEN WINDOW* (FAR LEFT) HANGS NEXT TO THE BAY WINDOWS; CONSTANTIN BRANCUSI'S *THE KISS* SITS ATOP HIS *BENCH*, NEXT TO AN AZTEC SERPENT; AND BRANCUSI'S *CHIMERA* (FAR RIGHT) STANDS BELOW FRANTIŠEK KUPKA'S *DISKS OF NEWTON (STUDY FOR "FUGUE IN TWO COLORS")*. PHILADELPHIA MUSEUM OF ART, LIBRARY AND ARCHIVES, ARENSBERG ARCHIVES (PMA-WLA), BOX 54, FOLDER 5. SEE ALSO PLATES 11, 12

important paintings by Delaunay in this country, not only physically speaking . . . [but because] it was painted in 1912 . . . the most revolutionary period in all art."[103] Walter responded:

> I know the painting and admire it immensely and should be happy to know the price. However, as to the question of date and originality, it is later than the Kupka *Disks of Newton* . . . which is in our collection. As I recall, this painting . . . is signed and dated on the back as of 1908.[104]

The Kupka work was in fact painted in 1912—just earlier than the Delaunay, but later than Arensberg believed or cared to prove.[105] Walter's response was typical of his personality: argumentative yet pliable (especially when a work he and Louise were interested in was for sale), simultaneously wrong and right, and stubbornly noncommittal. "I intend to verify my recollection as to the date next week," he wrote, "when I may have the opportunity to unscrew the board with which the back is now covered, and I will let you know then what I find."[106]

What other pleasures did the Arensbergs find in these works? What meanings did they assign to them? Did Walter, who had once been "'one of the cleverest chess-players in the university,' astounding his classmates with his ability to play the game mentally with neither board nor pieces,"[107] play imaginary games on Piet Mondrian's *Composition in Black and Gray* (see plate 17.1)? Or did he find a kindred cryptographer in Joan Miró, who seems to have hidden the letters of his own name in his painting *The Hermitage*

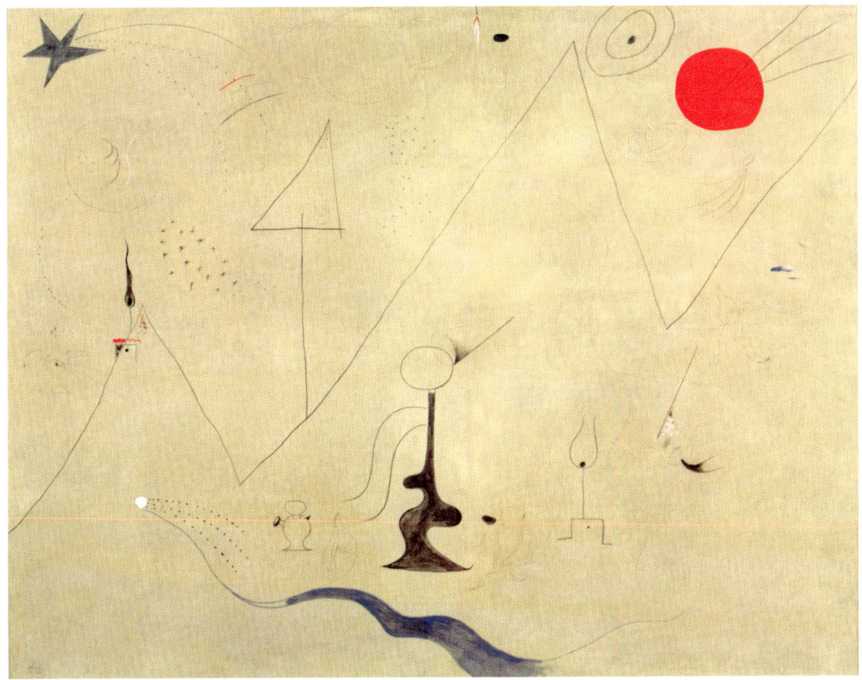

32. JOAN MIRÓ. *THE HERMITAGE*, 1924. OIL, CRAYON, AND GRAPHITE ON CANVAS, 114.3 × 146.2 CM. PHILADELPHIA MUSEUM OF ART, THE LOUISE AND WALTER ARENSBERG COLLECTION, 1950-134-141. SEE ALSO PLATES 13.5, 14.8

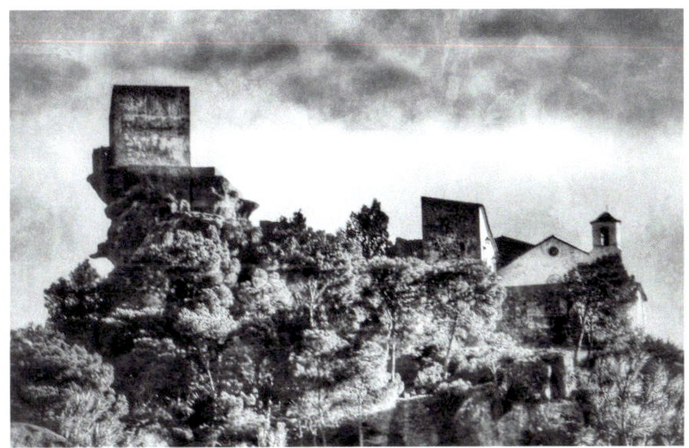

33. HERMITAGE OF SANT RAMON, MONTROIG, SPAIN. PHOTOGRAPH: RAMÓN CAMI / EYEEM / ALAMY STOCK

(fig. 32; see plate 13.5)?[108] With minimal effort, Walter might have seen an *M* spread across the mountain range; an *i* in the head and torso of the central female figure; an *r* in her bottom and legs; and, finally, an *o*, along with its diacritical accent, in the sun.[109]

Central to the dining room, *The Hermitage* hung over the Arensbergs' mantel on the opposite side of the wall that held Duchamp's *The King and Queen Surrounded by Swift Nudes*. Composed of flat graphic forms and simple lines, and conveying distance through a distorted approximation of three-point perspective, the painting was informed by Miró's personal feeling for the Hermitage of Sant Ramon, which sits spectacularly atop a cliff in Montroig, Spain (fig. 33).[110] The Arensbergs were perhaps not aware of the artwork's history, but they may well have noticed how its titular hermitage (on the mountain in the "background" of the painting) was echoed by the foyer of their own home a little farther beyond the wall on which it hung. Or that its central figure—depicted in exaggerated, cartoonish profile and perhaps wearing the *capirote* (pointed hat) of a penitent—suggested a sister of the foyer's principal occupant, Brancusi's *Princess X*.

As they had done with Duchamp's painting, Louise and Walter positioned *The Hermitage* across from two major sculptures by Brancusi—*The Kiss* and *Bench* (see fig. 31)—creating a mirroring effect between the four defined spaces along their home's principal horizontal axis (fig. 34). In this arrangement, Brancusi's kissing lovers were placed directly next to an Aztec sculpture of a coiled serpent. Did the Arensbergs perhaps see the little alcove that held them as the Garden of Eden? Walter had been interested in this subject since his early reading (while still at Harvard) of Sir James George Frazer's *Golden Bough*, and his research notes from 1946 indicate that he was still preoccupied with both the book and the biblical story:

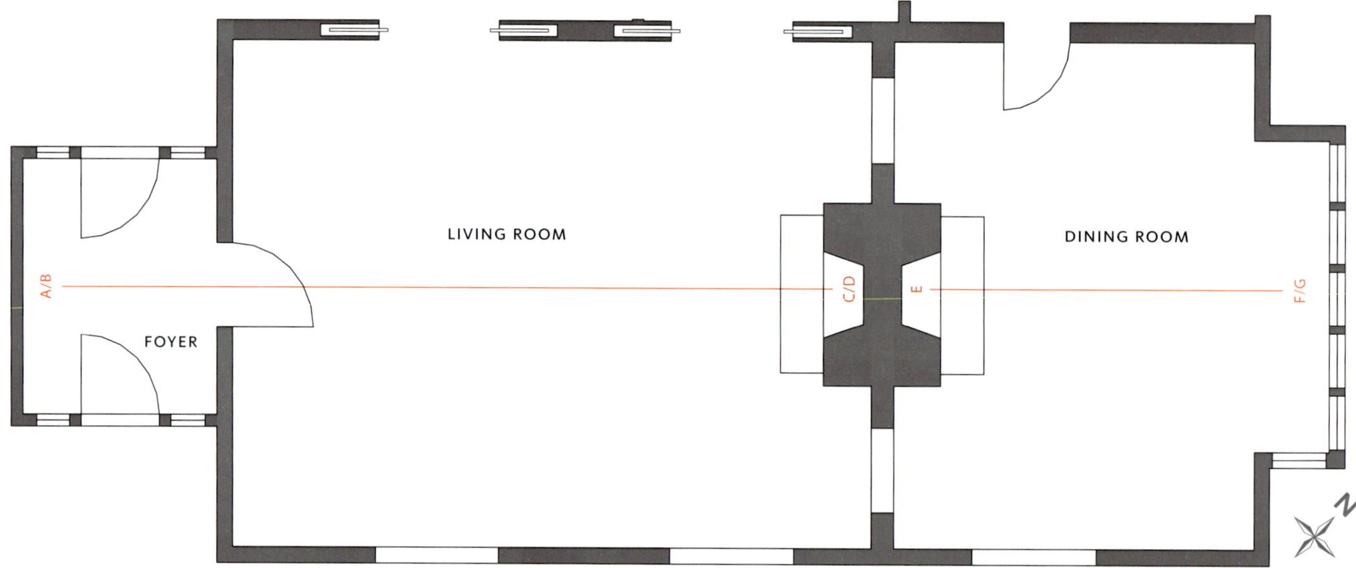

34. ARTWORKS IN OPPOSITION

A. CONSTANTIN BRANCUSI. *ARCH* (SEE PLATE 2.1)
B. CONSTANTIN BRANCUSI. *PRINCESS X* (SEE PLATE 2.2)
C/D. MARCEL DUCHAMP. FRONT: *THE KING AND QUEEN SURROUNDED BY SWIFT NUDES* (SEE FIG. 24; PLATE 5.24). BACK: *PARADISE (ADAM AND EVE)* (SEE FIG. 35)
E. JOAN MIRÓ. *THE HERMITAGE* (SEE FIGS. 30, 32; PLATE 13.5)
F. CONSTANTIN BRANCUSI. *THE KISS* (SEE PLATE 12.5)
G. CONSTANTIN BRANCUSI. *BENCH* (SEE PLATE 12.12)

> As I now see it the myth of the golden bough expresses the sequel to the myth of the Garden of Eden. A few weeks ago I gave an interpretation...which I thought then, and still think, maybe is original. The prohibition to pluck and eat of these trees is a prohibition to separate the fruit...as fetus from the mother in whose body it exists in the prenatal or paradisiacal state. As soon as Adam and Eve disobeyed and plucked and ate they [were] expelled from this paradisiacal condition from the garden into the world of sin and suffering outside. That is the birth, and that birth takes them from good to evil, from eternal life to certain death.[111]

Like so many of Walter's musings, the story of Adam and Eve also made him think of Duchamp: in 1949 he explained to Fiske Kimball, director of the Philadelphia Museum of Art, that he found "interesting allusions in Marcel's work to the Renaissance, as for instance in *The King and Queen* [*Surrounded by Swift Nudes*], where the subservient attitude of the Queen, whom Marcel once described to me as 'très putaine' [a big whore], suggests to me the Eve Tempting Adam of the Sistine ceiling."[112]

Whether Walter consciously linked these particular lines of reasoning to this display of Brancusi's works and the Aztec sculpture of the coiled serpent is, of course, speculative. Nevertheless, the doubling of displays across twinned rooms used key works to create a sequence of objects that activated the Arensberg circle's favorite dynamics—contrasting the royal with the religious, the chaste with the sexual, the overt with the concealed.

And, unbeknownst to most visitors (unless the Arensbergs let them in on the secret), along the invisible line drawn between these key works (see fig. 34), there was a third painting hidden between *The Hermitage* on one side of the wall and *The King and Queen Surrounded by Swift Nudes* on the other. In 1910–11, on the back of the latter, Duchamp had painted a picture of two figures in a garden. He titled it *Paradise (Adam and Eve)* (fig. 35).

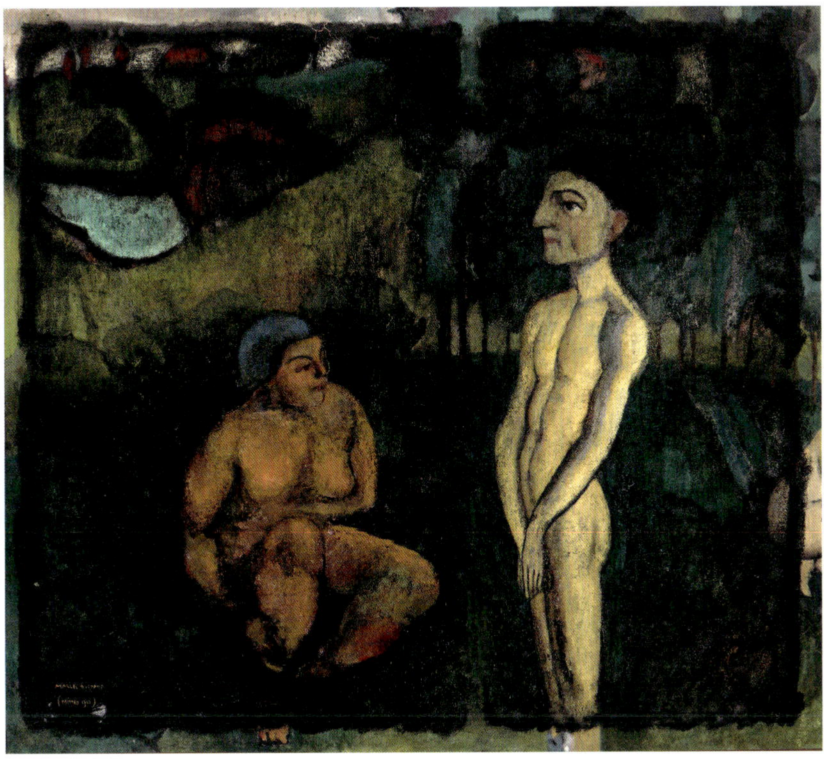

35. MARCEL DUCHAMP. *PARADISE (ADAM AND EVE)*, 1910–11. OIL ON CANVAS, 114.6 × 128.9 CM.
PHILADELPHIA MUSEUM OF ART, THE LOUISE AND WALTER ARENSBERG COLLECTION, 1950-134-63B

THE SUNROOM

After 1929, as many Americans were suffering through the Great Depression, the Arensbergs found their fortunes revived. The couple began purchasing art again after nearly a decade-long hiatus, buying so much so quickly that they ran out of places to put it. Thus, in 1933, they initiated another round of architectural modifications, commissioning Richard Neutra and his assistant Gregory Ain to design and oversee the construction of a spacious new "gallery room" at the rear of the house (fig. 36).[113]

The Arensbergs engaged Neutra just as he was beginning "to participate at the highest level in the international exchange of modernist ideas," following the success of his breakthrough work, the Lovell House of 1929, and his inclusion in the 1932 exhibition *Modern Architecture* at the Museum of Modern Art in New York.[114] Neutra's addition to 7065 Hillside featured nine large steel casement windows that allowed for a panoramic view of the fully enclosed brick patio,[115] which the architect refurbished "for placing variegated art objects with frequently changing positions for the private enjoyment of the collectors and their friends."[116] The Arensbergs celebrated its completion with a party, captured in the line-a-day diary of their old friend Beatrice Wood: "Exciting evening Arensbergs. Opening their new room by Neutra. Weston came down with photos."[117]

Along with the building of the sunroom (as it came to be called) came the attendant need to fill it, for the Arensbergs seemingly could not leave any surface bare. Though they quickly covered its walls, tables, and shelves with new possessions, they continued to lament the loss of the most significant piece in their New York collection, Duchamp's *The Bride Stripped Bare by Her Bachelors, Even*, otherwise known as *The Large Glass* (fig. 37).

Combining exquisite workmanship in unconventional materials, experiments with the effects of chance, and playful interpretations of contemporary scientific theories, *The Large Glass* synthesized many of Duchamp's long-gestating ideas and delivered them via a seductively inscrutable narrative. The artist had developed the principal ideas for this massive but fragile artwork in a series of notes he began making

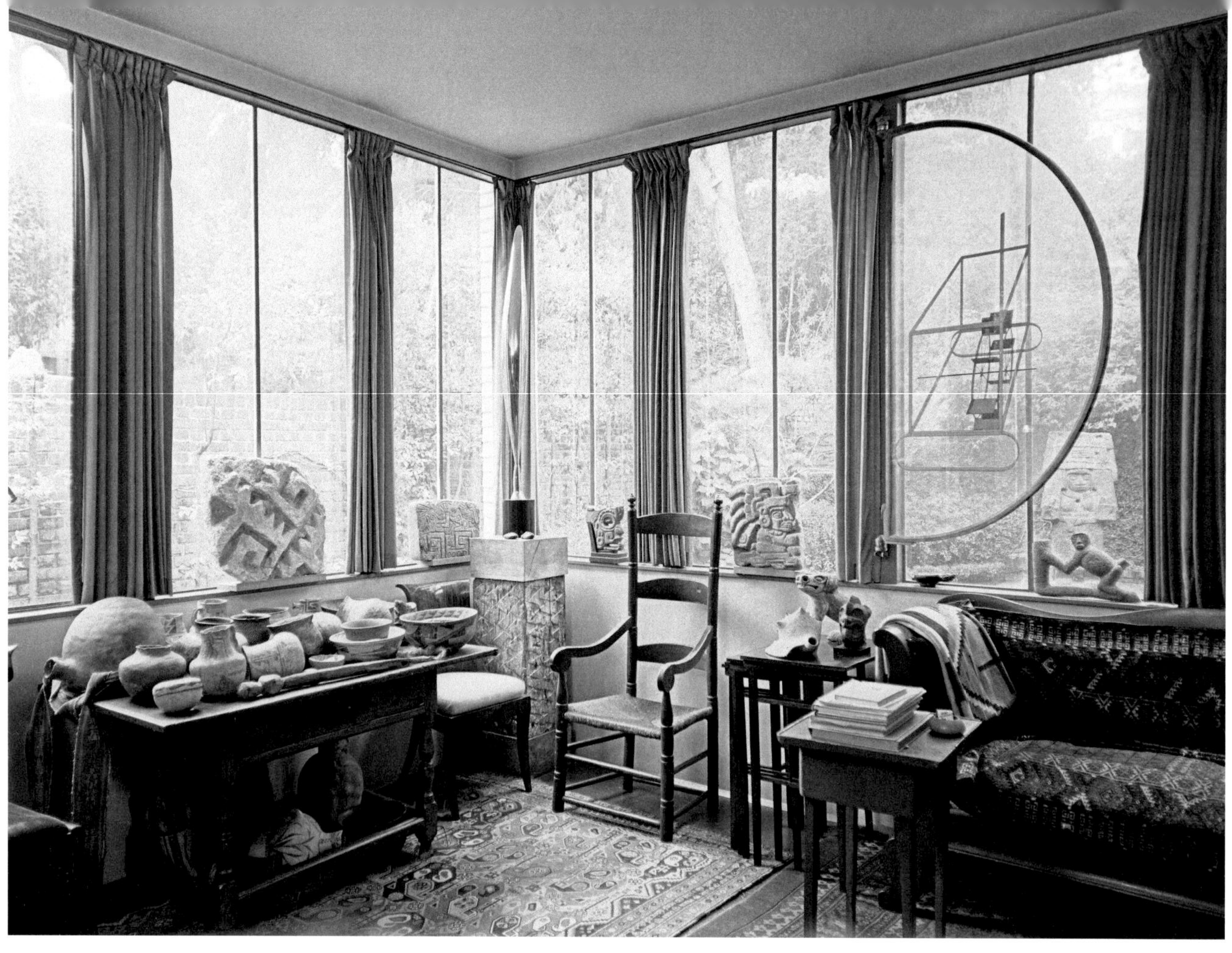

36. KARL BISSINGER. VIEW OF LOUISE AND WALTER ARENSBERG'S SUNROOM AT 7065 HILLSIDE AVENUE, LOS ANGELES, 16 MARCH 1950, SHOWING MARCEL DUCHAMP'S FIRST WORK ON GLASS, *GLIDER CONTAINING A WATER MILL IN NEIGHBORING METALS*. UNIVERSITY OF DELAWARE LIBRARY, NEWARK, SPECIAL COLLECTIONS, KARL BISSINGER ARCHIVE (MSS0682). © THE ESTATE OF KARL BISSINGER. SEE ALSO PLATES 24–26

in Paris in 1912, and had begun work on it soon after his arrival in New York in 1915. Laboring over its details intermittently for another eight years—first in the studio apartment owned by the Arensbergs, and later at Dreier's home after they had sold the work to her in 1921—Duchamp declared it "definitively unfinished" in 1923. The Arensbergs were devastated to learn, in 1931, that *The Large Glass* had shattered in its crate while in transit to Dreier's Connecticut home following its public exhibition at the Brooklyn Museum of Art.[118] Unperturbed, Duchamp found the cracks to be a delightful finishing touch when he returned five years later to mend the broken glass and secure it behind new panes in an aluminum frame (fig. 38).

Today the subject of voluminous published research and competing theories, *The Bride Stripped Bare by Her Bachelors, Even* is usually read (through interpretations of Duchamp's enigmatic notes) as an allegory for frustrated sexual desire, in which the "Bride" in her "Domain" (the upper pane) transmits commands that activate the operations of the "Bachelor Apparatus" in the lower pane.[119] In his text on *The Large Glass*, "Modern Machines from the Virgin to the Widow," David Joselit argues that "the Duchampian machine, and the Dada machine more generally, operate as switching stations between the modern rationalization of the body and newly developing techniques of disciplining the mind—particularly through the colonization or commodification of desire."[120]

In brief, the action of the Apparatus begins with the Malic Molds, residing in the Cemetery of Liveries, whose "gas castings" solidify into "rods," which then break into "spangles" and travel, via the Sieves, to the bottom of the lower pane. To "dazzle" the mirror reflection of the gas castings into the Bride's Domain is a job that falls to the Oculist Witnesses, while the nearby Glider slides back and forth reciting "litanies…

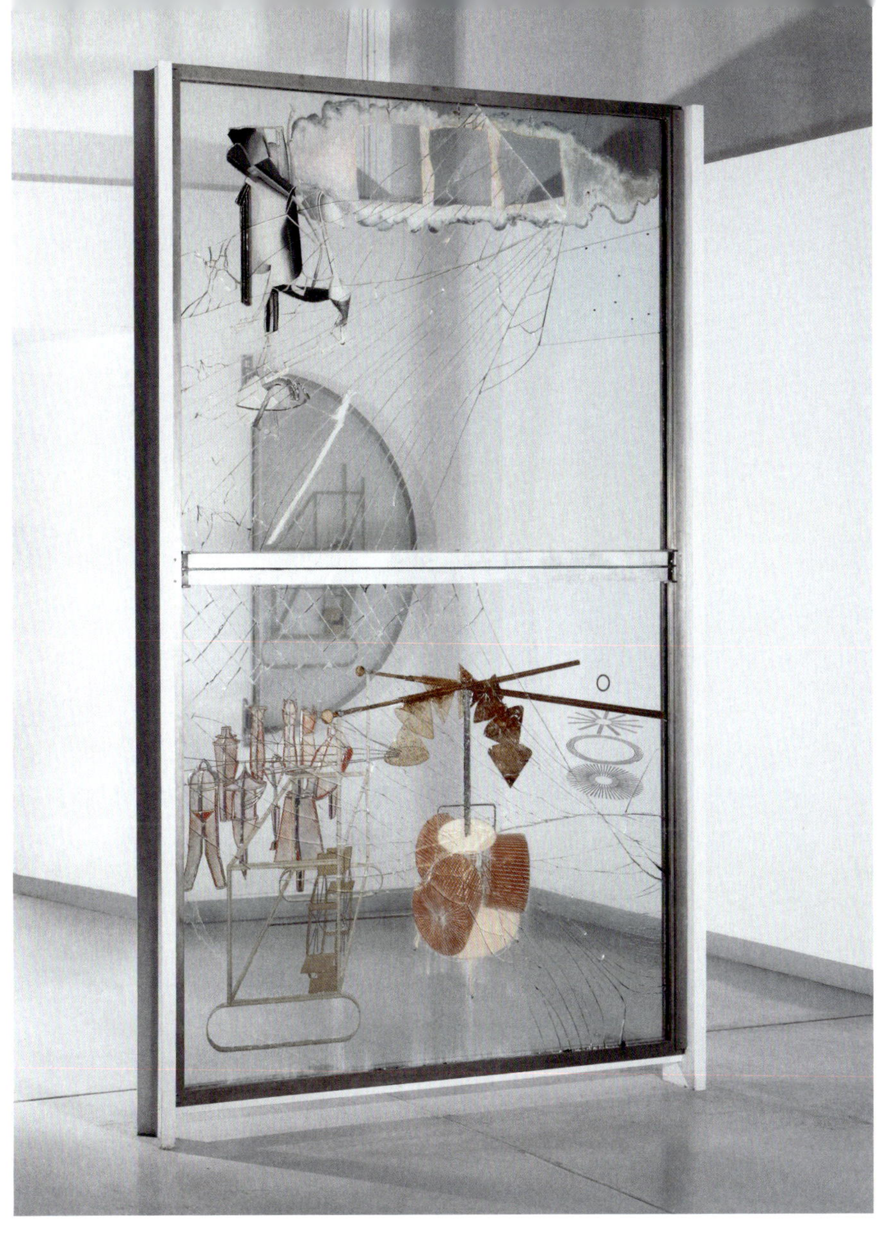

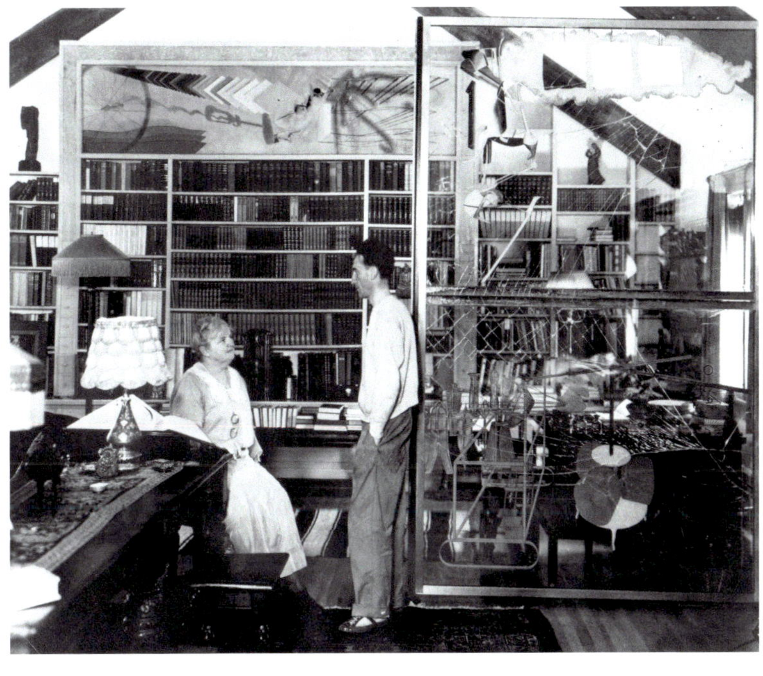

37. MARCEL DUCHAMP. *THE BRIDE STRIPPED BARE BY HER BACHELORS, EVEN (THE LARGE GLASS)*, 1915–23. OIL, VARNISH, LEAD FOIL, LEAD WIRE, AND DUST ON TWO GLASS PANELS, 277.5 × 177.8 × 8.6 CM. PHILADELPHIA MUSEUM OF ART. BEQUEST OF KATHERINE S. DREIER, 1952-98-1

DUCHAMP'S *GLIDER CONTAINING A WATER MILL IN NEIGHBORING METALS* CAN BE SEEN HANGING ON THE WALL BEHIND *THE LARGE GLASS* IN THIS INSTALLATION PHOTOGRAPH OF THE ARTWORKS IN THEIR PERMANENT HOME AT THE PHILADELPHIA MUSEUM OF ART.

38. LESLIE E. BOWMAN. *MARCEL DUCHAMP AND KATHERINE DREIER IN KATHERINE DREIER'S LIVING ROOM*, 1936. YALE UNIVERSITY ART GALLERY. BEQUEST OF KATHERINE S. DREIER, 1953.6.204

SHORTLY AFTER THIS PHOTOGRAPH WAS TAKEN, DUCHAMP DEPARTED FOR LOS ANGELES, WHERE HE SAW THE ARENSBERGS FOR THE FIRST TIME IN MORE THAN A DECADE.

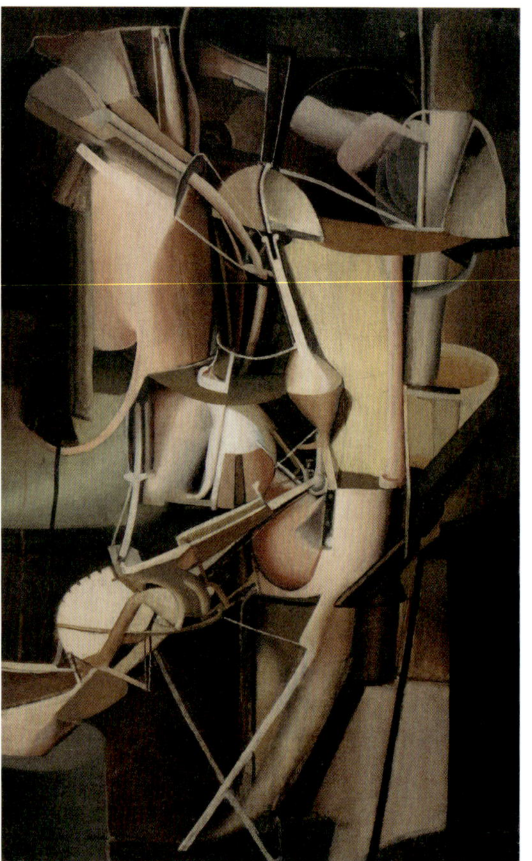

39. MARCEL DUCHAMP. *BRIDE*, 1912. OIL ON CANVAS, 89.5 × 55.6 CM. PHILADELPHIA MUSEUM OF ART, THE LOUISE AND WALTER ARENSBERG COLLECTION, 1950-134-65. SEE ALSO PLATES 15.1, 35.1

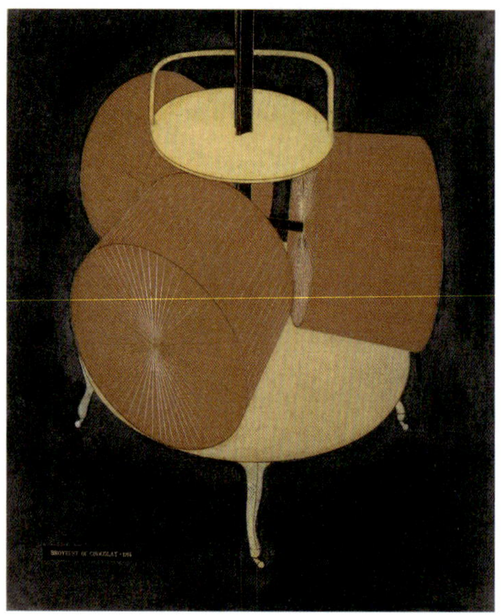

40. MARCEL DUCHAMP. *CHOCOLATE GRINDER (NO. 2)*, 1914. OIL, GRAPHITE, AND THREAD ON CANVAS, 65.4 × 54.3 CM. PHILADELPHIA MUSEUM OF ART, THE LOUISE AND WALTER ARENSBERG COLLECTION, 1950-134-70. SEE ALSO PLATES 32.21, 33.7

of . . . Onanism." Next to it, Duchamp's notes indicate, the Chocolate Grinder "grinds his chocolate himself," another euphemism for masturbation.[121]

Though the themes of *The Large Glass* were opaque—and the piece itself was no longer accessible to the Arensbergs—the couple had plenty of opportunity to continue cracking Duchamp's secretive codes. Over the years, they acquired at least seven works by the artist that contained representations of *The Large Glass*'s constituent parts. These included three paintings (*Bride* [fig. 39], *Chocolate Grinder (No. 1)*, and *Chocolate Grinder (No. 2)* [fig. 40]); a related work on glass, *Glider Containing a Water Mill in Neighboring Metals* (fig. 41); and three drawings (*Boxing Match*, *Cemetery of Uniforms and Liveries (No. 1)*, and *Oculist Witnesses*). Duchamp also gave the couple a deluxe edition of *The Green Box*, which he considered an instruction manual of sorts for interpreting *The Large Glass*,[122] and a deluxe edition of *Box in a Valise*, which contained a miniature facsimile of *The Large Glass* (see figs. 16a, b). Any of these works could be (and were) appreciated for their own artistic merits, but the Arensbergs' determined acquisition and display of them illustrates how proud they were of their own role in facilitating the work's creation and how thorough they were in preserving the range of materials—including studies, versions, and notes—needed to appreciate Duchamp's artistic methods.

It was probably in Neutra's new room made of glass, however, where the absence of *The Large Glass* was most keenly felt and its haunting presence in their lives most vividly shown. Years earlier, after missing their first chance to purchase Duchamp's *Nude Descending a Staircase* from the Armory Show, the Arensbergs had turned to the artist himself for an authorized copy (see plate 39.3). Now firmly settled in California but still regretting "the necessities of space and distance" that had forced them to sell *The Large Glass* to

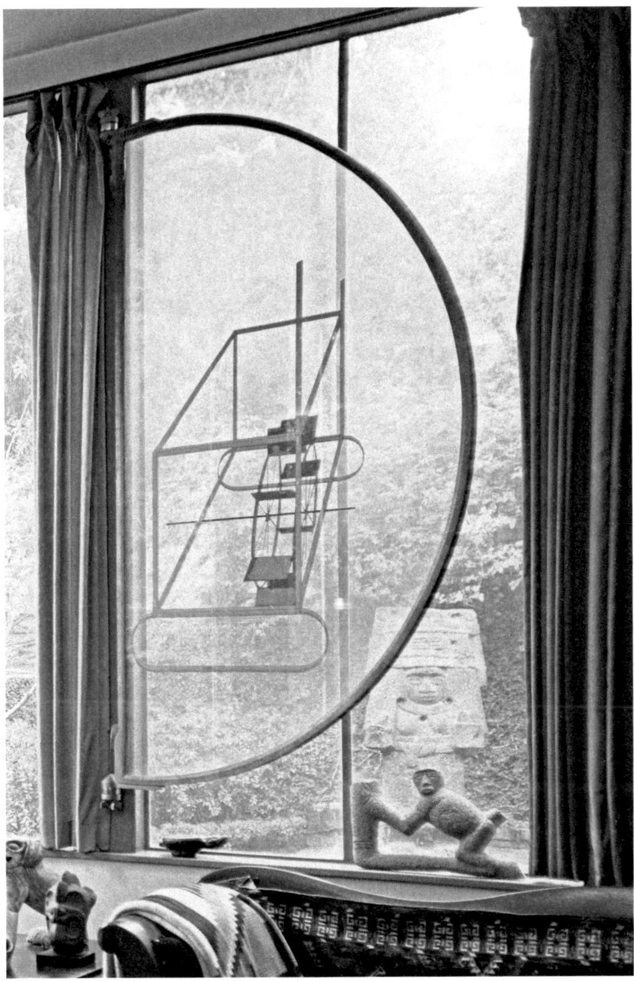

41. KARL BISSINGER. DETAIL OF FIG. 36, SHOWING A SCULPTURE OF THE AZTEC CORN GODDESS ON THE PATIO, SEEN THROUGH THE GLASS OF MARCEL DUCHAMP'S *GLIDER* AND THE STEEL-FRAMED CASEMENT WINDOWS DESIGNED BY RICHARD NEUTRA. UNIVERSITY OF DELAWARE LIBRARY, NEWARK, SPECIAL COLLECTIONS, KARL BISSINGER ARCHIVE (MSS0682). © THE ESTATE OF KARL BISSINGER

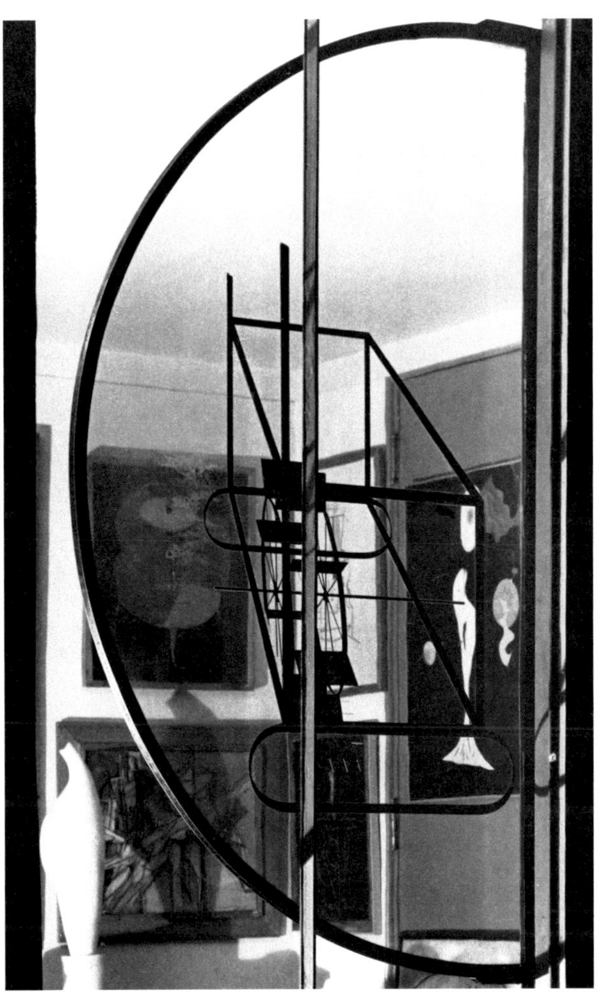

42. VIEW OF THE SUNROOM WALL, SEEN FROM THE GARDEN PATIO, THROUGH THE GLASS OF MARCEL DUCHAMP'S *GLIDER* AND THE STEEL-FRAMED CASEMENT WINDOWS DESIGNED BY RICHARD NEUTRA. PHOTOGRAPHER UNKNOWN. PHILADELPHIA MUSEUM OF ART, LIBRARY AND ARCHIVES, ARENSBERG ARCHIVES (PMA-WLA), BOX 54, FOLDER 22

Dreier,[123] Louise and Walter seem to have taken matters into their own hands: using *Glider Containing a Water Mill in Neighboring Metals*—in combination with other artworks, a large pre-Columbian sculpture, and the architecture of the room—they created a surrogate for *The Large Glass*, invoking the elaborate materials and meanings of that work in numerous ways.[124] Fastening *Glider* by its hinges to the steel sash of one of the Neutra-designed windows, they created a large rectangular frame around the existing curved one that echoed the design of *The Large Glass*. Seen from inside the sunroom, the Aztec corn goddess on the garden patio (already glimpsed once through the glass in the foyer door) was framed again by the window and *Glider*. This relationship, evident in photographs taken by Karl Bissinger (see fig. 41) and Fred Dapprich (see plate 26), suggests that, in the context of the sunroom, the ancient female figure could have served as proxy for the Bride, the figure invoked in the work's full title. Another photograph (by an unknown photographer) taken from the garden patio (fig. 42) allows us to look in through—rather than out from—*Glider* at the wall across from the window, on which hung Duchamp's painting *Chocolate Grinder (No. 2)*.[125] Duchamp had reworked his impressions of the chocolate grinder several times before etching it into the lower pane of *The Large Glass* alongside that work's version of the Glider. Had the photographer moved a few feet to the right in the courtyard and turned the camera slightly to the left, he or she could have captured *Chocolate Grinder (No. 1)* (see plate 30.17), invoking *The Large Glass* for a second time.

Significantly, it was Duchamp's early fixation on a chocolate grinder displayed in the window of a confectioner's shop in Rouen, France, that had marked, for him, a crucial juncture in his progress as an artist.[126] This experience, in 1913, inspired him to create the Chocolate Grinder paintings later owned by the Arensbergs, and it sparked his long-running investigation into the possibilities of windows and glass as media for artistic expression. As Duchamp started work that same year on *Glider*, the first of these works on glass, he composed a note related to this profoundly personal experience:

> The question of shop windows.∵
>
> To undergo the interrogation of shop windows.∵
>
> The exigency of the shop window.∵
>
> The shop window proof of the existence of the outside world.∵
>
> When one undergoes the examination of the shop window, one also pronounces one's own sentence. In fact, one's choice is round-trip. From the demands of the shop windows, from the inevitable response to shop windows, my choice is determined. No obstinacy, ad absurdum, of hiding the coition through a glass pane with one or many objects of the shop window. The penalty consists in cutting the pane and in feeling regret as soon as possession is consummated. Q.E.D.[127]

Writing of Duchamp's conflation of glass and eroticism, the art historian Charles Stuckey has observed that "the active role Duchamp gives to the window is noteworthy. The viewer is interrogated and examined … [and] is not particularly innocent but becomes a participant in some apparently sexual encounter."[128]

So it is hardly surprising that the Arensbergs chose a wall in their new glass room for their most explicit display of sexual symbolism, creating a tableau of artworks and artifacts that seemingly channeled the erotically charged narratives presented by the artist in *The Large Glass* and elsewhere. Comparing photographs of the sunroom (see plates 32, 33) with one of the living room (see plate 19), we can see that sometime in the late 1940s, the couple switched the locations of Picasso's *Man with a Guitar* (see plate 32.16) and Henri Matisse's *Mademoiselle Yvonne Landesberg*. The latter painting, which had long hung in the living room (see plate 19.12), was newly placed in the sunroom next to Duchamp's *Chocolate Grinder (No. 2)*. On the bureau below, Brancusi's *Maiastra* (see plate 33.6) was positioned to suggestively challenge both *Mademoiselle Yvonne Landesberg* (whose arms and posture, in this context, seem defensively chaste) and the athletically bent body depicted by a pre-Columbian vessel in the form of an acrobat (see plate 33.4). Was *Mademoiselle Yvonne Landesberg* now a bride being stripped bare by her bachelors? Next to the acrobat—and just below Matisse's painting—a nude pre-Columbian figure of a woman, with her legs open and her arms at rest on her stomach (see plate 33.2), also seems to have been placed in purposeful contradistinction to the Mademoiselle.

On the adjoining wall, innuendo gave way to explicitness. There, the Arensbergs positioned the oversize and graphically rendered male and female sexual organs depicted in Joan Miró's vibrant pastel *The Lovers* (see plate 33.15) directly below the open legs of Picasso's *Seated Female Nude* (see plate 33.14). Next to these paintings they hung Duchamp's *Virgin (No. 2)* (see plate 33.12) so that the "figure" in that drawing seems, by her implied motion, to be joining the sexual activity already under way. (This combination of artworks was perhaps a private reference to *The Passage from Virgin to Bride*, another painting by Duchamp that the Arensbergs were familiar with but did not own.) They also seem to have made an eroticized pairing of *The Lovers* with the anthropomorphized machine parts of Morton Livingston Schamberg's *Painting IV (Mechanical Abstraction)* (see plate 33.13).[129]

Though it is clear that the Arensbergs enjoyed combining artworks and artifacts to provocative effect, it would be impossible to ascribe precise meaning to these fetishized arrangements and rearrangements. And it would also be overly simplistic to read these "wall pictures" as purely pornographic. Walter had written the following many years earlier, in his preface to *The Cryptography of Dante*:

> Sex symbolism is not to be interpreted as symbolizing sex. The sex symbolism of the *Divina Commedia*, for example, is, in the last analysis, a representation of the *mental processes*, in which the mind is conceived as a trinity of will, intellect, and emotion, and which is represented accordingly as a family, as in the Trinity of the Christian Godhead, of father, son, and mother. The mutual relations of the three members of the family in a drama involving incest, death, and rebirth, are to be understood as a representation of the individual mind in conflict or in harmony with itself.[130]

Walter's insistence that sexual symbolism was as much a mental as a physical matter was certainly recognized by the curator Katharine Kuh, who also understood that the juxtaposition of works on the walls resembled the conversations that took place between Walter and Marcel. Kuh visited the Arensbergs while planning her 1949 exhibition of their collection for the Art Institute of Chicago. Her time in Hollywood coincided with Duchamp's second stay at the Arensbergs' California home, and in her memoir, *The Open Eye*, she described the deep rapport between the reacquainted men, finding that they still shared the secret language developed during their years together in New York:

> On and on they went, probing, questioning, and examining every ideographic nuance. Walter Arensberg searched for hidden meanings (usually erotic ones) in paintings and sculpture; Duchamp found them intuitively, for, after all, he was the artist par excellence who had created the climate for hidden meanings.[131]

Kuh wrote that though Walter's long separation from Duchamp had been a "serious deprivation" for the collector, the artist was "always present in principle if not in person."[132]

Duchamp was assuredly present in this room in the form of his most famous painting, *Nude Descending a Staircase (No. 2)*. It is unclear where in their Hollywood home the Arensbergs had displayed the *Nude* prior to Neutra's building of the sunroom, but the painting seems to have hung thereafter (except when on loan to exhibitions) on the room's northeast wall, its brownish hues naturally lit for almost two decades by California's afternoon sunshine (see plate 27.5). Surrounded by many other remarkable pieces—from delicately painted Native American bowls to the imposing stone sculpture representing an Easter Island deity that was later moved to the living room—and playfully flanked by two other major works, Salvador Dalí's *Soft Construction with Boiled Beans (Premonition of Civil War)* and Brancusi's *Mademoiselle Pogany [III]*, *Nude Descending a Staircase (No. 2)* never lost its power to provoke and excite (see plate 28).[133]

And if the story of *The Large Glass* (both of and in the work) was one of frustrated love, the story of the *Nude* can be told, inversely, as one in which the Arensbergs secured, through patience (and a little luck), the very first object of their affection. It is one best told, naturally, by moving to the stairway.

THE STAIRWAY

Though not sweeping or grand in the manner of other homes common to the wealthier neighborhoods of Los Angeles, the Arensbergs' stairway was nonetheless dramatic, serving not simply as a transitional space but as a focal point in its own right. Framed by three large walls built to the full height of two high-ceilinged floors, the space held at least thirty artworks, with almost no room left for more (see plates 36–38). And in the only known contemporary artistic impression of the Arensberg collection—a small, hand-drawn greeting card by Benjamin Dusanovich Kosich (fig. 43)—works from around the house are arranged in postcubist style around the staircase, invoking the kinetic action of Duchamp's descending *Nudes*. Kosich (who called himself "B. D. K. Ara," "D. Ara," and "Zorin," among other invented names) was a talented but struggling local artist whom the Arensbergs supported at the urging of Earl Stendahl.[134] Kosich no doubt chose this vantage point because it allowed him to highlight the fact that three of his own paintings hung in the stairway. But it also gave him artistic license to place his works in the company of acknowledged masterpieces whose reconfigured forms he blended seamlessly into the home's floor, ceiling, stairs, and walls—allowing us to imagine what Aline Louchheim meant when she wrote (in the *New York Times* article with which we began) that the Arensberg collection "submerged architecture and furnishings."[135]

For a start, as one might by now expect, the staircase offered rich opportunities for the couple to make visual puns that played on relations between art and house. For example, they tucked Duchamp's *Apolinère Enameled* under the rise of the staircase, creating visual continuity between the bedposts illustrated in that artwork and the balusters supporting the handrail above (fig. 44; see plate 38.22). And on the landing between the first and second floors, they added a third figure to Roberto Montenegro's *The Double* by placing an African sculpture of a woman in front of a self-portrait in which the artist had depicted himself with a similarly elongated neck and a mask-like face separating from his body (see fig. 44; plates 37.10, 37.11).

As noted elsewhere, the Arensbergs used their collection to conjure the presence of their absent friends, and it is clear from the couple's correspondence that Walter saw this particular painting as a kind of stand-in for Montenegro:

> Dear Roberto,
>
> What in the world is the news of you? Are you or are you not ever going to give us the pleasure of seeing you again? You have been away entirely too long, and I shouldn't be inclined to forgive you if I didn't have the painting of your Double to take your place.[136]

Francis M. Naumann has pointed out that Walter found similar consolation in Duchamp's works. Walter wrote to Duchamp in 1930 that "it is still the great lacuna that I never see you. There isn't a day that I don't pass some time with your pictures. They are your conversation."[137] On at least one occasion, prompted by another work in the staircase—*Woman at the Piano* by Albert Gleizes—Walter spoke directly to a painting rather than the artist who made it.[138] His unpublished poem, "Paroles devant une toile de Gleizes" (Words in front of a Gleizes canvas), hearkened back to his early poetic experiments while seemingly addressing the woman pictured in the painting via euphemism and wordplay.[139]

In another photograph, that of the soldiers touring the house, some of the men hanging over the staircase railing continue the "conversation" with Gino Severini's *Composition for Mosaic* (see plate 36.3). They are pictured laughing and pointing as the man in the foreground clenches his teeth to imitate the Italian mask depicted in that painting. Continuing up the stairs, the soldiers might have shared another laugh as they encountered yet another descending *Nude* (see fig. 44 and plate 39.3), this one a carefully

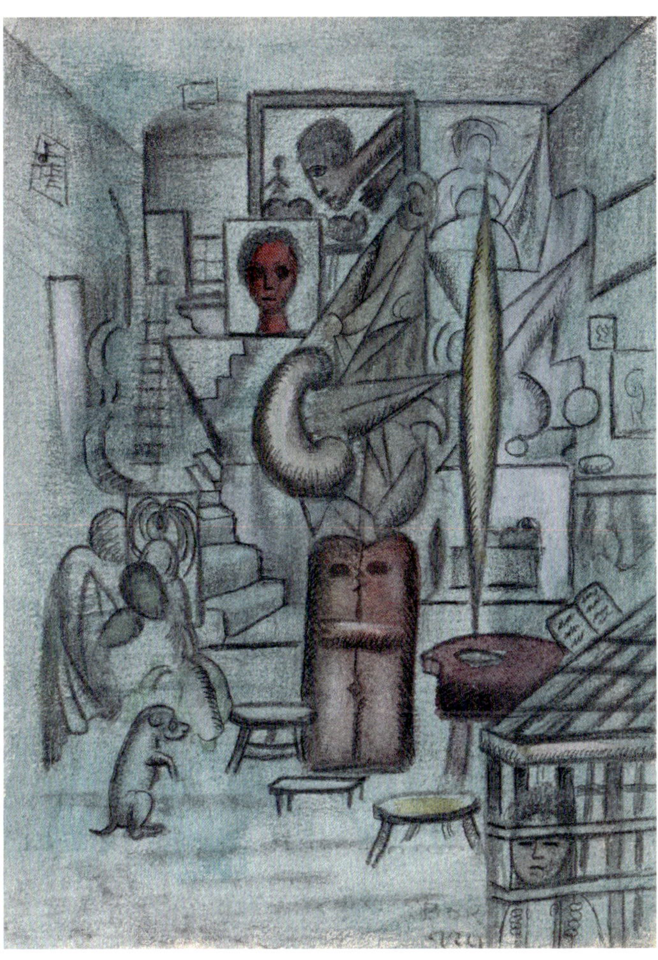

43. BENJAMIN DUSANOVICH KOSICH.
PERSONAL GREETING CARD TO THE ARENSBERGS, FEATURING A DRAWING OF THEIR HOME, CA. 1950. PENCIL AND WATERCOLOR SKETCH. PHILADELPHIA MUSEUM OF ART, LIBRARY AND ARCHIVES, ARENSBERG ARCHIVES (PMA-WLA), BOX 10, FOLDER 52

IN THIS SKETCH, PROBABLY DONE FROM MEMORY, REPRESENTATIONS OF AT LEAST TWO OF KOSICH'S PAINTINGS—*SELF-PORTRAIT* (SEE PLATE 38.2) AND *MOTHER AND CHILD STOOPING* (SEE PLATES 38.3, 39.6)—ARE FEATURED PROMINENTLY ALONGSIDE THOSE OF OTHER ARTWORKS IN THE ARENSBERG COLLECTION. WORKS BY CONSTANTIN BRANCUSI, GEORGES BRAQUE, GIORGIO DE CHIRICO, AND HENRI MATISSE ARE RECOGNIZABLE. IN AN ACCOMPANYING NOTE, KOSICH CRYPTICALLY CHALLENGED THE ARENSBERGS: "I BET YOU CANNOT GUESS WHAT THE THING IN THE CORNER REPRESENTS?"

executed photomechanical copy of *Nude Descending a Staircase (No. 2)*, which they had just seen in the sunroom. The Arensbergs had commissioned *Nude Descending a Staircase (No. 3)*—as it later became known—from Duchamp in 1916, after missing their chance to buy the original from the Armory Show.

Not yet understanding, in 1913, the impact the new art would have on their own lives, the Arensbergs had lost out to the San Francisco prints dealer Frederic C. Torrey, a man equally transfixed by the Armory Show and the commotion around Duchamp's *Nude*. He, too, had purchased only a few conventional works at the exhibition and seems to have been quite far along his somewhat circuitous route back to San Francisco when the importance of what he had seen overwhelmed him. Stopping in Albuquerque, New Mexico, Torrey sent an urgent telegram to the Armory Show organizers: "I WILL BUY DUCHAMP NUDE WOMAN DESCENDING STAIRWAY. PLEASE RESERVE."[140] A short time after *Nude Descending a Staircase (No. 2)* was shipped to him, he installed it—to the chagrin of his family—at the foot of the staircase in their home.[141]

It is tempting to think of this parallel punning as overly simplistic—as an all-too-obvious joke for visitors to their homes who were not yet attuned to more sophisticated forms of play. Yet it would be unfair to accuse Torrey or the Arensbergs of getting by on a nod and a wink. Torrey was a cultured and learned man who had bravely sailed into the headwinds of resistance to what he called the "new idiom."[142] He arranged his own exhibitions with the *Nude* as their centerpiece and lectured frequently to a baffled public on the merits of this art in its many forms, becoming, in Naumann's words, "one of the West Coast's greatest authorities on the new art, as well as one of its most articulate spokesmen and defenders."[143] He also traveled to Paris soon after purchasing the *Nude* to meet Duchamp, who gave him an early drawing of a figure ascending a staircase as a memento of their meeting and went on to describe him, in a letter to one of the Armory Show's organizers, Walter Pach, as "an excellent man."[144]

C. ALBERT GLEIZES
MAN ON A BALCONY (PORTRAIT OF DR. THÉO MORINAUD)
(SEE PLATE 38.1)

A. ROBERTO MONTENEGRO
THE DOUBLE
(SEE PLATE 37.10)

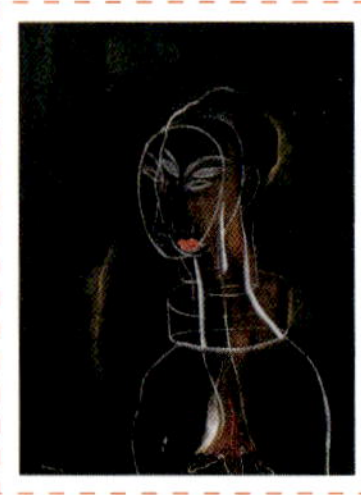

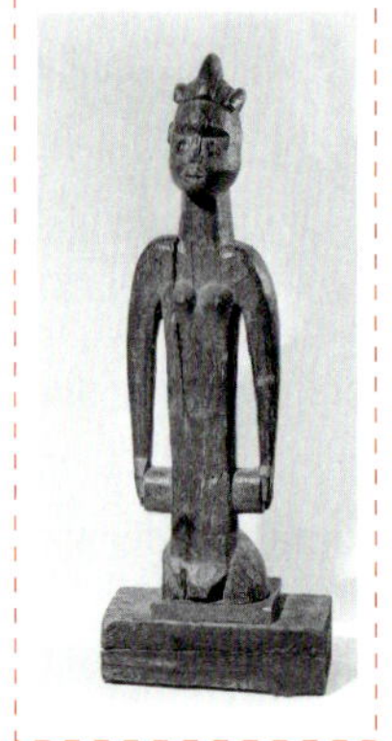

B. ARTIST/MAKER UNKNOWN (AFRICA)
FEMALE FIGURE
(SEE PLATE 37.11)

D. MARCEL DUCHAMP
APOLINÈRE ENAMELED
(SEE PLATE 38.22)

APOLINÈRE ENAMELED

44. SOME VISUAL PUNS IN THE STAIRWELL:
A. ROBERTO MONTENEGRO. *THE DOUBLE*, 1938. OIL ON PANEL, 66 × 50.8 CM. 1950-134-153
B. ARTIST/MAKER UNKNOWN (AFRICA). FEMALE FIGURE, DATE UNKNOWN. WOOD, 111.8 × 30.5 × 25.4 CM. 1950-134-203
C. ALBERT GLEIZES. *MAN ON A BALCONY (PORTRAIT OF DR. THÉO MORINAUD)*, 1912. OIL ON CANVAS, 195.6 × 114.9 CM. 1950-134-91
D. MARCEL DUCHAMP. *APOLINÈRE ENAMELED*, 1916–17. GOUACHE AND GRAPHITE ON PAINTED TIN, MOUNTED ON CARDBOARD, 24.4 × 34 CM. 1950-134-73
E. MARCEL DUCHAMP. *NUDE DESCENDING A STAIRCASE (NO. 3)*, 1916. GRAPHITE, PEN AND BLACK INK, BLACK PAINT, COLORED PENCIL OR CRAYON, AND BLUE WASH ON GELATIN SILVER PHOTOGRAPH, 148.1 × 91.8 CM. 1950-134-60
ALL ARE PHILADELPHIA MUSEUM OF ART, THE LOUISE AND WALTER ARENSBERG COLLECTION. SEE ALSO PLATES 36–39

As for the Arensbergs, their later decision to place *Nude Descending a Staircase (No. 3)* at the top of the stairs in their Hollywood home was much more nuanced than it seems at a glance, for it telegraphed a complex set of personal and historical relationships dating from the earliest days of Duchamp's work on the various versions of the *Nude*.

In 1911, Duchamp made his first iteration of the painting, *Nude Descending a Staircase (No. 1)*, which the Arensbergs also later owned and displayed for a time in their living room (see plate 7.16).[145] Influenced in part by the early chronophotographs of Etienne-Jules Marey and the stop-motion photographs of Eadweard Muybridge (including one of a nude woman descending stairs) published in his famous book, *The Human Figure in Motion*, this *Nude* was smaller and less radically abstract than *Nude Descending a Staircase (No. 2)*, which the artist completed in January of 1912.[146] In March of that year, Duchamp submitted the latter version—on which he had written "NU DESCENDANT UN ESCALIER" in capital letters at the bottom—to a group exhibition by members of the Salon des Indépendants. He became disenchanted, however, when fellow artists Jean Metzinger and Albert Gleizes, the leading proponents of cubism, took issue with his lack of adherence to cubist orthodoxy and asked him, via his brother Raymond Duchamp-Villon, to change its title or withdraw it from the exhibition. Duchamp sorely refused, later telling the artist Richard Hamilton, "I took the painting under my arm and went home with it."[147] That same year, Metzinger and Gleizes authored a crucial book on the movement, which Duchamp later described as having "clarified the mental chemistry of Cubism,"[148] and Gleizes's painting *Man on a Balcony (Portrait of Dr. Théo Morinaud)*

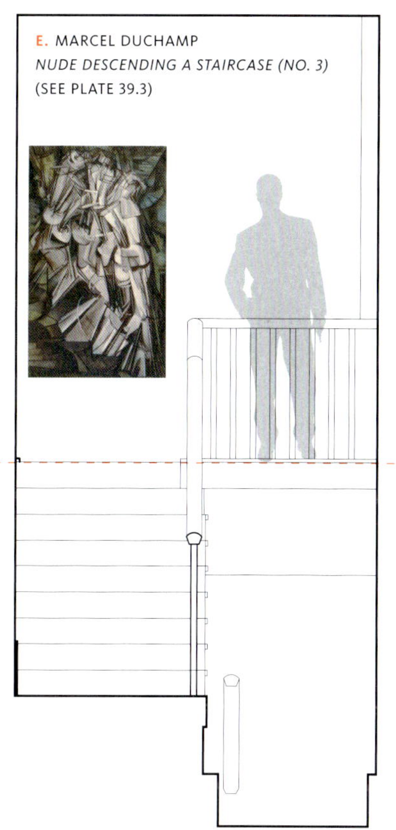

E. MARCEL DUCHAMP
NUDE DESCENDING A STAIRCASE (NO. 3)
(SEE PLATE 39.3)

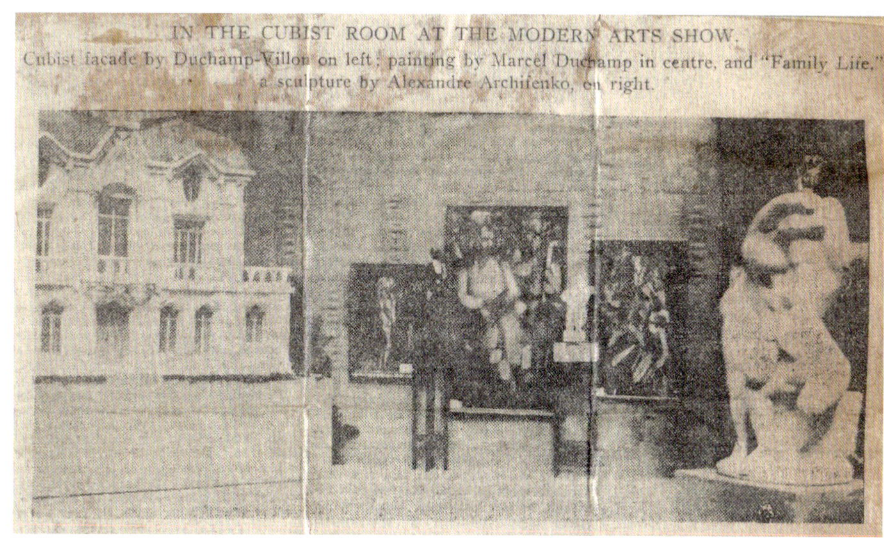

IN THE CUBIST ROOM AT THE MODERN ARTS SHOW.
Cubist facade by Duchamp-Villon on left; painting by Marcel Duchamp in centre, and "Family Life," a sculpture by Alexandre Archifenko, on right.

45. DETAIL OF A PAGE FROM WALT KUHN'S SCRAPBOOK OF PRESS CLIPPINGS DOCUMENTING THE ARMORY SHOW (VOL. 1, 1913, P. 123), FEATURING AN ARTICLE FROM THE *NEW YORK TRIBUNE* (17 FEBRUARY 1913, P. 7). THE CLIPPING SHOWS THE ONLY KNOWN PHOTOGRAPH, TAKEN BY THE HAGELSTEIN BROTHERS, OF THE ARMORY SHOW'S GALLERY I (ALSO KNOWN AS THE CUBIST ROOM OR THE CHAMBER OF HORRORS). MARCEL DUCHAMP'S *NUDE DESCENDING A STAIRCASE (NO. 2)* HANGS BESIDE ALBERT GLEIZES'S *MAN ON A BALCONY (PORTRAIT OF DR. THÉO MORINAUD)*. SMITHSONIAN INSTITUTION, ARCHIVES OF AMERICAN ART, WALT KUHN, KUHN FAMILY PAPERS, AND ARMORY SHOW RECORDS

came to be understood as "an open declaration of the principles of Cubist painting."[149] Ironically, *Nude Descending a Staircase (No. 2)* had hung beside *Man on a Balcony* at the Armory Show a year later, eclipsing that painting and all others as the exhibition's *succès de scandale* (fig. 45). The Arensbergs certainly understood the shared history of these artists when they hung *Nude Descending a Staircase (No. 3)* directly across the stairwell from *Man on a Balcony*.

In a nuanced exploitation of their home's construction, however, the Arensbergs did not give *Man on a Balcony* short shrift in this new configuration. They cleverly hung the large canvas so that Dr. Morinaud's feet were positioned at the floorline of the second floor. Seen across the stairwell from the upper landing, the painting would have conveyed the impression to its viewer that he or she was standing on a balcony looking at a man standing on a balcony (see fig. 44). This playful and historically resonant gesture illustrates how witty the Arensbergs could be, and it makes plain how paintings can be presented or perceived differently when they occupy a domestic space rather than an institutional one.

The couple might well have feared that this sense of play would be lost after they bequeathed their collection to a museum. They wrung their hands over that inevitability for more than a decade, exploring numerous schemes for the collection's disposition and making some surprising decisions late in life.[150] Writing to Katharine Kuh in 1949, Walter explained that a number of works Kuh had seen during her visit had been jettisoned and were no longer available for her planned exhibition. In addition to the Severini mentioned above, these included Diego Rivera's *The Flowered Canoe*, Marcel Gromaire's *The Night Watchman*, and José Clemente Orozco's *The Beggars*, all of which hung in the stairway. They had traded them, he explained, for "some absolutely superlative pre-Columbian pieces, and are we happy!"[151] Seen in the context of Walter's correspondence with Kuh, photographs of the stairway not only capture the passageway from the home's public spaces to its private ones but also provide a clear snapshot of the Arensbergs preparing their collection for posterity.

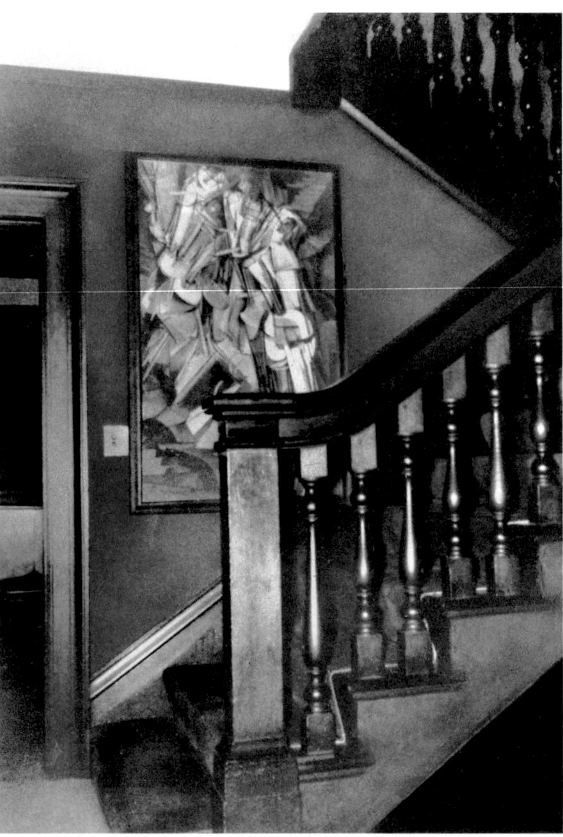

46. THE HALLWAY OF FREDERIC C. TORREY'S HOME IN BERKELEY, CALIFORNIA, CA. 1930, SHOWING A PHOTOGRAPHIC REPRODUCTION OF MARCEL DUCHAMP'S *NUDE DESCENDING A STAIRCASE (NO. 2)* HANGING IN THE SAME SPOT WHERE THE ORIGINAL HAD ONCE HUNG. PHOTOGRAPH BY *TIME* MAGAZINE. COLLECTION OF THE OAKLAND MUSEUM OF CALIFORNIA, ARCHIVES OF CALIFORNIA ART. GIFT OF DOROTHEA KELLEY

Descending or not, none of the three versions of the *Nude* was going anywhere, for they had long been integral to the Arensbergs' jointly created self-image (see fig. 4). What was it about the *Nude*s that so transfixed Louise and Walter? Was it their transgressive treatment of the nude—a subject that prior to Duchamp's intervention had been hallowed throughout the history of art? Was it because *Nude Descending a Staircase (No. 2)* and *Nude Descending a Staircase (No. 3)* had thrilled those who gathered at their New York apartment? Or was it simply that they knew and loved the artist who had shocked the world with what one scandalized critic called an "explosion in a shingle factory"?[152] Of the more than one million people other than the Arensbergs who saw *Nude Descending a Staircase (No. 2)* at the Armory Show, it is Torrey who might have best answered those questions. Having first offered the painting to John Quinn (who refused because he felt the asking price of $1,000 was too high), Torrey approached the Arensbergs, who agreed to buy it without hesitation. After selling the painting to the couple in February 1919, Torrey so regretted the loss that he, too, had a photomechanical copy made. He hung it at the foot of his staircase where the original had been (fig. 46).

THE OFFICES

To reach the rooms on the upper floor, the Arensbergs and their visitors used the art-filled interior staircase, and in 1933 the couple added a set of exterior stairs to take their employees directly into the rooms at the rear of the house. This addition, also by Neutra and Ain, gave private access to a pair of rooms that would house the couple's library and provide a home to Walter's research institute, soon to be established as the Francis Bacon Foundation.[153]

Incorporated as a nonprofit, tax-exempt company on 9 April 1937, the foundation became the umbrella organization for the perpetuation of Walter's research and for the management of the couple's collections. According to a note prepared by the foundation's secretary (the lawyer James Taylor) in 1947–48, the Arensbergs' holdings officially consisted of "five main divisions":

1. Works of Art
2. Pre-Columbian Collection
3. Eastern Carpets and Rugs
4. Antique Furniture, and
5. The Francis Bacon Library

The last of these, Taylor continued,

> has been built up by Mr. Arenberg [*sic*] with much thought and care and at great cost over a long period of years, for one purpose and one purpose only: to enable him to carry on research and studies in the Bacon-Shakespeare problem and, if possible, to give to the world the message that Bacon has, undoubtedly, left for posterity in the Shakespeare plays and poems.[154]

Like the art collection, both the library and the project it served grew dramatically during the couple's years in Hollywood, ultimately requiring a full-time staff. Many of the rare books were housed in the glass-fronted cases in Walter's personal office (see plates 40, 41), and there was ample room for more—along with a comprehensive reference library devoted to Renaissance literature and culture—in the large adjacent room that housed the secretaries who assisted his work. The group was led from 1944 by Walter's redoubtable assistant Elizabeth Wrigley, and after she was joined by Ruth Calder and Carol Bruns, they became affectionately known as the Three Graces. They spent every day with Walter, and their daily work followed a similar pattern (as Bruns's husband, Andrew Baker, recalled in an interview), with Walter dictating his latest thoughts and theories to all three women, who would then triple-check each other's transcripts and file an accurate record.[155]

At the beginning of 1954, in the weeks between the deaths of Louise and Walter, Wrigley produced a concise history of Walter's Baconian work to serve as an introduction to his account of the foundation's unfinished business.[156] She explained how his early efforts, published in *The Cryptography of Shakespeare* (1922), involved an arduous search for the anagrams and acrostics that he believed were hidden in the First Folio and other texts. Walter's copies of these books are covered with pencil notations, picking out with obvious enthusiasm the messages he found in them (figs. 47a, b). In pursuing this method, Walter was following in the footsteps of his Baconian mentor William Stone Booth (fig. 48), but he was also inspired by Bacon and other Renaissance writers who had developed powerful tools for concealing and revealing meaning.[157] Never content to work simply with received ideas or methods, Walter eventually developed hybrid forms such as the "anagrammatic acrotelestic" and the "compound anagrammatic acrostic." He described the latter as

> a method of constructing a spelling in another spelling, or text, by arranging the letters of the acrostic spelling in an anagrammatic sequence as an indefinite number of the acrostic letters of an indefinite number of consecutive words, beginning with either the first word or the last word of an indefinite number of consecutive lines.[158]

At the same time, Arensberg was pursuing a more outlandish theory that Bacon had "arranged for a secret grave at Lichfield Cathedral and a repository for the missing literary and historical documents of the times." He followed up a preliminary pamphlet on the subject, *The Secret Grave of Francis Bacon at Lichfield*

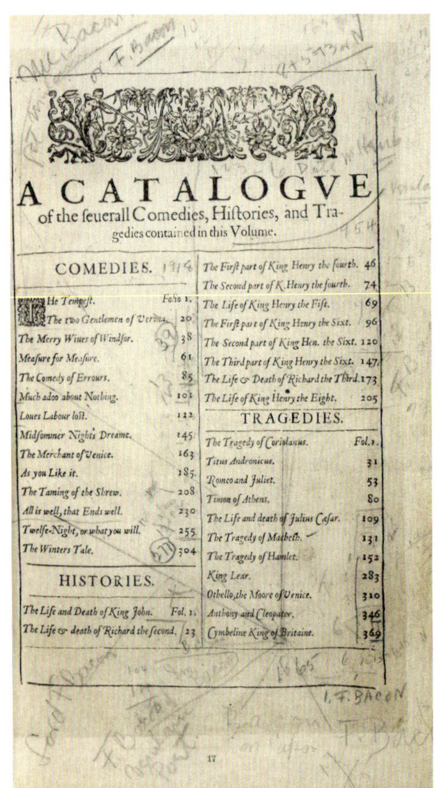

A CATALOGVE
of the ſeuerall Comedies, Hiſtories, and Tragedies contained in this Volume.

COMEDIES.	
The Tempeſt.	Folio 1.
The two Gentlemen of Verona.	20
The Merry Wiues of Windſor.	38
Meaſure for Meaſure.	61
The Comedy of Errours.	85
Much adoo about Nothing.	101
Loues Labour loſt.	122
Midſommer Nights Dreame.	145
The Merchant of Venice.	163
As you Like it.	185
The Taming of the Shrew.	208
All is well, that Ends well.	230
Twelfe-Night, or what you will.	255
The Winters Tale.	304

HISTORIES.	
The Life and Death of King John.	Fol. 1.
The Life & death of Richard the ſecond.	23
The First part of King Henry the fourth.	46
The Second part of K. Henry the fourth.	74
The Life of King Henry the Fift.	69
The First part of King Henry the Sixt.	96
The Second part of King Hen. the Sixt.	120
The Third part of King Henry the Sixt.	147
The Life & Death of Richard the Third.	173
The Life of King Henry the Eight.	205

TRAGEDIES.	
The Tragedy of Coriolanus.	Fol. 1.
Titus Andronicus.	31
Romeo and Juliet.	53
Timon of Athens.	80
The Life and death of Julius Cæsar.	109
The Tragedy of Macbeth.	131
The Tragedy of Hamlet.	152
King Lear.	283
Othello, the Moore of Venice.	310
Anthony and Cleopater.	346
Cymbeline King of Britaine.	369

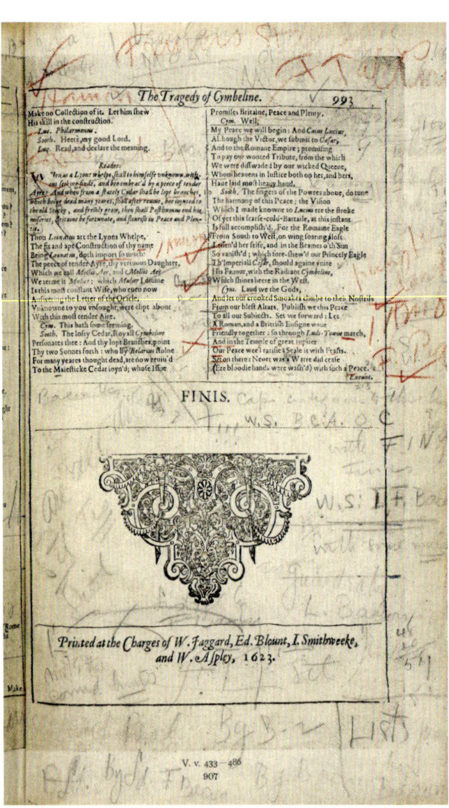

The Tragedy of Cymbeline. 993

FINIS.

Printed at the Charges of W. Jaggard, Ed. Blount, I. Smithweeke, and W. Aſpley, 1623.

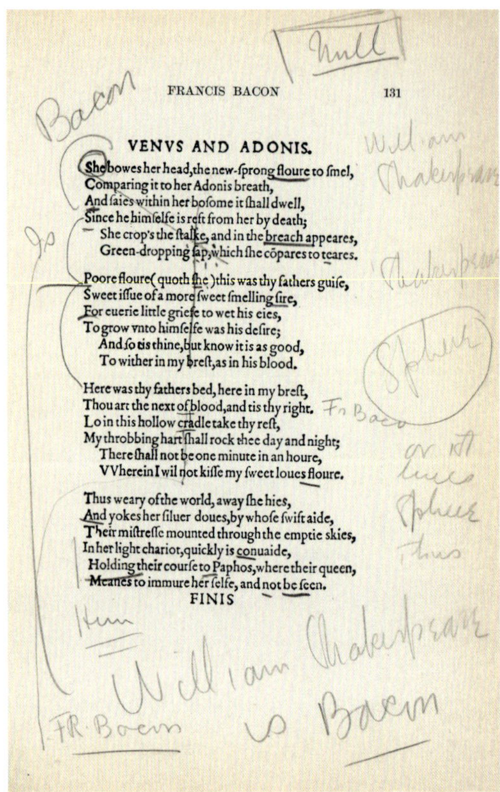

FRANCIS BACON 131

VENVS AND ADONIS.

She bowes her head, the new-ſprong floure to ſmel,
Comparing it to her Adonis breath,
And ſaies within her boſome it ſhall dwell,
Since he himſelfe is reft from her by death;
She crop's the ſtalke, and in the breach appeares,
Green-dropping ſap, which ſhe cōpares to teares.

Poore floure (quoth ſhe) this was thy fathers guiſe,
Sweet iſſue of a more ſweet ſmelling ſire,
For euerie little griefe to wet his eies,
To grow vnto himſelfe was his deſire;
And ſo tis thine, but know it is as good,
To wither in my breſt, as in his blood.

Here was thy fathers bed, here in my breſt,
Thou art the next of blood, and tis thy right.
Lo in this hollow cradle take thy reſt,
My throbbing hart ſhall rock thee day and night;
There ſhall not be one minute in an houre,
VVherein I wil not kiſſe my ſweet loues floure.

Thus weary of the world, away ſhe hies,
And yokes her ſiluer doues, by whoſe ſwift aide,
Their miſtreſſe mounted through the emptie skies,
In her light chariot, quickly is conuaide,
Holding their courſe to Paphos, where their queen,
Meanes to immure her ſelfe, and not be ſeen.

FINIS

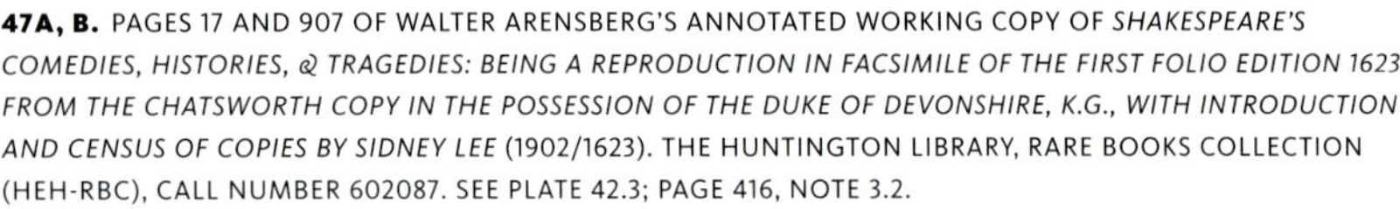

47A, B. PAGES 17 AND 907 OF WALTER ARENSBERG'S ANNOTATED WORKING COPY OF *SHAKESPEARE'S COMEDIES, HISTORIES, & TRAGEDIES: BEING A REPRODUCTION IN FACSIMILE OF THE FIRST FOLIO EDITION 1623 FROM THE CHATSWORTH COPY IN THE POSSESSION OF THE DUKE OF DEVONSHIRE, K.G., WITH INTRODUCTION AND CENSUS OF COPIES BY SIDNEY LEE* (1902/1623). THE HUNTINGTON LIBRARY, RARE BOOKS COLLECTION (HEH-RBC), CALL NUMBER 602087. SEE PLATE 42.3; PAGE 416, NOTE 3.2.

48. PAGE 131 OF WALTER ARENSBERG'S ANNOTATED WORKING COPY OF *SOME ACROSTIC SIGNATURES OF FRANCIS BACON* (1909) BY WILLIAM STONE BOOTH. AT THE BOTTOM, WALTER HAS EMPHATICALLY WRITTEN "WILLIAM SHAKESPEARE IS BACON." THE HUNTINGTON LIBRARY, RARE BOOKS COLLECTION (HEH-RBC), CALL NUMBER 613575

(1923), with deep reading in the history of the "Masonic and Rosicrucian Societies," who, he felt, would be the most likely keepers of such a secret. Persuaded that he was closing in on the location of the hidden vault in the Chapter House at Lichfield, Walter set off for England, where he made his case for excavation to the cathedral's dean. After a long wait (and an expensive one, since he was staying at the luxurious Savoy Hotel), the Chapter—or church council—met and shared its discouraging decision. Walter broke the bad news in a despondent letter to Louise:

> Darling:
>
> There is a London fog in my heart. This morning I received the letter from the Lichfield Chapter refusing my request to open the crypt which I believe, more strongly than ever, lies under the Chapter House. I should like to run home, like a beaten dog, with my tail between my legs. But the only thing to do—though I haven't any humor for it—is to do some work in the British Museum.[159]

Before returning home, Walter recovered his spirits and gathered enough material to publish a second pamphlet, *The Burial of Francis Bacon and His Mother in the Lichfield Chapter House* (1924). He continued to lobby the authorities at Lichfield for several decades, and as late as 1951 he was still working in vain to penetrate the mysteries of Bacon's secret grave.[160]

According to Wrigley, Arensberg responded to these setbacks by developing more systematic and mathematically rigorous approaches to the cryptographic structures he was searching for. Alongside his

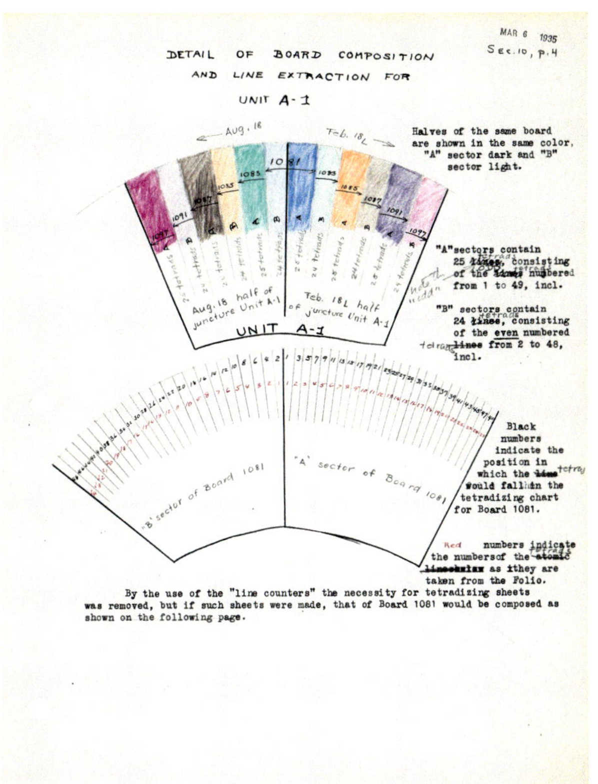

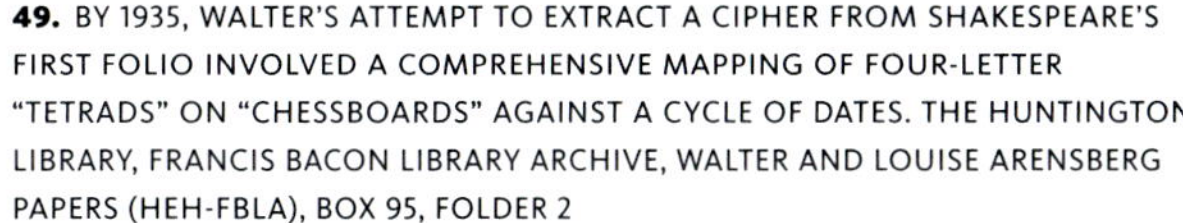

49. BY 1935, WALTER'S ATTEMPT TO EXTRACT A CIPHER FROM SHAKESPEARE'S FIRST FOLIO INVOLVED A COMPREHENSIVE MAPPING OF FOUR-LETTER "TETRADS" ON "CHESSBOARDS" AGAINST A CYCLE OF DATES. THE HUNTINGTON LIBRARY, FRANCIS BACON LIBRARY ARCHIVE, WALTER AND LOUISE ARENSBERG PAPERS (HEH-FBLA), BOX 95, FOLDER 2

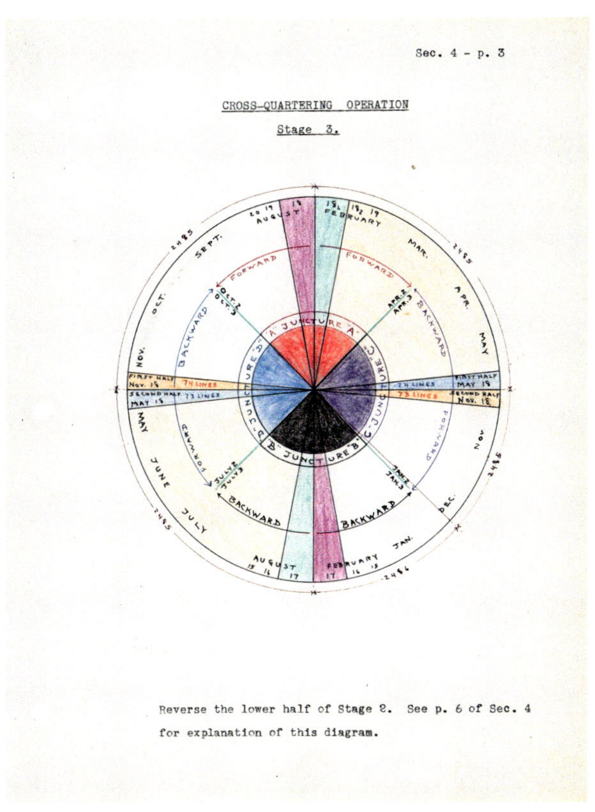

50. WALTER USED THIS SO-CALLED "CROSS-QUARTERING OPERATION" TO IDENTIFY KEY MOMENTS IN THE CYCLICAL CALENDAR THAT COULD THEN BE LINKED TO KEY LINES IN SHAKESPEARE'S TEXT. THE HUNTINGTON LIBRARY, FRANCIS BACON LIBRARY ARCHIVE, WALTER AND LOUISE ARENSBERG PAPERS (HEH-FBLA), BOX 95, FOLDER 2

ongoing research into key concepts and contextual clues, Arensberg renewed and refined his quest for a Baconian code: "As the research continued," Wrigley explained, "more and more indications of another code or cipher appeared, a cipher inflexible and capable of rigid mathematical application, one that would admit of conclusive proof." Once the foundation was up and running, "a full-time attack could be made on the problem. Assistants could be trained easily enough for tabulation work, mechanical coding and recording of tests."[161]

The ever-evolving plan subjected the texts of Shakespeare to increasingly elaborate calculations and reconfigurations, ranging from the fiendishly clever to the downright bizarre—involving "heptads" and "tetrads" (fig. 49); "locks," "watches," and "calendars"; "cross-quartering operations" (fig. 50); magic squares derived from Albrecht Dürer; and an array of grids called "chessboards." Arensberg developed so many different operations that his early assistants created a list of "code-words" to simplify his instructions: a key from 1935 included "ROT" for "Rotate," "PERM" for "Permute," "SER" for "Serial," "GRAV" for "Grave diagonal," and (of course) "ANA" for "Anagrammatize."[162]

The alphanumeric machinations became so convoluted that Arensberg hired expert consultants to help him with the math, among them Clyde Wolfe and Hervey Hicks from the mathematics department at the California Institute of Technology. Wolfe was so taken with the speculative structures produced by Arensberg that he went on to write a Baconian treatise of his own, but its complex notations were incomprehensible to Walter.[163] Even when Wolfe was working on the calculations that Walter himself had set for him, his math was too advanced for the literary scholar to follow: "Perhaps I am stupid," Walter wrote in December 1925, "but for the life of me I cannot understand the enclosed tables which you sent me. I am not a mathematician and am only a symbolist about sex. Please, in connection with all tables, consider me

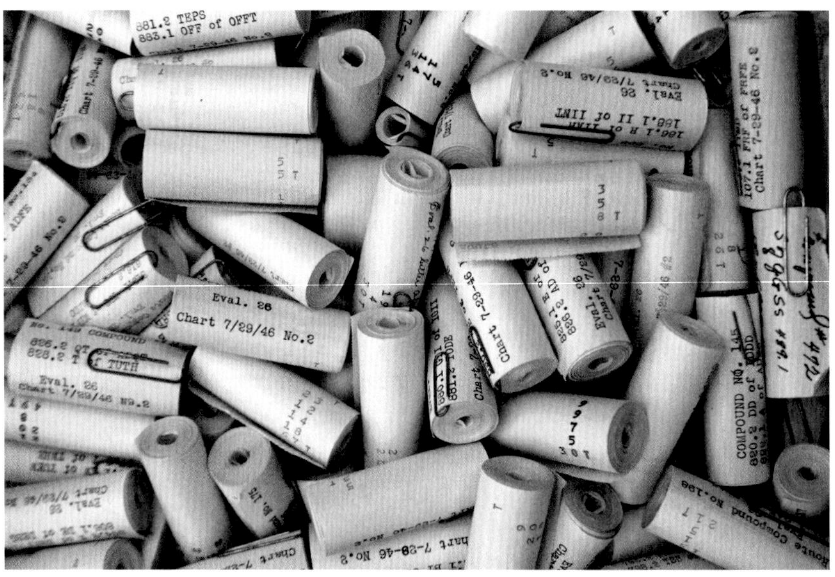

51. ROLLS OF TABULATIONS AND CALCULATIONS ON ADDING MACHINE PAPER (1945–59), GENERATED FIRST BY WALTER AND LATER BY EMPLOYEES OF THE FRANCIS BACON LIBRARY (BOTH BEFORE AND AFTER WALTER'S DEATH), IN PURSUIT OF PROOF THAT BACON WAS THE AUTHOR OF SHAKESPEARE'S WORKS. (THE ROLLS ARE NOW ORGANIZED INTO BOXES BY YEAR OF CREATION AT THE HUNTINGTON LIBRARY, SAN MARINO, CALIFORNIA.) THE HUNTINGTON LIBRARY, FRANCIS BACON LIBRARY ARCHIVE, WALTER AND LOUISE ARENSBERG PAPERS (HEH-FBLA), BOXES 129–32. PHOTOGRAPH BY WILLIAM H. SHERMAN

in the primary grade and spell it out in words."[164] Nonetheless, Walter clearly spent countless hours in front of his adding machine: when his working papers passed to the Huntington Library in 1995, they included several boxes containing nothing but tightly rolled tapes of calculations, each documenting one of the "indefinite" routes through the Shakespearean text, and none of them producing the key to unlock the secret he was looking for (fig. 51).

If the energy for the daily experiments waned, there was always, in these offices, a sense of new work to be done. Walter and his team continually filled index cards with ever more time-consuming tasks:

> 4/17/35
> Someday we ought to work out the value sums and juxtaposed value sums and consummated value sums of all our principal key words in the final alphabet that we are now using, as compared with what they are in the early alphabet. . . .
>
> 6/5/35
> Compile a chronological history of Bacon's life, giving the known dates for various events in his life.
>
> 2/11/39
> We should, someday, list and discuss the various treatments of the controversy in all the orthodox discussions of Shakespeare. We should make a list of all the early allusions to Bacon.[165]

Of these long-running endeavors, Walter had written earlier to his friend William Ivins:

> I am still digging in the same old mine, and the diggings are deeper than they used to be. All that I have published on the subject is essentially correct, though I now know that much of it is elementary. Within the last few months I have caught the tail—just the tip, alas—of the final form of the cryptographic structure. This structure involves a cryptographic

> game of chess, in which the cryptographic letters have to be arranged in the sixty-four cells of a chess board and then read in the order of a so-called endless, or reentrant, Knight's Tour which converts the chess board, by the numbers of the successive moves, into a Magic Square.[166]

Unfortunately, only a single photograph taken in one of the Arensbergs' earlier Californian residences captures Walter on his endless Tour around these Shakespearean chessboards (see fig. 2). But given that Walter's inquiries look more like games than scientific experiments, it is perhaps fitting that one of the desks he evidently used in the corner of the Francis Bacon Foundation office looks less like a Renaissance research library than a shrine to his old friend Duchamp (see plate 42).[167] Walter was supervised while working there by a Duchampian god and father (in the form of Morton Livingston Schamberg and Baroness Elsa von Freytag-Loringhoven's *God*, a provocative response to Duchamp's "readymade" sculptures; and Duchamp's *Portrait of the Artist's Father*).[168] And by surrounding himself with copies and originals of Duchamp's studies for paintings, Walter could continue his "conversation" with Marcel, even as he pursued his feverish encounters with Shakespeare and Bacon.

This photograph of Walter's workspace illustrates how the Francis Bacon Foundation office was animated by the same spirit of Duchamp—and the same oppositional dynamics—that we have traced throughout the house: the tensions between working processes and finished works; between open texts and hidden subtexts; between men and women; and, of course, between adversaries at chess. Many years after Walter's death, when questioned by Pierre Cabanne about his friend's Baconian project, Duchamp responded in a characteristically double-edged manner:

> Duchamp: [Walter's] system was to find, in the text, in every three lines, allusions to all sorts of things; it was a game for him, like chess, which he enjoyed immensely.
>
> Cabanne: Was his research really scientifically valuable?
>
> Duchamp: I don't believe so. I think it was mostly the conviction of a man at play.[169]

THE SITTING ROOM

Walter was evidently in a game-playing mood when he gave a tour of the collection to a group of eleventh graders from nearby Eagle Rock High School. When one of the students, Walter Hopps, inquired more deeply into the meaning of a painting by René Magritte called *The Six Elements* (fig. 52), Arensberg invited him back for another visit—the first of many that eventually led Hopps to see Louise and Walter as surrogate parents and that would shape his future career as a maverick museum director. In a 1991 *New Yorker* profile of Hopps, Calvin Tomkins (well known for his biography of Duchamp) relayed Hopps's recollection of this formative encounter:

> Arensberg took him upstairs to the library [i.e., the sitting room], gave him several books to read, and told him to think about the picture and its possible meaning for a couple of hours. He did that. "Then came the great moment," Hopps recall[ed]. "'All right,' Arensberg announced. 'I'm now going to tell you what it means. It means absolutely nothing.'"[170]

Relating the same anecdote a few years later to his biographers Deborah Treisman and Anne Doran, Hopps added:

> He gave me what is, in Zen Buddhism, called a hard lesson.... It was as if a master had asked me if I was ready for enlightenment and then thrown a glass of ice water in my face. For the next few days that was what constituted enlightenment. It became a laborious workout, intellectually: Why did he say that? What could it mean? I've never seen anyone teach a class more economically, with so few words. And the lesson I learned was not that the painting meant nothing but that there weren't going to be any easy answers about its meaning. I had to somehow sense or pick up on the curious poetry that Magritte was playing around with. I was thrilled.[171]

It was in the sitting room (which, ironically, had little room left for sitting) where Hopps first contemplated *The Six Elements* hanging among a group of other surrealist or surrealist-informed paintings, including Salvador Dalí's *Agnostic Symbol*; Joan Miró's *Man, Woman, and Child* and *Man and Woman*; and two works by Yves Tanguy, *The Parallels* and *The Storm (Black Landscape)*. This wall also held a major work the Arensbergs had first seen at the Armory Show, Francis Picabia's *Dances at the Spring*.

At first glance, then, this densely packed view presented a narrowly focused display of a kind unusual in the Hollywood house (see plate 46). But with a slight turn of the head in either direction, a visitor would have encountered some of the Arensbergs' most jarring juxtapositions. Indeed, if the most dramatic display of cross-cultural collage could be found in the living and dining rooms downstairs, the sitting room upstairs arguably covered more ground in less space. Just to the left of these pictures hung a cluster of ceremonial and metaphysical paintings, including a fifteenth-century Greek *Entombment of Saint Catherine of Alexandria*, a seventeenth-century Italian *Religious Procession to the Cathedral of Pisa*, and a twentieth-century copy, perhaps by Montenegro, of a nineteenth-century Mexican painting, *The Execution of Maximilian* (see plates 46.1, 46.3, 46.5). Continuing around the corner, in clever configurations of a more familiar kind, could be found a tableau of *retablos* around Picasso's *Table* (see plate 45). Duchamp's *Portrait of Chess Players*—the sketch for which could be found above Walter's desk in the Francis Bacon Foundation office (see plate 42.10)—hung above a bookcase containing rows of Renaissance texts, and against these shelves leaned a drawing by William Blake, appropriately titled *The Bard* (see plate 45.26).

On the opposite wall was a grouping of much older and mostly religious work, including the collection's only major forays into the art of the European Renaissance (see plates 47, 48). Among these were pictures attributed to Pietro di Miniato (*Crucifixion with the Mourning Virgin and Saint John the Evangelist*) and Palma il Giovane (*The Flagellation*); a *Virgin of Humility* by the Master of Carmignano and *Saints Benedict, Sebastian, Stephen, and John the Evangelist* by Arrigo di Niccolò; an anonymous Greek painting, *The Nativity and the Arrival of the Magi*; and a drawing/copy after Michelangelo of a nude youth from the Sistine Chapel ceiling.

The presence of such overtly Christian work is perhaps surprising given its proximity to Dalí's *Agnostic Symbol*. But Walter's approach to religion, like the couple's approach to collecting and displaying art, thrived on contradictions. One associate described Walter as "a complete agnostic [who] never failed to touch on that subject in his amusing and lively way";[172] but when he wrote to his friend the economic historian John Nef to critique Nef's recent book *The United States and Civilization* (1941), he both excoriated religious dogmatism and expressed his conviction that faith is vital: "In regard to your treatment of faith I feel, as you do, that it is an absolutely essential ingredient to life. It is what man lives by. But I profoundly object to your identification of faith with faith in a particular set of Christian dogmas."[173]

Walter's resistance to organized Christianity went hand in hand with an admiration for the cultures and accomplishments of so-called primitive peoples. On every flat surface, in a ring around the room,

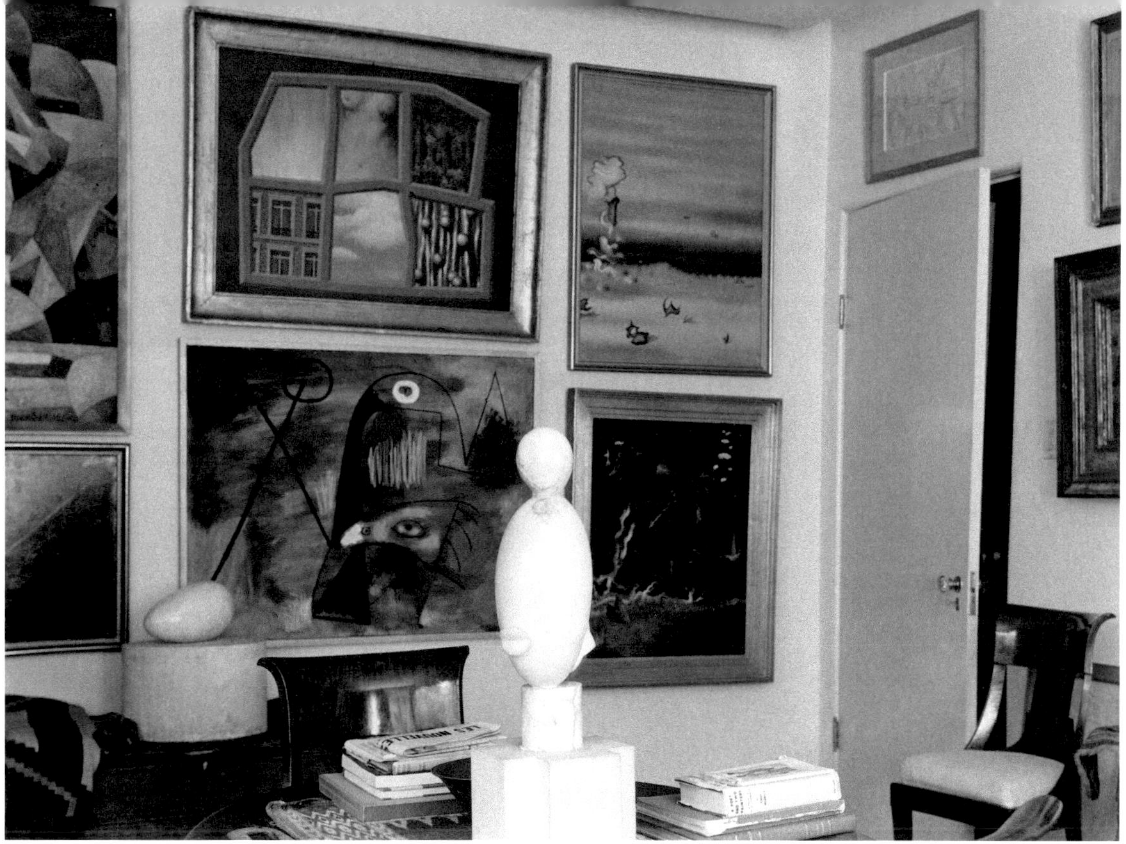

52. CHARLES SHEELER. VIEW OF LOUISE AND WALTER ARENSBERG'S SITTING ROOM, 7065 HILLSIDE AVENUE, LOS ANGELES, LATE OCTOBER 1939. PICTURED TO THE LEFT OF RENÉ MAGRITTE'S *THE SIX ELEMENTS* ARE FRANCIS PICABIA'S *DANCES AT THE SPRING* AND SALVADOR DALÍ'S *AGNOSTIC SYMBOL*. BELOW THE MAGRITTE HANGS JOAN MIRÓ'S *MAN, WOMAN, AND CHILD*; AND TO ITS RIGHT ARE TWO WORKS BY YVES TANGUY, *THE PARALLELS* AND *THE STORM (BLACK LANDSCAPE)*. TWO SCULPTURAL WORKS BY CONSTANTIN BRANCUSI, *WHITE NEGRESS [I]* AND *SCULPTURE FOR THE BLIND [I]*, ARE ALSO VISIBLE. PABLO PICASSO'S *THREE NUDES ON SHORE* IS ABOVE THE DOOR. MUSEUM OF FINE ARTS, BOSTON, THE LANE COLLECTION. PHOTOGRAPH © 2020, MUSEUM OF FINE ARTS, BOSTON. SEE ALSO PLATES 43–47

sat Native American and Mesoamerican objects in dialogue with sculptures by Brancusi. Brancusi's *White Negress [I]* stood as a beacon on the table in the center of the room (see plate 43); his *Sculpture for the Blind [I]*, flanked by symmetrical vessels sitting on rugs, served as a sort of altar beneath the object of Hopps's contemplation (see plate 46); and sometime between 1944 and early 1950, his *Prometheus* displaced Duchamp and Calder (cf. plates 48, 49), invoking the Greek creation myth and drawing together the room's transhistorical emphasis on cosmic birth and rebirth.

Inevitably, the Arensbergs brought Duchamp back into the room's final known configuration, bringing the portrait of the artist's father in from the nearby office to survey the scene and placing the late readymade *Why Not Sneeze, Rose Sélavy?* on a pedestal near the window, where the caged cubes of marble caught the California light (see plate 48.23). And they used one last piece by Duchamp to bring religious effigies into a game-within-a-game: on the dresser in the corner, they placed a Fang reliquary guardian from Gabon and eighteenth-century Native American statues of Christ and two saints, all seemingly punching the air, directly in front of Duchamp's drawing *Boxing Match* (cf. plates 48.10, 48.14, 48.15, 48.17 to 48.13).

It was also in the sitting room where Hopps met Duchamp for the first time. Tomkins writes:

> Once, when [Hopps] was reading in the Arensbergs' [sitting room], the door opened quietly and a man he didn't know looked in, said hello, and left. Later, he learned that it had been Marcel Duchamp, who was staying at the house on a visit to California.[174]

Two decades after his teenage education in the Arensberg home, Hopps organized the first major retrospective of Duchamp's work at the Pasadena Museum of Art.[175] It is easy to see, in Tomkins's final assessment of the curator's lifelong achievement, what Hopps had learned from the Arensbergs: "His sensitivity to works of art takes in not only the works of art themselves but the dialogue that he believes can and should occur between one work and another, provided that the placement, the lighting, and the sightlines are properly worked out."[176]

THE BEDROOMS

With Walter tapping away at his adding machines and issuing instructions simultaneously to three secretaries, it is safe to assume that the whole enterprise sometimes got a bit *loud*. On occasion this activity must have spread to the sitting room, which served as another reading room, or to the guest bedroom, where there was another worktable and a glass-paned corner cabinet that held among its treasures Walter's "shared secrets" with Duchamp, *Comb* and *With Hidden Noise* (see plates 56–58).[177] We might therefore expect that the master bedroom—the most private space in the house—would be a refuge for Louise from the noise generated by the Francis Bacon Foundation (see plates 50–55).

But while Louise did not participate directly in Walter's research, it would be wrong to imagine that she distanced herself entirely. It was largely Louise's money (and her judicious use of it) that had allowed the Francis Bacon Foundation—and by extension the art and book collections—to flourish. Had this endeavor bothered her, she could easily have insisted that it take place off-site. And in essence, if not always in appearance, *she* employed the people who worked for Walter. She utilized the service of his secretaries as necessary, especially where the management of the art, the organization of her correspondence, and the hiring of contractors for the home were concerned. Moreover, given that these employees entered their upstairs offices directly and that Walter seems to have spent most of his waking hours buried in books, Louise probably had the whole of the first floor to herself for much of the day. Support for this idea—with its inversion (architecturally speaking) of an upstairs, downstairs relationship between Louise and her husband's helpers—can be found in Andrew Baker's recollection that Walter's secretaries had to hang over the banister in order to hear the visiting actor Charles Laughton at a gathering in the Arensbergs' living room, as he read passages aloud from Walter's folios of Shakespeare.[178]

This is only to suggest that Louise found or created the space she needed in other parts of the house, not to imply that her manner was imperious. If anything, the opposite seems to have been true, with most accounts calling attention to her retiring personality and her nervous shyness, which, unless she was in the company of close friends, had been a noticeable trait since she was young. Louise's private correspondence projects an intelligent, affectionate, and generous demeanor. It also conveys quite clearly that she could be tough when necessary; that it was she who taught Walter to be a better negotiator, especially when she felt that Duchamp, in partnership with his good friend (and her former lover) Roché, had begun charging exorbitant prices as sales agents for works by Brancusi.[179]

Despite the fact Louise had been occasionally distrustful of Duchamp, she did not object to hanging his painting *Sonata* (see plate 53)—an early attempt at cubism, portraying Duchamp's mother and sisters during a music recital—above the bedroom reading table. Even in their most private spaces, it was Duchamp's family rather than their own that the couple chose to display.[180] Only a single framed photograph of an Arensberg relative (barely visible on Louise's bedroom vanity in the lower right corner of plate 54) appears anywhere in *Hollywood Arensberg*. If the Arensbergs did have pictures of their family in the bedroom, it is clear they did not want them to be documented as art or visible in any of the photographs taken over several decades to represent their collection. "Nothing personal," they had told Fiske Kimball when he was preparing a catalog of the works they had bequeathed to his museum, the Philadelphia Museum of Art (PMA).[181] When it came to their self-presentation, as we have seen throughout the house, the Arensbergs wanted their art to represent them.

That is not to say that the Arensbergs refrained from a more personal approach to the works displayed in this space, where they both spent long periods recovering from illness late in life. They played their by-now-familiar games around the bedroom bureau, where a Thai sculpture of a head makes a visual pun with the bell tower of Santo Spirito pictured in Giuseppe Zocchi's *The Arno River from the Rucellai Terrace* (see plate 52). Moreover, Picasso's *Seated Nude and Standing Nude* may seem incongruous with the two early American portraits placed next to it until we notice that all four of the characters in the three paintings pictured here have their elbows bent at right angles—and even the frolicking cherub inlaid into the chest-front seems to be in on the joke.

On the bedroom walls hung the "bits of Americana" described by Louchheim: Victorian still lifes, landscapes, and an assortment of other bric-a-brac. Perhaps these were pieces that Louise and Walter felt some sentimental attachment to: family heirlooms too nice to throw away but too out of character with the rest of their artworks to display more prominently, such as a head of a Buddha; the kind of view of Venice in oil paint sold to tourists; prints by Currier and Ives, including a Volunteer Fire Company Certificate of Membership and a portrait of someone named Eliza in a "fantastic frame" (see plates 50, 51).[182] Displayed alongside Charles Sheeler's precisionist *Cactus* (see plate 55), the arrangements of art in this room might be considered more surreal than the surrealist paintings hanging in the adjacent sitting room.

Given the prevalence of sexual symbolism in the collection, it may seem strange that this most intimate of rooms bears few if any indications of the couple's physical relationship. That may be because, as their friend and confidante Beatrice Wood acknowledged in her autobiography, *I Shock Myself*, they seemed to be more interested in her liaisons than in their own:

> I often wondered if they enjoyed hearing about my little romances because of the curious relationship they had. I could not fathom it.... During the night he and Lou shared a dark wooden bed together, circa Queen Victoria. And possibly their sexual relationship came from Victoria's period too, because somewhere there was a wall between them. In front of me they discussed Walter's amorous peccadilloes openly, referring to the fact that Walter had permission to visit these little chippies, whom he paid. I listened, thunderstruck at these revelations, but never asked questions.[183]

Sex begets children, of course, and it is unknown why the Arensbergs did not—or could not—have any. Walter at times seems to have had a tin ear for Louise's sensitivity to the subject. To the Mexico City art dealer Frances Toor, he wrote that he was "simply crazy" about Frida Kahlo's 1932 painting *My Birth*—an artwork graphically depicting Kahlo emerging newly born from the vagina of a woman whose head is covered by a sheet.[184] He added that it was "marvelous, and [I] should like to own it.... Unfortunately, the price [$400] seems high."[185] Later, after its price was lowered to $300, Walter wrote to Julien Levy, the New York dealer who had taken possession of it: "The Freda [*sic*] Rivera painting of childbirth I personally should like very much to add to our collection, but it so happens that Mrs. Arensberg is not of the same mind."[186] Just a month later he would purchase a "North American Indian" sculpture from Earl Stendahl, representing a woman giving birth, which he displayed at eye level on the shelf directly behind where he sat in his private office (see plate 41.3).[187]

Perhaps there is some significance in the fact that one of the collection's only portraits of a child hung in this room (see plate 54), but given their well-known fondness for their terrier, Lollie, they may have been more interested in the dog than in the young girl who cradles it. And there is little to be gained from speculating further about the couple's sex life (or lack thereof): marriages work for all kinds of reasons, and there

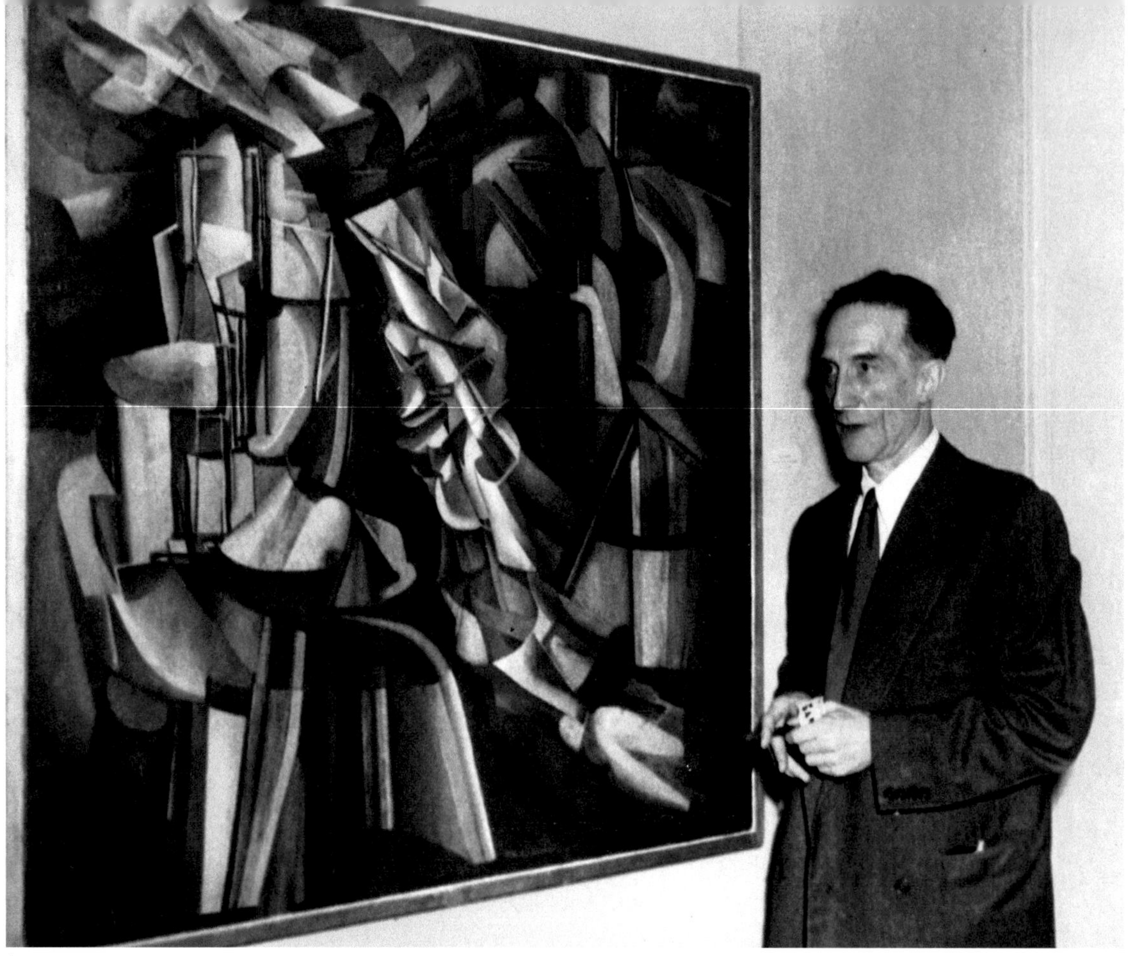

53. MARCEL DUCHAMP WITH *THE KING AND QUEEN SURROUNDED BY SWIFT NUDES*, AT THE ART INSTITUTE OF CHICAGO EXHIBITION *20TH CENTURY ART FROM THE LOUISE AND WALTER ARENSBERG COLLECTION*, CURATED BY KATHARINE KUH, 1949. PHOTOGRAPHER UNKNOWN. GELATIN SILVER PRINT, 17.5 × 21 CM. PHILADELPHIA MUSEUM OF ART, LIBRARY AND ARCHIVES, ALEXINA AND MARCEL DUCHAMP PAPERS (PMA-MDP), BOX 29, FOLDER 12. GIFT OF JACQUELINE, PAUL, AND PETER MATISSE IN MEMORY OF THEIR MOTHER, ALEXINA DUCHAMP

can be no question that Louise and Walter both provided deeply felt companionship to each other and left a precious bequest to the world. "I had the feeling that they cooperated on all sorts of levels," Walter Hopps said of them. "They were very close—each other's own best company, somehow."[188] Kuh's memoir, too, gives a glimpse of their shared passion:

> I was upstairs working on a projected catalogue of the collection. I heard shouts below—Walter calling his wife. "Lou, Lou, see what I've got!" He was beside himself, prancing around the living room in an absolute ecstasy. And there on a fine Oriental rug (the house was full of them and also of strange tattered curtains) stood two newly acquired [sculptures by] Brancusi.[189]

By 1949, however, the Arensbergs did not have much longer to enjoy their acquisitions. Nor did Kuh, who had been entertaining the expectation that her exhibition (and its richly illustrated catalog) at the Art Institute of Chicago would lead the couple to bequeath their collection to her museum (fig. 53). After this and other false starts with institutions across the United States, the couple finally acquiesced to the overtures of Fiske Kimball, officially bequeathing their collection to the PMA on 27 December 1950.

III

Endgames

THOUGH THE ARENSBERGS' art collection had found its final home, the fate of the Francis Bacon Foundation remained uncertain, with Walter urgently searching for a suitable successor to carry on his cryptographic research. On 7 December 1951, ten years to the day after the attack on Pearl Harbor, the U.S. government's top codebreaker was dispatched to the Arensbergs' Hollywood house for an unlikely job interview. The candidate was none other than William F. Friedman, who had begun his career in a Baconian think tank and then went on to lead the team that broke the Purple code used by the Japanese navy, eventually earning the Medal for Merit from President Harry S. Truman, the National Security Medal from President Dwight D. Eisenhower, and the title of world's greatest cryptologist from the historian David Kahn (fig. 54).[190]

Walter had first turned to Friedman for advice in 1925: the two men met twice in New York that autumn and exchanged dozens of letters over the following years. Their correspondence went quiet after 1930, but in June 1945 Walter wrote again to Friedman with a new plan for giving his Baconian books to the Library of Congress, along with the funds needed to support a team of researchers. Friedman agreed that Washington would be more likely than Los Angeles to attract expert codebreakers and asked for more information on the nature and aims of the Francis Bacon Foundation.[191] Arensberg said nothing more on the subject until October 1951, when he invited Friedman to Hollywood for a consultation on the future of the foundation and a glimpse of the art collection Friedman had heard so much about but had never seen.[192]

Friedman recorded his trip with characteristic precision in one of his few surviving diaries, noting that Walter put him up in a suite at the Knickerbocker Hotel ("$10.00 a day!") and comparing the cost of taxis in Los Angeles to those in Virginia ("highway robbery").[193] Arriving at the house on 8 December, Friedman received "a warm welcome from Arensberg, who looks much like he did 25 years ago . . . but a good deal more flabby and rather pin-point pupils with a glassy look in his eyes."[194] As in the earlier accounts by Louchheim and Wilson, Friedman's own eyes were quickly drawn from his host to the house:

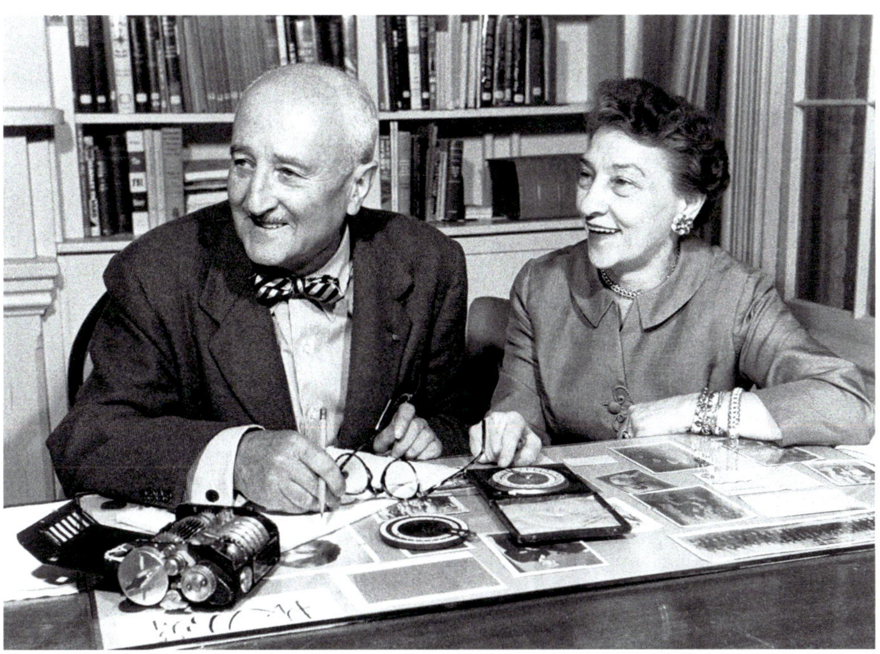

54. WILLIAM F. AND ELIZEBETH S. FRIEDMAN AT HOME IN WASHINGTON, DC. THIS PHOTOGRAPH WAS TAKEN IN 1957 TO PUBLICIZE THE COUPLE'S MAGNUM OPUS, *THE SHAKESPEAREAN CIPHERS EXAMINED*. COURTESY GEORGE C. MARSHALL FOUNDATION, LEXINGTON, VIRGINIA

> [The] home is quite an affair.... There isn't a room that doesn't have its walls covered—even the two bathrooms I visited, and I have no doubt the walls of the basement and garage are covered with paintings—all modernistic, Picassos, Duchamps, Rousseaus (4, the largest concentration of R's in the world), Matisses, etc, etc. It's really overwhelming, if you like & appreciate modern art.... The overall effect, except for the Oriental rugs on the floor, the pieces of furniture such as piano, easy chairs, and floor lamps, is that of living in an art gallery, a modern art gallery.[195]

Friedman's visit capped a particularly intense period for the Arensbergs, marked by the onset of physical illness and a growing anxiety about their artistic and intellectual legacies, which curtailed their once active social lives (fig. 55). Louise and Walter had entertained offers both serious and wishful from no fewer than thirty different organizations stretching across the continental United States and beyond; and from the beginning of 1948 through the end of 1950, as the situation became pressing, they met frequently with representatives from institutions of widely varying sizes and capabilities, each of them vying for the same prize. Even as Kuh was showing their collection in Chicago, the Arensbergs were secretly looking to place it elsewhere.[196] Among the contenders were the Fogg Art Museum at Harvard (Walter's alma mater); the National Gallery of Art in Washington, DC; the Instituto Nacional de Bellas Artes in Mexico City; and both of New York's premier museums, the Museum of Modern Art and the Metropolitan Museum of Art.

The main sticking point in these negotiations—as in others that had taken place in earlier years—was the couple's demand that the recipient of their art should also maintain their library and continue Walter's Baconian research. Hoping that their collections could stay in California ("nearby where I could enjoy them," Walter told Fiske Kimball and his wife, Marie, upon their first meeting in 1947[197]), the Arensbergs had initially signed a contract with UCLA in 1944. The university hired the architect Clarence Stein to draw up plans for a proposed complex combining an exhibition hall, library, and performance venue. Stein soon fell out with UCLA's supervising architect, David Allison, and relations broke down between the Arensbergs and the university's conservative Board of Regents, who annulled their agreement on 1 October 1947.[198]

Soon after, Louise and Walter briefly entertained the idea of giving their artworks to an ambitious new museum called the Modern Institute of Art, recently opened in Beverly Hills. A brainchild of the actor Vincent Price (who had conceived of it in part as a way to keep the Arensbergs' collection in California), the Modern Institute found initial success through a robust exhibition schedule and outreach program. In spite of its popularity in the community, however, the museum found few sponsors and failed spectacularly only two years after its incorporation.[199]

Throughout these turbulent years, Duchamp and Kimball, independently and jointly invested in the fate of the collection, proved adept at reading the Arensbergs' moods, understanding their changing demands, and sidestepping the various intrigues playing out between the couple and their suitors. Both men accepted what Walter seemingly could not: the Baconian project was a nonstarter at any credible academic institution. Duchamp, concerned about the ultimate destination for the majority of his most important artworks, maneuvered nimbly between all interested parties, joining the board of the Francis Bacon Foundation as the gift to Philadelphia was being negotiated; making detailed sketches with Kimball of how the Arensbergs' artworks could be hung in the PMA; and bequeathing *The Large Glass* to the museum on behalf of the executors of Katherine Dreier's estate.[200]

The breakthroughs in Kimball's campaign to secure the collection for Philadelphia were his promise to seek an arrangement with the nearby Free Library for the continuance of the Francis Bacon Foundation, and the set of small sketches he made in early 1949 suggesting to the Arensbergs that his museum would retain

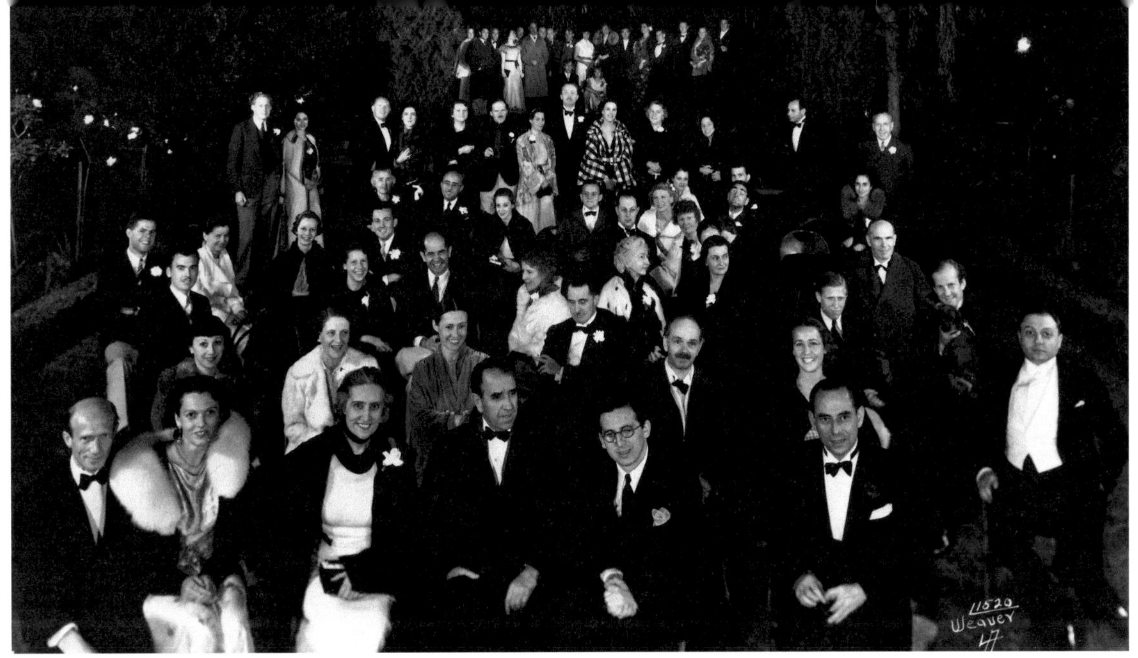

55. AN EVENING GARDEN PARTY, POSSIBLY FOR THE BENEFIT OF THE LOS ANGELES PHILHARMONIC, CA. 1935–36. PHOTOGRAPH BY WEAVER, LOS ANGELES. THE LOS ANGELES PHILHARMONIC WAS A GREAT PASSION OF LOUISE ARENSBERG'S; SHE IS SEATED BEHIND THE LEFT SHOULDER OF THE MAN IN THE MIDDLE OF THE PHOTOGRAPH. AMONG THE OTHERS PICTURED ARE RICHARD LERT, MUSIC DIRECTOR AND CONDUCTOR OF THE PASADENA SYMPHONY; THE COMPOSER FRANZ WAXMAN, WHO SCORED FILMS INCLUDING *THE BRIDE OF FRANKENSTEIN* (1935) AND *REBECCA* (1940); AND THE CHAMBER MUSIC PATRON ELIZABETH SPRAGUE COOLIDGE. PHILADELPHIA MUSEUM OF ART, NAOMI SAWELSON-GORSE RESEARCH COLLECTION, BOX 8, FOLDER 2

the essential elements of their domestic setting (figs. 56a, b).[201] He shared these drawings with the couple at their Hollywood home on 7 February 1949; they added their initials to the sketches as a sign of their early enthusiasm. Kimball sent a triumphant dispatch to PMA chairman Sturgis Ingersoll at the end of that day:

> I have the feeling we are winning.... [Art Institute of Chicago director Daniel Catton] Rich only offered him... a rotating partial showing... and this was not satisfactory.... I asked [Walter] if he would be content to put the pre-Columbian stuff elsewhere in the building, to gain more space. Yes, he would. I suggested somewhere between the Gothic, when America was unknown, and the Renaissance, when it was first discovered.... He liked this scheme. He said he felt the Gallatin gallery, of which I had a photograph, was too high.... I said, "Swell; of twelve rooms available in that area, eleven are of ordinary domestic proportions; the high one, though two stories, is a common feature of many private houses. I see just how to do it all."
>
> Marie said, "Fiske will draw and build you your dream house."[202]

Louise and Walter were not fully persuaded that Kimball's blueprint retained the essential features of their Hollywood house: two months later, Walter sent a telegram reminding Kimball that they were still considering other institutions able to build a new space "in which the collection could be housed in accordance with certain ideals that we have tried... to exemplify in our own home."[203] In particular, the Arensbergs were worried (as Walter put it in a backtracking letter of 27 April) about the "problems of circulation, perspective, and escape from the museum confinement, via side windows, into the surrounding daylight":

> We would like... a better setting for the Klees than the cribbed, cabined, and confined space to which you have allocated them—in a room, by the way, which is scarcely more than one-half the size of our own bedroom. And we would also like a better setting for our unique collection of the works of Duchamp. There is a make-shift character about the space for them... which—in our opinion—does nothing whatever to release and enhance their inner spirit.[204]

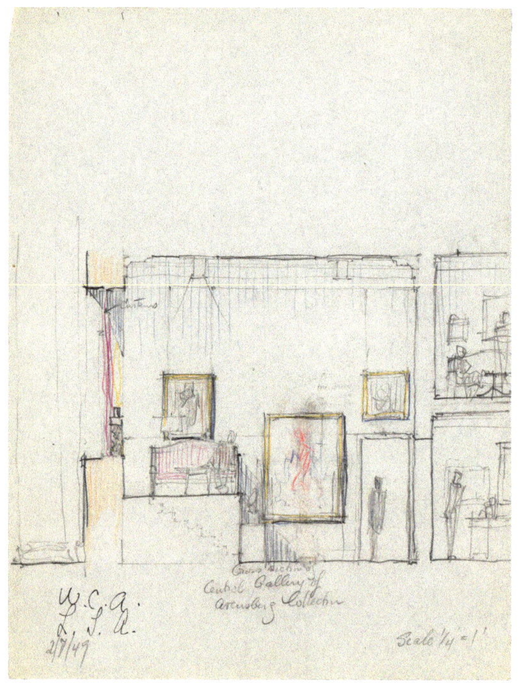

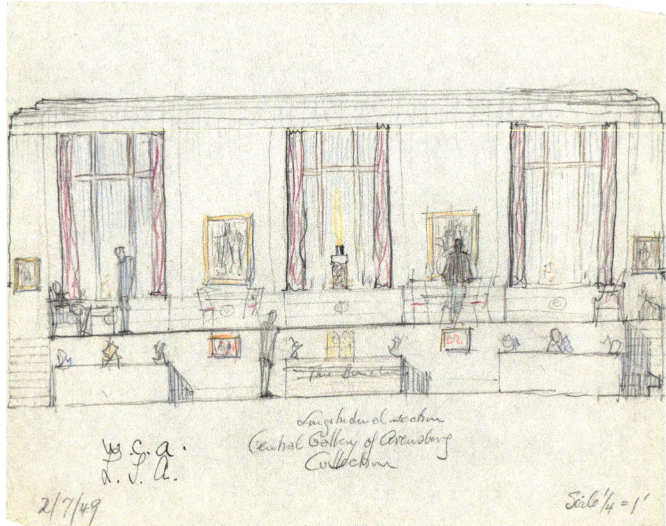

56A, B. FISKE KIMBALL. GALLERY SKETCHES, 7 FEBRUARY 1949. BOTH: COLORED PENCIL AND GRAPHITE ON PAPER, LEFT: 27.9 × 21.6 CM; RIGHT: 21.6 × 27.9 CM. KIMBALL USED THESE DRAWINGS TO CONVINCE THE ARENSBERGS THAT THEIR COLLECTION WOULD RETAIN ASPECTS OF ITS ORIGINAL DOMESTIC SETTING IF THEY GAVE IT TO THE PHILADELPHIA MUSEUM OF ART. PHILADELPHIA MUSEUM OF ART, LIBRARY AND ARCHIVES, FISKE KIMBALL RECORDS (PMA-FKR), BOX 181, FOLDER 3

Once again, Kimball and Duchamp worked together to find a way through the impasse. On 6 May, Kimball reported that Duchamp had visited the museum and suggested a multifloor option that would preserve the effect achieved by the Arensbergs in Hollywood: "Instead of spreading out, one can go up and down like a house; with the big windows upstairs as well as down. There is no reason the whole floor of the present downstairs north gallery shouldn't be raised, so that all of it looks out on the terraces and garden."[205] It took Kimball more than a year to resolve the challenges presented by this solution, and it was not until autumn 1950 that he secured the gift for his museum. In the end, he conceded additional galleries for the collection, but what sealed the deal was his proposal to install a glass-paned door from the galleries out to the balcony overlooking the museum's east terrace. This design built into the galleries in Philadelphia echoes what the Arensbergs were looking for in their Hollywood house.

With these problems fixed, the Arensbergs began, with some sadness, to pack up their collection. During their few remaining years at 7065 Hillside, "Louise and Walter grieved as they watched their art collection slowly depart...to its new home in Philadelphia. They agonized over which objects to send, finding it increasingly difficult to 'kiss [their] children good-bye.'"[206]

The couple's struggles with their deteriorating health, moreover, prevented them from visiting the works in Philadelphia. Louise wrote to Fiske Kimball in October 1950:

> It is stupid to be ill, particularly as we had been counting on a trip to Philadelphia in the middle of November—now it hardly looks possible. We look forward with such a feeling of satisfaction to the time when our "Collection" may enter into kingdom come in the Philadelphia Museum.[207]

In 1951 and 1952, Walter required surgery to treat ongoing problems stemming from an earlier cerebral hemorrhage that had caused the temporary loss of sight in one of his eyes. Louise underwent exploratory surgery in late September 1953, revealing a "terminal carcinoma" that was "widespread and much more

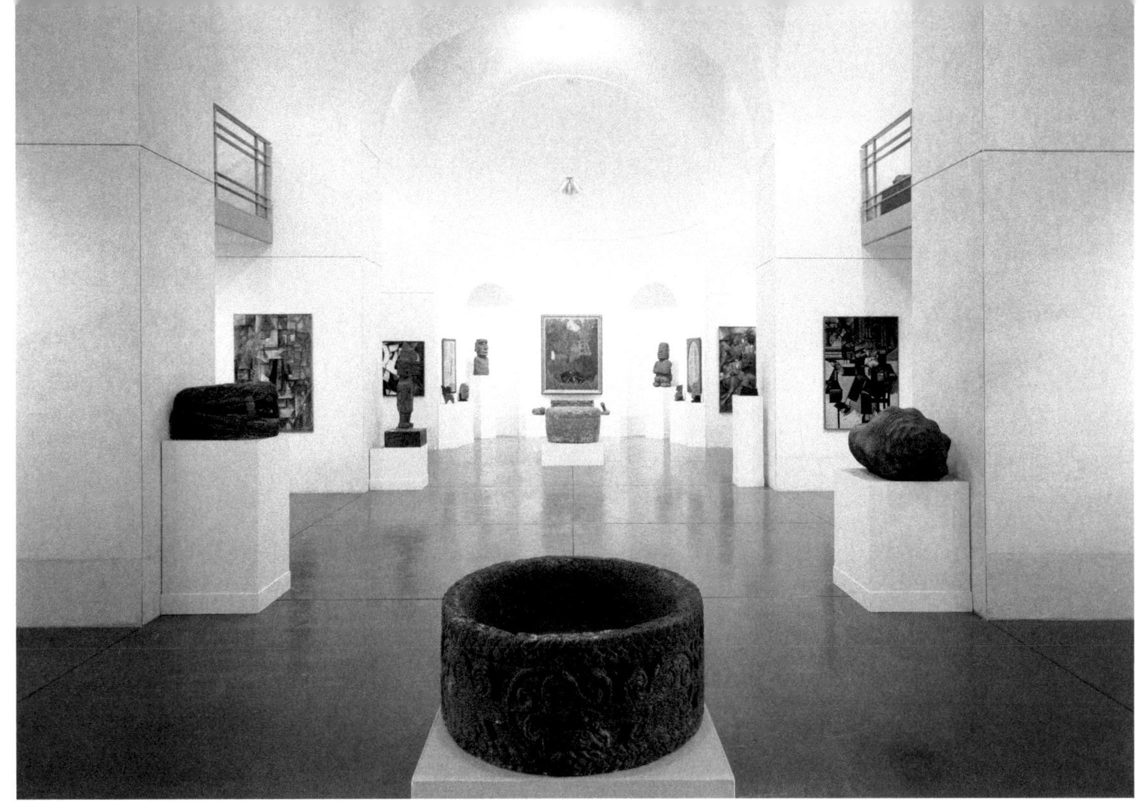

57. THE TRIBUNE OF THE ARENSBERG GALLERIES AT THE PHILADELPHIA MUSEUM OF ART, 29 JUNE 1954. PHOTOGRAPHER UNKNOWN. THE COLLECTION OPENED TO THE PUBLIC A FEW MONTHS LATER, ON 16 OCTOBER 1954. PHILADELPHIA MUSEUM OF ART, LIBRARY AND ARCHIVES, RIGHTS AND REPRODUCTIONS PHOTOGRAPH COLLECTION (PMA-RNR), BOX 64

advanced than expected."[208] In the weeks after her diagnosis, she received almost daily letters from her dearest friend, Beatrice Wood, then living and producing art in nearby Ojai. Attempting to take Louise's mind off her present pain, Wood reflected on the impact of her close access to the couple and their collection for nearly forty years:

> How much it has meant in my life, to sit with you, and absorb as part of daily living, the wonderful paintings and sculptures that you have had. How even much more it has meant to talk to you. After the narrowness of my mother's house, you opened the world for me.[209]

Louise died on 24 November 1953. Walter, inconsolable, followed shortly afterward, passing on 29 January 1954. As Wood later put it in her memoir, "He was all alone in the big house with ... fabulous treasures that had become meaningless to him. He did not want to live without Lou."[210]

After Louise died, a note she had written in relation to one of their artworks was found in the drawer of her bedroom dresser. Titled "Chagall: Le Poète," its prayer could have been addressed to the artist Marc Chagall, to the titular poet in his painting that had long hung in the Arensbergs' living room (*Half-Past Three [The Poet]*; see plate 22), or perhaps to her husband, the poet with whom she had shared her life:

> Every day I see the same thing
> I feel that I am dying
> The sacred tongue
> Trembles. Pray for me
> Every day the same thing
> My cursed tongue is trembling
> To you now I pray for help.[211]

Rare personal documents like this one passed into the silence of the Arensbergs' archive; after their deaths, it fell to Kimball to pay tribute to the couple when the museum's new galleries opened (fig. 57). His questions to Louise and Walter about the history and rationale of their collecting had been rebuffed, so the new custodian of the collection turned to those who knew the Arensbergs best, stitching their reminiscences into a glowing tribute published in the Christmas 1954 edition of *ARTnews*. Kimball gave the last word to his own wife, Marie, who painted a fond portrait of the couple they came to know well in the last years of their lives:

> Like so many before us, we had come to California with the specific intention of robbing them—of their collection.... No one could have been more gentle, more generous, or more eager to find an appropriate and permanent home for their noble pictures. Walter, who had stimulated the assemblage of the collection, was like a great, shaggy dog.... As he came dashing down the stairs from his library, with yet another drawing or document under discussion—as he was always doing—his merry smile illuminated the room and added to the lustre of the great paintings that adorned its walls.... Lou, a tiny, frail woman, with a mop of white curls and startling blue eyes, shared his every enthusiasm and prejudice.[212]

Other friends whose acquaintance stretched back to the couple's years in Cambridge and New York—Wallace Stevens, Walter Pach, Alfred Kreymborg, and Carl Van Vechten—contributed to Kimball's admiring account. But many of these friends had long since lost contact with the couple, and others had been privately expressing their doubts about Walter's artistic sensibility, and even his sanity, for several decades.

As early as 1917, William Ivins had written to Paul Sachs about the detrimental influence of psychoanalysis and avant-garde art on their former classmate: Walter, he complained, "is what the French call a verbomane, a person for whom words are things to be arranged, just as some of the Frenchmen of the period just before the war arranged pieces of newspaper and bits of rubber shoe with old match-boxes on a canvas and called it great painting."[213] By then settled in the Arensbergs' old house in Cambridge (Shady Hill), Sachs would soon launch his course in curating at Harvard that would run from 1921 to 1948 and shape the makers of American museums for several generations.[214]

In 1926, Ivins's complaint turned to lament, and when a meeting over dinner in New York revealed the extent of Walter's Baconian obsessions, Ivins gave a despairing account to the art historian Bernard Berenson:

> Last night I paid dearly at the altar of old friendship... with Walter Arensberg who twenty-five years ago was the sweetest, most sensitive, most subtle minded boy I ever knew—and now is fat and middle-aged and quite gaga on Bacon and Shakespeare and Egyptian mysteries and acrostics and phallic symbols and "Œdipus complexes," his feet way up in the clouds and his poor subtle complex brain deep in a muck pile.[215]

For Ivins, Walter was now best left to "Freud, Jung, Adler &al,"[216] and by the time Friedman had his own reunion with Walter twenty-five years later, he came to the same conclusion, finding Walter "very interesting and most lucid" on the topic of modern art but "quite mad on this subject [of Bacon and Shakespeare]."[217]

Concerns for Walter's fixation on Baconian conspiracy theories—as well as for his general emotional health—are recorded with differing degrees of anger, bewilderment, and even betrayal in the correspondence of many friends and associates during the Arensbergs' final years in Los Angeles. Among those compelled to document their thoughts was the psychiatrist and journalist Jules Langsner, who served as the Los Angeles

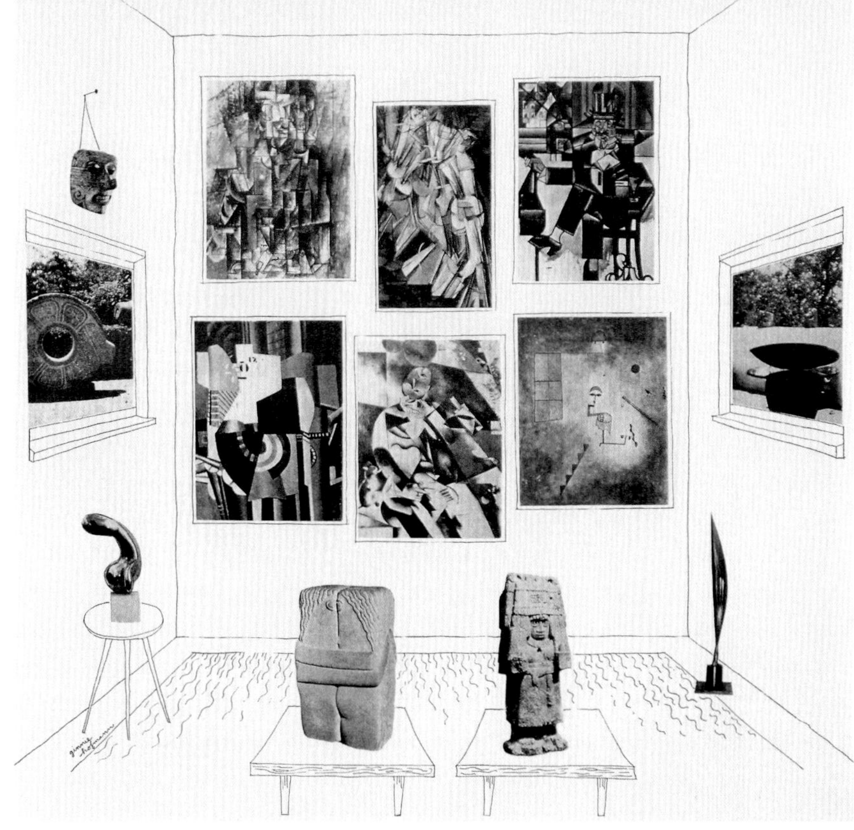

58. GINNIE HOFMANN. ILLUSTRATION ACCOMPANYING "THE ARENSBERG RICHES OF CUBISM," BY JULES LANGSNER, IN THE NOVEMBER 1949 ISSUE OF *ARTNEWS*

correspondent for *ARTnews*. Responding to his editor's futile plea for personal detail in the account he was writing of the Arensberg exhibition in Chicago (fig. 58), Langsner confided,

> It is my considered opinion, and you may not quote me, that [Walter's] abnormal reticence... is actually a grandiosity of considerable scale. He is willing to emerge, by implication, as a godlike figure, untarnished by humanizing description. He is a typical obsessive, compulsive type; perfectionist, fickle, suspicious, contentious, and brilliant.[218]

Around the same time, at Walter's urging, the scholar and curator Karl With had reluctantly replaced his friend Kenneth Ross as director of the Modern Institute of Art. He enjoyed his "frequent visits" with the Arensbergs, whose "home was like an oasis in the artistic desert of Los Angeles," but he found Walter's devotion to Duchamp hard to fathom and his Baconian research positively pathological:

> Arensberg's inclination to the absurd and eccentric seemed to me irreconcilable with his selective taste as evidenced in his painting collection. Still more incomprehensible to me were his obsessive and absorbing efforts to dethrone Shakespeare in favor of Francis Bacon's authorship.
>
> Walter Arensberg, as I see it, exhibited typical signs of a split personality. Strange as it may sound, one might have called him a "gregarious recluse," who one day appeared to be sociable, animated, even affectionate and talkative, on another day withdrawn, tense, inaccessible and even malevolent.[219]

Friedman, for his part, concluded that "the whole business is most curious and well worth writing up in psychiatric annals."[220] He did write it up, as it happens, as a cryptographic rather than a psychiatric case study: only three years after his visit, Friedman and his wife, Elizebeth (a gifted codebreaker in her own right), had finished their book-length rebuttal of the various methods proposed by Baconians to find secret ciphers in the texts of Shakespeare. Published in 1957 as *The Shakespearean Ciphers Examined*, the book featured a long chapter devoted to Walter's "*idée fixe*" and poured particular scorn on his lifelong faith in anagrams and acrostics.[221]

However, greater minds than Walter's had been passionate in their pursuit of the Baconian hypothesis (among them Mark Twain, Henry James, and Sigmund Freud himself[222]), and Walter was neither the only nor the most famous figure in the first half of the twentieth century to take the search for hidden alphabetical codes beyond the point of reason.[223] Between 1907 and 1911, Ferdinand de Saussure produced his foundational *Course of General Linguistics*, which prepared the ground for a new science of language. But a survey of his research notes for that project, some fifty years after his death, turned up a cache of 134 notebooks that uncovered another, more surprising line of inquiry. These rediscovered notes reveal that while he was writing *Course*, Saussure was also carrying out a feverish quest for anagrams in Indo-European literature. Convinced that hidden alphabetical patterns offered the key to a lost structural code in Latin, Greek, and Vedic poetry, he eventually filled 24 books with possible anagrams from Homer and another 19 with notes from Virgil. The more Saussure looked, the more he found, but instead of confirming his hunches, this proliferation of evidence unsettled him and led him to "wonder if one might not find definitive proof of all possible words in any text."[224] Saussure found himself relying upon a sense of intuition that he never fully trusted and, suffering from what he described as "a morbid horror of the pen," he finally set the project aside without publishing any of his findings. For some later linguists, these experiments were an episode of dementia that is best forgotten. For others, they were a ludic counterpoint to his orthodox work, serving as inspired glimpses of poetic meaning that pointed to different rules—and perhaps even different games—for language.[225]

Walking the line between the playful and the providential, and testing the boundary between method and madness, *anagrammateurs* are tireless in their discovery of the new words that lie buried within old ones. As the ultimate instrument of the *possible*, the anagram is rarely able to serve as evidence of intention or origin. When Walter's project is framed this way, it is easy to see why the Arensbergs were drawn so forcefully to the work of Duchamp, whose strategic development (as Aline Louchheim observed) could be clearly traced by walking through the rooms in their house:

> You can see how it all happened, how the Cézannesque portrait gave way to the multiple views in a painting of his sisters and how that in turn led to the famous *Nude Descending a Staircase* (which is present in four versions), with its "decomposition of forms." Finally you observe the stress on ideas in painting in *The King and Queen* [*Surrounded by Swift Nudes*] and the reference to the machine in *The Bride*.[226]

Even closer connections between Walter's work on anagrams and the objects in the couple's collection might be found in the dense network of carpets and other weavings that covered every floor and many pieces of furniture (fig. 59)—often commented on by visitors, but easy to overlook in the photographic record (particularly when captured in black and white).[227] The Arensbergs arranged these woven patterns from diverse cultures like pieces of a puzzle, adding another set of combinatorial grids to the worlds in which Walter worked. Here, too, as Marina Warner has shown, he was in good company. In her account of the carpet-covered couch on which Freud analyzed the dreams of his patients, Warner teases out the "relations between the structures of the unconscious and the patterning and weave of a rug" that struck psychoanalysts and poets alike at the turn of the twentieth century.[228]

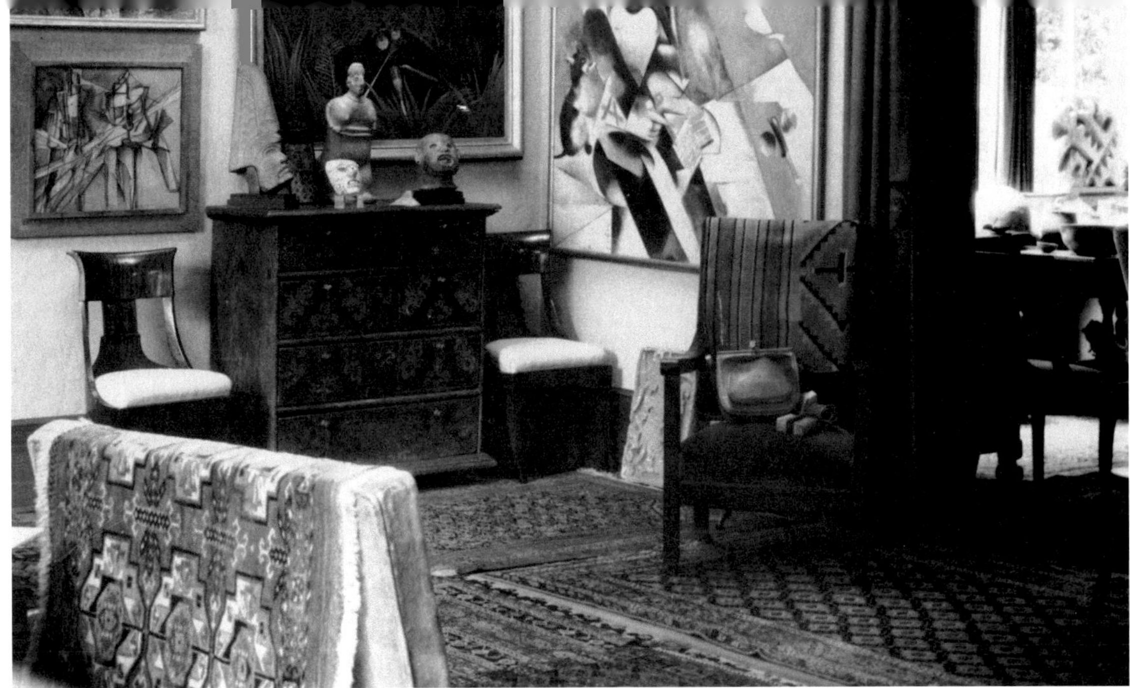

59. LEOPOLD (DICK) SEYFFERT JR. DETAIL OF A PHOTOGRAPH OF THE ARENSBERGS' LIVING ROOM, CA. 1945 (AFTER 15 MARCH). PHILADELPHIA MUSEUM OF ART, LIBRARY AND ARCHIVES, SEYFFERT PHOTOGRAPH COLLECTION. COURTESY ROBERT SEYFFERT

Like the interpretation of dreams and the production of poetry, searching for anagrams is more like playing out a series of possible moves than arriving at conclusive proof. And such games would not end, as Friedman observed during his final encounter with Walter in 1951, as long as there were new combinations still to be explored:

> He subconsciously knows, I believe, that his quest is hopeless but his system is such that for the rest of his life he can continue with the method, never finding positive proof—but never excluding the possibility that by continuous modification of his "alphabet" some day, somebody will find the right alphabet and good plain text . . . will be found.[229]

Sensing that there was little point in challenging Walter's "system," Friedman shifted the conversation to the Francis Bacon Foundation, with its deep resources for the study of the subject of their mutual admiration. After trying—and failing—to detach Walter's extraordinary library from his cryptographic project, Friedman cut his visit short and left feeling "sad at the thought of the utter waste of talent, effort, and money out chasing a will-o-wisp."[230]

Both the person who separated Walter's *ignis fatuus* from his valuable books and the institutions willing to house his library were ultimately found close to home. The Arensbergs' trusted assistant, Elizabeth Wrigley, took over the directorship of the Francis Bacon Foundation not long after Walter's death in 1954 and oversaw the construction of a dedicated building on the campus of the Claremont Colleges, opening it to the public in 1960. In many important ways, the environment Wrigley created there was a physical extension of the Arensbergs' lives and home—it was dedicated to the continuity of their foundation's mission and decorated with the books, rugs, furniture, and artifacts that had not been part of the original bequest to the PMA (figs. 60a–c). Using the cryptographic methods Walter had developed, Wrigley and her employees at the library continued his work on the Bacon/Shakespeare authorship question for several more years, ultimately deciding that it was not productive to continue without his input. Though "dreadfully pro-Bacon," Wrigley became increasingly agnostic on the authorship controversy, describing the library in 1981 simply as "a clearinghouse for Bacon scholarship."[231] Her modest declaration belied her growing accomplishment in expanding the library—which was already, during the Arensbergs' lifetime, the largest private collection of rare books related to Bacon—to more than 14,000 titles.

60A–C. FRANCIS BACON FOUNDATION LIBRARY, CA. 1960S. ELIZABETH WRIGLEY IS IN THE PHOTOGRAPH AT THE TOP LEFT. PHOTOGRAPH BY R. C. FRAMPTON PHOTO, CLAREMONT. THE HUNTINGTON LIBRARY, FRANCIS BACON LIBRARY ARCHIVE, WALTER AND LOUISE ARENSBERG PAPERS (HEH-FBLA), BOX 5, FOLDER 2

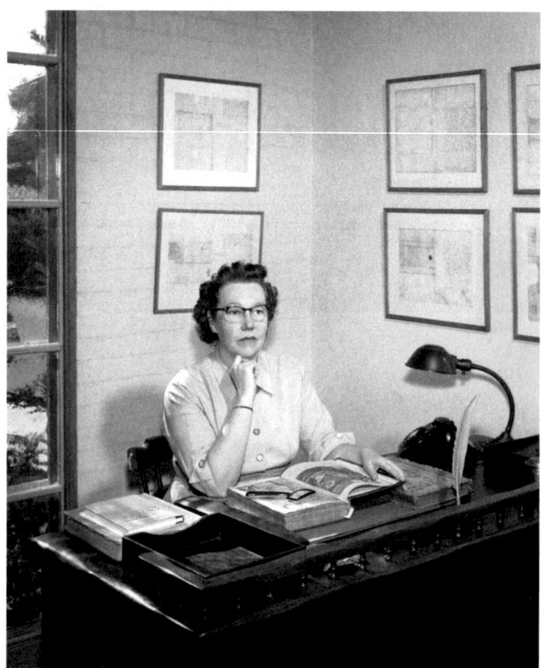

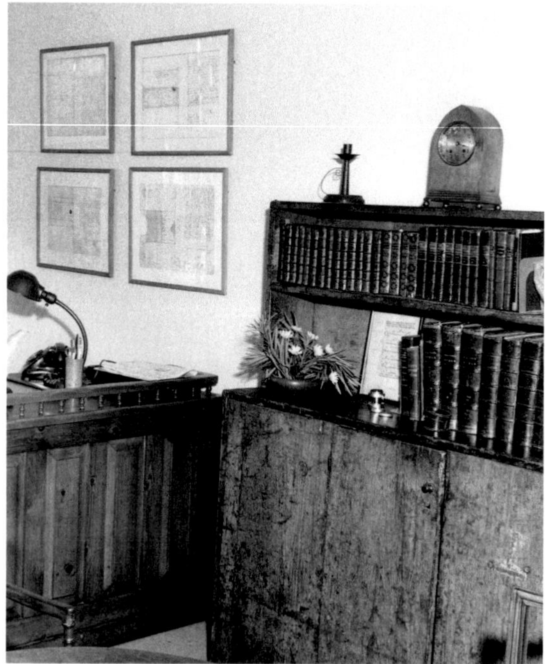

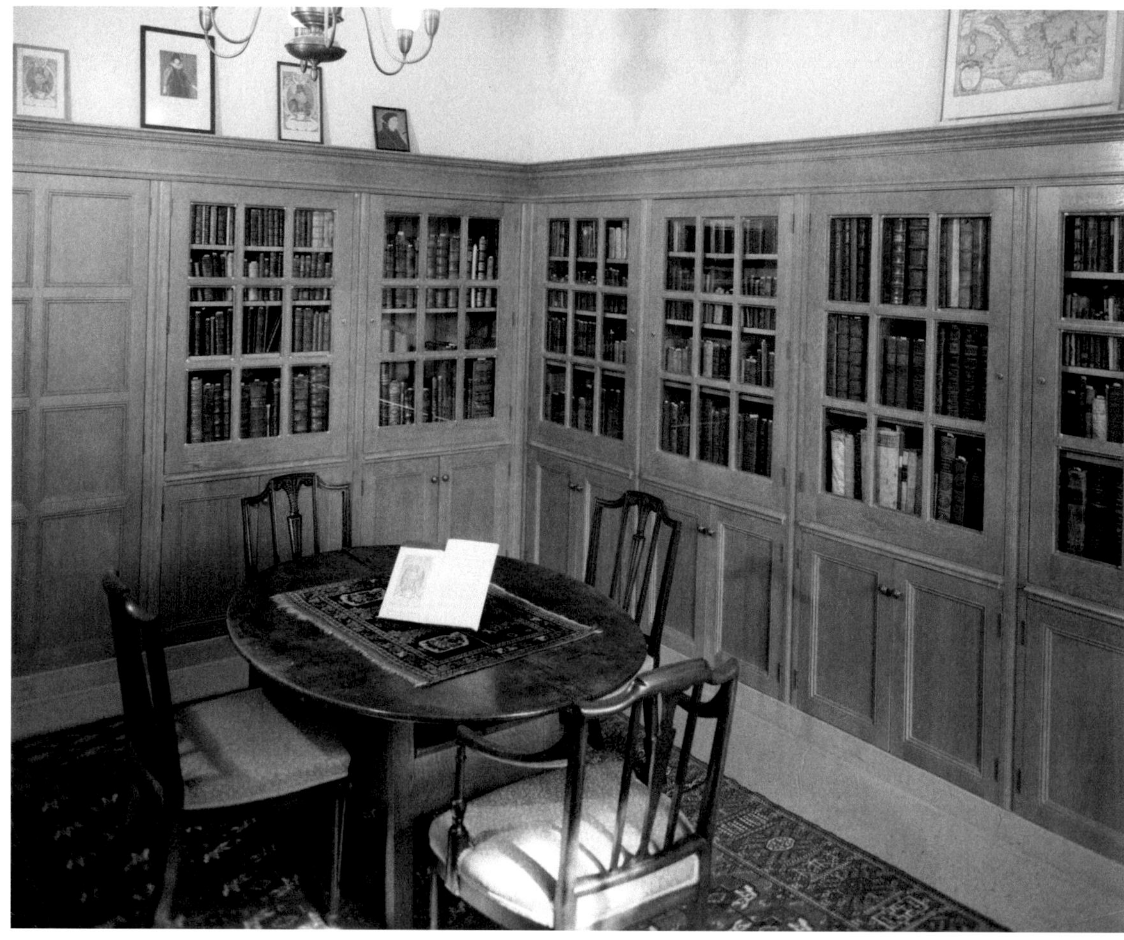

In 1995, with Wrigley's health failing and with financial pressure mounting, the foundation's board decided to close the library and give its contents to the Huntington Library in nearby San Marino. The successful transfer of this collection—along with funds for cataloging, for visiting fellowships, and for book prizes—completed the unfinished process begun by the Arensbergs more than forty years earlier when they signed their initial agreement with Kimball, allowing both the art and the books to be cared for by professionals, consulted by specialists, and enjoyed by the general public.

Bringing these divided collections back into a single frame (as we have attempted to do here) reopens the dialogue between Renaissance literature and modernist art, at once reinforcing the cognitive dissonance expressed so poignantly by Friedman and Ivins and reactivating the Royal Game that Louise and Walter played in their Hollywood home. After all, whether moving pictures around the house or rearranging the letters of the Shakespeare Folios, the Arensbergs are best seen as players of chess—which, as Stefan Zweig put it in his *Schachnovelle* (*Chess: A Novella*) of 1942, is much more than a game:

> Is it not also a science and an art, hovering between those categories as Muhammad's coffin hovered between heaven and earth, a unique link between pairs of opposites: ancient yet eternally new; mechanical in structure, yet made effective only by the imagination; limited to a geometrically fixed space, yet with unlimited combinations; constantly developing, yet sterile . . . but nonetheless shown to be more durable in its entity and existence than all books and works of art; the only game that belongs to all nations and all eras, although no one knows what god brought it down to earth to vanquish boredom, sharpen the senses and stretch the mind. Where does it begin and where does it end?[232]

Louise and Walter ultimately found a way to play chess with Francis Bacon and Marcel Duchamp in a game that would never end. The collections now housed by the Philadelphia Museum of Art and the Huntington Library allow new generations to keep playing too.

†

FORMER POSSESSIONS OF THE ARENSBERGS SHOWN IN THE TOP PHOTOGRAPHS, OPPOSITE, INCLUDE A CANDLESTICK AND SNUFFER (HEH-FBLA, FA-2/798); A MANTEL CLOCK MADE BY THE CHELSEA CLOCK CO., BOSTON, INSCRIBED WITH THE MODEL NUMBER 20556 (HEH-FBLA, FA-4/1025); A LEAF ON VELLUM FROM AN ITALIAN SERVICE BOOK, CA. 1475 (HUNTINGTON LIBRARY, FRANCIS BACON LIBRARY MANUSCRIPTS COLLECTION [HEH-FBLMC], BOX 1, CALL NUMBER FBL 1); AND A COPPER BOWL. FOR THE BOWL, SEE ALSO PAGE 417, NOTE 4.4.

AMONG THE AUTOGRAPH LETTERS HANGING ON THE WALLS (TOP LEFT AND RIGHT) IS ONE DATED 4 AUGUST 1606 FROM SIR FRANCIS BACON TO HIS COUSIN SIR THOMAS POSTHUMOUS HOBBY. IT WAS PARTICULARLY SIGNIFICANT TO WALTER BECAUSE IN IT BACON WROTE, "YOUR LOVING CONGRATULATION FOR MY DOUBLED LIFE, AS YOU CALL IT, I THANK YOU FOR." WALTER FELT THAT CRYPTIC LINE FURTHER VALIDATED THE IDEA THAT BACON WROTE THE PLAYS ATTRIBUTED TO WILLIAM SHAKESPEARE. FOR THE TEXT OF THIS LETTER, SEE *THE WORKS OF FRANCIS BACON*, VOL. 10, *THE LETTERS AND THE LIFE*, VOL. 3, ED. JAMES SPEDDING, ROBERT LESLIE ELLIS, AND DOUGLAS DENON HEATH (LONDON: LONGMANS, GREEN, READER, AND DYER, 1868), 298. FOR THE LETTER ITSELF, SEE HEH-FBLMC, BOX 1, CALL NUMBER FBL 7. THREE OTHER LETTERS ON THE WALL ARE AS FOLLOWS: A LETTER FROM NATHANIEL BACON TO ROGER TOWNSHEND OF 24 NOVEMBER 1619; A LETTER FROM THE PRIVY COUNCIL (GREAT BRITAIN) TO JOHN TEMPLE OF 4 AUGUST 1606; AND A LETTER FROM FRANCIS BACON TO SIR JULIUS CAESAR OF 13 JULY 1609. THESE ARE HEH-FBLMC, BOX 1, CALL NUMBERS FBL 5, FBL 6, AND FBL 9, RESPECTIVELY. THE OTHER TWO LETTERS PICTURED HERE ARE DESCRIBED ON PAGE 416, NOTES 2.1 AND 2.3.

OBJECTS IDENTIFIED IN THE BOTTOM PHOTOGRAPH INCLUDE A FRAMED ENGRAVING OF FRANCIS BACON BY WENCESLAS HOLLAR (HEH-FBLA, B-7/412); A FRAMED ENGRAVING OF FRANCIS BACON BY W. T. FRY, AFTER A DRAWING BY R. W. SATCHWELL FROM AN ORIGINAL BY VAN SOMER (NOT FOUND, SEE PMA-WLA, BOX 27, AIN 414/LATER LIBRARY "B" #9); A FRAMED PHOTOGRAPHIC COPY OF A PAINTING, AFTER HANS HOLBEIN THE YOUNGER, OF SIR WILLIAM BUTTS (HEH-FBLA, B-2/383); AND A MAP BY ABRAHAM ORTELIUS TITLED *ARGONAUTICA (ILLUSTRISSIMO PRINCIPI CAROLO COMITI ARENBERGIO, BARONI SEPTIMONTII, DOMINO MIRAVARTII, EQUITI AUREI VELLERIS, ETC.)* (HEH LIBRARY, NOT CATALOGED). MOST OF THE ANTIQUE CARPETS OWNED BY THE ARENSBERGS (AND LATER THE FBL), INCLUDING THE ONE SHOWN IN THIS PICTURE, ARE NOW IN THE HUNTINGTON ART COLLECTIONS. SEE ALSO PAGE 417, NOTE 5.

THE BOOKSHELF, TABLE, AND CHAIRS IN THESE PHOTOGRAPHS CAN BE SEEN IN PLATE 43.

Notes

1. Helen Freeman Corle, "Notes on the Work of Marcel Duchamp and Their Effect upon a Contemporary" (unpublished manuscript, July 1949–July 1950), Philadelphia Museum of Art, Library and Archives, Arensberg Archives (hereafter cited as PMA-WLA), box 43, folder 24, p. 21. Corle, a frequent guest at the Arensberg home, had small roles in film dramas of the 1930s—most notably D. W. Griffith's *Abraham Lincoln*. Her long essay was both a personal record of her friendship with Duchamp and an assessment of the role of the artist's work in the Arensberg collection. In the passage quoted here, Corle transcribes the title of Duchamp's painting *Le roi et la reine entourés de nus vites* as "Le Roi et La Reine entoure par le nues vites." In this volume, we use the English translation of the painting's title for ease of reading.

2. Aline B. Louchheim, "The Arensbergs Bought Cubists Then," *New York Times*, 23 October 1949, X9. Louchheim's tour provided the raw material for her survey *The Proud Possessors: The Lives, Times and Tastes of Some Adventurous American Art Collectors*, published under her married name, Aline B. Saarinen (New York: Random House, 1958).

3. See Naomi Sawelson-Gorse, "Hollywood Conversations: Duchamp and the Arensbergs," in *West Coast Duchamp*, ed. Bonnie Clearwater (Miami Beach: Grassfield in association with Shoshana Wayne Gallery, 1991), 26. One particularly fraught battle fought over a planned arts festival in 1951 pitted the Arensbergs' close acquaintance Kenneth Ross, director of the Los Angeles Municipal Arts Department, against city councilman Harold Harby, who decried modern art as Communist and anti-American. Of this dispute and others like it, the cultural historian D. J. Waldie has written: "Despite its aspects of comic hysteria, the culture war over modern art was real and serious. Arts administrators were cowed, instructors were hounded in the city's art academies, and public art works in modern styles were sequestered." Waldie, "Shock of the New: Los Angeles vs. Modernism," *KCET*, 21 July 2016, https://www.kcet.org/shows/lost-la/shock-of-the-new-los-angeles-vs-modernism. See also Sarah Schrank, "Painting the Town Red," in *Art and the City: Civic Imagination and Cultural Authority in Los Angeles* (Philadelphia: University of Pennsylvania Press, 2009), 64–96. For some rare exceptions in the fields of art, architecture, and photography, see Victoria Dailey, Natalie Shivers, and Michael Dawson, *LA's Early Moderns: Art, Architecture, Photography* (Los Angeles: Balcony, 2003).

4. Charis Wilson and Wendy Madar, *Through Another Lens: My Years with Edward Weston* (New York: North Point, 1998), 27–28. Wilson was introduced to the Arensbergs by the artist Beatrice Wood, whose autobiography, *I Shock Myself: The Autobiography of Beatrice Wood*, ed. Lindsay Smith, rev. ed. (San Francisco: Chronicle, 1985), described her own long friendship with the Arensbergs.

5. Not everyone found Walter's cryptic lessons so convincing. Charis Wilson's partner Edward Weston engaged with Walter in a long-running argument about the meaning of the natural forms he captured in his photographs: where Walter found phallic symbolism and saw "a pun for a torso," Weston saw "a rock fragment with a beautiful form, and [insisted] he had photographed it not to make a pun about something it might be thought to resemble but to reveal the essential structure and beauty of [a] particular rock." "For a long time," Wilson confessed, "I was secretly on Walter's side of the argument. It was he who had taught me to look for the hidden meanings in pictures, to pursue the clues an artist weaves into his work to define his intentions. My eyes would need a long re-education before I began to see Edward's photographs as he saw them." Wilson and Madar, *Through Another Lens*, 28, 82–83.

6. The vastness of this book collection is not well illustrated in this volume, mostly because there is little photographic documentation of the second-floor offices of the Francis Bacon Foundation. Today most of the Arensbergs' books are still accessible to the public, via the collections of the Huntington Library and the Philadelphia Museum of Art. At both institutions, the books are housed in either the rare books collections or the circulating stacks, depending on their rarity. A "list of books in Arensberg's [*sic*] private library" can be found at the Huntington Library, Francis Bacon Library Archive (hereafter cited as HEH-FBLA), Walter and Louise Arensberg Papers, box 132.1. An inventory of art-related books given to the Francis Bacon Foundation is located in PMA-WLA, box 32, folder 22. Lists of the books, magazines, and exhibition catalogs related to the Arensbergs' art collection that were given to the Philadelphia Museum of Art by the Francis Bacon Foundation, in six bulk shipments dated 8 May 1953; 13 October 1953; 1 March 1954; 12 March 1954; 17 March 1954; and June 1954, can be found in PMA-WLA, box 34, folder 25. See also PMA-WLA, box 35, folders 2 and 3. Additionally, a list of books purchased outside of California, assembled for tax purposes, is in PMA-WLA, box 30, folder 24.

7. Wilson and Madar, *Through Another Lens*, 28.

8. Louchheim, "The Arensbergs Bought Cubists Then."

9. Louchheim, "The Arensbergs Bought Cubists Then."

10. Louchheim, "The Arensbergs Bought Cubists Then."

11. On the early reception of the painting, see Isabelle Fleuriet, *The Grand Old Lady of Modern Art: Marcel Duchamp's "Nude Descending a Staircase"* (New York: Readymade, 2013). For a recent assessment of the impact of the International Exhibition of Modern Art, see *The Armory Show at 100: Modernism and Revolution*, ed. Marilyn Satin Kushner and Kimberly Orcutt, exh. cat. (New York: New-York Historical Society, 2013).

12. Both Ivins and Stevens are quoted in Fiske Kimball, "Cubism and the Arensbergs," *ARTnews Annual* 24 (1955): 120, 176. Ivins was the first curator of prints at the Metropolitan Museum of Art (from 1916 to 1946), and Stevens won the Pulitzer Prize for Poetry in 1955.

13. The Arensbergs had purchased Shady Hill from Harvard's first professor of art history, Charles Eliot Norton, and they sold it to the eminent director of Harvard's Fogg Art Museum, Walter's college classmate Paul Sachs. See John Voss, Conrad Wright, James Luther Adams, and Agnes Mongan, "Residents of Shady Hill," *Bulletin of the American Academy of Arts and Sciences* 35, no. 6 (1982): 6–25; and Naomi Sawelson-Gorse, "Marcel Duchamp's 'Silent Guard': A Critical Study of Walter and Louise Arensberg" (PhD diss., University of California, Santa Barbara, 1994), 103–4, 121.

14. Milton Brown, *The Story of the Armory Show* (New York: Joseph H. Hirshhorn Foundation, 1963), 102–3. On the closing day of the Armory Show, after it had moved on to Boston, its final venue, Walter purchased Jacques Villon's *Sketch for "Puteaux,"* which may have hung in the staircase of the Arensbergs' Hollywood home. In the years following the Armory Show, the Arensbergs went on to acquire six other works that had been exhibited there, including two by Duchamp—*Nude Descending a Staircase (No. 2)* (see plates 24.21, 27.5, 28.3, 29.1, 30.2) and *The King and Queen Surrounded by Swift Nudes* (see plates 3.12, 4.22, 5.24)—and Gleizes's *Man on a Balcony* (see plates 36.11, 37.13, 38.1), La Fresnaye's *Landscape* (see plate 35.11), Picabia's *Dances at the Spring* (see plates 43.23, 44.26, 45.31, 46.4, 47.1), and Villon's *Young Girl* (see plate 38.6). See also Francis M. Naumann, "Walter Conrad Arensberg: Poet, Patron, and Participant in the New York Avant-Garde, 1915–20," *Philadelphia Museum of Art Bulletin* 76, no. 328 (1980): 30.

15. Walter Arensberg to Katherine Dreier, 16 August 1923; quoted in Sawelson-Gorse, "'Silent Guard,'" 215.

16. Francis Picabia's phrase "Le vrai Dada de New York" is used by Tristan Tzara in a joint letter from Picabia and Tzara to Walter Arensberg, Paris, 8 November 1920 (PMA-WLA, box 15, folder 13); reproduced in Adrian Sudhalter, "Selected Documents," in *Dadaglobe Reconstructed* (Zurich: Scheidegger and Spiess, 2016), 72. See also Sawelson-Gorse, "'Silent Guard,'" 158–59; and Francis M. Naumann, *New York Dada, 1915–23* (New York: Abrams, 1994), 22–33.

17. In a playful exchange in *Dada*, no. 6 (edited by Tristan Tzara and issued on 5 February 1920), Duchamp replied to an entry purportedly authored by "Louise Margueritte and then and then," which asserted that he was "no longer producing art, having discovered a new queen check, check made with strings and a rubber bathing cap." Duchamp responded underneath: "Walter Conrad Arensberg hasn't yet discovered this mate [and] he contents himself for the moment with mating the king." Marcel Duchamp, "Walter Conrad Arensberg Hasn't Yet . . . ," in *Salt Seller: The Writings of Marcel Duchamp (Marchand du Sel)*, ed. Michel Sanouillet and Elmer Peterson (Oxford: Oxford University Press, 1973), 179.

18. At Harvard, Walter was a Class Day officer, an editor of the *Harvard Monthly*, secretary of the Jowett Club, vice president of the Chess Club, and president of Delta Upsilon; see Harvard Class Album of 1900, Harvard University Archives,

HUD 300.04.5. In June 1900, the *Harvard Advocate*, edited by none other than Wallace Stevens, printed the poem that Walter had written for that year's graduation. See Walter Arensberg, "Class Poem," *Harvard Advocate* 69, no. 9 (22 June 1900): 133–35, Harvard University archives, box 5.

19. In his two surviving passports, from 1923 and 1930, Walter lists his occupation as "Writer." See HEH-FBLA, box 82, folder 9.

20. See Suzanne W. Churchill, "Making Space for *Others*: A History of a Modernist Little Magazine," *Journal of Modern Literature* 22, no. 1 (1998): 47–67.

21. For the impact of experimental art on the formative work of the *Others* poets, see, for a start, Bram Dijkstra's *The Hieroglyphics of a New Speech: Cubism, Stieglitz, and the Early Poetry of William Carlos Williams* (Princeton: Princeton University Press, 1969); and Glen G. MacLeod's *Wallace Stevens and Company: The "Harmonium" Years, 1913–1923* (Ann Arbor: UMI Research Press, 1983). Cf. Francis M. Naumann, "The Dada Poetry of Walter Arensberg," *Tether* 4 (2018): 132–51.

22. Walter Arensberg, "For 'Shady Hill,' Cambridge, Mass.," in *Others: An Anthology of the New Verse*, ed. Alfred Kreymborg (New York: Alfred A. Knopf, 1917), 11.

23. See Molly Nesbit and Naomi Sawelson-Gorse, "Concept of Nothing: New Notes by Marcel Duchamp and Walter Arensberg," in *The Duchamp Effect: Essays, Interviews, Round Table*, ed. Martha Buskirk and Mignon Nixon (Cambridge: MIT Press, 1996), 131–75.

24. Marcel Duchamp, interview by James Johnson Sweeney, *Conversations with Elderly Wise Men*, NBC, broadcast 15 January 1956, https://www.youtube.com/watch?v=DzwADsrOEJk. The interview took place in the newly opened Arensberg galleries at the Philadelphia Museum of Art in 1955. An edited transcript of the interview can be found in Sanouillet and Peterson, *Salt Seller*, 127–37.

25. See Francis M. Naumann, "Cryptography and the Arensberg Circle," *Arts Magazine* 51 (May 1977): 127–33.

26. See Alan Stewart, "Francis Bacon's Bi-literal Cipher and the Materiality of Early Modern Diplomatic Writing," in *Diplomacy and Early Modern Culture*, ed. Robyn Adams and Rosanna Cox (Basingstoke, UK: Palgrave Macmillan, 2011), 120–37.

27. See Nesbit and Sawelson-Gorse, "Concept of Nothing."

28. Sawelson-Gorse, "'Silent Guard,'" 123–25. See also Naumann, "Walter Conrad Arensberg: Poet, Patron, and Participant," 11–15.

29. Robert M. Crunden, *American Salons: Encounters with European Modernism, 1885–1917* (New York: Oxford University Press, 1993), 409.

30. The date given for Sheeler's photographs is based on the Arensbergs' purchase of *Nude Descending a Staircase (No. 2)*, which was not yet in the apartment when the salon was in full swing. The *Nude* appears in Sheeler's photographs but was not purchased by the Arensbergs until early 1919 and shipped to them on 3 February of that year. See Francis M. Naumann, "Frederic C. Torrey and Duchamp's *Nude Descending a Staircase*," in *West Coast Duchamp*, ed. Bonnie Clearwater (Miami Beach: Grassfield in association with Shoshana Wayne Gallery, 1991), 20.

31. Sawelson-Gorse, "'Silent Guard,'" 123.

32. Henry McBride, "Modern Forms," *The Dial* 69 (July 1920): 61. Republished as "The Walter Arensbergs," in *The Flow of Art: Essays and Criticisms of Henry McBride*, ed. Daniel Catton Rich (New York: Atheneum, 1973; rev. ed., New Haven: Yale University Press, 1997), 156–59 in the 1997 edition.

33. See Sawelson-Gorse, "'Silent Guard,'" 117–18. Much of the biographical detail in the following paragraphs derives from Sawelson-Gorse's exhaustive account of these years in the Arensbergs' lives.

34. Pitts Sanborn, "Shakespeare's Cryptography," review of *The Cryptography of Shakespeare, Part One*, by Walter Arensberg, *The Measure: A Journal of Poetry* 27 (May 1923): 18.

35. See Kathryn Smith, *Frank Lloyd Wright: Hollyhock House and Olive Hill—Buildings and Projects for Aline Barnsdall* (New York: Rizzoli, 1992). For a brief discussion of the Arensbergs' short stay in the complex, see Smith's earlier article "Frank Lloyd Wright, Hollyhock House, and Olive Hill, 1914–1924," *Journal of the Society of Architectural Historians* 38, no. 1 (1979): 31.

36. Sawelson-Gorse, "'Silent Guard,'" 201.

37. Los Angeles Department of City Planning, Cultural Heritage Commission, *Historic-Cultural Monument Application for the Arensberg-Stendahl Home Gallery*, case no. CHC-2010-2948-HCM, ENV-2010-2949-CE, 13 January 2011, 2.

38. Los Angeles Department of City Planning, *Historic-Cultural Monument Application for the Arensberg-Stendahl Home Gallery*, 2.

39. The work's full name: *de ou par Marcel Duchamp ou Rrose Sélavy (Boîte-en-valise)* (*from or by Marcel Duchamp or Rrose Sélavy [Box in a Valise]*). Now considered a major work of art in its own right, its creation and many iterations are examined in depth in Ecke Bonk, *Marcel Duchamp: The Box in a Valise*, trans. David Britt (New York: Rizzoli, 1989).

40. Sawelson-Gorse, "Hollywood Conversations," 29.

41. Arthur Millier, "Painter Hits Art Theory: French Artist Visits City; Marcel Duchamp Views His 'Nude Descending the Stair,' in Hollywood Home," *Los Angeles Times*, 16 August 1936, 2.

42. Wilson and Madar, *Through Another Lens*, 100. Wilson and Weston attended a small party on 8 August 1936 with Wilson's brother Leon, Lloyd Wright (Frank Lloyd Wright's son), the photographer Sherill Schell, and Beatrice Wood. But the evening in question was almost certainly the much larger party thrown on 11 August 1936: see entry for 11 August 1936 in Jennifer Gough-Cooper and Jacques Caumont, "Ephemerides on and about Marcel Duchamp and Rrose Sélavy, 1887–1968," in *Marcel Duchamp: Work and Life*, ed. Pontus Hulten, exh. cat. (Cambridge: MIT Press, 1993), unpaginated.

43. See George Jelliss, "Introducing Knight's Tours," *Mayhematics*, 2004, http://www.mayhematics.com/t/1n.htm.

44. Philadelphia Museum of Art, Library and Archives, John Raphael Covert Papers, box 1, folders 28–31, containing Covert's notes on Magic Squares and Knight's Tours, intermingled with speculative research on the Bacon-Shakespeare controversy. On Covert's relationship with the Arensbergs and lifelong interest in codes, see Leo G. Mazow, *John Covert Rediscovered* (University Park: Palmer Museum of Art at Pennsylvania State University, 2003).

45. Man Ray lived in Hollywood from 1941 to 1951. He and Max Ernst (recently divorced from Peggy Guggenheim) married Juliet Browner and Dorothea Tanning, respectively, in a double wedding ceremony in Hollywood. The two couples celebrated afterward at the Arensberg home as well as at Earl Stendahl's home, located next door, but Man Ray's relationship with Louise and Walter became strained soon after. By the time of Duchamp's visit in 1949, Man Ray was considered persona non grata at the Arensberg home, and Duchamp had to sneak away from the Arensbergs to visit his friend.

46. Larry List, ed., *The Imagery of Chess Revisited*, exh. cat. (New York: Isamu Noguchi Foundation and Garden Museum and George Braziller, 2005), 17–21, 100–101.

47. Edward Alden Jewell, "'Inner Vision' and Out of Bounds," *New York Times*, 18 October 1942; quoted in John Vick, "A New Look: Marcel Duchamp, His Twine, and the 1942 First Papers of Surrealism Exhibition," *Tout-fait: The Marcel Duchamp Studies Online Journal*, 1 March 2008, https://www.toutfait.com/a-new-look-marcel-duchamp-his-twine-and-the-1942-first-papers-of-surrealism-exhibition.

48. Duchamp, interview by Sweeney, *Conversations with Elderly Wise Men*.

49. Elena Filipovic, "A Museum That Is Not," *e-flux journal* 4 (March 2009): 11, 14, https://www.e-flux.com/journal/04/68554/a-museum-that-is-not/. See also Filipovic's more recent account in *The Apparently Marginal Activities of Marcel Duchamp* (Cambridge: MIT Press, 2016), 73–154.

50. Naomi Sawelson-Gorse, "'For the Want of a Nail': The Disposition of the Louise and Walter Arensberg Collection" (master's thesis, University of California, Riverside, 1987), 23.

51. Jeremy Braddock, *Collecting as Modernist Practice* (Baltimore: Johns Hopkins University Press, 2012), 3.

52. See Braddock, *Collecting as Modernist Practice*, 106–55. On 8 July 1948, Walter wrote to Fiske Kimball, director of the Philadelphia Museum of Art, to explain his disinclination to send their collection to the city that was already home to the Barnes Foundation: "I am obliged to confess to a slight reluctance to entering the region that is so infected by the pollution of Dr. Barnes, and that will, somehow, as long as he continues, require to be quarantined. I should think that he would recognize that he is very bad advertising for his famous product, for he is himself a kind of running sore that even Argyrol [the drug for venereal disease that made Barnes his fortune] cannot cure." PMA-WLA, box 15, folder 2.

53. See Judith F. Dolkart, "To See as the Artist Sees: Albert C. Barnes and the Experiment in Education," in *The Barnes Foundation: Masterworks*, ed. Judith F. Dolkart and Martha Lucy (New York: Skira Rizzoli, 2012), 21.

54. Dolkart, "To See as the Artist Sees," 23–24.

55. Braddock, *Collecting as Modernist Practice*, 140–44.

56. Walter Arensberg, interview by Kenneth Ross, ca. 1951; this volume, 404–5.

57. Katherine Dreier made the same observation in her "Analytical Reflection" on *The Large Glass*: "Marcel Duchamp was the first to paint the image per se, to be completed by an act of consciousness on the part of the spectator. . . . To put our creative forces into action is the most important goal which the art of the present day can achieve. The spectator is no longer an onlooker—he is an actual participant." (Underscore is Dreier's.) "Duchamp's Glass: An Analytical Reflection" (unpublished manuscript, undated), Yale University, Katherine S. Dreier Papers, YCAL MSS 101 box 43, folder 1287, pp. 1–2. In Barnes's program too, "artist and audience would now be collaboratively engaged in the activity of creating meaning. The role of the viewer was no longer that of disinterested or passive contemplation, but recast [as Barnes put it in his *Art in Painting* of 1925] as necessarily 'involv[ing] effort and entail[ing] fatigue; work is done, the process is active and not passive.'" Braddock, *Collecting as Modernist Practice*, 113.

58. See Sawelson-Gorse, "'Silent Guard,'" 244–45.

59. For an exhaustive account of the techniques used in making the individual pieces of *Box in a Valise*, see Bonk, *Marcel Duchamp: The Box in a Valise*, 147–61; for specifics on the Arensbergs' role in 1936, see 150–51. See also Filipovic, *The Apparently Marginal Activities of Marcel Duchamp*, 73–154.

60. Susan Davidson, "Focusing an Instinct: The Collecting of Peggy Guggenheim," in *Peggy Guggenheim & Frederick Kiesler: The Story of Art of This Century*, ed. Susan Davidson and Philip Rylands (New York: Solomon R. Guggenheim Foundation, 2004), 60.

61. See Davidson, "Focusing an Instinct," 64; and Don Quaintance, Jasper Sharp, and Valentina Sonzogni, "Chronology," in *Peggy Guggenheim & Frederick Kiesler: The Story of Art of This Century*, ed. Susan Davidson and Philip Rylands (New York: Solomon R. Guggenheim Foundation, 2004), 369.

62. See Quaintance, Sharp, and Sonzogni, "Chronology," 369–70.

63. Jimmy Ernst, *A Not-So-Still Life: A Memoir* (New York: St. Martin's/Marek, 1984), 214.

64. Ernst, *A Not-So-Still Life*, 215.

65. Elise K. Kenney, "The Société Anonyme Collection Comes to Yale," in *The Société Anonyme: Modernism for America*, ed. Jennifer R. Gross, exh. cat. (New Haven: Yale University Press, 2006), 143–45.

66. Duchamp reworked *de ou par Marcel Duchamp ou Rrose Sélavy* many times over many years, producing some 300 total copies; only the first 24 were deluxe editions in valises. See Bonk, *Marcel Duchamp: The Box in a Valise*, 163–94.

67. Davidson, "Focusing an Instinct," 74.

68. Davidson, "Focusing an Instinct," 75.

69. Don Quaintance, "Modern Art in a Modern Setting: Frederick Kiesler's Design of Art of This Century," in *Peggy Guggenheim & Frederick Kiesler: The Story of Art of This Century*, ed. Susan Davidson and Philip Rylands (New York: Solomon R. Guggenheim Foundation, 2004), 207.

70. Quaintance, "Modern Art in a Modern Setting," 251.

71. Davidson, "Focusing an Instinct," 75.

72. A reproduction of the Arensbergs' copy of *Box in a Valise* (including the handmade collotype of *Virgin*) can be found in Bonk, *Marcel Duchamp: The Box in a Valise*, 276–77.

73. Walter Arensberg to Marcel Duchamp, 6 May 1943; quoted in Bonk, *Marcel Duchamp: The Box in a Valise*, 167. Bonk writes that "the letter is marked 'not sent,' which means according to Naomi Sawelson-Gorse that Duchamp never received it, or at least not in this form." Bonk, *Marcel Duchamp: The Box in a Valise*, 193n10.

74. Bonk, *Marcel Duchamp: The Box in a Valise*, 20.

75. Bonk, *Marcel Duchamp: The Box in a Valise*, 9.

76. Los Angeles Department of City Planning, *Historic-Cultural Monument Application for the Arensberg-Stendahl Home Gallery*, 2. Sabin's original drawings for the foyer are collected in the Henry Palmer Sabin Papers, 1920–1955, Architecture and Design Collection, Art, Design & Architecture Museum, University of California, Santa Barbara (hereafter cited as Sabin Papers, ADC, UCSB).

77. The curved lintel at the top of *Arch* and its weathered base (probably a fragment of crown molding) are held together by two vertical beams that Brancusi fitted as tenons into existing mortises on the top and bottom elements. *Arch* was not designed to be freestanding; the mortise-and-tenon joints cannot support the massive lintel. See Ann Temkin, entry for *Arch*, in Friedrich Teja Bach, Margit Rowell, and Ann Temkin, *Constantin Brancusi 1876–1957*, exh. cat. (Cambridge: MIT Press, 1995), 134.

78. Elaine Lustig Cohen, interview by Mark Nelson, New York, 10 June 2013. Her husband was the celebrated graphic designer Alvin Lustig, who designed the Francis Bacon Foundation stationery for Walter Arensberg as well as ephemera for Earl Stendahl's gallery next door.

79. For detailed information on Sabin, see Sabin Papers, ADC, UCSB.

80. See "Arensberg, W. C. house (Hollywood, Calif.)," 1927, Sabin Papers, ADC, UCSB, drawer 35, flat file 4.

81. See Sawelson-Gorse, "'Silent Guard,'" 214–15. We would expand upon this line of thinking by suggesting that the foyer might, in turn, have influenced Duchamp's posthumously revealed masterwork *Étant donnés: 1° La chute d'eau, 2° Le gaz d'éclairage*… The artist's ideas for this sculptural installation were just beginning to gel in 1948 and 1949, around the time of his last two extended stays in the Arensbergs' home. Though considerably different in their material execution, these two rooms—each aggressively presenting ambiguous genitalia in the display of a "woman" closed behind a heavy wooden door, and each designed to shock the viewer—resonate profoundly in their scale, thematic concerns, and relation to Duchamp.

82. The artist Beatrice Wood introduced Brancusi to the Arensbergs, who had already collected several of his sculptures. See "Chronology," in Friedrich Teja Bach, Margit Rowell, and Ann Temkin, *Constantin Brancusi 1876–1957*, exh. cat. (Cambridge: MIT Press, 1995), 380.

83. "Chronology," *Constantin Brancusi 1876–1957*, 377.

84. Sawelson-Gorse, "'Silent Guard,'" 215.

85. See Clarence John Laughlin, *The Voracious Princess* (photoprint), 20 June 1950, 1983.47.4.1765, Williams Research Center, the Clarence John Laughlin Archive at the Historic New Orleans Collection. See also Laughlin, *The Princess of Mlle. Bonaparte by Brancusi* (gelatin silver print), mid-twentieth century, Philadelphia Museum of Art (PMA) 1950-134-979, PMA-WLA, box 55, folder 14. The identification of *Study for "The Newborn"* (ca. 1914, PMA 1950-134-9) and *Study for "The Princess"* (ca. 1913–15, PMA 1950-134-11) from the reflection in Laughlin's photo is supported by Katharine Kuh's list of works and their locations in the Arensberg home. Kuh created the list while preparing for a 1949 exhibition at the Art Institute of Chicago; she wrote that the two drawings were located in the Arensbergs' "vestibule." See Kuh, notes and lists of works, July–December 1948, PMA-WLA, box 2, folder 4.

86. Clarence John Laughlin to Walter Arensberg, Washington, DC, 2 September 1945, PMA-WLA, box 21, folder 16. Laughlin introduced himself to Arensberg by sending a copy of his "symbolist" photobook *Ghosts along the Mississippi*. His photographic practice, as he described it in the book's prologue, would certainly have appealed to Walter: "The method of poetry is to abstract symbols from the stuff of living experience; to embody these symbols not only in emotive language, but, by means of the creative use of these symbols, to subtly penetrate beyond the tough outer skin of appearances, and give us a reality which is not only complexly sweetened or embittered by the perceiving mind, but *more extensive in time* than that reality which is immediately apprehensible; since now elements of the past and of the future play equal parts with that of the present. In the superior reality of poetic vision we enter a plane where symbols have a life of their own; and here perhaps we transcend, temporarily and incompletely, the limitations which time, or rather, our three-dimensional realization of time, places upon us." Clarence John Laughlin, prologue to *Ghosts along the Mississippi* (New York: Charles Scribner's Sons, 1948), unpaginated (italics in original).

87. Clarence John Laughlin, "Prints for Walter Conrad Arensberg," notes on photographic prints, MSS 563, Williams Research Center, the Clarence John Laughlin Archive at the Historic New Orleans Collection.

88. The soldiers shown in this photograph (and in others reproduced throughout this volume) were visiting the Arensbergs as part of an art therapy class provided by the hospital. Pictured in several of them is Don Schloat, who was captured by the Japanese while stationed in the Philippines in 1942. After three years as a prisoner of war in Bataan and Manila, he returned to Los Angeles and eventually became an artist and an animator of cartoons. Numerous articles about his tribulations appeared in the *Los Angeles Times*. See Schloat's memoir, *Freedom! Bataan—POW—PVT* (Valley Center, CA: Privately published, 1995).

89. Sawelson-Gorse, "'Silent Guard,'" 30, 115–16.

90. *Prodigal Son*, purchased in 1916, was the first Brancusi the Arensbergs owned; see "Chronology," in *Constantin Brancusi 1876–1957*, 376. Though Walter was never particularly religious, the parable of the prodigal son may have had some resonance for him, given his intellectual and geographic distance from his family.

91. Corle, "Notes on the Work of Marcel Duchamp," 22.

92. According to Jo Anne Van Tilburg, director of the Rock Art Archive at UCLA's Cotsen Institute of Archaeology, this sculpture was likely produced by a modern Rapa Nui artist in the 1920s or 1930s—an example of the type of work produced by the flourishing commercial arts industry that developed as modern archaeologists began to take interest in the statues and people of Easter Island.

93. We thank the art historian Charles Stuckey for this playful observation. Brancusi's *Three Penguins* (1911–12) was created after the sculptor was introduced to pictures and/or film footage of penguins by Jean-Baptiste Charcot, who gave a lecture in Paris on 12 December 1910 about his Antarctic expeditions. See Friedrich Teja Bach, entry for *Three Penguins*, in Friedrich Teja Bach, Margit Rowell, and Ann Temkin, *Constantin Brancusi 1876–1957*, exh. cat. (Cambridge: MIT Press, 1995), 114–15. By the time the Arensbergs purchased *Three Penguins* from the Quinn collection via Duchamp in 1934, they likely would have known the colloquial names of penguin species from articles in the popular press. See, for example, the explorer Frank Hurley's essay and photographs, "Life among the Penguins in Antarctica: The Birds That Walk Like a Man and Present a Natural Burlesque of Humanity," *New York Times Magazine*, 17 August 1924, https://nyti.ms/2zLtqdo.

94. The simple male-female, black-white contrasts of these polarities become more complex in later works, such as *The Large Glass*. See Francis M. Naumann, "A Reconciliation of Opposites," in *The Recurrent, Haunting Ghost: Essays on the Art, Life and Legacy of Marcel Duchamp* (New York: Readymade, 2012), 346.

95. "Je me suis tout à fait prêt à devenir le chess maniaque. Tour autour de moi prend le forme de cavalier ou de dame et le monde extérieur n'a pas d'autre interêt pour moi que dans la transposition en positions gagnantes ou perdantes." Marcel Duchamp to Walter and Louise Arensberg, Buenos Aires, 15 and 20 June 1919; published in Duchamp, *Affectionately, Marcel: The Selected Correspondence of Marcel Duchamp*, ed. Francis M. Naumann and Hector Obalk, trans. Jill Taylor (Ghent: Ludion, 2000), 85–86.

96. Walter Arensberg, interview by Ross; see this volume, 402.

97. The same was true of Duchamp: he authored a pamphlet of puns called *Rrose Sélavy* (Paris: GLM, 1939). Michel Sanouillet and Elmer Peterson, editors of Duchamp's collected writings, write that "Duchamp once called some of his sayings 'morceaux moisis' or 'wrotten writtens,' and there is a certain amount

of gaminess in many of his short sayings"; Sanouillet and Peterson, "Preface," in *Salt Seller: The Writings of Marcel Duchamp (Marchand du Sel)*, ed. Michel Sanouillet and Elmer Peterson (Oxford: Oxford University Press, 1973), vii. Many other authors have written on Duchamp's use of puns; see, for example, George H. Bauer, "Duchamp's Ubiquitous Puns," in *Marcel Duchamp: Artist of the Century*, ed. Rudolf Kuenzli and Francis M. Naumann (Cambridge: MIT Press, 1989), 127–48.

98. Michael Minelli, "The Want of a Nail . . . ," *X-Tra Contemporary Art Quarterly* 9, no. 4 (2007): 31.

99. Minelli, "The Want of a Nail," 31.

100. M. F. K. Fisher (Parrish) to Walter Arensberg, Hemet, CA, 6 March 1945, PMA-WLA, box 2, folder 40.

101. See entry for *Disks of Newton (Study for "Fugue in Two Colors")*, in *Twentieth Century Painting and Sculpture in the Philadelphia Museum of Art*, ed. Ann Temkin, Susan Rosenberg, and Michael Taylor (Philadelphia: Philadelphia Museum of Art, 2000), 24. For more on the inspiration Kupka took from Newton's color studies, see *Painting the Universe: František Kupka, Pioneer in Abstraction*, ed. Jaroslav Anděl and Dorothy Kosinski, exh. cat. (Berlin: Verlag Gerd Hatje, 1997), 71–76, 85–95.

102. See Alfred H. Barr, *Cubism and Abstract Art*, exh. cat. (New York: Museum of Modern Art, 1936), 73. Almost a century later, art historians still partake in robust discussions about this epochal development. It was the focus of Leah Dickerman's 2012–13 exhibition, *Inventing Abstraction, 1910–1925*, at the Museum of Modern Art.

103. Germain Seligman to Walter Arensberg, New York, 8 January 1946, PMA-WLA, box 10, folder 11.

104. Walter Arensberg to Germain Seligman, Los Angeles, 19 January 1946, PMA-WLA, box 10, folder 11.

105. See Barr, *Cubism and Abstract Art*, 73. Both *Disks of Newton* (PMA 1950-132-122) and Delaunay's *Simultaneous Contrasts: Sun and Moon* (Museum of Modern Art object no. 1.1954) are pictured in this foundational book. Barr called Delaunay's painting "*Disks*" and noted that it was painted in 1913—a date to which Seligman took exception.

106. Arensberg to Seligman, 19 January 1946.

107. "Music and Drama: 'The Shoemaker's Holiday,'" *Boston Evening Transcript*, 25 April 1898, 5; and Kimball, "Cubism and the Arensbergs," 119. Both cited in Sawelson-Gorse, "'Silent Guard,'" 18.

108. We are grateful to Charles Stuckey for making this perceptive observation, and to Teresa Montaner, chief curator at the Fundació Joan Miró, Barcelona, for further elucidating it. "Though Miró himself made no declaration on the subject," Montaner explained, "the information that Miró hid his own signature within his paintings is not new for me. Miró plays with the 'J' and 'M' of his name in a number of his works, either as a structuring element (using the 'J') or as a small detail of the composition with 'M.'" Email to Mark Nelson, 30 March 2017. Additionally, curator Carolyn Lanchner has written of "the near fetishistic care Miró customarily took in signing his paintings." See her essay "Peinture-Poésie, Its Logic and Logistics," in *Joan Miró*, exh. cat. (New York: Museum of Modern Art, 1993), 37.

109. We suggest it may be possible to read Miró's first name in the painting as well: the figure's bottom and legs might make an upside-down *J*; her head an *O*; either her cap or the triangular "tree" on the mountain might constitute an *A*; and finally, the line describing the mountains might also create an *N*.

110. Thanks here, again, to Montaner, who has answered our questions with great care and patience. Montaner, emails to Mark Nelson, 20 and 26 September and 10 October 2017. See also Margit Rowell, "Miró at the Museum: Works in the Philadelphia Museum of Art," *Philadelphia Museum of Art Bulletin* 83, no. 356/357 (1987): 3–38.

111. Walter Arensberg, "Golden Bough," 1 May 1946, HEH-FBLA, box 99, folder 13, p. 7.

112. Walter Arensberg to Fiske Kimball, Los Angeles, 5 January 1949, PMA-WLA, box 15, folder 3. The biblical creation myth had intrigued both Arensberg and Duchamp for more than thirty years and manifested itself in a number of ways. For example, though Arensberg was not in close contact with Duchamp in 1924, when the artist was living again in Paris, he likely would have known that Duchamp played Adam (opposite Bronia Perlmutter as Eve) on stage that year in a New Year's Eve sex farce called *Ciné-sketch*, organized by Francis Picabia and produced by René Clair. Man Ray took the only known photographs of Duchamp and Perlmutter "in costume" at a rehearsal. See Billy Klüver and Julie Martin, entry for "Bronia Perlmutter," *Dictionary of Artists' Models*, ed. Jill Berk Jiminez (New York: Routledge, 2013), 422.

113. Sawelson-Gorse, "'Silent Guard,'" 249–52. For a much more in-depth discussion of the Arensbergs' financial status, art acquisition, and commissioning of Neutra, see Sawelson-Gorse, "'Silent Guard,'" 238–58.

114. Thomas S. Hines, *Richard Neutra and the Search for Modern Architecture* (New York: Oxford University Press, 1982), 93.

115. Hines, *Richard Neutra*, 111. Hines notes that Neutra was "learning from the old Spanish practice of building to the property lines with rear interior courtyards for gardens and privacy," a design element he had just incorporated into his VDL Research house of 1932.

116. Richard Neutra and Gregory Ain, "Alteration of a House: Mr. and Mrs. Walter Arensberg," Richard and Dion Neutra Papers (Collection 1179), UCLA Library Special Collections, Charles E. Young Research Library, UCLA, box 20, folder 5.

117. Beatrice Wood, notation of 27 May 1933, in 1930–34 line-a-day diary, Beatrice Wood Papers, 1894–1998, Archives of American Art, Smithsonian Institution, box 17, folder 2, https://www.aaa.si.edu/collections/items/detail/line-day-diary-13122.

118. The Brooklyn Museum exhibition, in 1926, was the only public showing of *The Large Glass* before Duchamp installed it permanently at the Philadelphia Museum of Art in 1953. It was kept in a storage facility for four years after the Brooklyn exhibition, and then it broke. See Anne d'Harnoncourt, *Philadelphia Museum of Art: Handbook of the Collection*, ed. Sherry Babbitt (Philadelphia: Philadelphia Museum of Art, 1995), 316.

119. For a lucid study of the component parts of *The Large Glass*, see Linda Dalrymple Henderson, "Uncertainty, Chaos, and Chance in Early Twentieth-Century Art: The Cases of Wassily Kandinsky and Marcel Duchamp," *Étant donné Marcel Duchamp*, no. 4 (2002): 130–45. For a full exposition of *The Large Glass*, see Henderson, *Duchamp in Context: Science and Technology in "The Large Glass" and Related Works* (Princeton: Princeton University Press, 1998).

120. David Joselit, *Infinite Regress: Marcel Duchamp 1910–1941* (Cambridge: MIT Press, 1998), 6.

121. Henderson, "Uncertainty, Chaos, and Chance," 133–35.

122. Published in a limited edition of 300, this work was, as its title indicates, a green box. It contained ninety-four facsimiles of Duchamp's working notes and drawings for *The Large Glass*.

123. Walter Arensberg to Katherine Dreier, Los Angeles, 16 August 1923; quoted in Sawelson-Gorse, "'Silent Guard,'" 215.

124. The idea of reconstituting *The Large Glass* several years later might have appealed to Duchamp: it was in keeping with his description of the work as a "delay in glass"—a representation of a deferred and dynamic process rather than a static or finished work. This phrase is widely discussed in Duchamp scholarship, but for perhaps the fullest analysis, see Jerrold Seigel, *The Private Worlds of Marcel Duchamp: Desire, Liberation, and the Self in Modern Culture* (Berkeley: University of California Press, 1995), 87–115.

125. In this photograph, Dapprich also captures two major works that later moved to other locations in the house: Duchamp's *The King and Queen Traversed by Swift Nudes at High Speed*, and Joan Miró's *Female Nude* (PMA 1950-134-143), which, in this context, is strongly suggestive of Duchamp's "Bride."

126. Charles F. Stuckey, "Duchamp's Acephalic Symbolism," *Art in America*, January–February 1977, 96.

127. Marcel Duchamp, "À l'Infinitif," trans. Cleve Gray in collaboration with Duchamp, reprinted in *Salt Seller: The Writings of Marcel Duchamp (Marchand du Sel)*, ed. Michel Sanouillet and Elmer Peterson (Oxford: Oxford University Press, 1973), 74. Quoted in Stuckey, "Duchamp's Acephalic Symbolism," 96.

128. Stuckey, "Duchamp's Acephalic Symbolism," 96.

129. Though this 1916 work had been directly inspired by Duchamp's chocolate grinder paintings, Schamberg had never intended that any underlying meaning be found in his work the way his friends Duchamp, Picabia, and Covert had. See entry for *Painting VIII (Mechanical Abstraction)*, in Temkin, Rosenberg, and Taylor, *Twentieth Century Painting and Sculpture in the Philadelphia Museum of Art*, 50. See also Ben Wolf, who, in his monograph of Schamberg's paintings, notes that "although the artist's concern here is assumed to be (as elsewhere) in pure form—divorced from mechanomorphic fantasy—the unit possesses a curious portrait of 'mask quality.' It has the totemic feeling of a Baga shoulder mask from the Sudan, West Africa." Wolf, *Morton Livingston Schamberg* (Philadelphia: University of Pennsylvania Press, 1963), 53.

130. Walter Arensberg, *The Cryptography of Dante* (New York: Knopf, 1921), ix–x.

131. Katharine Kuh, *The Open Eye: In Pursuit of Art* (New York: Harper & Row, 1971), 61.

132. Kuh, *The Open Eye*, 56–57.

133. In 1947 Charles Eames informed Walter that he had requested that the proprietors of the Coronet Theatre (a venue for avant-garde film inaugurated that year in Los Angeles) send the Arensbergs information on a planned showing of "the Easter Island film." He might have been referring to Thor Heyerdahl's *Kon-Tiki*, filmed during a 1947 raft expedition; it won the Academy Award for best documentary in 1951. Shortly after receiving Eames's letter, the Arensbergs moved their Easter Island sculpture to a prominent position in the living room. Charles Eames to Walter Arensberg, 17 May 1947, PMA-WLA, box 7, folder 2.

134. See April Dammann, *Exhibitionist: Earl Stendahl, Art Dealer as Impresario* (Santa Monica, CA: Angel City, 2011), 115–17. For the drawing on page 43 of this volume and for Kosich's extensive correspondence to the Arensbergs, see PMA-WLA, box 10, folders 50–52.

135. Louchheim, "The Arensbergs Bought Cubists Then."

136. Walter Arensberg to Roberto Montenegro, Los Angeles, 22 May 1939, PMA-WLA, box 21, folder 18.

137. Walter Arensberg to Marcel Duchamp, Los Angeles, 23 May

1930, PMA-WLA, box 6, folder 21; quoted in Naumann, "Walter Conrad Arensberg: Poet, Patron, and Participant," 28.

138. This painting by Gleizes represented another double, constituting perhaps the only example where the Arensbergs hung an artist's initial study next to the finished work.

139. Walter Arensberg, "Paroles devant une toile de Gleizes" (unpublished typescript, undated), PMA-WLA, box 43, folder 13.

140. Torrey is quoted in Naumann, "Torrey and Duchamp's *Nude*," 11–12.

141. Naumann, "Torrey and Duchamp's *Nude*," 5.

142. Naumann, "Torrey and Duchamp's *Nude*," 20.

143. Naumann, "Torrey and Duchamp's *Nude*," 15.

144. Naumann, "Torrey and Duchamp's *Nude*," 15. Duchamp himself wrote that "in the drawing *Encore à cet astre* (PMA 1950-134-57; AC20-62), the figure is, of course, mounting the stairs. But while working on it, the idea of the Nude, or the title—I do not recall which—first came to my mind. I eventually gave the sketch to F. C. Torrey of San Francisco who bought the *Nude Descending a Staircase* [*(No. 2)*] from the 1913 New York Armory Show." Quoted in James Johnson Sweeney, ed., "Eleven Europeans in America," *The Museum of Modern Art Bulletin* 13, nos. 4–5 (1946): 19–20. Many years after Torrey had sold *Nude Descending a Staircase (No. 2)* to the Arensbergs, Torrey's wife and daughter sold this drawing to the Arensbergs through John Hatch in July 1939. See PMA-WLA, box 24, AIN 712.

145. *Nude Descending a Staircase (No. 1)* hung in the Arensberg living room until at least 1944, when Fred Dapprich photographed the room. Sometime before 1951 (when the living room was next photographed, by Floyd Harold Faxon) the *Nude* was replaced by Braque's 1912–13 canvas *Violin and Newspaper*. It is unclear where this version of the *Nude* hung after 1944.

146. For Duchamp's acknowledgment of Marey and Muybridge as influences, see his interviews with Sweeney ("Eleven Europeans in America," 10) and with Pierre Cabanne (*Dialogues with Marcel Duchamp*, trans. Ron Padgett [London: Thames and Hudson, 1971], 34–35). Many scholars have discussed Duchamp's indebtedness to chronophotography and similar imaging techniques being explored at the turn of the century. See, for example, Joselit, *Infinite Regress*, 53–55; Naumann, *The Recurrent, Haunting Ghost*, 16; and Henderson, *Duchamp in Context*, 10–11.

147. Fleuriet, *The Grand Old Lady of Modern Art*, 1–2.

148. Marcel Duchamp, entry for "Albert Gleizes," in Katherine S. Dreier and Duchamp, *Collection of the Société Anonyme: Museum of Modern Art 1920*, exh. cat. (New Haven: Yale University Art Gallery, 1950), 145. See Albert Gleizes and Jean Metzinger, *Du "Cubisme"* (Paris: Eugène Figuière, 1912).

149. Entry for *Man on a Balcony (Portrait of Dr. Théo Morinaud)*, in Temkin, Rosenberg, and Taylor, *Twentieth Century Painting and Sculpture in the Philadelphia Museum of Art*, 33.

150. For a thorough examination of the many schemes, see Sawelson-Gorse, "'For the Want of a Nail.'"

151. Walter Arensberg to Katharine Kuh, Los Angeles, 26 January 1949, PMA-WLA, box 2, folder 5. See also this volume, "Notes on Selected Objects," 414, specifically notes 1.7, 1.8, and 1.9.

152. For an overview of the response to the nude by the press at the time, see Fleuriet, *The Grand Old Lady of Modern Art*, 5–8.

153. See Los Angeles Department of City Planning, *Historic-Cultural Monument Application for the Arensberg-Stendahl Home Gallery*, 37.

154. Francis Bacon Foundation, "Notes and Plans," 1947–51, Philadelphia Museum of Art, Library and Archives, Francis Bacon Foundation (hereafter cited as PMA-FBF), box 4, folder 42.

155. Andrew Baker, interview by Mark Nelson and William H. Sherman, New York, 4 March 2013. Baker was the husband of Carol Bruns Baker (née Carol Bruns).

156. See Elizabeth S. Wrigley, "Brief History of the Research, 1922 to Present," PMA-FBF, box 4, folder 40. This text serves as an introduction to Walter Arensberg's "Plan of the Work," dictated to Wrigley on 6 January 1954.

157. See William H. Sherman, "Of Anagrammatology," *English Language Notes* 47, no. 2 (2009): 139–48.

158. Walter Arensberg, *The Cryptography of Shakespeare: Part One* (Los Angeles: Howard Bowen, 1922), 202–3.

159. Walter Arensberg to Louise Arensberg, London, ca. 29 April–2 May 1923, HEH-FBLA, box 77, folder 3.

160. Walter Arensberg to Maurice B. Cookson, Los Angeles, 30 August 1951, HEH-FBLA, box 77, folder 13.

161. Wrigley, "Brief History of the Research, 1922 to Present," PMA-FBF, box 4, folder 40.

162. Walter Arensberg, "Statements of Pattern Development, 1935," HEH-FBLA, box 95, folder 2.

163. Clyde Wolfe, "The Cryptographic Path" (unpublished manuscript, 1929–32), HEH-FBLA, box 86, folders 6–9.

164. Walter Arensberg to Clyde Wolfe, New York, 16 December 1925, HEH-FBLA, box 79, folder 7.

165. "Index to Miscellaneous Notes," "Projects," and "A–Z subjects" index cards, 17 April and 5 June 1935, and 11 February 1939, HEH-FBLA, box 106.

166. Walter Arensberg to William Ivins, 6 February 1930, PMA-WLA, box 10, folder 8. Little wonder, then, that Ivins later described Walter's approach as a scholar and collector in the following terms: "Walter was emancipated from all the normal obligations and responsibilities of life, and could turn night time into day time and devote his extremely good mind and time to chess and cryptic problems.... For him it sometimes seemed as though pictures were interesting just to the extent that they set him intellectual and psychological problems to speculate about—almost as though they were very complicated chess problems." William Ivins to Fiske Kimball, Woodbury, CT, 15 March 1954, William Mills Ivins Papers, 1878–1964, Archives of American Art, Smithsonian Institution, box 1, folder 6.

167. Inventories prepared by Mary Anne Adler (the couple's conservator) and Katharine Kuh (who carefully listed the location of all of the items sent to Chicago for her 1949 exhibition) provide a sense of some of the other artworks that would have been seen from the vantage point of someone sitting at this desk, including Vasily Kandinsky's *Circles in a Circle* (PMA 1950-134-104) and *Improvisation No. 29* [*The Swan*] (PMA 1950-134-102); Louis Marcoussis's *Portrait of Guillaume Apollinaire* (PMA 1950-134-128); and a second *Mechanical Abstraction* by Morton Livingston Schamberg (PMA 1950-134-181). According to the lists, Max Ernst's *The Forest* (see plate 58.8) and Roberto Montenegro's *The Double* (see plate 37.10) hung in this room circa 1948. Adler, list of works, 9 June 1951, PMA-WLA, box 1, folder 13; and Kuh, notes and lists of works, July–December 1948, PMA-WLA, box 2, folder 4.

168. Duchamp's *Portrait of the Artist's Father* (see plate 42.1) also hung for a time in the sitting room (see plate 48.21).

169. Cabanne, *Dialogues with Marcel Duchamp*, 52.

170. Calvin Tomkins, "A Touch for the Now," *New Yorker*, 29 July 1991, 35–36.

171. Walter Hopps, *The Dream Colony: A Life in Art*, ed. Deborah Treisman (New York: Bloomsbury USA, 2017), 32.

172. Marie Kimball, wife of Fiske Kimball, quoted in his *ARTnews* article, "Cubism and the Arensbergs," 178.

173. Walter continued: "I feel that you have completely misinterpreted the Baconian philosophy of prosperity as if he placed his emphasis on material things to the detriment of the development of the spirit. The exact converse of this view is in my opinion true, and the simplest and most obvious confirmation may be found in the *New Atlantis* where material prosperity, where the plenty of the biblical conception of the land of promise, is associated with the cultivation of the highest spiritual values." Walter Arensberg to John Nef, Los Angeles, 20 March 1943, PMA-WLA, box 13, folder 27.

174. Tomkins, "A Touch for the Now," 36.

175. See Walter Hopps, "Marcel Duchamp: A System of Paradox in Resonance," in *Marcel Duchamp, Pasadena Art Museum: A Retrospective Exhibition*, exh. cat. (Pasadena, CA: Pasadena Art Museum, 1963), unpaginated.

176. Tomkins, "A Touch for the Now," 34.

177. Though *Comb* does not appear in photographs of the guest bedroom, object records in the card catalog of the Arensberg collection confirm that both *Comb* and *With Hidden Noise* were kept in the guest bedroom cabinet (PMA-WLA, box 24, AINs 307 and 306, respectively). *With Hidden Noise* is clearly visible in the cabinet in plate 57.

178. Baker, interview by Nelson and Sherman.

179. Sawelson-Gorse, "'Silent Guard,'" 244–45.

180. In the office over Walter's desk, for example, hung *Portrait of the Artist's Father* (see plate 42.1); in the sitting room, *Portrait of Chess Players*, depicting Duchamp's two brothers, the artists Jacques Villon and Raymond Duchamp-Villon, held a prominent position over the bookcase (see plate 45.3); and in the living room, near *The King and Queen Surrounded by Swift Nudes*, hung *Yvonne and Magdeleine Torn in Tatters*, for which the artist had used his sisters as models (see plate 35.7).

181. Kimball, "Cubism and the Arensbergs," 117.

182. See PMA-WLA, box 26, AIN 515. For additional information, see this volume, "Notes on Selected Objects," 415.

183. Wood, *I Shock Myself*, 83.

184. Walter Arensberg to Frances Toor, Los Angeles, 12 September 1939, PMA-WLA, box 18, folder 46. We thank Ellen Hoobler for directing our attention to this painting and to the correspondence related to it.

185. Arensberg to Toor, 12 September 1939.

186. Walter Arensberg to Julien Levy, Los Angeles, 12 February 1940, PMA-WLA, box 10, folder 30.

187. Invoice no. 12584, Stendahl Galleries, 16 March 1940, PMA-WLA, box 28, folder 30.

188. Hopps, *The Dream Colony*, 34.

189. Kuh, *The Open Eye*, 58. The two sculptures Kuh refers to are *Torso of a Young Man [I]* (see plate 15.5) and *Fish* (see plate 6.23).

190. David Kahn, *The Codebreakers: The Story of Secret Writing* (New York: Macmillan, 1967), 393. Cf. Ronald Clark, *The Man Who Broke Purple: The Life of Colonel William F. Friedman, Who Deciphered the Japanese Code in World War II* (Boston: Little, Brown, 1977); and William H. Sherman, "How to Make Anything Signify Anything," *Cabinet* 40 (Winter 2010–11): 32–38.

191. William F. Friedman to Walter Arensberg, Washington, DC, 22 June 1945, HEH-WLA, box 77, folder 20. Friedman was replying to a letter from Walter of 17 June 1945, which does not survive.

192. See Walter Arensberg to William F. Friedman, 19 October 1951, HEH-WLA, box 77, folder 20. The silence had in fact been broken the year before: Friedman wrote to Walter on 1 June 1950 to thank him for sending "the very interesting and quite beautiful brochure of the Arensberg Collection which was on exhibit at the Chicago Art Institute a few months ago." HEH-WLA, box 77, folder 20.

193. William F. Friedman, "Diary of My Trip to Europe, 16 November 1951 to 4 December 1951, and to Hollywood, California, 7 Dec–12 Dec 1951," entries for 7 and 8 December 1951, William F. Friedman Papers, the George C. Marshall Research Library, item 881. In his diary, Friedman misdates the entry for 8 December as "Saturday 7 December."

194. Friedman, "Diary of My Trip . . . to Hollywood," entry for 8 December 1951.

195. Friedman, "Diary of My Trip . . . to Hollywood," entry for 8 December 1951.

196. For an in-depth account of the machinations surrounding the bequest to UCLA, see Sawelson-Gorse, "'For the Want of a Nail,'" 109–73.

197. George Roberts and Mary Roberts, *Triumph on Fairmount: Fiske Kimball and the Philadelphia Museum of Art* (Philadelphia: J. B. Lippincott, 1959), 257.

198. Sawelson-Gorse, "'For the Want of a Nail,'" 116.

199. Sawelson-Gorse, "'For the Want of a Nail,'" 125–31; see also Karl With, *Autobiography of Ideas: Memoirs of an Extraordinary Art Scholar*, ed. Roland Jaeger in cooperation with Gerda Becker-With, Dorothee von Berg, and Marion Philadelphia (Berlin: Gebr. Mann, 1997), 256–65.

200. Dreier had died in 1952; see Sawelson-Gorse, "'For the Want of a Nail,'" 200–202.

201. For a full understanding of the disposition of the collection and its various intrigues, see Kuh, *The Open Eye*, 56–64; and Kuh, *My Love Affair with Modern Art: Behind the Scenes with a Legendary Curator*, ed. Avis Berman (New York: Arcade, 2006), 17–23. See also Sawelson-Gorse, "'For the Want of a Nail'"; Roberts and Roberts, *Triumph on Fairmount*, 254–66 and 267–76; and a series of Kimball's letters to Sturgis Ingersoll, Pasadena, 6–13 February 1949, Philadelphia Museum of Art, Library and Archives, Fiske Kimball Papers (hereafter cited as PMA-FKP), box 162, folder 29.

202. Fiske Kimball to Sturgis Ingersoll, 7 February 1949, PMA-FKP, box 162, folder 29.

203. Walter Arensberg, telegram to Fiske Kimball, Los Angeles, 8 April 1949, Philadelphia Museum of Art, Library and Archives, Fiske Kimball Records (hereafter cited as PMA-FKR), box 179, folder 31.

204. Walter Arensberg to Fiske Kimball, Hollywood, 27 April 1949, PMA-FKR, box 179, folder 31.

205. Fiske Kimball to Walter Arensberg, Philadelphia, 6 May 1949, PMA-FKR, box 179, folder 31.

206. Sawelson-Gorse, "'For the Want of a Nail,'" 201–2, quoting in part Roberts and Roberts, *Triumph on Fairmount*, 275.

207. Louise Arensberg to Fiske Kimball, 15 October 1950, PMA-FKR, box 180, folder 3.

208. Ruth Calder to Gertrude Olney Stevens White, Los Angeles, 8 March 1954, HEH-FBLA, box 81, folder 30.

209. Beatrice Wood to Louise Arensberg, 29 September 1953, Beatrice Wood Papers, 1906–1998, Archives of American Art, Smithsonian Institution, box 8, folder 10.

210. Wood, *I Shock Myself*, 134–35.

211. See Louise Arensberg, *Chagall: Le Poète*, PMA-WLA, box 43, folder 7.

212. Kimball, "Cubism and the Arensbergs," 178.

213. William Ivins to Paul Sachs, 23 October 1917, transcribed in "Reminiscences of Paul Joseph Sachs," a 1958 interview by Saul Benison, the transcript of which is held in Butler Library, Columbia University; letter is quoted in Sawelson-Gorse, "'Silent Guard,'" 80. The comments were triggered by Walter's recent poem about Shady Hill (see this essay, page 7), the house he and Louise had sold to Sachs when leaving Cambridge for New York. Ivins was probably referring to Ossip-Lourié's book *Le langage et la verbomanie: Essai de psychologie morbide* (Paris: Librarie Félix Alcan, 1912).

214. See Sally Anne Duncan and Andrew McClellan, *The Art of Curating: Paul J. Sachs and the Museum Course at Harvard* (Los Angeles: Getty Research Institute, 2018).

215. William Ivins to Bernard Berenson, June 1926, Bernard Berenson Archive, Villa I Tatti, the Harvard University Center for Renaissance Studies; quoted in Sawelson-Gorse, "'Silent Guard,'" 213.

216. Ivins to Berenson, June 1926, Bernard Berenson Archive, Villa I Tatti, the Harvard University Center for Renaissance Studies; quoted in Sawelson-Gorse, "'Silent Guard,'" 213.

217. Friedman, "Diary of My Trip . . . to Hollywood," entry for 8 December 1951.

218. Jules Langsner to Thomas Hess, 3 October 1949, Jules Langsner Papers, circa 1910–1998, bulk 1950–1967, Archives of American Art, Smithsonian Institution; quoted in Sawelson-Gorse, "'Silent Guard,'" 345.

219. With, *Autobiography of Ideas*, 219.

220. Friedman, "Diary of My Trip . . . to Hollywood," entry for 8 December 1951. Another famous visitor a few years earlier, the expatriate British novelist Christopher Isherwood, described a similar experience: "Arensberg remained a charming enthusiastic sane host until you got onto the topic of Bacon; then he became wild-eyed and rather incoherent, with ruffled hair and gestures of frenzied excitement. I forgot what Arensberg looked like but I can remember his manner at such times—it was that of a madman as he reveals to you the existence of international conspiracies and speaks with smiling scorn of the enemies who are trying to outwit him." Christopher Isherwood, *Lost Years: A Memoir, 1945–1951*, ed. Katherine Bucknell (London: Chatto & Windus, 2000), 29–30, quoting Isherwood's diary entry for 8 April 1945.

221. *The Cryptologist Looks at Shakespeare*, Folger Shakespeare Library, Washington, DC, MS Y.d.76; published in revised form as William F. Friedman and Elizebeth S. Friedman, *The Shakespearean Ciphers Examined* (Cambridge: Cambridge University Press, 1957). The Friedmans describe Walter's life as an "academic rake's progress by which a promising scholar can become so enamoured of a single theory that he pursues it far beyond the bounds of good sense," comparing him to Gabriele Rossetti (father of Dante Gabriele, Christina, and William Michael): "[He] too had searched for, and found, acrostics in Dante's *Divine Comedy*; he too had gone on to the conviction that a secret society was at work, communicating in a secret language of their own." *The Shakespearean Ciphers*, 154.

222. See James Shapiro, *Contested Will: Who Wrote Shakespeare?* (New York: Simon & Schuster, 2010).

223. See William H. Sherman, "Walter Conrad Arensberg's Anagramania," *Cabinet* 45 (Spring 2012): 71–73.

224. Jean Starobinski, *Words upon Words: The Anagrams of Ferdinand de Saussure*, trans. Olivia Emmet (New Haven: Yale University Press, 1979), 100–101.

225. See Jonathan Culler, *Framing the Sign: Criticism and Its Institutions* (Norman: University of Oklahoma Press, 1989); and Jean-Jacques Lecercle, *The Violence of Language* (London: Routledge, 1990).

226. Louchheim, "The Arensbergs Bought Cubists Then."

227. The Huntington Art Collections include thirteen carpets of Persian, Chinese, and Kazakhstani origin and four decorative bag faces of Persian origin that were originally owned by the Arensbergs. The museum's object numbers for these items are 2007.3.1–2007.3.17.

228. Marina Warner, "Freud's Couch: A Case History," *Raritan* 31, no. 2 (2011): 155, 157. As Warner suggests, such connections depended on the verbal arts that made latent meanings visible and legible, but they shared with cryptography a concern with the science of permutation: "A carpet maker conjugates structural motifs 'in infinite combination,' as Freud wrote about his dream analysis, within a basic structure of frame, ground, and figure" (157).

229. Friedman, "Diary of My Trip . . . to Hollywood," entry for 8 December 1951.

230. Friedman, "Diary of My Trip . . . to Hollywood," entry for 8 December 1951.

231. Elizabeth Wrigley to Roberta Ballantine, 6 June 1981, HEH-FBLA, box 41, folder 7.

232. Stefan Zweig, *Chess: A Novella*, trans. Anthea Bell (London: Penguin, 2006), 12. Published in German as *Schachnovelle* (Buenos Aires: Pygmalión, 1942). The Royal Game—a long-serving nickname for the game of chess—was the alternate title for Zweig's novella, created for the first American publication in 1944.

THE LOUISE AND WALTER ARENSBERG COLLECTIONS OVER TIME

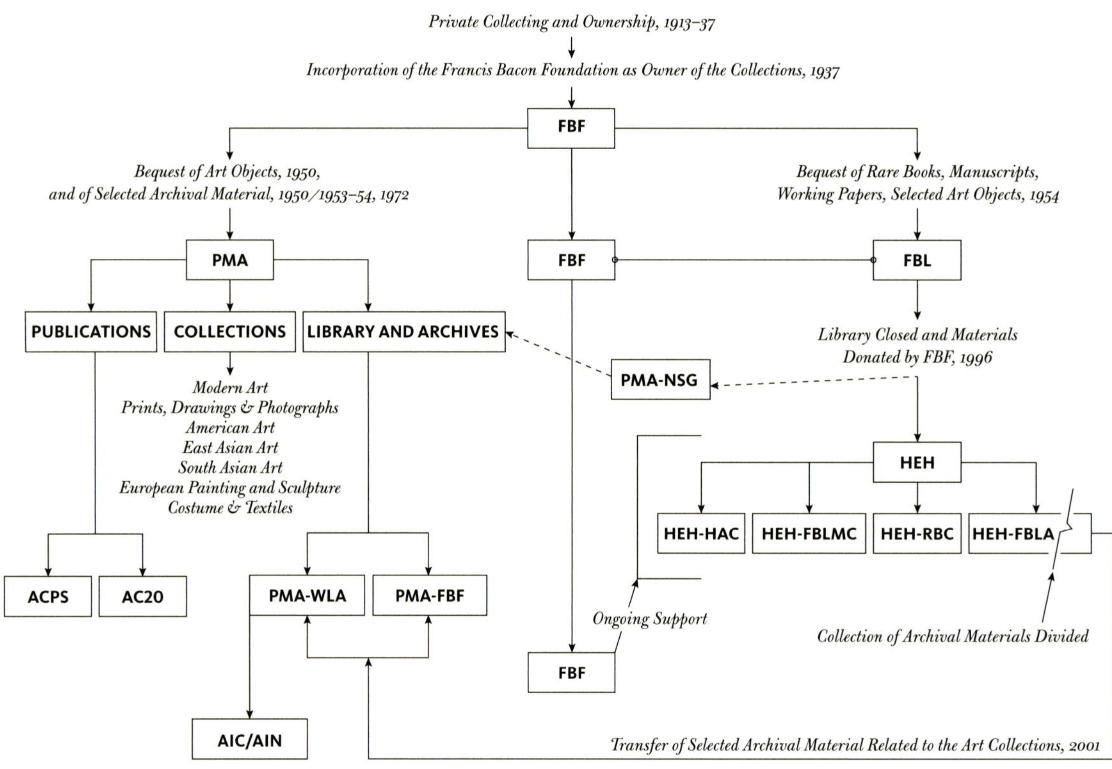

NOTES ON THE ABBREVIATIONS USED THROUGHOUT THIS BOOK

The following key to abbreviations directs readers to the primary repositories of art, books, and papers left behind by Louise and Walter Arensberg. Illustrated by the diagram opposite, it tracks the disposition of those materials as they traveled from private ownership to institutional stewardship.

FBF: FRANCIS BACON FOUNDATION

Established by Louise and Walter Arensberg in 1937 and run from an office located on the second floor of their home at 7065 Hillside Avenue in Los Angeles, the Francis Bacon Foundation served many functions for the couple. Its principal mission was "to promote study in science, literature, religion, history, and philosophy with special reference to the works of Francis Bacon, his character and life, and his influence on his own and succeeding times." The **FBF** was also the legal owner of the Arensbergs' collections of art, books, and manuscripts, granting these purchases tax-exempt status. **FBF** employees were charged not only with assisting Walter in his research on the authorship of Shakespeare's plays but also with managing the care of the collections, arranging loans to exhibitions, and (when the time came) attending to the collections' ultimate disposition. In 1950, Marcel Duchamp joined the **FBF**'s Board of Trustees and played a central role in formalizing the gift of its art-related collections to the Philadelphia Museum of Art. After the Arensbergs' deaths, the **FBF** continued its work from new bases in Pasadena and Claremont before bequeathing its library and archive to the Huntington in 1996 (see **FBL** and **HEH** below). The **FBF** today supports scholarly activities and public events at the Huntington.

PMA: PHILADELPHIA MUSEUM OF ART

In 1950, under the watchful eye of the Arensbergs and with the assistance of **FBF** trustee Marcel Duchamp, the foundation managed the transfer of more than one thousand art objects (along with a portion of corresponding archival material) to the Philadelphia Museum of Art, where these objects and materials formed the bedrock of the museum's modern and contemporary collections. As the Arensberg collection was received and processed by the **PMA**, objects were given accession numbers. All **PMA** accession numbers are a combination of three numbers: one denoting the year of an object's accession, one denoting the chronological position of an accession in relation to other accessions within a given year, and the last denoting an individual object within any given accession. The Arensberg collection was accession 134 of the year 1950. Hence, all accession numbers for the Arensberg collection begin 1950-134. Constantin Brancusi's *Arch* was the twenty-second Arensberg object cataloged, so its accession number is 1950-134-22. If an object or artwork pictured here is currently in the collection of the **PMA**, its corresponding accession number is included with its caption. Because the scholarship on any particular object may change over time, its accession number is the most reliable reference for further research at the **PMA** or when using the museum's searchable collections databases on-site or online at philamuseum.org.

PHILADELPHIA MUSEUM OF ART, LIBRARY AND ARCHIVES
PMA-WLA: ARENSBERG ARCHIVES
PMA-FBF: FRANCIS BACON FOUNDATION RECORDS
PMA-MDP: ALEXINA AND MARCEL DUCHAMP PAPERS
PMA-FKR: FISKE KIMBALL RECORDS
PMA-FKP: FISKE KIMBALL PAPERS
PMA-NSG: NAOMI SAWELSON-GORSE RESEARCH COLLECTION

In the **PMA** Library and Archives, the Arensberg Archives and Francis Bacon Foundation Records house many of the Arensbergs' personal and business papers. They include hundreds of photographs and much of the couple's voluminous correspondence, documenting both their art-collecting activities and their relationships with significant artists, writers, and scholars. Of particular interest are the letters from museum curators asking for temporary loans for exhibitions or making a case for their institution as a possible home for the entire collection. These archives also hold drafts of Walter's writings, materials related to his Baconian studies, and documents related to the founding of the **FBF**. After the closure of the Francis Bacon Library (see following page), some materials from the foundation were preserved by the art historian Naomi Sawelson-Gorse, who later deposited them at the **PMA**. The story of the Arensbergs' negotiations with the **PMA** can also be traced in the Fiske Kimball Records, which document the official business of Kimball's long period as the museum's director from 1925 to 1955, and particularly his courting of collectors and donors. There are also relevant materials in the Fiske Kimball Papers, which capture Kimball's personal and professional activities, documenting his family life and work as an architect and teacher as well as museum director. The Alexina and Marcel Duchamp Papers contain personal photographs, letters, lecture notes, transcripts of interviews, and published materials that illuminate Duchamp's relationship with the Arensbergs. Online finding aids for these archives can be accessed at https://pmalibrary.libraryhost.com. Digitized materials from the Alexina and Marcel Duchamp Papers, the Arensberg Archives, and the Fiske Kimball Papers are also available in the Duchamp Research Portal at https://duchamparchives.org/.

ACPS: *THE LOUISE AND WALTER ARENSBERG COLLECTION: PRE-COLUMBIAN SCULPTURE*
AC20: *THE LOUISE AND WALTER ARENSBERG COLLECTION: 20TH CENTURY SECTION*
When the Arensbergs made the bequest of their collection to the **PMA**, they requested that a catalog be published of their collection and allocated funds through the **FBF** for its realization. Published in 1954, the two resulting volumes, *The Louise and Walter Arensberg Collection: Pre-Columbian Sculpture* and *The Louise and Walter Arensberg Collection: 20th Century Section*, include a total of 393 black-and-white photographs representing only a small selection of the best objects and artworks owned by the couple. If an object pictured here was published in one of these two volumes, it has been given an **ACPS** number or an **AC20** number that corresponds to its plate number in the applicable book.

AIC: ARENSBERG INDEX CARD
AIN: ARENSBERG INVENTORY NUMBER
Before and after the Arensberg bequest to the **PMA**, the **FBF** kept a card catalog with an index card for every object owned by the couple. Written on each index card is an inventory number—no longer in official use—for the object it pictures and/or describes. The card catalog is now housed in **PMA-WLA**, where it is arranged by discipline and, within discipline, by the **AIN**s. The **AIC**s in this catalog are still filed in their original order. The **AIC** and **AIN** are cited in this book when an object is not in the collection of the **PMA**. On some documents originating from the **FBF**, **AIN**s are referred to as call numbers.

FBL: FRANCIS BACON LIBRARY
After Louise's death in November 1953 and Walter's in January 1954, the **FBF** transferred the couple's rare books and manuscripts, along with Walter's original research and working papers, to the Pashgian Building in Pasadena, where the foundation opened the newly instituted Francis Bacon Library to the public. In 1959, the **FBF** paid for the construction of a building for the **FBL** on the campus of the Claremont Colleges in Claremont, California. Both the **FBF** and the **FBL** were run by Elizabeth Wrigley, the Arensbergs' longest-serving employee, who had been in charge of many of the foundation's daily operations since 1945 and who was devoted to the perpetuation of Walter's projects.

HEH: THE HUNTINGTON LIBRARY, ART MUSEUM, AND BOTANICAL GARDENS, SAN MARINO, CALIFORNIA
Under mounting financial pressure, and needing a succession plan upon the illness and departure of Wrigley in 1995, the **FBF** closed the **FBL** and made a bequest of its holdings to the Huntington Library, one of the premier research institutes in the United States. The transfer of **FBL** materials to the Huntington Library was completed in 1996; Wrigley died the following year. A significant quantity of Arensberg-related materials from the **FBL**, including the couple's extensive collection of rare books and manuscripts, family photographs, foundation records, and Walter's original research notes and working papers, are now housed at the Huntington Library in one of three collections, accessible in the online catalog at https://catalog.huntington.org/:

- **HEH-FBLMC: FRANCIS BACON LIBRARY MANUSCRIPTS COLLECTION**
  See call number: mssFBL
- **HEH-RBC: RARE BOOKS COLLECTION**
  The more than four thousand books from the **FBL** in the Huntington Library can be found by searching for "Arensberg" or "Francis Bacon Library" as keyword.
- **HEH-FBLA: FRANCIS BACON LIBRARY ARCHIVE, WALTER AND LOUISE ARENSBERG PAPERS**
  See call number: 602120

The rare carpets and woven bag faces that had decorated the Arensberg home and later the **FBL** (see page 66) were also given to the Huntington Library but were later transferred to the Huntington Art Collections at the Huntington Art Museum:

- **HEH-HAC: HUNTINGTON ART COLLECTIONS**
  While the online finding aid for **HEH-HAC** can be accessed at http://emuseum.huntington.org/, these carpets and bag faces are not yet available for viewing online.

NOTES ON THE CAPTIONS USED THROUGHOUT THE PLATES

Captions and line drawings include any known information about a pictured object's maker, its title or description, and the date of its creation. To function most efficiently as signposts for further research, they forgo the annotations of medium and size typical to most art books and instead point readers to where these objects currently reside. That information is included in square brackets at the end of each caption and is more fully explained in the key to abbreviations (see pages 75, 76). No judgment is offered regarding the perceived monetary or cultural value of any particular artwork or artifact pictured in this book, and each has been captioned equally to acknowledge its individual contribution to the cacaphonous environment created by the Arensbergs.

MAKER AND PLACE OF ORIGIN

The proper attribution of artifacts to a named artist or maker is an ongoing endeavor. The following sample captions show a range of specificity regarding the creators of artworks, from a known and named artist (caption 1) through one for which no attribution is known or given (caption 12). When authorship can only be attributed to a broad group of people rather than to an individual, as many specifics as possible are provided (compare captions 3–10). When specific attribution of authorship has not yet been applied to a particular object, it has been designated "Artist/Maker unknown" (captions 11, 12), but if something is known of where an artifact was found and/or made, that location is provided in the parentheses that follow (caption 11).

1 MARCEL DUCHAMP, *The King and Queen Surrounded by Swift Nudes*, 1912 [1950-134-63A; AC20-68]

*2 PABLO PICASSO, *Seashore Scene*, 1905 [1950-134-159; AC20-162]

3 CHUMASH (POINT DUME, CALIFORNIA), Whale Form with Bone Blow Pipe, Date unknown [1950-134-477]

4 CHUMASH (CALIFORNIA), Boat Form, Date unknown [1950-134-792]

5–9 NATIVE AMERICAN, Baskets, Dates unknown [5: 1950-134-773; 6: *1950-134-772; 7: 1950-134-770; 8: 1950-134-771; 9: 1950-134-769]

10 *AZTEC (CENTRAL MEXICO), Serpent (Quetzalcoatl), 1300–1520 [1950-134-397; ACPS-29]

11 ARTIST/MAKER UNKNOWN (*CHINA), Couchant Animal, ca. 960–1279 [1950-134-499]

12 ARTIST/MAKER UNKNOWN, Gothic Chest Front, Date unknown [NOTE 1.10, PAGE 414]

ASTERISKS

Asterisks indicate that listed information is tentative (captions 10, 11).

An asterisk typeset in orange at the beginning of an entry (caption 2) indicates that an object's identification is tentative but strong enough to list, either because an educated guess can be made about it by looking at other photographs in this book or, in rare cases, because no other object known to have been in the Arensbergs' collection resembles it more.

An asterisk set within the ending brackets also indicates an educated guess at an object's identification. In the example shown (captions 5–9), five Native American baskets are nested together. Though only four baskets can be positively identified by markings visible in the photograph, the fifth basket (caption 6) falls within a logical progression of image acquisition numbers.

An asterisk set into a line drawing indicates that an object shown in its corresponding photograph could not be identified (see, for example, plate 41).

NOTES ON SELECTED OBJECTS

Objects not housed at the Philadelphia Museum of Art have been given an additional note, usually because their location is unknown (caption 12). See "Notes on Selected Objects," page 414.

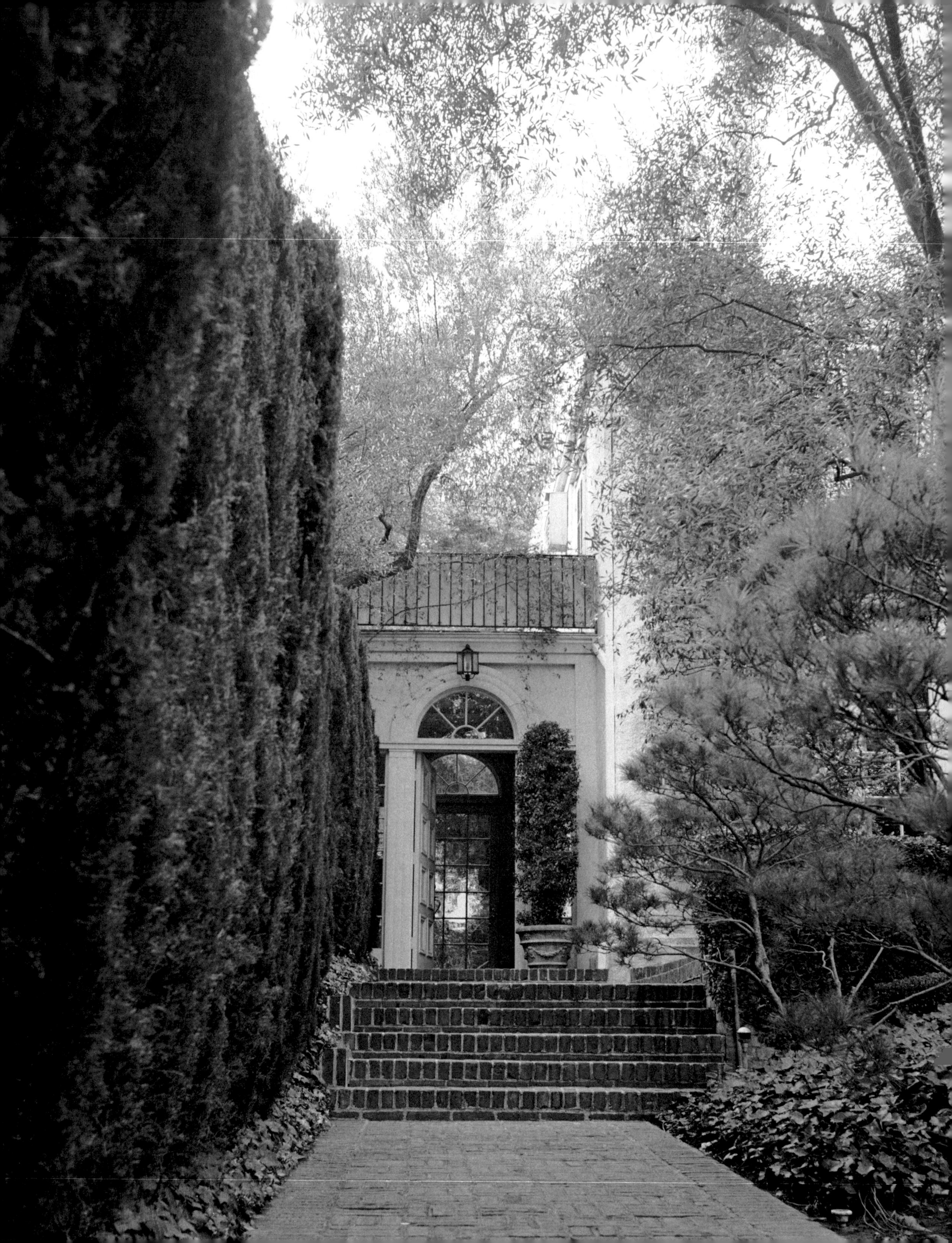

HOLLYWOOD ARENSBERG

A Reconstruction of the Home and Art Collection of Louise and Walter Arensberg, 7065 Hillside Avenue, Los Angeles, California, 1927–54

MARK NELSON

KARL BISSINGER. THE FRONT ENTRY OF THE LOUISE AND WALTER ARENSBERG RESIDENCE, 7065 HILLSIDE AVENUE, LOS ANGELES, 16 MARCH 1950. UNIVERSITY OF DELAWARE LIBRARY, NEWARK, SPECIAL COLLECTIONS, KARL BISSINGER ARCHIVE (MSS0682).

7065 HILLSIDE AVENUE, LOS ANGELES, CALIFORNIA
RESIDENCE OF LOUISE AND WALTER ARENSBERG, 1927–54

GROUND FLOOR

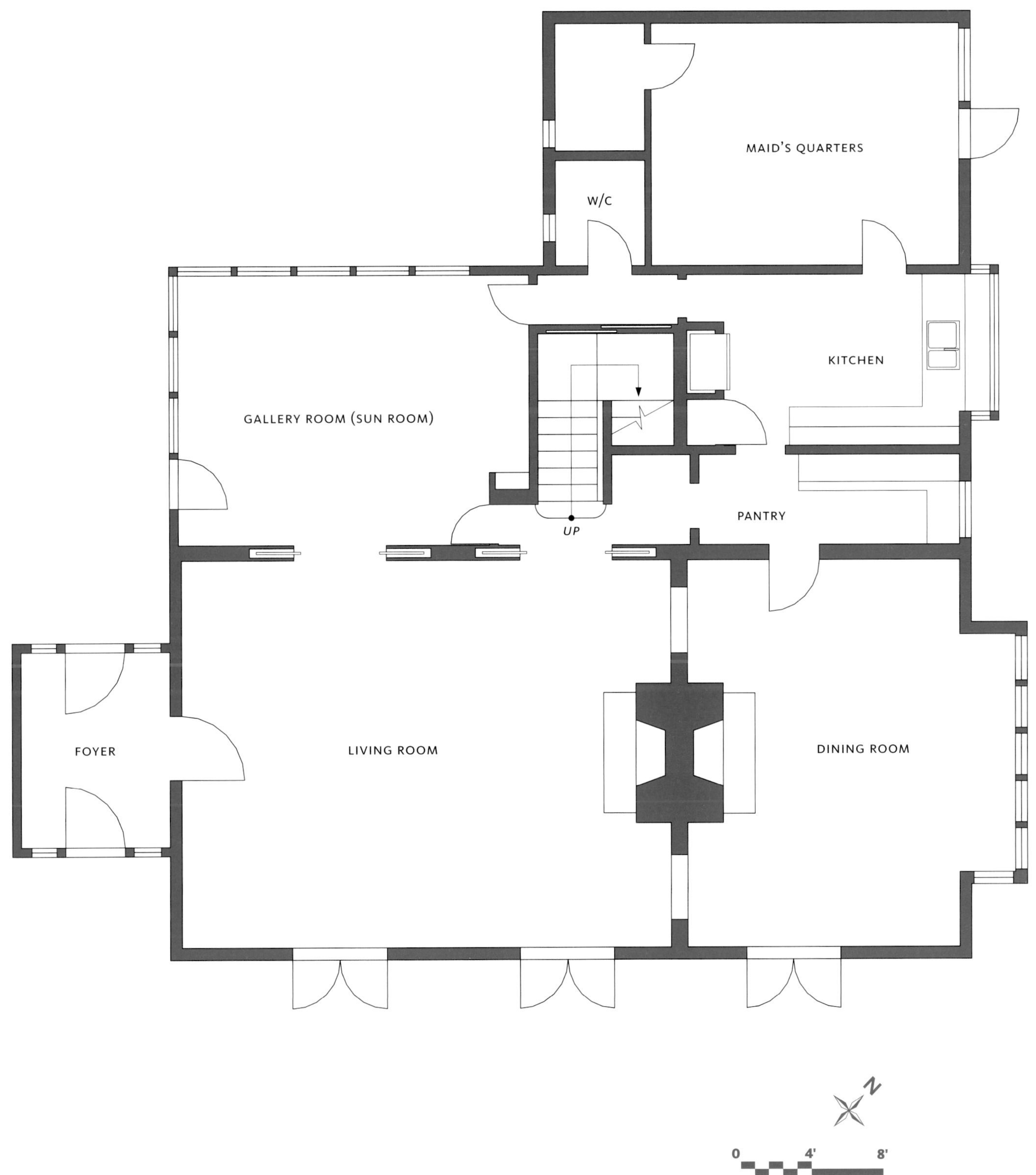
MAID'S QUARTERS
W/C
KITCHEN
GALLERY ROOM (SUN ROOM)
UP
PANTRY
FOYER
LIVING ROOM
DINING ROOM
N
0
4'
8'

PLATE 1

FRONT ENTRANCE

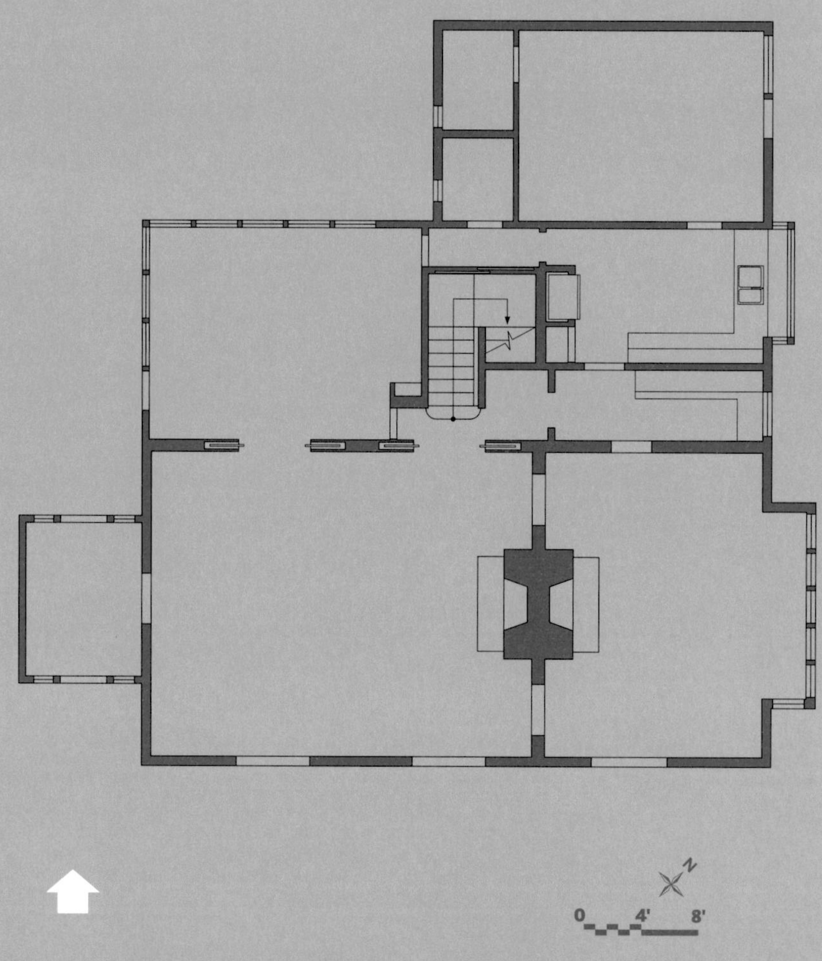

FRED R. DAPPRICH

CA. 1944

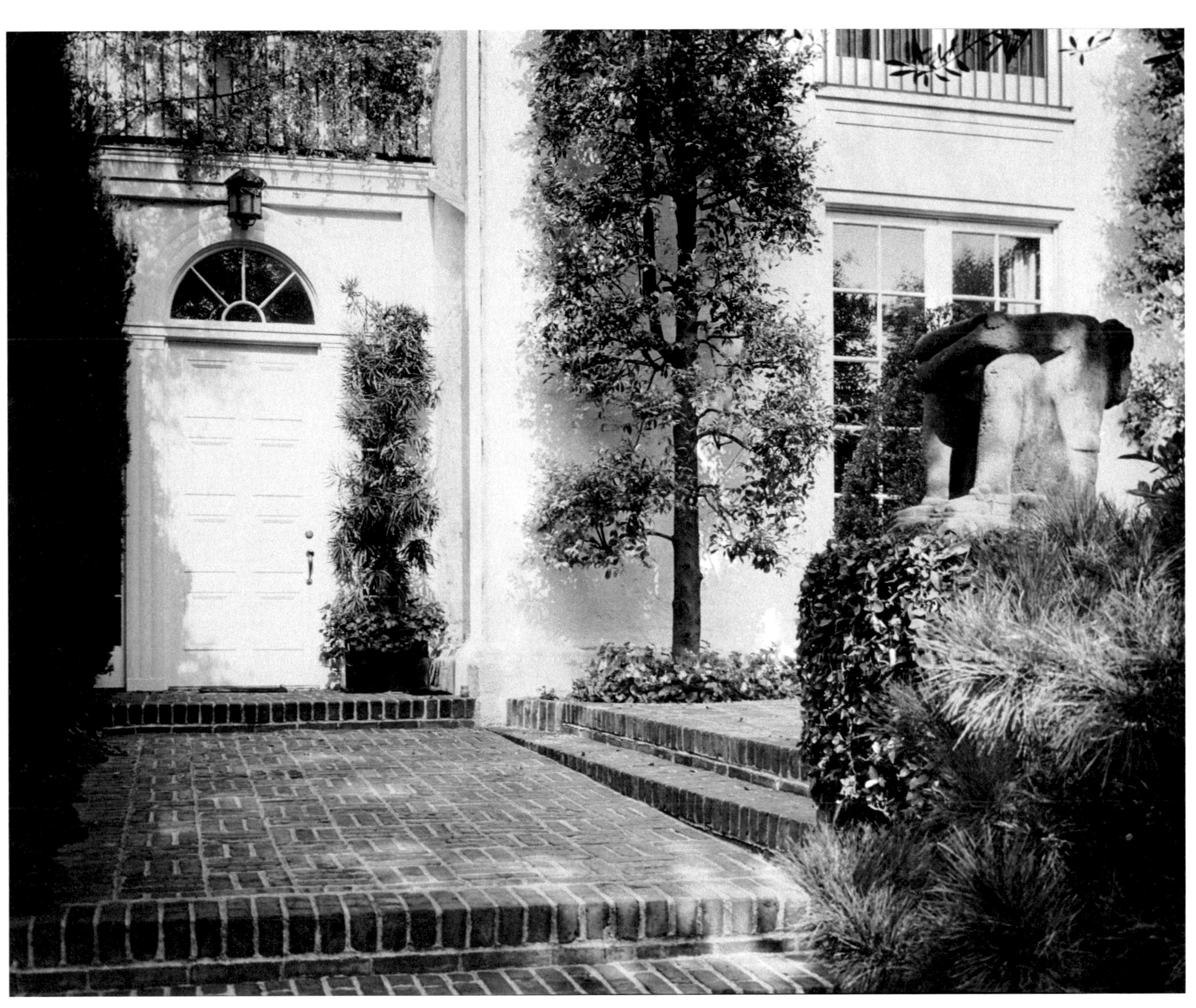

1 AZTEC (CENTRAL MEXICO), Figure of a Man, 1300–1520 [1950-134-305; ACPS-10]

PLATE 2

FOYER

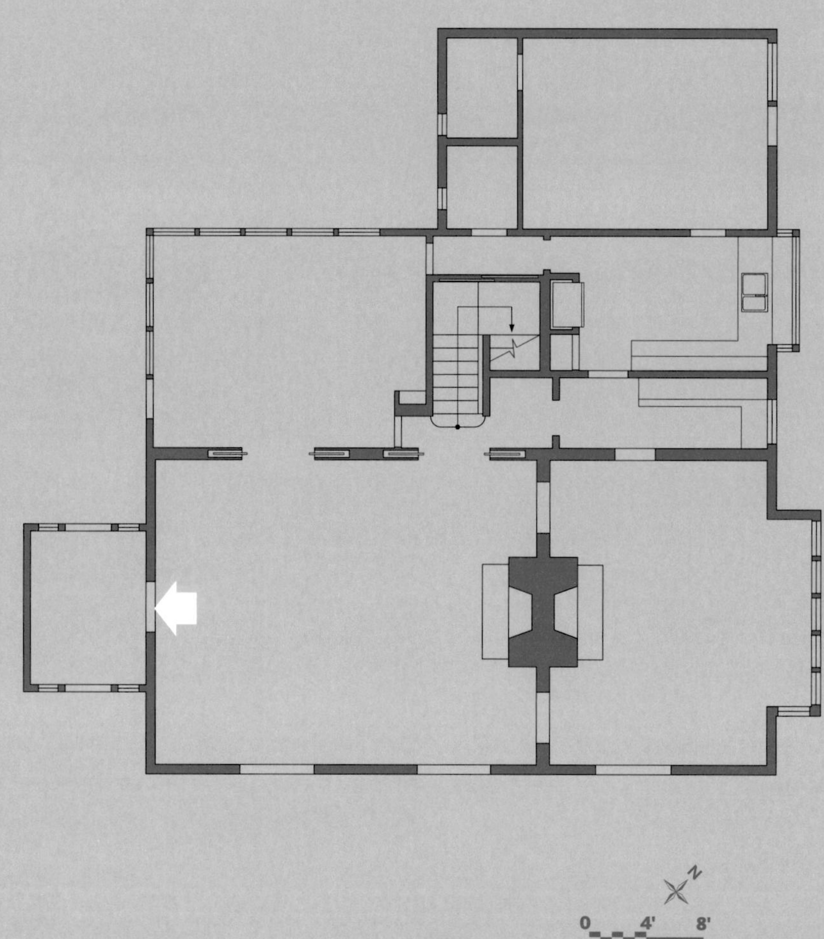

FLOYD FAXON
AFTER 25 SEPTEMBER BUT BEFORE 12 OCTOBER 1948

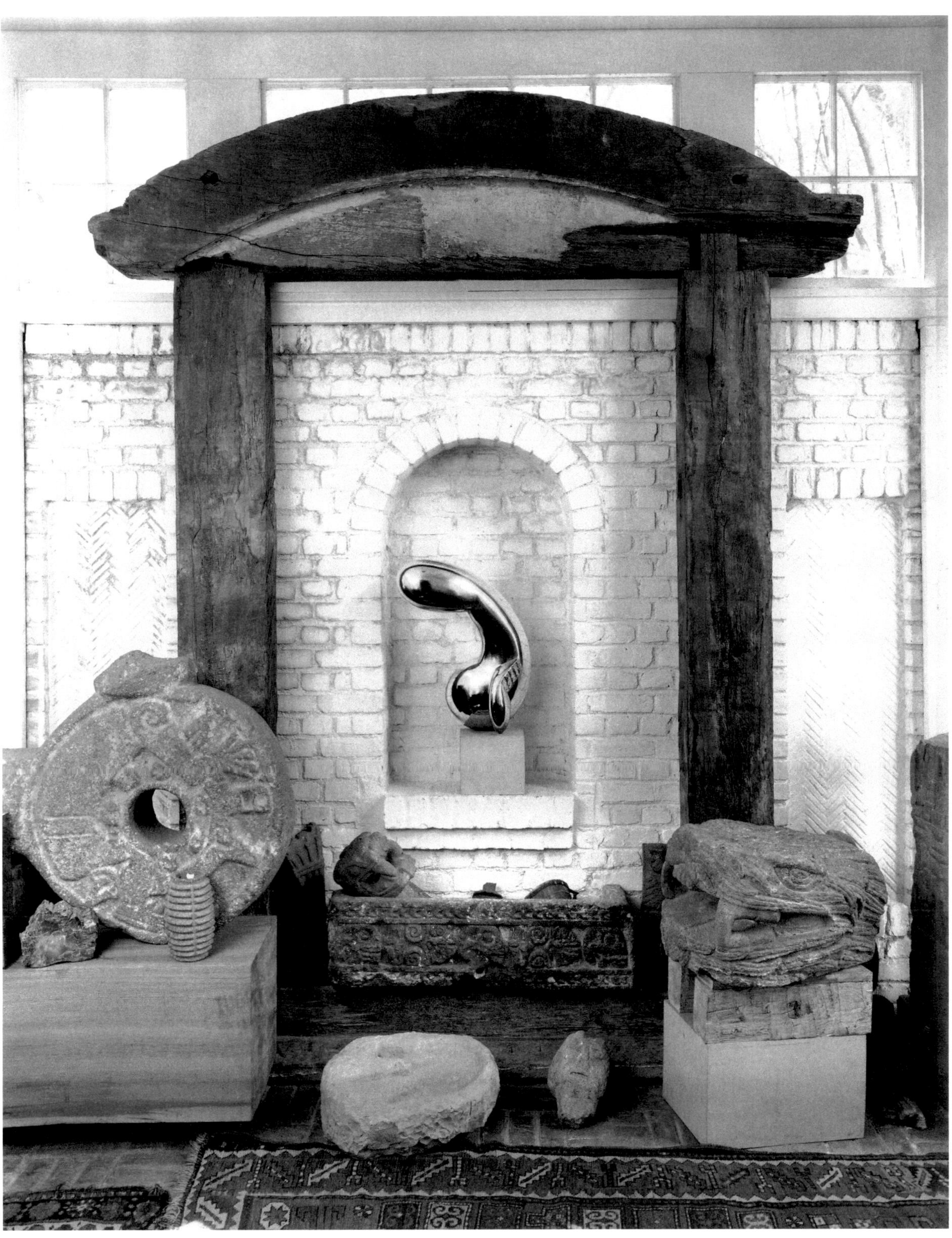

PLATE 2

1 CONSTANTIN BRANCUSI, *Arch*, ca. 1914–16 [1950-134-22; AC20-12]

2 CONSTANTIN BRANCUSI, *Princess X*, 1915–16 [1950-134-12; AC20-11]

3 Unidentified Geological Specimen (possibly petrified wood), Date unknown [NO EXTANT RECORD]

4 AZTEC (CENTRAL MEXICO), Ballcourt Ring with Monkey and Solar Motif, 1400–1520 [1950-134-225; ACPS-45]

5 COLIMA, JALISCO, MICHOACÁN, OR NAYARIT (WESTERN MEXICO), Mace Head, 200 BCE–300 CE [1950-134-290; ACPS-72]

6 CLASSIC VERACRUZ (EAST COAST MEXICO), Palma, 500–900 [1950-134-345; ACPS-158]

7 TOTONAC (EAST COAST MEXICO), Tenoned Head of a Jaguar, 600–900 [1950-134-289; ACPS-132]

8 AZTEC (CENTRAL MEXICO), Basin, 1300–1520 [1950-134-243; ACPS-42]

9 ARTIST/MAKER UNKNOWN, Leather Sap-Gathering Container and Natural Rubber (Latex) Ball, 20th century [1950-134-602]

THIS OBJECT MAY BE A REPLICA OF A PRE-COLUMBIAN BALL USED IN THE RITUAL BALLGAME.

10 CLASSIC VERACRUZ (EAST COAST MEXICO), Palma, 500–900 [1950-134-299; ACPS-152]

11 AZTEC (CENTRAL MEXICO), Head of a Serpent, 1300–1520 [1950-134-371; ACPS-37]

12 AZTEC (CENTRAL MEXICO), Fragment of an Upright Slab, 1300–1520 [1950-134-313; ACPS-50]

13 ARTIST/MAKER UNKNOWN, Dinosaur Print (fake), Date unknown [NOTE 1.1, PAGE 414]

14 NATIVE AMERICAN (NEW MEXICO), Figure/Head, Date unknown [1950-134-633]

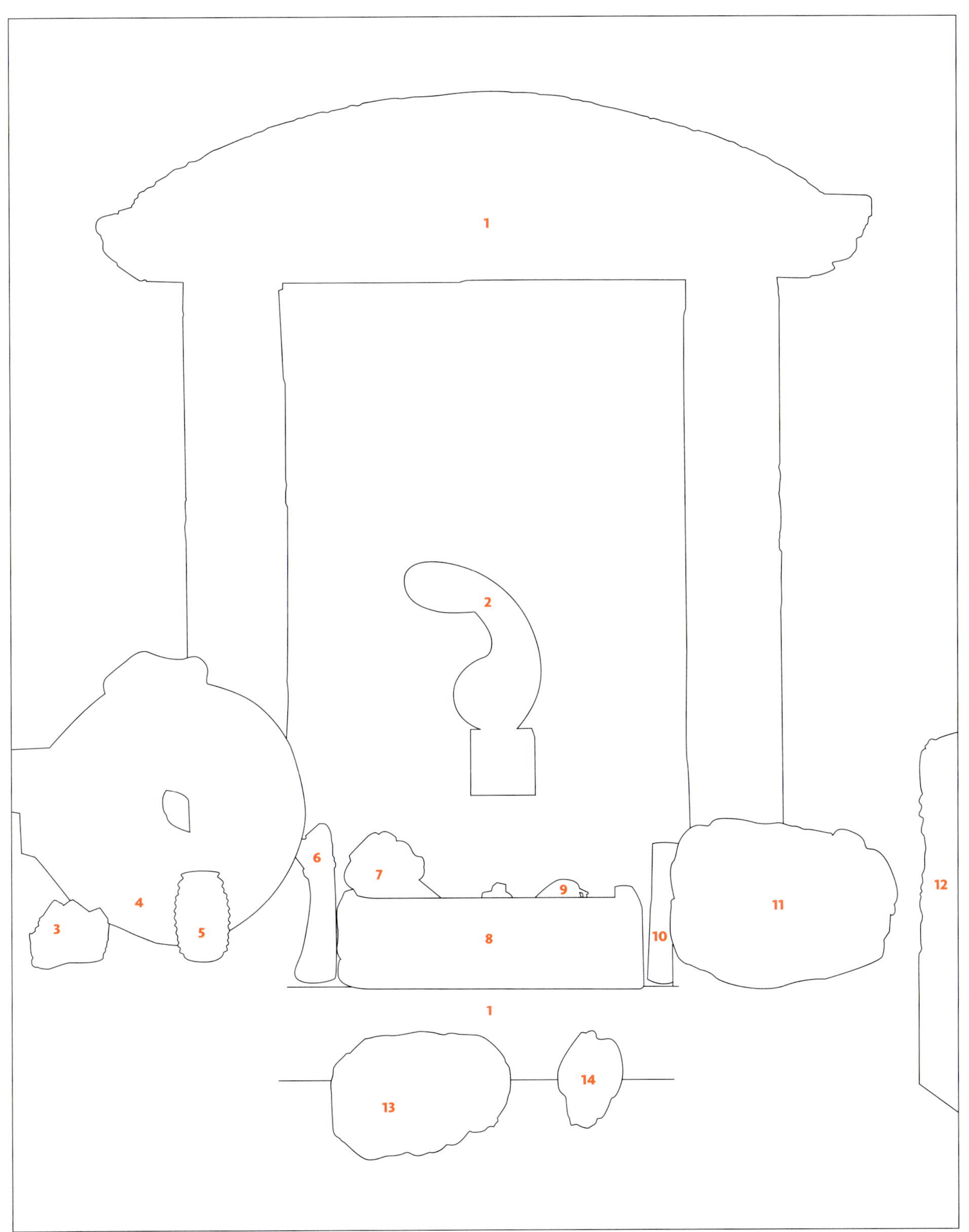
1
2
6
7
9
4
3
5
8
10
11
12
1
13
14

PLATE 3

LIVING ROOM

WITH VIEWS INTO THE DINING ROOM THROUGH THE NORTH AND SOUTH ARCHWAYS

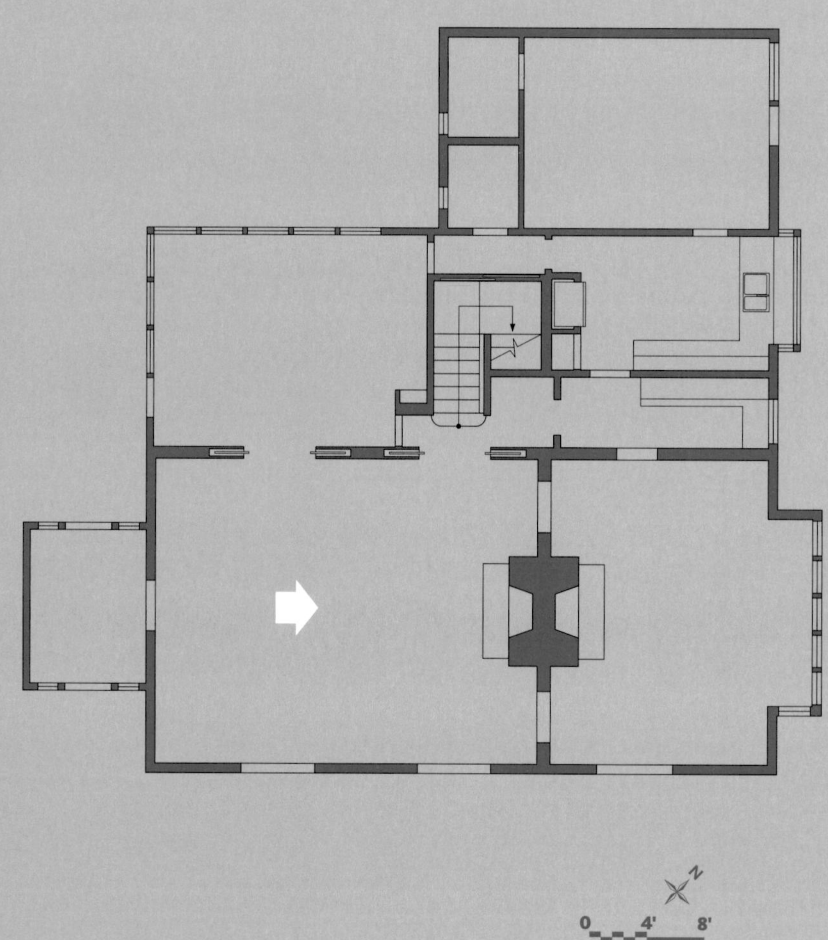

CORPORAL F. W. LUMBORD

CA. APRIL 1945

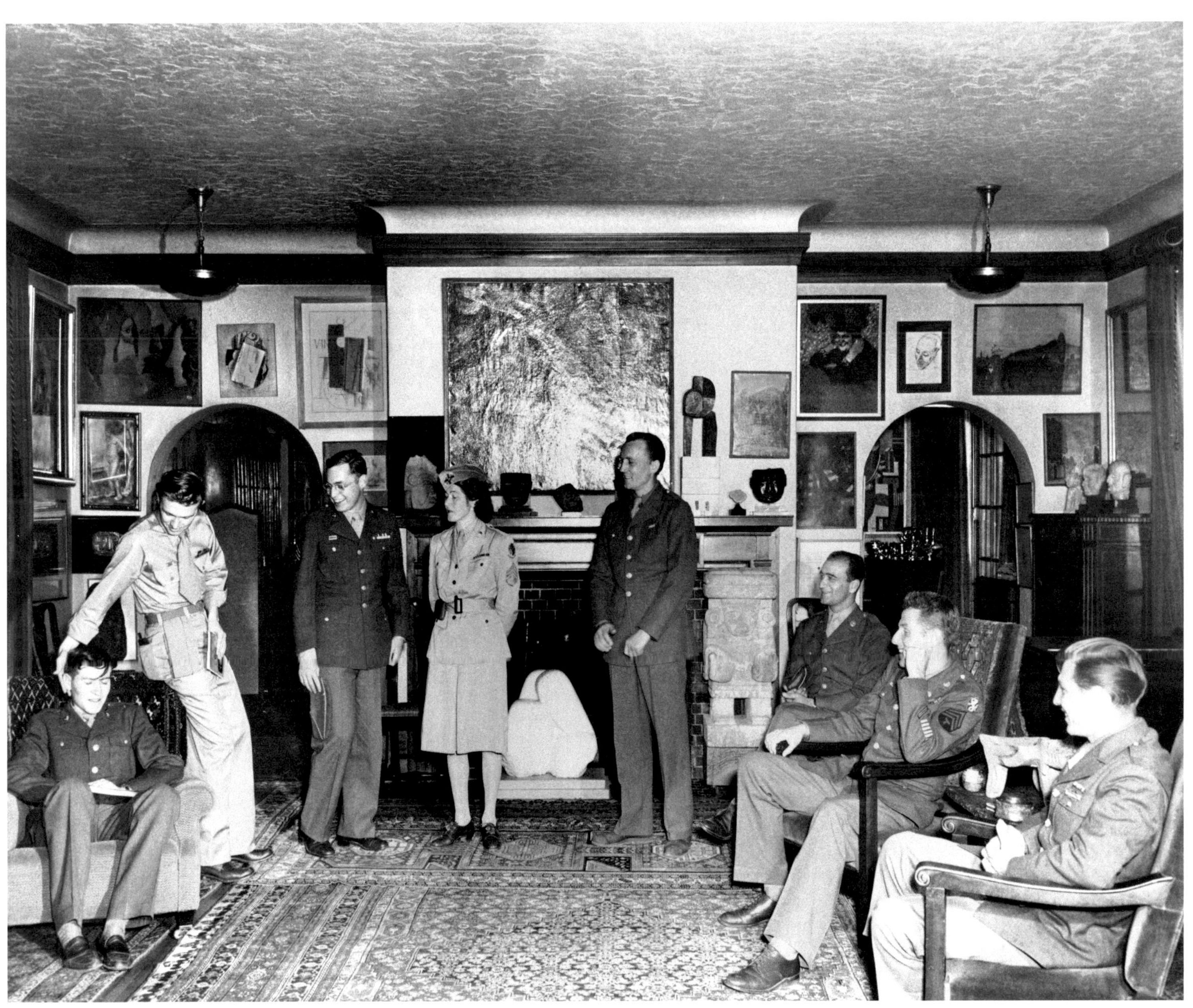

PLATE 3

1 MARCEL DUCHAMP, *Bride*, 1912 [1950-134-65; AC20-71]

*2 PAUL KLEE, *Demon as Pirate*, 1926 [1950-134-114; AC20-117]

3 MARCEL DUCHAMP, *Yvonne and Magdeleine Torn in Tatters*, 1911 [1950-134-53; AC20-58]

4 PIERRE-AUGUSTE RENOIR, *Bather*, ca. 1917–18 [1950-134-173; AC20-177]

5 CHIMÚ (PERU), Funerary Mask, 900–1470 [1950-134-284; ACPS-185]

*6 REPRODUCTION OF MARCEL DUCHAMP'S *Coffee Mill* (1911), Date unknown [NOTE 1.2, PAGE 414]

7 AZTEC (CENTRAL MEXICO), Figure (Quetzalcoatl), 1300–1520 [1950-134-251; ACPS-27]

8 GEORGES BRAQUE, *Still Life (Violin)*, 1913 [1950-134-25; AC20-25]

9 GEORGES BRAQUE, *Still Life (with the Word VIN)*, 1912–13 [1950-134-24; AC20-23]

10 GEORGES BRAQUE, *Paris* or *Still Life on a Table*, 1910 [1950-134-873]

11 CLASSIC VERACRUZ (EAST COAST MEXICO), Hacha in the Form of a Head, 500–900 [1950-134-337; ACPS-147]

12 MARCEL DUCHAMP, *The King and Queen Surrounded by Swift Nudes*, 1912 [1950-134-63A; AC20-68]

13 TEOTIHUACAN (CENTRAL MEXICO), Mask, 1st–9th century [1950-134-232; ACPS-15]

14 HUASTEC (EAST COAST MEXICO), Head, 900–1200 [1950-134-317; ACPS-129]

15 CONSTANTIN BRANCUSI, *Prodigal Son*, ca. 1914–15 [1950-134-8; AC20-7]

16, 17 MEZCALA (SOUTHWESTERN MEXICO), Seated Figures, 300 BCE–500 CE [16: 1950-134-542; 17: 1950-134-541]

18 MANTEÑO (ECUADOR), Stamp, 900–1500 [1950-134-307; ACPS-169]

19 ARTIST/MAKER UNKNOWN (MEXICO), Mask, Likely 20th century [1950-134-252]

20 HENRI ROUSSEAU, *Landscape*, 1905–10 [1950-134-177; AC20-181]

21 PABLO PICASSO, *Old Woman (Woman with Gloves)*, 1901 [1950-134-158; AC20-161]

22 PABLO PICASSO, *Head*, 1906 [1950-134-161; AC20-165]

23 HENRI ROUSSEAU, *Landscape with Cattle*, 1895–1900 [1950-134-175; AC20-180]

24 HENRI ROUSSEAU, *Village Street*, 1909–10 [1950-134-178; AC20-182]

*25 MARCEL DUCHAMP, *Nude Descending a Staircase (No. 1)*, 1911 [1950-134-58; AC20-63]

26 MEZCALA (SOUTHWESTERN MEXICO), Head, 300 BCE–500 CE [1950-134-208]

27 CLASSIC VERACRUZ (EAST COAST MEXICO), Hacha in the Form of a Head, 500–900 [1950-134-401; ACPS-136]

*28 ARTIST/MAKER UNKNOWN (MEXICO), Dog, Likely 20th century [1950-134-370; ACPS-197]

29 PABLO PICASSO, *Female Figure*, 1906 [1950-134-160A; AC20-163]

*30 PABLO PICASSO, *Seashore Scene*, 1905 [1950-134-159; AC20-162]

31 FERNAND LÉGER, *Typographer (Final State)*, 1919 [1950-134-125; AC20-128]

32 PAUL KLEE, *Village Carnival*, 1926 [1950-134-115; AC20-114]

33 SIR FRANCIS BACON, Autograph Letter Signed, to George Villiers, Earl (later Duke) of Buckingham, 22 September 1617 [NOTE 2.1, PAGE 416]

34 TEOTIHUACAN (CENTRAL MEXICO), Goddess Figure, 100–650 [1950-134-282; ACPS-2]

35 CONSTANTIN BRANCUSI, *Three Penguins*, 1911–12 [1950-134-7; AC20-6]

36 NATIVE AMERICAN (SOUTHWESTERN UNITED STATES), Jar, Date unknown [1950-134-648]

37 GUANACASTE-NICOYA (COSTA RICA), Metate, 300–800 [1950-134-319; ACPS-173]

38 TEOTIHUACAN (CENTRAL MEXICO), Vessel, 1st–9th century [1950-134-540]

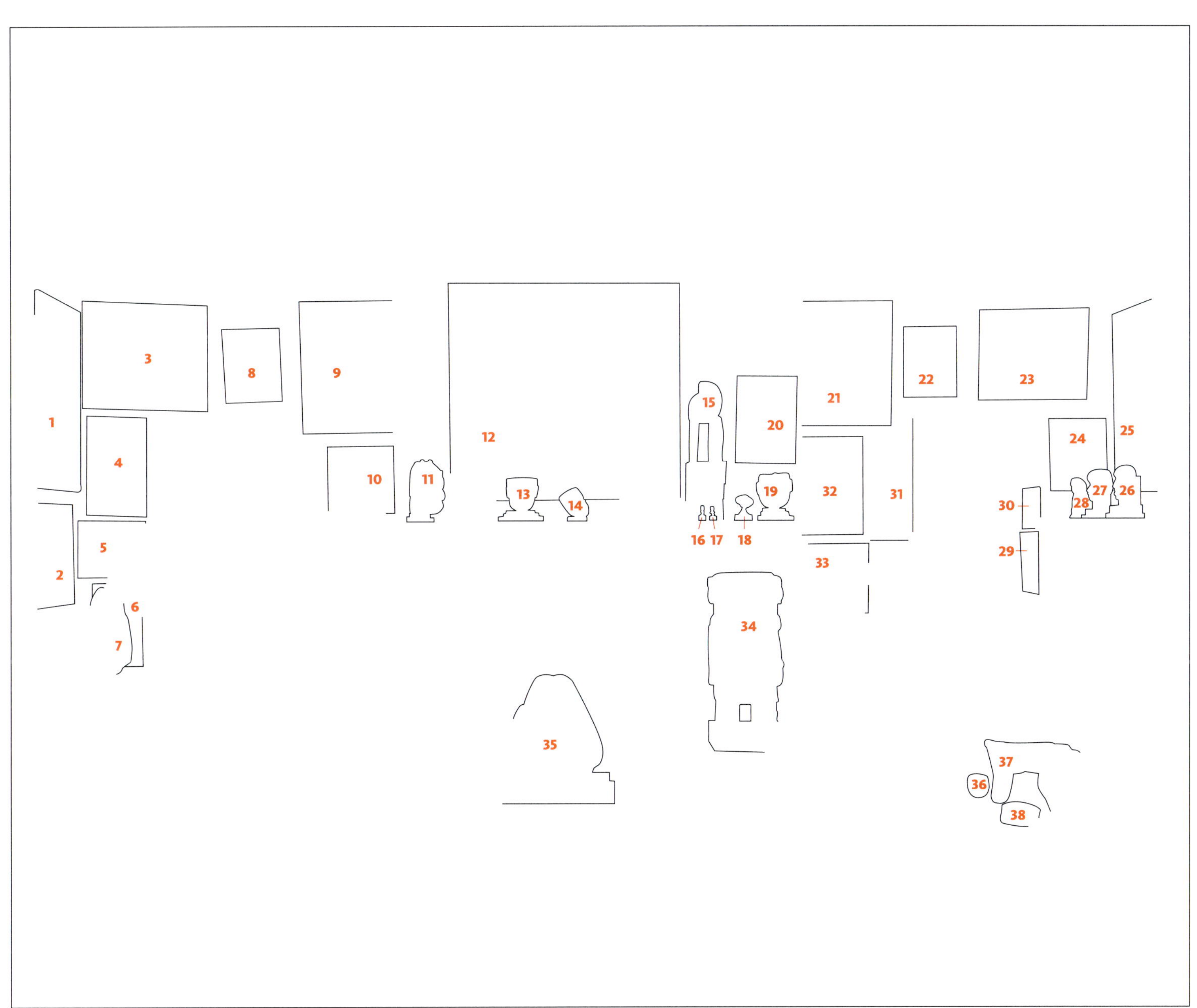
1
2
3
4
5
6
7
8
9
10
11
12
13
14
15
16
17
18
19
20
21
22
23
24
25
26
27
28
29
30
31
32
33
34
35
36
37
38

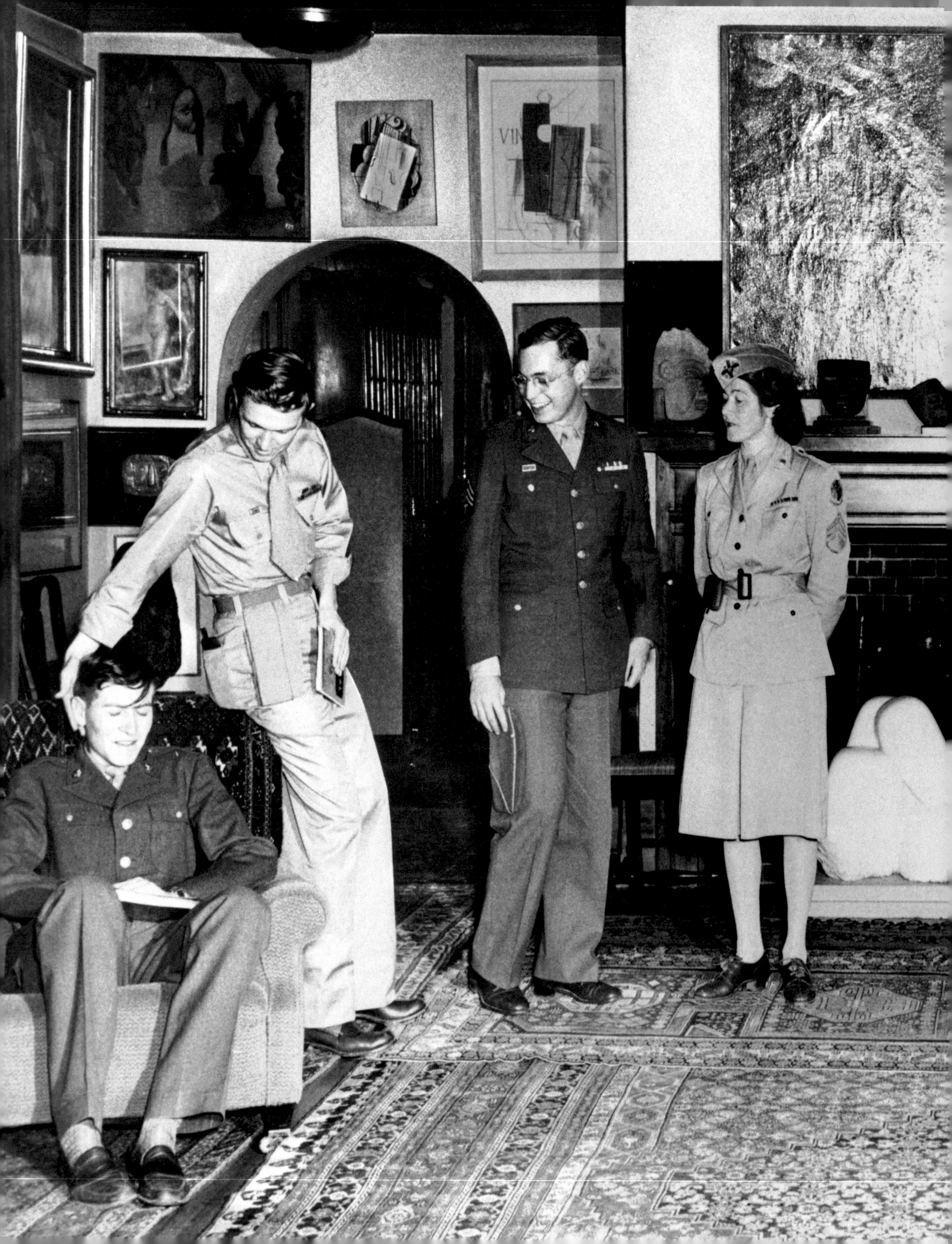

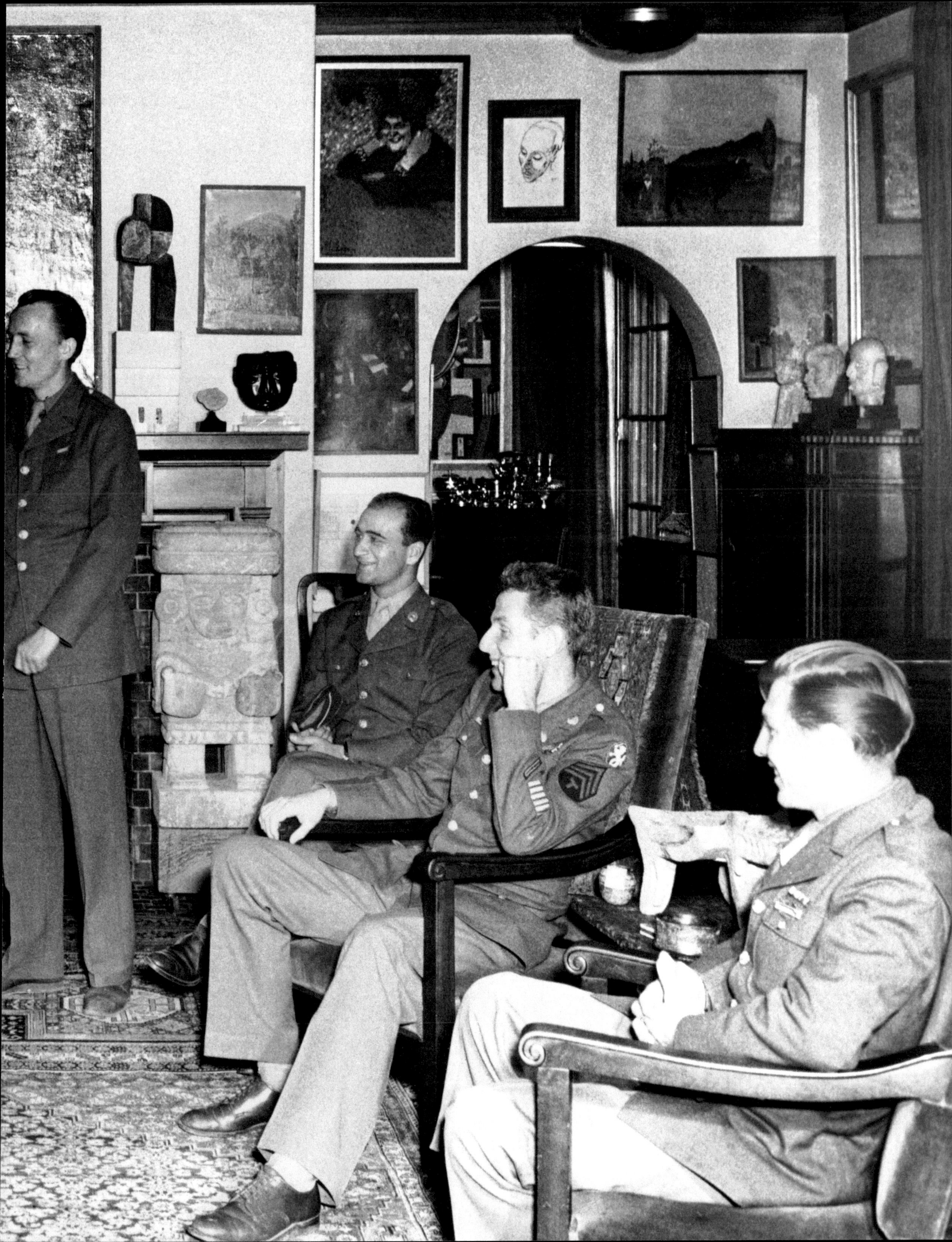

PLATE 4

LIVING ROOM

WITH VIEWS INTO THE DINING ROOM THROUGH THE NORTH AND SOUTH ARCHWAYS

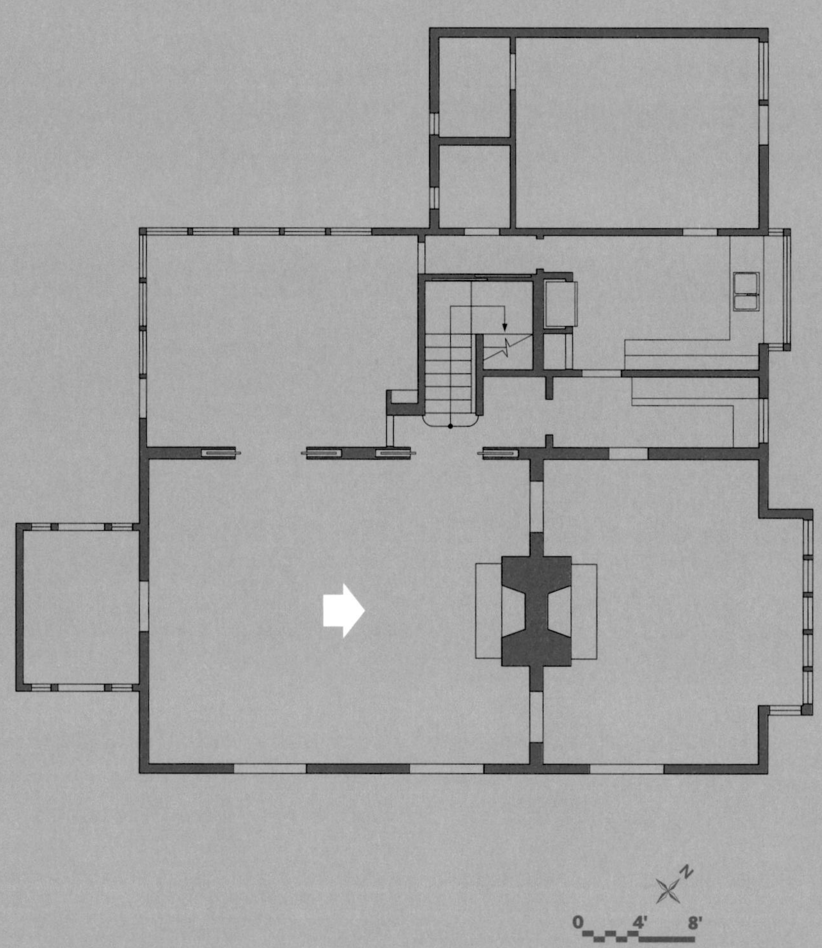

PROBABLY DICK SEYFFERT

CA. 1945, AFTER 15 MARCH

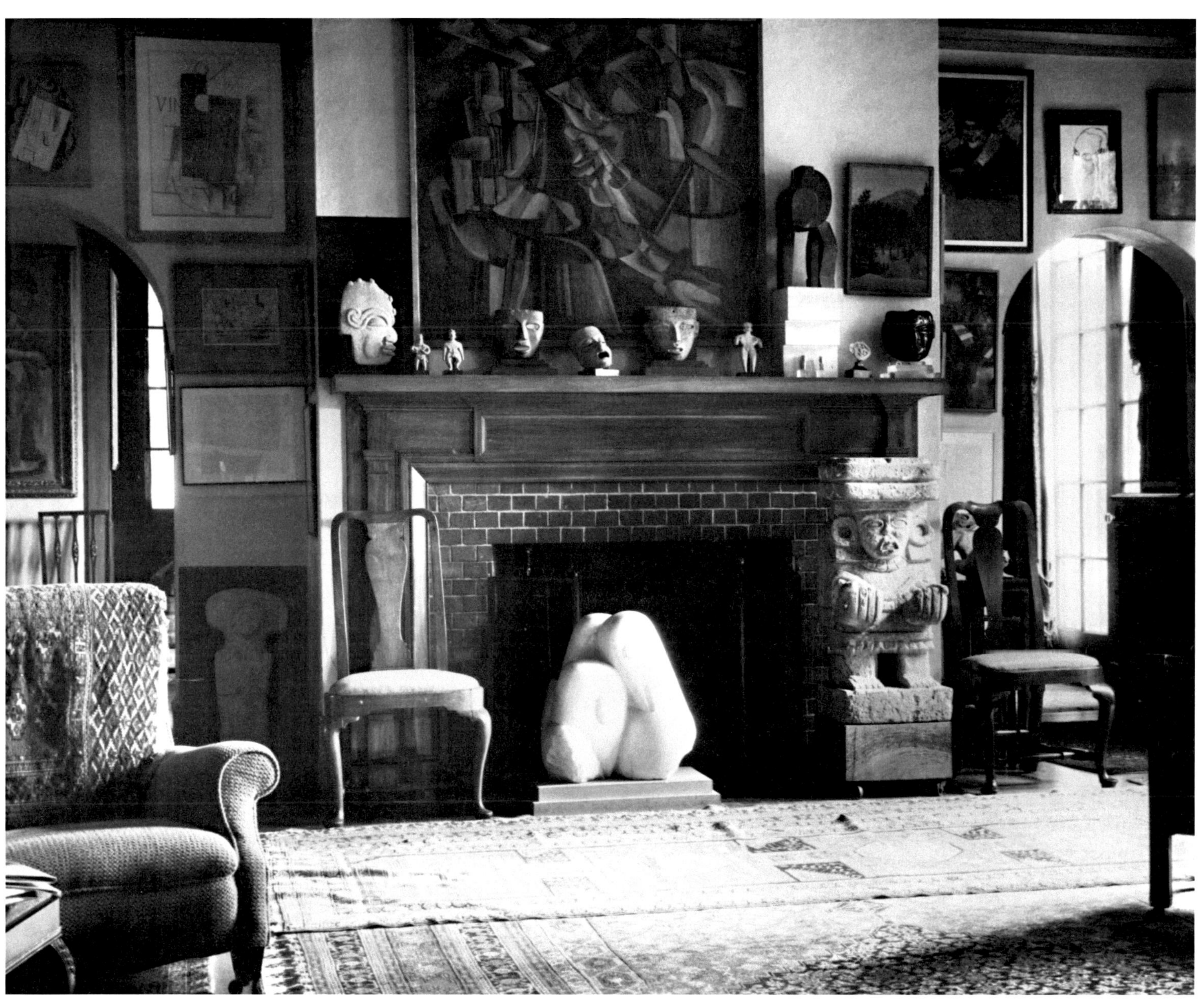

PLATE 4

1 GEORGES BRAQUE, *Still Life (Violin)*, 1913 [1950-134-25; AC20-25]

2 ROGER DE LA FRESNAYE, *Nude (The Italian Girl)*, 1911 [1950-134-89; AC20-124]

3 GEORGES BRAQUE, *Still Life (with the Word VIN)*, 1912–13 [1950-134-24; AC20-23]

4 GEORGES BRAQUE, *Paris* or *Still Life on a Table*, 1910 [1950-134-873]

*5 PABLO PICASSO, *The Jugglers*, 1905 (1913 edition) [1950-134-908]

6 HUASTEC (EAST COAST MEXICO), Figure of a Woman, 900–1200 [1950-134-330; ACPS-116]

7 CONSTANTIN BRANCUSI, *Three Penguins*, 1911–12 [1950-134-7; AC20-6]

8 TEOTIHUACAN (CENTRAL MEXICO), Goddess Figure, 100–650 [1950-134-282; ACPS-2]

9 ARTIST/MAKER UNKNOWN (MEXICO), Dog, Likely 20th century [1950-134-370; ACPS-197]

10 NATHANIEL BACON, Autograph Letter Signed, to Roger Townsend, 24 November 1619 [NOTE 2.2, PAGE 416]

11 PAUL KLEE, *Village Carnival*, 1926 [1950-134-115; AC20-114]

12 HENRI ROUSSEAU, *Landscape with Cattle*, 1895–1900 [1950-134-175; AC20-180]

13 PABLO PICASSO, *Head*, 1906 [1950-134-161; AC20-165]

14 PABLO PICASSO, *Old Woman (Woman with Gloves)*, 1901 [1950-134-158; AC20-161]

15 HENRI ROUSSEAU, *Landscape*, 1905–10 [1950-134-177; AC20-181]

16 ARTIST/MAKER UNKNOWN (MEXICO), Mask, Likely 20th century [1950-134-252]

17 MANTEÑO (ECUADOR), Stamp, 900–1500 [1950-134-307; ACPS-169]

18 CONSTANTIN BRANCUSI, *Prodigal Son*, ca. 1914–15 [1950-134-8; AC20-7]

19, 20 MEZCALA (SOUTHWESTERN MEXICO), Seated Figures, 300 BCE–500 CE [19: 1950-134-541; 20: 1950-134-542]

21 COLIMA (WEST MEXICO), Figurine, 300 BCE–300 CE [1950-134-621]

22 MARCEL DUCHAMP, *The King and Queen Surrounded by Swift Nudes*, 1912 [1950-134-63A; AC20-68]

23 TEOTIHUACAN (CENTRAL MEXICO), Mask, 1st–9th century [1950-134-233; ACPS-21]

24 HUASTEC (EAST COAST MEXICO), Head, 900–1200 [1950-134-317; ACPS-129]

25 TEOTIHUACAN (CENTRAL MEXICO), Mask, 1st–9th century [1950-134-232; ACPS-15]

26 COLIMA (WEST MEXICO), Figure, 300 BCE–300 CE [1950-134-627]

27 COLIMA (WEST MEXICO), Figure, 300 BCE–300 CE [1950-134-628]

28 CLASSIC VERACRUZ (EAST COAST MEXICO), Hacha in the Form of a Head, 500–900 [1950-134-337; ACPS-147]

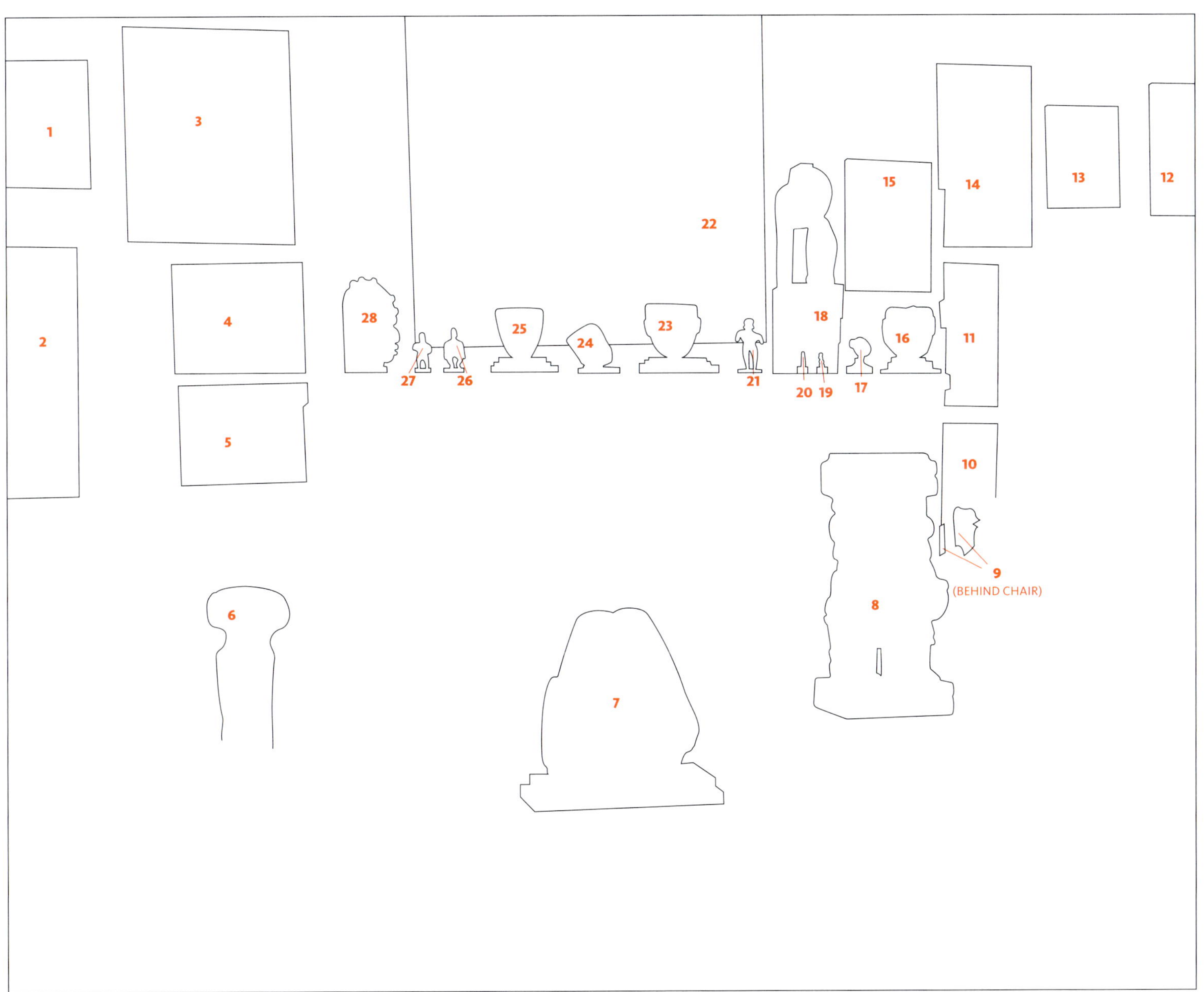
1
3
22
15
14
13
12
4
28
18
25
23
2
24
16
11
27
26
21
20
19
17
5
10
9
(BEHIND CHAIR)
8
6
7

PLATE 5

LIVING ROOM

WITH VIEWS INTO THE DINING ROOM THROUGH THE NORTH AND SOUTH ARCHWAYS

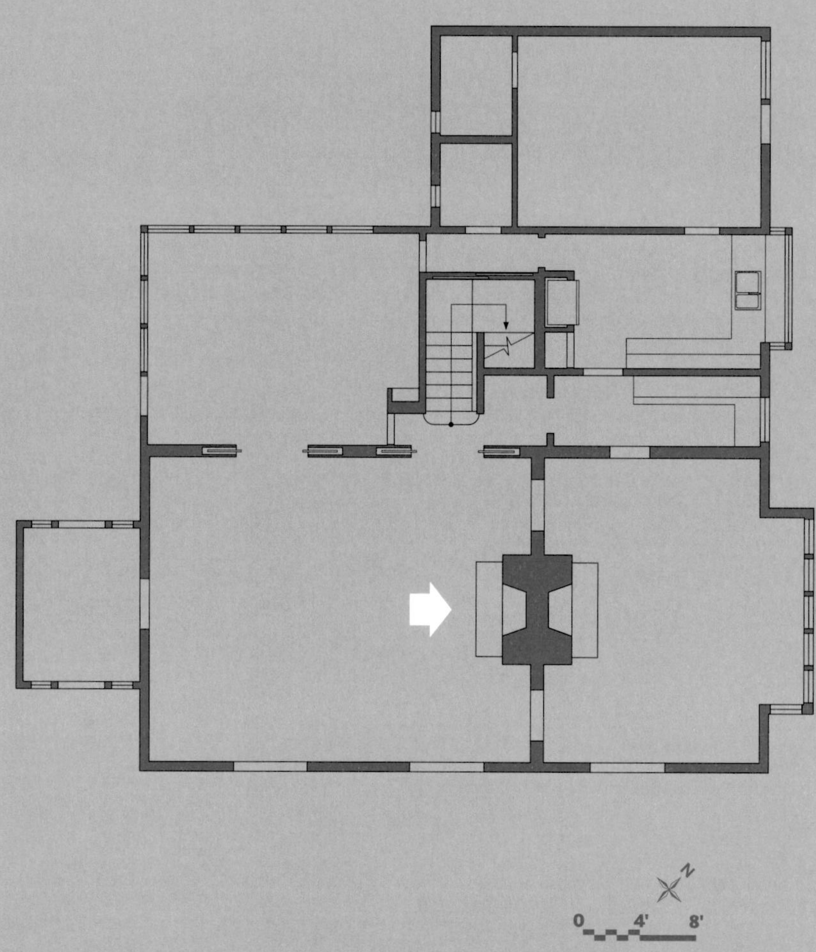

FLOYD FAXON

CA. JANUARY 1951

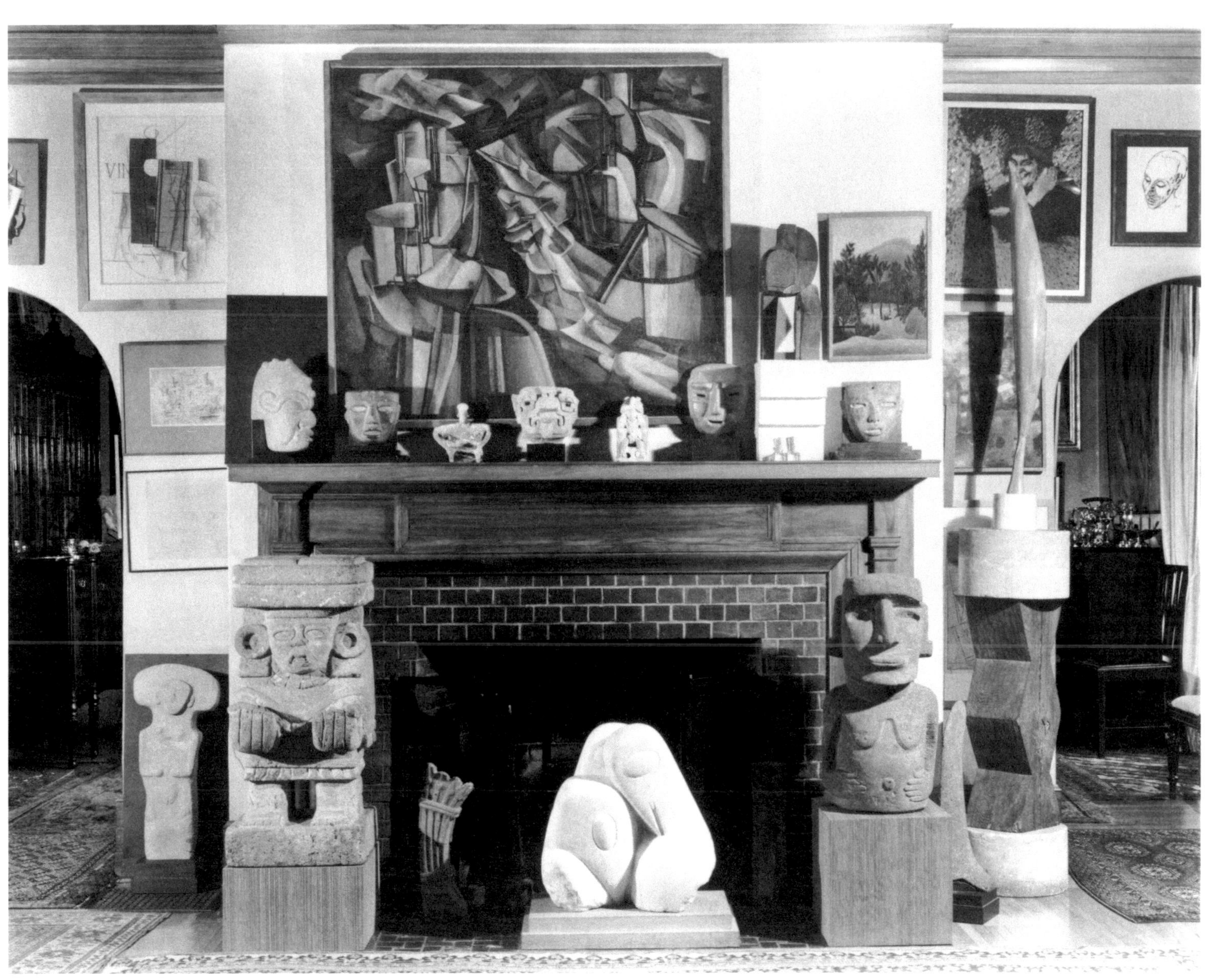

PLATE 5

1 GEORGES BRAQUE, *Still Life (Violin)*, 1913 [1950-134-25; AC20-25]

2 GEORGES BRAQUE, *Still Life (with the Word VIN)*, 1912–13 [1950-134-24; AC20-23]

3 GEORGES BRAQUE, *Paris* or *Still Life on a Table*, 1910 [1950-134-873]

4 PABLO PICASSO, *The Jugglers*, 1905 (1913 edition) [1950-134-908]

5 HUASTEC (EAST COAST MEXICO), Figure of a Woman, 900–1200 [1950-134-330; ACPS-116]

6 TEOTIHUACAN (CENTRAL MEXICO), Goddess Figure, 100–650 [1950-134-282; ACPS-2]

7 CLASSIC VERACRUZ (EAST COAST MEXICO), Palma, 500–900 [1950-134-345; ACPS-158]

8 CONSTANTIN BRANCUSI, *Three Penguins*, 1911–12 [1950-134-7; AC20-6]

9 ARTIST/MAKER UNKNOWN (EASTER ISLAND), Figure of a Man, 18th century [1950-134-408]

10 CLASSIC VERACRUZ (EAST COAST MEXICO), Palma, 500–900 [1950-134-384; ACPS-150]

11 LOUIS MARCOUSSIS, *Portrait of Guillaume Apollinaire*, 1912 [1950-134-128; AC20-131]

12 CONSTANTIN BRANCUSI, *Bird in Space (Yellow Bird)*, 1923–24 [1950-134-19; AC20-20]

13 MARCEL DUCHAMP, *Portrait (Dulcinea)*, 1911 [1950-134-54; AC20-59]

14 PABLO PICASSO, *Head*, 1906 [1950-134-161; AC20-165]

15 PABLO PICASSO, *Old Woman (Woman with Gloves)*, 1901 [1950-134-158; AC20-161]

16 GIORGIO DE CHIRICO, *The Poet and His Muse*, ca. 1925 [1950-134-39; AC20-37]

17 PAUL KLEE, *Village Carnival*, 1926 [1950-134-115; AC20-114]

18 TEOTIHUACAN (CENTRAL MEXICO), Mask, 1st–9th century [1950-134-233; ACPS-21]

19 HENRI ROUSSEAU, *Landscape*, 1905–10 [1950-134-177; AC20-181]

20 CONSTANTIN BRANCUSI, *Prodigal Son*, ca. 1914–15 [1950-134-8; AC20-7]

21, 22 MEZCALA (SOUTHWESTERN MEXICO), Seated Figures, 300 BCE–500 CE [21: 1950-134-541; 22: 1950-134-542]

23 MEZCALA (SOUTHWESTERN MEXICO), Mask, 300 BCE–500 CE [1950-134-268; ACPS-91]

24 MARCEL DUCHAMP, *The King and Queen Surrounded by Swift Nudes*, 1912 [1950-134-63A; AC20-68]

25 MAYA, Jaina Figure, 600–800 [1950-134-623]

26 ZAPOTEC (SOUTHERN MEXICO), Fragment of a Burial Urn, 500–900 [1950-134-394; ACPS-100]

27 COLIMA (WESTERN MEXICO), Seated Woman, 300 BCE–300 CE [1950-134-399; ACPS-58]

28 TEOTIHUACAN (CENTRAL MEXICO), Mask, 1st–9th century [1950-134-232; ACPS-15]

29 CLASSIC VERACRUZ (EAST COAST MEXICO), Hacha in the Form of a Head, 500–900 [1950-134-337; ACPS-147]

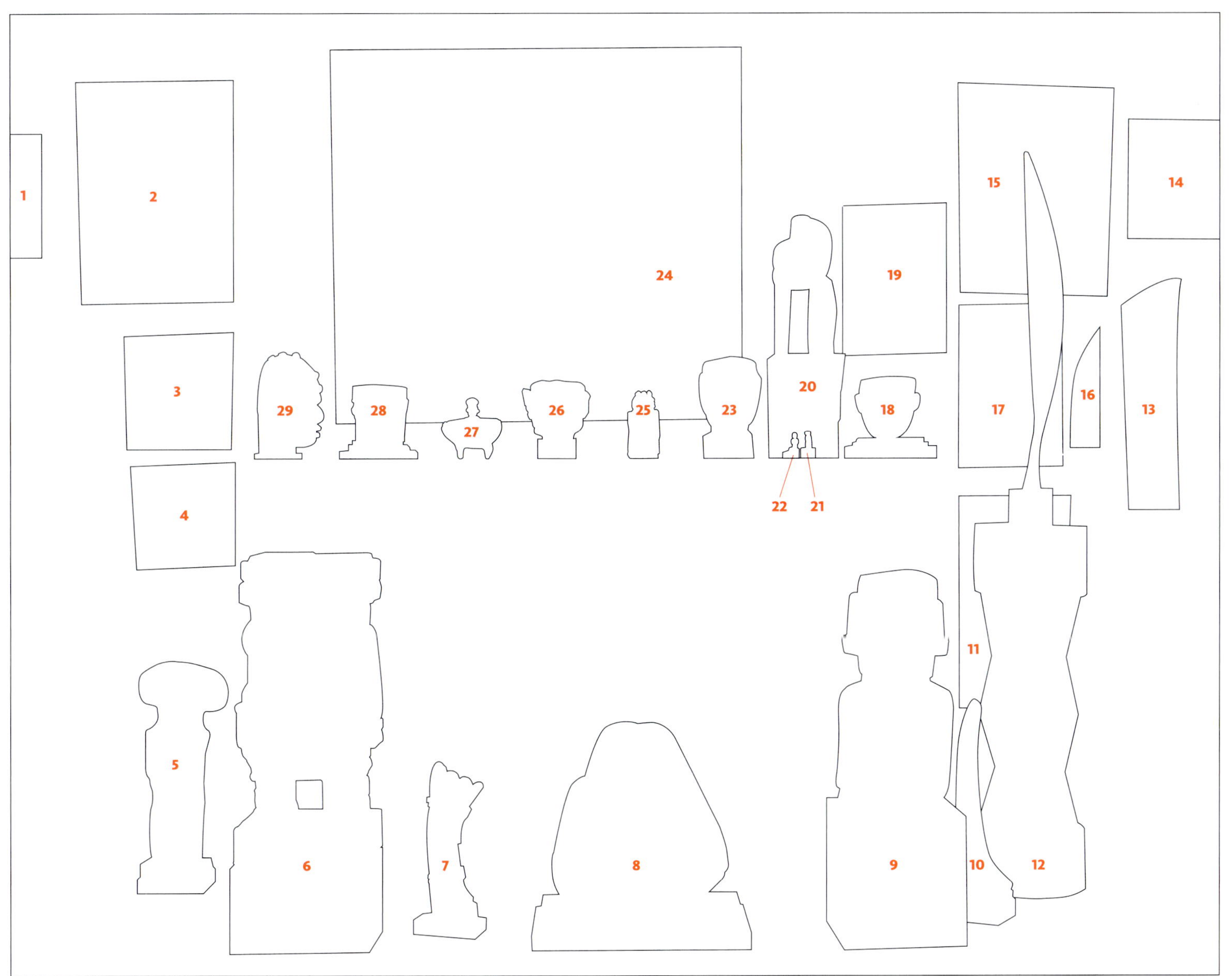
1
2
24
15
14
19
20
3
29
28
27
26
25
23
18
17
16
13
4
22
21
11
5
6
7
8
9
10
12

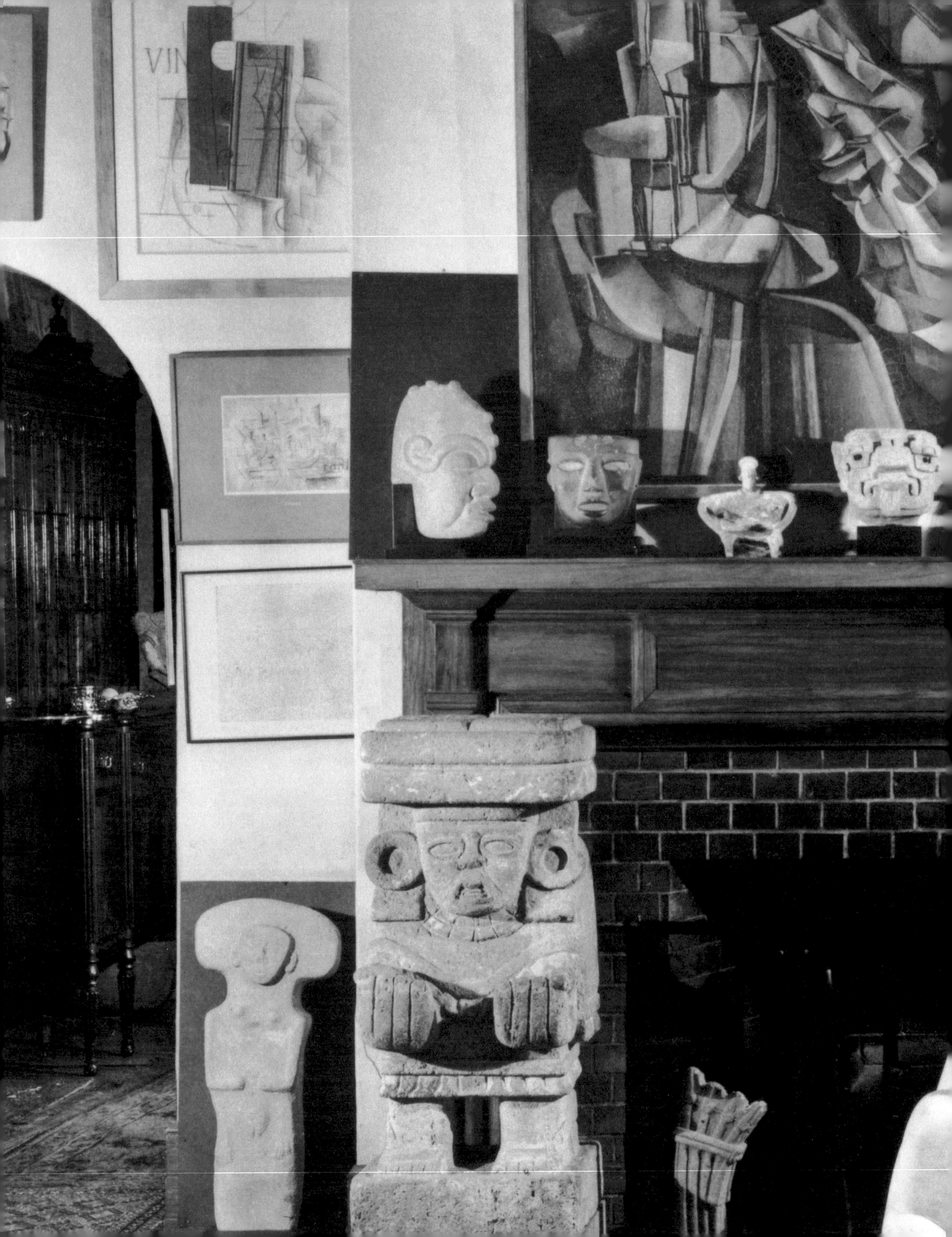
VIN

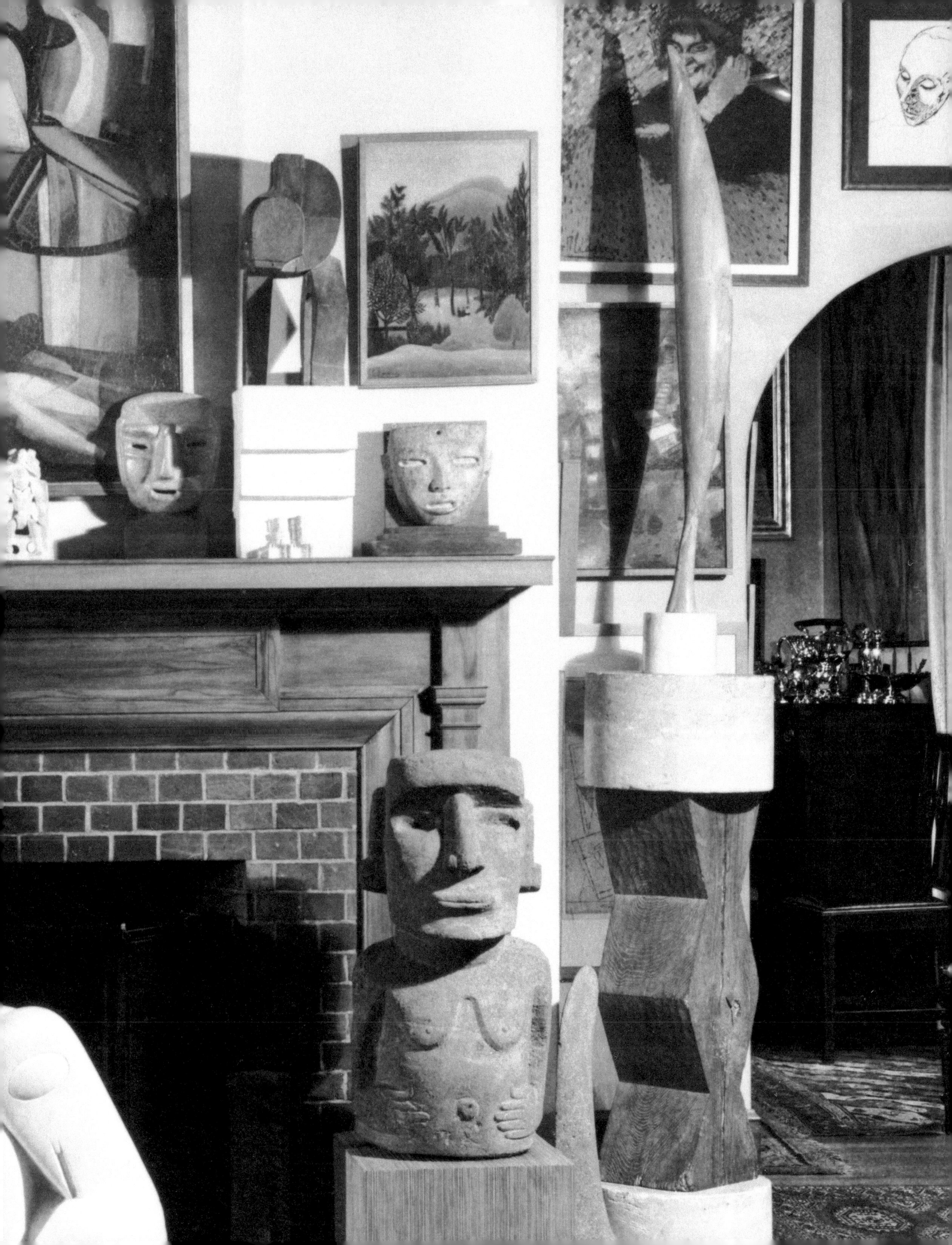

PLATE 6

LIVING ROOM

WITH A VIEW INTO THE DINING ROOM THROUGH THE SOUTH ARCHWAY

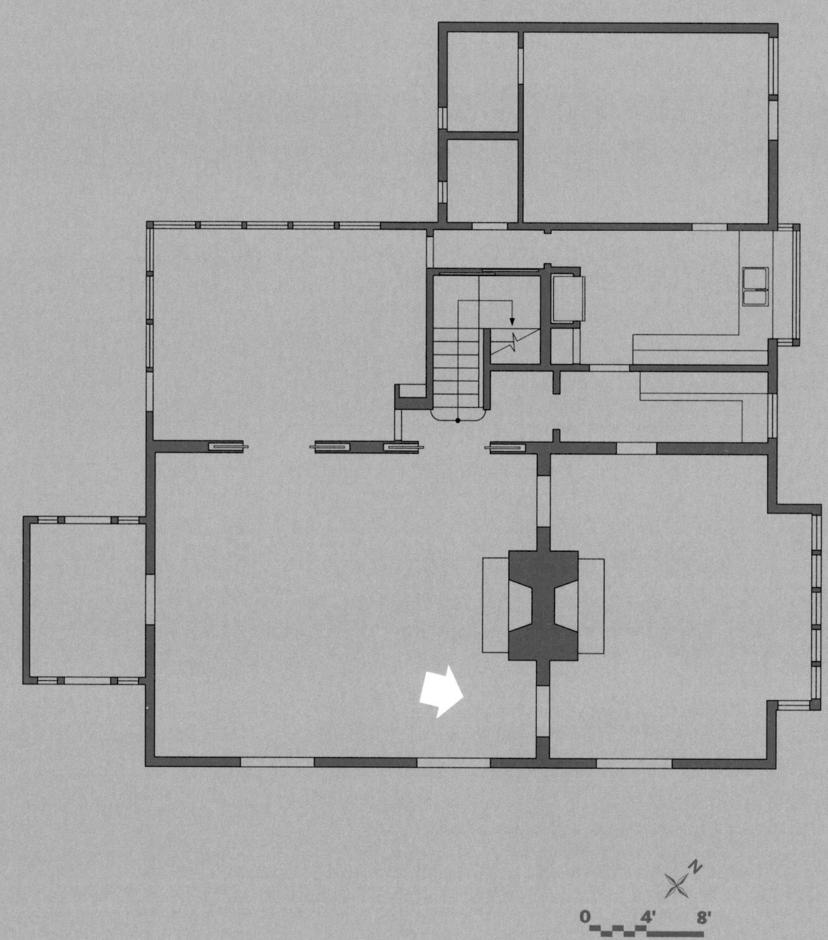

FLOYD FAXON

CA. JANUARY 1951

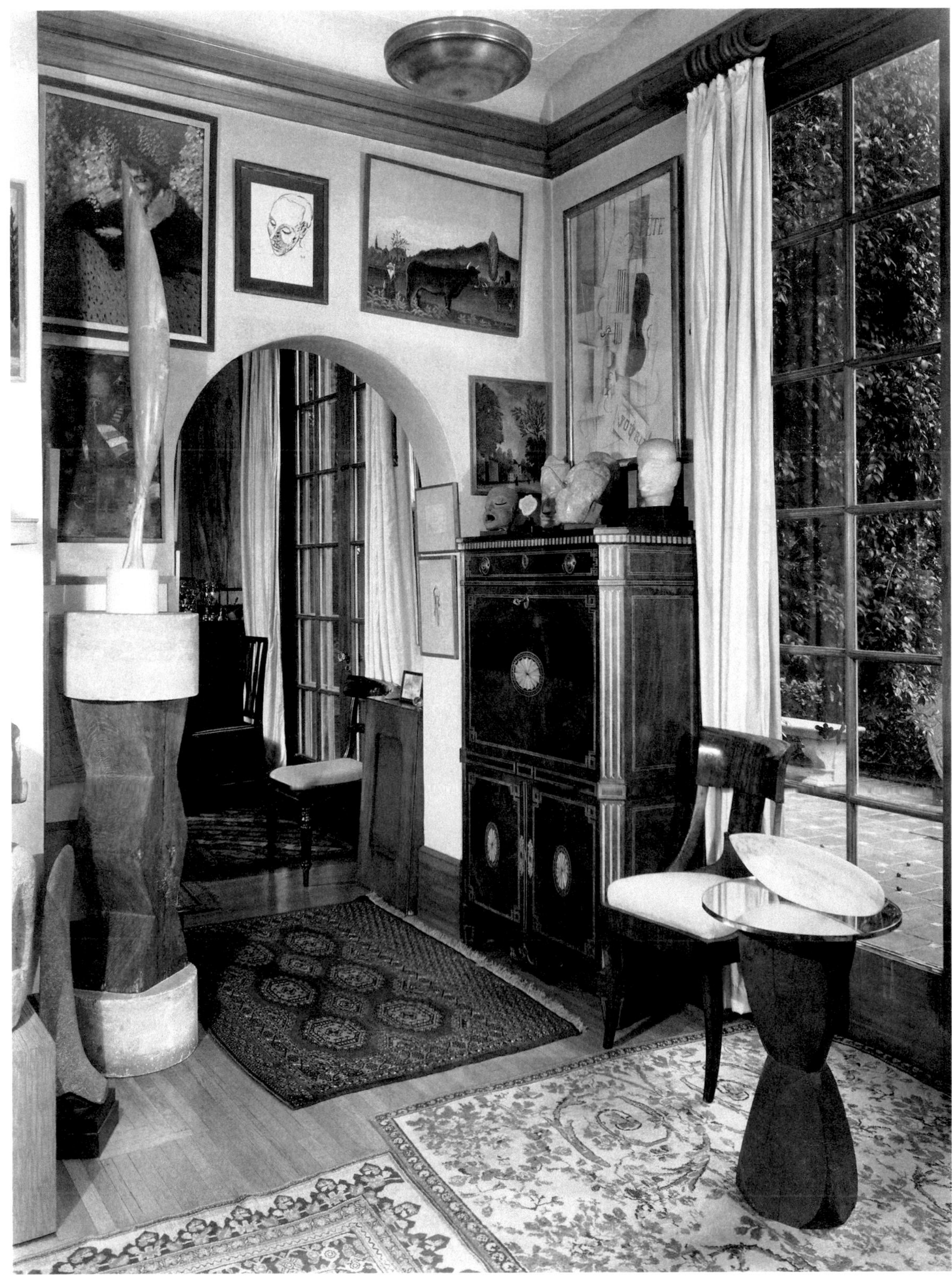

PLATE 6

1 HENRI ROUSSEAU, *Landscape*, 1905–10 [1950-134-177; AC20-181]

2 ARTIST/MAKER UNKNOWN (EASTER ISLAND), Figure of a Man, 18th century [1950-134-408]

3 PABLO PICASSO, *Old Woman (Woman with Gloves)*, 1901 [1950-134-158; AC20-161]

4 PAUL KLEE, *Village Carnival*, 1926 [1950-134-115; AC20-114]

5 LOUIS MARCOUSSIS, *Portrait of Guillaume Apollinaire*, 1912 [1950-134-128; AC20-131]

6 CLASSIC VERACRUZ (EAST COAST MEXICO), Palma, 500–900 [1950-134-384; ACPS-150]

7 CONSTANTIN BRANCUSI, *Bird in Space (Yellow Bird)*, 1923–24 [1950-134-19; AC20-20]

8 PABLO PICASSO, *Head*, 1906 [1950-134-161; AC20-165]

9 HENRI ROUSSEAU, *Landscape with Cattle*, 1895–1900 [1950-134-175; AC20-180]

10 MARCEL DUCHAMP, *Portrait (Dulcinea)*, 1911 [1950-134-54; AC20-59]

*11 MEZCALA (SOUTHWESTERN MEXICO), Mask, 300 BCE–500 CE [1950-134-380; ACPS-93]

12 KNUD MERRILD, *Abstraction*, 10 October 1935 [PMA-WLA BOX 72, FOLDER 9]

*13 ARTIST/MAKER UNKNOWN (*EUROPE OR NORTH AMERICA), Paperweight, Date unknown [NOTE 1.4, PAGE 414]

14 PABLO PICASSO, *Female Figure*, 1906 [1950-134-160A; AC20-163]

15 PABLO PICASSO, *Seashore Scene*, 1905 [1950-134-159; AC20-162]

16 HENRI ROUSSEAU, *Village Street*, 1909–10 [1950-134-178; AC20-182]

17 GEORGES BRAQUE, *Violin and Newspaper*, 1912–13 [1950-134-26; AC20-24]

18 HUASTEC (EAST COAST MEXICO), Head, 900–1200 [1950-134-317; ACPS-129]

19 MANTEÑO (ECUADOR), Stamp, 900–1500 [1950-134-307; ACPS-169]

20 JALISCO, AMECA-ETZATLÁN STYLE (WESTERN MEXICO), Fragment of a Head, 100 BCE–200 CE [1950-134-393; ACPS-65]

21 CLASSIC VERACRUZ (EAST COAST MEXICO), Hacha in the Form of a Head, 500–900 [1950-134-401; ACPS-136]

22 MEZCALA (SOUTHWESTERN MEXICO), Head, 300 BCE–500 CE [1950-134-208]

23 CONSTANTIN BRANCUSI, *Fish*, 1922 [1950-134-18; AC20-16]

24 AZTEC (CENTRAL MEXICO), Ballcourt Ring with Floral Motif, 1400–1520 [1950-134-372; ACPS-44]

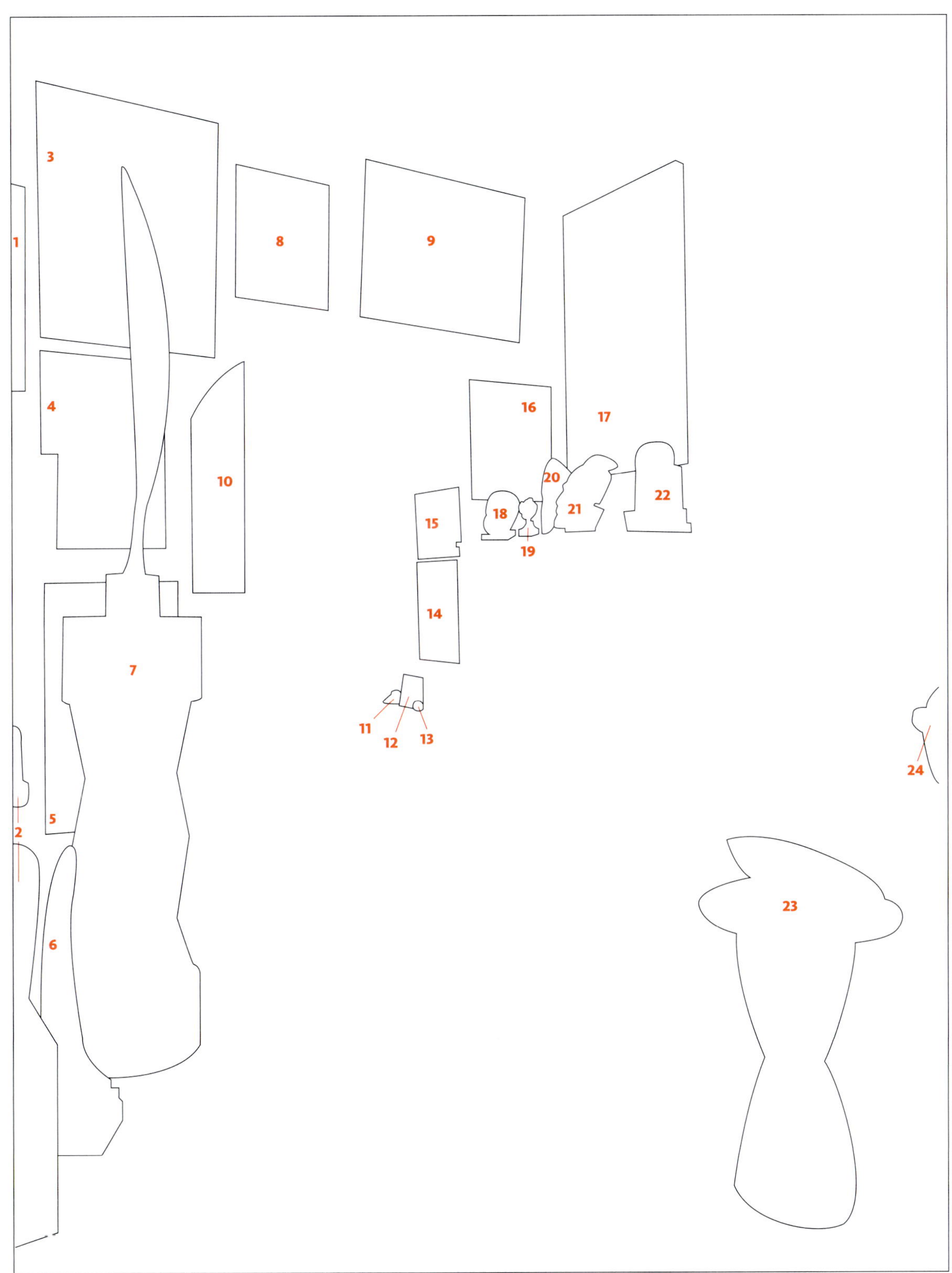

3
1
8
9
4
16
17
10
20
18
21
22
15
19
14
7
11
12
13
24
2
5
23
6

PLATE 7

LIVING ROOM

WITH A VIEW INTO THE DINING ROOM THROUGH THE SOUTH ARCHWAY

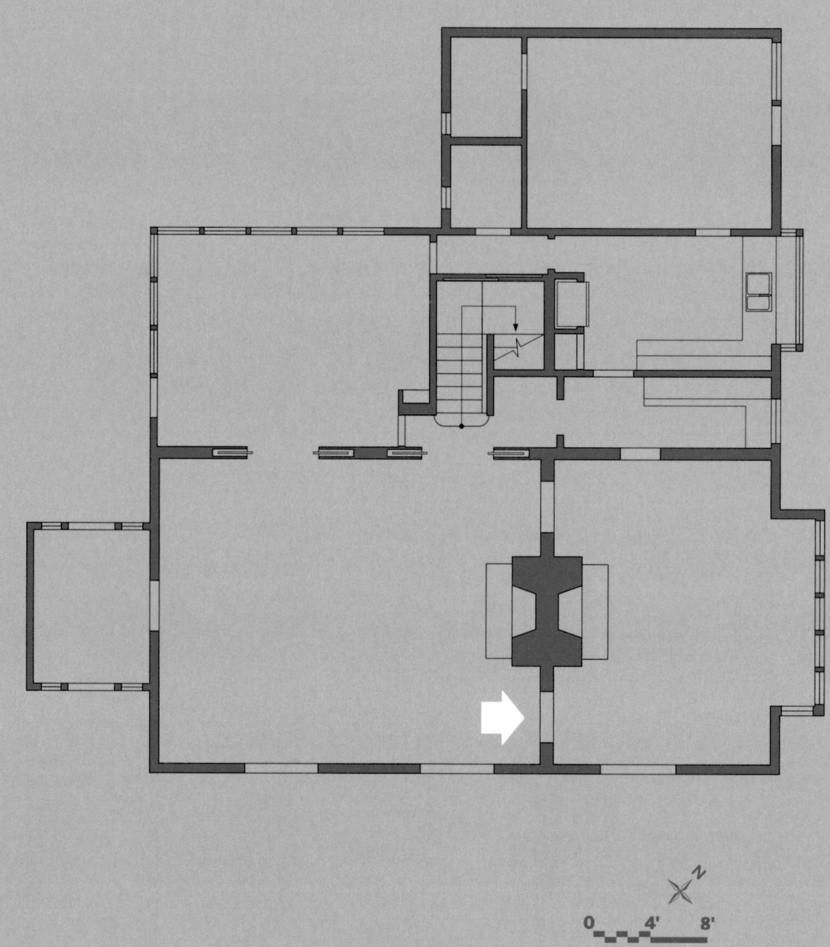

FRED R. DAPPRICH

CA. 1944

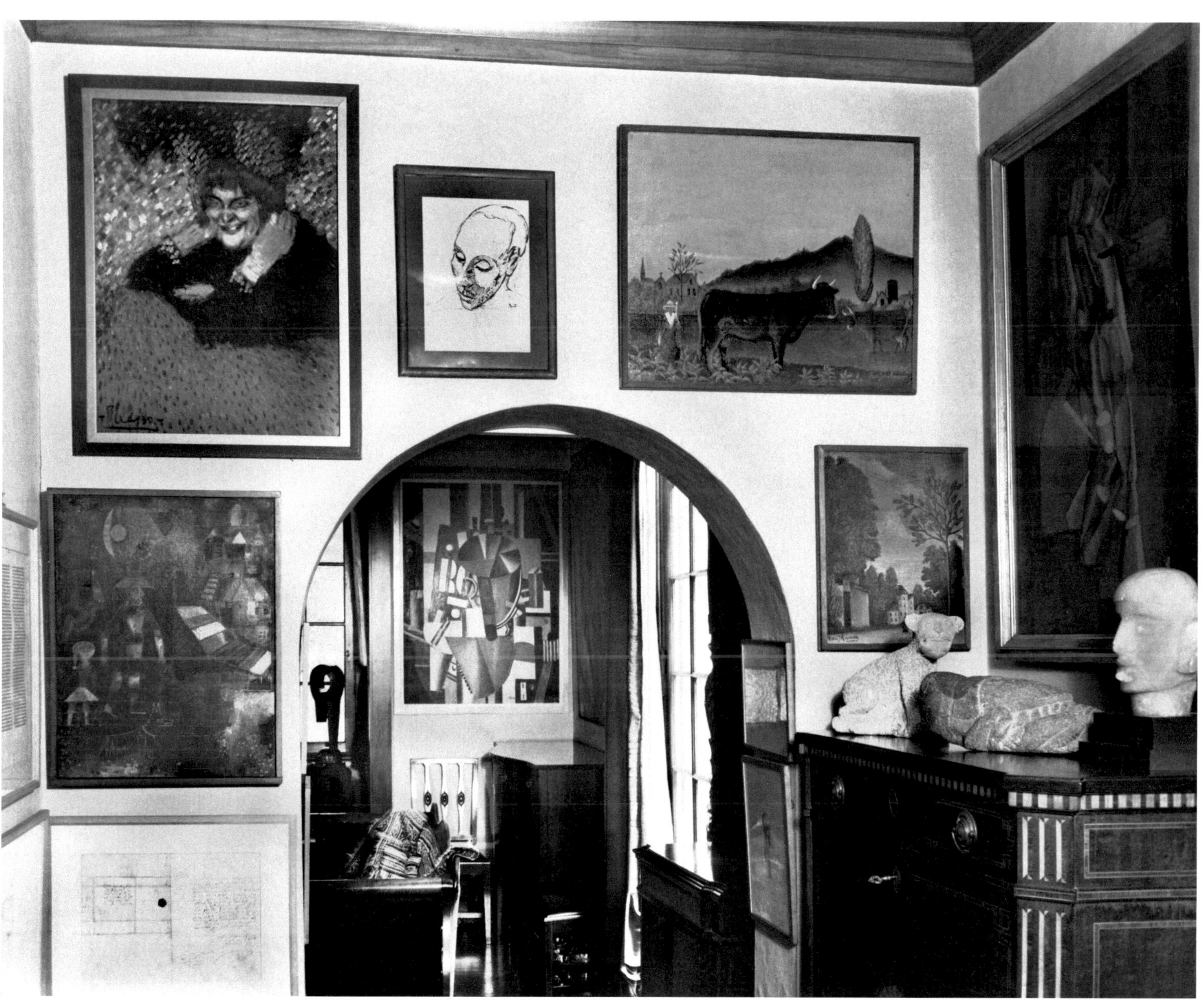

PLATE 7

1 JOHANN FUST AND PETER SCHOEFFER, Leaf from *Biblia Latina* (Latin Bible), Mainz, 1462 [NOTE 3.1, PAGE 416]

2 LADY ANNE COOKE BACON, Autograph Letter Signed, to Nathaniel Bacon, 6 August 1573 [NOTE 2.3, PAGE 416]

3 PABLO PICASSO, *Old Woman (Woman with Gloves)*, 1901 [1950-134-158; AC20-161]

4 PAUL KLEE, *Village Carnival*, 1926 [1950-134-115; AC20-114]

5 SIR FRANCIS BACON, Autograph Letter Signed, to George Villiers, Earl (later Duke) of Buckingham, 22 September 1617 [NOTE 2.1, PAGE 416]

6 CONSTANTIN BRANCUSI, *Chimera*, 1915–18 [1950-134-13; AC20-4]

7 PABLO PICASSO, *Head*, 1906 [1950-134-161; AC20-165]

8 FERNAND LÉGER, *Typographer (Final State)*, 1919 [1950-134-125; AC20-128]

9 MARCEL DUCHAMP, *Portrait (Dulcinea)*, 1911 [1950-134-54; AC20-59]

10 HENRI ROUSSEAU, *Landscape with Cattle*, 1895–1900 [1950-134-175; AC20-180]

*11 PABLO PICASSO, *Seashore Scene*, 1905 [1950-134-159; AC20-162]

12 PABLO PICASSO, *Female Figure*, 1906 [1950-134-160A; AC20-163]

13 HENRI ROUSSEAU, *Village Street*, 1909–10 [1950-134-178; AC20-182]

14 *MAYA (*SOUTHEASTERN MEXICO, YUCATÁN), Jaguar, *900–1250 [NOTE 1.3, PAGE 414]

15 AZTEC (CENTRAL MEXICO), Grasshopper, 1300–1520 [1950-134-340; ACPS-41]

16 MARCEL DUCHAMP, *Nude Descending a Staircase (No. 1)*, 1911 [1950-134-58; AC20-63]

17 MEZCALA (SOUTHWESTERN MEXICO), Head, 300 BCE–500 CE [1950-134-208]

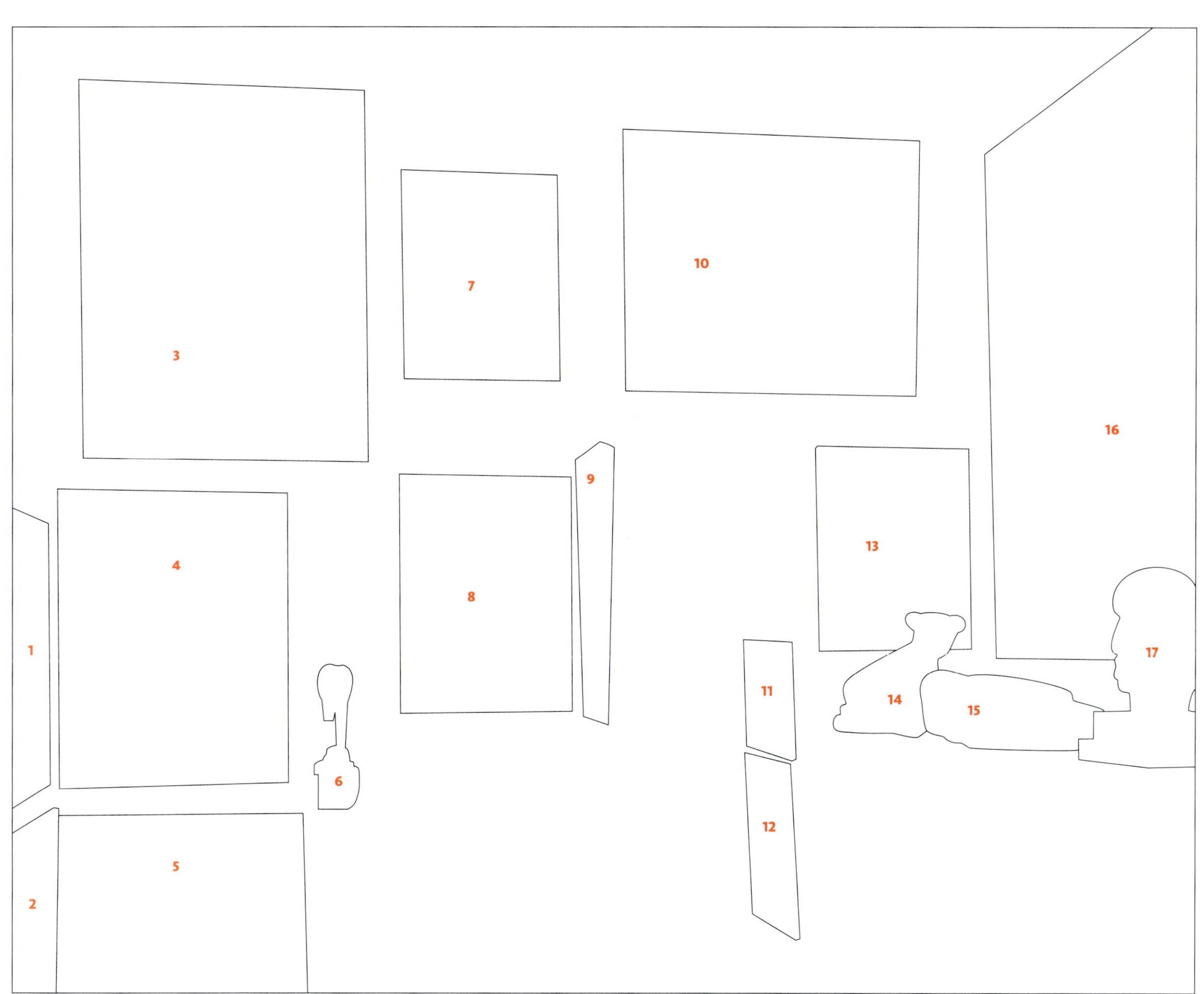
1
2
3
4
5
6
7
8
9
10
11
12
13
14
15
16
17

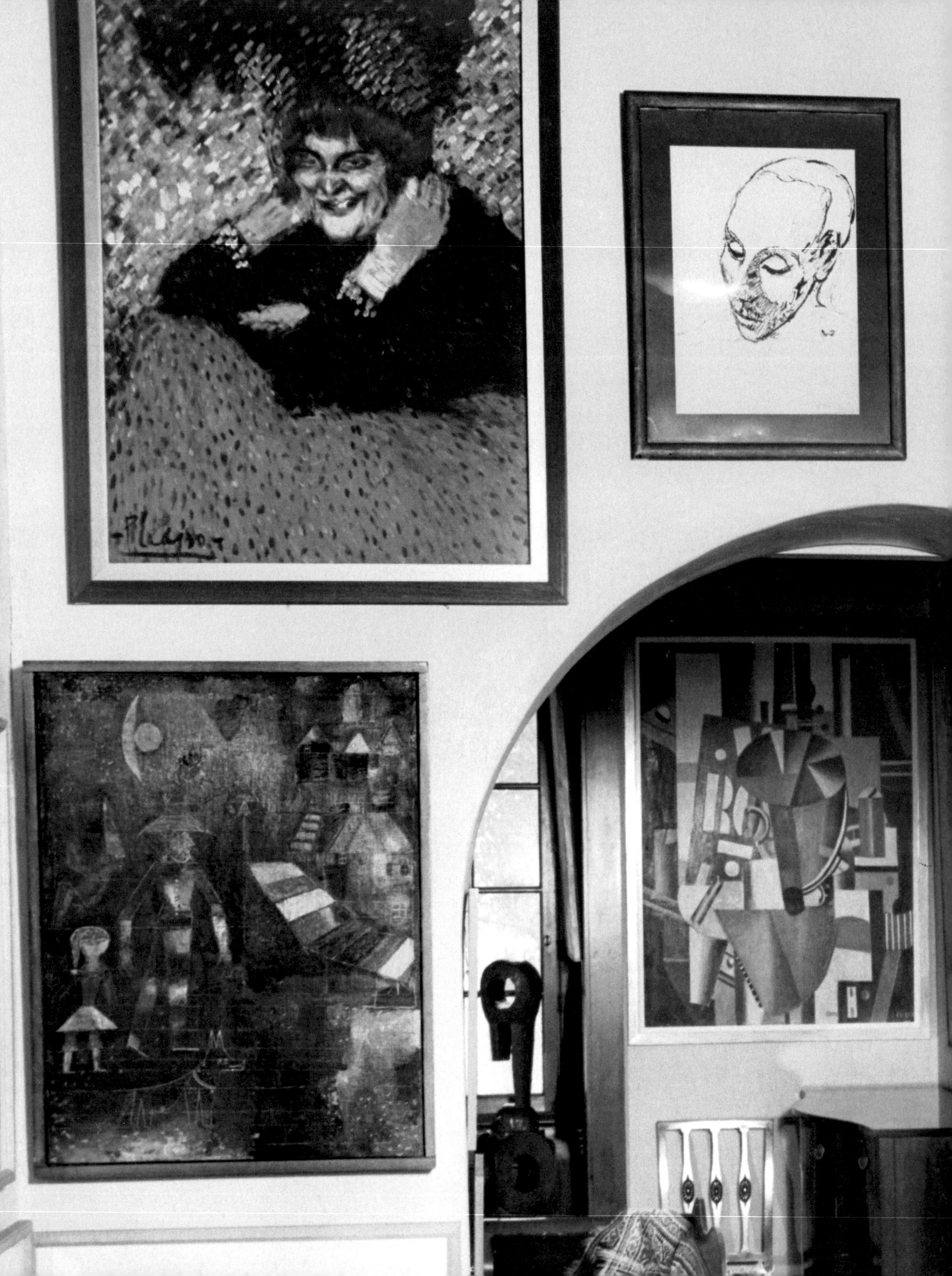
Picasso

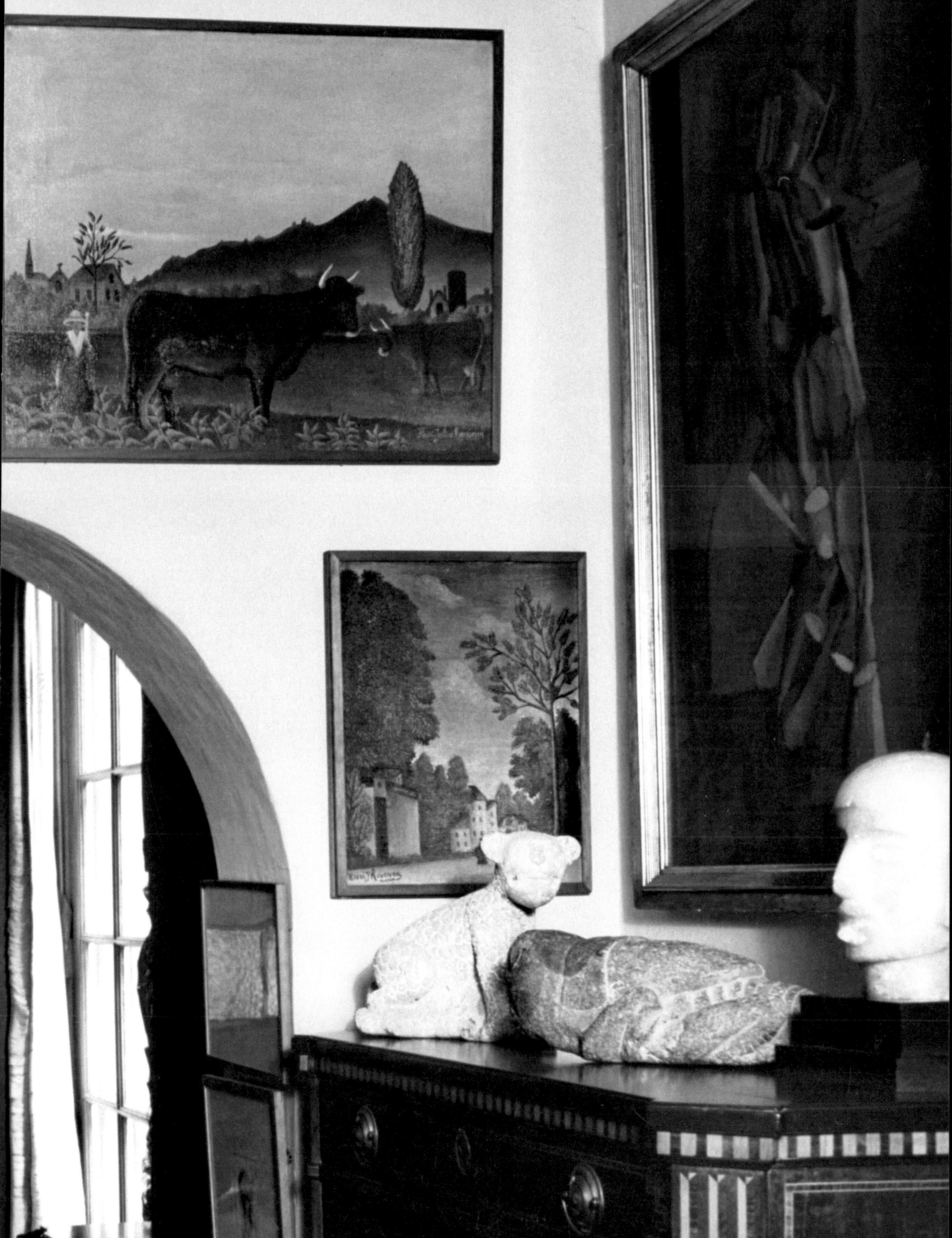

PLATES 8, 9, 10

DINING ROOM

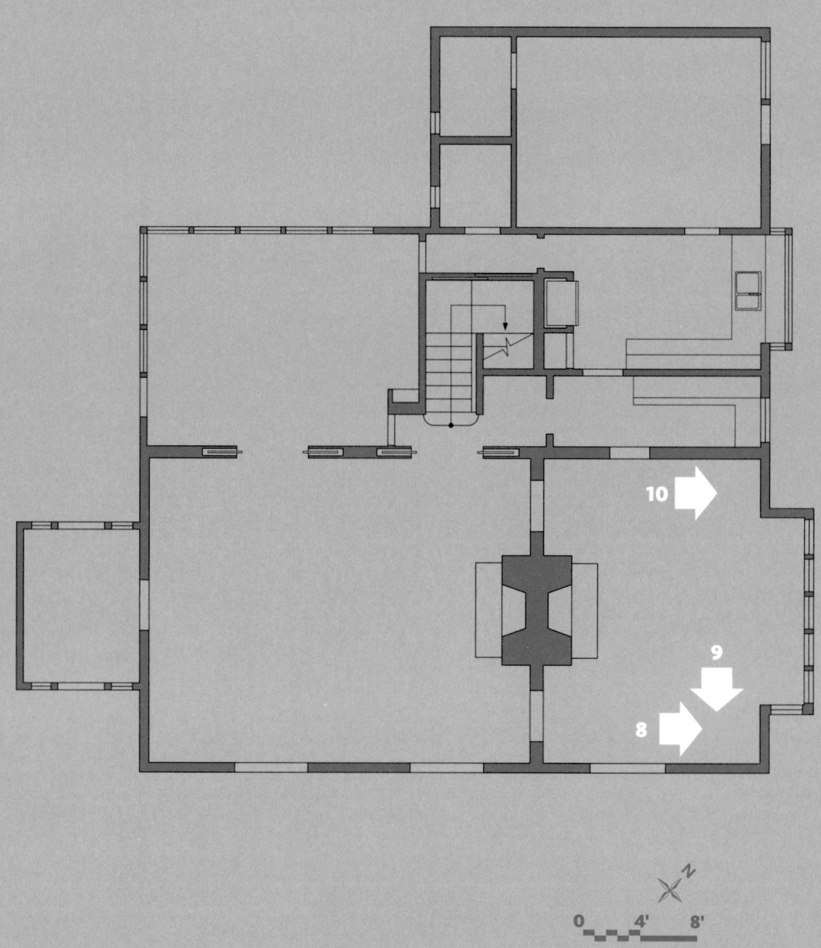

FLOYD FAXON

CA. 1948–49

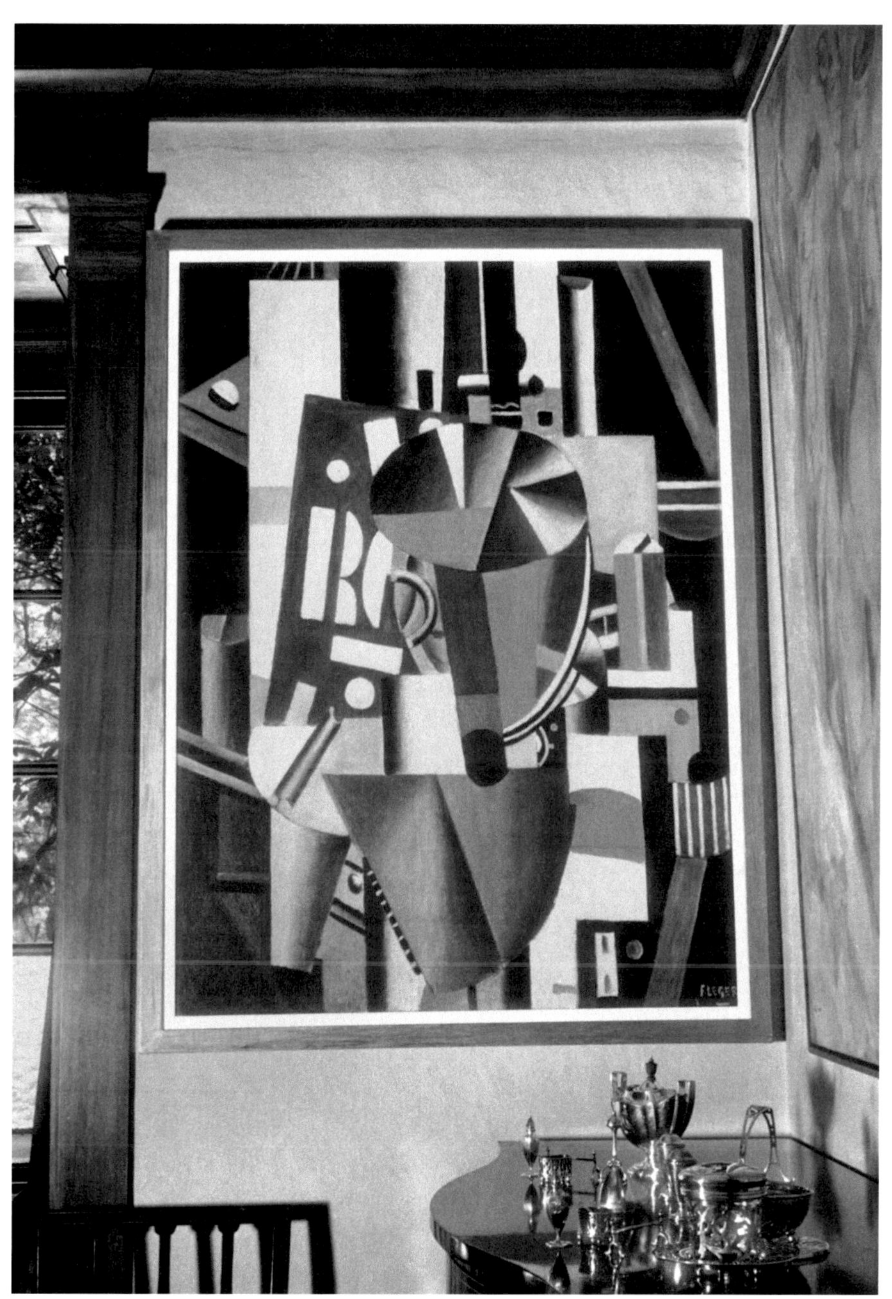

PLATE 8

1 FERNAND LÉGER, *Typographer (Final State)*, 1919 [1950-134-125; AC20-128]
2 (RIGHT) MARCEL DUCHAMP, *Portrait (Dulcinea)*, 1911 [1950-134-54; AC20-59; SEE PLATE 9.2]

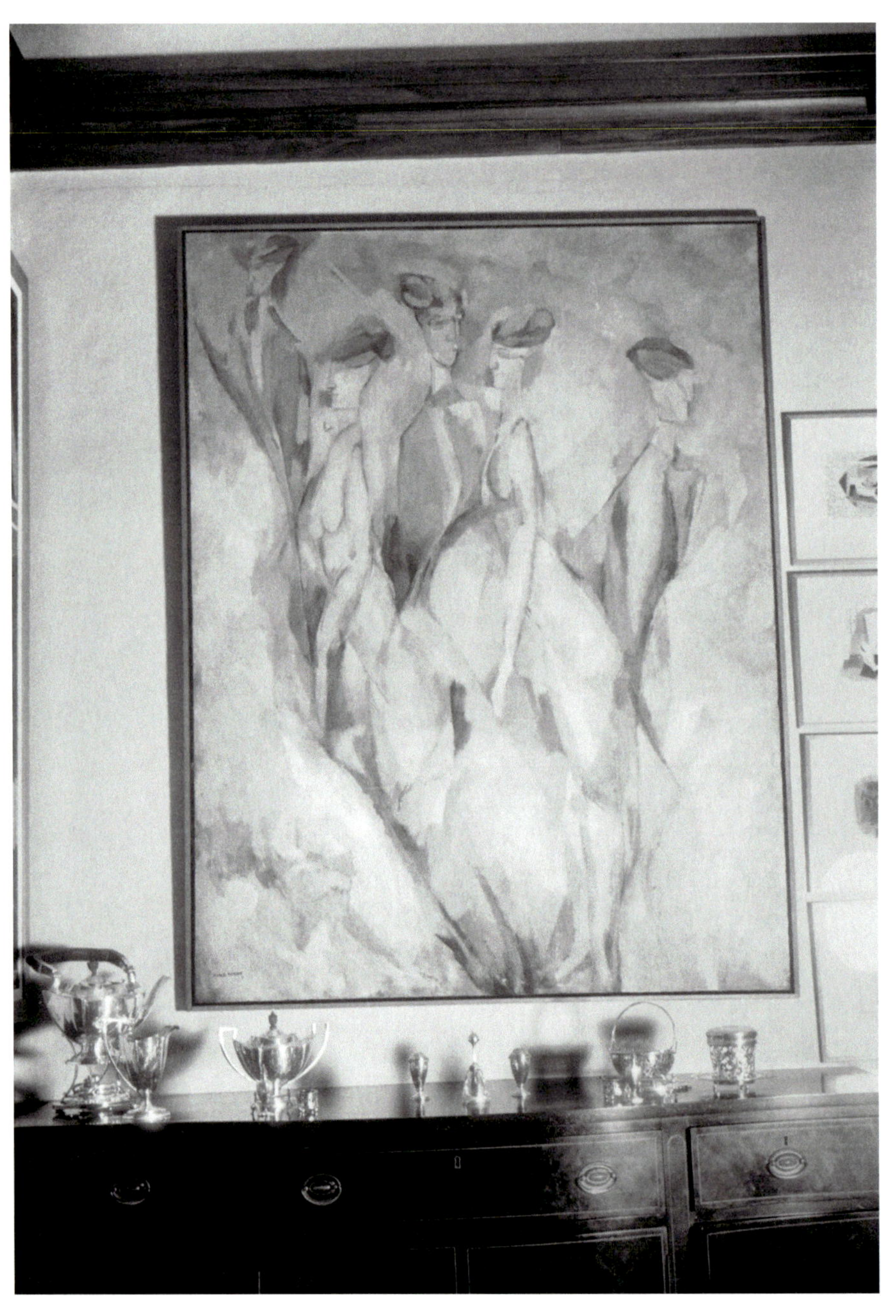

PLATE 9

1 (LEFT, BARELY VISIBLE) FERNAND LÉGER, *Typographer (Final State)*, 1919 [1950-134-125; AC20-128; SEE PLATE 8.1]

2 (CENTER) MARCEL DUCHAMP, *Portrait (Dulcinea)*, 1911 [1950-134-54; AC20-59]

3–6 (RIGHT, TOP TO BOTTOM) ARTIST/MAKER UNKNOWN, AFTER GEORGES BRAQUE, Still lifes, Dates unknown, before 1941 [1950-134-869, -870, -871, -872]

LITTLE IS CURRENTLY KNOWN ABOUT THE ORIGIN OF THESE FOUR PRINTS, WHICH UTILIZE COLLOTYPE AND POCHOIR TECHNIQUES AND LIKELY CONSTITUTE A SET. ADDITIONAL EXAMPLES CAN BE FOUND IN THE COLLECTIONS OF YALE UNIVERSITY ART GALLERY (ACQUISITION NUMBERS 1941.357, 1941.358, AND 1941.359) AND OF THE FRALIN MUSEUM OF ART AT THE UNIVERSITY OF VIRGINIA (ACQUISITION NUMBERS 1975.43.10, 1975.43.11, AND 1975.43.12).

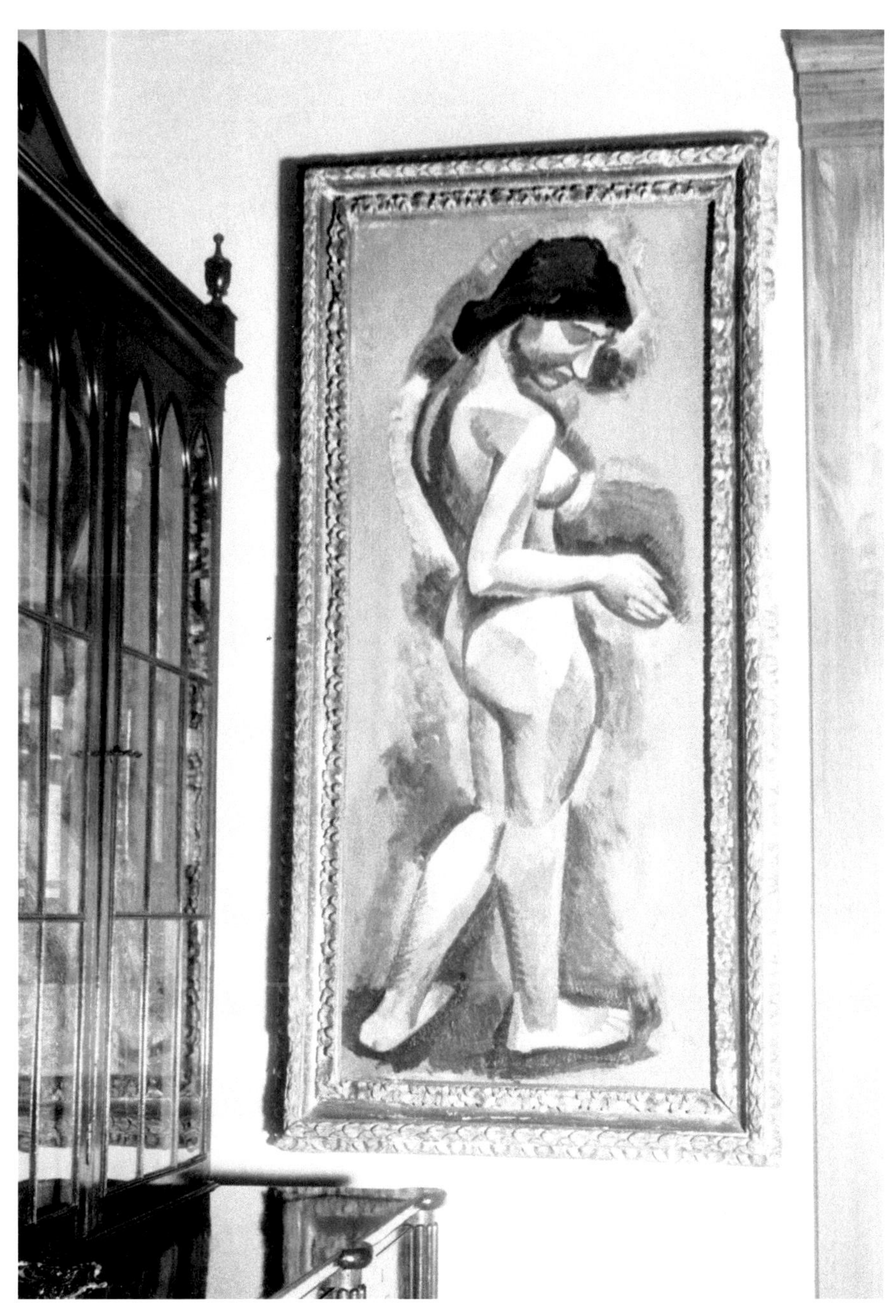

PLATE 10

1 ROGER DE LA FRESNAYE, *Nude (The Italian Girl)*, 1911 [1950-134-89; AC20-124]

PLATE 11

DINING ROOM

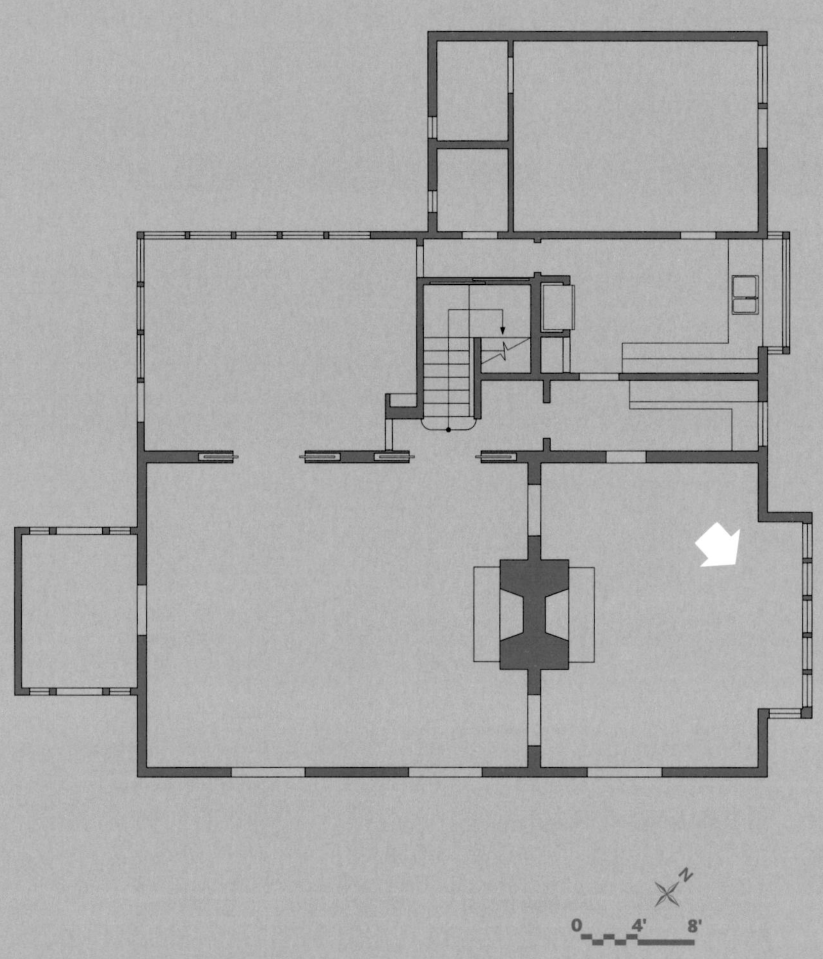

KARL BISSINGER

16 MARCH 1950

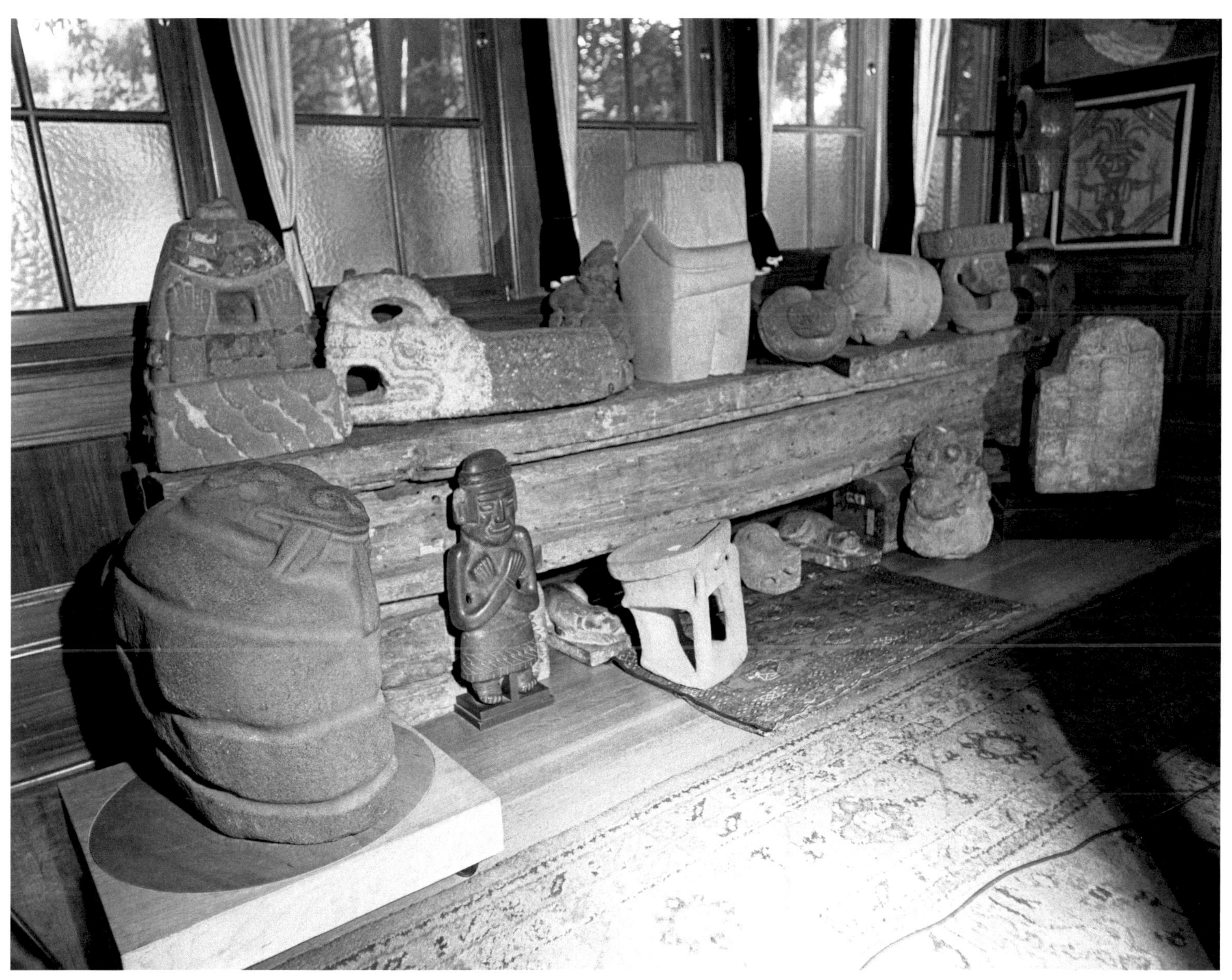

PLATE 11

1 AZTEC (CENTRAL MEXICO), Torso of Earth Goddess (Tlaltecuhtli), 1300–1520 [1950-134-603]

2 AZTEC (CENTRAL MEXICO), Tenoned Stone in Serpent Form, 1300–1520 [1950-134-334; ACPS-38]

3 AZTEC (CENTRAL MEXICO), Serpent (Quetzalcoatl), 1300–1520 [1950-134-349; ACPS-28]

4 CONSTANTIN BRANCUSI, *The Kiss*, 1916 [1950-134-4; AC20-3]

5 CONSTANTIN BRANCUSI, *Bench*, 1914–16 [1950-134-23; AC20-13]

6 AZTEC (CENTRAL MEXICO), Serpent, 1300–1520 [1950-134-315; ACPS-36]

7 DIQUÍS (COSTA RICA), Jaguar, 1000–1520 [1950-134-323; ACPS-182]

8 TEOTIHUACAN (CENTRAL MEXICO), Seated Figure (Old God of Fire), 1st–9th century [1950-134-301; ACPS-3]

9 CONSTANTIN BRANCUSI, *Chimera*, 1915–18 [1950-134-13; AC20-14]

10 FRANTIŠEK KUPKA, *Disks of Newton (Study for "Fugue in Two Colors")*, 1912 [1950-134-122; AC20-123]

11 CHIMÚ (PERU), Painting on Cloth of Figure Holding Staffs, 900–1470 [1950-134-342]

12 MAYA (MEXICO), Fragment of a Stela, 810 [1950-134-242; ACPS-164]

13 AZTEC (CENTRAL MEXICO), Rain God (Tlaloc), 1300–1520 [1950-134-948; ACPS-31]

14 ARTIST/MAKER UNKNOWN (*CHINA), Couchant Animal, ca. 960–1279 [1950-134-499]

15 AZTEC OR EARLY SPANISH COLONIAL (CENTRAL MEXICO), Animal Head, 1400–1600 [1950-134-605]

16 TARASCAN (WESTERN MEXICO), Metate or Stool, 800–1300 [1950-134-387; ACPS-57]

17 ARTIST/MAKER UNKNOWN (*CHINA), Couchant Animal, ca. 960–1279 [1950-134-498]

18 *AZTEC (CENTRAL MEXICO), Standing Figure of a Woman, 1300–1520 [1950-134-304]

19 AZTEC (CENTRAL MEXICO), Serpent, 1300–1520 [1950-134-294; ACPS-35]

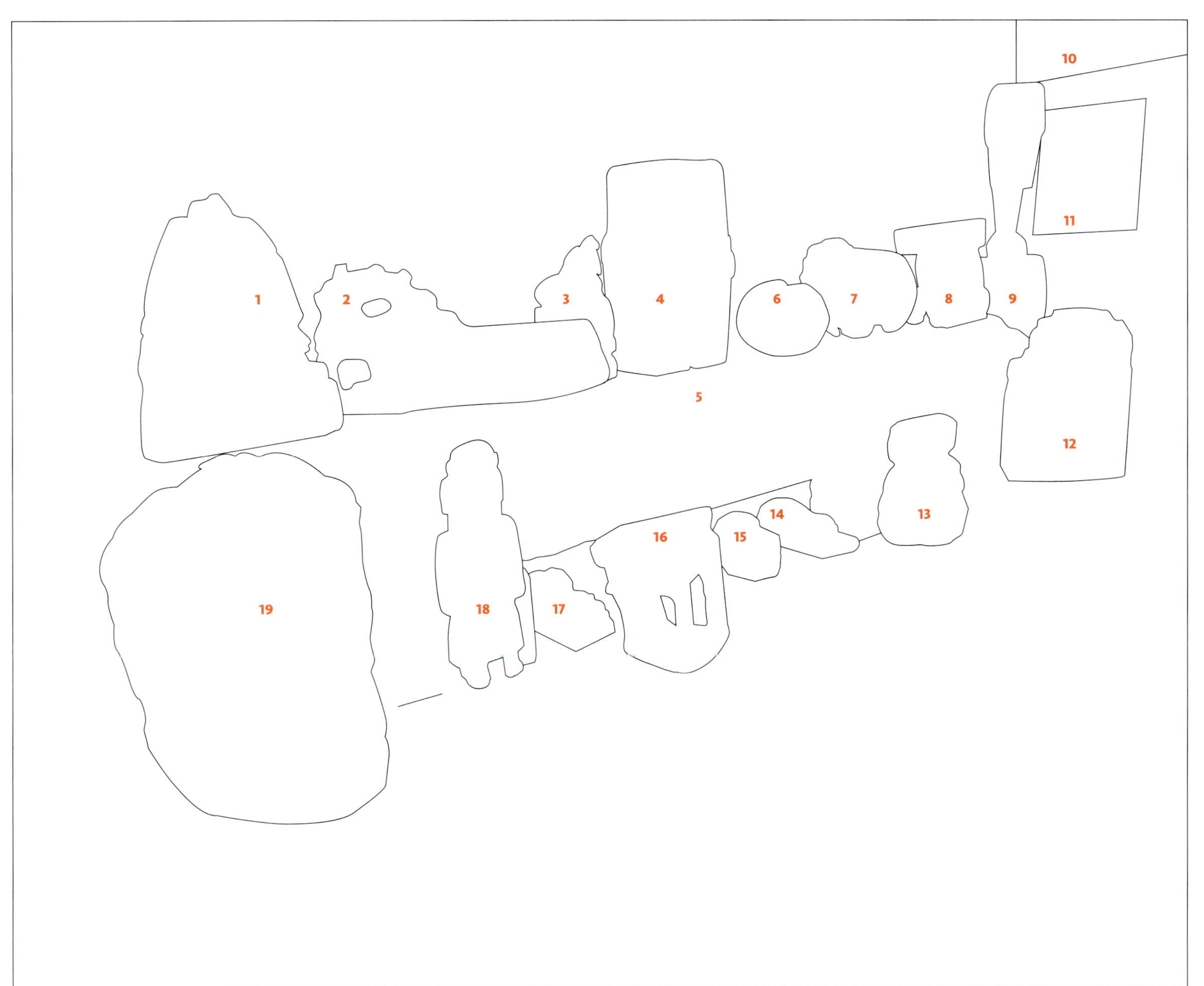

10
11
1
2
3
4
6
7
8
9
5
12
13
14
16
15
19
18
17

PLATE 12

DINING ROOM

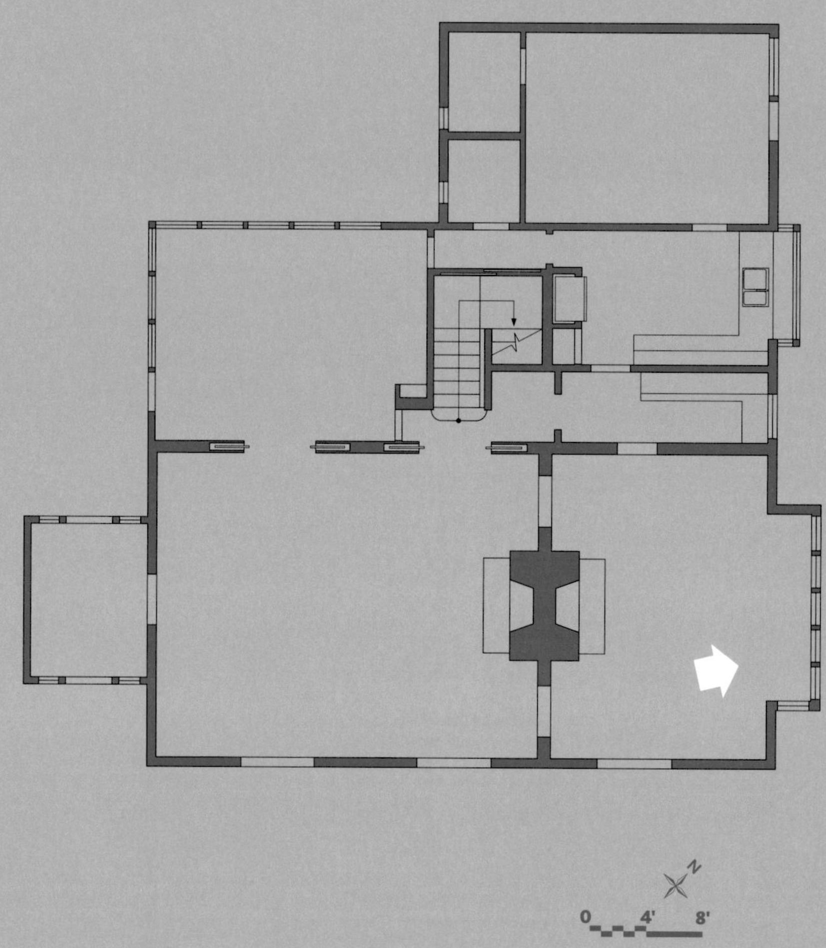

FLOYD FAXON

CA. LATE SEPTEMBER–LATE NOVEMBER 1948

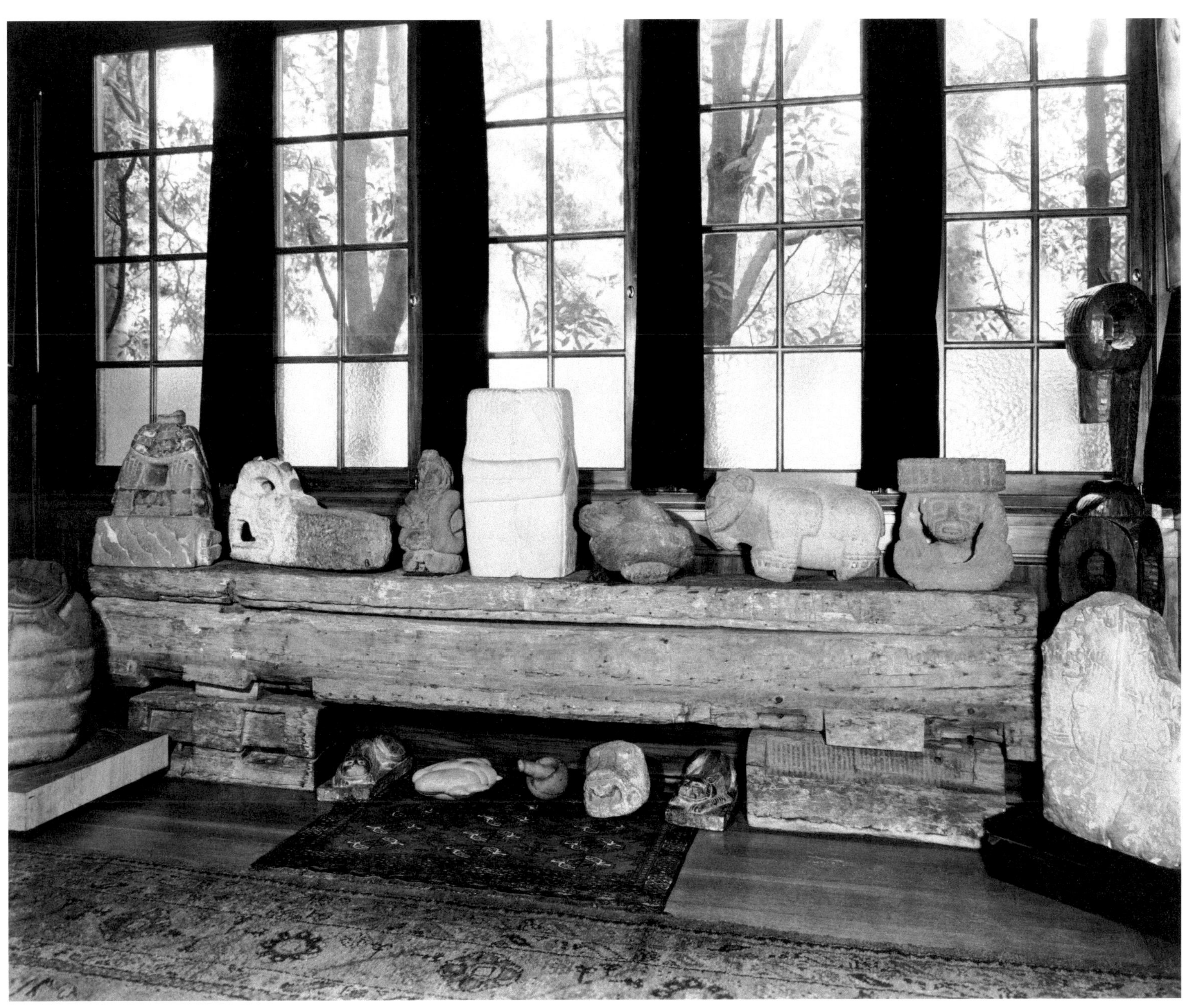

PLATE 12

1 JUAN GRIS, *Open Window*, 1917 [1950-134-97; AC20-98; SEE FIG. 31, PAGE 32]

2 AZTEC (CENTRAL MEXICO), Torso of Earth Goddess (Tlaltecuhtli), 1300–1520 [1950-134-603]

3 AZTEC (CENTRAL MEXICO), Tenoned Stone in Serpent Form, 1300–1520 [1950-134-334; ACPS-38]

4 AZTEC (CENTRAL MEXICO), Serpent (Quetzalcoatl), 1300–1520 [1950-134-349; ACPS-28]

5 CONSTANTIN BRANCUSI, *The Kiss*, 1916 [1950-134-4; AC20-3]

6 AZTEC (CENTRAL MEXICO), Serpent, 1300–1520 [1950-134-315; ACPS-36]

7 DIQUÍS (COSTA RICA), Jaguar, 1000–1520 [1950-134-323; ACPS-182]

8 TEOTIHUACAN (CENTRAL MEXICO), Seated Figure (Old God of Fire), 1st–9th century [1950-134-301; ACPS-3]

9 CONSTANTIN BRANCUSI, *Chimera*, 1915–18 [1950-134-13; AC20-14]

10 FRANTIŠEK KUPKA, *Disks of Newton (Study for "Fugue in Two Colors")*, 1912 [1950-134-122; AC20-123]

11 AZTEC (CENTRAL MEXICO), Serpent, 1300–1520 [1950-134-294; ACPS-35]

12 CONSTANTIN BRANCUSI, *Bench*, 1914–16 [1950-134-23; AC20-13]

13 ARTIST/MAKER UNKNOWN (*CHINA), Couchant Animal, ca. 960–1279 [1950-134-498]

14 NATIVE AMERICAN, Mortar and Pestle, Date unknown [1950-134-637A,B]

15 AZTEC OR EARLY SPANISH COLONIAL (CENTRAL MEXICO), Animal Head, 1400–1600 [1950-134-605]

16 ARTIST/MAKER UNKNOWN (*CHINA), Couchant Animal, ca. 960–1279 [1950-134-499]

17 MAYA (MEXICO), Fragment of a Stela, 810 [1950-134-242; ACPS-164]

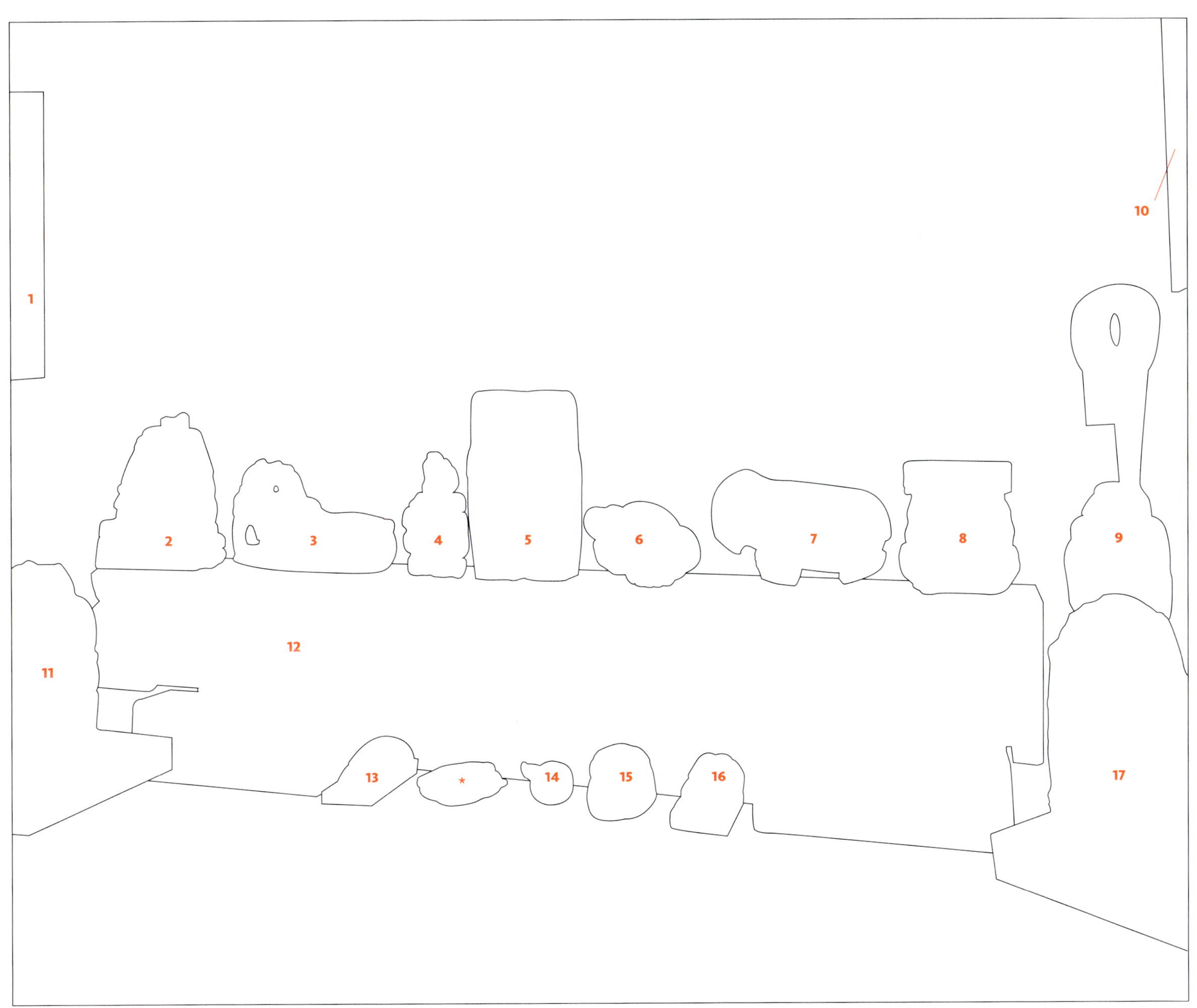
1
2
3
4
5
6
7
8
9
10
11
12
13
*
14
15
16
17

PLATE 13

DINING ROOM

WITH A VIEW INTO THE LIVING ROOM THROUGH THE SOUTH ARCHWAY

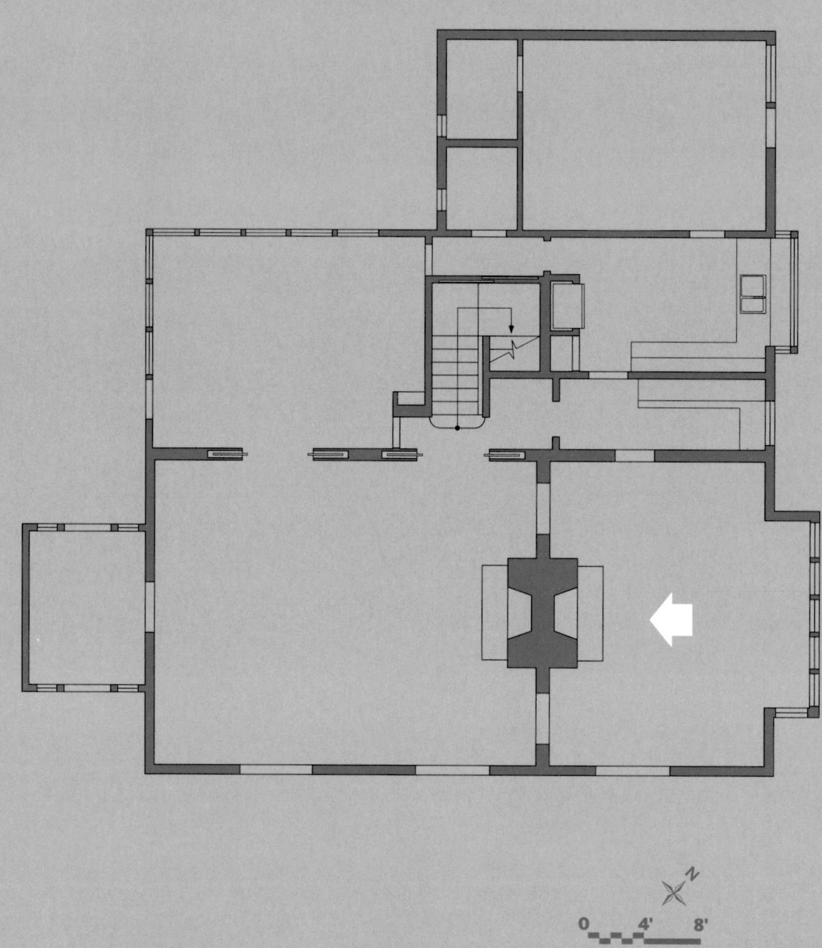

FRED R. DAPPRICH

CA. 1944

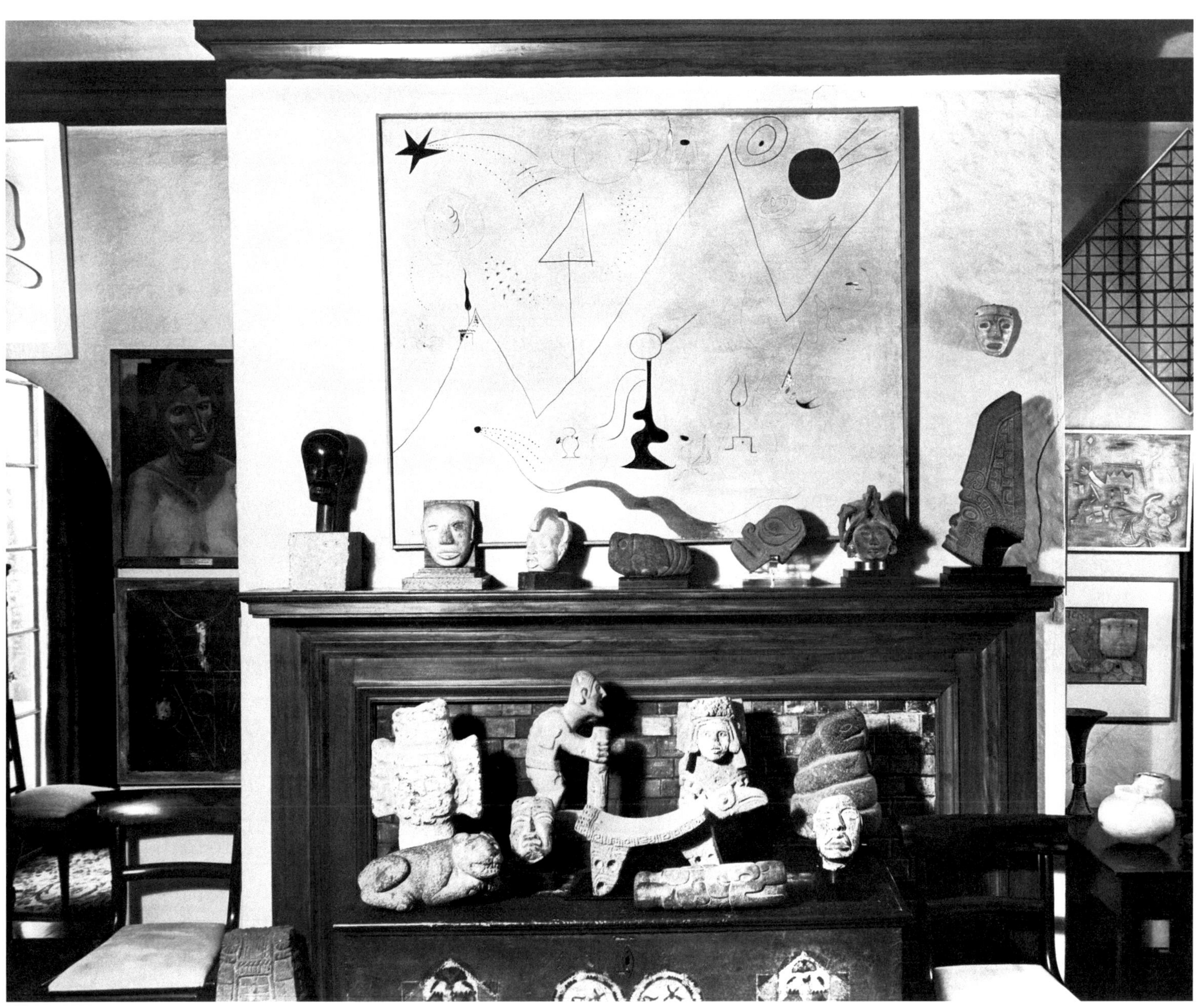

PLATE 13

1 JEAN (HANS) ARP, *Constellation*, 1932 [1950-134-2; AC20-2]

2 ANDRÉ DERAIN, *Woman*, ca. 1914 [1950-134-47; AC20-47]

3 CARLOS MÉRIDA, *Deer Dance*, 1935 [1950-134-134; AC20-138]

4 FANG (GABON), Head, Date unknown [1950-134-202]

5 JOAN MIRÓ, *The Hermitage*, 1924 [1950-134-141; AC20-144]

6 *HUASTEC OR TEOTIHUACAN (EAST COAST OR CENTRAL MEXICO), Mask, *1st–13th century [1950-134-234; ACPS-119]

7 CLASSIC VERACRUZ (EAST COAST MEXICO), Hacha in the Form of a Head, 500–900 [1950-134-285; ACPS-138]

8 AZTEC (CENTRAL MEXICO), Grasshopper Larva, 1300–1520 [1950-134-281; ACPS-40]

9 CLASSIC VERACRUZ (EAST COAST MEXICO), Hacha in the Form of a Head, 500–900 [1950-134-226; ACPS-145]

10 HUASTEC (EAST COAST MEXICO), Head, 1000–1500 [1950-134-298; ACPS-128]

11 CLASSIC VERACRUZ (EAST COAST MEXICO), Palma, 500–900 [1950-134-336; ACPS-154]

12 MEZCALA (SOUTHWESTERN MEXICO), Mask, 300 BCE–500 CE [1950-134-273; ACPS-87]

13 PIET MONDRIAN, *Composition in Black and Gray* or *Composition with Grid 4 (Lozenge)*, 1919 [1950-134-151; AC20-154]

14 PAUL KLEE, *Animal Terror*, 1926 [1950-134-113; AC20-115]

15 PAUL KLEE, *Jörg*, 1924 [1950-134-111; AC20-112]

16 ARTIST/MAKER UNKNOWN (CHINA), Bowl, Date unknown [PMA-WLA BOX 26, AIN 246]

17 MIXTEC (SOUTHEASTERN MEXICO), Vessel, 800–1300 [1950-134-316; ACPS-112]

18 ARTIST/MAKER UNKNOWN (*CHINA), Vase, Date unknown [NOTE 1.5, PAGE 414]

19 OLMEC (MEXICO), Mask, 1200–400 BCE [1950-134-339; ACPS-86]

20 AZTEC (CENTRAL MEXICO), Serpent, 1300–1520 [1950-134-215; ACPS-34]

21 CLASSIC VERACRUZ (EAST COAST MEXICO), Serpent Form, 500–900 [1950-134-331; ACPS-133]

22 GUANACASTE-NICOYA (COSTA RICA), Metate, 300–800 [1950-134-318; ACPS-172]

23 AZTEC (CENTRAL MEXICO), Water Goddess, 1300–1520 [1950-134-402; ACPS-8]

24 HUASTEC (EAST COAST MEXICO), Figure of a Man, 1000–1500 [1950-134-295; ACPS-113]

25 OLMEC (MEXICO), Head, 1200–600 BCE [1950-134-312; ACPS-124]

26 AZTEC (CENTRAL MEXICO), Jaguar, 1300–1520 [1950-134-333; ACPS-33]

27 AZTEC (CENTRAL MEXICO), Corn Goddess, 1300–1520 [1950-134-615]

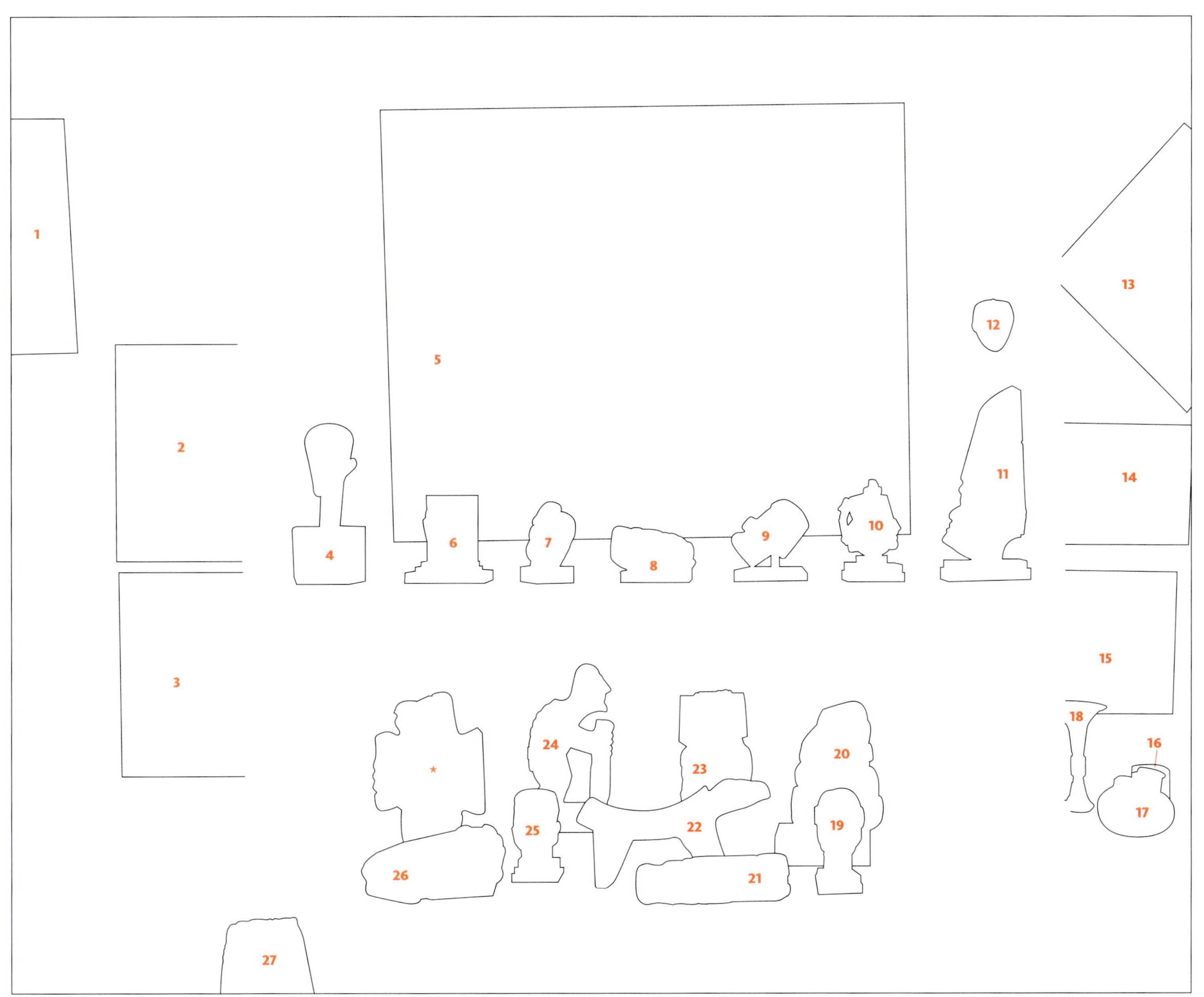
1
2
3
4
5
6
7
8
9
10
11
12
13
14
15
16
17
18
19
20
21
22
23
24
25
26
27
*

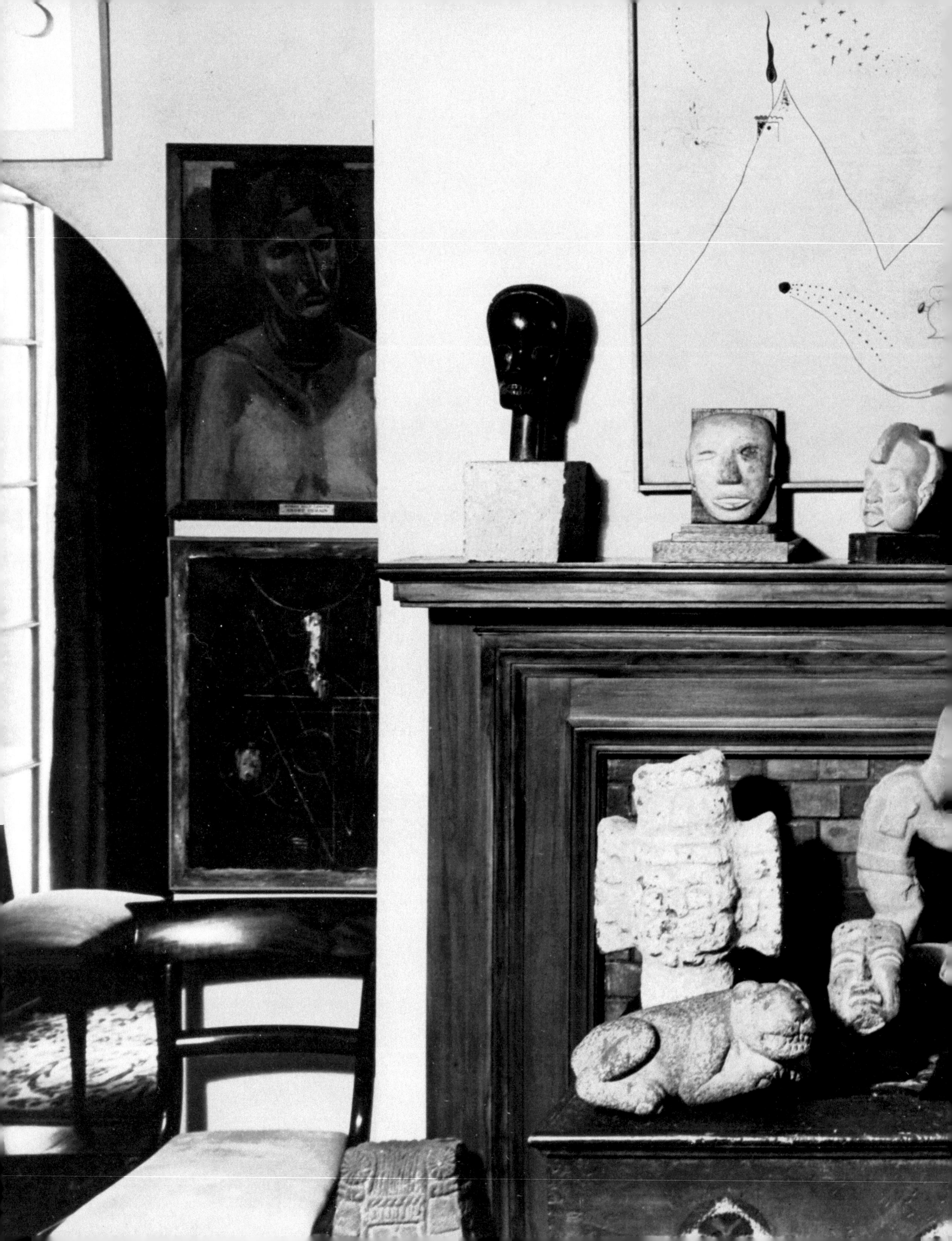

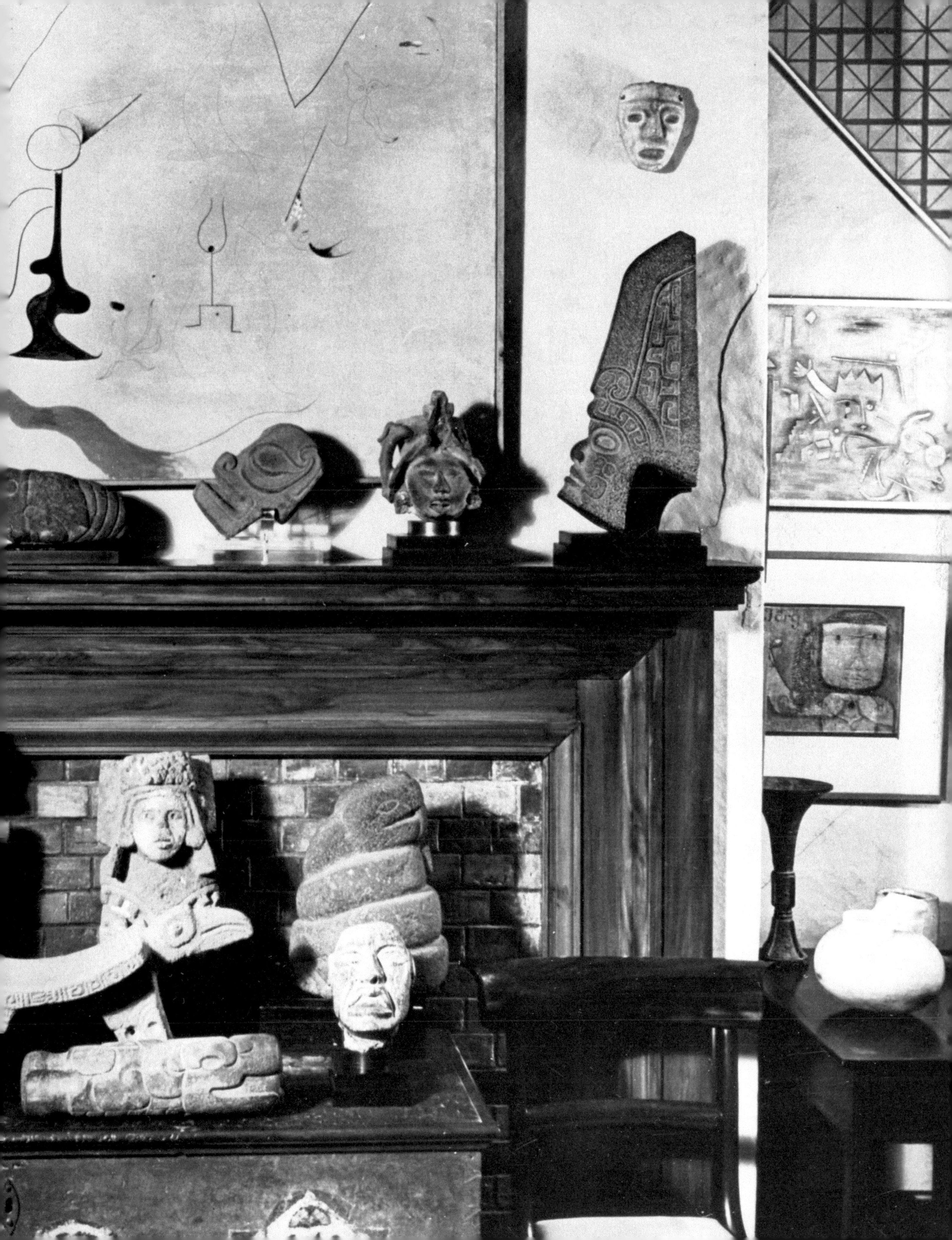

PLATE 14

DINING ROOM

WITH A VIEW INTO THE LIVING ROOM THROUGH THE SOUTH ARCHWAY

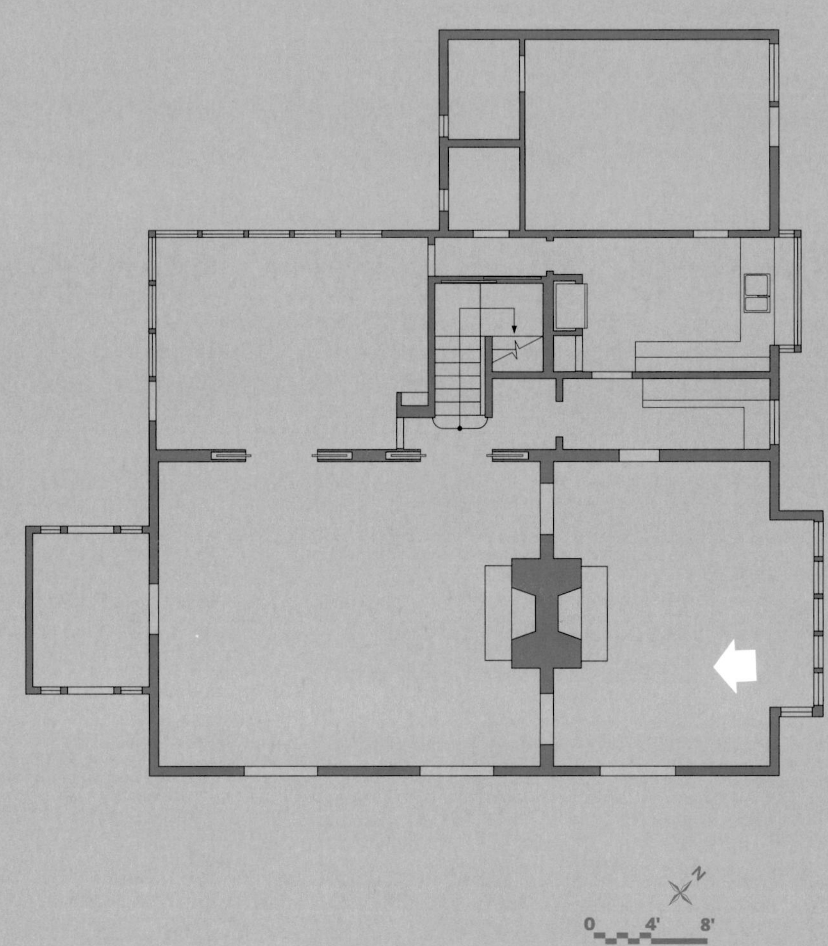

PROBABLY DICK SEYFFERT

CA. 1945, AFTER 15 MARCH

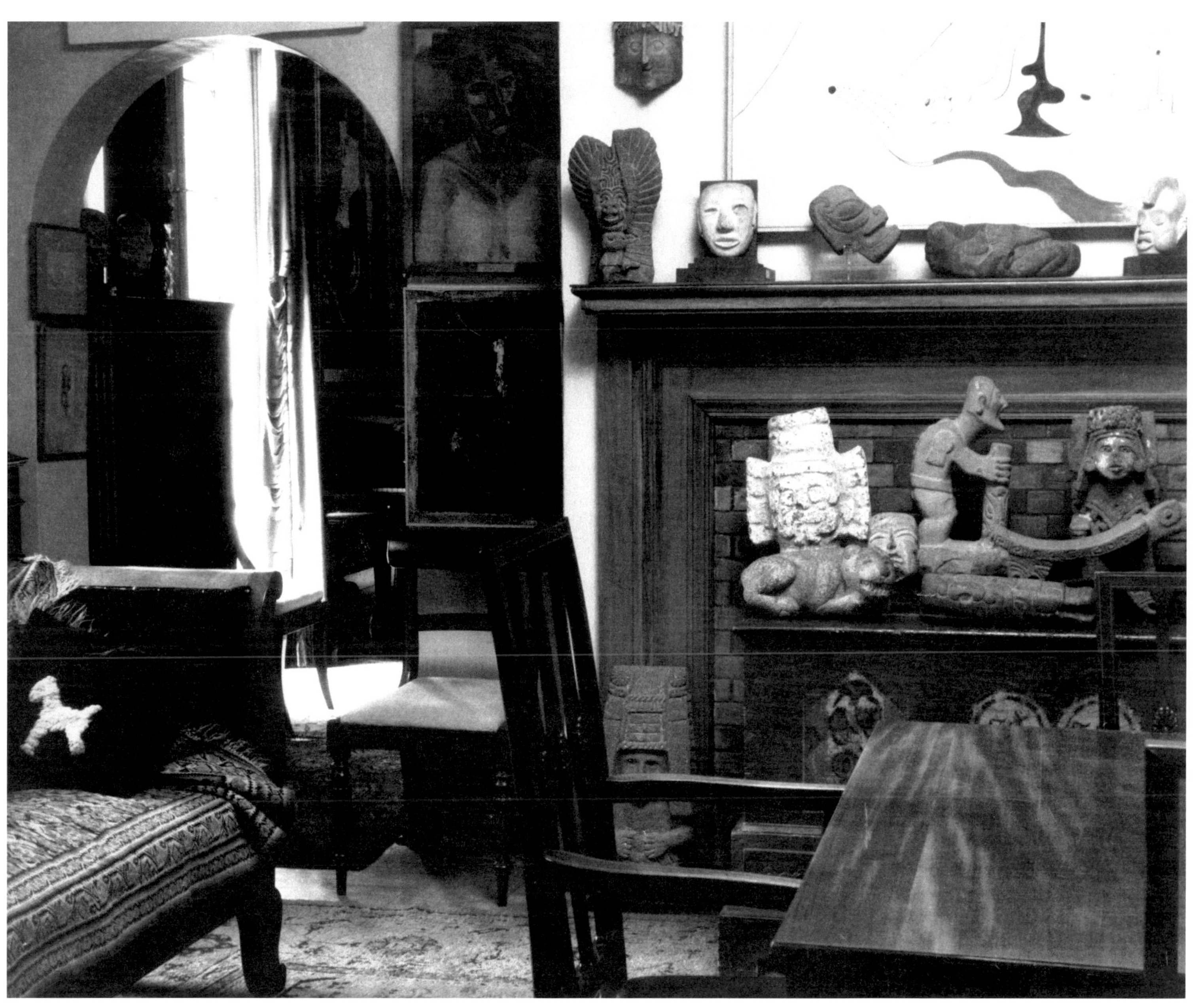

PLATE 14

1 JEAN (HANS) ARP, *Constellation*, 1932 [1950-134-2; AC20-2]

*2 PABLO PICASSO, *Seashore Scene*, 1905 [1950-134-159; AC20-162]

3 PABLO PICASSO, *Female Figure*, 1906 [1950-134-160A; AC20-163]

4 FERNAND LÉGER, *The City (Fragment, Third State)*, 1919 [1950-134-124; AC20-127]

5 ANDRÉ DERAIN, *Woman*, ca. 1914 [1950-134-47; AC20-47]

6 CARLOS MÉRIDA, *Deer Dance*, 1935 [1950-134-134; AC20-138]

7 CHANCAY (PERU), Mummy Mask, 1000–1450 [1950-134-363; ACPS-187]

8 JOAN MIRÓ, *The Hermitage*, 1924 [1950-134-141; AC20-144]

9 CLASSIC VERACRUZ (EAST COAST MEXICO), Palma, 500–900 [1950-134-328; ACPS-151]

10 *HUASTEC OR TEOTIHUACAN (EAST COAST OR CENTRAL MEXICO), Mask, *1st–13th century [1950-134-234; ACPS-119]

11 CLASSIC VERACRUZ (EAST COAST MEXICO), Hacha in the Form of a Head, 500–900 [1950-134-226; ACPS-145]

12 AZTEC (CENTRAL MEXICO), Grasshopper, 1300–1520 [1950-134-340; ACPS-41]

13 CLASSIC VERACRUZ (EAST COAST MEXICO), Hacha in the Form of a Head, 500–900 [1950-134-285; ACPS-138]

14 AZTEC (CENTRAL MEXICO), Corn Goddess, 1300–1520 [1950-134-615]

15 AZTEC (CENTRAL MEXICO), Jaguar, 1300–1520 [1950-134-333; ACPS-33]

16 OLMEC (MEXICO), Head, 1200–600 BCE [1950-134-312; ACPS-124]

17 HUASTEC (EAST COAST MEXICO), Figure of a Man, 1000–1500 [1950-134-295; ACPS-113]

18 CLASSIC VERACRUZ (EAST COAST MEXICO), Serpent Form, 500–900 [1950-134-331; ACPS-133]

19 GUANACASTE-NICOYA (COSTA RICA), Metate, 300–800 [1950-134-318; ACPS-172]

20 AZTEC (CENTRAL MEXICO), Water Goddess, 1300–1520 [1950-134-402; ACPS-8]

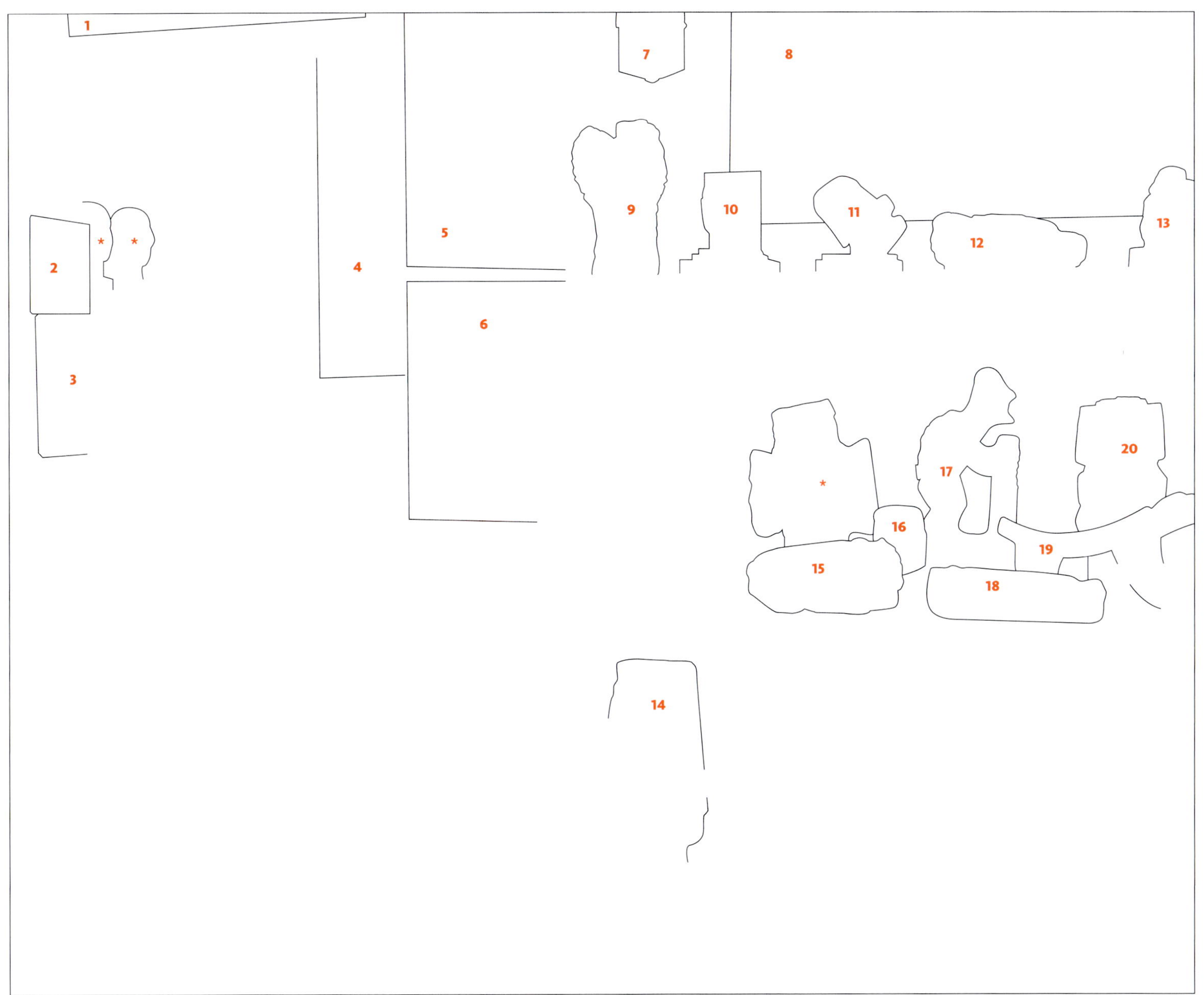
1
7
8
9
10
11
12
13
2
*
*
5
4
3
6
17
20
*
16
19
15
18
14

PLATE 15

DINING ROOM

WITH A VIEW INTO THE LIVING ROOM THROUGH THE SOUTH ARCHWAY

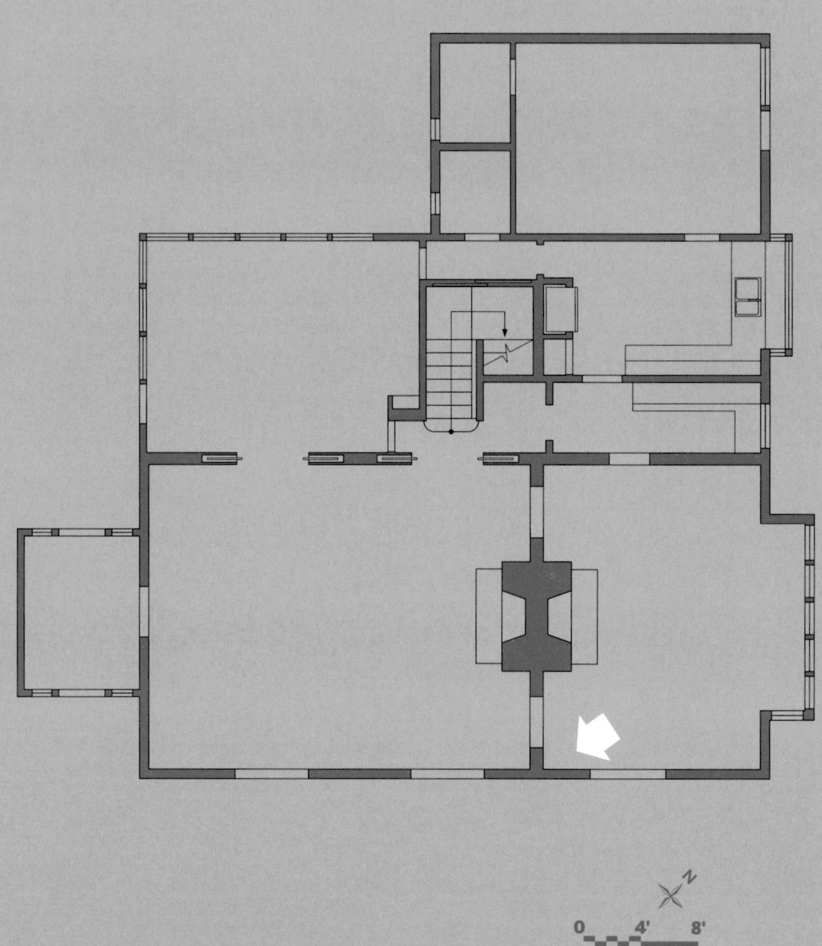

FLOYD FAXON

CA. JANUARY 1951

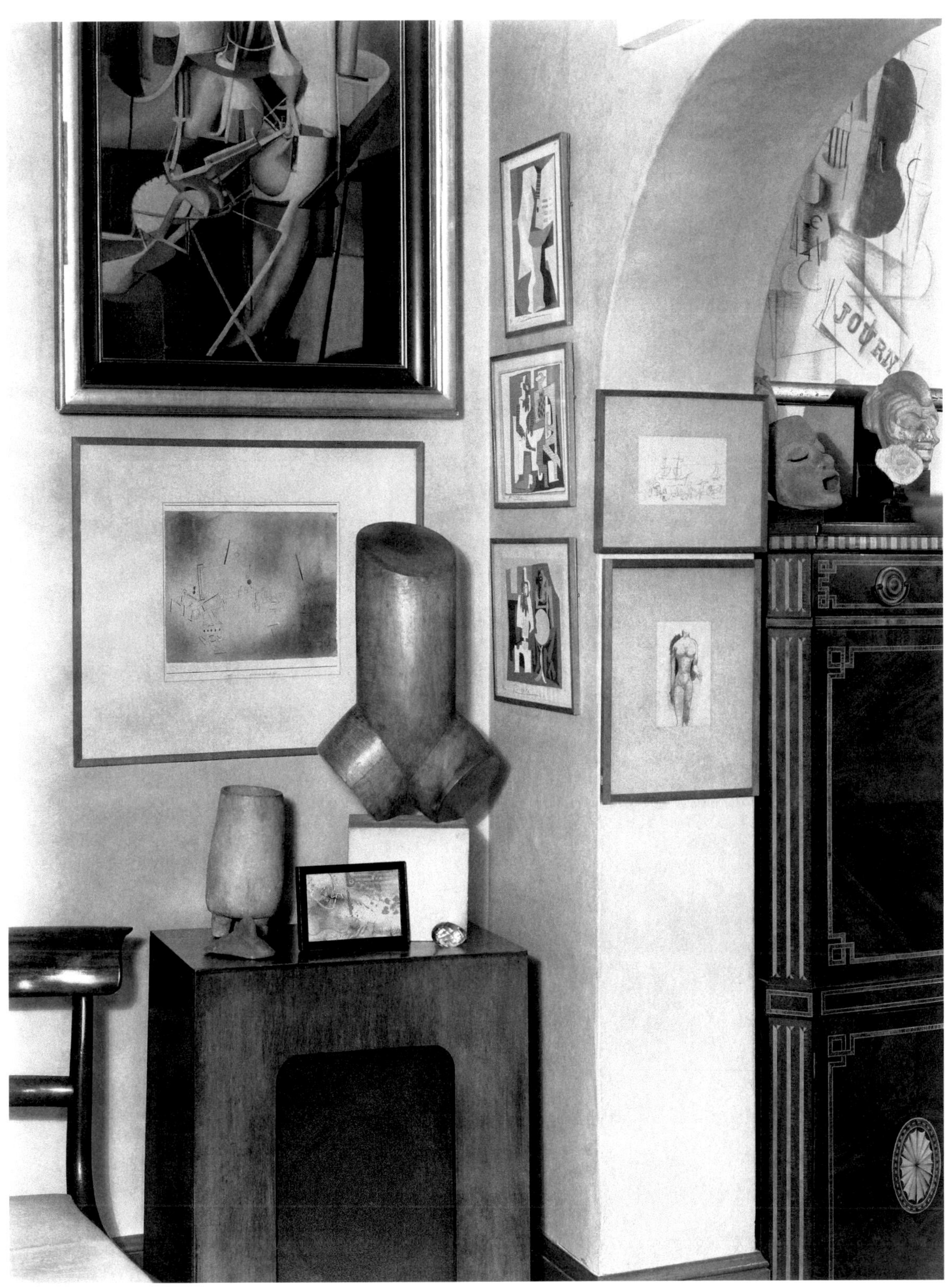

PLATE 15

1 MARCEL DUCHAMP, *Bride*, 1912 [1950-134-65; AC20-71]

2 PAUL KLEE, *Heavenly and Earthly Time*, 1927 [1950-134-117; AC20-118]

3 MIXTEC (SOUTHEASTERN MEXICO), Vessel, 800–1300 [1950-134-357; ACPS-111]

4 MEZCALA (SOUTHWESTERN MEXICO), Mask, 300 BCE–500 CE [1950-134-380; ACPS-93]

5 CONSTANTIN BRANCUSI, *Torso of a Young Man [I]*, ca. 1917–22 [1950-134-17; AC20-15]

6 KNUD MERRILD, *Abstraction*, 10 October 1935 [PMA-WLA BOX 72, FOLDER 9]

*7 ARTIST/MAKER UNKNOWN (*EUROPE OR NORTH AMERICA), Paperweight, Date unknown [NOTE 1.4, PAGE 414]

8 ARTIST/MAKER UNKNOWN, AFTER PABLO PICASSO, *Pedestal with Guitar and Score*, 1920 [1950-134-903]

9 ARTIST/MAKER UNKNOWN, AFTER PABLO PICASSO, *Pierrot and Harlequin*, 1920 [1950-134-900]

10 ARTIST/MAKER UNKNOWN, AFTER PABLO PICASSO, *Pierrot and Harlequin at the Café Terrace*, 1920 [1950-134-899]

11 JEAN (HANS) ARP, *Constellation*, 1932 [1950-134-2; AC20-2]

12 PABLO PICASSO, *Seashore Scene*, 1905 [1950-134-159; AC20-162]

13 PABLO PICASSO, *Female Figure*, 1906 [1950-134-160A; AC20-163]

14 GEORGES BRAQUE, *Violin and Newspaper*, 1912–13 [1950-134-26; AC20-24]

15 JALISCO, AMECA-ETZATLÁN STYLE (WESTERN MEXICO), Fragment of a Head, 100 BCE–200 CE [1950-134-393; ACPS-65]

16 HUASTEC (EAST COAST MEXICO), Head, 900–1200 [1950-134-317; ACPS-129]

17 CLASSIC VERACRUZ (EAST COAST MEXICO), Hacha in the Form of a Head, 500–900 [1950-134-206; ACPS-139]

18 MANTEÑO (ECUADOR), Stamp, 900–1500 [1950-134-307; ACPS-169]

PLATES 15.8–15.10 ARE FROM THE SERIES *DIX POCHOIRS*, PUBLISHED BY PAUL ROSENBERG, PARIS, CA. 1920.

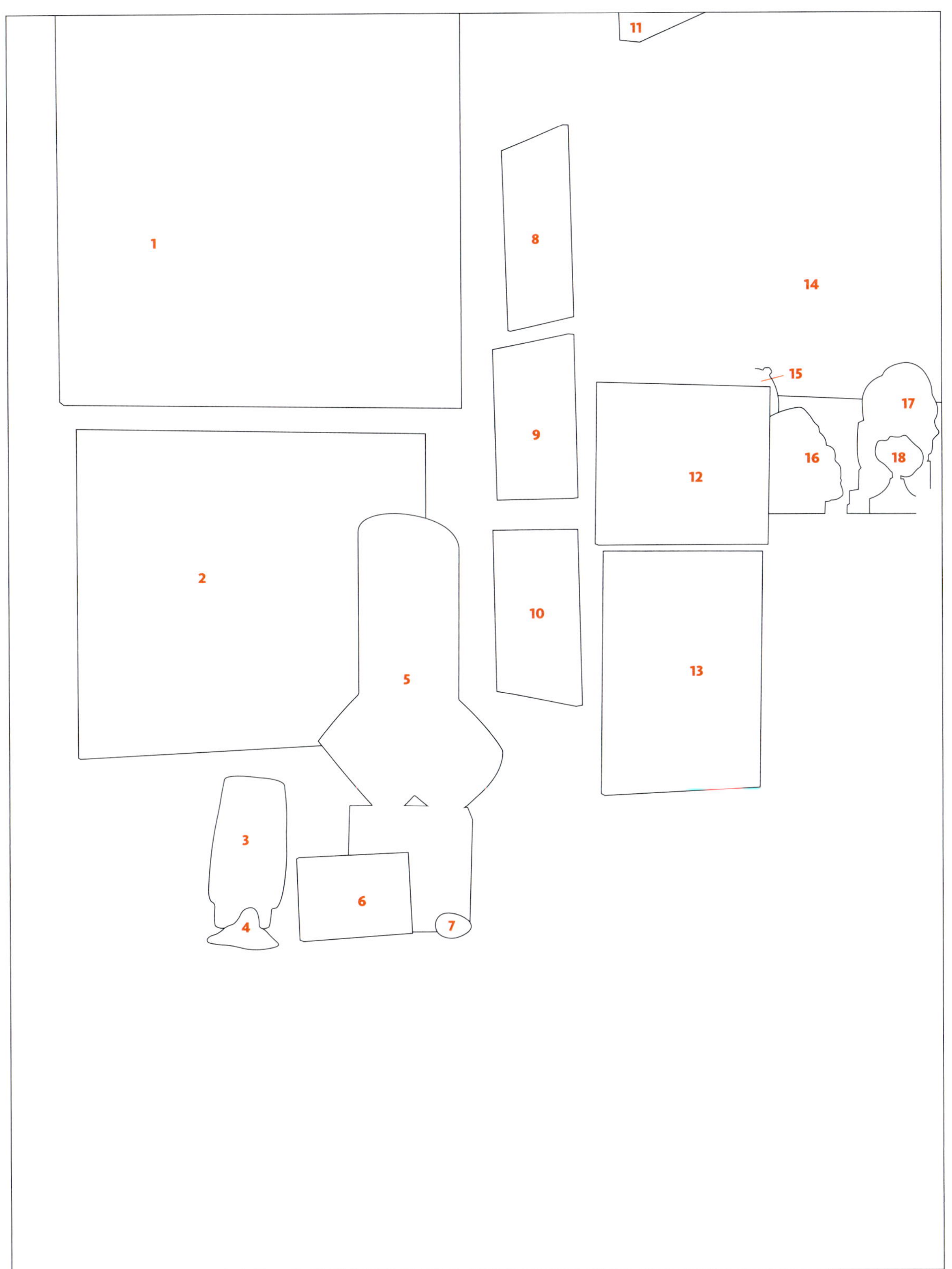
1
2
3
4
5
6
7
8
9
10
11
12
13
14
15
16
17
18

PLATE 16

DINING ROOM

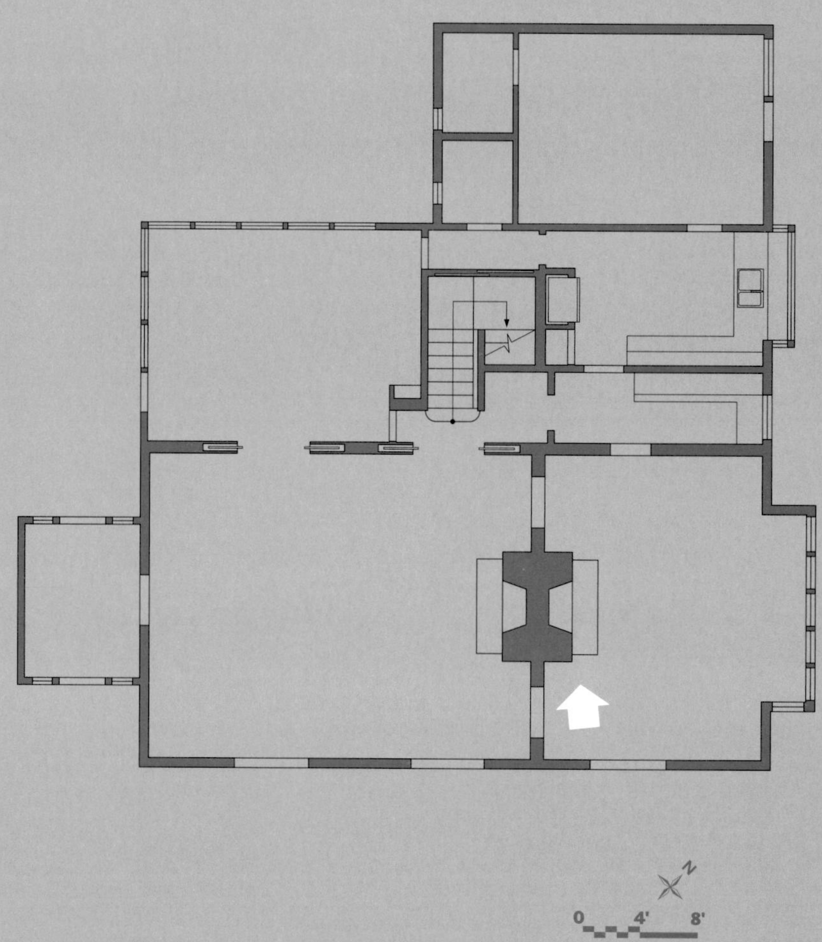

PROBABLY DICK SEYFFERT

CA. 1945, AFTER 15 MARCH

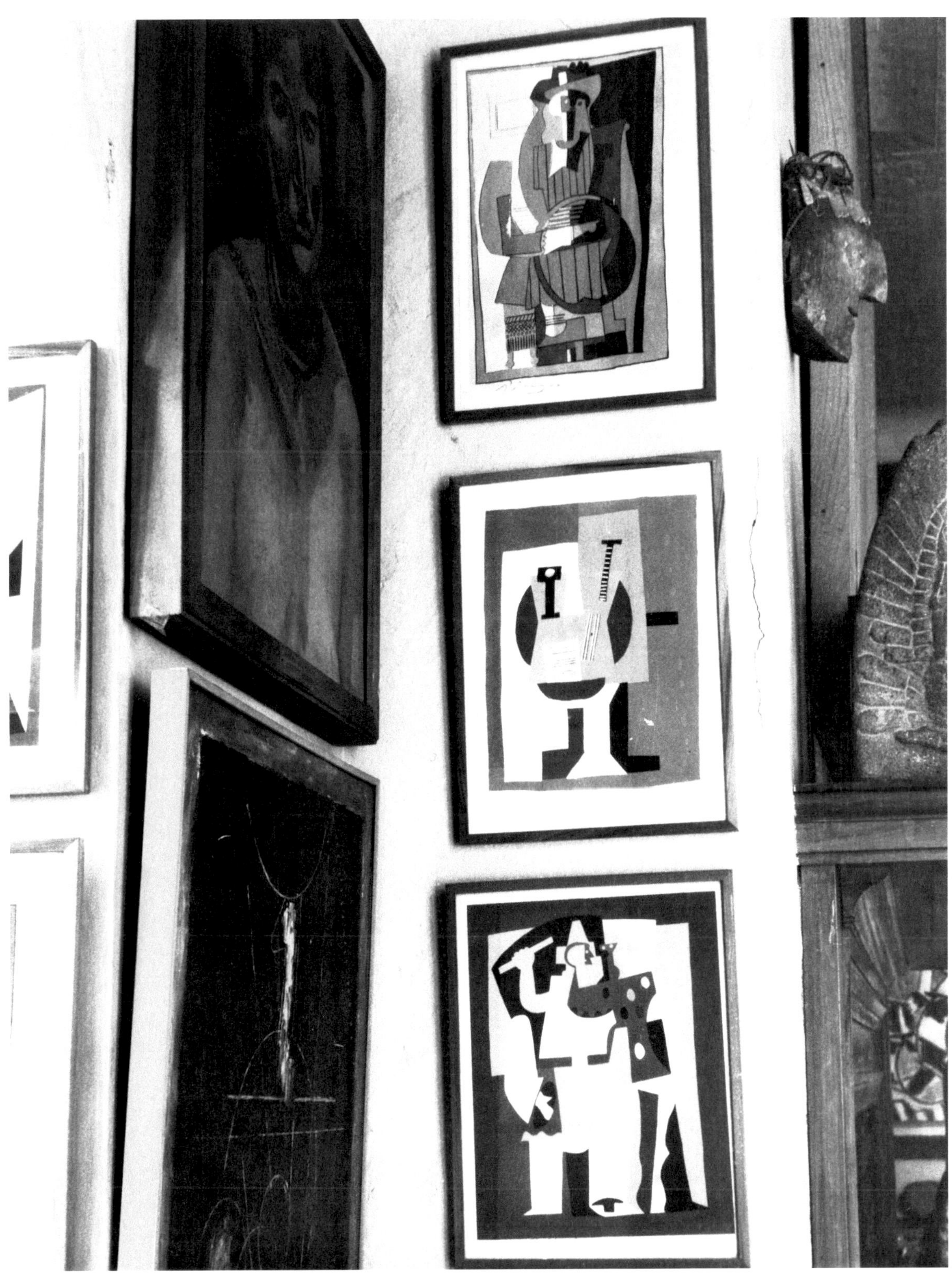

PLATE 16

1 ARTIST/MAKER UNKNOWN, AFTER PABLO PICASSO, *Pedestal with Guitar and Score*, 1920 [1950-134-903]

2 ANDRÉ DERAIN, *Woman*, ca. 1914 [1950-134-47; AC20-47]

3 CARLOS MÉRIDA, *Deer Dance*, 1935 [1950-134-134; AC20-138]

4 ARTIST/MAKER UNKNOWN, AFTER PABLO PICASSO, *Little Girl with a Hoop*, 1919 [1950-134-898]

5 ARTIST/MAKER UNKNOWN, AFTER PABLO PICASSO, *Guitar and Score*, 1920 [1950-134-907]

6 ARTIST/MAKER UNKNOWN, AFTER PABLO PICASSO, *Orchestra Conductor Pierrot*, 1920 [1950-134-902]

7 CHANCAY (PERU), Mummy Mask, 1000–1450 [1950-134-363; ACPS-187]

8 CLASSIC VERACRUZ (EAST COAST MEXICO), Palma, 500–900 [1950-134-328; ACPS-151]

9 FERNAND LÉGER, *Contrast of Forms*, 1913–14 [1950-134-123; AC20-126]

PLATES 16.1 AND 16.4–16.6 ARE FROM THE SERIES *DIX POCHOIRS*, PUBLISHED BY PAUL ROSENBERG, PARIS, CA. 1920.

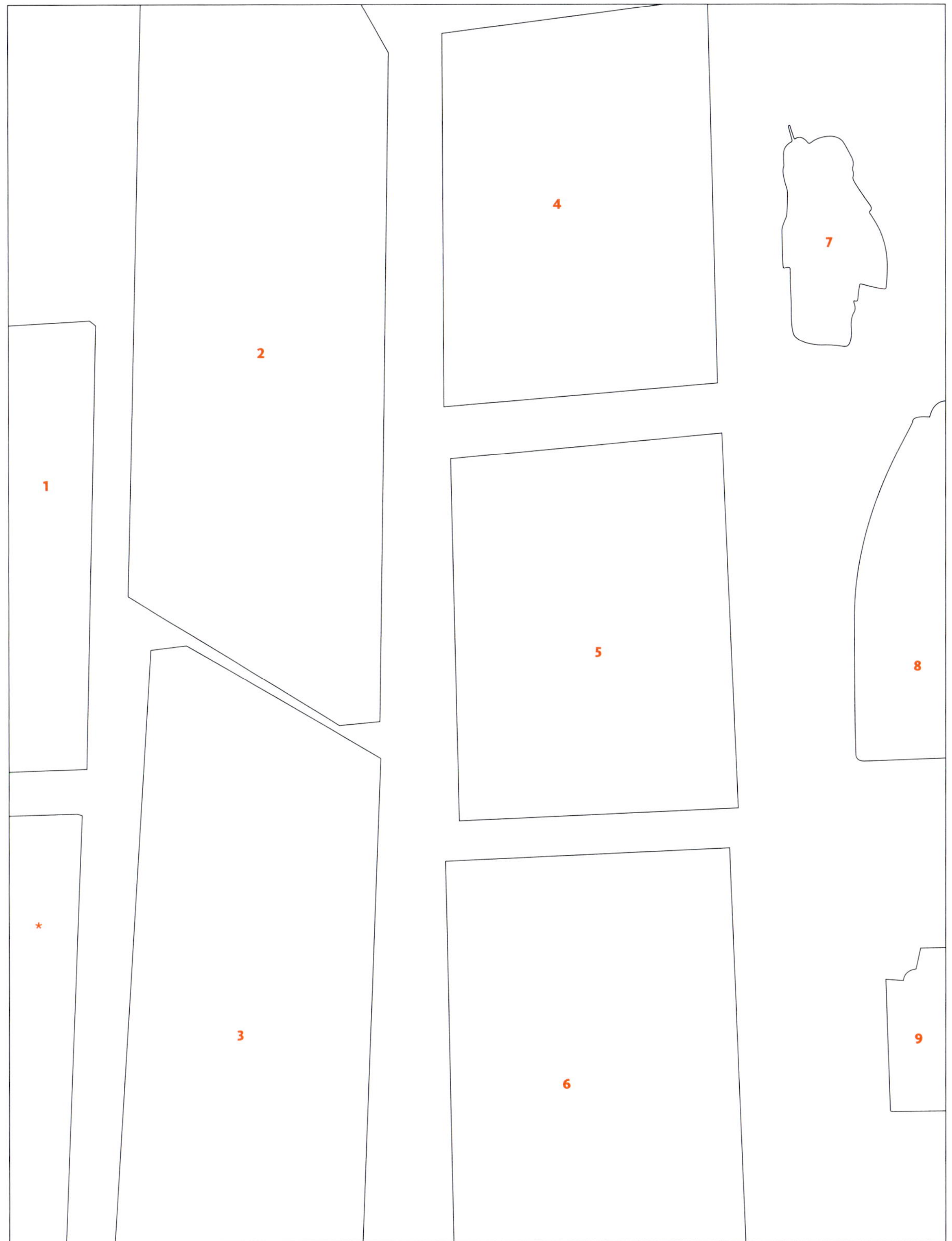
4
7
2
1
5
8
*
3
6
9

PLATE 17

DINING ROOM

WITH A VIEW INTO THE LIVING ROOM THROUGH THE NORTH ARCHWAY

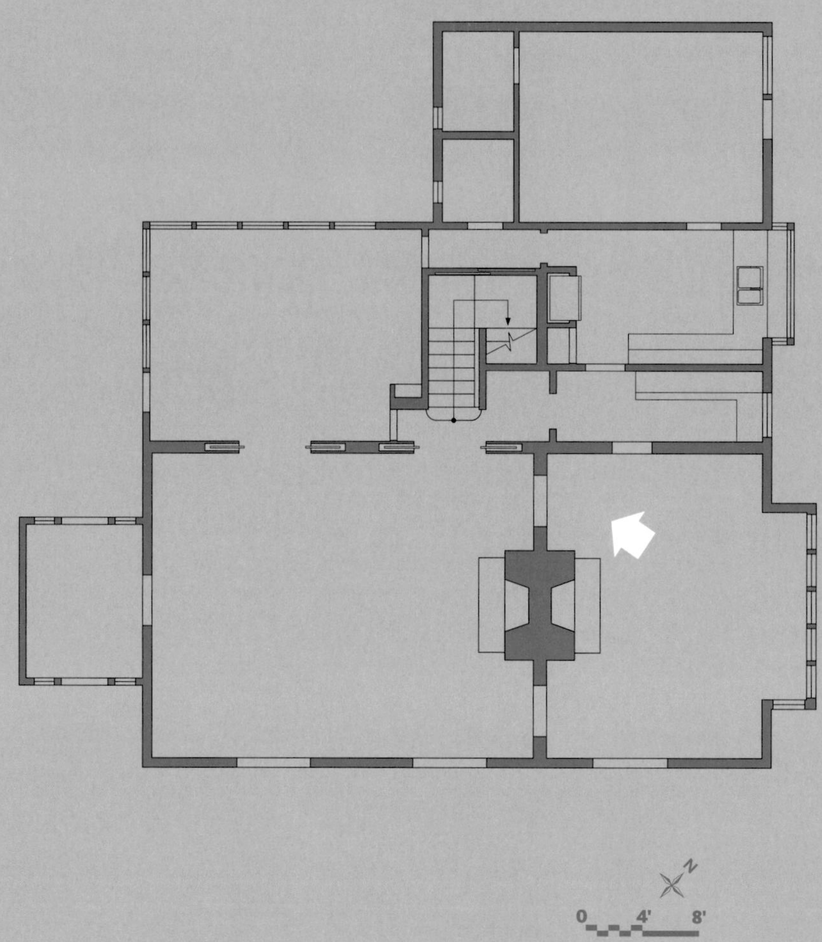

FRED R. DAPPRICH

CA. 1944

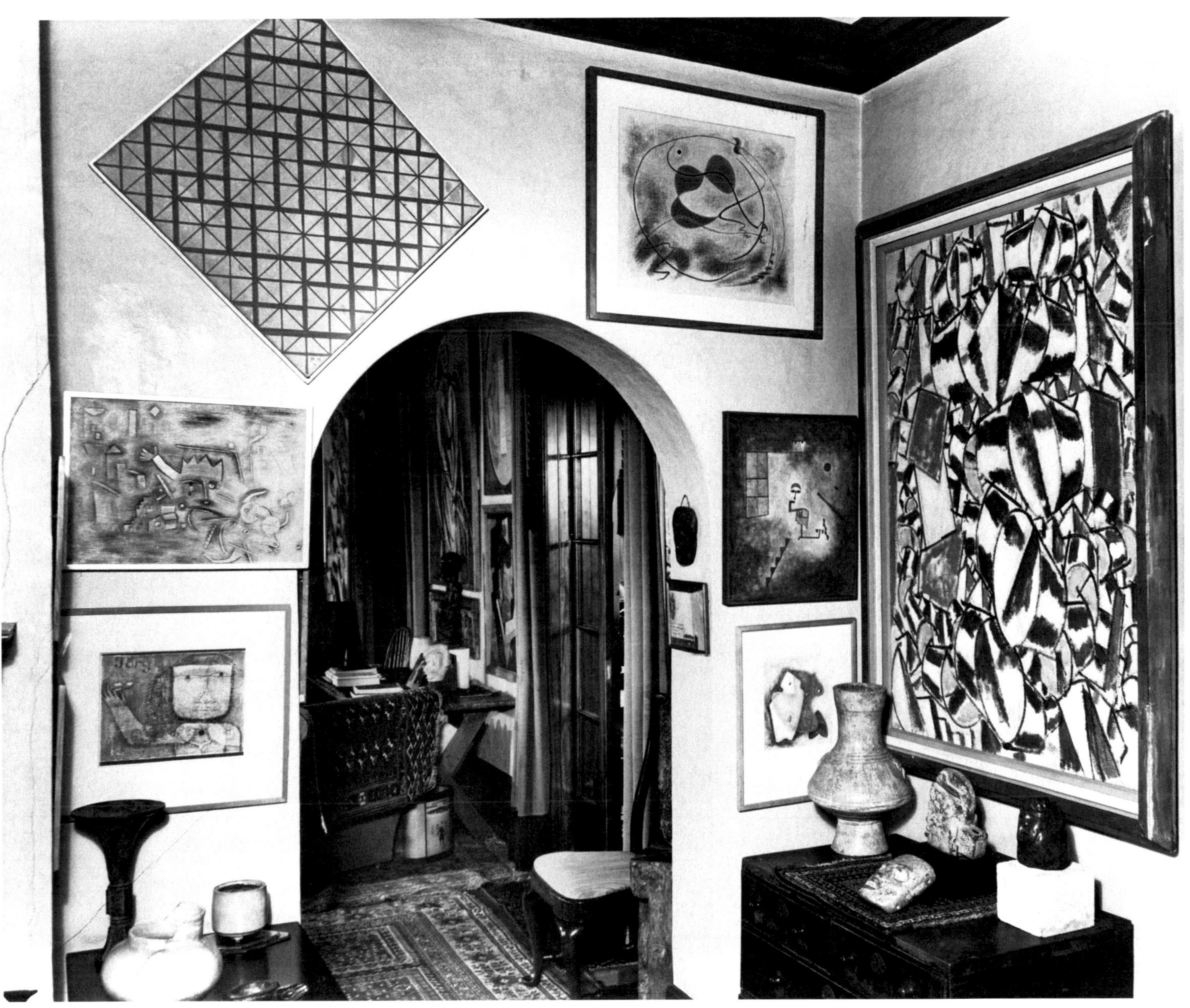

PLATE 17

1 PIET MONDRIAN, *Composition in Black and Gray* or *Composition with Grid 4 (Lozenge)*, 1919 [1950-134-151; AC20-154]

2 PAUL KLEE, *Animal Terror*, 1926 [1950-134-113; AC20-115]

3 PAUL KLEE, *Jörg*, 1924 [1950-134-111; AC20-112]

4 ARTIST/MAKER UNKNOWN (*CHINA), Vase, Date unknown [NOTE 1.5, PAGE 414]

5 MIXTEC (SOUTHEASTERN MEXICO), Vessel, 800–1300 [1950-134-316; ACPS-112]

6 ARTIST/MAKER UNKNOWN (CHINA), Bowl, Date unknown [PMA-WLA BOX 26, AIN 246]

7 GUANACASTE-NICOYA (COSTA RICA), Incense Burner or Vessel, 700–1350 [1950-134-227]

8 MARC CHAGALL, *Half-Past Three (The Poet)*, 1911 [1950-134-36; AC20-35]

9 HENRI MATISSE, *Mademoiselle Yvonne Landsberg*, 1914 [1950-134-130; AC20-133]

10 PAUL CÉZANNE, *Still Life with Apples and a Glass of Wine*, 1877–79 [1950-134-32; AC20-31]

11 FANG (GABON), Male Reliquary Guardian Figure, Mid-19th century [1950-134-200]

12 PAUL CÉZANNE, *Group of Bathers*, ca. 1895 [1950-134-34; AC20-33]

13 MIXTEC (SOUTHEASTERN MEXICO), Vessel, 800–1300 [1950-134-357; ACPS-111]

14 CLASSIC VERACRUZ (EAST COAST MEXICO), Hacha in the Form of a Head, 500–900 [1950-134-206; ACPS-139]

15 PABLO PICASSO, *Still Life with a Violin and a Guitar*, 1912–13 [1950-134-170; AC20-174]

16 JUAN GRIS, *Lamp*, 1916 [1950-134-96; AC20-97]

17 ANDRÉ MASSON, *Animal Caught in a Trap*, 1929 [1950-134-129; AC20-132]

18 ARTIST/MAKER UNKNOWN, Pre-Columbian Death Mask (fake), Date unknown [NOTE 4.1, PAGE 416]

19 ARTIST/MAKER UNKNOWN (MEXICO), *Recovery from an Illness*, 1927 [1950-134-493]

20 AZTEC (CENTRAL MEXICO), Figure (Quetzalcoatl), 1300–1520 [1950-134-251; ACPS-27]

21 PAUL KLEE, *Prestidigitator (Conjuring Trick)*, 1927 [1950-134-118; AC20-120]

22 KNUD MERRILD, *Arrowhead*, 1936 [1950-134-137; AC20-140]

23 FERNAND LÉGER, *Contrast of Forms*, 1913–14 [1950-134-123; AC20-126]

24 ARTIST/MAKER UNKNOWN (*CHINA), Burial Urn (fake), Date unknown [NOTE 4.2, PAGE 416]

25 TEOTIHUACAN (CENTRAL MEXICO), Mask, 1st–9th century [1950-134-359; ACPS-17]

26 CLASSIC VERACRUZ (EAST COAST MEXICO), Hacha in the Form of a Head of a Man, 500–900 [1950-134-212; ACPS-101]

27 AZTEC (CENTRAL MEXICO), Bust of Goddess, 1300–1520 [1950-134-236; ACPS-191]

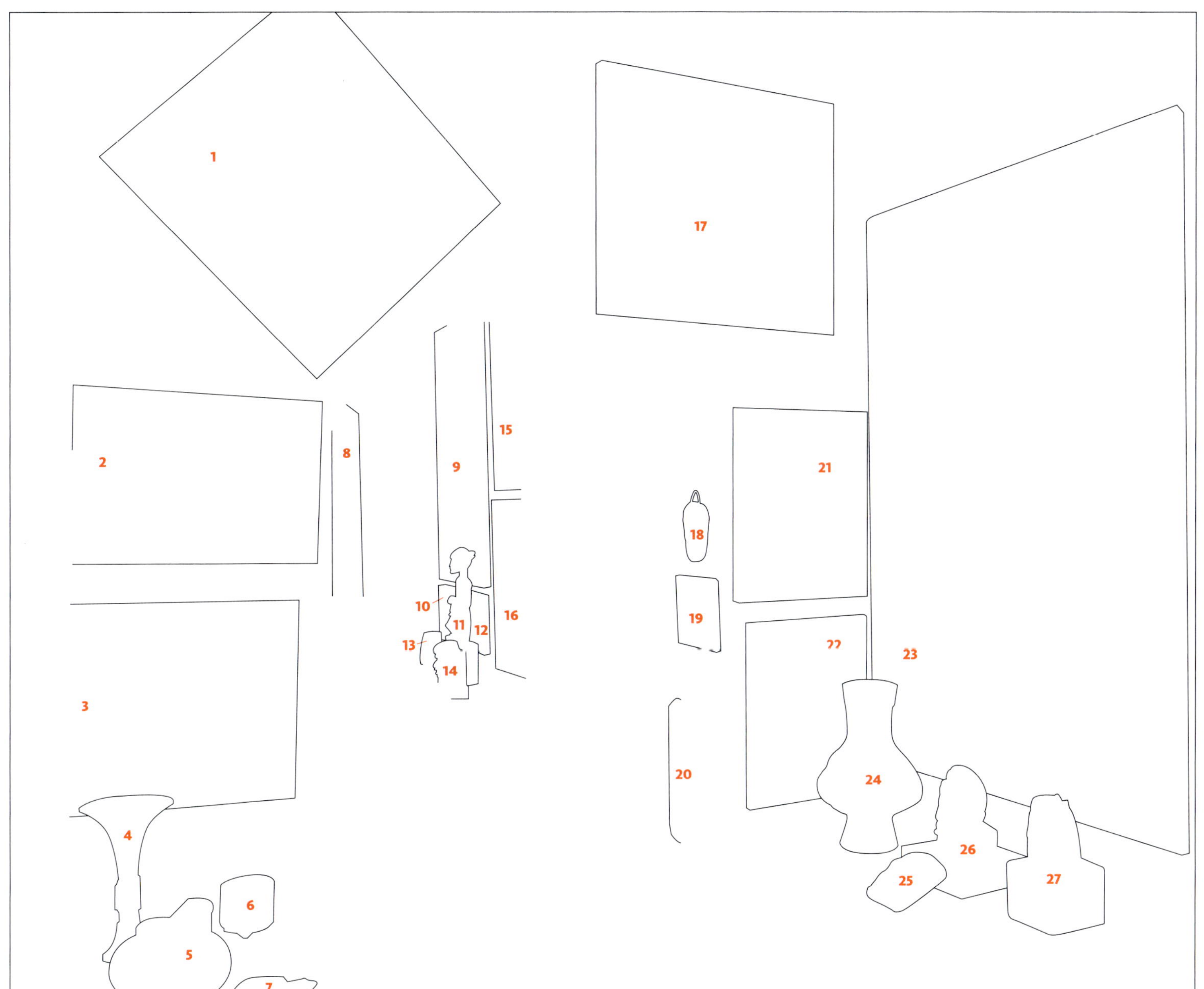

1
2
3
4
5
6
7
8
9
10
11
12
13
14
15
16
17
18
19
20
21
22
23
24
25
26
27

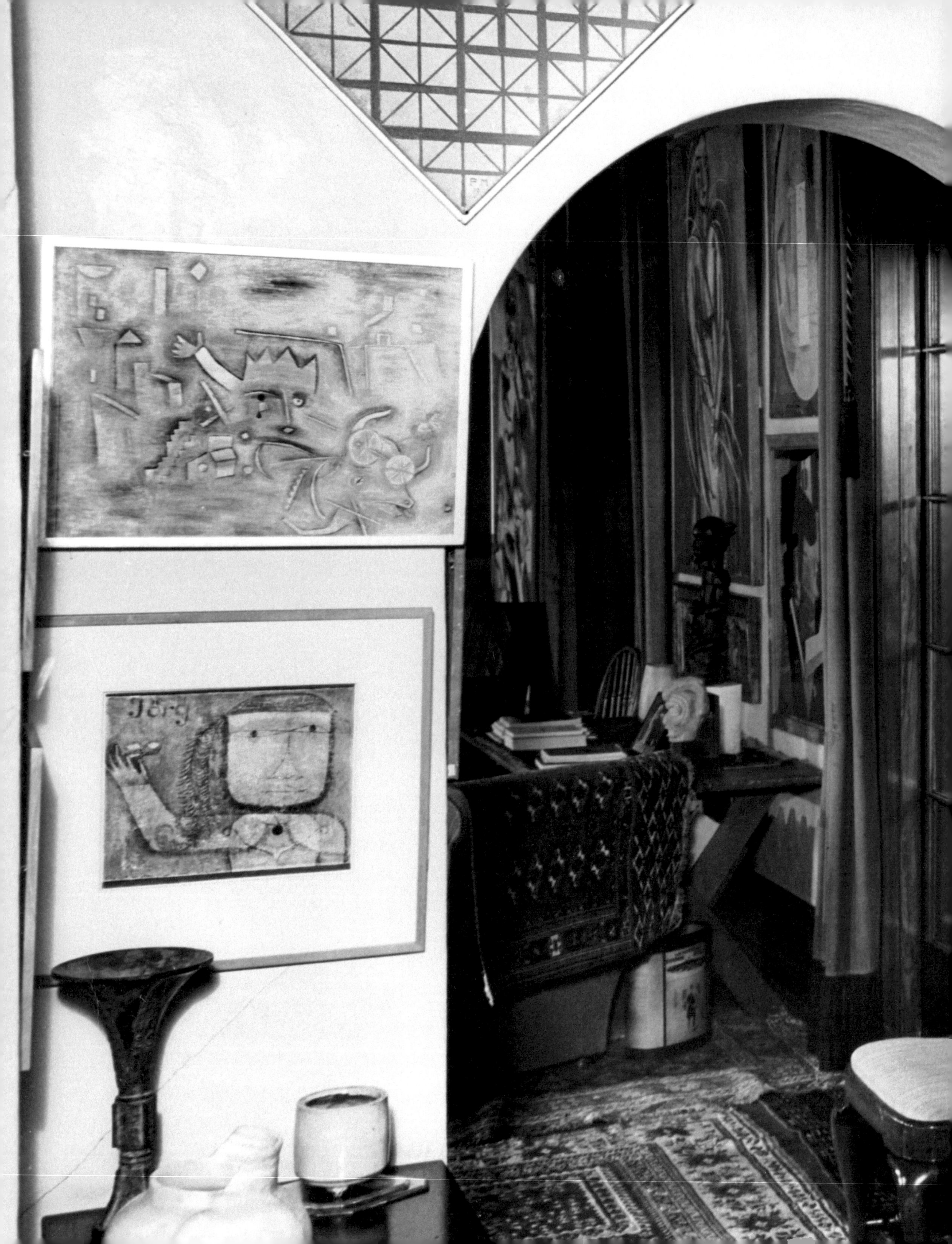
Jörg

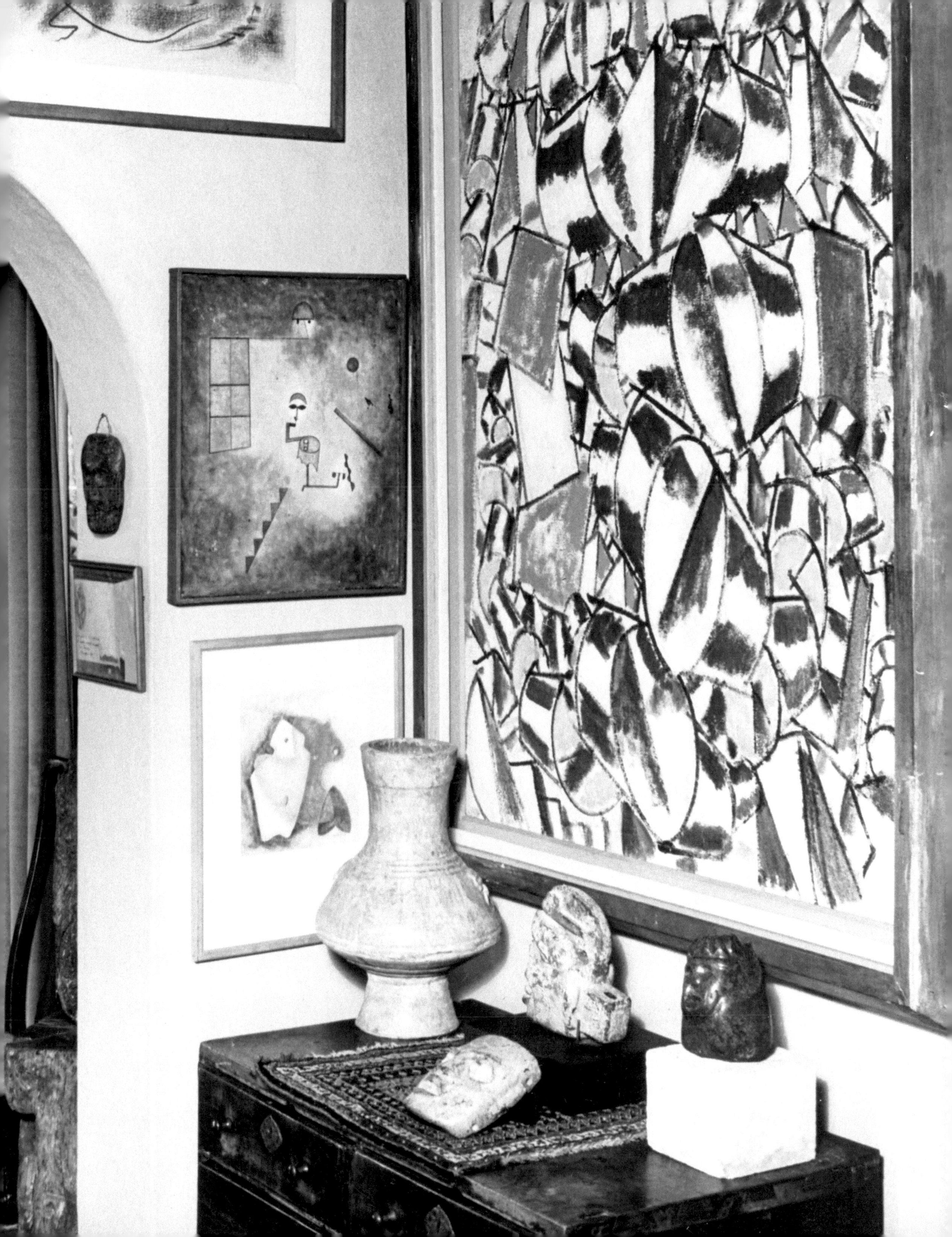

PLATE 18

LIVING ROOM AND FOYER

VIEWED FROM THE DINING ROOM

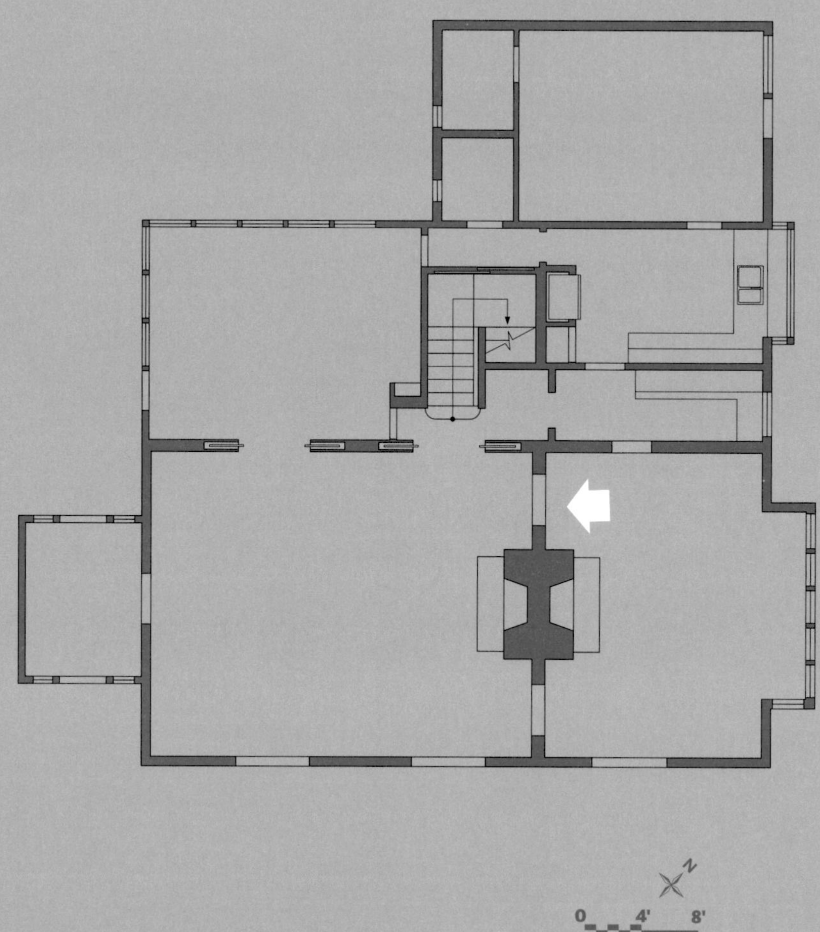

FRED R. DAPPRICH

CA. 1944

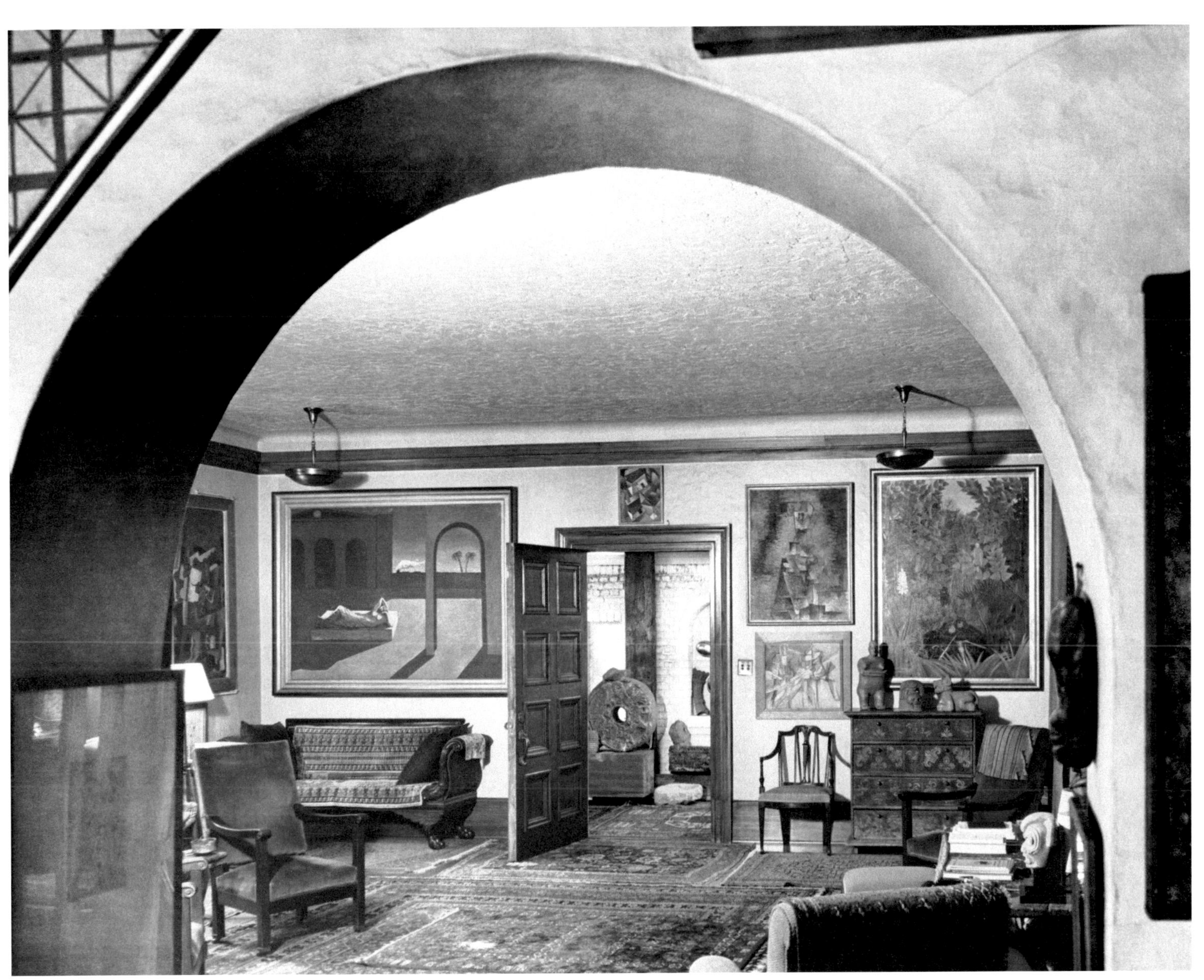

PLATE 18

1 PIET MONDRIAN, *Composition in Black and Gray* or *Composition with Grid 4 (Lozenge)*, 1919 [1950-134-151; AC20-154]

*2 ANDRÉ MASSON, *Animal Caught in a Trap*, 1929 [1950-134-129; AC20-132]

3 HENRI MATISSE, *Three Standing Nudes without Feet*, 1914 [1950-134-895]

4 GEORGES BRAQUE, *The Table*, 1918 [1950-134-29B; AC20-28]

5 GUANACASTE-NICOYA (COSTA RICA), Metate, 300–800 [1950-134-319; ACPS-173]

6 TEOTIHUACAN (CENTRAL MEXICO), Vessel, 1st–9th century [1950-134-540]

7 GIORGIO DE CHIRICO, *The Soothsayer's Recompense*, 1913 [1950-134-38; AC20-36]

8 JEAN METZINGER, *Landscape with Roofs*, ca. 1914 [1950-134-138; AC20-143]

9 CONSTANTIN BRANCUSI, *Arch*, ca. 1914–16 [1950-134-22; AC20-12]

10 COLIMA, JALISCO, MICHOACÁN, OR NAYARIT (WESTERN MEXICO), Mace Head, 200 BCE–300 CE [1950-134-290; ACPS-72]

11 AZTEC (CENTRAL MEXICO), Ballcourt Ring with Monkey and Solar Motif, 1400–1520 [1950-134-225; ACPS-45]

12 CLASSIC VERACRUZ (EAST COAST MEXICO), Palma, 500–900 [1950-134-345; ACPS-158]

13 TOTONAC (EAST COAST MEXICO), Tenoned Head of a Jaguar, 600–900 [1950-134-289; ACPS-132]

14 AZTEC (CENTRAL MEXICO), Basin, 1300–1520 [1950-134-243; ACPS-42]

15 ARTIST/MAKER UNKNOWN, Dinosaur Print (fake), Date unknown [NOTE 1.1, PAGE 414]

16 CONSTANTIN BRANCUSI, *Princess X*, 1915–16 [1950-134-12; AC20-11]

17 PABLO PICASSO, *Female Nude*, 1910 [1950-134-166; AC20-170]

18 MARCEL DUCHAMP, *The King and Queen Traversed by Swift Nudes at High Speed*, 1912 [1950-134-62; AC20-67]

19 HENRI ROUSSEAU, *The Merry Jesters*, 1906 [1950-134-176; AC20-179]

20 NAYARIT (WESTERN MEXICO), Figure of a Woman, 100 BCE–300 CE [1950-134-291; ACPS-75]

21 MAYA (GUATEMALA OR MEXICO), Hacha in the Form of Skull and Bird, 600–1200 [1950-134-360; ACPS-171]

22 AZTEC (CENTRAL MEXICO), Jaguar, 1300–1520 [1950-134-205]

23 ARTIST/MAKER UNKNOWN, Pre-Columbian Death Mask (fake), Date unknown [NOTE 4.1, PAGE 416]

24 CLASSIC VERACRUZ (EAST COAST MEXICO), Hacha in the Form of a Head, 500–900 [1950-134-206; ACPS-139]

*25 ARTIST/MAKER UNKNOWN (MEXICO), *Recovery from an Illness*, 1927 [1950-134-493]

*26 PAUL KLEE, *Prestidigitator (Conjuring Trick)*, 1927 [1950-134-118; AC20-120]

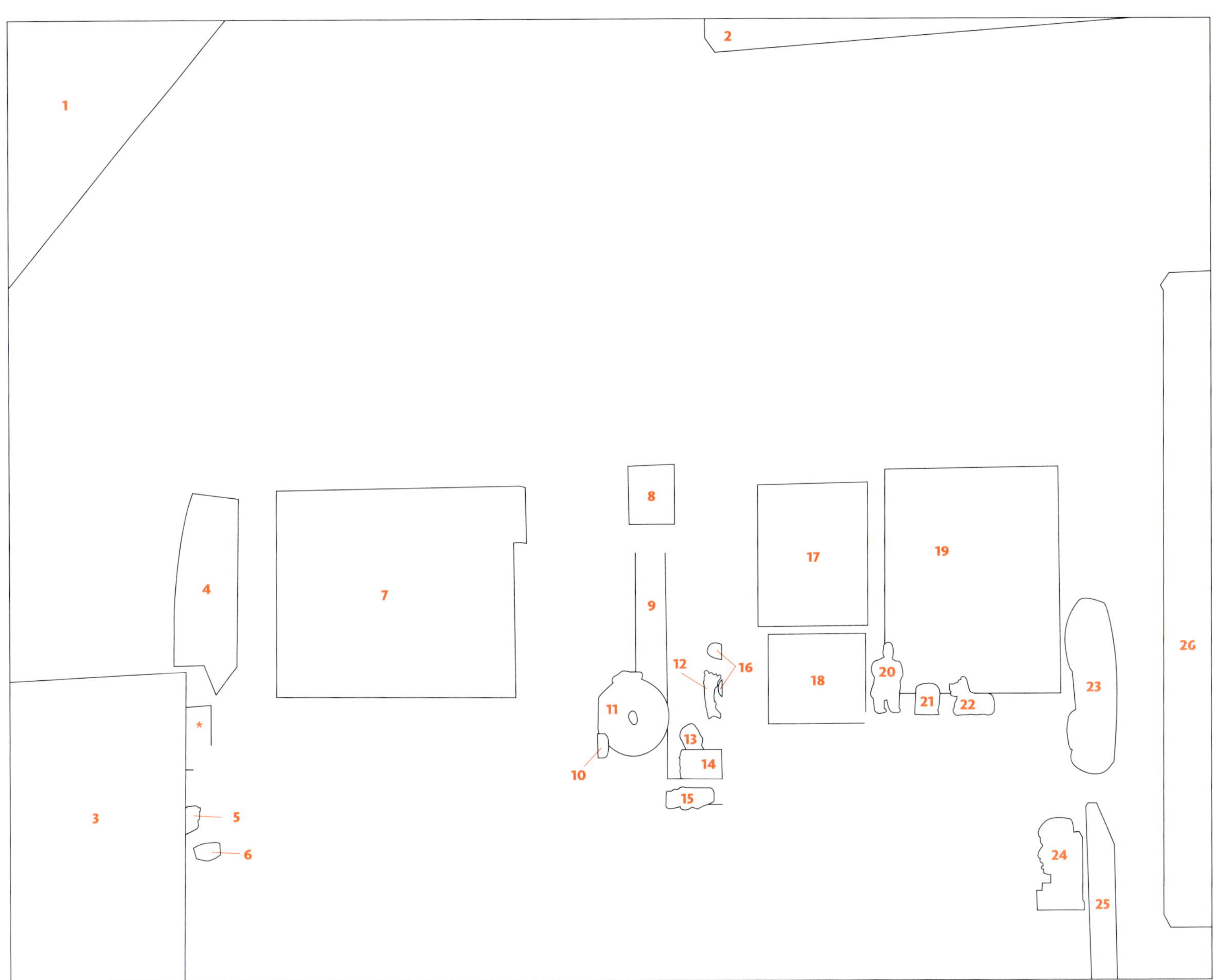
1
2
4
7
8
9
17
19
26
3
*
5
6
10
11
12
13
14
15
16
18
20
21
22
23
24
25

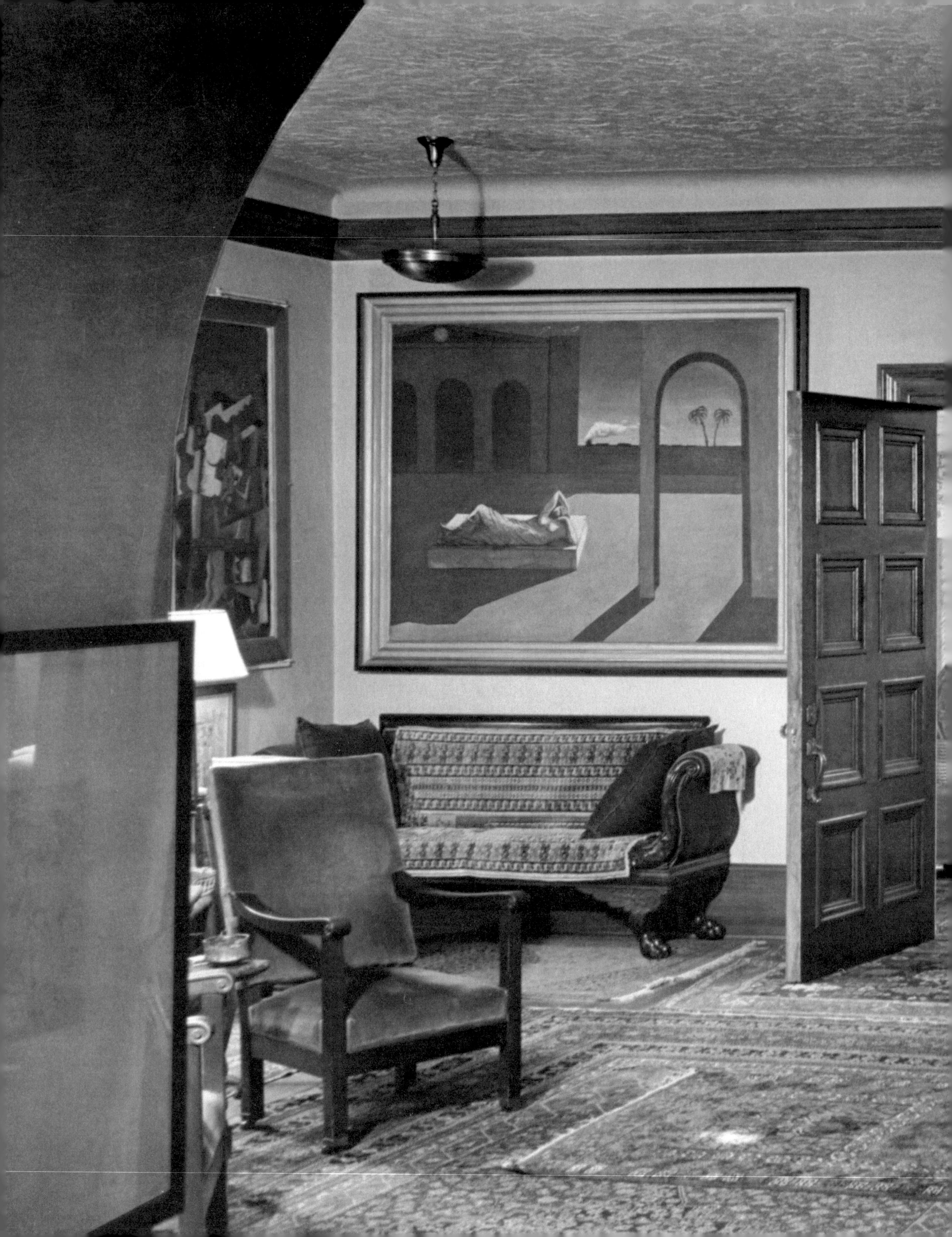

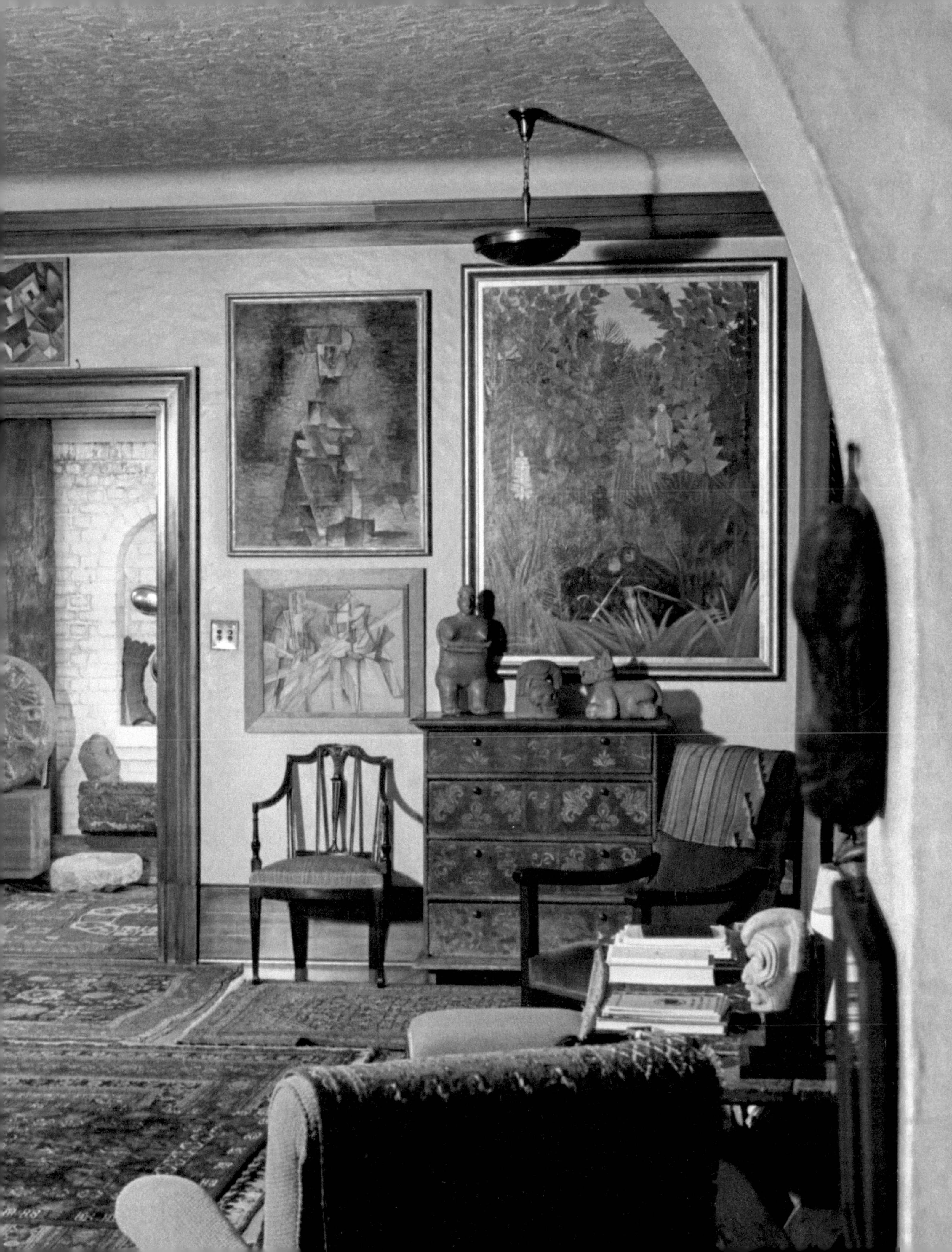

PLATE 19

LIVING ROOM

WITH VIEWS INTO THE SUNROOM (GALLERY ROOM) AND STAIRWAY HALL

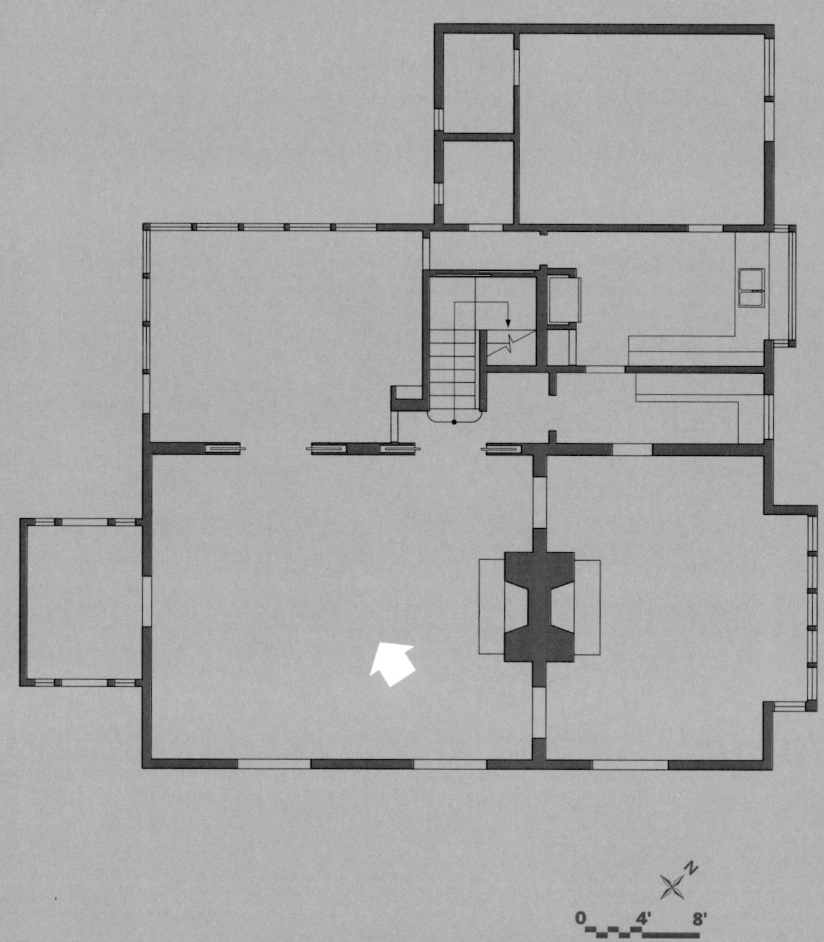

FRED R. DAPPRICH

CA. 1944

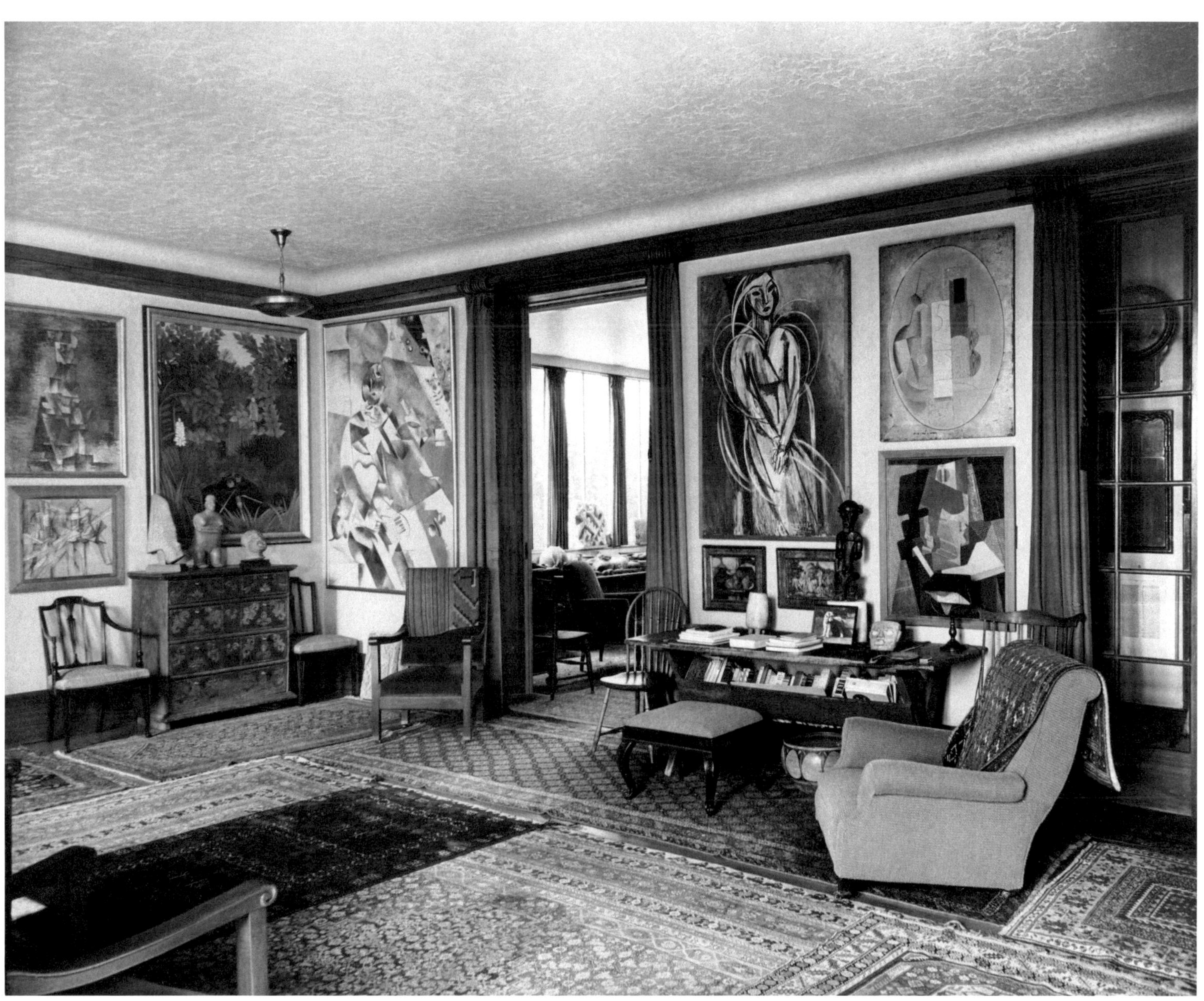

PLATE 19

1 PABLO PICASSO, *Female Nude*, 1910 [1950-134-166; AC20-170]

2 MARCEL DUCHAMP, *The King and Queen Traversed by Swift Nudes at High Speed*, 1912 [1950-134-62; AC20-67]

3 HENRI ROUSSEAU, *The Merry Jesters*, 1906 [1950-134-176; AC20-179]

4 CLASSIC VERACRUZ (EAST COAST MEXICO), Palma, 500–900 [1950-134-336; ACPS-154]

5 NAYARIT (WESTERN MEXICO), Figure of a Woman, 100 BCE–300 CE [1950-134-291; ACPS-75]

6 AZTEC (CENTRAL MEXICO), Head of Fertility God (Xipe Totec), 1300–1520 [1950-134-296; ACPS-13]

7 MARC CHAGALL, *Half-Past Three (The Poet)*, 1911 [1950-134-36; AC20-35]

8 TOLTEC (CENTRAL MEXICO), Relief, 800–1300 [1950-134-309; ACPS-5]

9 NATIVE AMERICAN (SOUTHWESTERN UNITED STATES), Vessel, Date unknown [1950-134-644]

10 ZAPOTEC (SOUTHERN MEXICO), Fragment of a Relief, 800–1500 [1950-134-245; ACPS-102]

11 MANTEÑO (ECUADOR), Relief, 500–1000 [1950-134-241; ACPS-190]

12 HENRI MATISSE, *Mademoiselle Yvonne Landsberg*, 1914 [1950-134-130; AC20-133]

13 PAUL CÉZANNE, *Still Life with Apples and a Glass of Wine*, 1877–79 [1950-134-32; AC20-31]

14 MIXTEC (SOUTHEASTERN MEXICO), Vessel, 800–1300 [1950-134-357; ACPS-111]

15 PAUL CÉZANNE, *Group of Bathers*, ca. 1895 [1950-134-34; AC20-33]

16 FANG (GABON), Male Reliquary Guardian Figure, Mid-19th century [1950-134-200]

17 TEOTIHUACAN (CENTRAL MEXICO), Mask, 1st–9th century [1950-134-359; ACPS-17]

18 JUAN GRIS, *Lamp*, 1916 [1950-134-96; AC20-97]

19 PABLO PICASSO, *Still Life with a Violin and a Guitar*, 1912–13 [1950-134-170; AC20-174]

20 JOHANN FUST AND PETER SCHOEFFER, Leaf from *Biblia Latina* (Latin Bible), Mainz, 1462 [NOTE 3.1, PAGE 416]

21 NATIVE AMERICAN, Bowl, Date unknown [1950-134-418]

FRED R. DAPPRICH ALMOST CERTAINLY RETURNED TO PHOTOGRAPH THE ARENSBERGS' HOME ON MORE THAN ONE OCCASION. THIS PICTURE BY DAPPRICH, FOR EXAMPLE, HAS MORE IN COMMON WITH PLATE 22 (BY AN UNKNOWN PHOTOGRAPHER) THAN IT DOES WITH PLATE 18 (WHICH WAS PUBLISHED IN *VOGUE* IN JANUARY 1945) OR PLATE 23, HIS OTHER PHOTOGRAPHS PICTURING DIFFERENT OBJECTS ON THE SAME BUREAU. THESE IMAGES CAN ALSO BE COMPARED TO THE IMAGE BY DICK SEYFFERT SHOWN ON PAGE 65, WHICH WAS KNOWN TO HAVE BEEN TAKEN AFTER 15 MARCH 1945.

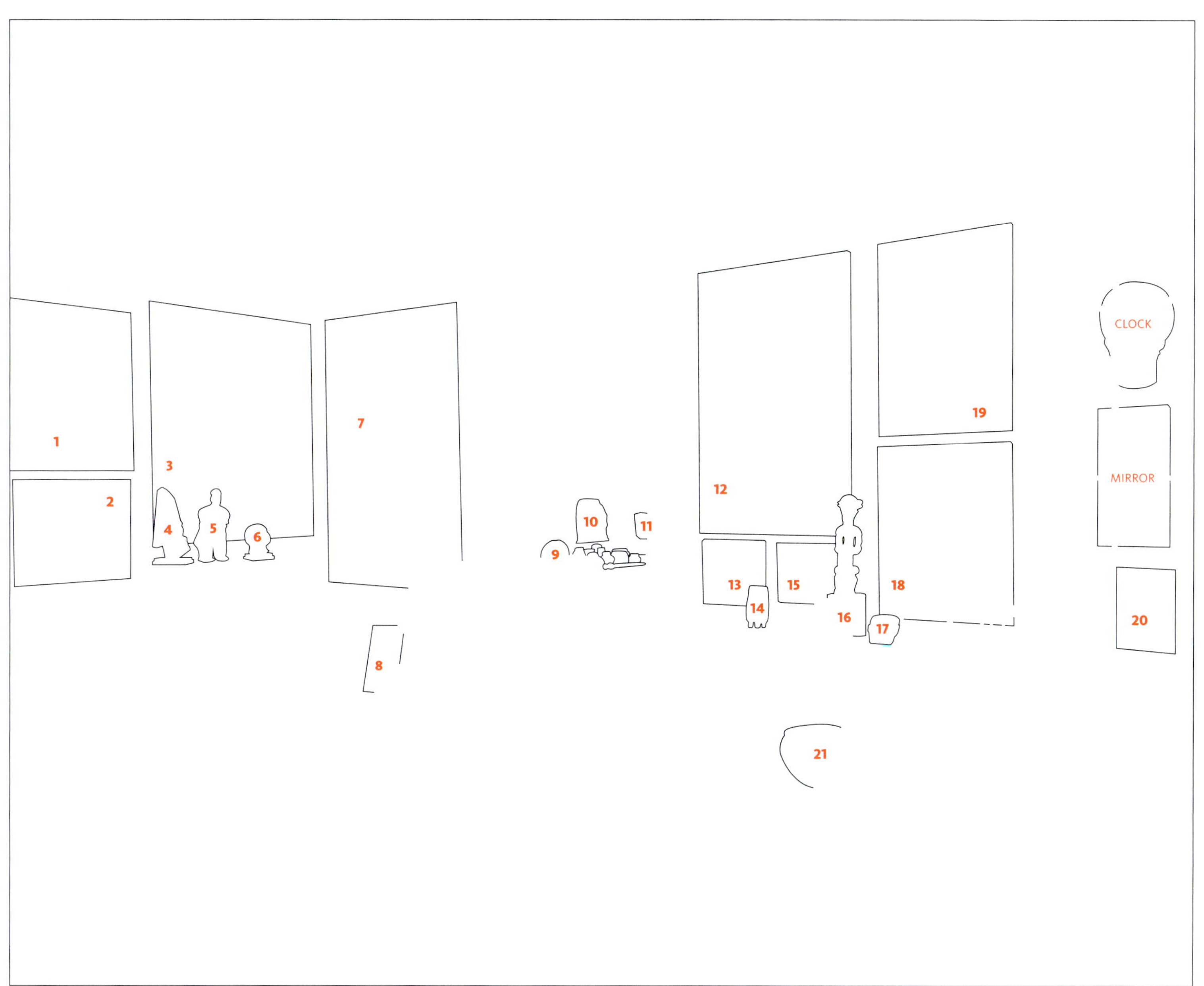
1
2
3
4
5
6
7
8
9
10
11
12
13
14
15
16
17
18
19
20
21
CLOCK
MIRROR

PLATE 20

LIVING ROOM

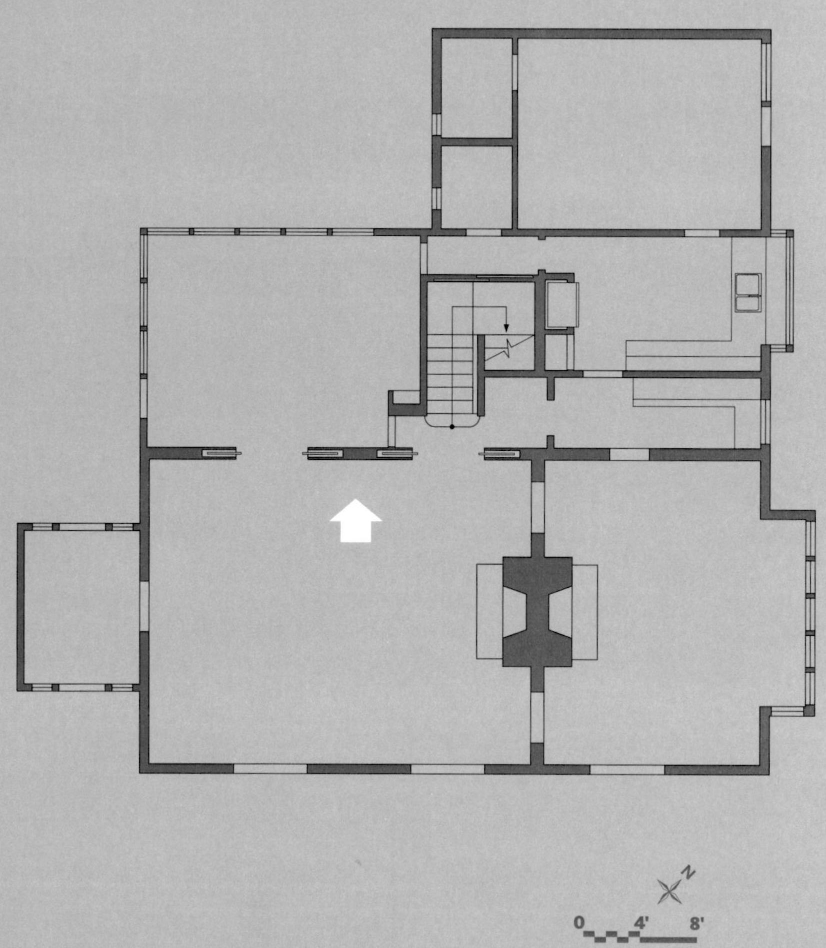

FRED R. DAPPRICH

CA. 1944

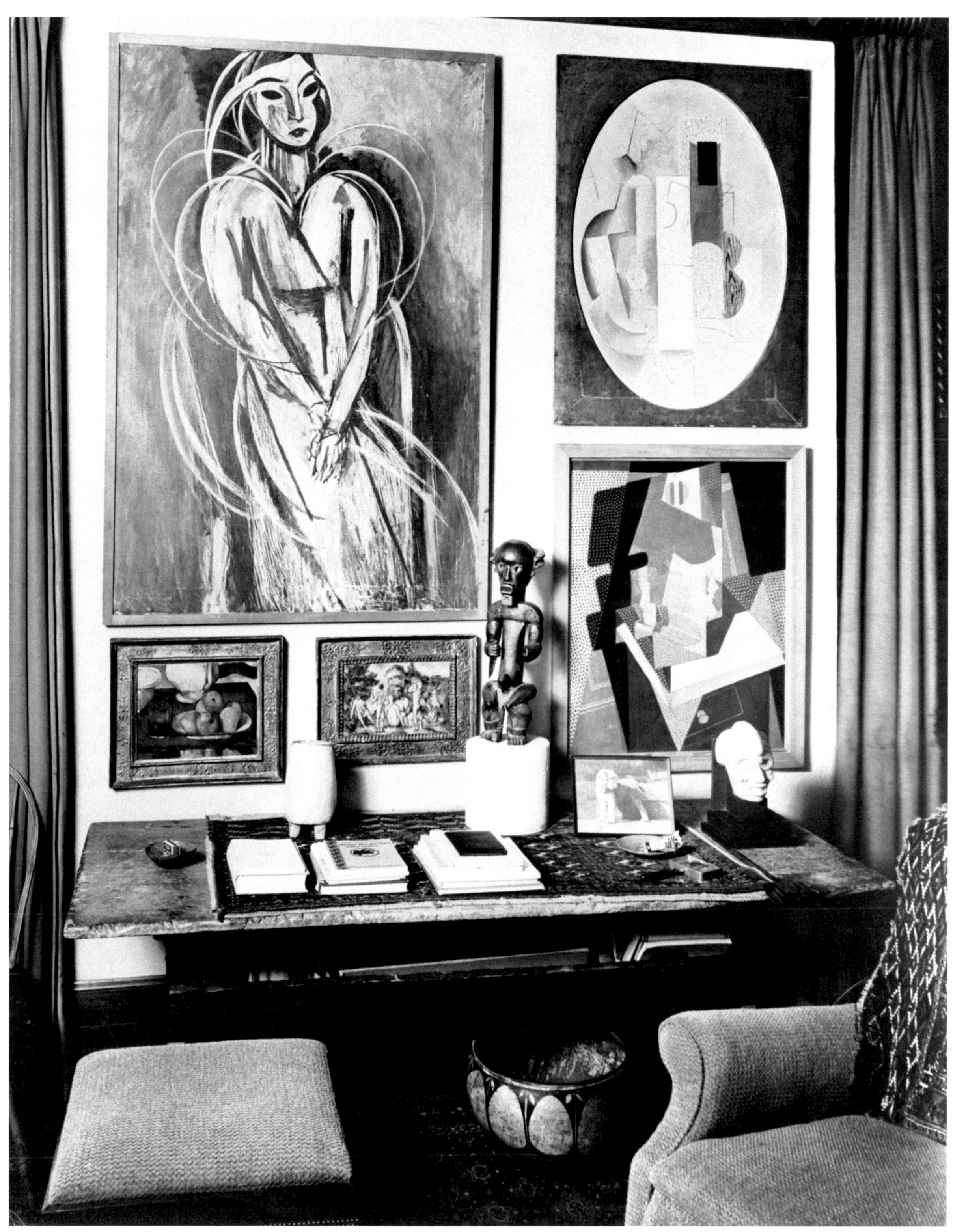

PLATE 20

1 HENRI MATISSE, *Mademoiselle Yvonne Landsberg*, 1914 [1950-134-130; AC20-133]
2 PABLO PICASSO, *Still Life with a Violin and a Guitar*, 1913 [1950-134-170; AC20-174]
3 PAUL CÉZANNE, *Still Life with Apples and a Glass of Wine*, 1877–79 [1950-134-32; AC20-31]
4 MIXTEC (SOUTHEASTERN MEXICO), Vessel, 800–1300 [1950-134-357; ACPS-111]
5 PAUL CÉZANNE, *Group of Bathers*, ca. 1895 [1950-134-34; AC20-33]
6 FANG (GABON), Male Reliquary Guardian Figure, Mid-19th century [1950-134-200]
7 JUAN GRIS, *Lamp*, 1916 [1950-134-96; AC20-97]
8 CLASSIC VERACRUZ (EAST COAST MEXICO), Hacha in the Form of a Head, 500–900 [1950-134-206; ACPS-139]
9 NATIVE AMERICAN, Bowl, Date unknown [1950-134-418]

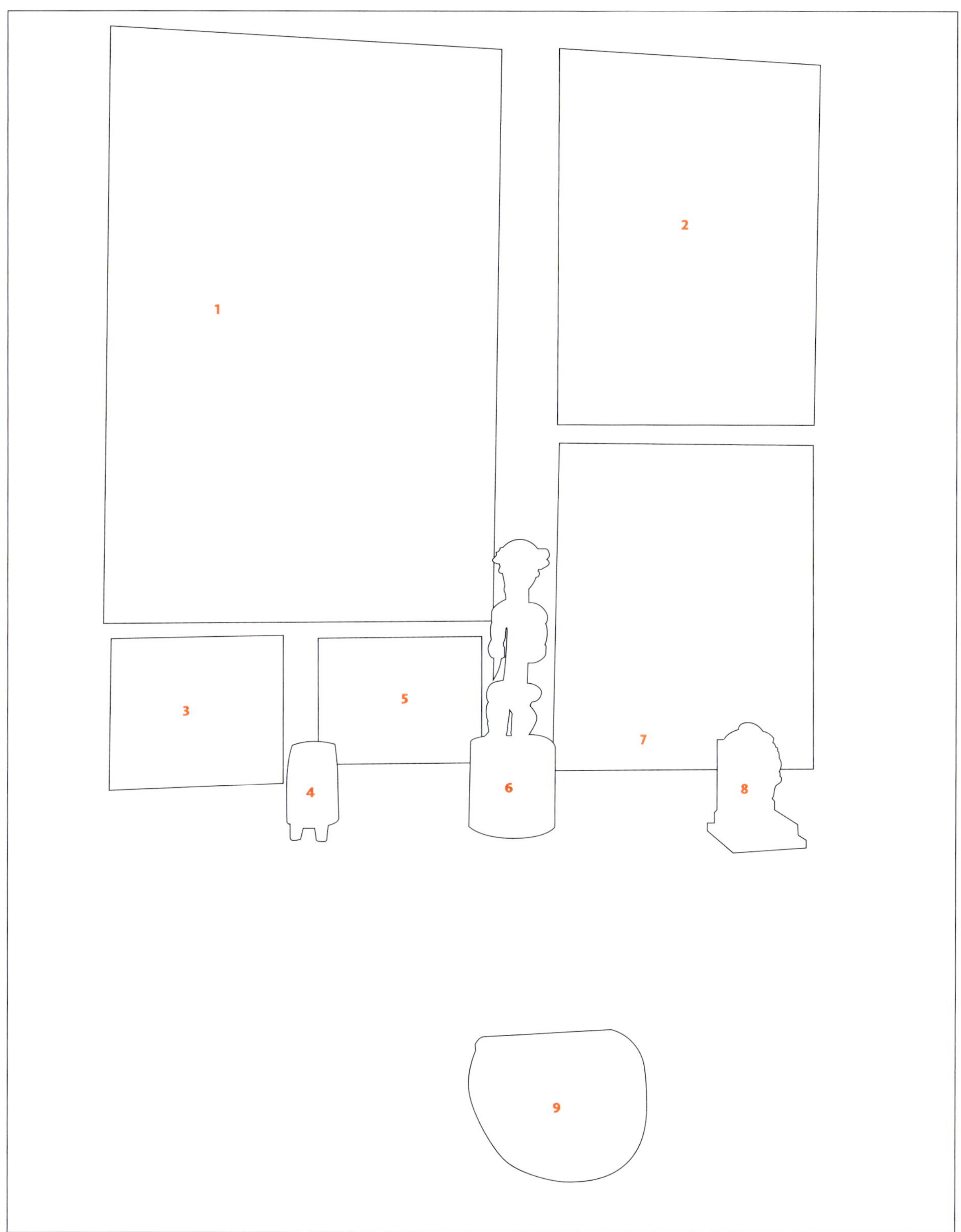

1
2
3
5
7
4
6
8
9

PLATE 21

LIVING ROOM

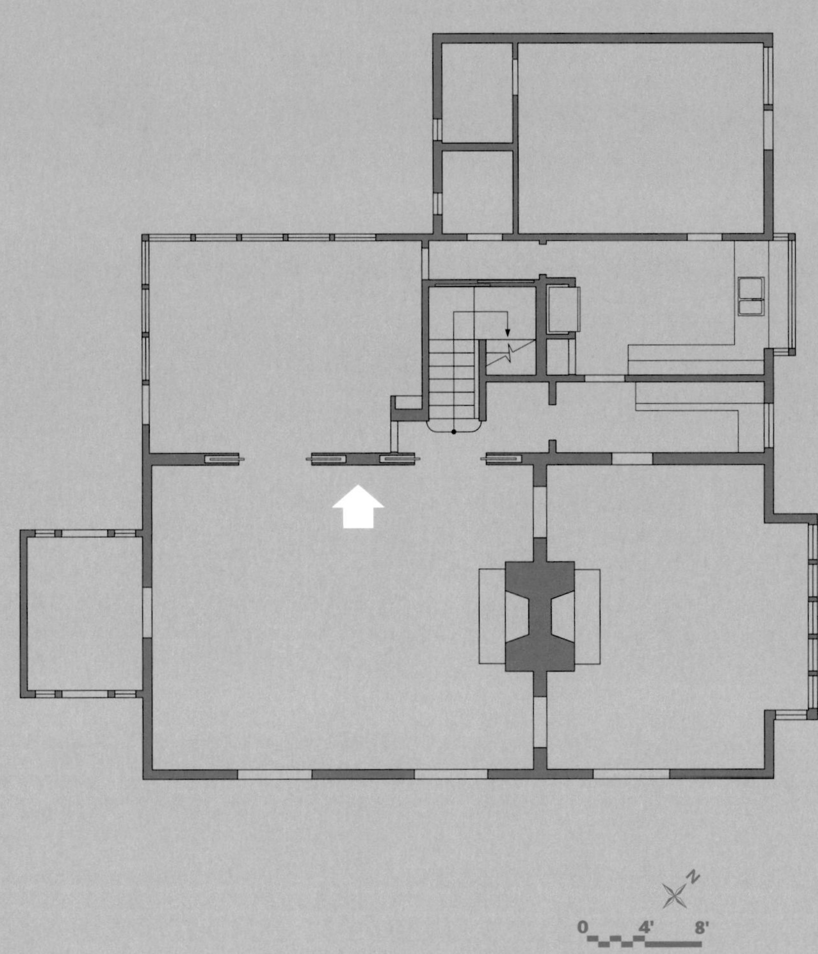

FRED R. DAPPRICH

CA. 1944

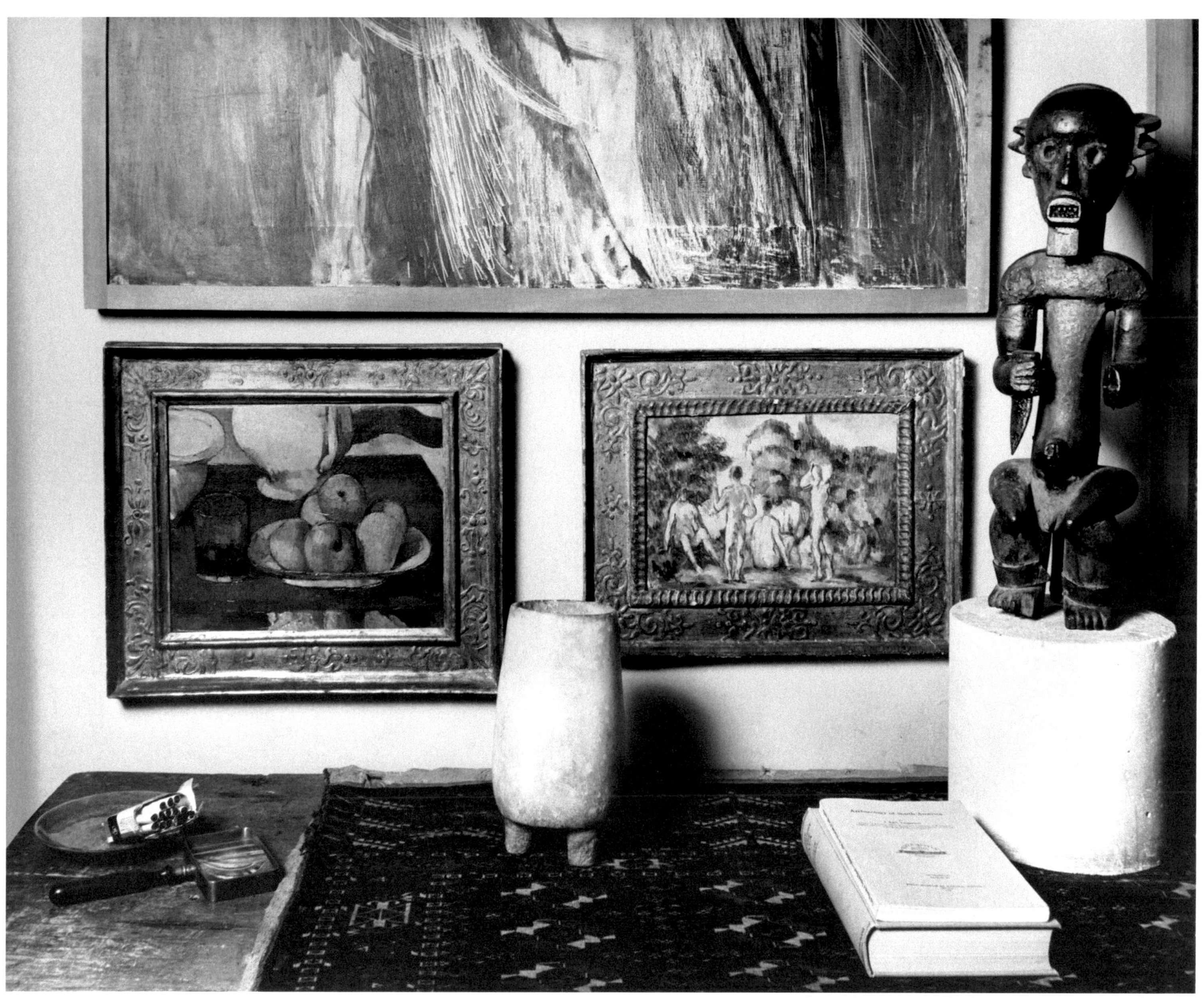

PLATE 21

1 HENRI MATISSE, *Mademoiselle Yvonne Landsberg*, 1914 [1950-134-130; AC20-133]

2 PAUL CÉZANNE, *Still Life with Apples and a Glass of Wine*, 1877–79 [1950-134-32; AC20-31]

3 MIXTEC (SOUTHEASTERN MEXICO), Vessel, 800–1300 [1950-134-357; ACPS-111]

4 PAUL CÉZANNE, *Group of Bathers*, ca. 1895 [1950-134-34; AC20-33]

5 FANG (GABON), Male Reliquary Guardian Figure, Mid-19th century [1950-134-200]

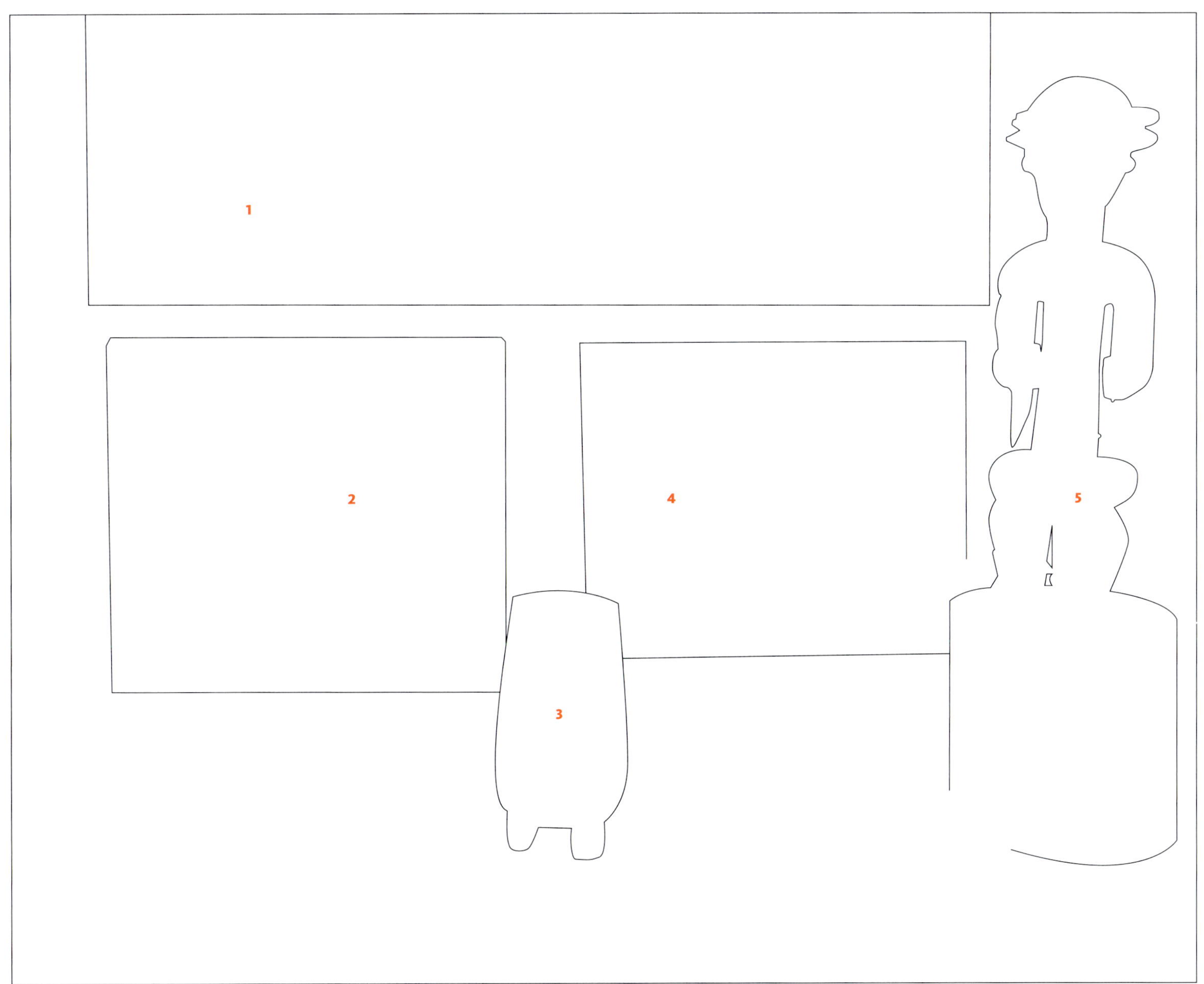
1
2
4
5
3

PLATE 22

LIVING ROOM

WITH A GLIMPSE INTO THE FOYER

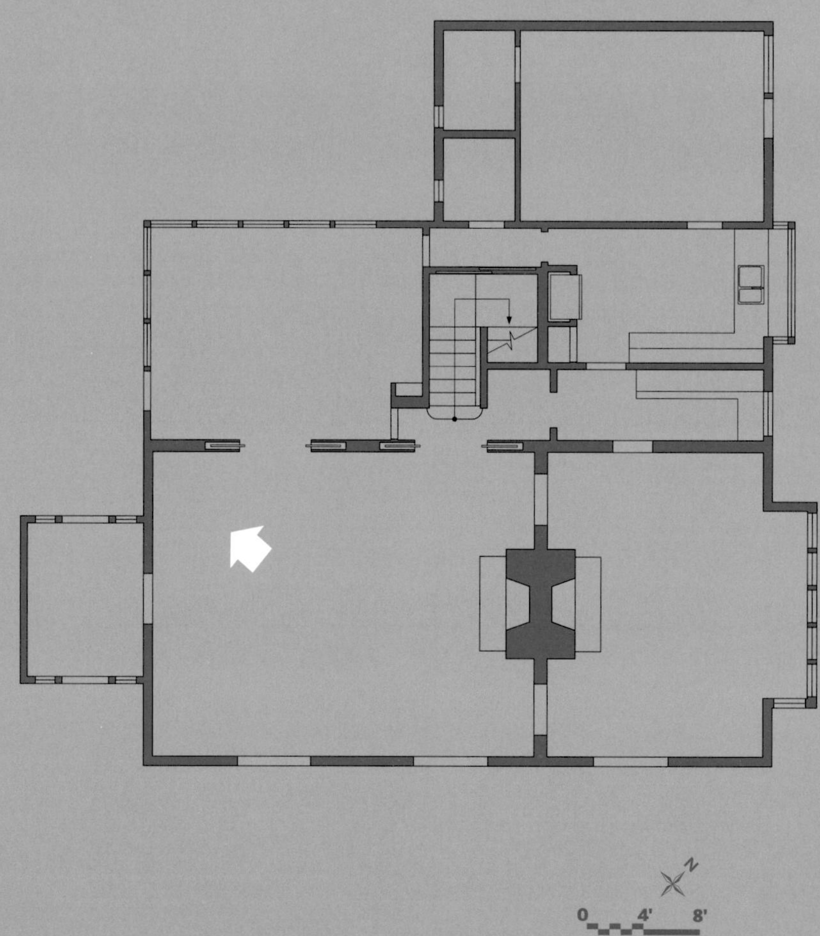

PHOTOGRAPHER UNKNOWN

CA. 1945

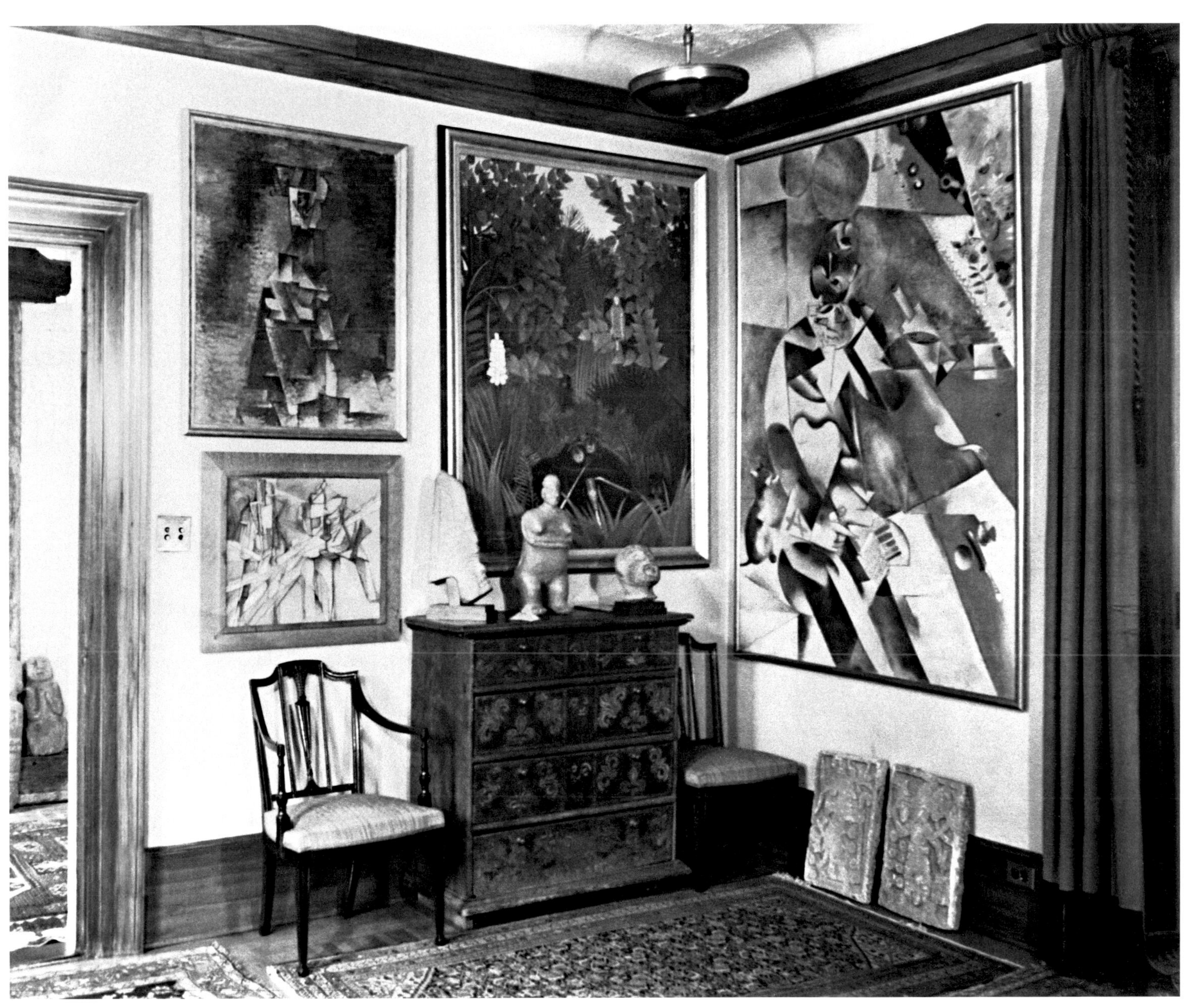

PLATE 22

1 CONSTANTIN BRANCUSI, *Arch*, ca. 1914–16 [1950-134-22; AC20-12]

2 DIQUÍS (COSTA RICA), Peg-Base Figure, 800–1520 [1950-134-288; ACPS-193]

3 ARTIST/MAKER UNKNOWN, Stone in Human Form, Date unknown [1950-134-547]

4 PABLO PICASSO, *Female Nude*, 1910 [1950-134-166; AC20-170]

5 MARCEL DUCHAMP, *The King and Queen Traversed by Swift Nudes at High Speed*, 1912 [1950-134-62; AC20-67]

6 HENRI ROUSSEAU, *The Merry Jesters*, 1906 [1950-134-176; AC20-179]

7 CLASSIC VERACRUZ (EAST COAST MEXICO), Palma, 500–900 [1950-134-336; ACPS-154]

8 NAYARIT (WESTERN MEXICO), Figure of a Woman, 100 BCE–300 CE [1950-134-291; ACPS-75]

9 AZTEC (CENTRAL MEXICO), Head of Fertility God (Xipe Totec), 1300–1520 [1950-134-296; ACPS-13]

10 MARC CHAGALL, *Half-Past Three (The Poet)*, 1911 [1950-134-36; AC20-35]

11, 12 TOLTEC (CENTRAL MEXICO), Reliefs, 800–1300 [11: 1950-134-309, ACPS-5; 12: 1950-134-310, ACPS-6]

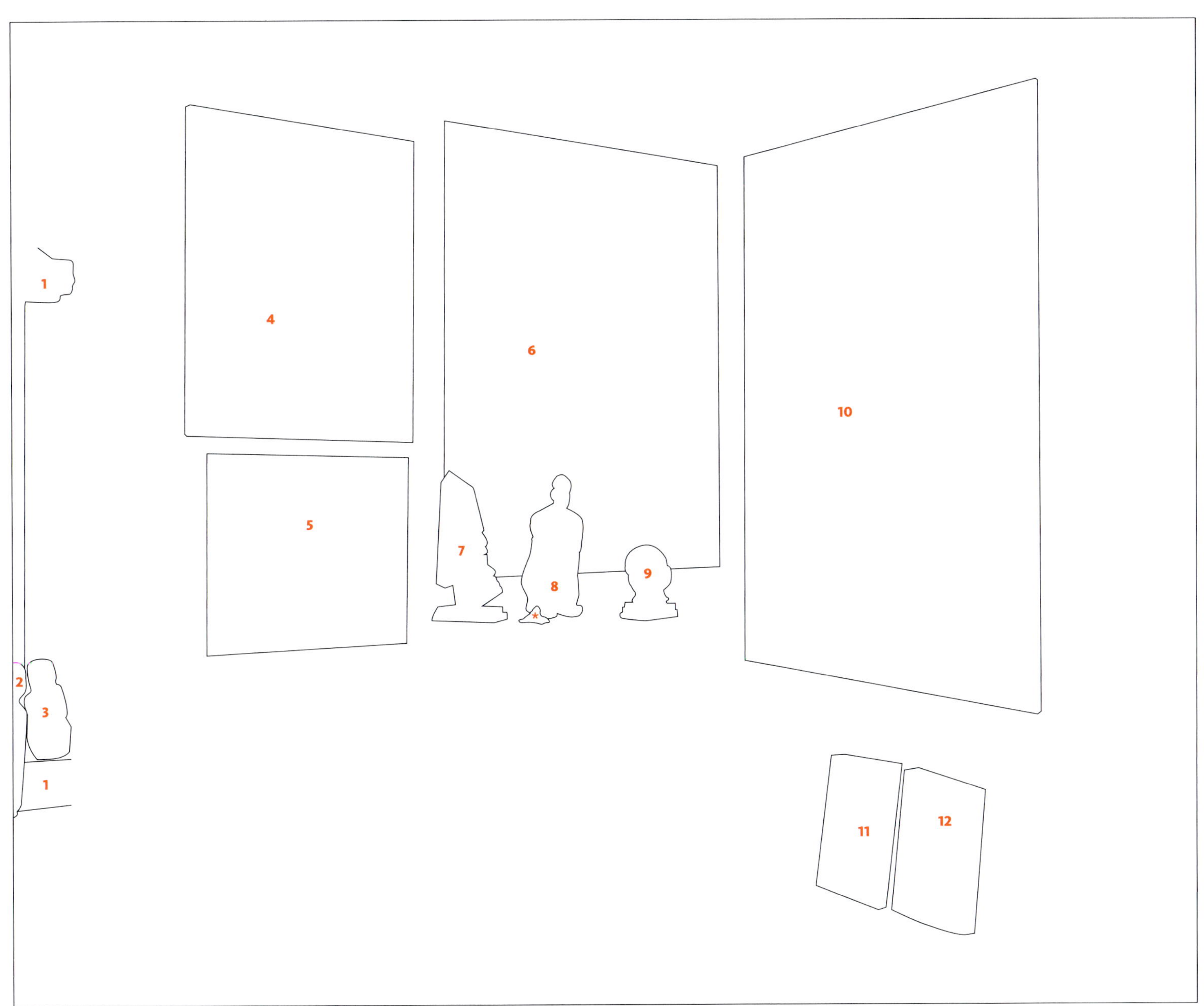
1
4
6
10
5
7
8
*
9
2
3
1
11
12

PLATE 23

LIVING ROOM

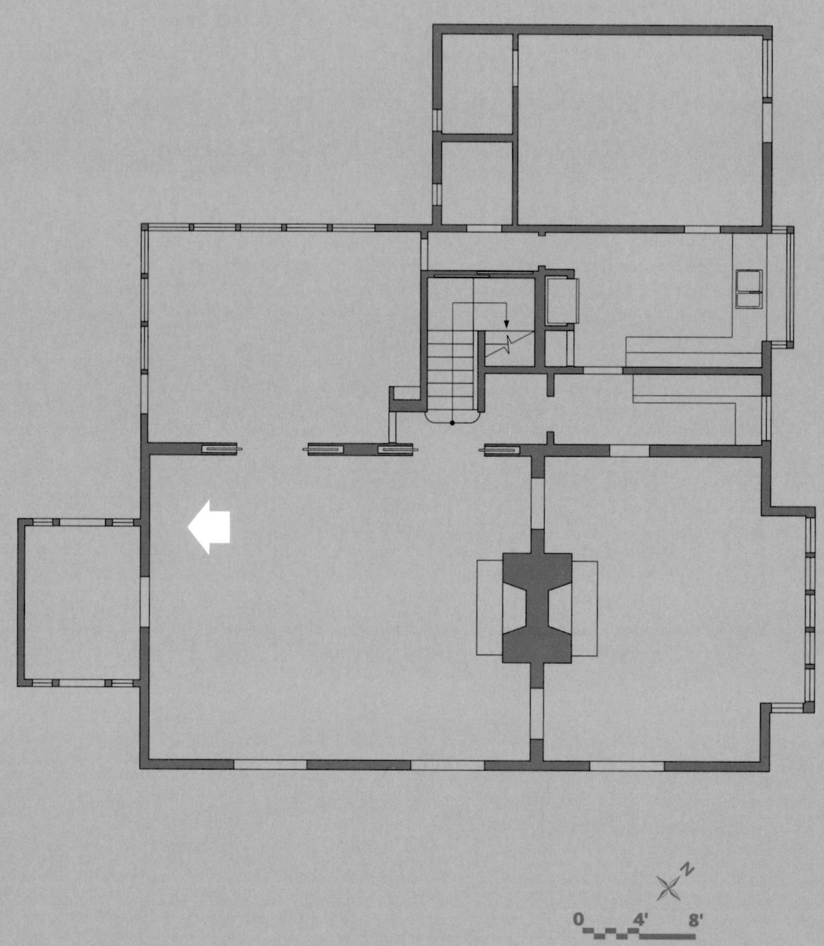

FRED R. DAPPRICH

CA. 1944

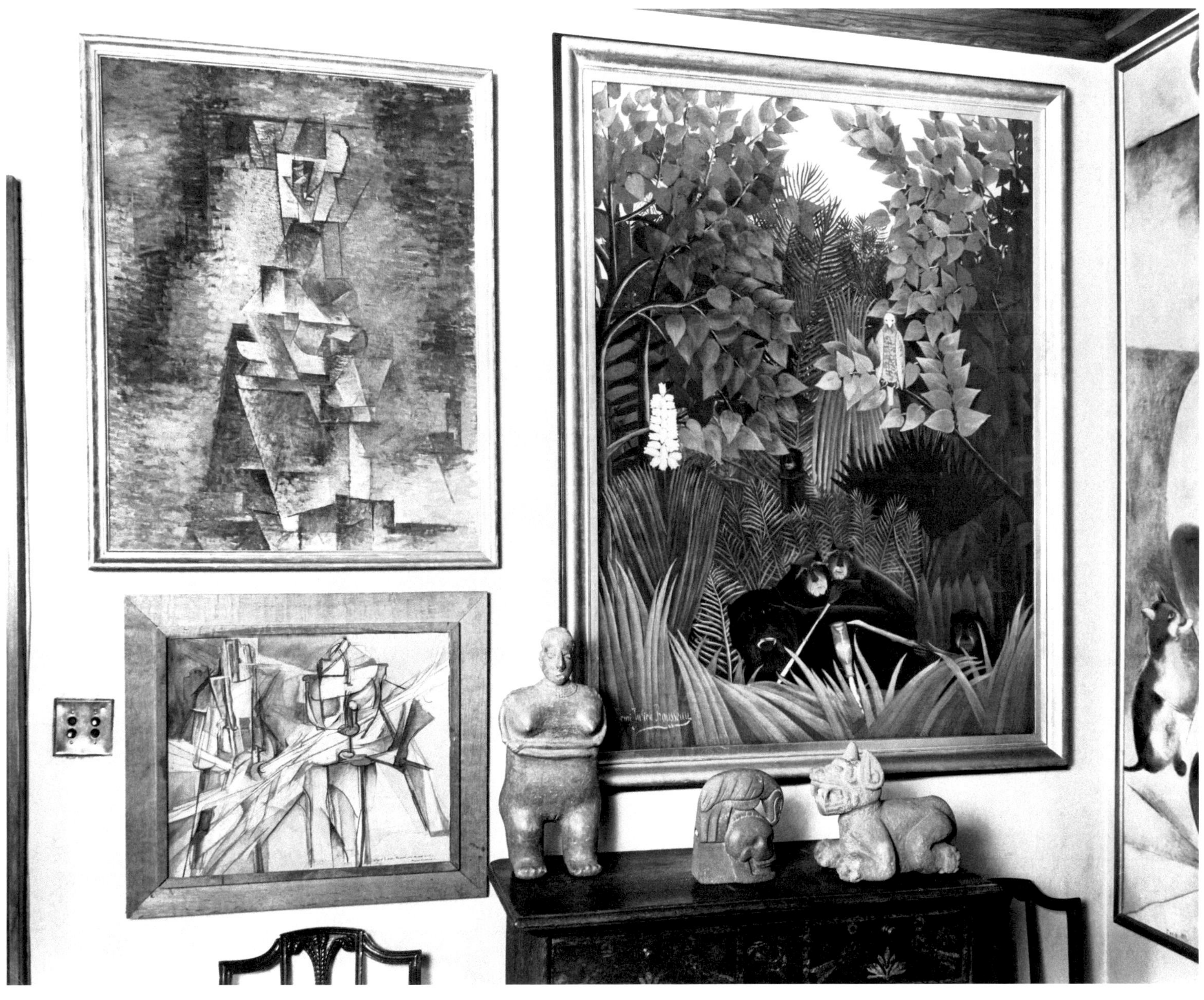

PLATE 23

1 PABLO PICASSO, *Female Nude*, 1910 [1950-134-166; AC20-170]
2 MARCEL DUCHAMP, *The King and Queen Traversed by Swift Nudes at High Speed*, 1912 [1950-134-62; AC20-67]
3 HENRI ROUSSEAU, *The Merry Jesters*, 1906 [1950-134-176; AC20-179]
4 NAYARIT (WESTERN MEXICO), Figure of a Woman, 100 BCE–300 CE [1950-134-291; ACPS-75]
5 MAYA (GUATEMALA OR MEXICO), Hacha in the Form of Skull and Bird, 600–1200 [1950-134-360; ACPS-171]
6 AZTEC (CENTRAL MEXICO), Jaguar, 1300–1520 [1950-134-205]
7 MARC CHAGALL, *Half-Past Three (The Poet)*, 1911 [1950-134-36; AC20-35]

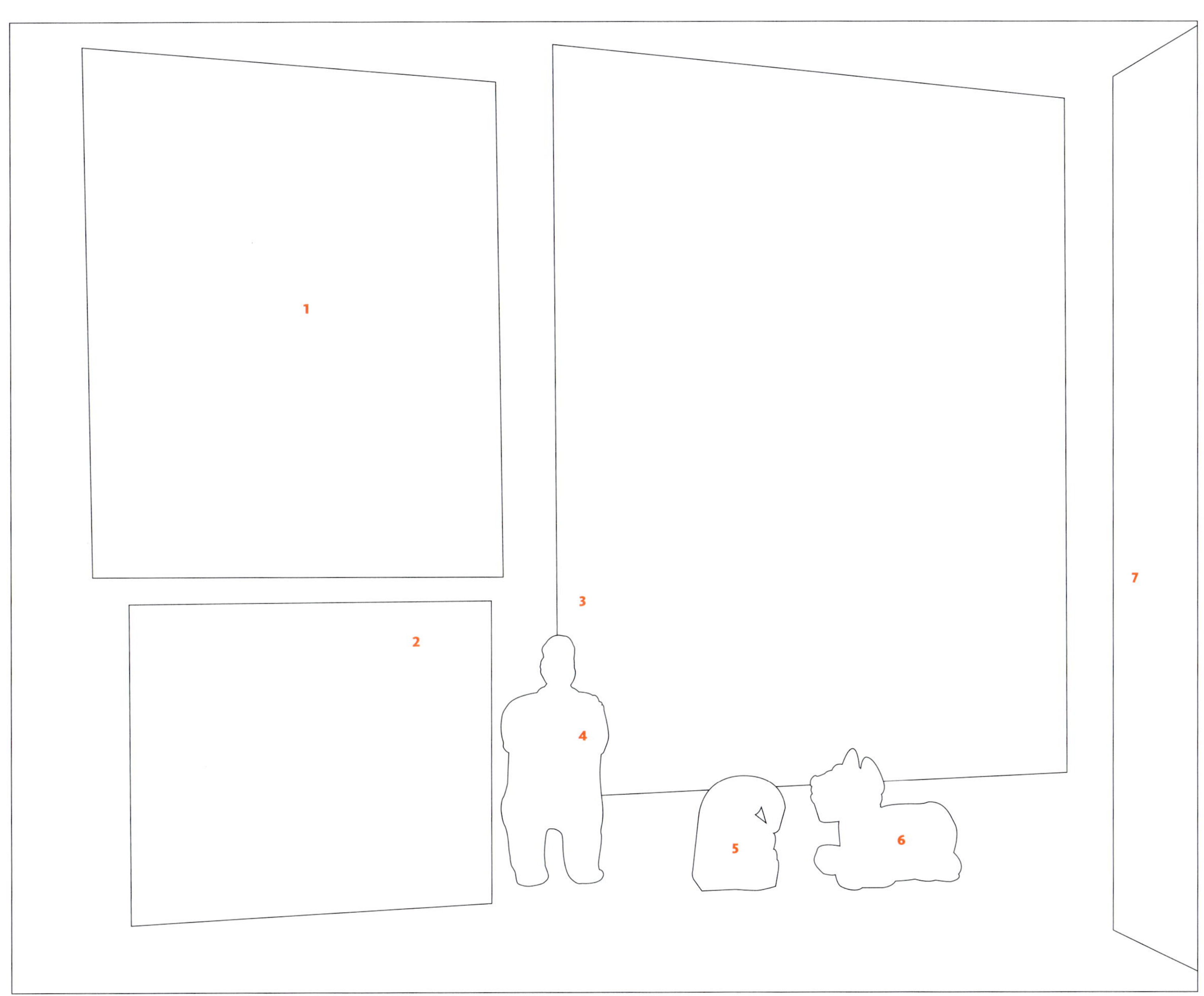
1
2
3
4
5
6
7

PLATE 24

SUNROOM (GALLERY ROOM)

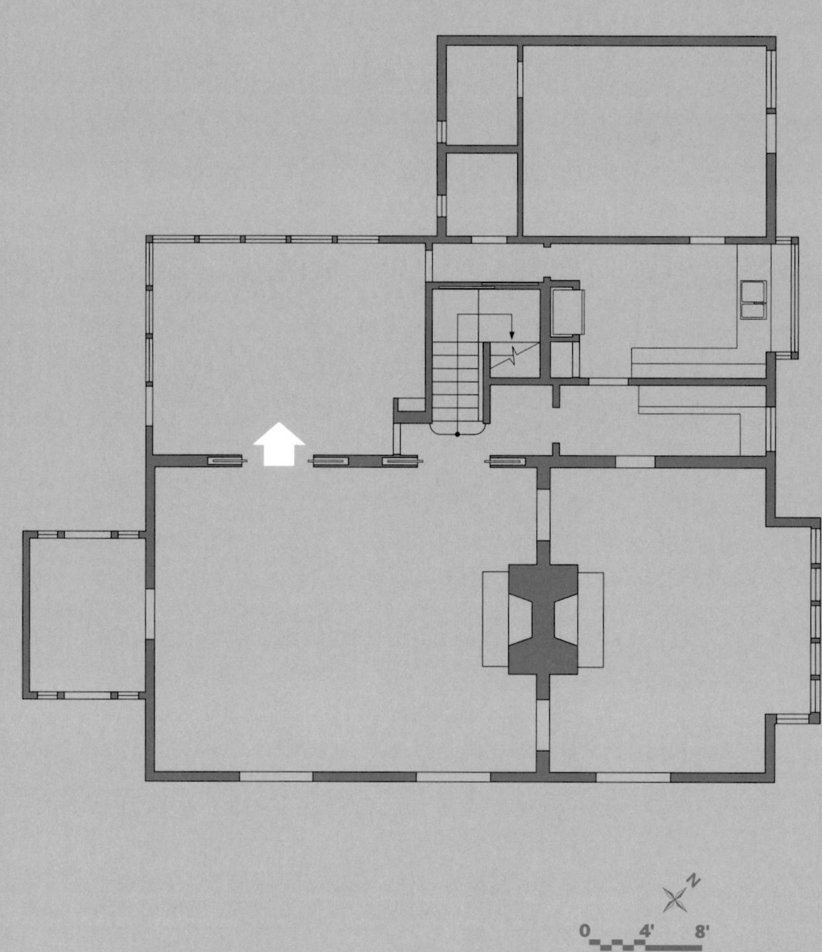

FRITZ (FRED) BLOCK

CA. 1942–43

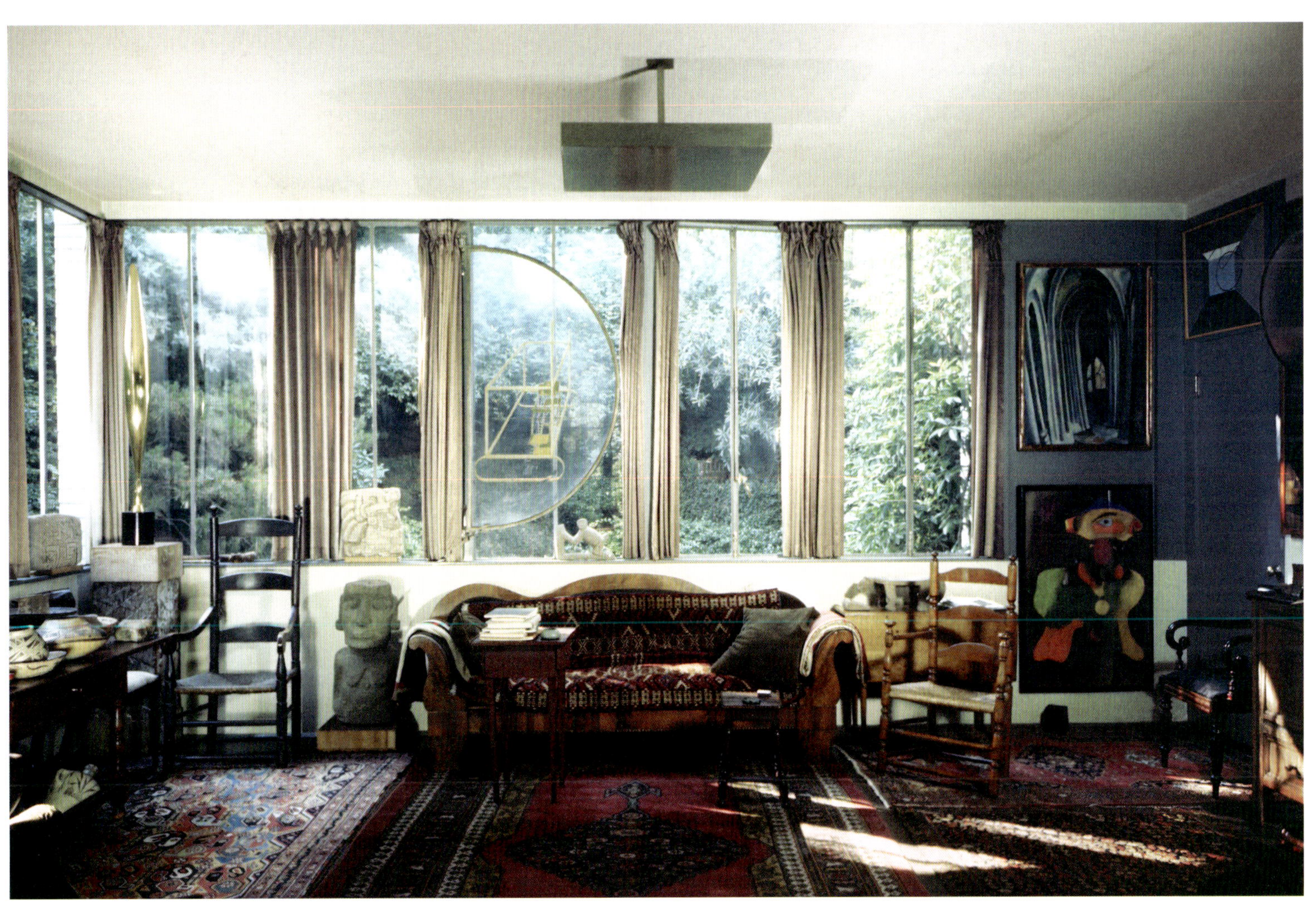

PLATE 24

1 MANTEÑO (ECUADOR), Relief, 500–1000 [1950-134-241; ACPS-190]

2 NATIVE AMERICAN (SOUTHWESTERN UNITED STATES), Vessel or Jar, Date unknown [1950-134-667]

3 NATIVE AMERICAN (SOUTHWESTERN UNITED STATES), Bowl, Date unknown [1950-134-645]

4 CASAS GRANDES (NORTHERN MEXICO OR SOUTHWESTERN UNITED STATES), Pot, 300–1500 [1950-134-548]

5 ARTIST/MAKER UNKNOWN, Bowl, 20th century [1950-134-807]

6 CASAS GRANDES (NORTHERN MEXICO OR SOUTHWESTERN UNITED STATES), Bowl, 300–1500 [1950-134-806]

7 CASAS GRANDES (NORTHERN MEXICO OR SOUTHWESTERN UNITED STATES), Pot, 300–1500 [1950-134-550]

8 NATIVE AMERICAN (SOUTHWESTERN UNITED STATES), Bowl, Date unknown [1950-134-737]

9 NATIVE AMERICAN, Incense Burner or Pipe, Date unknown [1950-134-642]

10 ARTIST/MAKER UNKNOWN, Water Jug, 20th century [1950-134-808]

11 CONSTANTIN BRANCUSI, *Bird in Space*, 1924 [1950-134-14, 15; AC20-19]

12A–C CONSTANTIN BRANCUSI, Three parts of the four-part base of *Mademoiselle Pogany [III]*, 1931
[1950-134-21; BECAUSE OF THE ARENSBERGS' DISPLAY, THESE PIECES WERE MISATTRIBUTED TO BRANCUSI'S *BIRD IN SPACE* IN AC20-19]

13 ZAPOTEC (SOUTHERN MEXICO), Fragment of a Relief, 300–600 [1950-134-244; ACPS-98]

14 ARTIST/MAKER UNKNOWN (EASTER ISLAND), Figure of a Man, 18th century [1950-134-408]

15 MARCEL DUCHAMP, *Glider Containing a Water Mill in Neighboring Metals*, 1913–15 [1950-134-68; AC20-76]

16 ATLANTIC WATERSHED (COSTA RICA), Fragment of a Metate, 1st–5th century [1950-134-322; ACPS-180]

17 GUANACASTE-NICOYA (COSTA RICA), Metate, 1–500 [1950-134-325; ACPS-178]

18 ROBERT DELAUNAY, *Saint-Séverin*, 1909 [1950-134-42A; AC20-41]

19 JOAN MIRÓ, *Woman*, 1934 [1950-134-146; AC20-150]

20 JACQUES VILLON (GASTON DUCHAMP), *Abstraction*, 1932 [1950-134-191; AC20-196]

21 MARCEL DUCHAMP, *Nude Descending a Staircase (No. 2)*, 1912 [1950-134-59; AC20-64]

22 MAYA (HONDURAS), Vessel, 650–1000 [1950-134-398; ACPS-168]

THE NORTHWEST WALL OF THE SUNROOM, PICTURED HERE, WAS ORIGINALLY BUILT IN 1933 AS RICHARD NEUTRA HAD DESIGNED IT, WITH STEEL CASEMENT WINDOWS SPANNING ITS ENTIRE WIDTH. WHEN GREGORY AIN ADDED THE SECOND-FLOOR SITTING ROOM IN 1936, HOWEVER, A STEEL I-BEAM WAS INSTALLED FOR SUPPORT IN THE SUNROOM'S NORTHEAST CORNER AND THE WINDOW WAS REMOVED. NO KNOWN PHOTOGRAPH DEPICTS THE ORIGINAL ARCHITECTURAL CONDITION.

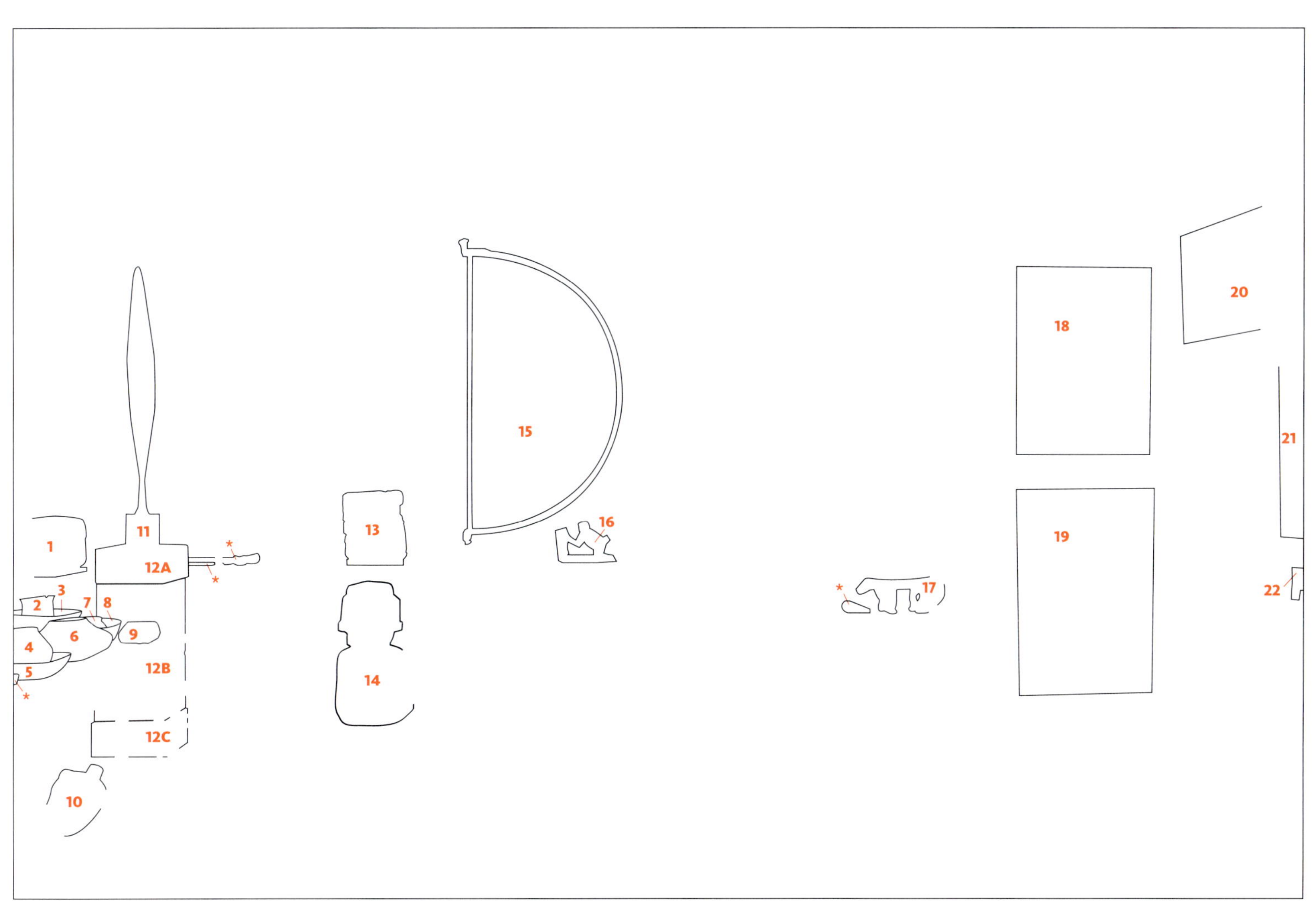
1
2
3
4
5
*
6
7
8
9
10
11
12A
*
*
12B
12C
13
14
15
16
17
*
18
19
20
21
22

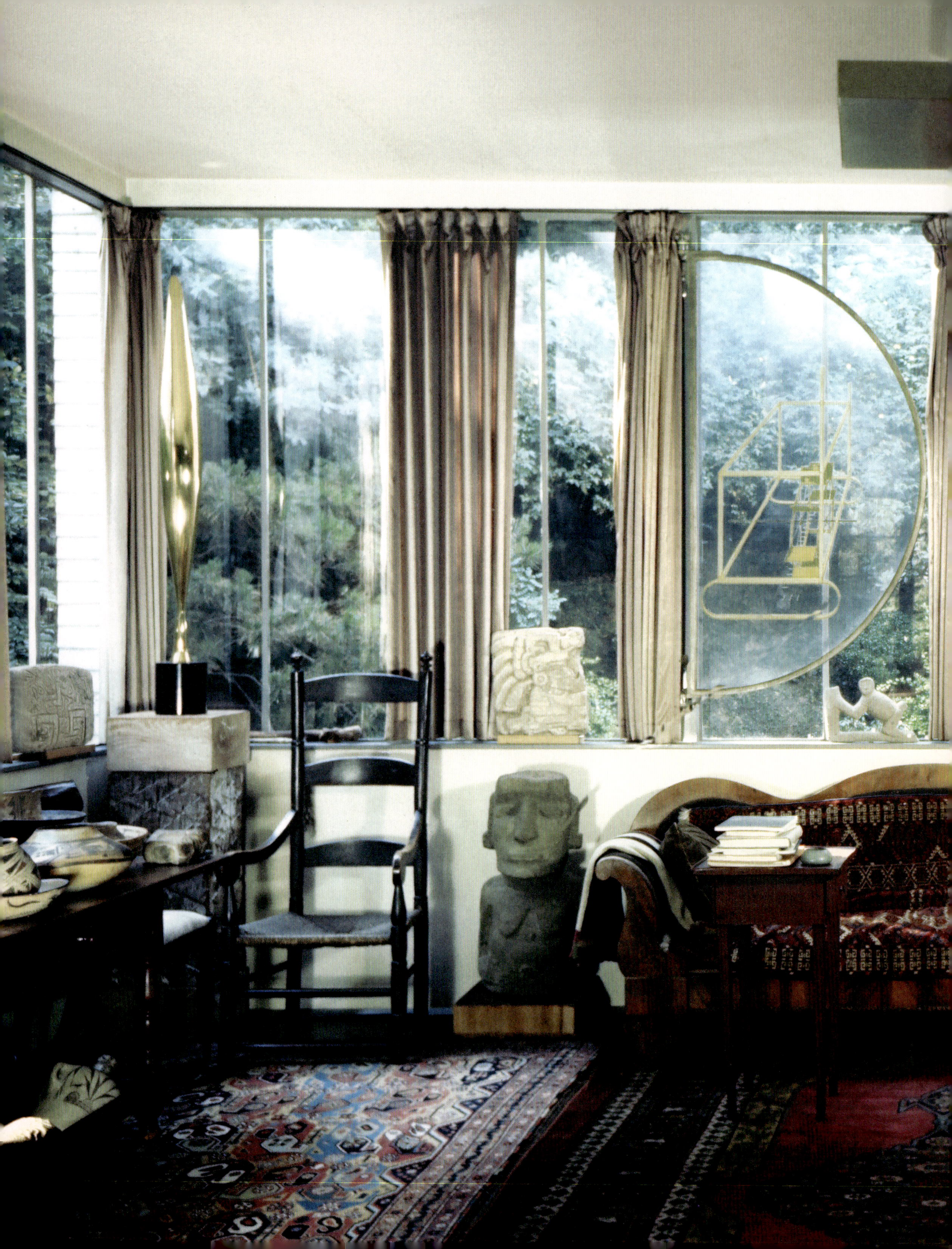

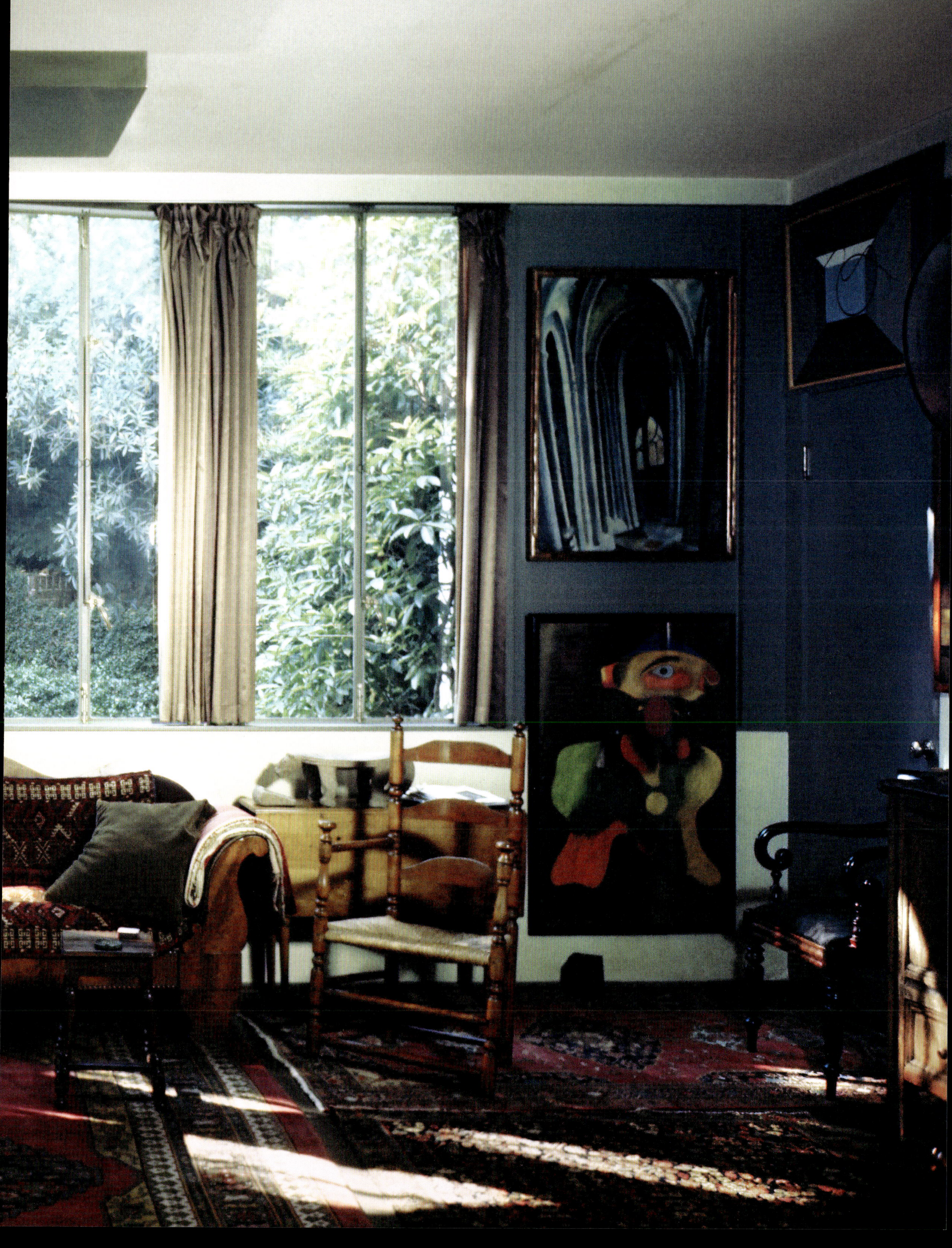

PLATE 25

SUNROOM (GALLERY ROOM)

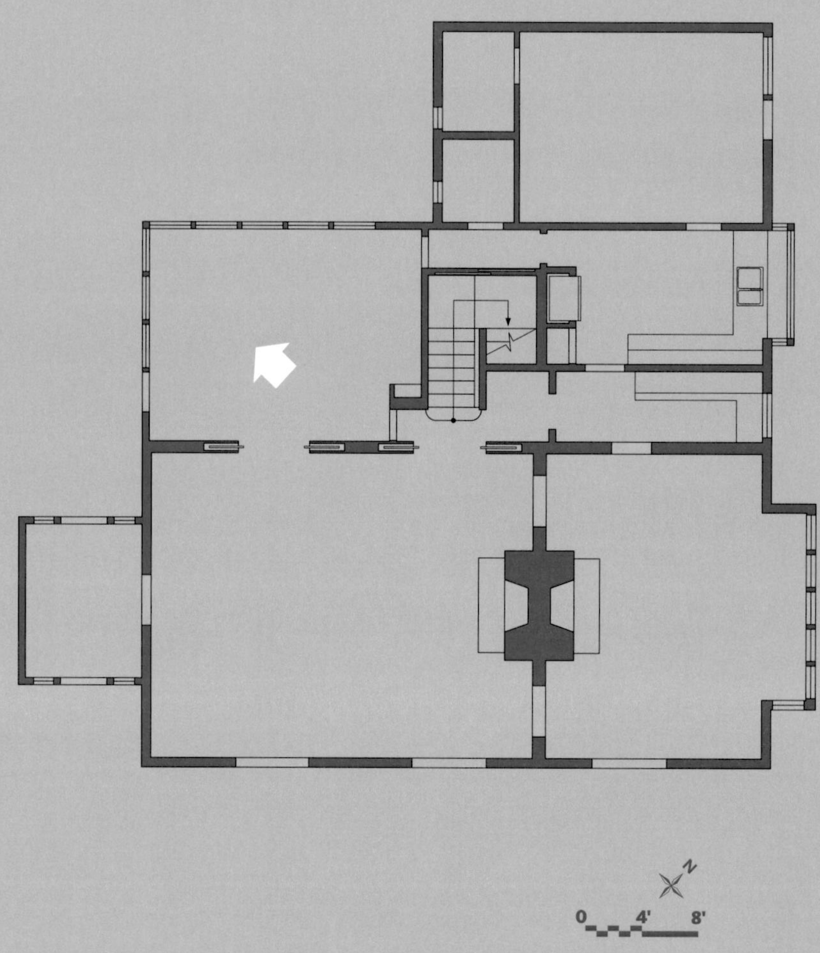

FRITZ (FRED) BLOCK

CA. 1942–43

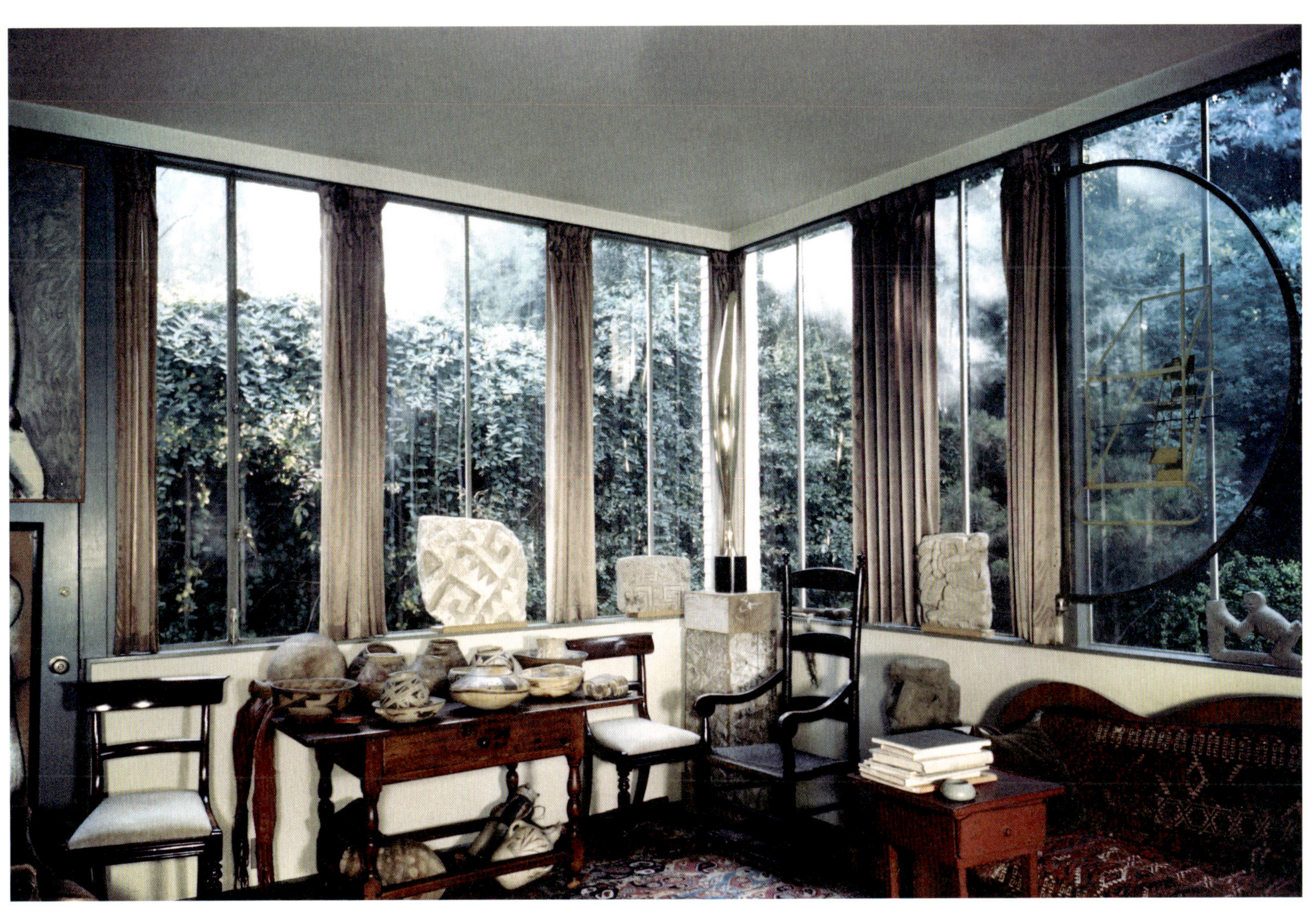

PLATE 25

1 PABLO PICASSO, *Seated Female Nude*, 1908–9 [1950-134-164; AC20-169]

2 JOAN MIRÓ, *The Lovers*, 1934 [1950-134-148; AC20-149]

3 ZAPOTEC (SOUTHERN MEXICO), Fragment of a Relief, 800–1500 [1950-134-245; ACPS-102]

4 NATIVE AMERICAN (SOUTHWESTERN UNITED STATES), Vessel, Date unknown [1950-134-644]

5 NATIVE AMERICAN (SOUTHWESTERN UNITED STATES), Bowl, Date unknown [1950-134-420]

6–8 CASAS GRANDES (NORTHERN MEXICO OR SOUTHWESTERN UNITED STATES), Pots, 300–1500 [6: 1950-134-600; 7: 1950-134-551; 8: 1950-134-548]

9 ARTIST/MAKER UNKNOWN, Bowl, 20th century [1950-134-807]

10–12 CASAS GRANDES (NORTHERN MEXICO OR SOUTHWESTERN UNITED STATES), Pots, 300–1500 [10: 1950-134-549; 11: 1950-134-552; 12: 1950-134-553]

13 CASAS GRANDES (NORTHERN MEXICO OR SOUTHWESTERN UNITED STATES), Pot, Date unknown [1950-134-257]

14 CASAS GRANDES (NORTHERN MEXICO OR SOUTHWESTERN UNITED STATES), Bowl, 300–1500 [1950-134-806]

15 NATIVE AMERICAN (SOUTHWESTERN UNITED STATES), Vessel or Jar, Date unknown [1950-134-667]

16 NATIVE AMERICAN (SOUTHWESTERN UNITED STATES), Bowl, Date unknown [1950-134-645]

17 CASAS GRANDES (NORTHERN MEXICO OR SOUTHWESTERN UNITED STATES), Pot, 300–1500 [1950-134-550]

18 NATIVE AMERICAN (SOUTHWESTERN UNITED STATES), Bowl, Date unknown [1950-134-737]

19 NATIVE AMERICAN, Incense Burner or Pipe, Date unknown [1950-134-642]

20 CHANCAY (PERU), Large Bottle in Figure Form, 1000–1470 [1950-134-306; ACPS-186]

21 NATIVE AMERICAN (SOUTHWESTERN UNITED STATES), Jar, Date unknown [1950-134-767]

22 ARTIST/MAKER UNKNOWN, Water Jug, 20th century [1950-134-808]

23 MANTEÑO (ECUADOR), Relief, 500–1000 [1950-134-241; ACPS-190]

24 CONSTANTIN BRANCUSI, *Bird in Space*, 1924 [1950-134-14, 15; AC20-19]

25A–C CONSTANTIN BRANCUSI, Three parts of the four-part base of *Mademoiselle Pogany [III]*, 1931 [1950-134-21; BECAUSE OF THE ARENSBERGS' DISPLAY, THESE PIECES WERE MISATTRIBUTED TO BRANCUSI'S *BIRD IN SPACE* IN AC20-19]

26 ZAPOTEC (SOUTHERN MEXICO), Fragment of a Relief, 300–600 [1950-134-244; ACPS-98]

27 ARTIST/MAKER UNKNOWN (EASTER ISLAND), Figure of a Man, 18th century [1950-134-408]

28 MARCEL DUCHAMP, *Glider Containing a Water Mill in Neighboring Metals*, 1913–15 [1950-134-68; AC20-76]

29 ATLANTIC WATERSHED (COSTA RICA), Fragment of a Metate, 1st–5th century [1950-134-322; ACPS-180]

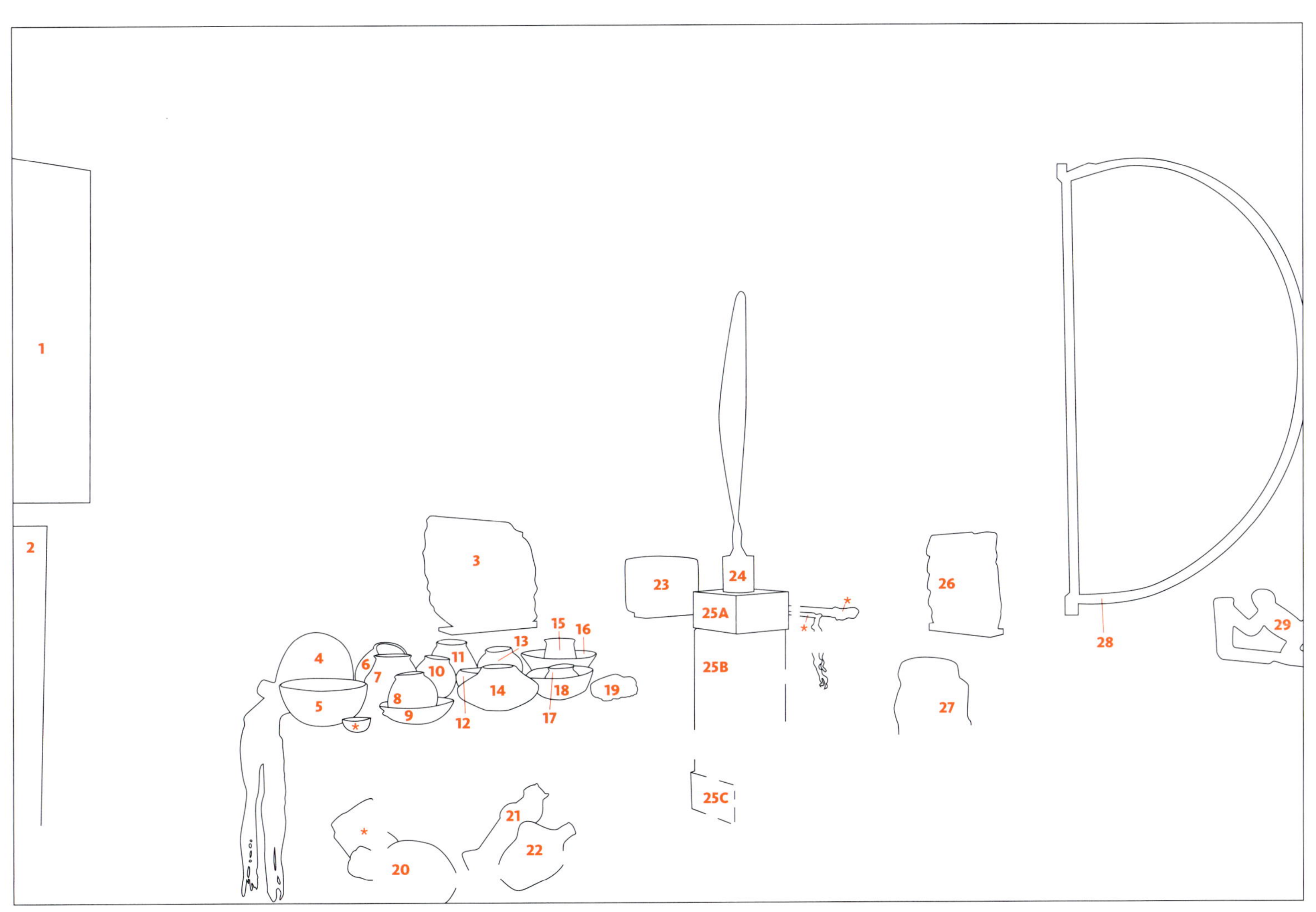

1
2
3
4
5
6
7
8
9
10
11
12
13
14
15
16
17
18
19
20
21
22
23
24
25A
25B
25C
26
27
28
29
*

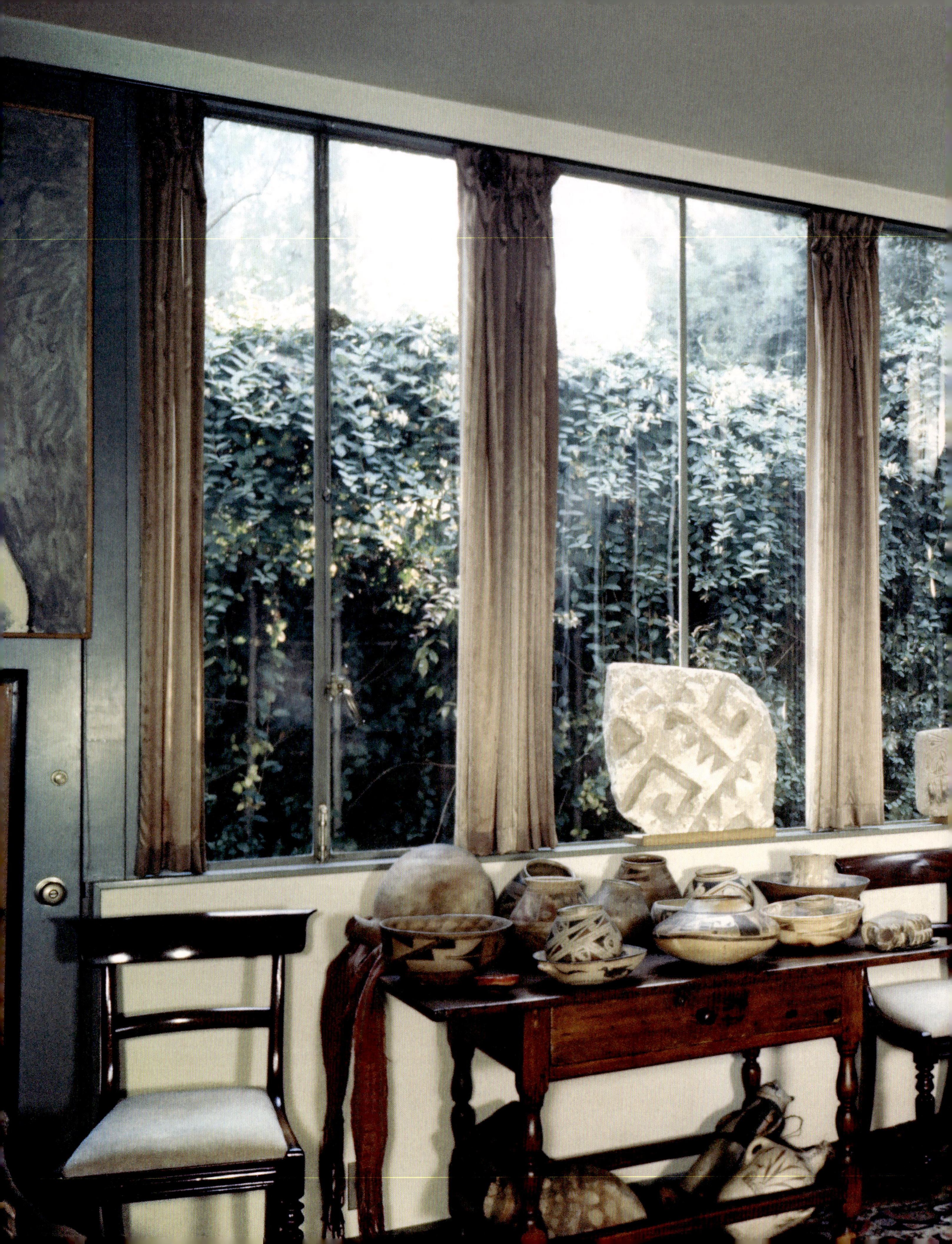

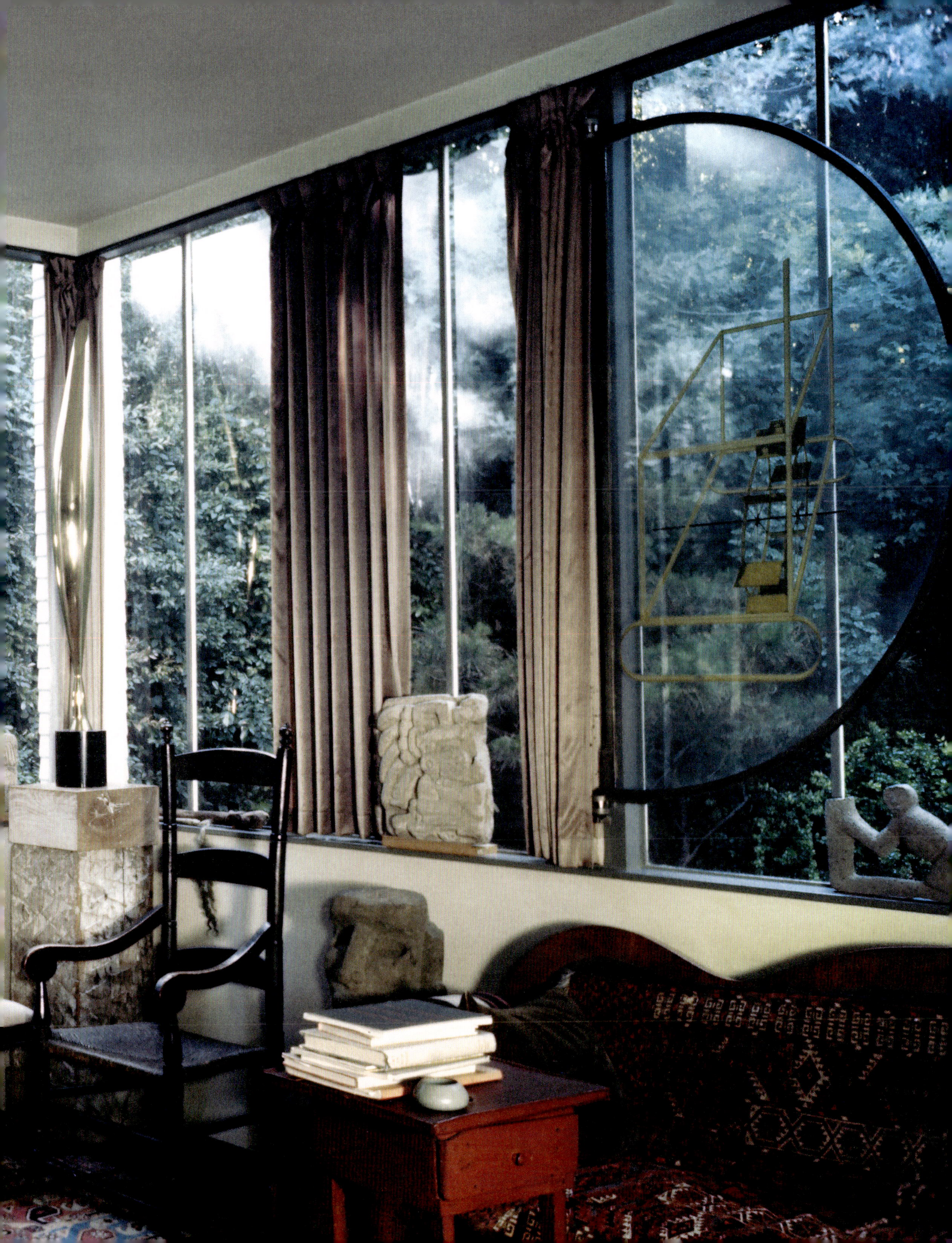

PLATE 26

SUNROOM (GALLERY ROOM)

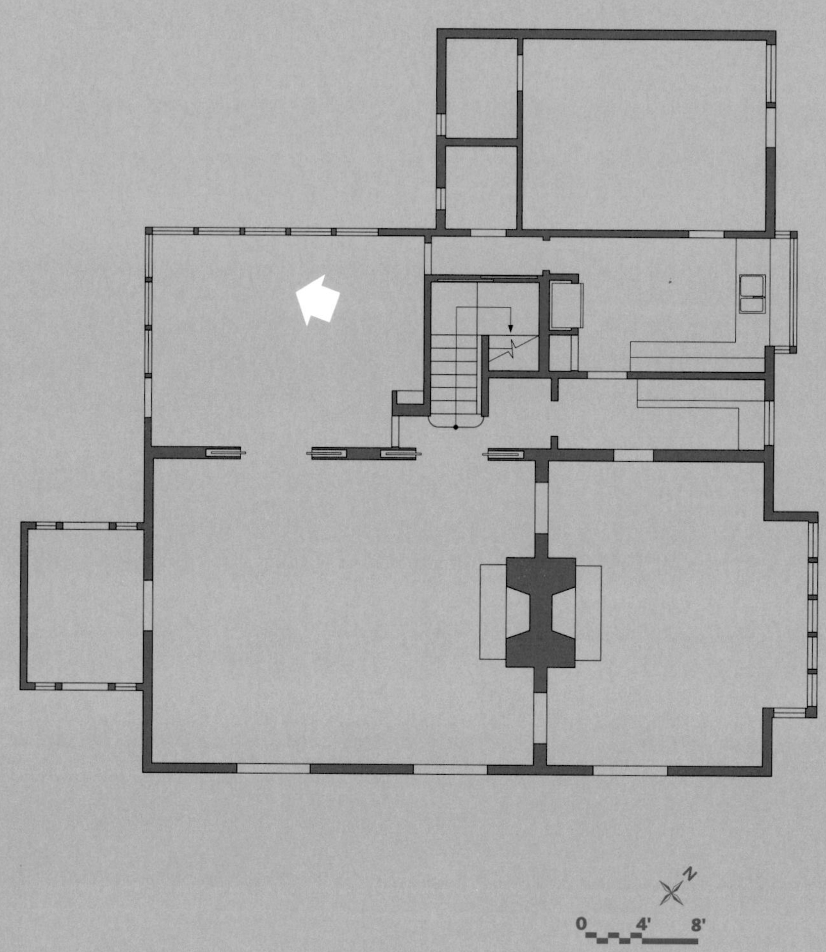

FRED R. DAPPRICH

CA. 1944

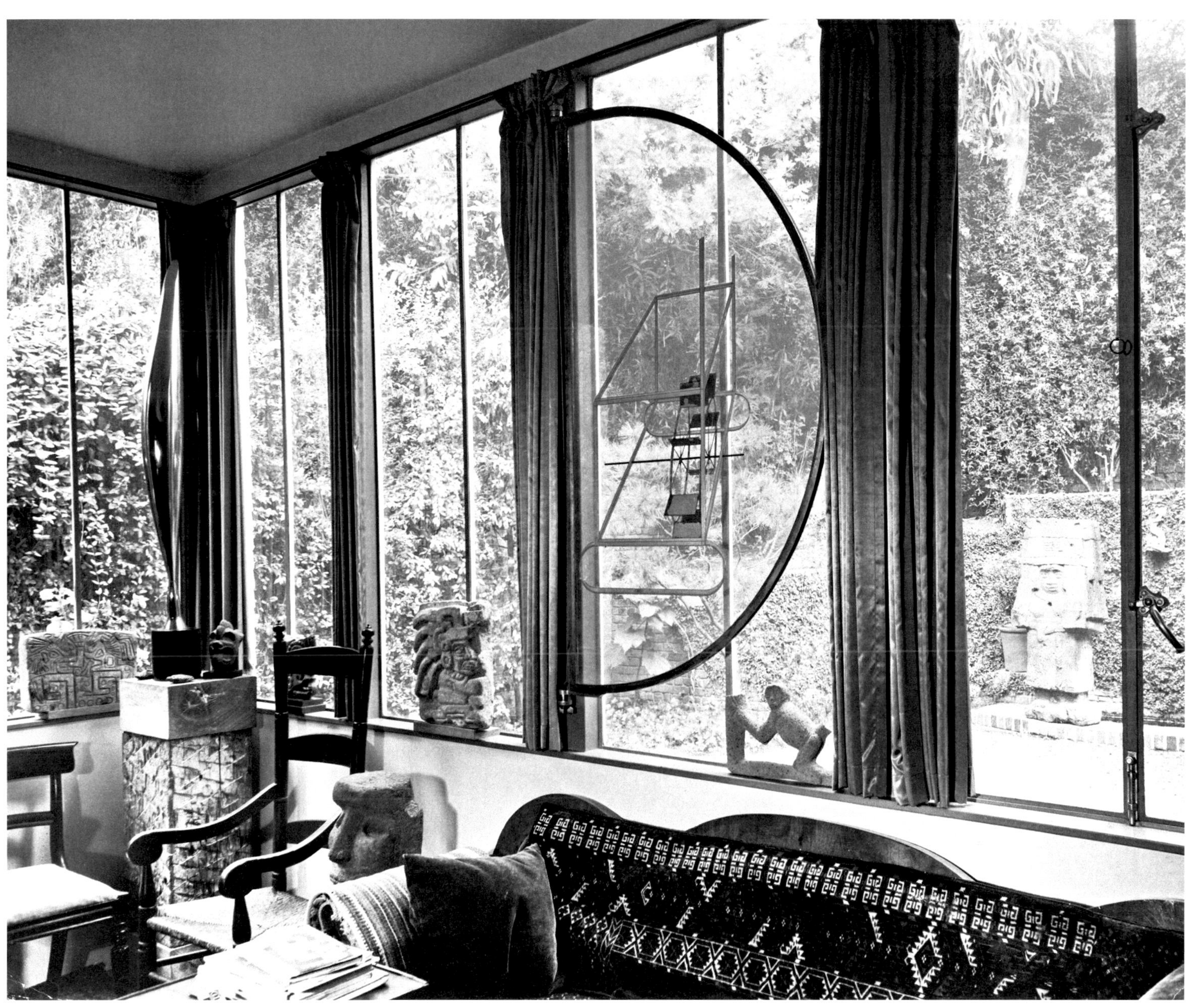

PLATE 26

1 MANTEÑO (ECUADOR), Relief, 500–1000 [1950-134-241; ACPS-190]

2 CONSTANTIN BRANCUSI, *Bird in Space*, 1924 [1950-134-14, 15; AC20-19]

3A–C CONSTANTIN BRANCUSI, Three parts of the four-part base of *Mademoiselle Pogany [III]*, 1931
[1950-134-21; BECAUSE OF THE ARENSBERGS' DISPLAY, THESE PIECES WERE MISATTRIBUTED TO BRANCUSI'S *BIRD IN SPACE* IN AC20-19]

4, 5 CLASSIC VERACRUZ (EAST COAST MEXICO), Hachas in the Form of Heads, 500–900 [4: 1950-134-335, ACPS-144; 5: 1950-134-341, ACPS-146]

6 ARTIST/MAKER UNKNOWN (EASTER ISLAND), Figure of a Man, 18th century [1950-134-408]

7 ZAPOTEC (SOUTHERN MEXICO), Fragment of a Relief, 300–600 [1950-134-244; ACPS-98]

8 MARCEL DUCHAMP, *Glider Containing a Water Mill in Neighboring Metals*, 1913–15 [1950-134-68; AC20-76]

9 ATLANTIC WATERSHED (COSTA RICA), Fragment of a Metate, 1st–5th century [1950-134-322; ACPS-180]

10 AZTEC (CENTRAL MEXICO), Corn Goddess, 1300–1520 [1950-134-347; ACPS-7]

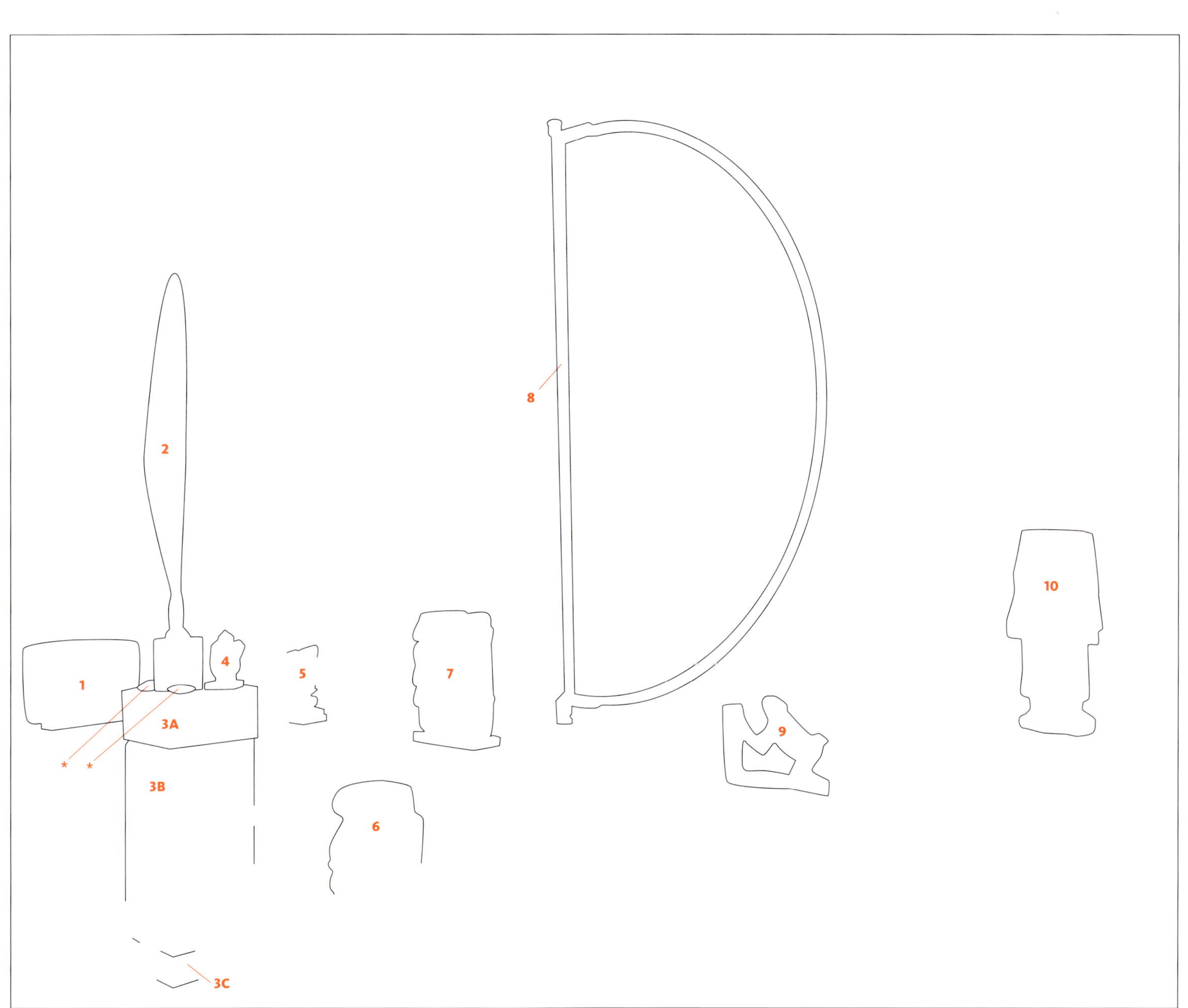
2
8
10
4
1
5
7
3A
9
* *
3B
6
3C

PLATE 27

SUNROOM (GALLERY ROOM)

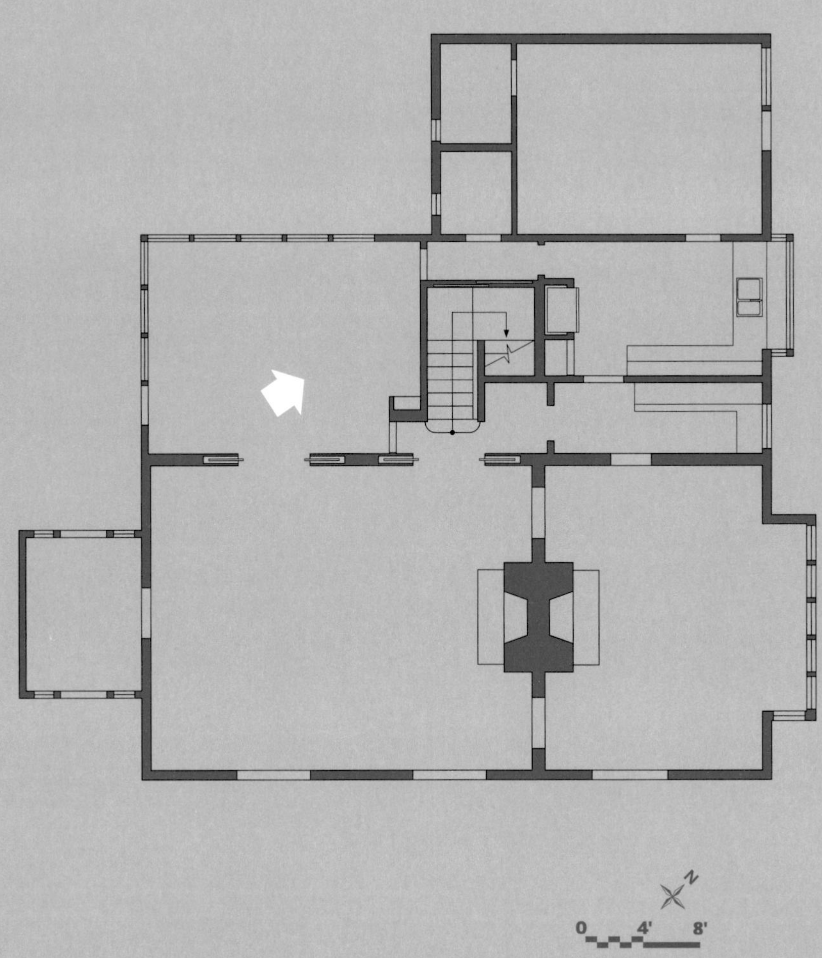

FRITZ (FRED) BLOCK
CA. 1942–43

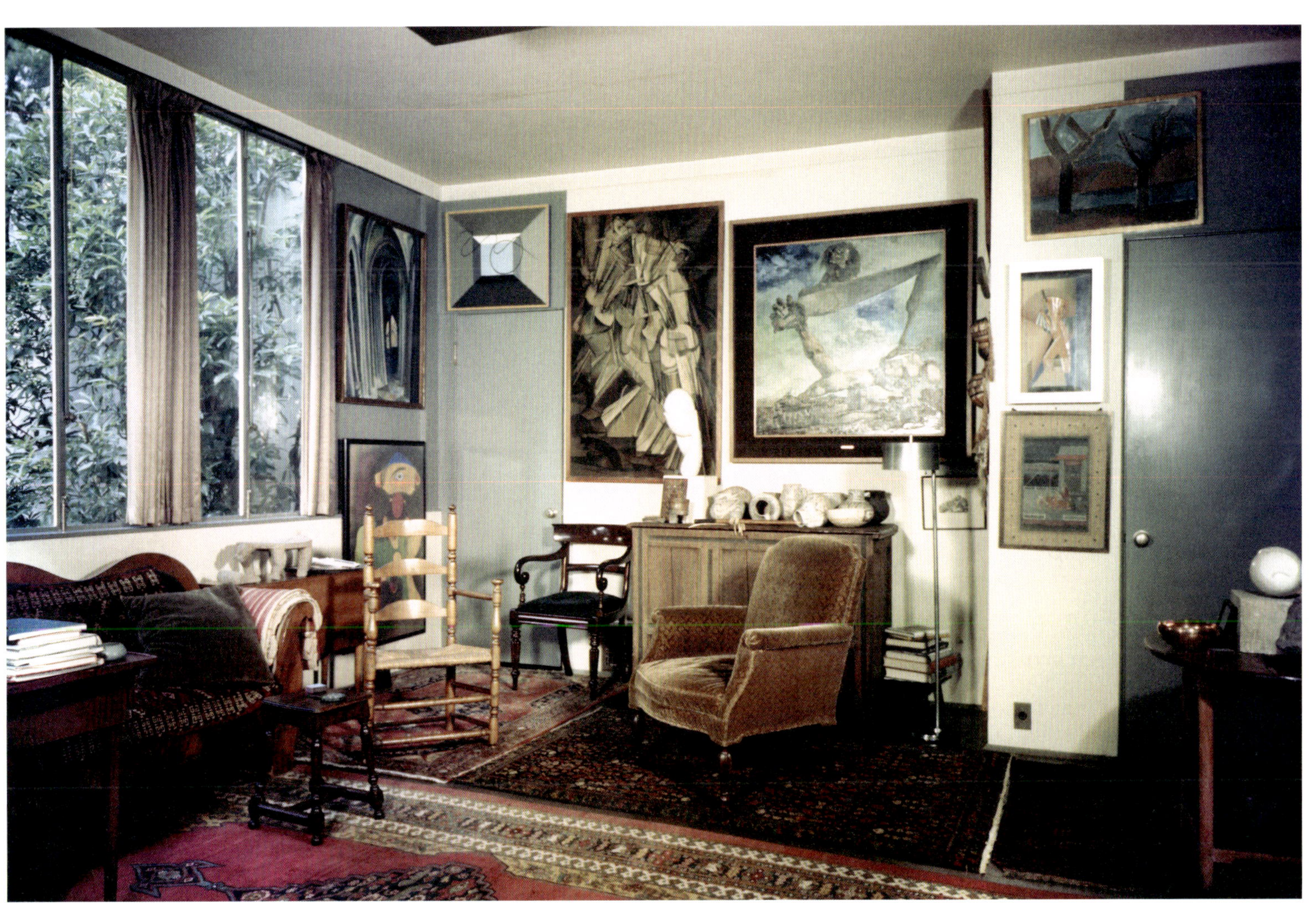

PLATE 27

1 GUANACASTE-NICOYA (COSTA RICA), Metate, 1–500 [1950-134-325; ACPS-178]

2 ROBERT DELAUNAY, *Saint-Séverin*, 1909 [1950-134-42A; AC20-41]

3 JOAN MIRÓ, *Woman*, 1934 [1950-134-146; AC20-150]

4 JACQUES VILLON (GASTON DUCHAMP), *Abstraction*, 1932 [1950-134-191; AC20-196]

5 MARCEL DUCHAMP, *Nude Descending a Staircase (No. 2)*, 1912 [1950-134-59; AC20-64]

6 CONSTANTIN BRANCUSI, *Mademoiselle Pogany [III]*, with one part of its base, 1931 [1950-134-21; AC20-21]

7 SALVADOR DALÍ, *Soft Construction with Boiled Beans (Premonition of Civil War)*, 1936 [1950-134-41; AC20-40]

8 WARI (SOUTH COAST PERU), Two Textile Fragments, 500–800 [1950-134-311]

9 TEOTIHUACAN (CENTRAL MEXICO), Tripod Vessel, 400–800 [1950-134-231; ACPS-54]

10 CASAS GRANDES (NORTHERN MEXICO OR SOUTHWESTERN UNITED STATES), Pot, 300–1500 [1950-134-258]

*11 NATIVE AMERICAN (SOUTHWESTERN UNITED STATES), Jug, Date unknown [1950-134-647]

12 CASAS GRANDES (NORTHERN MEXICO OR SOUTHWESTERN UNITED STATES), Pitcher, 300–1500 [1950-134-557]

13, 14 NATIVE AMERICAN (SOUTHWESTERN UNITED STATES), Jugs, Dates unknown [13: 1950-134-735; 14: 1950-134-646]

*15 MARCEL DUCHAMP, *Chocolate Grinder (No. 1)*, 1913 [1950-134-69; AC20-74]

16 IÑUPIAQ (NORTH COAST ALASKA), Mask, Late 19th–early 20th century [NOTE 4.3, PAGES 416–17]

17, 18 NATIVE AMERICAN, Masks, Dates unknown [17: 1950-134-430; 18: 1950-134-431]

19 PIMA (ARIZONA), Mask, Date unknown [1950-134-433]

20 REPRODUCTION OF ALBRECHT DÜRER'S ENGRAVING *Saint Anthony the Hermit* (1519), Date unknown [PMA-WLA BOX 72, FOLDER 6]

21 PABLO PICASSO, *Two Trees*, 1907–8 [1950-134-163; AC20-167]

22 ALEXANDER ARCHIPENKO, *The Bather*, 1915 [1950-134-1; AC20-1]

23 ARTIST/MAKER UNKNOWN (INDIA, *DELHI), *Woman Reading on a Terrace*, Late 18th century [1950-134-856]

24 ARTIST/MAKER UNKNOWN, Bowl, *ca. 1930s–1940s [NOTE 4.4, PAGE 417]

*25 KNUD MERRILD, *Abstraction*, 10 October 1935 [PMA-WLA BOX 72, FOLDER 9]

26 CONSTANTIN BRANCUSI, *Newborn [I]*, 1915 [1950-134-10; AC20-9]

27 NATIVE AMERICAN (SOUTHWESTERN UNITED STATES), Jar, Date unknown [1950-134-740]

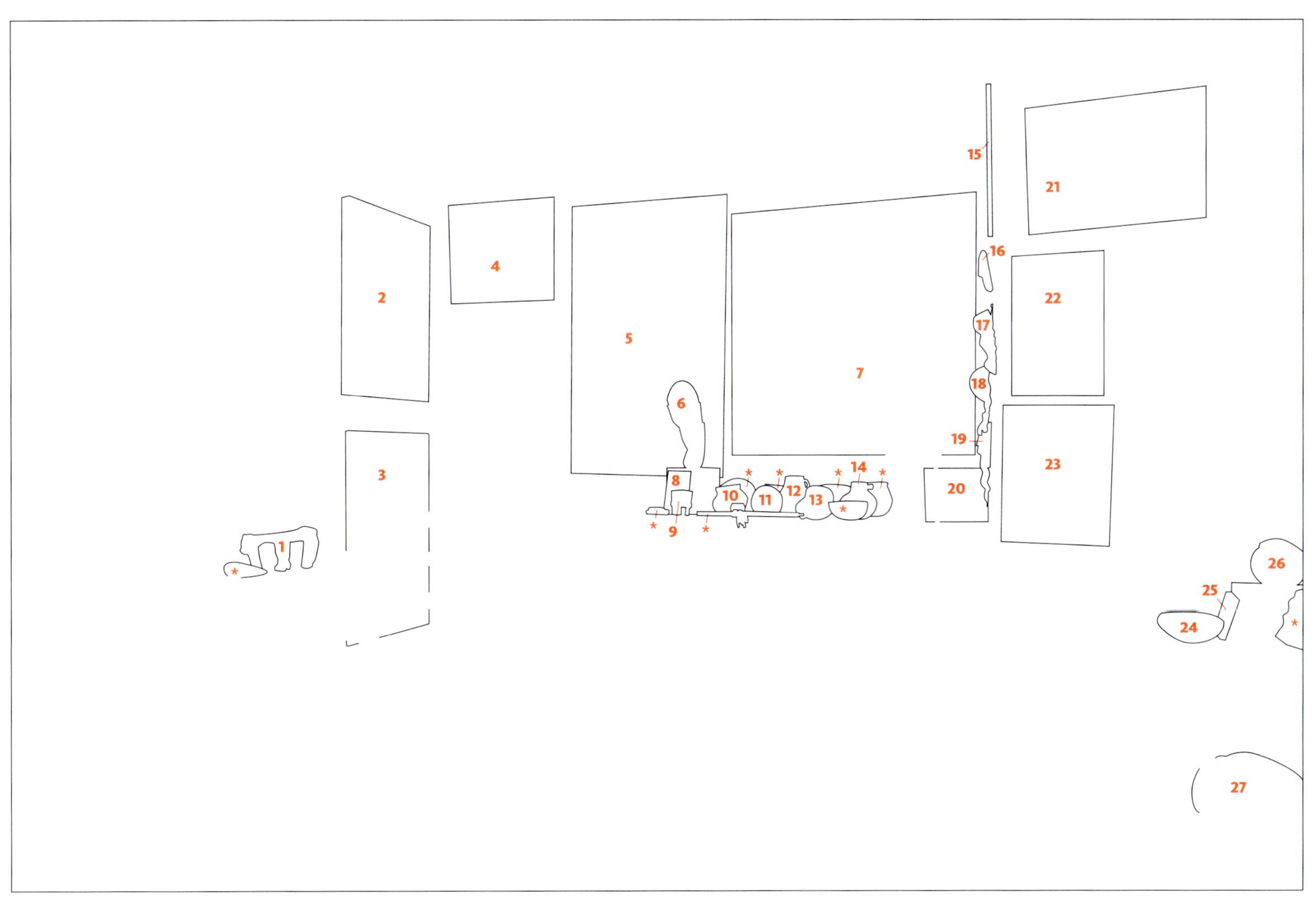
15
21
16
4
2
22
17
5
7
18
6
19
3
23
8
*
*
*
14
*
20
10
11
12
13
*
*
9
*
1
*
26
25
24
*
27

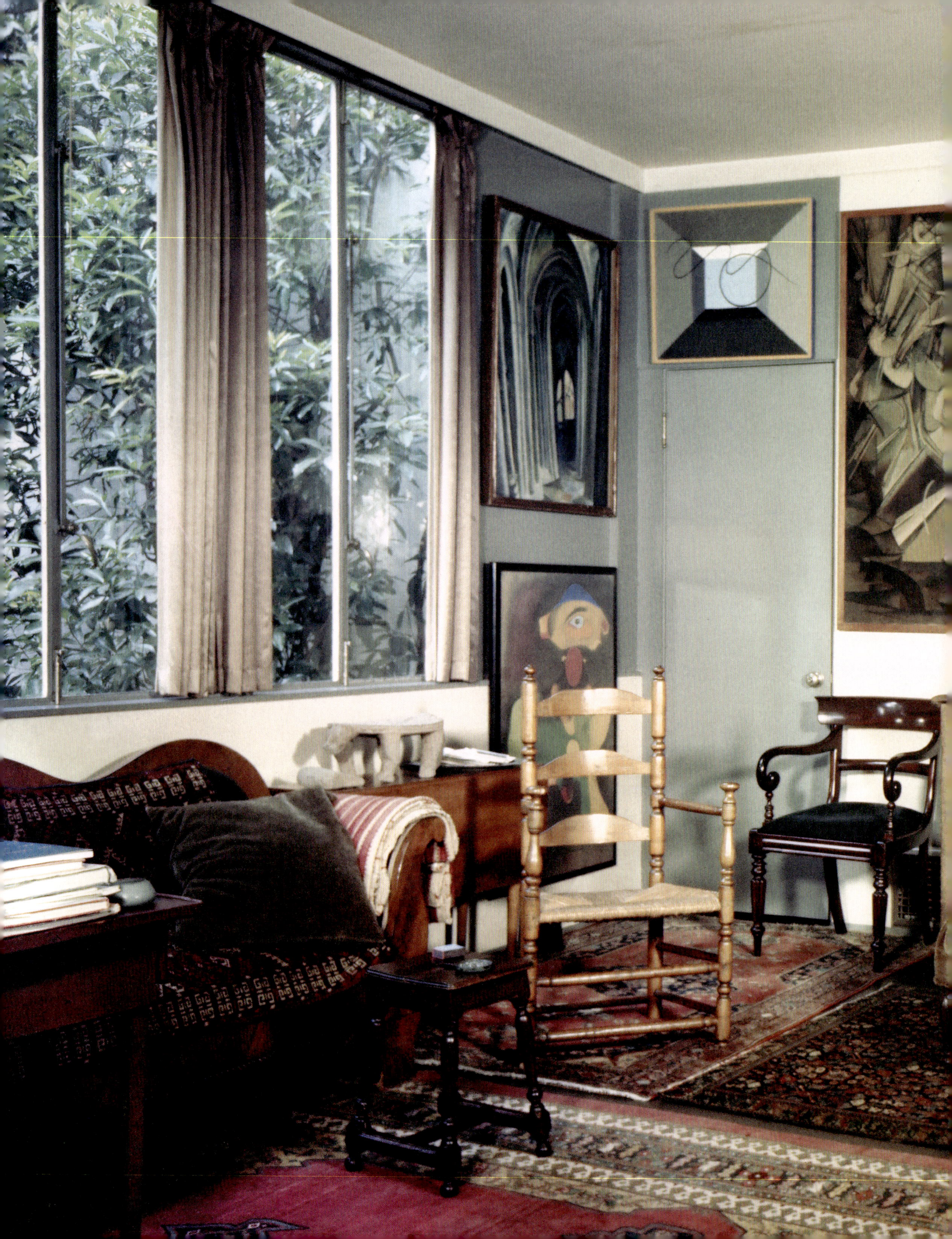

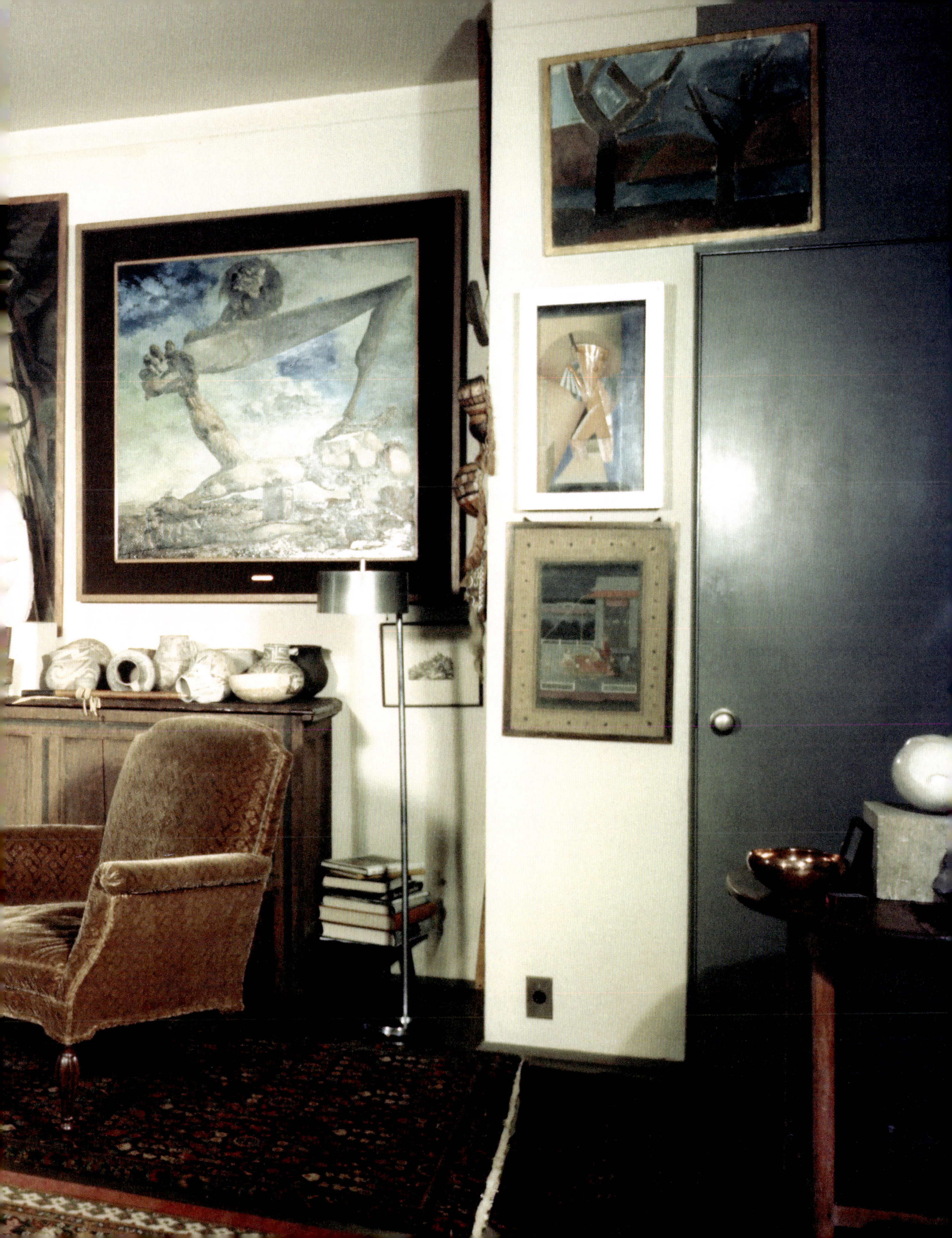

PLATE 28

SUNROOM (GALLERY ROOM)

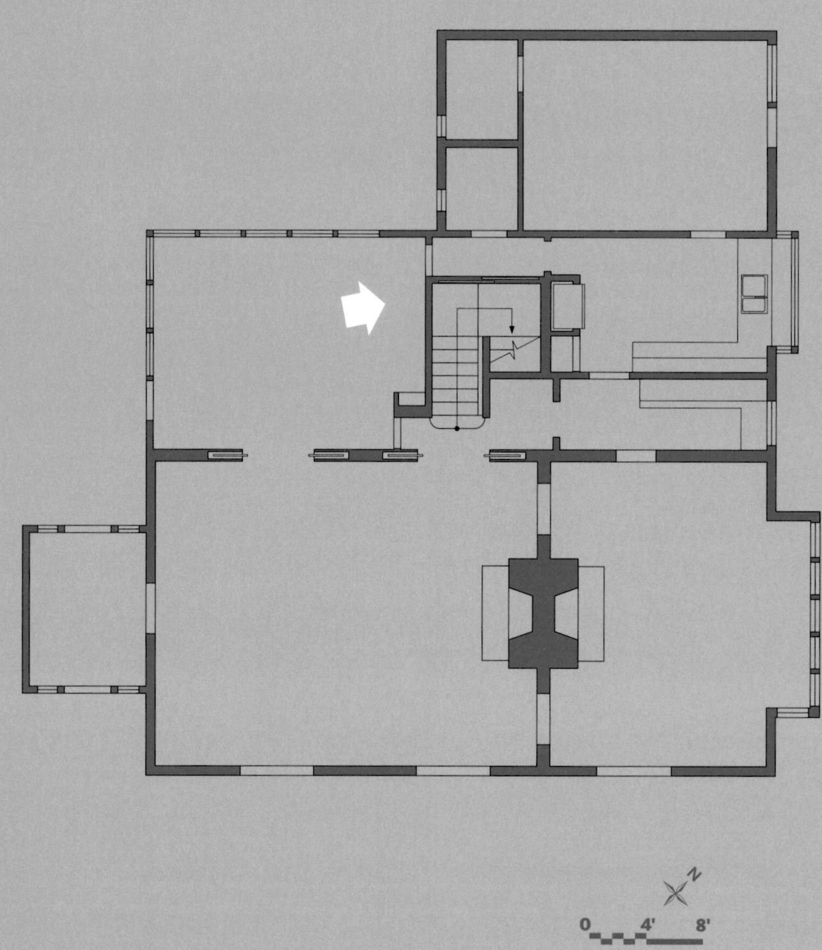

CORPORAL F. W. LUMBORD

CA. APRIL 1945

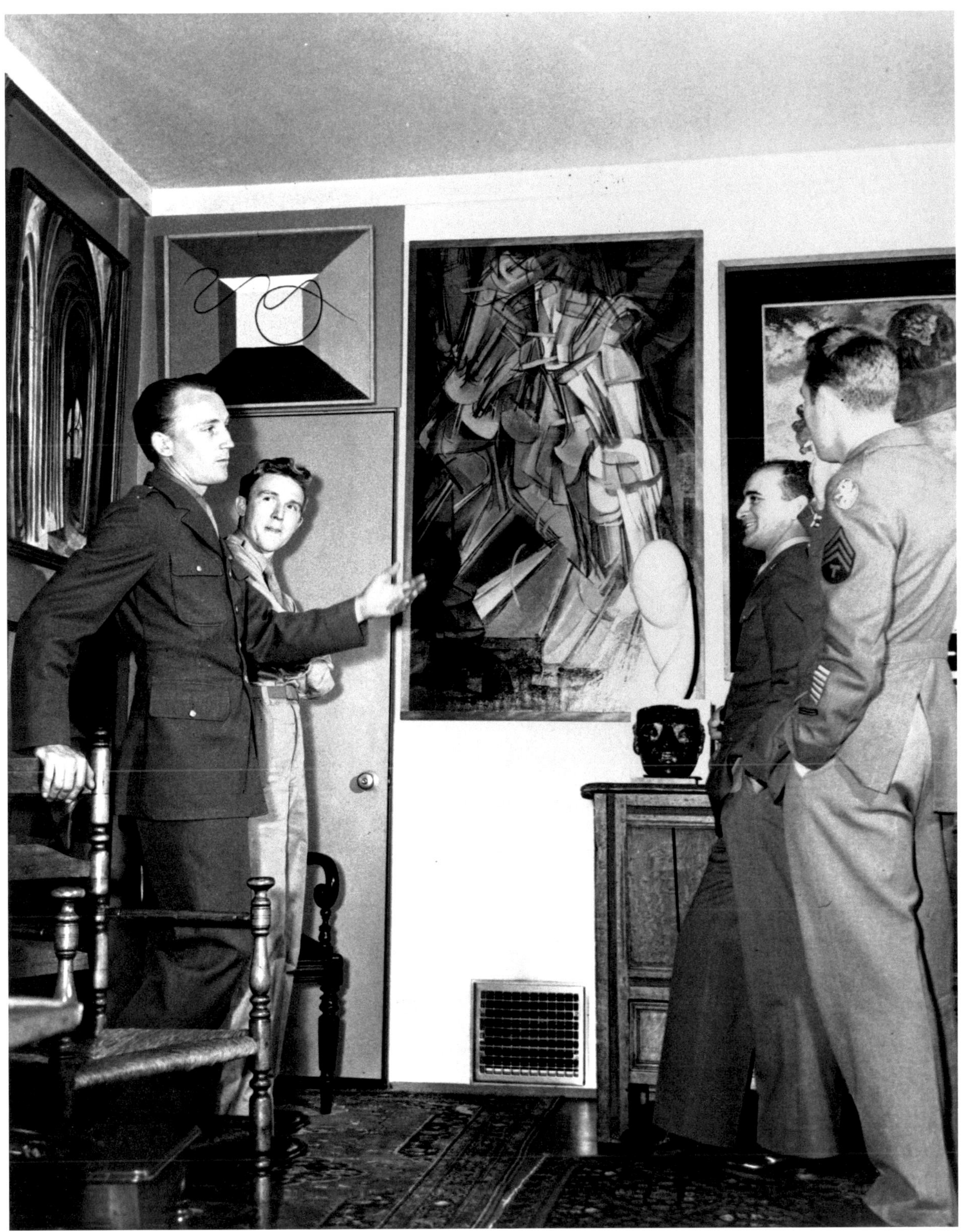

PLATE 28

1 ROBERT DELAUNAY, *Saint-Séverin*, 1909 [1950-134-42A; AC20-41]

2 JACQUES VILLON (GASTON DUCHAMP), *Abstraction*, 1932 [1950-134-191; AC20-196]

3 MARCEL DUCHAMP, *Nude Descending a Staircase (No. 2)*, 1912 [1950-134-59; AC20-64]

4 CONSTANTIN BRANCUSI, *Mademoiselle Pogany [III]*, with one part of its base, 1931 [1950-134-21; AC20-21]

5 TEOTIHUACAN (CENTRAL MEXICO), Mask, 1st–9th century [1950-134-395]

6 SALVADOR DALÍ, *Soft Construction with Boiled Beans (Premonition of Civil War)*, 1936 [1950-134-41; AC20-40]

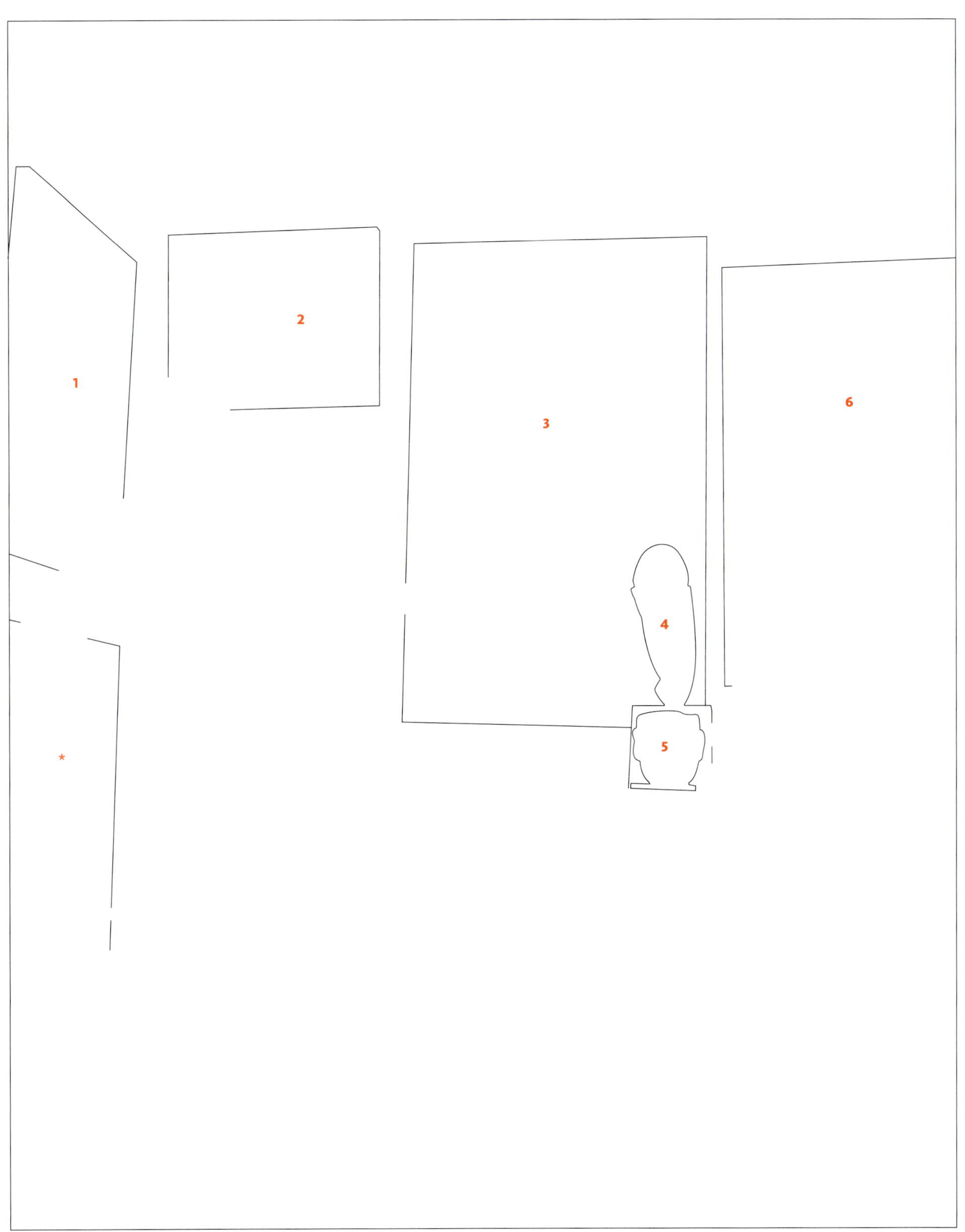
1
2
3
6
4
5
*

PLATE 29

SUNROOM (GALLERY ROOM)

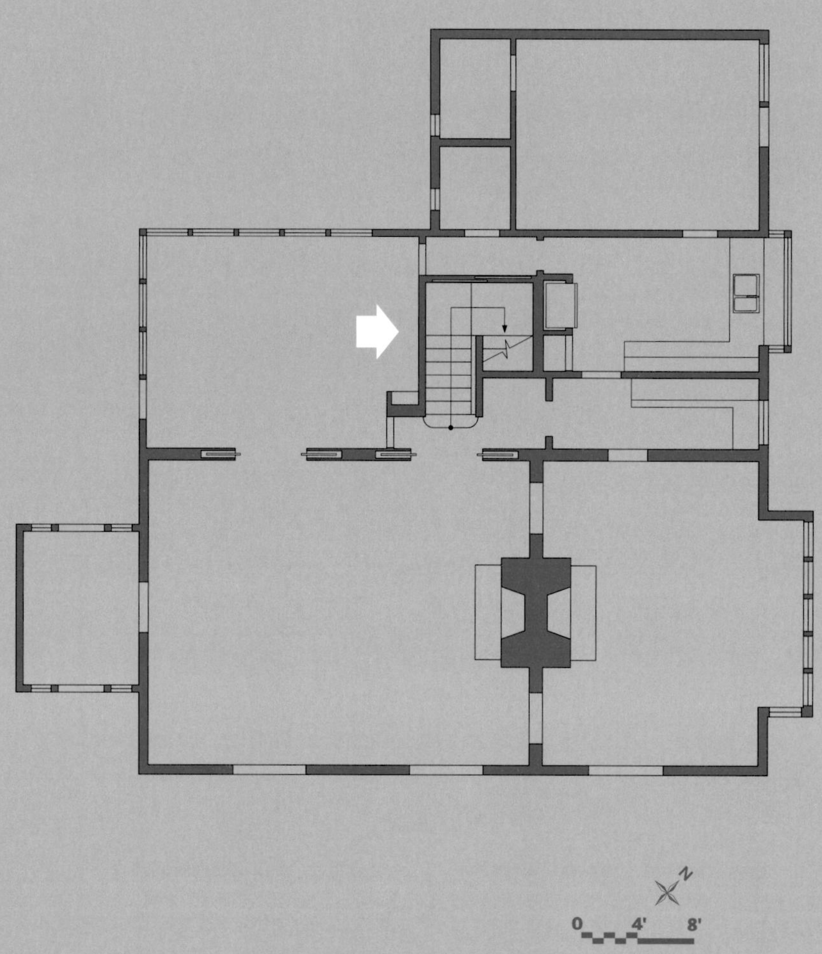

PHOTOGRAPHER UNKNOWN

CA. 1940S

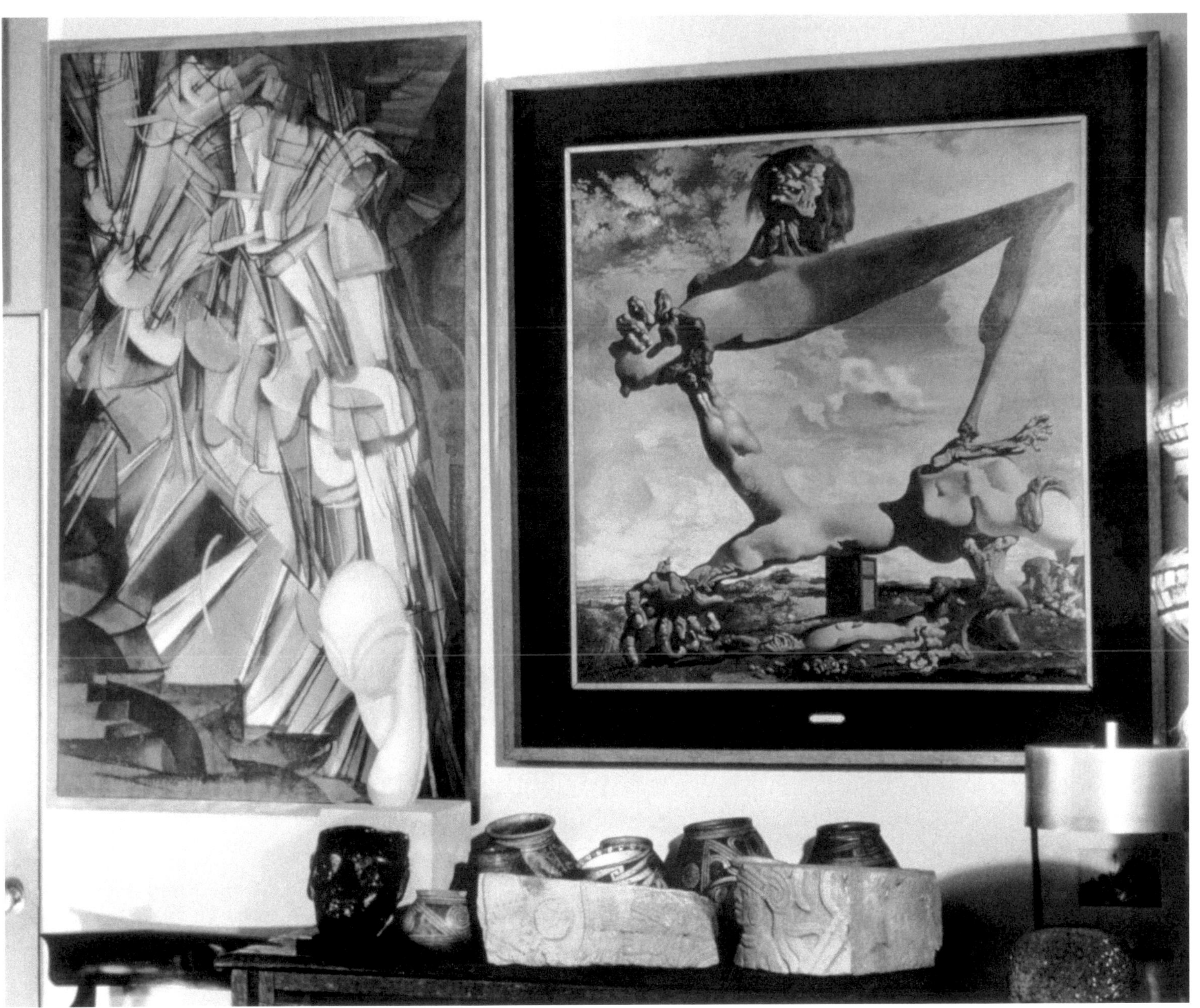

PLATE 29

1 MARCEL DUCHAMP, *Nude Descending a Staircase (No. 2)*, 1912 [1950-134-59; AC20-64]

2 CONSTANTIN BRANCUSI, *Mademoiselle Pogany [III]*, with one part of its base, 1931 [1950-134-21; AC20-21]

3 SALVADOR DALÍ, *Soft Construction with Boiled Beans (Premonition of Civil War)*, 1936 [1950-134-41; AC20-40]

4 TEOTIHUACAN (CENTRAL MEXICO), Mask, 1st–9th century [1950-134-395]

5–7 CASAS GRANDES (NORTHERN MEXICO OR SOUTHWESTERN UNITED STATES), Pots, 300–1500 [5: 1950-134-550; 6: 1950-134-549; 7: 1950-134-551]

8 CLASSIC VERACRUZ (EAST COAST MEXICO), Column Drum Fragment, 800–1300 [1950-134-302; ACPS-122]

9–12 CASAS GRANDES (NORTHERN MEXICO OR SOUTHWESTERN UNITED STATES), Pots, 300–1500 [9: 1950-134-258; 10: 1950-134-548; 11: 1950-134-600; 12: 1950-134-257]

13 CLASSIC VERACRUZ (EAST COAST MEXICO), Column Drum Fragment, 800–1300 [1950-134-303; ACPS-123]

14 CASAS GRANDES (NORTHERN MEXICO OR SOUTHWESTERN UNITED STATES), Pot, 300–1500 [1950-134-552]

15 OLMEC (MEXICO), Figure of a Man, 1200–600 BCE [1950-134-338; ACPS-1]

16 REPRODUCTION OF ALBRECHT DÜRER'S ENGRAVING *Saint Anthony the Hermit* (1519), Date unknown [PMA-WLA, BOX 72, FOLDER 6]

17, 18 NATIVE AMERICAN, Masks, Dates unknown [17: 1950-134-431; 18: 1950-134-430]

19 IÑUPIAQ (NORTH COAST ALASKA), Mask, Late 19th–early 20th century [NOTE 4.3, PAGES 416–17]

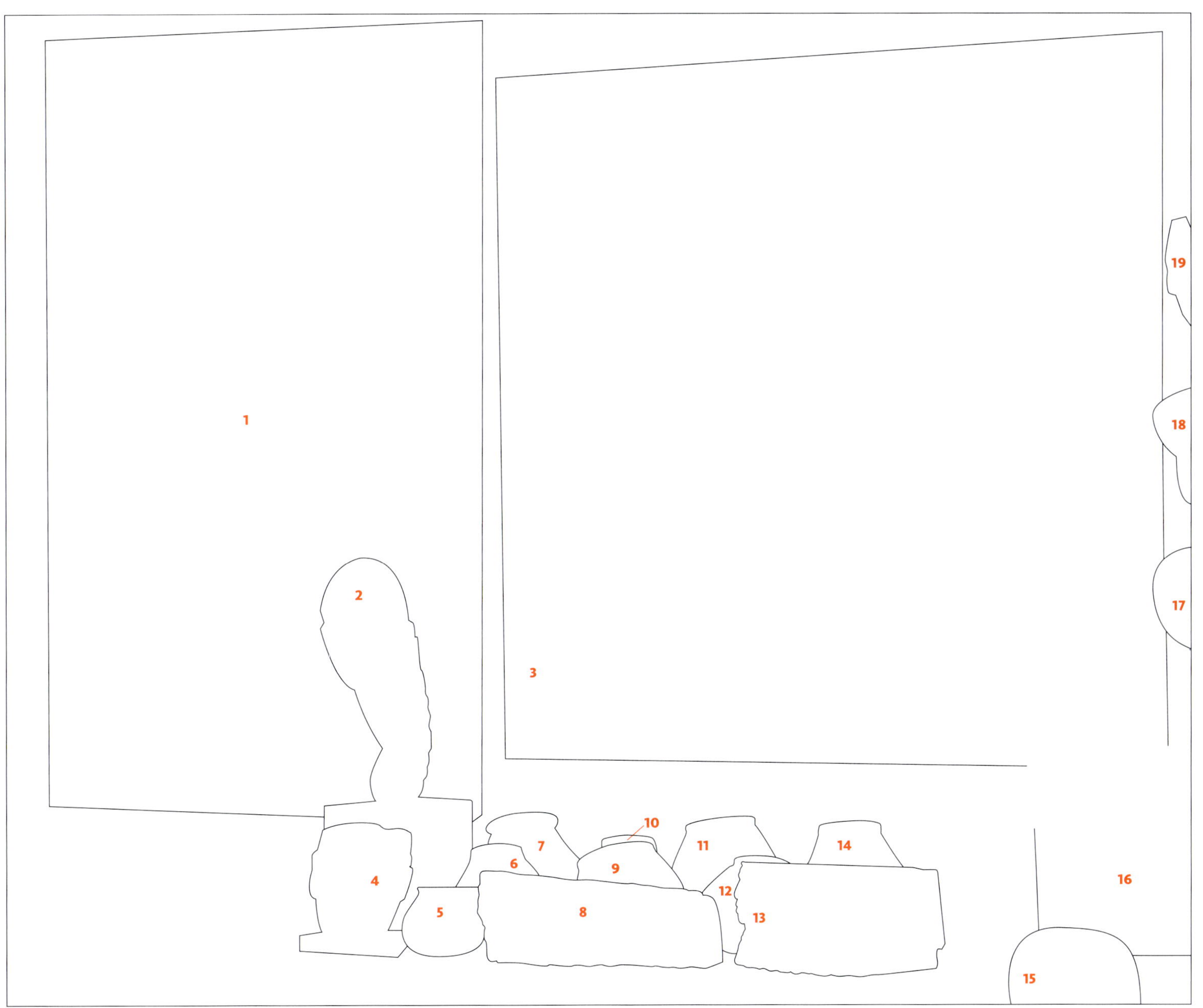
1
2
3
4
5
6
7
8
9
10
11
12
13
14
15
16
17
18
19

PLATE 30

SUNROOM (GALLERY ROOM)

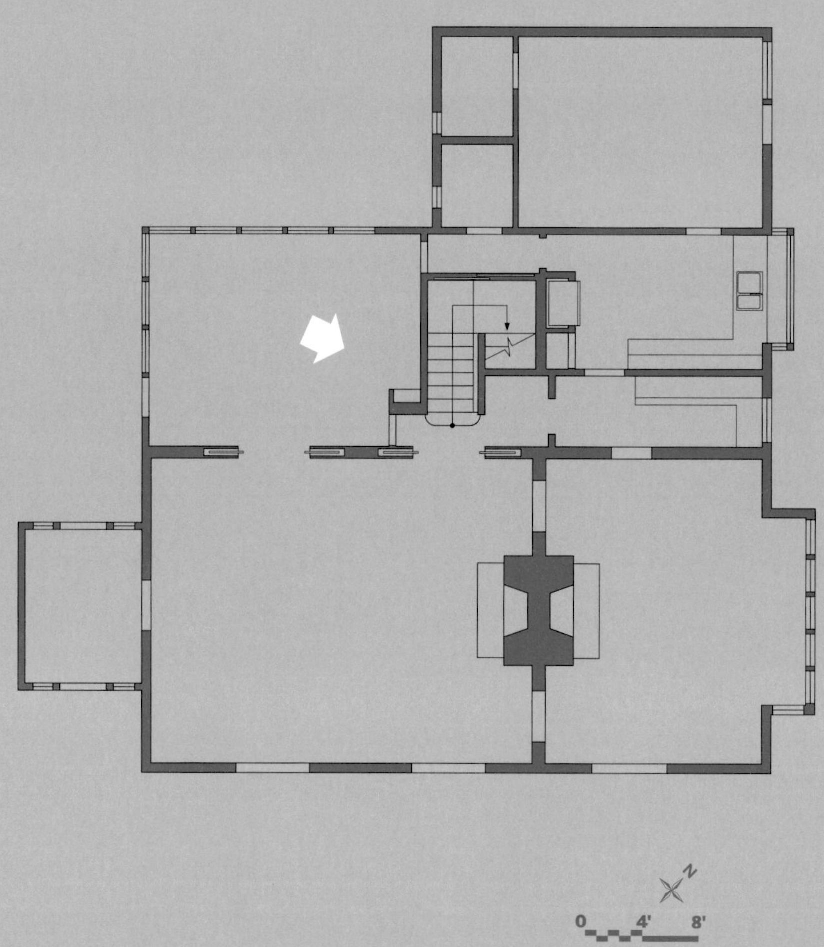

FRED R. DAPPRICH

CA. 1944

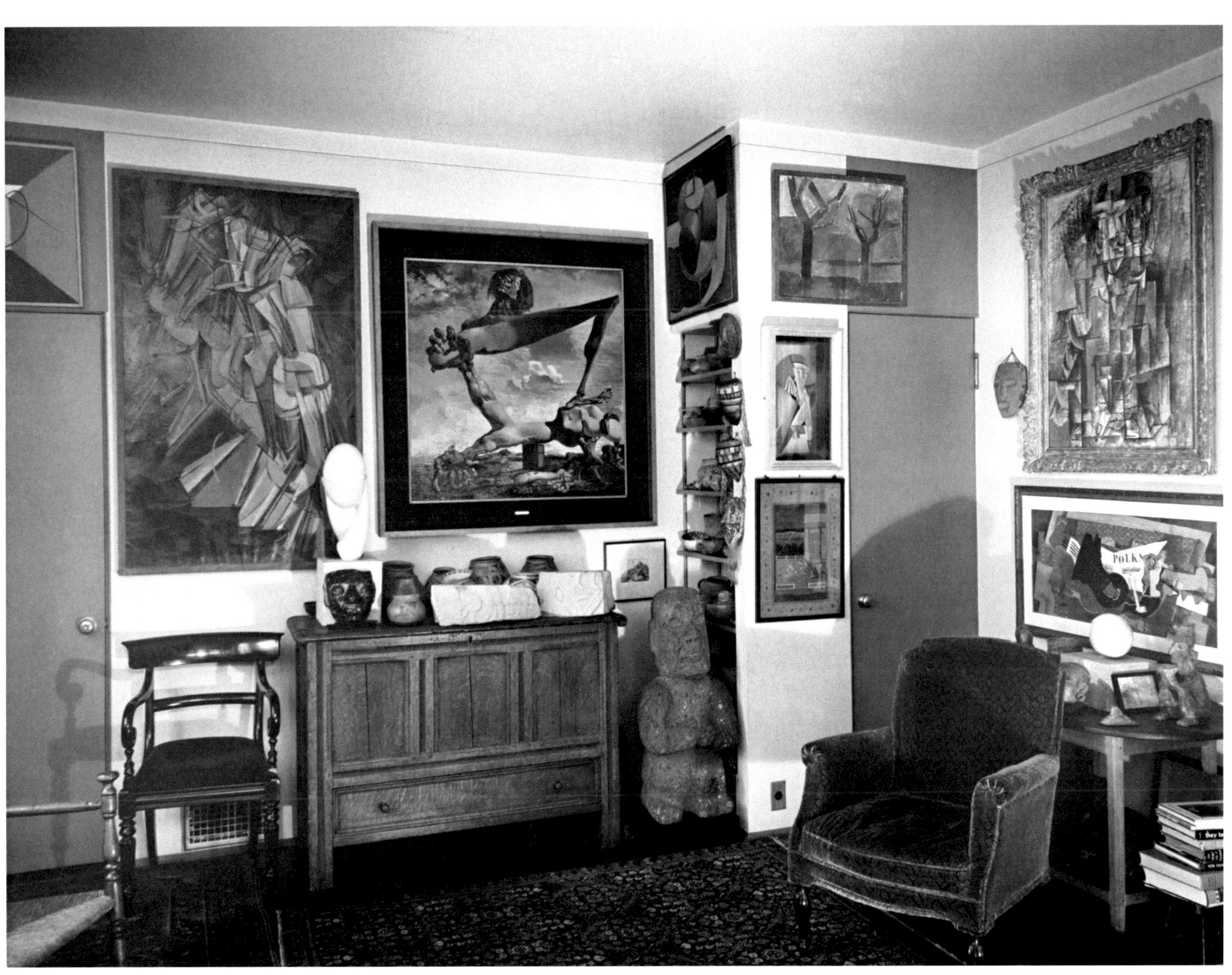
POLKA

PLATE 30

1 JACQUES VILLON (GASTON DUCHAMP), *Abstraction*, 1932 [1950-134-191; AC20-196]

2 MARCEL DUCHAMP, *Nude Descending a Staircase (No. 2)*, 1912 [1950-134-59; AC20-64]

3 CONSTANTIN BRANCUSI, *Mademoiselle Pogany [III]*, with one part of its base, 1931 [1950-134-21; AC20-21]

4 TEOTIHUACAN (CENTRAL MEXICO), Mask, 1st–9th century [1950-134-395]

5 SALVADOR DALÍ, *Soft Construction with Boiled Beans (Premonition of Civil War)*, 1936 [1950-134-41; AC20-40]

6–13 CASAS GRANDES (NORTHERN MEXICO OR SOUTHWESTERN UNITED STATES), Pots, 300–1500 [6: 1950-134-551; 7: 1950-134-549; 8: 1950-134-550; 9: 1950-134-548; 10: 1950-134-258; 11: 1950-134-600; 12: 1950-134-552; 13: 1950-134-257]

14, 15 CLASSIC VERACRUZ (EAST COAST MEXICO), Column Drum Fragments, 800–1300 [14: 1950-134-302, ACPS-122; 15: 1950-134-303, ACPS-123]

16 REPRODUCTION OF ALBRECHT DÜRER'S ENGRAVING *Saint Anthony the Hermit* (1519), Date unknown [PMA-WLA, BOX 72, FOLDER 6]

17 MARCEL DUCHAMP, *Chocolate Grinder (No. 1)*, 1913 [1950-134-69; AC20-74]

18 IÑUPIAQ (NORTH COAST ALASKA), Mask, Late 19th–early 20th century [NOTE 4.3, PAGES 416–17]

19, 20 NATIVE AMERICAN, Masks, Dates unknown [19: 1950-134-430; 20: 1950-134-431]

21 PIMA (ARIZONA), Mask, Date unknown [1950-134-433]

22 OLMEC (MEXICO), Figure of a Man, 1200–600 BCE [1950-134-338; ACPS-1]

23 PABLO PICASSO, *Two Trees*, 1907–8 [1950-134-163; AC20-167]

24 ALEXANDER ARCHIPENKO, *The Bather*, 1915 [1950-134-1; AC20-1]

25 ARTIST/MAKER UNKNOWN (INDIA, *DELHI), *Woman Reading on a Terrace*, Late 18th century [1950-134-856]

26 MEZCALA (SOUTHWESTERN MEXICO), Mask, 300 BCE–500 CE [1950-134-261; ACPS-94]

27 PABLO PICASSO, *Man with a Violin*, 1911–12 [1950-134-168; AC20-171]

28 GEORGES BRAQUE, *Guitar and Pipe (Polka)*, 1920–21 [1950-134-30; AC20-29]

29 NAYARIT (WESTERN MEXICO), Vessel in the Form of a Human Figure, 100 BCE–300 CE [1950-134-280; ACPS-73]

30 MAYA (HONDURAS), Vessel, 650–1000 [1950-134-398; ACPS-168]

31 HUASTEC (EAST COAST MEXICO), Head, 1st–9th century [1950-134-355; ACPS-121]

32 CONSTANTIN BRANCUSI, *Newborn [I]*, 1915 [1950-134-10; AC20-9]

33 MEZCALA (SOUTHWESTERN MEXICO), Mask, 300 BCE–500 CE [1950-134-380; ACPS-93]

34 KNUD MERRILD, *Abstraction*, 10 October 1935 [PMA-WLA, BOX 72, FOLDER 9]

35 COLIMA (WESTERN MEXICO), Vessel in the Form of a Seated Man, 300 BCE–300 CE [1950-134-379; ACPS-63]

*36 JOSEPH STELLA, *Landscape*, 1914 [1950-134-518]

37 NATIVE AMERICAN (SOUTHWESTERN UNITED STATES), Jar, Date unknown [1950-134-740]

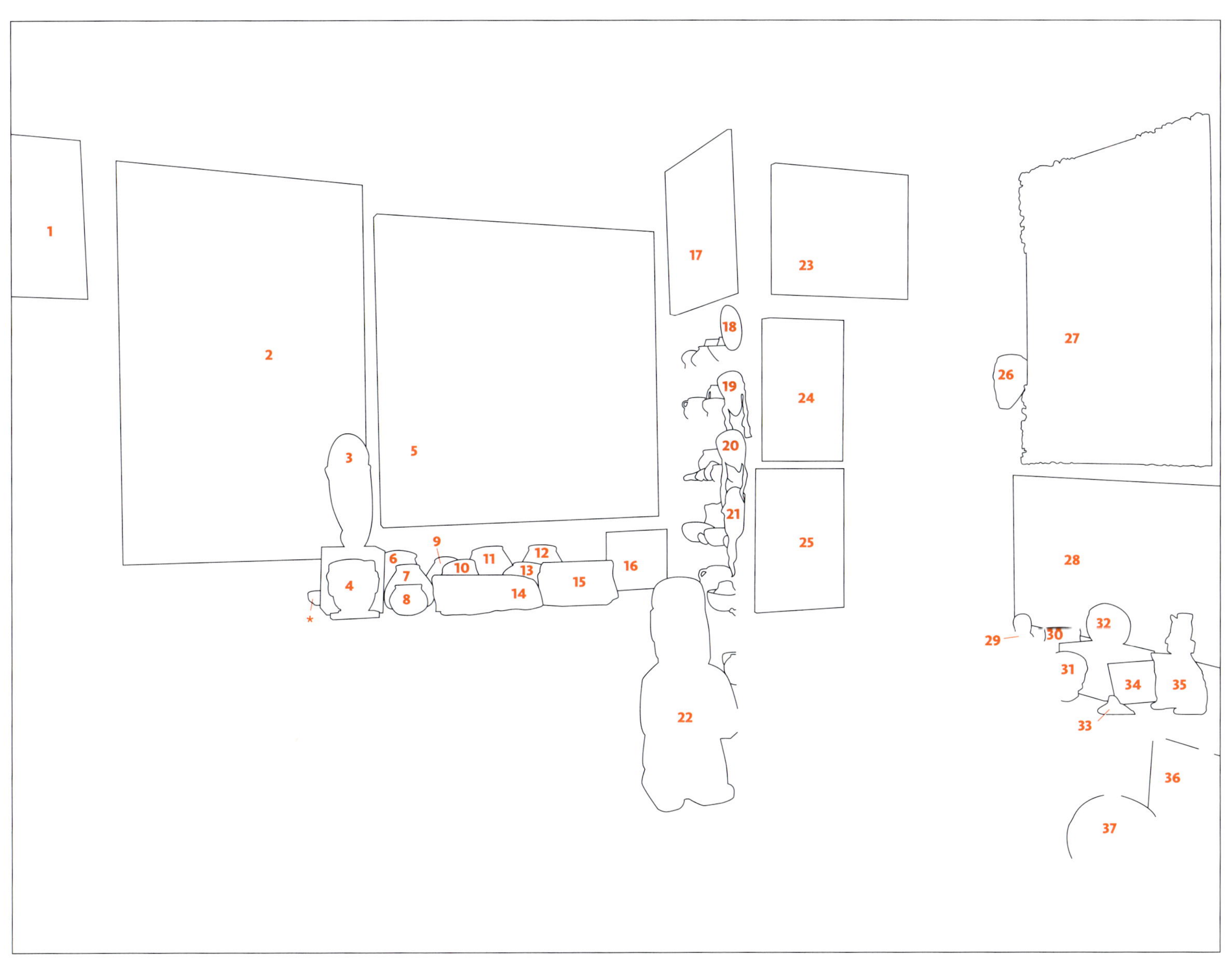
1
2
3
4
*
5
6
7
8
9
10
11
12
13
14
15
16
17
18
19
20
21
22
23
24
25
26
27
28
29
30
31
32
33
34
35
36
37

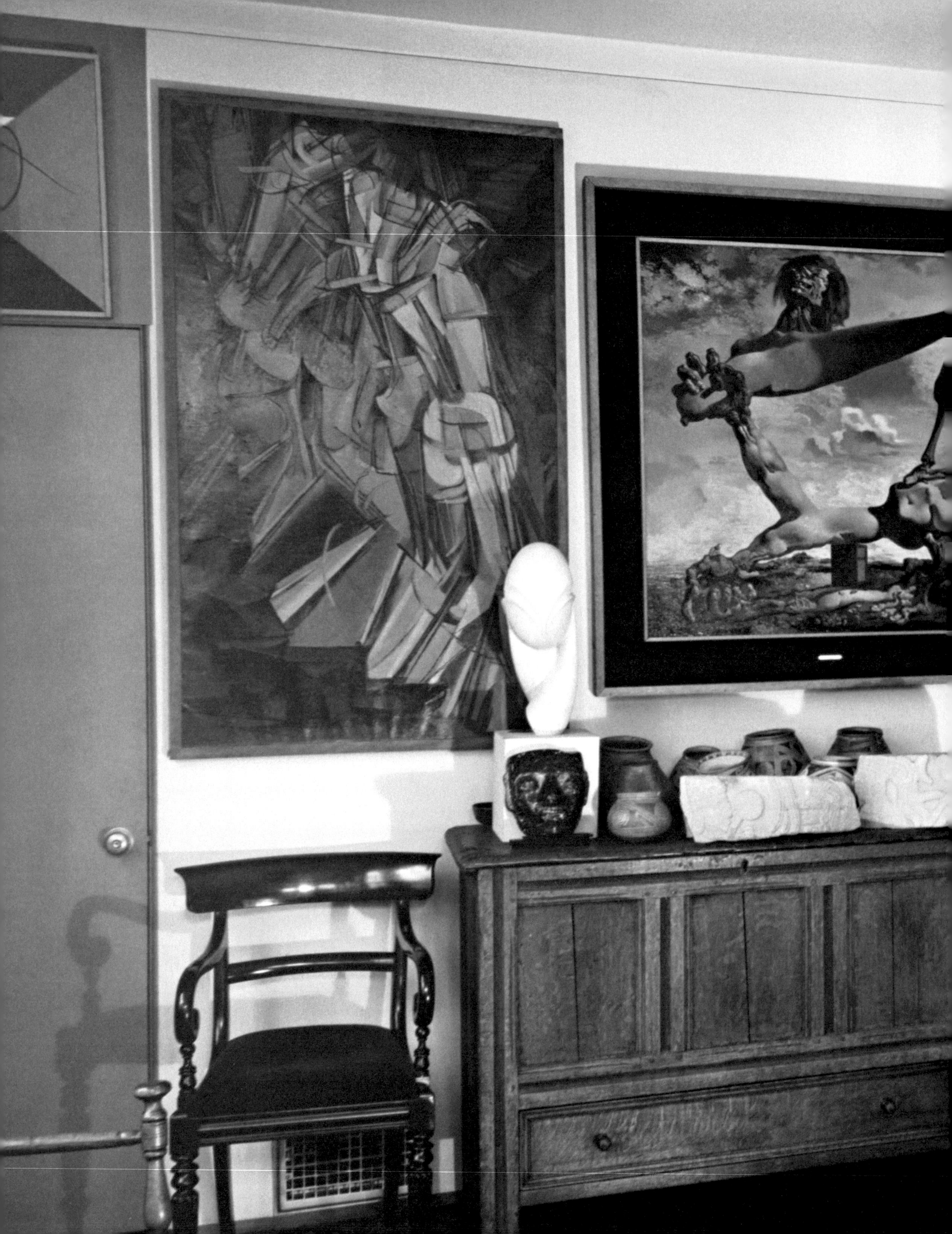

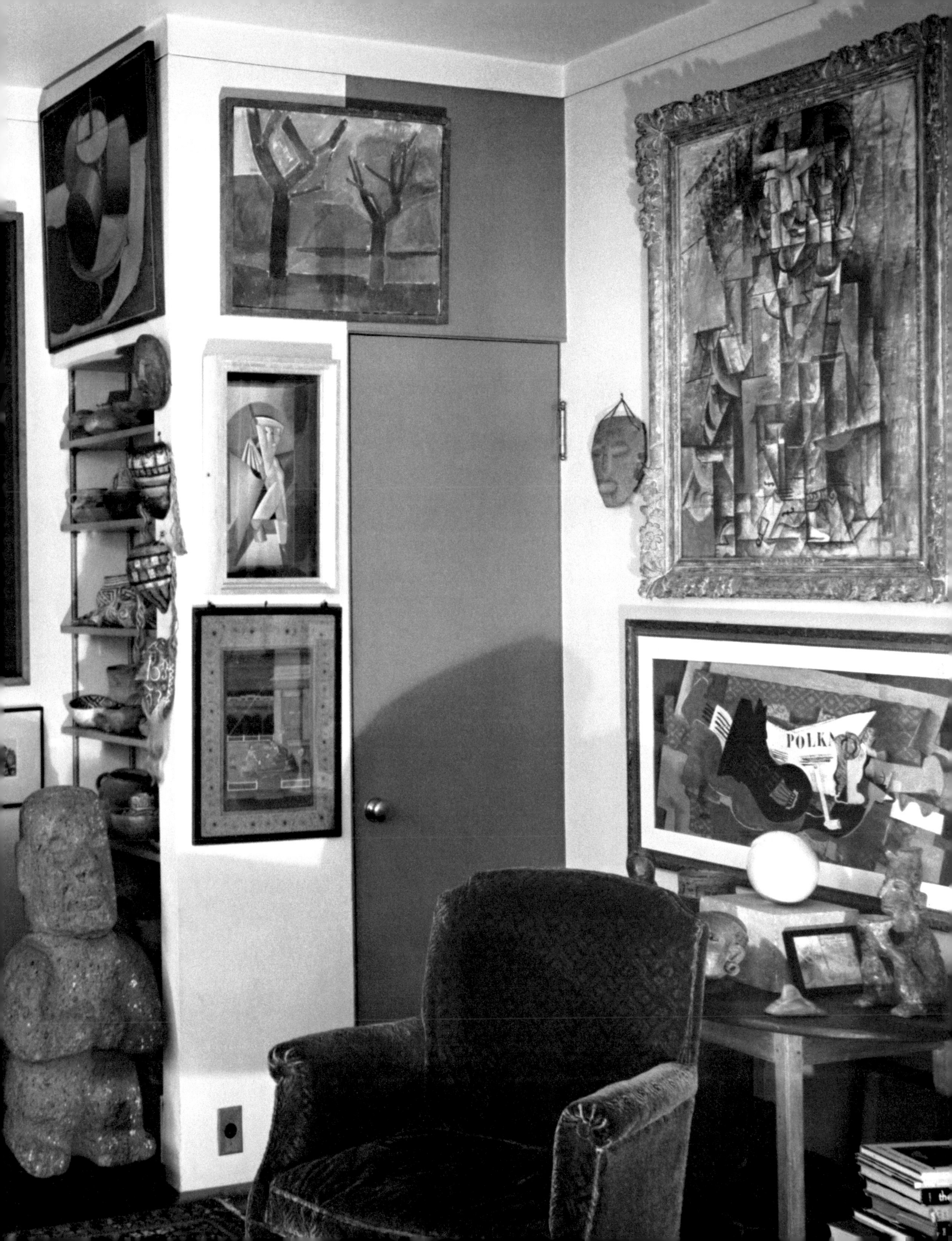
POLKA

PLATE 31

SUNROOM (GALLERY ROOM)

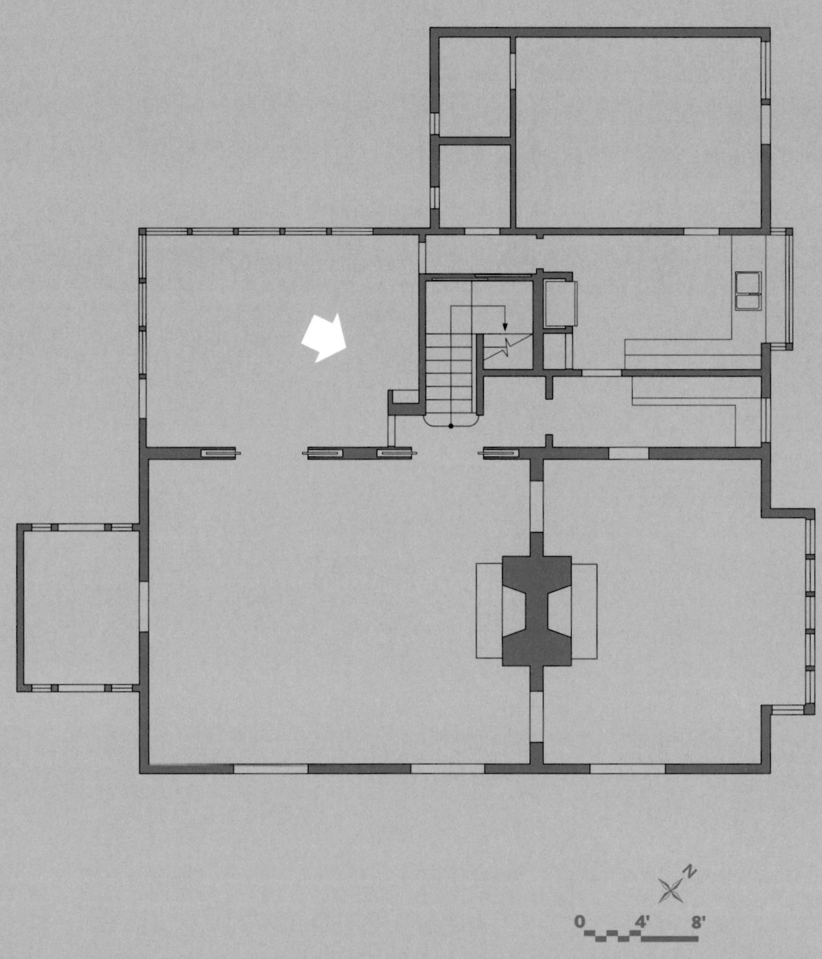

FLOYD FAXON

CA. JANUARY 1951

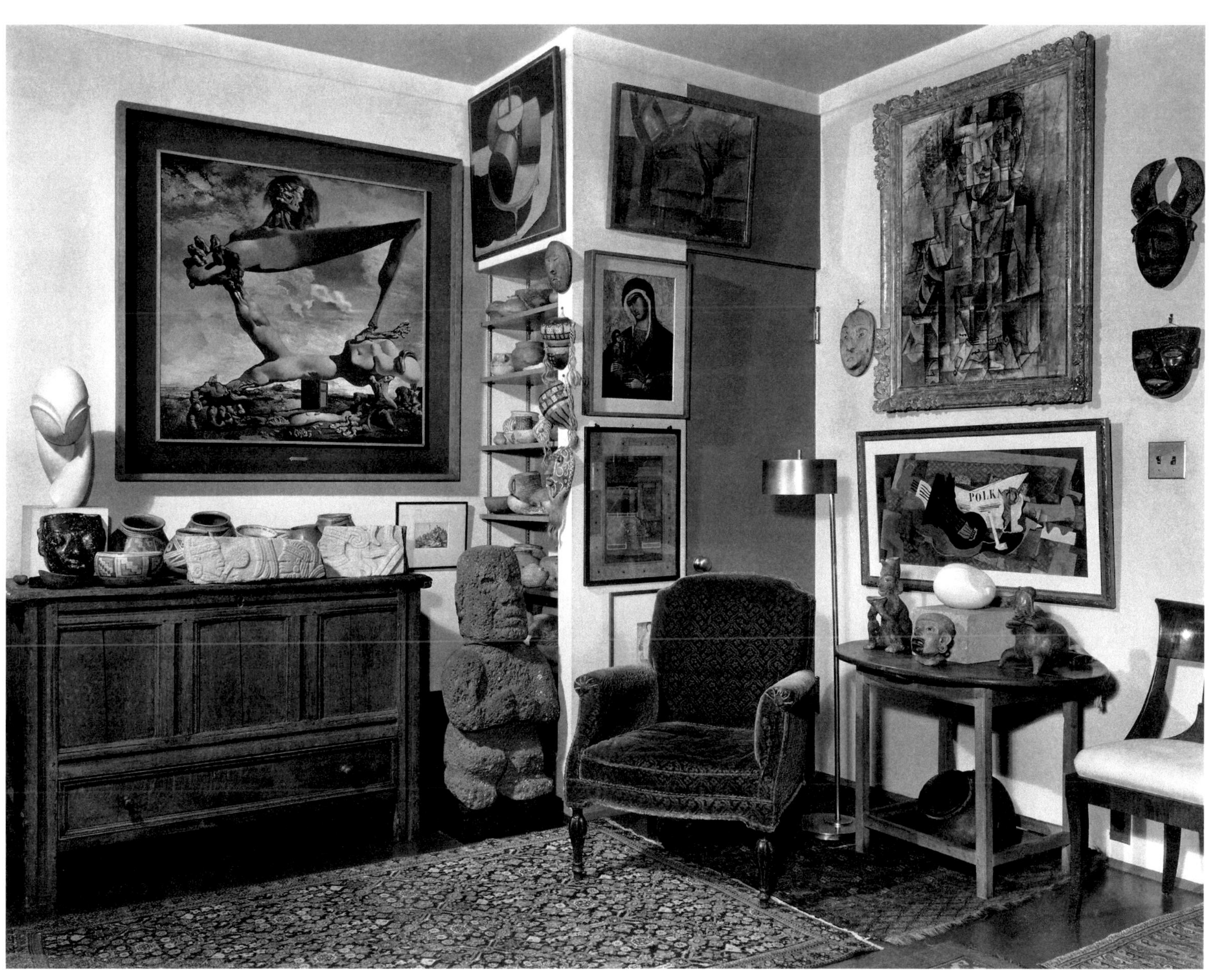

PLATE 31

1 SALVADOR DALÍ, *Soft Construction with Boiled Beans (Premonition of Civil War)*, 1936 [1950-134-41; AC20-40]

2 CONSTANTIN BRANCUSI, *Mademoiselle Pogany [III]*, with one part of its base, 1931 [1950-134-21; AC20-21]

3 TEOTIHUACAN (CENTRAL MEXICO), Mask, 1st–9th century [1950-134-395]

*4 NATIVE AMERICAN (SOUTHWESTERN UNITED STATES), Bowl, Date unknown [1950-134-730]

5–12 CASAS GRANDES (NORTHERN MEXICO OR SOUTHWESTERN UNITED STATES), Pots, 300–1500

[5: 1950-134-553; 6: 1950-134-551; 7: 1950-134-548; 8: 1950-134-600; 9: 1950-134-258; 10: 1950-134-257; 11: 1950-134-549; 12: 1950-134-552]

13, 14 CLASSIC VERACRUZ (EAST COAST MEXICO), Column Drum Fragments, 800–1300 [13: 1950-134-302, ACPS-122; 14: 1950-134-303, ACPS-123]

15 REPRODUCTION OF ALBRECHT DÜRER'S ENGRAVING *Saint Anthony the Hermit* (1519), Date unknown [PMA-WLA, BOX 72, FOLDER 6]

16 MARCEL DUCHAMP, *Chocolate Grinder (No. 1)*, 1913 [1950-134-69; AC20-74]

17 IÑUPIAQ (NORTH COAST ALASKA), Mask, Late 19th–early 20th century [NOTE 4.3, PAGES 416–17]

18–39 SEE DETAIL PAGES 216–17

40 OLMEC (MEXICO), Figure of a Man, 1200–600 BCE [1950-134-338; ACPS-1]

41 PABLO PICASSO, *Two Trees*, 1907–8 [1950-134-163; AC20-167]

42 ARTIST/MAKER UNKNOWN (ITALY), *Virgin and Child*, ca. 1340–60 [1950-134-195]

43 ARTIST/MAKER UNKNOWN (INDIA, *DELHI), *Woman Reading on a Terrace*, Late 18th century [1950-134-856]

44 ANDRÉ DERAIN, *Nude*, ca. 1909 [1950-134-46; AC20-46]

45 NATIVE AMERICAN (SOUTH ALASKA, KUSKOKWIN REGION), Mask, Date unknown [1950-134-489]

46 PABLO PICASSO, *Man with a Violin*, 1911–12 [1950-134-168; AC20-171]

47 GEORGES BRAQUE, *Guitar and Pipe (Polka)*, 1920–21 [1950-134-30; AC20-29]

48 COLIMA (WESTERN MEXICO), Vessel in the Form of a Seated Man, 300 BCE–300 CE [1950-134-379; ACPS-63]

49 HUASTEC (EAST COAST MEXICO), Head, 1st–9th century [1950-134-355; ACPS-121]

50 CONSTANTIN BRANCUSI, *Newborn [I]*, 1915 [1950-134-10; AC20-9]

51 NAYARIT (WESTERN MEXICO), Vessel in the Form of a Human Figure, 100 BCE–300 CE [1950-134-280; ACPS-73]

52 NATIVE AMERICAN, Pipe, Date unknown [1950-134-640]

53 NATIVE AMERICAN (SOUTHWESTERN UNITED STATES), Jar, Date unknown [1950-134-740]

54 FANG (GABON), Mask, Date unknown [1950-134-201]

55 TEOTIHUACAN (CENTRAL MEXICO), Mask, 1st–9th century [1950-134-314; ACPS-16]

THIS IMAGE IS NOTABLE FOR THE ABSENCE OF *NUDE DESCENDING A STAIRCASE (NO. 2)* (COMPARE TO PLATE 30). ON 14 OCTOBER 1950, THE ARENSBERGS LOANED THE PAINTING TO THE PHILADELPHIA MUSEUM OF ART, AT FISKE KIMBALL'S REQUEST, FOR *DIAMOND JUBILEE EXHIBITION: MASTERPIECES OF PAINTING*, WHICH WAS ON VIEW FROM 4 NOVEMBER 1950 TO 11 FEBRUARY 1951. THE WORK DID NOT RETURN TO CALIFORNIA. ACCIDENTALLY, AND APPROPRIATELY, IT BECAME THE FIRST PAINTING GIVEN OVER TO THE MUSEUM AS PART OF THE ARENSBERGS' BEQUEST OF 27 DECEMBER 1950. SEE PMA-WLA, BOX 24, AIN 706

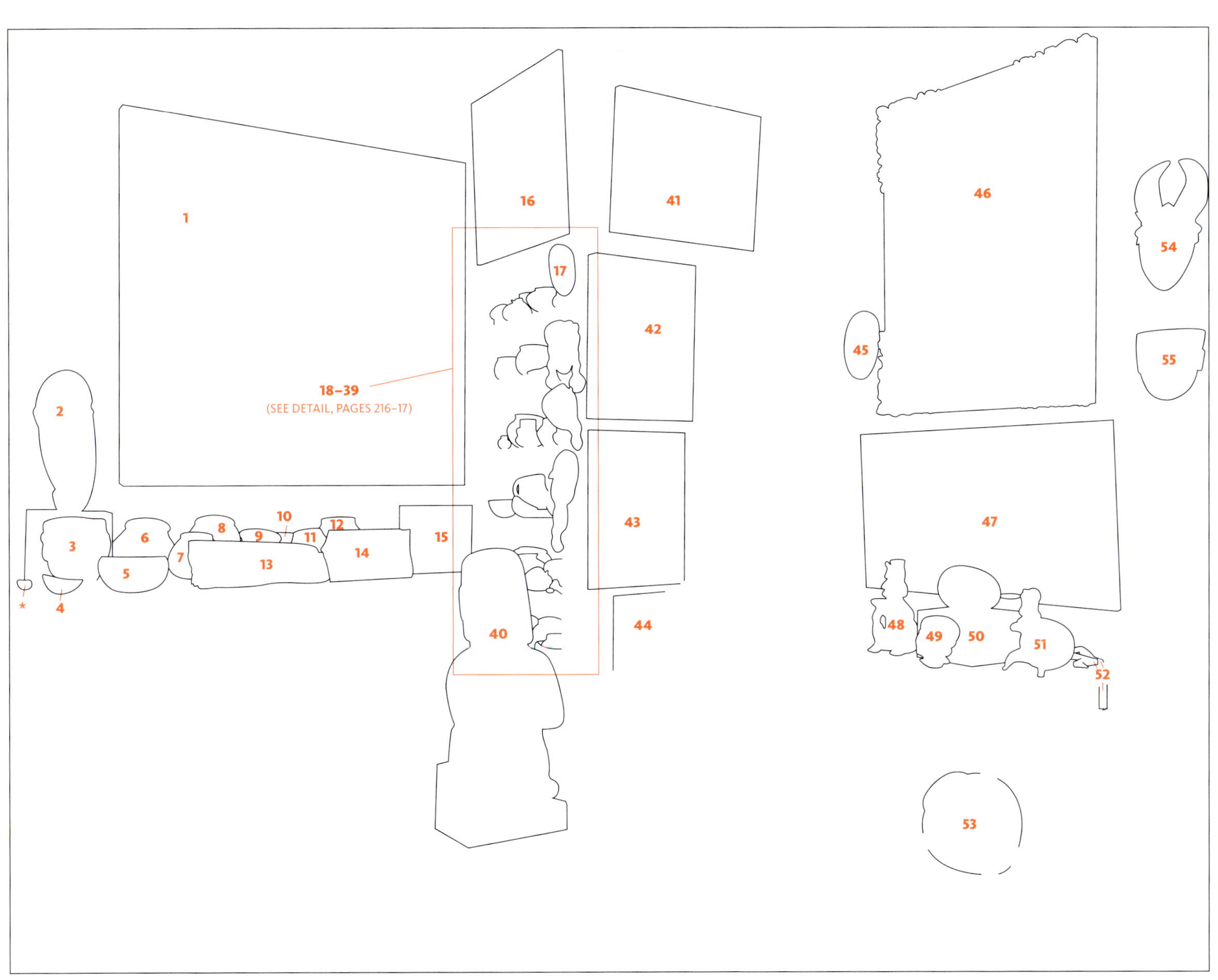
1
2
3
4
*
5
6
7
8
9
10
11
12
13
14
15
16
17
18–39
(SEE DETAIL, PAGES 216–17)
40
41
42
43
44
45
46
47
48
49
50
51
52
53
54
55

PLATE 31 (DETAIL)

18–22 NATIVE AMERICAN (SOUTHWESTERN UNITED STATES), Dates unknown

18: Vessel or Jar [1950-134-670] / 19: Pitcher [1950-134-712] / 20: Jar [1950-134-704]

21: Pitcher [1950-134-713] / 22: Vessel [1950-134-643]

23, 24 NATIVE AMERICAN, Masks, Dates unknown [23: 1950-134-430; 24: 1950-134-431]

25–32 NATIVE AMERICAN (SOUTHWESTERN UNITED STATES), Dates unknown

25: Jar [*1950-134-678] / 26: Jar [1950-134-428] / 27: Jug [1950-134-722] / 28: Jug [1950-134-692] / 29: Bowl [1950-134-716]

30: Pitcher [1950-134-427] / 31: Bowl [1950-134-689] / 32: Ladle [1950-134-694]

33 PIMA (ARIZONA), Mask, Date unknown [1950-134-433]

34 PUEBLO (SOUTHWEST, UPPER GILA), Jug, Date unknown [1950-134-424]

35–37 NATIVE AMERICAN (SOUTHWESTERN UNITED STATES), Dates unknown

35: Jar [1950-134-726] / 36: Jar [*1950-134-703] / 37: Vessel or Jug [1950-134-661]

38 CASAS GRANDES (NORTHERN MEXICO OR SOUTHWESTERN UNITED STATES), Pot, 300–1500 [1950-134-550]

39 NATIVE AMERICAN (SOUTHWESTERN UNITED STATES), Vessel, Date unknown [1950-134-666]

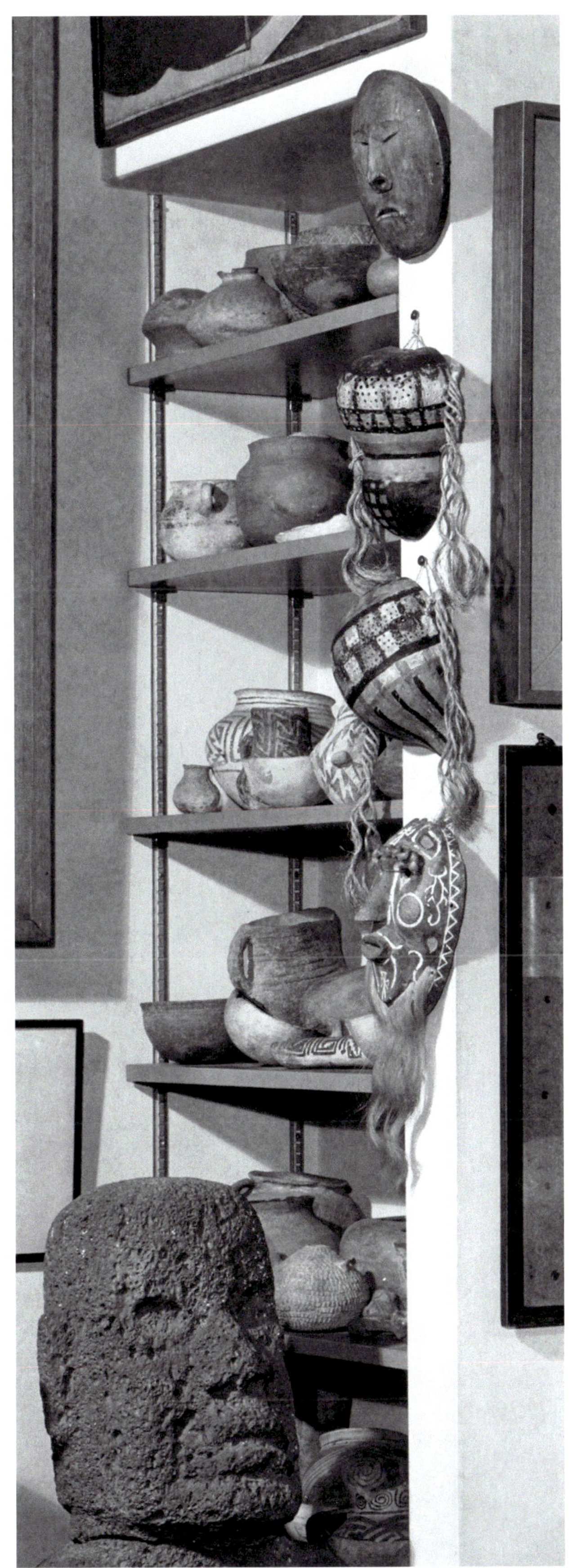

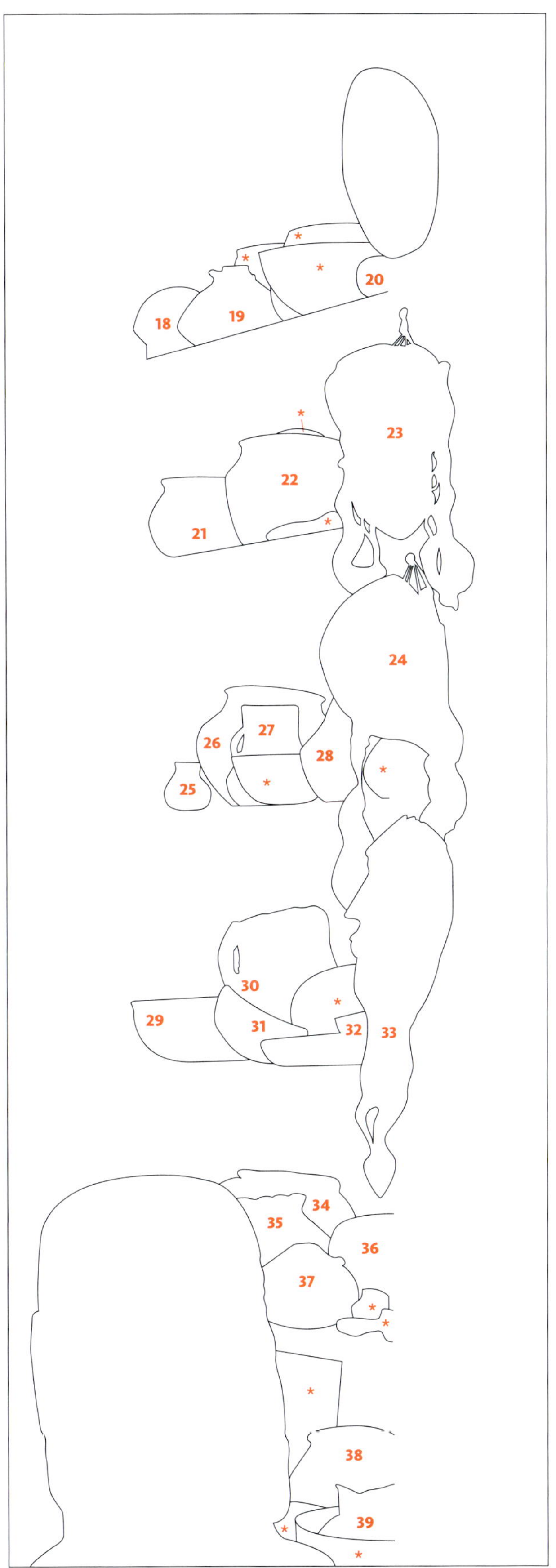
*
*
*
18
19
20
*
23
22
21
*
24
27
26
28
*
25
*
30
*
29
31
32
33
34
35
36
37
*
*
*
38
39
*
*

PLATE 32

SUNROOM (GALLERY ROOM)

WITH A VIEW INTO THE LIVING ROOM

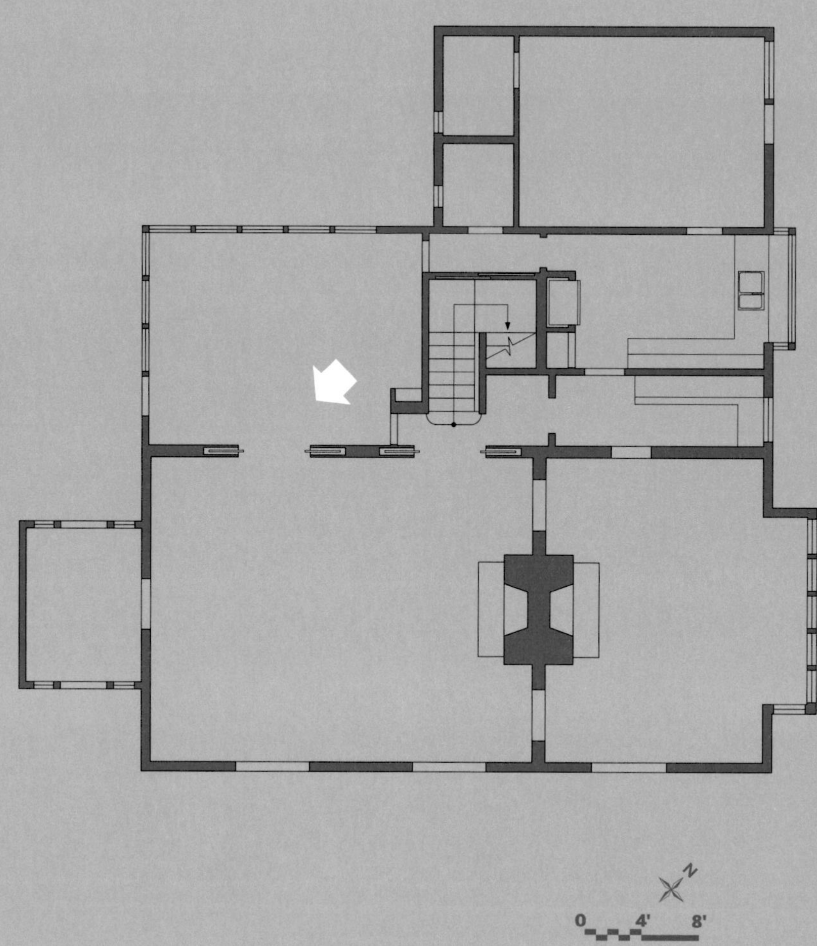

FRED R. DAPPRICH

CA. 1944

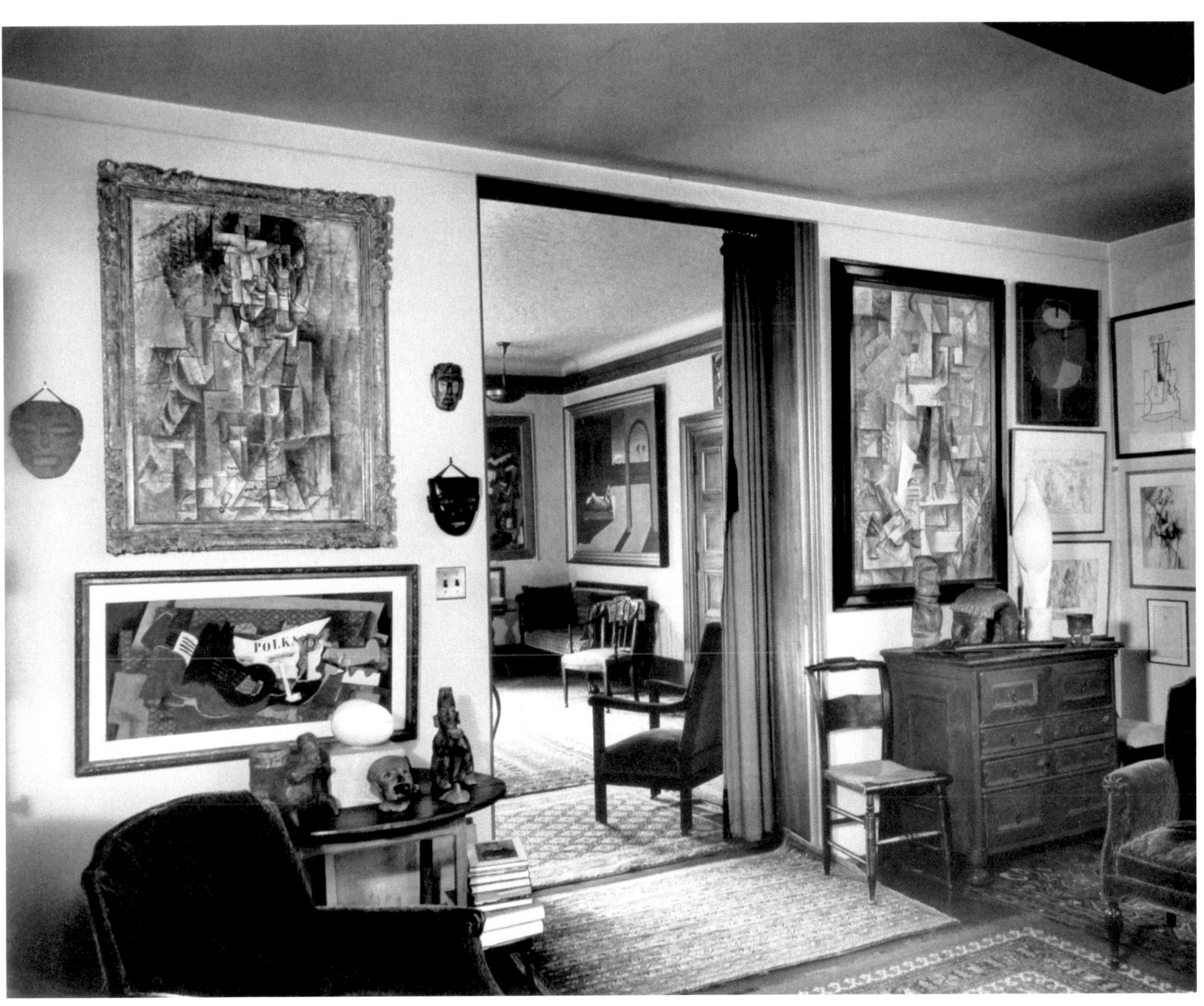
POLKA

PLATE 32

1 MEZCALA (SOUTHWESTERN MEXICO), Mask, 300 BCE–500 CE [1950-134-261; ACPS-94]

2 PABLO PICASSO, *Man with a Violin*, 1911–12 [1950-134-168; AC20-171]

3 GEORGES BRAQUE, *Guitar and Pipe (Polka)*, 1920–21 [1950-134-30; AC20-29]

4 MAYA (HONDURAS), Vessel, 650–1000 [1950-134-398; ACPS-168]

5 NAYARIT (WESTERN MEXICO), Vessel in the Form of a Human Figure, 100 BCE–300 CE [1950-134-280; ACPS-73]

6 CONSTANTIN BRANCUSI, *Newborn [I]*, 1915 [1950-134-10; AC20-9]

7 HUASTEC (EAST COAST MEXICO), Head, 1st–9th century [1950-134-355; ACPS-121]

8 COLIMA (WESTERN MEXICO), Vessel in the Form of a Seated Man, 300 BCE–300 CE [1950-134-379; ACPS-63]

9 MEZCALA (SOUTHWESTERN MEXICO), Mask, 300 BCE–500 CE [1950-134-380; ACPS-93]

10 JOSEPH STELLA, *Landscape*, 1914 [1950-134-518]

11 TEOTIHUACAN (CENTRAL MEXICO), Mask, 1st–9th century [1950-134-356; ACPS-89]

12 TEOTIHUACAN (CENTRAL MEXICO), Mask, 1st–9th century [1950-134-314; ACPS-16]

13 GEORGES BRAQUE, *The Table*, 1918 [1950-134-29B; AC20-28]

14 GIORGIO DE CHIRICO, *The Soothsayer's Recompense*, 1913 [1950-134-38; AC20-36]

15 JEAN METZINGER, *Landscape with Roofs*, ca. 1914 [1950-134-138; AC20-143]

16 PABLO PICASSO, *Man with a Guitar*, 1912 [1950-134-169; AC20-172]

17 ARTIST/MAKER UNKNOWN (EASTER ISLAND), Figure of a Man, Date unknown [1950-134-409]

18 ARTIST/MAKER UNKNOWN (NEW CALEDONIA), Club, Late 19th century [1950-134-495]

19 COLIMA (WESTERN MEXICO), Vessel in the Form of an Acrobat, 300 BCE–300 CE [1950-134-332; ACPS-64]

20 CONSTANTIN BRANCUSI, *Maiastra*, 1912 [1950-134-6; AC20-5]

21 MARCEL DUCHAMP, *Chocolate Grinder (No. 2)*, 1914 [1950-134-70; AC20-75]

22 PAUL CÉZANNE, *View of the Cathedral at Aix*, 1902–4 [1950-134-35; AC20-34]

23 PAUL CÉZANNE, *A Forest of Standing Timber*, ca. 1880–85 [1950-134-33; AC20-32]

24 TEOTIHUACAN (CENTRAL MEXICO), Tripod Vessel, 400–800 [1950-134-231; ACPS-54]

25 PABLO PICASSO, *Violin*, 1912 [1950-134-167; AC20-173]

26 MARCEL DUCHAMP, *Virgin (No. 2)*, 1912 [1950-134-64; AC20-70]

27 MARCEL DUCHAMP, *Once More to This Star*, 1911 [1950-134-57; AC20-62]

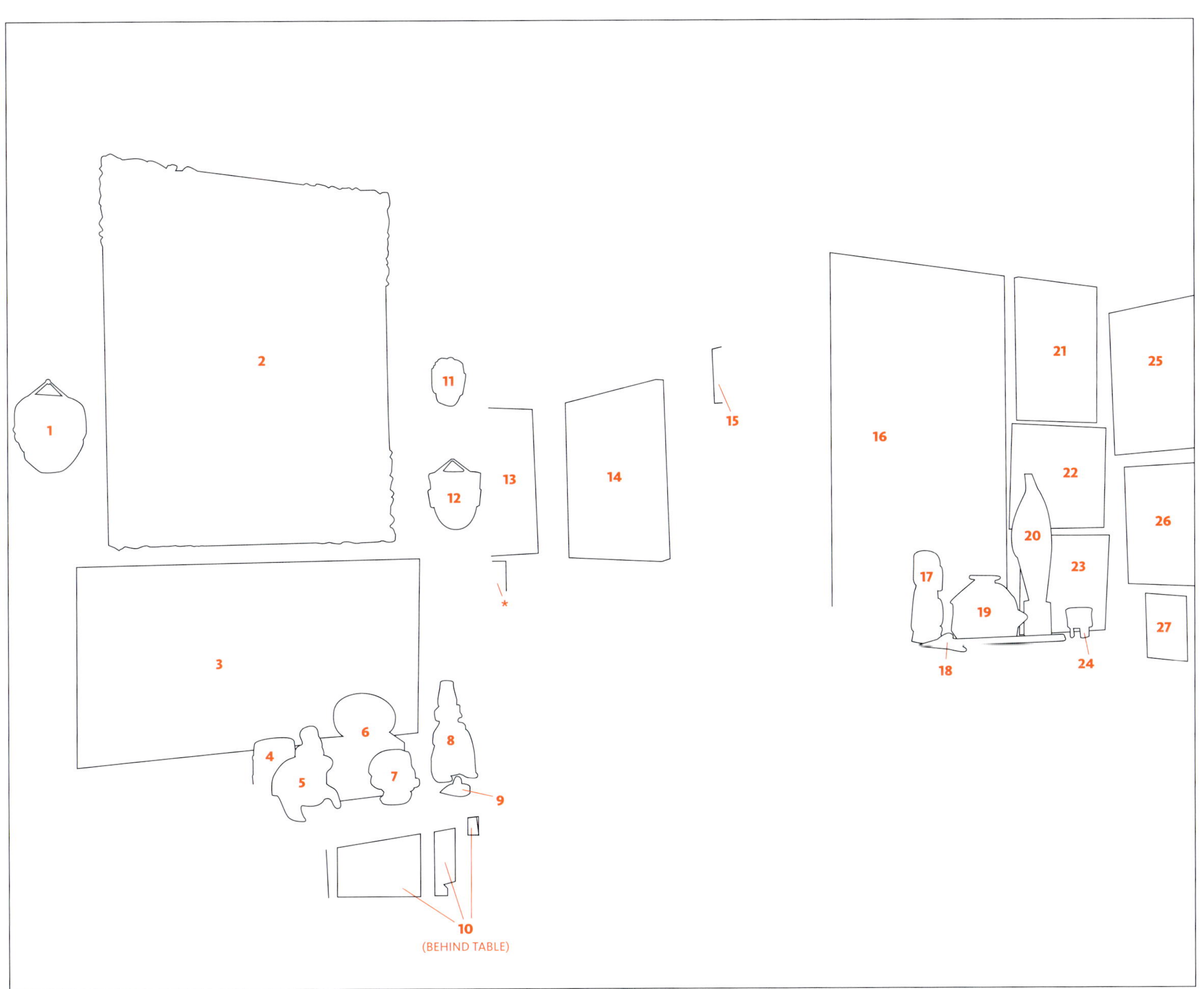
1
2
3
4
5
6
7
8
9
10
(BEHIND TABLE)
11
12
13
*
14
15
16
17
18
19
20
21
22
23
24
25
26
27

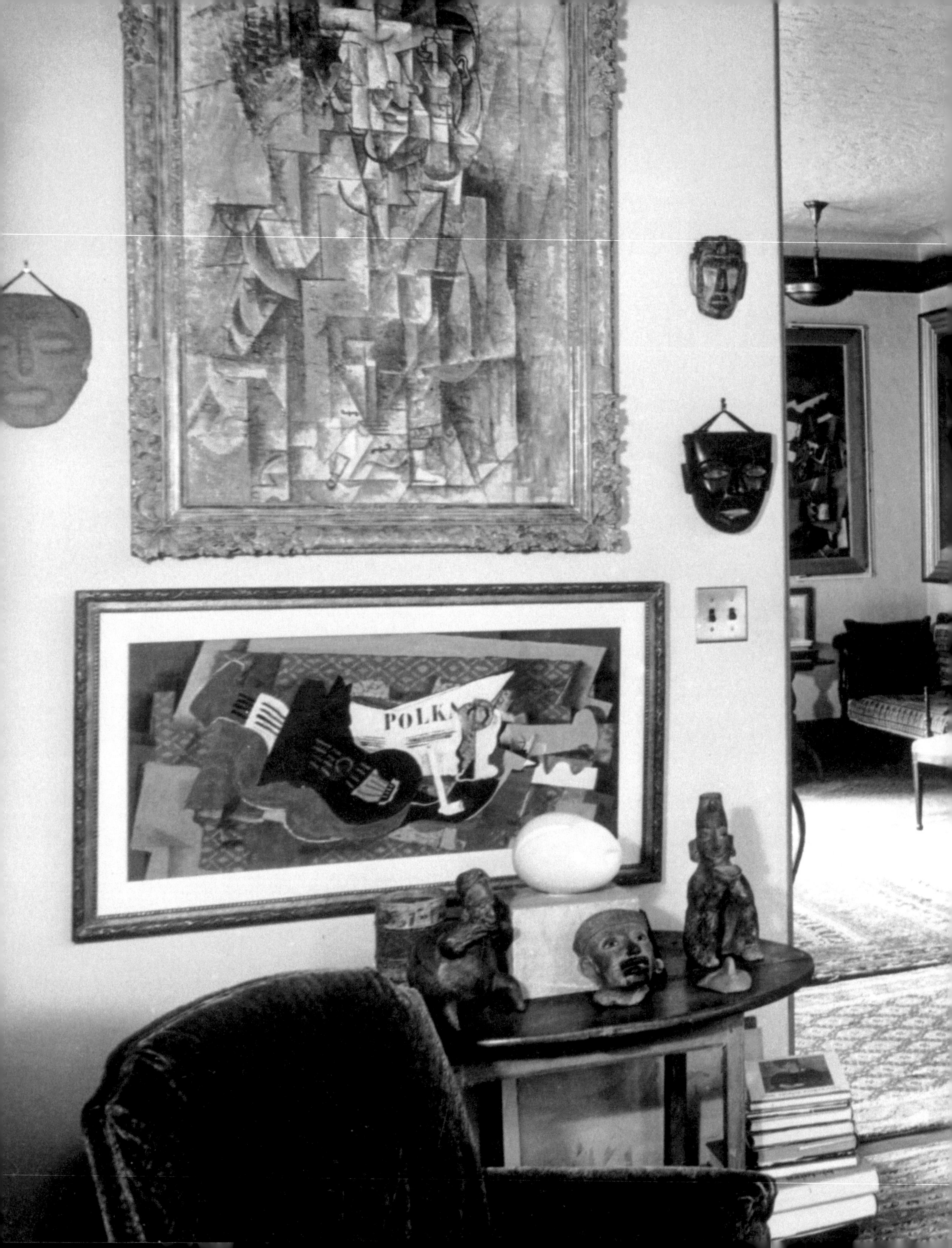
POLKA

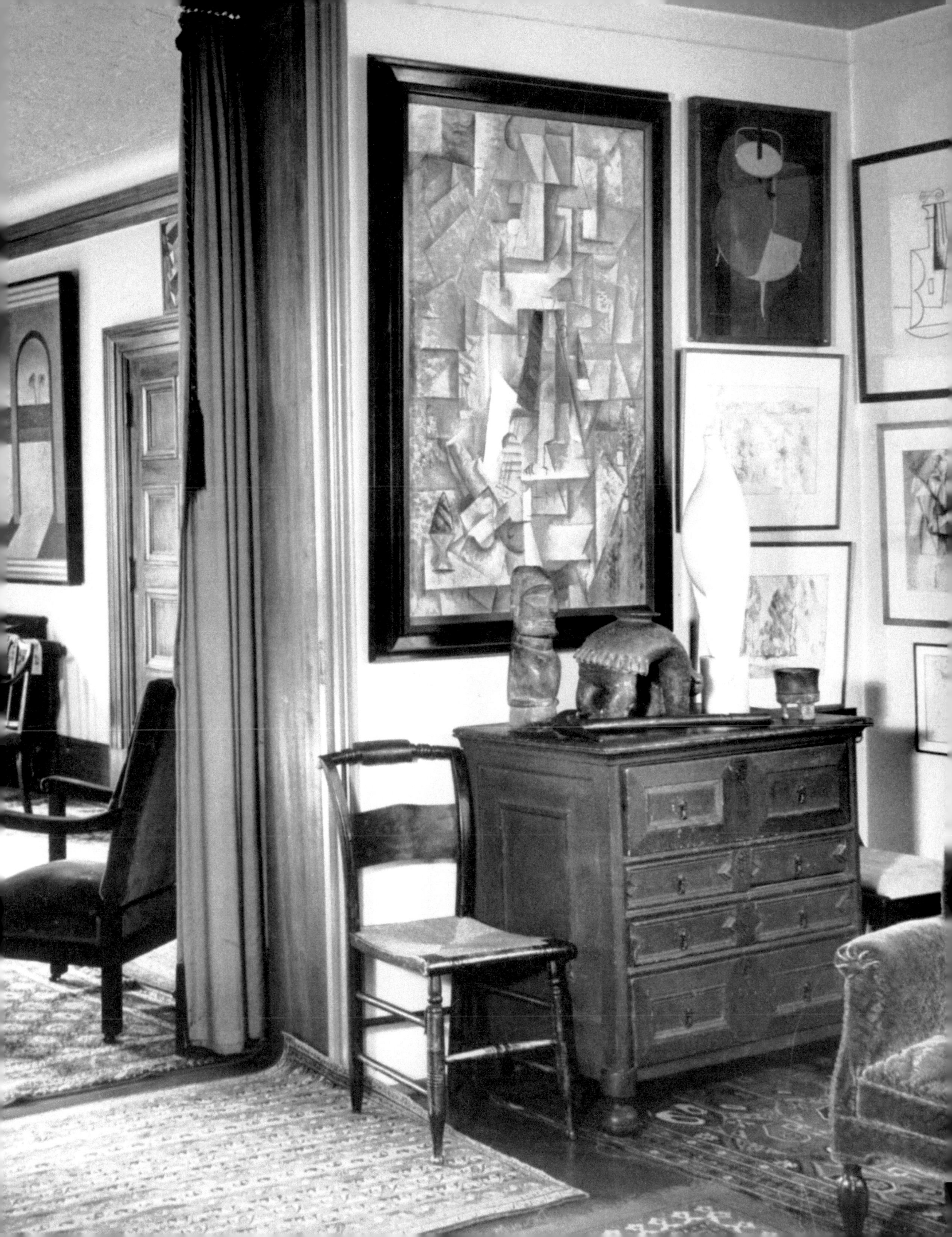

PLATE 33

SUNROOM (GALLERY ROOM)

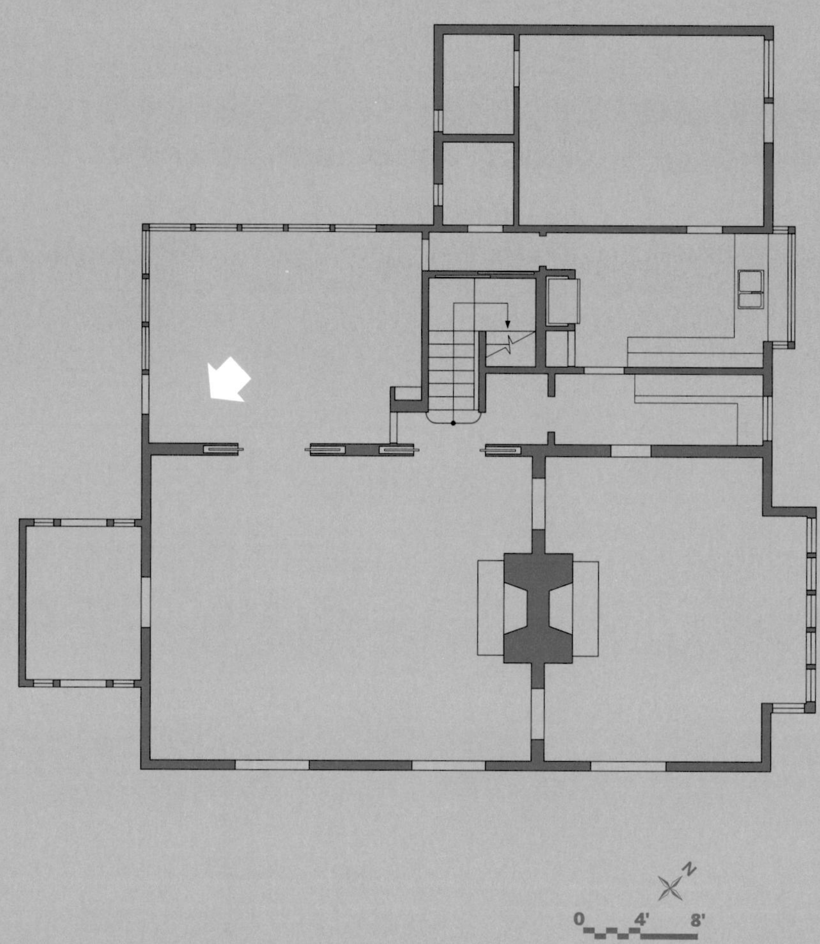

FLOYD FAXON

CA. JANUARY 1951

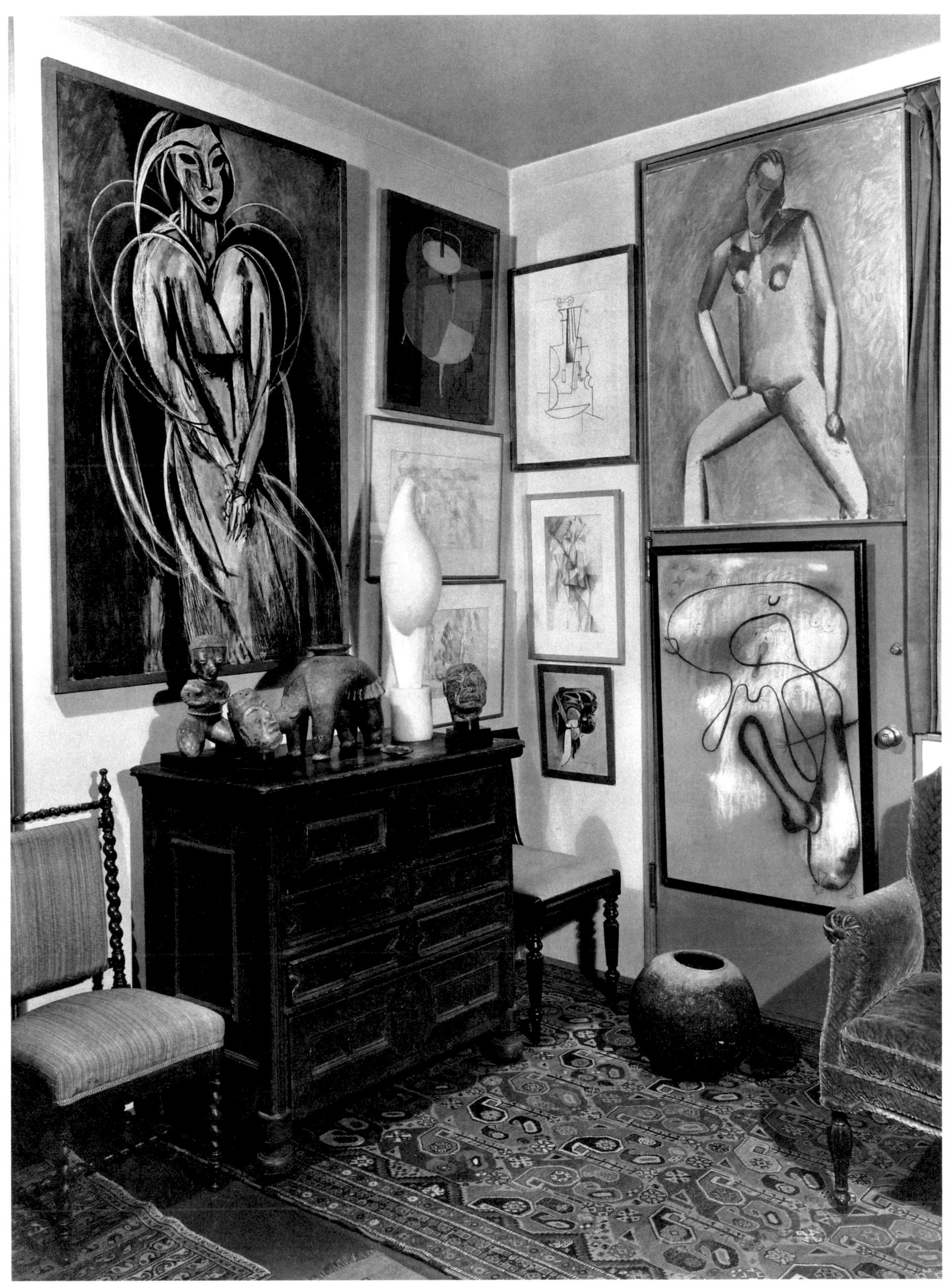

PLATE 33

1 HENRI MATISSE, *Mademoiselle Yvonne Landsberg*, 1914 [1950-134-130; AC20-133]

2 NAYARIT (WESTERN MEXICO), Figure of a Woman, 100 BCE–300 CE [1950-134-368; ACPS-74]

3 OLMEC (MEXICO), Head, 1200–600 BCE [1950-134-312; ACPS-124]

4 COLIMA (WESTERN MEXICO), Vessel in the Form of an Acrobat, 300 BCE–300 CE [1950-134-332; ACPS-64]

*5 ARTIST/MAKER UNKNOWN, Jade Dish, Date unknown [1950-134-855; SEE ALSO PMA-WLA, BOX 26, *AIN 657]

6 CONSTANTIN BRANCUSI, *Maiastra*, 1912 [1950-134-6; AC20-5]

7 MARCEL DUCHAMP, *Chocolate Grinder (No. 2)*, 1914 [1950-134-70; AC20-75]

8 PAUL CÉZANNE, *View of the Cathedral at Aix*, 1902–4 [1950-134-35; AC20-34]

9 PAUL CÉZANNE, *A Forest of Standing Timber*, ca. 1880–85 [1950-134-33; AC20-32]

10 OLMEC (MEXICO), Mask, 1200–400 BCE [1950-134-339; ACPS-86]

11 PABLO PICASSO, *Violin*, 1912 [1950-134-167; AC20-173]

12 MARCEL DUCHAMP, *Virgin (No. 2)*, 1912 [1950-134-64; AC20-70]

13 MORTON LIVINGSTON SCHAMBERG, *Painting IV (Mechanical Abstraction)*, 1916 [1950-134-180A; AC20-185]

14 PABLO PICASSO, *Seated Female Nude*, 1908–9 [1950-134-164; AC20-169]

15 JOAN MIRÓ, *The Lovers*, 1934 [1950-134-148; AC20-149]

16 CHUMASH (CALIFORNIA), Bowl, Date unknown [1950-134-476]

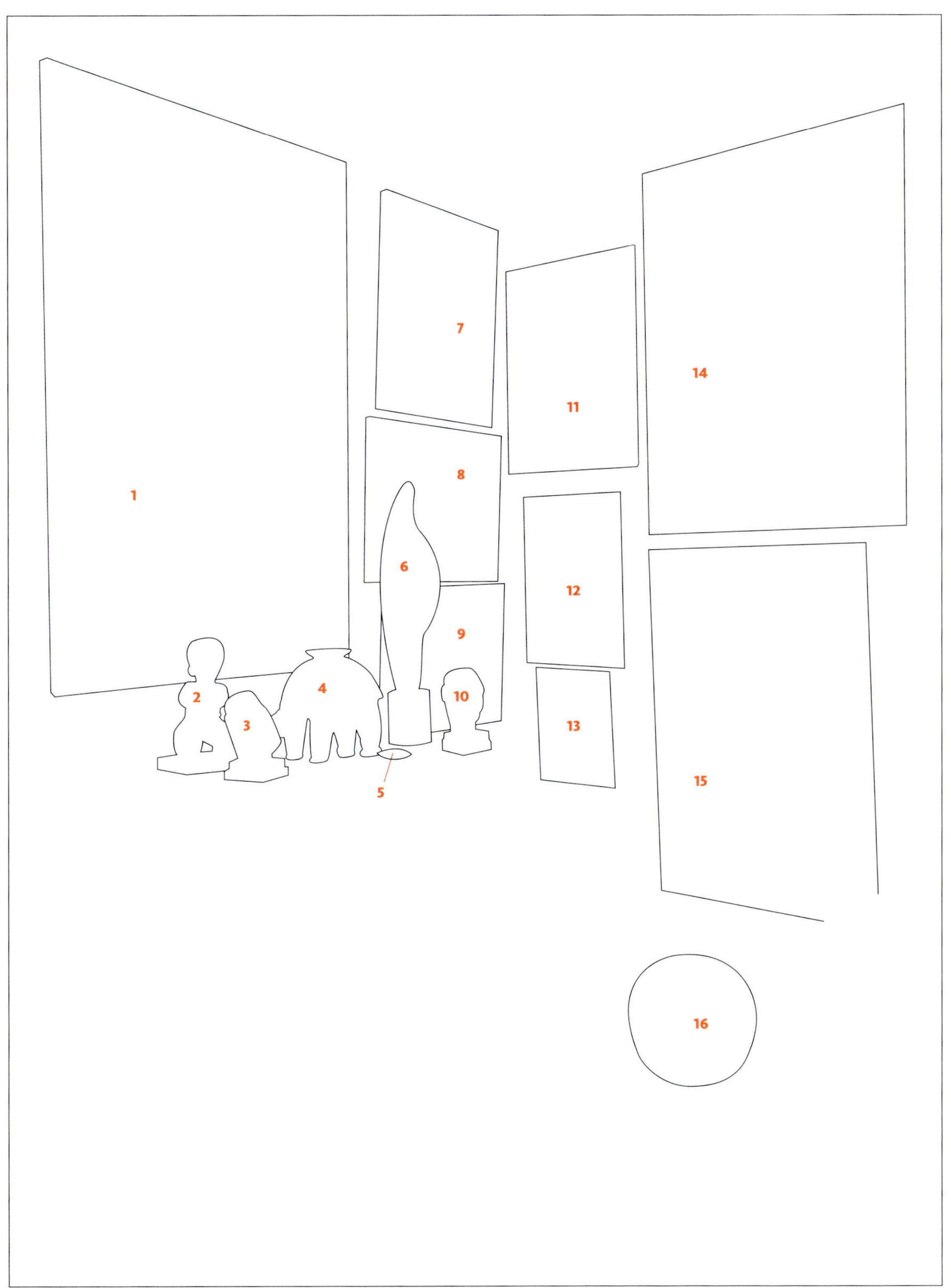
1
2
3
4
5
6
7
8
9
10
11
12
13
14
15
16

PLATE 34

LIVING ROOM

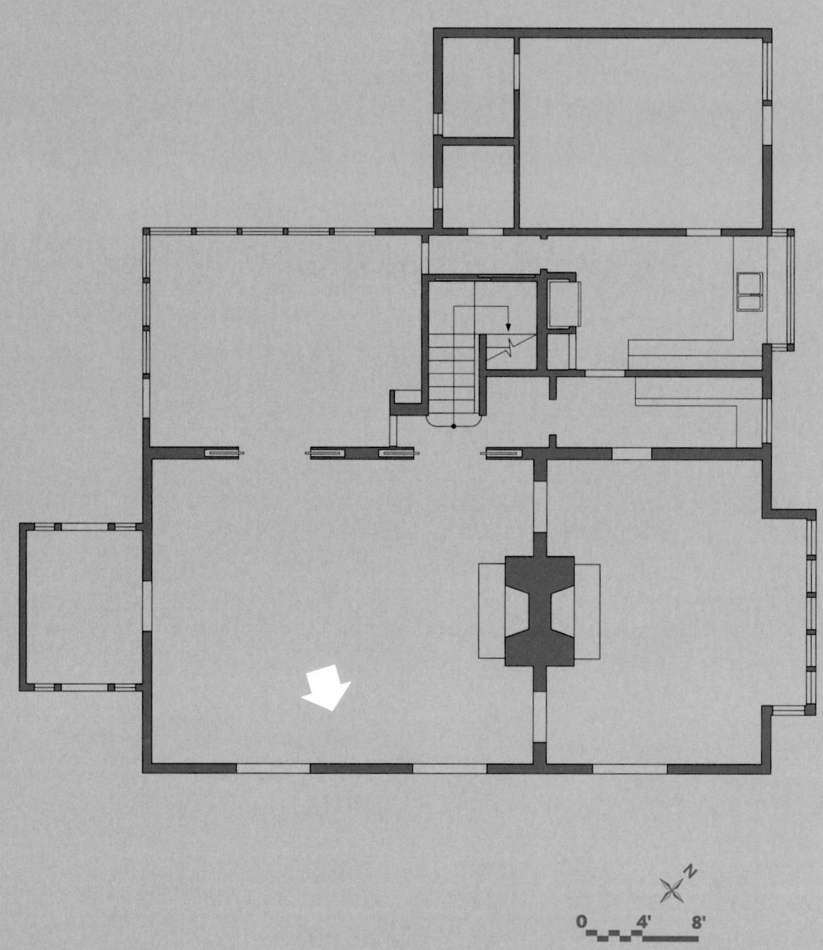

FRED R. DAPPRICH

CA. 1944

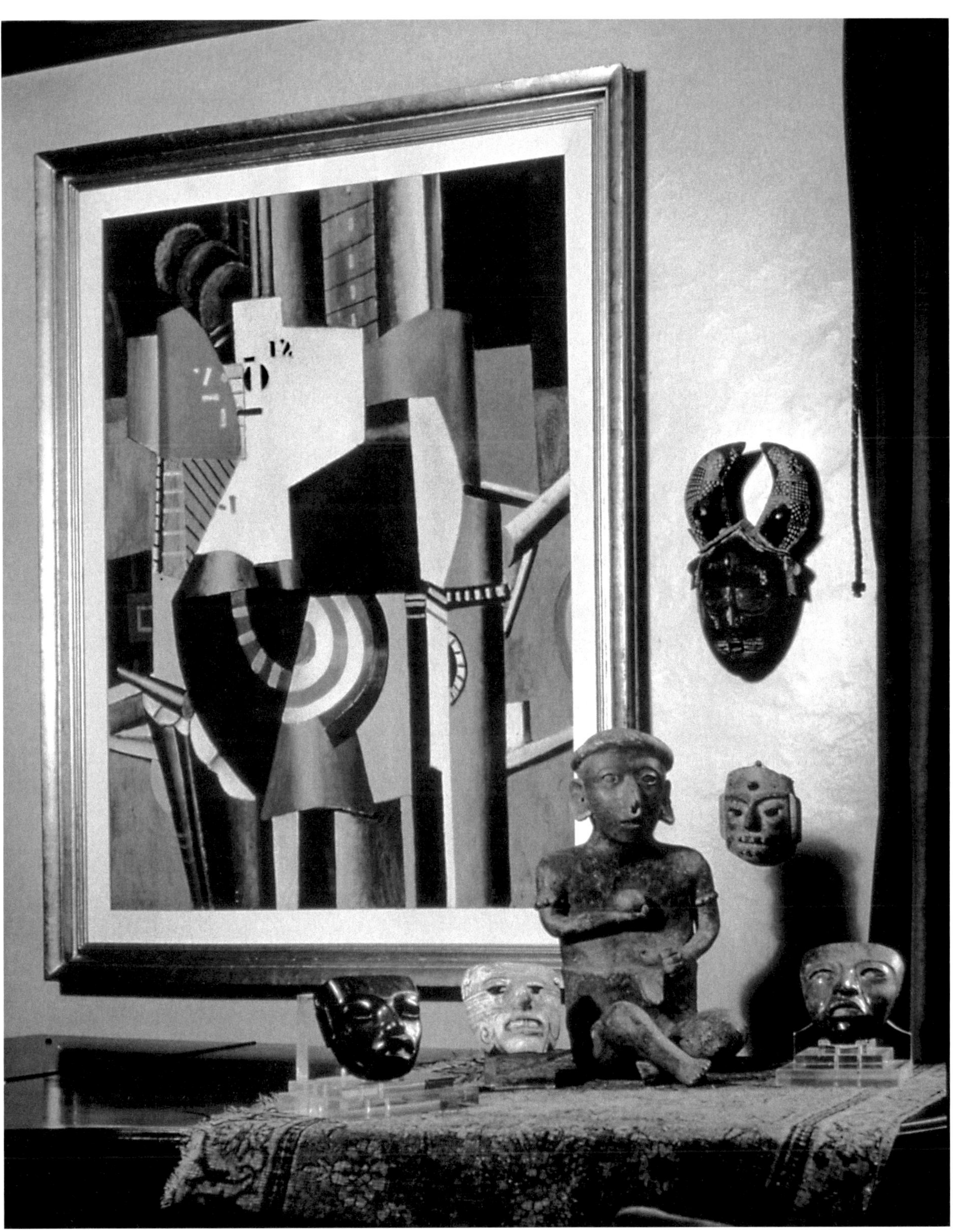

PLATE 34

1 FERNAND LÉGER, *The City (Fragment, Third State)*, 1919 [1950-134-124; AC20-127]

2 FANG (GABON), Mask, Date unknown [1950-134-201]

3 STEINWAY & SONS, Grand Piano, Date unknown [NOTE 1.6, PAGE 414]

4 TEOTIHUACAN (CENTRAL MEXICO), Mask, 1st–9th century [1950-134-249; ACPS-20]

5 MIXTEC (SOUTHEASTERN MEXICO), Mask, 800–1500 [1950-134-358; ACPS-25]

6 NAYARIT (WESTERN MEXICO), Seated Man, 100 BCE–300 CE [1950-134-308; ACPS-78]

7 MEZCALA (SOUTHWESTERN MEXICO), Mask, 300 BCE–500 CE [1950-134-262; ACPS-90]

8 TEOTIHUACAN (CENTRAL MEXICO), Mask, 1st–9th century [1950-134-293; ACPS-22]

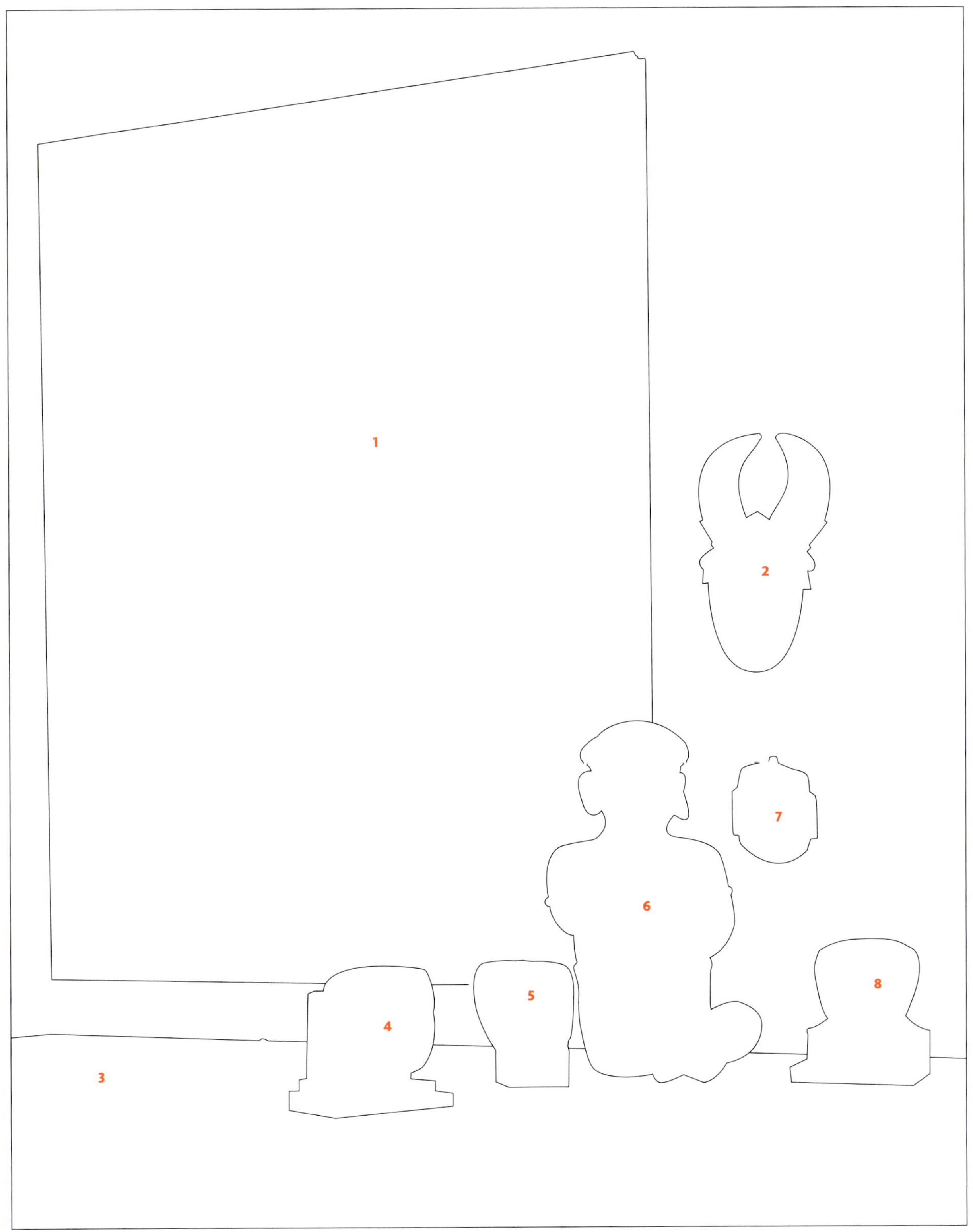
1
2
6
7
3
4
5
8

PLATE 35

LIVING ROOM

WITH A VIEW INTO THE DINING ROOM THROUGH THE NORTH ARCHWAY

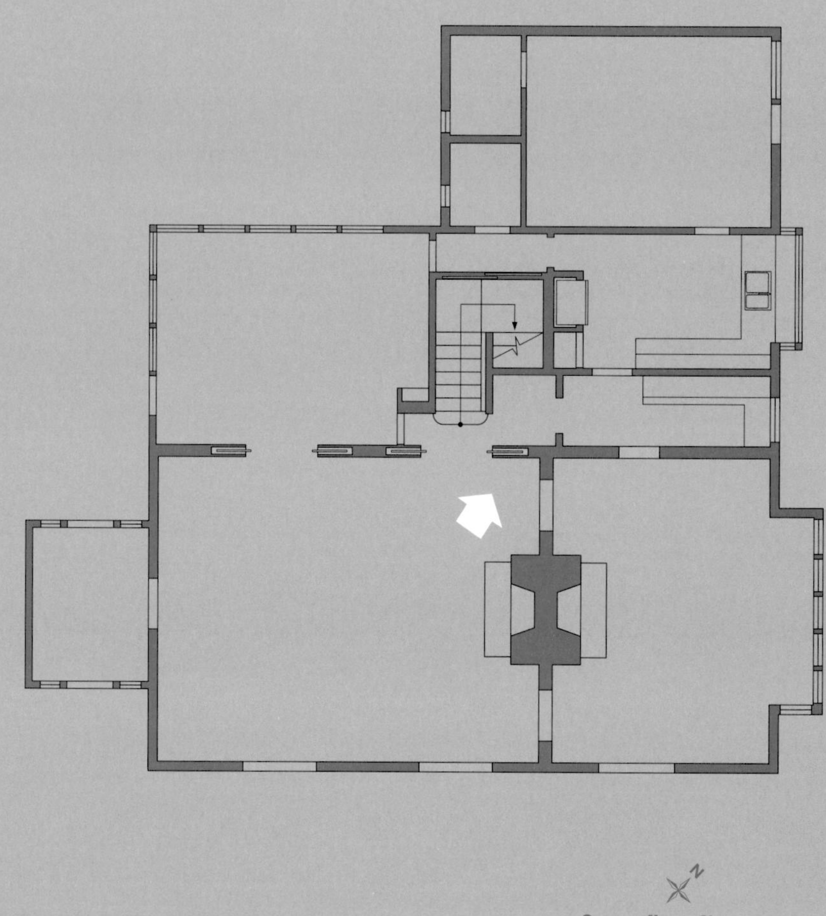

FRED R. DAPPRICH

CA. 1944

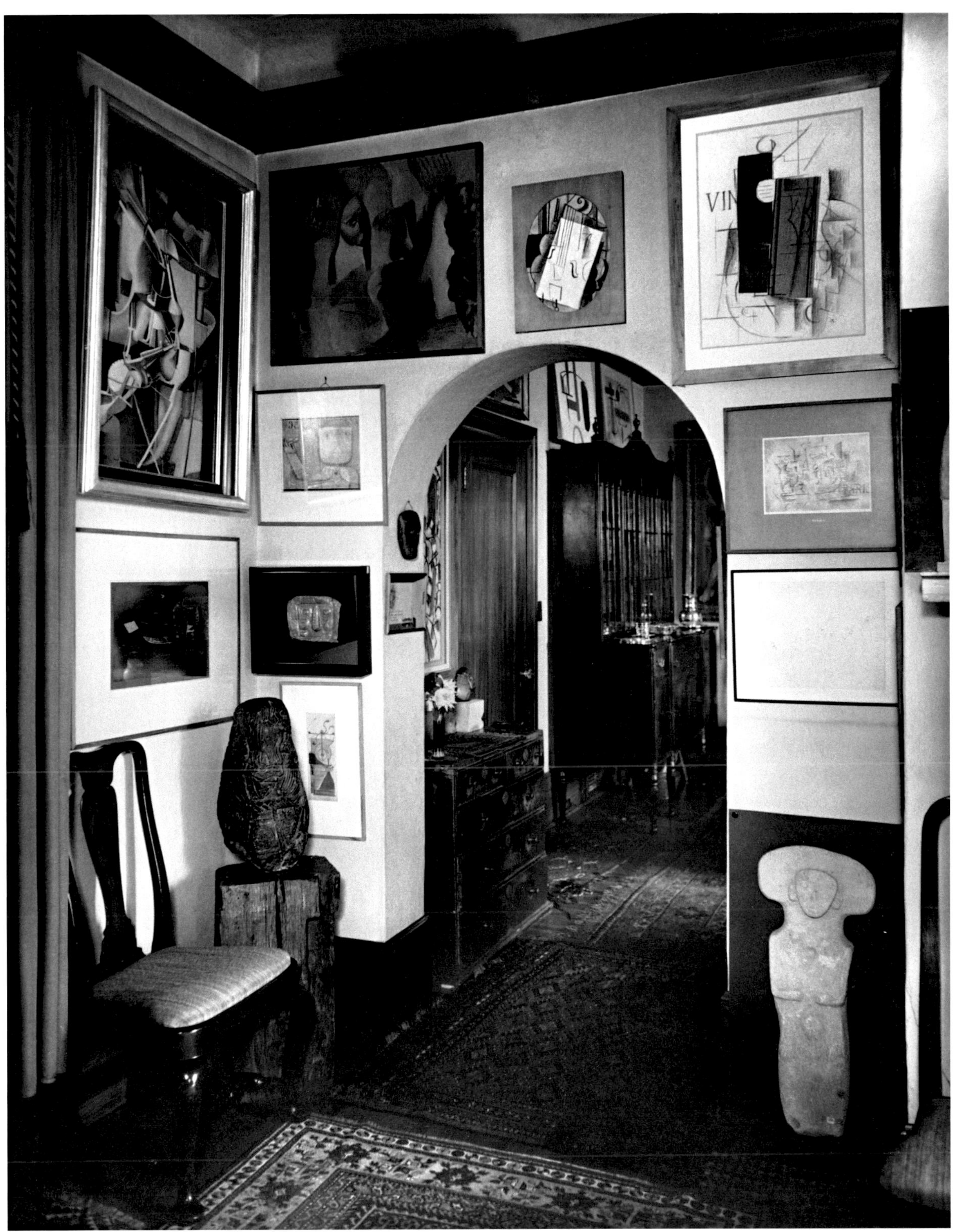
VIN

PLATE 35

1 MARCEL DUCHAMP, *Bride*, 1912 [1950-134-65; AC20-71]

2 PAUL KLEE, *Demon as Pirate*, 1926 [1950-134-114; AC20-117]

3 AZTEC (CENTRAL MEXICO), Figure (Quetzalcoatl), 1300–1520 [1950-134-251; ACPS-27]

4 REPRODUCTION OF MARCEL DUCHAMP'S *Coffee Mill* (1911), Date unknown [NOTE 1.2, PAGE 414]

5 CHIMÚ (PERU), Funerary Mask, 900–1470 [1950-134-284; ACPS-185]

6 PAUL KLEE, *Jörg*, 1924 [1950-134-111; AC20-112]

7 MARCEL DUCHAMP, *Yvonne and Magdeleine Torn in Tatters*, 1911 [1950-134-53; AC20-58]

8 GEORGES BRAQUE, *Still Life (Violin)*, 1913 [1950-134-25; AC20-25]

9 JOAN MIRÓ, *Female Torso*, 1931 [1950-134-145; AC20-148]

10 JEAN HÉLION, *Red Tensions*, 1933 [1950-134-99; AC20-100]

11 ROGER DE LA FRESNAYE, *Landscape*, 1912 [1950-134-90; AC20-125]

12 FERNAND LÉGER, *Contrast of Forms*, 1913–14 [1950-134-123; AC20-126]

13 ARTIST/MAKER UNKNOWN, Pre-Columbian Death Mask (fake), Date unknown [NOTE 4.1, PAGE 416]

14 ARTIST/MAKER UNKNOWN (MEXICO), *Recovery from an Illness*, 1927 [1950-134-493]

15 AZTEC (CENTRAL MEXICO), Bust of Goddess, 1300–1520 [1950-134-236; ACPS-191]

16 GUANACASTE-NICOYA (COSTA RICA), Incense Burner or Vessel, 700–1350 [1950-134-227]

17 ROGER DE LA FRESNAYE, *Nude (The Italian Girl)*, 1911 [1950-134-89; AC20-124]

18 GEORGES BRAQUE, *Still Life (with the Word VIN)*, 1912–13 [1950-134-24; AC20-23]

19 GEORGES BRAQUE, *Paris* or *Still Life on a Table*, 1910 [1950-134-873]

20 PABLO PICASSO, *The Jugglers*, 1905 (1913 edition) [1950-134-908]

21 HUASTEC (EAST COAST MEXICO), Figure of a Woman, 900–1200 [1950-134-330; ACPS-116]

22 CLASSIC VERACRUZ (EAST COAST MEXICO), Hacha in the Form of a Head, 500–900 [1950-134-337; ACPS-147]

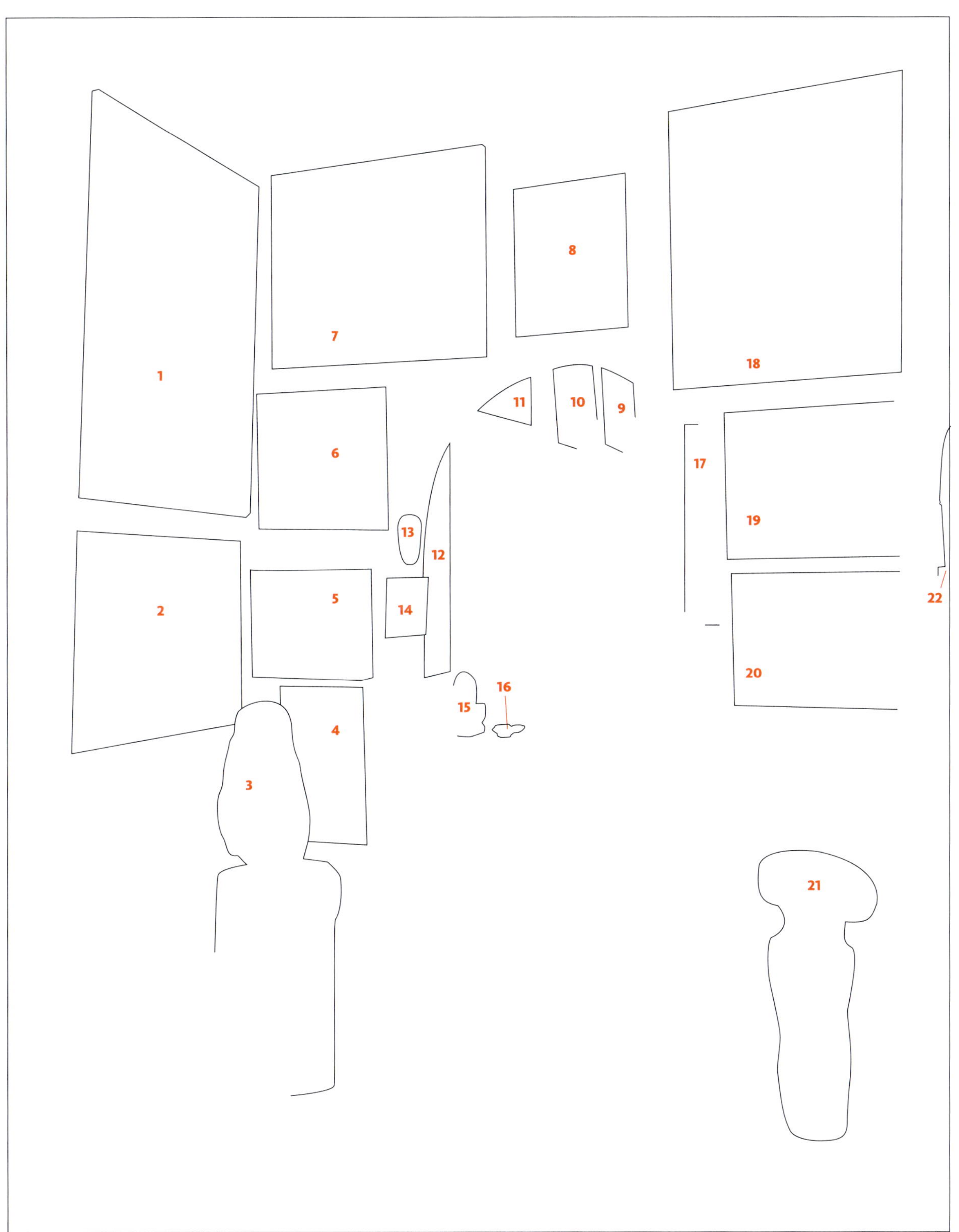

1
2
3
4
5
6
7
8
9
10
11
12
13
14
15
16
17
18
19
20
21
22

PLATE 36

STAIRWAY

VIEWED FROM THE GROUND FLOOR

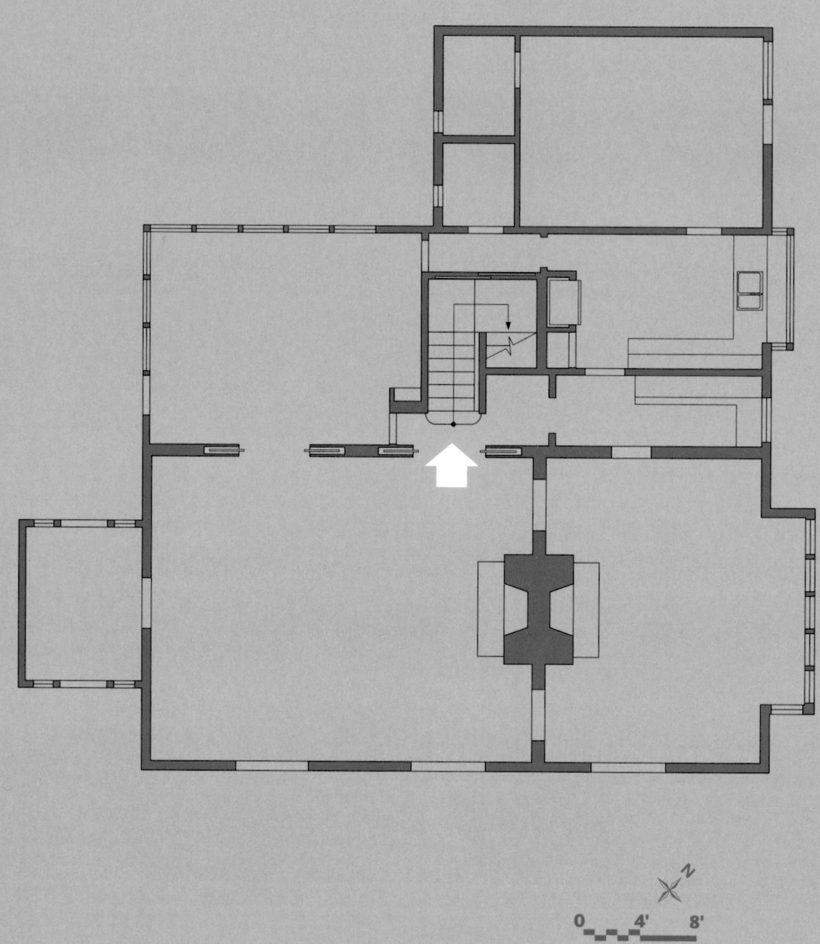

CORPORAL F. W. LUMBORD

CA. APRIL 1945

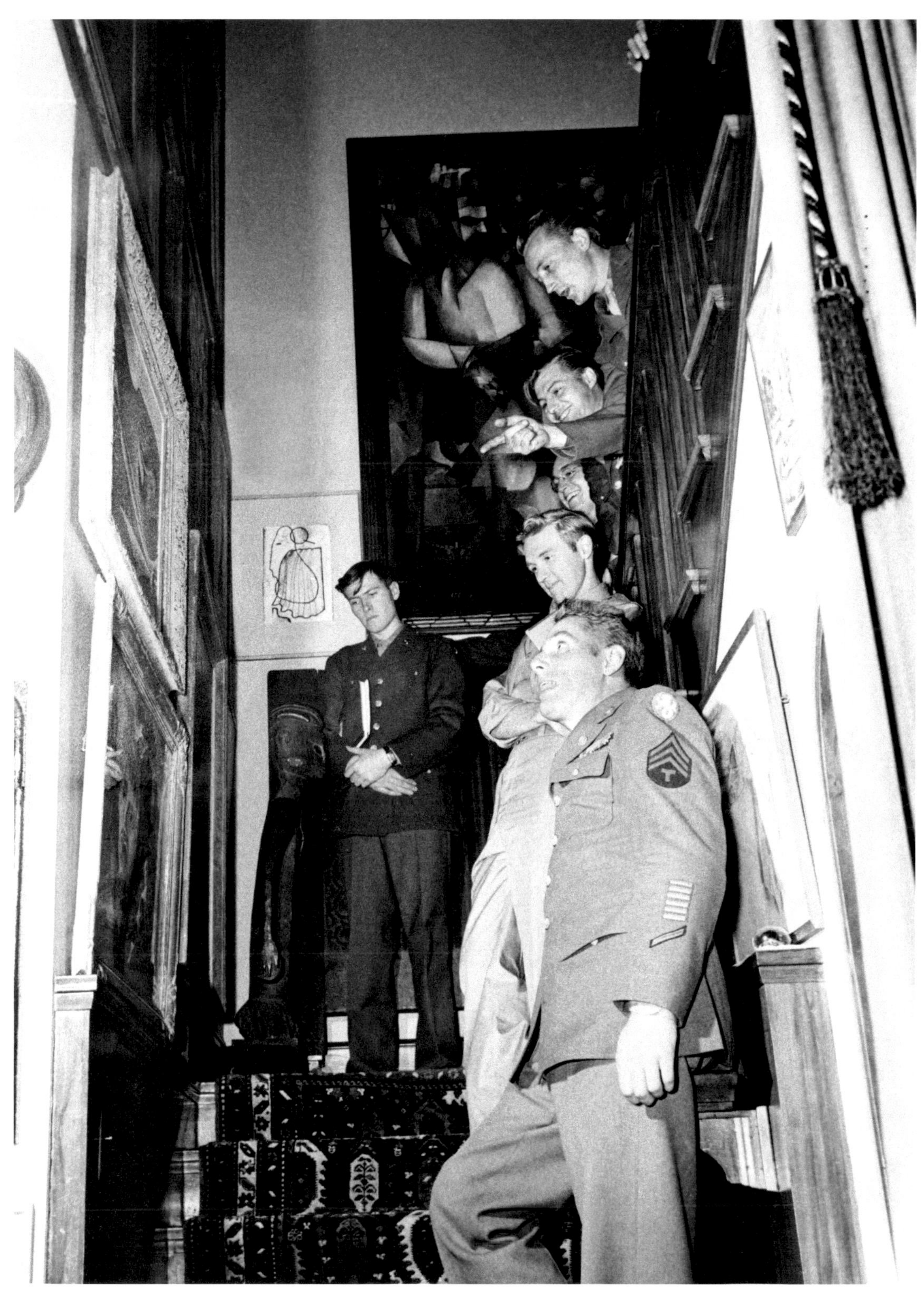

PLATE 36

*1 JUAN GRIS, *Chessboard, Glass, and Dish*, 1917 [1950-134-98; AC20-99; SEE PLATE 37.4]

2 MAX ERNST, *Garden Plane Trap*, 1934–35 [1950-134-87; AC20-90]

3 GINO SEVERINI, *Composition for Mosaic*, 1933 [NOTE 1.7, PAGE 414]

*4 DIEGO RIVERA, *The Flowered Canoe*, 1931 [NOTE 1.8, PAGE 414; SEE PLATE 37.6]

*5 LYONEL FEININGER, *Umpferstedt II*, 1914 [1950-134-88; AC20-91; SEE PLATE 37.7]

*6 GEORGES BRAQUE, *Violin and Newspaper*, 1912–13 [1950-134-26; AC20-24; SEE PLATE 37.9]

*7 MARCEL GROMAIRE, *The Night Watchman*, 1914 [NOTE 1.9, PAGE 414; SEE PLATE 37.8]

8 CARLOS MÉRIDA, *The Window*, 1933 [1950-134-133; AC20-137]

9 ARTIST/MAKER UNKNOWN (AFRICA), Female Figure, Date unknown [1950-134-203]

10 ARTIST/MAKER UNKNOWN, Gothic Chest Front, Date unknown [NOTE 1.10, PAGE 414]

11 ALBERT GLEIZES, *Man on a Balcony (Portrait of Dr. Théo Morinaud)*, 1912 [1950-134-91; AC20-92]

12 PAUL CÉZANNE, *The Bathers (Large Version)*, 1896–98 [1950-134-874]

13 HENRI MATISSE, *Study for Still Life after de Heem*, 1915 [1950-134-131; AC20-134]

14 ARTIST/MAKER UNKNOWN (*CHINA), Crystal Sphere, Date unknown [NOTE 4.5, PAGE 417]

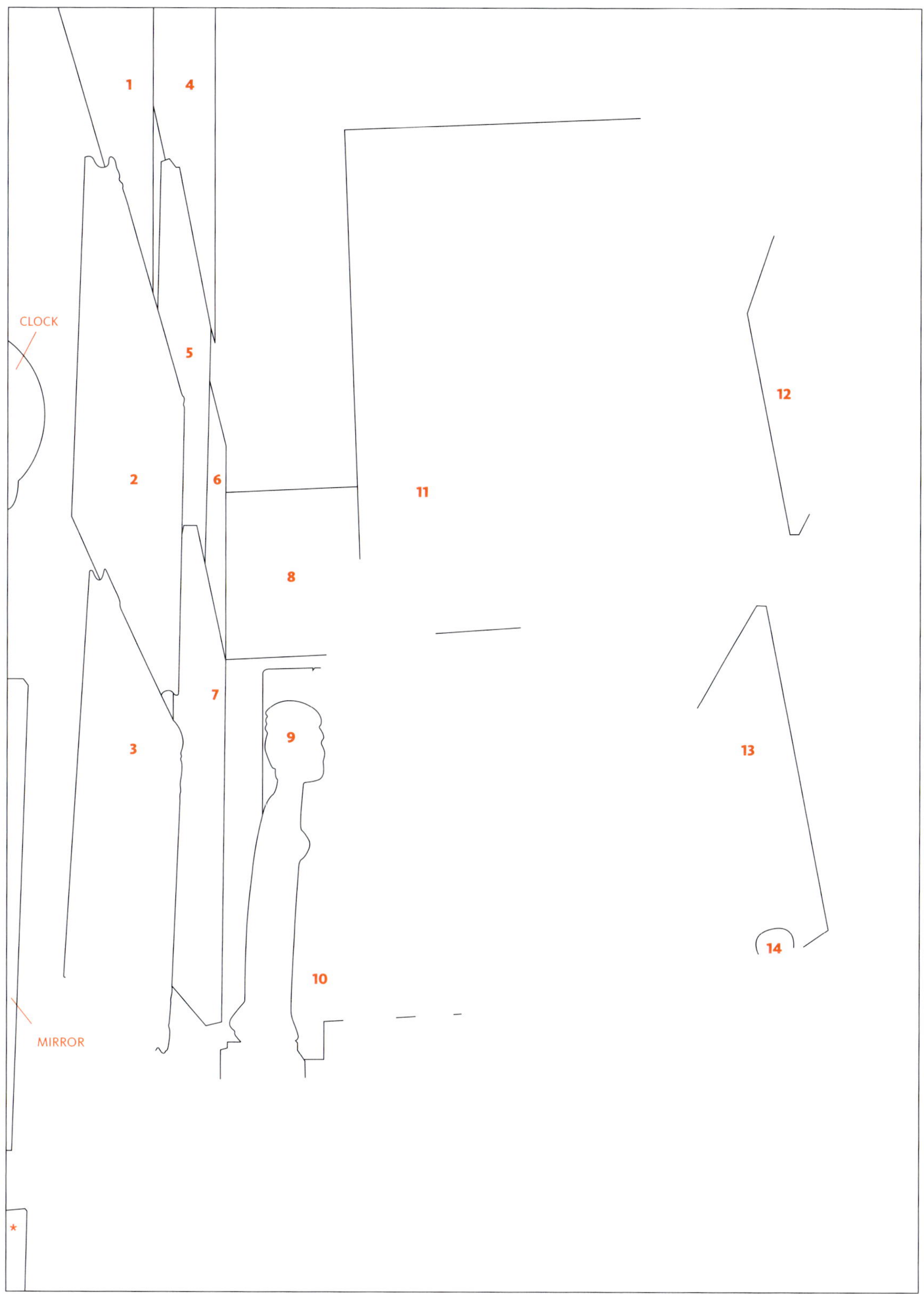
1
4
CLOCK
5
12
2
6
11
8
7
9
3
13
14
10
MIRROR
*

7065 HILLSIDE AVENUE, LOS ANGELES, CALIFORNIA
RESIDENCE OF LOUISE AND WALTER ARENSBERG, 1927–54

SECOND FLOOR

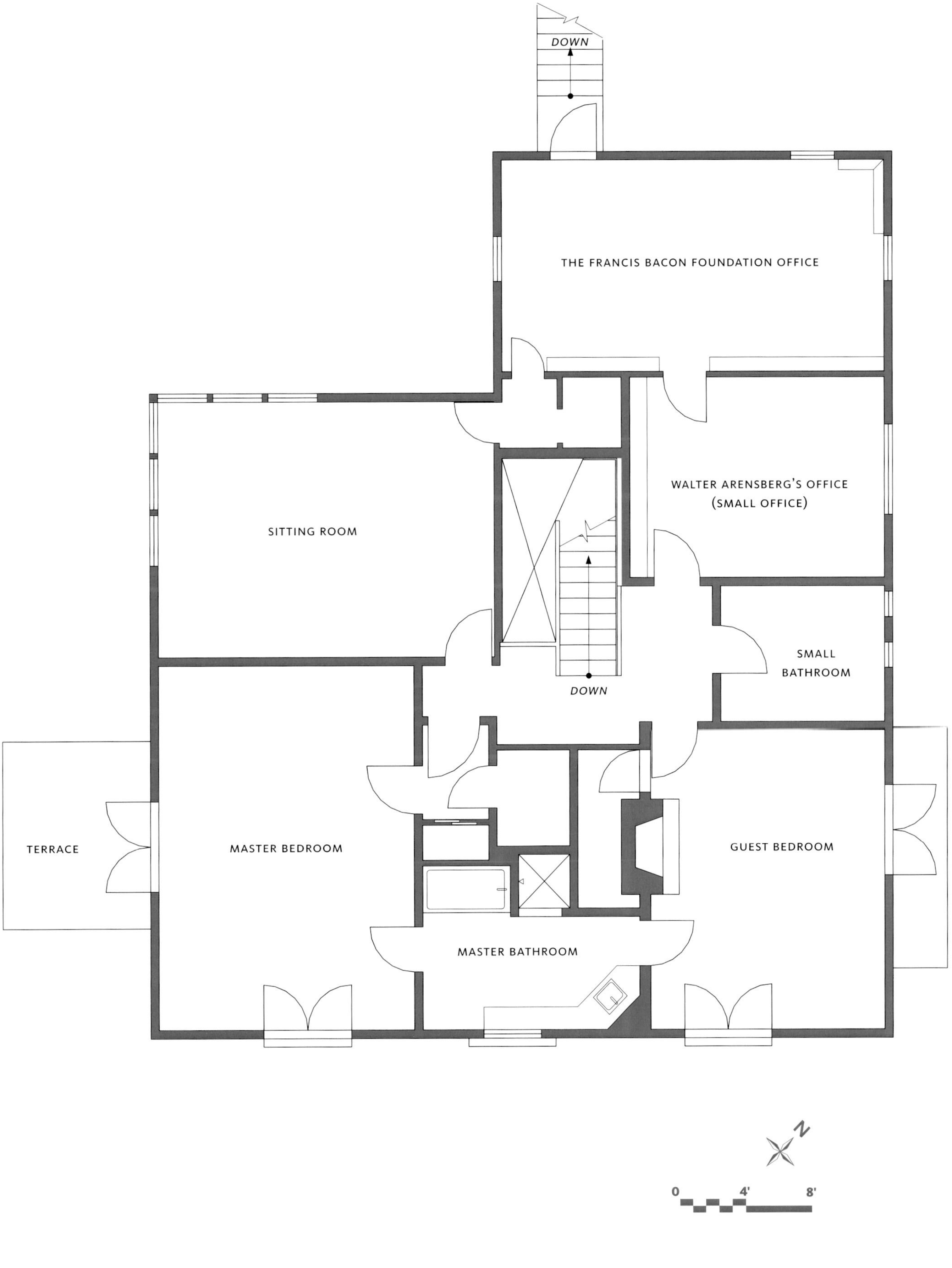

DOWN

THE FRANCIS BACON FOUNDATION OFFICE

WALTER ARENSBERG'S OFFICE
(SMALL OFFICE)

SITTING ROOM

SMALL
BATHROOM

DOWN

TERRACE

MASTER BEDROOM

GUEST BEDROOM

MASTER BATHROOM

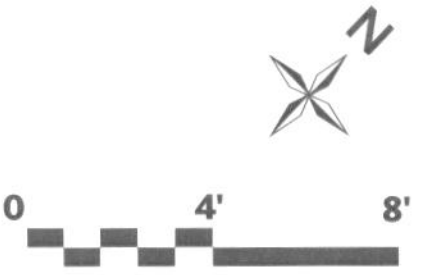

PLATE 37

STAIRWAY

VIEWED FROM THE SECOND FLOOR

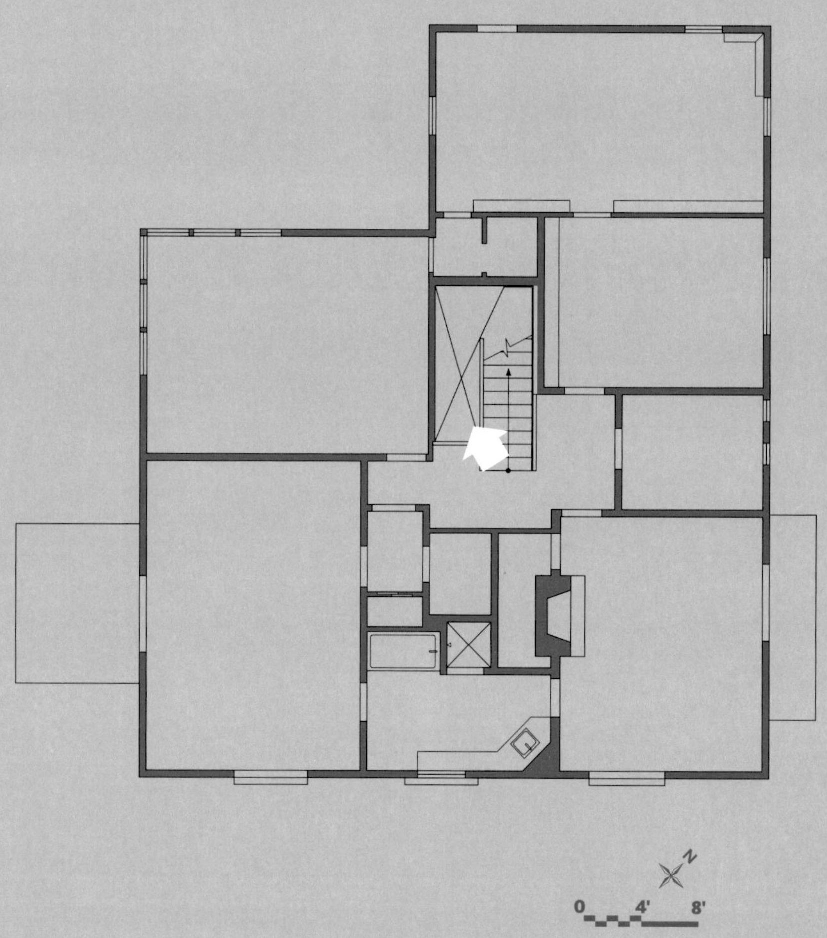

FRED R. DAPPRICH

CA. 1944 (NO LATER THAN JANUARY 1949)

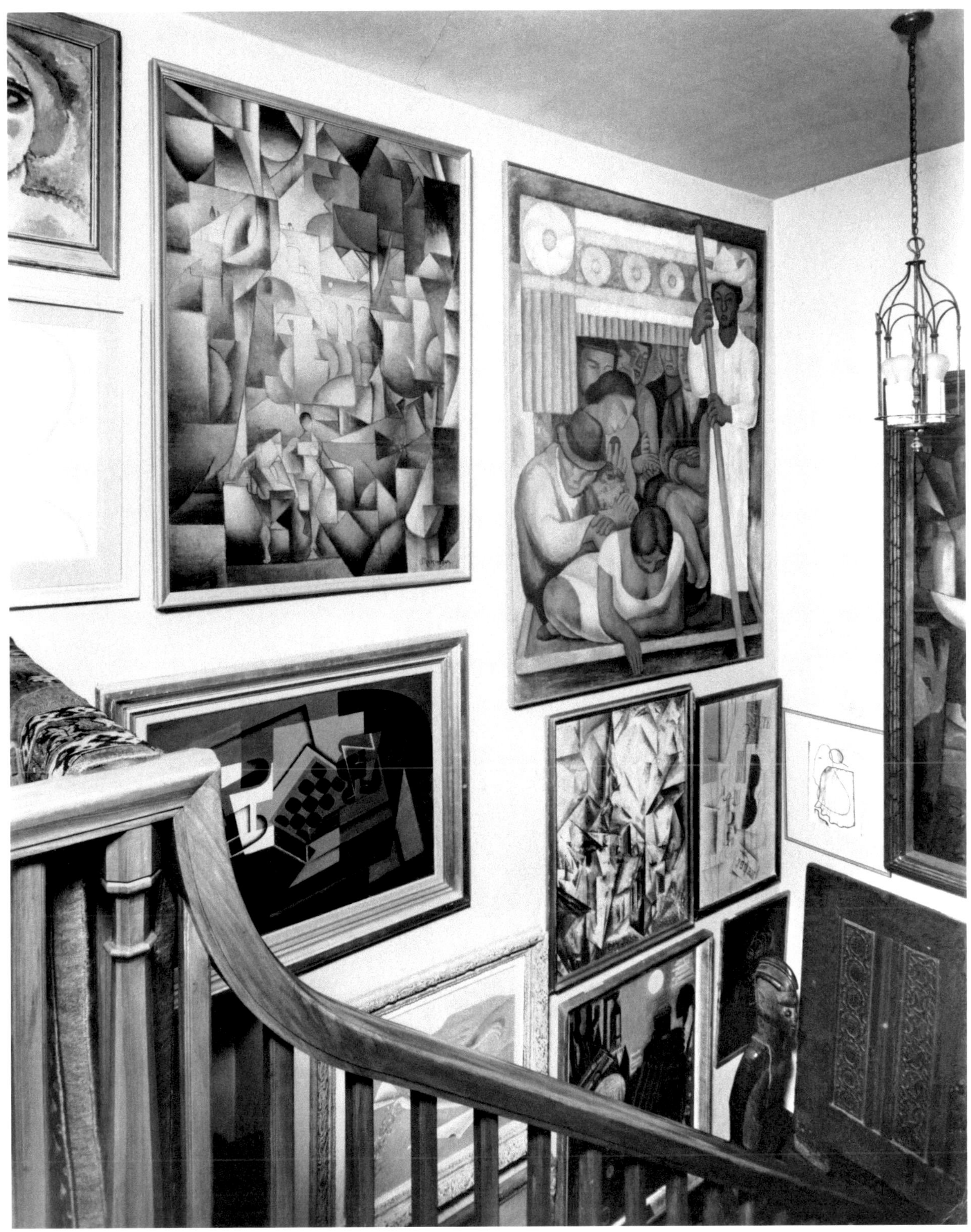

PLATE 37

1 ALEXEI JAWLENSKY, *Purple Lips*, 1912 [1950-134-512A; AC20-204 (LISTED, NOT PICTURED)]

2 AMEDEO MODIGLIANI, *Caryatid*, ca. 1912–14 [1950-134-150; AC20-153]

3 JEAN METZINGER, *The Bathers*, 1913 [1950-134-140; AC20-142]

4 JUAN GRIS, *Chessboard, Glass, and Dish*, 1917 [1950-134-98; AC20-99]

5 MAX ERNST, *Garden Plane Trap*, 1934–35 [1950-134-87; AC20-90]

6 DIEGO RIVERA, *The Flowered Canoe*, 1931 [NOTE 1.8, PAGE 414]

7 LYONEL FEININGER, *Umpferstedt II*, 1914 [1950-134-88; AC20-91]

8 MARCEL GROMAIRE, *The Night Watchman*, 1914 [NOTE 1.9, PAGE 414]

9 GEORGES BRAQUE, *Violin and Newspaper*, 1912–13 [1950-134-26; AC20-24]

10 ROBERTO MONTENEGRO, *The Double*, 1938 [1950-134-153; AC20-156]

11 ARTIST/MAKER UNKNOWN (AFRICA), Female Figure, Date unknown [1950-134-203]

12 CARLOS MÉRIDA, *The Window*, 1933 [1950-134-133; AC20-137]

13 ALBERT GLEIZES, *Man on a Balcony (Portrait of Dr. Théo Morinaud)*, 1912 [1950-134-91; AC20-92]

14 ARTIST/MAKER UNKNOWN, Gothic Chest Front, Date unknown [NOTE 1.10, PAGE 414]

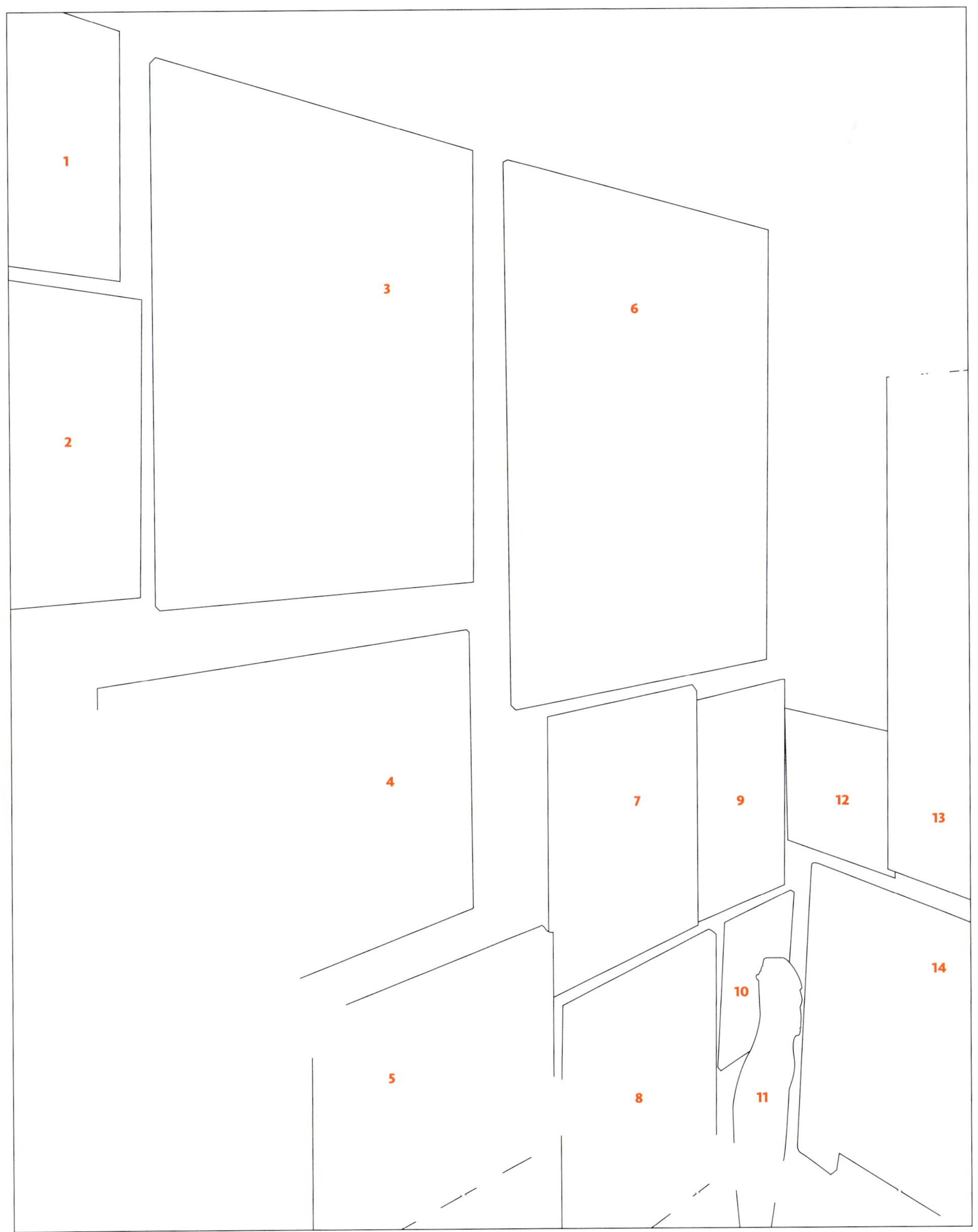
1
3
6
2
4
7
9
12
13
14
10
5
8
11

PLATE 38

STAIRWAY

VIEWED FROM THE SECOND FLOOR, WITH A GLIMPSE OF WALTER ARENSBERG'S OFFICE THROUGH THE DOOR AT THE RIGHT EDGE OF THE PHOTOGRAPH

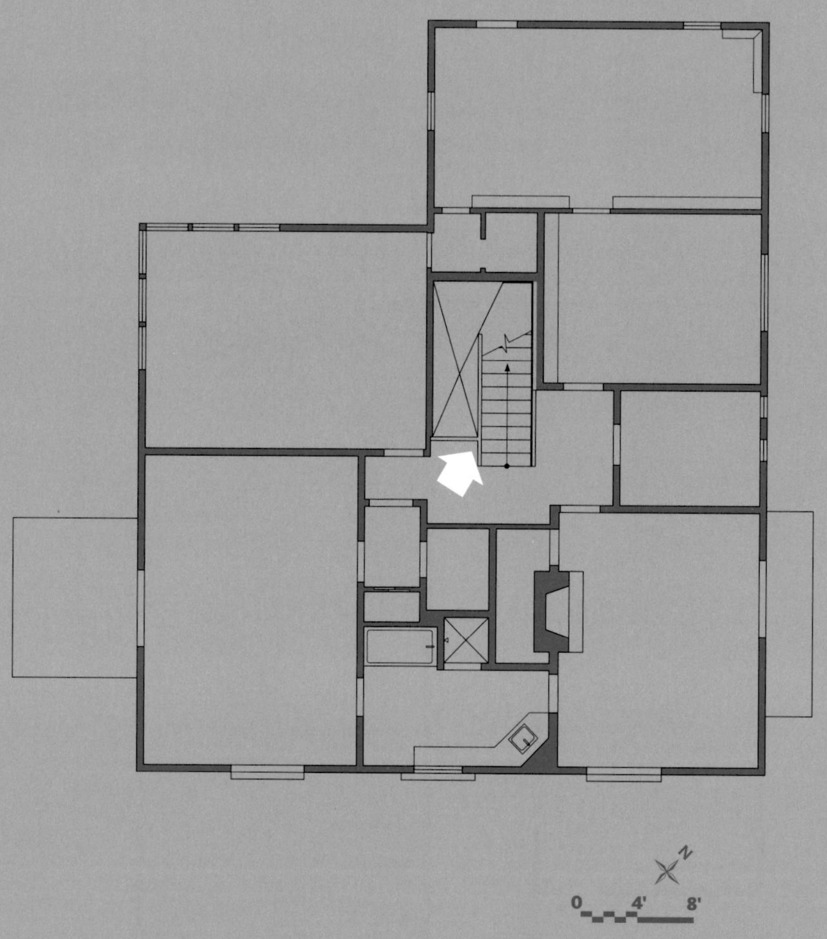

FRED R. DAPPRICH

CA. 1944 (NO LATER THAN JANUARY 1949)

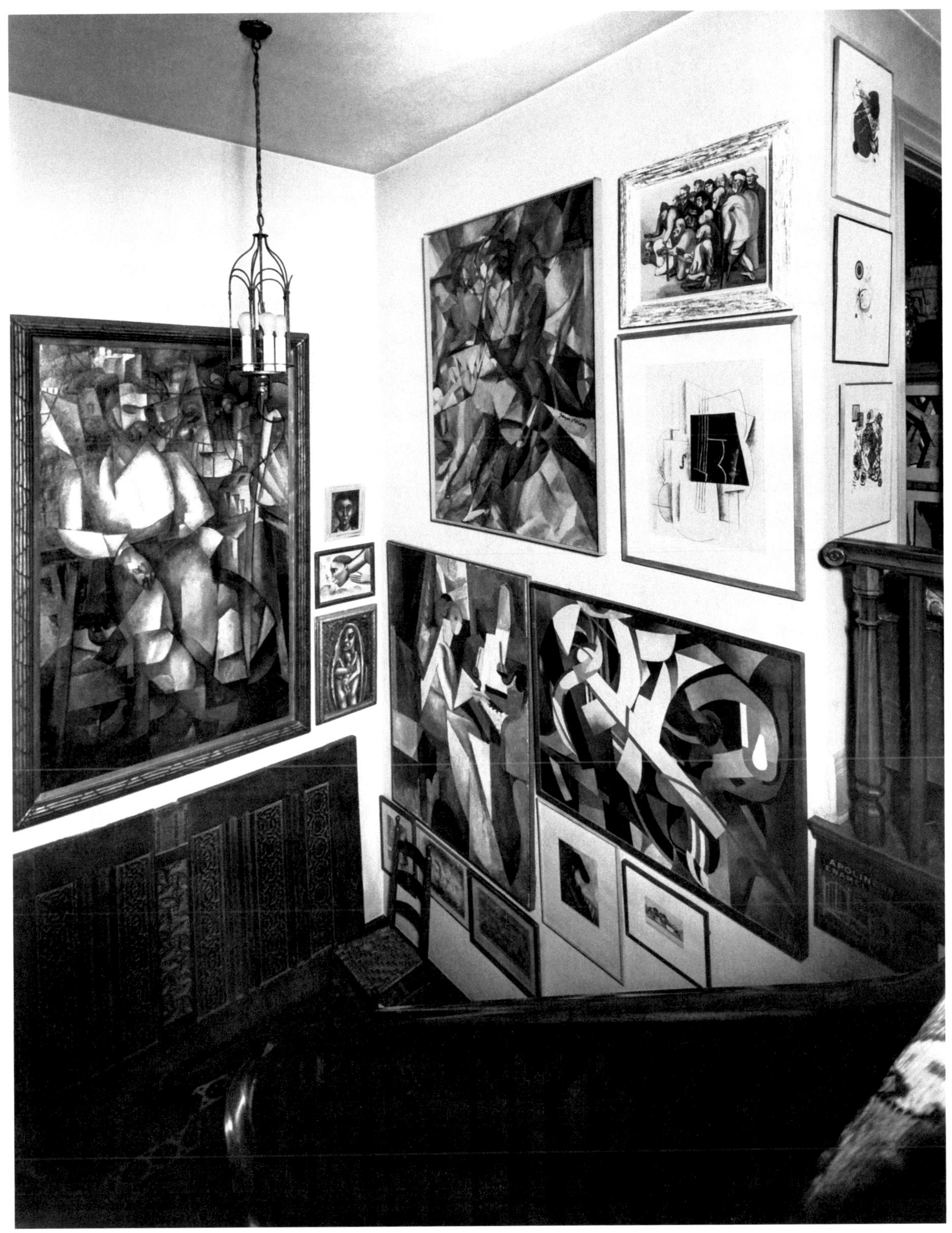

PLATE 38

1 ALBERT GLEIZES, *Man on a Balcony (Portrait of Dr. Théo Morinaud)*, 1912 [1950-134-91; AC20-92]

2 BENJAMIN DUSANOVICH KOSICH (ARA), *Self-Portrait*, ca. 1940 [1950-134-506]

3 BENJAMIN DUSANOVICH KOSICH (ARA), *Mother and Child Stooping*, ca. 1940 [1950-134-504]

4 BENJAMIN DUSANOVICH KOSICH (ARA), *Mother and Child Standing*, 1935 [1950-134-505]

5 ARTIST/MAKER UNKNOWN, Gothic Chest Front, Date unknown [NOTE 1.10, PAGE 414]

6 JACQUES VILLON (GASTON DUCHAMP), *Young Girl*, 1912 [1950-134-190; AC20-195]

7 ALBERT GLEIZES, *Woman at the Piano*, 1914 [1950-134-93; AC20-94]

8 ALBERT GLEIZES, *Study for "Woman at the Piano,"* ca. 1913 [1950-134-92; AC20-93]

9 PAUL KLEE, *Steamer before Lugano*, 1922 [1950-134-887]

10 KNUD MERRILD, *Portrait of D. H. Lawrence (1885–1930)*, 1923–24 [1950-134-136; AC20-139]

11 CHARLES SHEELER, *Landscape*, 1925 [1950-134-185; AC20-190]

12 FRANCIS PICABIA, *Physical Culture*, 1913 [1950-134-157; AC20-160]

13 GEORGES BRAQUE, *Still Life*, 1912 [1950-134-27; AC20-22]

14 JOSÉ CLEMENTE OROZCO, *The Beggars*, Date unknown [NOTE 1.11, PAGES 414–15]

15 VASILY KANDINSKY, *Small Worlds II*, 1922 [1950-134-881]

16 VASILY KANDINSKY, *Composition with Concentric Circles*, 1922 [1950-134-882]

17 VASILY KANDINSKY, *Small Worlds V*, 1922 [1950-134-883]

18 TOLTEC OR OTHER EPICLASSIC CULTURE (CENTRAL MEXICO), Head of a Ruler, with Hieroglyph 13-Reed on Reverse of Head, 600–900 [1950-134-207; ACPS-99]

19 SHERRIL SCHELL, *Construction in N.Y.*, ca. 1930 [1950-134-924]

20 SHERRIL SCHELL, *Window Reflection—Brick Presbyterian Church and Empire State Building*, 1931–32 [1950-134-923]

21 CLASSIC VERACRUZ (EAST COAST MEXICO), Yoke, 500–900 [1950-134-223; ACPS-159 OR 1950-134-224; ACPS-161]

22 MARCEL DUCHAMP, *Apolinère Enameled*, 1916–17 [1950-134-73; AC20-79]

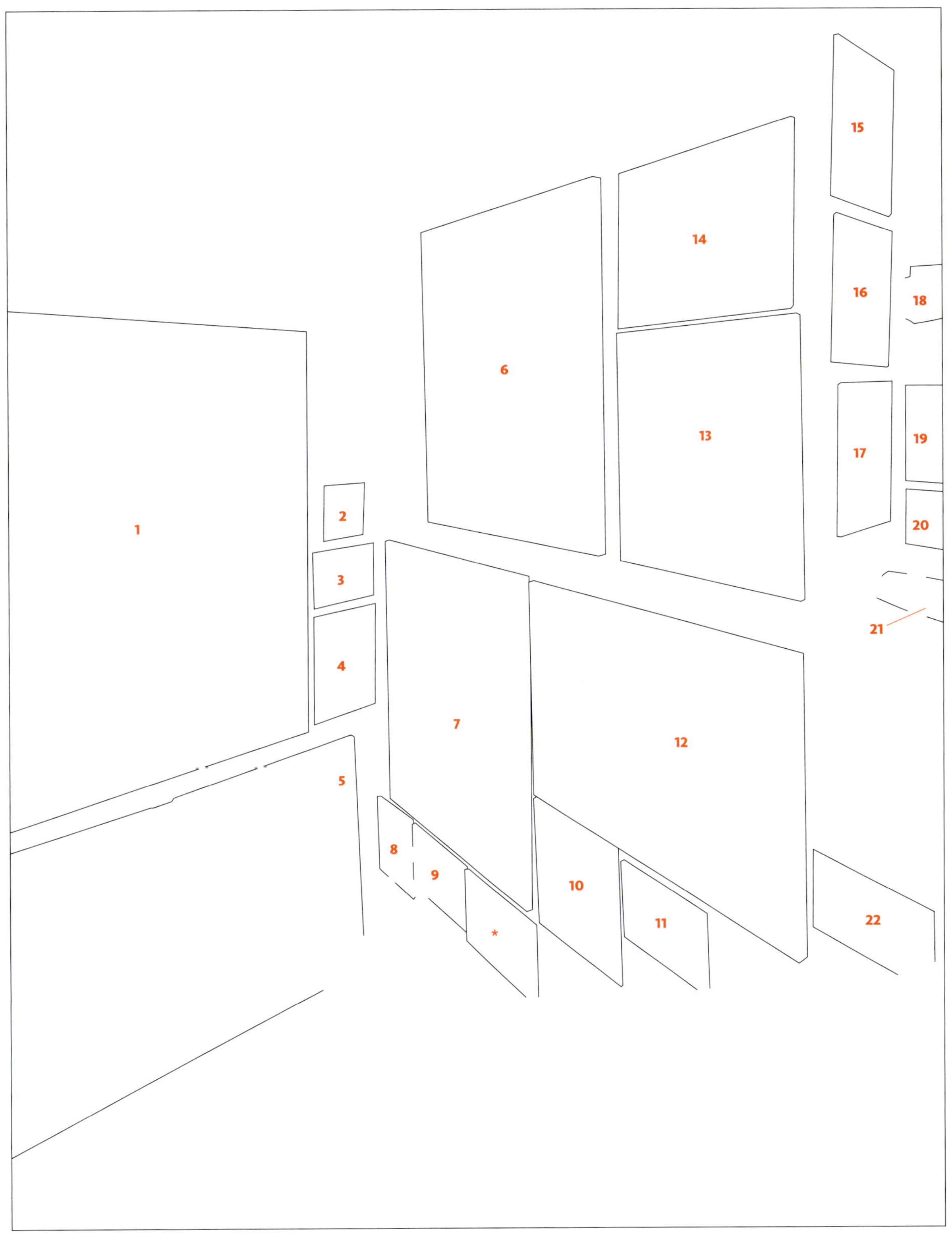

1
2
3
4
5
6
7
8
9
*
10
11
12
13
14
15
16
17
18
19
20
21
22

PLATE 39

LANDING

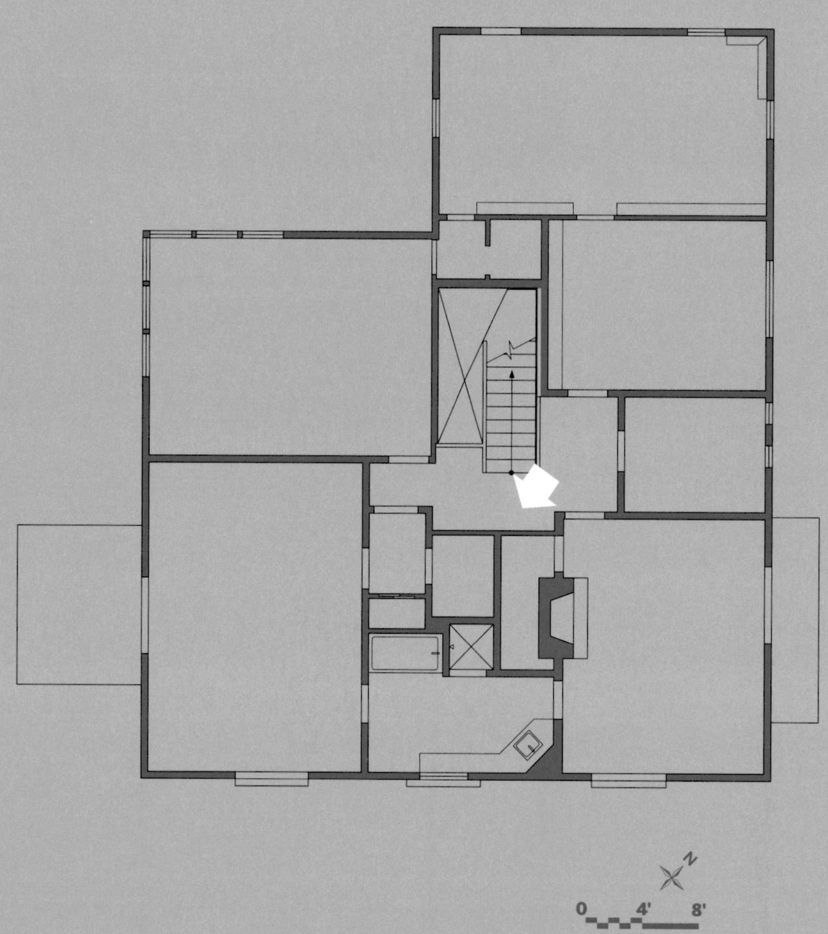

FLOYD FAXON

CA. 1948–49

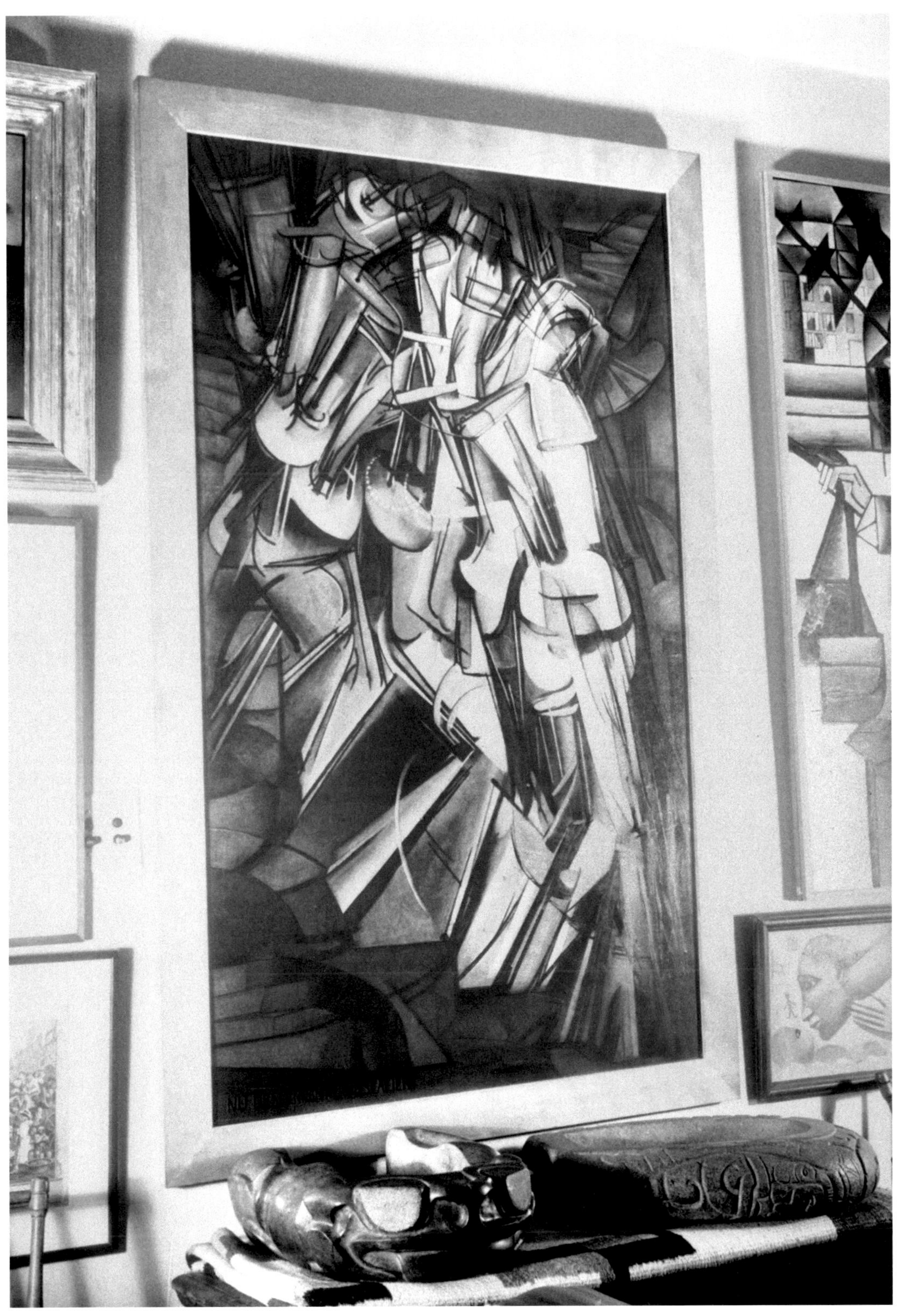

PLATE 39

1 ALEXEI JAWLENSKY, *Looking Within: Night*, 1923 [1950-134-101; AC20-102]

2 WILLIAM HOGARTH, *The Idle 'Prentice Executed at Tyburn*, after plate XI in the series *Industry and Idleness* (1747), Date unknown [NOTE 1.12, PAGE 415]

3 MARCEL DUCHAMP, *Nude Descending a Staircase (No. 3)*, 1916 [1950-134-60; AC20-65]

4, 5 CLASSIC VERACRUZ (EAST COAST MEXICO), Yokes, 500–900 [4: 1950-134-223, ACPS-159; 5: 1950-134-224, ACPS-161]

6 BENJAMIN DUSANOVICH KOSICH (ARA), *Mother and Child Stooping*, ca. 1940 [1950-134-504]

7 JUAN GRIS, *Man in a Café*, 1912 [1950-134-94; AC20-95]

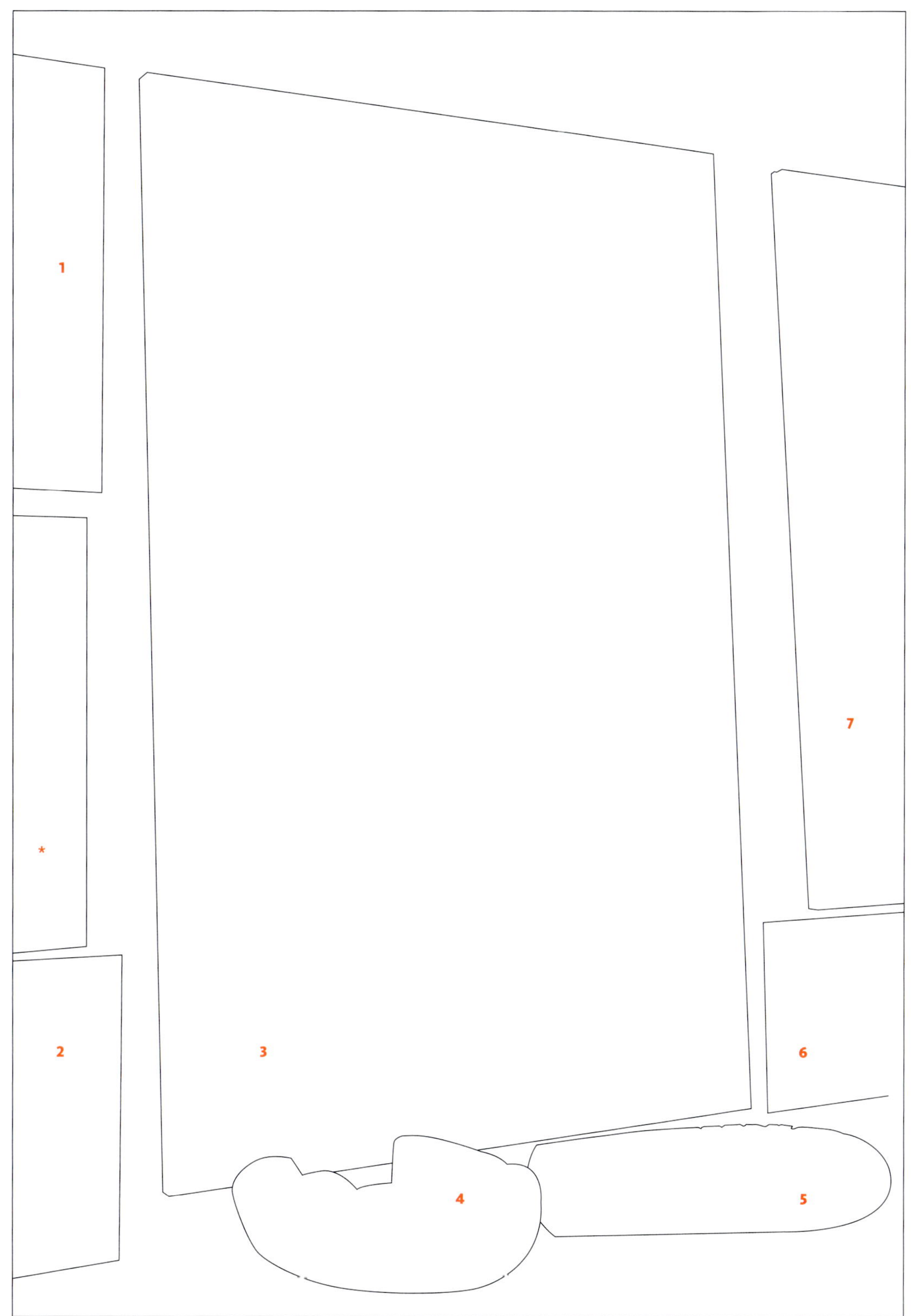
1
*
2
3
4
5
6
7

PLATE 40

WALTER ARENSBERG'S OFFICE (SMALL OFFICE)

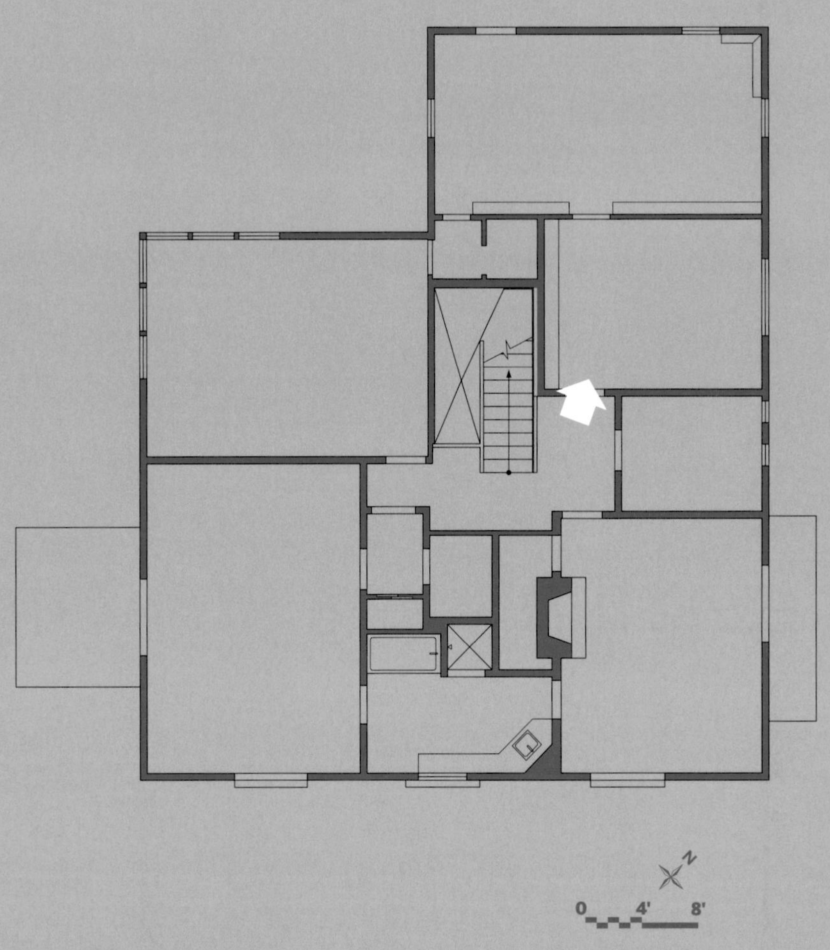

KARL BISSINGER
16 MARCH 1950

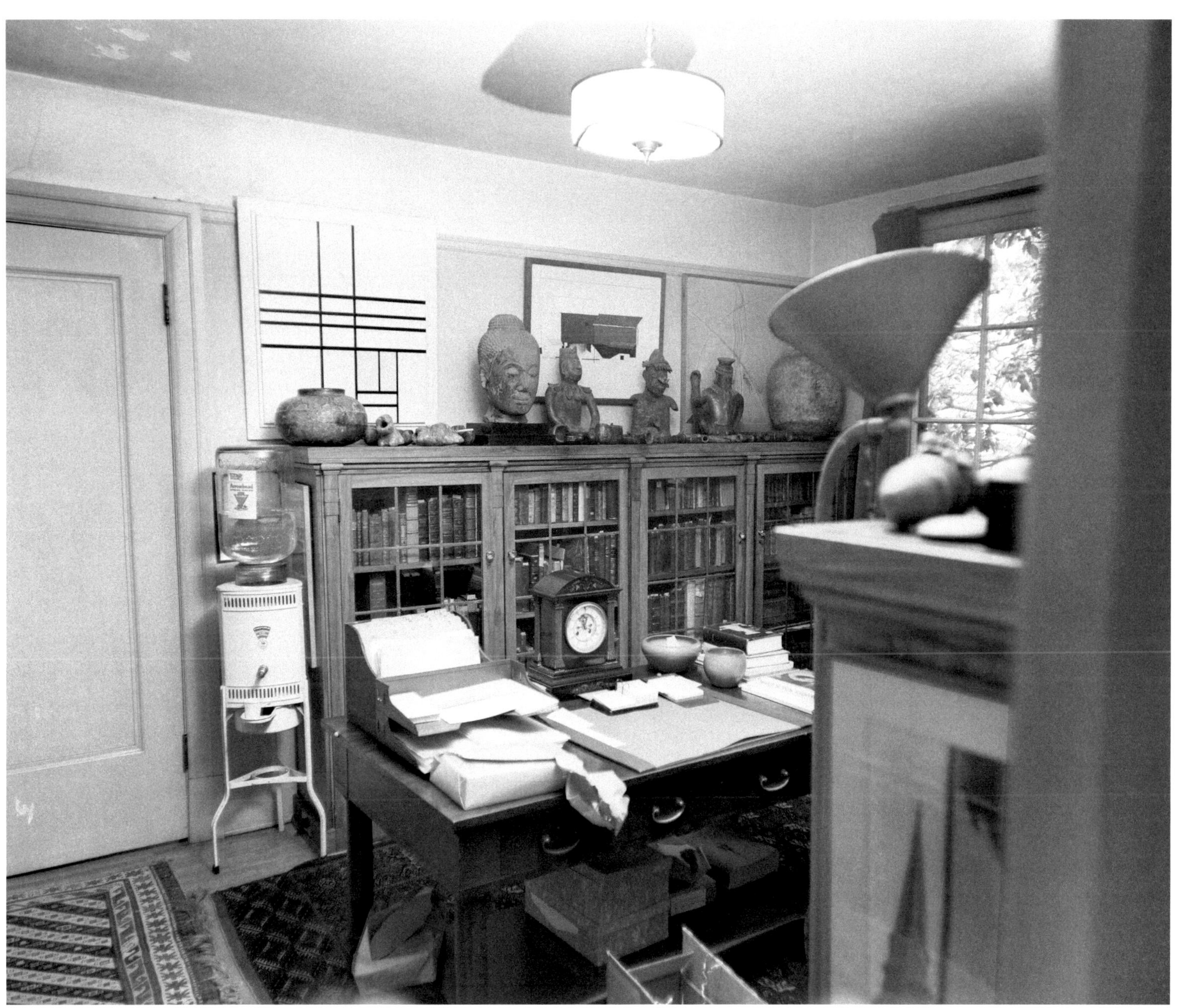

PLATE 40

1 PIET MONDRIAN, *Composition*, 1936 [1950-134-152; AC20-155]

2 CHARLES SHEELER, *Barn Abstraction*, 1918 [1950-134-184]

3 EDITH CLIFFORD WILLIAMS, *Two Rhythms*, 1916 [1950-134-524]

4 CHUMASH (CALIFORNIA), Vessel Carved with Frog Motif, Date unknown [1950-134-455]

5 CHUMASH (CALIFORNIA), Boat Form, Date unknown [1950-134-792]

6 CHUMASH (REMARIS CANYON, CALIFORNIA), Animal Form with Ridged Back, Date unknown [1950-134-803]

7 CHUMASH (CALIFORNIA), Boat Form, Date unknown [1950-134-774]

8 CHUMASH (ARROYO SEQUIT, CALIFORNIA), Pipe in Animal Form with Bone Pipestem and Horn, Date unknown [1950-134-48

9 CHUMASH (CALIFORNIA), Boat Form, Date unknown [1950-134-775]

10 ARTIST/MAKER UNKNOWN (THAILAND), Head of Buddha, 14th–15th century [1950-134-497]

11 COLIMA (WESTERN MEXICO), Vessel in the Form of a Seated Man, 300 BCE–300 CE [1950-134-248; ACPS-60]

*12 CHUMASH (CALIFORNIA), Dipper or Ladle, Date unknown [1950-134-416]

13 *CHUMASH (CALIFORNIA), Hook Form, Date unknown [1950-134-636]

14 CHUMASH (POINT DUME, CALIFORNIA), Boat Form, Date unknown [1950-134-445]

15 CHUMASH (CALIFORNIA), Pipe in Fish Form with One Fin, Date unknown [1950-134-440]

16 CHUMASH (CALIFORNIA), Pipe in Fish Form with Two Fins, Date unknown [1950-134-444]

*17 CHUMASH (CALIFORNIA), Dipper, Date unknown [1950-134-790]

18 NAYARIT (WESTERN MEXICO), Figure of a Man, 100 BCE–300 CE [1950-134-213; ACPS-77]

19 CHUMASH (*CHANNEL ISLANDS, CALIFORNIA), Pipe with Stone Mouthpiece, Date unknown [1950-134-784]

20 CHUMASH (CALIFORNIA), Pipe with Two Shell-Inlay Circles, Date unknown [1950-134-474]

21 COLIMA (WESTERN MEXICO), Vessel in Seated-Man Form, 300 BCE–300 CE [1950-134-247; ACPS-61]

22, 23 CHUMASH (CALIFORNIA), Pipes, Dates unknown [22: 1950-134-793; 23: 1950-134-780]

24 CHUMASH (CALIFORNIA), Pipe or Cloud Blower, Date unknown [1950-134-787]

25 CHUMASH (CALIFORNIA), Pipe or Cloud Maker in Fish Form, Date unknown [1950-134-473]

26 NATIVE AMERICAN (SOUTHWESTERN UNITED STATES), Bowl, Date unknown [1950-134-435]

*27 ZUNI (NEW MEXICO/ARIZONA), Animal Form with Beads and Arrowhead Attached, Date unknown [1950-134-415]

28 MARBLEHEAD POTTERY, Bowl, ca. 1908–36 [PMA 1996-3-2; NOTE 4.9, PAGE 417]

29 SHERRIL SCHELL, *Window Reflection—Brick Presbyterian Church and Empire State Building*, 1931–32 [1950-134-923]

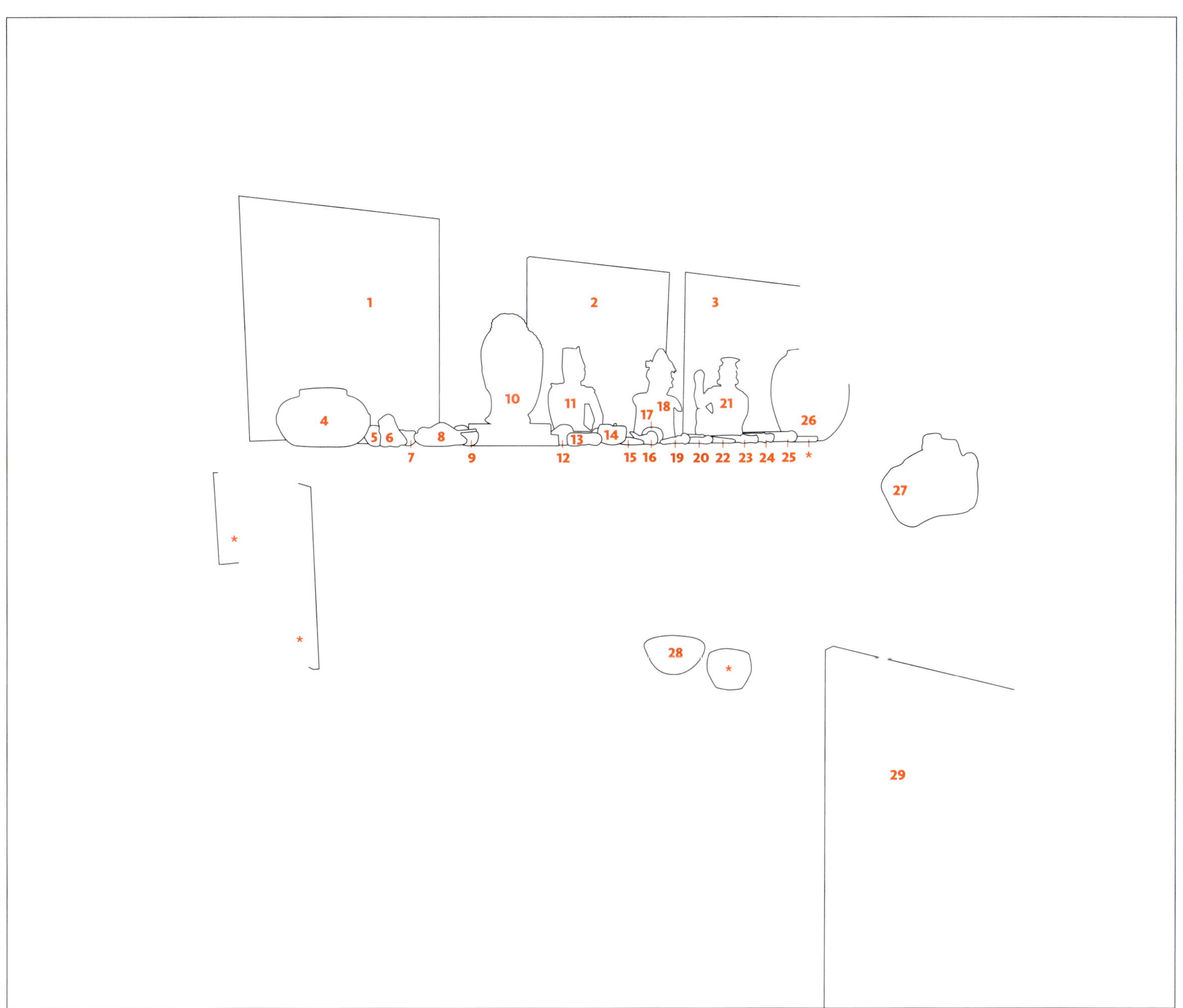
1
2
3
10
11
18
21
4
17
26
5
6
8
13
14
7
9
12
15
16
19
20
22
23
24
25
*
27
*
*
28
*
29

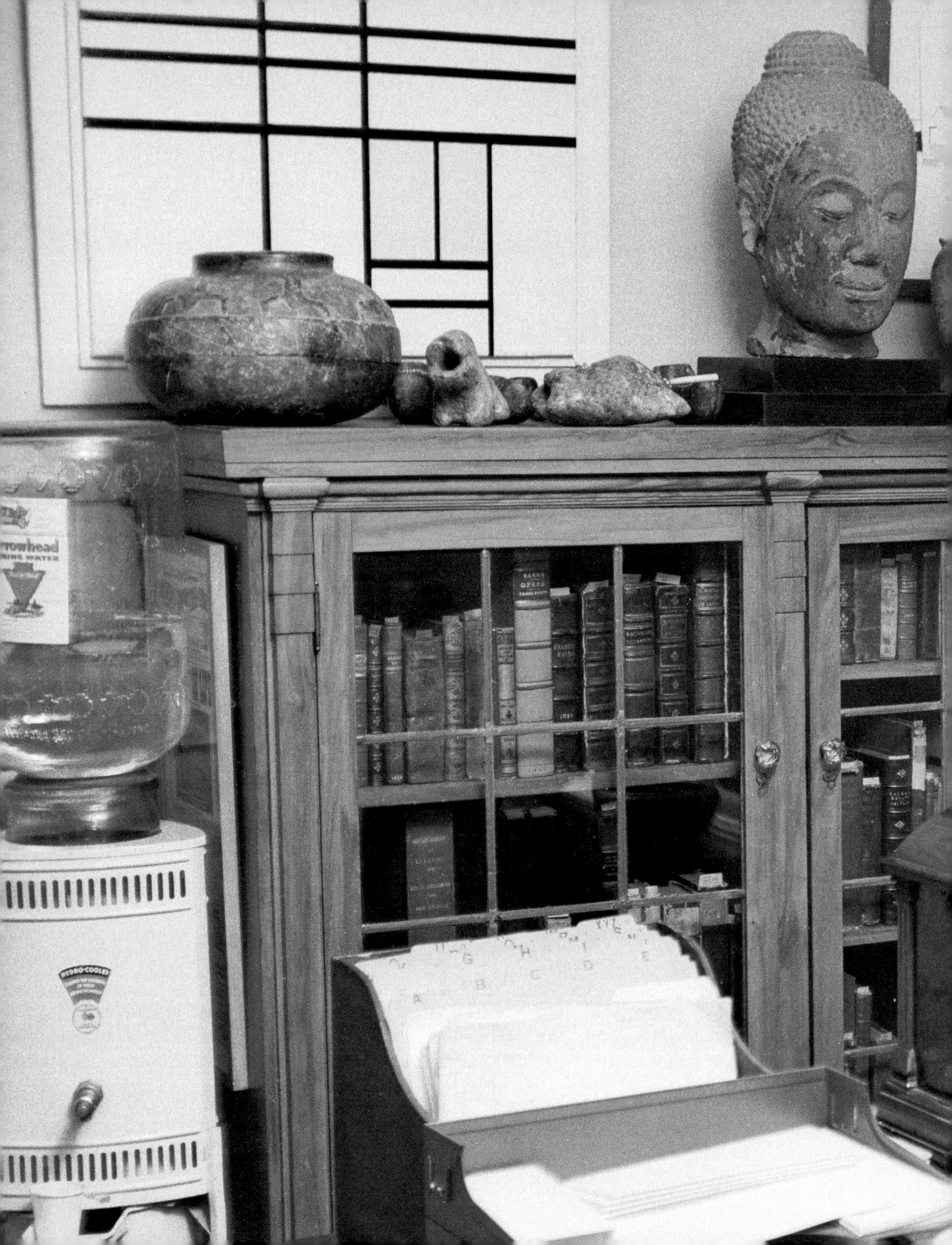
rrowhead
HYDRO-COOLER

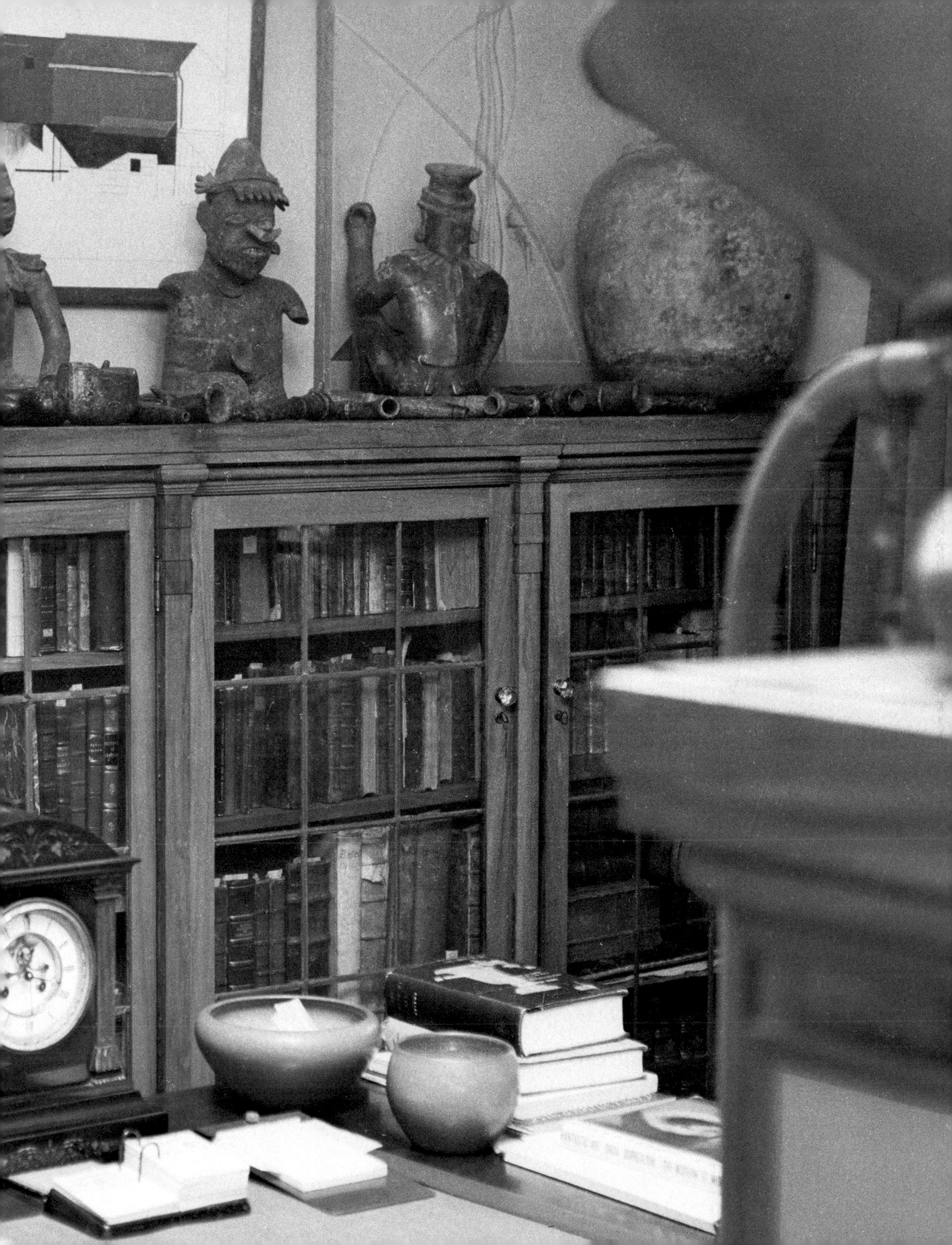

PLATE 41

WALTER ARENSBERG'S OFFICE (SMALL OFFICE)

WITH A VIEW OF THE LANDING THROUGH THE DOOR

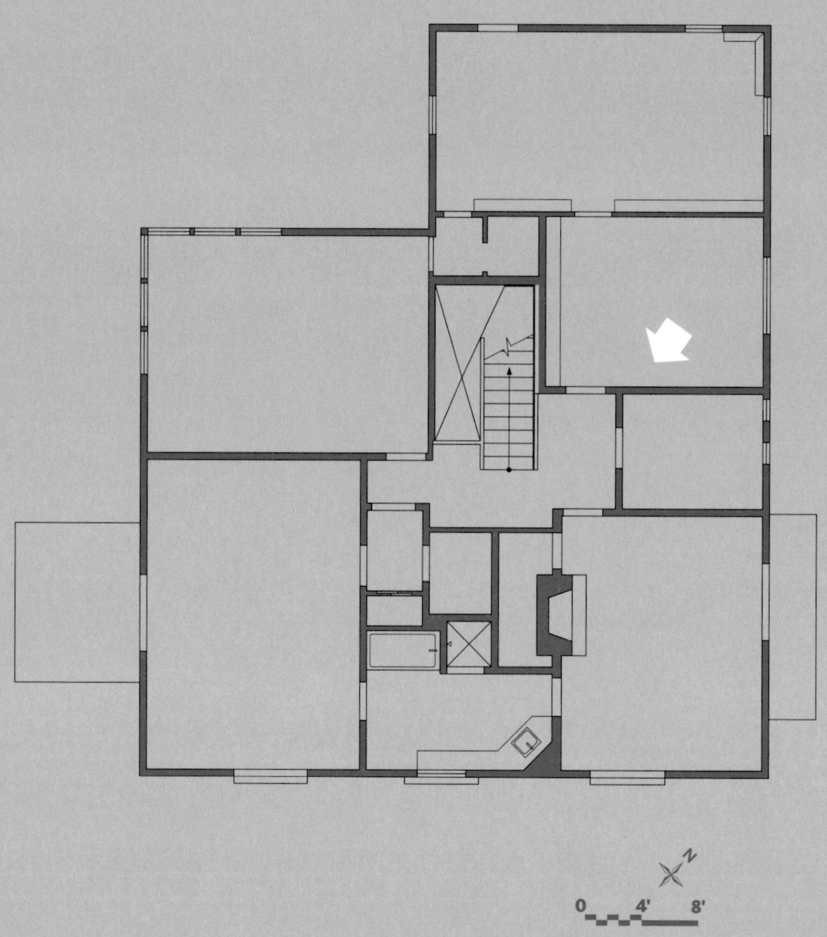

PROBABLY DICK SEYFFERT

CA. 1945, AFTER 15 MARCH

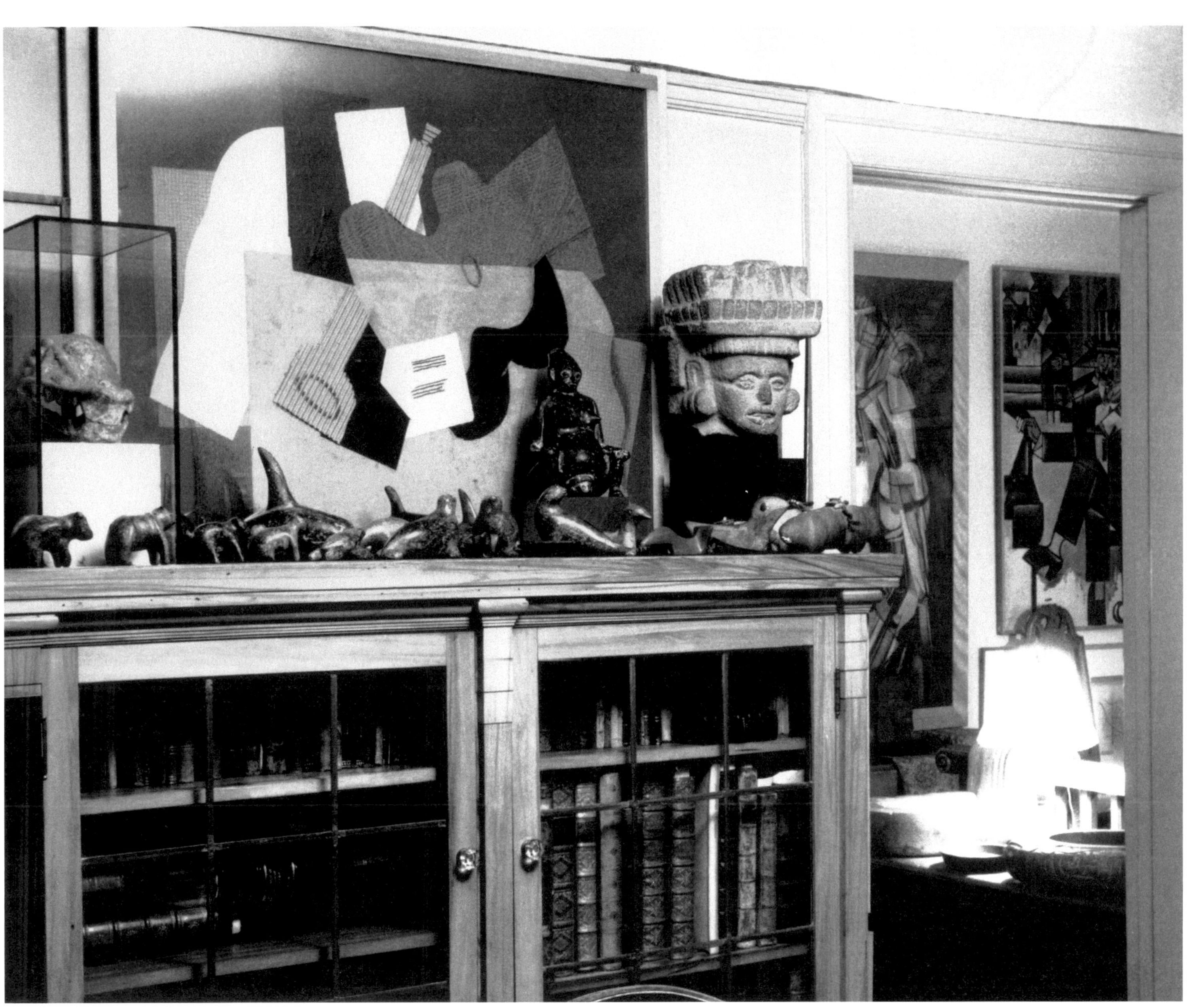

PLATE 41

1 GUANACASTE-NICOYA (COSTA RICA), Crocodile Head, 300–800 [1950-134-361; ACPS-176]

2 GEORGES BRAQUE, *Musical Forms*, 1918 [1950-134-28; AC20-26]

3 NATIVE AMERICAN (MISSISSIPPI RIVER VALLEY), Childbirth Figure with Pedestal, Date unknown [1950-134-448]

4 TOLTEC OR OTHER EPICLASSIC CULTURE (CENTRAL MEXICO), Head of a Ruler, with Hieroglyph 13-Reed on Reverse of Head, 600–900 [1950-134-207; ACPS-99]

5 MARCEL DUCHAMP, *Nude Descending a Staircase (No. 3)*, 1916 [1950-134-60; AC20-65]

6 JUAN GRIS, *Man in a Café*, 1912 [1950-134-94; AC20-95]

7 NATIVE AMERICAN, Animal Form with Four Legs and Curving Tail, Date unknown [1950-134-465]

8–18 CHUMASH (CALIFORNIA), Dates unknown

8: Bear Form [1950-134-452] / 9: Dog Form [1950-134-464] / 10: Squirrel Form [1950-134-451]
11: Whale Form [1950-134-791] / 12: Frog Form [1950-134-462] / 13: Bear Form [1950-134-463] / 14: Whale Form [1950-134-442]
15: Seal Form [1950-134-449] / 16: Whale Form [1950-134-786] / 17: Sea Lion Form [1950-134-450] / 18: Seal Form [1950-134-441]

19–21 NATIVE AMERICAN, Bird Forms, Dates unknown [19: *1950-134-458; 20: NOTE 1.13, PAGE 415; 21: 1950-134-414]

22 ZUNI (NEW MEXICO/ARIZONA), Bear Form with Two Arrowheads, Two Smaller Bear Forms with Green Eyes, and Beads Attached, Date unknown [1950-134-785]

23 ZUNI (NEW MEXICO/ARIZONA), Animal Form with Beads and Arrowhead Attached, Date unknown [1950-134-415]

24 MAYA (GUATEMALA OR MEXICO), Hacha in the Form of Skull and Bird, 600–1200 [1950-134-360; ACPS-171]

*25 CLASSIC VERACRUZ (EAST COAST MEXICO), Yoke, 500–900 [*1950-134-223, *1950-134-286, OR *1950-134-386]

26 VASILY KANDINSKY, *Pink (Rose)*, 1928 [1950-134-107; AC20-108]

27 CLASSIC VERACRUZ (EAST COAST MEXICO), Yoke, 500–900 [1950-134-283; ACPS-160]

*28 ARTIST/MAKER UNKNOWN (*CHINA), Platter, Date unknown [NOTE 4.6, PAGE 417]

29 CLASSIC VERACRUZ (EAST COAST MEXICO), Yoke, 500–900 [1950-134-224; ACPS-161]

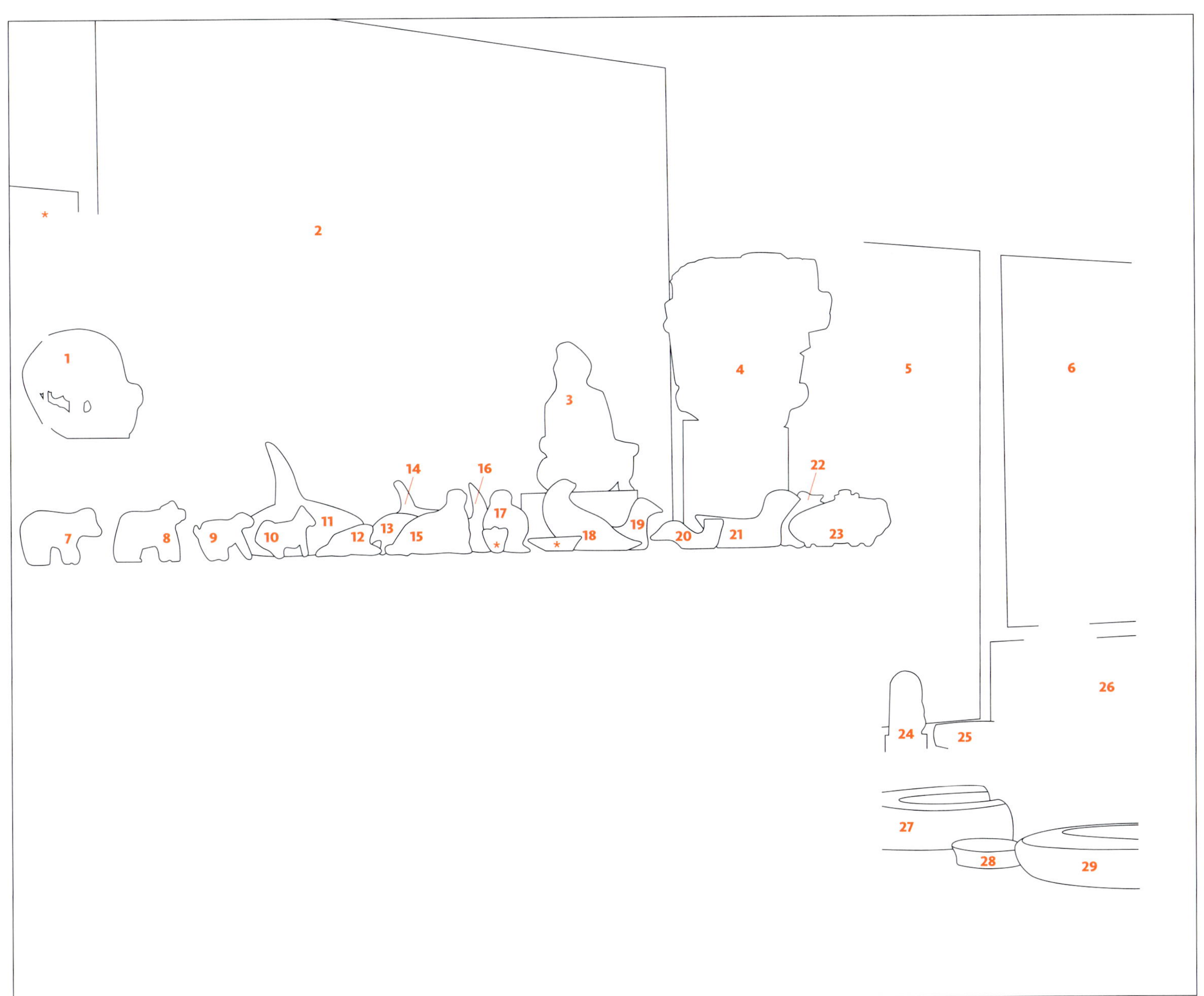
*
2
1
3
4
5
6
14
16
22
7
8
9
10
11
12
13
15
17
*
*
18
19
20
21
23
26
24
25
27
28
29

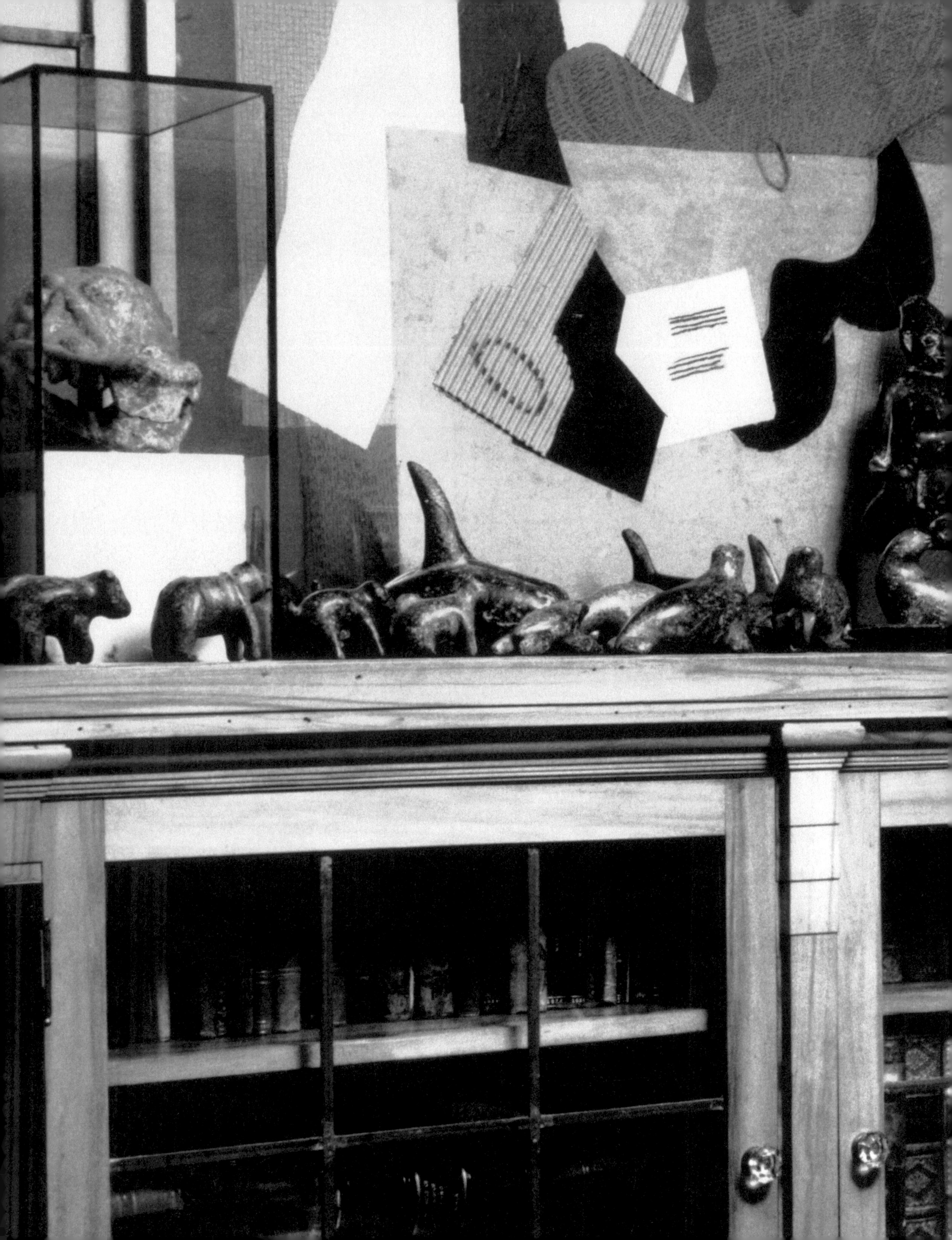

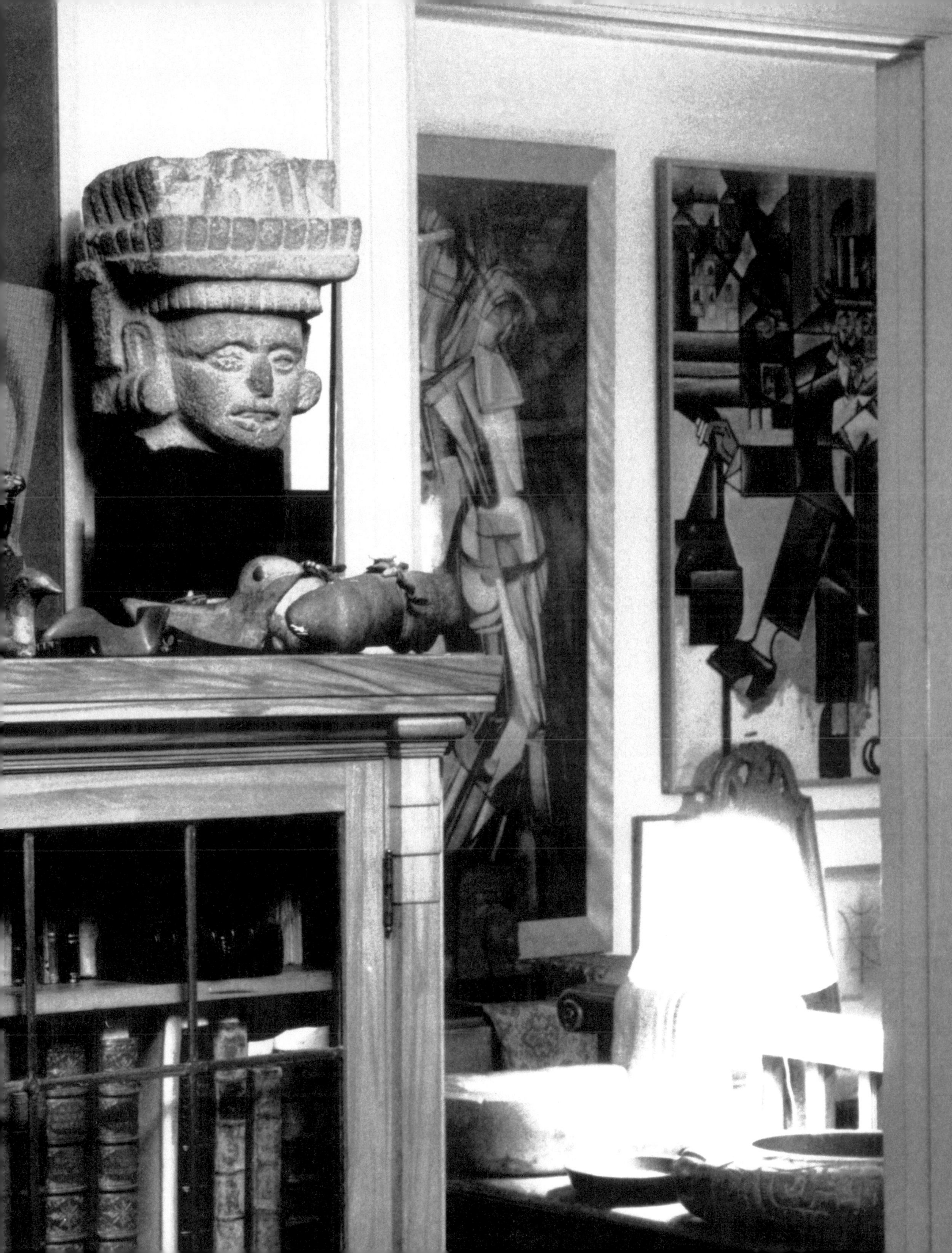

PLATE 42

THE FRANCIS BACON FOUNDATION OFFICE

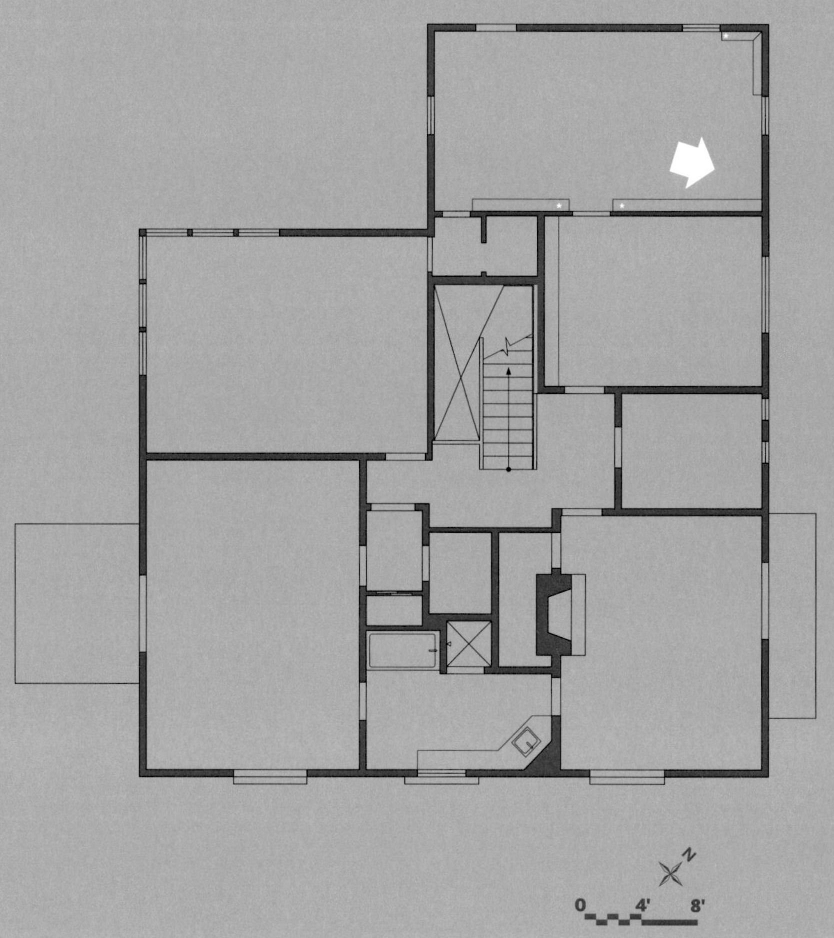

*EXTANT BUILT-IN BOOKCASES, NOT YET IN PLACE AT THE TIME THIS PHOTOGRAPH WAS TAKEN, ARE PARTIALLY VISIBLE IN FLOYD FAXON'S INVENTORY PHOTOGRAPHS OF CA. 1948 (NOT REPRODUCED IN THIS VOLUME; SEE PMA-WLA, BOX 65)

FRED R. DAPPRICH

CA. 1944

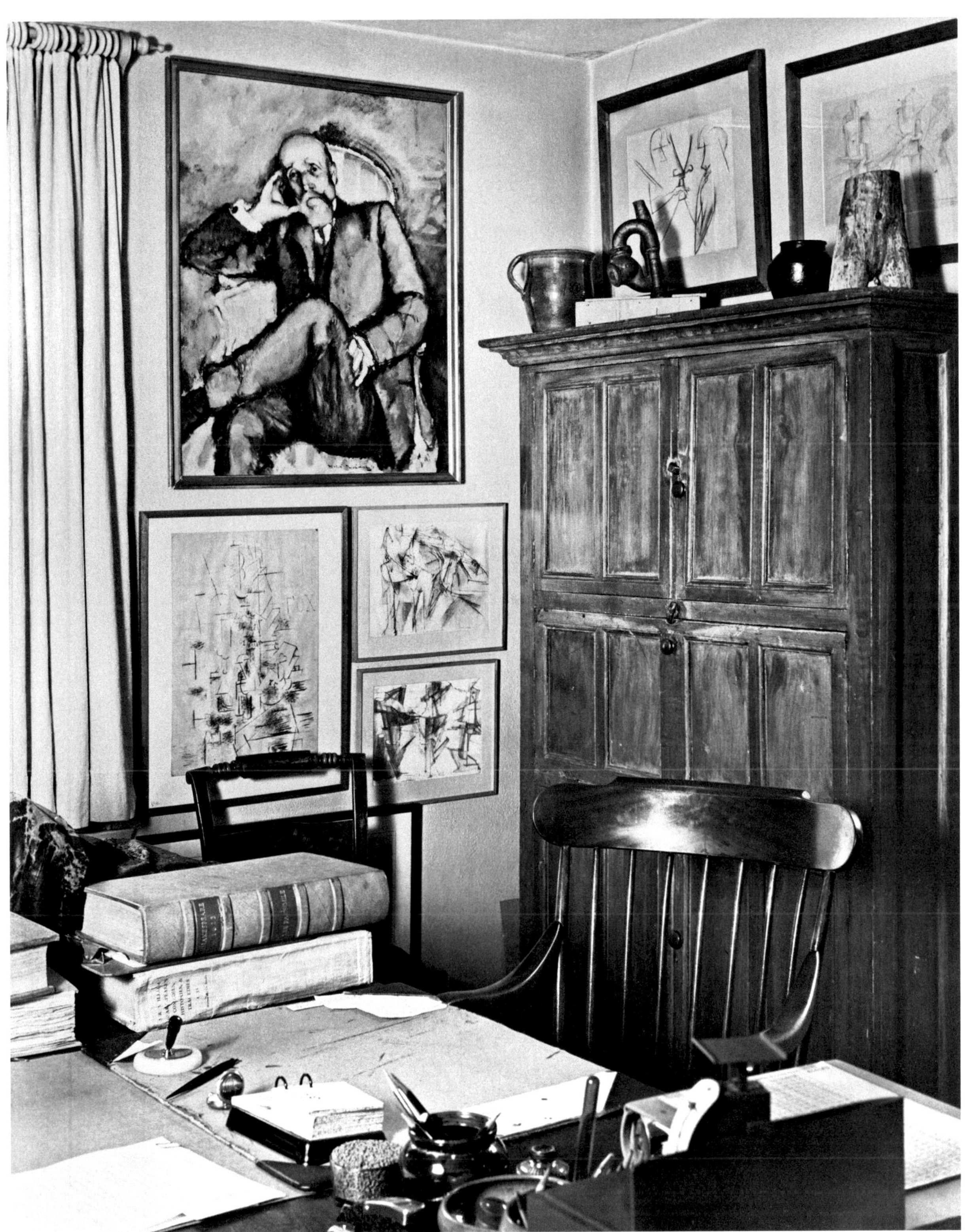

PLATE 42

1 MARCEL DUCHAMP, *Portrait of the Artist's Father*, 1910 [1950-134-49; AC20-54]

2 GEORGES BRAQUE, *Fox*, 1911 (printed 1912) [1950-134-868]

3 WILLIAM SHAKESPEARE, *Shakespeare's Comedies, Histories, & Tragedies: Being a Reproduction in Facsimile of the First Folio Edition 1623 from the Chatsworth Copy in the Possession of the Duke of Devonshire, K.G.*, ed. Sidney Lee (Oxford: Oxford University Press, 1902) [NOTE 3.2, PAGE 416]

4 WILLIAM SHAKESPEARE, *Mr. William Shakespeare's Comedies, Histories, and Tragedies: Faithfully Reproduced in Facsimile from the Edition of 1632* (London: Methuen & Co., 1909) [NOTE 3.3, PAGE 416]

5 REPRODUCTION OF MARCEL DUCHAMP'S DRAWING *Two Nudes: One Strong and One Swift* (1912), Date unknown, [1950-134-919]

6 REPRODUCTION OF MARCEL DUCHAMP'S DRAWING *The Bride Stripped Bare by the Bachelors* (1912), Date unknown [1950-134-920

7 DANIEL THOMAS EGERTON, *View of the City of Mexico*, 1840 [NOTE 1.14, PAGE 415]

8 ARTIST/MAKER UNKNOWN (NORTH AMERICA), Pitcher, Date unknown [NOTE 4.7, PAGE 417]

9 MORTON LIVINGSTON SCHAMBERG and ELSA VON FREYTAG-LORINGHOVEN, *God*, ca. 1917 [1950-134-182; AC20-187]

10 MARCEL DUCHAMP, *Study for "Portrait of Chess Players,"* 1911 [1950-134-55; AC20-60]

11 ARTIST/MAKER UNKNOWN (NORTH AMERICA OR EUROPE), Jar, Date unknown [NOTE 4.8, PAGE 417]

12 MARCEL DUCHAMP, *The King and Queen Traversed by Swift Nudes*, 1912
[1950-134-61; MISATTRIBUTED AS *STUDY FOR "THE KING AND QUEEN SURROUNDED BY SWIFT NUDES"* IN AC20-66]

13 ARTIST/MAKER UNKNOWN, "Found" Wood Sculpture, Date unknown [NOTE 1.15, PAGE 415]

14 MARBLEHEAD POTTERY, Bowl, ca. 1908–36 [NOTE 4.9, PAGE 417]

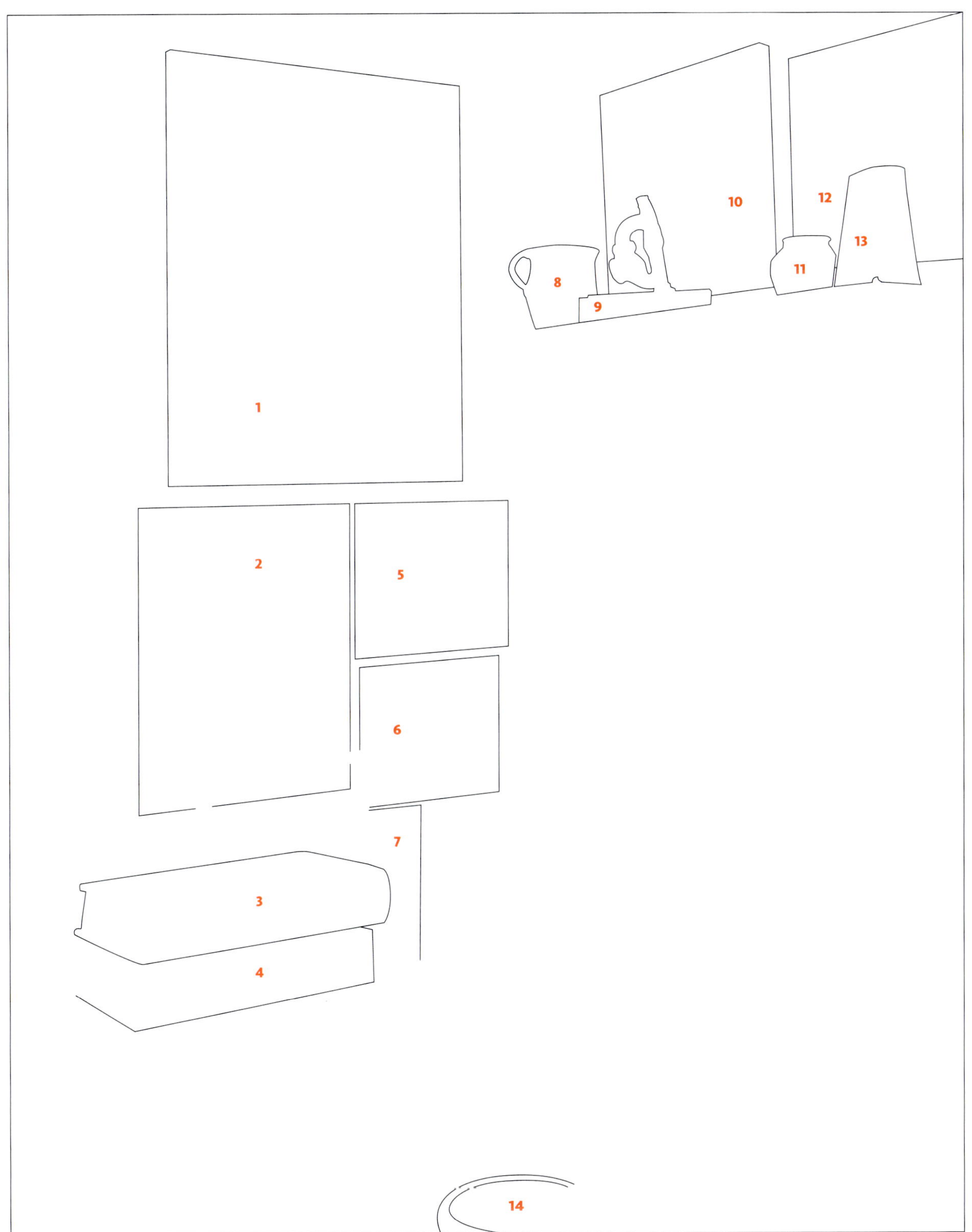
1
2
5
6
7
3
4
8
9
10
11
12
13
14

PLATE 43

SITTING ROOM

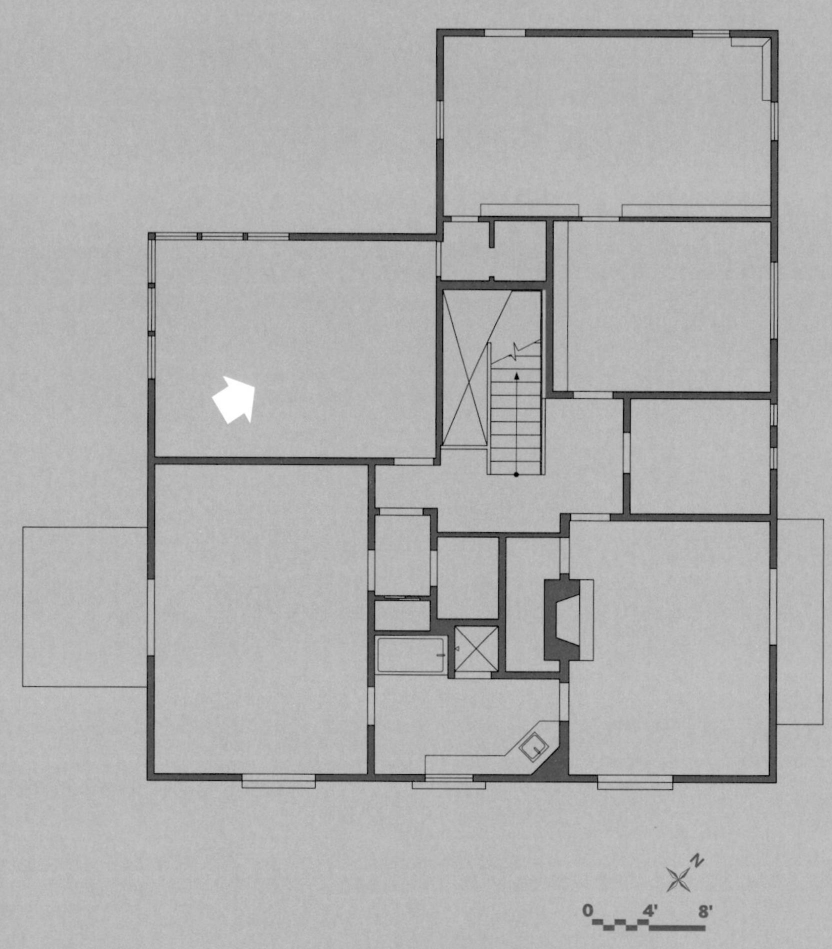

FLOYD FAXON
CA. JANUARY 1951

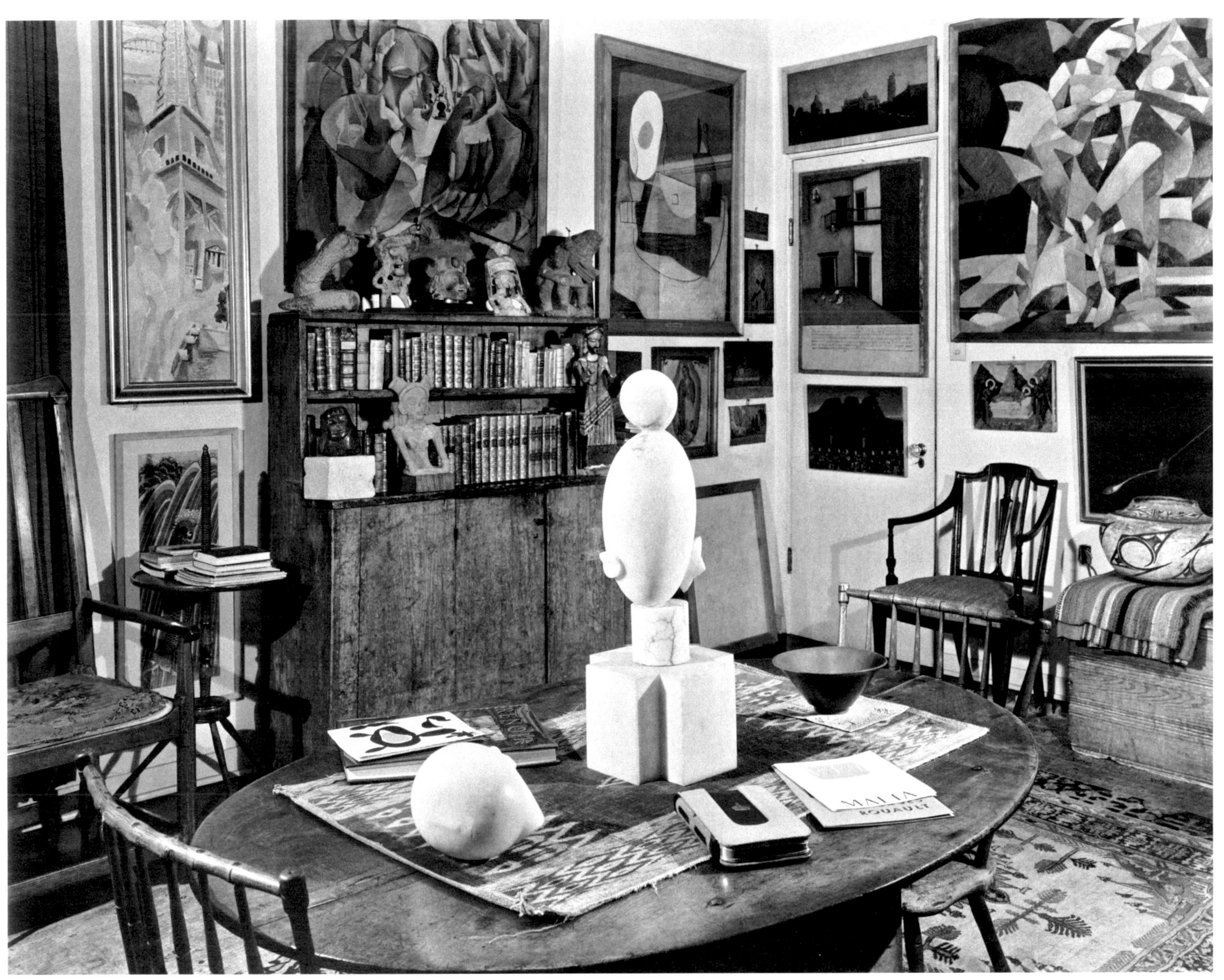
MALIA
ROUAULT

PLATE 43

1 ROBERT DELAUNAY, *Eiffel Tower*, ca. 1925 [1950-134-43A; AC20-43]

2 TOYOKUNI II, *A Carp Leaping a Waterfall*, ca. 1825–30 [NOTE 1.16, PAGE 415]

3 MARCEL DUCHAMP, *Portrait of Chess Players*, 1911 [1950-134-56; AC20-61]

4 *AZTEC (CENTRAL MEXICO), Serpent (Quetzalcoatl), 1300–1520 [1950-134-397; ACPS-29]

5 COLIMA (WESTERN MEXICO), Vessel in the Form of a Man, 300 BCE–300 CE [1950-134-263; ACPS-59]

6 HUASTEC (EAST COAST MEXICO), Head, 900–1200 [1950-134-606]

7 ZAPOTEC (SOUTHERN MEXICO), Effigy Vessel, 100–400 [1950-134-936; ACPS-97]

8 AZTEC (CENTRAL MEXICO), Wind God (Ehecatl), 1300–1520 [1950-134-235; ACPS-12]

9 AZTEC (CENTRAL MEXICO), Bust of Goddess, 1300–1520 [1950-134-236; ACPS-191]

10 HUASTEC (EAST COAST MEXICO), Figure of a Woman, 1000–1500 [1950-134-364; ACPS-130]

11 NATIVE AMERICAN (NEW MEXICO), *San José*, 18th century [1950-134-821]

12 ARTIST/MAKER UNKNOWN (MEXICO), *Joseph María de las Fuentes*, 19th century [1950-134-815]

13 PABLO PICASSO, *Still Life: The Table*, 1921 [1950-134-172; AC20-176]

14 ATTRIBUTED TO MIGUEL CABRERA (MEXICO), *Virgin of Guadalupe*, ca. 1740 [1950-134-817]

15 ARTIST/MAKER UNKNOWN (*MEXICO), Retablo, 7 December 1886 [1950-134-812]

16 ARTIST/MAKER UNKNOWN (*NEW MEXICO AREA), *Our Lady of the Immaculate Conception*, ca. 1820–50 [1950-134-826]

17 ARTIST/MAKER UNKNOWN (MEXICO), *Recovery from an Illness*, 1849 [1950-134-814]

18 ARTIST/MAKER UNKNOWN (MEXICO), *Delivery from Prison*, ca. 1902 [1950-134-813]

19 WILLIAM BLAKE, *The Bard*, ca. 1809 [1950-134-3, VERSO]

20 ARTIST/MAKER UNKNOWN (ITALY), *Religious Procession to the Cathedral of Pisa*, ca. 1675–1700 [1950-134-529]

21 ARTIST/MAKER UNKNOWN (MEXICO), *Fall from a Balcony*, ca. 1803 [1950-134-492]

22 ARTIST/MAKER UNKNOWN (MEXICO), *The Execution of Maximilian*, After 1867 [1950-134-827]

THE EXECUTION OF MAXIMILIAN MAY HAVE BEEN PAINTED BY ROBERTO MONTENEGRO FOR THE ARENSBERGS AFTER THEY TOLD HIM THEY ADMIRED THE 19TH-CENTURY ORIGINAL. SEE MONTENEGRO, LETTER TO THE ARENSBERGS, MEXICO CITY, 11 AUGUST 1948, PMA-WLA, BOX 12, FOLDER 62.

23 FRANCIS PICABIA, *Dances at the Spring*, 1912 [1950-134-155; AC20-158]

24 ARTIST/MAKER UNKNOWN (GREECE), *The Entombment of Saint Catherine of Alexandria*, Late 15th century [1950-134-194]

25 SALVADOR DALÍ, *Agnostic Symbol*, 1932 [1950-134-40; AC20-39]

26 NATIVE AMERICAN (SOUTHWESTERN UNITED STATES), Vessel, Date unknown [1950-134-419]

27 ARTIST/MAKER UNKNOWN (CHINA), Bowl, Date unknown [1950-134-863]

28 CONSTANTIN BRANCUSI, *White Negress [I]*, 1923 [1950-134-16; AC20-17]

29 DESIGNED BY MARCEL DUCHAMP, EXECUTED BY MARY REYNOLDS, Bookbinding for Alfred Jarry's *Ubu Roi*, 1935 [1950-134-77; AC20-85]

30 CONSTANTIN BRANCUSI, *Prometheus*, 1911 [1950-134-5; AC20-4]

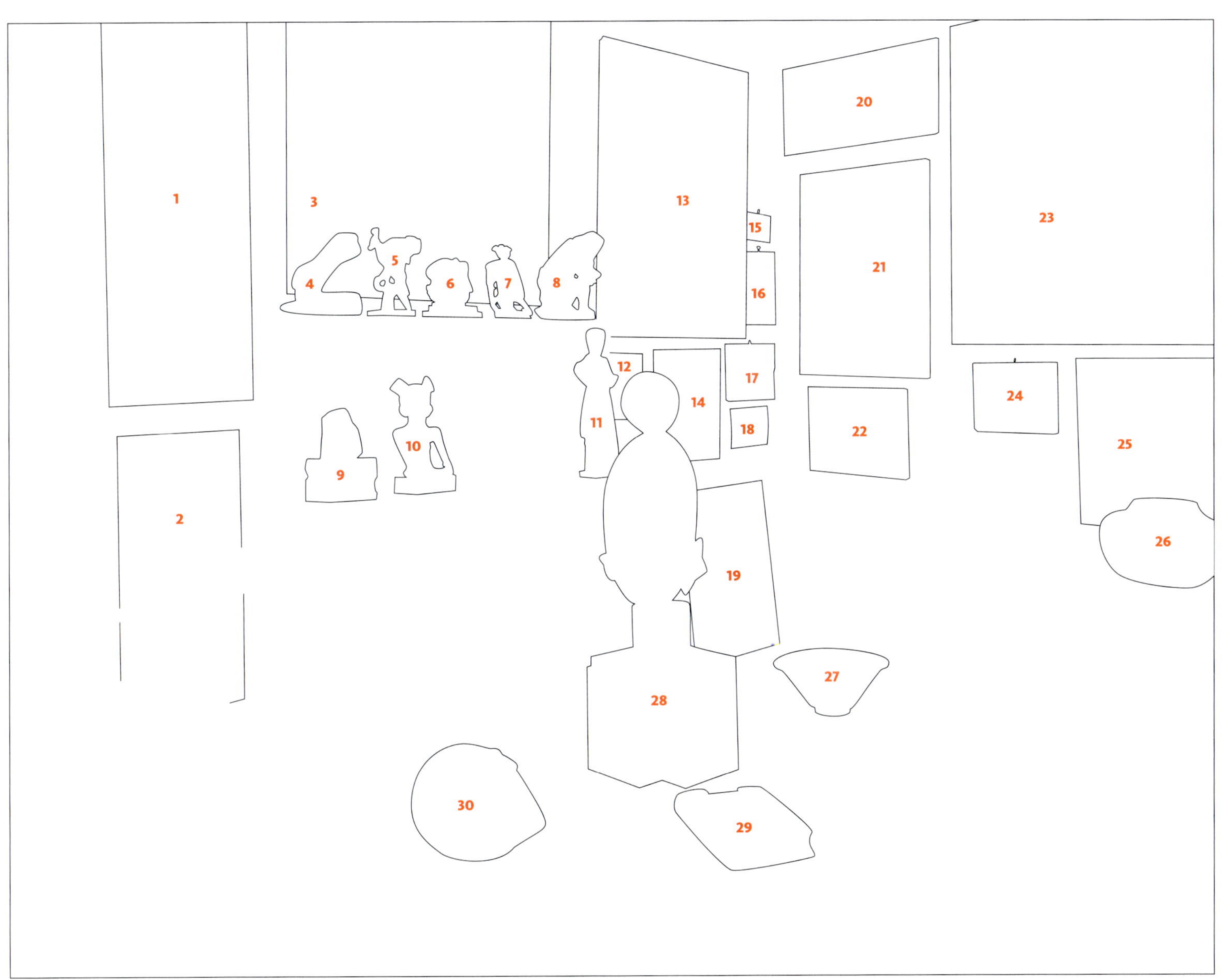
1
2
3
4
5
6
7
8
9
10
11
12
13
14
15
16
17
18
19
20
21
22
23
24
25
26
27
28
29
30

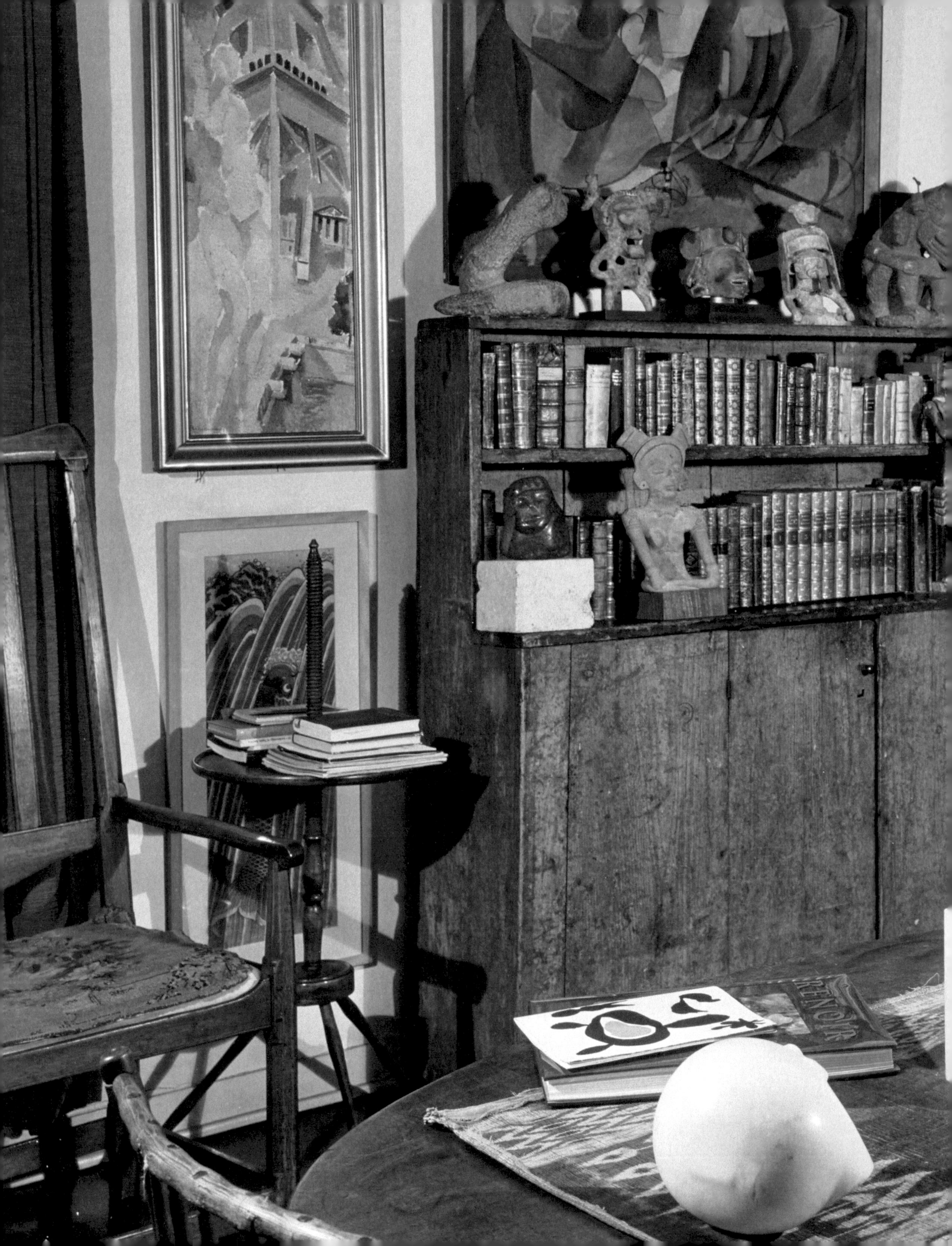
RENOIR

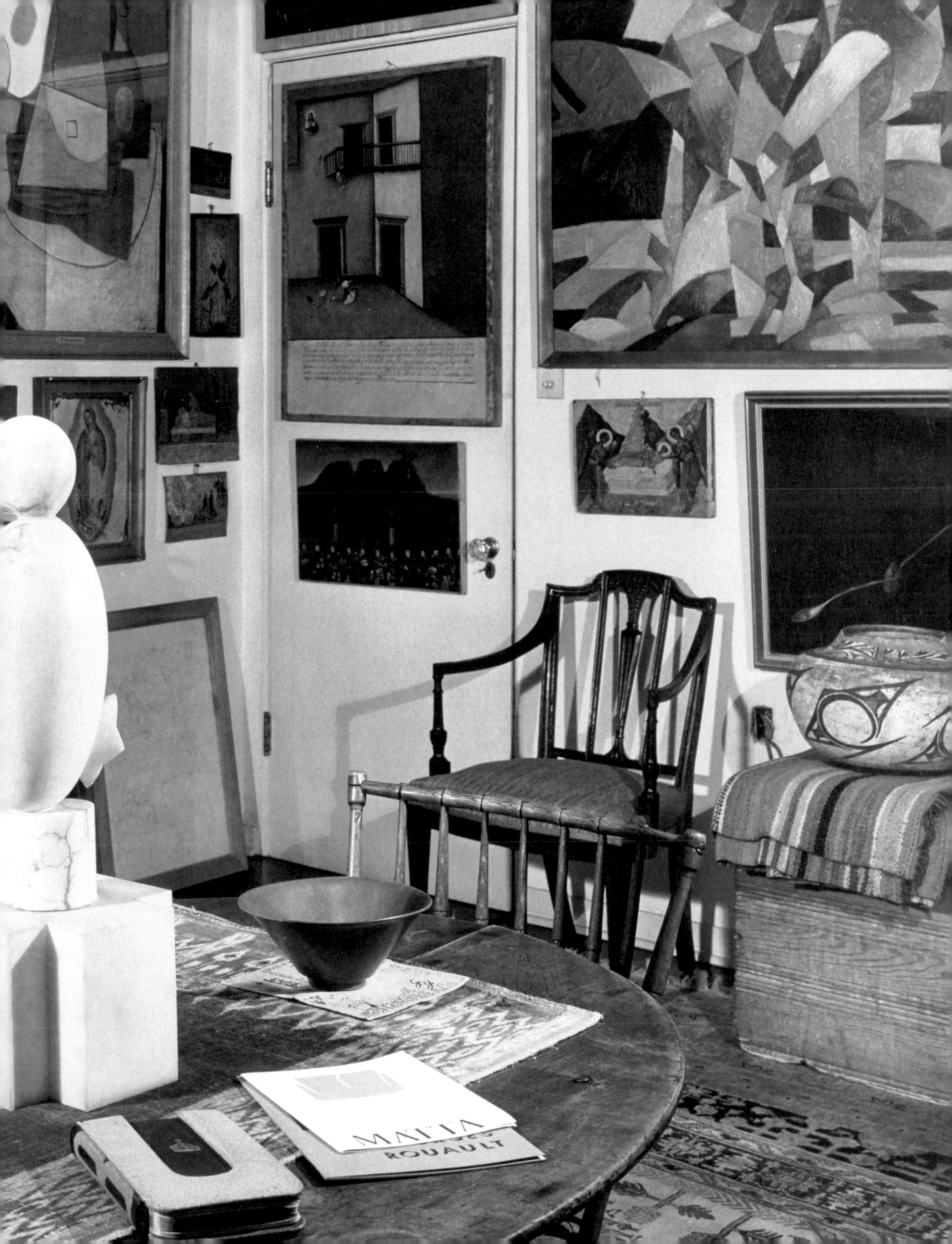
MATTA
ROUAULT

PLATE 44

SITTING ROOM

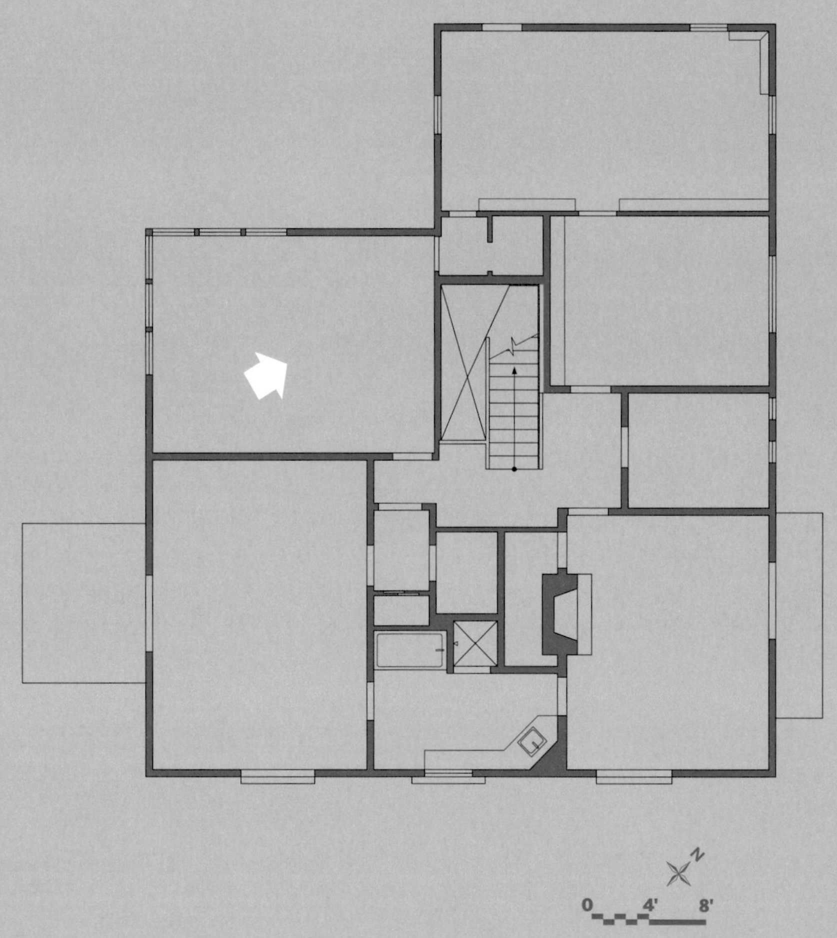

FRED R. DAPPRICH

CA. 1944

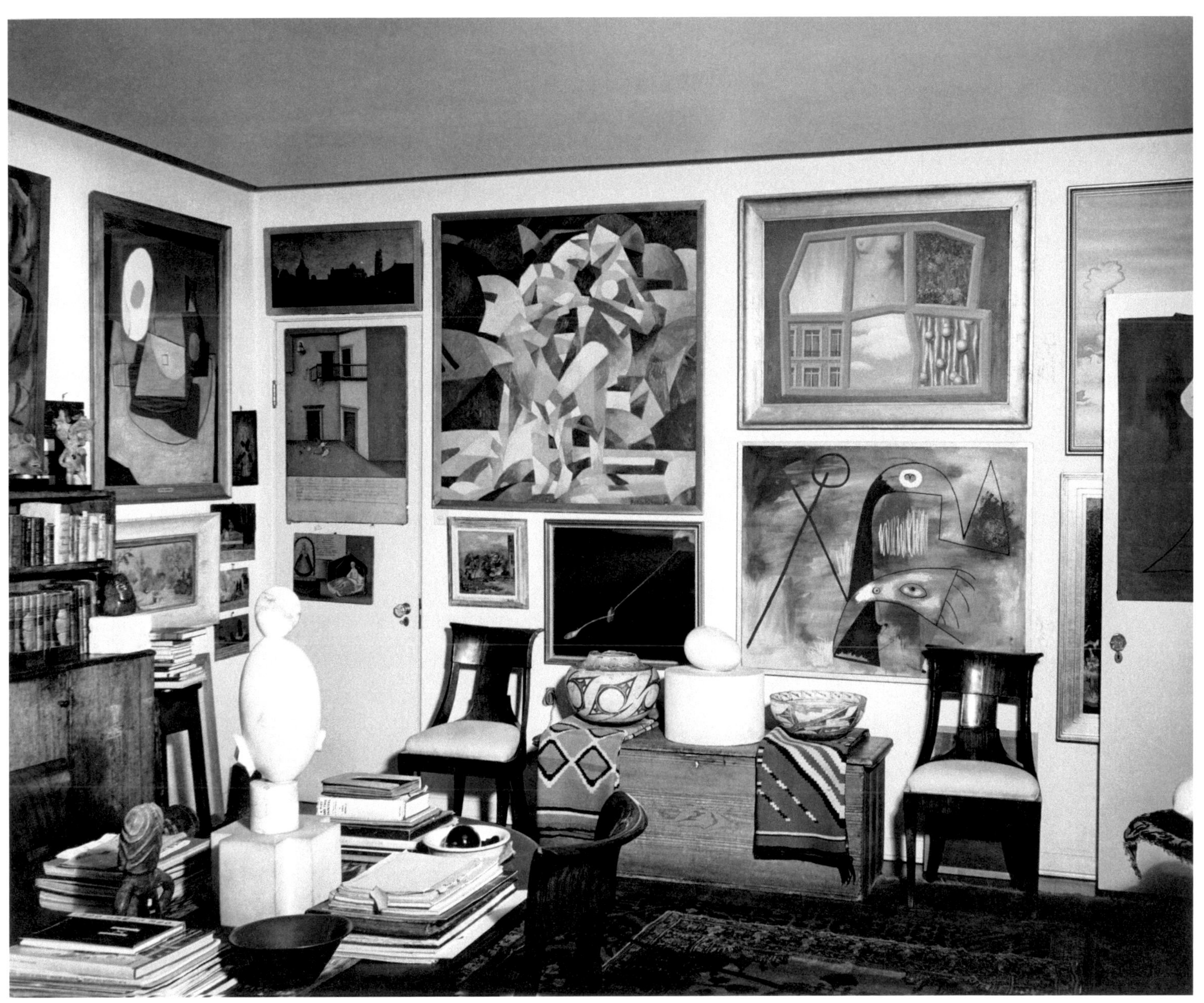

PLATE 44

1 MARCEL DUCHAMP, *Portrait of Chess Players*, 1911 [1950-134-56; AC20-61]

2 HUASTEC (EAST COAST MEXICO), Head, 900–1200 [1950-134-606]

3 ARTIST/MAKER UNKNOWN (MEXICO), *Recovery from an Illness*, ca. 1865 [1950-134-823]

4 ARTIST/MAKER UNKNOWN (*MEXICO), Retablo, Date unknown [1950-134-822]

5 COLIMA (WESTERN MEXICO), Vessel in the Form of a Man, 300 BCE–300 CE [1950-134-263; ACPS-59]

6 MEZCALA (SOUTHWESTERN MEXICO), Figure, 300 BCE–500 CE [1950-134-270; ACPS-82]

7 MEZCALA (SOUTHWESTERN MEXICO), Figure, 300 BCE–500 CE [1950-134-561]

8 AZTEC (CENTRAL MEXICO), Bust of Goddess, 1300–1520 [1950-134-236; ACPS-191]

9 COLIMA (WESTERN MEXICO), Fragmentary Figure of a Man with Headgear, 300 BCE–300 CE [1950-134-620]

10 PABLO PICASSO, *Still Life: The Table*, 1921 [1950-134-172; AC20-176]

11 LOUIS MICHEL EILSHEMIUS, *Landscape*, 1917 [1950-134-510]

*12 WILLIAM BLAKE, *The Bard*, ca. 1809 [1950-134-3, VERSO]

13 ARTIST/MAKER UNKNOWN (*NEW MEXICO AREA), *Our Lady of the Immaculate Conception*, ca. 1820–50 [1950-134-826]

14 ARTIST/MAKER UNKNOWN (MEXICO), *Recovery from an Illness*, 1849 [1950-134-814]

15 ARTIST/MAKER UNKNOWN (MEXICO), *Delivery from Prison*, ca. 1902 [1950-134-813]

16 ARTIST/MAKER UNKNOWN (MEXICO), *Accident in a Well*, ca. 1864 [1950-134-824]

17 CONSTANTIN BRANCUSI, *White Negress [I]*, 1923 [1950-134-16; AC20-17]

18 ARTIST/MAKER UNKNOWN (CHINA), Bowl, Date unknown [1950-134-863]

19 ARTIST/MAKER UNKNOWN (ITALY), *Religious Procession to the Cathedral of Pisa*, ca. 1675–1700 [1950-134-529]

20 ARTIST/MAKER UNKNOWN (MEXICO), *Fall from a Balcony*, ca. 1803 [1950-134-492]

21 ARTIST/MAKER UNKNOWN (MEXICO), *Joseph María de las Fuentes*, 19th century [1950-134-815]

22 DESIGNED BY MARCEL DUCHAMP, EXECUTED BY MARY REYNOLDS, Bookbinding for Alfred Jarry's *Ubu Roi*, 1935 [1950-134-77; AC20-85]

23 ARTIST/MAKER UNKNOWN (CHINA), Bowl, Date unknown [1950-134-850]

24 ARTIST/MAKER UNKNOWN (*CHINA), Crystal Sphere, Date unknown [NOTE 4.5, PAGE 417]

25 DAVID BURLIUK, *The Refugees*, Date unknown [NOTE 1.17, PAGE 415]

26 FRANCIS PICABIA, *Dances at the Spring*, 1912 [1950-134-155; AC20-158]

27 SALVADOR DALÍ, *Agnostic Symbol*, 1932 [1950-134-40; AC20-39]

28 NATIVE AMERICAN (SOUTHWESTERN UNITED STATES), Vessel, Date unknown [1950-134-419]

29 CONSTANTIN BRANCUSI, *Sculpture for the Blind [I]*, ca. 1920 [1950-134-20; AC20-18]

30 RENÉ MAGRITTE, *The Six Elements*, 1929 [1950-134-127; AC20-130]

31 JOAN MIRÓ, *Man, Woman, and Child*, 1931 [1950-134-144; AC20-147]

32 NATIVE AMERICAN (SOUTHWESTERN UNITED STATES), Bowl, Date unknown [1950-134-420]

33 YVES TANGUY, *The Parallels*, 1929 [1950-134-188; AC20-193]

34 YVES TANGUY, *The Storm (Black Landscape)*, 1926 [1950-134-187; AC20-192]

35 JOAN MIRÓ, *Man and Woman*, 1925 [1950-134-142; AC20-145]

36 CONSTANTIN BRANCUSI, *Prometheus*, 1911 [1950-134-5; AC20-4]

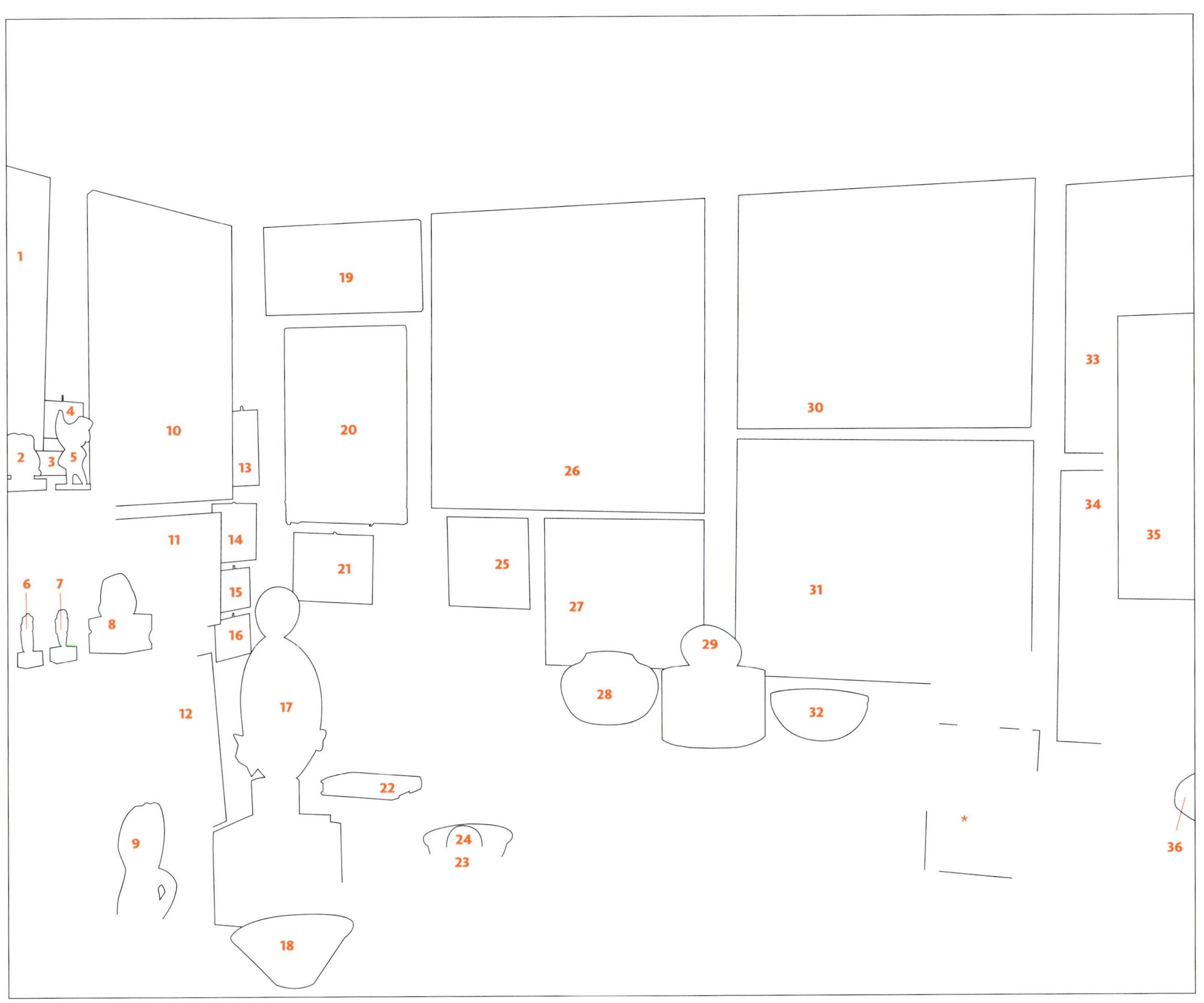
1
2
3
4
5
6
7
8
9
10
11
12
13
14
15
16
17
18
19
20
21
22
23
24
25
26
27
28
29
30
31
32
33
34
35
36
*

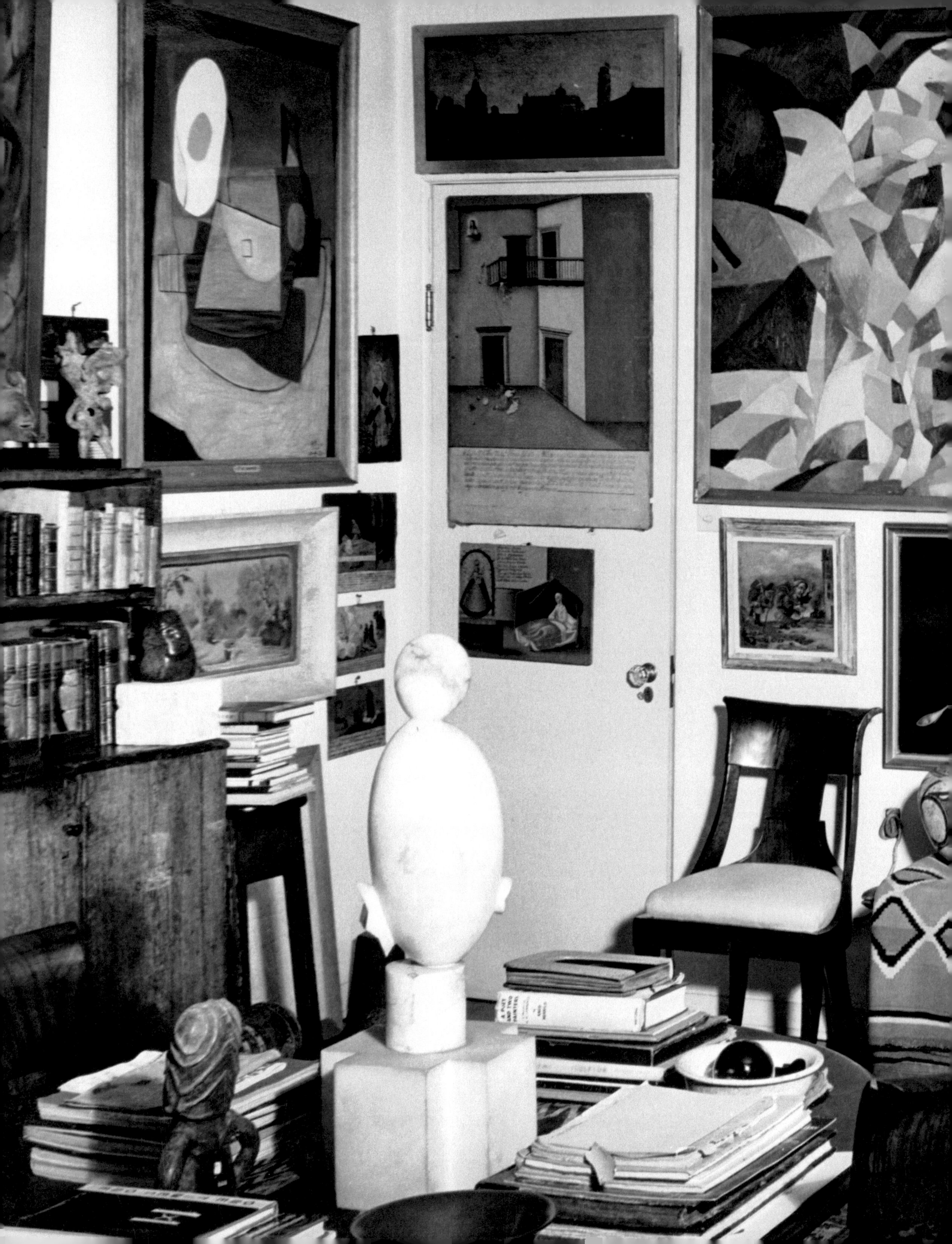

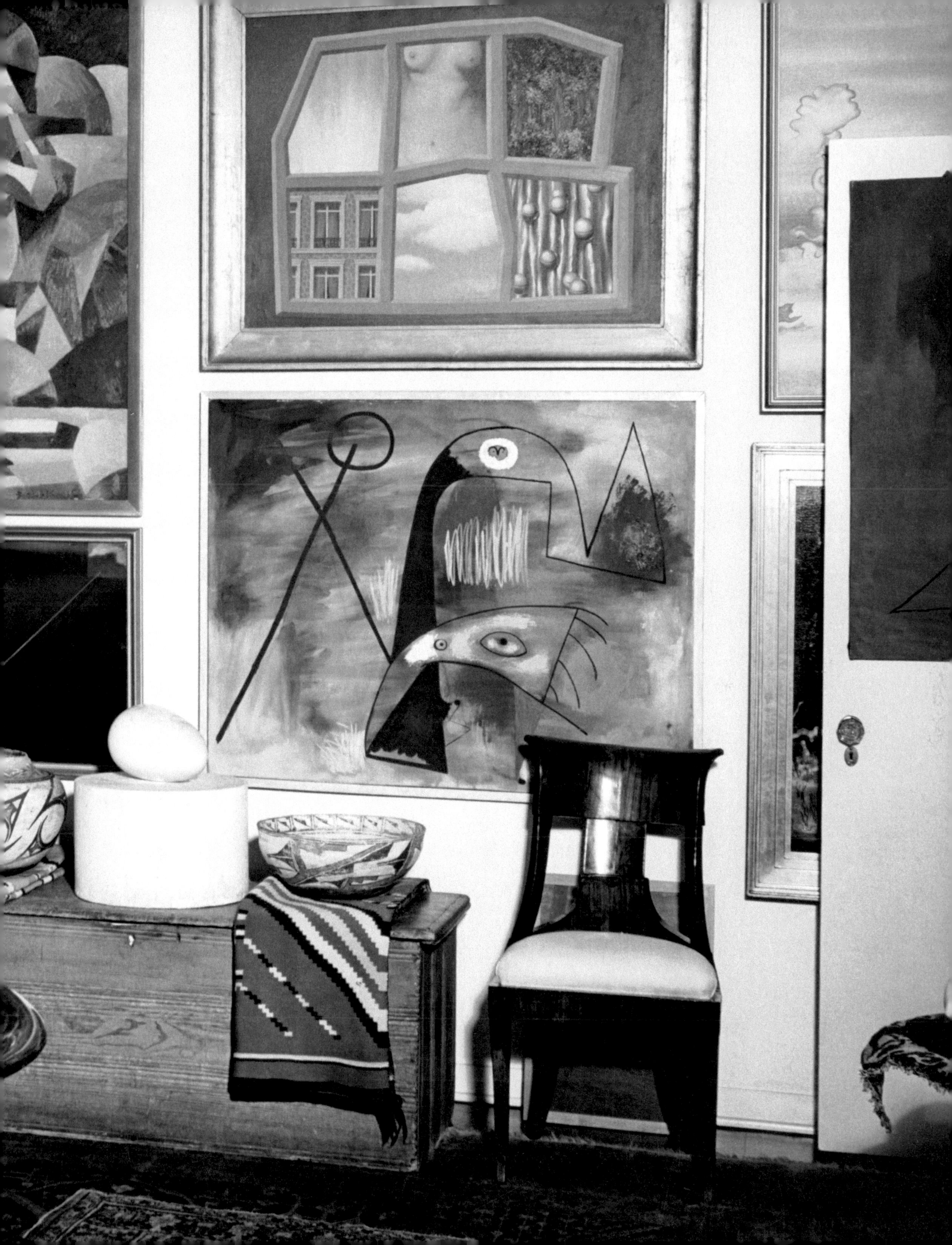

PLATE 45

SITTING ROOM

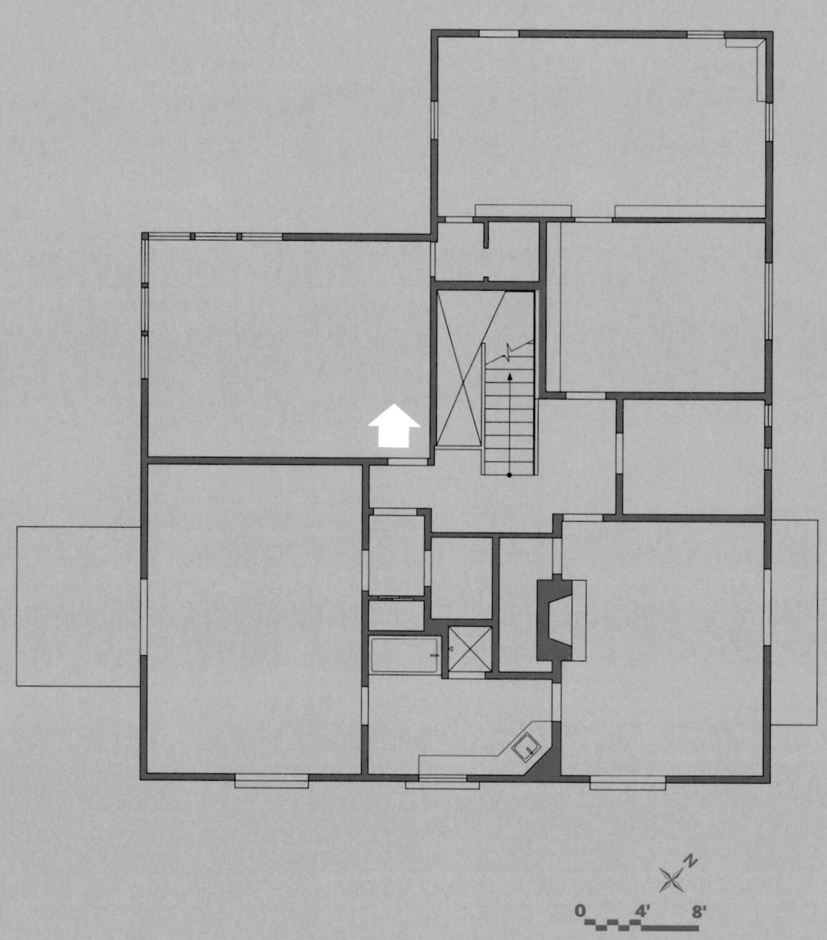

KARL BISSINGER
16 MARCH 1950

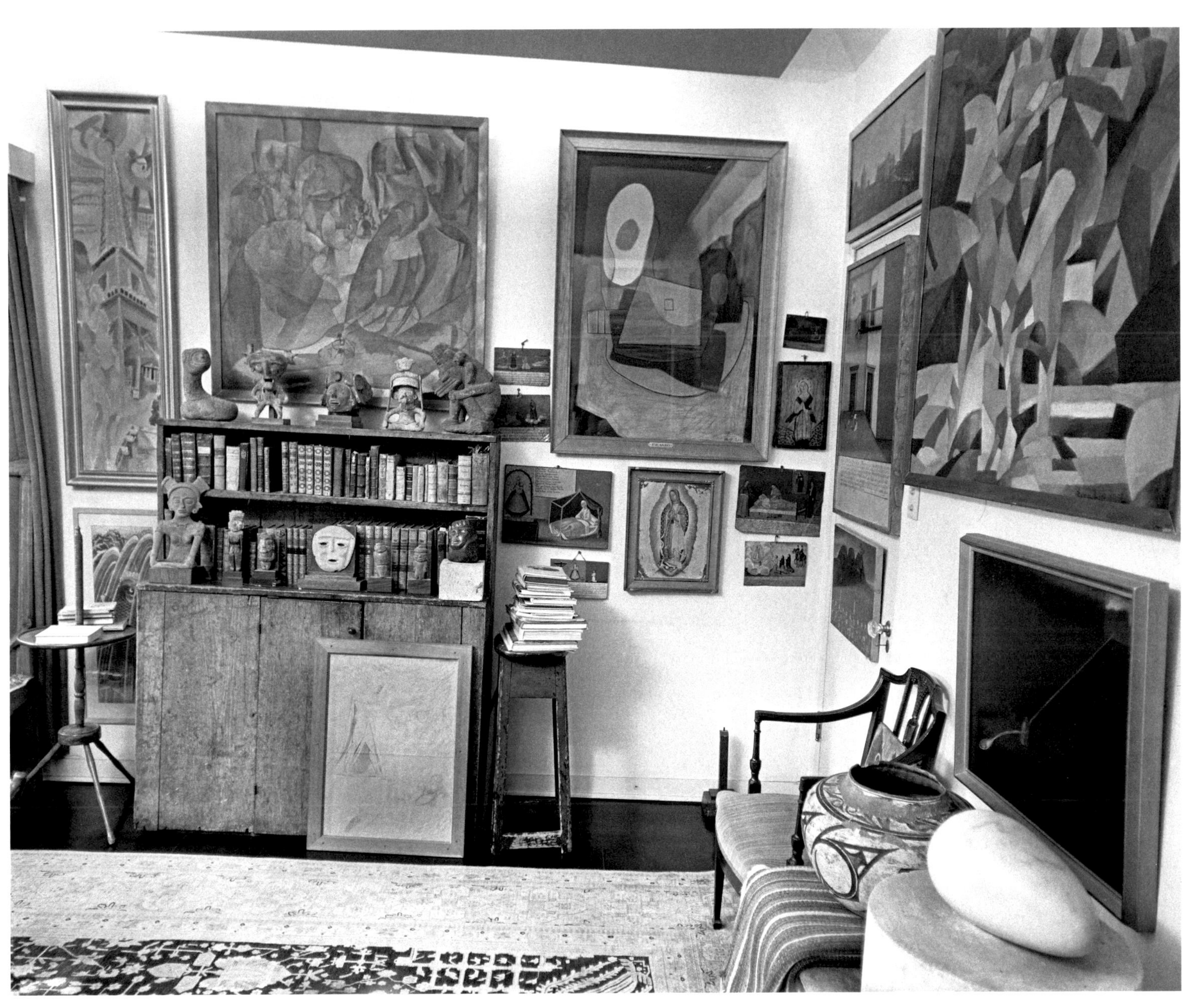

PLATE 45

1 ROBERT DELAUNAY, *Eiffel Tower*, ca. 1925 [1950-134-43A; AC20-43]

2 *AZTEC (CENTRAL MEXICO), Serpent (Quetzalcoatl), 1300–1520 [1950-134-397; ACPS-29]

3 MARCEL DUCHAMP, *Portrait of Chess Players*, 1911 [1950-134-56; AC20-61]

4 COLIMA (WESTERN MEXICO), Vessel in the Form of a Man, 300 BCE–300 CE [1950-134-263; ACPS-59]

5 HUASTEC (EAST COAST MEXICO), Head, 900–1200 [1950-134-606]

6 ZAPOTEC (SOUTHERN MEXICO), Effigy Vessel, 100–400 [1950-134-936; ACPS-97]

7 AZTEC (CENTRAL MEXICO), Wind God (Ehecatl), 1300–1520 [1950-134-235; ACPS-12]

8 ARTIST/MAKER UNKNOWN (MEXICO), *Accident in a Well*, ca. 1864 [1950-134-824]

9 ARTIST/MAKER UNKNOWN (MEXICO), Retablo, Date unknown [1950-134-822]

10 PABLO PICASSO, *Still Life: The Table*, 1921 [1950-134-172; AC20-176]

11 ARTIST/MAKER UNKNOWN (*MEXICO), Retablo, 7 December 1886 [1950-134-812]

12 ARTIST/MAKER UNKNOWN (*NEW MEXICO AREA), *Our Lady of the Immaculate Conception*, ca. 1820–50 [1950-134-826]

13 ARTIST/MAKER UNKNOWN (MEXICO), *Recovery from an Illness*, 1849 [1950-134-814]

14 ARTIST/MAKER UNKNOWN (MEXICO), *Delivery from Prison*, ca. 1902 [1950-134-813]

15 ATTRIBUTED TO MIGUEL CABRERA (MEXICO), *Virgin of Guadalupe*, ca. 1740 [1950-134-817]

16 ARTIST/MAKER UNKNOWN (MEXICO), *Recovery from an Illness*, ca. 1865 [1950-134-823]

17 ARTIST/MAKER UNKNOWN (MEXICO), *Joseph María de las Fuentes*, 19th century [1950-134-815]

18 AZTEC (CENTRAL MEXICO), Bust of Goddess, 1300–1520 [1950-134-236; ACPS-191]

19 MEZCALA (SOUTHWESTERN MEXICO), Figure, 300 BCE–500 CE [1950-134-270; ACPS-82]

20 MEZCALA (SOUTHWESTERN MEXICO), Figure, 300 BCE–500 CE [1950-134-561]

21 MEZCALA (SOUTHWESTERN MEXICO), Mask, 300 BCE–500 CE [1950-134-259; ACPS-95]

22 MEZCALA (SOUTHWESTERN MEXICO), Figure, 300 BCE–500 CE [1950-134-562]

23 MEZCALA (SOUTHWESTERN MEXICO), Standing Human Figure, 300 BCE–500 CE [1950-134-539]

24 HUASTEC (EAST COAST MEXICO), Figure of a Woman, 1000–1500 [1950-134-364; ACPS-130]

25 TOYOKUNI II, *A Carp Leaping a Waterfall*, ca. 1825–30 [NOTE 1.16, PAGE 415]

26 WILLIAM BLAKE, *The Bard*, ca. 1809 [1950-134-3, VERSO]

27 ARTIST/MAKER UNKNOWN (GREECE), *The Entombment of Saint Catherine of Alexandria*, Late 15th century [1950-134-194]

28 NATIVE AMERICAN (SOUTHWESTERN UNITED STATES), Vessel, Date unknown [1950-134-419]

29 CONSTANTIN BRANCUSI, *Sculpture for the Blind [I]*, ca. 1920 [1950-134-20; AC20-18]

30 SALVADOR DALÍ, *Agnostic Symbol*, 1932 [1950-134-40; AC20-39]

31 FRANCIS PICABIA, *Dances at the Spring*, 1912 [1950-134-155; AC20-158]

32 ARTIST/MAKER UNKNOWN (ITALY), *Religious Procession to the Cathedral of Pisa*, ca. 1675–1700 [1950-134-529]

33 ARTIST/MAKER UNKNOWN (MEXICO), *Fall from a Balcony*, ca. 1803 [1950-134-492]

34 ARTIST/MAKER UNKNOWN (MEXICO), *The Execution of Maximilian*, After 1867 [1950-134-827]

THE EXECUTION OF MAXIMILIAN MAY HAVE BEEN PAINTED BY ROBERTO MONTENEGRO FOR THE ARENSBERGS AFTER THEY TOLD HIM THEY ADMIRED THE 19TH-CENTURY ORIGINAL. SEE MONTENEGRO, LETTER TO THE ARENSBERGS, MEXICO CITY, 11 AUGUST 1948, PMA-WLA, BOX 12, FOLDER 62.

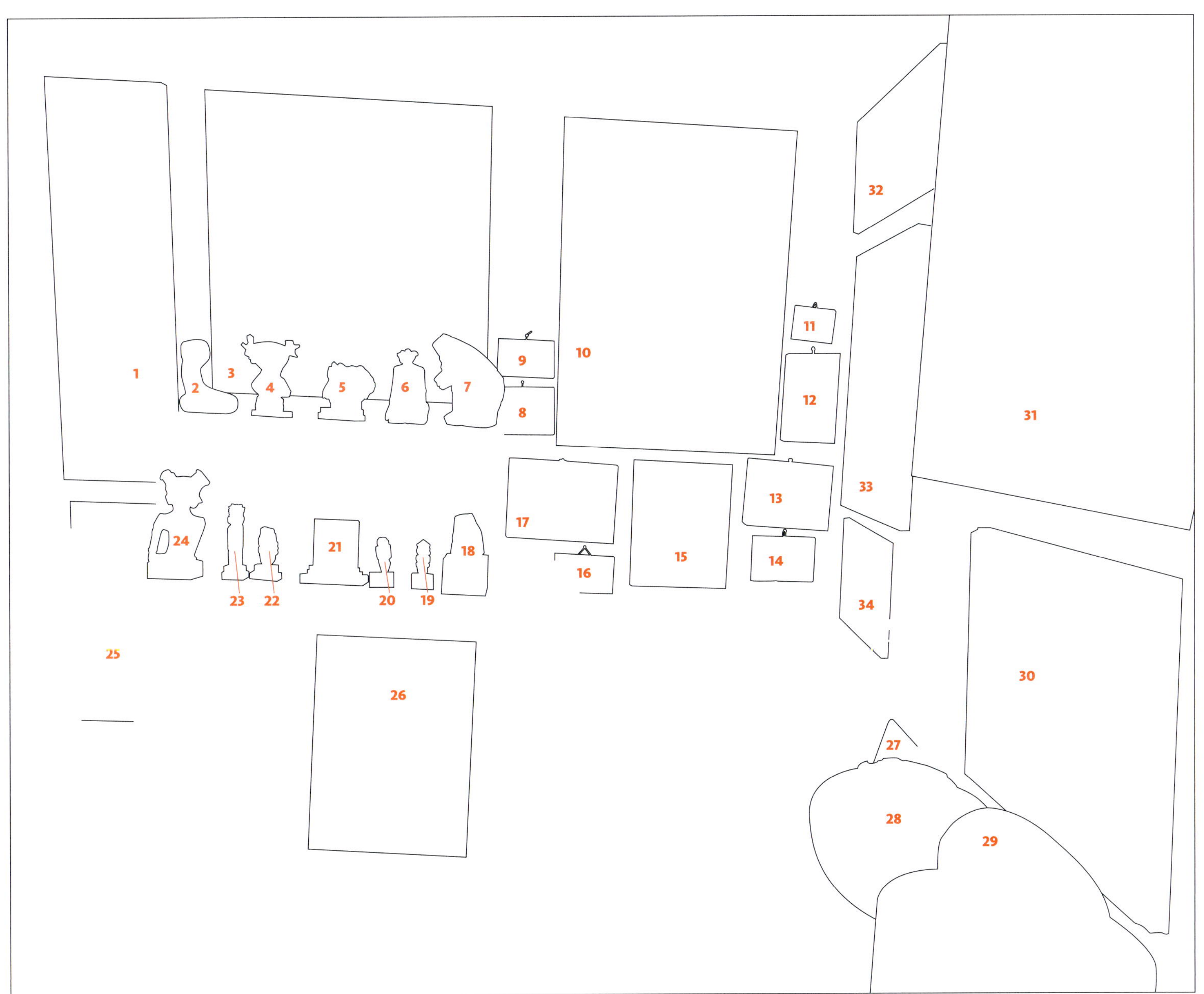
1
2
3
4
5
6
7
8
9
10
11
12
13
14
15
16
17
18
19
20
21
22
23
24
25
26
27
28
29
30
31
32
33
34

PLATE 46

SITTING ROOM

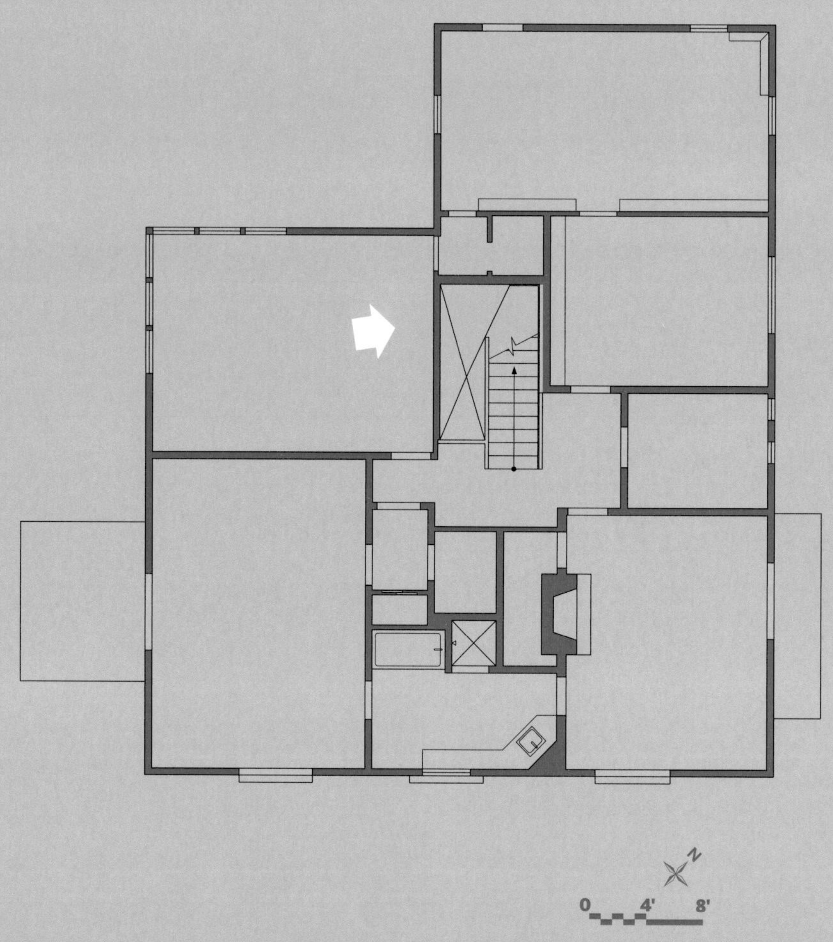

FLOYD FAXON

CA. JANUARY 1951

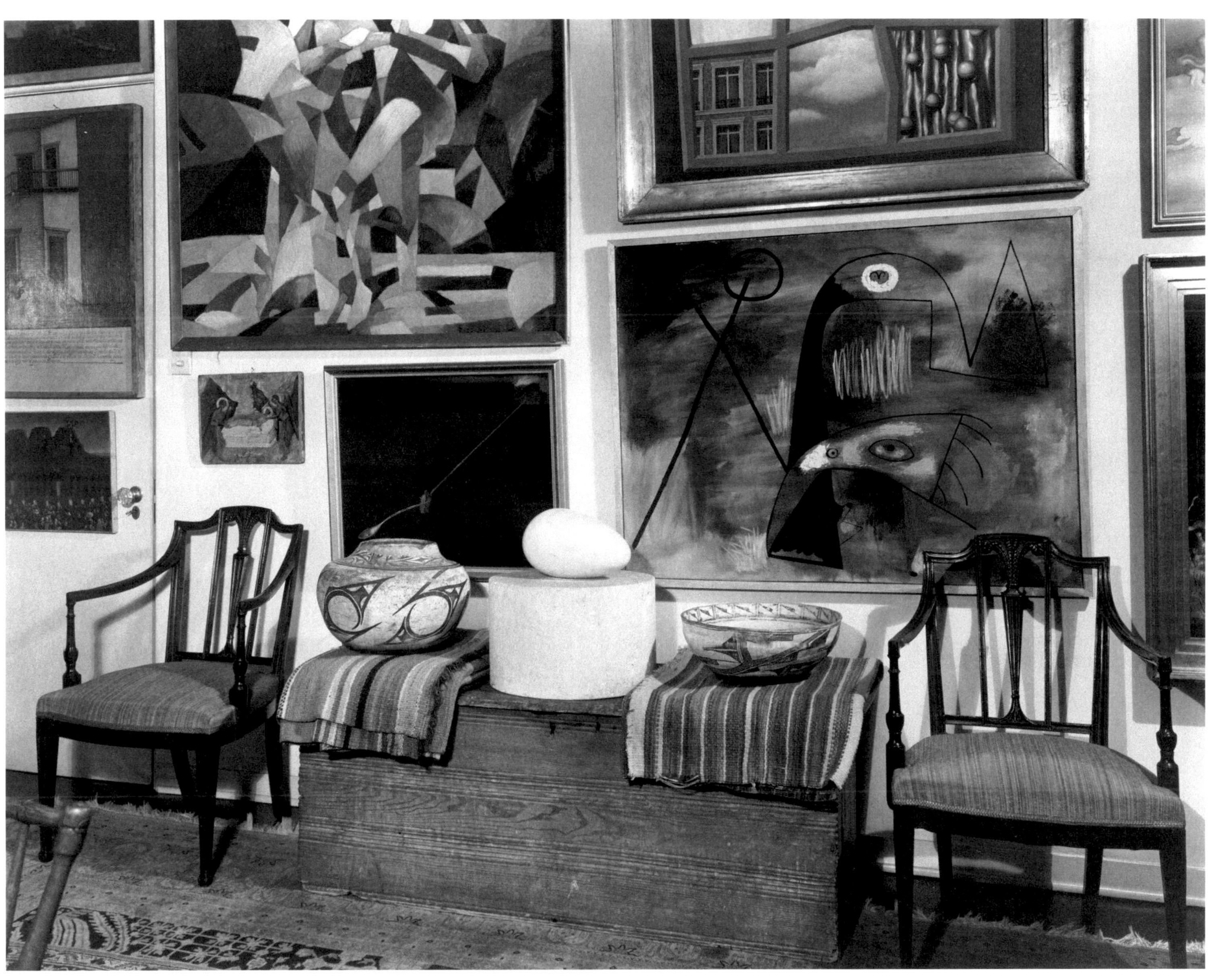

PLATE 46

1 ARTIST/MAKER UNKNOWN (ITALY), *Religious Procession to the Cathedral of Pisa*, ca. 1675–1700 [1950-134-529]

2 ARTIST/MAKER UNKNOWN (MEXICO), *Fall from a Balcony*, ca. 1803 [1950-134-492]

3 ARTIST/MAKER UNKNOWN (MEXICO), *The Execution of Maximilian*, After 1867 [1950-134-827]

THE EXECUTION OF MAXIMILIAN MAY HAVE BEEN PAINTED BY ROBERTO MONTENEGRO FOR THE ARENSBERGS AFTER THEY TOLD HIM THEY ADMIRED THE 19TH-CENTURY ORIGINAL. SEE MONTENEGRO, LETTER TO THE ARENSBERGS, MEXICO CITY, 11 AUGUST 1948, PMA-WLA, BOX 12, FOLDER 62.

4 FRANCIS PICABIA, *Dances at the Spring*, 1912 [1950-134-155; AC20-158]

5 ARTIST/MAKER UNKNOWN (GREECE), *The Entombment of Saint Catherine of Alexandria*, Late 15th century [1950-134-194]

6 SALVADOR DALÍ, *Agnostic Symbol*, 1932 [1950-134-40; AC20-39]

7 NATIVE AMERICAN (SOUTHWESTERN UNITED STATES), Vessel, Date unknown [1950-134-419]

8 CONSTANTIN BRANCUSI, *Sculpture for the Blind [I]*, ca. 1920 [1950-134-20; AC20-18]

9 RENÉ MAGRITTE, *The Six Elements*, 1929 [1950-134-127; AC20-130]

10 JOAN MIRÓ, *Man, Woman, and Child*, 1931 [1950-134-144; AC20-147]

11 NATIVE AMERICAN (SOUTHWESTERN UNITED STATES), Bowl, Date unknown [1950-134-420]

12 YVES TANGUY, *The Parallels*, 1929 [1950-134-188; AC20-193]

13 YVES TANGUY, *The Storm (Black Landscape)*, 1926 [1950-134-187; AC20-192]

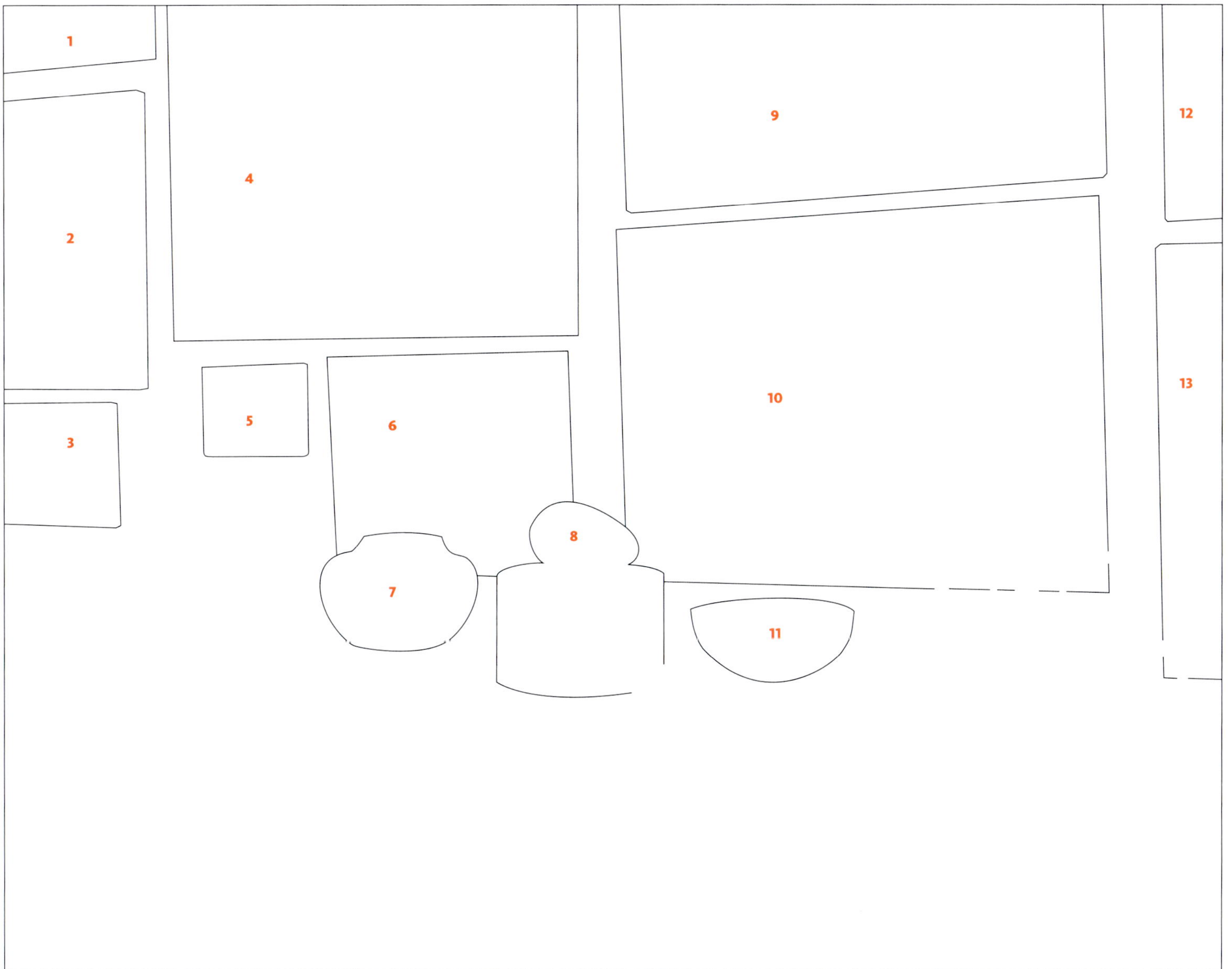
1
2
3
4
5
6
7
8
9
10
11
12
13

PLATE 47

SITTING ROOM

WITH A VIEW OF THE LANDING AND HALLWAY THROUGH THE DOOR

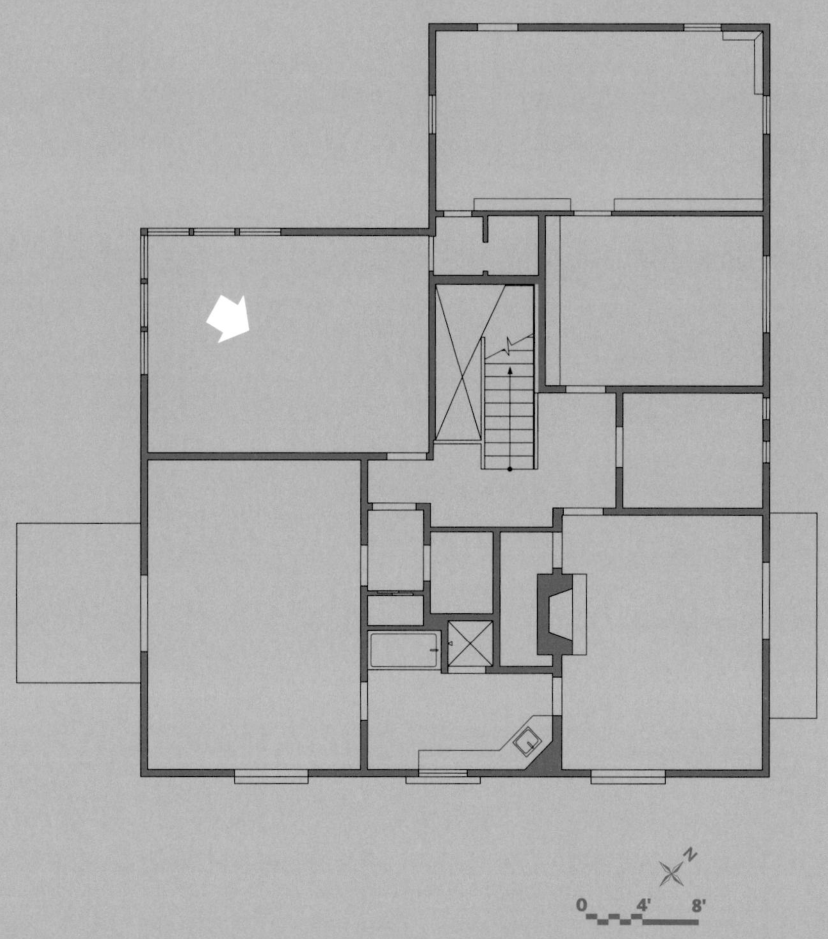

KARL BISSINGER
16 MARCH 1950

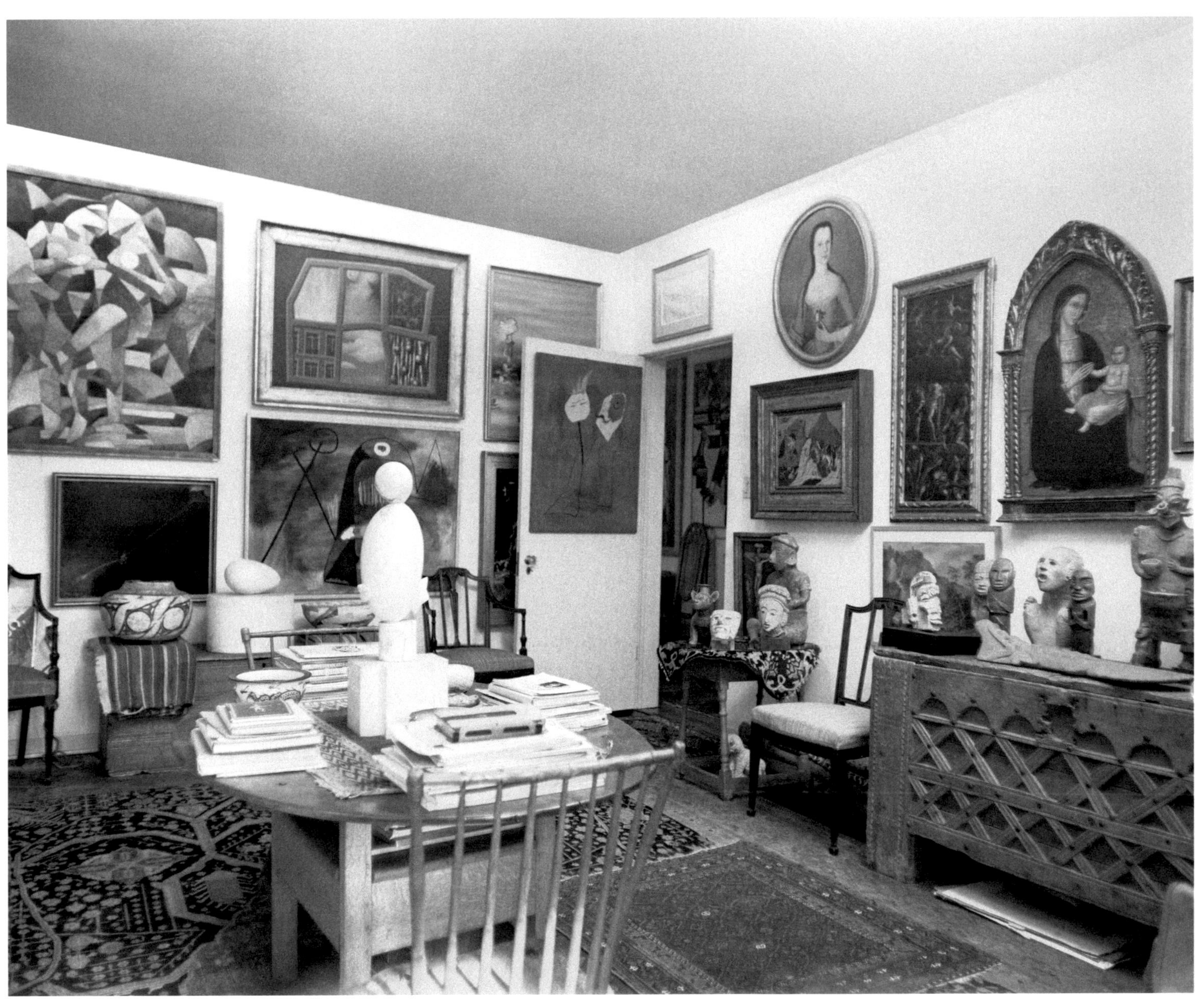

PLATE 47

1 FRANCIS PICABIA, *Dances at the Spring*, 1912 [1950-134-155; AC20-158]

2 SALVADOR DALÍ, *Agnostic Symbol*, 1932 [1950-134-40; AC20-39]

3 NATIVE AMERICAN (SOUTHWESTERN UNITED STATES), Vessel, Date unknown [1950-134-419]

4 CONSTANTIN BRANCUSI, *Sculpture for the Blind [I]*, ca. 1920 [1950-134-20; AC20-18]

5 NATIVE AMERICAN (SOUTHWESTERN UNITED STATES), Bowl, Date unknown [1950-134-420]

6 ARTIST/MAKER UNKNOWN (CHINA), Bowl, Date unknown [NOTE 4.10, PAGE 417]

7 CONSTANTIN BRANCUSI, *White Negress [I]*, 1923 [1950-134-16; AC20-17]

8 DESIGNED BY MARCEL DUCHAMP, EXECUTED BY MARY REYNOLDS, Bookbinding for Alfred Jarry's *Ubu Roi*, 1935 [1950-134-77; AC20-

9 ARTIST/MAKER UNKNOWN (NORTH AMERICA), Powder Horn, Date unknown [1950-134-199]

10 JOAN MIRÓ, *Man, Woman, and Child*, 1931 [1950-134-144; AC20-147]

11 RENÉ MAGRITTE, *The Six Elements*, 1929 [1950-134-127; AC20-130]

12 YVES TANGUY, *The Parallels*, 1929 [1950-134-188; AC20-193]

13 YVES TANGUY, *The Storm (Black Landscape)*, 1926 [1950-134-187; AC20-192]

14 JOAN MIRÓ, *Man and Woman*, 1925 [1950-134-142; AC20-145]

15 PABLO PICASSO, *Three Nudes on Shore*, 1920 [1950-134-171A]

16 MARCEL DUCHAMP, *Nude Descending a Staircase (No. 3)*, 1916 [1950-134-60; AC20-65]

17 FERNAND LÉGER, *Man with a Cane (First State)*, 1920 [1950-134-126; AC20-129]

18 COLIMA (WESTERN MEXICO), Vessel in the Form of a Dog, 300 BCE–300 CE [1950-134-329; ACPS-68]

19 MIXTEC (SOUTHEASTERN MEXICO), Mask, 800–1500 [1950-134-358; ACPS-25]

20 *MAYA (*SOUTHEASTERN MEXICO, YUCATÁN), Jaguar, *900–1250 [NOTE 1.3, PAGE 414]

21 HUASTEC (EAST COAST MEXICO), Head, 1st–9th century [1950-134-271; ACPS-120]

22 NAYARIT (WESTERN MEXICO), Seated Man, 100 BCE–300 CE [1950-134-308; ACPS-78]

23 ATTRIBUTED TO PIETRO DI MINIATO, *Crucifixion with the Mourning Virgin and Saint John the Evangelist*, ca. 1420 [1950-134-532]

24 ARTIST/MAKER UNKNOWN (GREECE), *The Nativity and the Arrival of the Magi*, Late 15th century [1950-134-192]

25 ARTIST/MAKER UNKNOWN (NORTH AMERICA), *Portrait of a Woman*, ca. 1750 [1950-134-196]

26 ATTRIBUTED TO PALMA IL GIOVANE (JACOPO NEGRETTI), *The Flagellation*, Late 16th century [1950-134-193]

27 MASTER OF CARMIGNANO, *Virgin of Humility*, ca. 1395–1400 [1950-134-527]

28 COPY AFTER MICHELANGELO BUONARROTI, *Nude Youth from Sistine Chapel Ceiling*, After 1512 [1950-134-530]

29 NAYARIT (WESTERN MEXICO), Figure of a Woman, 100 BCE–300 CE [1950-134-396; ACPS-76]

30 MEZCALA (SOUTHWESTERN MEXICO), Figure of a Woman, 300 BCE–500 CE [1950-134-219; ACPS-83]

31 CLASSIC VERACRUZ (EAST COAST MEXICO), Palma, 500–900 [1950-134-216; ACPS-153]

32 MEZCALA (SOUTHWESTERN MEXICO), Figure, 300 BCE–500 CE [1950-134-218; ACPS-84]

33 AZTEC (CENTRAL MEXICO), Seated Figure (*Xipe Totec), 1300–1520 [1950-134-297; ACPS-115]

34 MEZCALA (SOUTHWESTERN MEXICO), Figure, 300 BCE–500 CE [1950-134-220; ACPS-85]

35 TEOTIHUACAN (CENTRAL MEXICO), Figure of a Woman, 1st–9th century [1950-134-222]

36 CLASSIC VERACRUZ (EAST COAST MEXICO), Hacha in the Form of a Head of a Man, 500–900 [1950-134-212; ACPS-101]

37 ATTRIBUTED TO JOSEPH MALLORD WILLIAM TURNER, *The Falls at Tivoli*, *1803 [1950-134-522]

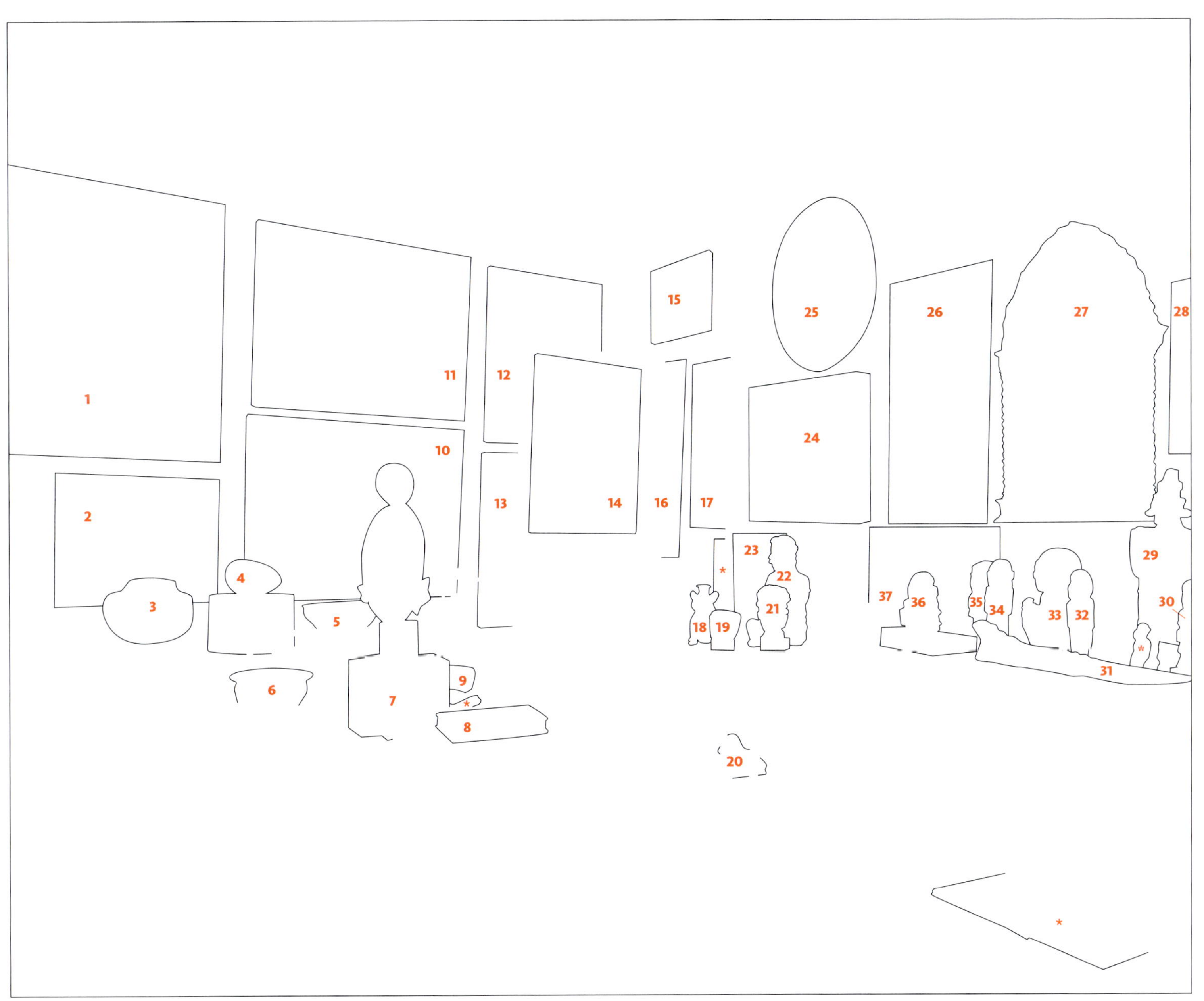
1
2
3
4
5
6
7
8
9
*
10
11
12
13
14
15
16
17
18
19
20
21
22
23
*
24
25
26
27
28
29
30
*
31
32
33
34
35
36
37
*

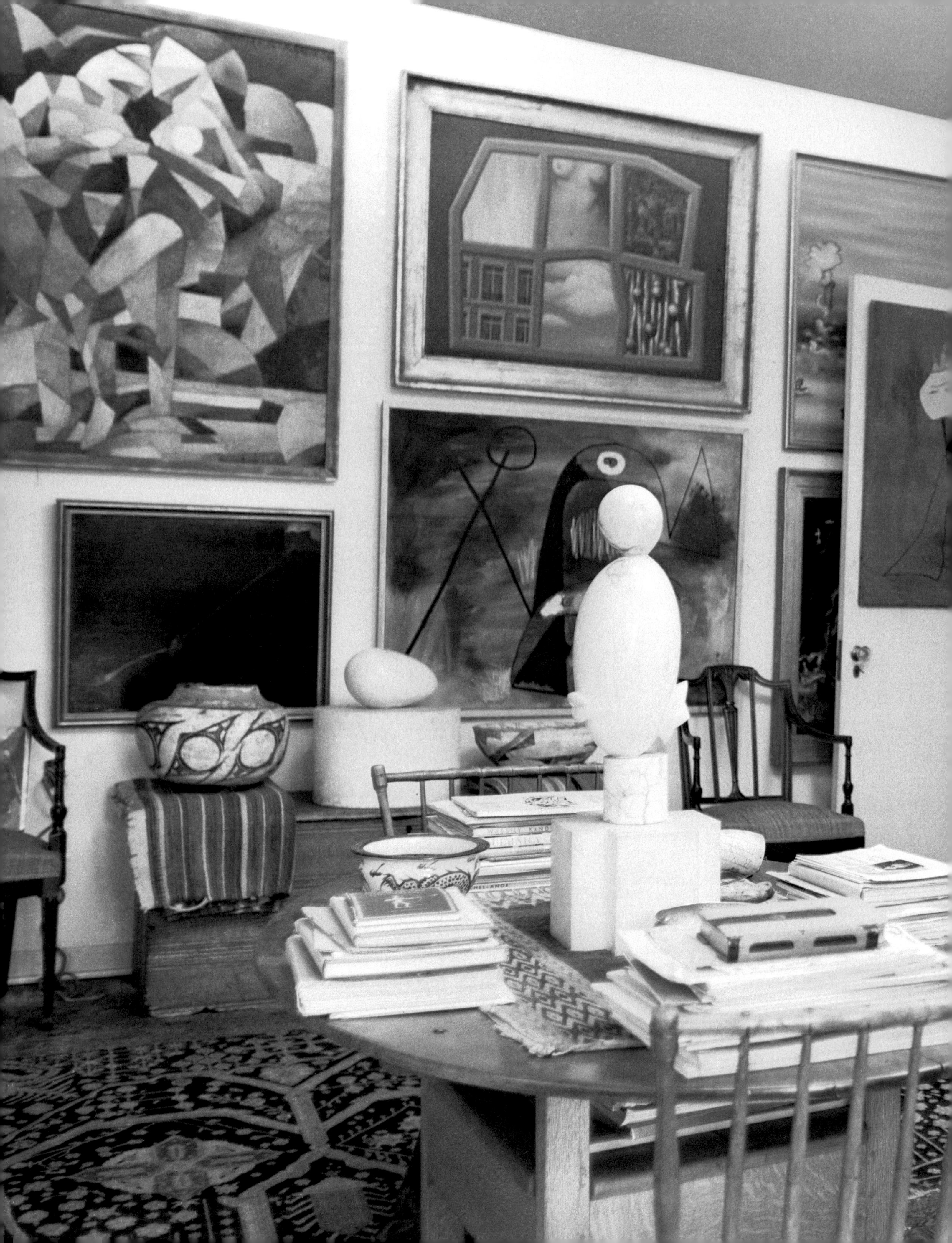

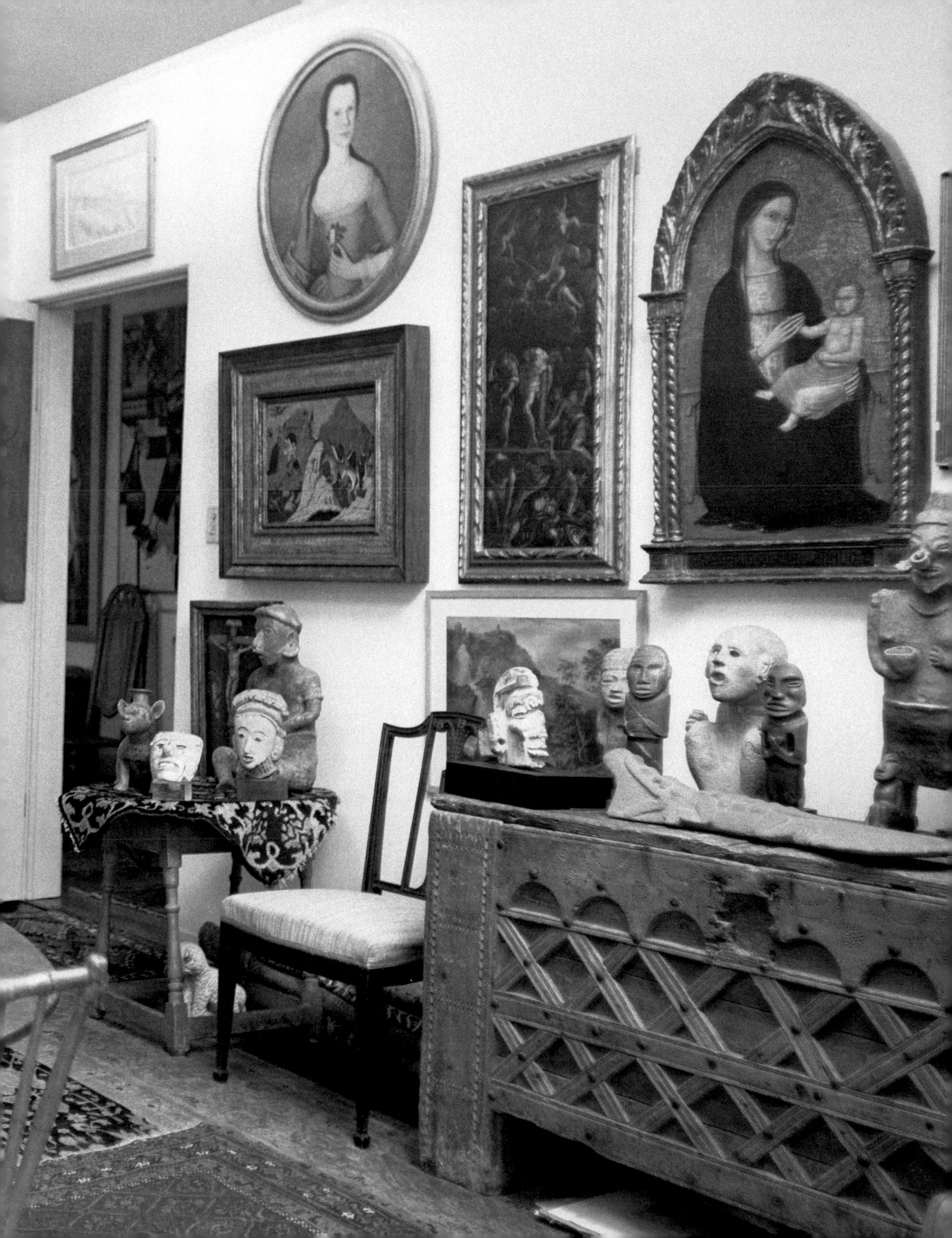

PLATE 48

SITTING ROOM

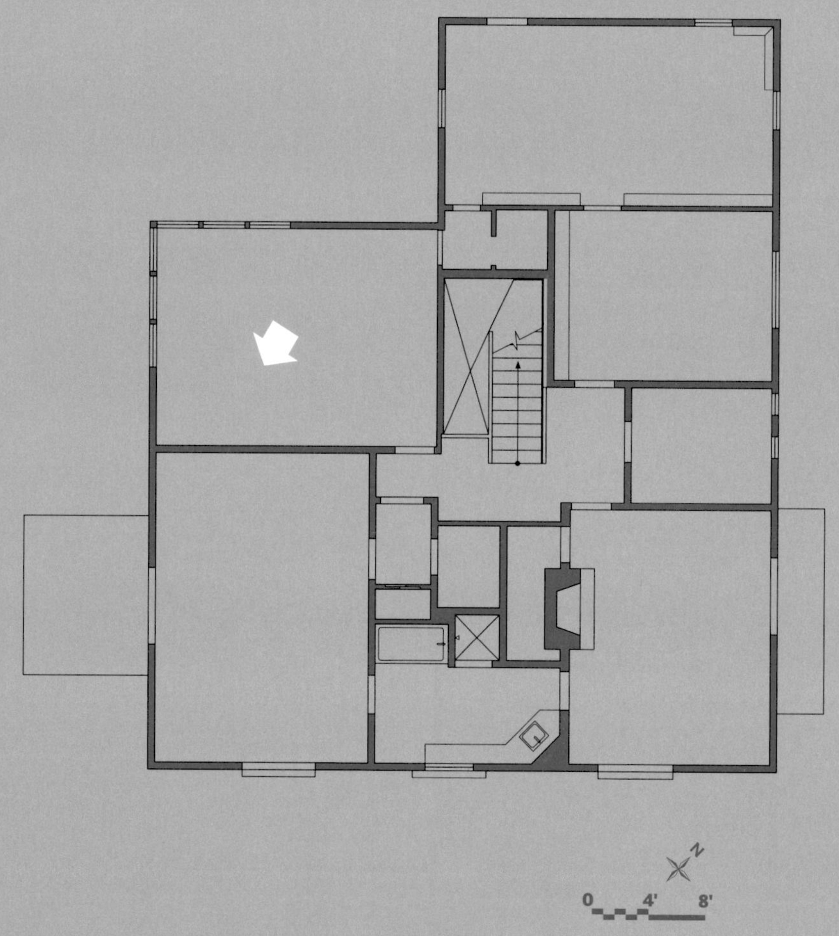

KARL BISSINGER
16 MARCH 1950

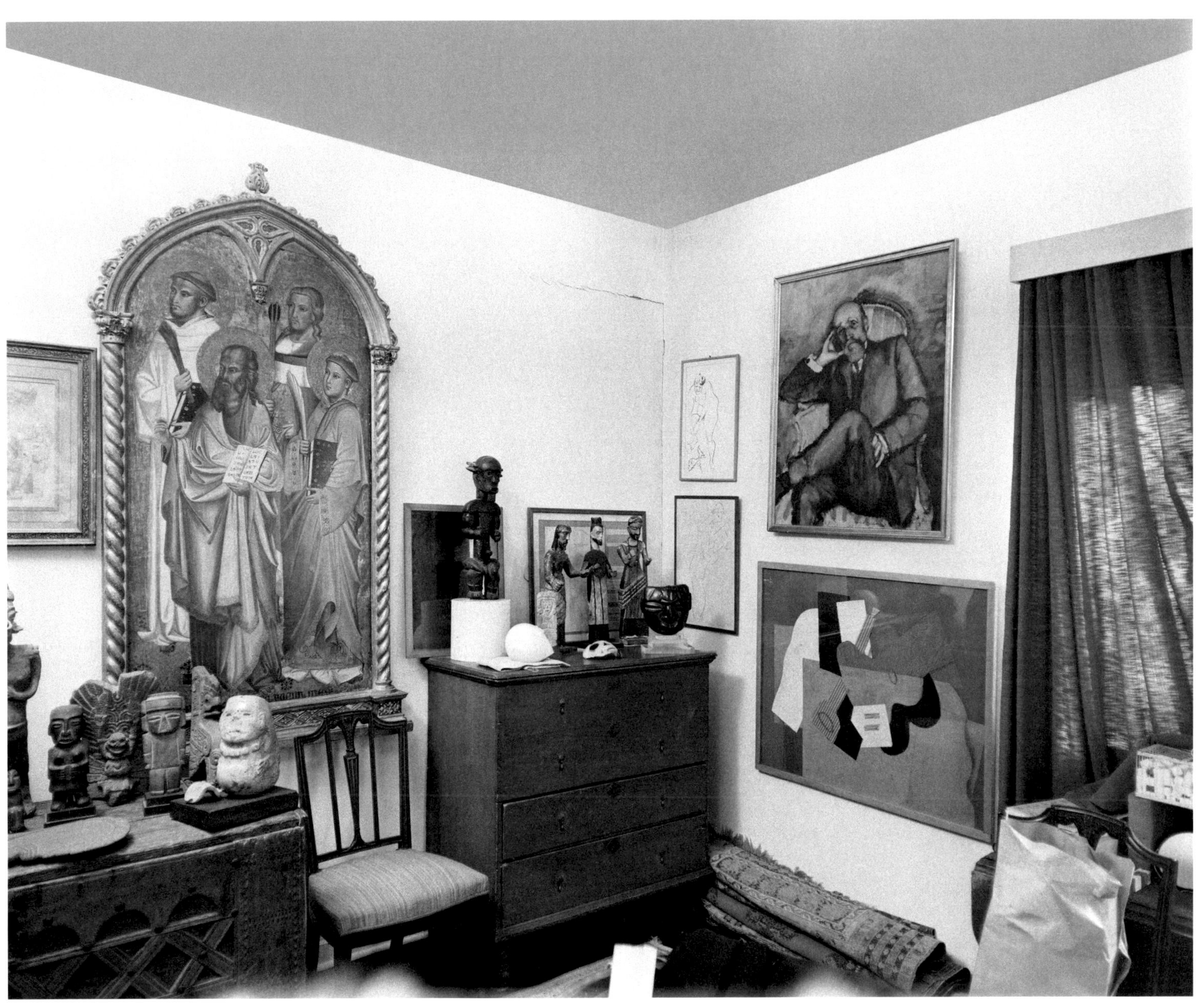

PLATE 48

1 COPY AFTER MICHELANGELO BUONARROTI, *Nude Youth from Sistine Chapel Ceiling*, After 1512 [1950-134-530]

2 NAYARIT (WESTERN MEXICO), Figure of a Woman, 100 BCE–300 CE [1950-134-396; ACPS-76]

3 CLASSIC VERACRUZ (EAST COAST MEXICO), Palma, 500–900 [1950-134-216; ACPS-153]

4 MEZCALA (SOUTHWESTERN MEXICO), Figure of a Woman, 300 BCE–500 CE [1950-134-219; ACPS-83]

5 CLASSIC VERACRUZ (EAST COAST MEXICO), Palma, 500–900 [1950-134-328; ACPS-151]

6 MEZCALA (SOUTHWESTERN MEXICO), Figure of a Man, 300 BCE–500 CE [1950-134-221; ACPS-81]

7 CLASSIC VERACRUZ (EAST COAST MEXICO), Palma, 500–900 [1950-134-214; ACPS-156]

8 AZTEC (CENTRAL MEXICO), Figure of a Woman, 1300–1520 [1950-134-292; ACPS-9]

9 ARRIGO DI NICCOLÒ (MASTER OF THE MANASSEI CHAPEL), *Saints Benedict, Sebastian, Stephen, and John the Evangelist*, ca. 1400–1410 [1950-134-528]

10 FANG (GABON), Male Reliquary Guardian Figure, Mid-19th century [1950-134-200]

11 CONSTANTIN BRANCUSI, *Prometheus*, 1911 [1950-134-5; AC20-4]

12 MIXTEC (SOUTHEASTERN MEXICO), Figure (Peñate), 1000–1520 [1950-134-240; ACPS-108]

13 MARCEL DUCHAMP, *Boxing Match*, 1913 [1950-134-67; AC20-73]

14 NATIVE AMERICAN (NEW MEXICO), *Christo*, 18th century [1950-134-820]

15 NATIVE AMERICAN (NEW MEXICO), *San Xavier*, 18th century [1950-134-819]

16 *MIXTEC (*SOUTHEASTERN MEXICO), Mask, 1000–1520 [1950-134-256; ACPS-110]

17 NATIVE AMERICAN (NEW MEXICO), *San José*, 18th century [1950-134-821]

18 ARTIST/MAKER UNKNOWN (MEXICO), Mask, Likely 20th century [1950-134-252]

19 HENRI MATISSE, *Reading—Nude in Profile*, 1913 [1950-134-893]

20 HENRI MATISSE, *Nude with Right Foot on Stool*, 1906 [1950-134-892]

21 MARCEL DUCHAMP, *Portrait of the Artist's Father*, 1910 [1950-134-49; AC20-54]

22 GEORGES BRAQUE, *Musical Forms*, 1918 [1950-134-28; AC20-26]

23 MARCEL DUCHAMP, *Why Not Sneeze, Rose Sélavy?*, 1921 [1950-134-75A–E; AC20-82]

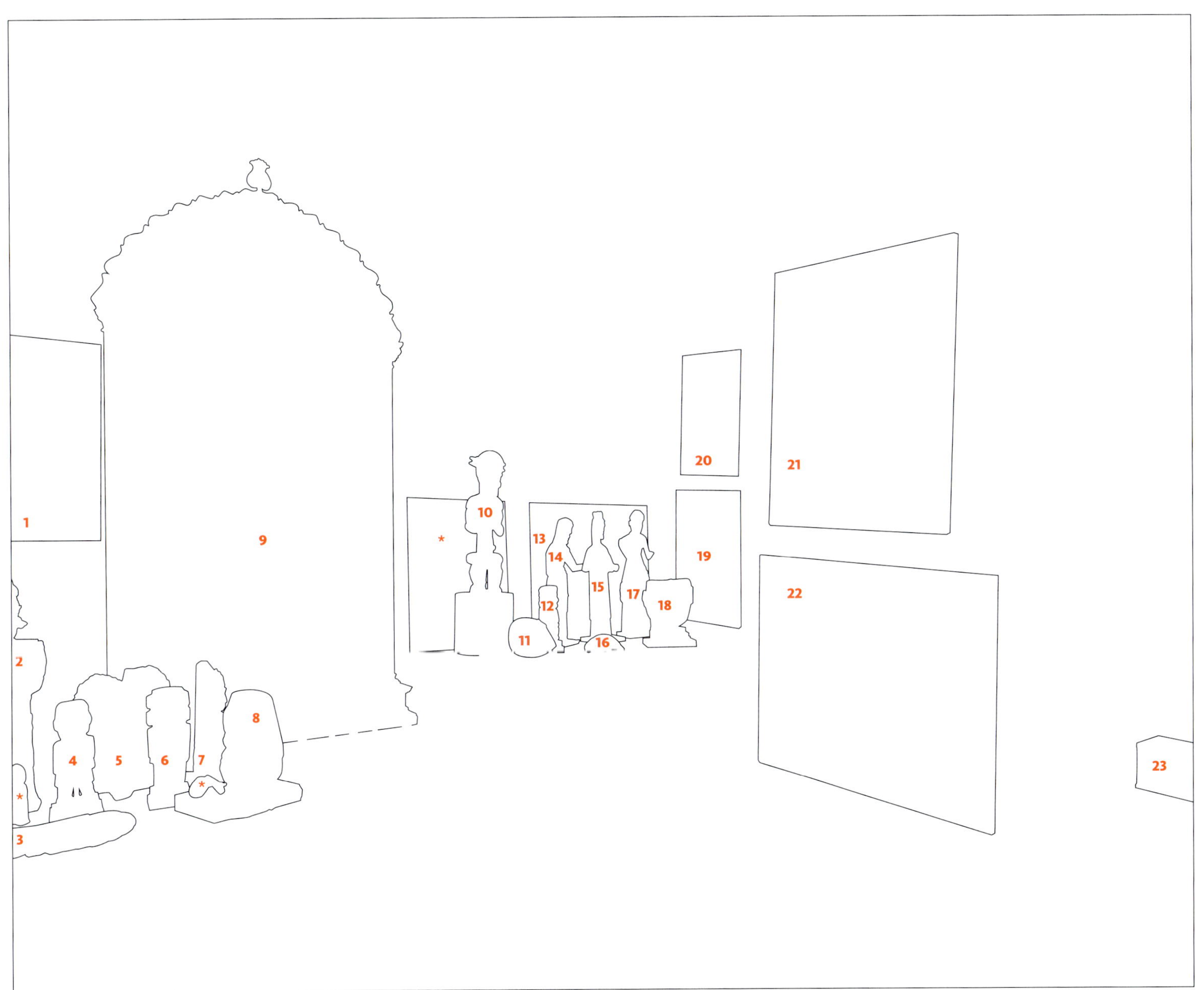
1
2
*
3
4
5
6
7
*
8
9
*
10
11
12
13
14
15
16
17
18
19
20
21
22
23

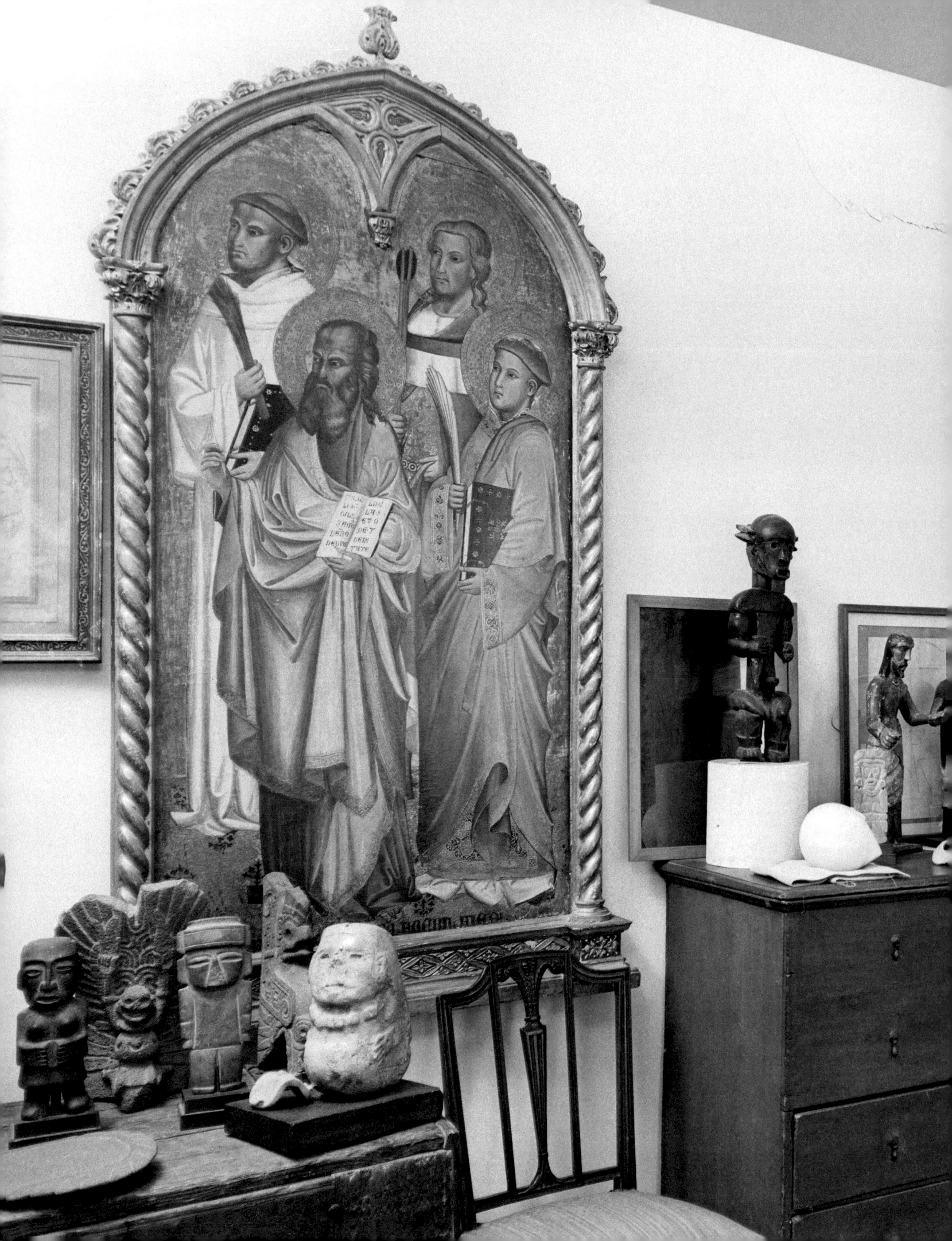

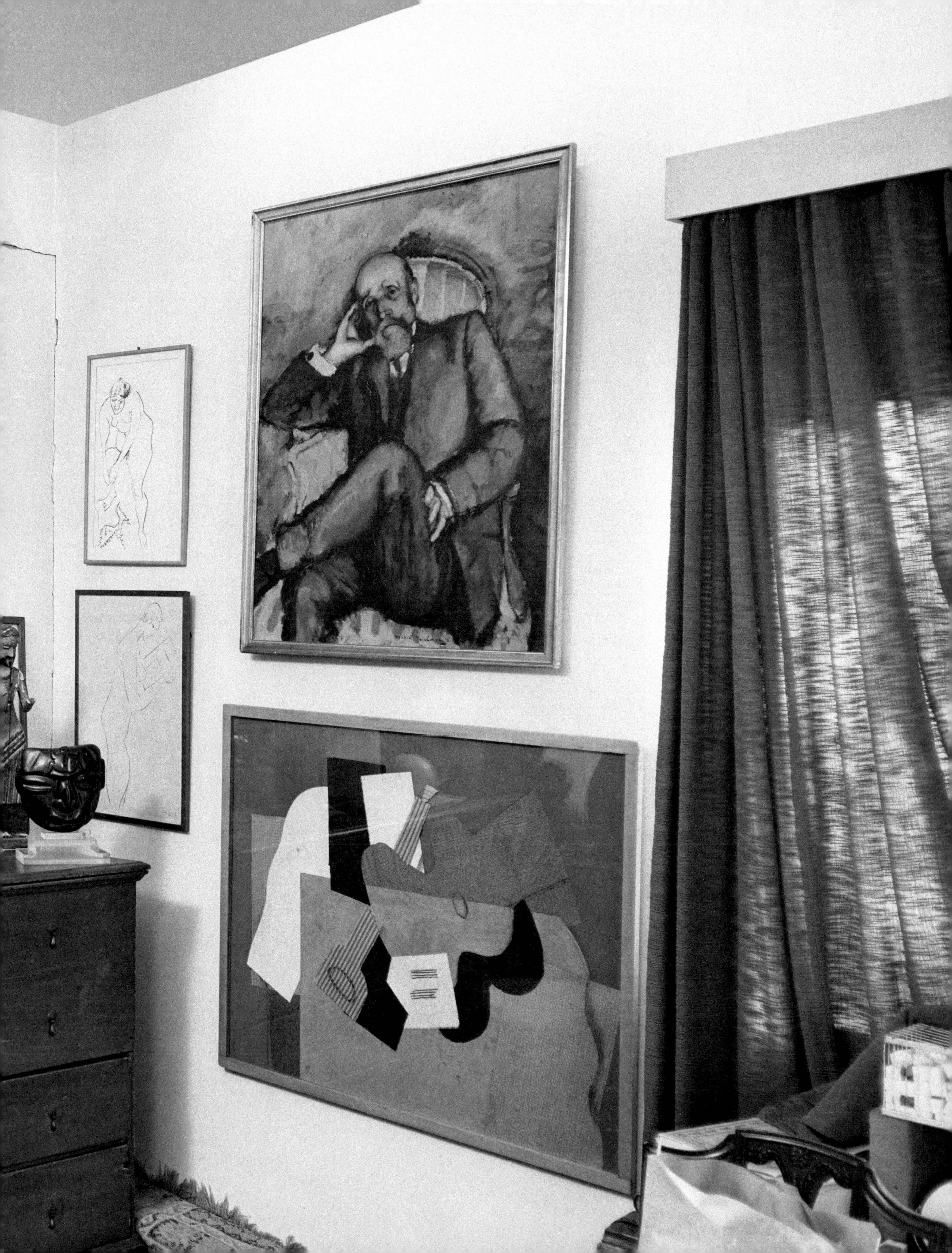

PLATE 49

SITTING ROOM

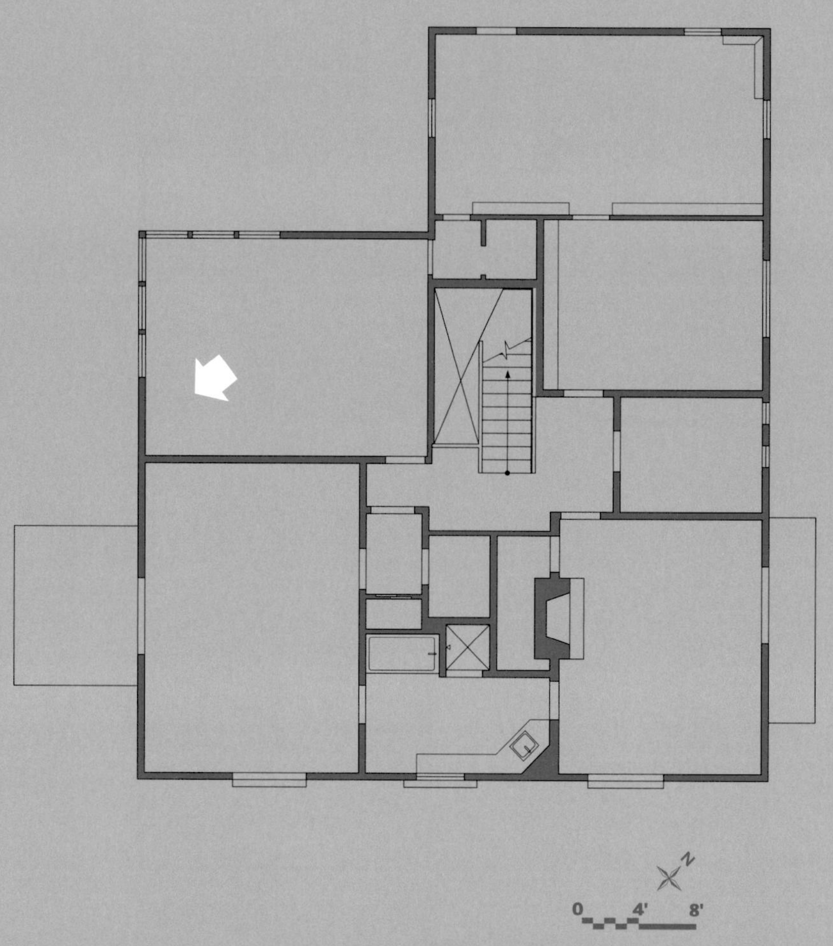

FRED R. DAPPRICH

CA. 1944

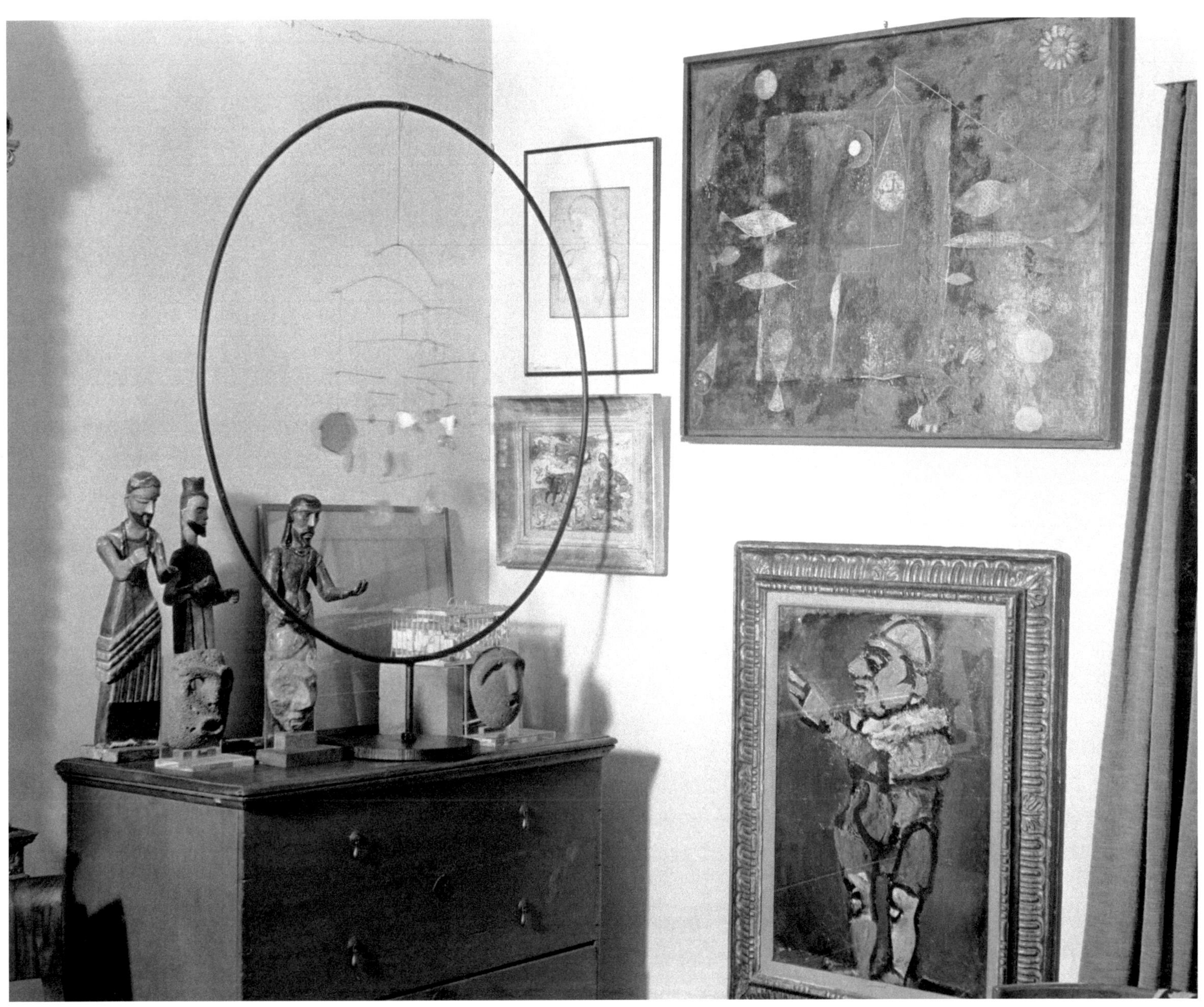

PLATE 49

1 ARRIGO DI NICCOLÒ (MASTER OF THE MANASSEI CHAPEL), *Saints Benedict, Sebastian, Stephen, and John the Evangelist*, ca. 1400–1410 [1950-134-528]

2 NATIVE AMERICAN (NEW MEXICO), *San José*, 18th century [1950-134-821]

3 NATIVE AMERICAN (NEW MEXICO), *San Xavier*, 18th century [1950-134-819]

4 *TARASCAN (WESTERN MEXICO), Mask, *1300–1520 [1950-134-265; ACPS-24]

5 NATIVE AMERICAN (NEW MEXICO), *Christo*, 18th century [1950-134-820]

6 ALEXANDER CALDER, *Mobile*, 1934 [1950-134-31; AC20-30]

7 MARCEL DUCHAMP, *Cemetery of Uniforms and Liveries (No. 1)*, 1913 [1950-134-66; AC20-72]

8 MARCEL DUCHAMP, *Why Not Sneeze, Rose Sélavy?*, 1921 [1950-134-75A–E; AC20-82]

9 TARASCAN (WESTERN MEXICO), Mask, 1300–1520 [1950-134-264; ACPS-92]

10 DAVID BURLIUK, *Woman with Cow*, Date unknown [NOTE 1.18, PAGE 415]

11 WILHELM LEHMBRUCK, *Female Torso, Tilted Head*, 1912 [1950-134-891]

12 PAUL KLEE, *Fish Magic*, 1925 [1950-134-112; AC20-113]

13 GEORGES ROUAULT, *Polichinelle*, ca. 1930 [1950-134-174; AC20-178]

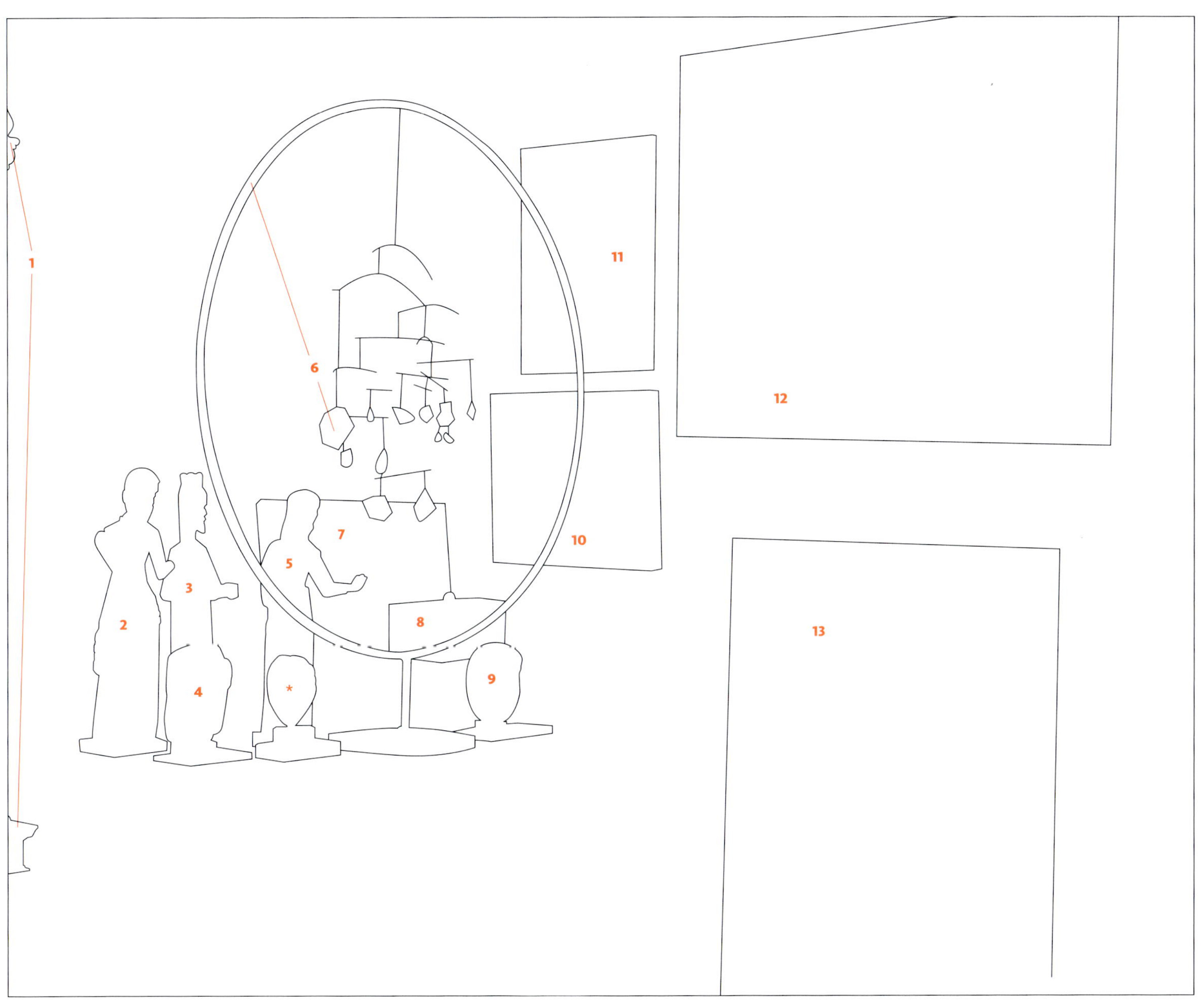
1
2
3
4
5
*
6
7
8
9
10
11
12
13

PLATES 50, 51

MASTER BEDROOM

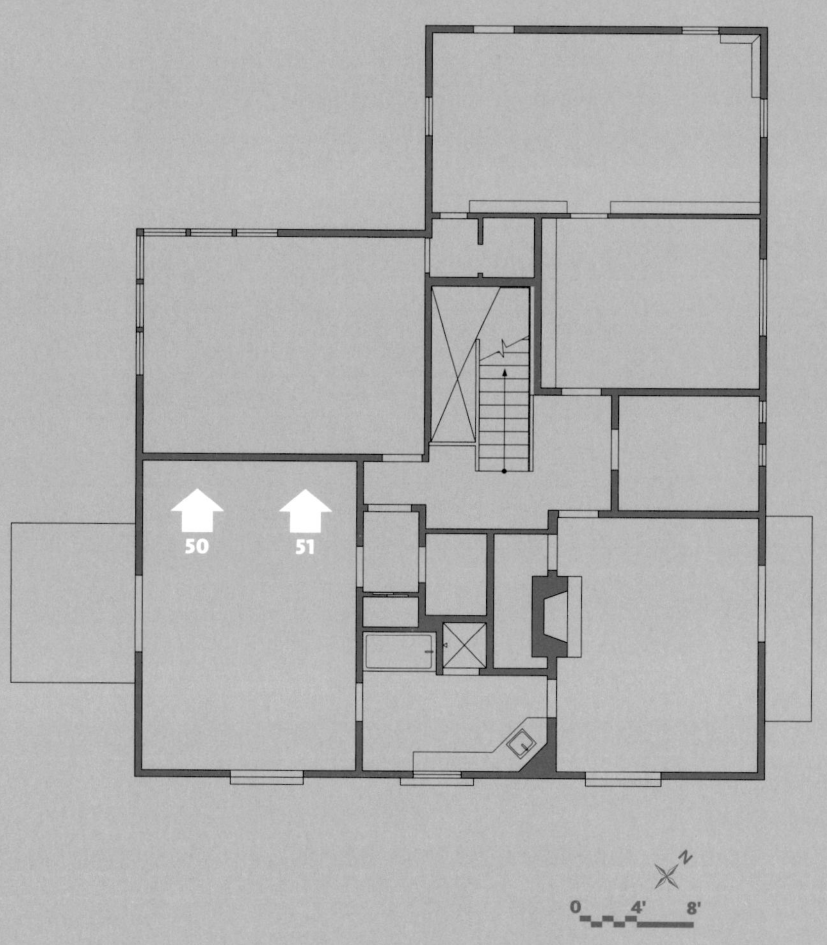

FLOYD FAXON
BOTH CA. 1948 (BEFORE 17 APRIL)

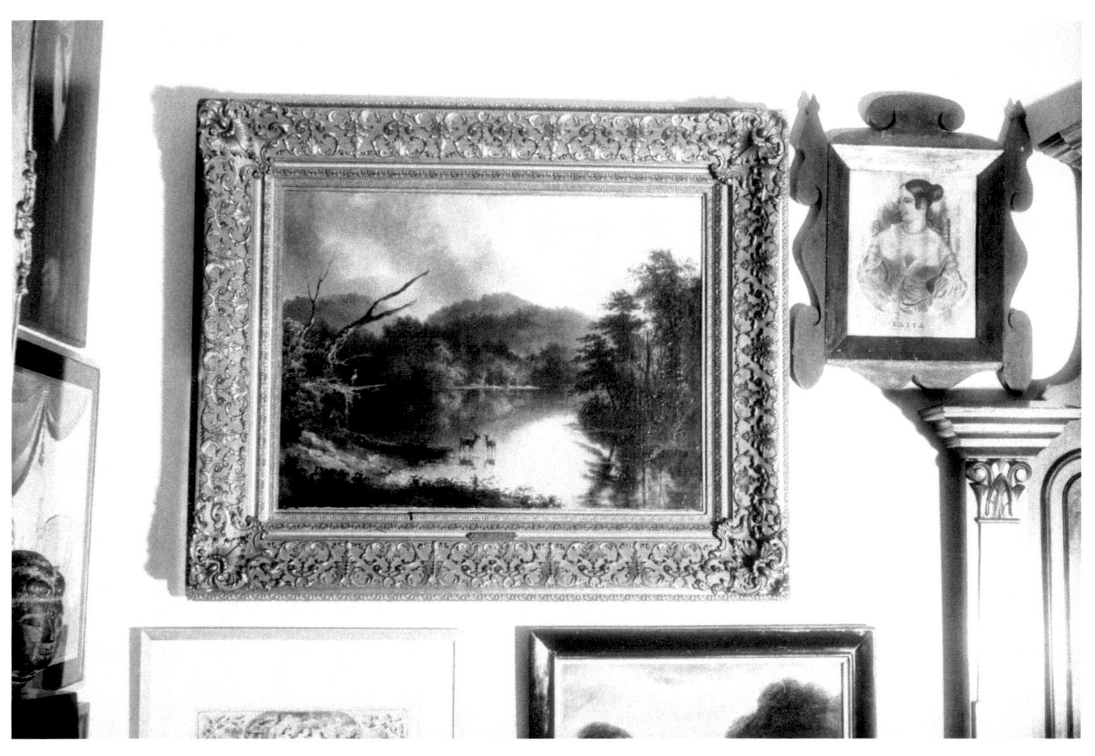

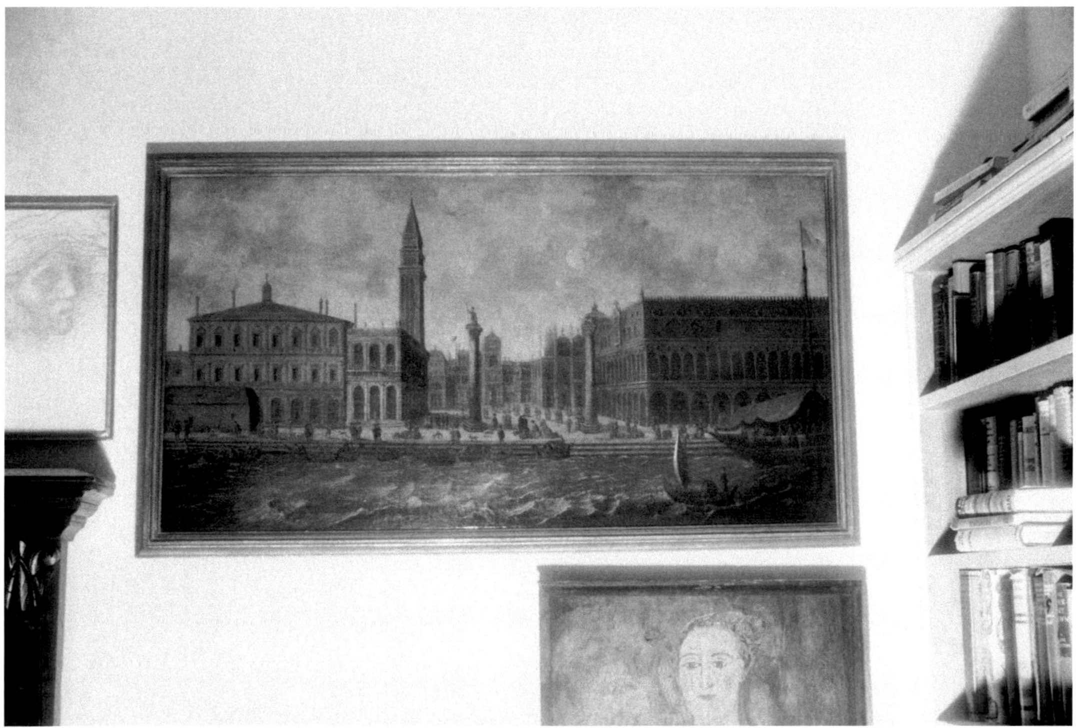

PLATE 50

1 ATTRIBUTED TO SYLVESTER WYCKOFF, *Self-Portrait*, ca. 1870s [1950-134-526]

2 ARTIST/MAKER UNKNOWN (NORTH AMERICA), *Several Figures—Domestic Scene*, Date unknown [1950-134-536]

3 ARTIST/MAKER UNKNOWN (CHINA), Head of Buddha, ca. 7th–8th century [1950-134-502]

4 *ALEXANDER HELWIG WYANT, Landscape, Late 1800s [NOTE 1.19, PAGE 415]

5 CURRIER & IVES, *Eliza*, Late 1800s [NOTE 1.20, PAGE 415]

6 CURRIER & IVES, Volunteer Fire Company Certificate of Membership, 1877 [NOTE 1.21, PAGE 415]

7 ARTIST/MAKER UNKNOWN (NORTH AMERICA), *Mount Vernon*, *19th century [1950-134-537]

PLATE 51

1 ALPHONSE LEGROS, Study of a Head, ca. 1720–30 [NOTE 1.22, PAGE 415]

2 ARTIST/MAKER UNKNOWN (*ITALY), View of Venice, Date unknown [NOTE 1.23, PAGE 415]

3 ARTIST/MAKER UNKNOWN (NORTH AMERICA), *Portrait of a Lady (Mrs. L. Nunt)*, 1720–30 [1950-134-198]

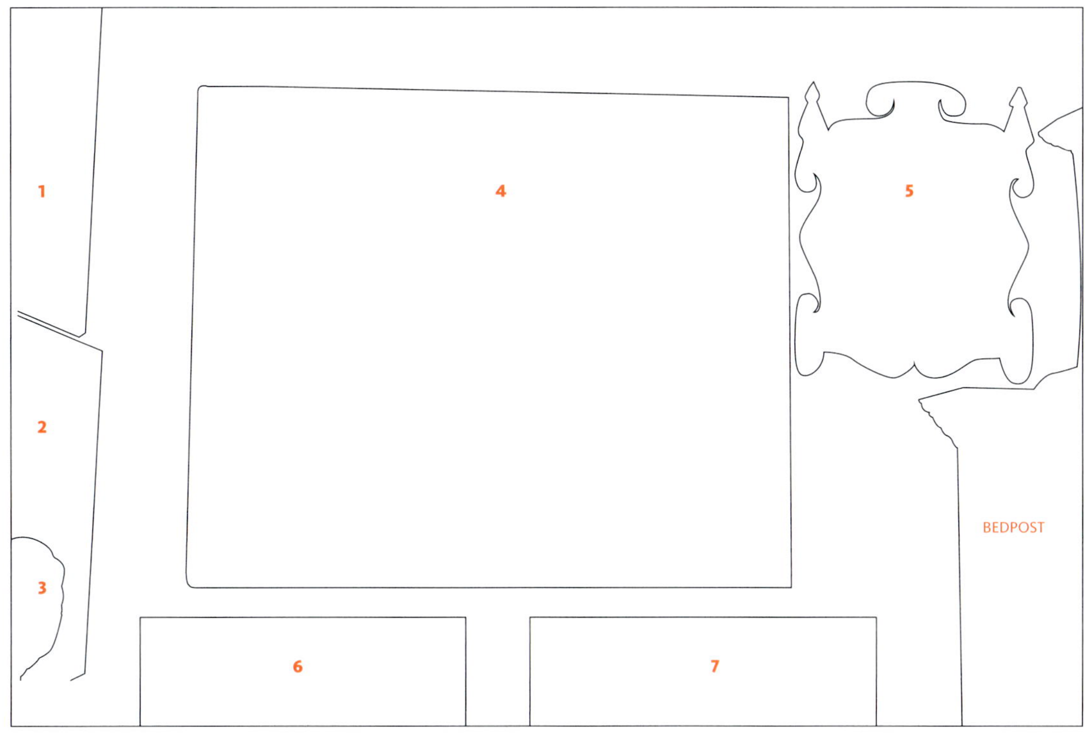
1
4
5
2
BEDPOST
3
6
7

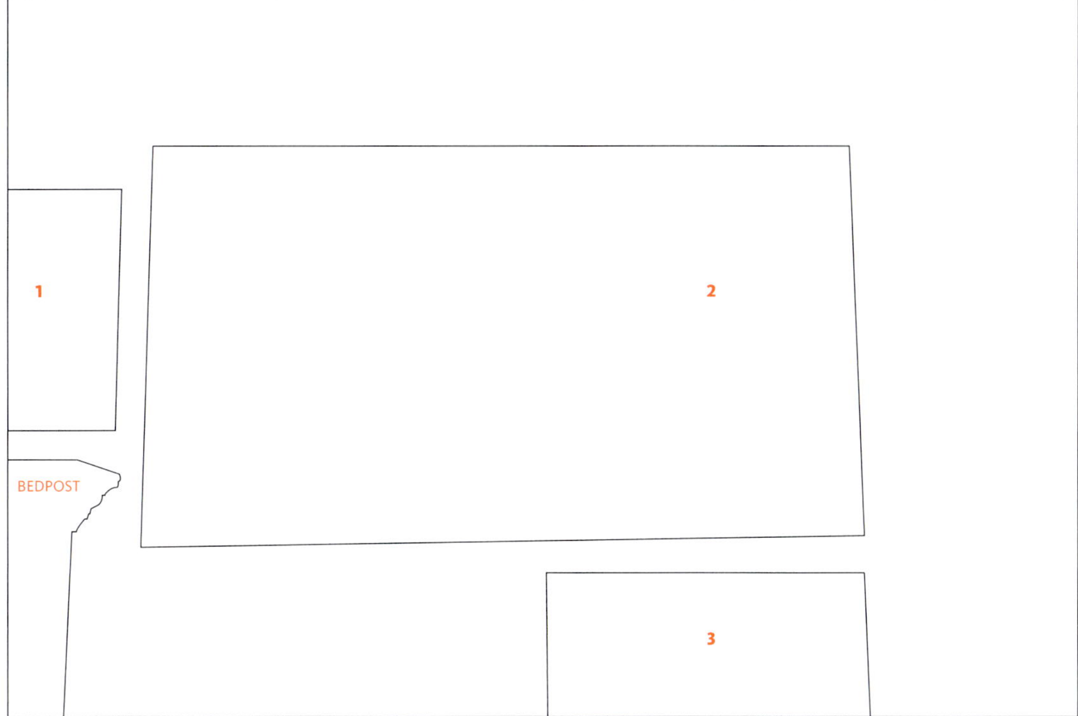
1
2
BEDPOST
3

PLATE 52

MASTER BEDROOM

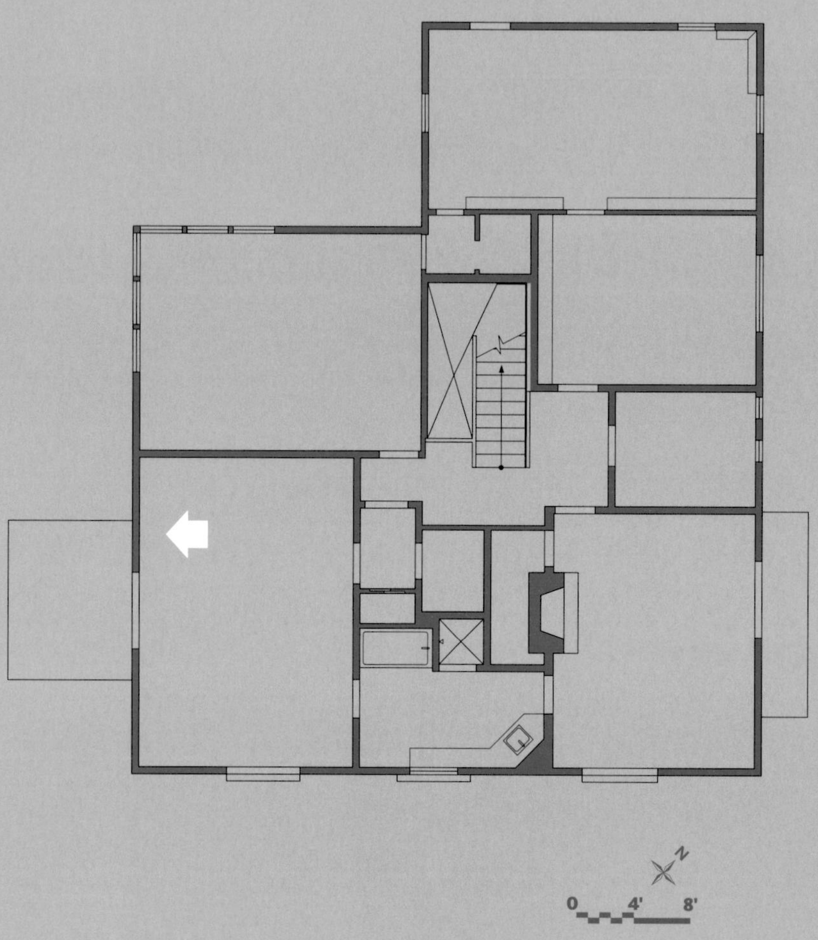

FRED R. DAPPRICH

CA. 1944

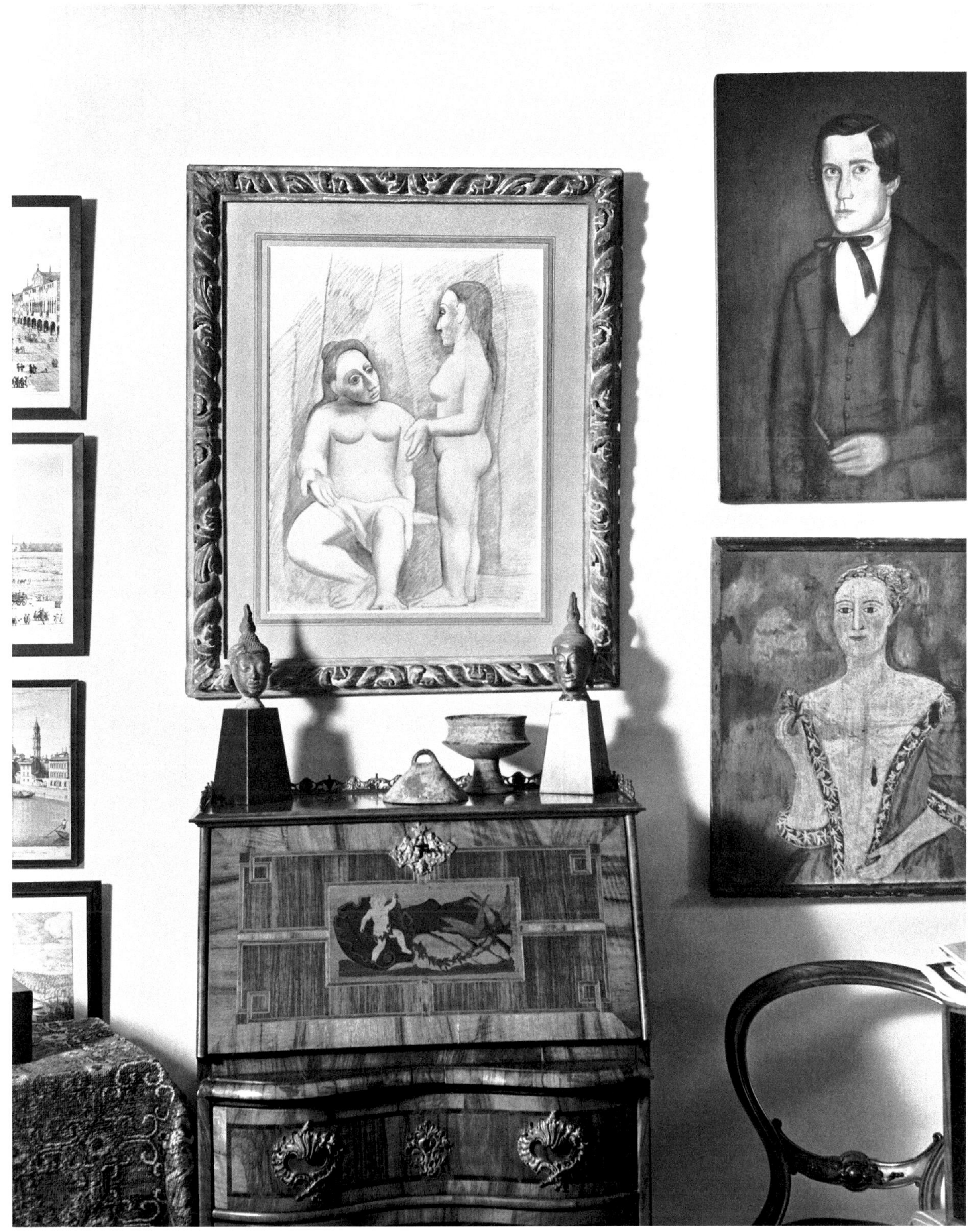

PLATE 52

1 REPRODUCTION OF CANALETTO'S *Prà della Valle* (right half, ca. 1741–44), Date unknown [NOTE 1.24, PAGE 415]

2 REPRODUCTION OF CANALETTO'S *S. Giustina in Prà della Valle* (left half, ca. 1741–44), Date unknown [NOTE 1.24, PAGE 415]

3 REPRODUCTION OF GIUSEPPE ZOCCHI'S *The Arno River from the Rucellai Terrace* (1744), Date unknown [NOTE 1.25, PAGES 415–16]

4 REPRODUCTION OF FRANZ HOGENBERG'S ENGRAVING AFTER A DRAWING BY GEORG HOEFNAGEL, *Cityscape of Arnsberg* (1588), Date unknown [NOTE 1.26, PAGE 416]

5 PABLO PICASSO, *Seated Nude and Standing Nude*, 1906 [1950-134-162; AC20-166]

6 ARTIST/MAKER UNKNOWN (THAILAND OR CAMBODIA), Head, Date unknown [1950-134-500]

7–8 ETRUSCAN (CENTRAL ITALY), Jar with Cover, Date unknown [1950-134-494]

9 ARTIST/MAKER UNKNOWN (THAILAND OR CAMBODIA), Head, Date unknown [1950-134-501]

10 ATTRIBUTED TO SYLVESTER WYCKOFF, *Self-Portrait*, ca. 1870s [1950-134-526]

11 ARTIST/MAKER UNKNOWN (NORTH AMERICA), *Portrait of a Lady (Mrs. L. Nunt)*, 1720–30 [1950-134-198]

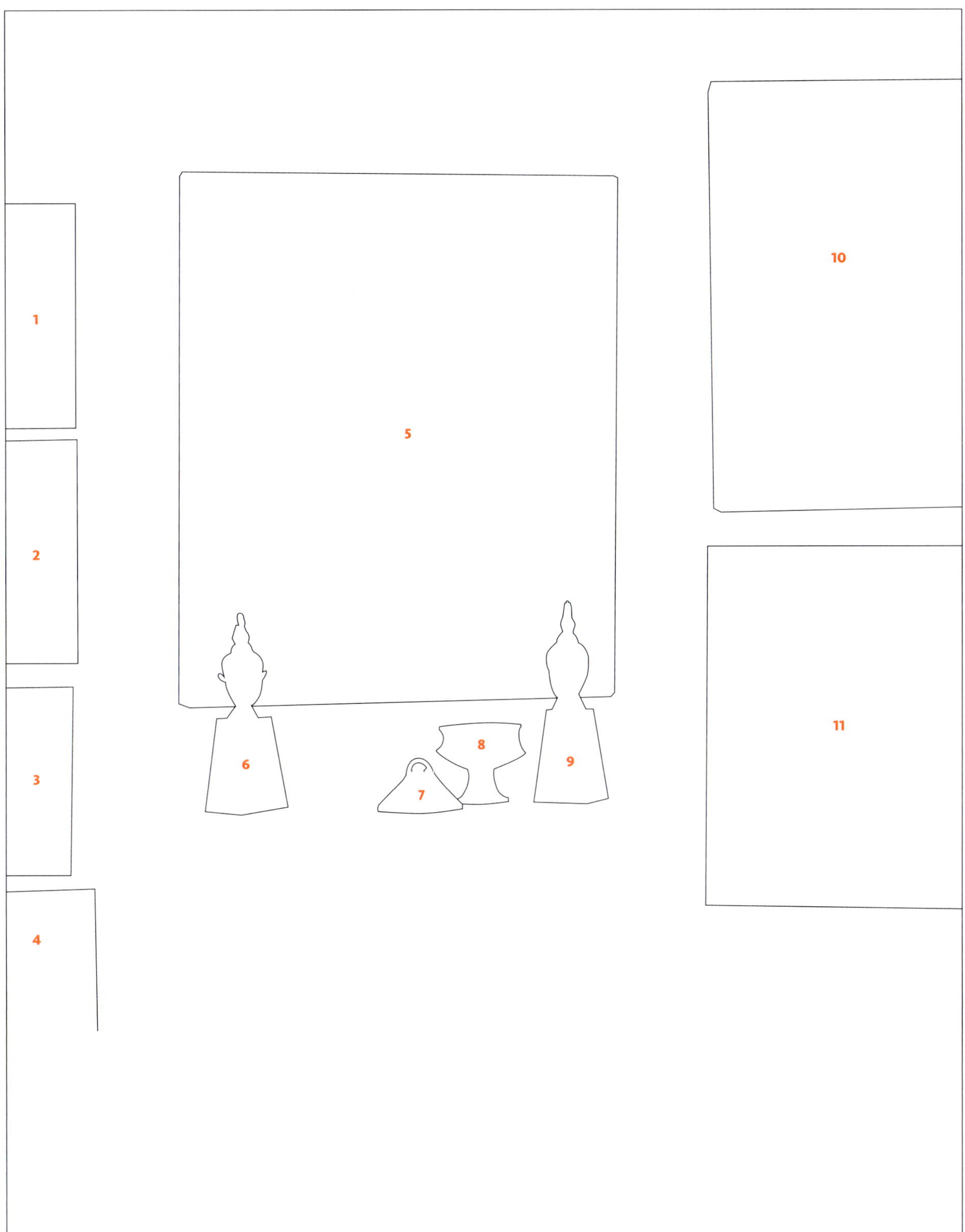
1
2
3
4
5
6
7
8
9
10
11

PLATES 53, 54, 55

MASTER BEDROOM

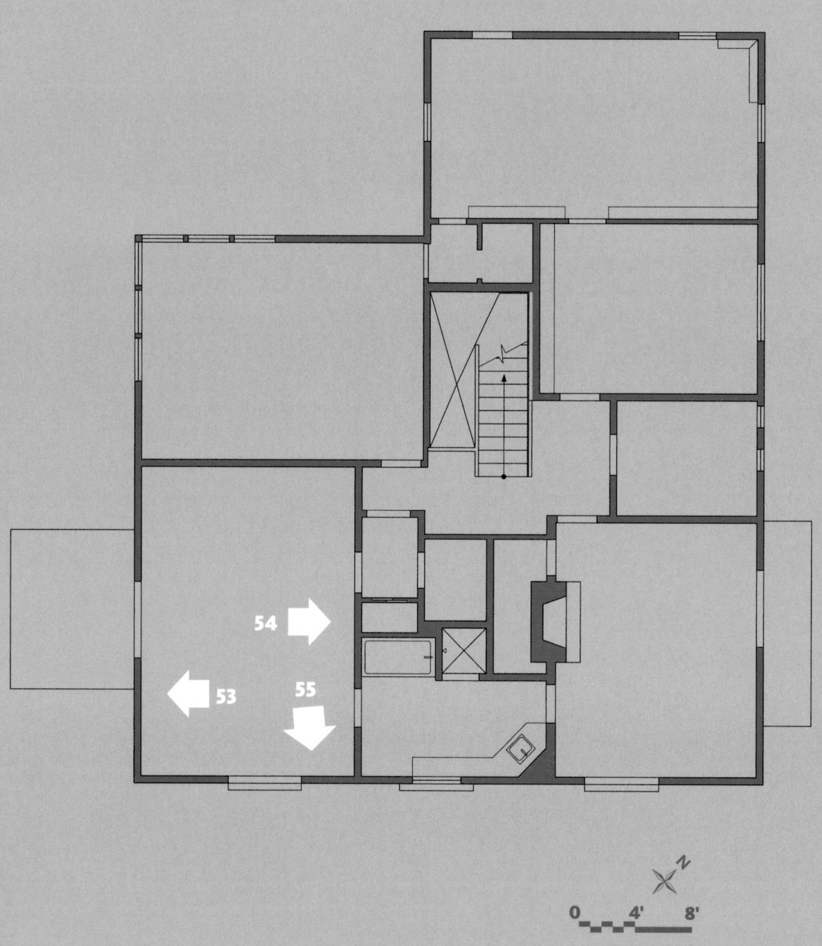

FLOYD FAXON

CA. 1948–49

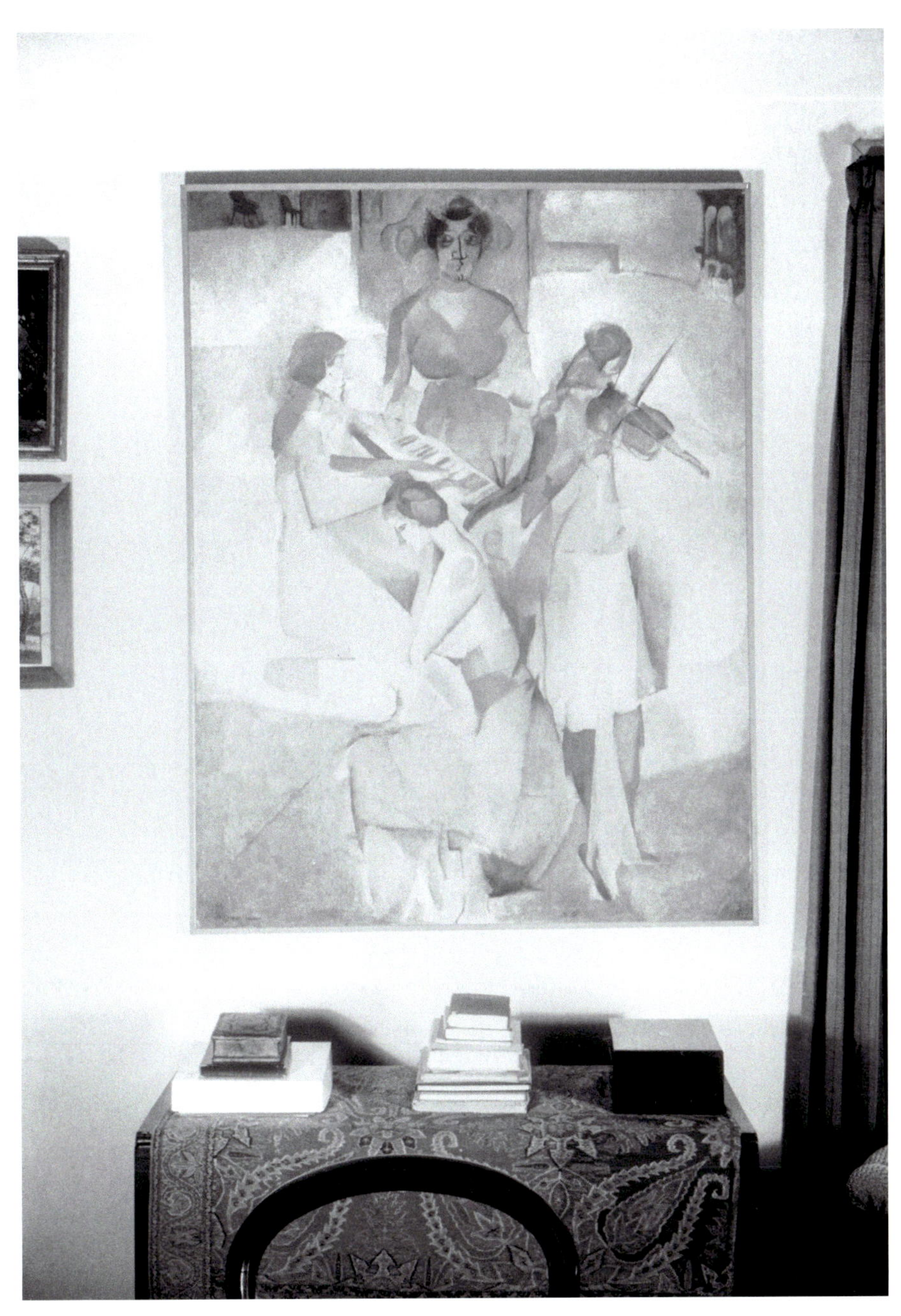

PLATE 53

1 (TOP LEFT) ARTIST/MAKER UNKNOWN (NORTH AMERICA), *Still Life with Flowers*, 19th century [1950-134-534]

2 (BOTTOM LEFT) ARTIST/MAKER UNKNOWN (NORTH AMERICA), Landscape, Early American [NOTE 1.27, PAGE 416]

3 (CENTER) MARCEL DUCHAMP, *Sonata*, 1911 [1950-134-52]

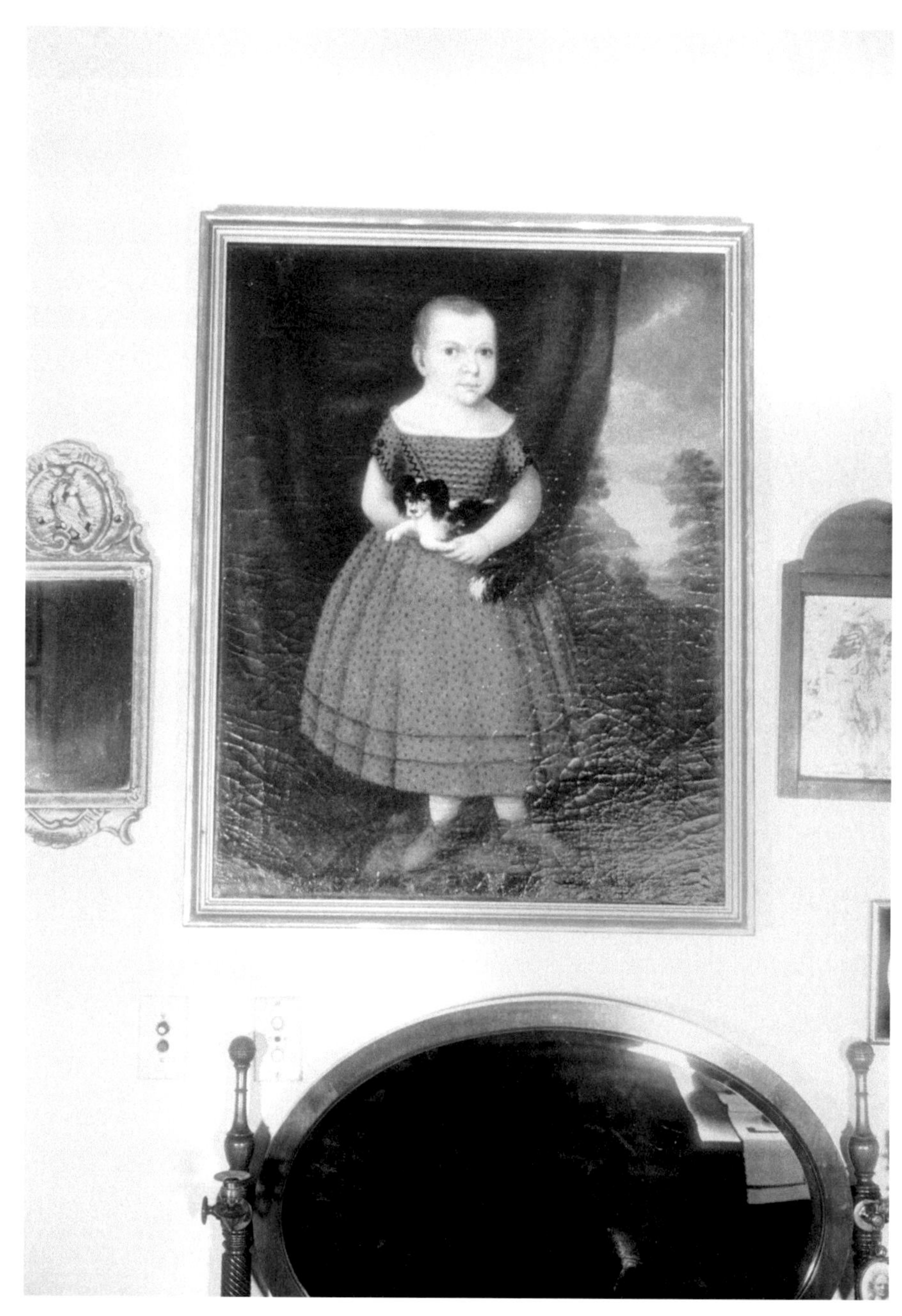

PLATE 54

1 (LEFT) NOT IDENTIFIED

2 (CENTER) ARTIST/MAKER UNKNOWN (NORTH AMERICA), *Portrait of a Child Holding a Dog*, Mid-19th century [1950-134-533]

3, 4 (TOP AND BOTTOM RIGHT) NOT IDENTIFIED

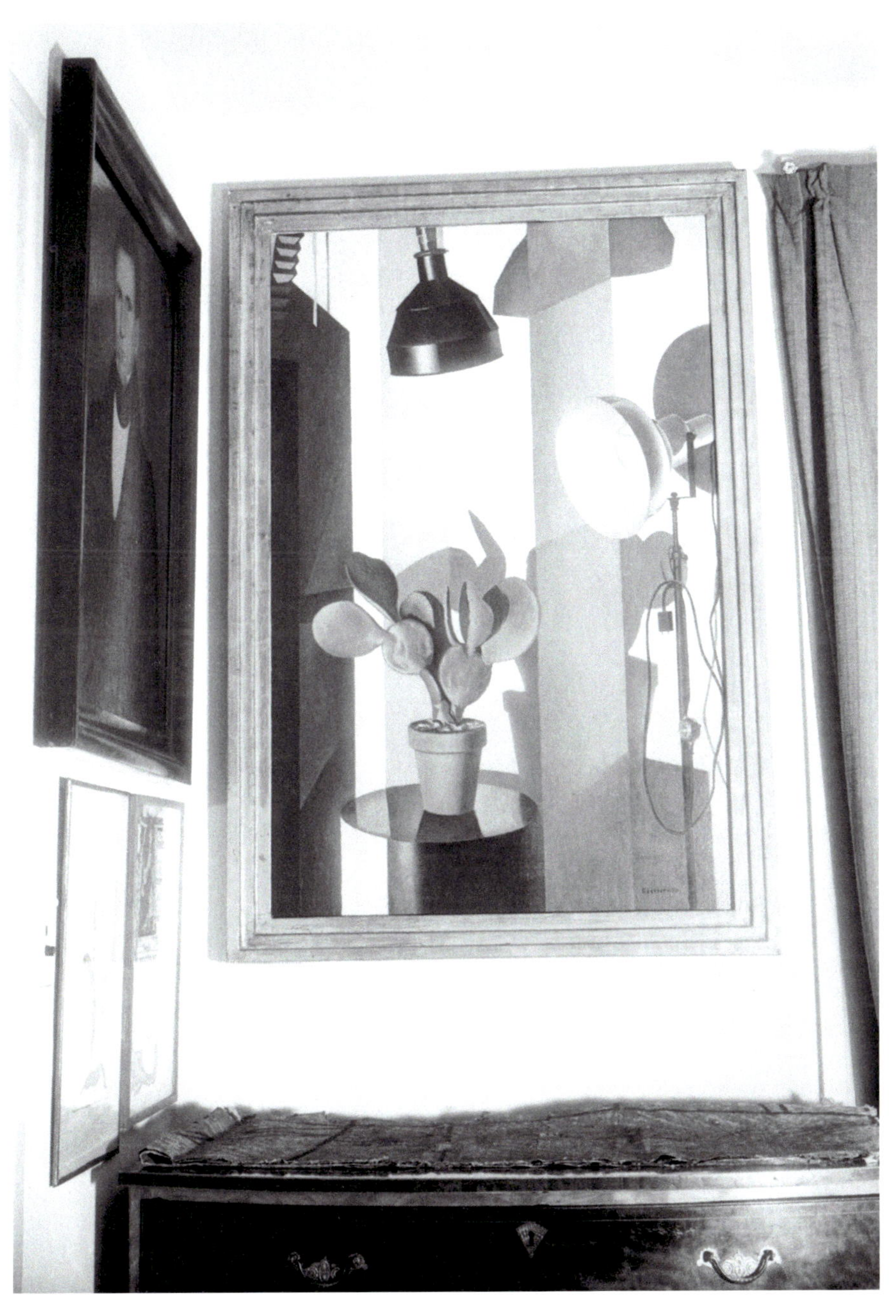

PLATE 55

1 (TOP LEFT) JOHN WILKIE, *Portrait of a Man*, 1836 [1950-134-523]

2 (BOTTOM LEFT, FRONT) ARTIST/MAKER UNKNOWN (GERMANY), *Tulip*, Date unknown [1950-134-531]

3 (BOTTOM LEFT, BACK) NOT IDENTIFIED

4 (CENTER) CHARLES SHEELER, *Cactus*, 1931 [1950-134-186]

PLATE 56

GUEST BEDROOM

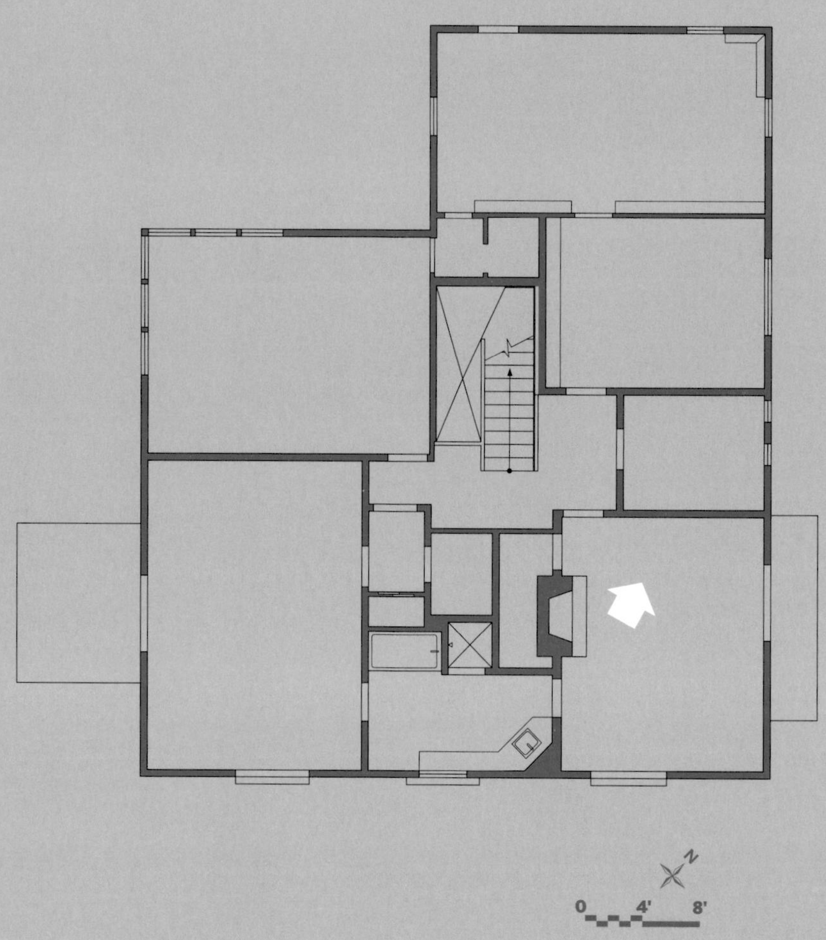

FRED R. DAPPRICH

CA. 1944

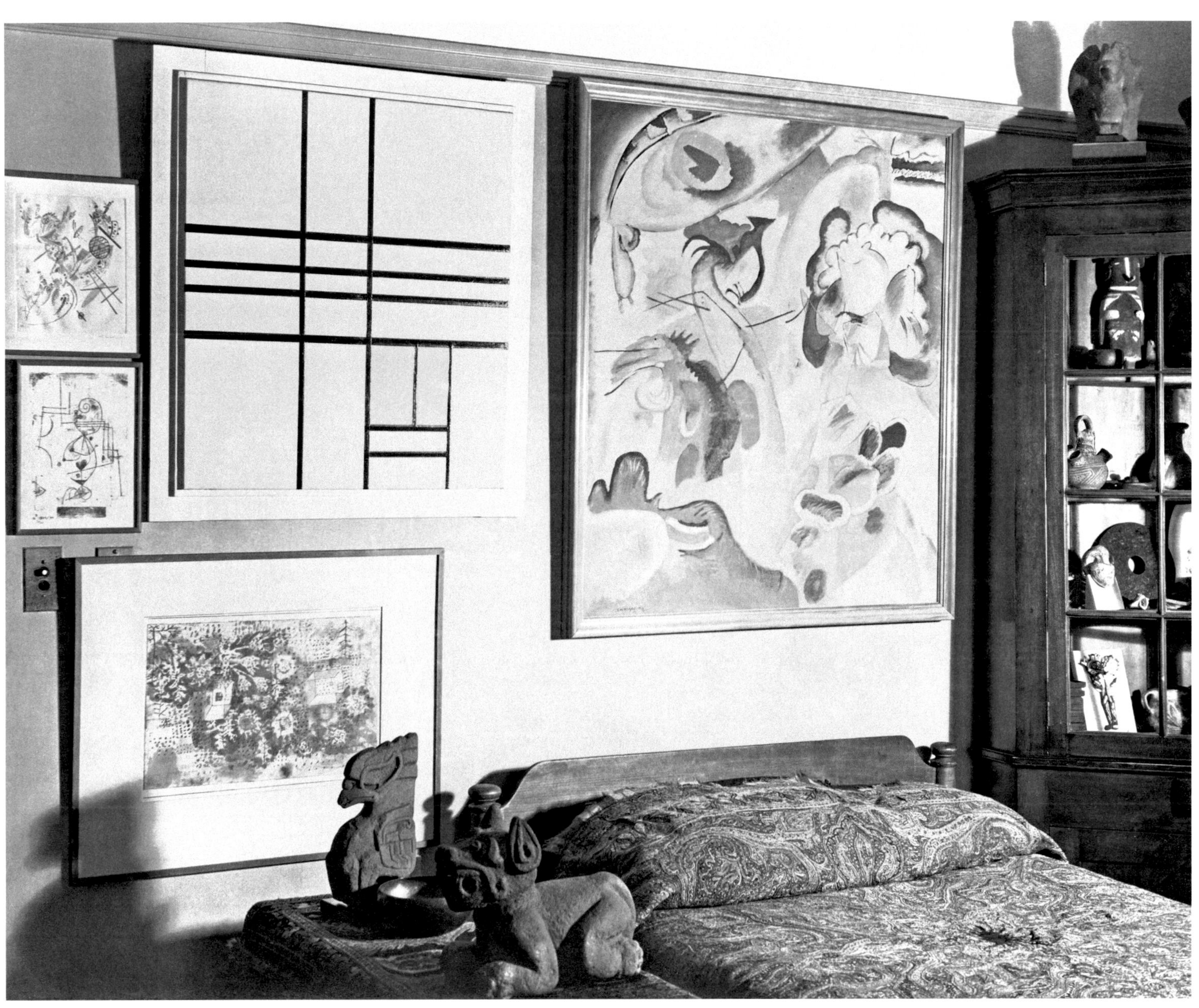

PLATE 56

1 VASILY KANDINSKY, *Small Worlds XII*, 1922 [1950-134-884]

2 PAUL KLEE, *Queen of Hearts*, 1921 [1950-134-885]

3 PAUL KLEE, *Small Houses in the Garden City*, 1928 [1950-134-119; AC20-121]

4 PIET MONDRIAN, *Composition*, 1936 [1950-134-152; AC20-155]

5 CLASSIC VERACRUZ (EAST COAST MEXICO), Palma, 500–900 [1950-134-346; ACPS-157]

6 ARTIST/MAKER UNKNOWN, Bowl, *ca. 1930s–1940s [NOTE 4.4, PAGE 417]

7 AZTEC (CENTRAL MEXICO), Jaguar, 1300–1520 [1950-134-205]

8 VASILY KANDINSKY, *Improvisation No. 29 (The Swan)*, 1912 [1950-134-102; AC20-103]

9 CLASSIC VERACRUZ (EAST COAST MEXICO), Palma, 500–900 [1950-134-601]

10 NATIVE AMERICAN (SOUTHWESTERN UNITED STATES), Kachina Doll, Date unknown [1950-134-437]

*11 INCA (PERU), Bowl, 1400–1532 [1950-134-564]

12 CHANCAY (PERU), Triple-Spouted Vessel, 1200–1470 [1950-134-610]

13 INCA (PERU), Pitcher, 1400–1532 [1950-134-584]

*14 INCA (PERU), Dish with Extended Handle, 1400–1532 [1950-134-569]

15 ARTIST/MAKER UNKNOWN (CHINA, POSSIBLY LIANGZHU CULTURE), Disk (Bi), ca. 3400–2250 BCE [1950-134-845]

16 RAYMOND DUCHAMP-VILLON, *Portrait of Professor Gosset* (REAR VIEW), ca. 1917–18 [1950-134-84; AC20-87]

17 ARTISTS/MAKERS UNKNOWN (CHINA), Seven Boxes Containing Calcified Jade Ornaments, Various dates [1950-134-832A–D; 1950-134-833A–E; 1950-134-834A–D; 1950-134-835A–E; 1950-134-836A–C (CA. 1700–800 BCE); 1950-134-837 (FISH FORM); 1950-134-838 (BIRD FORM, CA. 1050–800 BCE)]

18 ARTIST/MAKER UNKNOWN (BALI), Figure, Date unknown [1950-134-829]

19 NATIVE AMERICAN, Pitcher with Floral Decorations, Date unknown [1950-134-743]

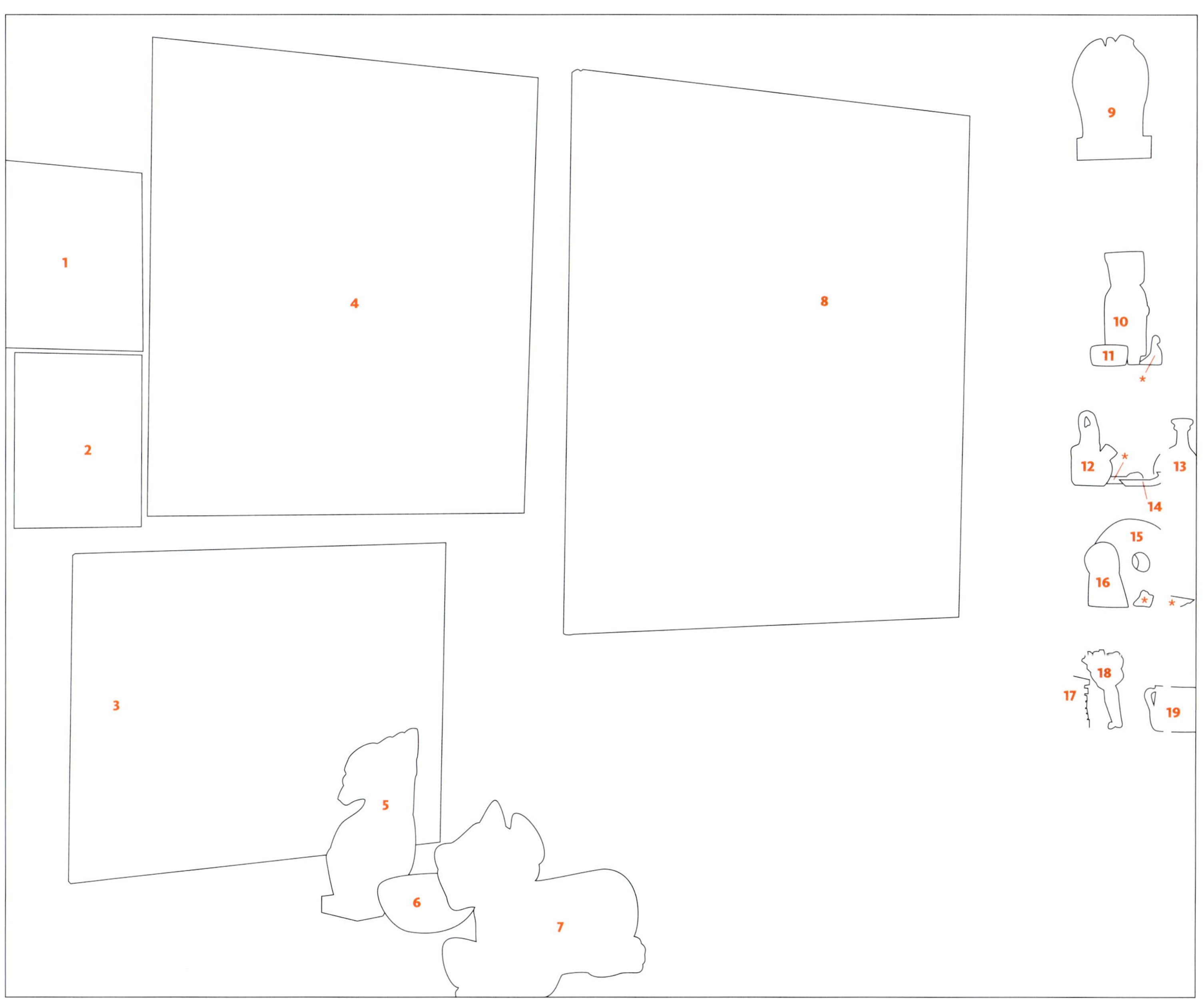

1
2
3
4
5
6
7
8
9
10
11
*
12
*
13
14
15
16
*
*
17
18
19

PLATE 57

GUEST BEDROOM

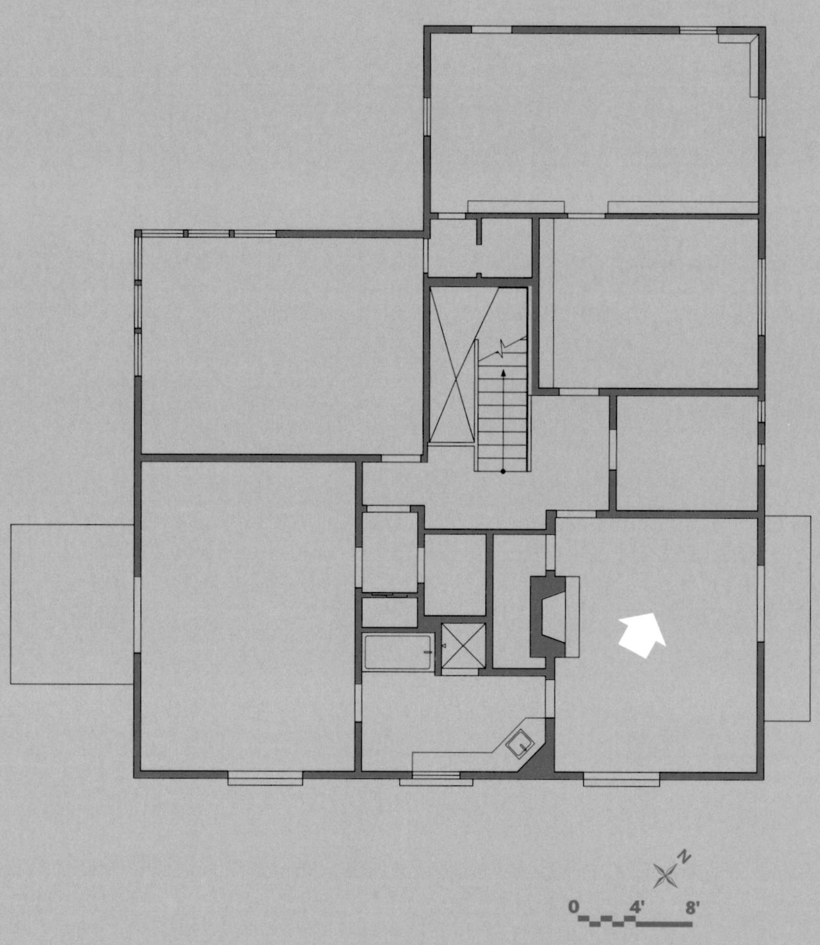

KARL BISSINGER

16 MARCH 1950

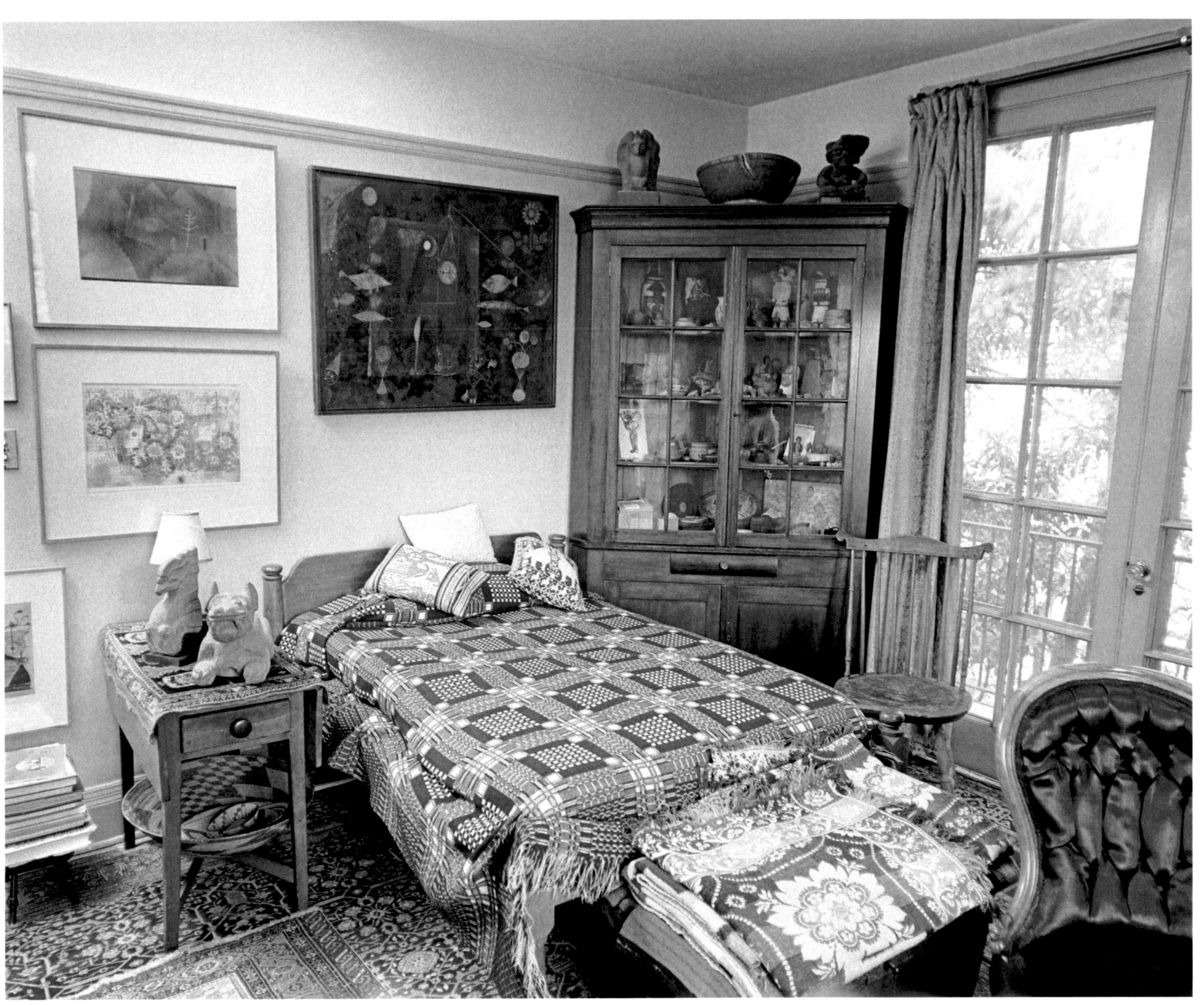

PLATE 57

1 PAUL KLEE, *Glance of a Landscape*, 1926 [1950-134-120; AC20-116]

2 PAUL KLEE, *Small Houses in the Garden City*, 1928 [1950-134-119; AC20-121]

3 REPRODUCTION OF MARCEL DUCHAMP'S *Coffee Mill* (1911), Date unknown [NOTE 1.2, PAGE 414]

4 CLASSIC VERACRUZ (EAST COAST MEXICO), Palma, 500–900 [1950-134-346; ACPS-157]

5 AZTEC (CENTRAL MEXICO), Jaguar, 1300–1520 [1950-134-205]

6–10 NATIVE AMERICAN, Baskets, Dates unknown [6: 1950-134-773; 7: *1950-134-772; 8: 1950-134-770; 9: 1950-134-771; 10: 1950-134-769]

11 PAUL KLEE, *Fish Magic*, 1925 [1950-134-112; AC20-113]

12 CLASSIC VERACRUZ (EAST COAST MEXICO), Palma, 500–900 [1950-134-601]

13 ARTIST/MAKER UNKNOWN (NORTH AMERICA), Bread Bowl, *Early U.S. [NOTE 4.11, PAGE 417]

14 TEOTIHUACAN (CENTRAL MEXICO), Seated Figure (Old God of Fire), 1st–9th century [1950-134-209; ACPS-4]

15, 16 NATIVE AMERICAN (SOUTHWESTERN UNITED STATES), Kachina Dolls, Dates unknown [15: 1950-134-437, 16: 1950-134-436]

17, 18 HOPI (SOUTHWESTERN UNITED STATES), Kachina Dolls, Dates unknown [17: 1950-134-744, 18: 1950-134-745]

19 INCA (PERU), Pitcher, 1400–1532 [1950-134-582]

20 NAZCA (PERU), Bowl with Seabird Designs (PICTURED UPSIDE DOWN), 200 BCE–600 CE [1950-134-608]

21 NATIVE AMERICAN (SOUTHWESTERN UNITED STATES), Pitcher with Floral Decorations, Date unknown [1950-134-743]

22 INCA (PERU), Container, 1400–1532 [1950-134-576]

23 MARCEL DUCHAMP, *With Hidden Noise*, 1916 [1950-134-71; AC20-77]

24 NAZCA (PERU), Bowl, 200 BCE–600 CE [1950-134-612]

25 NATIVE AMERICAN, Frog Form, Date unknown [1950-134-798]

26 INCA (PERU), Pitcher, 1400–1532 [1950-134-584]

27 CHUMASH (CALIFORNIA), Bowl in Turtle Form with Shell Rim Inlay, Date unknown [1950-134-443]

28 CHANCAY (PERU), Triple-Spouted Vessel, 1200–1470 [1950-134-610]

29 RAYMOND DUCHAMP-VILLON, *Portrait of Professor Gosset*, ca. 1917–18 [1950-134-84; AC20-87]

30 ARTIST/MAKER UNKNOWN (BALI), Figure, Date unknown [1950-134-829]

31 INCA (PERU), Pitcher, 1400–1532 [1950-134-583]

32 INCA (PERU), Container, 1400–1532 [1950-134-580]

33 CHUMASH (POINT DUME, CALIFORNIA), Whale Form with Bone Blow Pipe, Date unknown [1950-134-477]

34 INCA (PERU), Votive Container (Canopa), 1400–1532 [*1950-134-343]

35 CHUMASH (*CHANNEL ISLANDS, CALIFORNIA), Tarantula Form, Date unknown [1950-134-468]

36 ARTIST/MAKER UNKNOWN (POSSIBLY LIANGZHU CULTURE, CHINA), Disk (Bi), ca. 3400–2250 BCE [1950-134-845]

37 ARTIST/MAKER UNKNOWN (CHINA), Disk (Bi), ca. 2200–1800 BCE [1950-134-844]

38 ARTIST/MAKER UNKNOWN (CHINA), Semicircular Arc, Date unknown [1950-134-843]

39 ANCESTRAL PUEBLO, Pot, ca. 1000–1200 [1950-134-741]

40 ARTISTS/MAKERS UNKNOWN (CHINA), Seven Boxes Containing Calcified Jade Ornaments, Various dates [1950-134-832A–D; 1950-134-833A–E; 1950-134-834A–D; 1950-134-835A–E; 1950-134-836A–C (CA. 1700–800 BCE); 1950-134-837 (FISH FORM); 1950-134-838 (BIRD FORM, CA. 1050–800 BCE)]

41 ARTIST/MAKER UNKNOWN (BALI), Painted Cloth Fragment with Figures, Date unknown [1950-134-830]

42 NAZCA (PERU), Vessel Depicting the Anthropomorphic Mythical Being, 200–600 [1950-134-609]

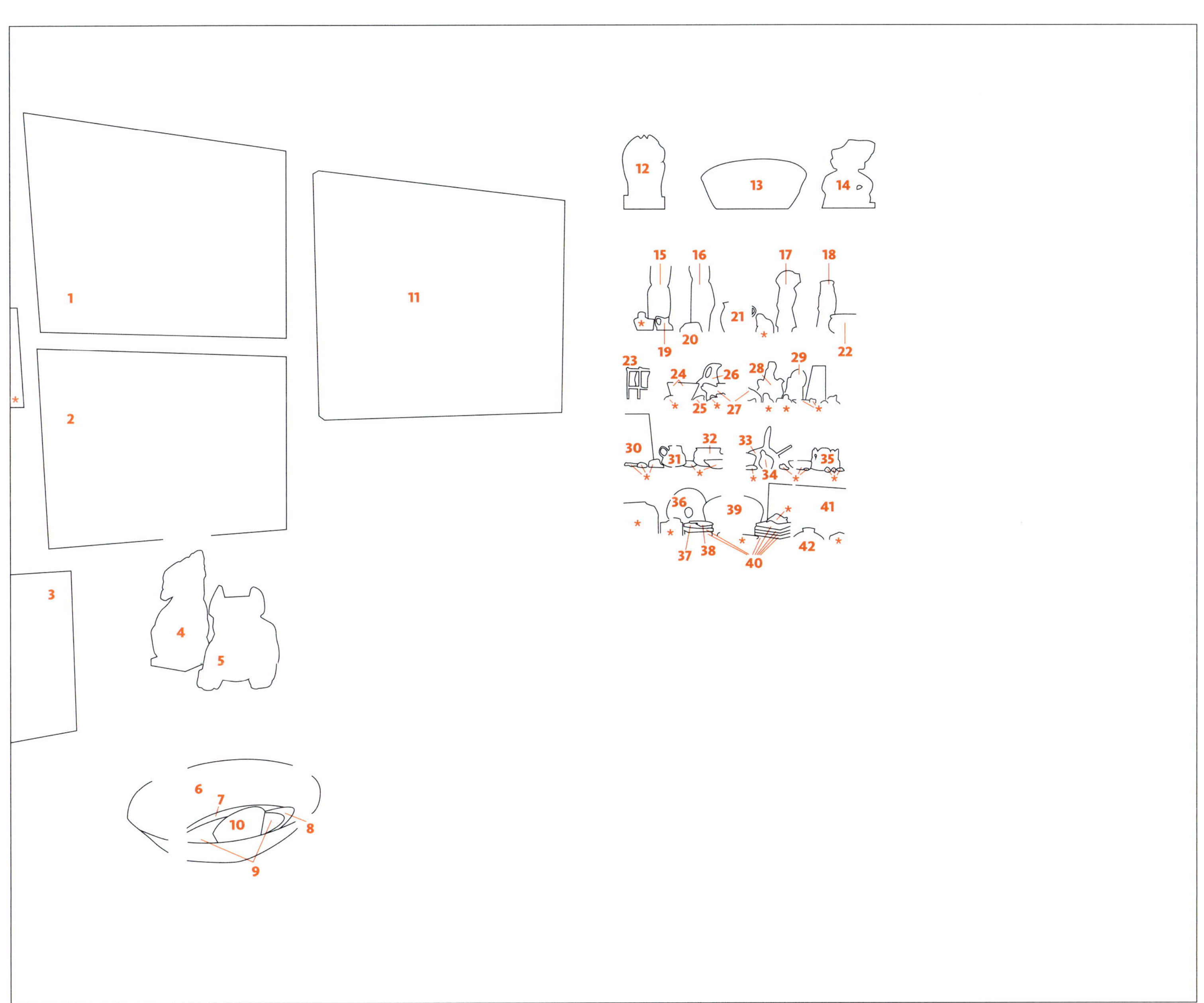
1
2
3
4
5
6
7
8
9
10
11
12
13
14
15
16
17
18
19
20
21
22
23
24
25
26
27
28
29
30
31
32
33
34
35
36
37
38
39
40
41
42

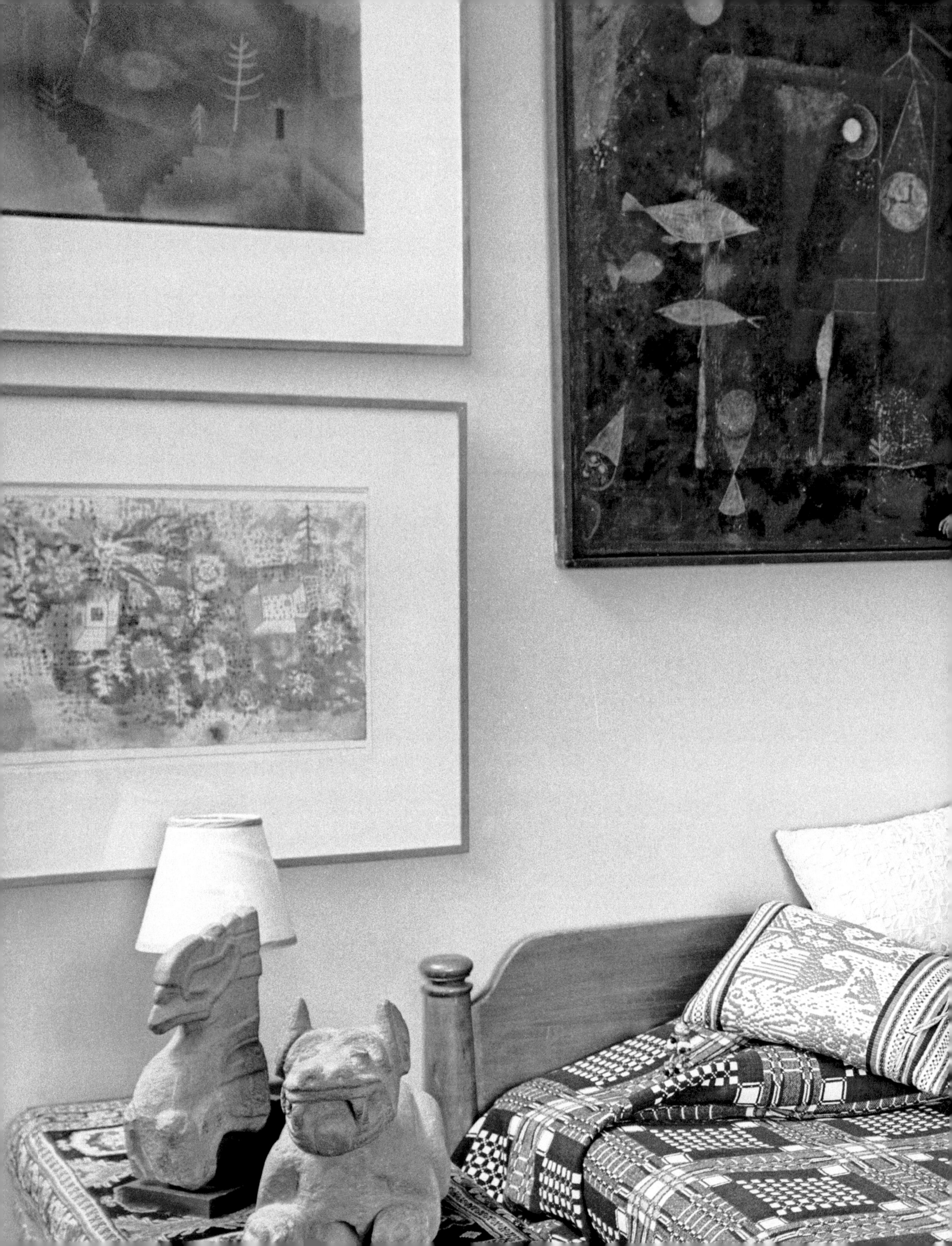

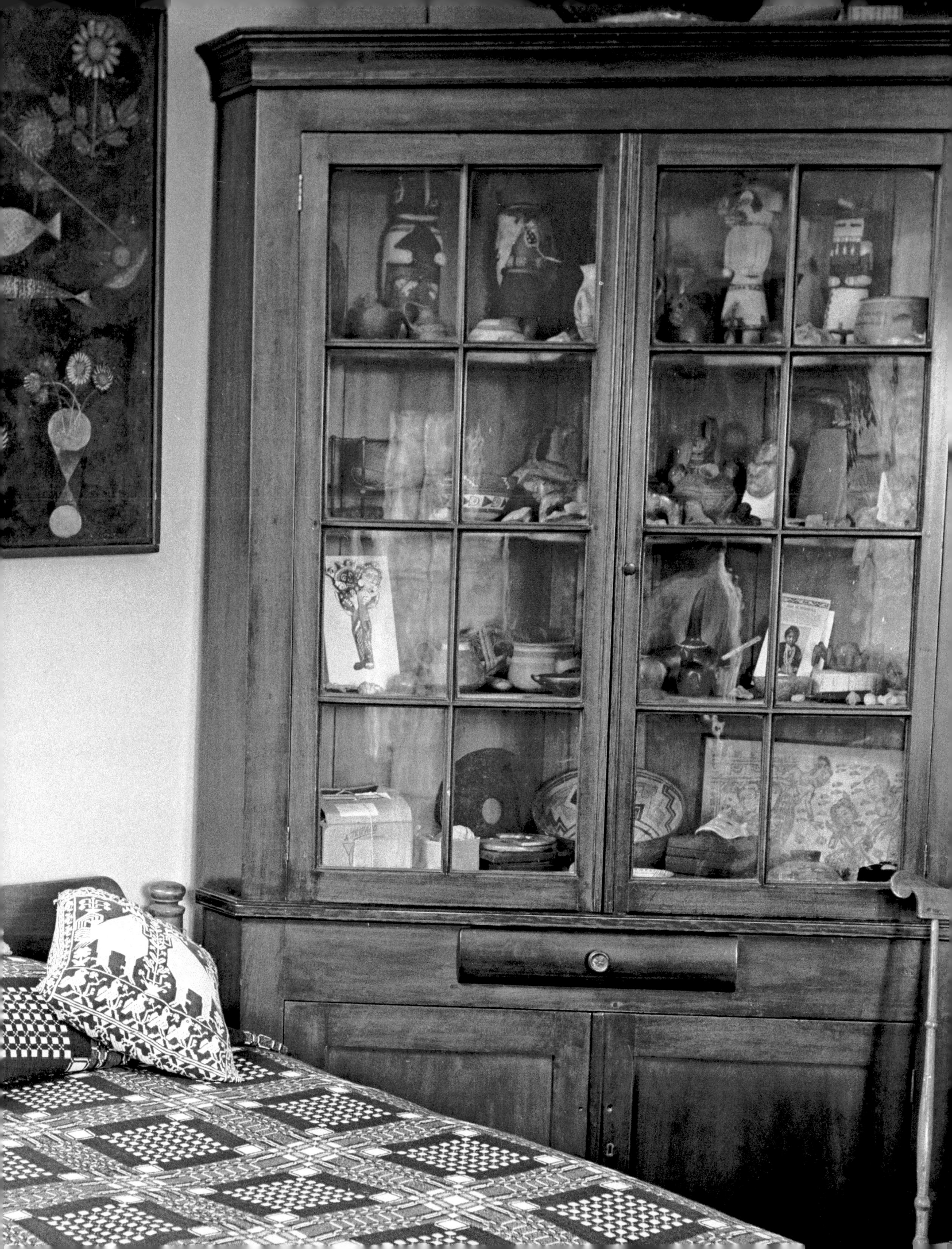

PLATE 58

GUEST BEDROOM

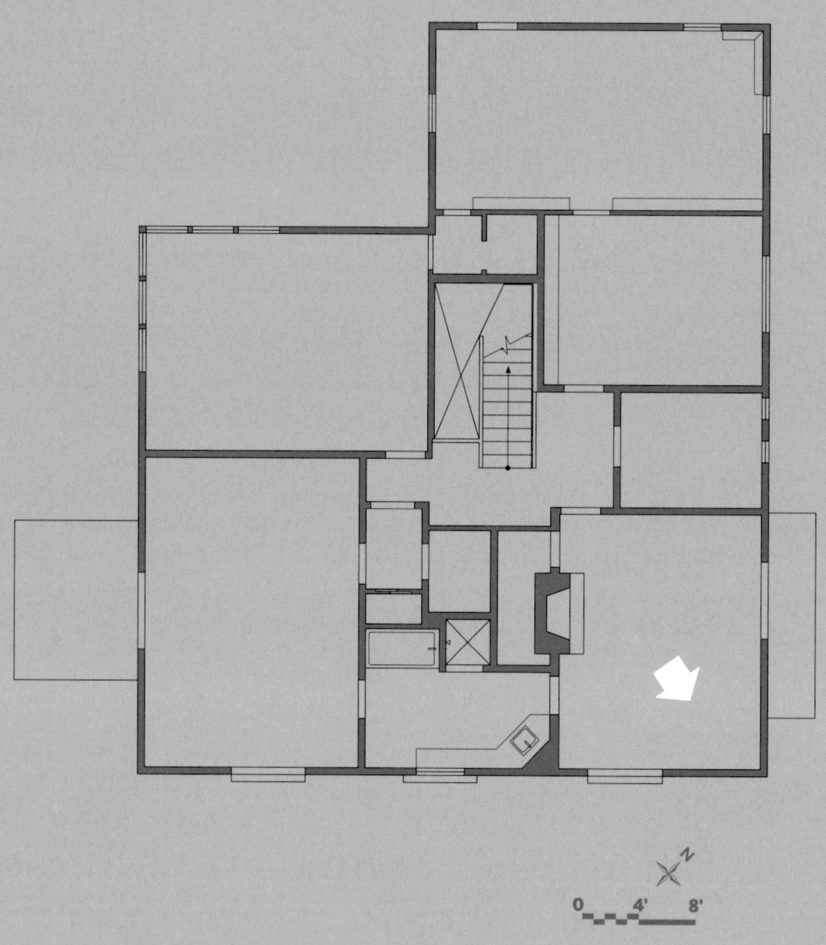

KARL BISSINGER
16 MARCH 1950

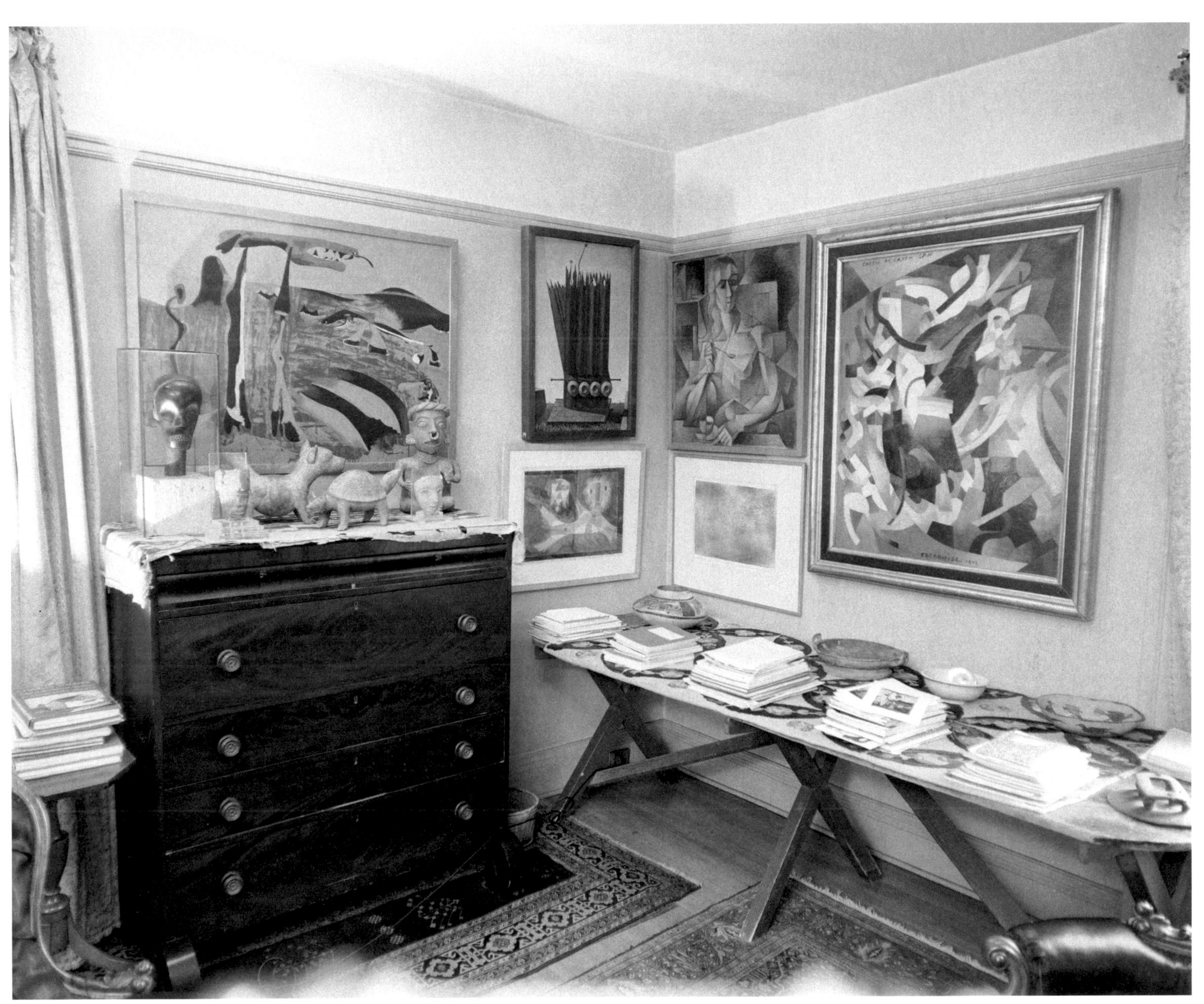

PLATE 58

1 JOAN MIRÓ, *Person in the Presence of Nature*, 1935 [1950-134-149; AC20-152]

2 FANG (GABON), Head, Date unknown [1950-134-202]

3 CLASSIC VERACRUZ (EAST COAST MEXICO), Hacha in the Form of a Head, 500–900 [1950-134-272; ACPS-141]

4 COLIMA (WESTERN MEXICO), Vessel in the Form of a Dog, 300 BCE–300 CE [1950-134-279; ACPS-67]

5 COLIMA (WESTERN MEXICO), Vessel in the Form of a Dog, 300 BCE–300 CE [1950-134-217; ACPS-70]

6 TEOTIHUACAN (CENTRAL MEXICO), Mask, 1st–9th century [1950-134-229; ACPS-23]

7 NAYARIT (WESTERN MEXICO), Seated Woman, 100 BCE–300 CE [1950-134-377; ACPS-79]

8 MAX ERNST, *The Forest*, 1923 [1950-134-85; AC20-88]

9 PAUL KLEE, *Goldfish Wife*, 1921 [1950-134-110; AC20-111]

10 JEAN METZINGER, *Tea Time (Woman with a Teaspoon)*, 1911 [1950-134-139; AC20-141]

11 PAUL KLEE, *Journey in Corsica*, 1927 [1950-134-116; AC20-119]

12 FRANCIS PICABIA, *Catch as Catch Can*, 1913 [1950-134-156; AC20-159]

13 CASAS GRANDES (NORTHERN MEXICO OR SOUTHWESTERN UNITED STATES), Bowl, 300–1500 [1950-134-806]

14 ARTIST/MAKER UNKNOWN (CHINA), Bronze Bowl, Date unknown [NOTE 4.12, PAGE 417]

15 ARTIST/MAKER UNKNOWN (*CHINA), Crystal Sphere, Date unknown [NOTE 4.5, PAGE 417]

16 ARTIST/MAKER UNKNOWN (CHINA), Bowl, Date unknown [1950-134-850]

17 ARTIST/MAKER UNKNOWN, Bowl, 20th century [1950-134-807]

18 ARTIST/MAKER UNKNOWN (*AFRICA), Stand, Date unknown [NOTE 4.13, PAGE 417]

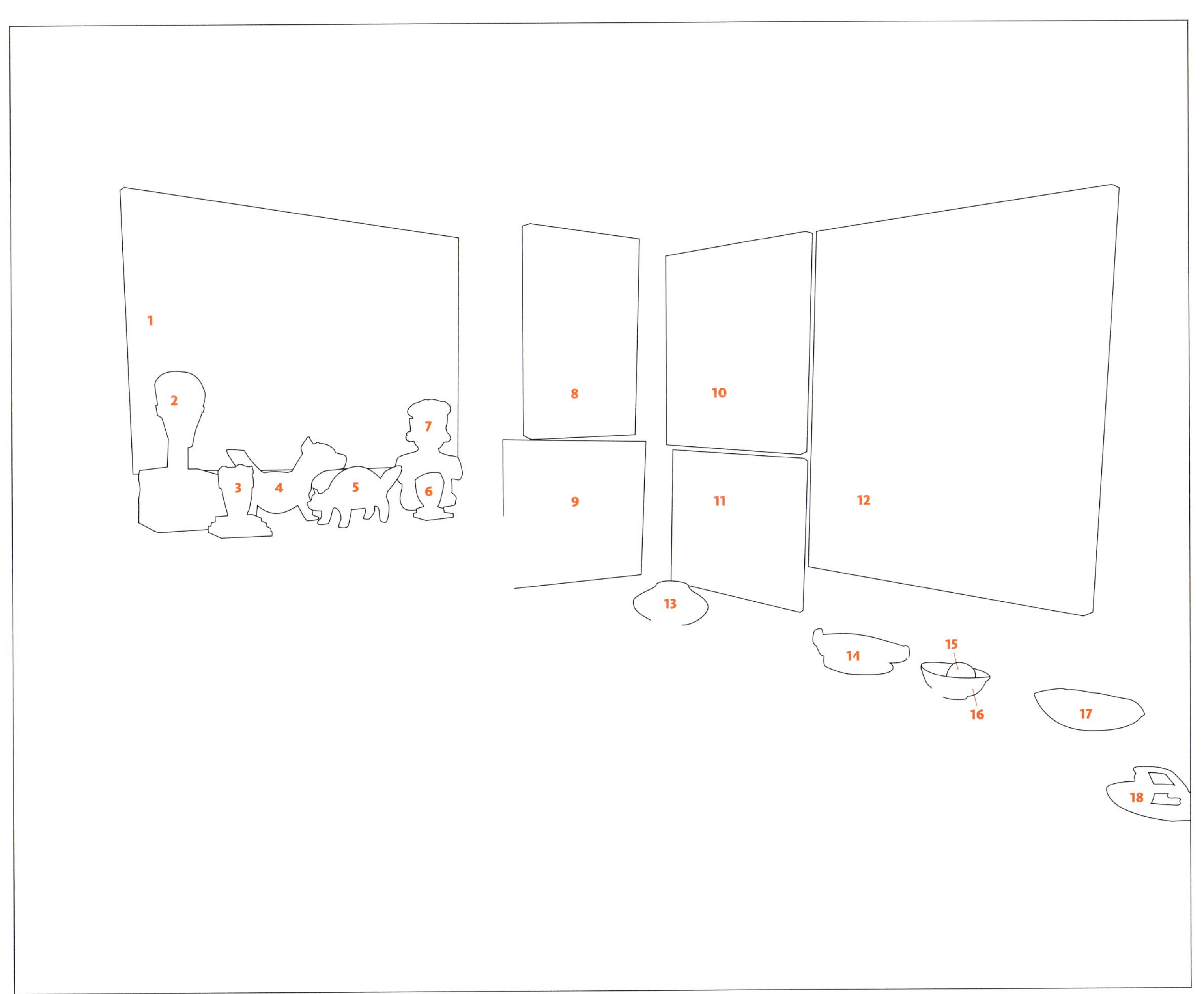

1
2
3
4
5
6
7
8
9
10
11
12
13
14
15
16
17
18

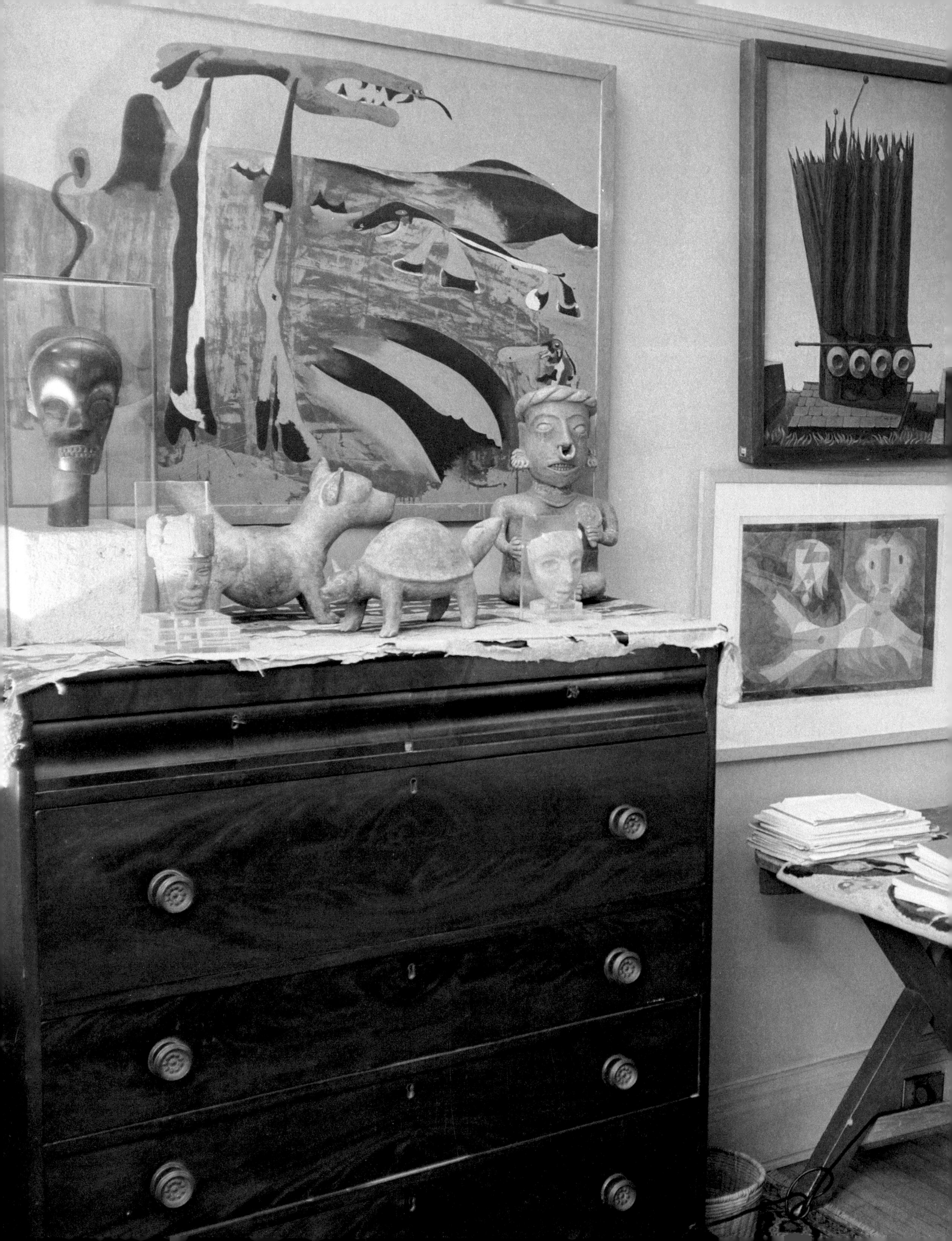

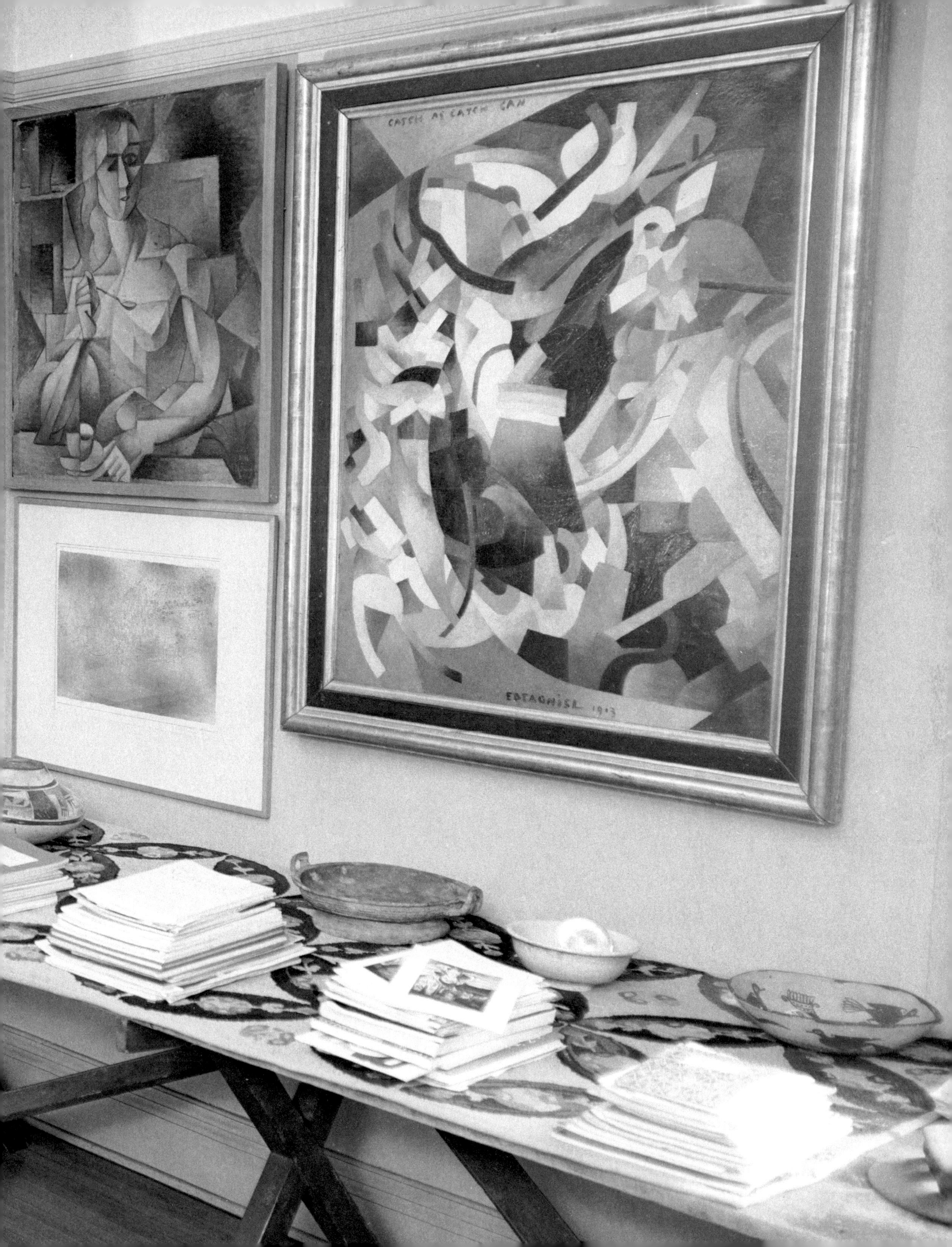
CATCH AS CATCH CAN

7065 HILLSIDE AVENUE, LOS ANGELES, CALIFORNIA
RESIDENCE OF LOUISE AND WALTER ARENSBERG, 1927–54

FRONT PATIO

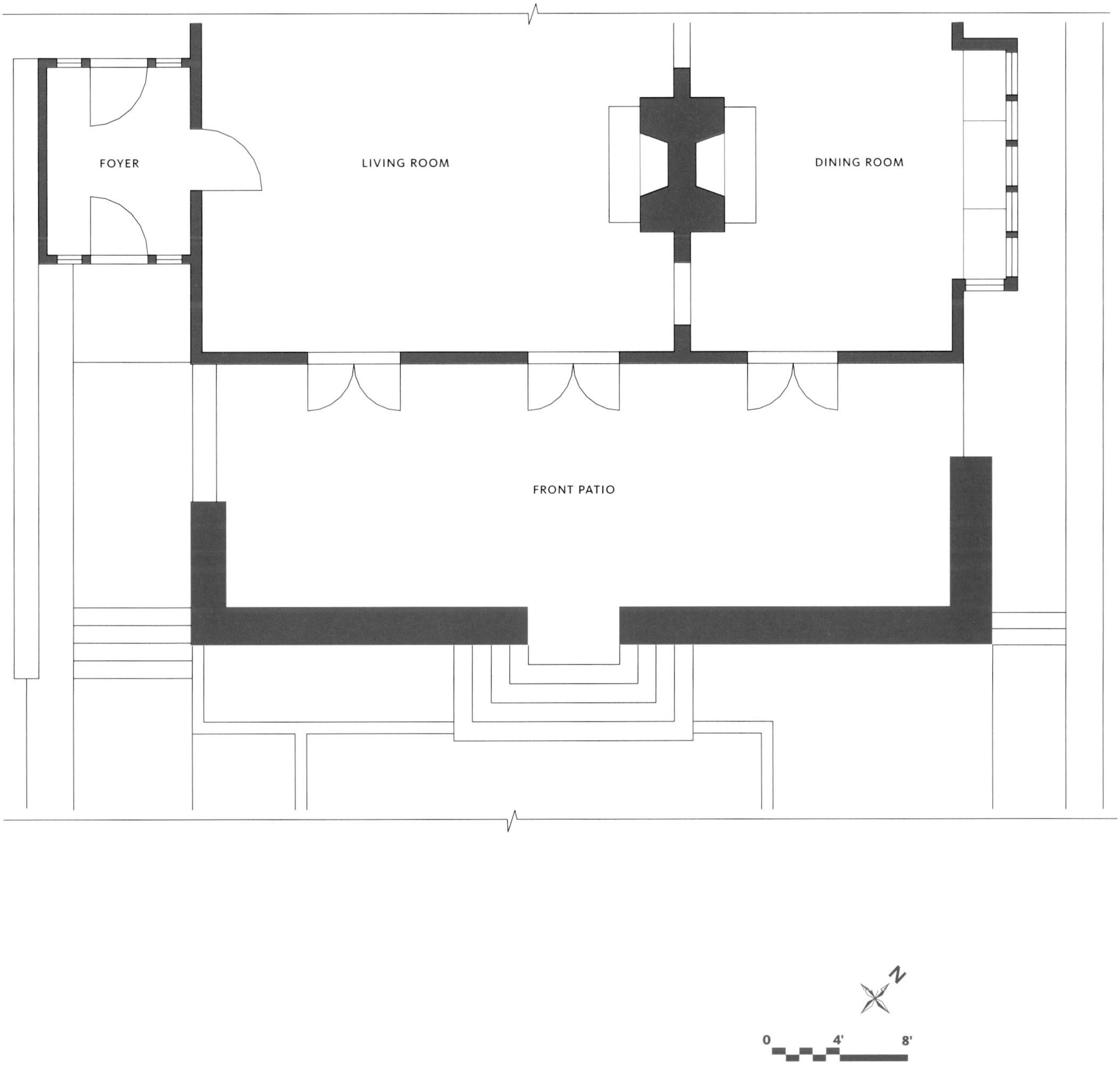

FOYER

LIVING ROOM

DINING ROOM

FRONT PATIO

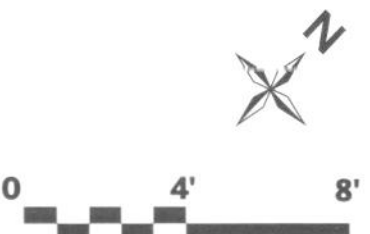

PLATE 59

FRONT PATIO

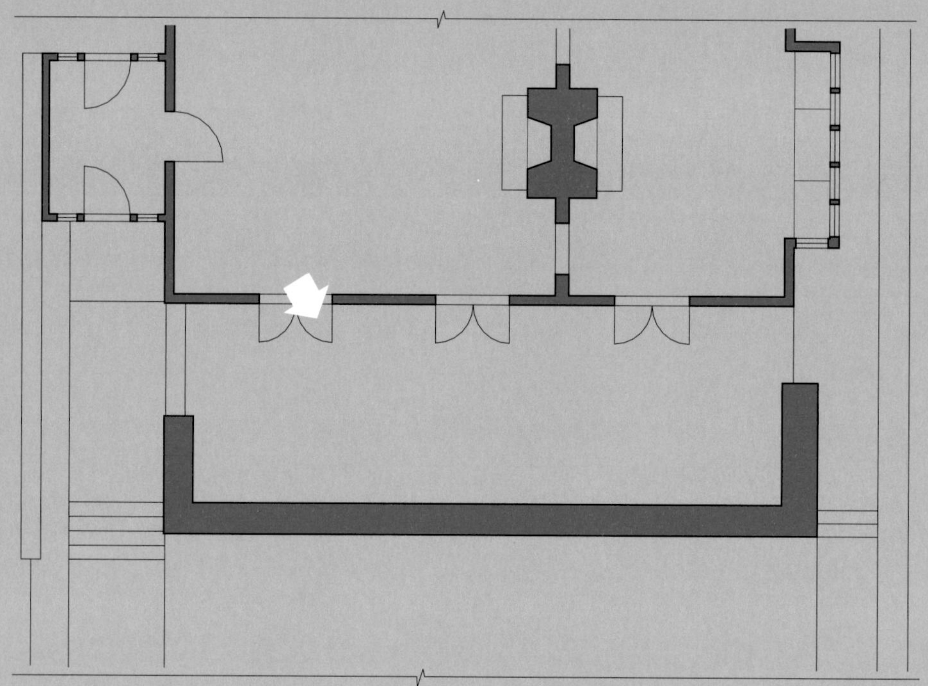

FLOYD FAXON
CA. FEBRUARY 1951

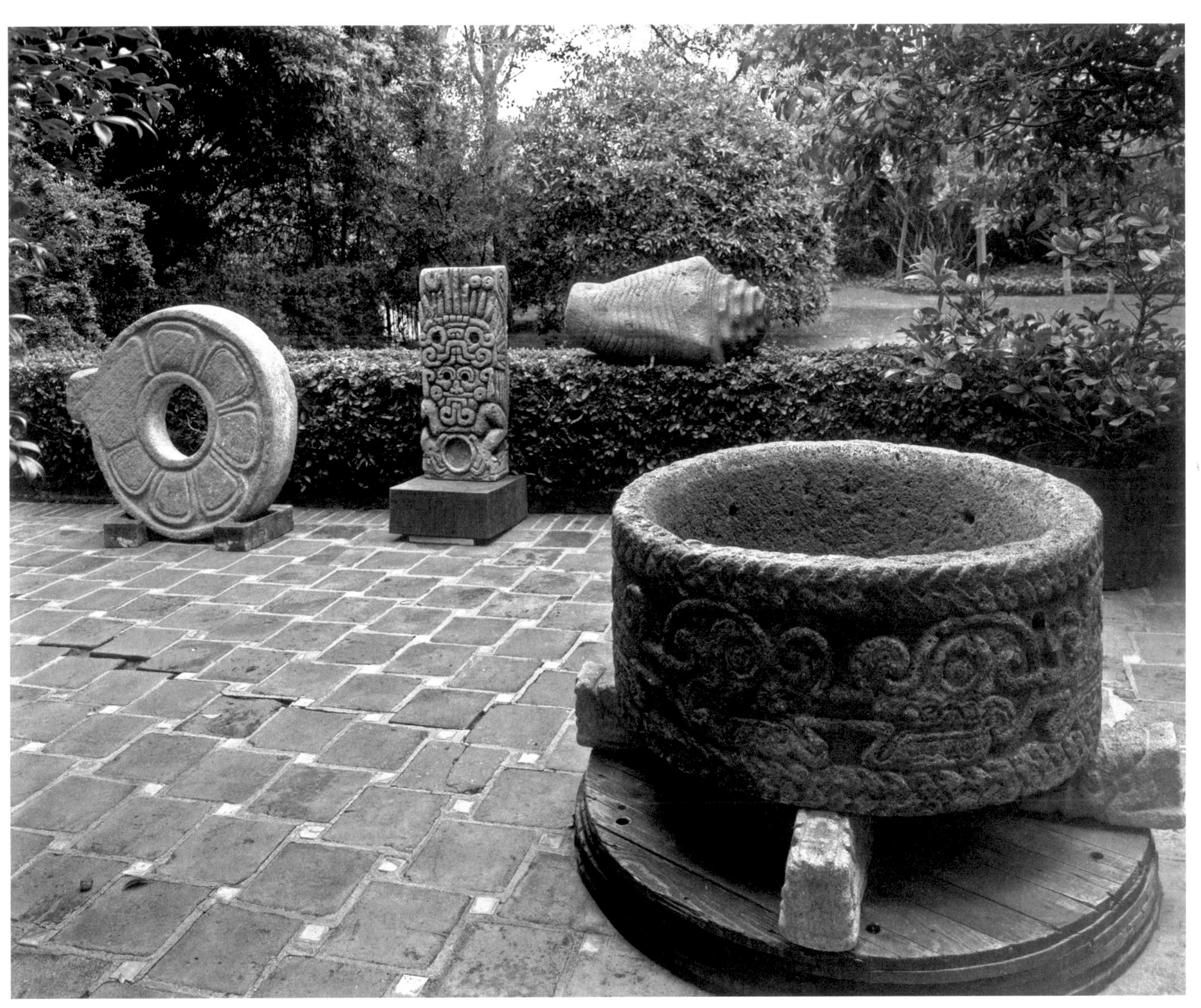

PLATE 59

1 AZTEC (CENTRAL MEXICO), Ballcourt Ring with Floral Motif, 1400–1520 [1950-134-372; ACPS-44]

2 TOLTEC OR OTHER EPICLASSIC/EARLY POSTCLASSIC CULTURE (CENTRAL MEXICO), Stela Showing Personage Holding Round Disk, Possibly a Mirror, 800–1200 [1950-134-406; ACPS-107]

3 AZTEC (CENTRAL MEXICO), Conch Shell, 1300–1520 [1950-134-348; ACPS-39]

4 AZTEC (CENTRAL MEXICO), Basin, 1300–1520 [1950-134-350; ACPS-43]

5–8 TOLTEC OR OTHER EPICLASSIC CULTURE (MEXICO), Tenoned Heads of Serpents, 600–900 [1950-134-351–354; ACPS-103–106]

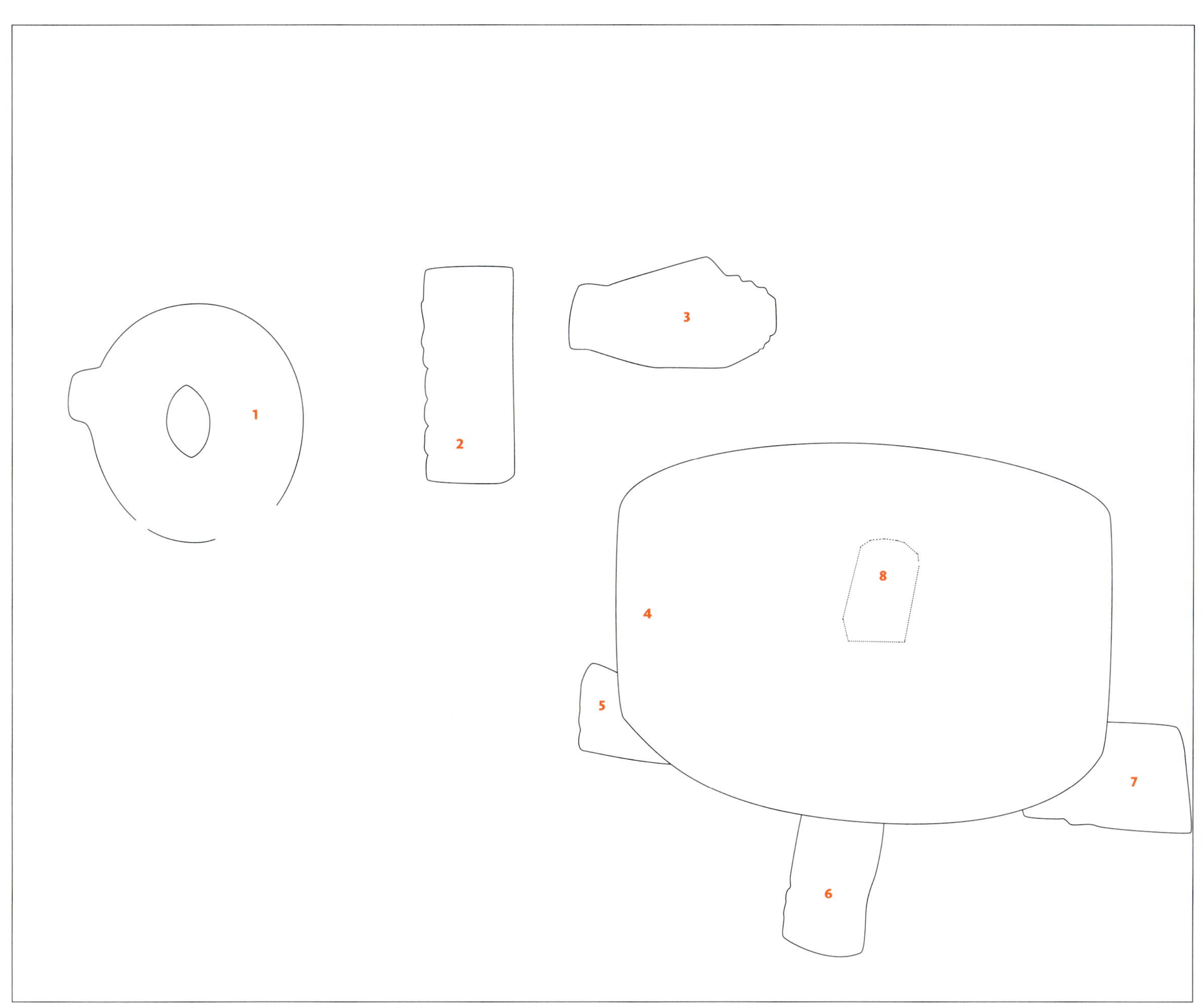
1
2
3
4
5
6
7
8

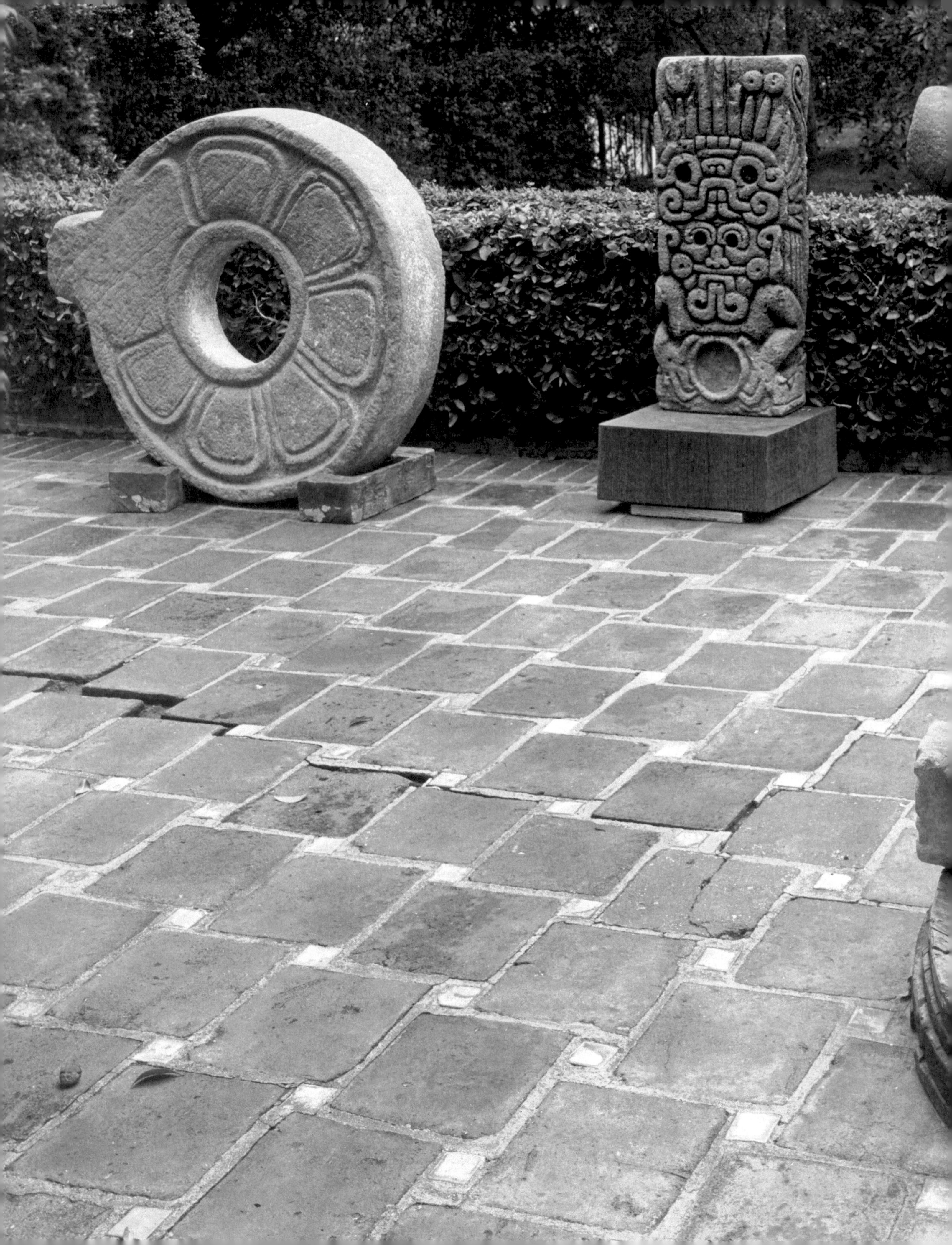

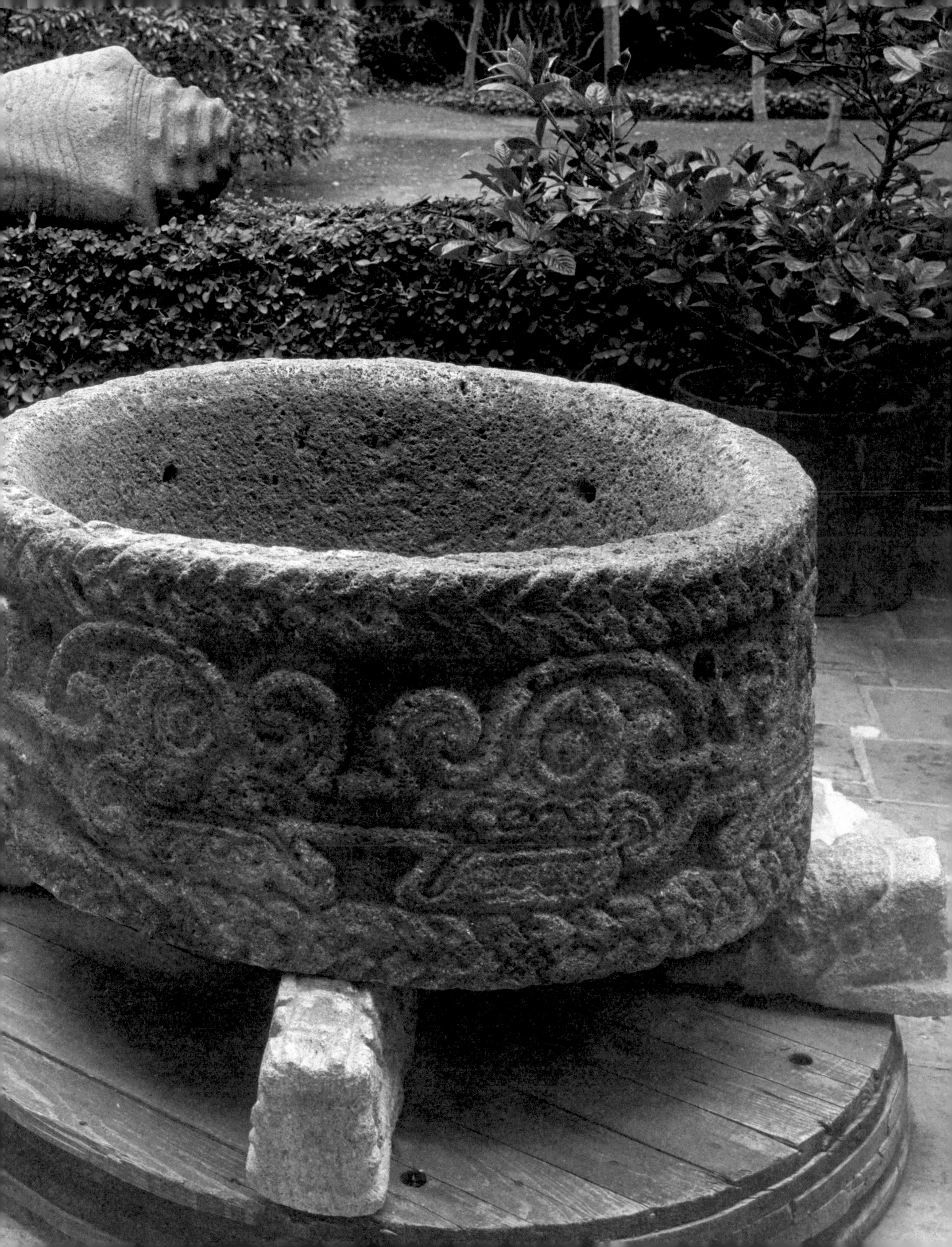

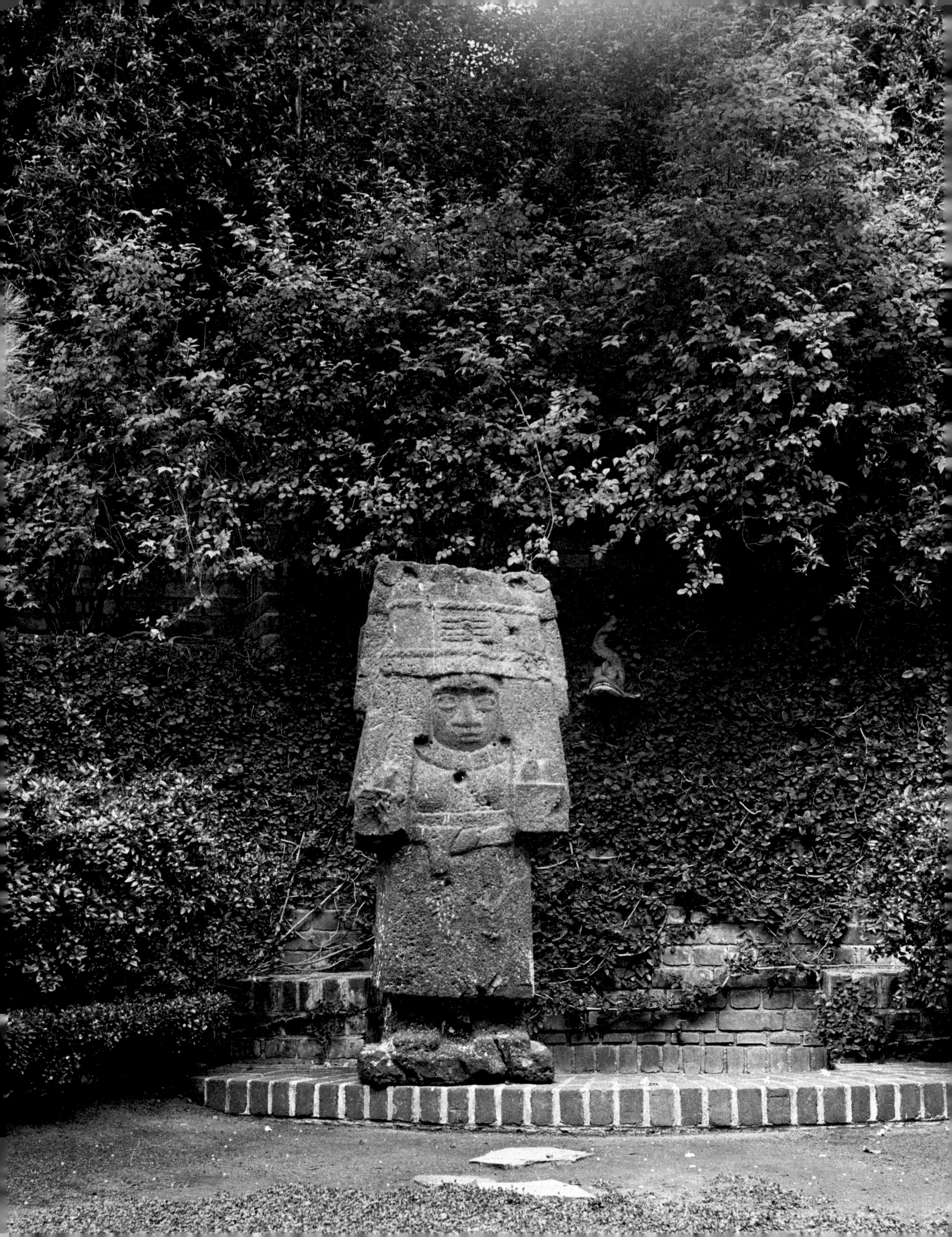

SMOOTHING THE PATH FOR ROUGH STONES

The Changing Role of Pre-Columbian Art in the Arensberg Collection

ELLEN HOOBLER

KARL BISSINGER. SCULPTURE OF AZTEC CORN GODDESS IN THE REAR PATIO GARDEN OF THE LOUISE AND WALTER ARENSBERG RESIDENCE, 7065 HILLSIDE AVENUE, LOS ANGELES, 16 MARCH 1950. UNIVERSITY OF DELAWARE LIBRARY, NEWARK, SPECIAL COLLECTIONS, KARL BISSINGER ARCHIVE (MSS0682). SEE ALSO PLATE 26.10 .

When one has to some extent recovered from the astonishment caused by the size of the Mexican monuments and by the skill needed for their execution by a people so primitively equipped, the sense of their meaning begins to form in one's mind, and one sees that the true wonder of this art is its intensity—its bare, direct statement of the idea.

—**WALTER PACH**[1]

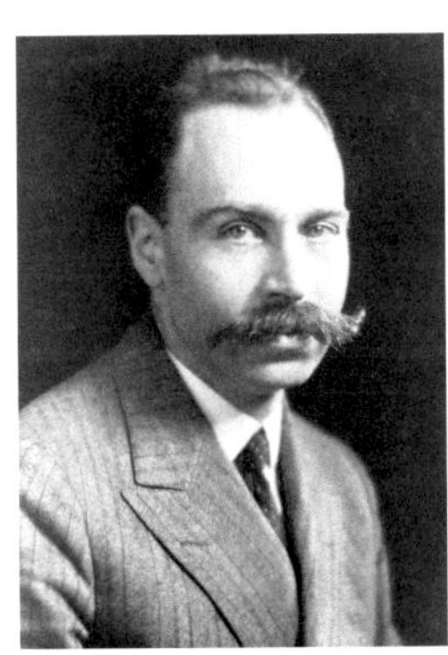

1. WALTER PACH, 1920. PHOTOGRAPHER UNKNOWN. COURTESY FRANCIS M. NAUMANN GALLERY

IN 1920, *The Dial* magazine ran an article titled "The Art of the American Indian," by the art critic Walter Pach (fig. 1). In the article, Pach contended that a unity existed in all the arts of the pre-Columbian Americas from north to south. This was not such an unusual attitude at the time, although it is less commonly held today.[2] Pach also pointed out the spirituality and artistic power he felt characterized Native American art:

> Familiar to most of us from childhood as the relics of a savage period, the Indian things reveal themselves in a startlingly new light if we think of them as art. To some it will seem at first that only by an extension of the term can it be applied to the work of the Indians. Let these people begin a new acquaintance with the sculpture and architecture of ancient Mexico—the greatest art which has yet been produced in the Western Hemisphere.[3]

In the next issue of *The Dial*, the art critic Henry McBride contributed the first installment of his Modern Forms column, largely devoted to Louise and Walter Arensberg's collection of modern, Dada, and primitive art. McBride did not mention the Aztec sculpture that then had pride of place before the Arensberg hearth (see Sherman and Nelson, figs. 9b, c), but he began the article with an assessment that he attributed to a traditionalist companion: "'Walter Arensberg is quite mad. Mrs. Arensberg is mad, too.'"[4] This statement was intended to convey the couple's preference for the modern art that was still, in 1920, incredibly shocking to the general public. While McBride did not explicitly say that ancient sculptures of Mexico could be art, as Pach did, or that cubist paintings could also be art, he was certainly fulfilling the column's stated mission to promote "exposition and consideration of the less traditional types of art."[5]

Indeed, when the "mad" Arensbergs first collected modern art, it was scandalous and unpalatable to most people. At the same time, they acquired several pre-Columbian pieces, which, along with African and Native American works, were more a foil for their modernist collection than an indication of a serious aesthetic interest. The couple had evolving motivations for the acquisition and display of their pre-Columbian collection during different phases of their lives, but their collecting habits continued to be influenced by the ideals of modernism, in that they often sought to collect art that did not conform to prevailing ideas of beauty and aesthetics. After their move to California in 1921 and a hiatus in collecting occasioned by financial pressures, the Arensbergs were ready to resume collecting at an increased pace in the early 1930s. By then, modern art was accepted by a significant portion of the population. But pre-Columbian works were still only rarely considered art; they were more frequently featured in anthropology museums. It is likely that the increase in importance of pre-Columbian art within the Arensbergs' collection was partially due to the couple's desire to continue to be tastemakers for works or areas of art that did not have broad acceptance.

There were practical reasons for the Arensbergs' marked interest in pre-Columbian art after they started collecting again in the 1930s. Works from Mexico and Central America were increasingly available in Los Angeles after the late 1930s, due to improvement in the reach of Mexican railways and the construction of the Mexican section of the Pan-American Highway. But there were also aesthetic reasons for the Arensbergs' renewed interest, as Walter later explained to Kenneth Ross—particularly the couple's attraction to what they called pre-Columbian art's "mysterious" quality.[6] They were not alone in being drawn to this art: by the late 1930s, pre-Columbian works were a significant source of inspiration for the surrealists centered in Mexico, and Walter, who was an early participant in the Dada movement (and who had purchased several surrealist paintings during these years; see, for example, plate 47), may have seen collecting pre-Columbian art as a material outgrowth of his own interests.

The Arensbergs' method of acquiring and displaying their pre-Columbian art is an important and, until now, little-examined chapter in the historiography of collecting such art in the United States, which has barely begun to be fleshed out. Some of the mentors and dealers key to the Arensberg collection have not yet been chronicled in the scant literature. While the Arensbergs' main Los Angeles dealer, Earl Stendahl, has been amply referenced in other books and essays, the Arensbergs' most important guide for non-Western art, Marius de Zayas Enríquez, has never been discussed in the context of pre-Columbian art dealing in the United States.[7] Other men in New York in the 1910s, notably Pach and John Quinn, were also influential for the Arensbergs, but de Zayas ushered the couple through their first purchases of pre-Columbian and African art. He was particularly key in developing the aesthetic principles that would guide the Arensbergs' collecting, being against the conventionally beautiful or highly finished and embracing the rough or broken, the monumental, and the esoteric. De Zayas sold the couple modern artworks, helping to build their collection during their New York years (1914–21), but was also largely responsible for the financial reversals that precipitated their move to California. Later, ensconced on the West Coast, the Arensbergs found new guides. Among them were the Mexican artist Roberto Montenegro and the drama critic turned Hollywood producer and sometime pre-Columbian scholar Kenneth Macgowan, as well as Stendahl, whose life and livelihood became enmeshed with the couple's own. Several works have been written on the best-known figure in the early history of collecting ancient art of the Americas, Robert Woods Bliss of Washington, DC.[8] Bliss was an influence on the Arensbergs but also a competitor for works, and, partly because of his geographic distance, his effect on shaping the collection was less important.

The art historian Naomi Sawelson-Gorse, the source of a significant body of scholarship on the Arensbergs, has written that their collecting of pre-Columbian art was "a passion typical of this era when such art was all the rage for avant-garde collectors."[9] This essay argues that the Arensbergs' pre-Columbian and Native American acquisitions certainly were a passion; at the same time, they were undertaken with sustained curiosity, appreciation, and, ultimately, a true respect for the formal qualities of these works and for the people who made them. However, these same formal qualities, in keeping with an aesthetic of the nonbeautiful, would prevent the Arensberg collection from receiving the attention it deserved after the couple's deaths.

I

The New York Years

NEW YORK 1914–21: RELATIONSHIPS AND INFLUENCES

As the previous sections of this book have already made clear, the Arensbergs were visionaries in the modernist acquisitions they made in the 1910s in New York, but they were ably guided by others who were already enmeshed in the avant-garde. Around the time the Arensbergs moved to New York in 1914, there were four men, all connected through the avant-garde network, who became touchstones in different ways for the couple: Marcel Duchamp (fig. 2), Walter Pach, John Quinn (fig. 3), and Marius de Zayas (fig. 4).[10] The Arensbergs received guidance in their acquisitions from each one of them, although through de Zayas and Duchamp the possibilities for actually purchasing art were more direct.

Marcel Duchamp was instrumental in shaping the couple's modernist collection and was an intellectual guide for Walter. However, Duchamp was never involved in the marketing of pre-Columbian art, and there is no evidence to suggest that he had significant knowledge or interest in "primitive" art. In fact, when he visited the Arensbergs decades later in Los Angeles, he was surprised by the growth of their collection in this area and discomfited by the restoration studio of their most prominent dealer.[11]

However, Pach, Quinn, and de Zayas all profoundly influenced the Arensbergs' pre-Columbian collection as well as their modern holdings. The role of Walter Pach, one of the organizers of the 1913 Armory Show, as an evangelist for (and facilitator of) modern art in New York has long been known and has been described in greater detail over the past few years.[12] For the Arensbergs, Pach served as a guide into a new aesthetic world. As the couple became fascinated by modern art, he encouraged their connoisseurship, first in Cambridge, then in New York after the Armory Show.[13] He recommended readings to the Arensbergs and introduced them to Marcel Duchamp, arranging for the French artist to stay in their New York apartment while the couple summered in Connecticut in 1915.[14] Walter held Pach in the highest esteem, valuing

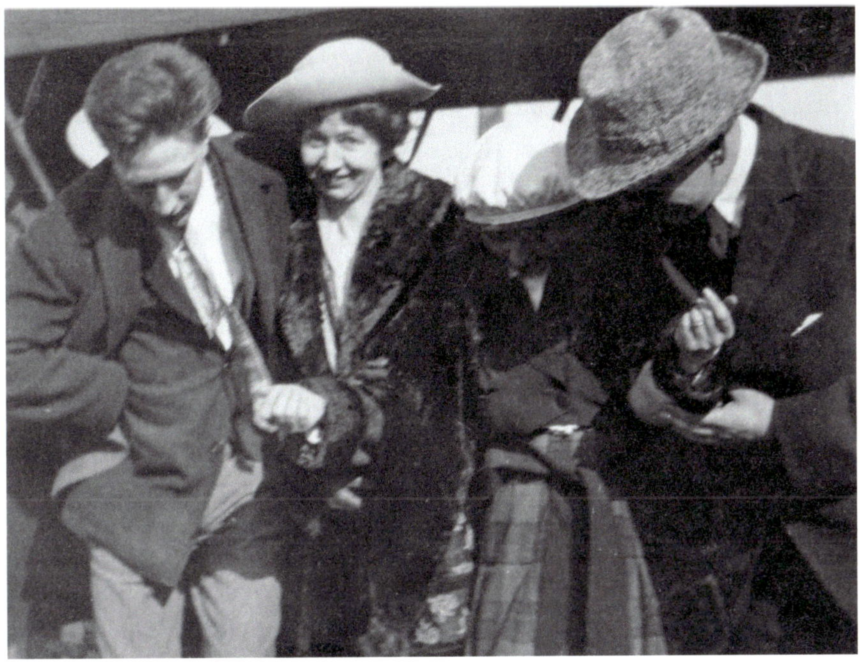

2. FROM LEFT: MARCEL DUCHAMP, LOUISE ARENSBERG, YVONNE CROTTI, AND WALTER ARENSBERG, NEW YORK, CA. 1916. PHOTOGRAPHER UNKNOWN. LOUISE ARENSBERG PHOTO ALBUMS, VOLUME 2, PAGE 2. PHILADELPHIA MUSEUM OF ART, LIBRARY AND ARCHIVES, ARENSBERG ARCHIVES (PMA-WLA), BOX 50, FOLDER 2

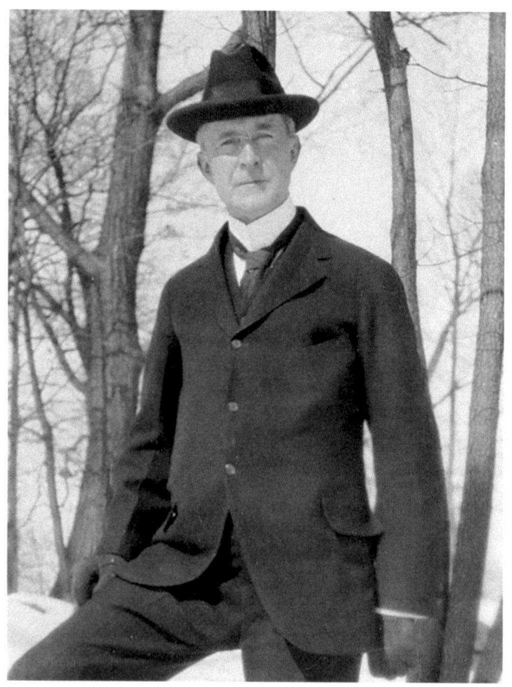

3. JOHN QUINN AT THE SLEEPY HOLLOW CLUB IN WESTCHESTER, NEW YORK, CA. 1915. PHOTOGRAPHER UNKNOWN. SMITHSONIAN INSTITUTION, ARCHIVES OF AMERICAN ART, ALINE AND EERO SAARINEN PAPERS, 1906–1977

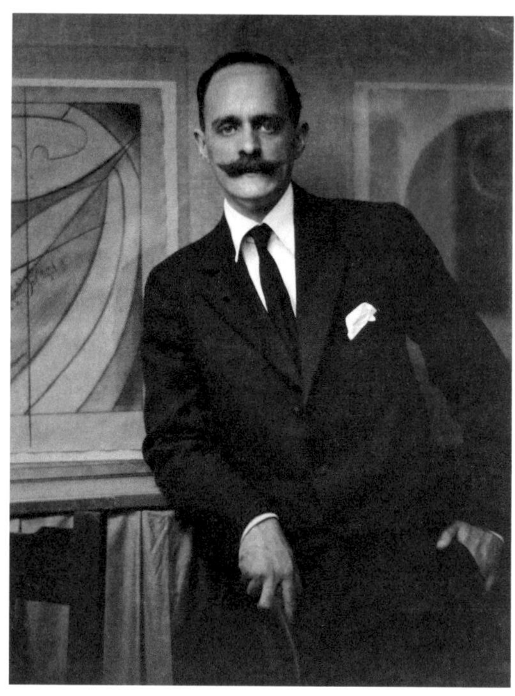

4. ALFRED STIEGLITZ. MARIUS DE ZAYAS, 1913. WAXED PLATINUM PRINT. SMITHSONIAN INSTITUTION, NATIONAL PORTRAIT GALLERY; GIFT OF AN ANONYMOUS DONOR

his opinion on all matters artistic and even his painting skills; he wrote to Pach in 1914, "I have been wondering if you are not the illusionist of the [modern art] movement. At any rate you bring to the study of appearance something incalculably more penetrating and faithful than mere observation."[15] There were relatively few letters exchanged between Pach and Arensberg in the 1910s, though, because apart from summer breaks spent by the Arensbergs in the country, Pach and the couple were likely interacting frequently in New York circles, at the Arensberg home, and at museums and exhibitions.

Best known for his work promoting French modernism, Pach was also one of the earliest boosters of the arts of the ancient Americas and their importance within the world's great aesthetic traditions. In his 1920 essay "The Art of the American Indian," Pach mentioned his attempts to persuade the Metropolitan Museum of Art in New York to mount a show of what was then called American Indian art. (The show was presented at the American Museum of Natural History instead.)[16] The struggle to persuade a broader audience of the importance of these works paralleled not only Pach's own efforts on behalf of modern art with the Metropolitan but also an intellectual quarrel taking place in France.[17] That same year, museum personnel, modern artists, anthropologists, and members of the avant-garde responded to a query circulated by the art critic Félix Fénéon about the appropriateness of including African art in the displays at the Louvre.[18] Curiously enough, although the questionnaire was on African art (*art Négre*), many of the respondents pointed to ancient American art as proof of the aesthetic abilities of non-Western peoples. One of Marius de Zayas's former associates, Charles Vignier, was among those weighing in, making it very likely that the Arensbergs were aware of this debate, which was published in the *Bulletin de la vie artistique*.

These discussions point to the odd position that pre-Columbian art has traditionally occupied within the field of "primitive" art. When juxtaposed with African art, whose imagery was liberally used in many works of modern art, pre-Columbian art has often been considered not truly primitive. Because of its precious materials and exquisite craftsmanship—the pristine finish of polished greenstone works, the exactingly detailed goldwork of Central and South America, the incredibly meticulous textiles of the Andes—or its complex iconography, particularly the clear and extensive narrative content of works adorned with

Maya or other hieroglyphs, pre-Columbian art was often deemed too sophisticated to be primitive. William Rubin, in the introduction to his 1985 catalog for *"Primitivism" in 20th Century Art: Affinity of the Tribal and the Modern* (an exhibition and catalog often deemed controversial because of its insistent pairing of modernist works by named artists with "primitive" works, accompanied by labels containing almost no contextualizing information), frames this distinction most succinctly. After reviewing the range of different art styles called "primitive" in Western society, Rubin asserts that pre-Columbian art was a "courtly" or "theocratic" art that should more properly be grouped with Egyptian or Persian art, half a step above "true" primitive art in his estimation.[19]

In fact, in the United States, the movement to embrace pre-Columbian and Native American symbolism had a deeper meaning than aesthetics. By the late 1910s, in the circles in which the Arensbergs moved, the question of what a truly "American art" was or could be was taking on a greater urgency.[20] One answer, particularly popular to different degrees in the interwar period, was that the specific place, or continent, of the Americas was as important to the formation of its artists as their heritage, and that there was an essential unity to the arts and artists of cultures across the Americas. This was the artistic face of a broader diplomatic and cultural movement known as pan-Americanism.[21] During the Arensbergs' New York years, Louise, recognized for her eccentric fashion sense and for dressing "to amuse herself," might have been just as interested in these themes as Walter, for early pan-Americanism in the New York of the 1910s was centered on the use of museum collections as inspiration for industrial design, notably fashion.[22] Pan-Americanism in art was a cause that Pach took up with a passion. It became a central preoccupation of his own writing and thinking, and he returned to it repeatedly for the rest of his life.[23] In 1922, just as the Mexican mural renaissance was beginning, Pach was invited to teach one session of Mexico's Escuela del Verano (summer school) program, an educational opportunity that allowed Mexicans to hear about the most up-to-date ideas in the arts and society and that also drew many Americans who wanted to learn Spanish.[24] During his first sojourn in Mexico, Pach became fascinated by pre-Columbian art and enamored of its artistic merits and ability to inspire modern artists. Upon his return, he wrote a manifesto, "The Greatest American Artists," published in *Harper's Monthly Magazine* in December 1923, from which the epigraph of this essay originates.

While residing in Mexico, Pach acquired pre-Columbian works, some of which he sold to the lawyer John Quinn.[25] A commercial attorney by trade, Quinn was also a significant figure within the modern art world, appearing before Congress in 1913 to request the lifting of tariffs on imported European art less than twenty years old, ostensibly to allow people of the middle or even lower economic classes to be able to purchase works of contemporary European art.[26] Congress assented, and in the same year as the tariffs were lifted, Quinn, a decisive purchaser who was probably "the primary beneficiary" of the Armory Show, reaped the rewards.[27] In all likelihood, the lawyer met the Arensbergs at this time through their shared association with Pach. Certainly they met socially and kept abreast of each other's movements in a general way, and in fact each acquired works from the other's collection at different times. Quinn was one of the earliest and most fervent collectors of the work of Constantin Brancusi, buying a number of works that later found their way into the Arensberg collection via de Zayas, including *Arch* (figs. 5, 6) and *Bench* (see Sherman and Nelson, fig. 31), which would later be prominently featured in the entryway and dining room alcove, respectively, of the Arensbergs' California home.[28]

Unlike the Arensbergs, who lived off the interest from large trust funds, Quinn worked as a lawyer to support himself and the formation of his collection. Although they moved in slightly different circles, the Arensbergs, as relatively young collectors observing the older man's acquisitions, likely took quite a few lessons from their interactions with Quinn, for they shared with him certain characteristics and collecting styles.

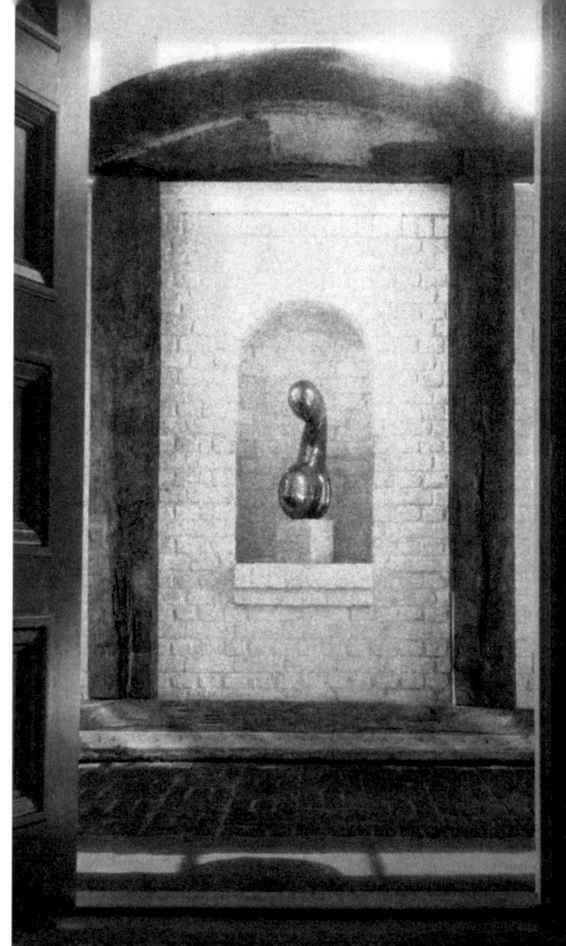

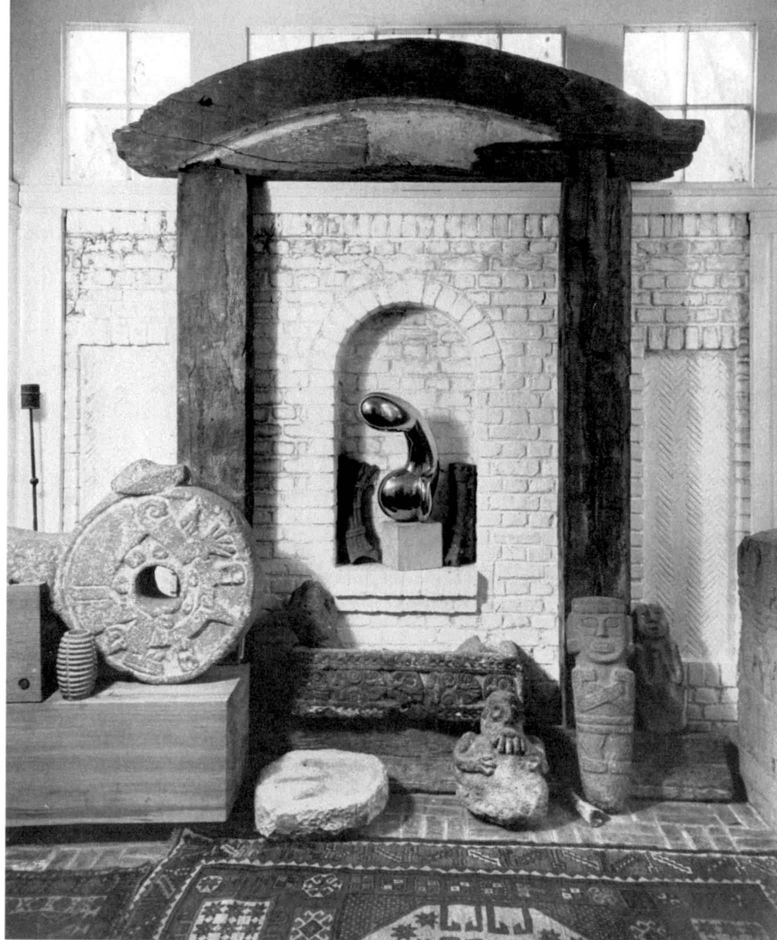

5. A VIEW FROM THE ARENSBERGS' LIVING ROOM OF HENRY PALMER SABIN'S NEWLY COMPLETED FOYER, 7065 HILLSIDE AVENUE, LOS ANGELES, CA. 1928. PHOTOGRAPHER UNKNOWN (POSSIBLY HENRY PALMER SABIN). UNIVERSITY OF CALIFORNIA, SANTA BARBARA, ART, DESIGN, & ARCHITECTURE MUSEUM, ARCHITECTURE AND DESIGN COLLECTION, HENRY PALMER SABIN PAPERS, 1920–1955, BOX 3, FOLDER 1

6. FRED R. DAPPRICH. VIEW OF THE ARENSBERGS' FOYER, 7065 HILLSIDE AVENUE, LOS ANGELES, CA. 1944. THIS PHOTOGRAPH OF THE FOYER, DATED SOME FIFTEEN YEARS AFTER FIG. 5, SHOWS THE GROWTH OF THE PRE-COLUMBIAN COLLECTION. PHILADELPHIA MUSEUM OF ART, LIBRARY AND ARCHIVES, ARENSBERG ARCHIVES (PMA-WLA), BOX 54, FOLDER 10

One such quirk was the Arensbergs' and Quinn's desire to own multiple versions of a single work, or works by the same artist that engaged with the same concepts in different ways over time. Notably, the Arensbergs became fixated on Marcel Duchamp's *Nude Descending a Staircase (No. 2)*, ultimately purchasing all three iterations of the work. The Arensbergs expressed their devotion to Duchamp by obsessively pursuing his works throughout their lives, while Quinn described his own motivations for acquiring many of Brancusi's sculptures in a letter to Brancusi himself: "Some people might say that I should have been content with only one example of the *Bird* and of *Mlle. Pogany*, either in marble or in bronze; but my reply would be that one can't have too much of a beautiful thing."[29] The Arensbergs also bought numerous Brancusi sculptures, most of which simplified the figure to near abstraction. And a couple of decades later, in the 1940s, the Arensbergs purchased many similar abstracted sculpted works from Veracruz (the *palma* stones, or palmate stones, as they are sometimes called; figs. 7, 8), as well as dozens of stone masks from the Teotihuacan civilization (figs. 9–14).

Some theories of collecting help to explain this type of acquisition. To accumulate objects and juxtapose them, the literary critic Susan Stewart tells us, is to replace "the narrative of production by the narrative of the collection, the replacement of the narrative of history with the narrative of the individual subject—that is, the collector himself."[30] Therefore, collections serve, as the theorist Russell Belk has put it, as "extensions of self," their formation a continual project of shaping and refining one's persona rather than merely acquiring, handling, and displaying objects.[31] Theorists of collecting have distinguished two main types of

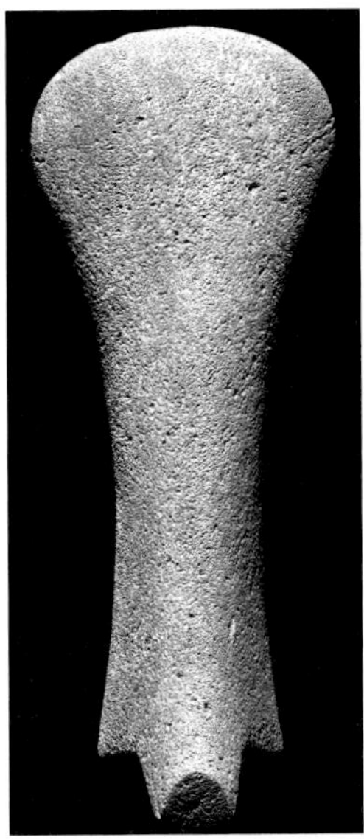

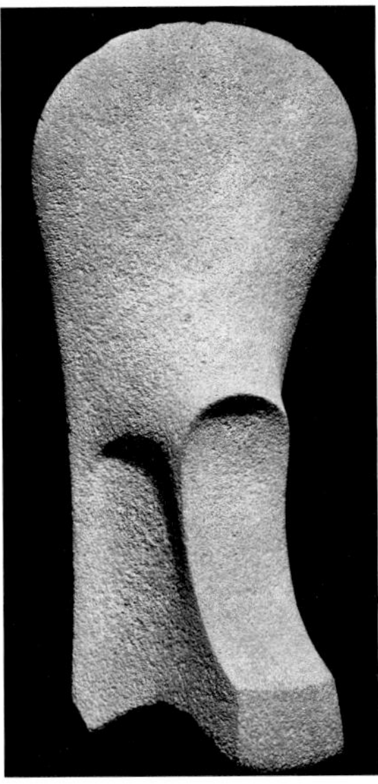

7, 8. CLASSIC VERACRUZ (EAST COAST MEXICO). PALMAS, 500–900. BASALTIC ROCK, LEFT: 43.2 × 24.8 × 14.3 CM; RIGHT: 58.4 × 25.4 × 15.2 CM. PHILADELPHIA MUSEUM OF ART, THE LOUISE AND WALTER ARENSBERG COLLECTION, 1950-134-384 (SEE ALSO PLATES 5.10, 6.6); 1950-134-390

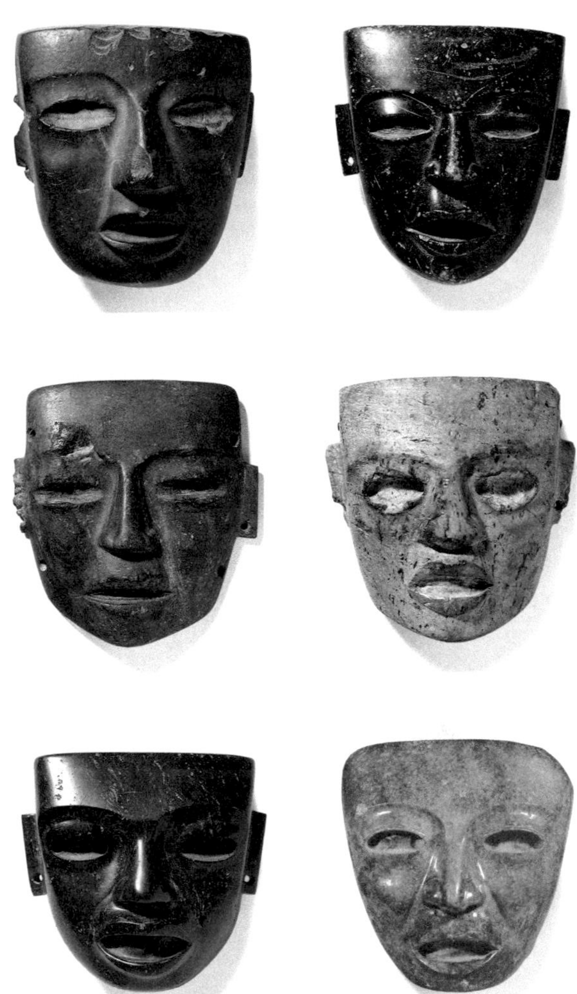

9–14. (LEFT TO RIGHT, TOP TO BOTTOM)
TEOTIHUACAN (CENTRAL MEXICO). MASKS, 1ST–9TH CENTURY. BASALT, SERPENTINE, OR JADE, VARIOUS SIZES, HEIGHT: BETWEEN 14 AND 21 CM. PHILADELPHIA MUSEUM OF ART, THE LOUISE AND WALTER ARENSBERG COLLECTION, 1950-134-232 (SEE PLATE 4.25); 1950-134-314 (SEE PLATE 31.55); 1950-134-267; 1950-134-359 (SEE PLATE 17.25); 1950-134-249 (SEE PLATE 34.4); 1950-134-293 (SEE PLATE 34.8)

collectors: those who form their assemblage from many unique objects, each valued on its own; and those who choose those things that add to a series, for which one might ultimately acquire all the possible iterations of that series (in the Arensbergs' case, their acquisition of works by Marcel Duchamp, perhaps).[32] However, Belk explains that while the desire to complete a collection or its subset may be strong, "at the same time there seems to be a paradoxical fear of completing a collection.... For if one is a collector and there is nothing left to collect, who is one then?"[33] Thus, many collectors will progressively raise (or lower) their standards of quality or adjust the boundaries of what conceptually constitutes being part of the collection, such that the collection can never be completed.

Quinn died in 1924 at the age of fifty-six, after fighting cancer for nearly a decade. Therefore, the Arensbergs in their last few years in New York bore witness to Quinn's living and collecting with a heightened awareness of his own mortality. Ultimately, for them Quinn may have become an example of what *not* to do, since he failed to make provisions for the disposition of his collection, and it was dispersed at auction.[34]

Quinn's diagnosis had led to a change in his acquisition habits, however; the lawyer had long collected in a scattershot fashion, at times to support and encourage young artists of the avant-garde, without a focused attention to the quality of an artwork. For several years, Walter Pach and others urged Quinn to buy fewer works, but ones that were more significant to the arc of his collection as a whole. Once Quinn became more aware of the passing of time, he explained to Marcel Duchamp that

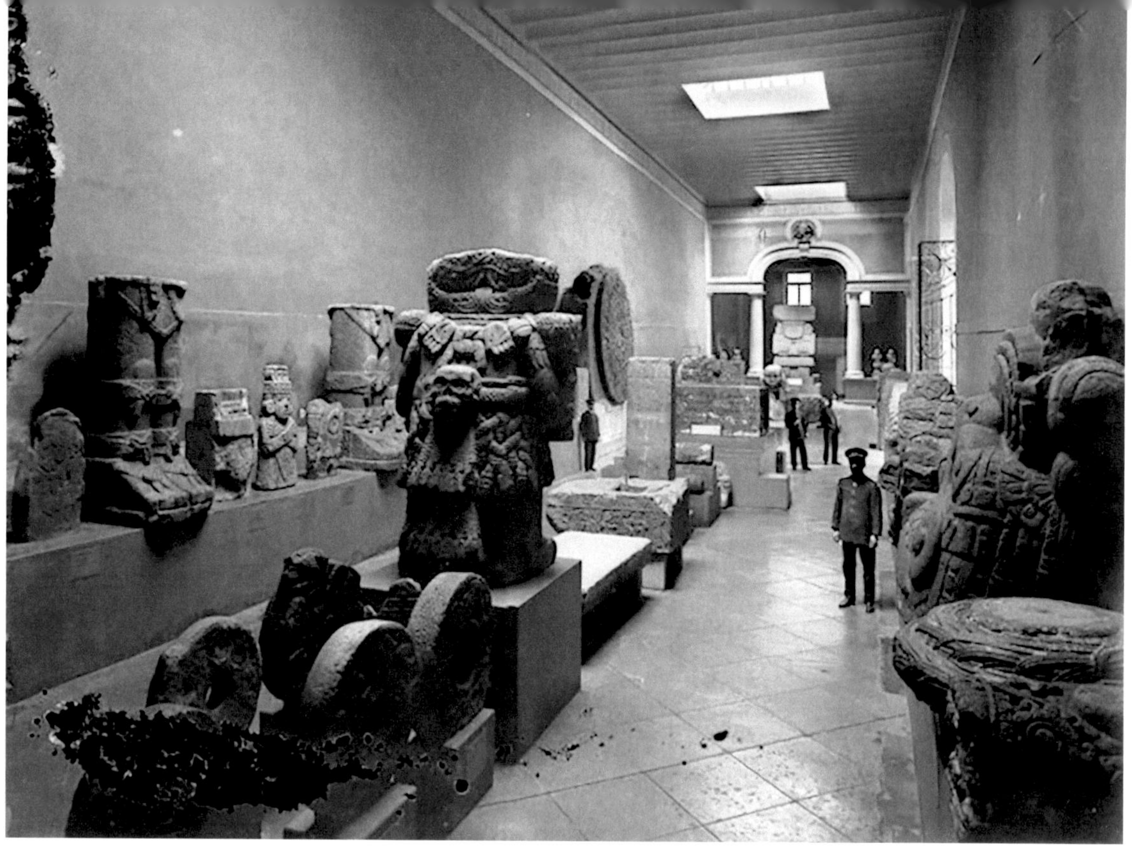

15. GALLERY OF MONOLITHS AT THE MUSEO NACIONAL; THE TEOTIHUACAN GREAT GODDESS STATUE (SIMILAR TO THE ARENSBERGS' SMALLER EXAMPLE) CAN BE SEEN FRAMED BY THE DOORWAY AT THE BACK OF THE ROOM. D.R. INSTITUTO NACIONAL DE ANTROPOLOGÍA E HISTORIA, MEXICO

> I have come to the time in my modest career of collector when I desire to add only works of first-rate importance and not more sketches or tentative work. This is a point that every collector, I imagine, arrives at sooner or later.[35]

Quinn sharpened his criteria further in the late 1910s and early 1920s, telling his French agent that he was only interested in acquiring "works of museum rank."[36] By the time of his death, Quinn had assembled an extensive grouping of art; he was one of the most important early collectors of modern art, but his acquisitions were diverse, and he was more interested in non-Western works than many have assumed. Letters between Pach and Quinn show that a "group of idols" Pach had bought in Mexico were being delivered to Quinn just prior to his death.[37]

Quinn also purchased pre-Columbian works from Marius de Zayas, the "radically Spanish, natally Mexican, residentially American, temperamentally universal" artist, critic, tastemaker, and sometime dealer of modern, African, and pre-Columbian art who was also the Arensbergs' seminal guide to "primitive" art.[38] While de Zayas's role in creating a market for African art in New York has, in recent years, begun to be more carefully delineated by scholars, his contribution to developing the taste for pre-Columbian art in New York has never been discussed.[39] Arensberg met de Zayas when the latter was a close collaborator of Alfred Stieglitz's at his Little Galleries of the Photo-Secession, better known as the 291 for its address on New York's Fifth Avenue. De Zayas sold his own works at 291 and traveled on Stieglitz's behalf to Paris from 1910 to 1911, returning with French modernist art to be offered for sale at 291 and many ideas to be published in *Camera Work*, the journal Stieglitz edited.

Marius de Zayas Enríquez y Calmet was born in 1880 to a family of Spanish descent that had lived in Mexico for two generations.[40] His entrepreneurial father owned two newspapers in the port city of Veracruz, but Marius was raised mostly in Coyoacán, a southern suburb of Mexico City.[41] In the capital city, young de Zayas frequented the Museo Nacional, which was filled with archaeological treasures from across

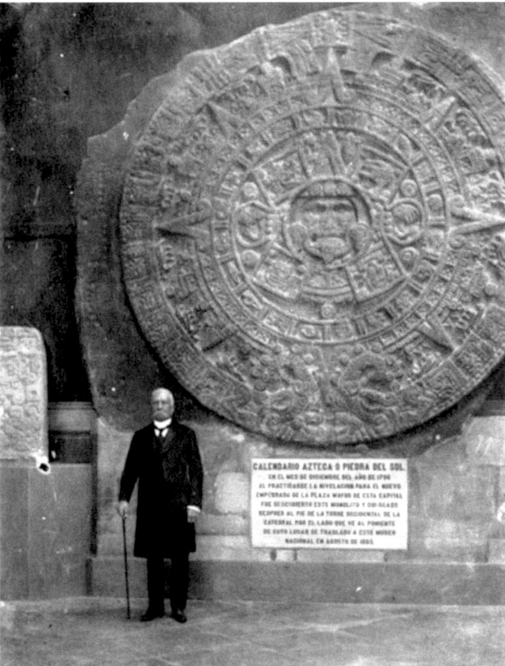

16. PORFIRIO DÍAZ (PRESIDENT OF MEXICO, 1876–80 AND 1884–1911), SHOWN IN FRONT OF THE AZTEC CALENDAR STONE IN THE MUSEO NACIONAL, CA. 1910. D.R. INSTITUTO NACIONAL DE ANTROPOLOGÍA E HISTORIA, MEXICO

Mexico (fig. 15).[42] De Zayas's father, Rafael, enthusiastically praised the Museo in an 1899 book, calling it "superior to that of any of its kind existing in the New World."[43] Thousands of images of this museum circulated, many showing the interior halls with numerous Aztec monoliths and some showing President Porfirio Díaz in attendance at this temple of culture (fig. 16).

Between 1899 and 1907, de Zayas moved back and forth between the United States and Mexico City, probably returning often to the Museo Nacional to seek inspiration. An anonymous profile of de Zayas in a 1908 article from Gustav Stickley's *Craftsman* magazine explained that

> [De Zayas's] first art studies were, of course, in Europe, but he is frank to say that in his accomplishments as an artist they have counted for little. His greatest art enthusiasms were found in the old museums in Mexico which are treasure houses of ancient Aztec art. In the strange carvings of these mysterious symbols he felt the greatest appeal to his imagination. And perhaps the sense of mystery always to be found in his more or less elaborate sketches may be traced to his early interest in and intimacy with the esoteric artistic expression of these long dead artists.[44]

Small wonder, then, that de Zayas and Walter Arensberg got on so well, given their shared love of the esoteric, the ancient, the anachronistic, and that which others termed "primitive."

In 1911, on his sojourn in France on behalf of Stieglitz and 291, de Zayas was at first doubtful upon seeing the African artworks that the European modernists sought out. He wrote to Stieglitz, "Some of the sculptors have merely copied [African art] without taking the trouble to translate it into French."[45] Still, de Zayas also told Stieglitz that it was imperative that 291 show such art, and he brought back with him African works—masks and a few sculptures in wood, to judge from photographs of the gallery's 1914 installation, which ran from 3 November to 8 December. It may have been at this exhibition that de Zayas sold the Arensbergs the Fang head (see plate 13.4) or the Fang male figure (see plate 20.6).[46] A second exhibition that opened in late 1914 at 291 featured works by Pablo Picasso and Georges Braque along with "Archaic Mexican pottery and carvings and experimental 'Kalograms' by the Mexican artist Torres Palomar" (fig. 17).[47]

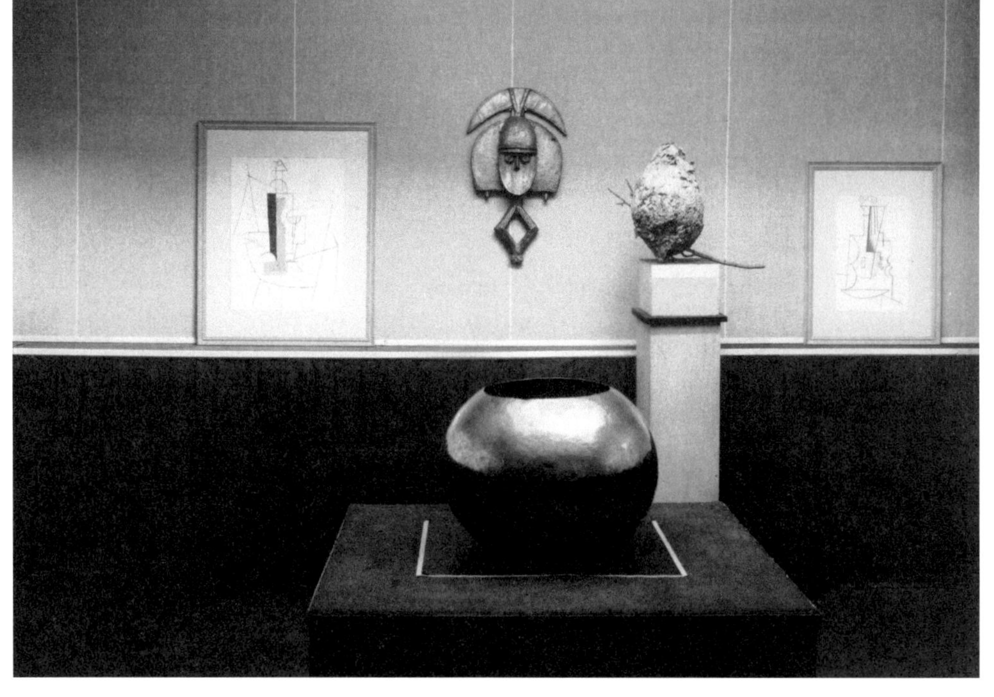

17. ALFRED STIEGLITZ. INSTALLATION VIEW OF THE *PICASSO–BRAQUE* EXHIBITION AT 291, 1915. PLATINUM PRINT, 19.4 × 24.4 CM. THE METROPOLITAN MUSEUM OF ART, ALFRED STIEGLITZ COLLECTION, 1949 (49.55.36). IMAGE © THE METROPOLITAN MUSEUM OF ART. IMAGE SOURCE: ART RESOURCE, NY

De Zayas's relationship with African art as well as ancient Mexican art, however, was complicated by the attitudes about race that he brought to their interpretation. His attitudes were clear from his 1914 text on African art, *Statuary in Wood by African Savages: The Root of Modern Art.*[48] De Zayas often used pseudo-scientific anthropological data to "prove" that African works, while beautiful, were devoid of an intellectual foundation. De Zayas also had the idea, likely passed to the Arensbergs to some degree, that each society had a type of art that was most natural to it and in which that society therefore excelled. One illustrative passage in his 1916 treatise *African Negro Art: Its Influence on Modern Art* hints at this:

> The expressive quality of Negro sculpture is due in great part to the manner in which the artist handles his material.... He seems to let his work be guided by the material, and instead of putting his feelings into wood, seems rather to draw them out of it. *Negro sculpture is as natural to wood as Mexican sculpture is to stone or Greek sculpture to marble.* Ivory, stone and iron are also sculptured by the African Negro, but in those materials he is unable to render his peculiar sense of plasticity and the expression of his sensibility.[49]

The emphatic contrast of Mexican (Aztec) stone with Greek marble seems to suggest that de Zayas considered the most characteristic medium of ancient Mexican art—that which most truly expressed its authentic and true character—to be sculpture made from a rough basalt, rather than a more polished material. Basalt is also the most common type of stone to be found in the Valley of Mexico region, where Mexico City and the former Aztec capital are located, and from which the region's architecture and monumental sculpture were wrought.

Many years later, Alfred Stendahl, son of the Arensbergs' main Los Angeles dealer, Earl Stendahl, commented (somewhat disparagingly) that Arensberg was a "rough stone man," in contrast to another collector, Robert Woods Bliss, who was a "polished stone man."[50] Stendahl, who also called the objects that Walter preferred "rugged, nonpretty things," perhaps did not understand that the preference for rough stones reflected a considered choice, not a lack of connoisseurship, on the Arensbergs' part.[51]

In general, de Zayas's greatest legacy for the Arensbergs seems to have been to pass along his strong and particular conviction that the greatest art of the American continent was Aztec sculpture in basalt. This was a major departure from accepted views in the United States at the time, which often exalted the Maya culture and looked down on the Aztecs as barbaric and primitive. A general preference for Maya statuary could have been reinforced for Walter during his years at Harvard; the Peabody Museum of Archaeology and Ethnology received a spate of treasures from Mexico and Central America while he was enrolled there.[52] When the Arensbergs lived in Cambridge, the Museum of Fine Arts, Boston, was one of the very first museums to show pre-Columbian works as art, in a 1912 exhibition that consisted mostly of Maya works.[53]

However, de Zayas could illustrate his assertion of the superiority of Aztec sculpture over that of the Maya to his clients in New York, and even offer comparisons between the two civilizations' monuments, by referring to the displays at the American Museum of Natural History (AMNH), located about half a mile from the Arensbergs' apartment on Manhattan's Upper West Side. Images of the AMNH's Hall of Mexico and Central America circa 1910 (figs. 18, 19) show that the halls were filled with some authentic antiquities but also with plaster casts of the monuments and architectural remains of ancient cultures, particularly the enormous, stony Aztec monuments of precisely the type that de Zayas praised, as well as Maya freestanding stelae, similar to the smaller stela the Arensbergs later owned (figs. 20a, b).[54] The early years of the twentieth century have been called the "golden age" for archaeological casts.[55] A curator of the ancient Americas at the AMNH observed in 1931 that the models of important temples of the ancient past, which the museum had exhibited for decades,

> offer one of the best ways at our command to recapture the spirit of the past in Middle America. They not only suggest the majesty of bygone times, but also . . . a thoughtful person, contemplating these models, can richly savor the past as he peoples the temples according to his fancy and equips the imagined ceremonials with the objects in the cases.[56]

Walter's "fancy" certainly would have appreciated the challenge of imagining the ways that real ancient people displayed and interacted with the objects on which the casts were based. He might even have attended some of the classes the AMNH offered on the motifs of Aztec art, taught by the curator Herbert Spinden.[57] And he was far from alone, even within his artistic and literary circle, in being inspired by the museum's collection: the artist and poet Max Weber, a frequent visitor to the Arensberg salon, wrote a poem dedicated to the form of a Maya offering vessel/throne, the *Chac-Mool*, declaring, "Thou art agent and medium of the infinity of all things."[58] Another *salonière*, the author William Carlos Williams, wrote a volume of poetry titled *The Destruction of Tenochtitlán*. While this book was not published until 1925, Williams composed a short draft with the same title for the avant-garde literary publication *Broom: An International Magazine of the Arts* a few years prior, inspired by his trips to the museum.[59] For his part, Walter Pach affirmed that he, too, had been impressed by the AMNH—until he had occasion to see the collections of the Museo Nacional when he taught in Mexico City in 1922.[60]

And remnants of the ancient Americas were more broadly present than one might suppose in early twentieth-century New York. The Brooklyn Museum's collection of ancient pre-Columbian works was another source of inspiration for many artists and thinkers, including, just a few years later, Walter Arensberg's future collaborator Kenneth Macgowan, then a drama critic.[61] In addition to the AMNH and Brooklyn Museum displays, the Arensbergs almost certainly saw the Louis Petich collection of ancient Mexican works, shown from 1895 to 1914 at the Metropolitan Museum of Art.[62] Formerly a minister of the Italian government to Peru and Mexico, Petich amassed a collection of more than sixteen hundred works from across Mexico, in different media. Perhaps most important for those who followed de Zayas's aesthetic, the Petich collection included

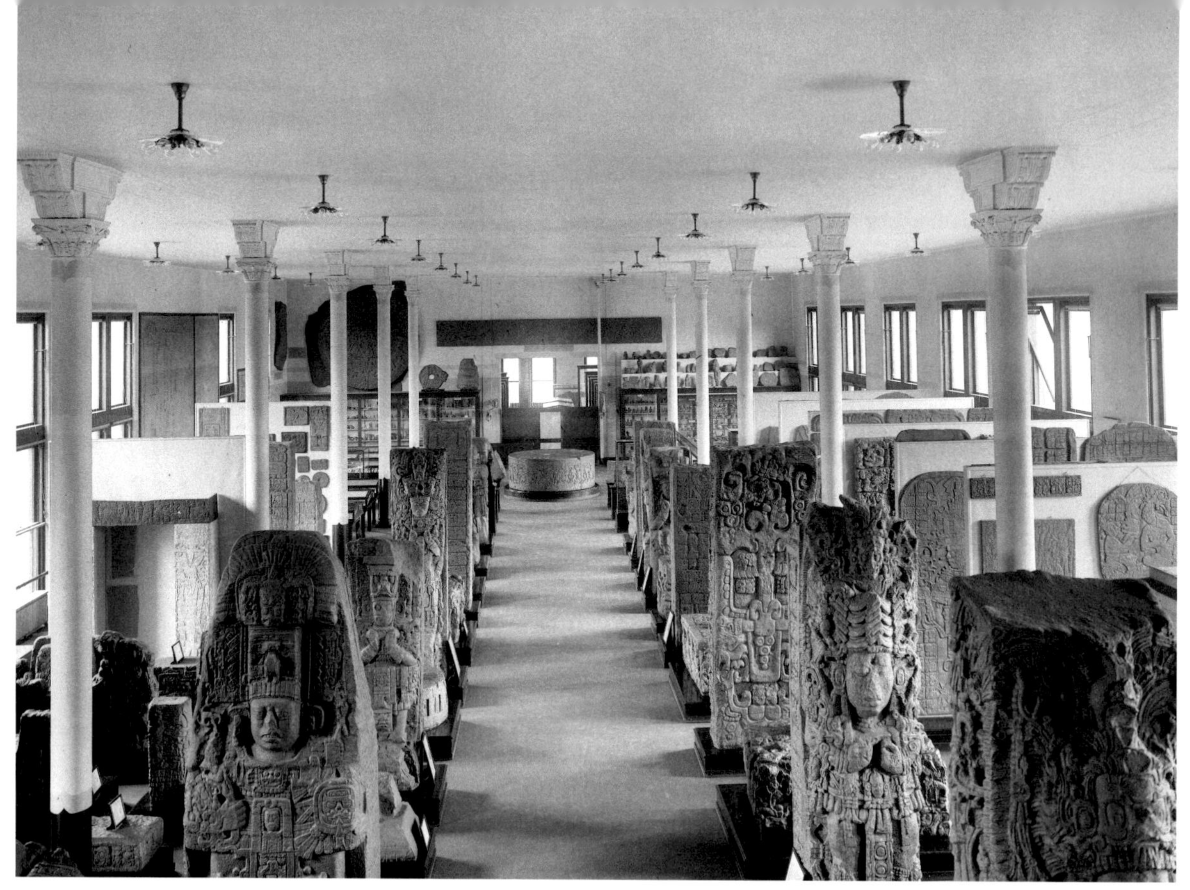

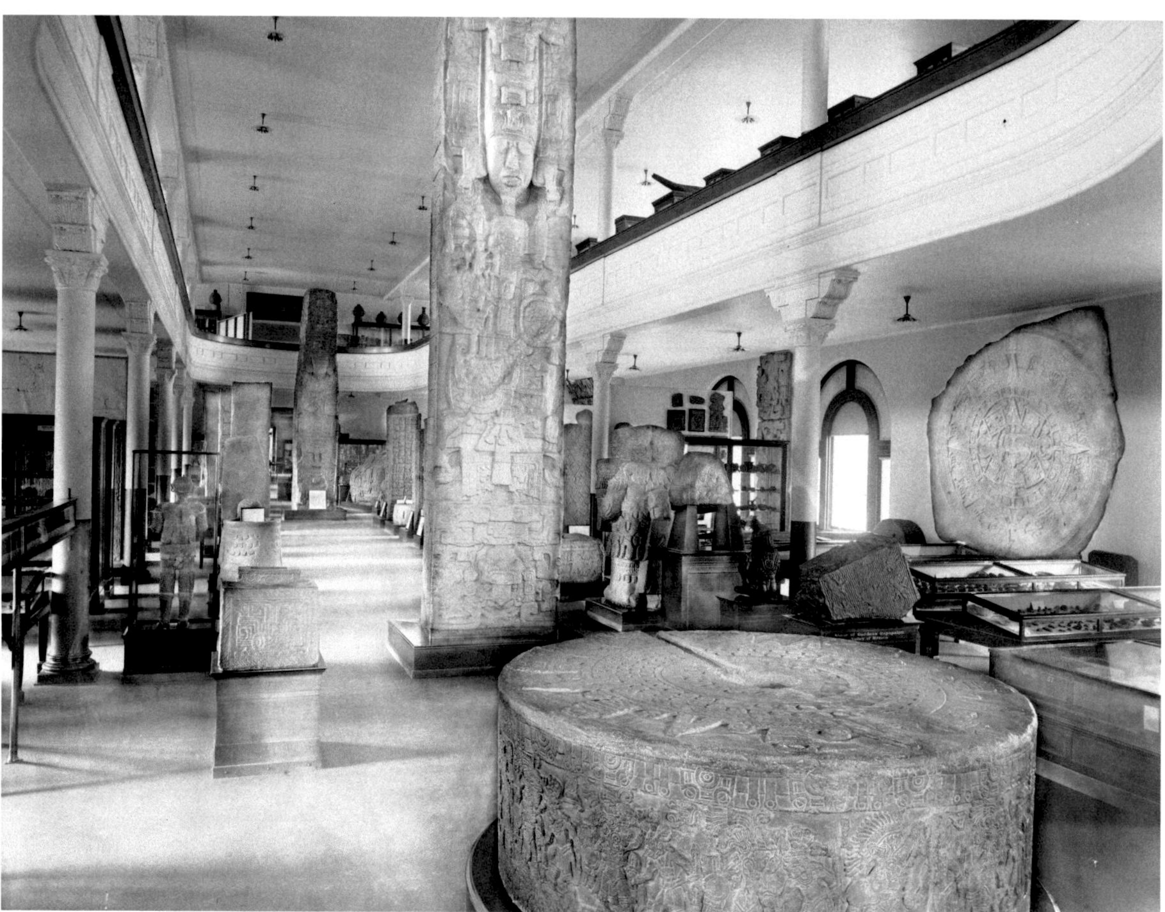

18, 19. CASTS AND OBJECTS IN THE MUSEUM OF NATURAL HISTORY, CA. 1910.
18: IMAGE #33037, AMERICAN MUSEUM OF NATURAL HISTORY
19: IMAGE #33392, AMERICAN MUSEUM OF NATURAL HISTORY

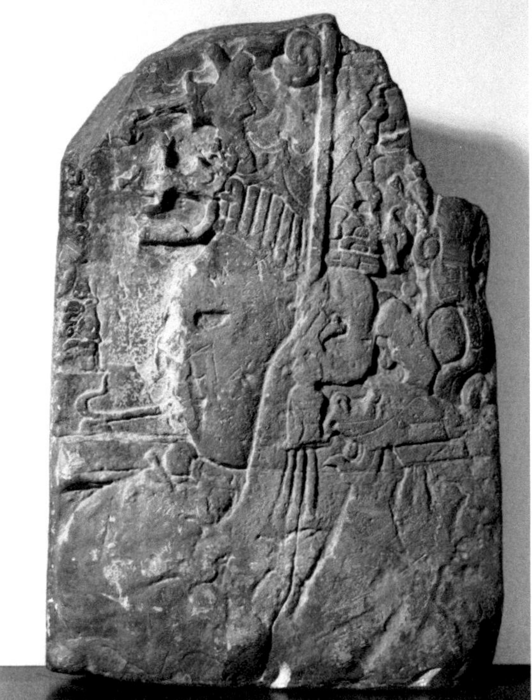

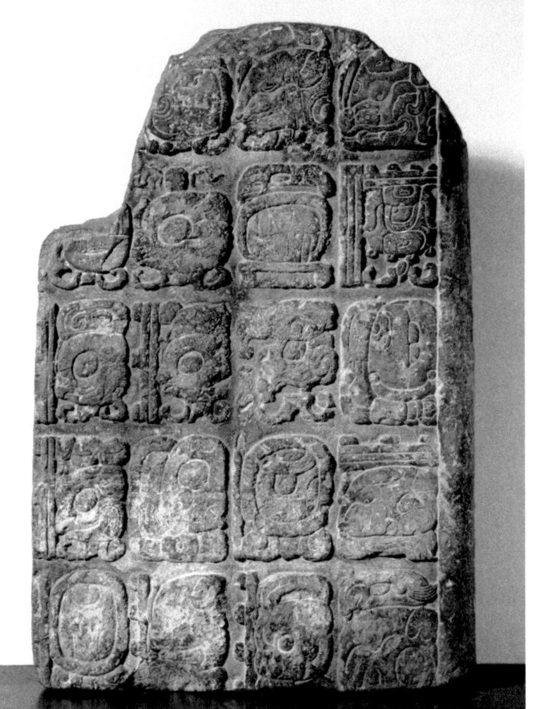

20A, B. MAYA (MEXICO). FRAGMENT OF A STELA (FRONT AND BACK), 810. FINE SANDSTONE, 58.4 × 39.4 × 14 CM. PHILADELPHIA MUSEUM OF ART, THE LOUISE AND WALTER ARENSBERG COLLECTION, 1950-134-242. SEE ALSO PLATE 11.12

> several rare and exquisite examples of Toltec modeling, a vast array of Aztec cast terra cottas and sculptured stone, rich even in its hideous grotesqueness, and varied enough to gratify even the most exacting student of archaeology.... These objects alone would be worthy of the best scholarly treatment; they are easily equal to the Greek product in exterior line and plane, and stand among the most remarkable specimens of ancient sculpture extant.[63]

When the *American Archaeologist* chronicled the collection in 1898, the central Mexican site of Tula had not yet been fully excavated, so the publication's use of the term *Toltec* is somewhat ambiguous, but it is possible that the evocation of rich yet "hideous grotesqueness" piqued the Arensbergs' curiosity, for they later owned several works thought to be Toltec.[64] In 1914, the Petich collection was transferred to the AMNH, located a short stroll from the Arensbergs' apartment, though not all of it was immediately put on view. While the collection includes some fairly large Aztec stone works, much of it had been carefully placed in wood-framed showcases, a display method totally contrary to that employed by the Arensbergs, who seemed to want to free the muscular, three-dimensional objects they were able to collect: they put the one medium-scale Aztec stone sculpture they owned at the time in front of their fireplace with only a simple pedestal.

Curiously enough, while the Arensbergs were collecting in New York, the Mexican Revolution was in full swing, bringing frequent reminders of Mexico to the pages of daily newspapers yet also making it very difficult to obtain large-scale works from the country. Perhaps for this reason, de Zayas seems to have arranged just two shows featuring pre-Columbian art: the December 1914–January 1915 exhibition at 291, and a second exhibition at his own Modern Gallery in October 1916.[65]

NEW YORK 1914–21: WORKS COLLECTED

Three examples of pre-Columbian art are visible in the extant photographs of the Arensbergs' New York apartment, all almost certainly bought through de Zayas's agency. One, a greenstone pebble roughly shaped into a bust-length female figure (figs. 21a, b), may have been an example of the "archaic Mexican carvings" sold at 291. It is a curious piece, being very lightly worked on the front, respecting the stone's natural contours and materiality, with eyes, nose, mouth, and a crown-like short headdress apparent on the front, but very eroded. Its carving style is in keeping with the indigenous cultures of Guerrero, on the Pacific coast of

Mexico, which produced some very ancient stone works (ca. 200 BCE–500 CE). However, the back of the work has more deeply and carefully etched diagonal lines springing out from its center line. This is a clear evocation of the pleated paper headdress that identified several goddesses of the Aztecs (ca. 1300–1521), a civilization dating to a millennium or more later, from central Mexico. Recent excavations have confirmed the Aztecs' tendency to appropriate works and styles of cultures that came before them, often when they conquered different parts of Mexico.[66] Possibly this piece was plundered in antiquity by the Aztecs during their conquests on the Pacific coast, then brought back and reworked in their capital. Since the offering caches featuring such works have only been excavated since the 1970s, the sculpture's history could not have been known. The Arensbergs would probably have loved this sculpture for its highly stylized human form and the enigmatic contrast of its two sides, one quite crisply carved and the other worked so lightly it appears almost molten.

The second pre-Columbian work seems to have been among examples for sale in a 1916 exhibition of works by Diego Rivera, where it was described as a "stone figure of Quetzalcoatl (Aztec)." This is almost certainly the one shown on a small base in front of the fireplace in the Arensbergs' living room (figs. 22a, b).[67] It also sat opposite Arensberg in his office in an early California rental house, seemingly accompanying him in his decipherment work (see Sherman and Nelson, fig. 2). The deity Quetzalcoatl, or the Plumed Serpent, had a certain cachet in popular culture even by the 1910s. One of the best-selling books of the mid-nineteenth century, which the Arensbergs might have read, was John Lloyd Stephens's *Incidents of Travel in Central America, Chiapas, and Yucatan* (1841). Richly illustrated with lithographs by the expedition artist Frederick Catherwood, this volume closely describes and illustrates El Castillo, the pyramid dedicated to the Plumed Serpent deity at Chichén Itzá in the Yucatán Peninsula.[68] The Quetzalcoatl figure seems to have had a special significance for de Zayas, who sought to buy it back from Walter a few years later.[69]

In the same exhibition as the Quetzalcoatl stone, de Zayas sold "Nahua pottery" or "Aztec pottery." Visible on the piano, a tripod vessel from the central Mexican site of Teotihuacan, featuring ceramic appliqués around the circumference of its bowl, may have been one such work (figs. 23a, b). It is likely that the Arensbergs appreciated the plastic simplicity of this bowl as contrasted with the symbol-filled surfaces of the Quetzalcoatl figure. Such ceramics were widely available in the late nineteenth and early twentieth centuries; because of their ubiquity and small size, they were easily taken out of Mexico. It's quite possible that members of the de Zayas family brought such works along in their baggage when they left Mexico.

Therefore, the pre-Columbian works the Arensbergs purchased in New York between about 1915 and 1920 seem to have been few, but they were choice. While large-scale rough stone figures were not available for purchase at this time, the Quetzalcoatl figure in particular was an archetype for much of the Arensbergs' later collecting.

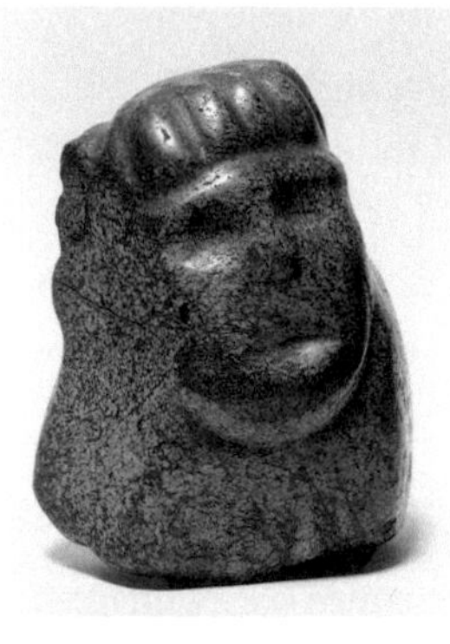

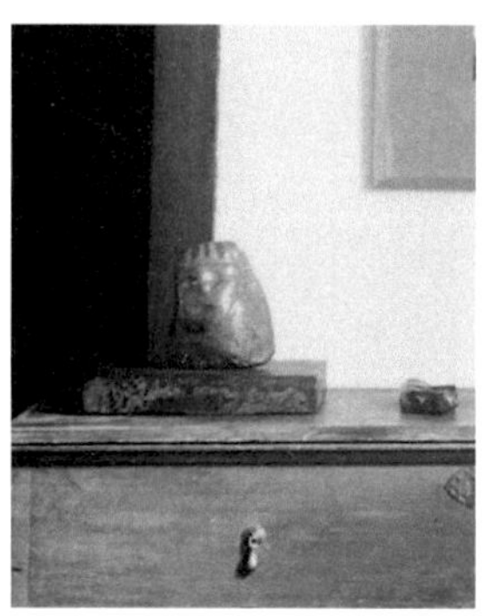

NEW YORK 1914–21: DISPLAY

Charles Sheeler's few existing photographs of the Arensbergs' living room on Sixty-Seventh Street show a densely hung display, already attempting to evoke contrasts and formal similarities between works of disparate times and places (see Sherman and Nelson, figs. 9a–d). As the art historian Francis M. Naumann points out, the Arensbergs seemed to purposefully invite their visitors to make comparisons between the "primitive" and the "modern" through provocative juxtapositions of art in their apartment.[70] Though these combinations were startling for the partygoers who frequented the Arensberg salon, the couple had undoubtedly

21A, B. AZTEC (CENTRAL MEXICO). BUST OF GODDESS, 1300–1520. GREEN IGNEOUS ROCK, HEIGHT: 14.6 CM. PHILADELPHIA MUSEUM OF ART, THE LOUISE AND WALTER ARENSBERG COLLECTION, 1950-134-236. COMPARED HERE WITH A DETAIL OF FIG. 9D ON PAGE 11. SEE ALSO PLATE 17.27

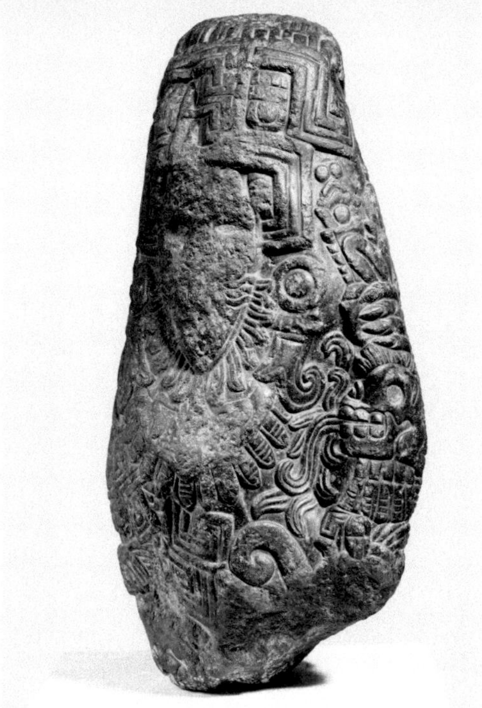

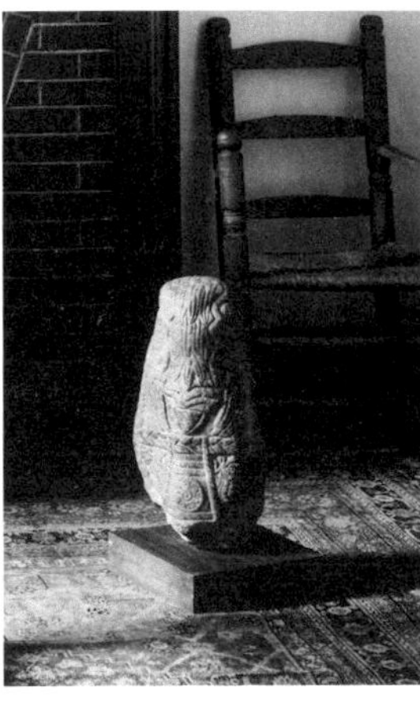

22A, B. AZTEC (CENTRAL MEXICO). FIGURE (QUETZALCOATL), 1300–1520. BASALTIC ROCK, 50.8 × 22.5 × 21.3 CM. PHILADELPHIA MUSEUM OF ART, THE LOUISE AND WALTER ARENSBERG COLLECTION, 1950-134-251. COMPARED HERE WITH A DETAIL OF FIG. 9B ON PAGE 11. SEE ALSO PLATE 35.3

taken cues from their contemporaries; indeed, the strategy of contrasting disparate works may have been at least partly due to de Zayas's influence. He employed similar techniques while working with Stieglitz at 291, contrasting the geometric forms of paintings' frames with rounded curves of African masks, for example, and, in one exhibition, with a bulbous wasp's nest (see fig. 17). Display techniques utilizing repeating and contrasting forms were also similar to those used by the curators of the African galleries at the AMNH.[71] As in these contemporaneous exhibition spaces, the arrangements in the Arensberg apartment played squares and rectangles (the paintings, straight-backed chair, oddly short door, and small desk) off of organic forms that included a tall African reliquary figure and the Aztec stone Quetzalcoatl on the floor.

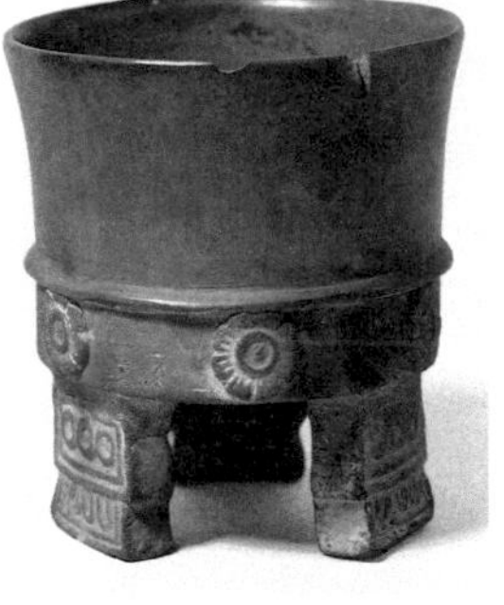

The Arensbergs may have been influenced by Quinn's display methods as well. While there are no known photographs showing how Quinn's collection looked when it hung in his apartment (also on Manhattan's Upper West Side), it has been described as being as crammed with art as the Arensberg house would be in later years, every wall filled with paintings. Quinn's companion Jeanne Robert Foster described the power of amassed works of art, particularly the display of Brancusi sculptures in the foyer of his home, which

> *hit* you when you [entered].... The ensemble was stupendous. The paintings behind them were the lovely...Redons [that] John owned.... Along between the pillars [which separated the foyer from the living and dining rooms] were Chinese ceramics.[72]

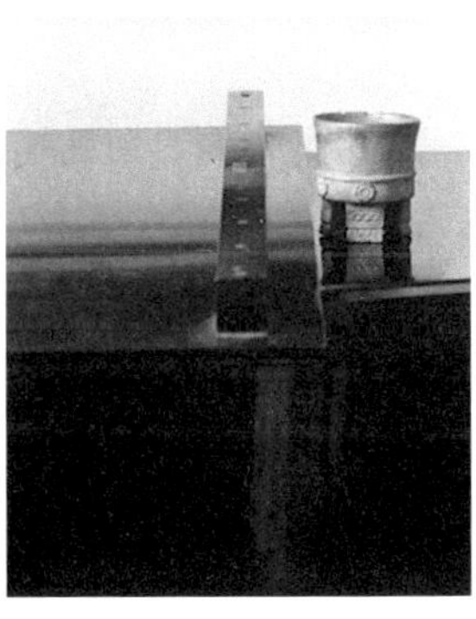

While the Arensbergs in the 1910s were only building up to the point that they might rotate their art frequently, as they seem to have done in their Hillside Avenue home, perhaps there, too, they took a lesson from Quinn's example. Quinn told the French collector Alphonse Kann in a letter, "I find, as the Japanese and Chinese long ago discovered, that it is interesting to put pictures away and to change the pictures that one has on one's walls, for a work of art that one has not seen for some time comes to one each new time one sees it with a fresh beauty."[73]

23A, B. TEOTIHUACAN (CENTRAL MEXICO). TRIPOD VESSEL, 400–800. CLAY, 12.1 × 11.4 × 11.7 CM. PHILADELPHIA MUSEUM OF ART, THE LOUISE AND WALTER ARENSBERG COLLECTION, 1950-134-231. COMPARED HERE WITH A DETAIL OF FIG. 9A ON PAGE 10. SEE ALSO PLATE 32.24

THE END OF THE NEW YORK YEARS

The Arensbergs might have been able to move modernist works around their walls frequently within a few years of the Armory Show, but they never collected much "primitive" art in the 1910s, seeming perhaps less engaged with it than was Quinn. In part this might have been related to the difficulty of acquiring such works. De Zayas owned one of several galleries selling this art at the time in New York, but pre-Columbian art, while visible at the Metropolitan and the AMNH, was not readily available for purchase. No other New York galleries of the era are known to have offered pre-Columbian art on a consistent basis, though several dealers in Paris were offering it alongside other types of primitive art.[74] Surprisingly, the only reliable purveyor of pre-Columbian works in New York around this time may have been Tiffany & Co. Their jeweler George Kunz traveled extensively in the Americas, searching for new stones to use. He often brought back pre-Columbian jade and gold objects, which he sold to collectors as well.[75]

Perhaps de Zayas was reluctant to begin selling a new and potentially lucrative genre of art in New York due to the anticommercial ethic he had absorbed from his mentor Stieglitz: while Stieglitz sold the art of photographers and avant-garde artists that he exhibited, he expressly wanted to avoid commercial success. Stieglitz was perpetually and vociferously opposed to artists promoting themselves and their work for monetary ends. De Zayas and one of his collaborators, fellow artist Paul Burty Haviland, tried to promote 291 by publishing *291*, a lavishly illustrated magazine about photography and art that was a work of art in its own right. Ultimately, however, they decided to split off and open the Modern Gallery in 1915. The opening was announced in a broadside inserted into *291*.[76]

The Modern Gallery was supported financially by Haviland, as well as by the wealthy collectors and patrons of the arts Eugene Meyer and Agnes Ernst Meyer, who together sought to promote modern art in New York and worldwide.[77] Just a few years after the French postimpressionists at the Armory Show caused such a scandal with their works, Haviland and de Zayas proposed selling works by artists such as Francis Picabia, André Derain, Henri de Toulouse-Lautrec, and others. The Modern Gallery's inaugural broadside in *291* promised "paintings of the most advanced character of the Modern Art Movement—Negro Sculptures—pre-Conquest Mexican Art—Photography."[78]

Many modern artists in Europe were desperate for new markets as World War I raged on the continent, and the Modern Gallery had every opportunity to corner a market of its own making for modern art. However, de Zayas in particular was an enthusiastic but extremely ineffective gallery owner. This may have had to do in part with his long association with the "anti-business" Stieglitz.[79] Also, raised in a wealthy family whose circumstances had changed drastically when they fled the Díaz regime in Mexico, de Zayas was never able to shed an aristocratic disinterest in money and profit. The art historian Douglas Hyland has said that

> De Zayas was not only a poor salesman, but also a poor accountant. His correspondence with [the primitive art dealer Paul] Guillaume and Haviland reveals that de Zayas was very lax in his attention to accounts and often frustrated his agents abroad.... De Zayas sold so few paintings and so little sculpture that it must have been discouraging for all concerned.[80]

The Modern Gallery closed in 1918, but de Zayas had a continuing interest in fomenting the appreciation of modern and primitive arts in New York, a focus that Walter Arensberg wanted to support. In October 1919, he opened the De Zayas Gallery, fully funded by his friend Arensberg. The gallery's stated objective was "looking into... the art production of the world for masterpieces and bringing them to America."[81] De Zayas depended heavily on his new or strengthened connection to the collector and dealer Charles Vignier; the first exhibition at the De Zayas Gallery was Chinese paintings, probably sourced from

Vignier's holdings.[82] De Zayas seems to have also gotten merchandise from Europe through Haviland and Paul Guillaume, as well as through Joseph Brummer, who had galleries in New York and Paris but only sold "primitive" art through the latter.

The De Zayas Gallery received a great deal of critical acclaim from the New York press, but it was not finding buyers. Even though de Zayas showed many of the most important European modernists of the time, he sold them to only a very small group; the Meyers, the Arensbergs, and Quinn seem to have composed the majority of his clientele.[83] Yet de Zayas's demand for the best-quality merchandise led him to seek a large amount of capital to create too large an inventory. When the gallery launched, de Zayas told Vignier that Arensberg had promised to "gather $500,000 and in one year the permanent capital of the institution would be one million dollars," a truly fantastic sum at the time.[84] (One million dollars would be the equivalent of nearly $13.3 million today.)[85] By contrast, just a few years earlier, Quinn had been unable to raise $10,000 with friends and a wealthy patron, Mrs. Rumsey, to create a new gallery for modernist art.[86] It is unclear whether de Zayas was delusional about the amount Arensberg could afford to invest, or if Arensberg had actually planned to put all of his own (and Louise's) and others' assets into the venture.[87]

However, having so few buyers, de Zayas could not make his endeavor profitable. In addition, according to the historian Antonio Saborit, he was swindled by Vignier, who chose to break off the partnership with de Zayas over the sale of two Paul Cézanne paintings (see plates 20.3, 20.5).[88] The paintings were sold to the Arensbergs at what Vignier judged to be too low a price. As he ended his association with de Zayas and Arensberg, Vignier also denied that he had any share in the stock of the gallery that had already been purchased and therefore refused to pay a debt of 360,000 francs—about $66,176 in 1921 dollars, or nearly $857,000 today—that he owed to the gallery.[89] De Zayas, notoriously hazy on details, seems not to have had a firm partnership agreement to which he could refer and could do nothing. In the end, the partnership and friendship dissolved, and it was clear that Arensberg had wildly overextended himself. Arensberg brought suit against the De Zayas Gallery in 1921, trying to recover the startling sum of $118,349 owed to him—equivalent to just over $1.5 million in today's dollars.[90] These financial reverses forced the Arensbergs to put their collection up for sale. Unfortunately for the couple (or fortunately, depending on one's perspective), this occurred just after a major sale of modern art by the dealer Dikran Kelekian, thus not much was sold, although Quinn was happy to purchase a Brancusi and a portrait by Henri Rousseau from the couple's collection.[91] Since so little was purchased, much of the Arensberg collection was put into storage, some of it not to reemerge for a few years, while some was sent "piece-meal" to California.[92] De Zayas was forced to liquidate his gallery (a difficult proposition when there were already insufficient buyers for his stock) and then sell his own collection a few years later, presumably in an attempt to repay the Arensbergs.[93] By this time, Marcel Duchamp had made an extended visit to Buenos Aires with Katherine Dreier and returned, but relations between Walter and him had cooled, and New York may have felt particularly bleak; at any rate, the "Arensberg Salon" began to close its doors (and its liquor cabinets) to guests, and the Arensbergs began the first of several long "sojourns" in California that eventually led to permanent residence there. The Arensbergs' New York years of collecting had ended.

II

The Los Angeles Years

LOS ANGELES 1921–36: REBUILDING FOR THE FUTURE

The Arensbergs bought very little artwork for several years after leaving New York, largely because Walter's ill-advised business venture with de Zayas (and loose loans to others) had brought them to the brink of financial disaster. During their first years in Los Angeles, they lived in a series of rental houses and stored their art collection in New York, uncertain whether they would live permanently in California.[94] They may have initially regretted the move; Louise Arensberg told a friend that "as soon as Walter comes to a good stopping place" (which he never reached), they would return to the East Coast.[95] However, at the same time, the couple were surrounded with seductive reminders that the land they lived on, while affording all the comforts of modern life, also had fragments of heritage that revealed its past as a part of Mexico.

For example, one of their first homes was Residence A of Aline Barnsdall's Olive Hill complex, which Frank Lloyd Wright had designed in Mayan Revival style (fig. 24).[96] Though they hated living there (complaining of the home's low ceilings and leaking roof), perhaps they felt that a creatively designed, anachronistic dwelling would recapture some of the energy of their New York apartment. And even with more limited financial resources, they may have furnished their Olive Hill home with some of the thousands of objects exhibited and sold in 1922 in Los Angeles as part of the first major exhibition of Mexican folk art in the United States (fig. 25).[97] This enormously successful exhibition featured demonstrations by contemporary artists of Mexico, as well as musical and dance performances.[98] It is estimated that during its height, the show's daily attendance was between three and four thousand people.[99] While the Arensbergs, like many non-Latino Angelenos, were enthusiasts of the pre-Columbian heritage of Mexico, there is little evidence that they engaged much with the contemporary Chicano culture of the city.

As promoters of Mexican folk art wound their way north to Los Angeles, the Arensbergs' friend Walter Pach found his way south to Mexico City. He returned home filled with wonder at the ancient art of the country. In his 1923 *Harper's* article, he praised "the height to which the art of ancient America had attained and the intimacy of its relationship with the America of to-day."[100] That year, pre-Columbian art was very much in vogue. The same issue of *Broom* that presented William Carlos Williams's first draft of "The Destruction of Tenochtitlan" also included an article by George Sacken on Maya art. The issue was illustrated throughout with motifs and designs from the culture, as well as drawings of pre-Columbian pieces. (Though the works pictured in the article were described as Maya, some were actually Native American, West Mexican, or Toltec.) Sacken discussed the American Museum of Natural History, in particular its gallery of Maya art, where, he asserted, "we feel distinctly the presence of a remarkable temperament, highly sophisticated yet essentially barbaric."[101] He concluded with a clarion call to contemporary artists to take inspiration from this ancient art:

> [Its] skillful opposition of vivid and of quiet forms, of horizontal and of vertical elements, produces an exquisite harmony—vivid but not crude, of utmost variety but absolute unity. All Maya works display this creative intelligence, and conscious use of definite aesthetic principles. Today, when a new order of artists is trying to rescue art from the morass of misused realism and to bring direction to an inchoate aesthetic, Maya art particularly recommends itself.[102]

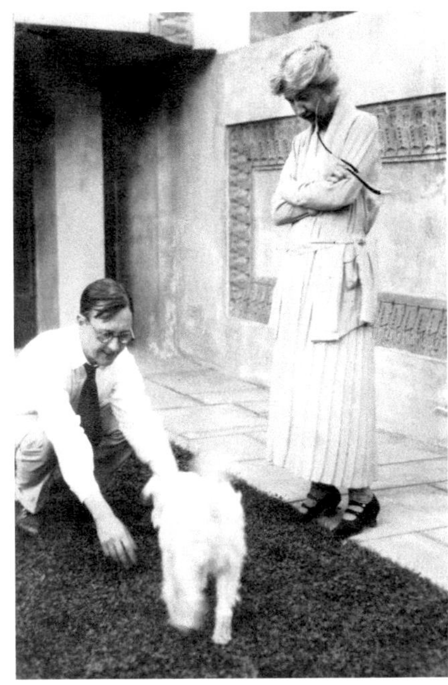

24. BEATRICE WOOD. WALTER AND LOUISE ARENSBERG IN FRONT OF RESIDENCE A, AT THE OLIVE HILL COMPLEX DESIGNED BY FRANK LLOYD WRIGHT FOR ALINE BARNSDALL, CA. SEPTEMBER 1922–JANUARY 1924. REPRODUCED COURTESY OF BEATRICE WOOD CENTER FOR THE ARTS / HAPPY VALLEY FOUNDATION. PHOTOGRAPH COURTESY FRANCIS M. NAUMANN

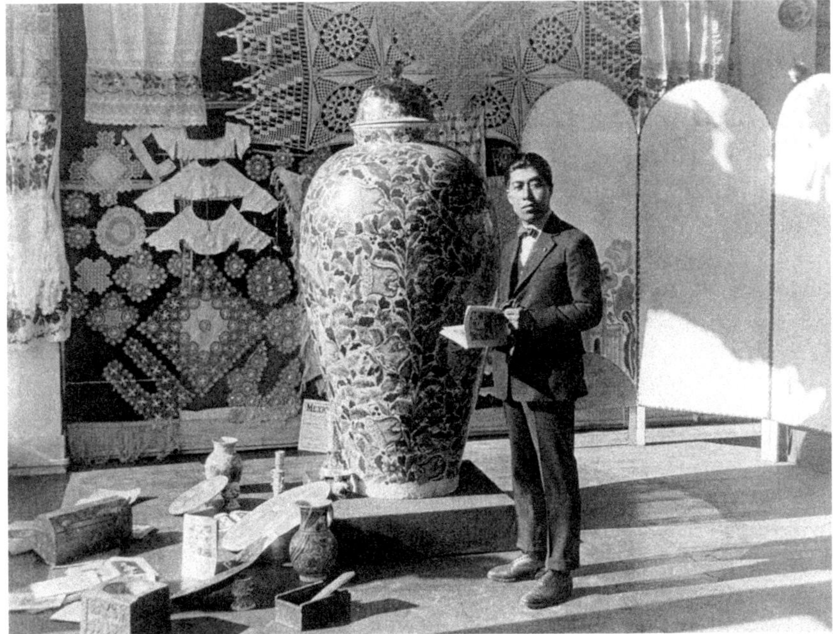

25. THE ARTIST XAVIER GUERRERO AT *EXHIBITION OF MEXICAN POPULAR ARTS*, LOS ANGELES, 1922. PHOTOGRAPHER UNKNOWN.

Articles like this one might well have opened the Arensbergs' minds to the potential of pre-Columbian art. Their improving finances couldn't have hurt either. The death of Walter's father in 1924 and of one of Louise's aunts in 1925 helped shore up the couple's previously precarious situation; by 1930 they were seeking both to buy back the few works they had sold and to acquire new ones with the assistance of Marcel Duchamp.[103] Dealers had begun to arrive in Los Angeles in the 1920s, drawn to the city by the flood of money from the movies. Among these dealers was Earl Stendahl, who had been in the area since 1913 and had begun selling art from the Ambassador Hotel by about 1921. Stendahl, the bookseller Jake Zeitlin, the gallerist Howard Putzel (director of the Stanley Rose gallery), and others probably began to include pre-Columbian art as part of their offerings by the 1930s.[104]

Many exhibitions of the early 1930s—originating in both California and New York—affirmed the Arensbergs' prior investments and growing interest in "primitive" works. The traveling exhibition *Mexican Arts*, for example, featuring colonial, nineteenth-century, and modern art, was first shown at the Metropolitan Museum of Art in 1930 and then sent across the country to San Antonio.[105] A more print-focused show of modern Mexican art, drawn from the Delphic Studios of New York, was exhibited in Los Angeles in 1931. Also in Southern California, Mexican muralists were producing large-scale works at Pomona College (José Clemente Orozco in 1930) and in Los Angeles itself (David Alfaro Siqueiros in 1932). These mural commissions sometimes featured ancient themes and imagery and often elicited disapproval and scandal, developments that perhaps endeared these works to the Arensbergs.[106]

However, the most important impetus for the Arensbergs' renewed interest in collecting pre-Columbian art was probably the 1933 exhibition *American Sources of Modern Art (Aztec, Mayan, Incan)*, organized by the Museum of Modern Art (MoMA) in New York (fig. 26). The Arensbergs owned the exhibition catalog, and the show included paintings by several artists whose work they would have known from their New York years (such as Rivera, Siqueiros, and Max Weber), as well as many ancient pieces, some that they had seen in the pre-Columbian collection at the AMNH.[107] The exhibition's gambit was to display works by the ancient cultures of the Americas in concert with works by modern artists of the hemisphere. The exhibition catalog

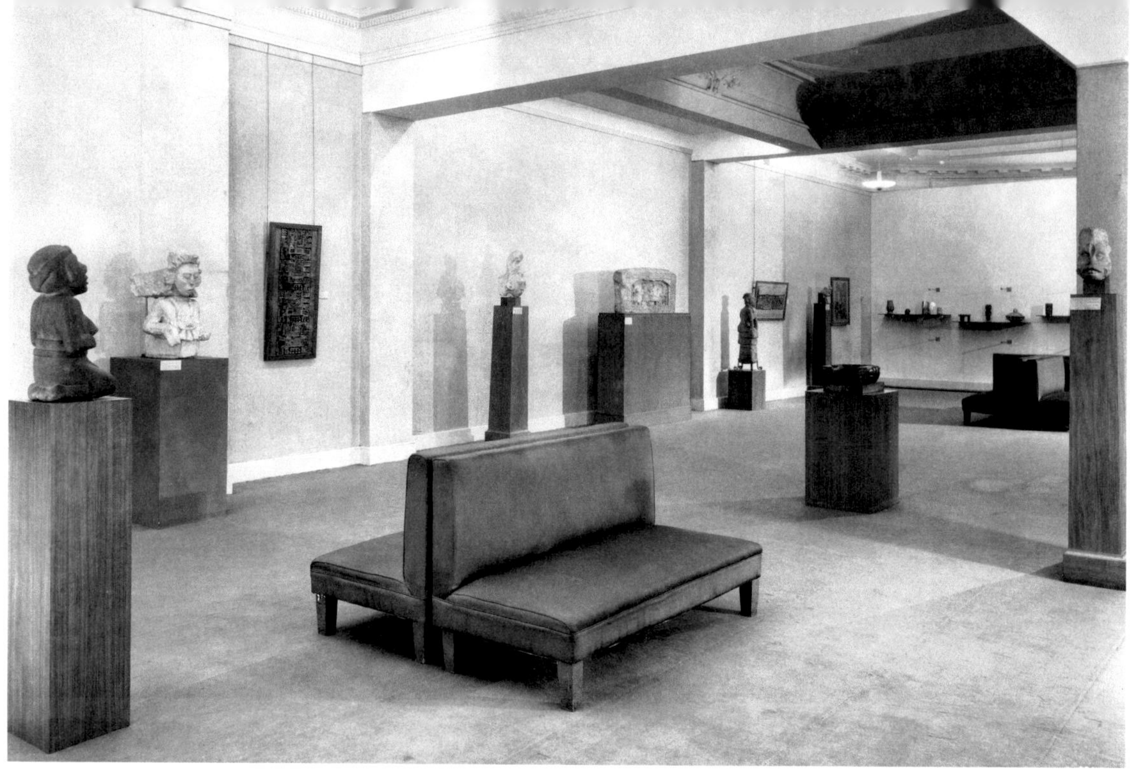

26. WURTS BROTHERS. INSTALLATION VIEW OF THE EXHIBITION *AMERICAN SOURCES OF MODERN ART (AZTEC, MAYAN, INCAN)*, AT THE MUSEUM OF MODERN ART, NEW YORK, 8 MAY–1 JULY 1933. GELATIN SILVER PRINT, 17.7 × 24.1 CM. PHOTOGRAPHIC ARCHIVE, THE MUSEUM OF MODERN ART ARCHIVES, NEW YORK. DIGITAL IMAGE © THE MUSEUM OF MODERN ART / LICENSED BY SCALA / ART RESOURCE, NY

stated that the show did not intend to promote pre-Columbian themes but instead "to show the high quality of ancient American art, and to indicate that its influence is present in modern art in the work of painters and sculptors."[108] Curator Holger Cahill's introductory essay tried to cover a lot of ground, giving modern art enthusiasts a primer in approximately three millennia of pre-Columbian creations that, he asserted, had "come to be looked upon as one of the great arts of the world, a profound and original expression of the spirit of man which has much to offer contemporary culture."[109] Cahill lavished extensive praise on the Aztecs:

> Aztec sculpture has density and bulk, a powerful simplicity, and exhibits great skill in the cutting.... In their choice and handling of subject the Aztec artists had a tendency to the fierce, the macabre, and the terrible.... [But] the ferocity of the Aztecs is never cold. It is passionate and human, just as their sacrificial rites were not an expression of mere cruelty but of a vivid sense of the awesome and overwhelming powers of the universe which man had to propitiate.[110]

Around the time *American Sources* was on view at MoMA, the museum was preparing for another exhibition investigating other "primitive" influences on modern art. *African Negro Art*, in 1935, included two of the Arensbergs' African works on loan, which thereafter were frequently requested for similar exhibitions organized by other institutions.[111] Much closer to home, the San Francisco Museum of Art (later known as SFMOMA) opened in 1935; in its inaugural year, it showed *African Negro Art*, *African Negro Textiles*, and *Oceanic Sculpture and Tapas*, among many other short-term exhibitions.[112]

These 1935 developments in the presentation of pre-Columbian art to the public and within the Arensberg collection were joined by the spectacle of the 1935 California Pacific International Exposition held in San Diego. One of the star exhibits, at the Palace of Fine Arts, was the Arensbergs' Brancusi sculpture *Bird in Space* (see plate 24.11) lent anonymously but reported as belonging to the Arensbergs by the *Los Angeles Times* columnist Arthur Millier.[113] If Louise and Walter had attended the fair and witnessed firsthand the public's reaction to their work, they would likely have seen the many pre-Columbian fragments and exhibits also on display. The California State Building, originally built for the 1915 Panama-California Exposition and centrally located on the fairgrounds, housed the San Diego Museum of Man, which featured a replica of the Temple of Quetzalcoatl at Chichén Itzá, on Mexico's Yucatán Peninsula, as its front entrance. The museum also displayed large and impressive casts of Maya stone monuments.[114] Another major draw was a selection from the "Jewels of Monte Albán," a golden treasure found in southern Mexico in 1932, which had riveted audiences (on both sides of the border) mired in the depths of the Great Depression.[115] Much of what was known about artmaking in Mexico and Central America was also synthesized that year by the archaeologist George Vaillant in a short pamphlet, *Artists and Craftsmen in Ancient Central America,* produced and illustrated by the AMNH. This easily digestible booklet was probably one of the first works in the Arensbergs' expanding library of pre-Columbian art.[116]

LOS ANGELES 1937–45: THE THRILL OF COLLECTING AGAIN

In 1937, after years of dabbling in pre-Columbian art, the Arensbergs suddenly began investing heavily in these newly popular creations. Walter was to turn sixty the next year, and the couple's financial situation was radically improving. (Their 1938 tax returns, for example, report an income of about $33,000—equivalent to about $575,000 today—almost solely due to bond payments on Louise's investments.)[117] Walter traveled to New York in May, purchasing six pre-Columbian works from the Brummer Gallery on 13 May and one from Pierre Matisse's gallery the next day.[118] Earlier in the year, Walter had purchased at least two modernist works from the dealer Theodore Schempp, and there may be a connection between the Brummer and Schempp transactions: one of the works Arensberg bought from Joseph Brummer had been sold to the gallery by Schempp himself, who dealt in pre-Columbian art throughout his career.[119] Alternatively, Walter's interest in doing business with the Brummer Gallery may have been sparked by a Duchamp-curated exhibition of Brancusi sculpture held there in November 1933. Duchamp had expressly requested that the Arensbergs' Brancusi sculpture *Prodigal Son* be included in the exhibition, and they had agreed to loan it for the show.[120]

Brummer was well known to the Arensbergs by the time of the Brancusi exhibition, as he had frequently sold works to John Quinn in the 1920s and had handled the sale of Quinn's estate in 1927. Duchamp had also arranged an exhibition of Brancusi's work at the Brummer Gallery in 1926, and had borrowed one of the Arensbergs' works for the show. However, it seems that the Arensbergs, who enjoyed personal relationships with artists and their dealers, had not purchased any pieces from the Hungarian-born Brummer prior to the 1930s.[121] This may have been because of Brummer's early association with Charles Vignier, de Zayas's former partner and a cause of major financial distress for the Arensbergs.[122] Furthermore, while de Zayas offered his clients a personal knowledge of Mexico (and, by extension, a greater ability to source from private collections), Brummer had no personal connection to his non-Western merchandise. Many of his clients, including Isabella Stewart Gardner, Henry Walters, and William Randolph Hearst, were creating their own museums. Others, including Robert Woods Bliss, Mildred Barnes Bliss, and Alastair Bradley Martin, were building collections for their personal enjoyment.[123] All of them expected delicate and precise craftsmanship in the non-Western works they purchased—criteria seemingly less interesting to the Arensbergs than the ideas imparted by the works themselves.

The Arensbergs' initial pre-Columbian purchases of 1937 make clear that de Zayas's influence on the couple had not waned: they were all sculptural works made from roughly hewn stone. For example, Walter's purchase from the Pierre Matisse Gallery, a coiled serpent wrought in rough red stone, illustrates the couple's continued preference for heavyset pieces (fig. 27; see also plate 13.20).[124] The Arensbergs would have had relatively easy access to West Mexican ceramic works in Los Angeles, but they had limited options for

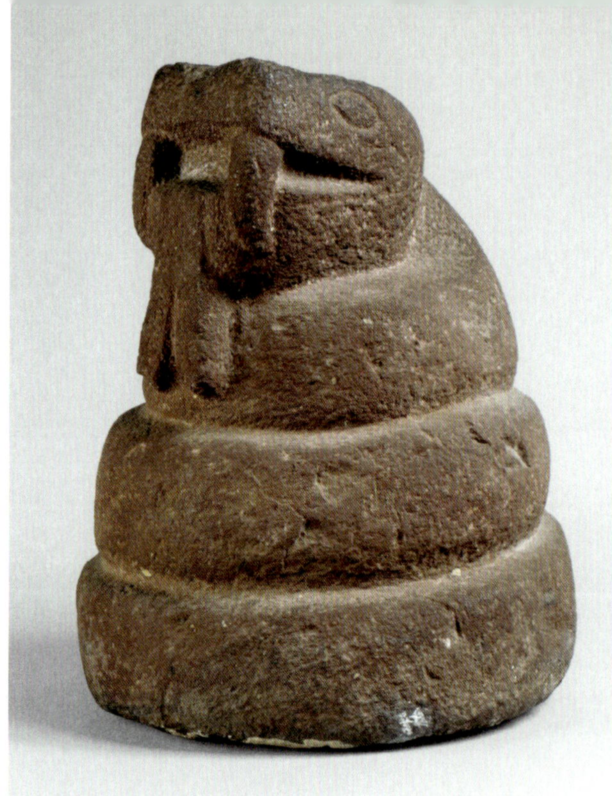

27. AZTEC (CENTRAL MEXICO). SERPENT, CA. 1300–1520. VOLCANIC STONE (TEZONTLE), 31.8 × 24.8 CM. PHILADELPHIA MUSEUM OF ART, THE LOUISE AND WALTER ARENSBERG COLLECTION, 1950-134-215. SEE ALSO PLATE 13.20

purchasing heavy stone works during these years. Earl Stendahl, who before then specialized in selling society portraits and plein air paintings, had not yet begun to sell much pre-Columbian art—at least not to the Arensbergs, who had purchased little in this area from him prior to this point. Somewhat surprisingly, the most active dealers in pre-Columbian art at this time were operating from Europe.[125]

The Brummer Gallery purchases also make clear that the Arensbergs were refining their taste: they show a marked preference for the human form—particularly for faces—which characterizes the couple's pre-Columbian collecting from that point on. Unlike Bliss, the Arensbergs were not so interested in sculpture featuring the perfected visages, elegantly shaped heads, and elaborate coiffures of Maya lords and ladies. Rather, they were attracted to masklike and abstracted faces. This purchase was no exception: it included three heads, two full-body figures, and a stone alligator (see plate 47.31), just the first of many palma sculptures that the Arensbergs would buy in the coming years. Now thought to have been paraphernalia in the sacred ballgame played across Mesoamerica, the palma was sold by Brummer as a standalone sculpture.[126] Many of the other works in the group were rough basalt or volcanic in composition, but the full-figure statue that Schempp sold to Brummer was worked in greenish jadeite (see plate 48.6), and one head was carved from white onyx, material known in Mexico as *tecali* (see plate 7.17).[127] The Brummer purchase also shows that by 1937, Walter was willing to spend a significant sum on a compelling piece. He bought the six works from Brummer in a lot for $4,000 (equivalent to nearly $72,000 today).[128] Most of this money was spent on a head with an elaborate headdress and a hieroglyph carved on the back, which Walter gave pride of place in his office (see plates 38.18, 41.4).[129]

At the end of 1937, there was another major development in the intellectual and physical expansion of the Arensbergs' pre-Columbian collection: the Mexican artist Roberto Montenegro (fig. 28) visited Hollywood, staying for some time with the Arensbergs in their home. Montenegro's reputation undoubtedly preceded him, since he had moved in the same circles as de Zayas in the 1910s.[130] An organizer of the previously mentioned 1922 folk art exhibition, he had also participated in building the cultural bureaucracy of Mexico beginning in the 1920s, painting murals in Mexico City and for the Mexican pavilion at the 1922 World's Fair in Rio de Janeiro. Montenegro's great respect for Mexican folk art and Mexican colonial art, about which he wrote books and curated exhibitions, fomented a broader appreciation for these less celebrated styles of art. (A copy of his 1926 book *Máscaras mexicanas* [Mexican masks], now held in the Philadelphia Museum of Art Library, is inscribed to Walter "with admiration.")[131]

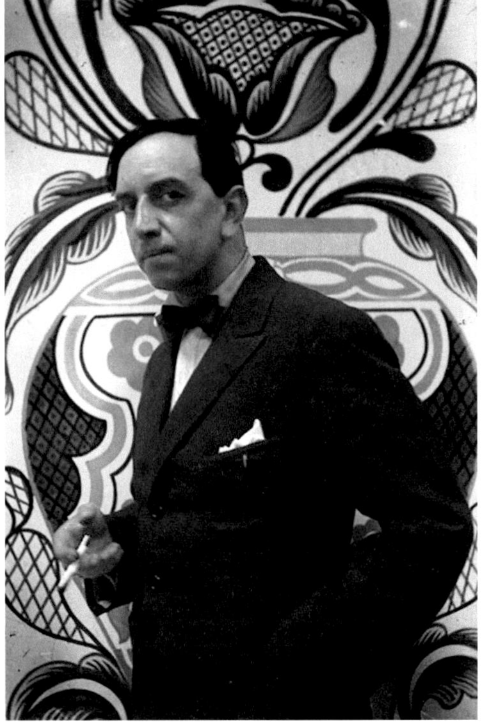

28. THE ARTIST ROBERTO MONTENEGRO, PICTURED IN FRONT OF PAINTED MOTIFS TAKEN FROM FOLK CERAMICS OF MEXICO. D.R. INSTITUTO NACIONAL DE ANTROPOLOGÍA E HISTORIA, MEXICO

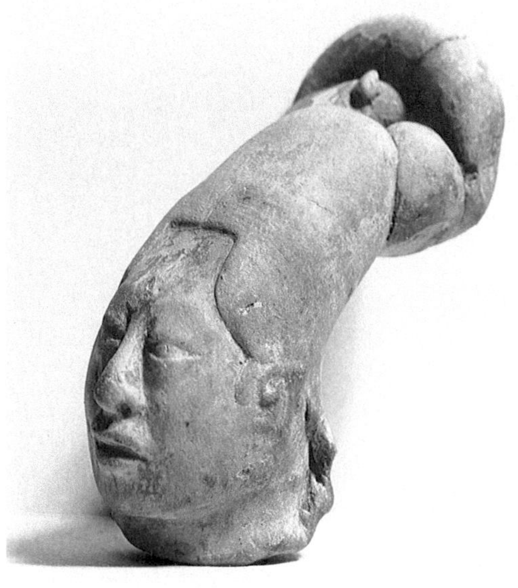

29. MAYA (ISLAND OF JAINA, MEXICO). HEAD, 1ST–9TH CENTURY. CLAY, HEIGHT: 9.8 CM. PHILADELPHIA MUSEUM OF ART, THE LOUISE AND WALTER ARENSBERG COLLECTION, 1950-134-277

Since the 1920s, Montenegro had been collecting and sometimes selling pre-Columbian and folk art from Mexico, so he may have naturally gravitated toward the Arensbergs.[132] Through his own acquisitions, he had become quite an expert on pre-Columbian art and was corresponding with Stendahl by at least as early as 1938, when he tentatively authenticated an obsidian mask for the dealer—a mask that may be the same one the Arensbergs bought and displayed on their living room mantel (see plate 3.19). In October 1938, Walter wrote Roberto a thank-you note for "sending the beautiful mask which is your portrait and all the other precious gifts."[133] The "mask which is your portrait" was likely Montenegro's painting *The Double* (see Sherman and Nelson, fig. 44a); the other gifts Walter referred to include a small pre-Columbian Maya head from a ceramic figurine (fig. 29), as well as one or two *retablo* paintings.[134] These devotional paintings seem to have been attractive for the Arensbergs; they bought many, including at least one or two more from Montenegro (several are pictured in plate 45). Retablos were shown along with ceramics, textiles, and wood works in the Popular (Folk) Art section that Montenegro organized in MoMA's 1940 exhibition *Twenty Centuries of Mexican Art*.[135] The show also featured Montenegro's own art in the Modern Art section, including *The Double*, which was lent by the Arensbergs.[136] This unsettling painting, showing a double outline of a head set against a black background, telegraphs Montenegro's association with the Mexican surrealists in the late 1930s.[137]

Montenegro was likely introduced to the Arensbergs by Earl Stendahl, who quickly became the couple's most important source of pre-Columbian art (fig. 30).[138] An inventive, resourceful dealer who offered chocolate and jigsaw puzzles for sale in lean times and modernist works in better ones, Stendahl sold the Arensbergs nearly all of the hundreds of pre-Columbian works that they ultimately owned. He essentially created and cornered a huge market for pre-Columbian art in Los Angeles beginning in the mid- to late 1930s. Stendahl was praised by many of his clients and associates, including Vincent Price, who later ran his own art gallery for a short time. Price wrote:

> No one has put Earl into his proper place in the history of great dealers, but I must say briefly that without him, we would know much less of the tremendous variety and brilliance of the art of Mexico, before Columbus. He is a real pioneer and an astute businessman.[139]

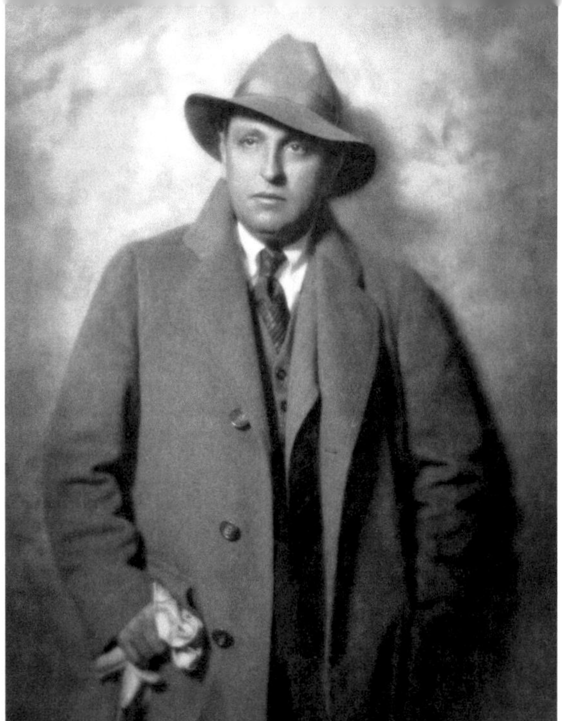

30. GEORGE HURRELL. EARL STENDAHL, 1928. COURTESY OF APRIL DAMMANN AND ANGEL CITY PRESS

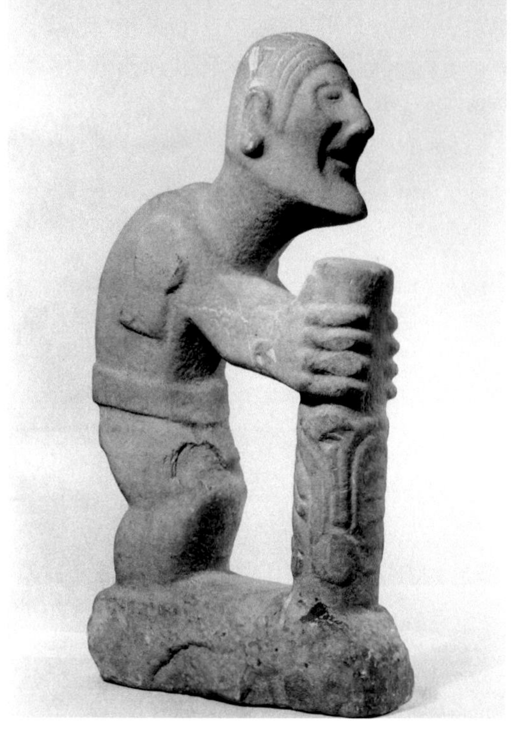

31. HUASTEC (EAST COAST MEXICO). FIGURE OF A MAN, 1000–1500. LIMESTONE, 44.5 × 22.9 × 8.3 CM. PHILADELPHIA MUSEUM OF ART, THE LOUISE AND WALTER ARENSBERG COLLECTION, 1950-134-295. SEE ALSO PLATES 13.24 AND 14.17

By contrast, Robert Woods Bliss, an avid but more skeptical customer, described him this way:

> He is not an archaeologist, and knows nothing really about Mexican archaeology; but he does have a flair for things and has learned to ask high prices.[140]

Indeed, Stendahl did not always have precise information as to the culture, much less the dates, of the works he sold, but he seems to have had a great capacity to know the desires of his clients, and to sell to them. He also seems to have exaggerated or invented a sexual connotation for some of the sculptures of the Gulf Coast that he sold to Walter, who was fixated on sexual symbolism (see Sherman and Nelson, pages 40–41). For example, a figure now known to be of the Huastec (sometimes spelled Huaxtec) civilization, showing an elderly man who grips a staff held in front of him (fig. 31), has no actual connection to any known sexually themed iconography, but is noted as phallic (with different spellings) in the invoices from Stendahl and on one of the index cards the Arensbergs used to catalog their collections.[141] On a separate occasion, Stendahl sold a stone basin to the couple, which he described in his invoice as an "Altar receptical [*sic*]—stone—Blood container."[142] Such round vessels were used for offerings of many kinds in ancient times, but certainly not exclusively to hold blood.

It is possible that Stendahl also emphasized the transgressive aspect of collecting this material—an idea that so far has been little discussed. One notion that may have made pre-Columbian art attractive to his clients, including Walter Arensberg, was the knowledge that Stendahl was removing these works illegally from Mexico and many other nations of Latin America. The sometimes illicit nature of Stendahl's transactions was tempered by the low probability that export laws would be enforced. His son, Alfred Stendahl, later said of the legality of importing pre-Columbian art at this time, "Well, we didn't know.... If you don't ask any questions, you don't know."[143] This simplistic rationale is belied by Stendahl's many self-aggrandizing stories, which often provided a narrative gloss compelling enough to justify the prices he asked or, in some cases, to compensate for merchandise that was either damaged or of lesser quality. As time went on, these tales were mythologized through their retelling by his clients and family members. Two examples of Stendahl's purported exploits include his posing as a movie producer in the Yucatán Peninsula

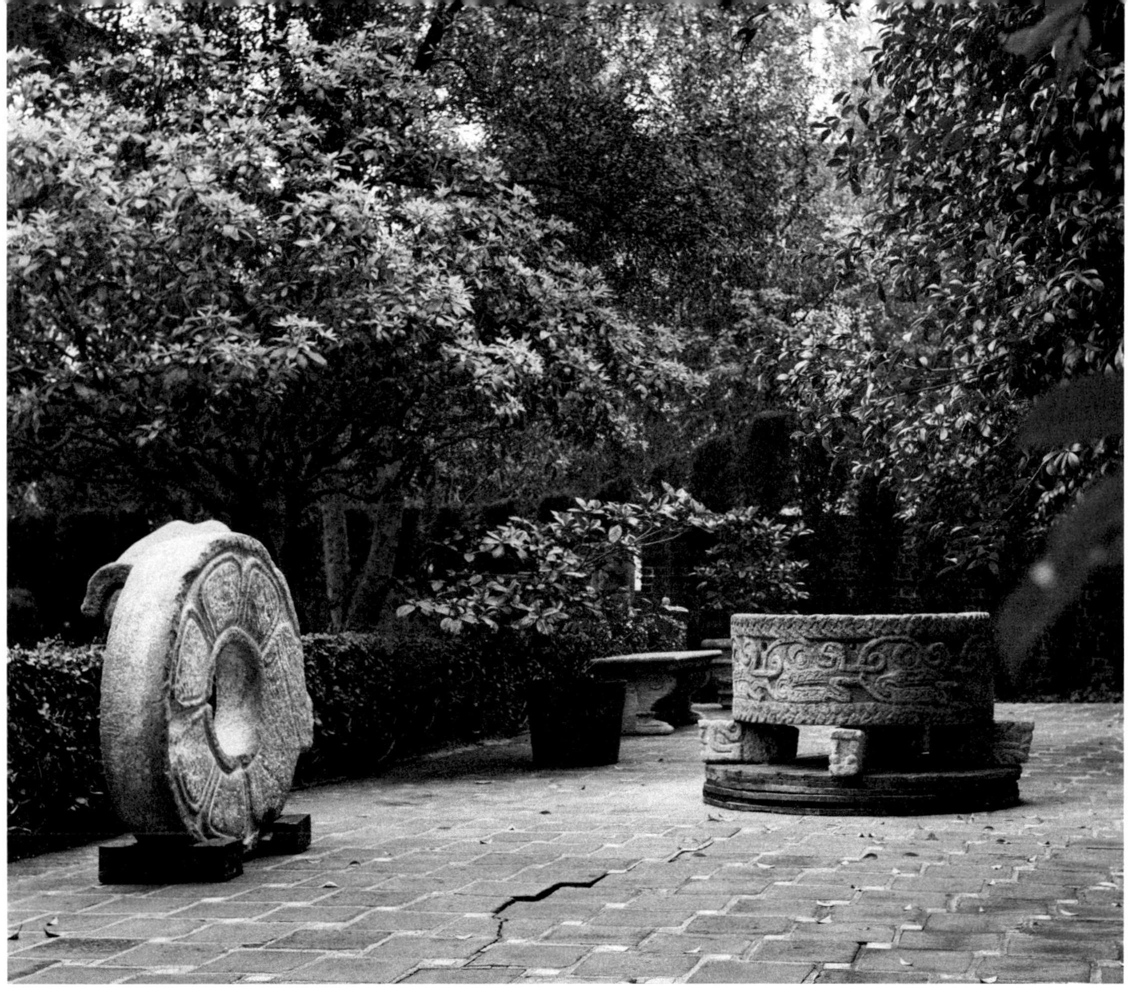

32. KARL BISSINGER. VIEW OF LOUISE AND WALTER ARENSBERG'S FRONT PATIO (DETAIL), 7065 HILLSIDE AVENUE, LOS ANGELES, 16 MARCH 1950, SHOWING THE LARGE AZTEC BASIN AT RIGHT. UNIVERSITY OF DELAWARE LIBRARY, NEWARK, SPECIAL COLLECTIONS, KARL BISSINGER ARCHIVE (MSS0682). © THE ESTATE OF KARL BISSINGER. SEE ALSO PLATE 59

to distract the Mexican army so his team could dig for pre-Columbian materials; and his visiting a local museum in Colima, West Mexico, selecting works of interest, and bribing its director to obtain the pieces.[144]

One of the major pieces Stendahl sold the Arensbergs brought these activities into nervous focus. When W. R. Valentiner, director of the Detroit Institute for the Arts, wrote to the Arensbergs in 1945 asking for permission to reproduce an image of their "Aztec serpent altar" (fig. 32), Walter replied:

> As for the serpent altar—I am not certain as to the piece you mean. We have two basins with death heads, one circular, and the smaller one rectangular. In any event, Stendahl advises that for reasons that may or may not be obscure, we should not have these objects published at present.[145]

Arensberg was clearly worried that Valentiner's request could cause problems with works for which he had paid a significant amount. Were Walter truly discreet, and not reveling in the air of secrecy created by the denial, he likely would not have mentioned the matter again. However, in a second letter accompanying a photograph of the other artwork that Valentiner had requested, Arensberg wrote, "I am sorry to have had to disappoint you about the photograph of the large basin.... I feel, however, that I had better follow Stendahl's advice in not having it published at present."[146]

The gallerist found the opportunity to become truly indispensable to the Arensbergs when he became their neighbor. In 1941, Stendahl acquired a property at 7055 Hillside Avenue that the couple owned, next door to the house they lived in. They had traded it to him for an unknown number of pre-Columbian works

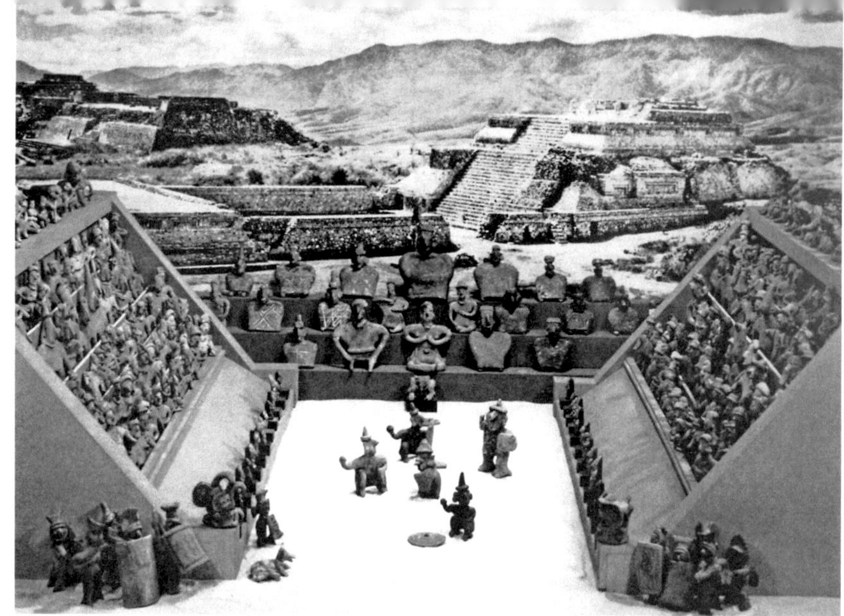

33. ALFRED STENDAHL. DIORAMA ON VIEW IN EARL STENDAHL'S CARPORT AT 7055 HILLSIDE AVENUE IN LOS ANGELES, CA. MID-1950S. GATHERING PRE-COLUMBIAN FIGURES TOGETHER IN TABLEAUX SUGGESTIVE OF MOMENTS OF DAILY LIFE WAS APPARENTLY AN EFFECTIVE SALES TECHNIQUE THAT STENDAHL HAD EMPLOYED SINCE AT LEAST THE LATE 1940S. THESE WORKS, FROM THE REGION OF WEST MEXICO, ARE GROUPED TO SUGGEST PLAYERS AND SPECTATORS OF THE RITUAL BALLGAME, WITH A LARGE-SCALE PHOTOGRAPH OF A PRE-COLUMBIAN BALLCOURT AS BACKDROP. COURTESY OF APRIL DAMMANN AND ANGEL CITY PRESS

whose value is still unclear.[147] This move to the neighborhood then known as the Outpost, in the Hollywood Hills, allowed Stendahl greater access to wealthy potential clients, including many who worked in the movie industry. It was a Machiavellian arrangement for Stendahl, because Walter, as Art Institute of Chicago curator Katharine Kuh wrote in her memoir, *The Open Eye*, "made daily excursions to the house next door and rarely came back empty-handed."[148] Stendahl himself boasted to his collaborator Guillermo M. Echániz:

> When you see the house and how I have arranged it to show the pre-Columbian things, you will agree with me that it was money well spent. There will be nothing like it in existence. It is right beside Mr. Arensberg's home and he is simply crazy about the place. Most of the magazines published for homes will use photographs of the rooms whereby the pre-Columbian things will be shown up to great advantage. This will mean money for us.[149]

Since Stendahl was willing to sell almost anything—raiding even the jewelry boxes of his daughter or wife to take back golden objects he had given them, if he had a prospective buyer—his own preferences are hard to discern.[150] He had an upstairs showroom at the gallery (an inner sanctum of sorts) where he curated displays that were devoted to polished jades, suggesting his own tastes were closer to Bliss's than to the Arensbergs'.[151] Yet Stendahl also spent much time and effort creating elaborate diorama-like environments, one simulating a pre-Columbian village and another showing a ballcourt (fig. 33). These tableaux were filled with rough ceramic figures from West Mexico, frequently touched up in the "restoration" studio he ran as well. The restoration operation was observed with great concern by some of the Arensbergs' associates, most notably Marcel Duchamp. Kuh, who spent time with the couple during Duchamp's 1948 visit to their home, explained:

> [One] day the three of us made a brief expedition to Walter's next-door neighbor, the dealer Earl Stendahl. Along with splendid examples of modern art, his gallery was the main source of Walter's pre-Columbian sculpture. Just how Stendahl maneuvered this vast, and I judge, forbidden cargo across the border was never explained. The visit was not entirely reassuring. Remedial treatment on early stone carvings was going on at quite a pace. As we left, Duchamp muttered, "*Dangereux*."[152]

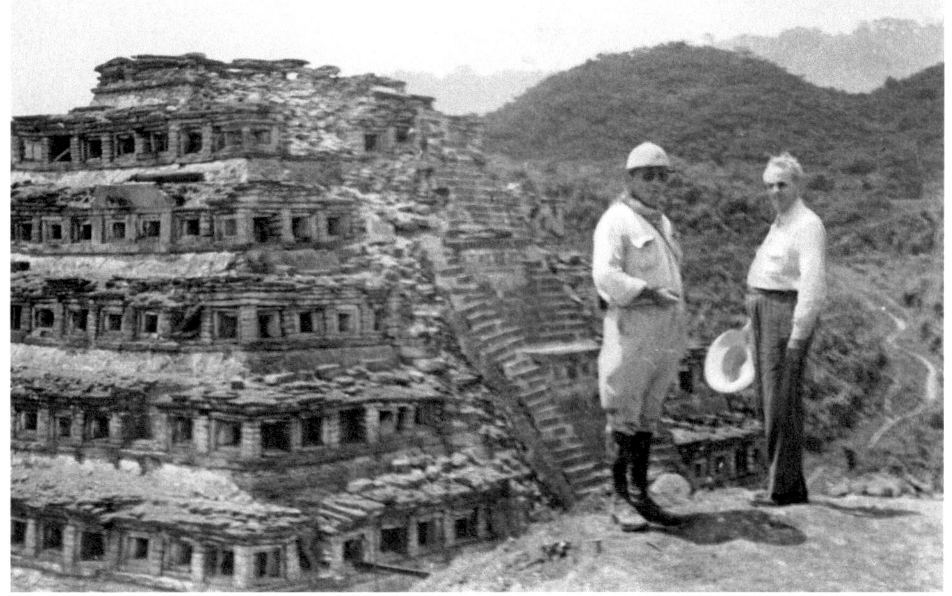

34. GUILLERMO M. ECHÁNIZ (LEFT) WITH EARL STENDAHL, CA. LATE 1940S.
PHOTOGRAPHER UNKNOWN. COURTESY OF APRIL DAMMANN AND ANGEL CITY PRESS

One of Stendahl's greatest strengths as a dealer was his ability to source pre-Columbian merchandise. In her book *Exhibitionist: Earl Stendahl, Art Dealer as Impresario*, Stendahl's granddaughter-in-law April Dammann wrote that Stendahl and members of his family have been "compared to Indiana Jones" (the larger-than-life action hero in Steven Spielberg's 1981 film *Raiders of the Lost Ark*) because of their often arduous buying trips throughout Latin America.[153] However, it is crucial to remember that Stendahl also had a well-developed network of contacts in the region who scouted, acquired, and sent him objects.[154] Echániz was one of Stendahl's most important agents in Latin America (fig. 34). Based in Mexico City, Echániz was a well-known collector, both of books and of pre-Columbian objects, and had a legitimate business as an antiquarian book dealer and printer.[155] While he is often associated only with pre-Columbian works, Echániz seems to have had wide interests and reach as an intermediary. According to one account of Echániz and Stendahl's first meeting, Echániz turned up in Los Angeles in 1935 with the intention of selling his printing press, which he claimed was the first one used on the American continent.[156] Reportedly, Stendahl gave him a tour of the Arensberg home and told Echániz that Walter "was proud of his small pre-Columbian collection, acquired in New York.... After a quick perusal, Echániz commented off-handedly to [Stendahl and Walter], 'Oh, I can get things like that.' This got Stendahl's attention. 'Well, get some!'"[157]

Echániz certainly was able to get pre-Columbian things: he had an uncanny ability to obtain unusual or important objects, and, at least in the 1930s, sometimes traded works with the Museo Nacional, when it still had fluid acquisition policies.[158] Like Stendahl, Echániz had a transactional outlook: in a pamphlet called "Thoughts about Collecting Mexican Archaeology," he even advocated for putting labels including the approximate monetary value of pre-Columbian works next to pieces in museums of Mexico.[159]

While the earliest invoice for a pre-Columbian work sold by Stendahl to the Arensbergs dates to February 1940, it is probable that Echániz was already sending works to Los Angeles before this.[160] Some were works from his personal collection—a yoke bought by the Arensbergs in 1941 (see plate 39.5), for example, was listed as having been published as part of the Echániz collection in the *Actas del Vigésimo-Séptimo Congreso de Americanistas* (*Acts of the Twenty-Seventh International Congress of Americanists*), held in Mexico City in 1939.[161]

There is no doubt that Echániz intersected with the anthropological and scholarly communities and, in some significant ways, helped to advance understanding of the pre-Columbian world in the first half of the twentieth century. However, he was also one of the boldest dealers trafficking in illegally exported pre-Columbian art and was good at offering conflicting versions of a story to throw doubt on his actual involvement in a matter. This was certainly the case for a Maya stela fragment owned by the Arensbergs, known to have gone through Echániz's hands (see figs. 20a, b). The stela fragment was called the Stone of Chiapa because it was found near the town of Chiapa de Corzo, Mexico, in the late nineteenth century. It passed through the collections of several owners and was reportedly even placed outside at the corner of Salamanca and Durango Streets in Mexico City for a time.[162] According to an article written by the Mexican journalist and cultural bureaucrat César Lizardi Ramos, Echániz acknowledged that he had sold the stone, but only in Mexico, to an unnamed foreign dealer.[163] Echániz also almost certainly had a hand in securing the enormous stone shell that the Arensbergs displayed—rather humorously, it should be added, since it gave the impression of having been set atop a hedgerow—on their front patio wall, which was covered by creeping fig (see page 337). This object is nearly identical to the three large conch shells excavated by archaeologists in 1979, in the patio of the Templo Mayor (Great Temple) of the Aztecs in downtown Mexico City—only five blocks from Echániz's bookstore, located at number 12 Donceles Street. When this piece came to light in the 1930s or 1940s, its possible relationship to the other monumental shells of the Templo Mayor would not have been recognized.[164]

Correspondence between the anthropologist Frederick Peterson and the collector Frank Boos in 1965, about a decade after the Arensbergs' deaths, includes a very skeptical assessment of Echániz's character. Peterson wrote of Echániz:

> He has been a dealer, and one of the foremost black-marketeers of Mexico, in antiquities, for about 50 years. He has also been responsible for aiding and encouraging and, I suspect, creating falsifications in about any branch of antiquities you care to name: codices, clay idols, stone sculpture, etc. etc.... [He] had about 25,000 archaeological pieces in his house when I saw him—of which all were for sale. He has an irritating knack of disclaiming all knowledge about places, events, and persons, when you know perfectly well that he perfectly recalls the incident or place or person. If he is in a coy mood you may get no information whatsoever from him, but if he is in an expansive mood he may give you some very valuable information. He tried to deliberately mislead me on several occasions when I asked for information, and is not above falsifying data or inventing it to suit the occasion.[165]

Despite having had similar difficulties in getting direct factual information from Stendahl and Echániz, the Arensbergs maintained a close relationship with the two men, particularly Stendahl, until their deaths. In fact, Stendahl's son, Alfred, asserted that Walter had great confidence in his father's ability to spot a fake:

> If someone came to him with an object of interest, Arensberg would direct the fellow next door to try and sell it to Stendahl. If Stendahl bought it, Arensberg would then buy the piece from him. Never mind that Arensberg had to pay Stendahl's mark-up.[166]

However, the couple did not offer Stendahl any exclusivity when it came to buying what they wanted. They purchased works they found compelling from other dealers when it suited them to do so. Montenegro was one such vendor. Another was the violinist Josef (or Joszef) Smilovits of the Léner Quartet, a well-known musical group who toured together, often in Mexico, from 1918 to 1942.[167] The quartet—or Smilovits at least—was hosted at the Arensbergs' house at some point in the late 1930s or 1940s and saw the couple's pre-Columbian collection there. In the 1940s, Smilovits had separated from the quartet and was living in Mexico, helping to found a chamber orchestra called Yolopatli ("Cure for the Heart" in the Aztecs' Nahuatl

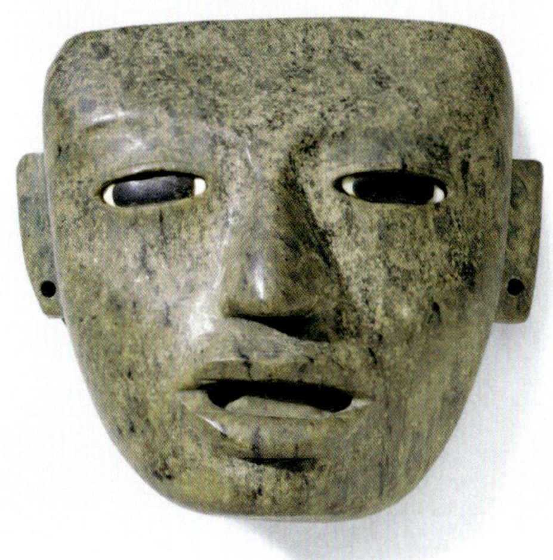

35. TEOTIHUACAN (CENTRAL MEXICO). MASK, 1ST–9TH CENTURY. GRANITIC ROCK WITH SHELL AND PYRITE INLAY. 21.6 × 24.1 × 10.2 CM. PHILADELPHIA MUSEUM OF ART, THE LOUISE AND WALTER ARENSBERG COLLECTION, 1950-134-947

language).[168] While traveling with his group in Mexico City and farther afield, Smilovits obtained many kinds of pre-Columbian works. He sold the Arensbergs several pieces, including a coiled snake and a jade mask. In fact, the polished granite "face panel" he procured for them from Teotihuacan was one of Walter's most prized acquisitions (fig. 35).[169] Of the many examples of this genre that the couple owned, only this one still had intact stone insets in the eyes. (In most known cases, these inlays were lost at some point during the approximately 1200–1800 years since they were made.) The mask was offered at $2,200, and Walter, having been schooled in the art of negotiation by Louise, telegraphed his offer of $2,000 (equivalent to nearly $21,000 today). Walter seems to have gotten nervous, however, when Smilovits did not reply immediately, and he quickly sent a follow-up letter in which he agreed to pay the asking price.[170]

The Arensbergs' dealings with Smilovits, Stendahl, and Echániz were not solely commercial—they also offered opportunities for education and information-sharing within a like-minded community that valued pre-Columbian art. The couple formed other groups as well: during the late 1930s and early 1940s, the Arensbergs began hosting a new salon (appropriately subdued, given their advancing age) for discussing the idea that Francis Bacon wrote the works attributed to Shakespeare. This group included the actors Charles Laughton and Edward G. Robinson, the violinist Louis Kaufman and his wife, Annette, the collector Ruth Maitland and her husband, Leslie, and others, many of whom collected pre-Columbian art.[171] Lloyd Wright (son of Frank Lloyd Wright), who had designed a Mayan Revival house for himself nearby on Doheny Drive, also participated.

Among the most influential members of the Arensbergs' California circle was the film producer Kenneth Macgowan (fig. 36), whose contributions to the pre-Columbian art field have been almost completely overlooked. Walter Arensberg and Macgowan seem to have lived nearly parallel lives about a decade apart. Both were Harvard men, and both became cub reporters, first in Boston and then in New York, soon after graduating. And just as Walter had become involved in the literary and artistic avant-garde, Macgowan immersed himself in theater, working as a drama critic for the *Evening Globe*, *Vogue*, and *Theater Arts*, and writing for publications such as *Shadowland*.[172] Arensberg and Macgowan had known each other in Cambridge and later in New York, and might have visited the American Museum of Natural History together.[173] In 1923, Macgowan wrote *Masks and Demons* with the artist and theatrical designer Herman Rosse. Heavily illustrated with both photographs and small designs of African, Native American, pre-Columbian, and ancient masks and motifs (many from the AMNH's collections), the book features sections with such suggestive titles as "Magic," "Awe," and "Legend." Macgowan and Rosse sought to examine "primitive" man's relationship with masks across cultures and time periods. *Masks and Demons* makes clear that Macgowan was, even in the 1920s, a serious, if budding, student of the ancient Americas. Macgowan's explanatory paragraph, for example, opposite an illustration of a Maya carving of a masked lord, includes citations of works by the sixteenth-century Spanish friar Bernardino de Sahagún and the French ethnographer Charles Étienne Brasseur de Bourbourg.[174] Macgowan also thanks a broad swath of anthropologists and administrators at many museums in Chicago and on the East Coast in the acknowledgments.[175] *Masks and Demons* is filled

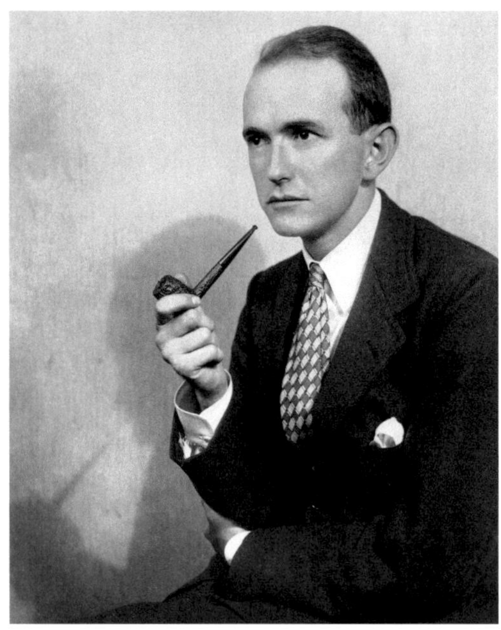

36. FLORENCE VANDAMM. PORTRAIT OF KENNETH MACGOWAN WITH PIPE IN HAND, 1927. SILVER GELATIN PHOTOPRINT, 24 × 19 CM. BOWDOIN COLLEGE LIBRARY, GEORGE T. MITCHELL DEPARTMENT OF SPECIAL COLLECTIONS & ARCHIVES, LOCAL CALL NUMBER 4278. COURTESY OF THE GEORGE J. MITCHELL DEPARTMENT OF SPECIAL COLLECTIONS & ARCHIVES, BOWDOIN COLLEGE LIBRARY, BRUNSWICK, MAINE

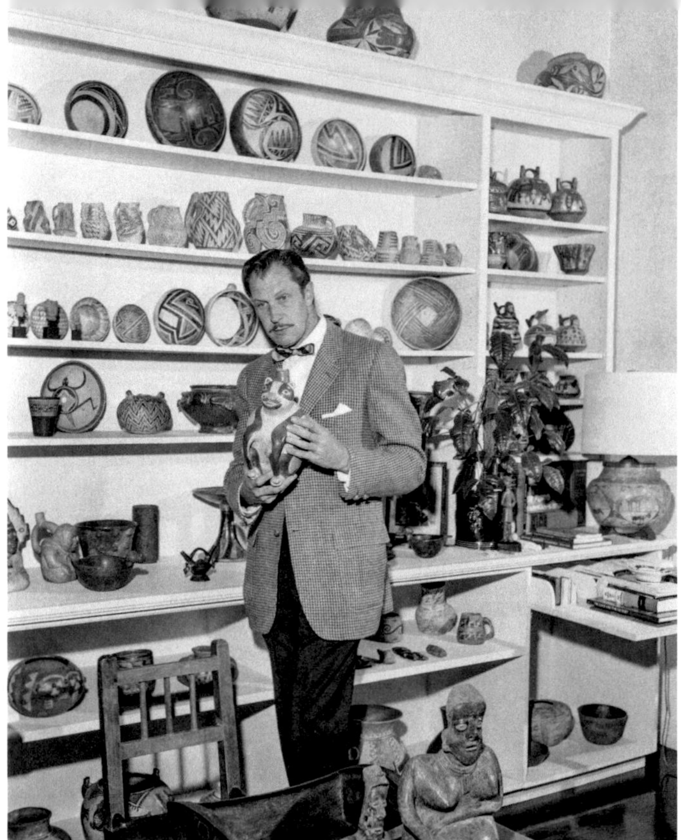

37. VINCENT PRICE WITH A DISPLAY OF CERAMICS FROM HIS ART COLLECTION, CA. 1955. COURTESY OF VICTORIA PRICE AND THE VINCENT PRICE ART MUSEUM

with poetic but unspecific musings on art that Walter might have appreciated. Next to an Olmec-style greenstone mask (of a type the Arensbergs owned in the 1950s), Macgowan wrote, "If a man may wear a mask, why not a god? Or, rather, if a mask can bring godhead to a man, will it not do something quite extraordinary for an idol?"[176] (Coincidentally—or not, given the ubiquitous challenge to previously held ideals and values presented by World War I—the title of Walter's 1916 volume of poems was *Idols*.) Macgowan, in the aforementioned passage, also references Quetzalcoatl, whom he calls a "culture-hero."[177] His early interest in the Aztec deity strongly suggests that he may have been the author of a short but meticulous research file maintained by the Arensbergs on the topic; it seems not to have been composed by Walter or Louise.[178]

Macgowan moved to Los Angeles around 1926 to work in Hollywood. He was an early pioneer in color film, winning an Oscar for the 1934 short *La Cucaracha*, which presented a stereotyped and idealized version of Mexican life. He had great commercial success as a producer in Hollywood, but his real passions were teaching theater and researching and writing about the pre-Columbian Americas. By the late 1940s, Macgowan had left the movie business to found the Department of Theater Arts at the University of California, Los Angeles (UCLA). Along with Vincent Price (fig. 37), Edward G. Robinson, and other Hollywood personalities, Macgowan was part of a group who sought to keep the Arensbergs' collection in California through the creation of a new museum, the short-lived Modern Institute of Art.[179]

A selection of Macgowan's personal collection of masks was shown at the Museum of Costume Art in 1943, and it included many Native American examples as well as masks from Africa, Asia, and Oceania. No pre-Columbian masks are evident in the available photographs of the exhibition.[180] While he was a connoisseur, Macgowan does not seem to have been a prolific collector of pre-Columbian art. He probably bought a few small works from Stendahl over the years and is reported to have patronized the Weyhe Gallery, which was not known as a dealer of pre-Columbian works.[181]

Macgowan was successful as both a mentor and a tutor for the Arensbergs in their nascent pre-Columbian studies, largely because of his ability to read deeply, synthesize great amounts of information, and simplify pre-Columbian themes for the layperson. In 1950, he authored *Early Man in the New World*, which dealt with the origins of civilizations in the Americas and explained several competing theories about how the Western Hemisphere was populated. The book was geared to the average reader, whom Macgowan reassured by emphasizing that he himself was not a professional archaeologist.[182] In this respect, the book may even have been influenced by his interactions with Walter: in 1944, at Arensberg's request, Macgowan sent him a "reading list on the archaeology of Middle America and South America," broken down by culture and including the Aztecs, Maya, and Incas, as well as some more general reading.[183] In an accompanying letter, Macgowan counseled Walter on how to begin his research: "I would suggest that in these three fields, you read the simpler books first."[184] The Arensbergs indeed bought most of the books Macgowan recommended and many others as well, some of which can be seen in piles or on shelves in pictures of their house, including George Vaillant's *Aztecs of Mexico* (1941; see plate 19), Herbert Joseph Spinden's *Ancient Civilizations of Mexico and Central America* (1922; see plate 20), J. Leslie Mitchell's *The Conquest of the Maya* (1935; see plate 21), and J. Eric Thompson's *Archaeology of South America* (1936; see plate 21).

Macgowan also combined his vocation, his knowledge of Latin America, and his patriotic feeling when he served during World War II as the chief of motion picture production for the Office of the Coordinator of Inter-American Affairs (OCIAA). There, as part of his duties, Macgowan prepared educational films on archaeological work in Mexico and South America.[185] Walter contributed to the war effort too, working with the Southern California branch of the OCIAA on diplomatic endeavors, frequently hosting Latin American visitors in his home and offering them tours of his collection.[186]

In 1949, Macgowan had another opportunity to use his movie-making skills in the service of his academic passions. With financial support from the United Fruit Company, and in collaboration with the adventurer and anthropologist Giles Healey, who shot footage in Mexico and Guatemala, Macgowan produced the short film *The Maya through the Ages*.[187] Drawing on Macgowan's Hollywood connections, the film was partially narrated by Price. The film's credits also acknowledge the assistance of the Mexican Instituto Nacional de Antropología e Historia (INAH; the National Institute of Anthropology and History), a crucial partner for Macgowan and Healey since it controlled access to archaeological sites and pre-Columbian collections in museums throughout the country.[188] A contrast can be drawn here between Macgowan, an important adviser to the Arensbergs who aided the Mexican government in promoting its ancient cultures, and Stendahl, who sought to avoid Mexico's scrutiny and potential penalties.

Like Macgowan, Vincent Price greatly influenced the Arensbergs and the trajectory of their collection. It had been his idea to form the Modern Institute of Art, promoting the idea that California could be more than a cultural backwater. When the museum failed, Walter and Louise led the effort to help pay off the debt Price had personally incurred when he leased the museum's building.[189] Price had formed a pre-Columbian collection even larger than the Arensbergs', and his collecting interests were similarly diverse, including modern art, Latin American colonial furniture, and religious sculpture.[190] Unlike the reticent Arensbergs, however, Price chose to detail his tastes and preferences with an actor's flair in *I Like What I Know: A Visual Autobiography*, a book recounting episodes from his life juxtaposed with works he owned. Having lived in New York and abroad, and having been part of an artistic avant-garde (in drama rather than the literary world), Price's experiences paralleled Walter's, though three decades later. In the book, he explains why he was attracted to "primitive" art:

> Most true primitive art is anything but untrained, and far from simple. Anthropologists define primitive art as the art of peoples without a written language, but their art is, in a sense, their language—hence the definition is invalid.... Understanding the appeal of primitive art has a great deal to do with understanding modern art, cubist art, abstract

38. FRONT COVER OF *AN EXHIBITION OF PRE-COLUMBIAN ART*, EXH. CAT. (CAMBRIDGE, MA: PEABODY MUSEUM AND THE WILLIAM HAYES FOGG ART MUSEUM, 1940)

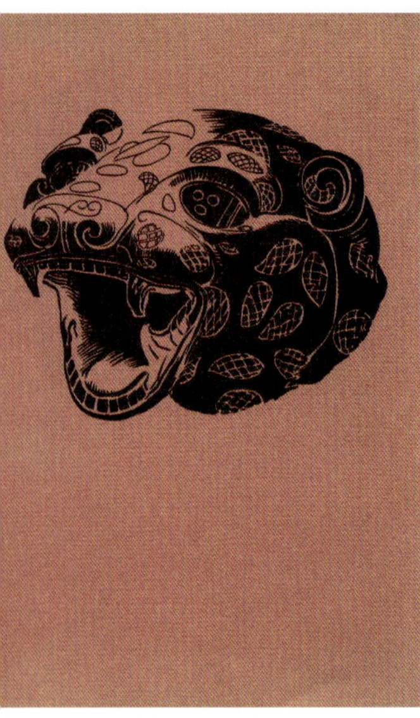

> art. It was the "discovery" of this art of simple people that helped bring about the modern Renaissance, just as the rediscovery of the art of Greece and Rome was a primal cause of the Italian Renaissance in the fourteenth or fifteenth century.... This desire to return to the simplicity of life...to the original vision, as it were... has perpetrated the creative urge of our time.[191]

Price and the Arensbergs seem to have had similar aesthetic sensibilities. This is illustrated, for example, by Price's assertion in *I Like What I Know* that a particular rough stone piece (albeit one from Costa Rica, not central Mexico) was pleasing because it was "carved in volcanic stone, giving it a lively surface texture in contrast to its massive, sit-down weight."[192] Price's writing perhaps provides some insight into why the Arensbergs made certain choices, given how little they said about their own collection of less conventionally beautiful works.

On the other side of the country, and at the opposite end of the aesthetic spectrum, was Walter's Harvard classmate Robert Woods Bliss, whose standards for objects were exacting—he only bought highly finished and largely complete pieces. In 1946, for example, Bliss returned photographs Stendahl had sent him of three works for sale; he told Stendahl that none of them tempted him and explained why:

> The bas relief (no. 2728) is a stone of much interest archaeologically, I should think, although it is much worn and the human figure is incomplete. Some day I shall hope to see it in a museum. You have never yet shown me a [ceramic West Mexican] dog which I want, and so the photograph goes back to you! The palma is not, I fear, up to my standard, nor does no. 2168 ["an important piece—human head in mouth of frog—Toltec"] appeal to me for my purposes.[193]

Although Bliss lived primarily in Washington, DC, he formed a great friendship with the Arensbergs, which seems to have been cemented between mid-1941 and May 1942, when Bliss and his wife, Mildred, lived in California.[194] Though he had previously been much more dependent on Brummer and European dealers, Bliss made Stendahl one of his primary conduits for acquiring art beginning at this time. The Arensbergs also seem to have seen Bliss as a resource for puzzling out the details of bequeathing their collection to an appropriate institution for posterity. In April 1939, as they were becoming preoccupied with the disposition of their collection, Walter wrote to Bliss, "I feel sure from what I hear vaguely of your own project in connection with Dumbarton Oaks that you must already know many of the answers for which I am still seeking."[195]

In the 1940s, works from the Arensbergs' pre-Columbian collection were being requested for various exhibitions, just as their modernist works had been for years. They lent a mask in 1940 to the *Pre-Columbian Art* show at Harvard's Fogg Art Museum, where the work was exhibited as fine art rather than a primitive curiosity. (The exhibition catalog [fig. 38] can be seen sitting atop a stool in plate 45.)[196] Soon afterward, Bliss was instrumental in encouraging the Arensbergs to loan many works from their collection to the exhibition *Ancient American Art*, which was held from April to June 1942 at the Santa Barbara Museum of Art (fig. 39). Bliss, who was eager to show the major collection he was forming at the time, was the largest lender by far to this show, contributing some sixty-two works; the Arensbergs lent thirty-eight pieces from their collection, including some larger stone works that would have been very difficult for Bliss to send from the East Coast.[197] Seven of the thirty-eight were shown when the exhibition traveled (at a reduced size) to San Francisco's de Young Museum later that year.[198] In 1943, the Pasadena Art Institute held an exhibition, *Latin American Art through 1000 Years*, featuring many works from the Arensbergs' collection, particularly a stone

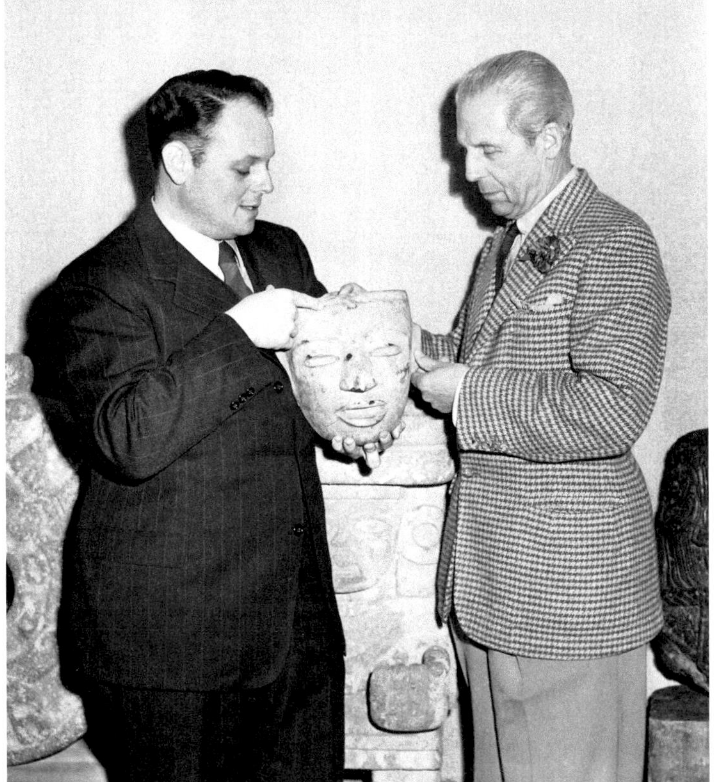

39. CURATOR MAURICE RIES (LEFT) AND ROBERT WOODS BLISS AT THE 1942 SANTA BARBARA EXHIBIT, EXAMINING A TEOTIHUACAN MASK THAT BLISS ACQUIRED IN 1940. BEHIND THEM ARE THREE LARGE-SCALE WORKS FROM THE ARENSBERG COLLECTION (LEFT TO RIGHT): AZTEC BALLCOURT RING (PMA 1950-134-225; SEE PLATE 2.4), TEOTIHUACAN GODDESS FIGURE (PMA 1950-134-282; SEE PLATE 3.34, AMONG MANY VIEWS), AND AZTEC FIGURE (PMA 1950-134-251; SEE PLATE 35.3). HARVARD UNIVERSITY ARCHIVES, HUGFP 76.74, BOX 15, OLVWORK373099

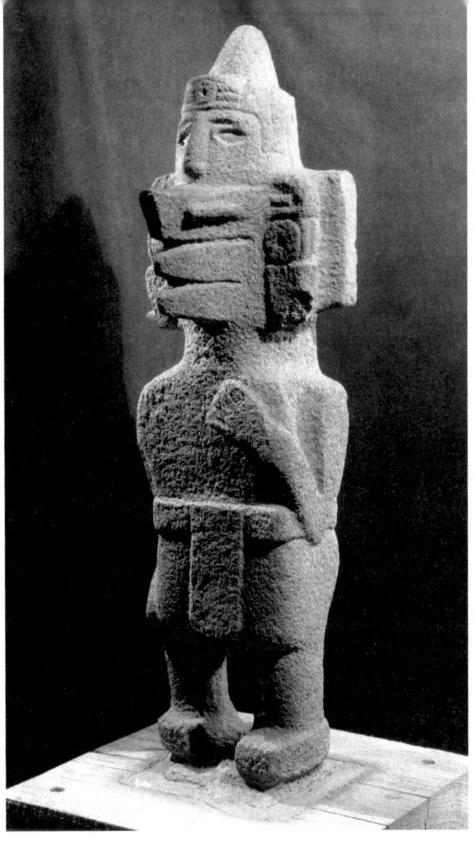

40. *AZTEC (CENTRAL MEXICO). WIND GOD (EHECATL), 1300–1520. VOLCANIC ROCK, 103.5 × 30.5 × 32.4 CM. PHILADELPHIA MUSEUM OF ART, THE LOUISE AND WALTER ARENSBERG COLLECTION, 1950-134-253

sculpture of Ehecatl, the Aztec wind god, which was described as "dominating the pre-Columbian room" at the exhibition (fig. 40).[199] Though that exhibition was a blockbuster, estimated to have attracted seven thousand visitors in seven weeks, the Arensbergs were very upset over the inclusion of some works they judged to be fakes.[200] Walter wrote a sternly worded rebuke to the Pasadena Art Institute's director, insisting that the works' "presence is a contamination, and for the sake of the reputation of the Institute and out of respect for the genuine materials which your friends have contributed, they should be removed."[201]

Bliss and Walter may have occasionally collaborated to acquire works of the highest quality. One of Stendahl's 1941 invoices reveals that they provided funds for the dealer, who was apparently short of cash, to bring a shipment of pre-Columbian works from Mexico or points south. Bliss and Walter each advanced Stendahl $3,000 to purchase works for them, paid $100 for his travel expenses, and agreed to pay a 20 percent commission above Stendahl's cost for the works.[202] Upon the dealer's return, each collector was able to choose from his finds, in an alternating fashion, rather like a draft pick of art objects.[203] Though the two men had very different aesthetics in their collections, they seem to have competed for artworks on a few occasions. (Soon after Bliss began to purchase from Stendahl, Echániz urged the dealer to create competition between Bliss and Walter in order to command the highest possible prices for his merchandise.)[204] And perhaps because he usually sought to negotiate over price, Walter sometimes lost out to Bliss. In 1941, for example, Bliss bought a Teotihuacan mural fragment that Walter wanted. Walter probably balked at the generally high cost of these works, which were difficult to export easily from Mexico.[205]

One point of difference between the Arensbergs and their peers Bliss, Price, and Macgowan (as well as other friends and collectors of Southern California) is that the couple never traveled to any of the countries from which their pre-Columbian objects originated. In contrast, Price, writing about the importance of his experiences in Mexico and Central America, said, "One day I quietly decided to go deeper into Mexico and see for myself. Stendahl's storerooms had convinced me that Mexico must be one of the most provocative countries in the world, inhabited by one of the most versatile, art-producing people who ever lived."[206]

The Arensbergs received many invitations to visit Mexico, both from the Mexican government when it courted the couple for the donation of their collection to the Instituto Nacional de Bellas Artes and from many of their friends.[207] Roberto Montenegro, the architect Juan O'Gorman, and the author Frances Toor (who had written a popular guidebook on touring Mexico, *Mexican Folkways*) tried many times to convince the Arensbergs to travel south of the border.[208] However, Louise was afraid of flying and both she and Walter suffered from ill health, which made traveling difficult, especially in later years. It is also possible that the Arensbergs' lack of any firsthand knowledge of contemporary Mexican reality was purposeful, allowing them to construct their own fantasy of ancient Mexico. Their home was a refuge, one in which they had created a whole imagined world for themselves; to link the remains of ancient Mexico that populated their house with the experience of the real country might have ruined the enigmatic qualities of the art they owned.

While the Arensbergs never visited Latin America, they were surrounded by artists, scholars, design, and objects from the region. Their friendships and alliances were formed against a backdrop of intensifying pan-American cooperation that quickly waned after World War II. In the late 1930s and early 1940s, the United States, concerned about rising fascism in Europe, used soft power and cultural diplomacy to draw closer to Latin America, especially Mexico. Many exhibitions, such as MoMA's 1940 show *Twenty Centuries of Mexican Art*, were organized or cosponsored by governmental bodies.[209] However, pan-Americanism in the years prior to World War II was not just an official policy but a lived reality for many in the United States: people across the country had unprecedented opportunities to read books and magazines, listen to radio shows, and watch movies inspired by Latin American themes.[210] The Arensbergs, with their neighbors and friends, took this vogue for all things Mexican to the extreme—debating the controversial murals painted by Siqueiros and Orozco in and around Los Angeles, attending cocktail parties with the likes of Dolores del Río and Diego Rivera, and spending large amounts of discretionary income on pre-Columbian art.

1937–45: WORKS COLLECTED

After 1937, the Arensbergs bought modernist works sparingly but were seemingly delighted by the novelty of their pre-Columbian collecting. The ancient American objects they acquired probably gained importance in their minds slowly; in 1940, Walter told an acquaintance, "In spite of my good resolutions, [I have] gone off the deep end in purchasing some pre-Columbian stones," a reference whose phrasing is not particularly complimentary.[211] However, the couple continued their purchases in this area, acquiring the great bulk of their pre-Columbian objects between 1937 and 1945, purchasing about 260 works during these eight years for a total of over $60,000 (more than a million dollars today, accounting for inflation).[212] The number of works purchased and dollars spent per year fluctuated wildly in the early 1940s, from a high of 81 objects totaling about $23,500 in 1941, to just 8 works purchased in 1943 for a total of $1,350.[213] During this period, the Arensbergs also began collecting Native American works with greater frequency and discrimination as well, acquiring some 80 pieces by the time they died.[214]

The non-Western portion of the Arensberg art collection is extraordinary not only for its scale but also for the breadth of objects and aesthetics that it encompasses. It includes pre-Columbian works from Mexico, Central America, and Peru, as well as African, Native American, Chinese, and colonial Latin American works. The pre-Columbian collection includes at least a few high-quality, representative works from each of the major civilizations and regions of Mesoamerica: Maya, Mezcala, Mixtec, Olmec, Teotihuacan, Toltec, Veracruz, West Mexican, Zapotec, and, of course, Aztec. While Arensberg was described by Stendahl as preferring rough stones—and indeed, the couple purchased an unprecedented number of sculptures in basalt, often in large format—they also purchased quite a few ceramics, some polished stone works, a handful of metal objects, and a few Peruvian textile fragments.[215]

Where some stone works, like the palmas, verged on being as abstract as the couple's favorite Brancusi sculptures, others, elaborately glyph-covered, seemed to vibrate in the same way their many cubist paintings did. Many of these palmas from Veracruz can be seen throughout the Arensberg home. So named because early archaeologists thought their shape recalled the form of a palm frond, the palmas tend to have an upswept paddle form, with graceful squared or rounded lines at the top that taper near the bottom. Usually there is a specific organic form, often a bird or animal, portrayed on the front of the statues.[216] Many collectors seemed to instinctively appreciate them—Stendahl told Echániz regarding acquisitions that "if you can get ahold of any palma it would be swell."[217] The Arensbergs owned at least ten palmas, including the alligator they bought from Brummer in 1937 (see plate 47.31); there were also three depicting birds (see plates 48.7, 56.5, and one not pictured [PMA 1950-134-375]), two with skeletal or supernatural figures (see plates 2.10, 14.9), one with a man's face (see plate 13.11), and one showing a tied bundle of reeds (see plates 5.7, 18.12). Although abstract palmas decorated only by the graceful lines of the stone are less common, the Arensbergs sought these out, buying two (see figs. 7, 8). (They may have been inspired by their visits to the Metropolitan Museum of Art years before—at least one similarly abstract statue was part of the Petich collection there.)[218] It seems likely that the Arensbergs felt these simplified palmas resonated formally with some of their Brancusi sculptures, which Walter, in a 1949 article, described to Jules Langsner as exemplifying the Platonic ideal of form.[219]

Photographs make clear that palmas were displayed in various rooms: in the foyer (see plate 2.6), below the mantelpiece in their living room (see plates 5.7, 5.10), on the mantelpiece in the dining room (see plate 14.9), and on the night table in the guest bedroom (see plate 56.5). Although we now know that palmas were sometimes worn on the belts, or yokes, of players in rituals related to the ceremonial ballgame, their function was unknown when the Arensbergs collected them. Over time, the couple purchased a large number of other stone works from Veracruz, now also thought to have been related to the ballgame, such as *hachas* (axes) and *yugos* (yokes).[220] Iconography-laden yokes were sometimes particularly expensive. In 1940, for example, the Arensbergs spent $900 for one they displayed on a low table on the second-floor landing (see plate 39.5); perhaps the couple felt that the mystery of the yoke's function warranted their purchase.[221] One of the few early catalogs to feature such paraphernalia—although without offering a full explanation of their purpose—accompanied the exhibition *Twenty Centuries of Mexican Art* at MoMA, in 1940. Alfonso Caso, curator of the exhibition's pre-Columbian section, said the creators of these works were "more skillful than any others in carving basalt and other hard stones."[222] In the catalog, the Arensbergs would have learned that yokes, at least in some cases, were placed in tombs around the heads of the dead. The catalog also included a palma depicting bound reeds, very similar to the one they later bought (see plate 5.7).[223]

Another object type illustrated in the *Twenty Centuries* catalog, undoubtedly of great interest to the Arensbergs, was the stone mask of Teotihuacan. Today there are still few definite explanations of its use or meaning.[224] As they did with the palmas, Louise and Walter purchased many similar examples of the mask, buying about a dozen of them over the years.[225] Two are shown together on top of Louise's piano in the living room, displayed with masks from other regions of Mexico and one from Africa (see plate 34). Perhaps these masks were presented together because of their similar squared forms; they seem to have afforded the Arensbergs the pleasure that comes from closely observing small differences among a group of similar works. (This is also a tactic of the museum curator: to invite sustained contemplation by filling a case with similar things.)[226] The Arensbergs must have understood, innately or through practice, how an archetypal grouping—in this example, of square-faced masks with nonnaturalistic features—could effectively enhance the experience of viewing them by calling attention to differences of material, greater or lesser definition of line, and the widening or narrowing of facial features such as the nose and mouth. In general, masks and

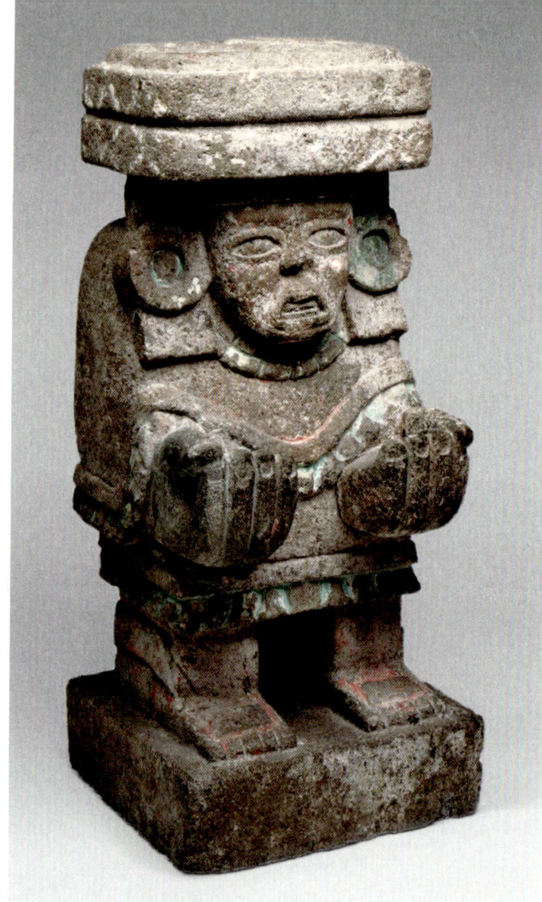

41. TEOTIHUACAN (CENTRAL MEXICO). GODDESS FIGURE, 100–650. VOLCANIC STONE WITH TRACES OF PIGMENT, 92.1 × 41.3 × 40.6 CM. PHILADELPHIA MUSEUM OF ART, THE LOUISE AND WALTER ARENSBERG COLLECTION, 1950-134-282. SEE ALSO PLATE 5.6

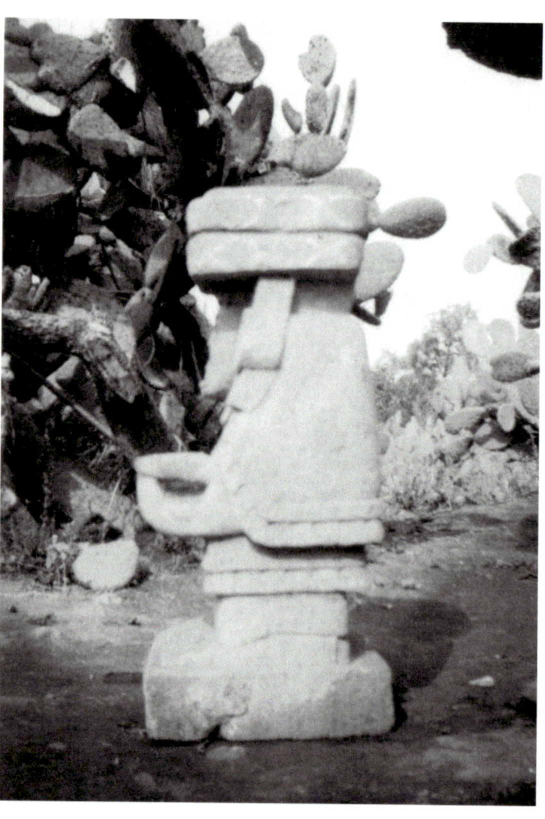

42. THE GODDESS FIGURE IN A MEXICAN LANDSCAPE WITH CACTI. FROM THE PRIVATE COLLECTION OF MIGUEL COVARRUBIAS, CA. LATE 1930S. PHOTOGRAPHER UNKNOWN. ARCHIVO MIGUEL COVARRUBIAS. SALA DE ARCHIVOS Y COLECCIONES ESPECIALES, DIRECCIÓN DE BIBLIOTECAS, UNIVERSIDAD DE LAS AMÉRICAS PUEBLA

masklike faces were a major preoccupation of the Arensbergs. The purpose of a mask in traditional societies is to disguise or completely transform its wearer, and perhaps the Arensbergs saw in these works a fascinating image of transformation.[227] Probably encouraged in this interest by Macgowan and possibly by Montenegro, both of whom had written entire books on masks, the Arensbergs owned nearly thirty pre-Columbian masks and "face panels," dozens of representations of heads, and many more objects whose faces seem to be looking directly at the viewer.

Also purportedly originating from the central Mexican site of Teotihuacan, as many of the masks did, was a medium-format stone figure depicting a goddess, which was displayed at the center of the Arensberg home by the hearth (fig. 41). This was probably the "large Toltec stone figure" sold to the couple for $2,500 by Stendahl in November 1940, fairly soon after the Arensbergs' return to collecting.[228] It seems to have been acquired from Echániz shortly before its sale.[229] The goddess is similar to, but much smaller than, a monumental figure of a deity from Teotihuacan, which the Arensbergs would have known through illustrations in books. (The original is also visible at Mexico's Museo Nacional; see fig. 15.)[230] The statue was exceptionally striking and clearly important to the Arensbergs, given its central placement in their living room. It may have been offered to buyers in Mexico prior to being brought to the United States: a photograph of the work outdoors in a landscape with cacti is in the archives of the Mexican artist and collector Miguel Covarrubias (fig. 42). The goddess, noteworthy for having small remnants of red and green stucco on it, would have seemed to be a rare prize when considered against the generally gray and brown palette of rough stones. Its large hands, disproportionate to the rest of the figure, extend out toward the viewer, adding great visual interest to a piece mostly worked in flat planes of low relief. However, the three-dimensionality of this detail is also unusual in the corpus of Teotihuacan sculpture. The figure's authenticity

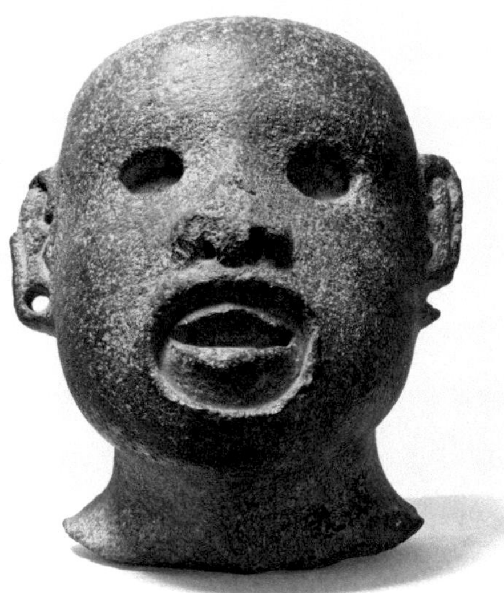

43. AZTEC (CENTRAL MEXICO). HEAD OF FERTILITY GOD / OUR LORD THE FLAYED ONE (XIPE TOTEC), 1300–1520. BASALTIC ROCK, 21.6 × 17.8 × 19.1 CM. PHILADELPHIA MUSEUM OF ART, THE LOUISE AND WALTER ARENSBERG COLLECTION, 1950-134-296. SEE ALSO PLATE 22.9

has been questioned in recent years, but recent excavations at the site have revealed that Teotihuacan's material culture may have been much more diverse than scholars have realized.[231]

Another recognizable deity of central Mexico found in the Arensberg collection was the god Xipe Totec (Our Lord the Flayed One).[232] Symbolizing the sprouting of green shoots from decayed kernels of corn that had been planted in the ground, Xipe was embodied on earth by priests who would sacrifice a human victim, strip off his or her skin, and then wear it as a kind of costume until it rotted off. Patron god of goldsmiths, Xipe is discussed at length in some colonial manuscripts, such as the Florentine Codex, to which at least Macgowan seems to have had access.[233] Xipe is depicted most frequently in the rough stone sculptures of the Aztecs but seems to be a god of great antiquity whose representations appear in many cultures. Two ceramic effigy vessels from the Zapotec culture of southern Mexico depicting Xipe were included, for example, in the *Twenty Centuries* catalog.[234] Montenegro may have discussed the deity with the Arensbergs; shortly after his stay with them, in 1939, the Mexican artist painted a work titled *Síntesis* (Synthesis) that includes what may be a Gulf Coast–style figure of Xipe, depicted above a scene of death and destruction.[235] Montenegro returned to the theme more directly in 1952, producing a series of haunting prints where a man looks poignantly out at viewers from behind a mask of skin.[236] While some images of Xipe are ambiguous or hard to identify, the Arensbergs owned at least one that clearly shows a mask of skin on a human head (fig. 43). (Stendahl, of course, embellished this, calling it the head of a "high priest.")[237] This likely interest in Xipe may have been part of a larger fascination for figures in transformation that is still prevalent among many collectors of pre-Columbian art.[238]

A preference that has endured since the 1920s among collectors of pre-Columbian art is one for West Mexican ceramics. Alfonso Caso has written that pre-Columbian art in general has a "strong religious and even hieratic nature," but these works run completely counter to that characterization, offering a seemingly light and happy vision of paired couples with children, dogs and other animals, and small scenes of village life (three can be seen in plate 40).[239] Ceramics of this type were characteristic of most California collections of pre-Columbian art starting in the late 1930s, as they were not expensive compared to other objects, amply available at Stendahl's shop, and probably sold at many other venues as well (fig. 44). Although the Arensbergs usually opted for more intellectually stimulating works, they succumbed to the charms of these ceramics in the same way their friends did. They bought several red ceramic dogs from Colima (see plate 58.4, for example), which often functioned as vessels as well as sculpture. They also purchased exuberant, adorned women and men from Nayarit. However, the couple did not own any of a very common variety, those depicting mothers with children.[240]

West Mexican ceramics are often some of the most reconstructed or over-restored creations of the pre-Columbian world. These figures are mostly found in groups, often in underground shaft tombs. At the time the Arensbergs were collecting, the antiquity of the works was unknown, but they can now be dated to circa

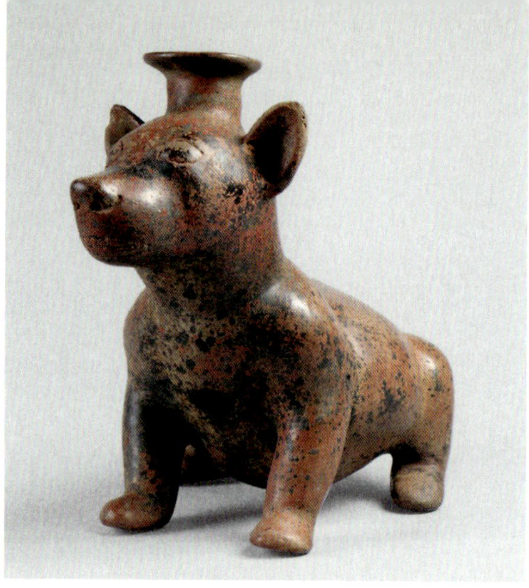

44. COLIMA (WESTERN MEXICO). VESSEL IN THE FORM OF A DOG, 300 BCE–300 CE. CLAY, 35.6 × 27.9 CM. PHILADELPHIA MUSEUM OF ART, THE LOUISE AND WALTER ARENSBERG COLLECTION, 1950-134-329. SEE ALSO PLATE 47.18

300 BCE–300 CE. Since they are often found in assemblage, made of the same clay and fired at the same time, many works from a grouping typically have the same color and texture. Even if these ceramic statues were broken in pieces when shipped over long distances from small towns in Mexico to cities in the United States, the many fragments could be reassembled or reconfigured by art dealers like Stendahl. Dealers might have joined the best-preserved head to the most complete body, for example, and embellished the finished piece with extra detailing. With a little wet clay and a good eye for mixing paint, they could create an impressive and seemingly well-preserved figure, such as the seated man holding a sphere from Nayarit (see plate 34.6). On closer inspection, this work—which is very similar to others in major American art museums that originally came from Stendahl—has been repaired and may have originally looked very different.[241] Stendahl was very proud of his capacities for restoration, documented in a 1955 article from the *Los Angeles Times*, when reporter Bill Henry visited him. Henry wrote, "Since much of this ancient stuff comes to him in bits and pieces, cracked and broken by the ravages of time, Stendahl has had to develop not only perception and patience to pick out the matching fragments but an amazing technical skill at putting them back together."[242]

1945–51: PRE-COLUMBIAN COMES INTO ITS OWN IN THE COLLECTION

Like many avid collectors, and perhaps due to their friendship with Quinn, whose collection had been posthumously dispersed, the Arensbergs were deeply concerned about securing a permanent home for their collection, even signing a deed of gift and approving a tentative set of architectural plans for a separate gallery to display their art at UCLA in 1940—a plan that ultimately failed. However, they vacillated to an unusual degree, entertaining inquiries from more than thirty institutions, including major museums; several universities; and the government of Mexico, through its cultural arm, the Instituto Nacional de Bellas Artes (INBA). The institute's representative, the musician and ethnomusicologist Carlos Chávez (a close colleague of Montenegro's), visited the Arensbergs in 1950 to urge them to consider donating their collection to the INBA. Chávez, fluent in English and a celebrity in his own right, was a shrewd choice of emissary to negotiate the Mexican proposal because he was a member of the musical avant-garde and fully engaged with the pre-Columbian world.[243]

Chávez invited the Arensbergs to visit Mexico so they could explore the possibility of leaving the collection to the Museo Nacional, where their pre-Columbian holdings could be displayed alongside the greatest works of their kind. He noted that "if your [modern] collection would eventually be donated to Mexico it will be the first such collection that we would have and we all think it would create not only great interest but real sensation and furore."[244] The Arensbergs cautiously expressed to Chávez their desire "to give expression to [their] profound reverence for pre-Columbian art."[245] Thus, they couched their ultimate rejection in terms of the difficulties of leaving a predominantly English library dedicated to Francis Bacon to an institution in Mexico City, but it is more likely that they were uncomfortable with their collection leaving the United States.[246]

Another strong contender was the Art Institute of Chicago. The couple were initially entranced by Daniel Catton Rich, the museum's director of fine arts, and his curator Katharine Kuh, who first visited California in 1945. After seeing their holdings, Rich wrote to the couple that their pre-Columbian collection "deserves intense study.... I am more and more certain that for us these objects have the liberating and inspiring power that classic art had for the Renaissance."[247] Walter enjoyed this turn of phrase so much that he repeated it in a letter to his friend and fellow collector Ruth Maitland.[248]

What soured the Art Institute's relationship with the Arensbergs was, in part, Rich's and Kuh's lack of sensitivity to the couple's aspirations for the ancient American part of their collection. Kuh believed there were many fakes among these objects, and later recalled that

> I didn't want to take the pre-Columbian works for the Art Institute and I refused. I said that I didn't know enough about them, which I didn't, and that this wasn't my field and I didn't know how to handle it. Walter wanted the exhibition to be seen just as it was in his home.[249]

In spite of these difficulties, about forty-five pre-Columbian works were initially selected by Kuh for a show to be held at the Art Institute in late 1949. Tatiana Proskouriakoff of Harvard University, a well-respected Mayanist, was chosen to catalog the pre-Columbian section.[250] However, the Art Institute, somewhat hostile to the inclusion of these works in the show (and well aware that the Arensbergs were still being courted by other institutions), did not allocate ample resources for this exhibition. The couple, likely eager for a fresh scholarly perspective on their collection, were enthusiastic about the prospect of having someone as well regarded as Proskouriakoff catalog all of the approximately three hundred major pre-Columbian works in their collection. But the museum declined to cover the full cost of this work, offering instead to pay "for a sixth or a seventh of the total expenses involved," since so few works were to come to Chicago; they also asked to reduce the number of works in the show, to fewer than forty-three.[251]

Walter responded angrily:

> This is a reduction in an original selection which was itself a very drastic reduction, and which was never really satisfactory to us. Your first selection excluded...many of the pieces which we considered of first rate importance.... We have therefore come to the decision to confine our loan to the art from the twentieth century.[252]

While the exhibition did take place, in October–December 1949, the Arensbergs were displeased with its presentation and felt that the Art Institute showed a lack of respect for their wishes with regard to the ancient American works. Needless to say, Kuh and Rich did not win the collection for Chicago.[253]

However, for the Arensbergs, the experience of sending away the modernist paintings allowed them to see their art in new ways. In 1950, Walter wrote the following to Duchamp about their collection as it had been displayed in the house:

> [It] was a very exciting experience for us for many years, because it created so many interesting juxtapositions.... But we came to feel, at the time of the Chicago exhibition, when the paintings were all out of the house, that the [pre-Columbian] sculpture that remained in solitary possession became much more impressive, and actually filled in all the space that the paintings had left empty. In a sense, we were actually...seeing the sculpture for the first time.[254]

In addition, this fresh perspective convinced the couple that their collection did not need to be displayed in its entirety as it had been in their house and "should be shown in the museum in a separate gallery."[255] At the same time as they were reevaluating their collection, Fiske Kimball, director of the Philadelphia Museum of Art, was courting the Arensbergs. Although he was not particularly enthusiastic about pre-Columbian sculpture, he wanted the modern works badly enough to embrace all parts of their collection.[256] In February 1949, a few months before the modernist paintings were to go to the Art Institute, Kimball visited the Arensbergs in Los Angeles. Kimball was trained as a draftsman and architect, and one of his strengths was his ability to visualize and sketch out a gallery in detail. He discussed with the couple how Philadelphia might show their collection and whether Walter would "be content to put the pre-Columbian stuff elsewhere in the building to gain more space. Yes, he would. I suggested somewhere in the central section of the building, between the Gothic, when America was unknown, and the Renaissance, when it was discovered.... He liked this scheme."[257]

Kimball's reference to the pre-Columbian sculpture as "stuff" rather than art and his immediate need to classify it in a chronological scheme give a sense of Kimball's incomprehension of the works he was requesting. However, the Arensbergs' requirement that these works be displayed to confirm their importance demanded a diplomatic touch from Kimball. Later, in a letter to Sturgis Ingersoll, president of the Philadelphia Museum of Art's board, Kimball confirmed the placement of pre-Columbian art at the museum and wrote, "[Walter] particularly liked putting this stuff in the center after it has been so long (and still in Chicago and New York) been regarded as not art at all."[258]

By 1950, the Arensbergs, long plagued by bad health, knew that time was running out and decided to entrust their collection to Kimball and Philadelphia. At the museum, the pre-Columbian collection was divided into two categories: those works deemed by the institution to be of sufficient quality for showing in the museum (the display collection); and a study collection including works of lower aesthetic or historical value, or of doubtful authenticity.[259] Of the 208 works in the display collection, 197 were cataloged and illustrated in a 1954 catalog authored by George Kubler, a well-respected professor of art history at Yale University.[260] The great majority were from Mesoamerica, Kubler's specialty, which encompasses much of today's Mexico, Guatemala, and Belize, and parts of Honduras and El Salvador.[261] Today the catalog has some limitations from a scholarly point of view, in part because so much time has elapsed since its publication; many major advances have been made in the field due to archaeological finds and the development of Maya epigraphy.

LOS ANGELES 1948–51: ACQUISITION OF FINAL MASTERWORKS

Even as they struggled to coordinate final details for the disposition of their collection, from 1949 until about 1951, the Arensbergs were coming to terms with what their pre-Columbian works meant to them. Surprisingly, they made quite a few purchases of major works they had been interested in acquiring for years, sometimes decades, even as the agreement they had negotiated with the Philadelphia Museum of Art was being finalized. In about 1951, Walter told Kenneth Ross, director of Los Angeles's Municipal Arts Department, that

> the interest in pre-Columbian in the first place is to show that there is a culture that at least holds its own and possibly outranks the other cultures of antiquity. Before our time it was never recognized as art. Now it may outrank all other cultures. It is certainly the most mysterious.[262]

Ross's interview with Walter succinctly expresses the attraction the Arensbergs felt for this art, and Walter claimed that they "began to collect pre-Columbian stuff almost as soon as we began to collect paint-

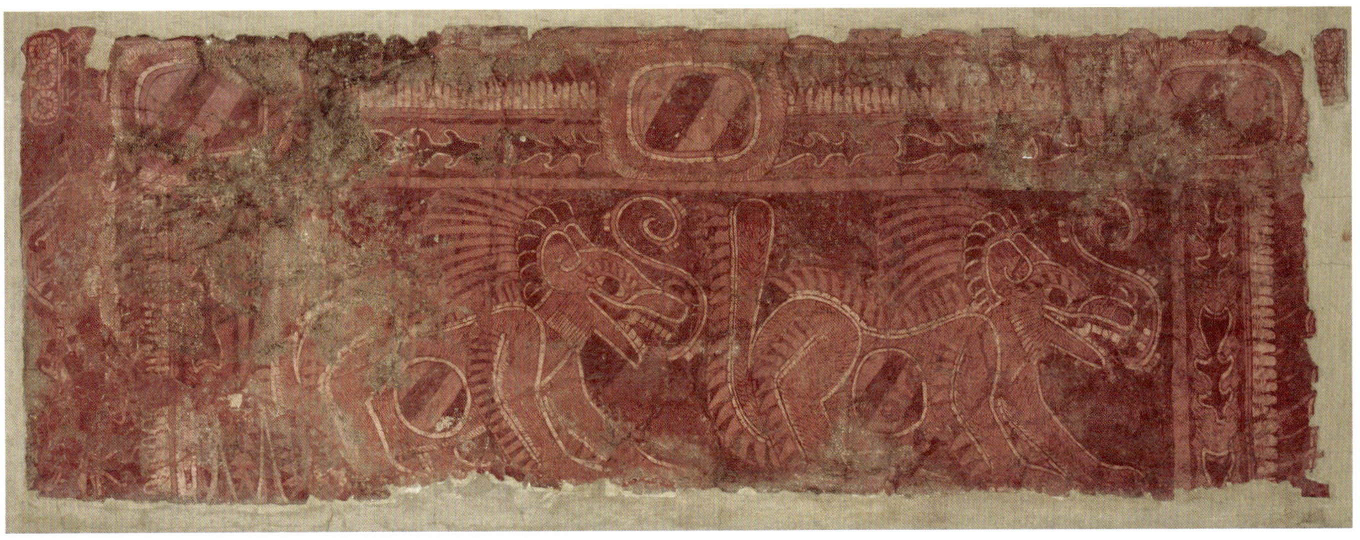

45. TEOTIHUACAN (CENTRAL MEXICO). FRESCO, 100–650. 73.7 × 198.1 CM. PHILADELPHIA MUSEUM OF ART, THE LOUISE AND WALTER ARENSBERG COLLECTION, 1950-134-404

ings, way back in the teens."[263] A bit of revisionist history, but it suggests that by this point, the Arensbergs felt they needed to generate a creation myth for their love of ancient American works.

The works the Arensbergs purchased late in life were of the highest quality. The couple committed to acquiring only the finest works they could find, as their friend John Quinn had done many years earlier when he realized that his illness would be terminal. This seems to be a tacit acknowledgment on the Arensbergs' part that their collection's future had been mostly secured and their money would not have to sustain the couple much longer. They probably found great joy in purchasing grand works they had admired for years.

One of the first and most significant works purchased from Stendahl with this new mindset was a fragment of a mural painted in the fresco technique, from the central Mexican site of Teotihuacan, for which they paid $5,000 in 1950 (fig. 45).[264] It was very slightly smaller, less well preserved, and simpler in its imagery and color scheme than the example that Bliss was able to buy from Stendahl in 1941.[265]

By 1950, extensive excavations were under way at Teotihuacan, and the Arensbergs would have been able to learn more about this exceptional place in the pre-Columbian Americas, famed for its enormous population (perhaps as large as 125,000 at the civilization's height). The city's people had lived in large multifamily dwellings of one or two stories in height, featuring stucco walls often painted with elaborate murals. When the city was abandoned circa 650 CE, the homes fell into disuse and their walls broke into pieces.

The Arensbergs' fragment—larger than many other known examples—comes from the residential complex known as Atetelco, to the west of the city's ceremonial center.[266] The mural shows two jaguars strutting across a landscape, eating or carrying stylized human hearts in their mouths. Scrolls, indicating speech, song, or communication, emanate from their jaws. The work was probably painted fairly late in the chronology of Teotihuacan (350–550 CE), and its subject matter reflects what may have been a trend toward militarization as the city passed its apogee and went into decline. The complex began to be excavated by archaeologists affiliated with the government of Mexico in the mid-1940s; because it was an uncovered site, many fragments were removed during these years. A few years after seeing the Arensbergs' fragment at their house, journalist César Lizardi Ramos wrote an article on the occasion of Mexico's hosting the Congress of Americanists in 1962, describing the Arensbergs' fragment and noting that he had been able to identify the person—a sculptor he described only as a foreigner—who was hired to remove this fragment from the wall at the site.[267] Lizardi Ramos reported that the sculptor said he wanted nothing more to do with looting after this episode. The fragment presumably went through Echániz's hands to Stendahl. A photograph of Stendahl's gallery taken circa 1948 shows another mural section for sale on the back wall, indicating that Stendahl had an effective network for obtaining such prizes (fig. 46).[268] Many like these were smuggled out

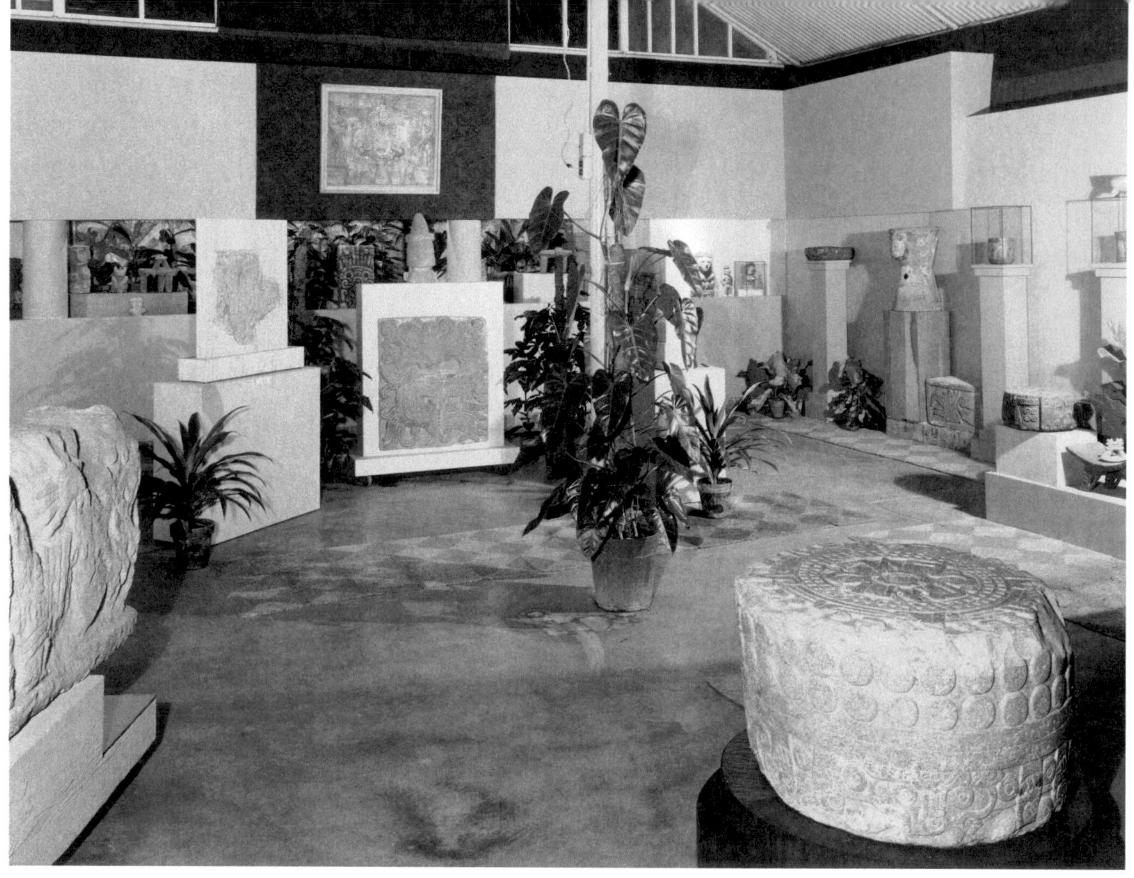

46. FLOYD FAXON. A STENDAHL GALLERIES DISPLAY OF PRE-COLUMBIAN ART, CA. 1948, SHOWING A TEOTIHUACAN MURAL FRAGMENT DISPLAYED AGAINST THE BLACK PANEL ON THE BACK WALL, CENTER; AND THE ARENSBERGS' CALENDAR STONE IN THE FOREGROUND, RIGHT (SEE FIG. 47). A NUMBER OF OTHER WORKS PURCHASED BY THE ARENSBERGS ARE VISIBLE IN THE IMAGE. COURTESY OF APRIL DAMMANN AND ANGEL CITY PRESS

of Mexico before the 1970s, when the United States and other countries became more stringent about prohibiting their import.[269]

Another of the Arensbergs' most cherished works was the calendar stone that they also bought from Stendahl in 1950 (fig. 47). They arranged to purchase it for the astounding price of $20,000 (over $210,000 adjusted for inflation), paying in yearly installments of $5,000, beginning in January 1951.[270] This was almost certainly the highest price they paid for any single work in their collection at any time, and it leaves no doubt that by the end of their lives, they took ancient American art very seriously. It ultimately became one of the highlights of the installation of their collection at the Philadelphia Museum of Art (see Sherman and Nelson, fig. 57, showing calendar stone in background).

Like the Quetzalcoatl statue (see fig. 22a), the calendar stone is not a unique genre of object. It is a smaller, simpler, yet more luxurious iteration of what is probably the most famous pre-Columbian object in the world: the monumental calendar stone that is today displayed in the Museo Nacional de Antropología e Historia in Mexico City. This work can be seen in Mexico printed on everything from T-shirts and postcards to coffee mugs and keychains. It has come to represent Mexican national identity in a general way, although most people are not familiar with the precise meanings of its symbols. Having returned home from Los Angeles, Lizardi Ramos wrote a detailed letter to the Arensbergs, explaining the significance of the stone and including a diagram of its parts, for which they thanked him profusely.[271]

The INAH stone is made of volcanic basalt, plentiful in the region and the most common material used to create Aztec sculpture. The Arensbergs' work, by contrast, is carved from a greenish stone—possibly igneous rock—and was polished after being carved. This material was much harder to work than basalt and infinitely more precious to the Aztecs. Their preference for greenstone over other materials, even gold, was so strong that they were said to have willingly traded golden objects for cheap green glass beads when the Spanish invaded in 1519.[272]

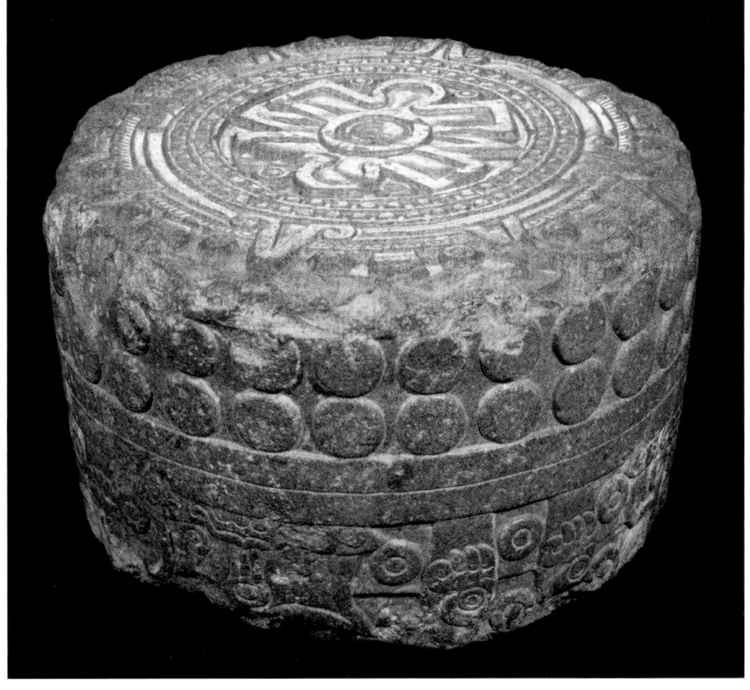

47. AZTEC (CENTRAL MEXICO). CALENDAR STONE, 1400–1520. GREEN IGNEOUS ROCK, 49.5 × 83.8 CM. PHILADELPHIA MUSEUM OF ART, THE LOUISE AND WALTER ARENSBERG COLLECTION, 1950-134-403

Like the "phallic" Huastec figure, the stone acquired additional cachet from Stendahl's inventive marketing. He conveyed a highly speculative—and, in retrospect, quite amusing—provenance for this work to potential buyers, including the Arensbergs and Robert Woods Bliss. In Stendahl's legend, the stone was "used on [the] main pyramid in Mexico City and damaged by Spaniards when rolled down the staircase."[273] The Arensbergs believed this story; it was passed on to the Philadelphia Museum of Art on the index cards they used to inventory their works. Suffice to say, the damage to the work would have been far more extensive if it had, in fact, been rolled down an enormous flight of stone steps. Stendahl purchased the object, which he called "the most important stone in these United States," in January 1944, and first tried to sell it to Robert Woods Bliss. He told Bliss, "[My] price to a museum would be about $20,000. My price to you is $15,000. I am not offering it for sale locally." Stendahl continued, with some condescension, "Charles Laughton is now a collector, and [Walter] Arensberg's mouth is watering, but he is not in [a] posi tion to handle a piece of this importance."[274] However, it took Stendahl years to sell the work, during which time he installed it as a showpiece, first in his garden and then in his gallery (see fig. 46).[275] In an earlier letter of late 1943, Stendahl told Bliss that the work "was brought to this country many years ago into the port of New Orleans and has been in a family of minor importance until a few years ago."[276] It seems very possible that this was part of the collection imported by the Mexican government to be shown at the World's Industrial and Cotton Centennial of 1884, held in New Orleans. Mexico's pavilion was touted as one of the fair's most elaborate and successful exhibits, and it definitely included pre-Columbian works.[277] According to the art historian Mary Miller, at the close of the Centennial, Mexico decided it was too expensive to ship the works back and sold them off instead.[278] This might explain how a work of this quality made its way with relative ease to the Arensbergs' collection.[279]

THE ENDURING IMPORTANCE OF THE ARENSBERG PRE-COLUMBIAN COLLECTION

The Arensbergs were an inspiration for many others building pre-Columbian collections in the mid-twentieth century. Louise and Walter began acquiring these objects before most people considered them valuable, built significantly larger holdings than most of their peers, and benefited from their emotional, financial, and physical closeness to Earl Stendahl. At the same time that Nelson Rockefeller struggled to place his pre-Columbian and non-Western holdings at the Metropolitan Museum of Art, the Arensbergs' gift to the Philadelphia Museum of Art was celebrated, and it inspired other individuals to donate the holdings they had acquired.[280] In some cases, there were also regional considerations: Vincent Price's donation of many pre-Columbian works to East Los Angeles College was a visceral response to California's loss of the Arensberg collection.[281] However, there were other collectors who, despite being out of state, nonetheless corresponded with and purchased from Stendahl and who kept abreast of the Arensberg collection through him. Frequently, these were couples, often a generation younger, whose collections were modeled after the Arensbergs'. Alan and Janet Wurtzburger of Baltimore, for example, collected "primitive" art, although they seem to have done so knowing that they would donate their holdings to the Baltimore Museum of Art, which they did throughout the 1950s. While the Wurtzburgers were more interested in African art than pre-Columbian, they modeled themselves on the Arensbergs in their belief that American museums needed to present a truly comprehensive exhibition of the world's cultures.[282] The catalog entries for the Wurtzburgers' collection were written by George Kubler, shortly after he had authored the Philadelphia Museum of Art's volume on the Arensberg pre-Columbian holdings. Like Louise and Walter, the Wurtzburgers acquired a comprehensive collection of pre-Columbian art, including works from most major cultures of the region. Ultimately totaling 107 works, including a Teotihuacan mural fragment (albeit smaller and in poorer condition than the Arensbergs' example), the Wurtzburger collection clearly shows the influence of Stendahl and the Arensbergs.[283]

In a similar vein, James and Florence Gruener of Cleveland purchased many pre-Columbian artworks from Stendahl's gallery about a decade after the Arensbergs. Like many other collectors of Latin American art in the middle decades of the twentieth century, the Grueners took a trip to Mexico, which sparked their interest in pre-Columbian artwork. They returned to Latin America many times, acquiring pre-Columbian works and filming village life, craft production, and archaeological sites. Later, from the 1950s until about 1970, the Grueners also purchased from dealers in New York, Texas, and California. Ultimately, their pre-Columbian holdings were donated to the Cleveland Museum of Art, although no formal catalog was published for the collection. The objects they owned, also drawn from many cultures, reflected not only their aesthetic tastes but also a nostalgia for their travels in Mexico.[284]

Finally, a lesser-known collection, formed at least in part through Stendahl, was amassed by Fred and Florence Olsen and is today part of Yale University Art Gallery's holdings. The Olsens made donations to Yale in 1958 and 1960, and the Art Gallery purchased additional works from them in 1973. The Olsens' collection contains many more finely crafted ceramics and polished Maya jades than the Arensbergs' did, but it is also notable for its Aztec stone sculptures, including a corn goddess purchased from Stendahl that would not have been out of place in the Arensbergs' garden.[285]

Each of these collections imparts the legacy of Louise and Walter Arensberg in different ways. The couple's preferences in pre-Columbian art, and the pieces Stendahl correspondingly made available for sale, have been a huge influence on the tastes of those who came after them. Though Robert Woods Bliss and his collection have largely dominated the historical narrative about pre-Columbian collecting, the Arensbergs, in fact, may have been more broadly influential on collectors. However, since the Arensbergs did not generally seek out input from scholars or encourage academic research on their collection as Bliss did, Bliss's collection and others that foregrounded works with a more traditional, finished aesthetic have commanded most of the scholarly attention in the field since then. Notwithstanding the one research file among the Arensberg papers that details sources on the deity Quetzalcoatl, the couple were mostly content to appreciate their works' conceptual and aesthetic sophistication, rather than researching them from a strictly scholarly standpoint.[286] Although Walter was involved with the Southwest Museum in Los Angeles, in general the couple did not solicit expertise from the few academics and curators who may have known these materials, as Robert Woods Bliss did, to the detriment of their collection's reputation after their deaths.[287]

In popular culture, the couple's collection set an aesthetic standard for works that were rugged and aesthetically powerful—but not always beautiful. This model was replicated more widely and popularized through advertisements, movies (and, later, television shows), and interior design. Megan O'Neil and Mary Miller have directed our attention to the aesthetic of the Kahlúa ads that began circulating in 1955, the year after the Arensbergs died, and Matthew H. Robb has pointed out a half-dozen movies made between 1948 and 1964 in which pre-Columbian objects anchored a plot twist, all illustrating how these "rugged, nonpretty things" became a staple of commercial culture.[288]

Over the past few years, there has been a growing interest in the historiography of art collecting in California, with the advent of the Getty-organized Pacific Standard Time (PST) series of exhibitions in 2011, 2013, and 2017. The PST initiative has sparked renewed interest in the Arensberg collection, an assemblage of works formed in Los Angeles (perhaps it could only have been formed there) but dispersed to Philadelphia. Due to a dearth of research material about the Arensbergs' pre-Columbian collection until now, many of the essays in PST-related publications only briefly discuss the couple.[289]

While the Arensberg collection was often imitated, for many it simply could not be replicated. Of the installation at the Philadelphia Museum of Art, Beatrice Wood, Louise's closest friend, said: "I was terribly disappointed because, after seeing the collection in their home where it was lived with, with all kinds of primitive furniture…Oriental rugs, Mayan princesses, Mayan masks, the whole thing was so alive and so marvelous that it was cold and dead in a museum."[290]

Wood's view was far from the consensus, however, among visitors to the Philadelphia Museum of Art who had never seen the Arensberg collection in its original context. An anonymous reviewer from the *New York Herald Tribune* wrote, "The point that the museum is emphasizing—and no visitor can miss it—is that the inhabitants of America before the Spanish conquest were great artists."[291]

Perhaps more than any of the good press this new installation received, the Arensbergs would have relished their old friend Walter Pach's assessment, affirming the choices they had made about what to buy and how to show it. After his last visit to California, in 1953, Pach wrote to Walter:

> [I] was astonished at the number and importance of the pieces you have added since my last visit to you in 1943. There were some things that just got me by the throat… and I don't know whether it isn't more important for the public to see than the modern pictures that are cropping up on every hand now.… Every socialite and her boyfriend are talking modern art now (which doesn't spoil it for me), whereas the grandeur of those old Mexicans is still unappreciated by all but the fewest people.[292]

It is certain that the Arensbergs would have appreciated their pre-Columbian collection catching more than just a few people "by the throat." Had the couple lived to walk through the tribune of the Philadelphia Museum of Art on the night their life's work was given over to the public—perhaps running their hands along the cool surface of the calendar stone one final time as they did so—they might have been startled to find, some forty years into their collecting, that they were once again on the cutting edge.

†

Notes

1. Walter Pach, "The Greatest American Artists," *Harper's Monthly Magazine*, 1 December 1923, 257.

2. In 1916, the archaeologist Edgar Lee Hewett had asserted, "It is necessary to repeat again and again that all native American remains, whether of plains tribes, mound-builders, cliff-dwellers, Pueblo, Navaho, Toltec, Aztec, Maya, Inca, are just the works of the Indian." This was meant not to be disparaging but to comment on the unity of native cultures across the Americas. Edgar L. Hewett, "America's Archaeological Heritage," *Art and Archaeology*, December 1916, 257–66; reprinted in Jack Flam and Miriam Deutch, eds., *Primitivism and Twentieth-Century Art: A Documentary History* (Berkeley: University of California Press, 2003), 103.

3. Walter Pach, "The Art of the American Indian," *The Dial* 68 (January 1920): 57–65; reprinted in Flam and Deutch, *Primitivism and Twentieth-Century Art*, 171.

4. Henry McBride, "Modern Forms," *The Dial* 69 (July 1920): 61.

5. McBride, "Modern Forms," 61. This was the tagline for McBride's column.

6. Walter Arensberg, interview by Kenneth Ross, ca. 1951; this volume, 405.

7. Stendahl has been most fully described in April Dammann, *Exhibitionist: Earl Stendahl, Art Dealer as Impresario* (Santa Monica, CA: Angel City Press, 2011). A briefer introduction can be found in Michael D. Coe's essay on the system of dealing in pre-Columbian art, "From *Huaquero* to Connoisseur: The Early Market in Pre-Columbian Art," in *Collecting the Pre-Columbian Past: A Symposium at Dumbarton Oaks, 6th and 7th October 1990*, ed. Elizabeth Hill Boone (Washington, DC: Dumbarton Oaks Research Library and Collection, 1993), 271–90. The contributions of Marius de Zayas (1880–1961) have been described in Antonio Saborit, "Marius de Zayas: Transatlantic Visionary of Modern Art," in *Nexus New York: Latin/American Artists in the Modern Metropolis*, ed. Deborah Cullen (New York: El Museo del Barrio, 2009), 86–103; and in Francis M. Naumann, introduction to Marius de Zayas, *How, When, and Why Modern Art Came to New York*, ed. Francis M. Naumann (Cambridge: MIT Press, 1996), vii–xiv.

8. Bliss has been described in Coe, "From *Huaquero* to Connoisseur," 271–90, as well as in Julie Jones, "Mildred and Robert Woods Bliss and the Pre-Columbian Collection at Dumbarton Oaks," in *A Home of the Humanities: The Collecting and Patronage of Mildred and Robert Woods Bliss*, ed. James N. Carder (Washington, DC: Dumbarton Oaks Research Library and Collection, 2010), 53–74; and in Joanne Pillsbury and Miriam Doutriaux, "Incidents of Travel: Robert Woods Bliss and the Creation of the Maya Collection at Dumbarton Oaks," in *Ancient Maya Art at Dumbarton Oaks*, ed. Joanne Pillsbury, Miriam Doutriaux, Reiko Ishihara-Brito, and Alexandre Tokovinine (Washington, DC: Dumbarton Oaks Research Library and Collection, 2012), 1–25.

9. Naomi Sawelson-Gorse, "Marcel Duchamp's 'Silent Guard': A Critical Study of Walter and Louise Arensberg" (PhD diss., University of California, Santa Barbara, 1994), 349.

10. While the correspondence between Walter Arensberg and these men is voluminous, the evidence of their connection to Louise, or Louise's connection to any of this art, is much more difficult to analyze. For ease of use, the term *Arensbergs* will be used in most cases in this essay, unless referring to direct correspondence with only one member of the couple. All scholars who have written about the Arensbergs have grappled with this same issue, as Sawelson-Gorse describes in "'Silent Guard,'" 5–6.

11. During Duchamp's April 1949 trip to California, he visited Stendahl's gallery with Walter Arensberg and Katharine Kuh. Kuh described the visit, noting that Duchamp came away from Stendahl's workshop feeling uneasy about how much work was going on there. Katharine Kuh, *My Love Affair with Modern Art*, ed. Avis Berman (New York: Arcade, 2006), 22.

12. See Laurette E. McCarthy, *The Paintings of Walter Pach*, exh. cat. (New York: Francis M. Naumann Fine Art, 2011); and Marilyn Satin Kushner and Kimberly Orcutt, eds., *The Armory Show at 100: Modernism and Revolution*, exh. cat. (New York: New-York Historical Society, 2013).

13. The story of their meeting and Pach's tutoring of the couple is told in greater detail in Sawelson-Gorse, "'Silent Guard,'" 98–100.

14. See Walter Pach, postcard to Walter Arensberg, New York, 24 February 1914; Arensberg to Pach, Boston, 2 March 1914; and Pach to John Quinn, New York, 4 October 1915; all three in Bennard B. Perlman, ed., *American Artists, Authors, and Collectors: The Walter Pach Letters, 1906–1958* (Albany: State University of New York Press, 2002), 33–34, 269.

15. Walter Arensberg to Walter Pach, Boston, 2 March 1914, in Perlman, *Walter Pach Letters*, 34. Arensberg asks again after Pach's own painting in several other letters: see Arensberg to Pach, summer 1915; and Pach to Arensberg, Brewster, New York, 11 September 1947; both in Perlman, *Walter Pach Letters*, 34–35, 38–39. While not as celebrated for his oeuvre as many of the artists he promoted, Pach was a prolific painter. However, critics such as Bernard Berenson urged Pach to concentrate his energies on writing: see Berenson to Pach, Florence, 11 August 1924; Berenson to Pach, Florence, 9 June 1926; and Berenson to Pach, Florence, 19 August 1926; all three in Perlman, *Walter Pach Letters*, 60, 62–63. The Arensbergs had a more positive assessment of Pach's talent and in fact owned one of his paintings, a watercolor of a landscape (Philadelphia Museum of Art [PMA], accession no. 1950-134-516).

16. Pach, "The Art of the American Indian," 171.

17. On Pach's, Quinn's, and others' struggle to get the Metropolitan Museum to host a loan exhibition of modern art, see Judith Zilczer, *"The Noble Buyer": John Quinn, Patron of the Avant-Garde*, exh. cat. (Washington, DC: Smithsonian Institution Press, 1978), 54. When finally shown in 1921 (grudgingly), the Metropolitan Museum's exhibition of modern art included works lent by Walter Arensberg.

18. Félix Fénéon, ed., "Will Arts from Remote Places Be Admitted into the Louvre?," *Bulletin de la vie artistique* 1 (15 November and 1 and 15 December 1920); reprinted in Flam and Deutch, *Primitivism and Twentieth-Century Art*, 148–66.

19. William Rubin, "Modernist Primitivism: An Introduction," in *"Primitivism" in 20th Century Art: Affinity of the Tribal and the Modern*, vol. 1, exh. cat. (New York: Museum of Modern Art, 1984), 3: "To be sure, pre-Columbian court styles such as the Aztec, Olmec, and Incan continued to be called Primitive (and artists did not always distinguish between them and tribal art). But this was an inconsistency and should now be recognized as such. In their style, character, and implications, the pre-Columbian court and theocratic arts of Mesoamerica and South America should be grouped with the Egyptian, Javanese, Persian, and other styles that together with them had constituted the definition of the Primitive during the later nineteenth century."

20. Although he came to far different conclusions than Pach ultimately did, Robert J. Coady, owner of several downtown art galleries and editor of *The Soil* magazine, looked to technology as an answer to what "truly American" art would be. See Menno Hubregtse, "Robert J. Coady's 'The Soil' and Marcel Duchamp's 'Fountain': Taste, Nationalism, Capitalism, and New York Dada," *RACAR: Revue d'art canadienne / Canadian Art Review* 34, no. 2 (2009): 28–42. Sandra S. Phillips also suggests that Pach intimated that echoes of technology, engineering, and industry might pervade a truly American style; Phillips, "The Art Criticism of Walter Pach," *The Art Bulletin* 65, no. 1 (1983): 117.

21. Pach was critical to this, in articles that he wrote from the 1920s through the 1940s. See also Holly Barnet-Sánchez, "The Necessity of Pre-Columbian Art: U.S. Museums and the Role of Foreign Policy in the Appropriation and Transformation of Mexican Heritage, 1933–1944" (PhD diss., University of California, Los Angeles, 1993); and Helen Delpar, *The Enormous Vogue of Things Mexican: Cultural Relations between the United States and Mexico, 1920–1935* (Tuscaloosa: University of Alabama Press, 1992).

22. Wallace Stevens to Fiske Kimball, 23 February 1954; published in Wallace Stevens, *Letters of Wallace Stevens*, ed. Holly Stevens (New York: Knopf, 1966), 822; cited in Sawelson-Gorse, "'Silent Guard,'" 114. Louise's style was noteworthy enough that she was caricatured in Clara Tice, "Who's Who in Manhattan," *Cartoons Magazine*, 1917, 178–79; a clipping is in Philadelphia Museum of Art, Library and Archives, Arensberg Archives (hereafter cited as PMA-WLA), box 74, folder 9. On the use of museum collections for fashion and industrial design in the early twentieth century, see Ann Marguerite Tartsinis, *An American Style: Global Sources for New York Textile and Fashion Design, 1915–1928* (New York: Bard Graduate Center, 2013).

23. Phillips links this as well to the interest of Elie Faure, the French art historian whose work Pach was translating at this time. See Phillips, "The Art Criticism of Walter Pach," 113, 117.

24. On the importance of the summer school, see Delpar, *The Enormous Vogue of Things Mexican*, 18–20.

25. Phillips contends that Pach acquired pre-Columbian art for both Quinn and Arensberg; see Phillips, "The Art Criticism of Walter Pach," 117n73. While Pach certainly made acquisitions for John Quinn (1870–1924), particularly in his last decade of collecting, as documented in the letters between them (see Perlman, *Walter Pach Letters*, 245–321), I have not found information indicating the same offers to the Arensbergs.

26. See Judith Zilczer, "John Quinn and Modern Art Collectors in America, 1913–1924," *American Art Journal* 14, no. 1 (1982): 57.

27. Zilczer, *"The Noble Buyer,"* 25.

28. Quinn bought these through Marius de Zayas; see B. L. Reid, *The Man from New York: John Quinn and His Friends* (New York: Oxford University Press, 1968), 398, 579.

29. John Quinn to Constantin Brancusi, 22 May 1921; cited in Zilczer, *"The Noble Buyer,"* 41.

30. Susan Stewart, *On Longing: Narratives of the Miniature, the Gigantic, the Souvenir, the Collection* (Durham, NC: Duke University Press, 1993), 156.

31. Russell W. Belk, "Collectors and Collecting," in *Interpreting Objects and Collections*, ed. Susan M. Pearce (London: Routledge, 1994), 321. See also Stewart, *On Longing*, 157, for a discussion of collections as extensions of self.

32. See Belk, "Collectors and Collecting," 320, on what he calls "Type A" and "Type B" collectors.

33. Belk, "Collectors and Collecting," 324.

34. The Quinn collection was sold at auctions at the Hôtel Drouot in Paris in 1926 and the American Art Galleries in New York in 1927. See Judith Zilczer, "Dispersal of the John Quinn Collection," *Archives of American Art Journal* 30, no. 1/4 (1990): 35–40.

35. John Quinn to Marcel Duchamp, 28 May 1920; cited in Zilczer, *"The Noble Buyer,"* 45.

36. John Quinn to Henri Pierre Roché, 17 September 1919; cited in Zilczer, *"The Noble Buyer,"* 50. In contrast to Quinn, the Arensbergs often sought out sketches or studies that would illuminate the ideas behind their more finished works.

37. See Walter Pach to John Quinn, New York, 28 January 1923; 5 March 1923; and 13 June 1923; plus Pach to Quinn, Paris, 15 July 1924; all in Perlman, *Walter Pach Letters*, 313–14, 315, 318–19.

38. Description of de Zayas by unknown author in contemporary periodical *The Bang* 2 (28 October 1907): 1; cited in Douglas Hyland, *Marius de Zayas: Conjurer of Souls*, exh. cat. (Lawrence, KS: Spencer Museum of Art, 1981), 13.

39. On de Zayas and the New York market for African art, see Yaëlle Biro, "Avant Charles Ratton: Commerce et diffusion des arts africains des années 1900 aux années 1920," in *Charles Ratton: L'invention des arts "primitifs,"* ed. Philippe Dagen and Maureen Murphy, exh. cat. (Paris: Flammarion, 2013), 42–57.

40. This is indicated by the description as "radically Spanish." One of de Zayas's earliest biographers, Douglas Hyland, notes that the de Zayas family can trace its roots to the seventh century in Spain. This is not a meaningless distinction. Even today, families of Spanish descent in Mexico may emphasize their aristocratic roots, and they frequently socialize in different circles than mestizo, or more mixed, Mexicans.

41. See Saborit, "Marius de Zayas," 86, 101; and Hyland, *Marius de Zayas: Conjurer of Souls*, 11.

42. This museum has changed names and locations over time. From 1825 to 1910, it was known as the Museo Nacional. In 1910, the museum split from the natural history collections and was called the Museo Nacional de Arqueología, Historia y Etnografía. In 1939, it was renamed the Museo Nacional de Antropología. Ultimately, in 1964, it became the Museo Nacional de Antropología e Historia, which remains its name today.

43. Rafael de Zayas Enríquez, *Los Estados Unidos Mexicanos: Sus progresos en veinte años de paz, 1877–1897; Estudio histórico y estadístico, fundado en los datos oficiales más recientes y completos* (New York: H. A. Rost, 1899), 208.

44. "Marius de Zayas: A Kindly Caricaturist of the Emotions," *The Craftsman* 8, no. 4 (1908): 390, https://digital.library.wisc.edu/1711.dl/DLDecArts.hdv13n04.

45. Marius de Zayas to Alfred Stieglitz, New York, 21 April 1911, Alfred Stieglitz / Georgia O'Keeffe Archive, Beinecke Rare Book and Manuscript Library, Yale University, YCAL MSS 85 Series I, box 12, folders 309–310; cited in Hyland, *Marius de Zayas: Conjurer of Souls*, 32.

46. On the Arensbergs' acquisition of the Fang head and male figure, see Yaëlle Biro, "Works Acquired by Walter and Louise Arensberg," on the webpage for *African Art, New York, and the Avant-Garde*, exhibition at the Metropolitan Museum of Art, New York, November 2012–September 2013, https://www.metmuseum.org/exhibitions/listings/2012/african-art/sources-dealers-collectors/arensberg.

47. See William Innes Homer, "Appendix I: Exhibitions at 291," in idem, *Alfred Stieglitz and the American Avant-Garde* (Boston: New York Graphic Society, 1977), 298. On Torres Palomar and de Zayas, see also José Juan Tablada, "Tres artistas mexicanos en Nueva York: Marius de Zayas, Palomar, Juan Olaguíbel," *El Universal Ilustrado*, 17 January 1919, 3, https://icaadocs.mfah.org/icaadocs/THEARCHIVE/FullRecord/tabid/88/doc/737391/language/en-US/Default.aspx.

48. Marius de Zayas, *Statuary in Wood by African Savages: The Root of Modern Art*, exh. cat. (New York: 291, 1914); reprinted in Flam and Deutch, *Primitivism and Twentieth-Century Art*, 70.

49. Marius de Zayas, *African Negro Art: Its Influence on Modern Art*, exh. cat. (New York, Modern Gallery, 1916); excerpt reprinted in Flam and Deutch, *Primitivism and Twentieth-Century Art*, 97. Italics are mine.

50. See Coe, "From *Huaquero* to Connoisseur," 280.

51. Alfred Stendahl, interview by George M. Goodwin, 26 August 1967, Oral History Program, University of California, Los Angeles, 48.

52. For instance, the Peabody Museum received Chichén Itzá artifacts from alumnus Edward Thompson, the American consul to Mexico. Thompson, while stationed in the Yucatán Peninsula, had purchased a hacienda there that contained the pre-Columbian site of Chichén Itzá. For more on the objects received from Thompson, see Clemency Chase Coggins and Orrin C. Shane III, eds., *Cenote of Sacrifice: Maya Treasures from the Sacred Well at Chichén Itza* (Austin: University of Texas Press, 1984).

53. See A. M. T., "Exhibition of Maya Art," *Museum of Fine Arts Bulletin* (Boston) 10, no. 56 (1912): 13–14.

54. See plates 11.12 and 12.17 for the Maya stela fragment. The Arensbergs also owned an Aztec stela fragment (see plate 2.12).

55. Fabienne de Pierrebourg, "Moulages et collections, moulages et vestiges mésoaméricains, un dialogue?," *In Situ* 28 (2016): 26, https://journals.openedition.org/insitu/12731. However, it is worth noting that casts of all kinds were "the central attractions in American museums between 1874 and 1905," according to the art historian Pamela Born in "The Canon Is Cast: Plaster Casts in American Museum and University Collections," *Art Documentation: Journal of the Art Libraries Society of North America* 21, no. 2 (2002): 8.

56. George Vaillant (AMNH associate curator of Mexican archaeology), "Enlivening the Past," *Natural History* 31, no. 5 (1931): 531; cited in Diana Fane, "Reproducing the Pre-Columbian Past: Casts and Models in Exhibitions of Ancient America, 1824–1935," in *Collecting the Pre-Columbian Past: A Symposium at Dumbarton Oaks, 6th and 7th October 1990*, ed. Elizabeth Hill Boone (Washington, DC: Dumbarton Oaks Research Library and Collection, 1993), 141. It is interesting to note that even the AMNH's tearoom was designed in pre-Columbian style that riffed off of the southern Mexican site of Mitla. (The Arensbergs later owned a relief from the site.) See, for example, a view of tables and chairs in the museum's Mitla Restaurant, November 1909, photograph by Thomas Lunt, AMNH Negative Logbook 17, American Museum of Natural History Research Library, image 32593, http://images.library.amnh.org/photos/ptm/catalog/desc/151686/3.

57. See Tartsinis, *An American Style*, 39. It seems likely that Walter, who was fascinated even during the couple's New York years by ciphers and codes, might have appreciated references to Aztec glyphs and writing, especially since he was at the time working on poetry that included phonetic and symbolic aspects.

58. Max Weber, "Chac-Mool of Chichen-Itza," in *Cubist Poems* (London: E. Mathews, 1914), 23–24.

59. William Carlos Williams, "Symposium: The Destruction of Tenochtitlan," *Broom: An International Magazine of the Arts* 4, no. 2 (1923): 112–20, available at http://bluemountain.princeton.edu.

60. See Walter Pach, *Queer Thing, Painting: Forty Years in the World of Art* (New York: Harper & Brothers, 1938), 282.

61. See Kenneth Macgowan and Herman Rosse, *Masks and Demons* ([New York]: Harcourt, Brace, 1923), 167.

62. See Joanne Pillsbury, "Recovering the Missing Chapters," in *Making the Met*, ed. Andrea Bayer (New York: Metropolitan Museum of Art, forthcoming), 203–9; and "Notes," *American Archaeologist* 2, part 2 (November 1898): 304.

63. "Notes," *American Archaeologist*, 304.

64. See the Toltec reliefs (plates 22.11 and 22.12), for example, although the "Toltec" classification had changed meanings in the half century between 1898 and the Arensbergs' purchase of the reliefs.

65. For the mission statement of the Modern Gallery, see "'291' and the Modern Gallery," *Camera Work*, no. 48 (October 1916): 63; reproduced in Homer, *Alfred Stieglitz and the American Avant-Garde*, 195. The founding statement of the Modern Gallery was first printed, in part, as a broadside that was slipped into copies of *291*, nos. 7–8 (September–October 1915). The statement had emphasized "pre-conquest Mexican art."

66. See, for example, Leonardo López Luján, *The Offerings of the Templo Mayor of Tenochtitlan* (Boulder: University Press of Colorado, 1994), 316–23.

67. Naumann, "Appendix A: Exhibitions at the Modern and De Zayas Galleries," in Marius de Zayas, *How, When, and Why Modern Art Came to New York*, ed. Francis M. Naumann (Cambridge: MIT Press, 1998), 142.

68. For more on Stephens and Catherwood's influence on American culture, see R. Tripp Evans, *Romancing the Maya: Mexican Antiquity in the American Imagination, 1820–1915* (Austin: University of Texas Press, 2004), 44–87. If the Arensbergs had missed reading *Incidents of Travel in Central America, Chiapas, and Yucatan* in their school days, it was on a list of suggested readings from their friend Kenneth Macgowan in 1944. See Macgowan to Walter Arensberg, 30 June 1944, PMA-WLA, box 12, folder 12. See also John L. Stephens, *Incidents of Travel in Central America, Chiapas, and Yucatan*, 2 vols. (London: John Murray, 1841).

69. See Marius de Zayas to Walter Arensberg, New York, 29 October 1921, De Zayas Archives, Seville; transcription courtesy of Antonio Saborit. In the letter, after a discussion of storage and the finances of the failing gallery, de Zayas asked Arensberg, "Will you consider saling [*sic*] the Mexican stone?" Leonardo López Luján has shown that Coyoacán, the Mexico City suburb where the de Zayas family lived at the turn of the century, was a center in antiquity for the veneration of Quetzalcoatl in particular, and that several of the statues of this deity discovered in the nineteenth and early twentieth centuries were found there. See López Luján, "Reflexiones sobre el arte escultórico y el culto a Quetzalcóatl en el Coyoacán posclásico," *Estudios de Cultura Náhuatl* 51 (January–June 2016): 43–65, http://www.historicas.unam.mx/publicaciones/revistas/nahuatl/pdf/ecn51/1016.pdf.

70. See Francis M. Naumann, "Walter Conrad Arensberg: Poet, Patron, and Participant in the New York Avant-Garde," *Philadelphia Museum of Art Bulletin* 26, no. 328 (1980): 8–10 (figs. 6–9).

71. See, for example, the view of the African Hall at the American Museum of Natural History, September 1910, photograph by Julius Kirschner, AMNH Negative Logbook 17, American Museum of Natural History Research Library, image 32926, http://images.library.amnh.org/photos/ptm/catalog/desc/152018/3.

72. Jeanne Robert Foster to Aline Saarinen, 20 May 1957; cited in Zilczer, *"The Noble Buyer,"* 38.

73. John Quinn to Alphonse Kann, 15 June 1922, Thomas F. Conroy Collection; cited in Zilczer, *"The Noble Buyer,"* 39.

74. In Paris, the Brummer and Ratton galleries were selling pre-Columbian art by the early 1910s, and there were periodic auctions in Paris of collections that included pre-Columbian art. On Brummer, see Coe, "From *Huaquero* to Connoisseur," 278–79. On Ratton, see Dagen and Murphy, *Charles Ratton: L'invention des arts "primitifs."*

75. George Kunz sold pre-Columbian objects to Henry Walters of Baltimore, as documented in William R. Johnston, *William and Henry Walters, The Reticent Collectors* (Baltimore: Johns Hopkins University Press and Walters Art Gallery, 1999), 142, 190–91. See also Tiffany & Co. to Henry Walters, New York, 21 December 1911, which can be found online at the Digital Archaeological Record, Archaeology of Highland Chiriqui, Panama—Documents, Images, and Datasets, Holmberg fig. 11-1910-1912, tDAR id: 365550, doi:10.6067/XCV8MS3QVM; and Ellen Hoobler, forthcoming, on Kunz as a pre-Columbian dealer. However, it is likely that in the Dadaist, often anti-capitalist, circles in which the Arensbergs moved, gold objects bought from a luxury jeweler would not have been of much interest.

76. The Arensbergs saved a copy of the Modern Gallery broadside; see PMA-WLA, box 73, folder 10.

77. See Saborit, "Marius de Zayas," 99. For more on the Modern Gallery, see de Zayas, *How, When, and Why Modern Art Came to New York*. Agnes Ernst Meyer was a pioneering journalist in New York. In 1933, the Meyers bought the *Washington Post*, which would be run for decades by their daughter Katharine Graham. See https://womenofeverycomplexionandcomplexity.weebly.com/mother-and-daughter-journalists-agnes-meyer-and-katharine-graham-shaped-journalism.html.

78. From its founding, the Modern Gallery published catalogs promoting its exhibitions of modern art, African sculpture, and pre-Columbian art; see a list of its catalogs in archives related to Modern Gallery, Archives Directory for the History of Collecting in America, Frick Art Reference Library, https://research.frick.org/directory/detail/1463.

79. Robert M. Crunden, *American Salons: Encounters with European Modernism, 1885–1917* (New York: Oxford University Press, 1993), 340.

80. Hyland, *Marius de Zayas: Conjurer of Souls*, 48.

81. Marius de Zayas to Charles Vignier, New York, 3 January 1920, Fondo Marius de Zayas, Charles Vignier file, De Zayas Archives, Seville; cited in Saborit, "Marius de Zayas," 100.

82. Hyland, *Marius de Zayas: Conjurer of Souls*, 50.

83. Information on the De Zayas Gallery's clientele from unpublished gallery ledgers, De Zayas Archives, Seville. My thanks to Antonio Saborit for giving me scans of some of these ledgers.

84. Marius de Zayas to Charles Vignier, New York, 3 January 1920; cited in Saborit, "Marius de Zayas," 100.

85. For conversion to 2019 dollars, see https://www.dollartimes.com/inflation, accessed 20 January 2020.

86. See Zilczer, "John Quinn and Modern Art Collectors in America," 59.

87. See PMA-WLA, box 46, folder 5, for letters to Walter from his bank, People's Pittsburgh Trust Company, regarding his sales of stocks and bonds during the years following the Great Depression. Walter had been advised by his brother and his banker not to make such sales, but on 30 December 1933, for instance, he sold some stock and had over $1,000 deposited in his account—the equivalent of about $20,000 today. Beatrice Wood has observed that Walter Arensberg seemed to love lending large sums of money to people who had no possible means of repaying it to him. See Wood, *I Shock Myself: The Autobiography of Beatrice Wood*, ed. Lindsay Smith, rev. ed. (San Francisco: Chronicle, 1985), 54–55.

88. See Saborit, "Marius de Zayas," 100–101; and Sawelson-Gorse, "'Silent Guard,'" 201, 225–27n14.

89. See Saborit, "Marius de Zayas," 100; conversion to 2019 dollars based on https://fred.stlouisfed.org/series/M1404BUSM306NNBR, with an exchange rate of 5.4 francs to the dollar, and then $66,176.00 USD with inflation based on https://www.dollartimes.com/inflation, accessed 20 January 2020.

90. See de Zayas, *How, When, and Why Modern Art Came to New York*, 234n3; conversion to 2019 dollars based on https://www.dollartimes.com/inflation, accessed 20 January 2020. This story is recounted in greater detail in Sawelson-Gorse, "'Silent Guard,'" 205–9.

91. See John Quinn to Henri Pierre Roché, 19 February 1922, John Quinn Papers, New York Public Library, box 38, folder 2; cited in Zilczer, "John Quinn and Modern Art Collectors in America," 71. See also Zilczer, "Dispersal of the John Quinn Collection," 39; and Sawelson-Gorse, "'Silent Guard,'" 209. In a letter to Marcel Duchamp on 23 May 1930, Walter Arensberg asked for help recovering the Brancusi, *Newborn [I]* (see plate 32.6), which he had sold to Quinn (Walter calls the sculpture *Tête d'enfant* in the letter); PMA-WLA, box 6, folder 21. A full accounting of *Newborn*'s provenance is in Ann Temkin, entry for *Newborn*, in Friedrich Teja Bach, Margit Rowell, and Ann Temkin, *Constantin Brancusi 1876–1957*, exh. cat. (Cambridge: MIT Press, 1995), 136. Later, the Arensbergs may have bought some of Quinn's pre-Columbian works, possibly including a Costa Rican jaguar (see plate 12.7). Its description is similar to object no. 659 from the sale of John Quinn's property at the American Art Galleries on 12 February 1927. See *Paintings and Sculptures: The Renowned Collection of Modern and Ultra-Modern Art Formed by the Late John Quinn* (New York: American Art Association, 1927), 227, https://archive.org/details/paintingssculptu00amer. Naomi Sawelson-Gorse asserts that the Arensbergs acquired from Quinn's collection fifteen works in total, which may have included pre-Columbian works. See Naomi Sawelson-Gorse, "'For the Want of a Nail': The Disposition of the Louise and Walter Arensberg Collection" (master's thesis, University of California, Riverside, 1987), 244.

92. Sawelson-Gorse, "'Silent Guard,'" 209.

93. De Zayas sold his collection at auction in New York on 23 March 1923. See the sale catalog by the Anderson Galleries, *The Collection of Marius de Zayas of New York City* (New York: Anderson Galleries, 1923), https://archive.org/details/collectionofmario0ande.

94. During their early years in California, the Arensbergs seem to have been deeply unsettled. They first rented 2012 La Brea Terrace, in Hollywood, in April 1921. By September of that year they had moved to 2062 Highland Avenue. Just a year later, in September 1922, they moved to 1645 North Vermont Avenue (Residence A of Aline Barnsdall's Frank Lloyd Wright–designed Olive Hill complex). In early 1924, they moved to 1820 Whitley Avenue. After a yearlong return to New York in the fall of 1925 (where they stayed first at the Harvard Club and then in an apartment at 40 West Fifty-Ninth Street), they returned to Los Angeles and rerented the house on Whitley Avenue. They occupied one last rental house, at 7887 Hillside Avenue, before settling into their permanent home at 7065 Hillside Avenue in September 1927. See Naomi Sawelson-Gorse, "'For the Want of a Nail,'" 241–45.

95. Louise Arensberg to John Davis Hatch, ca. 24 April 1934, John Davis Hatch Papers, 1790–1995, Archives of American Art, Smithsonian Institution, box 9, folder 12; cited in Paul J. Karlstrom, "Modernism in Southern California, 1920–1956: Reflections on the Art and the Times," in *Turning the Tide: Early Los Angeles Modernists 1920–1956*, ed. Paul J. Karlstrom and Susan Ehrlich, exh. cat. (Santa Barbara, CA: Santa Barbara Museum of Art, 1990), 14.

96. On the Mayan Revival style and Frank Lloyd Wright's Barnsdall house complex, see Marjorie Ingle, *The Mayan Revival Style: Art Deco Mayan Fantasy* (Salt Lake City: Peregrine Smith, 1984). After living in the Barnsdall house, whose proportions and leaking roof they disliked, the Arensbergs became virulently anti–Frank Lloyd Wright, which may have hampered their enjoyment of his other Mayan Revival projects. Lloyd Wright (Frank's son, who also designed homes in the Mayan Revival style), however, was a close friend of the Arensbergs for many years.

97. See James Oles, "For Business of Pleasure: Exhibiting Mexican Folk Art, 1820–1930," in *Casa Mañana: The Morrow Collection of Mexican Popular Arts*, ed. Susan Danly, exh. cat. (Albuquerque: University of New Mexico Press, 2001), 20–22.

98. One of the artists who demonstrated his talent live in front of an audience there was a good friend of Diego Rivera's, the relatively less-known Adolfo Best-Maugard. Best-Maugard lived in Paris in the early 1910s and was very likely known to Marius de Zayas as well.

99. See "Mexican Folk Music Planned at Art Exhibit," *Los Angeles Times*, 19 November 1922, section 2, page 1; cited in Oles, "Exhibiting Mexican Folk Art, 1820–1930," 21, 177n26.

100. Pach, "The Greatest American Artists," 252.

101. George Sacken, "Maya Art," *Broom* 4, no. 2 (1923): 86, available at http://bluemountain.princeton.edu. I am grateful to Antonio Saborit for bringing this article to my attention.

102. Sacken, "Maya Art," 88.

103. This is an interesting aspect of the Arensbergs' personalities—though they claimed to march exclusively to the beat of their own drummer, they often sought the approbation of people whose opinion they esteemed. In this case, Walter wrote to Duchamp in 1930, asking the provocative question, "Would it interest you to hear that Mrs. Eddy has just agreed to sell us your Chess Players?" Arensberg to Duchamp, Hollywood, 23 May 1930.

104. On Stendahl, see Dammann, *Exhibitionist: Earl Stendahl*, 22, 27. On Zeitlin and Putzel, among others, see Margarita Nieto, "Mexican Art and Los Angeles, 1920–1940," in *On the Edge of America: California Modernist Art, 1900–1950*, ed. Paul J. Karlstrom (Berkeley: University of California Press, 1996), 136, http://ark.cdlib.org/ark:/13030/ft5p30070c/. Walter had a falling-out with Zeitlin in 1941, accusing him of "telling a story derogatory to the character of [Arensberg's] work." Walter Arensberg to Jake Zeitlin, Hollywood, 8 August 1941, PMA-WLA, box 20, folder 48. Zeitlin wrote to Walter to apologize (Los Angeles, 9 August 1941, PMA-WLA, box 20, folder 48); however, that was the last known correspondence between the pair, so it is unclear if Walter ever forgave him. It is hard to imagine that the Arensbergs would not have acquired a few of the ceramics of West Mexico that were probably amply available in Los Angeles, promoted by the Mexican muralists and artists working in California at this time, which certainly could be found at Stendahl's and at Altman Antiques, as well as probably at other merchants. On the movements and inspiration of Mexican muralists working in the United States at this time, see Anna Indych-López, "Mural Gambits: Mexican Muralism in the United States and the 'Portable' Fresco," *The Art Bulletin* 89, no. 2 (2007): 287–305.

105. See Indych-López, "Mural Gambits."

106. Orozco's *Prometheus* mural at Pomona had no explicitly pre-Columbian themes, but Siqueiros's work *América Tropical* included Latin American and possibly pre-Columbian imagery. For more on these murals, see Nieto, "Mexican Art in Los Angeles," 127, 130, 132.

107. The Modern Gallery and De Zayas Gallery had sold the paintings by Rivera, whom de Zayas knew personally; Siqueiros had just painted his controversial murals in Los Angeles that the Arensbergs must have been aware of; and Weber, as mentioned above, had been a part of their nightly salon.

108. Holger Cahill, *American Sources of Modern Art*, exh. cat. (New York: Museum of Modern Art, 1933), 5, https://www.moma.org/documents/moma_catalogue_2932_300061865.pdf.

109. Cahill, *American Sources of Modern Art*, 8–9.

110. Cahill, *American Sources of Modern Art*, 13.

111. See James Johnson Sweeney, ed., *African Negro Art*, exh. cat. (New York: Museum of Modern Art, 1935), https://www.moma.org/documents/moma_catalogue_2937_300086871.pdf, 31, 47, plate 12. The Arensbergs lent to the MoMA exhibition a figure of a woman from "French Sudan" (plate 12, which is illustrated in Sweeney's catalog) and a Gabonese head (cat. 368). In 1944, the Denver Art Museum asked to borrow these two works; see Kate Kent to Walter Arensberg, Denver, 19 September 1944, PMA-WLA, box 5, folder 73. Walter replied, "I regret to have to tell you that one of the pieces to which you refer is lost or stolen, and the other has received an injury so that I feel it is too risky to let it out again on loan"; Arensberg to Kent, Hollywood, 9 November 1944, PMA-WLA, box 5, folder 73. In 1947, the Pasadena Art Institute also asked to borrow these two works and were told the same thing. See Alice M. Goudy to Walter Arensberg, Pasadena, 18 August 1947; and Arensberg to Goudy, Hollywood, 6 September 1947, both PMA-WLA, box 14, folder 35. Walter seems to have remained interested in African works in the late 1930s: he corresponded with Kenneth Macgowan regarding African masks in 1938 and implied that he was thinking of buying a mask from Carl Zigrosser of New York's Weyhe Gallery; Walter Arensberg to Macgowan, Hollywood, 22 November 1938, PMA-WLA, box 12, folder 11.

112. For a list of SFMOMA exhibitions, see Janine Gericke, Jessica Lemieux, and Peggy Tran-Le, "Finding Aid to the San Francisco Museum of Modern Art Exhibition Records, 1934–ongoing" (last modified December 2015), 28–29, https://s3-us-west-2.amazonaws.com/sfmomamedia/media/uploads/files/ARCH.EXH.001_findingaid.pdf.

113. See Arthur Millier, "Fine Art of Many Centuries and Countries at San Diego," *Los Angeles Times*, 26 May 1935, A1, A7.

114. For more on the architecture of Balboa Park and the replica of the Temple of Quetzalcoatl, see "The California Building—San Diego Museum of Man," San Diego Museum of Man, https://www.museumofman.org/california-building. On the impact of such spectacles and immersive environments on patrons whose fascination long outlasted the fairs, see Guilhem Olivier, "Dr. H. B. Nicholson: 'Grandfather' of Aztecs Studies," trans. Michel Besson, http://www.mexicolore.co.uk/aztecs/home/henry-nicholson-grandfather-of-aztecs-studies; first published in English as "A Born Raconteur and Warm Human Being," in *Codex Nicholson*, ed. Brian Dervin Dillon and Matthew A. Boxt (Costa Mesa, CA: Pacific Coast Archaeological Society, 2012).

115. The golden objects had been called "an American Tutankhamun" by the *New York Times* in 1932, and then featured at the Chicago World's Fair of 1932 and exhibited in other venues in the United States. See Ellen Hoobler, "An 'Artistic Discovery' of Antiquity: Alfonso Caso, the Archaeologist as Curator at the New York World's Fair and MoMA's *Twenty Centuries of Mexican Art*, 1939–1940," in *Visual Culture of the Ancient Americas: Contemporary Perspectives*, ed. Ellen Hoobler and Andrew Finegold (Norman: University of Oklahoma Press, 2017), 119–34.

116. The Arensbergs owned a copy of Vaillant's pamphlet; it is included in a list of books, magazines, and exhibition catalogs that were given to the Philadelphia Museum of Art by the Francis Bacon Foundation. See "Third shipment of art books to Philadelphia," 1 March 1954, PMA-WLA, box 34, folder 25, p. 7.

117. See the Arensbergs' 1938 federal income tax return, PMA-WLA, box 74, folder 11; conversion to 2019 dollars based on https://www.dollartimes.com/inflation, accessed 20 January 2020. It's interesting to note that about $32,000 of their income came from dividends on Louise's bonds, compared to $194.33 from Walter's dividends.

118. See Brummer Gallery, invoice to Walter Arensberg, 13 May 1937, PMA-WLA, box 28, folder 7; and Pierre Matisse Gallery, invoice to Walter Arensberg, 14 May 1937, PMA-WLA, box 28, folder 7.

119. See Theodore Schempp, receipts from Walter Arensberg, 19 January and 3 February 1937, PMA-WLA, box 28, folder 25. Though Brummer may have connected Walter to Schempp, Schempp seems to have been well known to Earl Stendahl as well. In 1940, the Stendahls and the Schempps vacationed together for two months in Mexico and Central America; see Earl Stendahl to Jere Abbott, 27 May 1940, Stendahl Art Galleries Records, 1907–1971, Archives of American Art, Smithsonian Institution, box 1, folder 17. In this letter, Stendahl writes, "My agents in the South were able to gather up some magnificent things in the pre-Columbian things." I am grateful to Alanna Radlo-Dzur for bringing this correspondence to my attention.

120. See Paola Mola, "5 Photographs Sent by Duchamp to," in *The Brancusi Effect: An Archival Impulse*, ed. Vanessa Joan Müller and Nicolaus Schafhausen, exh. cat. (Berlin: Sternberg, 2015), 5.

121. The Arensbergs made a single purchase of six works of pre-Columbian art from the Brummer Gallery in 1937. See card for "Arensberg, Walter C." in Active Clients Address Cards, the Brummer Gallery Records, Cloisters Archives, Metropolitan Museum of Art, https://libmma.contentdm.oclc.org/digital/collection/p16028coll9/id/42128/rec/2.

122. See Yaëlle Biro, "African Arts between Curios, Antiquities, and Avant-Garde at the *Maison Brummer*, Paris (1908–1914)," *Journal of Art Historiography* 12 (June 2015): 13, https://arthistoriography.files.wordpress.com/2015/06/biro1.pdf.

123. See Christine Brennan, "The Brummer Gallery and the Business of Art," *Journal of the History of Collections* 27, no. 3 (2015): 455.

124. The Pierre Matisse Gallery, founded in New York by the youngest son of the artist Henri Matisse, opened in 1931, a decade after the Arensbergs had decamped for California. Walter Arensberg may have been steered to the gallery by his friend (and Mexico booster) Walter Pach, who was a supporter of Pierre Matisse's enterprise; see Anna Jozefacka, "Pierre Matisse Gallery," in *Index of Historic Collectors and Dealers of Cubism*, Leonard A. Lauder Research Center for Modern Art, Metropolitan Museum of Art, https://www.metmuseum.org/art/libraries-and-research-centers/leonard-lauder-research-center/research/index-of-cubist-art-collectors/matisse-gallery. The Arensbergs eventually purchased a number of other works from the Pierre Matisse Gallery.

125. In Europe, Joseph Brummer (who also had a New York gallery) and Charles Ratton were the major dealers in Paris. Charles Vignier seems to have sold pre-Columbian works from time to time. Additionally, pre-Columbian collections formed by individuals were sold with some frequency at European auctions in the 1920s and 1930s. By the 1940s in the United States, John Wise of New York had become a major competing dealer, but he was patronized much more frequently by Robert Woods Bliss. Even in the early 1940s, Stendahl considered Joseph Brummer and Pierre Matisse of New York as competitors but also potential consignees. The Carlebach Gallery of New York may have served as a source.

126. On the definition of Mesoamerica and other basic terms of pre-Columbian culture, including the sacred ballgame, a good resource is Mary Ellen Miller, *The Art of Mesoamerica: From Olmec to Aztec*, 6th rev. ed. (London: Thames & Hudson, 2019).

127. The jadeite statue's corresponding inventory card in the Brummer Gallery Records is no. N3374, https://libmma.contentdm.oclc.org/digital/collection/p16028coll9/id/11303. For the tecali head (PMA 1950-134-208), see inventory card no. N4103 in the Brummer Gallery Records, https://libmma.contentdm.oclc.org/digital/collection/p16028coll9/id/13858. Like the greenstone pebble that was one of the first works the Arensbergs purchased through de Zayas, jadeite is a very hard stone to work, and its green color, associated with water and agricultural fertility, made it sacred for the ancient Mexicans. The Arensbergs may have learned of these associations from de Zayas.

128. Conversion to 2019 dollars based on https://www.dollartimes.com/inflation, accessed 20 January 2020. Brummer, always shrewd, made a tidy profit; the Brummer Gallery records show that he paid about $1,200 for the works and sold them for more than three times as much.

129. The head with headdress's corresponding inventory card in the Brummer Gallery Records is no. P11021, https://libmma.contentdm.oclc.org/digital/collection/p16028coll9/id/39187. Brummer classified this piece as Zapotec, but it is actually central Mexican, dating to the Postclassic period, circa 1300–1500; it is possibly either Mixtec or Aztec. For an exhibition that was part of the 1937 Greater Texas & Pan-American Exposition, the head was cataloged as Aztec; see *Catalogue of the Exhibition of Art of the Americas: Pre-Columbian and Contemporary*, exh. cat. (Dallas: Dallas Museum of Fine Arts, 1937), 37 (no. 268), https://texashistory.unt.edu/ark:/67531/metapth183291. The head shows on one side a person with elaborate headdress (presumably a lord). On the back, the head bears the glyph 13-Reed/Dart, which is likely a date; this is also probably the portrait subject's name. (People were often named for the date of their birth in the Mesoamerican calendar.) Many thanks to Javier Urcid for his assistance in classifying this work. The head was sold to Brummer by Charles Ratton of Paris, a source of many "primitive" works that had resonance for the surrealists.

130. Montenegro (1885–1968) had been close to the Mexican literary community since the early 1900s, making illustrations for the Mexican publication *La Revista Moderna de México* at the request of de Zayas's close friend José Juan Tablada. Like many Mexican artists yearning to be a part of the avant-garde, Montenegro had lived in Paris and other parts of Europe at the same time as de Zayas did. For more on Montenegro, see Rodrigo Gutiérrez Viñuales, "Roberto Montenegro y los artistas americanos en Mallorca (1914–1919)," *Anales del Instituto de Investigaciones Estéticas* 25, no. 82 (2003): 93–121, http://www.scielo.org.mx/pdf/aiie/v25n82/v25n82a4.pdf; and Ida Rodríguez Prampolini, *El Surrealismo y el arte fantástico de México* (Mexico City: UNAM, Instituto de Investigaciones Estéticas, 1983), 48–51.

131. Apart from *Máscaras mexicanas*, Montenegro was the author of, among other books, a bilingual volume *Mexican Painting (1800–1860) / Pintura mexicana (1800–1860)* (1933); an essay in MoMA's *Twenty Centuries of Mexican Art* catalog (1940); a catalog of Mexico's Museo de Artes Populares (1948); and *Retablos de Mexico* (1950, with translations by Irene Nicholson).

132. Roberto Montenegro seems to have at least known of Stendahl's agent Guillermo M. Echániz since 1932, when he wrote to the artist Miguel Covarrubias complaining that "Chano" (presumably Echániz) and "Willy" (probably the American expatriate silver designer William Spratling) were buying up all the available pre-Columbian works found in the southern state of Guerrero. Montenegro to Covarrubias, Mexico, 15 November 1932, Archivo Miguel Covarrubias, Sala de Archivos y Colecciones Especiales, Dirección de Bibliotecas, Universidad de las Américas Puebla, archivero 2/6, cajón 3/3, C.C. 54, no. 185 (Correspondencia M II). While Chano is usually a nickname for a person whose name ends in *-iano*, Covarrubias and Montenegro bestowed nicknames on many people in their circle, and the Chano in Montenegro's letter is probably referring to Echániz. That Echániz, Spratling, and Stendahl were in close contact and traded and sold pieces among themselves is demonstrated in many letters and other documents in the Stendahl Art Galleries Records at the Getty Research Institute (GRI), Los Angeles. See, for instance, William Spratling to Earl Stendahl, 14 June 1948, Stendahl Art Galleries Records, GRI, box 91, folder 1; and Earl Stendahl to Bill [Guillermo] Echániz, 8 January 1942, Stendahl Art Galleries Records, GRI, box 10, folder 3.

133. Walter Arensberg to Roberto Montenegro, Hollywood, 29 October 1938, PMA-WLA, box 21, folder 18.

134. The head is illustrated in the Philadelphia Museum of Art's 1954 catalog of the Arensberg collection: Philadelphia Museum of Art, *Pre-Columbian Sculpture*, vol. 2 of *The Louise and Walter Arensberg Collection*, classified and annotated by George Kubler (Philadelphia: Philadelphia Museum of Art, 1954), no. 166. Retablos, sometimes called ex-votos, are paintings, often small, that are offered to a saint, the Virgin, or the like, usually in thanks for a favor believed to have been received through the intercession of the religious figure. In Mexico, retablos are frequently painted on tin. The Arensbergs acquired several retablos from Roberto Montenegro by gift or purchase; one is *Fall from a Balcony* (see plate 44.20). Several of the retablos acquired from Montenegro were made in thanks for convalescences; interestingly, the Arensbergs frequently complained of ailments in letters to Montenegro and cited their infirmities as reasons why they could not visit Mexico. See plates 35.14 and 45.13 for two retablos titled *Recovery from an Illness*.

135. See Roberto Montenegro, "Folk Art / Arte Popular," in *Twenty Centuries of Mexican Art / Veinte siglos de arte mexicano*, exh. cat. (New York: Museum of Modern Art and the Instituto de Antropología e Historia de México, 1940), 109–36, https://www.moma.org/documents/moma_catalogue_2985_300061951.pdf.

136. Montenegro's painting *Maya Women* was also included in *Twenty Centuries of Mexican Art* and was acquired by MoMA (acc. 560.1941). See *Twenty Centuries of Mexican Art*, 155. *The Double* was not illustrated in the exhibition catalog.

137. Montenegro contributed two works to the surrealism exhibition organized in Mexico City in 1940 by André Breton, Wolfgang Paalen, and César Moro; see *Exposición Internacional del Surrealismo*, exh. cat. (Mexico City: Galeria de Arte Mexicano, 1940), unpaginated. The Arensbergs sold most of the modern Mexican paintings in their collection by 1946, but even then they retained works by Montenegro and the Guatemalan painter Carlos Mérida, who also exhibited in the *Exposición Internacional del Surrealismo*. The exhibition cocoordinator Paalen, an Austrian artist living in exile in Mexico, was aware of the Arensbergs' collection. He once asked to reproduce a work they owned for an issue of *Dyn*, the journal he founded and published in Mexico from 1942 to 1944; see Paalen to Louise and Walter Arensberg, Mexico City, 26 September 1944, PMA-WLA, box 14, folder 19.

138. Montenegro had an exhibition at Stendahl's gallery around 1937; see the exhibition file for *Paintings by Roberto Montenegro*, Stendahl Art Galleries Records, 1907–1971, Archives of American Art, Smithsonian Institution, box 3, folder 17. Apparently at that time, Montenegro painted a portrait of Earl's daughter Eleanor; she was not happy with the portrait and kept it in storage. See Dammann, *Exhibitionist: Earl Stendahl*, 110–11.

139. Vincent Price, *I Like What I Know: A Visual Autobiography* (Garden City, NY: Doubleday, 1959), 183.

140. Robert Wood Bliss to the archaeologist A. V. Kidder, 4 February 1944, © Dumbarton Oaks, House Collection, Washington, DC.

141. See PMA-WLA, box 25, AIN 1145. Stendahl's invoice to Arensberg for the sculpture calls it a "falic [*sic*] god"; Stendahl Art Galleries, invoice to Walter Arensberg, 27 February 1939, PMA-WLA, box 28, folder 28. It is true that from the Huasteca region originate large stones representing erect penises, known to have been placed at temples (some images of these, especially the "Phallus of Yahualica," circulated in the early twentieth century on postcards and stereo cards). Objects from the region were part of a *salón secreto*, or secret gallery, at the museum of anthropology in Mexico City. Montenegro might have mentioned this gallery to the Arensbergs or perhaps even showed them the difficult-to-obtain catalog; see Ramón Mena, *Catálogo del salón secreto (culto al falo)* (Mexico City: Imprenta del Museo Nacional de Arqueología, Historia y Etnografía, 1926). But these particular works of the Arensbergs seem to have no real phallic connection.

142. Stendahl Art Galleries, invoice to Walter Arensberg, 1 April 1940, PMA-WLA, box 28, folder 30.

143. Alfred Stendahl, interview by Goodwin, 31.

144. See William Jerome Gill, "Art from Nobody Knows Where," *Saturday Evening Post*, 8 February 1964, 58; and Dammann, *Exhibitionist: Earl Stendahl*, 140–42. The story about the Colima museum, at least, is fully corroborated in two letters from Echániz (who signed himself "Agent B 52") to Stendahl, Mexico City, 14 February and 8 July 1941, Stendahl Art Galleries Records, GRI, Los Angeles, box 10, folder 3, subject file: Echániz, G. M., 1940–42.

145. See W. R. Valentiner to Walter Arensberg, Detroit, 24 May 1945; and Walter Arensberg to Valentiner, Hollywood, 31 May 1945; both PMA-WLA, box 5, folder 76.

146. Walter Arensberg to W. R. Valentiner, Hollywood, 7 June 1945, PMA-WLA, box 5, folder 76.

147. See Stendahl Art Galleries, invoices to Walter and Louise Arensberg, 1940–41, PMA-WLA, box 28, folder 21. For more information on the Arensberg–Stendahl trade, see Sawelson-Gorse, "'For the Want of a Nail,'" 252, 254. There are numerous invoices for purchases in 1941 in the Arensberg and Stendahl archives; frustratingly, however, no correspondence makes clear which works were considered to be part of this trade. One handwritten note suggests that the amount may have been about $6,000, but this is far from certain.

148. Katharine Kuh, *The Open Eye: In Pursuit of Art* (New York: Harper & Row, 1971), 58.

149. Earl Stendahl to Bill [Guillermo] Echániz, Los Angeles, 23 March 1942, Stendahl Art Galleries Records, GRI, box 10, folder 3.

150. See Dammann, *Exhibitionist: Earl Stendahl*, 156–57.

151. See Dammann, *Exhibitionist: Earl Stendahl*, 133.

152. Kuh, *My Love Affair with Modern Art*, 22.

153. Dammann, *Exhibitionist: Earl Stendahl*, 140.

154. See Coe, "From *Huaquero* to Connoisseur," 279–81.

155. See Miguel Palacios Beltrán, "Introducción de la imprenta en México," 27–28; and Palacios Beltrán, "Otros impresores del siglo XVI en México," 54, both in *Bibliotecas y archivos*, no. 2 (1971); see https://biblat.unam.mx/es/buscar/palacios-beltran. From the 1930s until the 1960s, the Librería Anticuaria G. M. Echániz produced small runs (approximately twenty-five copies each) of super-deluxe editions of pre-Columbian codices, including the Codices Laud (1937), Zouche-Nuttall (1939), Fejérváry-Mayer (1945), and Cortesiano (1949), as well as a book on stamps of ancient Mexico. Echániz (?–1965) displayed his collection of colonial books and printing presses in his home in Mexico City.

156. See Dammann, *Exhibitionist: Earl Stendahl*, 130. There was considerable doubt among prospective buyers that the press was as Echániz represented it, so it was never sold and remained in Echániz's possession until his death; see Palacios Beltrán, "Otros impresores del siglo XVI en México," 53–54.

157. Dammann, *Exhibitionist: Earl Stendahl*, 130.

158. In 1935, for instance, Echániz sold two ceramic vessels to the Museo Nacional de Antropología for 14 pesos; see Archivo Histórico del Museo Nacional de Antropología, Mexico City, vol. 94, document 3151, 5 July–14 August 1935. Also in 1935, the museum negotiated an exchange of objects with him; see Archivo Histórico del Museo Nacional de Antropología, Mexico City, vol. 95, document 3182, 19 February–7 November 1935. See also Museo Nacional de Antropología, *Catálogo del Archivo Histórico*, vol. 1, *1831–1936* (Mexico City: Consejo Nacional para la Cultura y las Artes, 1992), 298, 301. Echániz often asked to be credited as the source of these objects in the museum's annals or other publications, but this request was not always accommodated.

159. See Guillermo Echániz, "Consideraciones sobre coleccionismo de arqueología mexicana" (Mexico: printed by the author, 1958), 9. Advertising the value of museums' pre-Columbian collections would probably have increased the flow of pre-Columbian objects from the nondealer public who uncovered artifacts in Mexico to dealers like Echániz. Echániz also told Stendahl that he had encouraged a friend in state government to pursue the construction of a museum in the western Mexican state of Colima "to show the people those things have real value so they do not sell so cheap" (except, presumably, when they sold to Echániz himself). Guillermo Echániz [he signed the letter "Agent B 52"] to Earl Stendahl, 14 February 1941, Stendahl Art Galleries Records, GRI, box 10, folder 3.

160. The Arensbergs' $4,000 purchase of pre-Columbian art from the Brummer Gallery in May 1937, mentioned above, seems to have radically focused Stendahl's intention to acquire similar works. A document signed by Echániz certifying the authenticity of a group of Zapotec urns that Stendahl acquired (which were later determined to be falsifications) is dated 24 October 1938; Stendahl Art Galleries Records, GRI, box 10, folder 3. However, the earliest Stendahl Art Galleries invoice for a purchase by the Arensbergs of pre-Columbian works is from 13 February 1940; PMA-WLA, box 28, folder 30. Walter Arensberg was aware of Echániz's work in Mexico on behalf of Stendahl. In June 1941 he asked Echániz, through Stendahl, to obtain several copies of the unexpurgated version of Henry Miller's *Tropic of Capricorn*, which had been censored in the United States for its sexual content; Arensberg to Stendahl, Hollywood, 2 June 1941, PMA-WLA, box 18, folder 11. Echániz informed Stendahl in July that the book was sold out in Mexico but that he was advertising to buy used copies, without much

success; Echániz to Stendahl, 8 July 1941, Stendahl Art Galleries Records, GRI, box 10, folder 3.

161. See PMA-WLA, box 35, AIN 32; and *Vigésimo Séptimo Congreso Internacional de Americanistas: Actas de la primera sesión, celebrada en la ciudad de México en 1939* (Mexico: Instituto Nacional de Antropología e Historia, Secretaría de Educación Pública, 1947), fig. 23.

162. The story of the Stone of Chiapa is convoluted and involves its publication by the noted Mayanist Sylvanus G. Morley, its possible sale by René d'Harnoncourt, and various other details. Why the stone would have been placed on a street corner in the residential district of Roma in Mexico City is a mystery. For a full description of the stela's movements, see Karl Herbert Mayer, *Maya Monuments: Sculptures of Unknown Provenance in the United States*, trans. Sandra L. Brizée (Ramona, CA: Acoma, 1980), 57–58.

163. See César Lizardi Ramos, "Importante monumento mexicano se halla en Estados Unidos," *Revista de Revistas*, 9 September 1951, 22–24. An English translation of the article is in PMA-WLA, box 11, folder 33; Lizardi Ramos apparently sent the Arensbergs a copy of the article and the couple had it translated and annotated. Had they lived longer, the Arensbergs might have formed a friendly relationship with Lizardi Ramos; they exchanged very cordial letters with him, in which it is clear that Walter was impressed by Lizardi Ramos's knowledge. See PMA-WLA, box 11, folder 33. For more information on Lizardi Ramos, see J. Eric S. Thompson, "César Lizardi Ramos (1895–1971)," *Estudios de Cultura Maya* 9 (1973): 381–91, https://revistas-filologicas.unam.mx/estudios-cultura-maya/index.php/ecm/article/view/376/377.

164. On the Templo Mayor monumental shells, see Leonardo López Luján and Simon Martin, "Los caracoles monumentales del recinto sagrado de Tenochtitlan," *Arqueología Mexicana* 27, no. 160 (2019): 26–35. The shell sculptures would almost certainly have been made in groups of four or five for placement in and near the Templo Mayor.

165. Frederick Peterson to Frank Boos, 8 May 1965, Frederick A. Peterson Papers, Center for Southwest Research, University Libraries, University of New Mexico, box 1, folder 4. In one letter to Echániz, Stendahl seems to joke that Echániz had created a "copy" of a *palma* in the shape of a turkey, but it's unclear whether he meant to use it for advertising or to sell as authentic. In a second letter, Stendahl asks whether Echániz has "unloaded" his *palma* yet on the "French boy" of their acquaintance (possibly a reference to Pierre Matisse); Stendahl to Echániz, 2 January 1942 and 8 January 1942 (the 2 January letter is incorrectly dated 1941), Stendahl Art Galleries Records, GRI, box 10, folder 3.

166. Dammann, *Exhibitionist: Earl Stendahl*, 170. In a 7 May 1941 letter to Walter Arensberg and Robert Woods Bliss, Stendahl claimed that he would sell the works to them at the cost of the works plus a 20 percent markup, but in reality his profit may have been much more substantial. PMA-WLA, box 18, folder 11.

167. On Josef Smilovits (1898–1987), see finding aid for Léner Quartet Papers, Music Division, New York Public Library, http://archives.nypl.org/20198#overview.

168. Yolopatli would later become the first professional chamber orchestra in Mexico; see Orquestra de Cámara de Bellas Artes, "Integrantes," https://ocba.bellasartes.gob.mx/integrantes.html.

169. Kubler referred to the Teotihuacan masks as "face panels" in Philadelphia Museum of Art, *Pre-Columbian Sculpture*, figs. 15–23. He used the term *face panels*, not *masks*, because the eyeholes in the Teotihuacan masks are not drilled through, making it impossible to use them as masks.

170. In the end, Walter Arensberg was able to buy the granite mask for $2,000. For a small mask that could be easily smuggled out of Mexico in luggage, this sale was a financial coup for Smilovits, although he claimed to be selling the mask "for a friend." See the correspondence between Josef Smilovits and Walter Arensberg, from 11 December 1950 to 21 February 1951, PMA-WLA, box 17, folder 42.

171. See Sawelson-Gorse, "'Silent Guard,'" 253–55, 323n41. Thanks to auction catalogs, we know something of the scope of the other *salonières*' collections, and there is sometimes other documentation. On Edward G. Robinson's collection, see the catalog from its exhibition at the Museum of Modern Art, *Forty Paintings from the Edward G. Robinson Collection, March 4–April 12, 1953* (New York: Museum of Modern Art, 1953), https://www.moma.org/documents/moma_catalogue_3301_300062120.pdf. The exhibition traveled to the National Gallery of Art; see Museum of Modern Art, "Paintings from Well-Known Edward G. Robinson Collection to Go on View at Museum," press release no. 530224-15, 1 March 1953, https://www.moma.org/momaorg/shared/pdfs/docs/press_archives/1685/releases/MOMA_1953_0015_15.pdf?2010. Much of Robinson's pre-Columbian collection was included in *Catalogue of Primitive Art from the Edward G. Robinson Collection* (London: Sotheby & Co., 1973). On Charles Laughton's collection, see David Wallace, *Exiles in Hollywood* (Pompton Plains, NJ: Limelight Editions, 2006), 160–61; and *Pre-Columbian and North-American Indian Art: Properties from Various Owners, Including the Charles Laughton–Elsa Lanchester Collection* (New York: Parke-Bernet Galleries, 1966). Less is known about Ruth Maitland's collection; a short synopsis is available at the Frick Collection, Archives Directory for the History of Consulting in America, https://research.frick.org/directory/detail/1317.

172. See the obituary for Macgowan (1888–1963) in *University of California: In Memoriam* (April 1964): 39–44, https://oac.cdlib.org/ark:/13030/hb6g500784/?brand=oac4. One of Macgowan's essays in *Shadowland* was "Expressionism on Broadway," *Shadowland* 8, no. 4 (1923): 48–49, 72; reprinted in *The Best of "Shadowland,"* ed. Anna Kate Sterling (Metuchen, NJ: Scarecrow, 1987), 183–87.

173. See Sawelson-Gorse, "'Silent Guard,'" 61.

174. See Macgowan and Rosse, *Masks and Demons*, 53.

175. See Macgowan and Rosse, *Masks and Demons*, 165–66.

176. Macgowan and Rosse, *Masks and Demons*, 49. The authors mistakenly describe this mask as an Aztec piece—an attribution that probably came from the American Museum of Natural History, where they say the mask was held; see Macgowan and Rosse, *Masks and Demons*, 167.

177. Macgowan and Rosse, *Masks and Demons*, 49.

178. The Arensbergs' Quetzalcoatl research file makes direct reference to the stone figure believed to depict Quetzalcoatl that was in the Arensbergs' living room (see plate 35.3). See "Quetzalcoatl: God of the Air, Lord of Life," unattributed and undated research notes, PMA-WLA, box 23, folder 15.

179. Victoria Price, daughter of Vincent Price, claims that Macgowan was chosen, at her father's suggestion, as the first president of the Modern Institute of Art's board of trustees. See Victoria Price, *Vincent Price: A Daughter's Biography* (New York: St. Martin's, 1999), 139. Vincent Price, but not Macgowan, is named as a founder of the Modern Institute in a 1947 newspaper article; see "New Museum to Put Modern Art on Show," *Los Angeles Times*, 25 November 1947, A18. For more on the founding of the Modern Institute of Art, see Naomi Sawelson-Gorse, "Hollywood Conversations: Duchamp and the Arensbergs," in *West Coast Duchamp*, ed. Bonnie Clearwater (Miami Beach: Grassfield in association with Shoshana Wayne Gallery, 1991), 26.

180. Installation photographs of the exhibition *Masks from the Collection of Kenneth Macgowan*, Museum of Costume Art, 10 February–31 March 1943, are available at https://libmma.contentdm.oclc.org/digital/collection/p16028coll1/id/23945.

181. See entry for Kenneth Macgowan, SNAC (Social Networks and Archival Context), http://n2t.net/ark:/99166/w6tb1pmf. From Stendahl he bought a very inexpensive ($1) obsidian lip plug around 1940; "Pre-Hispanic Stockbook with Prices," Stendahl Art Galleries Records, GRI, box 91, folder 6, item 271 (page 8).

182. See J. N. Emerson, review of *Early Man in the New World*, by Kenneth Macgowan, *Canadian Historical Review* 32, no. 4 (1951): 391–92.

183. Macgowan to Walter Arensberg, 30 June 1944.

184. Macgowan to Walter Arensberg, 30 June 1944.

185. See William W. Melnitz and Jack Morrison, "Kenneth Macgowan (1888–1963): A Memorial Tribute Presented to the American Educational Theatre Association," *Educational Theatre Journal* 15, no. 3 (1963): 209–11. On Kenneth Macgowan's archaeological films, see Macgowan, *Early Man in the New World* (New York: Macmillan, 1950), vii.

186. In December 1943, the Arensbergs welcomed Raymond G. McKelvey, executive secretary of the Southern California Council of Inter-American Affairs, and his Argentinian guest, Mrs. Abraham Scheps, for a tour of their collection. See McKelvey to Walter Arensberg, Los Angeles, 6 December 1943; Walter Arensberg to McKelvey, Hollywood, 8 December 1943; and McKelvey to Walter Arensberg, Los Angeles, 9 December 1943; all in PMA-WLA, box 17, folder 53.

187. Giles Healey was a charismatic adventurer who, in 1946, discovered the Maya ruins of Bonampak with relatively intact polychrome frescoes. The find was chronicled in dramatic fashion in *Life* magazine, making Healey a minor celebrity. "Maya Murals: Great Discovery Sheds Light on Culture of Ancient Race," *Life*, 21 November 1949, 80–84.

188. *The Maya through the Ages* is online at https://www.youtube.com/watch?v=67DRwY3KZUA.

189. See Kenneth Macgowan to Walter Arensberg, Los Angeles, 5 July, 22 August, and 31 August 1949; and Walter Arensberg to Macgowan, Hollywood, 15 July 1949; all in PMA-WLA, box 12, folder 58.

190. Rebeca Vega (registrar, Vincent Price Art Museum), personal communication with Ellen Hoobler, June 2019.

191. Price, *I Like What I Know*, 130.

192. Price, *I Like What I Know*, 166.

193. Robert Woods Bliss to Earl Stendahl, 6 May 1946; cited in "A California Sojourn and the Robert Woods Bliss Collection of Pre-Columbian Art," *Dumbarton Oaks Archives 75th Anniversary Blog*, 15 June 2017, https://www.doaks.org/research/library-archives/dumbarton-oaks-archives/historical-records/75th-anniversary/blog/a-california-sojourn-and-the-robert-woods-bliss-collection-of-pre-columbian-art.

194. See "A California Sojourn and the Robert Woods Bliss Collection of Pre-Columbian Art."

195. Walter Arensberg to Robert Woods Bliss, Hollywood, 1 June 1940, PMA-WLA, box 3, folder 23.

196. See Edward W. Forbes, *William Hayes Fogg Art Museum Annual Report, 1939–40*, 4–5, 17, https://www.jstor.org/stable/4301227 (registration required); and William

Hayes Fogg Art Museum, *An Exhibition of Pre-Columbian Art*, exh. cat. (Cambridge, MA: Fogg Art Museum, Harvard University, 1940), 3, 29, https://hdl.handle.net/2027/mdp.39015010997065. The Arensbergs' loan to the exhibition is listed in the catalog as a jadeite mask of "late Toltec style."

197. Bliss urged the Arensbergs to join him in lending works to the exhibition; see Bliss to Walter Arensberg, Santa Barbara, CA, 11 August 1942, PMA-WLA, box 3, folder 23.

198. See the joint catalog for the Santa Barbara and San Francisco exhibitions: Maurice Ries, *Arts of America before Columbus, 500 B.C.–A.D. 1500*, exh. cat. (Santa Barbara, CA: Santa Barbara Museum of Art; San Francisco: M. H. de Young Memorial Museum, 1942).

199. "Ancient Stone God Exhibited," newspaper unknown, date unknown; a clipping of this article, sans publication details, is in PMA-WLA, box 41, folder 37.

200. The estimate of exhibition attendance is from "Latin American Exhibition to Close Sunday," *Pasadena Star-News*, 25 November 1943; clipping located in PMA-WLA, box 41, folder 37. On presence of fakes, see Walter Arensberg to Jarvis Barlow (director of the Pasadena Art Institute), 13 October 1943, PMA-WLA, box 21, folder 21.

201. Arensberg to Barlow, 13 October 1943. Walter believed that the source of the Pasadena exhibition's fake works was Albert Ruddock, a benefactor and board member of many Pasadena institutions. Walter wrote to Kenneth Macgowan: "The objectionable objects, as we learned, were things that Ruddock found in his own garden, and simply brought to the Institute and put in place without a by-your-leave, with the idea that they were just as good as all the others." Walter Arensberg to Macgowan, Hollywood, 15 October 1943, PMA-WLA, box 12, folder 11.

202. See Earl Stendahl to Walter Arensberg and Robert Woods Bliss, Los Angeles, 7 May 1941, PMA-WLA, box 18, folder 11. Stendahl references the 20 percent cost basis in other correspondence with Walter Arensberg, but how he proved the "original cost" is unknown.

203. See Stendahl Art Galleries, invoice to Walter Arensberg, 19 February 1941, PMA-WLA, box 28, folder 31; Earl Stendahl to Walter Arensberg and Robert Woods Bliss, Los Angeles, 7 May 1941, PMA-WLA, box 18, folder 11; and Sawelson-Gorse, "'For the Want of a Nail,'" 254. Bliss got his first choice of the objects and Walter got the second and third choices; after that, the two men alternated picking from the remaining pieces. It's unclear whether collectors commonly advanced Stendahl the money to acquire objects. His son suggested it was an isolated incident; see Alfred Stendahl, interview by Goodwin, 47–48. Documents from the Stendahl Art Galleries Records suggest that Stendahl had considered repeating this fundraising technique in 1942 but told Echániz that "Mrs. Arensberg doesn't want to advance money on a gamble," which gives reason to believe that the results of the 1941 arrangement may not have been entirely satisfactory to eitther Bliss or the Arensbergs. Stendahl to Echániz, 31 January 1942, Stendahl Art Galleries Records, GRI, box 10, folder 3.

204. Echániz urged Stendahl in a letter to "establish a competence [*sic*] between A and B." "B. 52" [Guillermo Echániz] to Earl Stendahl, 5 May 1941, Stendahl Art Galleries Records, GRI, box 10, folder 3.

205. See Teotihuacan (Central Mexico), Net-Jaguar Mural, 400–600, Dumbarton Oaks Research Library and Collection, Pre-Columbian Collection, Washington, DC, accession no. PC.B.062, http://museum.doaks.org/Obj23026.

206. Price, *I Like What I Know*, 200.

207. Carlos Chávez, general director of the Instituto Nacional de Bellas Artes, invited the Arensbergs to visit Mexico in a letter to Walter, 19 April 1950, PMA-WLA, box 10, folder 2.

208. See Roberto Montenegro to Walter and Louise Arensberg, Mexico City, 3 February 1940, and 9 November 1942, PMA-WLA, box 21, folder 19; and Juan O'Gorman to Walter Arensberg, 20 January 1946, PMA-WLA, box 14, folder 7. Frances Toor, who occasionally visited a brother in Los Angeles, invited the Arensbergs to Mexico several times; see her letters to Walter from Mexico City, on 5 August, 22 September, and 27 November 1939, all in PMA-WLA, box 18, folder 46.

209. For the fullest account of this history, see Holly Barnet-Sánchez, "The Necessity of Pre-Columbian Art in the United States: Appropriations and Transformations of Heritage," in *Collecting the Pre-Columbian Past: A Symposium at Dumbarton Oaks, 6th and 7th October 1990*, ed. Elizabeth Hill Boone (Washington, DC: Dumbarton Oaks Research Library and Collection, 1993), 177–208. See also Barnet-Sánchez, "The Necessity of Pre-Columbian Art: U.S. Museums and the Role of Foreign Policy," 177–208; and Hoobler, "An 'Artistic Discovery' of Antiquity," 119–34.

210. See James Oles, *South of the Border: Mexico in the American Imagination 1914–1947*, exh. cat. (Washington, DC: Smithsonian Institution Press, 1993), 137–45.

211. Walter Arensberg to Curt Valentin, Hollywood, 20 June 1940, PMA-WLA, box 3, folder 54.

212. Conversion to 2019 dollars based on https://www.dollartimes.com/inflation, accessed 20 January 2020.

213. See Stendahl Art Galleries, invoices to Walter and Louise Arensberg, 1937–45, PMA-WLA, box 28, folders 28, 30–33.

214. The Native American objects in the Arensberg collection are deserving of more in-depth study.

215. This contrasts with Alfred Stendahl's simplistic assessment of the Arensbergs as being almost solely interested in stone works; see Stendahl, interview by Goodwin, 42. A full listing of the Arensberg collection at the Philadelphia Museum of Art shows they owned sixteen Andean works (from Peru and Ecuador), as well as a few Central American gold, stone, and ceramic works.

216. See John F. Scott, "Dressed to Kill: Stone Regalia of the Mesoamerican Ballgame," in *The Sport of Life and Death: The Mesoamerican Ballgame*, ed. E. Michael Whittington (London: Thames & Hudson, 2001), 50–63.

217. Earl Stendahl to Bill [Guillermo] Echániz, Los Angeles, 2 November 1940, Stendahl Art Galleries Records, GRI, box 10, folder 3.

218. See Veracruz (Mexico), Palma, 7th–10th century, Metropolitan Museum of Art, New York, Museum Purchase, 1900, 00.5.56, https://www.metmuseum.org/art/collection/search/318675.

219. Jules Langsner, "The Arensberg Riches of Cubism," *ARTnews*, November 1949, 62.

220. Some of the Arensbergs' hachas are pictured in plates 4.28, 6.21, 13.9, 14.13, 20.8, 26.4, 26.5, and 58.3. Yokes are pictured in plates 39.4, 39.5, and 41.27. See also Philadelphia Museum of Art, *Pre-Columbian Sculpture*, nos. 136–48 (hachas) and 159–63 (yokes).

221. Stendahl Art Galleries, invoice to Walter Arensberg, 1 April 1940, PMA-WLA, box 28, folder 30. The $900 the Arensbergs paid for the yoke in 1940 would equal about $16,000 today; conversion based on https://www.dollartimes.com/inflation, accessed 20 January 2020.

222. Alfonso Caso, "Pre-Spanish Art / Arte Prehispanico," in *Twenty Centuries of Mexican Art / Veinte siglos de arte mexicano*, exh. cat. (Mexico City: Museum of Modern Art and the Instituto de Antropología e Historia de México, 1940), 25–26, https://www.moma.org/documents/moma_catalogue_2985_300061951.pdf. The yoke that Caso was likely citing has been revealed to be a fake, as detailed in Michel Krutt, "Un Yugo 'in situ' en Omealca, Veracruz," *Boletín del INAH* 36 (June 1969): 16–19. I am very grateful to Rex Koontz for his input on the actual use of the ballgame paraphernalia and for bringing this article to my attention.

223. See Caso, "Pre-Spanish Art," 63, 66.

224. Teotihuacan masks have been described by the art historian Matthew H. Robb as "one of the most common yet enigmatic object types in Teotihuacan culture." They may have been attached to funerary bundles, but their precise meaning and use is not clear. Matthew H. Robb, "Introduction to Teotihuacan," in *Teotihuacan: City of Water, City of Fire*, ed. Matthew H. Robb, exh. cat. (San Francisco: Fine Arts Museums of San Francisco, 2017), 236–37. Robb has expanded on his hypotheses about the function and significance of these works in his essay "The 500 Faces of Teotihuacan: Masks and the Formation of Mesoamerican Canons," in *Canons and Values: Ancient to Modern*, ed. Larry Silver and Kevin Terraciano (Los Angeles: Getty Research Institute, 2019), 114–37.

225. Eight Teotihuacan masks are illustrated in Philadelphia Museum of Art, *Pre-Columbian Sculpture*, nos. 15–22. Other Teotihuacan masks are in an Arensberg pre-Columbian study collection at the Philadelphia Museum of Art; see note 259 in this essay for more on the study collection.

226. While the Arensbergs were collecting and displaying Teotihuacan masks, gestalt psychology was being formulated and popularized in Germany by the psychologist Max Wertheimer. One of its principles is that people innately tend toward "similarity grouping," or mentally grouping together objects that share commonalities of design, color, size, and so on; and that these groupings can feel particularly harmonious. See Roy R. Behrens, "Art Design and Gestalt Theory," *Leonardo* 31, no. 4 (1998): 299–303.

227. In the 1960s (years after the Arensbergs collected pre-Columbian art), the concept of shamanic transformation became popular for understanding the imagery of pre-Columbian objects, and it remains a topic of enduring fascination for many collectors today. For a critical review of the use of shamanism to interpret pre-Columbian art, see Cecelia F. Klein, Eulogio Guzmán, Elisa C. Mandell, and Maya Stanfield-Mazzi, "The Role of Shamanism in Mesoamerican Art: A Reassessment," *Current Anthropology* 43, no. 3 (2002): 383–419.

228. Stendahl Art Galleries, invoice to Walter Arensberg, 7 November 1940, PMA-WLA, box 28, folder 30.

229. Echániz and Stendahl seem to refer to the Arensbergs' stone goddess figure in their correspondence. Stendahl asks Echániz to reassure him that the works he sold to Arensberg were "absolutely genuine." Echániz replied, "There is a ranch near Teotihuacan. The farmer found a pyramid and in an underground chamber there was the fresco and the two pieces, the large woman with thumbs up and the other figure." Stendahl to Echániz, Los Angeles, 11 November 1940, and Echániz to Stendahl, 13 November 1940; both Stendahl Art Galleries Records, GRI, box 10, folder 3. Recent excavations at the site to which Echániz refers have revealed underground tunnels filled with precious works under pyramids, but the provenance of the Arensbergs' stone goddess is still unknown.

230. The monumental Teotihuacan goddess (similar to the Arensbergs' smaller goddess) is mentioned in many major books on pre-Columbian art published pre-1940, such as Lucien Biart, *The Aztecs: Their History, Manners, and Customs*, trans. J. L. Garner (Chicago: McClurg, 1887), 149–50, which claimed that the statue was originally covered in gold that was looted by the Spanish conquistadors. The goddess is also mentioned in Herbert J. Spinden, *Ancient Civilizations of Mexico and Central America* (New York: American Museum of Natural History, 1917).

231. The art historian Esther Pasztory has raised questions about the authenticity of the figure, in personal communication with Ellen Hoobler, October 2004. However, other art historians, including Matthew H. Robb, assert that the figure is not particularly anomalous, pointing to the diverse materials found over the past ten years in subterranean tunnels at the site. Robb, personal communication with Hoobler, September 2019.

232. See Mary Miller and Karl Taube, *An Illustrated Dictionary of the Gods and Symbols of Ancient Mexico and the Maya* (London: Thames & Hudson, 1993), 188–89.

233. The 1905 Spanish-language edition of the Florentine Codex would have been difficult, but not impossible, to obtain. Since portions of the Arensbergs' research file on Quetzalcoatl refer to the Florentine Codex, it is probable that Macgowan owned some version of the codex. For the 1905 edition, see Bernardino de Sahagún, *Historia general de las cosas de Nueva España*, ed. Francisco del Paso y Troncoso, 4 vols. (nos. 6–8) (Madrid: Fototipia de Hauser y Menet, 1905). Arthur J. O. Anderson and Charles E. Dibble, translators of an English version of Sahagún's codex that was published in twelve volumes between 1948 and 1982, cite a microfilm version of the Florentine Codex that has been available since 1938 at the School for American Research in Santa Fe, New Mexico; it is likely that this was only one of several microfilm copies of the codex. See Sahagún, *General History of the Things of New Spain*, vol. 12, *The War of Conquest: How It Was Waged Here in Mexico*, trans. Arthur J. O. Anderson and Charles E. Dibble (Salt Lake City: University of Utah Press, 1978), vi. Many thanks to Charles B. Dibble, nephew of the translator Dibble, for bringing this note in Anderson and Dibble's translation to my attention.

234. See Caso, "Pre-Spanish Art," 59–60.

235. Montenegro's *Síntesis* is in the collection of the Museo Colección Blaisten in Mexico City; see http://museoblaisten.com/Obra/2243/Sintesis. His depiction of Xipe Totec resembles the Huastec head in the Arensberg collection (see plate 32.7).

236. Montenegro's print *Xipe* is in the collection of the Museo Colección Blaisten; see http://museoblaisten.com/Obra/46/Xipe.

237. See Stendahl Art Galleries, invoice to Walter Arensberg, 9 July 1941, PMA-WLA, box 28, folder 31.

238. See Peter T. Markman and Roberta H. Markman, *Masks of the Spirit: Image and Metaphor in Mesoamerica* (Berkeley: University of California Press, 1989). See also the human-serpent combination figures in the Arensberg collection (plates 12.4, 35.3, and 43.4).

239. Caso, "Pre-Spanish Art," 26. On West Mexico, see Christopher S. Beekman and Robert B. Pickering, eds., *Shaft Tombs and Figures in West Mexican Society: A Reassessment*, exh. cat. (Tulsa, OK: Thomas Gilcrease Institute of American History and Art, 2016).

240. For a Colima woman figure, see plate 5.27. For Colima men, see plates 40.11 and 40.21. For Colima dogs, see plates 47.18, 58.4, and 58.5.

241. For other seated figures that were purchased from Stendahl, see Nayarit (Mexico), Seated Female Figure, 300 BCE–200 CE, The Walters Art Museum (2009.20.40), Gift of John Bourne, 2009; Nayarit (Mexico), Seated Male Ancestor, 1st–4th century, Metropolitan Museum of Art (2005.91.2), Gift of The Andrall and Joanne Pearson Collection, 2005; and Nayarit (Mexico), Seated Male Figure with Fringed Headdress, 200 BCE–500 CE, Los Angeles County Museum of Art (M.86.296.15), The Proctor Stafford Collection, purchased with funds provided by Mr. and Mrs. Allan C. Balch.

242. Bill Henry, "By the Way with Bill Henry," *Los Angeles Times*, 17 June 1955, A1.

243. For more on Carlos Chávez and his celebrity in the United States, see Leonora Saavedra, ed., *Carlos Chávez and His World* (Princeton: Princeton University Press, 2015)—in particular, see the following chapters: Leonora Saavedra, "Carlos Chávez and the Myth of the Aztec Renaissance," 134–63; Helen Delpar, "Carlos Chávez and the Mexican 'Vogue,' 1925–1940," 204–19; and Antonio Saborit, "Masters Carlos Chávez and Miguel Covarrubias: A Puppet Show," trans. Rebecca Levi, 237–53.

244. Carlos Chávez to Walter Arensberg, Mexico City, 8 August 1950, PMA-WLA, box 10, folder 2.

245. Walter Arensberg to Carlos Chavez, 26 April 1950, PMA-WLA, box 10, folder 2.

246. Walter expresses the Arensbergs' concern about the viability of a Francis Bacon library in Mexico in a letter to Benjamin "Ap" Fuller, 13 March 1950, PMA-WLA, box 7, folder 56.

247. Daniel Catton Rich to Walter Arensberg, Chicago, 29 April 1945, PMA-WLA, box 2, folder 1.

248. Walter Arensberg to Ruth Maitland, Hollywood, 5 May 1945, PMA-WLA, box 12, folder 18. Maitland's home and collection were featured alongside the Arensbergs' in "Great Art ... in Four California Houses," in the February 1945 issue of *Vogue*.

249. Katharine Kuh, "An Interview with Katharine Kuh," by Avis Berman, ed. William McNaught, *Archives of American Art Journal* 27, no. 3 (1987): 28.

250. See Daniel Catton Rich to Walter Arensberg, Chicago, 6 October 1948, PMA-WLA, box 2, folder 4. Tatiana Proskouriakoff's research mainly focused on the Maya, particularly on the decipherment of their glyphs, so Rich may have felt that the Arensbergs would be interested in her experience.

251. Rich to Arensberg, 6 October 1948. He explained to Walter: "On our list for the exhibit, we chose approximately 43 pieces. In that way, the Art Institute would be responsible for a sixth or a seventh of the total expenses involved" in the creation of a catalog of the Arensbergs' pre-Columbian collection. Rich wrote that Proskouriakoff would charge $20 a day for her work, and crating and shipping the exhibition's 43 pre-Columbian works would cost about $2,500. "This strikes Katharine and me as a little high in connection with our budget," he continued, "and it may be necessary to eliminate one or two of the largest pre-Columbian pieces which will require special and complex boxes and handling."

252. Walter Arensberg to Daniel Catton Rich, Hollywood, 14 October 1948, PMA-WLA, box 2, folder 4.

253. Alfred Stendahl, who noted that his father acted at times as an agent for the Arensbergs in the distribution of their collection, was surprised by this turn of events. He seems to have been unaware that the disposition of their pre-Columbian collection was important for them. Stendahl claimed that Arensberg "wanted the cubist collection of his kept together for, say, fifteen years—maybe it was twenty, I don't know. The other material, which is mostly pre-Columbian, I don't believe he had any desires one way or the other, except that he did want to prove that the cubists were a significant period. He wanted it kept together for that reason." Apparently the Stendahls underestimated the Arensbergs' commitment to pre-Columbian art. Stendahl, interview by Goodwin, 35.

254. Walter Arensberg to Marcel Duchamp, 8 April 1950, PMA-WLA, box 6, folder 32. The importance for the Arensbergs of having their pre-Columbian and modern collections displayed together is also noted in Walter's correspondence with the Peabody Museum of Archaeology and Ethnology at Harvard University. The Peabody Museum was interested in acquiring the Arensbergs' pre-Columbian collection, but Walter told its director, Donald Scott, "We have always felt that the pre-Columbian material and the art of the twentieth century are illuminated by their juxtaposition in the collection as it now stands." Walter Arensberg to Donald Scott, Hollywood, 19 November 1948, PMA-WLA, box 14, folder 41.

255. Arensberg to Duchamp, 8 April 1950.

256. See George Roberts and Mary Roberts, *Triumph on Fairmount: Fiske Kimball and the Philadelphia Museum of Art* (Philadelphia: J. B. Lippincott, 1959), 257.

257. Fiske Kimball to Sturgis Ingersoll, 7 February 1949, Philadelphia Museum of Art, Library and Archives, Fiske Kimball Papers (hereafter cited as PMA-FKP), box 162, folder 29.

258. Fiske Kimball to Sturgis Ingersoll, 9 February 1949, PMA-FKP, box 162, folder 29.

259. The Arensberg display collection at the Philadelphia Museum of Art comprises 5 African objects (including an "Egyptian mummy cloth"); 208 pre-Columbian objects; 82 Native American objects; 2 Latin American colonial objects; 3 "miscellaneous" (Greek, Etruscan, and Melanesian) objects; and 7 Asian objects. The study collection includes 94 pre-Columbian objects; 173 Native American objects; 23 works of colonial and modern Latin American folk and religious art; 3 "miscellaneous" objects (2 Balinese, 1 Melanesian); and 39 Asian objects from China, Japan, Korea, and India.

260. See Philadelphia Museum of Art, *Pre-Columbian Sculpture*.

261. Mesoamerica has some shared cultural characteristics across the region, such as the use of a 260-day ritual calendar, the playing of a sacred ballgame, and some deities in common, even though it was populated by diverse peoples who developed in different ways in disparate parts of the region.

262. Arensberg, interview by Ross; this volume, 405.

263. Arensberg, interview by Ross; this volume, 405.

264. Stendahl Art Galleries, invoice to Walter Arensberg, 19 June 1950, PMA-WLA, box 28, folder 35. The $5,000 that the Arensbergs paid for the Teotihuacan mural fragment would equal about $52,000 today; conversion based on https://www.dollartimes.com/inflation, accessed 20 January 2020. It would be worth much more than that in today's art market; a Teotihuacan mural fragment with a pre-1970 provenance is now usually worth at least several hundred thousand dollars, if not over a million dollars.

265. Bliss's 1941 purchase from Stendahl was the Net-Jaguar Mural that is now in the Dumbarton Oaks Research Library and Collection (accession no. PC.B.062).

266. There are other mural fragments from Teotihuacan in private collections and museums, including the Fine Arts Museums of San Francisco, Dumbarton Oaks, Duke University, the Baltimore Museum of Art, and the University of Missouri at Columbia. For a fascinating account of the network of dealers and collectors who removed and exported these murals from Teotihuacan, see Matthew H. Robb, "Tracing the History of the Techinantitla Murals," *Ixiptla*, no. 4 (2018): 80–91.

267. César Lizardi Ramos, "Murales Mexicanos en Estados Unidos," *Excelsior* (Mexico City), 24 September 1962, 14; located in Fondo Alfonso Caso Andrade,

Archivo Técnico de la Biblioteca Nacional de Antropología e Historia, Museo Nacional de Antropología, box 12, folder 21. The foreign sculptor that Lizardi Ramos referred to may have been (among many possibilities) the Colombian-born Rómulo Rozo, who lived in Mexico until his death. Rozo's son, Rómulo Rozo Krauss, writes that the sculptor was impoverished in Mexico—so much so that he slept under a coverlet made from Mexican Postal Service sacks. Rómulo Rozo Krauss, *Rómulo Rozo: Escultor Indoamericano*, 2nd ed. (Mexico City: Ediciones Universidades de Latinoamérica, 1974; Mexico City: Delfos Editor, 1990), 74. Citation refers to the Delfos edition.

268. The mural fragment in the photograph of Stendahl's gallery (see fig. 46) is now in the collection of the Denver Art Museum (accession no. 1965.202). It is reproduced in Linda R. Manzanilla, "The Xalla Palace in Teotihuacan," in *Teotihuacan: City of Water, City of Fire*, ed. Matthew H. Robb, exh. cat. (San Francisco: Fine Arts Museums of San Francisco, 2017), 121 (fig. 15.4).

269. In 1970, UNESCO finalized the *Convention on the Means of Prohibiting and Preventing the Illicit Import, Export and Transfer of Ownership of Cultural Property*. On the implementation of the 1970 UNESCO convention in the United States (a process managed in part by Alfred Stendahl) and the effects of subsequent legislation on the trade in pre-Columbian art, see Patty Gerstenblith, "The Meaning of 1970 for the Acquisition of Archaeological Objects," *Journal of Field Archaeology* 38, no. 4 (2013): 364–73.

270. See Stendahl Art Galleries, sales agreement to Louise Arensberg, Hollywood, 4 March 1950, PMA-WLA, box 28, folder 35. Conversion to 2019 dollars based on https://www.dollartimes.com/inflation, accessed 20 January 2020. The Arensbergs began making payments in January 1951; see Stendahl Art Galleries, receipt to Louise Arensberg, Hollywood, 24 January 1951, PMA-WLA, box 28, folder 35. However, a document in the Stendahl Art Galleries archives shows that the dealer may have relented after three installments, because the 5 March 1953 receipt is marked "paid in full." Stendahl Art Galleries Records, GRI, box 90, folder 5.

271. The diagram of the calendar stone is in César Lizardi Ramos to Walter Arensberg, Mexico City, 16 August 1951, PMA-WLA, box 11, folder 33. Earlier in the summer, Walter had sent Lizardi Ramos a letter with some photographs he had requested. In it, Walter wrote, "It was a great experience to meet you and learn from you the significance of so many of the signs and symbols. I had never before come across a comparable wealth of knowledge in this field." Walter Arensberg to Lizardi Ramos, 26 June 1951, PMA-WLA, box 11, folder 33. Disappointingly, we don't know where the calendar stone was located in the Arensberg home. Lizardi Ramos said that during his visit to the home, Walter "showed [him] the mark that the precious monolith left on the floor." Lizardi Ramos, "Tesoros Arqueológicos Mexicanos en Los Angeles," *Excélsior*, 29 July 1951, 1, 4.

272. On the preciousness of greenstones in pre-Columbian cultures, see Miller and Taube, *Dictionary of the Gods and Symbols of Ancient Mexico and the Maya*, 101–2. Miller and Taube write that "jade was the most precious rock or mineral" in pre-Columbian Mexico and note that Spaniards traded green glass beads to the Aztecs in return for gold.

273. This phrase is on the Arensbergs' inventory index card for the calendar stone; PMA-WLA, box 25, AIN 1430.

274. Earl Stendahl to Robert Woods Bliss, Los Angeles, 29 January 1944, © Dumbarton Oaks, House Collection, Washington, DC. In this letter, he also wrote, "[The calendar stone] was evidently placed in one of the most sacred temples of the high priest, and at the time of destruction of the Aztecan capital, it was dislodged from its pedestal and rolled down the stairway of the pyramid, as it shows this kind of treatment by the chipped edges."

275. An undated photograph of the calendar stone in Stendahl's garden appears in Dammann, *Exhibitionist: Earl Stendahl*, 183.

276. Earl Stendahl to Robert Woods Bliss, Los Angeles, 25 October 1943, © Dumbarton Oaks, House Collection, Washington, DC.

277. See Janice Lee Jayes, "Minerals and Aztec Villages: Mexico on the American Fairground," in *The Illusion of Ignorance: Constructing the American Encounter with Mexico, 1877–1920* (Lanham, MD: University Press of America, 2011), 181–94.

278. Many thanks to Mary Miller for this information. For the Cotton Centennial, the Smithsonian Institution had the Treasury give duty-free entry to foreign objects that exhibitors agreed to donate or sell to the Smithsonian. This supports Miller's argument about the sale of works from Mexico's Cotton Centennial presentation. See Michael Shane Powers, "The Smithsonian Institution in the 1884 New Orleans World's Fair," *The Bigger Picture* (blog), Smithsonian Institution Archives, 3 October 2017, https://siarchives.si.edu/blog/smithsonian-insitution-1884-new-orleans-world's-fair.

279. Further research will hopefully allow us to better understand the complex provenance of the Arensberg collection calendar stone.

280. On Nelson Rockefeller's attempts to place his collection at the Metropolitan Museum of Art, see Joanne Pillsbury, "The Pan-American: Nelson Rockefeller and the Arts of Ancient Latin America," in "The Nelson A. Rockefeller Vision: Arts of Africa, Oceania, and the Americas," special issue, *Metropolitan Museum of Art Bulletin* 72, no. 1 (2014): 18–27.

281. Price's donation to East Los Angeles College led to the creation of the college's Vincent Price Art Museum.

282. Information on Alan and Janet Wurtzburger's collection comes from Kevin Tervala (associate curator of African and non-Western art, Baltimore Museum of Art), personal communication with Ellen Hoobler, July 2018.

283. For more on the Wurtzburger collection, see Baltimore Museum of Art, *The Alan Wurtzburger Collection of Pre-Columbian Art* (Baltimore: Baltimore Museum of Art, 1958).

284. See Margaret Young-Sánchez, "The Gruener Collection of Pre-Columbian Art," *Bulletin of the Cleveland Museum of Art* 79, no. 7 (1992): 234–75.

285. On the Olsen collection, see "About Art of the Ancient Americas," Yale University Art Gallery, https://artgallery.yale.edu/art-ancient-americas; Richard R. Brettell, "Mezcala Stone Sculpture in the Olsen Collection," *Yale University Art Gallery Bulletin* 35, no. 1 (1974): 14–19; and "Acquisitions 1973," *Yale University Art Gallery Bulletin* 35, no. 1 (1974): 52–58, 76–79, where the corn goddess is called "Figure of Woman, Wearing Cubical Headdress" (1973.88.44).

286. The couple's purported guide, Stendahl, often lacked knowledge or even the ability to consult sources. At least as of 1940, he noted that he could only look at the pages of books in Spanish, for he did not read the language; Stendahl to Bill [Guillermo] Echániz, Los Angeles, 2 November 1940, Stendahl Art Galleries Records, GRI, box 10, folder 3. Perhaps for this reason, the unpaid adviser Kenneth Macgowan became much more important. Many collectors prefer not to do scholarly research or reading on their holdings, for a variety of reasons. However, the Arensbergs seem to have developed a profound appreciation for the works' formal qualities.

287. Walter's association with the Southwest Museum began with a request for loans of his works in 1939 (denied) and intensified with his election as a trustee of the museum in 1944, despite his claim, in an 8 December 1943 letter to F. W. Hodge, the museum's director, that "my interest in your field is very keen, almost exclusively however from the esthetic point of view and I should warn you that I have no knowledge of archaeology." Walter's association with the museum continued until his death, although he stepped down as trustee after Louise's death. All correspondence is in PMA-WLA, box 17, folder 55.

288. Megan E. O'Neil and Mary Ellen Miller, "An Artistic Discovery of America: Exhibiting and Collecting Mexican Pre-Hispanic Art in Los Angeles from 1940 to the 1960s," in *Found in Translation: Design in California and Mexico, 1915–1985*, ed. Wendy Kaplan, exh. cat. (Los Angeles: Los Angeles County Museum of Art, 2017), 166; and Matthew H. Robb, "The Pre-Columbian as MacGuffin in Mid-Century Los Angeles," in *L.A. Collects L.A.: Latin America in Southern California Collections*, ed. Jesse Lerner and Rubén Ortiz Torres (Berlin: Bom Dia Boa Tarde Boa Noite, 2017), 49–64.

289. See, for example, Andrew Perchuk and Catherine Taft, "Floating Structures: Building the Modern in Postwar Los Angeles," in *Pacific Standard Time: Los Angeles Art, 1945–1980*, ed. Rebecca Peabody et al., exh. cat. (Los Angeles: Getty Research Institute and J. Paul Getty Museum, 2011), 10–11; William Hackman, *Out of Sight: The Los Angeles Art Scene of the Sixties* (New York: Other, 2015), 1–3; and O'Neil and Miller, "An Artistic Discovery," 162, 166. Two Pacific Standard Time essays focus on the Arensbergs: Jesse Lerner, "The Tlaloc Stripped Bare by the Bachelors, Even: Modernism and Latin American Archaeology in the Arensberg Collection," in *L.A. Collects L.A.: Latin America in Southern California Collections*, ed. Lerner and Rubén Ortiz Torres (Berlin: Bom Dia Boa Tarde Boa Noite, 2017), 87–96; and Robb, "The Pre-Columbian as MacGuffin in Mid-Century Los Angeles." Neither contains much information about the specific works in the Arensbergs' pre-Columbian collection.

290. Beatrice Wood, oral history interview by Paul Karlstrom, 26 August 1976, Archives of American Art, https://www.aaa.si.edu/collections/interviews/oral-history-interview-beatrice-wood-12423#transcript.

291. "Pre-Columbus American Art," *New York Herald Tribune*, 4 October 1953, section 4, page 7; clipping located in PMA-WLA, box 41, folder 40.

292. Walter Pach to Walter Arensberg, New York, 2 December 1953, PMA-WLA, box 14, folder 21; published in Perlman, *Walter Pach Letters*, 51–52.

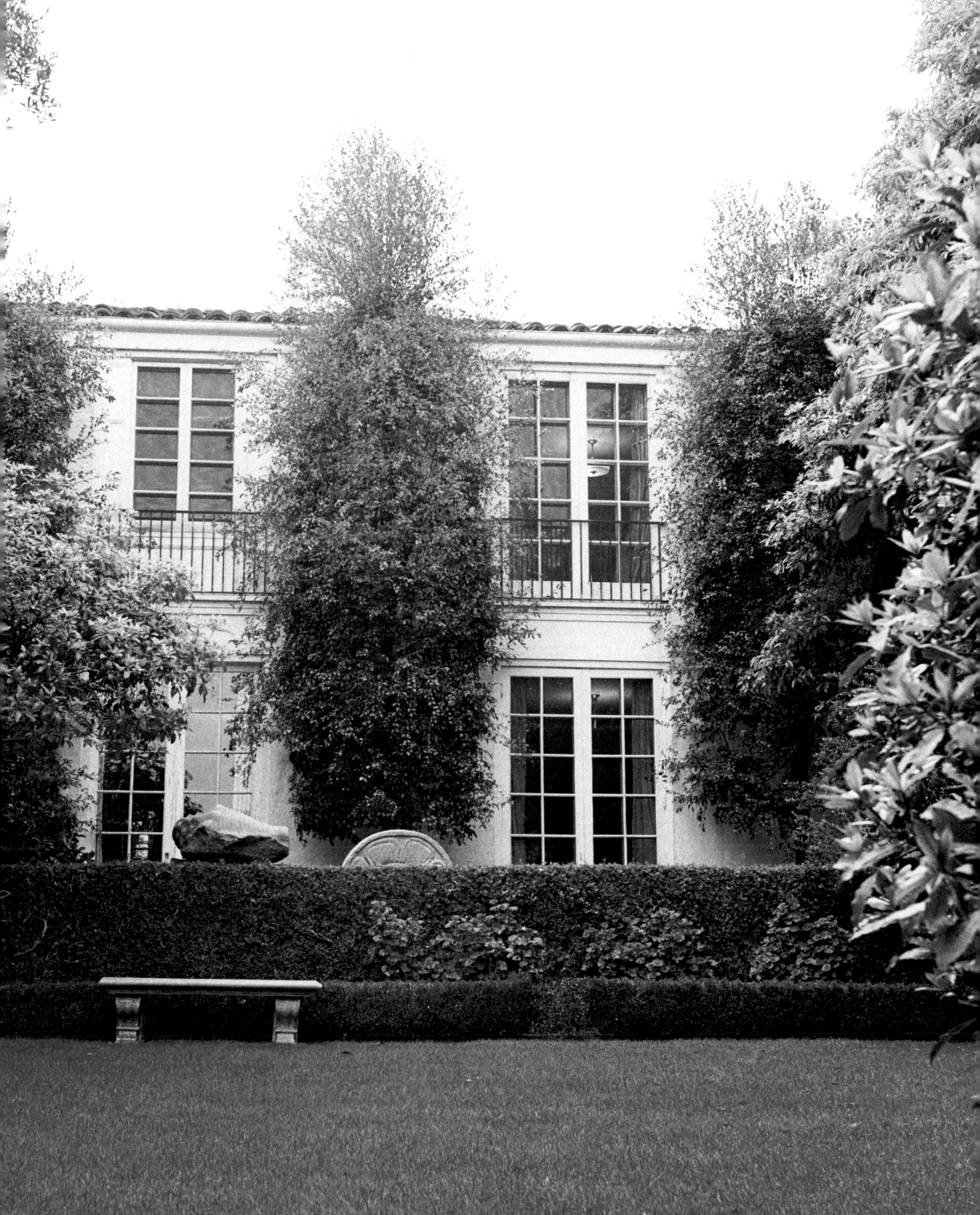

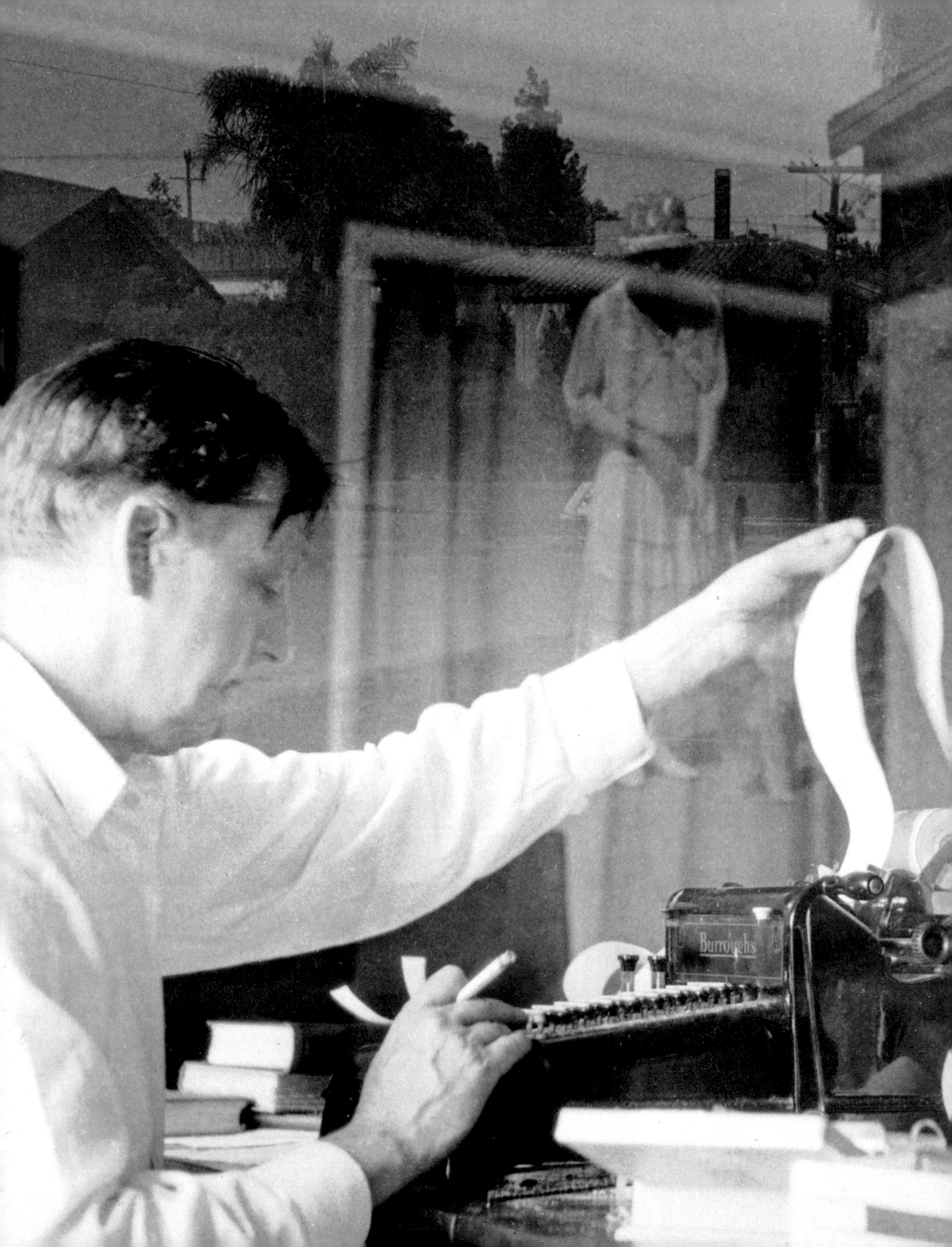
Burroughs

AN INTERVIEW WITH WALTER ARENSBERG

Undated, ca. 1951

KENNETH ROSS

with notes by **MARK NELSON** *and* **WILLIAM H. SHERMAN**

BEATRICE WOOD. ACCIDENTAL DOUBLE EXPOSURE SHOWING WALTER ARENSBERG USING HIS ADDING MACHINE IN HIS HOME OFFICE AND LOUISE ARENSBERG STANDING ON A HOLLYWOOD SIDEWALK WITH THE COUPLE'S DOG, LOLLIE. BOTH EXPOSURES, CA. 1924–26. THESE OVERLAPPING PHOTOGRAPHS WERE TAKEN AT ONE OF THE HOUSES THAT THE COUPLE RENTED BEFORE PURCHASING 7065 HILLSIDE AVENUE IN 1927. THE HUNTINGTON LIBRARY, FRANCIS BACON LIBRARY ARCHIVE, WALTER AND LOUISE ARENSBERG PAPERS (HEH-FBLA), BOX 104, FOLDER 9. REPRODUCED COURTESY OF BEATRICE WOOD CENTER FOR THE ARTS / HAPPY VALLEY FOUNDATION

KENNETH ROSS was an early and important advocate for modern art in California, occupying a variety of key positions during the 1940s, including the directorships of the Pasadena Art Institute and the ill-fated Modern Institute of Art, which had been created in an attempt to keep the Arensberg collection in Los Angeles. From 1949 through the late 1970s, Ross made his most significant contributions as director of the fledgling Municipal Arts Department (now the Los Angeles Department of Cultural Affairs) by greatly expanding its arts programming and community outreach and by spearheading many notable public projects, among them the restoration of Frank Lloyd Wright's Hollyhock House and the preservation of Simon Rodia's Watts Towers.

KENNETH ROSS: I think the thing of interest is the relation between the Baconian research and the collection as they developed hand in hand. You feel they do have a relationship, I know, and your views would be interesting.[1]

WALTER ARENSBERG: Well, I have felt for many years that the so-called Baconian method for the interpretation of nature was applicable to the interpretation of art, and that it was intended by Bacon to be particularly applicable to the interpretation of the Shakespearean plays. Bacon wanted to create a practical experiment by means of which it would be possible to apply his method of interpretation to a body of literature and to prove the validity of that method by having it prove to be the tool that would uncover the hidden meaning of this body of literature. The body of literature to which I refer is the Shakespearean Opus, particularly the Shakespearean plays as collected in the First Folio. It was Bacon's intention that the First Folio should constitute a kind of microcosm or little model of the Universe and that the method for the interpretation of the Universe—the Macrocosm—would be equally applicable to this microcosm, the Shakespeare plays. In making this microcosm in the form of the Shakespeare First Folio, Bacon conceived that the form of expression that he used in the play was identical with that poetry which he calls parabolical or allusive poetry.[2] In defining this kind of poetry—parabolical or allusive—Bacon was using a tradition which he inherited from Dante, who defined the *Divina Commedia* as a kind of poetry that had four concurrent, simultaneous meanings—he called those meanings first, the literal, the allegorical, and he subdivided this into allegorical proper, moral and mystical. Dante got that idea from Aquinas, who felt that the Holy Scripture also had four concurrent meanings. Aquinas got the idea from Aristotle, who had the conception of four forms of existence, and he must have got that from Pythagoras with the doctrine of the sacred four. Thus this method of interpretation really constitutes the most ancient of all literary tradition. It goes clear back to the dawn of pre-Socratic philosophy.

KR: This method then not only applies to literature but to life in general?

WA: I came to feel that the identical method to which we are now referring for the interpretation of nature and for the interpretation of literature was equally applicable for the interpretation of art, and particularly for the interpretation of contemporary art. Perhaps the closest example of work that can be interpreted by this Baconian method of interpretation is the work of Paul Klee.

Now what is the essential character of the poetry or art that can be interpreted by the Baconian method of interpretation—its essential character is its systematic use of allusion rather than direct reference. Bacon calls the kind of poetry he is speaking about parabolical or allusive, and he is referring to the use of allusion, and that involves a consideration of the context rather than any direct exposition or literal statement.

KR: Did this theory influence you in collecting a specific kind of art or have you simply collected what you liked regardless of any particular theory? Your collection has definite character.

WA: I think we collected what we liked. We found that what we were collecting, without any a priori intention, conformed in general to the type of artistic expression which paralleled Bacon's definition of parabolical or allusive poetry. It is particularly true of Klee, of Duchamp, and I think it is particularly true of Brancusi.

KR: Were you aware of this philosophy at the time you started [the] collection or did it come later—sometime after you had been collecting?

This interview has been lightly edited for ease of reading. The original typescript carbon is in the Philadelphia Museum of Art, Library and Archives, Arensberg Archives (hereafter cited as PMA-WLA), box 44, folder 7. It is difficult to pin down precisely the circumstances under which Walter agreed to be interviewed, but a clue can perhaps be found in his letter to Ross of 21 February 1951, in which Walter laments: "When I consented to your request for an 'exclusive' it was with the idea of enabling you to take advantage of any possible demand for an article that might grow out of the publication of the story about the gift." Ross responded politely, "I do appreciate your thoughtfulness in considering me in this and in referring *Time* magazine to me. I am sorry that no requests for feature stories developed and that the pressure of my two jobs has made it impossible for me to initate a story." (Both letters, PMA-WLA box 11, folder 41.)

1. Sir Francis Bacon (1561–1626) was the leading scholar-statesman of Renaissance England. He ushered in a new age of experimental science based on both the observation of nature and the study of ancient mysteries. In applying Bacon's scientific method to the study of art, Arensberg was following the lead of Delia Bacon (no relation), whose *Philosophy of the Plays of Shakespere Unfolded* (1857) opened the case for Baconian authorship of the plays collected in the so-called First Folio (published posthumously in 1623).

2. In his *Advancement of Learning* (1605), Bacon described three kinds of poetry: narrative, dramatic, and allusive or parabolic. The last of these included fables, myths, and allegories, and their symbols and stories carried deeper truths for those who knew how to read them.

WA: No, I was interested in the Baconian work and in the problem of the authorship of the Shakespeare plays really very early in life. The Baconian work was the direct outgrowth, though I was interested in it from a point of view of curiosity, of my work on the *Divina Commedia* in which I tried to apply to my interpretation of the *Divina Commedia* the definition of meaning and the description of the kind of poetry that Dante gave.[3] I began to see after that was finished, in spite of the fact that scholars think there is little or no Dante influence in Shakespeare, that Dante is probably the profoundest influence in the Shakespearean work, and the method of interpretation that Bacon defines is practically identical with what Dante uses.

The idea of creating a little model of the universe, a microcosm, which could prove the validity of his method by showing that it was valid for the microcosm and that would show that it would be valid for all the universe. Modern science is really based on this theory.

KR: Is this method taken up by modern philosophers?

WA: It is very curious that there is very little reference in modern books on Semantics to this traditional method of interpretation that came from Aristotle, Aquinas, to Dante and Bacon.

KR: Does it seem to be overlooked or discounted?

WA: It seems to be overlooked, I don't know why. There is an awfully nice passage here where Bacon speaks of having made a little model. It is on the basis of an application of that method that I discovered an autobiographical meaning in the plays, and that Bacon refers to a location at which he intends to be buried with his mother, and that is the Chapter House of Lichfield Cathedral.[4] There are other autobiographical allusions in the plays that you can work out. Right or wrong, my hypothesis is a completely independent one which has nothing to do with any of the hypotheses on which any other Baconian is working. What I call the orthodox heresy is the so-called Biliteral Cypher of Mrs. Gallup.[5] In my opinion, that simply doesn't exist. She has managed, and her disciples have managed, to believe that it exists without giving any proof that it exists. It is in accordance with that theory that Bacon is supposed to be the son of Queen Elizabeth.

KR: That is what she is trying to prove?

WA: That is her theory. By the way, this is very important. Many people who don't want to argue the point and aren't interested in the question say, "What does it matter, so long as we have the works?" Walter Prichard Eaton, when he was here just a few weeks ago, made use of that very reply.[6] It is my opinion that the identity of the author is of the utmost importance to know, and that the real importance of the inquiry is not to establish the identity of the author, but to find out what the meaning of the plays is. The orthodox theory that the author of the plays was the actor does a terrible damage to every reader of the Shakespeare plays because it obliges him to limit what he is able to see in the plays to what could have been within the range of the experience of the author as the ignorant actor.

KR: On the other hand, would it not be possible that the grandeur of the play might not be automatically transferred to the actor?

WA: Look what happens. If you believe that the author of the plays was the actor of Stratford and then you read the plays and find allusions to the *Divina Commedia*, to Paradiso [Canto] 18, to the Eagle of Paradiso and the Temple of Jupiter, if you find allusions to the *Aeneid*, and the myth of the Golden Bough, and *Oedipus at Colonus*, or to *The Persians* of Aeschylus—if you think you found those and you are an orthodox believer that the author was an actor, you have to consider

3. Arensberg's interest in Dante stretched back to his undergraduate studies at Harvard, where he also acquired the grounding in allegory, psychology, and cryptography that would mark his later work on Bacon. But the publication of *The Cryptography of Dante* by Alfred A. Knopf in 1921 marked a turning point in Arensberg's life: it would be his last work written before moving from New York to California, his last book to be released by a mainstream publisher, and his last study of a subject outside the Shakespeare authorship debate.

4. Like many other advocates for Bacon's authorship of Shakespeare's plays, Arensberg was obsessed with the possibility that buried manuscripts would settle the question. He traveled twice to England in the early 1920s in search of documents that he believed had been hidden in a secret tomb in Lichfield Cathedral. In his privately published pamphlet on this topic, *The Burial of Francis Bacon and His Mother in the Lichfield Chapter House* (1924), Arensberg implores the cathedral administration to exhume Bacon's body.

5. Elizabeth Wells Gallup was a schoolteacher from Michigan who became the main proponent of the theory that Bacon had left hidden cryptograms in the works attributed to Shakespeare. Her book *The Bi-literal Cypher of Sir Francis Bacon* (1899) attracted many followers. The preeminent codebreakers William and Elizebeth Friedman got their start in the field working for Gallup, and William would later serve as Arensberg's chief cryptographic consultant; however, the couple would ultimately pour scorn on the work of both Gallup and Arensberg in *The Shakespearean Ciphers Examined* (1957).

6. Walter Prichard Eaton was Arensberg's classmate at Harvard. He served as drama critic for several major newspapers and taught playwriting at Yale.

7. Sir Sidney Lee was the author of the standard biography of Shakespeare in Arensberg's day, and editor of the most scholarly facsimile of the First Folio.

8. One of the United States' most influential philosophers, George Santayana wrote widely on the relationships between art, literature, and religion. Walter took Santayana's course on aesthetics during his final year at Harvard.

yourself wrong in believing that these allusions exist. You are obliged to pauperize the plays in order to make [them] fit with the hypothesis that the author of the plays was an inexperienced and ignorant actor.

KR: Could you not say that this actor could have been an extraordinary man?

WA: There is nothing that is known about the life of William Shakespeare that gives any evidence that he had anything but an extremely limited experience of social life or of education.

KR: There is a pretty good background on Bacon, then?

WA: Yes, he travelled in Europe, was practically the head of the English State.

KR: Is there much known about Shakespeare?

WA: A great deal of it that is supposed to be known is just put there by guess. The device of Sidney Lee, who wrote the best-known of the Lives of Shakespeare, was to say, "Doubtless, such and such was true," when he came to a statement which had no evidence.[7]

This shows the kind of association of ideas that have influenced Mrs. A. and me in making a collection and the Baconian research.

KR: I can see one link in your concern of the importance of finding the true author must be directly related to your concern to correctly attributing the paintings, then.

WA: That is true. All art is autobiographical, every painting is autobiographical, and the real importance of being sure that so-and-so did do such-and-such a picture is to be able to correlate it with the rest of the artist's work. In no single work of art does an artist express himself entirely, and you can only understand a certain painting, say, by Cézanne in context with the rest of his total opus. It is the same thing with a picture by Duchamp or by Klee—you can only really understand that single painting if you can correlate it with the rest of his work.

KR: That is one reason that you have been particularly interested in acquiring as much of the entire work output of Duchamp as possible.

WA: I think it adds enormously to our ability to appraise him, and to give him the actual great status he has as an artist, to hang the works together, and to see—though they are few—how they are built into a kind of single unit of expression. That is certainly true of Brancusi.

KR: What is it as a rule that first interests you in a picture? What quality?

WA: I think in any great work of art the intellectual context ought to be as great as the emotional, and I like to remember in that connection the line that Dante wrote as the beginning of one canzone—"Oh, ladies who have the intellect of love." That is, he thinks of love as having an intellectual as well as emotional component, and all art has to have the same component of intellect and emotion.

KR: That is why you were not drawn to the Impressionists?

WA: To me that was an intellectual challenge—to see the Impressionists for the first time, and to correlate that with the kind of imagination of the world that prior academic art had given. It was a good deal of achievement to see what they were doing.

KR: Did it seem more emotional than intellectual?

WA: Of course Santayana had the idea that it was a kind of emotion.[8] As I recall, he said that Impressionist painting is like the work of a person with the top of his head cut off above the eyes. It is as if it were a particularly visionary thing, but it really is an intellectual analysis of the emotion.

There is one thing about Cubist art—I think to a certain degree the artist intends the work to be difficult. He intends to compel the spectators to engage in an active cooperation of interpretation. It is an attempt

9. The idea that it is the spectator rather than the artist who completes a work of art was very important to Marcel Duchamp. He first discussed this concept publicly in April 1957, in a short paper titled "The Creative Act," which he delivered to the American Federation of Arts in Houston. His speech was subsequently printed in *ARTnews* 56, no. 4 (1957): 28–29. In "The King and Queen Surrounded," we suggest that this idea "is frequently credited to Duchamp, but it seems to have been part of the broader conversation around art in the years when modernism was becoming more readily accepted." See p. 19 and 69n57 in this volume.

10. The Arensbergs did own a copy of Paul Klee's 1923 lithograph *Tightrope Walker* (PMA 1950-134-530), but it is not pictured in any of the photographs reproduced in this book.

11. Klee's gouache and watercolor painting *Glance of a Landscape* hung for a time over the nightstand in the Arensbergs' guest room (plate 57.1).

12. The concept of the zoon (from the Greek for "living being") was popularized by the nineteenth-century philosopher and evolutionary biologist Herbert Spencer. It signifies a complete animal, particularly one growing from a single fertilized egg.

to make the spectator a co-creator, because the spectator who really penetrates this mystery of forms that, say, Picasso gave us in his Cubist work is becoming active instead of passive. He is no longer a photographic plate that receives something that is lined up and already digested for him. This is very true of all the great Cubists, and is particularly true of Duchamp too.[9]

KR: What about a man like Klee?

WA: In the case of Klee it is obviously true. He often propounds the problem that you have to solve in the form of giving you a title to a painting and then obliging you, as an otherwise uninstructed person, to find the relevance of the title to the painting. A good example is Klee's *Tightrope Walker* which shows a man on a precarious balance on a tightrope.[10] Then behind all the apparatus which looks something like a Sandy Calder "mobile" is a great white cross. Klee propounds this problem—what is the relevance of associating a tightrope walker with a cross? He obliges us to come out at the end with the answer that he is giving us a little parable in which he uses the tightrope as the Christian "straight and narrow" path. There is no path that is straighter or narrower or more uncertain than a tightrope.

Another thing of Klee's where the allusive idea comes out is the one that he calls *Glance at* [*sic*] *a Landscape*.[11] It is a landscape with a great red setting sun that looks like an eye. He is trying to tell us that the eye is looking at us. It is in terms of that kind of allusion that he is really conveying to us that the earth is a zoon—it is the living creature that is looking at us.[12]

KR: Your collection seems to take in a certain period following the Post-Impressionists, say up to 1920—this was the foundation and beginning of modern art as we know it now. Did you collect with the idea of forming this type of collection?

WA: We never proposed or thought to make a collection. We suddenly found ourselves in a fix. We had a lot of things we liked, but we didn't buy them on a logical scheme or program. If it turned out to be a logical scheme, it was subconscious. I think it was this subconscious element that I have been talking about this afternoon that guided us.

KR: You haven't collected much in recent years?

WA: We have been buying mostly Pre-Columbian things. The interest in Pre-Columbian in the first place is to show that there is a culture that at least holds its own and possibly outranks the other cultures of antiquity. Before our time it was never recognized as art. Now it may outrank all other cultures. It is certainly the most mysterious.

KR: It is again that quality of mystery or magic that appeals to you?

WA: Maybe it is something about the exploring or the discovering that appeals to us.

KR: In collecting the Pre-Columbian did you have a specific purpose to bring together a large group of important work to indicate that it was one of the great cultures?

WA: We began to collect Pre-Columbian stuff almost as soon as we began to collect paintings, way back in the teens.

KR: In the last ten or fifteen years you have not purchased anything of the contemporary school?

WA: I think that we felt that there was nothing actually coming out in painting on the same level of novelty and importance as what had come out in the past and what we had collected. I still feel that.

KR: Don't you occasionally see something that has a bit of that feeling?

WA: Yes, yes indeed, but…

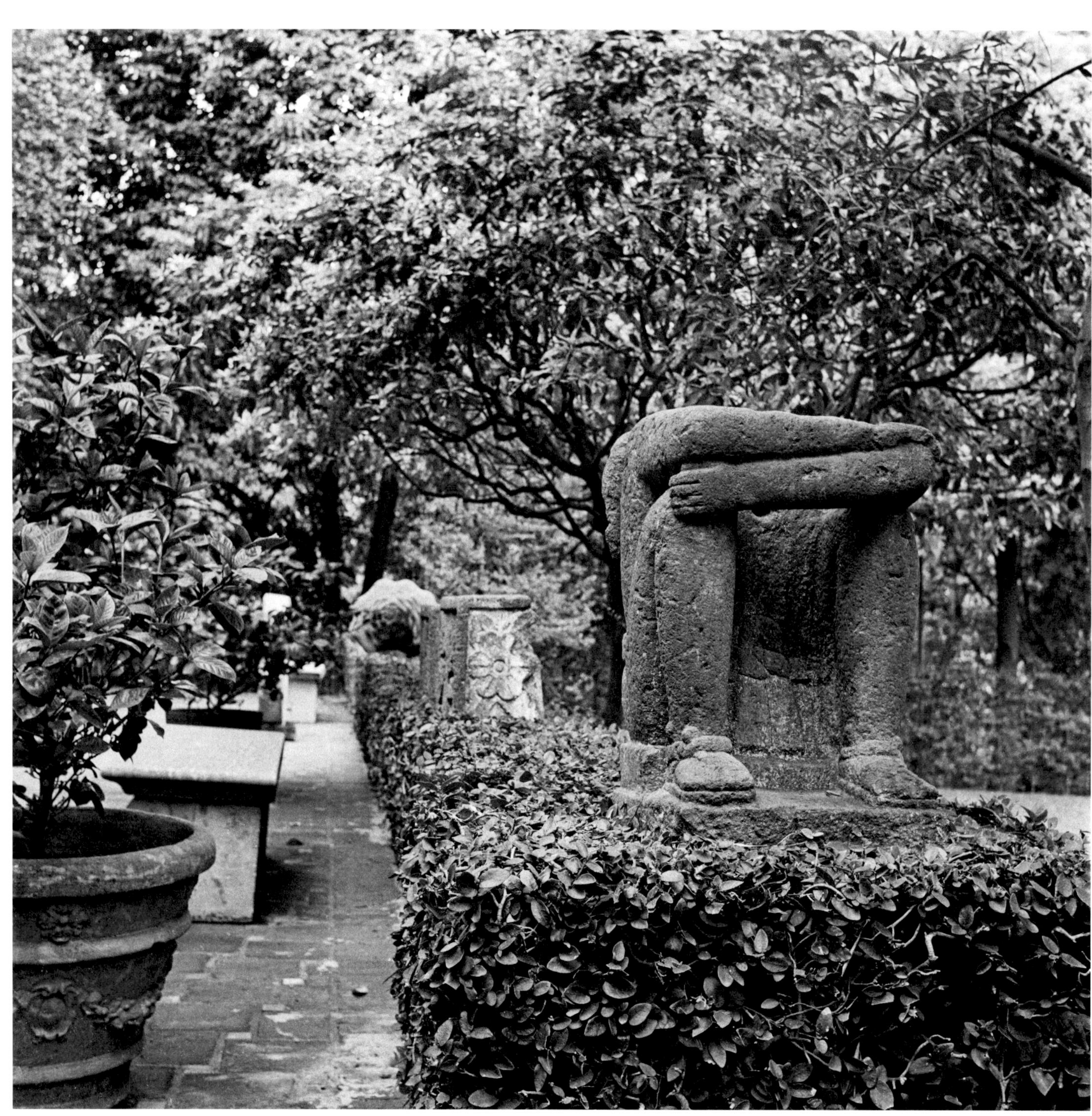

KARL BISSINGER. A VIEW OF LOUISE AND WALTER ARENSBERG'S FRONT PATIO, 7065 HILLSIDE AVENUE, LOS ANGELES, 16 MARCH 1950. UNIVERSITY OF DELAWARE LIBRARY, NEWARK, SPECIAL COLLECTIONS, KARL BISSINGER ARCHIVE (MSS0682). SEE ALSO PLATES 1, 59

PICTURED LEFT TO RIGHT:
AZTEC (CENTRAL MEXICO). BALLCOURT RING WITH FLORAL MOTIF (BARELY VISIBLE AT LEFT) (SEE PLATE 59.1; PAGES 340, 369, 399)
AZTEC (CENTRAL MEXICO). CONCH SHELL (SEE PLATE 59.3; PAGES 340–41, 369 [BARELY VISIBLE], 399)
AZTEC (CENTRAL MEXICO). RELIEFS (PMA 1950-134-365 AND PMA 1950-134-366; NOT SHOWN ELSEWHERE IN THIS VOLUME). ANOTHER IMAGE BY BISSINGER, NOT PRINTED IN THIS VOLUME, SHOWS PMA 1950-134-365 MORE CLEARLY.
AZTEC (CENTRAL MEXICO). FIGURE OF A MAN (SEE PLATE 1)

BIOGRAPHICAL NOTES ON THE PHOTOGRAPHERS

MARK NELSON | WILLIAM H. SHERMAN

LOUISE AND WALTER ARENSBERG had a conflicted relationship with photography, both as a medium for artistic expression and as an engine for publicity. They were in close contact with some of the most esteemed photographers of the twentieth century, yet they displayed virtually nothing by them alongside their paintings and sculptures. And while the Arensbergs allowed their collection to be photographed for popular publications, they always insisted on being left out of the frame.

In 1950, when Fleur Cowles requested that the Arensbergs allow their collection to be photographed for her new magazine, *Flair*, they responded that they would "under no circumstances consent to the article if we personally are involved in the photography."[1] Yet when Cowles's photographer Karl Bissinger arrived in Los Angeles, he was treated well by the couple and given access to some of their more private spaces.[2] The Arensbergs agreed to four similar projects during their lifetimes: a 1945 photo essay in *Vogue* that included five pictures by Fred Dapprich; a profile in *View* (also 1945) illustrated with images of individual artworks and a single unattributed photograph of Marcel Duchamp's *Glider* hanging in their sunroom; a 1949 profile in *ARTnews* containing only one image, a bizarre illustration of their home created by Ginnie Hofmann, who had obviously not seen it in person (see page 63 of this volume); and a book published in 1951, *Modern Artists in America*, again featuring several photographs by Dapprich. Through the years, the Arensbergs were also the subject of newspaper articles from time to time. None of these publications included a picture of the collectors.

Paradoxically, the Arensbergs were not camera shy. Throughout her life, Louise engaged with the lens whenever she was being photographed, especially in her early years, when she posed for many playful pictures taken by Walter's cousin John Covert. Walter, too, was capable of adopting different personae for the camera, from the theatrical pictures in his class yearbook at Harvard to the moody portrait that served as the frontispiece for the Philadelphia Museum of Art's official catalog of the Arensberg collection.

None of these photographs was taken by Alfred Stieglitz, Man Ray, Edward Weston, or Sherril Schell, all of whom were part of the Arensbergs' circle at various times. Indeed, the more famous a photographer was, the less likely he or she would photograph the Arensbergs. Bissinger and Charles Sheeler achieved renown as photographers in their lifetimes but photographed the Arensbergs' art collection and not the couple themselves. Only Beatrice Wood, whose fame came later and in a different field (ceramics), was allowed that intimacy.

Moreover, it is difficult to say whether the Arensbergs considered photographs to be "art." Walter frequently engaged in conversations with Weston about the content and meaning of his pictures, taking special pleasure in Weston's photograph *Bedpan* and letting him know he would hang it in his study.[3] The couple acquired beautifully composed and printed photographs by Stieglitz, Sheeler, Schell, and Clarence John Laughlin as well as by Florence Homolka, George E. Holton, and Constantin Brancusi, but they seem not to have displayed many of these in their home. Merely a handful of photographs appear among the hundreds of artworks shown in *Hollywood Arensberg*: two by Schell hang on the side of a cabinet in Walter's office (see plates 38, 40); two by an unknown photographer showing the Mexican archaeological sites of Tulum and Chichén Itzá appear in a later image of the foyer (see page 23); and a picture of the Arensbergs' dog (possibly taken by the artist Knud Merrild) sits on a living room table (see plate 20). Otherwise, only a portrait of Marcel Duchamp, taken by Edward Steichen, is recorded as having hung in the Arensbergs' bedroom.[4]

1. Walter and Louise Arensberg, telegram to Fleur Cowles, 3 March 1950, Philadelphia Museum of Art, Library and Archives, Arensberg Archives (hereafter cited as PMA-WLA), box 7, folder 42. Cowles had proposed that Karl Bissinger photograph the collection; Cowles to the Arensbergs, New York, 30 January 1950, PMA-WLA, box 7, folder 42.

2. *Flair*'s editor, Patrick O'Higgins, who accompanied Bissinger to the Arensbergs' house, thanked the couple afterward for their cooperation on the shoot; O'Higgins to Walter Arensberg, New York, 28 March 1950, PMA-WLA, box 7, folder 42.

3. See Charis Wilson and Wendy Madar, *Through Another Lens: My Years with Edward Weston* (New York: North Point, 1998), 82–83. See also the correspondence between Walter Arensberg and Edward Weston (PMA-WLA, box 20, folder 16, and box 42, folder 17), Brett Weston (PMA-WLA, box 20, folder 15), Charis Wilson (PMA-WLA, box 20, folder 29), and Harry Leon Wilson (PMA-WLA, box 20, folder 28). For Walter's response to *Bedpan*, see his letter to Edward Weston, Hollywood, 24 February 1930, PMA-WLA, box 20, folder 16.

4. The AIC for this object (1950-134-918) contains a pencil notation indicating that it hung in the bedroom; see PMA-WLA, box 24, AIN 382.

These images may have been displayed as much for their subject matter as for their photographic merit.

Of course, the Arensbergs commissioned photography sporadically in service of their collection (when museum curators and publications editors requested images of their artworks, for example, or when Marcel Duchamp needed pictures of his own works to create his *Box in a Valise*), but they seem not to have fully embraced its documentary power until quite late in their lives (around 1945) when they hired Floyd Faxon to capture every individual object they owned, for inventory purposes. Yet if the Arensbergs were ambivalent about photography, the opposite was true of their attitude toward photographers. Louise and Walter maintained warm relations with the men and women who contributed to the record of their lives. They wrote letters of support for Weston when he applied for a grant from the John Simon Guggenheim Memorial Foundation, and they generated interest in his prints among visitors to their home and bought a number of his pictures.[5] They allowed military photographer Corporal F. W. Lumbord to document a group of injured soldiers visiting from nearby Birmingham Hospital, and, most poignantly, they intervened with the U.S. government on behalf of the German expatriate Fritz (Fred) Block, making a lasting impact on his life and livelihood.[6]

The following pages offer brief profiles of the photographers whose work more than half a century ago made this book possible.

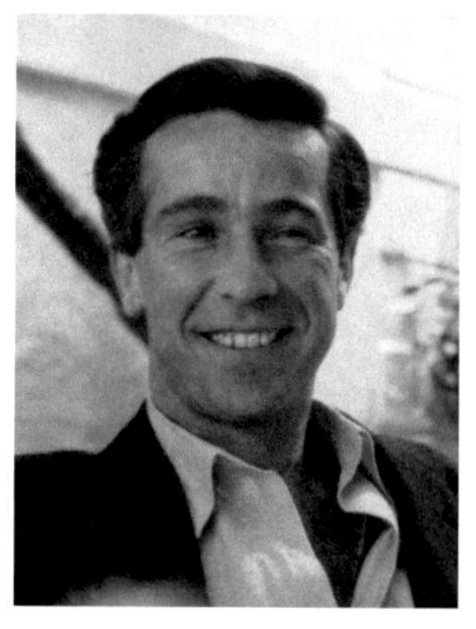

KARL BISSINGER was born in 1914 in Cincinnati, where he showed an early aptitude for art. As a young adult, he moved to New York to study at the Art Students League, and he worked after graduation as a property stylist for the Condé Nast photography studios. There he met Irving Penn, Cecil Beaton, and Richard Avedon, who first loaned him a camera and encouraged him to use it. Bissinger began taking pictures for *Harper's Bazaar*, *Vogue*, and many other magazines, soon catching the eye of Fleur Cowles, who was launching a new magazine called *Flair*. Cowles sent Bissinger to Los Angeles in service of a planned "California issue," for which she envisioned an article on the Arensbergs and their collection. She described Bissinger to the couple as "potentially one of the great photographers of our time [with a] tender, poetic camera."[7]

Flair soon sank under the weight of production extravagance, investor turmoil, and industry intrigue, but through 1950 and into the beginning of 1951, Cowles and her staff assembled twelve issues of a magazine now considered a classic of midcentury design and taste-making. Bissinger printed several enlargements of the best brackets from his set of eighteen photographs of the Arensberg home, but as is often the case in publishing, neither the imagined article nor its accompanying photographs ever ran. Instead, for more than sixty years, the pictures sat in an envelope unceremoniously labeled "Job 163. 3/16/50."

The unearthing of these photographs at the University of Delaware Library was among the most exciting discoveries of *Hollywood Arensberg*'s many historical excavations. Bissinger's pictures—probably the last taken before the Arensberg collection was dismantled—provide new views of key walls and rooms and of previously unknown perspectives on the home's second floor and exterior landscaping.

Not long after *Flair* folded, Bissinger abandoned photography to pursue his interest in pacifism and radical politics, working at the American Friends Service Committee and later at the War Resisters League. A survey of his work, *The Luminous Years: Portraits at Mid-Century*, was published by Abrams in 2003. Bissinger died in Manhattan in 2008.

5. See Walter Arensberg to Henry Allen Moe (secretary of the John Guggenheim Memorial Foundation), Hollywood, 30 December 1937, PMA-WLA, box 10, folder 21; and Walter Arensberg to Edward Weston, 24 June 1932 and 21 June 1951, Hollywood, PMA-WLA, box 20, folder 16.

6. See Walter Arensberg to William Fleet Palmer (U.S. Attorney, Southern District of California), Hollywood, 23 January 1942, PMA-WLA, box 3, folder 26. We thank the art historian Roland Jaeger for additional information on the assistance the Arensbergs provided to Block and his wife, Anna-Sophie, when they were under duress.

7. Fleur Cowles to Louise Arensberg, 30 January 1950.

8. The tentative dating of Block's color photos of the Arensberg sunroom is based on significant study of Block's archive by Roland Jaeger. We thank Jaeger for his long-running engagement with our project generally and with this problem specifically.

9. For a comprehensive biographical portrait of Block, see Roland Jaeger, *Photo-Eye Fritz Block: New Photography, Modern Color Slides*, trans. Maka/Magill Translations and Laura Schleussner (Zurich: Scheidegger & Speiss, 2018); and Roland Jaeger, *Block & Hochfeld, die Architekten des Deutschlandhauses: Bauten und Projekte in Hamburg 1921–1938, Exil in Los Angeles* (Berlin: Gebr. Mann, 1966).

10. See United States World War II Draft Registration Card for Frederick Richard Dapprich, 1942, https://www.familysearch.org/ark:/61903/1:1:V4DW-P7Y (registration required).

11. See the advertisement for the Fred R. Dapprich Advertising Agency in *Printers' Ink*, 16 September 1920, 157, https://hdl.handle.net/2027/mdp.39015064566360.

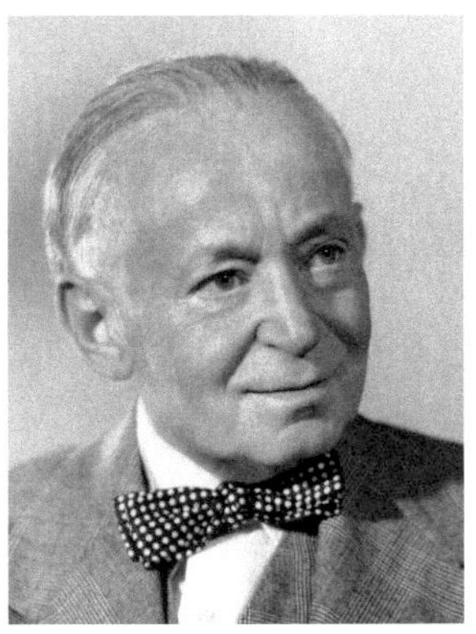

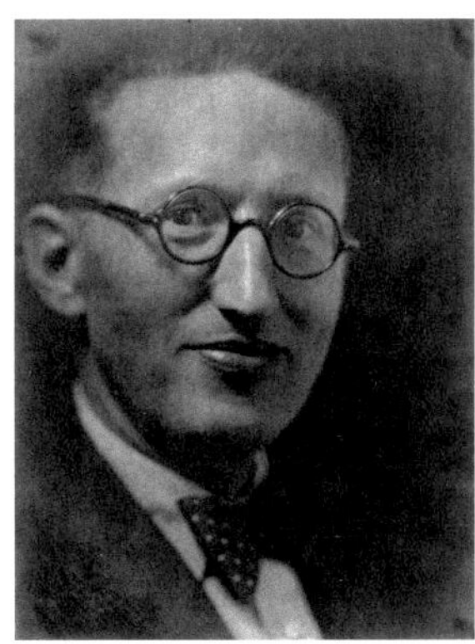

FRITZ (FRED) BLOCK was born in Warburg, Westphalia, in 1889. His training as an architect, begun in 1908, culminated in a doctorate from the Technische Hochschule Dresden in 1915. With a university friend, Ernst Hochfeld, Block opened the Hamburg-based architectural office Dr. Block & Hochfeld in 1921. The firm's largest and most important commission, Deutschlandhaus (1928–29), was a modern commercial building in the center of Hamburg that exemplified Block's advocacy of the Neues Bauen (New Building) movement then emerging in central Europe. Block initially taught himself photography to document that building's construction, but his ease with a Leica camera was soon supplemented by an awareness of the artistic avant-garde, an eye for diverse subject matter, and a love of travel.

As the international financial crisis shook Europe in the early 1930s, Block began exhibiting his photographs and selling them to magazines and photo agencies. When the National Socialist Party rose to power in 1933, however, he was no longer allowed to practice architecture or photojournalism in Germany because of his Jewish heritage. Over the next five years, Block and his wife, Anna-Sophie, traveled extensively to avoid the deteriorating conditions in Germany before making the risky decision to return to Hamburg in 1938 to prepare for emigration. Fritz endured a brief but harrowing imprisonment following the November pogrom of that year, but, remarkably, Anna-Sophie secured his release and the pair finally managed to immigrate to the United States.

It is unclear how or when the Blocks first met the Arensbergs, but the two couples developed a lasting rapport soon after the Blocks' 1939 arrival in Los Angeles. In 1942, as American involvement in World War II intensified, Block was declared an "enemy alien" by the U.S. government until Walter intervened on his behalf. Walter later sponsored Block's application for American citizenship.

In Los Angeles, Block turned his efforts to color photography, developing thematic slide presentations for progressive art education that formed the basis of a new business, Dr. Block Color Productions. His first series of slides, completed in 1943, focused on California's new modernist architecture. It is likely that his pictures of the Arensberg sunroom date from this time.[8]

Block died in Los Angeles in 1955. His architectural work and photography are well documented in two monographs by the art historian Roland Jaeger.[9]

FREDERICK RICHARD DAPPRICH (seen here in a portrait taken by his friend Milton M. Inman) was born in Belleville, Illinois, in 1880.[10] He began his career as an advertising copywriter in New York and then moved to Virginia, where he generated and published ad industry data analysis that he sold through his own agency.[11] Dapprich transitioned to a career in photography around the time of his relocation to California in the early 1920s[12] and was successful enough by 1923 for his work to be featured in John Wallace Gillies's book *Principles of Pictorial Photography*.[13] Dapper and well educated, he traveled with ease among Hollywood's elite and made a name for himself (as his business stationery proclaimed) working as a "photographer of interesting people."[14]

By the early 1930s, Dapprich was firmly established as an innovator in the burgeoning field of architectural photography, creating the work that he is best remembered for today. His pictures were published through the 1940s in lifestyle magazines, including *Vogue*, *House and Garden*, and *Architectural Digest*. As a member of both the Camera Club and the Camera Pictorialists of Los Angeles, Dapprich was also well known to readers of the *Los Angeles Times* arts columns, where his photographs were regularly published.[15]

A preferred photographer of the architects Rudolf M. Schindler and Harwell Hamilton Harris, Dapprich was influential to Julius Shulman and other up-and-coming photographers as modernism took hold in California.[16] Harris's biographer, Lisa Germany, has written that Dapprich's "soft, very painterly, sepia-toned prints ... were as romantic as the International Style photographs were classical. They were never frontal and symmetrical; rather the camera's eye looked in and around angles, pushing its way into the depths of space. In their rich gradations of tone, one might also feel the presence of color."[17]

A small printed card in the Arensberg archives (sent to clients after Dapprich had presumably undergone some type of medical procedure) reflects his dry sense of humor. It reads: "Fred R. Dapprich, Architectural Photographer and Teacher, is 'in circulation again,' having graduated 'magna cum laude' from St. Luke's Hospital with the aid of Drs. Belknap, Jacobsen and Robb."[18] Dapprich died in California in 1965.

12. See United States Census for 1920, Richmond City, VA, ED 112; and United States Census, 1930, Los Angeles, CA, ED 720; U.S. National Archives and Records Administration, accessed through https://www.familysearch.org/ark:/61903/1:1:MJV3-JC8 (registration required); and https://www.familysearch.org/ark:/61903/1:1:XC8Z-ZJ4 (registration required).

13. See John Wallace Gillies, *Principles of Pictorial Photography* (New York: Falk, 1923).

14. Thank you to Carl Mautz for supplying us with a photograph of Dapprich's stationery.

15. See, for instance, Dapprich's photograph *The White Bridge*, printed in "Prize-Winners at the Exhibit of the Southern California Camera Club at the Southwest Museum," *Los Angeles Times*, 3 February 1924, 3; as well as *Hauschen in Walde*, in "Shown at the Exhibit of the Southern California Camera Club at the Southwest Museum," *Los Angeles Times*, 25 January 1925, 7; *Early Morning in the Park*, in "Cameracraft," *Los Angeles Times*, 2 August 1925, 4; *Introspection*, in "At All-American Photographic Salon 1927," *Los Angeles Times*, 23 October 1927, 4; *Christmas*, in "By Camera Pictorialists," *Los Angeles Times*, 19 October 1930, 5; and *Living Room, David R. Barnett Residence*, in "House and Garden," *Los Angeles Times*, 19 November 1933, 5.

16. See Julius Shulman, oral history interview by Taina Rikala De Noreiga, 12 January–3 February 1990, Archives of American Art, Smithsonian Institution, https://www.aaa.si.edu/collections/interviews/oral-history-interview-julius-shulman-11964#transcript.

17. Lisa Germany, *Harwell Hamilton Harris* (Austin: University of Texas Press, 1991), 78.

18. Fred R. Dapprich graduation announcement, undated, PMA-WLA, box 38, folder 38.

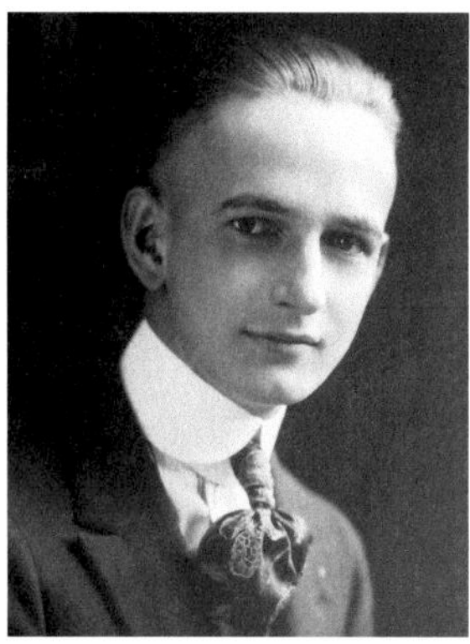

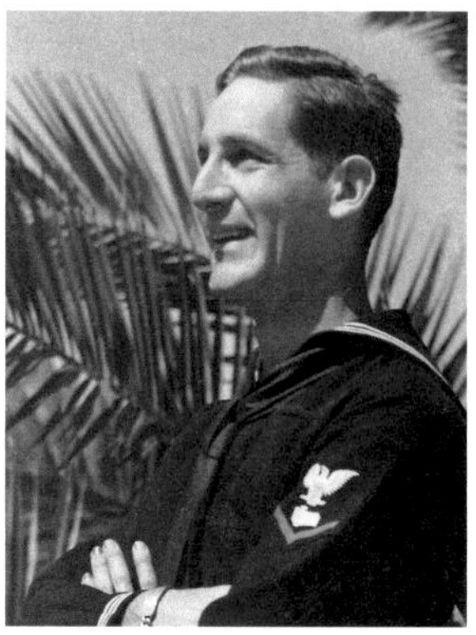

FLOYD HAROLD FAXON was born in Greenfield, New York, to a commercial merchant named Walter Faxon and his wife, Lydia, in 1897.[19] In 1905, Floyd and his three brothers—Walter Jr., Frank, and Webster—moved with their parents to Burbank, California. Floyd attended high school there before serving in the United States Navy during World War I, attaining the rank of Printer Petty Officer 1st Class. By 1920, Faxon had set up shop as a photographer, finding success over the next three decades working for a diverse roster of clients. He took pictures for the *Los Angeles Herald Examiner*, for example, and for Metro-Goldwyn-Mayer Studios, where, as the 1940 census records, he was employed as "cameraman."[20]

Faxon was equally comfortable photographing people, objects, and architectural environments. His early photographs include images of Hugo Ballin's murals for Griffith Observatory and Dean Cornwell's murals for the Central Rotunda in the Los Angeles Public Library.[21]

The Arensbergs contracted Faxon regularly between 1945 and 1951, and he remained in their favor through the end of their lives. (Correspondence in their archives indicates that other photographers whom the couple hired did not fare as well.) Many of the photographs Faxon took for them were quickly rendered inventory shots, and while a number of these pictures have been reproduced in this volume (because they provide the only record of a particular wall or artwork in the Arensberg collection), their inclusion should not suggest to the reader that Faxon was anything less than a gifted technician with a keen eye for composition.

A survey of Faxon's extant photographs indicates at least professional relationships with many in the Arensberg circle, including the actor Edward G. Robinson and his wife, Gladys, who helped establish the Modern Institute of Art; the artist Philip Guston, who credited the Arensbergs with introducing him to modern art; Earl Stendahl; and Kenneth Ross.

Faxon retired to Oceanside, California, where he died in 1978. There is still much to be learned of his crucial contributions to the historical record of Los Angeles.[22]

LEOPOLD (DICK) SEYFFERT JR. was born in Philadelphia in 1915. Seyffert's parents—the well-known portrait painter Leopold Seyffert and the modernist landscape painter Helen Fleck—met as students at the Pennsylvania Academy of the Fine Arts and married in 1911. Though the Seyffert family had initially settled in Missouri from their native Germany in the 1850s, they moved to Colorado Springs in the 1880s and later to Pittsburgh, where Seyffert's father began his career as an artist. Leopold Sr.'s many artistic successes allowed for frequent travel to Europe. While visiting France during the summer of 1924, the Seyfferts were photographed by Man Ray, whom they likely met while socializing with other artists and expatriates. After Leopold Jr.'s parents divorced in 1930 and his mother married the art dealer Jean Goriany, he shuttled between La Châtaigneraie boarding school in Geneva, his mother's new home in Senlis, France, and his father's homes in New York and Easton, Connecticut.

Seyffert served in the Navy as a photographer from 1944 to 1946, and the pictures of the Arensberg collection most likely taken by him would have been produced shortly after March 1945. Perhaps to distinguish himself professionally from his famous father, Leopold Jr. became known at this time as Dick.

The younger Seyffert's professional career as an artist began in earnest in the late 1940s, when he lived in Bolivia and Peru. In the 1950s, he returned to the United States and established a studio first in Chicago and, later, in New York City at the National Arts Club, where he had close ties with Portraits, Inc., and with Grand Central Gallery. Like his father, Seyffert (now known as Richard) became a painter of choice for America's cultural and political elite: his portraits included the poet W. H. Auden, Illinois governor John Stelle, Nobel Prize winner Dr. George H. Whipple, and Air Force general Lawrence S. Sister. Among the institutions where Seyffert's work is represented are the Pentagon, the University of Chicago, the Century Association, the Overseas Press Club, and the National Arts Club (on whose board of governors he served). In Seyffert's later years, he became a popular teacher at the Art Students League and also began painting landscapes during his frequent trips. He died in New York in 1979.[23]

19. See New York State Census for 1905, Greenfield, Saratoga County, NY, ED 1, U.S. National Archives and Records Administration, accessed through https://www.familysearch.org/ark:/61903/1:1:MKMV-N3Y (registration required).

20. See United States Census for 1940, Los Angeles, CA, ED 60-892, U.S. National Archives and Records Administration, accessed through https://www.familysearch.org/ark:/61903/1:1:K9CY-9ND (registration required).

21. See Faxon's photographs in the Los Angeles Public Library Photo Collection, https://tessa.lapl.org/cdm/landingpage/collection/photos.

22. We thank Mary Faxon (Floyd Faxon's granddaughter-in-law) and Bob Faxon (Floyd Faxon's grand nephew) for providing biographical detail.

23. We thank Robert Seyffert for providing biographical detail on his uncle, Dick Seyffert. Robert gave nine photographs of the Arensberg home to the Philadelphia Museum of Art Library and Archives, where they are now held in the Seyffert Photograph Collection.

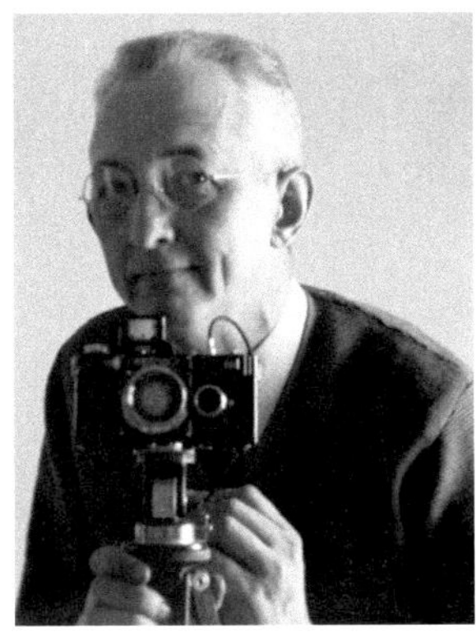

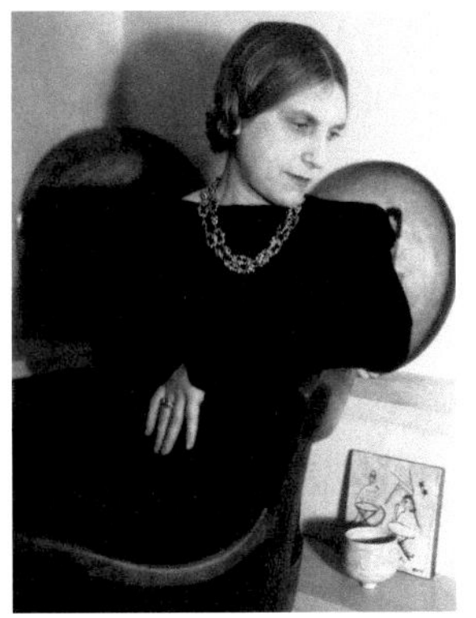

24. Charles Sheeler, oral history interview by Bartlett Cowdrey, 9 December 1958, Archives of American Art, Smithsonian Institution, https://www.aaa.si.edu/collections/interviews/oral-history-interview-charles-sheeler-12883#transcript.

25. *Mama of Dada*, a documentary film about Wood written and directed by Tom Neff, was released in 1993.

CHARLES SHEELER was born in 1883. A native Pennsylvanian like Walter Arensberg, he studied at the School of Industrial Art and the Academy of Fine Arts in Philadelphia.

Sheeler achieved his fame as a painter but earned his living as a photographer. By 1912, he was photographing buildings for Philadelphia architects, and in 1916 he was hired as staff photographer by Marius de Zayas for the Modern Gallery in New York, where he worked until 1924. During these years, Sheeler captured art-filled buildings for some of the country's wealthiest collectors, including Albert Barnes and John Quinn. In 1926, Edward Steichen hired him to work for *Vogue* and *Vanity Fair*, and his industrial images were in demand with the leading U.S. advertising agencies. While Sheeler focused on painting, drawing, and etching from the 1930s onward, his so-called precisionist style drew on photography for its source material and representational techniques. He continued to make and exhibit photographs until he suffered a debilitating stroke in 1959.

The Arensbergs first encountered Sheeler's work at the Armory Show in 1913, where the artist showed at least six paintings. He became a close friend of the Arensbergs and a regular participant in the artistic salon in their New York apartment. Sheeler's photographs of that space were taken sometime after March 1919 and have become the most familiar images of the Arensberg collection in its domestic setting (see pages 10–11). In an interview from 1958, Sheeler described the Arensbergs as the period's most successful collectors and singled out Walter for particular praise: "[He] had that great ability, radar eye, that is he could look right through a picture and back through the canvas again and come up with an opinion of it."[24]

Long after his death in 1965, Sheeler's photographic archive was given to the Museum of Fine Arts in Boston by MFA trustee Saundra Lane. The Lane Collection contains the photographic record of Sheeler's visit to the Arensbergs' Hollywood house in October 1939 (see pages iv, 53), making Sheeler the only photographer who captured the couple's collection in both homes.

BEATRICE WOOD was born in 1893 to wealthy parents in San Francisco. In the late 1890s, the family moved to New York, where Wood was educated at private schools. After training as an actress and dancer in Paris, she returned to New York when war broke out in 1914. She joined the French National Repertory Theatre and met many of the French artists who had taken up residence in the United States.

Through the writer Henri Pierre Roché and the composer Edgard Varèse, Wood met Marcel Duchamp in 1917, who in turn introduced her to the Arensbergs. Wood was involved in several Arensberg-related projects, including the Society of Independent Artists' exhibition (where her drawings and paintings were displayed alongside Duchamp's notorious *Fountain*) and avant-garde journals funded by Walter—earning her the moniker "the Mama of Dada."[25]

Wood remained the Arensbergs' closest friend after the couple moved to California: they feature prominently in her diaries (now housed at the Smithsonian's Archives of American Art) and are a significant presence in her autobiography, *I Shock Myself*. She was the first to photograph the couple's new home at 7065 Hillside Avenue before the walls were filled with art (which gives them limited value for the kind of photographic tour presented in this book), and her intimacy with both Duchamp and the Arensbergs put her in a unique position to capture the only photos of all three figures together (see front cover and page xvi).

In 1927, the year the Arensbergs moved into their Hillside Avenue home, Wood followed them to California. There she developed an interest in ceramics that occupied her for the rest of her life. She created a studio and arts center in Ojai, where the Indian philosopher J. Krishnamurti had set up a branch of the Theosophical Society. Wood's social, spiritual, and artistic life continued until 1998, when she died nine days after her 105th birthday.

PAGES 408–11, LEFT TO RIGHT. **KARL BISSINGER** (DETAIL), CA. EARLY 1950S. PHOTOGRAPHER UNKNOWN. UNIVERSITY OF DELAWARE LIBRARY, NEWARK, SPECIAL COLLECTIONS, KARL BISSINGER ARCHIVE (MSS0682). **FRITZ (FRED) BLOCK**, UNDATED. PHOTOGRAPHER UNKNOWN. PHILADELPHIA MUSEUM OF ART, LIBRARY AND ARCHIVES, ARENSBERG ARCHIVES (PMA-WLA), BOX 53, FOLDER 18. **FREDERICK RICHARD DAPPRICH**, CA. 1928. PHOTOGRAPH BY MILTON M. INMAN. COURTESY CATHARINE KARL MILLIKAN, GRANDDAUGHTER OF MILTON M. INMAN, LONG BEACH, CALIFORNIA. **FLOYD HAROLD FAXON**, UNDATED. PHOTOGRAPHER UNKNOWN. COURTESY BOB FAXON. **LEOPOLD (DICK) SEYFFERT JR.** IN THE NAVY, CA. 1944–46. COURTESY ROBERT SEYFFERT. **CHARLES SHEELER**, SELF-PORTRAIT, NOT BEFORE 1932. DOWNTOWN GALLERY RECORDS, 1824–1974, BULK 1926–1969, ARCHIVES OF AMERICAN ART, SMITHSONIAN INSTITUTION. **BEATRICE WOOD** AT AMERICA HOUSE EXHIBITION, 1947. PHOTOGRAPHER UNKNOWN. COURTESY BEATRICE WOOD CENTER FOR THE ARTS / HAPPY VALLEY FOUNDATION.

NOTES ON THE DATING AND LOCATIONS OF PHOTOGRAPHS

MARK NELSON *with contributions from* **WILLIAM H. SHERMAN**

This book is not intended to present a complete visual record of artworks and objects owned by Louise and Walter Arensberg. Similarly, it has not been designed to show all extant photographs of the couple or their house. The following notes provide a guide for further access to the photographic record of the Arensbergs' home, hopefully illuminating what has been learned by studying these pictures and highlighting what might still be discovered by further examining them.

The Philadelphia Museum of Art, Library and Archives, Arensberg Archives (hereafter cited as PMA-WLA), holds both original prints and copy-prints of images by Fred R. Dapprich and Floyd Faxon intermingled in folders loosely organized by the rooms they show in the Arensberg house (PMA-WLA, box 54). Prints by Floyd Faxon in these folders (see plates 2, 5, 6, 15, 31, 33, 43, 46, 59) include his maker's stamp and are dateable to within a month of their creation because they have inventory numbers written on their backs that correspond to invoices he sent the Arensbergs (PMA-WLA, box 28, folders 10–15). One image has a Faxon inventory number, but no maker's mark (see plate 12). Another forty-three rolls of uncut negatives by Faxon, picturing individual objects in the Arensbergs' collection and used by the couple for cataloging purposes, can also be found in the PMA archives (PMA-WLA, box 65). Quickly composed and varying in quality, a few of these images have been used in this volume because they offer the only view of a particular wall (see plates 8–10, 39, 50, 51, 53–55). Some of the negatives in this expansive set include tantalizing glimpses of rooms in the Arensbergs' house but were not suitable for publication in this book. Notably, they show the bookshelves that were built along three walls of the Francis Bacon Foundation office sometime after circa 1944 and picture a number of artworks hanging on a wall in that room: John Covert's *Hydro Cell* (PMA 1950-134-509); Jacques Villon's sketch for *Puteaux (Smoke and Trees in Bloom, No. 2)* (PMA 1950-134-189); and a map by Abraham Ortelius (see page 66).

Fred R. Dapprich also put a maker's stamp on his original prints, and the pictures attributed to him in this volume can be verified against those markings (see pages 27, 32; plates 1, 7, 13, 17–21, 23, 26, 30, 32, 34, 35, 37, 38, 42, 44, 49, 52, 56). The five pictures by Dapprich that appeared in the January 1945 feature on the Arensbergs' home in *Vogue* can be dated, with relative certainty, to circa late 1944 (see plates 7, 18, 20, 30; page 350). Plate 18, for example, shows an object known to have been purchased in September 1944 ("No. 1959, Skull Head with Eagle," in Stendahl Art Galleries invoice to Walter Arensberg, 27 September 1944 (PMA-WLA, box 28, folder 32). Plate 23 was likely taken that same day because the three objects on the bureau have not moved—it was part of a set of thirteen pictures by Dapprich of the Arensberg home (all duplicates of those at the PMA) that can be found in the Special Collections of the Museum of Modern Art (MoMA) Library (call number N6490.A674.1940; see plates 1, 7, 13, 21, 34, 35, 37, 38, 42, 49, 52, 56). Presumably, all of the pictures in this set also date to late 1944, since one of them was included in the *Vogue* article.

The set was sent, at an unknown date, to MoMA librarian Bernard Karpel by either Dapprich or Walter Arensberg. Karpel later contacted Dapprich directly while working with Ad Reinhardt and Robert Motherwell on their 1951 publication *Modern Artists in America* (see Karpel to Dapprich, New York, 17 August 1950, PMA-WLA, box 22, folder 20). *Modern Artists in America* used four of the five *Vogue* images from 1944 and none from the MoMA set. It also featured several pictures of the Arensberg home that Dapprich likely took at a later date (see plates 19, 26, 32, 44). Because artworks pictured in the *Modern Artists in America* set occupy different positions than they do in the MoMA or *Vogue* sets (cf. plates 18 and 19, for example), we presume that Dapprich took more pictures inside the Arensbergs' home sometime between 1945 and 1950. In his letter, Karpel thanks Dapprich for sending two negatives, a curiosity considering the emphasis photographers usually place on retaining their originals. Starting prepress work from a provided negative rather than a print—combined with a lack of familiarity with the actual house on Reinhardt's or Motherwell's part—may have been what caused one of Dapprich's images to be flopped when it appeared in *Modern Artists in America* (cf. plate 32 and page 137 of *Modern Artists in America*).

Condé Nast has scanned four of Dapprich's original prints (from the set of five that appeared in *Vogue*) and now offers them for editorial reproduction through Getty Images.

Included in PMA-WLA, box 54, along with the Dapprich and Faxon photographs were several photographs that long remained unattributed. We learned quite late in the process of writing this book that those pictures were probably taken by Leopold (Richard) Seyffert Jr., who, in his capacity as a professional photographer, went by the name Dick Seyffert. Dick's nephew, Robert Seyffert, donated a set of nine pictures to the PMA Library and Archives where they can now be found in the Seyffert Photograph Collection. In addition to duplicates of the Seyffert prints in PMA-WLA, box 54 (which Dick perhaps gave to the Arensbergs at some point), are others that are unique to this collection. We have used five of the probable Seyffert photographs in this volume (see page 65; plates 4, 14, 16, 41). These pictures must have been taken after 15 March 1945 because an object known to have been invoiced that day appears on the living room chest of drawers in Seyffert's photograph on page 65 ("No. 2084, Inca Bundle Mask with Fabric," in Stendahl Art Galleries invoice to Walter Arensberg, 15 March 1945, PMA-WLA, box 28, folder 32 [cf. PMA 1950-134-311]), and they likely were not taken much later than 1946, when Seyffert's Navy service concluded.

Four of Charles Sheeler's five pictures of the Arensbergs' New York apartment (see pages 10–11), along with another four pictures of their Hollywood home (see, for example, pages iv, 53) that he took during a 1939 visit to California with his wife, Musya, are housed in the Lane Collection, Museum of Fine Arts, Boston. Original prints of the same four New York images can be found in the collection of the Whitney Museum of American Art. Part of a 1980 gift to the Whitney by James Maroney and Suzanne Fredericks, they are viewable online (https://whitney.org/artists/1209). An additional image by Sheeler of the New York apartment can be found in PMA-WLA, box 54, folder 3. Sheeler's 1939 image of the living room desk at 7065 Hillside Avenue (see page iv) bridges the years and distance that separate the New York apartment and the Hollywood home. The earliest interior image in the photographic tour presented by *Hollywood Arensberg*, it pictures the only arrangement of art in the Hollywood house that bears similarities to one in the New York apartment (cf. page 11, top). Capturing the Arensbergs' interest in books as well as art, the 1939 image also illustrates one of the most familiar tropes of early twentieth-century collecting: the juxtaposition of an African sculpture with a cubist painting. The Arensbergs later moved that painting, Jean Metzinger's *Tea Time (Woman with a Teaspoon)*, to the guest bedroom (see plate 58.10). They replaced it in the living room with Juan Gris's painting *Lamp*, making a simple pun between that work and the desk lamp in front of it (see plate 19.18).

The only known color pictures of the Arensberg house, taken by Fritz (Fred) Block (see plates 24, 25, 27), were provided by the art historian Roland Jaeger, who manages the photographer's estate. Though there is no official record of when the images were taken, we thank Jaeger for considering their history so thoroughly on our behalf. These images are numbered 179, 180, and 181 in the archive's set of master slides for Block's series Modern Architecture I, which was completed in 1943 and does not feature any architecture built after 1943. Buildings created after 1943 were included in the series Modern Architecture II (1952). Jaeger notes that the three Arensberg images were removed from the circa 1948–50 list of the Modern Architecture I series—a common practice for Block. It is unclear whether the Arensbergs asked him to remove them or he simply felt they no longer belonged in the set.

Over the course of her long relationship with the Arensbergs, Beatrice Wood took many photographs of the couple and their homes, photographs that are now spread across multiple archives, including those of the Huntington Library, the Philadelphia Museum of Art, and, especially, the Archives of American Art (AAA) at the Smithsonian Institution, Washington, DC. The Beatrice Wood Papers, at the latter institution, include many significant objects related to her relationship with the Arensbergs, Marcel Duchamp, and others in their circle. In her autobiography, *I Shock Myself*, Wood published her photographs of the Arensbergs' early days in New York, including some of their New York apartment; their Hollywood home; and their brief time living in Residence A of Frank Lloyd Wright's Olive Hill complex. Photocopies of a first draft of Wood's book show other Wood photographs that were not included in the final book (see Beatrice Wood Papers, Archives of American Art, Smithsonian Institution, series 4, subseries 4.1, box 11, folders 60, 61). The original prints of Wood's photographs of Duchamp's 1936 visit to the Arensbergs—sourced for this volume from copies in the PMA archive (see front cover and page xvi)—can also be found in the

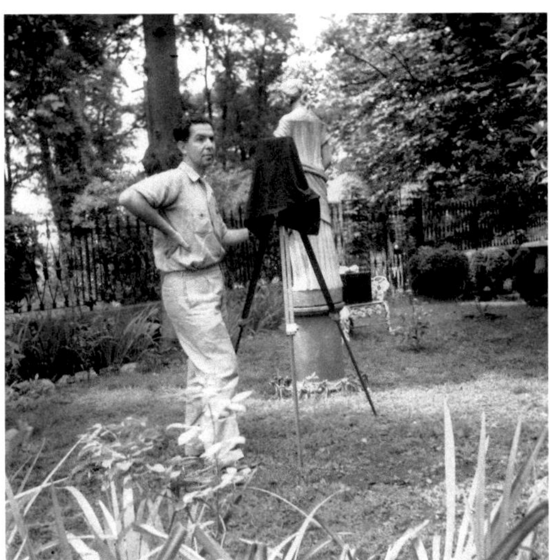

CLARENCE JOHN LAUGHLIN. *DONALDSONVILLE R. C. CHURCH YARD,* CA. 1952. THE CLARENCE JOHN LAUGHLIN ARCHIVE AT THE HISTORIC NEW ORLEANS COLLECTION, CALL NUMBER 1981.247.12.10

AAA (series 8, box 24, folder 10). Francis M. Naumann owns one of Beatrice Wood's original albums of her own photographs, many of which feature the Arensbergs. We thank him for sharing this resource with us (see page 363).

After reading correspondence between the Arensbergs and *Flair* magazine's publisher, Fleur Cowles, and editor, Patrick O'Higgins (PMA-WLA, box 7, folder 42), we began to suspect that other images of the Arensberg home might exist. Photographs taken by Karl Bissinger for *Flair* were found after Bissinger's son, David Fechheimer, suggested they might be housed with his father's photographic archive at the University of Delaware Library. We are extremely grateful to Mr. Fechheimer, and to L. Rebecca Johnson Melvin, manuscripts librarian and curator, Joseph R. Biden Jr. Senatorial Papers, Special Collections and Museums at the University of Delaware Library, for locating these photographs and for facilitating their professional imaging and allowing us to publish them (see pages 23, 25, 31, 36, 39, 78, 342, 369, 406; plates 11, 40, 45, 47, 48, 57, 58). These photographs and their original negatives are housed at the Karl Bissinger Archive, University of Delaware Library.

We were unable to track down any information on Corporal F. W. Lumbord (first name unknown), who took five photographs, four of which are printed here, of wounded soldiers visiting the Arensberg home while participating in an art therapy class at nearby Birmingham Hospital (see page 24; plates 3, 28, 36). These images can be found in PMA-WLA, box 53, folder 51, and the enclosure envelope that originally held them can be found among the correspondence between the Arensbergs and David Glusker (PMA-WLA, box 8, folder 13). The image by Lumbord of four men standing next to Marcel Duchamp's *Nude Descending a Staircase (No. 2)* (see plate 28) bears a stamp that reads "Official Photograph, Birmingham General Hospital, Van Nuys, California," and an attached handwritten note reads "L to R: Pfc [Private First Class] Dick Rembrandt; Birmingham staff instructor, S/Sgt. [Staff Sergeant] Robert Elin; Air Corps casualty, Pvt. [Private] Luis Romano; & T/4 [Technician Fourth Grade (Sergeant)] Don Schloat, Phillippine [*sic*] prison returnee." The tentative dating of these photographs is based on Schloat's rescue from a Japanese prison camp (featured in several *Los Angeles Times* articles) after he narrowly escaped the Palawan massacre of 1944; he first returned to Los Angeles in March of 1945.

Finally, special mention should be made of the work of Clarence John Laughlin, who produced nearly one hundred photographs of the Arensberg sculptures and paintings, first in Los Angeles and later in Philadelphia. These pictures, with titles ranging from the didactic to the poetic, were sometimes cut by Laughlin into collages and often included elaborate captions written on carefully prepared note cards. Though only one of them is featured in this book (see page 24), the images in their entirety provide fascinating insight into a photographer who was transfixed by the artworks in the Arensberg collection. These pictures are now housed at the Historic New Orleans Collection (THNOC) in Louisiana. Though most are not viewable online as of this writing, lists of these photographs and their accession numbers can be found by searching THNOC's online catalog using the keyword "Arensberg."

NOTES ON SELECTED OBJECTS

MARK NELSON *with contributions from* **WILLIAM H. SHERMAN**

ABBREVIATED KEY TO ACRONYMS

(FOR COMPLETE KEY, SEE PAGES 75–76)

AIC: ARENSBERG INDEX CARD
AIN: ARENSBERG INVENTORY NUMBER
FBF: FRANCIS BACON FOUNDATION
FBL: FRANCIS BACON LIBRARY
HEH: HENRY E. HUNTINGTON LIBRARY, ART MUSEUM, AND BOTANICAL GARDENS, SAN MARINO, CALIFORNIA (THE HUNTINGTON)
HEH-FBLMC: HUNTINGTON LIBRARY, FRANCIS BACON LIBRARY MANUSCRIPTS COLLECTION
HEH-RBC: HUNTINGTON LIBRARY, RARE BOOKS COLLECTION
HEH-FBLA: HUNTINGTON LIBRARY, FRANCIS BACON LIBRARY ARCHIVE
HEH-HAC: HUNTINGTON ART COLLECTIONS
PMA: PHILADELPHIA MUSEUM OF ART
PMA-WLA: PHILADELPHIA MUSEUM OF ART, ARENSBERG ARCHIVES
PMA-FBF: PHILADELPHIA MUSEUM OF ART, FRANCIS BACON FOUNDATION RECORDS

1. NOTES ON SELECTED PICTURED OBJECTS TRADED OR SOLD BEFORE OR SHORTLY AFTER THE BEQUEST OF THE ARENSBERG COLLECTION TO THE PHILADELPHIA MUSEUM OF ART

1.1 (PLATES 2.13, 18.15): DINOSAUR PRINT (FAKE)
The AIC for this object (PMA-WLA, box 27, AIN 35) has no picture attached but reads: "Dinosaur Print. Purchased from Watron Long Beach. Gift to Dept. of Vertebrate Paleontology of Calif. Inst of Tech. 10–27–54. Not to Phila." In the 1980s, the Natural History Museum of Los Angeles County (then known as the Los Angeles County Museum of Natural History) accessioned the invertebrate paleontology collections of the California Institute of Technology (Caltech), the University of Southern California (USC), and the University of California, Los Angeles (UCLA). Transferring the massive amount of data contained on file cards and in archival paper records for those collections into a digital resource, the Invertebrate Paleontology Collections Database (IPCD), is part of the ongoing work of the museum's Invertebrate Paleontology Department (LACMIP). Though this specimen does have an accession number, P.300.57-35 (the same general accession number given to all of the Caltech specimens), it is not in the IPCD and was never given a catalog number. While locating and photographing this object for me, the staff at the Natural History Museum of Los Angeles County determined that it was a fake. For their generosity and their patience in answering my many questions about this object, I am extremely grateful to Dr. Luis M. Chiappe, director, Dinosaur Institute; Doug Goodreau, lab supervisor, Dinosaur Institute; Dr. Sam McLeod, collections manager, Vertebrate Paleontology; Mary Stecheson, former curatorial assistant, Invertebrate Paleontology; and Paige Johnson, former curatorial assistant, Dinosaur Institute. I would also like to extend my gratitude to Jennifer Kerr, vice president (and former president) of the Southern California Paleontological Society, for facilitating these conversations.

1.2 (PLATES *3.6, 35.4, 57.3): REPRODUCTION OF MARCEL DUCHAMP'S *COFFEE MILL*
Marcel Duchamp's original *Coffee Mill*—a small work of oil and graphite on board—was made in 1911 as a gift for his brother the sculptor Raymond Duchamp-Villon. Because the Arensbergs could not purchase the original, they likely asked Duchamp to make this copy for them. The AIC for this "colored" reproduction (PMA-WLA, box 26, AIN 732) notes that it was "Sold to H. Linthural [sp?] for $3.00 in 1960–61."

1.3 (PLATES 7.14, 47.20): *MAYA (*SOUTHEASTERN MEXICO, YUCATÁN), JAGUAR
The AIC for this object (PMA-WLA, box 26, AIN 1114) includes a photograph and reads "Tiger, Mayan, Stone, Yucatan," and notes that it was "Traded for [AIN] 1432 and $672.75." In *Diego Rivera: Murals for the Museum of Modern Art* (New York: Museum of Modern Art, 2011), Anna Indych-López rightly notes that "there are of course no tigers in Mexico, but the word *tigre* is used colloquially for the jaguar, an animal considered sacred by the Aztecs" (p. 52). This suggests one possible explanation for how the Arensbergs came to use the word *tiger* in this context and provides a rationale for the change of title for this object to "jaguar" in this volume.

1.4 (PLATES *6.13, *15.7): ARTIST/MAKER UNKNOWN (*EUROPE OR NORTH AMERICA), PAPERWEIGHT
The AIC for an object (PMA-WLA, box 27, AIN 1112) with no picture attached reads "Paper Weight, Cut Glass, Egg-shaped. Victorian. Lost? Stolen?" Though it cannot be confirmed that the object pictured here is a match to this card, the description seems to fit the object better than any other in the collection.

1.5 (PLATES 13.18, 17.4): ARTIST/MAKER UNKNOWN (*CHINA), VASE
The AIC for this object (PMA-WLA, box 26, AIN 250/previously 247) includes a photograph and reads "Vase. Bronze. Ming." The card notes that the vase was "Swapped in 1949 (Stendahl) for [AIN] 1402 and [AIN] 1407." Because the whereabouts of this object are currently unknown, its attribution to the Ming dynasty on the AIC cannot be verified.

1.6 (PLATE 34.3): STEINWAY & SONS, GRAND PIANO
Louise Arensberg's piano (PMA-WLA, box 26, AIN 1060) is still in use at a private home in Los Angeles.

1.7 (PLATE 36.3): GINO SEVERINI, *COMPOSITION FOR MOSAIC*
The AIC for this painting (PMA-WLA, box 26, AIN 613) includes a photograph and lists its title as "Birds & Still Life." In a January 1949 letter to Katharine Kuh, associate curator of painting and sculpture at the Art Institute of Chicago, Walter Arensberg explains that he and Louise have traded this painting—along with eight other works, including Diego Rivera's *The Flowered Canoe* (note 1.8), Marcel Gromaire's *The Night Watchman* (note 1.9), and José Clemente Orozco's *The Beggars* (note 1.11)—for "some absolutely superlative Pre-Columbian pieces, and are we happy!" See Walter Arensberg to Katharine Kuh, Art Institute of Chicago, 26 January 1949 (PMA-WLA, box 2, folder 5). An image of the painting can be found on page 424 of *Gino Severini: Catalogo ragionato* by Daniela Fonti (Milan: Arnoldo Mondadori, 1988). Fonti gives the proper title of the work as *Composizione per mosaico* (on which the English title here is based). She dates the piece to 1933 and notes that it came to the United States in 1935 (p. 424). Because of a foreshortening effect in the photograph printed here, this very horizontal work appears to be vertical. The location of the painting could not be ascertained before the publication of this volume.

1.8 (PLATES *36.4, 37.6): DIEGO RIVERA, *THE FLOWERED CANOE*
The Arensbergs loaned this painting to the Museum of Modern Art for Rivera's first retrospective in the United States, where it was on view from 23 December 1931 through 27 January 1932. The painting is plate 46 in *Diego Rivera*, the catalog for that exhibition (New York: Museum of Modern Art, 1931), where it is titled *The Canoe*. The AIC for this painting (PMA-WLA, box 26, AIN 595) includes a photograph, lists its title as *Le Canot*, and notes that it was exhibited at "San Diego Gallery," "2/12–3/31/36 approx." The Arensbergs traded the painting for pre-Columbian works (see note 1.7). It is now in the collection of Museo Dolores Olmedo, Xochimilco, Mexico, where it is known as *La canoa enflorada*.

1.9 (PLATES *36.7, 37.8): MARCEL GROMAIRE, *THE NIGHT WATCHMAN*
The AIC for this "oil on canvas" (PMA-WLA, box 26, AIN 612) includes a photograph and notes that it was titled *The Night Watchman*. The Arensbergs traded the painting for pre-Columbian works (see note 1.7). The location of this work could not be ascertained before the publication of this volume.

1.10 (PLATES 36.10, 37.14, 38.5): ARTIST/MAKER UNKNOWN, GOTHIC CHEST FRONT
The AIC for this carved wood object (PMA-WLA, box 26, AIN 620) includes a photograph. Its whereabouts are not currently known.

1.11 (PLATE 38.14): JOSÉ CLEMENTE OROZCO, *THE BEGGARS*
The AIC for this "Tempera?" painting (PMA-WLA, box 26, AIN 605) includes a photograph

and notes that the work measured 16 7/8 × 20 1/2 inches. The card also notes that the painting was exhibited at the "San Fran. Museum of Art from 10/25/36–??/36." Clearly misdated, the card refers to the *Exhibition of Mexican Paintings and Drawings*, held at the San Francisco Museum of Art—now the San Francisco Museum of Modern Art (SFMOMA)—from 30 October through 2 December 1935. Though the exhibition traveled afterward to the San Diego Museum (also known as the Fine Arts Gallery of San Diego), the organizers of that show decided against asking for a continuance of the loan, and the painting was sent back to the Arensbergs "express prepaid" on 11 December 1935. See Reginald Poland to Dr. Alma Reed, 5 December 1935, and Grace L. McCann Morley to Walter Arensberg, 12 December 1935; both in *Exhibition of Mexican Paintings and Drawings*, 30 October–2 December, Exhibition Records (box 3, folder 3), San Francisco Museum of Modern Art Archives. The Arensbergs' painting *The Flowered Canoe* by Diego Rivera was exhibited instead (see note 1.8). The Arensbergs traded this painting for pre-Columbian works (see note 1.7). The current location of this work could not be ascertained before the printing of this volume. I am extremely grateful to Barbara Rominski, former head of the Research Library and Archives, SFMOMA, for providing me with these archival records.

1.12 (PLATE 39.2): WILLIAM HOGARTH, *THE IDLE 'PRENTICE EXECUTED AT TYBURN*
William Hogarth's "progresses," or "modern moral Subjects" as he described them, were sets of popular and widely distributed serial engravings communicating didactic messages of reform on a variety of topical subjects. Among these was the 1747 series *Industry and Idleness*, which contrasted the lives and fates of two imagined apprentices—one lazy, the other industrious. *The Idle 'Prentice Executed at Tyburn* was the eleventh of twelve plates in that series. An image of the etching is plate 190 (cat. no. 178) in *Hogarth's Graphic Works, First Complete Edition*, vol. 2, *Plates* by Ronald Paulson (New Haven: Yale University Press, 1965). The AIC for this engraving (PMA-WLA, box 26, AIN 570) includes a photograph.

1.13 (PLATE 41.20): NATIVE AMERICAN, BIRD FORM
The AIC for this object (PMA-WLA, box 26, AIN 1344) includes a photograph and notes that this "Bird Stone" of "Grey Green Rock" from "Doc Lyle farm. Jefferson County, Ohio," was returned to Earl Stendahl.

1.14 (PLATE 42.7): DANIEL THOMAS EGERTON, *VIEW OF THE CITY OF MEXICO*
Vista de la ciudad de México (*View of the City of Mexico*) is plate 10 in *Vistas de México*, a volume of twelve lithographs Egerton published in 1840. The lithograph was possibly based, in part, on Egerton's painting *The Valley of Mexico*, which was lot 92 in *Selected Quality Pictures, 15/07/2011*, the catalog of an an auction organized by Keys, Norfolk. The AIC for this work (PMA-WLA, box 26, AIN 392) includes a photograph and reads "D. I. Edgerton [*sic*]. Lithographs. Mexican Landscape. 1840. Colored. Not to Phila." No other information is available regarding from whom the Arensbergs acquired this picture or where it later went.

1.15 (PLATE 42.13): ARTIST/MAKER UNKNOWN, "FOUND" WOOD SCULPTURE
The Arensbergs owned several sculptures made of wood or mutated garden vegetables (PMA-WLA, box 64, folder 28). Though described in the archival documentation as "found," they were possibly somewhat manipulated to accentuate their anthropomorphic qualities. Perhaps kept more as amusement than as art, they nonetheless had a certain visual harmony with the couple's works by Constantin Brancusi and with some of their pre-Columbian artifacts. The location of these objects is not currently known.

1.16 (PLATES 43.2, 45.25): TOYOKUNI II, *A CARP LEAPING A WATERFALL*
The AIC for this print (PMA-WLA, box 26, AIN 1160) reads only "Toyokuni Japanese Print. Salmon Swimming Upstream." The card does not have a photograph attached, and the location of the actual print owned by the Arensbergs could not be ascertained before the publication of this volume. However, an impression of this image was offered by Christie's in its auction catalog *Japanese Screens, Paintings and Prints, New York, Tuesday October 25, 1994* (sale 7986; lot 292). An image of the print appears on page 71, described as "Toyokuni II: Kakemono-e (71.2 × 24.5 cm.); A double-*Oban* vertical diptych of a carp leaping a waterfall, signed Gototei Toyokuni ga and sealed Toyokuni and published by Yamamotoya Heikichi." I am extremely grateful to Paula Doe of Fuji Arts, Ann Arbor, Michigan, for her initial identification of this work and for her patience fielding my many questions about it.

1.17 (PLATE 44.25): DAVID BURLIUK, *THE REFUGEES*
The AIC for this painting (PMA-WLA, box 26, AIN 1191) includes a photograph and notes only that this "oil" painting was titled *The Refugees*, that it was "11 × 11," and that it was "Sold to ASV" for $75 in September 1963. The location of the painting could not be ascertained before the publication of this volume.

1.18 (PLATE 49.10): DAVID BURLIUK, *WOMAN WITH COW*
This painting is reproduced on page 27 of the 1944 book *Burliuk* by Katherine S. Dreier, with reproductions selected by Dreier and Marcel Duchamp (New York: Société Anonyme and *Color and Rhyme*, 1944). The book notes that David and Mary Burliuk visited the Arensbergs in Los Angeles in April of 1942, and that David's works were already in their collection by the time of that visit (p. 165). The AIC for this painting (PMA-WLA, box 26, AIN 1190) includes a photograph, gives the painting's title as *The Beloved Cow*, and notes that it was "Sold to ASV" for $75 in September 1963. The location of the painting could not be ascertained before the publication of this volume.

1.19 (PLATE 50.4): *ALEXANDER HELWIG WYANT, LANDSCAPE
The AIC for this "oil painting" (PMA-WLA, box 26, AIN 512) includes a photograph and notes that it was "traded 4/17/48." The location of the painting could not be ascertained before the publication of this volume.

1.20 (PLATE 50.5): CURRIER & IVES, *ELIZA*
The AIC for this "print" (PMA-WLA box 26, AIN 515) includes a photograph and notes that it was "Colored, with fantastic frame." The location of the print could not be ascertained before the publication of this volume.

1.21 (PLATE 50.6): CURRIER & IVES, VOLUNTEER FIRE COMPANY CERTIFICATE OF MEMBERSHIP
The AIC for this "Print–Engraving?" (PMA-WLA, box 26, AIN 513) includes a photograph. The location of this print could not be ascertained before the publication of this volume.

1.22 (PLATE 51.1): ALPHONSE LEGROS, STUDY OF A HEAD
The AIC for this "Drawing" in "Red Crayon" (PMA-WLA, box 26, AIN 516) includes a photograph and notes that the picture was "Given to sister, Mrs. Price." ("Mrs. Price" was Walter's sister, Edith Arensberg Price; their correspondence can be found in HEH-FBLA, box 81.) The location of the drawing could not be ascertained before the publication of this volume.

1.23 (PLATE 51.2): ARTIST/MAKER UNKNOWN (*ITALY), VIEW OF VENICE
The AIC for this "Italian" "Oil" (PMA-WLA, box 26, AIN 517) includes a photograph and notes that it was "traded 4/17/48." The location of this painting could not be ascertained before the publication of this volume.

1.24 (PLATES 52.1 AND 52.2): REPRODUCTION OF CANALETTO'S *PRÀ DELLA VALLE* (RIGHT HALF) AND *S. GIUSTINA IN PRÀ DELLA VALLE* (LEFT HALF)
The AICs for these prints (PMA-WLA, box 26, AIN 506 and AIN 507) include photographs and greatly abbreviated descriptions. The prints have origins in *Vedute: Altre prese da i Inoghi altre ideate* (Views: Some taken from places, others imagined) (1741–44), a portfolio of thirty-five etchings by Canaletto (Giovanni Antonio Canal) picturing Venice and surrounding locations (they are plates 7 and 8, respectively). See Ruth Bromberg, *Canaletto's Etchings: Revised and Enlarged Edition of the Catalogue Raisonné* (San Francisco: Alan Wofsy Fine Arts, 1993). These prints form a panoramic view when hung side by side, but for whatever reason, the Arensbergs displayed one above the other.

1.25 (PLATE 52.3): REPRODUCTION OF GIUSEPPE ZOCCHI'S *THE ARNO RIVER FROM THE RUCELLAI TERRACE*
This engraving is included in *Scelta di XXIV vedute delle principali contrade, piazze, chiese,*

e palazzi della città di Firenze (Selection of twenty-four views of the main neighborhoods, piazzas, churches, and palaces of the city of Florence), a copy of which can be found in the collection of the Morgan Library (call number 49013; record ID 174302; accession number PML49013). The Morgan owns all of the prepatory drawings for the engravings in this volume as well, including *Veduta di Lung'Arno e del Ponte a S. Trinita, presa dal terrazzo de SS.ʳⁱ Rucellai* (View of the Arno River from the Rucellai terrace) (call number B3 FF 064 07; record ID 191917; accession number: 1952.30:9). A reproduction of the work can also be seen in Elaine Evans Dee, *Views of Florence and Tuscany by Giuseppe Zocchi, 1711–1767: Seventy-seven Drawings from the Collection of the Pierpont Morgan Library, New York* (Meriden, CT: Meriden Gravure and Steinhour Press, 1971), plate 9. The AIC for this print (PMA-WLA, box 26, AIN 505) reads "Parr (Engraver). 1850. Colored." The date given on the card perhaps relates to the date of the particular edition of the print that the Arensbergs owned.

1.26 (PLATE 52.4): REPRODUCTION OF FRANZ HOGENBERG'S ENGRAVING AFTER A DRAWING BY GEORG HOEFNAGEL, *CITYSCAPE OF ARNSBERG*

Civitates orbis terrarum (Cities of the world) was an immensely successful early atlas that greatly influenced cartography and bookmaking for many years afterward. All six volumes, published in Cologne between 1572 and 1617, were overseen by a principal editor, Georg Braun. For an excellent reproduction of *Cityscape of Arnsberg*, see pages 298–99 of the Taschen facsimile, Georg Braun and Franz Hogenberg, *Cities of the World: Complete Edition of the Colour Plates of 1572–1617* (Cologne: Taschen, 2008). Stephan Füssel's essay in the same volume provides historical perspective on the significance of this early tome and its creators. The AIC for this object (PMA-WLA, box 26, AIN 504) reads: "Print . . . colored, by hand . . . Returned to Mr and Mrs A in return for items of equal value. 3–30–53; Sent to Arensbergs in East." The original map is now in the collection of Charles C. M. Arensberg, VMD.

1.27 (PLATE 53.2): ARTIST/MAKER UNKNOWN (NORTH AMERICAN), LANDSCAPE

The AIC for this "Early American" "Water color" (PMA-WLA, box 26, AIN 501) includes a photograph. The location of the painting could not be ascertained before the publication of this volume.

2. NOTES ON SELECTED PICTURED ARTIFACTS NOW HOUSED IN THE FRANCIS BACON LIBRARY MANUSCRIPTS COLLECTION, THE HUNTINGTON LIBRARY (HEH-FBLMC)

2.1 (PLATES 3.33, 7.5, AND PP. 66–67): SIR FRANCIS BACON, AUTOGRAPH LETTER SIGNED, TO GEORGE VILLIERS, EARL (LATER DUKE) OF BUCKINGHAM

This letter is pictured and briefly mentioned in the 1944 *Vogue* article featuring the Arensbergs, "Great Art . . . in Four California Houses." For the letter itself, see HEH-FBLMC, box 1, call number FBL 4. For the text of the letter, see *The Works of Francis Bacon*, vol. 13, *The Letters and The Life*, vol. 6, collected and edited by James Spedding, Robert Leslie Ellis, and Douglas Denon Heath (London: Longmans, Green, Reader, and Dyer, 1868), 292.

2.2 (PLATE 4.10, AND PP. 66–67): NATHANIEL BACON, AUTOGRAPH LETTER SIGNED, TO ROGER TOWNSEND

For the letter itself, see HEH-FBLMC, box 1, call number FBL 5.

2.3 (PLATE 7.2, AND PP. 66–67): LADY ANNE COOKE BACON, AUTOGRAPH LETTER SIGNED, TO NATHANIEL BACON

For the letter itself, see HEH-FBLMC, box 1, call number FBL 3.

3. NOTES ON SELECTED PICTURED ARTIFACTS NOW HOUSED IN THE RARE BOOKS COLLECTION, THE HUNTINGTON LIBRARY (HEH-RBC)

Significant assistance with the notes in this section was provided by William H. Sherman.

3.1 (PLATES 7.1, 19.20): JOHANN FUST AND PETER SCHOEFFER, LEAF FROM *BIBLIA LATINA* (LATIN BIBLE)

Sometimes known as the "Mainz Bible" or the "1462 Bible," Fust and Schoeffer's *Biblia Latina* was the fourth printed edition of the Latin Bible. Its innovative use of a text type designed for extended private reading made it one of the most influential books of its time. For historical perspective, see Eric Marshall White, *Peter Schoeffer: Printer of Mainz* (Dallas: Bridwell Library, 2003). The AICs for this framed page (PMA-WLA, box 27, AIN 623) note that it was moved "to HEH 16. Jan. 1996." Photographs of the object attached to the cards are credited to Al Stendahl (son of the Arensbergs' neighbor Earl Stendahl). For the leaf itself, see HEH-RBC, call number 602125.

3.2 (PLATE 42.3): *SHAKESPEARE'S COMEDIES, HISTORIES, & TRAGEDIES* (SIR SIDNEY LEE'S OXFORD FACSIMILE OF THE FIRST FOLIO OF 1623)

This was the best available photographic facsimile of the so-called First Folio, the earliest complete collection of Shakespeare's plays, published in 1623. It was probably the most heavily used book in the Arensbergs' library: like many Baconians, Walter believed that its pages contained systematic (if cryptic) evidence for Bacon's authorship of the plays, and he spent countless hours poring over its pages. He and his team worked through two copies of the book, covering the margins with pencil notations and filling many boxes with interpretations derived from words, punctuation marks, and typographical ornaments. Walter does not seem to have sought out original copies of Shakespeare's works, as he did with Bacon's, but he took pains to acquire the most reliable reproductions. Lee's 1902 edition, printed by Oxford University Press and limited to 1,000 copies, was considered the most accurate facsimile and became the text of choice for Shakespeareans and Baconians alike. The entire volume is available online at oll.libertyfund.org/people/sir-sidney-lee. For the Arensbergs' copies, see HEH-RBC, call numbers 602087 and 602088.

3.3 (PLATE 42.4): *MR. WILLIAM SHAKESPEARE'S COMEDIES, HISTORIES, AND TRAGEDIES* (THE METHUEN FACSIMILE OF THE SECOND FOLIO OF 1632)

This was (and remains) the standard reproduction of the so-called Second Folio, the new version of Shakespeare's complete plays printed in 1632. The Arensbergs' copy is now HEH-RBC, call number PR2751.A25 1909B.

4. NOTES ON SELECTED PICTURED OBJECTS NOW HOUSED IN THE FRANCIS BACON LIBRARY ARCHIVE, THE HUNTINGTON LIBRARY (HEH-FBLA)

Significant assistance with the notes in this section was provided by June Li, formerly curator of the Chinese Garden at the Huntington Botanical Gardens, now curator emerita. I am extremely grateful to Ms. Li for examining these objects and discussing them with me on many occasions. Her notes have now been incorporated into the HEH-FBLA online finding aid.

4.1 (PLATES 17.18, 18.23, 35.13): ARTIST/MAKER UNKNOWN, PRE-COLUMBIAN DEATH MASK (FAKE)

The AIC for this object (PMA-WLA, box 27, A&A 27/AIN 1468) reads: "Mask. Stone. Pre-Colombian [*sic*]. Aztec Valley of Mexico Death Mask." After examining a high-resolution photograph of this object, Ronald W. Dammann of Stendahl Galleries, Los Angeles, stated that the object is unequivocally fake. For the mask itself, see HEH-FBLA, box 149, call number A&A 27/1468.

4.2 (PLATE 17.24): ARTIST/MAKER UNKNOWN (*CHINA), BURIAL URN (FAKE)

The AIC for this object (PMA-WLA, box 27, A&A 8/AIN 245) includes a photograph and reads "Han Burial Urn. Clay." June Li observes: "This object is not aesthetically pleasing and probably not authentic. Its surface is too evenly encrusted with soil or some strange clay-like material—a telltale method of antiquing something. Its shape and finish are unlike most burial vessels of the Han period, when ceramic vessels were often covered in brown or green lead glaze to mimic more expensive vessels made of bronze." According to handwritten notations by Francis M. Naumann on a photograph of the urn given to him by Elizabeth Wrigley, the Arensbergs kept the cremated remains of their dog, Lollie, in the urn. For the urn itself, see HEH-FBLA, box 137, call number A&A 8/245.

4.3 (PLATES 27.16, 29.19, 30.18, 31.17): IÑUPIAQ (NORTH COAST ALASKA), MASK

The AIC for this object (PMA-WLA, box 27, A&A 28/AIN 1469) reads "mask. Wood. Eskimo." A tentative identification of this mask as Iñupiaq was provided by Dr. Aron Crowell, Alaska director of the Arctic Studies Center,

Smithsonian National Museum of Natural History. After examining a high-resolution photograph of the mask provided by HEH, Dr. Crowell noted in an email of 6 October 2011 that "the simple portrait style, round, relatively flat shape without attachments, and minimal painting except red or black highlights are all consistent with masks from that area. The down-turned mouth means it represents a woman." I am extremely grateful to Dr. Crowell for discussing this object with me, and to Dr. Ann Fienup-Riordan and Dr. Aaron Glass for facilitating my conversation with him. For the mask itself, see HEH-FBLA, box 149, call number A&A 28/1469.

4.4 (PLATES 27.24, 56.6): ARTIST/MAKER UNKNOWN, BOWL
The AIC for this object (PMA-WLA, box 27, A&A 23/AIN 1106) includes a photograph. For the bowl itself, see HEH-FBLA, box 139, call number A&A 23/1106.

4.5 (PLATES 36.14, 44.24, 58.15): ARTIST/MAKER UNKNOWN (*CHINA), CRYSTAL SPHERE
The AIC for this object (PMA-WLA, box 27, A&A 16/AIN 488, previously 490) includes a photograph and reads "Sphere. (Crystal) Chinese." According to June Li, "Crystal balls are precious objects often placed on stands of bronze or other precious metals made in the form of clouds or dragons. The balls themselves represent the 'pearls' pursued by dragons in Chinese mythology." She notes that there are two other Chinese crystal balls in prominent Pennsylvania collections: one in the General William Crozier Collection at the Philadelphia Museum of Art (PMA accession number 1944-20-2a, b) and another, famous for its bizarre story of theft and retrieval, at the University of Pennsylvania Museum of Archaeology and Anthropology. Li suggests that the object might be of Chinese origin, but cautions that without any documents of provenance, proper attribution of this object is unlikely. For the crystal ball itself, see HEH-FBLA, box 141, call number A&A 16/488.

4.6 (PLATE 41.28): ARTIST/MAKER UNKNOWN (*CHINA), PLATTER
The AIC for this object (PMA-WLA, box 27, A&A 10/AIN 274) includes a photograph. June Li's opinion that "this object does not appear to be typically Chinese" challenges the description written on the AIC. For the platter itself, see HEH-FBLA, box 141, call number A&A 10/274.

4.7 (PLATE 42.8): ARTIST/MAKER UNKNOWN (NORTH AMERICA), PITCHER
The AIC for this object (PMA-WLA, box 27, A&A 1/AIN 2) includes a photograph and reads "North American—Colonial or Federal." For the pitcher itself, see HEH-FBLA, box 139, call number A&A 1/2.

4.8 (PLATE 42.11): ARTIST/MAKER UNKNOWN (NORTH AMERICA OR EUROPE), JAR
The AIC for this object (PMA-WLA, box 27, A&A 2/AIN 4) includes a photograph and reads "North American—Early European Culture." For the jar itself, see HEH-FBLA, box 139, call number A&A 2/4.

4.9 (PLATES 40.28, 42.14): MARBLEHEAD POTTERY, BOWL
Dr. Herbert Hall established Marblehead Pottery in 1904, in Marblehead, Massachusetts, as part of a therapeutic program designed to treat patients with nervous disorders. Later commercialized, the pottery was sold from a local handicraft shop and by mail-order catalog until 1936, when production ended. Though Marblehead pieces are now highly collectible artifacts associated with the Arts and Crafts movement, the photograph printed here suggests that the Arensbergs bought the bowl for purely utilitarian purposes. This bowl has a Marblehead maker's mark (initiated ca. 1908, but used only sporadically). The AIC for the object (PMA-WLA, box 27, A&A 25/AIN 1172) does not have a photograph attached. For the bowl itself, see HEH-FBLA, box 147, call number A&A 25/1172. I am extremely grateful to Pam Peterson, former director of the Marblehead Museum and Historical Society, Marblehead, Massachusetts, for discussing this object with me. She also confirmed that another Arensberg-owned bowl in the FBLA (with a distinctive Marblehead color and glaze, but lacking a maker's mark) was also made by Marblehead Pottery. The AIC for that object (PMA-WLA, box 27, A&A 22/AIN 983) does not have a photograph attached. For the bowl itself, see HEH-FBLA, box 146, call number A&A 22/983. A third Marblehead piece owned by the Arensbergs (plate 40.28; 1996-3-2) was given to the PMA by the FBF in 1996.

4.10 (PLATE 47.6): ARTIST/MAKER UNKNOWN (CHINA), BOWL
This white bowl decorated with blue dragons has a foot rim and flattened mouth-rim glazed in brown with incised patterns. June Li notes that the bowl was quite thickly thrown, that it appears to be stoneware rather than porcelain, and that the dragons are painted in a practiced and easy manner. She further notes that the dark brown glaze may indicate Southeast Asian (perhaps Vietnamese) rather than Chinese origins, and suggests that it may date from the nineteenth century. The AIC for this object (PMA-WLA, box 27, A&A 11/AIN 279) includes a photograph and reads: "Bowl—Chinese. Porcelain. With blue figures on white background. Not to Phila." For the bowl itself, see HEH, A&A 11/AIN 279.

4.11 (PLATE 57.13): ARTIST/MAKER UNKNOWN (NORTH AMERICA), BREAD BOWL
The AIC for this object (PMA-WLA, box 27, A&A 14/AIN 339) includes a photograph and reads: "Bread bowl. Wooden. Early U.S. 16½ Diameter." For the bowl itself, see HEH, A&A 14/339.

4.12 (PLATE 58.14): ARTIST/MAKER UNKNOWN (CHINA), BRONZE BOWL
According to June Li, this metal (bronze?) vessel is very crudely cast and has a large quantity of rust and hardened earth on its surface. The decorative style evokes the Western Zhou period (about 1100 to 771 BCE), but it is probably not of that vintage. The rust and the heavy weight seem to point to the presence of iron—something that would not have been used that early and is more common in the cast sculpture of later periods (especially Ming and Qing onward). It may be a later attempt to create an object that looked much older than it actually was. The AIC for this object (PMA-WLA, box 27, A&A 9/AIN 247) includes a photograph and reads: "Bowl — Chinese — Asiatic. Early. Chou[*sic*]? Bronze." For the bowl itself, see HEH, A&A 9/247.

4.13 (PLATE 58.18): ARTIST/MAKER UNKNOWN (*AFRICA), STAND
The AIC for this object (PMA-WLA, box 27, A&A 3/AIN 30) includes a photograph and reads: "African—Negro. Stand, Brown wood. Oval 8½ Dia[meter]." For the stand itself, see HEH, A&A 3/30.

5. A NOTE ON THE CARPETS AND FURNITURE PICTURED THROUGHOUT THIS BOOK

The Huntington Art Collections include thirteen carpets of Persian, Chinese, and Kazakhstani origin and four decorative bag faces of Persian origin that were originally owned by the Arensbergs. The museum's object numbers for these items are 2007.3.1–2007.3.17. As of this writing, images of these artifacts are not yet available for viewing online.

Several pieces of furniture owned by the Arensbergs are in private collections. Others are still in use at the Huntington Library.

SELECTED BIBLIOGRAPHY

Affron, Matthew. *The Essential Duchamp*. Philadelphia: Philadelphia Museum of Art; New Haven: Yale University Press, 2018.

"African Art: New York and the Avant-Garde." Special issue 3 of *Tribal Art*, 1 December 2012.

Agee, William C. *Morton Livingston Schamberg (1881–1918)*. Exh. cat. New York: Salander-O'Reilly Galleries, 1982.

Altshuler, Bruce, ed. *Salon to Biennial—Exhibitions that Made Art History*. Vol. 1, *1863–1959*. London: Phaidon, 2008.

Anděl, Jaroslav, and Dorothy Kosinski, eds. *Painting the Universe: František Kupka, Pioneer in Abstraction*. Berlin: Verlag Gerd Hatje, 1997.

Arensberg, Walter Conrad. *The Baconian Keys*. Pittsburgh: Privately published, 1928.

———. *The Burial of Francis Bacon and His Mother in the Lichfield Chapter House: An Open Communication to the Dean and Chapter of Lichfield Concerning the Rosicrucians*. Pittsburgh: Privately published, 1924.

———. *The Cryptography of Dante*. New York: Alfred A. Knopf, 1921.

———. *The Cryptography of Shakespeare: Part One*. Los Angeles: Howard Bowen, 1922.

———. *Francis Bacon, William Butts, and the Pagets of Beaudesert*. Pittsburgh: Privately published, 1929.

———. *Idols*. Boston: Houghton Mifflin, 1916.

———. "Ing," "Arithmetical Progression of the Verb 'To Be,'" "For 'Shady Hill,' Cambridge, Mass.," "Axiom," and "Theorem." In *Others: An Anthology of the New Verse*, edited by Alfred Kreymborg, 9–13. New York: Alfred A. Knopf, 1917.

———. *The Magic Ring of Francis Bacon*. Pittsburgh: Privately published, 1930.

———. *Mr. Pennell's Etchings of London*. New York: F. Keppel, 1906.

———. *Poems*. Boston: Houghton Mifflin, 1914.

———. *The Secret Grave of Francis Bacon at Lichfield*. San Francisco: J. Howell, 1923.

———. *The Shakespearean Mystery*. Pittsburgh: Privately published, 1928.

———. *The Skeleton Text of the Shakespeare Folio*. Los Angeles: Francis Bacon Foundation, ca. 1952.

———. "Vacuum Tires: A Formula for the Digestion of Figments à la la." *TNT* (March 1919): unpaginated.

Art Institute of Chicago. *20th Century Art from the Louise and Walter Arensberg Collection*. Chicago: Art Institute of Chicago, 1949.

Bach, Friedrich Teja, Margit Rowell, and Ann Temkin. *Constantin Brancusi 1876–1957*. Exh. cat. Cambridge: MIT Press, 1995.

Barnett, Vivian Endicott, and Josef Helfenstein, eds. *The Blue Four: Feininger, Jawlensky, Kandinsky, and Klee in the New World*. Cologne: DuMont Buchverlag, 1997.

Barr, Alfred H. *Cubism and Abstract Art*. Exh. cat. New York: Museum of Modern Art, 1936.

Bauer, George H. "Duchamp's Ubiquitous Puns." In *Marcel Duchamp: Artist of the Century*, edited by Rudolf Kuenzli and Francis M. Naumann, 127–48. Cambridge: MIT Press, 1989.

Belk, Russell W. "Collectors and Collecting." In *Interpreting Objects and Collections*, edited by Susan M. Pearce, 317–26. London: Routledge, 1994.

Bissinger, Karl. *The Luminous Years: Portraits at Mid-Century*. New York: Harry N. Abrams, 2003.

Bonk, Ecke. *Marcel Duchamp: The Box in a Valise*. Translated by David Britt. New York: Rizzoli, 1989.

Boone, Elizabeth Hill, ed. *Collecting the Pre-Columbian Past: A Symposium at Dumbarton Oaks, 6th and 7th October 1990*. Washington, DC: Dumbarton Oaks Research Library and Collection, 1993.

Braddock, Jeremy. "Barnes without Barnes: On Philadelphia's New Barnes Foundation." *Los Angeles Review of Books*, 23 August 2012.

———. *Collecting as Modernist Practice*. Baltimore: Johns Hopkins University Press, 2012.

Bridwell Library. *Peter Schoeffer: Printer of Mainz; A Quincentenary Exhibition at Bridwell Library*. Exh. cat. Dallas: Bridwell Library, 2003.

Brown, Milton W. *American Painting from the Armory Show to the Depression*. Princeton: Princeton University Press, 1955.

———. *The Story of the Armory Show*. New York: Joseph H. Hirshhorn Foundation, 1963.

Cabanne, Pierre. *Dialogues with Marcel Duchamp*. Translated by Ron Padgett. London: Thames and Hudson, 1971.

Cahill, Holger. *American Sources of Modern Art*. Exh. cat. New York: Museum of Modern Art, 1933.

Churchill, Suzanne W. "Making Space for *Others*: A History of a Modernist Little Magazine." *Journal of Modern Literature* 22, no. 1 (1998): 47–67.

Covarrubias, Miguel. "La Venta: Colossal Heads and Jaguar Gods." *DYN*, no. 6 (November 1944): 24–33. Reprinted in Christian Kloyber, ed., *Wolfgang Paalen's "DYN": The Complete Reprint*. Vienna: Springer-Verlag, 2000.

Crunden, Robert M. *American Salons: Encounters with European Modernism, 1885–1917*. New York: Oxford University Press, 1993.

Curran, Kathleen. *The Invention of the American Art Museum: From Craft to Kulturgeschichte,*

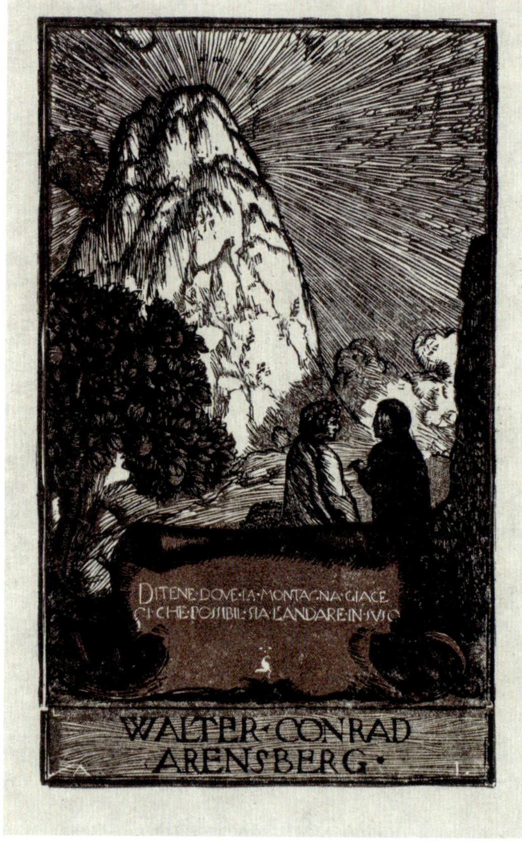

WALTER ARENSBERG'S BOOKPLATE (DATE UNKNOWN), DEPICTING DANTE AND VIRGIL SEATED ON A LEDGE OR SARCOPHAGUS BEHIND A CARTOUCHE WITH AN INSCRIPTION FROM DANTE'S *DIVINA COMMEDIA*. LOOSELY TRANSLATED, THE INSCRIPTION READS: "SHOW ME HOW TO ASCEND THE MOUNTAIN, THAT I MAY REACH, IF POSSIBLE, THE SUMMIT." PRIVATE COLLECTION

1870–1930. Los Angeles: Getty Research Institute, 2016.
Dailey, Victoria. "L.A. Now and Then, or South by North West." *The Book Club of California Quarterly News-Letter* 71, no. 1 (2005): 3–8.
Dailey, Victoria, Natalie Shivers, and Michael Dawson. *LA's Early Moderns: Art, Architecture, Photography*. Los Angeles: Balcony, 2003.
Dammann, April. *Exhibitionist: Earl Stendahl, Art Dealer as Impresario*. Santa Monica, CA: Angel City Press, 2011.
Davidson, Susan, and Philip Rylands, eds. *Peggy Guggenheim & Frederick Kiesler: The Story of Art of This Century*. Exh. cat. New York: Solomon R. Guggenheim Foundation, 2004.
Dee, Elaine Evans. *Views of Florence and Tuscany by Giuseppe Zocchi, 1711–1767; Seventy-Seven Drawings from the Collection of the Pierpont Morgan Library, New York*. Exh. cat. 2nd ed. Washington, DC: International Exhibitions Foundation, 1971.
Delpar, Helen. *The Enormous Vogue of Things Mexican: Cultural Relations between the United States and Mexico, 1920–1935*. Tuscaloosa: University of Alabama Press, 1992.
Delson, Susan B. *Dudley Murphy, Hollywood Wild Card*. Minneapolis: University of Minnesota Press, 2006.
de Zayas, Marius. *How, When, and Why Modern Art Came to New York*. Edited by Francis M. Naumann. Cambridge: MIT Press, 1998.
d'Harnoncourt, Anne. "A. E. Gallatin and the Arensbergs: Pioneer Collectors of Twentieth-Century Art." *Apollo*, n.s., 100, no. 149 (1974): 52–61.
———. *Philadelphia Museum of Art: Handbook of the Collection*. Philadelphia: Philadelphia Museum of Art, 1995.
d'Harnoncourt, Anne, and Kynaston McShine, eds. *Marcel Duchamp*. Munich: Prestel-Verlag with Museum of Modern Art, New York, and Philadelphia Museum of Art, 1989.
d'Harnoncourt, Anne, and Walter Hopps. "*Étant donnés: 1° la chute d'eau, 2° le gaz d'éclairage*. Reflections on a New Work by Marcel Duchamp." *Philadelphia Museum of Art Bulletin* 64, nos. 299–300 (1969): 1–58.
Dickerman, Leah. *Dada: Zurich, Berlin, Hannover, Cologne, New York, Paris*. Exh. cat. Washington, DC: National Gallery of Art, 2005.
———, ed. *Inventing Abstraction, 1910–1925: How a Radical Idea Changed Modern Art*. Exh. cat. New York: Museum of Modern Art, 2012.
Dijkstra, Bram. *The Hieroglyphics of a New Speech: Cubism, Stieglitz, and the Early Poetry of William Carlos Williams*. Princeton: Princeton University Press, 1969.
Dolkart, Judith F., and Martha Lucy, eds. *The Barnes Foundation: Masterworks*. New York: Skira Rizzoli, 2012.
Dreier, Katherine S., and Marcel Duchamp. *Collection of the Société Anonyme: Museum of Modern Art 1920*. Exh. cat. New Haven: Yale University Art Gallery, 1950.
Eggers, George W. "Dr. Fred Block's Sets of Color Slides." *College Art Journal* 8, no. 2 (1948–49): 95–100.
Elsner, John, and Roger Cardinal, eds. *The Cultures of Collecting*. Cambridge: Harvard University Press, 1994.
Felleman, Susan. *Botticelli in Hollywood: The Films of Albert Lewin*. New York: Twayne, 1997.
Flam, Jack, and Miriam Deutch, eds. *Primitivism and Twentieth-Century Art: A Documentary History*. Berkeley: University of California Press, 2003.
Fleuriet, Isabelle. *The Grand Old Lady of Modern Art: Marcel Duchamp's "Nude Descending a Staircase."* New York: Readymade, 2013.
Friedman, William F., and Elizebeth S. Friedman. *The Shakespearean Ciphers Examined: An Analysis of Cryptographic Systems Used as Evidence that Some Author Other than William Shakespeare Wrote the Plays Commonly Attributed to Him*. Cambridge: Cambridge University Press, 1957.
Gough-Cooper, Jennifer, and Jacques Caumont. "Ephemerides on and about Marcel Duchamp and Rrose Sélavy 1887–1958," n.p. In *Marcel Duchamp: Work and Life*. Edited by Pontus Hulten. Cambridge: MIT Press, 1993.
"Great Art … in Four California Houses." *Vogue*, Americana issue, 1 February 1945, 128–37.
Gross, Jennifer R., ed. *The Société Anonyme: Modernism for America*. Exh. cat. New Haven: Yale University Press, 2006.
Henderson, Linda Dalrymple. *Duchamp in Context: Science and Technology in "The Large Glass" and Related Works*. Princeton: Princeton University Press, 1998.
———. "Uncertainty, Chaos, and Chance in Early Twentieth-Century Art: The Cases of Wassily Kandinsky and Marcel Duchamp." *Étant donné Marcel Duchamp*, no. 4 (2002): 130–45.
Hines, Thomas S. *Richard Neutra and the Search for Modern Architecture*. New York: Oxford University Press, 1982.
Hopps, Walter. *The Dream Colony: A Life in Art*. Edited by Deborah Treisman, from interviews with Anne Doran. New York: Bloomsbury USA, 2017.
Hulten, Pontus, ed. *Marcel Duchamp: Work and Life*. Exh. cat. Cambridge: MIT Press, 1993.
Hyland, Douglas. *Marius de Zayas: Conjurer of Souls*. Exh. cat. Lawrence, KS: Spencer Museum of Art, 1981.
Jaeger, Roland. *Block & Hochfeld: Die Architekten des Deutschlandhauses: Bauten und Projekte in Hamburg, 1921–1938, Exil in Los Angeles*. Berlin: Gebr. Mann, 1996.
———. "Fritz Block: Around the World with Leica." *LFI* 4 (May 2005): 6–17.
———. *Photo-Eye Fritz Block: New Photography, Modern Color Slides*. Translated by Maka/Magill Translations and Laura Schleussner. Zurich: Scheidegger & Speiss, 2018.
Joselit, David. *Infinite Regress: Marcel Duchamp 1910–1941*. Cambridge: MIT Press, 1998.
Kachur, Lewis. *Displaying the Marvelous: Marcel Duchamp, Salvador Dalí, and Surrealist Exhibition Installations*. Cambridge: MIT Press, 2001.
Kahn, David. *The Codebreakers: The Story of Secret Writing*. New York: Macmillan, 1967.
Kahnweiler, Daniel-Henry. "Cubism: The Creative Years." *ARTnews Annual* 24 (1955): 97–106, 107–16.
Kaplan, Wendy, ed. *California Design, 1930–1965: Living in a Modern Way*. Exh. cat. Los Angeles: Los Angeles County Museum of Art, 2011.
———. *Found in Translation: Design in California and Mexico, 1915–1985*. Exh. cat. Los Angeles: Los Angeles County Museum of Art, 2017.
Karlstrom, Paul J., ed. *On the Edge of America: California Modernist Art, 1900–1950*. Berkeley: University of California Press, 1996. http://ark.cdlib.org/ark:/13030/ft5p30070c.
Kaufman, Louis, and Annette Kaufman. *A Fiddler's Tale: How Hollywood and Vivaldi Discovered Me*. Madison: University of Wisconsin Press, 2003.
Kimball, Fiske. "Before Columbus: Selections from the Louise and Walter Arensberg Collection." *Philadelphia Museum of Art Bulletin* 49, no. 239 (1953): 3–15.
———. "Cubism and the Arensbergs." *ARTnews Annual* 24 (1955): 117–22, 174–78.
———. "Opening of the Louise and Walter Arensberg Collection: The 'Modern Museum' of the Philadelphia Museum of Art." *Philadelphia Museum of Art Bulletin* 50, no. 243 (1954): 3–15.
Klein, Michael. *John Covert, 1882–1960*. Exh. cat. Washington, DC: Smithsonian Institution Press, 1976.
Knud Merrild: Works from the 1930's & 1940's. Exh. cat. Los Angeles: Steve Turner Gallery, 1991.
Kuenzli, Rudolf, and Francis M. Naumann, eds. *Marcel Duchamp: Artist of the Century*. Cambridge: MIT Press, 1990.
Kuh, Katharine. "An Interview with Katharine Kuh." By Avis Berman. Edited by William McNaught. *Archives of American Art Journal* 27, no. 3 (1987): 2–36.
———. *My Love Affair with Modern Art: Behind the Scenes with a Legendary Curator*. Edited by Avis Berman. New York: Arcade, 2006.
———. *The Open Eye: In Pursuit of Art*. New York: Harper & Row, 1971.
Kushner, Marilyn Satin, and Kimberly Orcutt, eds. *The Armory Show at 100: Modernism and Revolution*. Exh. cat. New York: New-York Historical Society, 2013.
Lanchner, Carolyn. *Joan Miró*. Exh. cat. New York: Museum of Modern Art, 1993.
Langsner, Jules. "The Arensberg Riches of Cubism." *ARTnews*, November 1949, 24–25, 61–62.
Laughlin, Clarence John. *Ghosts along the Mississippi*. New York: Charles Scribner's Sons, 1948.
Lawrence, John H., Jude Solomon, and Mallory Taylor. *Clarence John Laughlin and His Contemporaries*. Exh. cat. New Orleans: Historic New Orleans Collection, 2016.
List, Larry, ed. *The Imagery of Chess Revisited*. Exh. cat. New York: Isamu Noguchi Foundation and Garden Museum and George Braziller, 2005.
Los Angeles County Museum. *Pre-Columbian Art*. Exh. cat. Los Angeles: Los Angeles County Museum, 1940.
Louchheim, Aline B. "The Arensbergs Bought Cubists Then." *New York Times*, 23 October 1949, X9.

———. "Art of America before Columbus: Part of the Arensberg Collection Installed in Philadelphia." *New York Times*, 4 October 1953, X10.

Macgowan, Kenneth, and Herman Rosse. *Masks and Demons*. [New York]: Harcourt, Brace, 1923.

MacLeod, Glen G. *Wallace Stevens and Company: The "Harmonium" Years, 1913–1923*. Ann Arbor: UMI Research Press, 1983.

Mazow, Leo G. *John Covert Rediscovered*. University Park: Palmer Museum of Art at Pennsylvania State University, 2003.

McBride, Henry. "Modern Forms." *The Dial* 69 (July 1920). Republished as "The Walter Arensbergs." In *The Flow of Art: Essays and Criticisms of Henry McBride*, edited by Daniel Catton Rich, 156–59. New York: Atheneum, 1973. Rev. ed., New Haven: Yale University Press, 1997.

McCarthy, Laurette E. *The Paintings of Walter Pach*. Exh. cat. New York: Francis M. Naumann Fine Art, 2011.

Miller, Mary Ellen. *The Art of Mesoamerica: From Olmec to Aztec*. 6th rev. ed. London: Thames & Hudson, 2019.

Minelli, Michael. "The Want of a Nail…" Review of *Enigma Variations: Philip Guston and Giorgio di Chirico*, Santa Monica Museum of Art. *X-TRA* 9, no. 4 (2007): 30–33.

Modern Institute of Art. *Klee: 30 Years of Paintings, Water Colors, Drawings and Lithographs by Paul Klee and in a Klee-Like-Mood, 2000 Years of Coptic, Persian, Chines, European and Peruvian Textiles*. Exh. cat. Westwood, CA: Campbell's Bookstore, 1948.

———. *Knud Merrild: Twenty Five Year Retrospective*. Exh. cat. Beverly Hills, CA: Modern Institute of Art, 1948.

———. *Modern Artists in Transition*. Exh. cat. Beverly Hills, CA: Modern Institute of Art, 1948.

———. *Schools of Twentieth Century Art*. Exh. cat. Beverly Hills, CA: Modern Institute of Art, 1948.

Motherwell, Robert, Ad Reinhardt, and Bernard Karpel, eds. *Modern Artists in America*. 1st series. New York: Wittenborn, Schultz, 1951.

Museum of Modern Art. *Twenty Centuries of Mexican Art / Veinte siglos de arte méxicano*, exh. cat. New York: Museum of Modern Art and Instituto de Antropología e Historia de México, 1940.

Naumann, Francis M. "Cryptography and the Arensberg Circle." *Arts Magazine* 51 (May 1977): 127–33.

———. "The Dada Poetry of Walter Arensberg." *Tether* 4 (2018): 132–51.

———. "Frederic C. Torrey and Duchamp's *Nude Descending a Staircase*." In *West Coast Duchamp*, edited by Bonnie Clearwater, 10–23. Miami Beach: Grassfield in association with Shoshana Wayne Gallery, 1991.

———, ed. and trans. "Marcel Duchamp's Letters to Walter and Louise Arensberg, 1917–1921." In *Marcel Duchamp: Artist of the Century*, edited by Rudolf Kuenzli and Francis M. Naumann, 203–27. Cambridge: MIT Press, 1989. First published in *Dada/Surrealism* 16 (1987), 203–27.

———. *New York Dada, 1915–23*. New York: Abrams, 1994.

———. *New York Dada: The Arensberg Circle of Artists*. Exh. cat. New York: Francis M. Naumann Fine Art, 2019.

———. *The Recurrent, Haunting Ghost: Essays on the Art, Life and Legacy of Marcel Duchamp*. New York: Readymade, 2012.

———. "Walter Conrad Arensberg: Poet, Patron, and Participant in the New York Avant-Garde." *Philadelphia Museum of Art Bulletin* 76, no. 328 (1980): 2–32.

Naumann, Francis M., and Beth Venn. *Making Mischief: Dada Invades New York*. Exh. cat. New York: Whitney Museum of American Art, 1996.

Naumann, Francis M., and Bradley Bailey. *Marcel Duchamp: The Art of Chess*. New York: Readymade, 2009.

Naumann, Francis M., and Hector Obalk, eds. *Affectionately, Marcel: The Selected Correspondence of Marcel Duchamp*. Translated by Jill Taylor. Ghent: Ludion, 2000.

Nesbit, Molly, and Naomi Sawelson-Gorse. "Concept of Nothing: New Notes by Marcel Duchamp and Walter Arensberg." In *The Duchamp Effect: Essays, Interviews, Round Table*, edited by Martha Buskirk and Mignon Nixon, 131–75. Cambridge: MIT Press, 1996.

Oles, James. *South of the Border: Mexico in the American Imagination 1914–1947*. Exh. cat. Washington, DC: Smithsonian Institution Press, 1993.

Pach, Walter. "The Art of the American Indian." *The Dial* 68 (January 1920): 57–65. Reprinted in *Primitivism and Twentieth-Century Art: A Documentary History*, edited by Jack Flam and Miriam Deutch, 167–73. Berkeley: University of California Press, 2003.

———. "The Greatest American Artists." *Harper's Monthly Magazine*, 1 December 1923, 252–62.

———. *Queer Thing, Painting: Forty Years in the World of Art*. New York: Harper & Brothers, 1938.

Peabody Museum and William Hayes Fogg Art Museum. *An Exhibition of Pre-Columbian Art*. Exh. cat. Cambridge: Harvard University Press, 1940.

Peabody, Rebecca, et al., eds. *Pacific Standard Time: Los Angeles Art, 1945–1980*. Exh. cat. Los Angeles: Getty Research Institute and J. Paul Getty Museum, 2011.

Perchuk, Andrew, and Catherine Taft. "Floating Structures: Building the Modern in Postwar Los Angeles." In *Pacific Standard Time: Los Angeles Art, 1945–1980*, edited by Rebecca Peabody et al., 4–62. Exh. cat. Los Angeles: Getty Research Institute and J. Paul Getty Museum, 2011.

Perlman, Bennard B., ed. *American Artists, Authors, and Collectors: The Walter Pach Letters, 1906–1958*. Albany: State University of New York Press, 2002.

"The Philadelphia Museum." *Life*, 3 September 1951, 66–74.

Philadelphia Museum of Art. *20th Century Section*. Vol. 1 of *The Louise and Walter Arensberg Collection*. Philadelphia: Philadelphia Museum of Art, 1954.

———. *Pre-Columbian Sculpture*. Vol. 2 of *The Louise and Walter Arensberg Collection*. Classified and annotated by George Kubler. Philadelphia: Philadelphia Museum of Art, 1954.

Price, Vincent. *I Like What I Know: A Visual Autobiography*. Garden City, NY: Doubleday, 1959.

Rawlinson, Mark. *Charles Sheeler: Modernism, Precisionism and the Borders of Abstraction*. London: I. B. Tauris, 2007.

Reid, B. L. *The Man from New York: John Quinn and His Friends*. New York: Oxford University Press, 1968.

Roberts, George, and Mary Roberts. *Triumph on Fairmount: Fiske Kimball and the Philadelphia Museum of Art*. Philadelphia: J. B. Lippincott, 1959.

Rowell, Margit. "Miró at the Museum: Works in the Philadelphia Museum of Art." *Philadelphia Museum of Art Bulletin* 83, no. 356/357 (1987): 3–38.

Saarinen, Aline B. *The Proud Possessors: The Lives, Times and Tastes of Some Adventurous American Art Collectors*. New York: Random House, 1958.

Saborit, Antonio. "Marius de Zayas: Transatlantic Visionary of Modern Art." In *Nexus New York: Latin/American Artists in the Modern Metropolis*, edited by Deborah Cullen, 86–103. New York: El Museo del Barrio, 2009.

Sanborn, Pitts. "Shakespeare's Cryptography." Review of *The Cryptography of Shakespeare, Part One*, by Walter Arensberg. In *The Measure: A Journal of Poetry* 27 (May 1923): 18.

Sanouillet, Michel, and Elmer Peterson, eds. *Salt Seller: The Writings of Marcel Duchamp (Marchand du Sel)*. Oxford: Oxford University Press, 1973.

Santa Barbara Museum of Art. *Pasadena to Santa Barbara: A Selected History of Art in Southern California, 1951–1969*. Exh. cat. Santa Barbara, CA: Santa Barbara Museum of Art, 2012.

Sawelson-Gorse, Naomi. "The Art Institute of Chicago and the Arensberg Collection." *One Hundred Years at the Art Institute: A Centennial Celebration*. Special issue of *The Art Institute of Chicago Museum Studies* 19, no. 1 (1993): 80–101, 107–11.

———. "'For the Want of a Nail': The Disposition of the Louise and Walter Arensberg Collection." Master's thesis, University of California, Riverside, 1987.

———. "Hollywood Conversations: Duchamp and the Arensbergs." In *West Coast Duchamp*, edited by Bonnie Clearwater, 24–45. Miami Beach: Grassfield in association with Shoshana Wayne Gallery, 1991.

———. "Marcel Duchamp's 'Silent Guard': A Critical Study of Louise and Walter Arensberg." PhD diss., University of California, Santa Barbara, 1994.

———. "Sex, Alcohol, Soufflés, with Chess, Accompanied by Music." In *Dada New York: New World for Old*, edited by Martin Ignatius Gaughan, 78–111. Farmington Hills, MI: G. K. Hall, 2003.

Schloat, Don. *Freedom! Bataan—POW—PVT*. Valley Center, CA: Privately published, 1995.

Schrank, Sarah. "Painting the Town Red." In *Art and the City: Civic Imagination and Cultural Authority in Los Angeles*, 64–96. Philadelphia: University of Pennsylvania Press, 2009.

Schwarz, Arturo. *The Complete Works of Marcel Duchamp*. New York: Harry N. Abrams, 1969.

Scripps College. *Arts of the North American Indian*. Exh. cat. Claremont, CA: Scripps College, 1950.

Seigel, Jerrold. *The Private Worlds of Marcel Duchamp: Desire, Liberation, and the Self in Modern Culture*. Berkeley: University of California Press, 1995. http://ark.cdlib.org/ark:/13030/ft9h4nb688/.

Sherman, William H. "How to Make Anything Signify Anything." *Cabinet* 40 (Winter 2010–11): 32–38.

———. "Of Anagrammatology." *English Language Notes* 47, no. 2 (2009): 139–48.

———. "Walter Conrad Arensberg's Anagramania." *Cabinet* 45 (Spring 2012): 71–73.

Smith, Kathryn. "Frank Lloyd Wright, Hollyhock House, and Olive Hill, 1914–1924." *Journal of the Society of Architectural Historians* 38, no. 1 (1979): 15–33.

———. *Frank Lloyd Wright: Hollyhock House and Olive Hill—Buildings and Projects for Aline Barnsdall*. New York: Rizzoli, 1992.

Soby, James Thrall. "Marcel Duchamp in the Arensberg Collection." *View: The Modern Magazine*, Marcel Duchamp issue, series 5, no. 1 (1945): 10–12.

Solomon R. Guggenheim Museum. *Paintings from the Arensberg and Gallatin Collections of the Philadelphia Museum of Art*. Exh. cat. New York: Solomon R. Guggenheim Museum, 1961.

Starobinski, Jean. *Words upon Words: The Anagrams of Ferdinand de Saussure*. Translated by Olivia Emmet. New Haven: Yale University Press, 1979.

Starr, Kevin. *Material Dreams: Southern California through the 1920s*. New York: Oxford University Press, 1990.

Stebbins, Theodore E., Jr., and Norman Keyes Jr. *Charles Sheeler: The Photographs*. Exh. cat. Boston: Little, Brown, 1987.

Stendahl, Alfred. *Pre-Columbian Art*. Exh. cat. Dallas: Dallas Museum of Fine Arts, 1950.

Stewart, Alan. "Francis Bacon's Biliteral Cipher and the Materiality of Early Modern Diplomatic Writing." In *Diplomacy and Early Modern Culture*, edited by Robyn Adams and Rosanna Cox, 120–37. Basingstoke, UK: Palgrave Macmillan, 2011.

Stuckey, Charles F. "Duchamp's Acephalic Symbolism." *Art in America*, January–February 1977, 94–99.

Sweeney, James Johnson, ed. *African Negro Art*. Exh. cat. New York: Museum of Modern Art, 1935.

———, ed. "Eleven Europeans in America." *The Bulletin of the Museum of Modern Art* 13, nos. 4–5 (1946): 2–39.

Tanning, Dorothea. *Between Lives: An Artist and Her World*. New York: W. W. Norton, 2001.

Temkin, Ann, Susan Rosenberg, and Michael Taylor, eds. *Twentieth Century Painting and Sculpture in the Philadelphia Museum of Art*. Philadelphia: Philadelphia Museum of Art, 2000.

Tice, Clara. "Who's Who in Manhattan" (caricature of Louise Arensberg). *Cartoons Magazine*, August 1917, 178–79. Clipping in PMA-WLA, box 74, folder 9.

Tomkins, Calvin. *Duchamp: A Biography*. New York: Henry Holt, 1996.

———. "A Touch for the Now" (profile of Walter Hopps). *New Yorker*, 29 July 1991, 33–57.

Track 16 Gallery and Robert Berman Gallery. *Man Ray: Paris—LA*. Santa Monica, CA: Smart Art, 1996.

Umland, Anne. *Joan Miró: Painting and Anti-Painting, 1927–1937*. New York: Museum of Modern Art, 2008.

Voss, John, Conrad Wright, James Luther Adams, and Agnes Mongan. "Residents of Shady Hill." *Bulletin of the American Academy of Arts and Sciences* 35, no. 6 (1982): 6–25.

Voyce, Stephen. "'Make the World Your Salon': Poetry and the Community at the Arensberg Apartment." *Modernism/modernity* 15, no. 4 (2008): 627–46.

Waldie, D. J. "Shock of the New: Los Angeles vs. Modernism." *KCET*, 21 July 2016, https://www.kcet.org/shows/lost-la/shock-of-the-new-los-angeles-vs-modernism.

Warner, Marina. "Freud's Couch: A Case History." *Raritan* 31, no. 2 (2011): 146–63.

Weschler, Lawrence. "Paradise: The Southern California Idyll of Hitler's Cultural Exiles." In *Exiles & Emigrés: The Flight of European Artists from Hitler*, edited by Stephanie Barron and Sabine Eckmann, 341–61. Los Angeles: Los Angeles County Museum of Art and Harry N. Abrams, 1997.

Wilson, Charis, and Wendy Madar. *Through Another Lens: My Years with Edward Weston*. New York: North Point, 1998.

With, Karl. *Autobiography of Ideas: Memoirs of an Extraordinary Art Scholar*. Edited by Roland Jaeger in cooperation with Gerda Becker-With, Dorothee von Berg, and Marion Philadelphia. Berlin: Gebr. Mann, 1997.

Wolf, Ben. *Morton Livingston Schamberg*. Philadelphia: University of Pennsylvania Press, 1963.

Wood, Beatrice. *I Shock Myself: The Autobiography of Beatrice Wood*. Edited by Lindsay Smith. Rev. ed. San Francisco: Chronicle, 1985.

———. "Visit to Brancusi." *Archives of American Art Journal* 32, no. 4 (1992), 19–24.

Zilczer, Judith. *"The Noble Buyer": John Quinn, Patron of the Avant-Garde*. Exh. cat. Washington, DC: Smithsonian Institution Press, 1978.

Zweig, Stefan. *Chess: A Novella*. Translated by Anthea Bell. London: Penguin, 2006. Published in German as *Schachnovelle*. Buenos Aires: Pygmalión, 1942.

ARCHIVES AND ARCHIVAL MATERIAL

Arensberg, Walter and Louise. Papers. Arensberg Archives. Philadelphia Museum of Art, Library and Archives, PA.

Bissinger, Karl. Papers (MSS0682). Special Collections, University of Delaware Library, Newark.

Bliss, Robert Woods. Papers. House Collection. Dumbarton Oaks Research Library and Collection, Washington, DC.

Block, Fritz. Estate Archive. Stockholm and Hamburg.

Brummer Gallery Records. The Cloisters Library and Archives, Metropolitan Museum of Art, New York.

Corle, Helen Freeman. "Notes on the Work of Marcel Duchamp and Their Effect upon a Contemporary" (unpublished manuscript). Arensberg Archives. Philadelphia Museum of Art, Library and Archives, PA.

Covert, John Raphael. Papers. Philadelphia Museum of Art, Library and Archives, PA.

Dreier, Katherine S. Papers / Société Anonyme Archive. Yale Collection of American Literature, Beinecke Rare Book and Manuscript Library, Yale University, New Haven, CT.

Duchamp, Alexina and Marcel. Papers. Philadelphia Museum of Art, Library and Archives, PA.

Fisher, Charles J. Recommendation Report. Los Angeles Department of City Planning, Cultural Heritage Commission, case no. CHC-2010-2948-HCM/ENV-2010-2949-CE, 2010.

Friedman, William F. Papers. The George C. Marshall Foundation, Lexington, VA.

Francis Bacon Foundation Records. Philadelphia Museum of Art, Library and Archives, PA.

Francis Bacon Library Archive. The Huntington Library, Art Museum, and Botanical Gardens, San Marino, CA.

Francis Bacon Library Manuscripts Collection. The Huntington Library, Art Museum, and Botanical Gardens, San Marino, CA.

Huntington Art Collections. The Huntington Library, Art Museum, and Botanical Gardens, San Marino, CA.

Ivins, William Mills. Papers, 1878–1964. Archives of American Art, Smithsonian Institution, Washington, DC.

Kimball, Fiske. Memoirs and supporting letters describing the acquisition of the Arensberg Collection, 1947–51. Fiske Kimball Papers, box 162, folder 28, 29. Philadelphia Museum of Art Library and Archives, Philadelphia, PA.

Kubler, George. George Kubler Records of the Arensberg Collection Catalog. Philadelphia Museum of Art, Library and Archives, PA.

Laughlin, Clarence John. Clarence John Laughlin Archive. The Historic New Orleans Collection, LA.

Neutra, Richard. Richard and Dion Neutra Papers (Collection 1179). UCLA Library Special Collections, Charles E. Young Research Library, University of California, Los Angeles.

Pach, Walter. Papers, 1883–1980. Archives of American Art, Smithsonian Institution, Washington, DC.

———. "The Politer, the Cutt'n'er" (manuscript memoir). Arensberg Archives. Philadelphia Museum of Art, Library and Archives, PA.

Rare Books Collection. The Huntington Library, Art Museum, and Botanical Gardens, San Marino, CA.

Sabin, Henry Palmer. Papers. Architecture and Design Collection; Art, Design & Architecture Museum; University of California, Santa Barbara.

Sawelson-Gorse, Naomi. Naomi Sawelson-Gorse Research Collection. Philadelphia Museum of Art, Library and Archives, PA.

Stendahl, Alfred. Interview by George M. Goodwin, 26 August 1967. Oral History Program, University of California, Los Angeles. Original transcript from UCLA Department of Special Collections, Oral History Collection.

Stendahl, Earl. Papers. Stendahl Art Galleries Records. Getty Research Institute, Los Angeles.

Wood, Beatrice. Papers, 1894–1998. Archives of American Art, Smithsonian Institution, Washington, DC.

INDEX

Note: page numbers in italics refer to figures; those in bold refer to plates. Numbers in brackets following object descriptions refer to Philadelphia Museum of Art accession numbers.

ILLUSTRATION CREDITS

Every effort has been made to identify and contact the copyright holders of images published in this book. Should you discover what you consider to be a photo by a known photographer, please contact the publisher. The following sources have granted additional permission to reproduce illustrations in this volume.

Front cover: Beatrice Wood. Louise Arensberg, Walter Arensberg, and Marcel Duchamp in the garden at 7065 Hillside Avenue, Los Angeles, 17 August 1936. Philadelphia Museum of Art, Library and Archives, Alexina and Marcel Duchamp Papers (PMA-MDP), box 30, folder 17. Gift of Jacqueline, Paul, and Peter Matisse in memory of their mother, Alexina Duchamp. Reproduced courtesy of Beatrice Wood Center for the Arts / Happy Valley Foundation

Back cover: Floyd Faxon. View of Louise and Walter Arensberg's living room at 7065 Hillside Avenue, ca. January 1951. See plate 5, page 99

Frontispiece (left): Beatrice Wood. Portrait of Walter Arensberg. Philadelphia Museum of Art, Library and Archives, Arensberg Archives (PMA-WLA), box 53, folder 12. Reproduced courtesy of Beatrice Wood Center for the Arts / Happy Valley Foundation

Frontispiece (right): Portrait of Louise Arensberg. Photographer unknown, possibly Beatrice Wood. Philadelphia Museum of Art, Library and Archives, Arensberg Archives (PMA-WLA), box 50, folder 16

page iv: Charles Sheeler. Living room of Louise and Walter Arensberg's house, 7065 Hillside Avenue, Los Angeles, October 1939 (detail). Museum of Fine Arts Boston, Lane Collection. Photograph © 2020, Museum of Fine Arts, Boston

page 363 (fig. 25): From Margaret Hooks, *Tina Modotti, Photographer and Revolutionary* (London: HarperCollins, 1995)

PHOTOGRAPHER CREDITS

Karl Bissinger
Plates 11, 40, 45, 47, 48, 57, 58; page 401; details on pages 300–301, 258–59, 294–95, 326–27, 332–33: University of Delaware Library, Newark, Special Collections, Karl Bissinger Archive (MSS0682). © The Estate of Karl Bissinger

Fritz (Fred) Block
Plates 24, 25, and 27; details on pages 180–81, 186–87, 196–97: © Fritz Block Estate Archive, Stockholm/Hamburg

Fred R. Dapprich
Plates 1, 7, 13, 17, 18, 19, 20, 21, 22 (possibly), 23, 26, 30, 32, 34, 35, 37, 38, 42, 44, 49, 52, 56; details on pages 112–13, 130–31, 148–49, 154–55, 210–11, 222–23, 280–81: Philadelphia Museum of Art, Library and Archives, Arensberg Archives (PMA-WLA), box 54

Floyd Faxon
Plates 2, 5, 6, 12, 15, 31, 33, 43, 46, 59; details on pages 102–3, 217, 274–75, 340–41: Philadelphia Museum of Art, Library and Archives, Arensberg Archives (PMA-WLA), box 54
Plates 8, 9, 10, 39, 50, 51, 53–55: Philadelphia Museum of Art, Library and Archives, Arensberg Archives (PMA-WLA), box 65

Corporal F. W. Lumbord
Plates 3, 28, 36; details on pages 89, 92–93: Lumbord / Birmingham General Hospital Official Photograph. Philadelphia Museum of Art, Library and Archives, Arensberg Archives (PMA-WLA), box 53, folder 51

Leopold (Dick) Seyffert Jr.
Plates 4, 14, 16, 41; detail on pages 264–65: Philadelphia Museum of Art, Library and Archives, Seyffert Photograph Collection. Permission courtesy of Robert Seyffert

ADDITIONAL CREDITS

Alexander Archipenko: © 2020 Estate of Alexander Archipenko / Artists Rights Society (ARS), New York

Constantin Brancusi: © Succession Brancusi – All rights reserved (ARS) 2020

Georges Braque: © 2020 Artists Rights Society (ARS), New York / ADAGP, Paris

Alexander Calder: © 2020 Calder Foundation, New York / Artists Rights Society (ARS), New York

Marc Chagall: © 2020 Artists Rights Society (ARS), New York / ADAGP, Paris

Giorgio de Chirico: © 2020 Artists Rights Society (ARS), New York / SIAE, Rome

Salvador Dalí: © 2020 Salvador Dalí, Fundació Gala-Salvador Dalí, Artists Rights Society

André Derain: © 2020 Artists Rights Society (ARS), New York / ADAGP, Paris

Marcel Duchamp: © Association Marcel Duchamp / ADAGP, Paris / Artists Rights Society (ARS), New York 2020

Max Ernst: © 2020 Artists Rights Society (ARS), New York / ADAGP, Paris

Lyonel Feininger: © 2020 Artists Rights Society (ARS), New York / VG Bild-Kunst, Bonn

Albert Gleizes: © 2020 Artists Rights Society (ARS), New York / ADAGP, Paris

Paul Klee: © 2020 Artists Rights Society (ARS), New York

Fernand Léger: © 2020 Artists Rights Society (ARS), New York / ADAGP, Paris

René Magritte: © 2020 C. Herscovici / Artists Rights Society (ARS), New York

André Masson: © 2020 Artists Rights Society (ARS), New York / ADAGP, Paris

Henri Matisse: © 2020 Succession H. Matisse / Artists Rights Society (ARS), New York

Carlos Mérida: © 2020 Artists Rights Society (ARS), New York / SOMAAP, Mexico City

Jean Metzinger: © 2020 Artists Rights Society (ARS), New York / ADAGP, Paris

Joan Miró: © Successió Miró / Artists Rights Society (ARS), New York / ADAGP, Paris 2020

Francis Picabia: © 2020 Artists Rights Society (ARS), New York / ADAGP, Paris

Pablo Picasso: © 2020 Estate of Pablo Picasso / Artists Rights Society (ARS), New York

Diego Rivera: © 2020 Banco de México Diego Rivera Frida Kahlo Museums Trust, Mexico, D.F. / Artists Rights Society (ARS), New York

Georges Rouault: © 2020 Artists Rights Society (ARS), New York / ADAGP, Paris

Jacques Villon: © 2020 Artists Rights Society (ARS), New York / ADAGP, Paris

MARK NELSON is a partner at McCall Associates, New York, where he designs books for museums, galleries, and artists. His clients include the Metropolitan Museum of Art, the Museum of Modern Art, the Philadelphia Museum of Art, and the Whitney Museum of American Art. Over the course of his career, Nelson has worked closely with many leading artists, including Vija Celmins, Jenny Holzer, Sherrie Levine, and Richard Serra. He is the author, with Sarah Hudson Bayliss, of *Exquisite Corpse: Surrealism and the Black Dahlia Murder* (2006).

WILLIAM H. SHERMAN is director of the Warburg Institute and professor of cultural history at the University of London's School of Advanced Study. Before moving to the Warburg, he served as director of research and collections at the Victoria and Albert Museum and founded the Centre for Renaissance & Early Modern Studies at the University of York. Sherman has published widely on the history of books and readers and the plays of Shakespeare and his contemporaries, and his recent work has focused on the relationship between word and image and the history of codes and ciphers.

ELLEN HOOBLER is the William B. Ziff, Jr., Associate Curator of Art of the Americas at the Walters Art Museum in Baltimore, Maryland. A specialist on pre-Columbian art and its historiography, Hoobler most recently was coeditor of *Visual Culture in the Ancient Americas: Contemporary Perspectives* (2017). She has also published recent articles in the *Journal of the Walters Art Museum* and the *Journal of Interactive Technology and Pedagogy* (CUNY).

THE GETTY RESEARCH INSTITUTE PUBLICATIONS PROGRAM
Mary Miller, *Director, Getty Research Institute*
Gail Feigenbaum, *Associate Director*

PUBLISHED BY THE GETTY RESEARCH INSTITUTE, LOS ANGELES
Getty Publications
1200 Getty Center Drive, Suite 500
Los Angeles, California 90049-1682
www.getty.edu/publications

Laura Santiago, *Editor*
Mark Nelson, McCall Associates, New York, *Designer*
Mark Nelson with Amita Molloy and Victoria Gallina, *Production*
Allison McCann and Karen Ehrmann, *Image and Rights Acquisition*

Type composed in Monotype Bulmer and FF Kievit

Distributed in the United States and Canada by the University of Chicago Press
Distributed outside the United States and Canada by Yale University Press, London

Printed in Italy at Trifolio SRL, Verona

This publication has been generously supported by

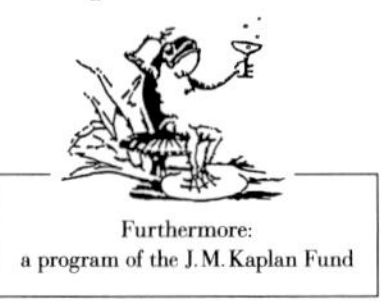

LIBRARY OF CONGRESS CATALOGING-IN-PUBLICATION DATA
Names: Nelson, Mark, 1967– author. | Sherman, William H. (William Howard), author. | Hoobler, Ellen, 1976– author. | Getty Research Institute, issuing body.
Title: Hollywood Arensberg : avant-garde collecting in midcentury L.A. / Mark Nelson, William H. Sherman, Ellen Hoobler.
Description: Los Angeles : Getty Research Institute, [2020] | Includes bibliographical references and index. | Summary: "Hollywood Arensberg presents the first comprehensive reconstruction and interpretation of Louise and Walter Arensberg's groundbreaking collection of modern and pre-Columbian art, giving readers a room-by-room, object-by-object tour of the couple's home in Los Angeles"— Provided by publisher.
Identifiers: LCCN 2020010654 | ISBN 9781606066669 (hardcover)
Subjects: LCSH: Arensberg, Walter, 1878–1954—Art collections. | Arensberg, Louise S. (Louise Stevens), 1879–1953—Art collections. | Art—Private collections—California—Los Angeles. | Art—Collectors and collecting—California—Los Angeles. | Art, Modern—20th century. | Indian art.
Classification: LCC N5220.A65 N45 2020 | DDC 708.1794/94—dc23
LC record available at https://lccn.loc.gov/2020010654